Operations Management
A Process Approach with Spreadsheets

Scott M. Shafer

Jack R. Meredith

John Wiley & Sons, Inc.

New York ❖ Chichester ❖ Weinheim ❖ Brisbane ❖ Singapore ❖ Toronto

Acquisitions Editor: Beth Lang Golub
Marketing Manager: Carlise Paulson
Production Editor: Tony VenGraitis
Outside Production Coordination: Janet Nuciforo
Designer: Nancy Field
Photo Editor: Hilary Newman
Illustration Coordinator: Anna Melhorn
Cover Photo: © 1997 Jose L. Pelaez/The Stock Market
Cover Illustration: Michael Jung

This book was set in Garamond by Ruttle, Shaw & Wetherill, Inc. and printed and bound by Hamilton Printing Company.
The cover was printed by Phoenix Color.

This book is printed on acid-free paper.

The paper in this book was manufactured by a mill whose forest management programs include sustained yield harvesting of its timberlands. Sustained yield harvesting principles ensure that the numbers of trees cut each year does not exceed the amount of new growth.

ISBN 0-471-16545-X

Printed in the United States of America

10 9 8 7 6 5 4 3 2 1

Dedicated with love to our wives
Nikki Shafer and Carol Meredith

About the Authors

Scott M. Shafer is an Associate Professor of Operations Management in the Department of Management at Auburn University. He received a BS in Industrial Management, a BBA in Marketing, and a PhD in Operations Management from the University of Cincinnati.

His current research interests are in the areas of cellular manufacturing, operations strategy, business process design, production scheduling, and information technology. Recently, a study investigating the productivity of 738 researchers in the field of operations management ranked Dr. Shafer in the top 20 in terms of both publication quality and research productivity. His publications have appeared in journals such as the *Journal of Operations Management, Decision Sciences, International Journal of Production Research, OMEGA, IEEE Transactions on Engineering Management, International Journal of Operations and Production Management, International Journal of Purchasing and Materials Management, Production and Inventory Management Journal, Journal of Corporate Accounting and Finance,* and *Project Management Journal.* Dr. Shafer is active in several professional societies including the Decision Sciences Institute, the Institute for Operations Research and the Management Sciences, and the Production Operations Management Society, and has made over a dozen presentations at the national meetings of these organizations. Additionally, he is a former member of the Board of Advisors of SOLE—The International Society of Logistics, is the current Membership Services Coordinator of the Decision Sciences Institute, and is certified in Production and Inventory Management (CPIM) by the American Production and Inventory Control Society. Dr. Shafer is a native of Cincinnati, Ohio. For fun he enjoys working out, tennis, golf, snow skiing, concerts, and playing guitar. Scott and his wife Nikki had their first child, Brianna Regan, in November 1997.

Jack R. Meredith is Professor of Management and Broyhill Distinguished Scholar and Chair in Operations at the Babcock Graduate School of Management at Wake Forest University. He received his undergraduate degrees in engineering and mathematics from Oregon State University and his PhD and MBA from University of California, Berkeley. During his undergraduate studies he worked for Ampex Corporation and Hewlett-Packard Company as a mechanical engineer. Following the award of his undergraduate degrees he worked as an astrodynamicist for Douglas Aircraft Company, and then TRW Systems Group on the Apollo Space Program.

His current research interests are in the areas of research methodology and the strategic planning, justification, and implementation of advanced manufacturing technologies. His recent articles in these areas have been published in *Decision Sciences, Journal of Operations Management, Sloan Management Review, Strategic Management Journal,* and others. He has two other textbooks that are currently popular for college classes: *Fundamentals of Management Science* (R. D. Irwin) and *Project Management* (John Wiley & Sons). He is currently the Editor-in-Chief of the *Journal of Operations Management,* an area editor for *Production and Operations Management,* was the founding editor of *Operations Management Review,* and was the production/operations management series editor for John Wiley & Sons, Inc.

Jack and his family are new residents of Winston-Salem, North Carolina. His wife Carol is a freelance writer and his daughter, Kiersten Dart, lives in Chicago with husband Clint and grandson Avery. His oldest son, Brandon, is a senior at the University of Illinois, Champaign-Urbana, majoring in Computer Engineering and his youngest son, Jeremy, is also a senior at the University of Illinois majoring in Computer Science.

Preface

The mission of this book is to provide students with an applied and contemporary introduction to the field of operations management that is also well-grounded in theory. To accomplish this objective, the traditional approaches for organizing operations management topics in textbooks were abandoned in favor of a new approach that emphasizes two major themes. First, the material is organized on the basis of business processes. Thus, the book's emphasis is on how traditional operations management activities support overall business processes rather than the performance of these activities independent of the other functional areas. Second, the use of spreadsheets, arguably the most powerful decision support tool available, is integrated throughout the text.

It is widely acknowledged that today's business environment is increasingly competitive. This is the result of the globalization of markets, the accelerating pace of technological advances, dramatically shorter product life cycles, and increases in the education and sophistication of customers. One implication of these trends is that today's business graduates need additional skills beyond those of the graduates of only a few years ago. As an example, the trend away from vertical hierarchical organizations toward horizontal process-centered ones creates a need for individuals who can also work as part of a team and who understand how technology can be used to better meet customer needs. This book has been written to help students understand these trends.

ORGANIZATION

To achieve the above stated mission, the book has been organized into four parts.

❖ *Part One: Operations in a Global Market.* Part One provides the setting, context, and background material for the remainder of the book. It begins with an introduction to the field of operations management. Next, issues related to strategy and international competitiveness are discussed. These are followed by a discussion of how quality management activities support the business strategy and enhance competitiveness. Finally, using quality management as a backdrop, Part One concludes with a discussion of business process design. Because the remainder of the book is organized around three primary business processes, this material provides the foundation for the rest of the book.

❖ *Part Two: Product and Transformation System Design.* Since it is highly undesirable to isolate decisions about product/service design from transformation system design, these activities are combined into a single business process. Major topics include product/services selection and design, the transformation system, and facility layout.

❖ *Part Three: Resource Management Processes.* Managing organizational resources includes activities such as obtaining and managing capital resources, human resource management, facilities location and design, and the management of technology. Operations management activities such as forecasting, capacity planning, and facility location are discussed in Part Three.

❖ *Part Four: Product Supply Processes.* Most of the traditional operations management activities support the organization's efforts to supply products and services to the customer. The activities in this process begin with the acquisition of raw materials and end with delivering the finished product to the customer. The operations management topics that support the product supply process include aggregate and master scheduling, inventory management, planning material requirements, just-in-time systems, purchasing/procurement, detailed scheduling, project management, and quality control.

EATURES _____

We have incorporated a number of unique features into the book in an effort to facilitate and enhance the educational experience.

❖ *Organization Within Chapters.* In addition to organizing the major topics on the basis of the business processes as opposed to more traditional approaches (e.g., system design versus system operation, or strategic operations, tactical operations, and detailed operations), the material within the chapters also has a rather unique organization. First, since psychologists have argued that the best way to master material is to begin by reading summaries, each chapter begins with a ***Chapter Overview*** that summarizes the entire chapter. Then, directly following the Chapter Overview, each Introduction section opens with several ***short examples*** of actual companies that demonstrate the importance and relevance of the topic or highlight some of the critical issues related to the topic. Key points related to these examples are discussed to further introduce the student to the topic. Additional examples are integrated throughout the chapters in ***Operations in Practice*** sidebars. Since the chapter summaries have been moved to the beginning of each chapter, the chapters conclude with ***Chapter in Perspective***. These sections provide a road map for the student, highlighting how the material in a particular chapter is related to both the material before and after it.

Another feature of the book is that the end-of-chapter questions and problems have been renamed to be more positive and better reflect their purpose. Questions in ***Check Your Understanding*** provide students with an opportunity to assess how well they mastered the material in the text while questions in the ***Expand Your Understanding*** provide the opportunity to go beyond what was presented in the text. Thus, the questions in Check Your Understanding are typical of what other books call review questions, and those in Expand Your Understanding correspond to discussion-type questions.

Apply Your Understanding continues this theme and provides end-of-chapter class-tested mini-cases. Finally, the traditional problems are now called ***Exercises*** (*problem* refers to something that is difficult to deal with, whereas *exercise* implies practice and training). This section provides a variety of exercises ranging from some that can be worked using only a calculator to ones that require the use of spreadsheets.

❖ *Integrated Spreadsheet Analysis.* In addition to fostering the development of spreadsheet skills, integrating spreadsheets significantly enhances the introductory operations management course by allowing students to analyze more meaningful exercises, rather than simply solving traditional homework-type problems. For example, one of the primary assumptions of the basic economic order quantity (EOQ) model is that only one item is involved. Although this assumption is not very realistic, the reason for it is that the calculations become overly complicated when multiple products interact (e.g., are stored in the same warehouse, are produced on the same machine, are purchased using a common budget.). However, a spreadsheet's built-in optimization capability provides a very straightforward and intuitive approach for handling this situation. Table 1 lists the operations management topics addressed with spreadsheet analysis and Table 2 identifies the specific spreadsheet skills that are fostered in this book, respectively.

❖ *Contemporary Topics.* In addition to illustrating many contemporary topics with the chapter opening examples and the Operations in Practice sidebars, numerous sections in the book are dedicated to timely topics including business process design (reengineering), mission and vision statements, core competencies, mass customization, benchmarking, quality function deployment, the Baldrige Award, ISO 9000, service defections, information technology, supply chain management, ERP (including SAP), supply chain management, process capability, and outsourcing.

❖ *Instructor Friendly.* All teaching supplements were developed by the authors of the book and were designed to make the book easy to teach from. The PowerPoint slides are comprehensive including solutions to all end of chapter exercises and are easy to use or modify.

❖ *Student Friendly.* Students will appreciate the cost savings of a trim, one-color book. Also, less computer-literate students will appreciate the step-by-step detailed explanations given in the **Spreadsheet Analysis** sections. Finally, students should benefit from the numerous real-world examples used to introduce and illustrate the material.

$\mathscr{S}$UPPLEMENTS

A range of supplements accompanies this text.

❖ *Instructor's Resource Guide:* A comprehensive instructor's resource guide features teaching suggestions and answers to end of chapter questions and exercises.

❖ *Web Site:* As an additional resource for instructors, a Web site supporting the book is available. The Web site provides additional up-to-date references, cases, teaching suggestions, Web links, and sample course syllabi.

❖ *PowerPoint Presentations:* Comprehensive PowerPoint slide shows have been developed for each chapter. The slides include the vast majority of figures and tables in the text, bulleted slides to lecture from, and solutions to all exercises. Having the slides in PowerPoint provides instructors with the flexibility to add, delete, modify, print out, change the style, reorder, and upload the files.

$\mathcal{T}$ABLE 1 ❖ O M Topics Addressed With Spreadsheet Analysis

Topic	Chapter
ABC Analysis	12
Aggregate Scheduling	11
Assignment Model	11S
Breakeven Analysis (Capacity Planning)	9
Breakeven Analysis (Facility Location)	10
Breakeven Analysis (New Product)	5
Cell Formation (Rank Order Clustering Algorithm)	7
Center of Gravity Method	10
Control Charts	17
EOQ Model	12
Forecasting: Exponential Smoothing	8
Forecasting: Linear Trend Model	8
Forecasting: Moving Averages	8
Forecasting: Weighted Moving Averages	8
Learning Curves	9
Lot Sizing	13
Master Scheduling	11
MRP Explosion	13
Quality Function Deployment	5
Reorder Point Policies	12S
Priority Rules	15
Project Management	16
Seasonal Values	8
Sequencing Heuristics	15
Simulation	12S, 16
Waiting Line Analysis	15S
Weighted Score Method	10

$\mathcal{T}$ABLE 2 ❖ Spreadsheet Skills Developed

Skill	Chapter(s)
ABS (absolute value) Function	8
Absolute Cell References	8, 9, 10, 11, 12
Array Functions	8
AVERAGE Function	8, 10, 12S, 15, 17
ChartWizard	8, 9
Fitting Trend Line to Plotted Data	8
Formulas with Exponents	9, 15S
Generating Random Numbers	12S
Goal Seek Feature	5
IF Function	11, 12S, 13
Linear Programming	9S
LINEST Function	8
LN Function	9
MAX Function	11, 12S, 13, 15, 16
MIN Function	16
Random Number Generation	12S, 16
ROUNDUP Function	9, 11
Solver (Optimization)	8, 9S, 11, 11S, 12, 16
Sorting Spreadsheet	7, 12, 15
SQRT Function	12, 16
TREND Function	8

- ❖ *Test Bank:* The test bank includes numerous true/false, multiple choice, and open ended exercise questions.
- ❖ *Computerized Test Bank:* The entire test bank has been computerized to facilitate the task of creating examinations. It is available in Windows format.
- ❖ *Video Tape:* the Wiley/Nightly Business Report Video contains applicable segments from the highly respected Nightly Business Report. The segments are approximately 3 to 5 minutes in length. They are particularly well suited to introducing a topic and providing additional real-world examples.

$\mathscr{A}$CKNOWLEDGMENTS _____

Last, we would like to thank the following reviewers of this textbook for their extensive and valuable feedback: Terri Friel, Eastern Kentucky University; Robert Handfield, Michigan State University; Janet L. Hartley, Bowling Green State University; Gerhard Plenart, Brigham Young University; William R. Sherrard, San Diego State University; David Sparling, University of Guelph (Ontario, Canada); Janet M. Wagner, University of Massachusetts; Elliot Weiss, University of Virginia; Craig H. Wood, University of New Hampshire.

Scott M. Shafer
Jack R. Meredith

Contents

Part Two:
Product and Transformation System Design /145

Part Three:
Resource Management Processes /265

Part Four:
Product Supply Processes /415

Appendix A:
Area Under the Normal Distribution   /794

Appendix B:
Random Numbers   /795

Bibliography   /796

Photo and Illustration Credits   /819

Index   /821

❖ ❖ ❖

Operations in a Global Market

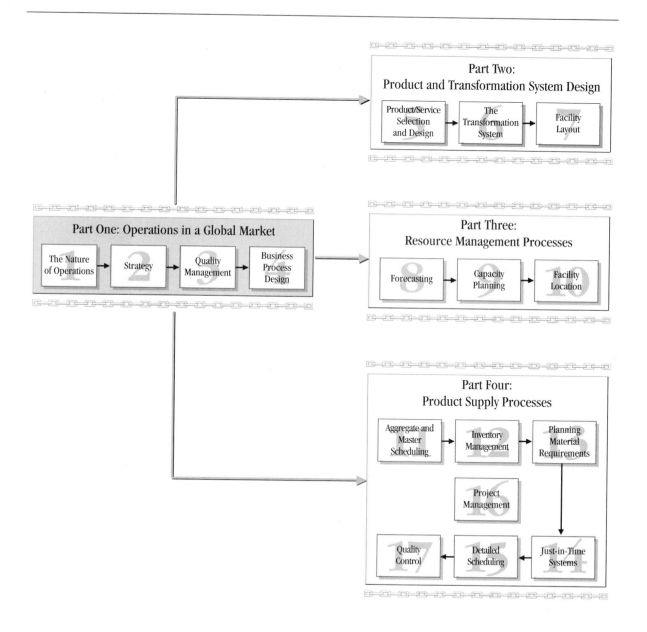

Chapter 1

The Nature of Operations

C HAPTER OVERVIEW

❖ Operational activities are the tasks within an organization that create value for the customer.

❖ Operations includes a number of subareas such as operations strategy, transformation system design, inventory management, and scheduling.

❖ Operations, as an organizational necessity, has always been with us, but its more formal beginnings can probably be traced to the publication of Frederick Taylor's book on scientific management in 1911. Conceptually, operations has now moved out of the factory and into all forms of organizations; it has thus taken the name *operations management*.

❖ In the functional view, all organizations must perform three core functions: operations, finance, and marketing. The operations function is commonly responsible for 80 percent of all the physical assets of the organization as well as 60 to 80 percent of all the human resources.

❖ Organizational structures are currently evolving from a functional (or vertical) structure to a process-centered (or horizontal) structure. With the process-centered arrangement, companies organize activities on the basis of specific value-creating processes.

❖ The production system is where the inputs (capital, materials, labor, etc.) are converted or transformed into outputs: services or products. The production system operates in an environment consisting of the economy, government regulations, competitors, technology, and so on.

❖ The heart of the production system is the transformation system, which adds value to the inputs through a wide variety of activities such as altering, transporting, storing, and inspecting.

❖ The production system monitors data from the inputs, transformation system, outputs, and environment and provides control by altering the inputs and transformation system (thereby, it is hoped, affecting the outputs).

❖ Every organization that adds value is considered to be a service. Any physical entity accompanying a transformation that adds value is a facilitating good. Production systems that provide no facilitating good are called *pure services*.

INTRODUCTION

❖ Facing increased competition and customers who are smarter, more demanding, and less brand-loyal, McDonald's is reevaluating the way it makes some of the items on its menu. For example, it is considering a switch to a hamburger bun that does not require toasting. In trial tests, customers seemed to prefer the new bun's taste and texture. Furthermore, not toasting buns should translate into substantial cost savings due to reduced preparation time and the elimination of commercial toasting equipment. At first, such savings may seem trivial; however, consider that McDonald's processes several billion buns for its hamburgers, chicken, and fish sandwiches (Gibson, 1995).

❖ Kodak's traditional approach to increasing sales was to encourage consumers to take more pictures. However, an enormous market opportunity exists, given that 98 percent of the photographs taken are never copied or enlarged. To capitalize on this market opportunity Kodak developed the CopyPrint Station. With the CopyPrint Station, photographs are scanned in and copies are printed out on a high-quality thermal printer. Kodak's goal for the CopyPrint Station is to make copying photographs easier and more enjoyable, thus increasing the use of photos as gifts. The primary benefits of the CopyPrint Station are that consumers don't need negatives to make copies or enlargements, and they don't have the hassle associated with dropping off and picking up their pictures. In a test-market study conducted in Australia, the average photo processing shop quadrupled its weekly enlargement sales (Maremont, 1995).

❖ Getting the Olympic flame to Atlanta for the summer Olympics of 1996 was a major undertaking. Ten thousand runners carried the flame 15,000 miles, passing through 42 states in 84 days. More than two years of planning went into this operation. For example, plans had to be coordinated with 2970 local police jurisdictions. Additionally, plans had to be made to deal with rush-hour traffic, no-show runners, or runners who were not able to complete their leg of the relay. In all, it was estimated that the Olympic flame relay cost in the neighborhood of $20 million, not including transportation, computers, and communication equipment used to support the project (Ruffenach, 1996).

4

❖ It is not well known that the Kmart and Wal-Mart chains both date back to 1962. By 1987 Kmart was clearly dominating the discount chain race, with almost twice as many stores (2223 to 1198) and sales of $25.63 billion to Wal-Mart's $15.96 billion. However, for the retail year that ended in January 1991, Wal-Mart had overtaken Kmart, with sales of $32.6 billion to Kmart's sales of $29.7 billion. Interestingly, although Wal-Mart had taken the lead in sales in 1991, it still had fewer stores—1721 to Kmart's 2330. By the retail year that ended in January 1996, Wal-Mart had clearly established itself as the dominant discount chain, with sales of $93.6 billion to Kmart's $34.6 billion. Perhaps equally telling is the shift in market share experienced by these two companies. For the period from 1987 to 1995 Kmart's market share declined from 34.5 percent to 22.7 percent while Wal-Mart's increased from 20.1 percent to 41.6 percent.

What accounts for this reversal in fortunes? Kmart's response to the competition from Wal-Mart was to build on its marketing and merchandising strengths and invest heavily in national television campaigns using high profile spokespeople such as Jaclyn Smith (a former Charlie's Angel). Wal-Mart took an entirely different approach and invested millions of dollars in operations in an effort to lower costs. For example, Wal-Mart developed a companywide computer system to link cash registers to headquarters, thereby greatly facilitating inventory control at the stores. Also, Wal-Mart developed a sophisticated distribution system. The integration of the computer system and the distribution system meant that customers would rarely encounter out-of-stock items. Further, the use of scanners at the checkout stations eliminated the need for price checks. By Kmart's own admission, its employees were seriously lacking the skills needed to plan and control inventory effectively (Duff and Ortega, 1995).

These brief examples serve to highlight the diversity and importance of operations. Take the description of McDonald's. This example provides a glimpse of two themes that are central to operations: *customer satisfaction* and *competitiveness*. This example also illustrates a more subtle point—that improvements made in operations can simultaneously increase customer satisfaction and lower costs. The Kodak example illustrates another central theme: that advances in technology often support improving operations. Finally, the Wal-Mart example demonstrates how a company obtained a substantial competitive advantage by improving some basic operational activities such as controlling its inventory.

In terms of the diversity inherent in operations, note that McDonald's and Wal-Mart are traditional service organizations, whereas Kodak is an operation that focuses on creating a product. Also, note the diversity in the durations of the operations. McDonald's, Kodak's, and Wal-Mart's operations are ongoing whereas transporting the Olympic flame has a finite duration. Finally, note that transporting the Olympic flame is a not-for-profit activity, while McDonald's, Kodak, and Wal-Mart are very much concerned with generating a profit.

Pause for a moment and consider other products and services you use today. You may be doing your homework assignments on a Japanese notebook computer, driving to the store in a German automobile, and watching a sitcom on a television made in Taiwan while cooking your food in a Korean microwave. The marketplace has definitely become international, and consumers purchase their products from the provider that offers them the most value for their money. However, most of your *services*—banking, insurance, personal care—are probably domestic, although some of these may also be owned by foreign corporations. There is a reason why most services are produced by domestic firms while products may be produced in part, or wholly, by foreign firms, and it concerns an area of business known as operations.

A great many societal changes that are occurring today intimately involve activities associated with operations. For example, there is great pressure among competing nations to increase national productivity, and many politicians and national leaders decry America's poor progress in improving productivity growth in comparison with that of other nations. Similarly, businesses are conducting a national crusade to improve the quality of their offerings in both products and services (though sometimes we consumers wonder if this isn't just another marketing gimmick). As we will see, increasing productivity and improving quality are primary objectives of operations management.

Another characteristic of our modern society is the explosion of new technologies that surround and, sometimes, confound us. We almost take for granted the automatic teller machines (ATMs) that give us money when the bank is closed and the word-processor dictionaries that check the spelling in our term papers. But now and then an ATM balks just when we are desperate for cash, and we can't get a simple computer error corrected on a utility bill without seven phone calls. Our industries also rely increasingly on technology: robots carry and weld parts; workerless, dark "factories of the future" turn out a continuing stream of products; banks transfer funds instantly across cities, states, and oceans. Yet here too, we occasionally read about robots painting each other instead of the cars, or a clerk receiving a weekly paycheck made out for $10 million. These are the successes, and the failures, of operations.

This exciting, competitive world of operations is at the heart of every organization and, more than anything else, determines whether the organization survives in the international marketplace or disappears into bankruptcy or a takeover. It is this world that we will be covering in the following chapters.

In what way can operations be considered to be at the heart of every organization? Basically, operations involves tasks that create value for someone, and that is why organizations exist. The organization may be very big, like General Motors, or just a one-person sole proprietorship; both exist to make money through the creation of value. Moreover, this has always been true, from the earliest days of bartering to the modern world and corporations. Even nonprofit organizations like the Red Cross strive to create value for the recipients of their services in excess of their cost.

Consider McDonald's again. This firm uses a number of inputs including ingredients, labor, equipment, and facilities; transforms them in a way that adds value to them (e.g., by frying); and obtains an output, such as a chicken sandwich, that can be sold at a profit. This conversion process, termed a *production system,* is illustrated in Figure 1.1. The elements of the figure represent what is known as a **system**[1]: *a purposeful collection of people, objects, and procedures for operating within an environment.* Note the word *purposeful;* systems are not merely arbitrary groupings but goal-directed or purposeful collections. Managing and running a production system efficiently and effectively is at the heart of the operations activities that will be discussed in this text. Since we will be using this term throughout the text, let us formally define it. **Operations** is concerned with transforming inputs into useful outputs and thereby adding value to some entity; this constitutes the primary activity of virtually every organization.

❖ Systems Perspective

As Figure 1.1 illustrates, a production system is defined in terms of environment, inputs, transformation system, outputs, and the mechanism used for monitoring and control. The environment includes those things that are outside the actual production system but influence it in some way. Because of its influence, we need to consider the environment even though it is beyond the control of decision makers within the system. For example, a large portion of the inputs to a production system are acquired from the environment. Also, consider the impact that government regulations related to pollution control and workplace safety have on the transformation system. Or think about how changes in customers' needs, a competitor's new product, or a new advance in technology can influence the level of satisfaction with a production system's current outputs. As these examples show, the environment exerts a great deal of influence on the production system.

---

[1]Note that the word *system* is being used here in a broad sense and should not be confused with more narrow usages such as information systems, planning and control systems, or performance evaluation systems.

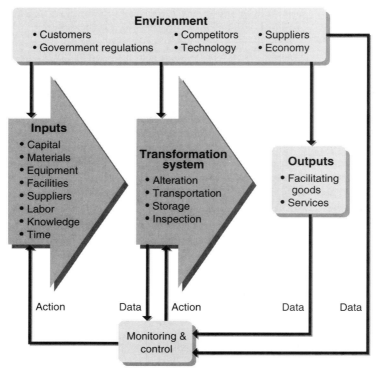

Figure 1.1   The production system.

Because the world around us is constantly changing, it is necessary to continuously monitor the production system and take action when the system is not meeting its goals. Of course, it may be that the current goals are no longer appropriate, indicating a need to revise the goals. On the other hand, it may be determined that the goals are fine but that the inputs or transformation system or both should be acted upon in some way. In either case, it is important to continuously monitor the performance of a system by collecting data from the environment, the transformation system, and the outputs. Then, on the basis of an analysis of these data, appropriate actions can be devised to enhance the system's overall performance.

Thinking in terms of systems provides decision makers with numerous advantages. To begin, the systems perspective focuses on how the individual components that make up a system interact. Thus, the systems perspective provides decision makers with a broad and complete picture of an entire situation. Furthermore, the systems perspective emphasizes the relationships between the various system components. Without considering these relationships, decision makers are prone to a problem called *suboptimization*. Suboptimization occurs when one part of the system is improved to the detriment of other parts of the system, and perhaps the organization as a whole. As an example of suboptimization, assume that an organization decides to broaden its product line in an effort to increase sales. Such a decision could actually end up hurting the organization as a whole if the organization does not have the capacity or capability to produce the broader product line, or if the broader product line increases inventory-related costs more than profits from the increased sales. The point of this example is that decisions need to be evaluated in terms of their effect on the entire system, not simply in terms of how they will affect one component of the system.

It is interesting to note that the components of systems are often themselves systems, called *subsystems*. For example, a factory that assembles personal computers is a system. Within this system there are many subsystems, such as the system that reports financial information, the system for assembling the computers, the system for ordering the raw materials, the system for designing new products, and the system for recruiting and hiring workers. And many of these subsystems could be further divided into sub-subsystems. To illustrate, the system that reports financial information may be composed of a system that reports information to sources outside the organization and another system that provides financial information to employees within the organization.

It also stands to reason that since systems can be divided into component subsystems, it should also be possible to combine them into larger systems. This is indeed the case. Consider the example of the personal computer assembly plant. This plant may be just one of a number of plants making up a particular division of the company. Thus, combining these plants would form a system corresponding to the division of this company. Furthermore, combining the divisions of the company would create a system for the whole company. This logic could be extended to creating systems for the entire industry, and all the way up to creating a system for the entire economy.

This discussion highlights the importance of defining a system's boundary appropriately. Specifically, defining a boundary determines what a decision maker will and will not consider, since things outside the system boundary are considered to be part of the environment and beyond the decision maker's control. Defining a system boundary is important because if it is defined too narrowly, important relationships among system components may be omitted. On the other hand, extending the boundary increases the complexity and costs associated with developing and using the model. Unfortunately, determining the system boundary is more of an art than a science and is based on the experience, skill, and judgment of the analyst.

Regardless of where the system boundary is defined, all production systems receive inputs from their environment, transform these inputs, and create value in the form of outputs. In the remainder of this section we elaborate on inputs, the transformation system, outputs, and the environment.

❖ Inputs

The set of inputs used in a production system is more complex than might be supposed. We require facilities in which to work, light to see, shelter from rain, a workplace to support our activities, and so on. We may also need equipment and supplies to aid in the transformation of the raw materials. Supplies are distinguished from raw materials by the fact that they are not usually a part of the final output. Oil, paper clips, pens, tape, and other such items are commonly classified as supplies because they only aid in producing the output.

Another very important input is knowledge of how to transform the inputs into outputs. The employees of the organization, of course, hold this knowledge, and let us not forget the last input, which is always mandatory—sufficient time to accomplish the operations. Indeed, the operations function quite frequently fails in its task because it cannot complete the ***transformation activities*** within the required time limit.

❖ Transformation System

The transformation system is the part of the system that adds value to the inputs. Value can be added to an entity in a number of ways. Four major ways are described below.

1. *Alter.* Something can be changed structurally. That would be a *physical* change, and this approach is basic to our manufacturing industries where goods are cut, stamped, formed, assembled, and so on. We then go out and buy the shirt, or computer, or whatever the good is. But it need not be a separate object or entity; for example, what is altered may be *us.* We may get our hair cut, or we may have our appendix removed.

   Other, more subtle, alterations may also have value. *Sensual* alterations, such as heat when we are cold, or music, or beauty may be highly valued on certain occasions. Beyond this, even *psychological* alterations can have value, such as the feeling of worth from obtaining a college degree or the feeling of friendship from a long-distance phone call.

2. *Transport.* An entity, again including ourselves, may have more value if it is located somewhere other than where it currently is. We may appreciate having things brought to us, such as flowers, or removed from us, such as garbage.

3. *Store.* The value of an entity may be enhanced for us if it is kept in a protected environment for some period of time. Some examples are stock certificates kept in a safe-deposit box, our pet boarded at a kennel while we go on vacation, or ourselves staying in a motel.

4. *Inspect.* Last, an entity may be more valued because we better understand its properties. This may apply to something we own, plan to use, or are considering purchasing, or, again, even to ourselves. Medical exams, elevator certifications, and jewelry appraisals fall into this category.

Thus, we see that value may be added to an entity in a number of different ways. The entity may be changed directly, in space, in time, or even just in our mind. Additionally, value may be added using a combination of these methods. To illustrate, an appliance store may create value by both storing merchandise and transporting (delivering) it. There are other, less frequent, ways of adding value as well, such as by "guaranteeing" something. These many varieties of transformations, and how they are managed, constitute some of the major issues to be discussed in this text.

❖ Outputs

Two types of outputs commonly result from a production system: services and products. Generally, products are physical goods, such as a copy of a photograph produced by the CopyPrint Station, and services are abstract or nonphysical. More

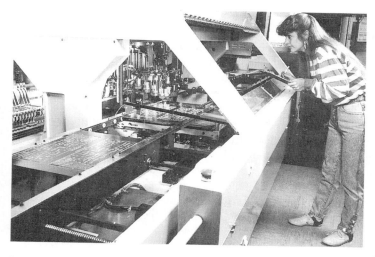

Inspecting the production system in a manufacturing firm.

specifically, we can consider the characteristics in Table 1.1 to help us distinguish between the two.

However, this classification may be more confusing than helpful. For example, consider a pizza delivery chain. Does this organization produce a product or provide a service? If you answered "a service," suppose that instead of delivering its pizzas to the actual consumer, it made the pizzas in a factory and sold them in the frozen-food section of grocery stores. Clearly the actual process of making pizzas for immediate consumption or to be frozen involves basically the same tasks, although one may be done on a larger scale and use more automated equipment. The point is, however, that both organizations produce a pizza, and defining one organization as a service and the other as a manufacturer seems to be a little arbitrary. As another example, consider visiting a dentist. Is having a cavity filled a product or a service? What if the dentist pulls the tooth instead?

You should be starting to see the possible confusion. Let's take another example. You want a load of sand for your child's sandbox. Your neighbor, whose yard is entirely sand, is digging a large hole in which to plant a tree. You negotiate, and your

$\mathcal{T}$ABLE 1.1 ❖ Characteristics of Products and Services

Products	Services
Tangible	Intangible
Minimal contact with customer	Extensive contact with customer
Minimal participation by customer in the delivery	Extensive participation by customer in the delivery
Delayed consumption	Immediate consumption
Equipment-intense production	Labor-intense production
Quality easily measured	Quality difficult to measure

neighbor shovels the sand from the hole into your sandbox for $10. Is this a product or a service?

We avoid this ambiguity by adopting the point of view *that any physical entity accompanying a transformation that adds value is a **facilitating good*** (the pizza, the filling, the sand). In many cases, of course, there may be no facilitating good; we refer to these cases as *pure services.*

The advantage of this interpretation is that every transformation that adds value is simply a service, either with or without facilitating goods! If you buy a piece of lumber, you have not purchased a product. Rather, you have purchased a bundle of services, many of them embodied in a facilitating good: a tree-cutting service, a saw mill service, a transportation service, a storage service, and perhaps even an advertising service that told you where lumber was on sale. We refer to these services as a bundle of "benefits," of which some are tangible (the sawed length of lumber, the type of tree) and others are intangible (courteous salesclerks, a convenient location, payment by charge card). Some services may of course, even be negative, such as an audit of your tax return. In summary, ***services*** *are bundles of benefits, some of which may be tangible and others intangible, and they may be accompanied by a facilitating good or goods.*

Firms often run into major difficulties when they ignore this aspect of their operations. They may think of themselves as only a "lumberyard" and not as providing a bundle of services. They may recognize that they have to include certain tangible services (such as cutting lumber to the length desired by the customer) but ignore the intangible services (charge sales, having a sufficient number of clerks).

Another reason for not making a distinction between manufacturing and services is that making such a distinction can be harmful. Specifically, when a company thinks of itself as a manufacturer it tends to focus on measures of internal performance such as efficiency and utilization; and when companies classify themselves as services they tend to focus externally and ask questions such as, "How can we serve our customers better?" This is not to imply that improving internal performance measures is not desirable. Rather, it suggests that improved customer service should be the primary impetus for all improvement efforts. It is generally not advisable to seek internal improvements if these improvements do not ultimately lead to corresponding improvements in customer service and customer satisfaction.

In this text we will adopt the point of view that all value-adding transformations (i.e., operations) are services, and there may or may not be a set of accompanying facilitating goods. Figure 1.2 illustrates a variety of outputs that range from virtually pure services to what would be known as products. Although we work with "products" as extensively as with services throughout the chapters in this book, bear in mind that in these cases we are working with only a *portion* of the total service, the facilitating good. In general, we will use the nonspecific term *outputs* to mean either products or services.

❖ Monitoring and Control

Suppose that in our production system we make a mistake. We must be able to observe this (monitor) and change our system to correct for it (control). The activities of monitoring and control, as illustrated in Figure 1.1, are used extensively in systems, including management systems, and will be encountered throughout this text. In essence, the monitoring process must tell the manager when significant changes

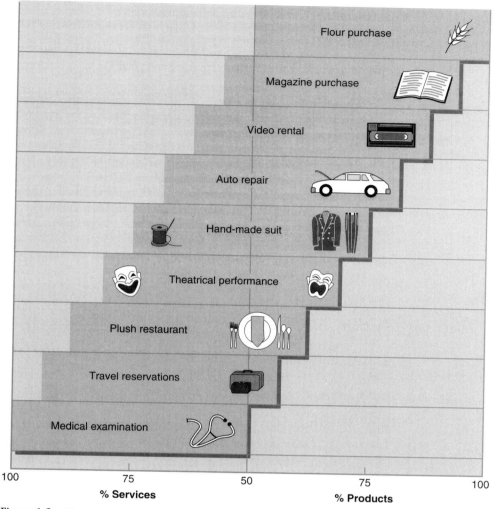

Figure 1.2 The range from services to products.

are occurring in any part of the production system. If the changes are not significantly affecting the outputs, then no control actions need be taken. But if they are, management must intercede and *apply corrective control* to alter the inputs or the transformation system and, thereby, the outputs.

Table 1.2 lists some components of the five elements of the production system for a variety of common organizations.

*O*PERATIONS ACTIVITIES

Operations include not only those activities associated specifically with the production system but also a variety of other activities. For example, purchasing or procurement activities are concerned with obtaining many of the inputs needed in the

*T*ABLE 1.2 ❖ Examples of Organizations and Their Components

Organization	Inputs	Transformation System	Outputs	Monitor/Control	Environment
Bank	Checks Deposits Vault ATMs	Safekeeping Investment Statement preparations	Interest Storage Loans Statements	Interest rates Wage rates Loan default rates	Federal Reserve Economy
Cinema	Films Food People Theater	Film projection Food preparation	Entertainment Snacks	Film popularity Disposable incomes	Economy Entertainment industry
Manufacturer	Materials Equipment Labor Technology	Cutting Forming Joining Mixing	Machines Chemicals Consumer goods Scrap	Material flows Production volumes	Economy Commodity prices Consumer market
Hospital	Drugs Patients Equipment Beds	Care Fill prescriptions Surgery	Lab tests Cures Removed organs	Government regulations New treatments Training	Medical community Drug control laws
Retailer	Merchandise Clerks Display cases Facility	Ordering Stocking Advising Selling	Goods transfers Exchanges Advertising	Complaints Fashions Disposable income	Economy Goods markets Credit bureaus
School	Books Teachers Facility Students	Learning Counseling Motivating	Education Skills Research	Demographics Grievances	State and county boards Tax system
Post office	Labor Equipment Trucks	Transportation Printing	Safe deliveries Stamps	Weather Mail volumes Sorting/loss errors	Transportation network Weather Civil service
Garbage service	Labor Trucks Landfill Trash	Trash; garbage removal Landfilling/ recycling	Clean space Cleaned streets	Truck condition Holidays/events	Street; highway network County regulations

production system. Similarly, shipping and distribution are sometimes considered marketing activities and sometimes considered operations activities.

As organizations begin to adopt new organizational structures based on business processes and abandon the traditional functional organization, it is becoming less important to classify activities as operations or nonoperations. However, for ease of description, we divide the field of operations into a series of subject areas as shown

$\mathcal{T}$ABLE 1.3 ❖ **Major Subject Areas in Operations**

❖ *Strategy:* Determining the critical operations tasks to support the organization's overall mission.

❖ *Output planning:* Selecting and designing the services and products the organization will offer to customers, patrons, or recipients.

❖ *Capacity planning:* Determining when to have facilities, equipment, and labor available and in what amounts.

❖ *Facility location:* Deciding where to locate production, storage, and other major facilities.

❖ *Transformation system design:* Determining the physical transformation aspects of the production activities.

❖ *Facility layout:* Devising an appropriate material flow and equipment layout within the facility to efficiently and effectively accommodate the transformation activities.

❖ *Aggregate planning:* Anticipating the yearly needs for labor, materials, and facilities by month or week within the year.

❖ *Inventory management:* Deciding what amounts of raw materials, work-in-process, and finished goods to hold.

❖ *Project management:* Learning how to plan and control project activities to meet specifications for performance, schedule, and cost.

❖ *Material requirements planning:* Determining when to order or produce materials, and in what amounts, to meet a master delivery schedule.

❖ *Scheduling:* Determining when each activity or task in the transformation system is to be done and where all the inputs should be.

❖ *Quality control:* Determining how quality standards are to be developed and maintained.

❖ *Reliability and maintenance:* Determining how the proper performance of both the output and the transformation system itself is to be maintained.

in Table 1.3. These areas are quite interdependent, but to make their workings more understandable we discuss them as though they were easily separable from each other. In some areas, a full-fledged department may be responsible for the activities, such as quality control or scheduling, but in other areas the activities (such as facility location) may be infrequent and simply assigned to a particular group or project team. Moreover, some of the subareas are critically important because they are a part of a larger business process or because other areas depend on them. Some subareas, such as inventory management, quality, and scheduling, have received an extensive amount of attention, so considerable written material is available about them. Finally, since we consider all operations to be services, these subject areas are equally applicable to organizations that have traditionally been classified as manufacturers and services.

$\mathcal{T}$HE FUNCTIONAL VIEW OF ORGANIZATIONS

Traditionally, companies have been organized on the basis of the type of work performed. Thus, organizations were divided into marketing, finance, accounting, engineering, operations, and other departments. This type of organization is referred

Layout, capacity, and teller schedules are critical decisions for banks.

to as a *functional organization* because work is organized on the basis of the function performed.

In the functional view, all organizations must perform three core functions: operations, finance, and marketing. Clearly, if they are to continue to exist all organizations must create value (operations), get the output to the customer (marketing), and raise capital to support their operations (finance). Additionally, organizations perform a number of other important functional activities such as reporting financial information (accounting) and designing new products (engineering)—to name just two. Below we briefly overview the generic functions that make up the functional organization.

❖ Operations

Operations is the part of the organization concerned with transforming inputs into outputs. In most service and manufacturing organizations, the operations function is responsible for about 80 percent of the physical assets of the firm such as buildings, equipment, supplies, raw materials, work-in-process, and finished goods. Moreover, operations is generally responsible for 60 to 80 percent of all the human resources as well.

Because of its key role in a functional organization, operations has important interfaces with the other areas in the organization. The smooth and efficient execution of these interactions is extremely important to maintaining the competitiveness of firms and the effective performance of all organizations. Among the more important interfaces are the following.

❖ Marketing

The marketing function is oriented toward matching the firm's strengths and abilities to the needs of the marketplace. Major points of contact between marketing and operations occur throughout the production system. At the front end, marketing is involved in acquiring information to be used in the design of the product or service to meet customers' needs and selling customers on the operations capabilities of the firm (e.g., high quality, fast response, extensive variety, unique customization). Operations needs to know from marketing what characteristics of the output are important to customers, what each characteristic is worth, and what the forecast of demand for the outputs will be. Marketing needs to know from operations what outputs will be available, when they will be ready, what they will cost, and what characteristics they will have.

With service outputs, production and consumption often occur at the same time, so that operations and marketing are a joint activity. With products, the distribution function is commonly another joint activity coordinated between operations and marketing.

Common areas of conflict between operations and marketing have typically been the breadth of the product line; the stocking of expensive finished goods; and alterations of, additions to, and cancellations of orders. A broad product line is advantageous for marketing, since a complete line of goods can be offered to customers. However, the variety required from operations makes for an expensive, troublesome, and time-consuming production system. It is no accident that Japanese automobiles gained market share through their reputation for quality and low cost, even though almost no choice was available to the customer.

❖ Finance

The finance function in business is responsible for obtaining and conserving funds to operate the firm. Thus there are a number of points of interface with operations, which is responsible for managing some 80 percent of the physical resources of the firm. Major points of contact occur during acquisition of capital assets (equipment, facilities) and determination of inventory policy (particularly stocking levels, where significant capital is tied up). Finance needs to know from operations what capital assets are going to be needed in the future and when high inventories are expected. Operations needs to know from finance any limitations and restrictions on its use of funds.

Another major area of contact is cash flow, where operations is expending funds for materials and then generating funds from completed goods. Finance needs to know from operations when outputs will be produced, thereby generating funds from sales, and what funds are needed to support the production system.

Finance and operations also work closely together in implementing the firm's business strategy. If offering higher quality or improved performance to customers will result in higher profit margins, finance helps operations identify equipment and investments that will provide these improvements, and then makes sure the funds are available when needed. Operations includes finance in its strategic planning, since virtually everything operations does—utilization of labor, investment in equipment, purchase of materials—involves the expenditure and, ultimately, the recovery of funds.

❖ Accounting

Accounting, overseen by the firm's controller, is responsible for reporting financial information and for maintaining day-to-day control of the firm's assets. Major interfaces with operations occur in two areas:

❖ *Cost reporting:* Here, operations reports usage of assets to accounting.

❖ *Variance reporting:* Variance reports concerning labor, purchased materials, and so on identify deviations from plan that may require corrective feedback actions.

Accounting needs to know from operations how many resources were used in the production process, by type and time period. Accounting also monitors the use of capital and other assets, in order to report them accurately. In turn, operations needs information from accounting regarding how efficiently it is using the firm's resources so that it can take measures to lower costs or improve other characteristics desired by customers. Conflicts between operations and accounting typically arise when operations does not want to take the time to report use of resources to accounting and accounting delivers reports to management that inaccurately allocate use of resources to individual departments.

Accounting and operations cooperate on developing and reporting measures that help managers make intelligent decisions. For example, with automation and the other advanced technologies in use today, existing methods of job costing are becoming inadequate for managerial decision making and firms are moving to new costing systems such as activity-based costing.

❖ Human Resources/Personnel

Human resources (HR) is responsible for obtaining properly skilled labor and managers for the organization. It needs to know from operations of upcoming needs—in terms of both number of people and levels of skills—in order to properly support the production system. HR is also responsible for upgrading the firm's skills through employee training and development. In addition, it monitors and recommends changes in pay scales and incentive plans.

The competitive advantage of firms in our global economy clearly rests in the capabilities of their people. To the extent that employees are well educated, intensively trained, experienced, and knowledgeable about the firm's competitive advantages and procedures, the firm will continue to prosper. HR and operations therefore closely coordinate their plans for hiring, attrition, and retirement, as well as their training, education, and development programs, to acquire and retain the most capable people to conduct the firm's business. Operations informs HR of its long-term strategy so that the best people will be available to execute it. And HR communicates to operations the problems and opportunities it is facing.

❖ Information Systems

Operations activities are closely tied to computerized information systems. This relatively new function in the organization acquires, writes, and supports the software systems used throughout the production system. Thus, information systems (IS) needs to know from operations what information it requires to conduct its activities, and operations needs to know from IS what information is feasible and how long it will take to get. One interesting area that operations and IS must continually address in every firm is whether to attempt to simplify the organization and its policies or build a more complex information system to cope with the increasing complexity.

As firms have become more integrated and responsive to the customer, the role of information has become critical to survival. Knowing what the customer needs and how to get it to market quickly is an information problem. Operations and IS bridge this problem by frequent and close communication of their needs and difficulties.

❖ Engineering

Operations has two major ties with engineering. Operations works with *product (or design) engineering* to facilitate the efficient, high-quality production of the services and products being designed (to be discussed in greater detail in Chapter 5). Too often in the past, design engineers gave no thought to how the output would be produced, with the result that a new product or service was inadequate, too expensive, or too late for the marketplace. Operations also works with *manufacturing engineering* to devise the best way to produce the service or product in the minimum time, to specifications, and at the least cost.

Engineering and operations are the up-front functions for delivering value to the customer. As they work together on the design and production of products and services, the problems of producing what has been designed are minimized and the customer receives better quality, performance, price, and value. It is estimated that 70 percent of the cost of a product or service is locked in when engineering finishes designing it, so when operations has a role in that process, the cost (not to mention the quality or performance) is significantly improved.

A PROCESS VIEW OF ORGANIZATIONS

The previous section described the traditional functional organizational structure, in which activities are grouped on the basis of functional similarity (e.g., marketing activities or accounting activities). However, as a result of recent advances in technology and increased international competition, many organizations have recognized a need for better methods of grouping and integrating organizational activities. Figure 1.3 illustrates how organizational structures are currently evolving to meet this need. Figure 1.3*a* depicts the traditional functional organization discussed above. In the functional organization, employees at any level are coordinated by having a common supervisor, who controls the information that is shared across the groups and resolves problems that arise between groups.

In the 1980s Michael Porter, a professor at the Harvard Business School, developed the concept of a *value chain* as a way to improve the coordination among various functional groups. The value-chain approach (Figure 1.3*b*) emphasized the organization as a system of interdependent activities that create value for the customer. Superimposing the value chain over the functional hierarchy provides a coordinating mechanism for linking sequentially related organizational activities. In

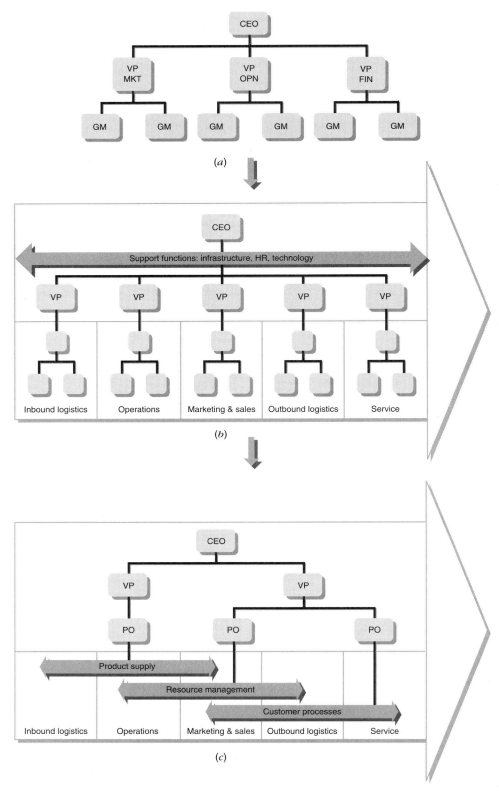

Figure 1.3 Evolution of organizational structures: (a) traditional functional organization; (b) value-chain approach; (c) process-centered structure.

effect, this is accomplished by organizational groups viewing subsequent organizational groups along the value chain as their "internal" customers. Thus, Porter's value chain presented a new view of management depicting the organization as a system of value-creating vertical processes rather than a collection of independent activities.

As business became increasingly globalized and competition fiercer, organizations were forced to become even more efficient and effective. The present phase of the evolution is shown in Figure 1.3c: organizations are now adopting organizational structures based on specific value-creating processes rather than simply using the value chain to coordinate separated functional groups. Thus, the traditional horizontal structure based on functional specialists is being abandoned in favor of a vertical structure based on process generalists. Furthermore, in comparing Figure 1.3b and c, we observe that the traditional management positions are also evolving. For example, vice president (VP) and general management (GM) positions that were responsible for specific functional activities such as operations, marketing, and finance, are evolving to become managers of processes. Managers of processes, often referred to as process owners (PO), have responsibility for entire value-creating processes such as supplying a product from the receipt of raw materials to the distribution of the final product.

The evolution to process organizational structures makes the topics in this course all the more relevant. Specifically, in the old functional organizational structure, only people in the operations area thought in terms of value-creating processes. However, in the new process-centered organization, all employees are organized on the basis of specific value-creating process. Thus, all employees must now think in terms of how their efforts fit into and support a particular value-creating process.

In a fashion similar to defining three generic functions (i.e., marketing, finance, and operations), it is possible to identify generic value-creating processes that are applicable to most organizations. In this book we demonstrate how operations management activities support three generic business processes:

❖ **Product and Transformation System Design.** As we will see, it is undesirable to isolate decisions about product/service design from decisions about the design of transformation systems; hence, these activities are combined into a single business process. Part Two of this book focuses on how operations management activities support this business process.

❖ **Resource Management Processes.** Managing organizational resources includes activities such as obtaining and managing capital resources, human resource management, the location and design of facilities, and the management of technology. The operations management activities that support resource management processes are discussed in Part Three.

❖ **Product Supply Processes.** Most of the traditional operations management activities support supplying the organization's outputs (including both products and services) to the customer. The activities in this process begin with the acquisition of raw materials and end with delivering the finished product/service to the customer. The operations management activities that support product/service supply processes are discussed in Part Four.

$\mathcal{T}$HE EVOLUTION OF OPERATIONS MANAGEMENT _____

We conclude this chapter with a discussion of organizations and management, the development of the field of operations management, and the emergence and growth of the service sector.

❖ Organizations and Management

Humans learned early in their evolution that cooperation with each other was the only way to satisfy desires that they could not achieve alone—desires for special food, certain belongings, acceptance and fellowship, safety, and so on. The instruments for such cooperation to achieve these desires are *organizations,* which, broadly defined, are *groups abiding by certain policies that guide the members in their activities.* We can envision some typical productive organizations, from Viking explorers to the Aztec Indian nation to modern international businesses. But children's play groups and "TGIF" parties are also organizations for satisfying human desires, although their duration is limited.

Throughout history people have formed organizations to satisfy individual or collective goals and disbanded or left those organizations when they were no longer of use or when organizational goals conflicted with personal goals. As civilization advanced from a family-centered farming economy to a handicraft-trading economy,[2] people began to recognize the advantages of specialization and trade. Rather than produce all of its own goods and services, a family could often produce, with less total effort, an excess of a commodity for which it had a special advantage and trade the excess for other desired commodities. Trade thus bound neighboring families closer together, since each family became more dependent on the others' commodities. As people making compatible commodities naturally began working with each other, the informal handicraft organizations evolved into the craft guilds of the Middle Ages and then into factories.

Any group endeavor requires **management** if it is to be effective in attaining its goals. Coordination of effort is the key to group success, and management performs this activity, among others. We know that the early Egyptian, Chinese, and Greek scholars conversed at length regarding management and administration. The need in early times for management becomes obvious when one considers such projects as the pyramids, the Great Wall of China, and the wars of Alexander. Nevertheless, the *function* of management received little recognition in these early times, and reports of notable achievements in management were the exception rather than the rule.

As the early handicraft system evolved into craft guilds and then factories, however, the role of management as a necessary function gained new importance and recognition. Peter Drucker, a management scholar, has commented:

> The emergence of management as an essential, a distinct and a leading institution is a pivotal event in social history. Rarely, if ever, has a new basic institution, a new leading group, emerged as fast as has management since the turn of this century. Rarely in hu-

---

[2]That is, before mass production.

man history has a new institution proven indispensable so quickly; and even less often has a new institution arrived with so little opposition, so little disturbance, so little controversy. . . . Management, which is the organ of society specifically charged with making resources productive, that is, with the responsibility for organized economic advance, therefore, reflects the basic spirit of the modern age. It is, in fact, indispensable—and this explains why, once begotten, it grew so fast and with so little opposition (pp. 3–4).

❖ The Development of Operations Management

The roots of operations as a distinct function go back to the Industrial Revolution, which started in the 1770s with the following important developments:

- ❖ The concept of division of labor, espoused by Adam Smith.
- ❖ The steam engine, invented by James Watt.
- ❖ The concept of interchangeable parts, developed by Eli Whitney.

Adam Smith, in *An Inquiry into the Nature and Causes of the Wealth of Nations* (1776), pointed out that where workers are organized to produce large quantities of an item the labor required should be divided into discrete tasks. He believed that this division of labor would produce several benefits:

- ❖ Workers who continually performed the same task would acquire greater skill at that task.
- ❖ Time would be saved that is normally lost in switching from one task to another.
- ❖ A worker's increased concentration on the same task frequently would lead to the development of special tools and techniques for easier or faster accomplishment of that task.

Then, in 1878, an American tennis champion turned his attention to factories and began a movement that eventually earned him a reputation as the father of scientific management. His name was Frederick Winslow Taylor. Taylor's philosophy was that successful management was the result not of applying individual management "techniques" to the job but rather of a comprehensive approach to business operations. He believed that improved efficiency in a business could be obtained by

1. Using managers as *planners* of work, gathering traditional knowledge about the work, and reducing it to standardized procedures for the workers.
2. Methodically *selecting, training,* and *developing* each worker on an individual basis.
3. Striving for *cooperation* between management and workers to simultaneously obtain both maximum production and high workers' wages.
4. *Dividing* the work between managers and the workers so that both are working on what they are most proficient at.

Taylor described his new management philosophy in a book, *The Principles of Scientific Management,* published in 1911. This event, more than any other, can be considered the beginning of the field of operations management.

The 1950s saw the development of systems theory, operations research, and the computer, each of which furthered the field. As was discussed earlier, *systems theory* emphasized the interrelationships in operations problems. *Operations research,* also known as *management science,* employed a quantitative decision focus for operations problems. The computer allowed the fast, inexpensive development of management information, provided support for business functions such as payroll, and formed a basis for automation.

With so much attention being devoted to the management of factories, by the 1950s this special area of management came to be known as *manufacturing management.* (Other terms such as *industrial management* and *factory management* were used synonymously.) In the late 1950s scholars and researchers in the field began to generalize the problems and techniques of manufacturing management to other productive organizations as well, such as petroleum and chemical processors and wholesalers, and the name for the field evolved into *production management.* This term was intended to stress the fact that the field had become a functional management discipline in itself and not just a set of manufacturing techniques. In the late 1960s the field expanded even further, this time into the *service sector* of the economy. Since the word *production* seemed to connote product organizations, the more general term *operations* was substituted to emphasize the *generic* (or general) basis of the field. This transition from production to operations is still occurring today.

By the end of World War II, many managers in this country believed that the concept of mass production had been mastered. Consider the environment at the end of World War II:

- ❖ Manufacturers in the United States produced the highest-quality products at the lowest possible prices.

- ❖ Manufacturers in the United States had little or no foreign competition, as the Japanese and European economies had been destroyed during the war.

- ❖ Demand in the United States for products exceeded the capacity to supply them, largely because the majority of productive capacity during the war was used to support the war effort, and by the time the war ended, there was a great deal of pent-up demand.

Thus, manufacturers in the United States were in a comfortable position. They had the best products, they had no foreign competition, and they were able to sell whatever they produced. This is why many managers came to the conclusion that the concept of mass production had been mastered.

Consider what you would do if you ran a business with the goal of maximizing profits and were selling your products as fast as you could produce them. One alternative would be to expand capacity so that you could make more of the product. This is exactly what many businesses did during the late 1940s and 1950s. By the 1960s, productive capacity had pretty much caught up with demand and now manufacturers were in the unfortunate position of not being able to sell all they could produce. As a result, in the 1960s managers turned their attention to developing new and innovative ways to sell their products. Hence, the 1960s are often referred to as the "marketing era." It was during this period that concepts such as market segmentation, target marketing, and consumer behavior were developed. Television was used to bring marketing messages to large audiences, and marketing strategy became synonymous with corporate strategy.

Having mastered manufacturing in the 1940s and 1950s, and marketing in the 1960s, businesses turned their attention to the last core functional area, and the 1970s began the "era of finance." It was during this era that concepts such as running business units as profit centers evolved. Also, the use of financial performance measures such as return on investment and payback period became prevalent. The attention of top management was directed toward managing the portfolio of businesses the company owned and operated. Becoming a large conglomerate appeared to be the overriding objective.

In the meantime, while companies in the United States were focusing on marketing in the 1960s and finance in the 1970s, its international competitors, especially in West Germany and Japan, were focusing their efforts on improving operations. Even a cursory look at any of a number of industries such as automobiles or consumer electronics suggests the impact of this trend. Take the auto industry, for example. In 1980, General Motors had a market share of 46 percent; this dropped below 32 percent in October and November of 1989 (Ingrassia and White, 1989). The point is not that marketing and finance activities are not important. Rather, it is that all three activities are vital, and they all must play a role in developing corporate strategy.

Currently, because of the continuing growth of services in our economy, and their poor record of productivity, it appears that services will command an increasing amount of attention from operations management. For example, McDonald's innovation in fast food involved improved operations: consistent quality, fast service, low price. Let us then take a closer look at the role of services in our economy.

❖ The Emergence and Growth of the Service Sector

With the rise in the standard of living resulting from increased factory productivity came changes in the needs and demands of the population. A person could use just so many pairs of shoes, so many easy chairs, and so many cars. Rather than spend their income on more goods, people decided to see a movie, eat out more often, pay someone else to clean their houses or cut their lawns, improve their education or health, travel abroad, or just invest their surplus income.

Figures 1.4 and 1.5 dramatically illustrate that, since 1950, services (including transportation, trade, utilities, government, finance, insurance, real estate, and gen-

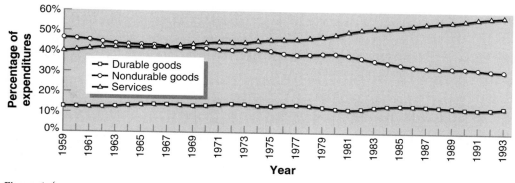

Figure 1.4 Expenditures on services as a proportion of personal consumption. *Source:* Economic Report of the President, February 1996.

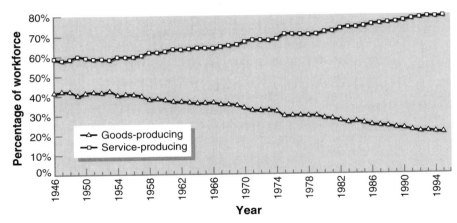

Figure 1.5 Employment in services as a proportion of the workforce.
Source: Economic Report of the President, February 1996.

eral services) have been rapidly increasing as a proportion of both *expenditures* for personal consumption and *employers* of the workforce. Note that less than 20 percent of the workforce is now employed in manufacturing (including mining and construction). Paralleling the growth in private-sector services, there has also been a significant increase in public-sector (government) services such as fire protection, welfare, and defense.

Although the demand for services has increased markedly, one reason for the tremendous growth in service-sector employment has been negative: its lack of growth in productivity. The inefficiency of services is evidenced by the constant and often bitter criticism of the post office, the railroads, the health care system, public schools, and many other such systems.

Only in recent years have service-sector organizations received the same attention from researchers as had been paid to manufacturers. Many of the concepts and ideas developed for the manufacturing sector can be modified and applied to service industries. For example, the problems of routing school buses, locating fire and rescue stations, and laying out health centers and scheduling their activities have been addressed through modifications of manufacturing management methods, with encouraging results. But society is still struggling under the weight of numerous problems of design, improvement, and development of systems of welfare, health delivery, criminal justice, solid waste disposal, pollution control, urban renewal, and land use. These problems are ripe for the application of operations management methods.

❖ Critical Issues in Operations

The field of operations management is facing a number of critical issues today that are inherent in our dynamic economy and global markets. First, as just noted, the management of the service sector is a large and important challenge. The productivity of both private and public services is poor and poses a formidable challenge to the field. As services increase in both employment and expenditures, they will absorb productive resources that are needed elsewhere in our economy, unless we can significantly improve their productivity.

Second, the computer is everywhere, offering great opportunities for improved management, particularly of operations. As an outgrowth of the wide use of the computer, automation and technology are changing our lives every day. Indeed, the movement of designing business processes (reengineering), which is the basis for the new process-centered organizational structures, is concerned with developing organizational structures that best meet the needs of customers and are based on the capabilities offered by new technologies.

OPERATIONS IN PRACTICE

Allen-Bradley Competes Internationally with Automation

Allen-Bradley manufactures electric motor contactors, or switches, and sells them by the millions. It had a profitable domestic market until Americans started buying foreign machinery and motors with tiny foreign-made contactors that seemed to do the job just about as well as Allen-Bradley's big, expensive contactors. Tracy O'Rourke, then Allen-Bradley's chief executive officer, clearly saw the threat that was coming.

In response, he initiated a study to determine the lowest worldwide price for these little contactors. The firm found that they were being sold in Australia at that time for only $8 apiece, half of what they were going for in Europe ($16, and even that was cheaper than the American price). O'Rourke concluded that if Allen-Bradley wanted to stay in the market, it would have to be able to make a profit at $8; at any higher price, it would constantly be undercut by the competition.

According to O'Rourke, Allen-Bradley constructed a "little" pilot (test) plant, relatively automated, to see if the contactors could be profitable at $8. The company found out that, in spite of the smoothness and speed of production in this small, integrated plant, "we would absolutely lose our shirt" at a selling price of $8. Even if there was no direct labor at all—zero, zip, nil—Allen-Bradley would still lose money. The executives looked at the numbers: $5 million to redesign their product and another $15 million to retool the plant, all so they could lose money at $8 per unit. It didn't make sense.

But they worked at it some more and found that if they could get rid of all the people (indirect as well) and all the paperwork, and all the end-of-the-day inventory too, they could justify the investment at the $8 price. That meant a completely automated, integrated, top-quality factory. Though this was difficult to do, it was what they did. This plant now produces 600 contactors per hour, in 777 variations and lot sizes of one or two, with virtually no people, paper, or final inventory. The quality cost due to defects was previously 3.5 percent of sales (equivalent to over 35,000 rejects per million produced) but now runs 15 rejects per million!

This is what it takes to compete successfully in today's worldwide marketplace. It isn't a matter of slightly higher productivity here and slightly better quality there. By and large, we need improvements on the order of 10 to 20 times better than now, just to stay in business. Without that, today's businesses won't be around for the long run (Avishai, 1989; O'Rourke, 1989).

There is also a "quality crusade," both service and product firms across the globe are joining. Quality is one of the major concerns of operations management, and designing for quality, as well as building quality, is of critical importance to operations managers. Similarly, there has been a surge of interest in fast response to customers, another concern of operations. Quick, timely delivery of outputs, as well as fast design of services and products, is clearly the next competitive battleground for international firms.

Another critical issue for operations is capitalizing on the organization's human assets, employing people for their brainpower instead of their muscle power. Although most firms acknowledge that people are their most valuable assets, they still treat their employees as though they were expendable. Measures such as utilization (of both people and machines) and short-term profitability encourage inappropriate behavior on the part of all employees. New means and measures of motivation are needed that will do a better job of tying individual behaviors to organizational goals.

Perhaps most critical of all, global competitiveness is the essence of operations. As we move into the future, the worldwide markets of Europe, Asia, and America will be selecting the best products and services among those offered. Operations plays the major role in that competition. The sidebar on Operations in Practice describes the success of Allen-Bradley in rejuvenating its operations through automation. This issue of global competitiveness is the next topic we will study, in Chapter 2.

$\mathcal{C}$HAPTER IN PERSPECTIVE _____

This first chapter serves as an introduction to the field of operations management. At the beginning of the chapter, *operations* was defined as the activities associated with transforming inputs into useful outputs in order to create a result of value. It was also shown that the actual production system is defined in terms of environment, inputs, transformation system, outputs, and the mechanism used for monitoring and control. The four primary ways that value can be added to an entity and the major subject areas within operations were also discussed.

The chapter overviewed two alternative ways for organizing work activities. In the traditional functional approach, companies organize activities on the basis of the type of work performed. With this approach, operations, marketing, and finance are defined as the three core functions. Recently, however, many companies have found that they can significantly improve organizational efficiency and effectiveness by organizing activities on the basis of specific value-creating processes. As a result of the evolution from functional to process-centered organizational structures, this book has been organized on the basis of three generic business processes: design of product and transformation systems, resource management, and product supply. Finally, this chapter closed with a discussion of the development of operations management, the emergence and growth of the service sector, and some critical issues in operations.

Chapter 2 will continue our introduction to operations with a discussion of business strategy and international competitiveness. Chapter 3 then follows with a discussion of how quality management activities support a business strategy and enhance competitiveness. Chapter 4 provides the foundation for the remainder of the book and concludes Part One with an overview of designing business processes.

❖ CHECK YOUR UNDERSTANDING _____

1. Define the following: operations, services, system, system boundary, environment, facilitating goods.

2. List several examples of each of the four primary ways of creating value. Also, list several examples of organizations that create value by combining two or more of these approaches.

3. What is the operations function in a trucking firm? An advertising agency? Identify the components of each element of the production system.

4. How does the concept of a facilitating good clarify the distinction between products and services?

5. Name the tangible and intangible benefits of purchasing an antique and of going to the theater.

6. What is the benefit of describing the activities of an organization in terms of a production system as in Figure 1.1?

7. What are the services embodied in the following products: water piped into your house, *Fortune* magazine, a restaurant meal, a bank loan?

8. Contrast a functional organizational structure and a process-centered one.

9. What is the concept of division of labor?

❖ EXPAND YOUR UNDERSTANDING _____

1. Since value is always in the mind of the beholder, how does altering a product differ from advertising or guarantees in terms of added value?

2. How does the way a system's boundary is defined affect the results of a systems analysis?

3. Which functional area of business is it most important for operations to interface with smoothly? Why?

4. Why is it so hard to increase productivity in the service sector?

5. Why is it important for managers in functional areas such as finance, marketing, and personnel to understand operations?

6. Can you identify some other types of transformations besides those listed in Figure 1.1, such as "guarantees"?

7. Identify some other major differences between services and products besides those listed in Table 1.1.

8. Why, in Figure 1.4, are only the nondurable goods declining as a percentage of expenditures instead of both durable and nondurable goods?

9. In the sidebar about Allen-Bradley, the firm found contactors being sold at half the price in Australia as compared with Europe. How ethical is it for a firm to charge a lower price in one country than another? How ethical is it for a firm to sell a product at less than what it costs to make (this is called *dumping*), particularly if another firm goes bankrupt as a result?

10. Which of the major areas in Table 1.3 is most influenced by new technology? What kinds of technologies have an impact on this area?

11. The United States government has strict laws regarding pollution, antitrust activities, and bribery by American firms. Yet many other countries have no such laws. Indeed, firms and individuals in those countries may well expect to receive a kickback (return of cash) for orders placed or delivered. How ethical is it for a firm based in the United States to meet foreigners' expectations? How ethical is it for the United States government to restrict the activities of domestic firms but not those of foreign firms operating in the United States?

12. Since pure services are nonphysical (i.e., have no facilitating good), does technology offer anything for competitiveness in this area?

13. Many foreign firms have been successful in the following areas: steel, autos, cameras, radios, and televisions. Are services more protected from foreign competition? How?

14. It is commonly said that Japanese firms employ 10 times as many engineers per operations worker as American firms and 10 times fewer accountants. What impact would you expect this to have on their competitiveness? Why?

15. Projects are composed of representatives from each of several functional areas. What might be the role of a representative from your functional area in a project team whose goal was to develop a new product or service for a firm?

16. Develop an organization chart for a school of business that you plan to open next year.

❖ APPLY YOUR UNDERSTANDING _____
Taracare, Inc.

Taracare, Inc., operates a single factory in Miami, where it fabricates and assembles a wide range of outdoor furniture including chairs, tables, and matching accessories. Taracare's primary production activities include extruding the aluminum furniture parts, bending and shaping the extruded parts, finishing and painting the parts, and then assembling the parts into completed furniture. Upholstery, glass tabletops, and all hardware are purchased from outside suppliers.

Craig Johnson purchased Taracare in 1993. Before that, Craig had distinguished himself as a top sales rep of outdoor furniture for one of the leading national manufacturers. However, after spending 10 years on the road, Craig decided to pursue other opportunities. After searching for a couple of months, he came across what he believed to be an ideal opportunity. Not only was it in an industry that he had a great deal of knowledge about, but he would be his own boss. Unfortunately, the asking price was well beyond Craig's means. However, after a month of negotiation, Craig convinced Jeff Lewis, Taracare's founder, to maintain a 25 percent stake in the business. Although Jeff had originally intended to sell out completely, he was impressed with Craig's knowledge of the business, his extensive contacts, and his enthusiasm. He therefore agreed to sell Craig 75 percent of Taracare and retain 25 percent as an investment.

Craig's ambition for Taracare was to expand it from a small regional manufacturer to one that sold to major national retailers. To accomplish this objective, Craig's first initiative was to triple Taracare's sales force in 1994. As sales began to increase, Craig increased the support staff by hiring an accountant, a comptroller, two new designers, and a purchasing agent.

By the middle of 1997, Taracare's line was carried by several national retailers on a trial basis. However, Taracare was having difficulty meeting the deliveries its sales reps were promising and difficulty satisfying the national retailers' standards for quality. To respond to this problem, Craig hired Sam Davis as the new manufacturing manager. Before accepting Craig's offer, Sam was the plant manager of a factory that manufactured replacement windows sold by large regional and national retailers.

After several months on the job—and after making little progress toward improving on-time delivery and quality—Sam scheduled a meeting with Craig to discuss his major concerns. Sam began:

I requested this meeting with you, Craig, because I am not satisfied with the progress we are making toward improving our delivery performance and quality. The bottom line is that I feel I'm getting very little cooperation from the other department heads. For example, last month purchasing switched to a new supplier for paint; and although it is true that the new paint costs less per gallon, we have to apply a thicker coat to give the furniture the same protection. I haven't actually run the numbers, but I know it is actually costing us more, in both materials and labor. Another problem is that we typically run a special promotion to coincide with launching new product lines. I understand that the sales guys want to get the product into the stores as quickly as possible, but they are making promises about delivery that we can't meet. It takes time to work out the bugs and get things running smoothly. Then there is the problem with the designers. They are constantly adding features to the product that make it almost impossible for us to produce. At the very least, they make it much more expensive for us to produce. For example, on the new "Destiny" line, they designed table legs that required a new die at a cost of $25,000. Why couldn't they have left the legs alone so that we could have used one of our existing dies? On top of this, we have the accounting department telling us that our equipment utilization is too low. Then, when we increase our equipment utilization and make more product, the finance guys tell us we have too much capital tied up in inventory. To be honest, I really don't feel that I'm getting very much support.

Rising from his chair, Craig commented

You have raised some important issues. Unfortunately, I have to run to another meeting. Why don't you send me a memo outlining these issues and your recommendations? Then perhaps I will call a meeting and we can discuss these issues with the other department heads. At any rate, our production problems are really no worse than that of our competitors, and we don't expect you to solve all of our problems overnight. Keep up the good work and send me that memo at your earliest convenience.

Questions

1. Does Sam's previous experience running a plant that made replacement windows qualify him to run a plant that makes outdoor furniture?

2. What recommendations would you make if you were in Sam's shoes?

3. Given Craig's background and apparent priorities, how is he likely to respond to your recommendations? On the basis of this likely response, is it possible to rephrase your recommendations so that they may be more appealing to Craig?

Chapter *2*

Business Strategy and International Competitiveness

$\mathscr{C}$ HAPTER OVERVIEW

❖ An organization's business strategy specifies what its competitive advantage will be and how this advantage will be achieved and sustained.

❖ A large number of factors are considered in deriving a business strategy: the firm's strengths and weaknesses, its core competencies, the environment, the markets, competitors, and so on.

❖ A common starting point in the formulation of strategy is the development of vision and mission statements. Vision statements are used to express the organization's values and its aspirations. Mission statements express the organization's purpose or reason for existence.

❖ One important part of developing a business strategy is identifying the organization's core competencies. Core competencies are the collective knowledge and skills an organization has that distinguish it from the competition.

❖ Four major business strategies are: first-to-market, second-to-market, cost minimization or late-to-market, and market segmentation.

❖ Successful firms typically focus on one or two areas in which they excel such as innovation; cus-

tomization; flexibility of products, services, and volumes; performance; quality; reliability of products, services, and delivery; responsiveness; after-sales service; and price.

❖ Focus can be lost very easily if management adds new outputs to the mix, requires new attributes from the existing outputs, adds new tasks to the production system, does not alter the operations tasks to fit the products' life cycles, allows departmental professionalism to guide actions, or just never makes the focus explicit in the first place.

❖ The areas a firm should focus on are normally the *order winners* for that market. Other factors are considered to be simply *order qualifiers* in that without acceptable levels of these factors, the firm is not even in the running.

❖ The three major trading regions are Europe, North America, and the Pacific rim. Exchange rates between currencies are quoted as the number of one currency to buy a unit, such as a dollar, of another currency. A country runs a trade deficit when its imports exceed its exports, as has been happening with increasing frequency in the United States since the early 1970s.

❖ Outsourcing is the practice of buying parts or entire products from an external, especially foreign, source and then assembling or branding them under your nameplate. When the primary value-added activities required to produce a product are outsourced, the firm is called *hollow.*

❖ The primary characteristics of the transformation system are its efficiency, effectiveness, capacity, quality, lead time, and flexibility.

❖ The engineering design of a product or service determines about 70 percent of the resulting cost of the output.

❖ Productivity is normally defined as output per worker-hour, but this is a *partial factor measure.* If two or more factors are considered in the denominator, it is known as a *multifactor measure,* and if all the inputs—labor, capital, materials, and energy—are included, it is known as a *total factor measure.*

❖ Although the United States currently has the highest overall productivity among the industrialized nations, its rate of growth in productivity is less than that of several other industrialized nations.

❖ Responsiveness is a combination of customization, response time, and quality that goes beyond the expectations of customers.

❖ Customization, derived from production flexibility, is a continuum that ranges from standard, world-class products on one end to options, then variants, then alternative models, and finally complete customization on the other end.

❖ The mass customization strategy emerged in response to the discovery that efficiency and flexibility can be improved simultaneously and may not have to be traded off for one another. Organizations pursuing a mass customization strategy seek to produce low-cost, high-quality outputs in high variety.

❖ The benefits of flexibility, in addition to the ability to customize, include faster response, greater volume capacity, shorter design-to-market lead times, lower cost of changes, lower cost of offering a full line, and protection against delays in production and distribution.

❖ The major advantages of fast response time to customers are a reduced opportunity for changing orders, better focus on the customer and the production system, faster generation of revenue, higher quality, more efficient production, and better communication and morale.

❖ Twelve dimensions of quality are: (1) conformance to specifications, (2) performance, (3) quick response, (4) quick-change expertise, (5) features, (6) reliability, (7) durability, (8) serviceability, (9) aesthetics, (10) perceived quality, (11) humanity, and (12) value.

❖ The benefits of high quality include better profit margins, higher market shares, protection from competition, reduced risks to health and safety, less waste, more efficient production, and up to 25 percent lower costs.

INTRODUCTION

❖ Concerned about a shortage of labor, Manor Care is designing its Sleep Inns the way an industrial engineer designs an assembly line. To minimize the size of the housekeeping staff, nightstands are attached to the wall so there are no legs to be vacuumed around. The closets have no doors to open and close. Rounded shower stalls are used to eliminate corners, which collect dirt and are difficult to clean. An advanced security system logs the time a maid inserts her card and enters a room and is used to track the maid's time. The same system permits guests to use their credit cards to enter the room, thus eliminating the need for the hotel to handle keys. Asphalt and shrubbery are used to limit the amount of lawn mowing required. The result of these efforts is that cleaning a room takes 20 minutes versus the industry standard of 30 minutes. Furthermore, an entire 92-room hotel is operated with the equivalent of 11 full-time workers (Wessel, 1989).

❖ In the early 1980s, the biggest threat to the largest American steelmakers was foreign competition. However, after closing inefficient plants, modernizing others, and reducing payrolls during the 1980s, large American steelmakers can now go toe to toe with these foreign competitors. As an example, in 1982 in the United States it took 10.59 labor hours to produce and ship 1 metric ton of steel; in Japan it took 10.01 hours. By the early 1990s, American producers reversed this advantage. As a result of improving their productivity faster than their foreign counterparts, by the middle of 1991 American steelmakers were able to produce 1 metric ton with 5.4 labor hours, compared with 5.6 hours for Japanese steelmakers. Furthermore, in addition to improving their productivity, large American steelmakers have simultaneously improved their quality. To illustrate, in the early 1980s Ford rejected about 8 percent of its domestic steel shipments, and 20 percent of its steel shipments were late. By the early 1990s, its steel rejects had been reduced to less than 1 percent and 99 percent of its shipments were delivered on time (Pare, 1991).

❖ In early 1995, Kansas City Power and Light began installing automatic meter readers in its 420,000 meters. An automatic meter reader is a small electronic device that broadcasts data on electricity usage every few minutes and eliminates the need for $15-an-hour human meter readers. Coca-Cola is testing a similar technology to be used in the millions of vending machines that stock its product. Using such a device, Coca-Cola will be able to reduce costs by scheduling deliveries for only those vending machines that are out of stock. Without the devices, delivery schedules and quantities are based primarily on hunches. Also, Coca-Cola anticipates that the use of these devices will lead to increased sales through more timely restocking of the machines. Finally, the data collected will be used to help Coca-Cola evaluate the effectiveness of various advertising campaigns (Zachary, 1995).

For a wide variety of reasons, numerous companies are investing substantial amounts of time and other resources in improving organizational efficiency or productivity. In the case of Manor Care, a shortage of labor required it to find ways to operate its hotels with fewer employees. In the case of domestic steel producers, the impetus for improving productivity was a desire to remain competitive in a global marketplace. The opportunities that new technologies often provide to improve organizational efficiency and effectiveness are illustrated by Kansas City Power and Light and Coca-Cola. Regardless of the specific reasons a particular organization cites for improving productivity, such programs are almost always undertaken with the intent of sustaining or improving the organization's competitive position in the marketplace.

Making and keeping an organization competitive is top management's job, and this is accomplished partly through the business strategy that top management adopts. This strategy gives the firm its direction and vision for the future and guides its decisions in both the short term and the long term. A common strategy in the recent past, particularly for small firms, was to be a local supplier who could react quickly to the immediate needs of its customers.

But global producers are now competing in virtually all markets, whether local, domestic, or foreign. Thus, even if a firm sees itself as only a small, local business, it must be globally competitive to survive. For example, small regional foundries have been driven out of business by the thousands and replaced by international competitors. Thus, it is incumbent on every firm's top management to consider international competition in its business strategy.

In the traditional functional organization discussed in Chapter 1, top management needed to draw the expertise of all the functional areas together to focus on the needs of the market. Marketing needed to know and be in touch with the organization's customers; research and development (R&D) needed to direct creative efforts toward satisfying the needs of this market; and operations needed to produce and deliver responsively. Support and staff functions such as finance, personnel, and data processing needed to provide the resources the other functions required in a timely and effective manner. In contrast to the functional organization, one advantage of companies organized on the basis of their value-creating processes is that this coordination among the different functions occurs somewhat automatically.

Our description of the production system in Chapter 1 assumed that the organization had some specific, well-defined goal—for example, such a goal might be making gourmet cookies for an upscale market. This goal implies awareness of marketing: What services and facilitating goods do customers want? But any independent financial goal (to make the company rich) or marketing goal (to increase sales 10 percent) is only wishful thinking unless the operations of the organization can deliver what is needed with the resources that are available. What transformation activities are needed? What level of quality is required? Is transportation necessary?

The organization's strategy—known as its *business strategy*—provides the information needed to design business processes for the firm to achieve its goals. The business strategy also provides the information for all activities carried out in the organization to support the production system in its task. In the functional organization, this specification of how each function is going to support the overall business strategy was known as a *functional strategy*. Thus, there was a marketing strategy, a finance strategy, an operations strategy, and so on. In organizations structured on the basis of business processes, separate functional strategies specifying how each functional area will support the overall business strategy are not needed. Rather, a strategy for how each business process supports the overall business strategy is developed. Along these lines, a **business process strategy** is a set of objectives, plans, and policies describing how a particular business process will support the business strategy of the organization.

This chapter explores the development of the business strategy and international competitiveness in more detail. We first look at the process of forming the business strategy and some common results of this process. We then consider the need to focus the strategy on a few key aspects of the output—the service or product—to satisfy a unique market. Finally, we turn our attention to the global competitiveness of the organization. Here we focus primarily on the two factors: cost, which includes the issue of productivity; and responsiveness, which includes the attributes of customization (or variety), quality, and response time.

STRATEGY FORMULATION

The organization's business strategy is a set of objectives, plans, and policies for the organization to compete successfully in its markets. In effect, the business strategy specifies what an organization's competitive advantage will be and how this advantage will be achieved and sustained. As we will see, a key aspect of the business strategy is defining the organization's core competencies and focus. The actual strategic plan that details the business strategy is typically formulated at the executive committee level (CEO, president, vice presidents). It is usually long-range, in the neighborhood of 3 to 5 years.

In fact, however, the decisions that are made over time are the long-range strategy. In too many firms, these decisions show no pattern at all, reflecting the truth that they have no active business strategy, even if they have gone through a process of strategic planning. In other cases these decisions bear little or no relationship to the organization's stated or official business strategy. The point is that an organization's actions often tell more about its true business strategy than its public statements.

❖ Formulating the Business Strategy

The general process of formulating a business strategy is illustrated in Figure 2.1. Relevant inputs to the strategic planning process are the products and services needed by customers; the strengths and weaknesses of the competition; the environment in general; and the organization's own strengths, weaknesses, culture, and resources.

After collectively considering these inputs, strategic planning is often initiated by developing a vision statement, a mission statement, or both. **Vision statements** are used to express the organization's values and aspirations. **Mission statements** express the organization's purpose or reason for existence. In some cases, organizations may choose to combine the vision and mission statements into a single statement. Regardless of whether separate statements or combined statements are developed, the intent is to communicate the organization's values, aspirations, and

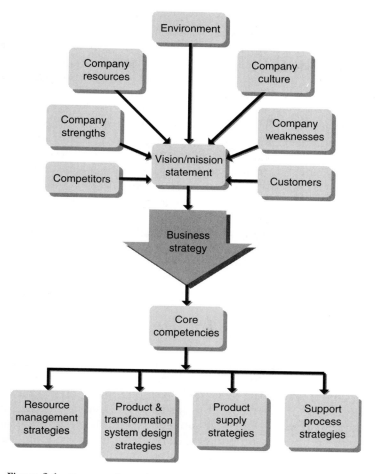

Figure 2.1 Strategy formulation.

purpose so that employees can make decisions that are consistent with and support these objectives.

Effective vision and mission statements tend to be written using language that inspires employees to high levels of performance. Further, to foster employees' commitment, it is advisable to include a wide variety of employees in the development of the vision or mission statement, rather than enforcing top management's view by edict. Once the vision and mission statements are developed for the organization as a whole, divisions, departments, process teams, project teams, work groups, and so on can develop individual vision-mission statements that support the organization's overall statement. For example, after a university develops its overall vision-mission statement, each college could develop its own unique statements specifying the role that it will play in supporting the overall mission of the university. Likewise, once each school develops its own vision-mission statement, the departments within the school can develop unique statements. Having each organizational unit develop its own unique statements promotes wider participation in the process, helps employees think in terms of how their work supports the overall mission, and results in statements that are more meaningful to a select group of employees. Some examples of actual vision-mission statements are provided in Figure 2.2.

Once the vision-mission statement is drafted, a business strategy is formulated specifying how the vision and mission will be accomplished. One important result of developing a business strategy is identifying the organization's core competencies. ***Core competencies*** are the collective knowledge and skills an organization has that distinguish it from the competition. Typically, core competencies center on an organization's ability to integrate a variety of specific technologies and skills in the development of new products and services. Clearly, one of top management's most important activities is to identify and develop the core competencies the organization will need to successfully execute the business strategy. Given this importance, we discuss core competencies in more detail in the next section.

Once a business strategy is formulated, and the core competencies are specified, each business process develops its own strategy to guide its activities so that they are consistent and support the organization's overall business strategy. Although formulating the business strategy is displayed as rather straightforward in Figure 2.1, in reality it is very iterative.

❖ Core Competencies

As previously mentioned, core competencies are the collective knowledge and skills that distinguish an organization from the competition. In effect, core competencies provide the basis for developing new products and services, and they are a primary factor in determining an organization's long-term competitiveness. Therefore, an important part of strategic planning is identifying and predicting the core competencies that are critical to sustaining and enhancing the organization's competitive position. On this basis, an assessment can be made of suppliers' and competitors' capabilities. If the organization finds that it is not the leader, it must determine the cost and risks of catching up with the best versus the cost and risks of losing the core competency.

Often, it is more useful to think of an organization in terms of its portfolio of core competencies, rather than its portfolio of businesses or products. For instance, Sony is known for its expertise in miniaturization; 3M for its knowledge of substrates, coatings, and adhesives; Black and Decker for small electrical motors and industrial design; Boeing for its ability to integrate large-scale complex systems; and Honda for engines and power trains. Had Sony initially viewed itself as primarily a manufacturer of Walkmans, rather than as a company with expertise in miniaturization, it might have overlooked several profitable opportunities such as entering the camcorder business. As another example, Boeing has successfully leveraged its core competency related to integrating large-scale systems in its production of commercial jetliners, space stations, fighter-bombers, and missiles.

As these examples illustrate, core competencies are often used to gain access to a wide variety of markets. Cannon used its core competencies in optics, imaging, and electronic controls to enter the markets for copiers, laser printers, cameras, and image scanners. In a similar fashion, Honda's core competencies in engines and power trains are the basis for its entry into other businesses: automobiles, motorcycles, lawn mowers, and generators.

In addition to providing access to a variety of markets, a core competence should be strongly related to the key benefits provided by the product or service.

Coca-Cola Company's Mission Statement

Our Mission

We exist to create value for our share owners on a long-term basis by building a business that enhances the Coca-Cola Company's trademarks. This also is our ultimate commitment.

As the world's largest beverage company, we refresh the world. We do this by developing superior soft drinks, both carbonated and non-carbonated, and profitable non-alcoholic beverage systems that create value for our Company, our bottling partners and our customers.

In creating value, we succeed or fail based on our ability to perform as stewards of several key assets:

1. Coca-Cola, the world's most powerful trademark, and other highly valuable trademarks.
2. The world's most effective and pervasive distribution system.
3. Satisfied customers, who make a good profit selling our products.
4. Our people, who are ultimately responsible for building this enterprise.
5. Our abundant resources, which must be intelligently allocated.
6. Our strong global leadership in the beverage industry in particular and in the business world in general.

The Central Intelligence Agency

Our Vision

To be the keystone of a U.S. Intelligence Community that is pre-eminent in the world, known for both the high quality of our work and the excellence of our people.

Our Mission

We support the President, the National Security Council, and all who make and execute U.S. national security policy by:
- Providing accurate, evidence-based, comprehensive, and timely foreign intelligence related to national security; and
- Conducting counterintelligence activities, special activities, and other functions related to foreign intelligence and national security as directed by the President.

APICS—The Educational Society for Resource Management

Vision

To inspire individuals and organizations toward lifelong learning and to enhance individual and organizational success.

Mission

To be the premier provider and global leader in individual and organizational education, standards of excellence, and information in integrated resource management.

Sources: http://www.cocacola.com/co/mission.html, http://www.odci.gov/cia/information/mission.html, http://www.industry.net/c/orgunpro/apics/plan (February 12, 1997).

Figure 2.2   Examples of vision and mission statements.

In Sony's case, its expertise in miniaturization translates directly into important product features such as portability and aesthetic designs. Alternatively, suppose that Sony developed a core competence in writing understandable user manuals. Since people who purchase a Walkman or camcorder rarely base their decision on the quality of the user manual (when was the last time you read a user manual?), this competence would provide little if any competitive advantage.

Another characteristic of a core competence is that it should be difficult to imitate. Clearly, no sustainable competitive advantage is provided by a core competence that is easily imitated. For example, Sony's expertise in miniaturization would mean little if other electronics manufacturers could match it simply by purchasing and taking apart Sony's products (this is called *reverse engineering*).

The topic of core competence is also strongly related to outsourcing. **Outsourcing**—an approach that is being increasingly used—involves subcontracting out certain activities such as the production of parts to an external supplier. For example, a manufacturer might outsource the production of certain components, the management and maintenance of its computer resources, or the processing of its payroll.

When we consider the concept of core competence, it is important to recognize that not all parts or activities are equal. Rather, activities and parts can be thought of as a continuum ranging from strategically unimportant to strategically important. Parts and activities are considered strategically important when

- ❖ They are strongly related to what customers perceive to be the key characteristics of the product.
- ❖ They require highly specialized knowledge and skill.
- ❖ They require highly specialized physical assets, and few other suppliers possess these assets.
- ❖ The organization has a technological lead or is likely to obtain one.

Activities that are not strategic are candidates for outsourcing. These parts or activities are not strongly linked to key product characteristics, do not require highly specialized knowledge, do not need special physical assets, and the organization does not have the technological lead in this area. Thus, if it is beneficial to outsource these parts or activities—perhaps because of lower cost or higher quality—no loss in competitiveness should result.

On the other hand, when most of a firm's complex parts and production are outsourced, particularly to a foreign supplier, the firm is called *hollow*. As we have discussed, the wise firm will outsource only nonstrategic, simple, relatively standard parts such as nuts and bolts that are not worth the firm's time to produce itself; the complex, proprietary parts that give their products an edge in the marketplace are produced internally. If the firm outsources these parts as well, it soon finds that the engineering design talent follows the production of the part outside the firm, too. Then, the firm has been **hollowed out,** becoming merely a distributor of its supplier's products.

So what is the problem? If a supplier can deliver the parts at lower cost and better quality when they are needed, why not use them? The problem is that the supplier gains the expertise to produce the critical parts your firm needs. After a while, when the supplier has improved on the process and you have forgotten how to make the parts, it is likely to start producing the products you have been selling in competition with you and drop you as a customer. This is even more dangerous if, as noted above, the product and transformation system has also been hollowed out, following the production activities to the supplier. This happened extensively in the television industry, where the Japanese learned first how to produce, and then how to engineer black-and-white and later color television sets. They then started tentatively introducing their own brands, to see if American customers would buy them. Their products were inexpensive, were of high quality, and caught on quickly in the free-enterprise American markets. The Japanese now virtually control this industry.

❖ Business Strategy and the Product Life Cycle

A wide variety of common business strategies are described in this section and the following section. A number of them are tied to the stages in the standard *life cycle* of products and services, shown in Figure 2.3. Studies of the introduction of new products indicate that the life cycle (or *stretched-S growth curve,* as it is also known) provides a good pattern for the growth of demand for a new output. The curve can be divided into three major segments: introduction and early adoption, acceptance and growth of the market, and maturity with market saturation. After market saturation, demand may remain high or decline; or the output may be improved and possibly start on a new growth curve.

The length of product and service life cycles has been shrinking significantly in the last decade or so. In the past, a life cycle might have been five years, but it is now six months. This places a tremendous burden on the firm to constantly monitor its strategy and quickly change a strategy that becomes inappropriate to the market.

The life cycle begins with an *innovation*—a new output or process for the market. The innovation may be a patented product or process, a new combination of existing elements that has created a unique product or process, or some service that was previously unavailable. Initial versions of the product or service may change relatively frequently; production volumes are small, since the output has not caught on yet; and margins are high. As volume increases, the design of the output stabilizes and more competitors enter the market, frequently with more capital-intensive

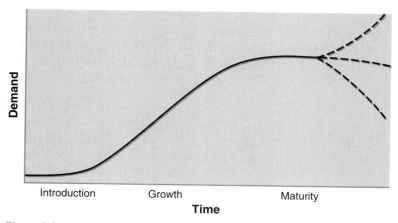

Figure 2.3 The life-cycle curve.

equipment. In the mature phase, the now high-volume output is a virtual commodity, and the firm that can produce an acceptable version at the lowest cost usually controls the market.

Clearly, a firm's business strategy should match the life-cycle stages of its products and services. If a firm is good at innovation—as, for example, Hewlett-Packard is—it may choose to focus only on the introduction and acceptance phases of the product's life cycle and then sell or license production to others as the product moves beyond the introduction stage. If its strength is in high-volume, low-cost production, the company should stick with proven products that are in the maturity stage. Most common, perhaps, are firms that attempt to stick with products throughout their life cycle, changing their strategy with each stage.

❖ Categories of Business Strategies

One approach to categorizing an organization's business strategy is based on its timing of introductions of new outputs. Two researchers, Maidique and Patch, suggest the following four product development strategies:

- ❖ *First-to-market.* Organizations that use this strategy attempt to have their products available before the competition. To achieve this, strong applied research is needed. If a company is first-to-market, it has to decide if it wants to price its products high and thus skim the market to achieve large short-term profits or set a lower initial price to obtain a higher market share and perhaps larger long-term profits.

- ❖ *Second-to-market.* Organizations that use this strategy try to quickly imitate successful outputs offered by first-to-market organizations. This strategy requires less emphasis on applied research and more emphasis on fast development. Often, firms that use the second-to-market strategy attempt to learn from the mistakes of the first-to-market firm and offer improved or enhanced versions of the original products.

- ❖ *Cost minimization or late-to-market.* Organizations that use this strategy wait until a product becomes fairly standardized and is demanded in large volumes. They then attempt to compete on the basis of costs as opposed to features of the product. These organizations focus most of their research and development on improving the production system, as opposed to focusing on product development.

- ❖ *Market segmentation.* This strategy focuses on serving niche markets with specific needs. Applied engineering skills and flexible manufacturing system are often needed for the market-segmentation strategy.

Be aware that a number of implicit trade-offs are involved in developing a strategy. Let us use the first-to-market strategy to demonstrate. A first-to-market strategy requires large investments in product development in an effort to stay ahead of the competition. Typically, organizations that pursue this strategy expect to achieve relatively higher profit margins, larger market shares, or both as a result of initially having the market to themselves. The strategy is somewhat risky because a competitor may end up beating them to the market. Also, even if a company succeeds in getting to the market first, it may end up simply creating an opportunity for the competition to learn from its mistakes and overtake it in the market. To illustrate, although Sony introduced its Betamax format for VCRs in 1975, JVC's VHS format—introduced the following year—is the standard that ultimately gained widespread market acceptance.

Such trade-offs are basic to the concept of selecting a business strategy. Although specific tasks must be done well to execute the selected strategy, not everything needs to be particularly outstanding—only a few things. And of course, strategies based on anything else—acquisitions, mergers, tax loss carry-forwards, even streams of high-technology products—will not be successful if the customer is ignored in the process.

OCUS

In the previous section, we discussed the issue of core competence. Now we look in more depth at the basic aim of the strategy. The goal of each strategy is to utilize an organization's core competencies to establish and maintain a unique strength, or **focus,** for the firm that leads to a sustainable competitive advantage. A number of industry studies have found that, over time, the successful companies are the ones that have demonstrated a continuous, single-minded determination to achieve one or both of the following competitive positions within their respective industries:

1. Have the *lowest cost* compared with the competition. If the quality of the output is acceptable, then the firm can adopt a very competitive pricing policy that will gain profitable volume and increase market share.

2. Have an *outstanding strength* (short lead time, advanced technology, high quality, and so on) that differentiates a firm from the competition and is valued in the marketplace. Then, if the firm has an acceptable cost structure, it can adopt a pricing policy to gain large margins and fund reinvestment in its differentiated strength.

❖ Areas of Focus

McKinsey & Company, a top management consulting firm, studied 27 outstanding successful firms to find their common attributes. Two of the major attributes reported in *Business Week* are directly related to the formulation of the business strategy:

1. *Stressing one key business value.* At Hewlett-Packard, it is developing new products; at Dana Corporation, it is improving productivity.

2. *Sticking to what they know best.* All the outstanding firms define their core competencies (or strengths) and then build on them. They resist the temptation to move into new areas or diversify.

When an organization chooses to stress one or two key areas of strength, it is referred to as a *focused organization.* For example, IBM is known for its customer service, General Electric for its technology, and Procter and Gamble for its consumer marketing. In general, most but not all areas of focus relate to product supply processes. Some firms, such as those in the insurance industry, focus on financial strength and others on marketing strengths. Kenner Toys, for example, considers its strength to be a legal one: the ability to win contracts for exclusive production of popular children's toys.

Table 2.1 identifies several areas of focus that organizations commonly choose when forming their competitive strategy; all are various forms of differentiation. Note that the concept of focus applies to pure service organizations as well as product firms. The sidebar about Rolm Telecommunications describes how that company achieves its focus on quality and also provides an example of a company that needed to work around its traditional functional structure.

❖ Order Qualifiers and Winners

Recent competitive behavior among firms seems to be dividing most of the factors in Table 2.1 into two sets that Terry Hill, an operations strategist and researcher in England, calls *order qualifiers* and *order winners*. An **order qualifier** is a characteristic of the product or service that is required if the product is even to be considered or in the running. In other words, it is a prerequisite for entering the market. An **order winner** is a characteristic that will win the bid or the purchase. These qualifiers and winners vary with the market, of course, but some general commonalties exist across markets. For example, response time, performance, customization, innovation, quality, and price seem to be frequent order winners, and the other factors (e.g., reliability and flexibility) tend to be order qualifiers.

❖ Loss of Focus

An organization can sometimes lose its focus. For example, in the traditional functional organization purchasing may buy the cheapest materials it can. This requires buying large quantities with advance notice. Scheduling, however, is trying to reduce inventories so it orders materials on short notice and in small quantities. Quality control is trying to improve the output, so it carefully inspects every item, creating delays and extensive rework. In this example, each functional department is pursuing its own objectives but is not focusing on how it can support the organization's overall business strategy. In an effort to eliminate these types of problems, many organizations are adopting organizational structures based on specific value-creating processes, as opposed to organizing work on the basis of the type of activity performed. Organizing work on the basis of value-creating processes enables each employee to focus on the desired end result.

There may even be a loss of focus at the top management level. For example, one firm decided to consolidate its production of made-to-order products in a remodeled central plant. Previously, the products were made in three separate plants that were obsolete and inefficient. One plant produced high volumes of cheap fasteners (screws, nails) on demand for the construction industry. It used large, dirty equipment to stamp out the fasteners in short lead times with minimal quality control. The second plant produced expensive, high-quality microwave ovens. Engineering design was the critical function, with long lead times, extensive testing, and purchases in small lots. The third plant produced custom integrated circuits in clean rooms with expensive computerized equipment. The consolidation proved to be a

𝒯ABLE 2.1 ❖ Common Areas of Organizational Focus

❖ *Innovation:* Bringing a range of new products and services to market quickly.

❖ *Customization:* Being able to quickly redesign and produce a product or service to meet customers' unique needs.

❖ *Flexibility of products and services:* Switching between different models or variants quickly to satisfy a customer or market.

❖ *Flexibility of volume:* Changing quickly and economically from low-volume production to high volumes and vice versa.

❖ *Performance:* Offering products and services with unique, valuable features.

❖ *Quality:* Having better craftsmanship or consistency.

❖ *Reliability of the product or service:* Always working acceptably, enabling customers to count on the performance.

❖ *Reliability of delivery:* Always fulfilling promises with a product or service that is never late.

❖ *Response:* Offering very short lead times to obtain products and services.

❖ *After-sale service:* Making available extensive, continuing help.

❖ *Price:* Having the lowest price.

---

disaster. Although this is an extreme example, many firms do exactly the same thing with a variety of product lines that have grown up in the same plant. Clearly, these firms once had some competitive advantage, or they never would have survived.

How do organizations lose their focus and get into trouble? There are a number of ways this can happen.

❖ *New outputs:* This is the situation in the example above. Managers, in an attempt to reap what they feel will be economies of scale, add products or services to the organization's offerings that require expertise in a wide variety of areas. Unable to control the variety of expertise required of each line, the organization becomes unfocused.

❖ *New attributes:* This occurs when management adds a new twist to the output that conflicts with the existing focus, or the market demands a new twist that the firm cannot meet. For example, the firm may have been producing a high-quality custom product, and a competitor develops a new process to produce a standard item at a cheap price. Management might decree that a low-cost version of the item is now needed in the marketplace, but operations cannot meet this requirement and also stay focused on high-quality custom products.

❖ *New tasks:* Management may add new tasks to operations, such as reducing costs, raising quality, or improving product safety. Such requirements may come about because of new laws or regulations, union contracts, or other such reasons. But the requirement will compromise the firm's existing focus and may make it uncompetitive in the marketplace.

❖ *Life-cycle changes:* As products go through their life cycle, the task of operations often changes, as shown in Figure 2.4. Initially, the task is to get an adequate-quality item into a market that has just discovered this new output. The form of the output often changes at this early, experimental stage, so the organization must be flexible enough to accept changes in design. As the

OPERATIONS IN PRACTICE

Rolm Telecommunications

A major building block in Rolm's business strategy is "vision." Rolm has found that the critical factor in companies' performance is largely the employees' image of what the business is, where it is going, and how each of the parts fits into the whole. As Wayne Mehl, Rolm's general manager, says, "That image determines the outcome."

In working with their people to better understand the whole of what Rolm is, managers found it necessary to break down the walls between functions, to let people see the entire organization and what it was about. They involved their people more closely with management, with other functions, and even with suppliers and customers. Rolm considers its primary unit of value to be its people. The people make things happen—people have the vision and carry out the plans. Without people, nothing happens.

One example of this interplay between vision and people is in the area of quality. In too many firms, poor quality is expected and accepted. Only 1 percent defective goods is considered excellent in many manufacturing firms.

But Mehl asks us to consider some examples where poor quality is unacceptable, such as banking and music. What would you think about a bank that had 99 percent accurate statements? Of every 100 entries on your statement, one would be wrong, on average. For many people that would mean an average of one error on every statement. What would you think about a bank that sent you a statement that was wrong every month, and was proud of its quality? Or suppose you went to a concert with a date and the orchestra played 99 percent of the notes correctly. Would you be embarrassed?

Some of the results of this attention to Rolm's employees and their vision of the firm are clearly evident. For example, inventories have been cut in half, defective products in process have been reduced by a factor of six, and rework has almost been eliminated. Mehl quotes a production supervisor as saying, "I used to have seven people doing rework, and now I have one. My goal is none" (Mehl, 1983).

market accepts the item, the task becomes dual: meeting the growing demand in the marketplace while remaining somewhat flexible in terms of minor design modifications. Finally, as the design solidifies and more and more competitors enter the market, the pressure to cut cost becomes paramount. At this stage the output may be fairly classified as a commodity. Throughout this life cycle, the focus of the organization has to change, if it stays with the same output. Many firms, however, choose to compete at only one stage of the life cycle and abandon other stages, so that they can keep the strength of their original focus.

❖ *Departmental professionalism:* Sometimes an organization loses its focus when particular specialties (e.g., finance and marketing) are allowed to follow the guidelines of their profession rather than the needs of the organization. Although the professional guidelines are always admirable, they may not apply at a particular time in a particular firm. For example, finance may

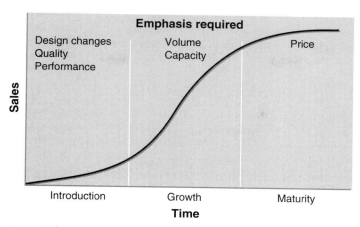

Figure 2.4 Product life cycle: stages and emphasis.

pressure production to reduce inventory levels in an effort to lower inventory-related costs while marketing may simultaneously pressure production to increase inventory levels so that delivery dates can be shortened and sales increased. Clearly, allowing each functional area to pursue its own professional guidelines independently can severely compromise the organization's overall focus.

❖ *Ignorance and noncommunication:* The most common reason a firm loses its focus is simply that the focus was never clearly identified in the first place. Never having been well defined, it could not be communicated to the employees, could therefore not gain their support, and thus was lost. Sometimes a focus is identified but not communicated throughout the organization, because management thinks that lower-level employees don't need to know the strategic focus of the firm in order to do their jobs.

In addition to the advantages of being "focused," there are also some dangers. A narrowly focused firm can easily become uncompetitive in the market if the customers' requirements change. In addition to being focused, a firm must also be flexible enough to alter its focus when the need changes and to spot the change in time. Frequently, a focus in one area can be used to advantage in another way, if there is enough time to adapt—for example, to move into a new product line or alter the application of the focus.

GLOBAL COMPETITIVENESS

The previous sections have overviewed the formulation of a business strategy and areas of focus. In this section we build on that foundation as we investigate global competitiveness. **Competitiveness** can be defined in a number of ways. We may think of it as the long-term viability of a firm or organization; or we may define it in a short-term context such as the current success of a firm in the marketplace as measured by its market share or its profitability. We can also talk about the competitiveness of a nation, in the sense of its aggregate competitive success in all markets. The President's Council on Industrial Competitiveness gave this definition in 1985:

Competitiveness for a nation is the degree to which it can, under free and fair market conditions, produce goods and services that meet the test of international markets while simultaneously maintaining and expanding the real incomes of its citizens.

❖ Global Trends

The trend in merchandise trade for the United States is illustrated in Figure 2.5. Although it may seem that foreign competition has been taking markets away from American producers only in the past decade, this figure indicates that the nation's merchandise imports have been growing considerably for the last 30 years and have almost exploded since 1970. Although *exports* have increased over this period as well, they have not increased as fast as imports; the result is a growing trade deficit with foreign countries. Partly as a result of this deficit, the United States is now the biggest debtor nation in the world. Although the trade deficit has received major attention only since it burgeoned in the early 1980s, Figure 2.5 indicates that it is actually part of a long-term trend and will not be easily or swiftly changed.

Newspapers and network news programs often report on the bilateral trade deficit of the United States with various foreign countries. These stories frequently focus on the bilateral trade gap between the United States and Japan. There are a number of problems, however, with bilateral trade statistics. For instance, when Japan shifts some of its production to other countries such as China or Thailand, it appears that the trade gap between the United States and Japan has decreased. Similarly, Japanese-owned companies operating in the United States are partly responsible for the increase in exports to Japan. Both of these occurrences tend to distort the true nature of the balance of trade between the United States and Japan.

❖ Exchange Rates

As the United States buys more imports from overseas with dollars, and foreigners buy fewer American exports, a surplus of dollars accumulates abroad that tends to

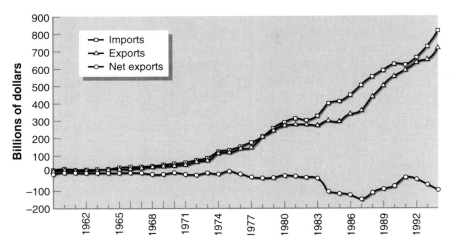

Figure 2.5 The United States' merchandise trade. *Source:* Economic Report of the President, February 1996.

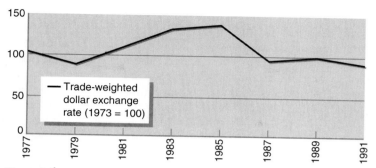

Figure 2.6 Purchasing power of the dollar. *Source:* Federal Reserve Board.

reduce the desirability of holding dollars and thus their value. This is illustrated in the trade-weighted dollar exchange rate plotted in Figure 2.6. The trade-weighted dollar exchange rate is the average price of the United States dollar to foreign currencies. A large value of the trade-weighted dollar exchange rate indicates a strong dollar, making it easier for Americans to afford imports but also making it more difficult for people in other countries to afford American exports. Although other factors, such as intervention by a central bank and changes in national interest rates, can alter the exchange rate in the short term, the basic economic factors of competitiveness tend to show through over the long term. As Figure 2.6 indicates, the dollar has lost about 35 percent of its value relative to the currencies of other countries over the six-year period from 1985 to 1991.

What does this mean to you, and to the average foreign consumer? What it means is that in 1991, Americans needed to pay about 35 percent more for products produced overseas and imported than they had paid in 1985. Meanwhile, however, the prices for products produced in the United States and exported to other countries declined by 35 percent over this same period. Thus, a decline in the value of the dollar is a double-edged sword. Such a decline makes imported goods more expensive for Americans to purchase but at the same time makes exports less expensive for foreign consumers, increasing the demand for domestic products.

According to economic theory, this shift should make American products more desirable (or competitive) in foreign markets, and imports less desirable in American markets. However, some market actions that governments and businesses often take to keep from losing customers can alter this perfect economic relationship. For instance, when the price of Japanese products in the United States started increasing in terms of dollars, Japanese firms initiated huge cost-cutting drives to reduce the cost (and thereby the dollar price) of their products, to keep from losing American customers. This strategy has largely been successful.

Instead of American products becoming significantly cheaper in Japan, some claim that many of these products have been politically blocked from access to Japanese markets by the Japanese government, which tries to protect domestic firms from foreign competition. When a government does this to protect a developing domestic industry while it is struggling to become competitive in world markets, the short-run strategy may be wise. But in Europe, a result of protectionism has been that consumers buy only half as many electronic components (TV sets, etc.) as Americans and yet pay two to three times as much for them.

Not all foreign currencies have improved, relative to the dollar, as steeply as Japan. For example, the currencies of the "four tigers" of Asia—Korea, Singapore, Hong Kong, and Taiwan—were kept in relative proportion to the dollar. As a result, these countries are now "low-wage" producers and are replacing Japan in the production of basic commodities such as clothing, steel, toys, and even electronics. Given their low domestic wages in combination with the easy availability of machinery for high-volume production, we even see Brazil, the Philippines, Malaysia, and Mexico (particularly with its free-trade "Maquiladora" zone near the United States border) moving into the production of major durable goods such as automobiles and television sets. Meanwhile, Japan, Germany, and other traditionally export-oriented nations are moving upscale and producing technically advanced, higher-priced goods for sale around the world.

❖ International Markets and Producers

The way current trends are developing, it now seems that there will soon be three major trading regions in the world: Europe, North America, and the Pacific rim, as illustrated in Figure 2.7. Note that Africa, middle Asia, and Latin America are not included. It was thought that by 1992 "fortress Europe" would emerge, under the sponsorship of the European Economic Community (EEC), as one of the largest unified markets in the world; all existing labor, paperwork, and trade barriers would fall as the giant free-trade region emerged. This region is even larger than the North American region, which consists primarily of the United States and Canada. However, there are still several issues that need to be resolved, such as currency and sovereignty, be-

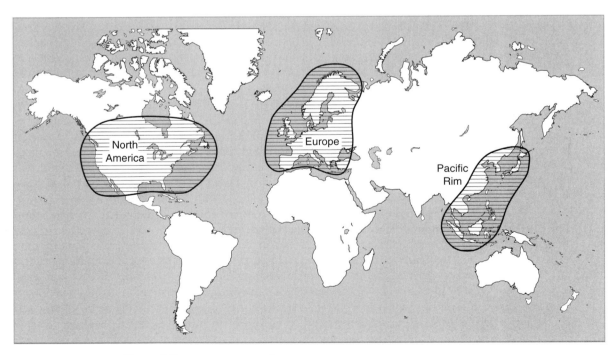

Figure 2.7   Three major trading regions.

fore the goal of a unified European market is realized. The Pacific rim is composed of the Asian countries, including Japan, Korea, Taiwan, Hong Kong, and Singapore. These countries currently are major exporters of goods, but not importers.

International competition has grown very complex in the last few years. Previously, firms were either domestic, exporters, or international. A domestic firm produced and sold in the same country. An exporter sold goods, often someone else's, abroad. An international firm sold domestically produced as well as foreign-produced goods both domestically and in foreign countries. However, domestic sales were usually produced domestically, and foreign sales were made either in the home country or in a plant in the foreign country, typically altered to suit national regulations, needs, and tastes.

Now, however, there are global firms, joint ventures, partial ownerships, foreign subsidiaries, and other types of international producers. For example, Canon is a global producer that sells a standard "world-class" camera with options and add-ons available through the local dealer. And the "big three" American automobile producers—Ford, Chrysler, and General Motors—all own stock in foreign automobile companies. Mazak, a fast-growing machine tool company, is the American subsidiary of Yamazaki Machinery Company of Japan. Part of the reason for cross-ownerships and cross-endeavors is the spiraling cost of bringing out new products. A new drug can cost $200 million to develop and bring to market. Even more expensive are new computers, at $1 billion, or new memory chips, at $4 billion for those introduced in the early 1990s. By using joint ventures and other such approaches to share costs (and thereby lower risks), firms can remain competitive.

Whether to build offshore, assemble offshore, use foreign parts, employ a joint venture, and so on is a complex decision for any firm and depends on a multitude of factors. For example, the Japanese are expanding many of their automobile manufacturing plants in the United States. The reasons are many: to circumvent American governmental regulation of importers, to avoid the high yen cost of Japanese-produced products, to avoid import fees and quotas, to placate American consumers, and so on. Of course, other considerations are involved in producing in foreign countries: culture (e.g., if women are part of the labor force), political stability, laws, taxes, regulations, and image.

Other complex arrangements of suppliers can result in hidden international competition. For example, many products that bear an American nameplate have been totally produced and assembled in a foreign country and simply shipped in under the American manufacturer's or retailer's nameplate, such as IBM's original Epson printers or Nike shoes. Even more confusing, many products contain a significant proportion of foreign parts, or may be composed entirely of foreign parts and only assembled in the United States (e.g., toasters, mixers, hand tools).

❖ Operations and Global Competitiveness

Operations commonly plays a critical role in international competitiveness. Its activities are concerned with such factors as the efficiency and effectiveness of domestic production compared with outsourcing, the appropriate locations for international facilities, the output capacities needed for various plants, and the labor-machinery tradeoffs in each facility. For example, in some countries there may be an excess of low-cost labor and a high cost of capital to buy equipment, so the transformation system should be designed to be labor-intensive.

In general, six primary characteristics of the transformation system are critical.

1. *Efficiency:* This is usually measured as output per unit of input. The problem in trying to compare different transformation systems, of course, is choosing good measures for outputs and inputs. In a store, it might be dollars of sales per square foot. In a maternity suite, it might be deliveries per day.

2. *Effectiveness:* Whereas efficiency is known as "doing the thing right," effectiveness is known as "doing the right thing." That is, is the right set of outputs being produced? Are we focused on the right task?

3. *Capacity:* Capacity, too, is different from efficiency in that it specifies the maximum production volume that is attainable. Equipment and tools tend to significantly increase capacity, though if their cost is too high, they may reduce overall efficiency.

4. *Quality:* The output may not work well or last long, in which case we say it is of poor quality.

5. *Response time:* How quickly can the output be produced? If a custom output or a totally new output is desired, *response time* refers to the time needed to produce the first unit of this different output.

6. *Flexibility:* Can the transformation system be used to produce other, different outputs? How easily? How fast? What variety or level of customization can be achieved?

Operations must provide, through the transformation system, products and services that embody the factors critical to success in the market. In general, customers seek to maximize the value of their transactions; they desire the most performance for the lowest possible price. In the vast majority of global markets today, only a few factors can differentiate between producers because the other factors are relatively standard for a given product or service. For example, on-time delivery, multiple product functions, friendly service, and credit are all expected and are commonly offered by the competing suppliers; those without these order qualifiers are not even in the running.

The critical order-winning factors that are emphasized by the competing producers are price and what we refer to as **responsiveness:** customization, quality, and response time. These factors vary in importance for each market, and the most successful producer will be closest to striking the proper balance between them.

In the next two sections we discuss these factors in detail. We start with the basic driver of the price to the customer—cost—and the role of productivity in determining the cost of a product or service. The following section moves into a discussion of responsiveness.

$\mathscr{C}$OST AND THE ROLE OF PRODUCTIVITY

Operational activities play a major role in determining the cost of a product or service, particularly during the up-front design for the output. It is commonly said that approximately 70 percent of the cost is built in at the design engineering stage.

OPERATIONS IN PRACTICE

Black & Decker Pushes Back

In 1985 Black & Decker was offering professional tools for specialized markets and held 20 percent of the world market share. But Japan's Makita Electric Works stole a good portion of that market by offering lower-cost, standardized, high-quality products.

Black & Decker responded by completely redesigning its power tools to control costs, meet safety requirements, use common parts wherever possible, employ standardized components, and be producible by automation. On one major component, the standardized motor, the redesign was so effective that only one-third the number of people were required to produce it. But the $17 million project was estimated to have a long (seven-year) payback.

In spite of the long estimated payback, the product redesign clearly kept Black & Decker from losing a major market to foreign competition. The problem with calculating long payback periods for strategic investments such as this is that they assume things will remain as they are—market shares, profit margins, and so on (Eklund, 1985).

That is, anything happening after this point can affect the cost by only about 30 percent. Thus, in the traditional functional organization, it is important for all interested parties—research and development, marketing, engineering, and especially operations—to be represented on the design team. Such integration is the foundation upon which activities are grouped together in process-centered organizations. At any rate, the importance of such a joint effort is illustrated in the sidebar about Black & Decker. This topic will be discussed in considerable detail in Chapter 5.

It is worth noting that cost to the producer and price to the customer are two very different factors. You might expect that the price would always be set greater than the cost, but in many situations it is not. For example, in a recession or an oversupply situation, a producer may dump its product on the market to salvage any revenue it can. Or a firm may try to break into a market by offering a product at a low price as a "come-on" to encourage consumers to become familiar with its brand. Or a producer may even try to capture an entire market by driving competitors out with its low prices, planning to raise prices after the competition has left the market.

Yet it is not always clear when a firm is dumping, because costs are never a clear-cut issue. First, on many occasions American firms have claimed that foreign firms were dumping when, in fact, the foreign firms were simply more productive and were able to offer the same goods at much lower prices while still making a profit. Second, if a firm is producing one product successfully but has excess capacity on some of its resources (e.g., machines), it may be able to produce another product for simply the additional cost of the raw materials and then make a nice profit at a much lower price to the consumer. That is, the "marginal contribution" becomes the full profit, since the normally fixed expenses were available free.

Nevertheless, it is always to the producers' advantage to keep their absolute costs as low as possible. This allows them the flexibility of reducing price and still making a profit if competition moves into the market, or simply making an excellent profit on a reasonable price if competition is minimal. The primary method of keeping costs low entails a concept called *productivity,* which we discuss in the remainder of this section.

❖ Productivity Definitions and Measures

Productivity is a special measure of efficiency and is normally defined as output per worker-hour. Note that there are two major ways to increase a firm's productivity: increase the numerator (output) or decrease the denominator (worker-hours). Also, of course, productivity would increase slightly if both increased but output increased faster than worker-hours, or if both decreased but worker-hours decreased faster than output.

This definition of productivity is actually what is known as a *partial factor* measure of productivity, in the sense that it considers only worker-hours as the productive factor. Productivity could easily be increased by substituting machinery for labor, but that doesn't mean that this is a wise decision. We can also define a variety of other partial productivity measures such as capital productivity (using machine-hours or dollars invested), energy productivity (using kilowatt-hours), and materials productivity (using inventory dollars).

A *multifactor* productivity measure uses more than a single factor, such as both labor and capital. Obviously, the different factors must be measured in the same units, such as dollars. An even broader gauge of productivity, called *total factor* productivity, is measured by including *all* the factors of production—labor, capital, materials, and energy—in the denominator. This measure is to be preferred in making any comparisons of productivity.

Perhaps the best use of a productivity measure is to track changes over time. Investigating how productivity changes over time usually provides more useful managerial information than simply comparing the same measure at a specific point in time for different organizational units within the same company, or comparing the productivity of the entire organization with other organizations. Ideally, productivity should exhibit a general upward trend over time. A drop in productivity should be investigated so that corrective action can be taken if necessary.

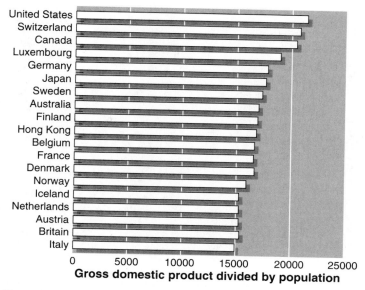

Figure 2.8 International comparisons of productivity. *Source:* "The World Economy in Charts," *Fortune,* 128(2), 1993, p. 96.

❖ Improving Productivity Rates

Improving productivity is important because for a society to increase its standard of living, it must first increase its productivity. Figure 2.8 shows overall productivity for several countries and Hong Kong. In Figure 2.8 productivity is calculated by dividing output (as measured by GDP or GNP) by its total population. Thus, productivity is measured as the dollar value (in 1990 American dollars) of per capita outputs. For example, the United States produced just over $21,500 worth of goods and services per capita. An increase in this measure of productivity means that on average each person in the country produced more goods and services. Figure 2.9 shows annual rates of growth in productivity. Note that although the United States currently enjoys the highest productivity, productivity is growing almost three times as fast in Japan and Hong Kong.

How can the United States improve its productivity growth? It has been estimated that technology has been responsible for at least half of the growth in productivity in the United States between 1948 and 1966. It would appear, then, that this one approach holds the most promise for continuing increases in productivity. Technology in the past resulted in the substitution of mechanical power for human physical labor **(mechanization).** This trend is continuing even faster today, where electronic equipment is replacing human sensing skills **(automation).** Every day we read in magazines and newspapers about new "factories of the future" that are improving productivity and, frequently, replacing factory workers. It is not hard to imagine complex equipment doing much of the work that occupies humans in today's jobs.

Mechanization, automation, and computerization are commonplace and expected in our society. In fact, as consumers we get irritated and indignant on the few occasions when a computer bills us inaccurately or loses our reservations,

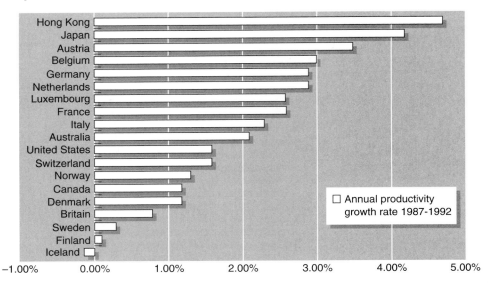

Figure 2.9 International comparisons of growth in productivity. *Source:* "The World Economy in Charts," *Fortune,* 128(2), 1993, p. 96.

when a vending machine dispenses coffee but no cup, or when a traffic signal gets stuck on red. We forget the savings in cost, increase in speed, and enlarged service capacity this equipment has also provided.

We must be careful, however, not to focus solely on productivity as the problem but rather to consider overall competitive ability. Any solution must include quality, lead time, innovation, and a host of other such factors aimed at improving customers' satisfaction. Furthermore, since 50 to 60 percent of a typical manufacturer's cost is for materials, improved sourcing is also critical to long-term competitiveness.

But some people fear that the United States is not yet ready for such a solution. Productivity has improved since the late 1970s, largely by such drastic measures as plant closings, pay cuts, union givebacks, and massive layoffs. Managers are still looking for faster machines and less labor expense to solve their problems, having in too many cases bargained away to tough unions every other response.

In the next section, we will look at this bigger picture of competitiveness and the various components that go into it. Productivity's major competitive impact is through cost, but this is not the only factor in a firm's competitiveness.

$\mathcal{R}$ESPONSIVENESS: CUSTOMIZATION, RESPONSE TIME, AND QUALITY

In addition to *price*, attained through productive cost reductions, the other primary factor in competitiveness is responsiveness to the needs of the customer. This concept of responsiveness goes beyond the usual order qualifiers such as meeting promised delivery dates, offering the features that are normally expected, and providing the expected after-sales service. Firms these days are winning markets by being particularly responsive to customers in terms of higher levels of customization

OPERATIONS IN PRACTICE

Responsiveness at First National Bank of Chicago

In the 1980s, Lawrence C. Russell, executive vice president and head of the service products group of First National Bank of Chicago, commissioned a study to determine what customers of banking services valued most. First Chicago had decided it would investigate the possibility of making a profit on normally free noncredit services such as corporate checking, funds transfer, shareholder services, and so on.

These services are usually provided by banks to build a stronger customer "relationship" to encourage deposits and loans. In order to make such services profitable, First Chicago needed to know what its customers valued in these services—hence the need for a survey.

The result was surprising. Customers said they valued timeliness, accuracy, and responsiveness. First Chicago now considers these to be the primary facets of any high-quality banking service. "What we've learned is that a strategy focused on quality is the best way any company can respond to competition," says its president, Richard L. Thomas. First Chicago's corporate cash management program is now considered to be one of the best in American business (Bowles, 1986).

to fit a customer's particular needs, extremely fast response to a customer's requests, and outstanding quality. The sidebar on First National Bank of Chicago illustrates the potential of this level of responsiveness. We will discuss each of these aspects of responsiveness.

❖ Customization

Customization, in the sense that we are using it, refers to offering a product or service exactly suited to a customer's desires or needs. However, many needs are relatively nonspecific, such as a toaster or an oil change for your car, and total customization is not particularly necessary or desirable. In these cases, "variety" to meet the need may be completely adequate, as long as customers get about the right kind of oil (10W—30 or 5W—40) put into the proper hole in the engine.

Thus, there is a range of accommodation to the customer's needs, as illustrated in Figure 2.10. At the left, there is the completely standard, world-class (suitable for all markets) product or service. Moving to the right is the standard with options, continuing on to variants and alternative models, and ending at the right with made-to-order customization. In general, the more customization the better, if it can be provided quickly, with acceptable quality and economy.

Advantages of Customization

To offer different levels of variety or customization requires flexibility on the part of the producer, commonly obtained through advanced technologies or particularly skilled workers. There are over a dozen different types of flexibility that we will not

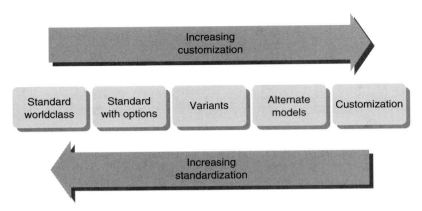

Figure 2.10   Continuum of customization.

pursue here—design, volume, routing through the production system, product mix, and many others. But having the right types of flexibility can offer a producer the following major competitive advantages:

- ❖ Faster matches to customers' needs because changeover time from one product or service to another is quicker.
- ❖ Closer matches to customers' needs.
- ❖ Ability to supply the needed items in the volumes required for the markets as they develop.
- ❖ Faster design-to-market time to meet new customer needs.
- ❖ Lower cost of changing production to meet needs.
- ❖ Ability to offer a full line of products or services without the attendant cost of stocking large inventories.
- ❖ Ability to meet market demands even if delays develop in the production or distribution process.

Mass Customization

Until recently, it was widely believed that producing low-cost standard products (at the far left in Figure 2.10) required one type of transformation system and producing higher-cost customized products (far right) required another type of system. However, in addition to vast improvements in operating efficiency, an unexpected by-product of continuous improvement programs of the 1980s was substantial improvement in flexibility. Indeed, prior to this, efficiency and flexibility were thought to be trade-offs. Increasing efficiency meant that flexibility had to be sacrificed, and vice versa.

Thus, with the emphasis on continuous improvement came the realization that increasing operating efficiency could also enhance flexibility. For example, many manufacturers initiated efforts to reduce the amount of time required to set up (or change over) equipment from the production of one product to another. Obviously, all time spent setting up equipment is wasteful, since the equipment is not being used during this time to produce outputs that ultimately create revenues for the organization. Consequently, improving the amount of time a resource is used productively directly translates into improved efficiency. Interestingly, these same reductions in equipment setup times also resulted in improved flexibility. Specifically, with shorter equipment setup times, manufacturers could produce economically in smaller-size batches, making it easier to switch from the production of one product to another.

In response to the discovery that efficiency and flexibility can be improved simultaneously and may not have to be traded off, the strategy of mass customization emerged. Organizations pursuing **mass customization** seek to produce low-cost, high-quality outputs in high variety. Of course, as was mentioned earlier, not all products and services lend themselves to being customized. This is particularly true of commodities such as sugar, gas, electricity, and flour. On the other hand, mass customization is often quite applicable to products characterized by short life cycles, rapidly advancing technology, or changing customer requirements. However, recent research suggests that successfully employing mass customization requires an organization to first develop a transformation system that can consistently deliver high-quality outputs at a low cost. With this foundation in place, the organization can then seek ways to increase the variety of its offerings while at the same time ensuring that quality and cost are not compromised.

In an article published in *Harvard Business Review*, James Gilmore and Joseph Pine II identified four categories of mass customization:

1. *Collaborative customizers.* These organizations establish a dialogue to help customers articulate their needs and then develop customized outputs to meet these needs. For example, purchasing eyewear is often a difficult task for the typical customer. Because these customers often have little knowledge about what type of frame will best fit their face, they are forced to try on an endless number of frames. To address this problem one Japanese eyewear retailer developed a computerized system to help customers select eyewear. The system combines a digital image of the customer's face and customers' statements about their desires and then develops a recommended lens size and shape. The recommended lens is displayed on the digital image of the customer's face. This allows the optician and the customer to collaborate and modify the lens. The system contains similar features for selecting the nose bridge, hinges, and arms. Once the customer is satisfied, the customized glasses are produced at the retail store within an hour.

2. *Adaptive customizers.* These organizations offer a standard product that customers can modify themselves. For example, many home improvement stores sell closet organizers. Each closet organizer package is the same but includes instructions and tools to cut the shelving and clothes rods so that the unit can fit a wide variety of closet sizes. Also, each customer can specify the dimensions of the various components of the closet organizer on the basis of his or her needs: some customers may want more shelf space; others may need more rod space.

3. *Cosmetic customizers.* These organizations produce a standard product but present it differently to different customers. For example, Planters packages its peanuts and mixed nuts in a variety of containers on the basis of specific needs of its retailing customers including Wal-Mart, 7-Eleven, and Safeway.

OPERATIONS IN PRACTICE

Mass Customization at Hewlett-Packard

Faced with increasing pressure from its customers for quicker order fulfillment and for more highly customized products, Hewlett-Packard (HP) wondered whether it was really possible to deliver mass-customized products rapidly, while at the same time continuing to reduce costs. On the basis of recent experiences in several of its key businesses, including computers, printers, and medical products, HP has concluded that this is indeed possible. HP's approach to mass customization can be summarized as effectively delaying tasks that customize a product as long as possible in the product supply process.

More specifically, HP's mass customization program is based on three principles:

❖ Products should be designed around a number of independent modules that can be easily combined in a variety of ways.

❖ Manufacturing tasks should also be designed and performed as independent modules that can be relocated or rearranged to support new production requirements.

❖ The product supply process must perform two functions. First, it must cost-effectively supply the basic product to the locations that complete the customization activities. Second, it must have the requisite flexibility to process individual customers' orders.

HP has discovered that modular design provides three primary benefits. First, components that differentiate the product can be added during the later stages of production. For example, the company designed its DeskJet printers so that country-specific power supplies are combined with the printers at local distribution centers and actually plugged in by the customer when the printer is set up. Second, production time can be significantly reduced by simultaneously producing the required modules. Third, producing in modules facilitates the identification of production and quality problems.

A primary benefit of this modular production system is that it allows HP to change the sequence in which production activities are performed. For example, HP's disk drive division was having difficulty matching supply and demand. The problem was that customers would often change their orders at the last minute. These changes required inserting different printed circuit boards into the drive. Inserting these circuit boards into the drives did not itself create much of a problem, but the time-consuming test procedures that followed did. After adopting its modular production system, HP addressed this problem by dividing test procedures into two subprocesses. One subprocess was concerned with performing the standard tests that all disk drives undergo. The second subprocess performed all the tests required for a particular printed circuit board. By dividing the testing activities in this fashion, HP could perform all the standard tests before inserting the circuit boards and then needed to conduct unique tests only after the customers' requirements were known (Feitzinger and Lee, 1997).

4. *Transparent customizers.* These organizations provide custom products without the customers' knowing that a product has been customized for them. For example, an on-line computer service may track how each customer uses its service and then suggest additional features that the customer may find useful.

❖ Response Time

The competitive advantages of faster response to new markets or to the individual customer's needs have only recently been noted in the business media. For example, in a recent study of the American and Japanese robotics industry, the National Science Foundation found that the Japanese tend to be about 25 percent faster than Americans, and to spend 10 percent less, in developing and marketing new robots. The major difference is that the Americans spend more time and money on marketing, whereas the Japanese spend five times more than the Americans on developing more efficient production methods.

Table 2.2 identifies a number of prerequisites for, and advantages of, fast response. These include higher quality, faster revenue generation, and lower costs through elimination of overhead, reduction of inventories, greater efficiency, and fewer errors and scrap. One of the most important but least recognized advantages for managers is that by responding faster, they can allow a customer to delay an order until the *exact* need is known. Thus the customer does not have to change the order—a perennial headache for most operations managers.

$\mathcal{T}$ABLE 2.2 ❖ Prerequisites for and Advantages of Rapid Response

1. *Sharper focus on the customer.* Faster response for both standard and custom-designed items places the customer at the center of attention.

2. *Better management.* Attention shifts to management's real job, improving the firm's infrastructure and systems.

3. *Efficient processing.* Efficient processing reduces inventories, eliminates non–value-added processing steps, smoothes flows, and eliminates bottlenecks.

4. *Higher quality.* Since there is no time for rework, the production system must be sufficiently improved to make parts accurately, reliably, consistently, and correctly.

5. *Elimination of overhead.* More efficient, faster flows through fewer steps eliminate the overhead needed to support the eliminated steps, processes, and systems.

6. *Improved focus.* A customer-based focus is provided for strategy, investment, and general attention (instead of an internal focus on surrogate measures such as utilization).

7. *Reduced changes.* With less time to delivery, there is less time for changes in product mix, engineering changes, and especially changes to the order by the customer who just wanted to get in the queue in the first place.

8. *Faster revenue generation.* With faster deliveries, orders can be billed faster, thereby improving cash flows and reducing the need for working capital.

9. *Better communication.* More direct communication lines result in fewer mistakes, oversights, and lost orders.

10. *Improved morale.* The reduced processing steps and overhead allow workers to see the results of their efforts, giving a feeling of working for a smaller firm, with its greater visibility and responsibility.

Faster response to a customer also seems to reduce the unit costs of the product or service significantly. On the basis of the empirical studies illustrated in Figure 2.11, it seems that there is about a 2:1 relationship between response time and unit cost. That is, a 50 percent reduction in response time results in a corresponding 25 percent reduction in unit cost. The actual empirical data indicated a range between about 5:3 and 5:1, so for a 50 percent reduction in response time there could be a cost reduction from a high of 30 percent to a low of 10 percent. This is an overwhelming benefit because if corresponding price reductions are made, it improves the value delivered to the customer through both higher responsiveness and lower price. The result for the producer is a much higher market share. If the producer chooses not to reduce the price, then the result is both higher margins and higher sales, for significantly increased profitability.

❖ Quality

In the long run, the most important single factor affecting a business unit's competitive ability is the quality of its products and services, relative to those of competitors. In the days of the craftspeople and guilds, the quality of an individual's output was *advertising*, a declaration of *skill*, and a source of *personal pride*. With the coming of the Industrial Revolution and its infinite degree of specialization and interchangeability of parts (and workers), pride in one's work became secondary to effective functioning of the individual as simply one cog in an enormous organizational system. Quite naturally, quality deteriorated and therefore had to be specifically identified and controlled as a functional aspect of the output.

This recognition of the need to specifically consider the quality of an output was given impetus during World War II, when the military adopted statistical sampling procedures through Military Standard 105. The result was a significant increase in interest in quality control in firms supplying arms and materials to the armed forces, which then spread to firms in the general economy.

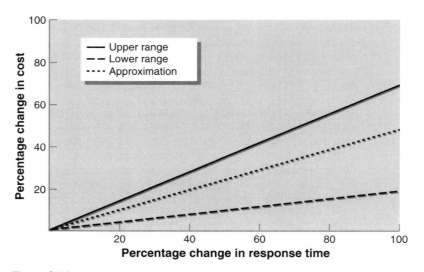

Figure 2.11   Cost reductions with decreases in response time.

In addition, this interest spread to Japan, which by the middle 1950s was producing cheap imitations of American and other foreign goods and exporting them around the world. This interest culminated in an invitation from Japan to W. Edwards Deming, an American expert in quality control, to come to Japan and speak on his ideas about using teams of workers to improve quality.

Defining and Measuring Quality

Quality is a relative term, meaning different things to different people at different times. Richard J. Schonberger has compiled a list of 12 dimensions that customers perceive as associated with products and services:

1. *Conformance to specifications.* Conformance to specifications is the extent to which the actual product matches the design specifications. An example of nonconformance would be a pizza delivery operation that consistently required 35 minutes or more to make and deliver pizzas when the company advertised that pizzas would be delivered in 30 minutes or less.

2. *Performance.* Surveys suggest that customers most frequently equate the quality of products and services with their performance.[1] Examples of performance include how quickly a sports car accelerates from zero to 60 miles per hour, how good a steak tastes at a restaurant, and the range and clarity of a wireless phone.

3. *Quick response.* Quick response is associated with the amount of time required to react to customers' demands. Examples of quick response include travel agencies that can produce boarding passes at the time airline reservations are made, mail-order catalogues that ship from inventory overnight, automobile manufacturers that can design a new model in less than three years, and fire and rescue services that are on the scene within minutes of a 911 call.

4. *Quick-change expertise.* Examples of quick-change expertise include a 10-minute oil change, a motorcycle assembly line that can switch over and make any model with little or no delay, and costume and set changes in the theater.

5. *Features.* Features are the attributes that a product or service offers. Examples of features include a videocassette recorder with on-screen programming, airbags in automobiles, and a salad bar with more than 50 ingredients.

6. *Reliability.* Reliability is the probability that a product will perform as intended on any given trial or the probability that a product will continue to perform for some period of time. Examples of reliability are the probability that a car will start on any given morning, and the probability that a car will not break down in less than four years.

7. *Durability.* Durability refers to how tough a product is. Examples of durability include a notebook computer that still functions after being dropped,

---

[1]Spencer, Hutches, Jr., "What Customers Want: Results of ASQC/Gallop Survey," *Quality Progress,* February 1989, pp. 33–35.

watches that are waterproof 100 meters underwater, and a knife that can cut through steel and not need sharpening.

8. *Serviceability.* Serviceability refers to the ease with which maintenance or a repair can be performed. A product for which serviceability is important is a copier machine. Have you ever been in an office when the copier was down?

9. *Aesthetics.* Aesthetics are factors that appeal to human senses. Aesthetic factors associated with an automobile, for instance, include its shape, its color, and the sound of its engine.

10. *Perceived quality.* Quality is not an absolute but rather is based on customers' perceptions. Customers' impressions can be influenced by a number of factors including brand loyalty and an organization's reputation.

11. *Humanity.* Humanity has to do with how the customer is treated. An example of humanity is a private university that maintains small classes so students are not treated like numbers by the professors.

12. *Value.* The value of a product or service relates to how much of the preceding 11 dimensions of quality customers get relative to what they pay. The value dimension of quality suggests that enhancing one or more of the dimensions of quality does not automatically lead to perceived higher quality. Rather, enhancements of quality are evaluated by customers relative to their effect on cost.

It is worth noting that not all the dimensions of quality are relevant to all products. Thus, organizations need to identify the dimensions of quality that are relevant to the products and services they offer. Market research about customers' needs is the primary input for determining which dimensions are important. Once the important dimensions have been determined, how the organization and its competitors rate on these dimensions should be assessed. If an organization rates lower on a given dimension than the competition, it can either try to improve on that dimension or attempt to shift customers' attitudes so that the customers will place more emphasis on the dimensions the organization rates highest on. Of course, measuring the quality of a service can often be more difficult than measuring the quality of a product or facilitating good. However, the dimensions of quality apply to both.

Benefits of High Quality

Many benefits are associated with providing products and services that have high quality. Obviously, customers are more pleased with a high-quality product or service. They are more apt to encourage their friends to patronize the firm, as well as giving the firm their own repeat business. Top quality also establishes a reputation for the firm that is very difficult to obtain in any other manner, and it allows the firm to charge a premium price. This was verified in the Profit Impact of Market Strategy (PIMS) study conducted by the Strategic Planning Institute: it was found that high-quality products and services were not only the most profitable but also garnered the largest market shares.

High quality also tends to protect the firm from competition, which may have to offer competing outputs at an especially low price (with correspondingly low margins) in order to stay in business. It enhances the attractiveness of follow-up products or services so that their chances of success are much improved. And, of course, high quality minimizes risks to safety and health, and reduces liability.

High quality has implications for production as well. If quality is built into the production system, it improves workers' morale, reduces scrap and waste, smooths work flows, improves control, and reduces a variety of costs. As a result, Philip Crosby, a well-known quality consultant, and others state that "quality is free." Crosby estimates that firms are losing up to 25 percent of the amount of their sales because of poor quality. Similarly, the American Society for Quality Control estimates that for American products and services, poor quality consumes between 15 and 35 cents of every sales dollar. By comparison, the corresponding figure for Japanese products is between 5 and 10 cents. A study conducted by Ken Matson of Litton's Industrial Automation Systems Division verified these estimates, finding that the annual cost of nonconformance in quality, by itself, was about 14 cents for every dollar of equipment assets.

Clearly, the link between quality and productivity can be mutually beneficial. The traditional view was that improvements in quality come at the expense of lower productivity. However, Japanese companies have demonstrated that improvements in quality usually lead to improvements in productivity. To draw an analogy, if you try to work faster on a mathematics test, you are likely to make more errors. This is the case in production too, but it depends on what has been invested up front to improve overall quality. For instance, if processes have been simplified and improved, workers and machines can work both faster *and* with fewer errors. Analogously, a student with a solid understanding of both math principles and the operation of a calculator can work faster on a math test than one with limited knowledge of the functioning of a calculator. Further, a calculator solves much more complicated problems than can be done by hand.

CHAPTER IN PERSPECTIVE

This chapter has continued our introduction to operations management. In the first part of the chapter, business strategy was defined and the process of formulating business strategy was overviewed. Next, four major business strategies and core competence were discussed. Following this, focus was discussed, including areas of focus, the distinction between order qualifiers and order winners, and how organizations lose their focus.

The second part of this chapter was concerned with issues related to global competitiveness. Here the discussion centered on international competitiveness, the impact of exchange rates, and six primary characteristics of the transformation system. Next, productivity was defined and the productivity (and growth in productivity) of several industrialized nations was discussed. Finally, the chapter concluded with a discussion of how customization, response time, and quality each affect an organization's responsiveness.

Chapter 3 extends the material presented in this chapter and addresses the role of *quality management* in supporting the business strategy and enhancing organizational competitiveness. Chapter 4 will build on quality management's focus on the customer and overviews business process design.

❖ CHECK YOUR UNDERSTANDING _____

1. Define the following terms: order winners, order qualifiers, focus, core competence, life cycle, productivity, business process strategy, outsourcing, responsiveness.

2. Briefly overview the process of formulating strategy.

3. What roles do an organization's vision and mission statements play in the formulation of strategy?

4. Review the four major business strategies in terms of their relation to the life cycle.

5. Provide examples for each of the four major business strategies, using organizations you are familiar with.

6. Provide examples for the common areas of focus listed in Table 2.1, using organizations you are familiar with.

7. Briefly describe the ways an organization can lose its focus.

8. Explain the relationship between exchange rates and global competitiveness.

9. Describe *hollowing out*. Why is it dangerous for a firm? Could a service firm become hollow?

10. How do each of the six characteristics of the transformation system translate into added output value for the customer?

11. Contrast high productivity and high growth in productivity.

12. What country has the highest productivity? The highest growth in productivity.

13. Contrast mechanization and automation.

14. Briefly overview the components of responsiveness.

15. Briefly explain mass customization.

16. List several examples of each of the twelve dimensions of quality.

❖ EXPAND YOUR UNDERSTANDING _____

1. It is said that a firm's strategic plan is the one locked in the safe. Contrast this concept with that of the strategic plan as a series of decisions made by the firm over time.

2. Is there any commonality in the three generic strategies of low cost, differentiated product or service, and niche position?

3. What well-known firms might be considered to have lost their original focus?

4. Is it wise for a firm to stick to what it knows best, or should it expand its market by moving into adjoining products or services? How can it avoid losing its focus?

5. With regard to the sidebar on Rolm Telecommunications, do you think that perfect quality, or at least a significantly higher level of quality, is expected more in services than in products?

6. Would service strategies have the same areas of focus as in Table 2.1?

7. Which means of losing focus do you think is most typical?

8. As international competition increases and weaker firms go out of business, what will order qualifiers and winners be in the future?

9. Why are trade-offs necessary? Why not just be excellent in all areas of focus? Is this not what the Japanese do?

10. Contrast the philosophy of the holding company with that of the focused firm. How can two such contradictory views each have successful proponents?

11. Can you think of any other areas of possible focus for a firm besides those identified in Table 2.1?

12. Is it ethical to employ a strategy whose aim is to bankrupt your competitors?

13. It is commonly said that the reason for short-term management perspectives in American firms is the short-term perspective of the stock market—the stockholders who own these firms. But Japan and other countries have their own stock markets too; why aren't they focused on the short term?

14. Some countries, it is charged, subsidize their foreign sales at low prices by keeping prices higher in their domestic market. Is this ethical? What do you think is the suspected strategy here?

15. Companies typically advertise products and production systems to improve their general image with the public. Is it ethical for a firm to advertise

quality in one product line when its other products have nowhere near the same quality? What do firms often do in this case?

16. What trade-offs are involved in employing more automation in a plant?

17. How might the addition of equipment to a production system lower efficiency? What does this say about replacing labor with equipment to increase productivity?

18. How could the productivity of resources such as a pump, a warehouse, $1000 of capital, a market survey, and a kilowatt-hour be measured?

19. What hard decisions might have to be made to increase a firm's productivity? Are firms willing to make them? When would and wouldn't they be willing?

20. What are some possible quality measures of a theatrical performance?

21. What types of outputs do not require high quality?

22. If a plastic imitation cannot be distinguished from the real thing, what difference does it make?

23. According to K. Blanchard and N. V. Peale (1988), the following three ethical tests may be useful: (1) Is it legal or within company policy? (2) Is it balanced and fair in the short and long term? (3) Would you be proud if the public or your family knew about it? Apply these tests to the following situations:

a. A foreign firm subsidizes its sales in another country.

b. A foreign firm dumps its products (sells them for less than cost) in another country.

c. A country imports products that, had they been made domestically, would have violated domestic laws (e.g., laws against pollution).

24. Will the trade deficit illustrated in Figure 2.5 continue forever? What will logically happen?

25. Will the trend in exchange rates in Figure 2.6 continue down to zero? What will logically happen?

26. When is national protectionism a wise policy? A foolish policy? Consider Japan, the United States, and Europe.

27. How would you define world-class quality? Could a service be considered world-class?

28. How ethical is it for a supplier to compete against its original customer when it obtained its expertise from that customer?

29. Why do Americans invest more in marketing new products while the Japanese invest more in engineering? What advantages accrue to each investment?

30. Where might the cost savings in faster response to a customer's need come from?

31. Which of the 12 dimensions of quality typifies a meal in a gourmet restaurant? A CD player? A surgical operation?

32. Define three operational measures of quality for a college course such as this one. Be specific.

❖ APPLY YOUR UNDERSTANDING
Kateland Metropolitan University

Kateland Metropolitan University (KMU) was chartered as a state university in 1990. The university opened its doors in 1994 and grew rapidly during its first three years. By 1997, the enrollment reached just over 9300 students. However, with this rapid growth came a number of problems. For example, because the faculty had to be hired so quickly, there was no real organization. Curriculum seemed to be decided on the basis of which adviser a student happened to consult. The administrative offices resembled "organizational musical chairs," with vague responsibilities and short tenures.

The faculty of the Business School was typical of the confusion that gripped the entire university. The 26 faculty members were mostly recent graduates of Ph.D. programs at major universities. There were 21 assistant professors and instructors, 3 associate professors, and 2 full professors. In addition, funds were available to hire 3 additional faculty members, either assistant or associate professors. The newly recruited dean of the Business School was recently promoted to associate professor after five years of teaching at a large northeastern university.

Upon arriving at the Business School, the dean asked the faculty to E-mail their concerns to her so that she could begin to get a handle on the major issues confronting the school. Her office assistant selected the following comments as representative of the sentiments expressed.

"Our student-teacher ratio is much higher than what it was at my former university. We need to fill those open slots as quickly as possible and get the provost to fund at least two more faculty positions."

"If we don't get the quality of enrollments up in the MBA program, the Graduate School will never approve our application for a Ph.D. program. We need the Ph.D. program to attract the best faculty, and we need the Ph.D. students to cover our courses."

"Given that research is our primary mission, we need to fund more graduate research assistants."

"The travel budget isn't sufficient to allow me to attend the meetings I'm interested in. How can we improve and maintain our visibility if we get funding for only one to two meetings per year?"

"We need better secretarial support. Faculty members are required to submit their exams for copying five days before they are needed. However, doing this makes it difficult to test the students on the material covered in class right before the exam, since it's difficult to know ahead of time exactly how far we will get."

"I think far too much emphasis is placed on research. We are here to teach."

"Being limited to consulting one day a week is far too restrictive. How are we supposed to stay current without consulting on a more frequent basis?"

"We need a voice mail system. I never get my important messages."

Questions

1. What do the comments by the faculty tell you about KMU's strategy?

2. What would you recommend the dean do regarding the Business School's strategic planning process? What role would you recommend the dean play in this process?

3. *Productivity* is defined as the ratio of output (including both goods and services) to the input used to produce it. How could the productivity of the Business School be measured? What would the impact be on productivity if the professors all received a 10 percent raise but continued to teach the same number of classes and students?

❖ EXERCISES

1. Compare the productivity of the companies below. Which firm is the most productive?

Firm	Output, Units/Year	Annual Worker-Hours
Estec	432	217,328
Teckore	756	428,926
Stekpro	584	331,817

2. Able Electronics produces 1700 items with $3.5 million of equipment. Micron Devices produces 2500 items using $4.5 million worth of equipment.

   a. Compare the capital productivity of Able and Micron.

   b. If the equipment in both firms is new but is depreciated linearly over 10 years at Able and 8 years at Micron, recalculate capital productivity on an annual basis. What does this tell you about pitfalls in calculating capital productivity?

3. **a.** Calculate the multifactor productivity of Reynard Shoes, which uses 10 workers and 500,000 francs of equipment to produce 10,000 pairs of shoes a year. Assume that the workers are paid 25 francs an hour and work a 50-hour week, 50 weeks a year.

b. Recalculate the multifactor productivity by including the cost of materials: 700,000 francs a year.

c. How would you compare Reynard's productivity with American Shoes, which produces 20,000 pairs of shoes a year with 15 workers, $200,000 of equipment, and $300,000 of materials a year? Assume a 40-hour week and 50 weeks a year. What information do you still need?

4. The printed circuit board (PCB) industry in one state produced $1,783,457,850 worth of product last year and paid $372,876,515 for labor, $490,313,297 for materials, and $511,387,216 for equipment. Compare the multifactor productivities of the PCB industry with the state's chip industry, which produced $2,318,746,019 worth of silicon computer chips and paid $518,255,899 for labor, $711,341,866 for materials, and $686,377,103 for equipment.

5. a. Calculate the total factor productivity of HiTeck International assuming that workers earn $15 per hour and work fifty 40-hour weeks per year, capital usage runs $1 million a year, material usage is $10 million a year, and energy costs are $300,000 per year. HiTeck runs a full double shift half the year for its seasonal product and a single shift of 90 workers the other half of the year. Annual output is 15,000 appliances.

b. Compare the total factor productivity of HiTeck with Fastec, which subcontracts all its work, paying $10 million for 9500 appliances. What is a potential danger to Fastec?

6. Suppose you knew, in Exercise 5, that HiTeck's 15,000 appliances consisted of 5000 toasters, 6000 ovens, and 4000 dishwashers. If you now wanted to calculate HiTech's productivity, what additional information would you like to have?

7. A company has collected the data on the spreadsheet below for the two plants it operates. The plants are of similar size and capacity. All data are in thousands of dollars.

a. Using a spreadsheet, calculate the labor, capital, and multifactor (including labor, capital and materials) productivity for each plant for all years.

b. Using a spreadsheet, plot Plant A's and B's labor productivity on the same graph.

c. Using a spreadsheet, plot Plant A's and B's capital productivity on the same graph.

d. Using a spreadsheet, plot Plant A's and B's multifactor productivity on the same graph.

e. Evaluate each plant's performance overtime both independent of the other plant and relative to the other plant. (Refer to *b–d* above.)

8. Referring to Exercise 7, use a spreadsheet to calculate the percent change in labor, capital, and multifactor productivity for each plant for all years. Using a spreadsheet, plot the percentage change in multifactor productivity for both plants on the same graph. How do the plants' performances compare?

Exercise 7 Spreadsheet

	A	B	C	D	E	F	G	H	I
1		Plant A	Plant A	Plant A	Plant A	Plant B	Plant B	Plant B	Plant B
2	Year	Sales	Labor	Capital	Materials	Sales	Labor	Capital	Materials
3	1986	35100	1800	8780	20800	34800	1780	8705	17800
4	1987	38200	1950	10230	20600	37900	1910	9670	20300
5	1988	39600	2000	10800	21050	40300	2005	10500	22100
6	1989	41000	2150	11170	23300	40600	1990	10800	21800
7	1990	42900	2175	12570	24300	42700	2060	11600	21900
8	1991	46500	2325	12000	26600	45800	2180	12600	24100
9	1992	47500	2400	12100	24400	48300	2260	13600	28500
10	1993	47900	2495	12900	27600	48900	2255	14050	27500
11	1994	50400	2520	13800	29200	50200	2280	14700	29700
12	1995	53400	2700	14500	31200	50500	2260	15100	29900
13	1996	56300	2900	15300	29600	55100	2430	16800	31000

Quality Management

𝒞HAPTER OVERVIEW

- ❖ In spite of the importance of quality, a cost is associated with obtaining and maintaining high quality, and it is important for a firm to identify the appropriate level of quality for the market. Historically, American firms have underestimated the value of high quality.

- ❖ The four major cost categories of quality are prevention costs, appraisal costs, internal costs of defects, and external costs of defects. The first two are the costs of good quality, and the last two are the costs of poor quality.

- ❖ Some of the quality programs currently being used include total quality management (TQM), quality circles (with their problem-solving tools such as process analysis and fishbone charts), Taguchi methods, and quality function deployment (QFD).

- ❖ In conjunction with efforts to improve their products and key processes, many organizations are en-

gaging in a relatively new activity called *benchmarking*. Essentially, benchmarking involves comparing an organization's performance with the performance of other organizations.

- ❖ Quality is a major issue in services and is often the basis for a strong competitive advantage. Frequently, this *quality advantage* is instilled in employees by a specialized training program.

- ❖ W. Edwards Deming, Joseph Juran, and Philip Crosby are often credited with being key contributors to modern quality management approaches.

- ❖ Two of the most coveted quality awards are the Deming Prize and the Malcolm Baldrige National Quality Award. The International Organization for Standardization's ISO 9000 quality standard has emerged as the most widely recognized standard in the world.

INTRODUCTION

❖ It was not that long ago that IBM's very survival was questioned by industry experts and investors. One indication of this sentiment was the drop in IBM's stock price from $175 per share in August 1987 to $51.50 at the end of January 1993. However, by the end of 1996, it appeared as though IBM had reversed its fortunes. For example, in the last quarter of 1996, IBM won four out of five computer-services contracts it went after; it was sold out of its new mainframe computer model; sales of its PCs increased 25 percent; and it was having difficulty meeting the demand for its new line of home PCs.

Perhaps somewhat surprisingly, IBM's turnaround was not the result of advanced technology, price reductions, or fancy marketing campaigns. Rather, it was due to the fact that Louis V. Gerstner, Jr., its chairman and CEO, focused on customers. Gerstner's philosophy is that before you can satisfy customers' needs, you first have to talk to them to learn about their needs. In an interview, Gerstner stated, "I came here with a view that you start the day with customers, that you start thinking about a company around its customers, and you organize around customers." Thus, according to Gerstner, the primary problems facing IBM when he took the helm had to do not with technology but with customer relations.

In his role as chairman and CEO, Gerstner practices what he preaches. He makes it a point to meet regularly with customers and estimates that 40 percent of his time is spent listening to customers' complaints and plans. For example, when customers expressed concerns about having to invest in proprietary hardware and software, Gerstner responded by increasing IBM's support for more industry standards such as the Java language developed by Sun Microsystems (Sager, 1996).

❖ In 1991, the West Babylon school district of Long Island, New York, began applying continuous improvement and quality to its administrative and education processes. The objectives of these initiatives were to affirm the district's commitment to providing high-quality education, to emphasize the importance of lifelong learning, and to provide students with opportunities to take pride in their work. Given these objectives, the district adopted the term *total quality education* (TQE) to describe the initiatives. Initially, the district's superintendent and board of education agreed to apply W. Edwards Deming's "14 Points for management" to the administration process. To facilitate this, the superintendent attended quality training programs taught by two of the leading experts in quality management, Joseph Juran and Deming himself. Numerous improvements were made throughout the district, ranging from creating more appealing lunch menus to placing less emphasis on exams to changing students' report cards in order to better evaluate actual learning (Manley and Manley, 1996).

❖ National Semiconductor was an early proponent of total quality. Its first quality circles were created in 1981; it began a preventive maintenance program in 1982; it began using statistical process control in 1983; it used design of experiment techniques in 1984; and in 1986 it implemented design for manufacturing techniques. In the 1990s, National Semiconductor initiated a second stage of total quality by submitting an application to be considered for the Malcolm Baldrige National Quality Award. During its second stage, National Semiconductor focused its attention on customer-supplier relationships, customers' satisfaction, developing scorecards for customers, analyzing its processes, empowering its employees, and developing team strategies, problem-solving techniques, and "visioning." Also, National Semiconductor worked on becoming ISO 9000–certified during this period. In its third and present stage, National Semiconductor is focusing on becoming a learning organization. In this phase the company is concerned with concepts such as personal mastery, shared vision, systems thinking, and team learning (Rau, 1995).

❖ "Quality is one of the keys to the continued competitive success of U.S. businesses. The Malcolm Baldrige National Quality Award, which highlights customer satisfaction, workforce empowerment and increased productivity, has come to symbolize America's commitment to excellence. This year's Award winners join an ever-growing and diverse family of companies showing the world that quality pays" (President Clinton, October 16, 1996).

Chapter 2 ended with a brief discussion of quality as a factor in international competitiveness. Because of its direct link to competitiveness, quality management is clearly one of the most timely topics in business today, as the above examples—including the quotation from the president of the United States—illustrate. Furthermore, quality management is applicable to all organizations, whether they exist to make a profit (IBM and National Semiconductor), or are nonprofit organizations (West Babylon school district), and whether or not a tangible output is produced.

In this chapter we build on the material in Chapter 2 related to the important role of quality in competitiveness and discuss quality management in greater detail. We begin with a review of the trade-offs between the benefits of quality and its costs. Next, the philosophies of several experts on quality are presented. Then we describe some common quality programs in the United States and Japan such as total quality management and quality circles. Finally, we tie these pieces together and conclude the chapter with an overview of the major quality awards and certifications.

$\mathcal{Q}$UALITY COSTS AND TRADE-OFFS

An often neglected issue in marketing is that customers are frequently willing to pay for excellent quality. In the traditional view it was thought that products and services of excellent quality would translate into higher costs. Of course this view neglects the negative consequences of gaining a reputation for producing shoddy outputs. Also, the Japanese have demonstrated across numerous industries that it is often possible to improve quality and lower costs at the same time. One explanation for this phenomenon is that it is simply cheaper to do a job right the first time than to try to fix it or rework it later. Philip B. Crosby, an author and expert on quality, expressed this view in the title of a book, *Quality Is Free*, which sold approximately 1 million copies.

Two primary sets of costs are involved in quality: control costs and failure costs. The aggregate of these costs runs between 15 and 35 percent of sales for many American firms. Traditionally, these costs are broken down into four categories, as shown in Table 3.1: prevention costs, appraisal costs, internal costs of defects, and external costs of defects. The first two costs are incurred in attempting to control quality, and the last two are the costs of failing to control quality. Costs of defects (or nonconformance) can run from 50 to 90 percent of the total cost of quality.

By plotting, for a given market, the two sets of expected costs identified above—the expected cost of controlling quality and the expected cost of *not* controlling quality (i.e., the cost of defects)—and adding them together, we can determine the expected total cost of quality. This would then give us an indication, at least for these costs, of the best level of quality for that market.

Figure 3.1 presents two extreme situations that might occur using this approach. Figure 3.1*a* is typical of commonplace products, such as nails, for which the expected cost of controlling quality increases with the resulting level of quality and the expected cost of probable defects decreases slightly with higher levels of quality. Since the cost of probable defects is relatively low and does not change significantly as the level of quality is changed, the lowest total quality cost is found at low levels of quality.

$\mathcal{T}$ABLE 3.1 ❖ Four Categories of Quality Costs

Category 1: Prevention costs. These costs are incurred in the process of trying to prevent defects and errors from occurring. They consist of such elements as

❖ Planning the quality control process.
❖ Training for quality.
❖ Educating the firm's suppliers.
❖ Designing the product for quality.
❖ Designing the production system for quality.
❖ Preventive maintenance.

Category 2: Appraisal costs. These are the costs of determining the current quality of the production system. They consist of factors such as

❖ Measuring and testing parts and materials.
❖ Running special test laboratories.
❖ Acquiring special testing equipment.
❖ Conducting statistical process control programs.
❖ Receiving inspection.
❖ Reporting on quality.

Category 3: Internal costs of defects. These costs are incurred when defects and errors are found before shipment or delivery to the customer. They consist of elements such as

❖ Labor and materials that go into scrap.
❖ Engineering change notices.
❖ Reworking and retesting to correct defects.
❖ Lost profits on downgraded products and services.
❖ Lost yield from malfunctioning equipment or improperly trained workers.
❖ Downtime of equipment and labor sitting idle while waiting for repairs.
❖ Expediting to get orders of appropriate quality delivered on time.

Category 4: External costs of defects. These are the costs of trying to correct defects and errors after receipt by the customer. They include items such as

❖ Quick response to complaints.
❖ Adjustments to correct the problem.
❖ Lost goodwill.
❖ Recalls to correct the problem for other customers.
❖ Warranties, insurance, and settlements of lawsuits.

Figure 3.1*b* is most appropriate for much more important items such as elevators, spaceships, and large computers. Here, all the costs are much larger—say, by a factor of 1 million. Again, the expected cost of quality increases with increasing quality. But the expected cost of probable defects is much more steeply sloped, so that this expected cost is extremely high at low levels of quality (where defects are likely) and is low at high levels of quality (where defects are unlikely and few, if any, are expected).

The question for most producers—who offer outputs that are probably somewhere between nails and spaceships—is: What is the appropriate level of quality for their situation? In the past, American producers assumed that their situation was more akin to that of nails (Figure 3.1*a*), that is, they assumed that defects (or qual-

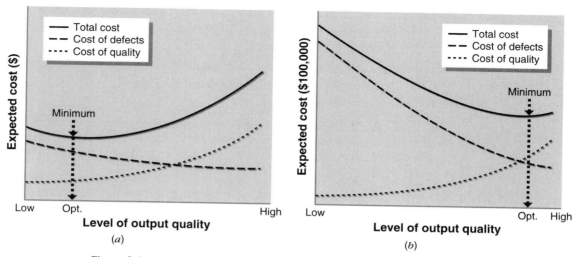

Figure 3.1 Optimum quality levels for two types of products.

ity levels) were not particularly important. Since Japanese products with high quality have entered and captured American markets, American producers are finding that the cost of defects may be considerably higher than they had thought and that their situation is really more like spaceships (Figure 3.1*b*).

Part of the reason for the change, of course, may simply be that consumers' expectations have been raised. But there are other factors that need to be considered, as well as determining the most appropriate, and most attainable, quality level for a firm's outputs. Some of these are listed below:

❖ *The market:* Competition is often the major factor in determining the appropriate, and necessary, level of quality.

❖ *Production objectives:* Is the output to be a high-volume, low-priced item or an exclusive, expensive item?

❖ *Product testing:* Insufficient testing of the output may fail to reveal important flaws.

❖ *Output design:* How the output is designed may itself doom quality from the start.

❖ *Production system:* The procedure for producing the output may also adversely affect quality.

❖ *Quality of inputs:* If poor materials, insufficiently trained workers, or inappropriate equipment must be used, quality will suffer.

❖ *Maintenance:* If equipment is not properly maintained, parts are not available in inventories, or communications are not kept open within the organization, quality will be less than it should be.

❖ *Quality standards:* If concern for quality is not apparent throughout the organization, no economically feasible amount of final testing or inspection will result in a high-quality output.

❖ *Customer feedback:* If the organization is insensitive to complaints and requests for repairs or service, quality will not significantly improve.

How to Make Quality Pay

Many companies have learned a painful lesson—that improving quality does not always pay. Take Varian Associates, for example. Varian, a maker of scientific equipment, had 1000 of its managers attend a four-day course on quality. Indeed, the company achieved some impressive results as a result of its quality initiatives. For instance, its vacuum systems unit for computer clean rooms improved on-time delivery performance from 42 percent to 92 percent. Unfortunately, however, the division was so focused on meeting production schedules that it failed to return customers' phone calls, and its market share eventually declined. The bottom line was that in 1990 the company lost $4.1 million, compared with a profit of $32 million in the previous year. The executive vice president for quality commented, "All of the quality-based charts went up and to the right, but everything else went down."

To take another example, the oil equipment producer Wallace Company, won the Malcolm Baldrige National Quality Award in 1990. Two years later it was filing for Chapter 11 bankruptcy protection as the cost of its quality programs continued to increase and oil prices plummeted.

The key to avoiding such negative outcomes is to make sure that quality initiatives are directly related to improving customers' satisfaction, which then should translate into higher sales, higher profits, and a higher market share. Efforts that do not lead to improved customer satisfaction simply add cost and waste effort.

One approach to ensuring that efforts to improve quality will be related to what customers actually want is the concept of *return on quality*. With this approach, sophisticated financial tools are used to assess the payoff of quality programs. For example, NationsBank uses this approach to measure the effect on revenues of improvements such as adding tellers and offering new mortgage products. And at AT&T, each of the 53 business units reports quarterly on the financial impact of its quality improvement projects (Greising, 1994).

PHILOSOPHIES OF QUALITY MANAGEMENT

Although you may think that "made in Japan" signifies a product of superior quality, it may surprise you to learn that many of the techniques and philosophies Japanese companies employ today were actually developed in the United States, usually around the end of World War II. Unfortunately, as we noted in Chapter 1, the sentiment among domestic manufacturers at the end of World War II was that they already produced the highest-quality products in the world at the lowest cost. Thus, they were not particularly interested in or concerned with improving quality. Japan was an entirely different story. Its products had a reputation for poor quality and after it lost the war its economy was a shambles. As a result, Japanese manufacturers were eager for help related to quality improvement. In this section, we briefly overview the philosophies of three of the leading gurus of quality: Deming, Juran, and Crosby.

❖ W. Edwards Deming

According to W. Edwards Deming, the major cause of poor quality is *variation*. Thus, a key tenet of Deming's approach is to reduce variability in the manufacturing process. Deming also stressed that improving quality was the responsibility of top management. However, he also believed that all employees should be trained in the use of problem-solving tools and especially statistical techniques.

Perhaps the contribution that Deming is most associated with is his *14 Points*, summarized in Table 3.2.

Deming believed that improvements in quality created a chain reaction. According to this theory, improved quality leads to lower costs, which then translate into higher productivity. The resulting better quality and lower prices lead to increased market share. Higher market share means that the company can stay in business and create more jobs.

❖ Joseph Juran

In 1951 Joseph Juran wrote the *Quality Control Handbook,* which was considered by many to be the "bible" of quality and continues to be a useful reference to this day. In contrast to Deming, Juran tended to work more within the existing system rather than trying to effect major cultural changes. Juran argued that employees at different levels spoke different languages. Thus, according to Juran, managers

*T*ABLE 3.2 ❖ Deming's 14 Points
___

1. Create constancy of purpose toward improvement of product and service, with a plan to become competitive, stay in business, and provide jobs.
2. Adopt the new philosophy. We are in a new economic age. We can no longer live with commonly accepted levels of delays, mistakes, defective materials, and defective workmanship.
3. Cease dependence on mass inspection. Require, instead, statistical evidence that quality is built in to eliminate the need for inspection on a mass basis.
4. End the practice of awarding business on the basis of price tags. Instead, depend on meaningful measures of quality, along with price.
5. Improve constantly and forever the system of production and service, to improve quality and productivity, and thus constantly decrease costs.
6. Institute modern methods of training.
7. Institute modern methods of supervision.
8. Drive out fear, so that everyone may work effectively for the company.
9. Break down the organizational barriers—everyone must work as a team to foresee and solve problems.
10. Eliminate arbitrary numerical goals, posters, and slogans for the workforce which seek new levels of productivity without providing the methods.
11. Eliminate work standards and numerical quotas.
12. Remove barriers that rob employees of pride of workmanship.
13. Institute a vigorous program of education and training.
14. Create a structure which will push the 13 prior points every day.
___

Source: Deming, W. Edwards. *Quality, Productivity, and Competitive Position* (Cambridge, Mass.: MIT, Center for Advanced Engineering Study, 1982), pp. 16–17.

OPERATIONS IN PRACTICE

Applying Deming's 14 Points in Services

The table here illustrates how the West Babylon school district and a law firm applied Deming's 14 Points to their operations. West Babylon was discussed at the beginning of the chapter. The law firm—Turner, Padget, Graham, and Laney—operates a general trial practice and employs 41 lawyers. Its offices are located in three cities in South Carolina. Not only do these examples illustrate the applicability of Deming's 14 Points to service-oriented organizations, but they also illustrate the applicability of the points to nonprofit organizations.

Deming's 14 Points	School District	Law Firm
1. Constancy of purpose.	Developed a mission statement for the school district.	Committed to quality for long term.
2. Adopt new philosophy.	Cross-functional teams set up as quality circles.	Recognized a need for better management.
3. Cease dependence on mass inspection.	Less emphasis on exams.	Emphasized quality of inputs (e.g., staff) and improved processes (e.g., research, filing, billing).
4. Don't make decisions based purely on cost.	Suppliers who delivered poor quality were taken off list of bidders.	Applied this to purchases of computer systems and office supplies.
5. Improve constantly.	Quality circles continued to work toward improving the delivery of services.	Improved all processes, measured them by maintaining records, and reduced variation.
6. Methods of training.	Quality circle used to help select training materials. Teachers trained in use of new classroom technologies.	Improved training material and facilities. Reduced amount of job training by coworkers.
7. Methods of supervision.	All supervisors received training five times a year on advanced techniques in cooperative supervision. Emphasis was that leading means helping others do their jobs better.	Managed more by coaching and mentoring.
8. Drive out fear.	Developed new solutions and encouraged experimentation.	Made staff feel secure. Didn't manage by fear.
9. Work as a team.	Superintendent's quality council created with representatives from personnel, student services, testing, finance, transportation, and lunch programs.	Created teams of partners, associates, secretaries, and support staff.

Deming's 14 Points	School District	Law Firm
10. Eliminate slogans and posters.	Transportation staff was responsible for reducing waste and accidents in a quota-free environment.	Provided employees with the means, including training and equipment, to do the job.
11. Eliminate numerical quotas.	Bell-shaped curve was not used to force grade distribution.	Placed less emphasis on billable hours. Rewarded employees for client services.
12. Pride of workmanship.	Focused on how to prevent defects, not fix them after the fact.	Improved communications. Recognized that staff wanted to do a good job.
13. Education and training.	Teachers received regular training in computer technology and multimedia technology.	Emphasized education and training. Trained staff on teamwork and problem solving.
14. Push 13 points every day.	Each semester, employees developed one to three goals and a plan to accomplish these goals.	Management pushed plans and vision.

Sources: Manley, R. and J. Manley. "Sharing the Wealth: TQM Spreads from Business to Education." *Quality Progress* (June 1996): 51–55. Blodget, N. "Law Firm Pioneers Explore New Territory." *Quality Progress* (August 1996): 90–94.

spoke in terms of dollars, workers spoke in terms of things, and middle management spoke in terms of both. (Deming addressed this issue by proposing that statistics be used as the common language across all organizational levels.)

Juran and Deming agreed on a number of issues. For example, they both advocated that employees know who the users of their product were. Also, Juran advocated the use of statistical tools to help improve conformance to specifications.

But there were also a number of areas where Juran and Deming disagreed. For example, Juran disagreed with Deming's Point 8, about the need to drive fear out of the system. Also, at the top management level, Juran focused more on quality cost accounting and Pareto analysis than on statistical techniques of process control. Finally, Juran's definition of quality was "fitness for use" whereas Deming never offered a specific definition.

Deming is probably best remembered for his 14 points, and Juran is probably best remembered for his *quality trilogy:*

1. *Quality planning.* This is the process of preparing to meet quality goals. During this process customers are identified and products that meet their needs are developed.

2. *Quality control.* This is the process of meeting quality goals during operations. Quality control involves five steps: (1) deciding what should be controlled, (2) deciding on the units of measure, (3) developing performance

standards, (4) measuring performance, and (5) taking appropriate actions based on an analysis of the gap between actual and standard performance.

3. *Quality improvement.* This is the activities directed toward achieving higher levels of performance.

Juran believed that most companies did not place enough emphasis on quality planning and quality improvement.

Juran viewed the collection of information on quality costs a critical component of quality deployment. Along these lines, he suggested that organizations typically progress through four phases. In the first phase, organizations seek to minimize their prevention and appraisal costs. However, because a large number of defects are produced, these organizations incur large external failure costs. To alleviate this problem, the organization increases its appraisal costs in the second phase. This effectively lowers the shipment of defects but increases internal failure costs because defects are discovered earlier. Typically, however, overall total quality costs decrease. In the third phase the organization introduces process control, thereby increasing its appraisal costs but lowering internal and external failure costs even more. Finally, in the fourth phase, the organization increases prevention costs in an effort to decrease total quality costs once again.

❖ Philip B. Crosby

According to Philip Crosby, quality meant not elegance but conformance to requirements. He believed that a problem with quality did not exist per se, but rather that the organization had functional problems. Crosby also argued that it was always more cost-effective to perform an activity right the first time. Given this, Crosby suggested that zero defects was the only meaningful performance standard and the cost of quality (including the cost of nonconformance) the only performance measure. In contrast to Deming, Crosby focused more on management, organizational processes, and changing corporate culture than on the use of statistical techniques.

𝒬UALITY PROGRAMS

We will overview some of the more common quality programs here and describe their benefits. Before doing so, however, let us first look more closely at the difference between traditional attitudes toward quality in American and Japanese management.

❖ American versus Japanese Approaches

Although quality is crucial to competitiveness in both international and domestic markets, close attention to quality, as noted above, has not been characteristic of American firms. Some of the reasons are the following:

1. Inadequate assignment of responsibility for quality to the worker performing the task. Rarely is this responsibility specified; it is more or less assumed to be part of the task.

2. Workers' lack of familiarity with methods and procedures of quality control.

3. Piece-rate and other pay incentives that emphasize and reward quantity rather than quality.

4. Work-in-process and buffer inventories, which bury poor quality in the system until a later time when these items are reissued for further processing.

5. Long supplier lead times, which prohibit the rejection of defective incoming materials. This is a common problem today in the United States, particularly in the case of castings. Frequently, the lead time on castings is 6 to 18 months. After waiting this long, the manufacturer *cannot* wait any longer for a defective casting to be recast or to order from another foundry—the customer would cancel the order. Manufacturers must repair castings as best they can and proceed with the job. They cannot even threaten to switch to another foundry in the future, because foundries have closed up in droves over the last two decades.

As was previously mentioned, the Japanese once had a reputation for poor quality. In the 1950s, "made in Japan" meant "cheap imitation goods" that invariably broke after minimal use. (It was even rumored that the Japanese had renamed one of their major manufacturing regions "Usa" so they could stamp "MADE IN USA" on their products.) It is doubtful if any country before or since has had such a worldwide reputation for bad quality. Clearly, the turnaround, which started with the visit by W. Edwards Deming, is barely short of miraculous.

In 1950 the Japanese government invited Deming (then a professor at New York University) to give a series of lectures on quality control to help Japanese engineers reindustrialize the country. But Deming insisted that the heads of the companies attend the talks too. As a result, the top Japanese managers were also invited, and they all showed up. Deming promised them that if they followed his advice, they

---

OPERATIONS IN PRACTICE

The Deming Award to Yokogawa– Hewlett-Packard (YHP)

In 1975, when Kenzo Sasaoka took over the joint venture between Yokogawa Electric Corporation of Japan and Hewlett-Packard, YHP had been at the bottom of HP's operations in product quality and profitability. Sasaoka initiated a pilot total quality control program and immediately reduced defects on one line by several orders of magnitude.

The program spread through the rest of manufacturing; into administration, research, and development; and even into sales. In 1982, YHP won the Deming Prize for high quality. More significantly, YHP jumped from last in profitability to the top of the list. Between 1975 and 1985, manufacturing costs decreased 42 percent and product defects overall dropped 79 percent. In addition, the time to market for new products was cut by one-third. Meanwhile, revenue per employee climbed 120 percent, market share jumped 193 percent, and profits shot up 244 percent (Port, 1987).

would be able to compete with the west within just a few years. They did! Now the most prestigious award given in Japan each year for industrial quality is named the Deming award. (See the sidebar about one American winner of this award.) In response to Japan's Deming award, the United States in 1987 established its own award to promote and recognize outstanding quality, the Malcolm Baldrige National Quality Award. We discuss these awards in more detail in the next section.

But the Japanese did not stop there. They tied the concept of quality control directly into their production system—and now they have even tied it into their entire economy through inspections to guarantee the quality of exports. The natural inclinations of Japanese culture and traditions were exploited in this quality crusade:

❖ Quality circles (described below), were based on natural teamwork procedures and individual workers' responsibility for results. Behavioral and attitudinal factors were considered of primary importance in improving quality levels.

❖ Extensive training for all levels of workers, as well as suppliers, helped instruct them in the use of quality control procedures.

❖ Cross-training and job rotation were used to demonstrate the importance of quality.

❖ Lifetime employment made clear the necessity of living with the product's reputation.

❖ The disinclination to store unneeded materials fostered the development of just-in-time operations, which furthered the quality concept through immediate inspection, processing, and use. If a product was defective, that was *immediately* clear.

❖ Patience was exercised in testing and checking components extensively before installing them in products—and then in taking the time to check the products again before shipping them to customers.

After nearly two decades of a national emphasis on quality, Japan's reputation for producing shoddy goods was totally reversed. Now, by comparison, it is the United States (along with other countries, it might be noted) that seems to be producing "shoddy" goods. In fact, the quality levels of the United States and others may not have actually fallen that much. Nevertheless, when high quality is combined with competitive pricing—another strength of the Japanese system—the result is extremely strong competition for existing producers.

A number of programs, some successful and some unsuccessful, have been instituted in the United States over the years to help improve quality. Traditional methods for improving quality, especially in service organizations, have involved the establishment of goals, or standards, to guide workers. These goals are then periodically reemphasized through organizational programs, contests, posters, and the annual budget. Typical of such programs is "zero defects," a program developed in the aerospace industry in 1962. This program attempted to *prevent* errors by eliminating their cause, rather than remedying them after they had been made. Better training and motivation on the part of both the worker and the manager are primary ingredients of such a program. Committees are formed, the union is involved, training review sessions are sponsored, posters are hung, contests are run, banners are pinned up, achievement dinners are given, and so forth.

❖ Total Quality Management

A more recent concept, similar to zero defects, that the Japanese and some American firms have embraced is called *total quality management* (TQM) or *total quality control* (TQC). The basic idea of TQM is that it is extremely expensive to "inspect" quality into a company's products and much more efficient and effective to build items right in the first place. As a result, responsibility for quality has been taken away from the quality control department and placed where it belongs—with the workers who produce the parts in the first place. This is called *quality at the source.* It is the heart of *statistical quality control* (SQC), sometimes called *statistical process control* (SPC)—programs being implemented in many firms in the United States today.

The beginning of TQM dates back to the 1930s, when Dr. W. A. Shewart began using statistical control at the Bell Institute. In fact, both Juran and Deming were students of Shewart's. In the early 1950s, military standards were developed for quality and applied to the aerospace industry and at nuclear facilities. The objective of these military standards was to make sure that prescribed manufacturing procedures were followed and to establish procedures for inspecting parts. After World War II, the Japanese Union of Scientists and Engineers (JUSE) began consulting with Deming. In 1951, the Deming Prize was introduced in Japan to reward organizations that excelled at implementing Deming's principles.

In 1952 the concept of *quality assurance* was proposed. Its proponents argued that in contrast to quality control, which relies on inspection, quality assurance is better because it develops a system that can produce high-quality products in the first place. Quality control and TQM are further contrasted in Table 3.3. In 1954 Juran made his first trip to Japan, and in 1956 Japan adopted quality as its national slogan.

The first *quality circles* were created in Japan in 1957. In 1966, Japan celebrated the creation of the 10,000th quality circle, and in 1977 the creation of the 100,000th

𝒯ABLE 3.3 ❖ Quality Control versus TQM

Quality Control	Total Quality Management
Inspection after the fact.	Design quality into the product and production system.
Focus on consequences of poor quality.	Focus on identifying and eliminating causes of poor quality.
Customer is purchaser.	Customer is user.
Some number of defects is normal.	Goal is zero defects.
Responsibility for quality control is assigned to individuals or departments.	Quality is the responsibility of everyone.
Improving quality increases cost.	Improving quality typically pays for itself.

quality circle was celebrated. The first quality circle in the United States appeared in 1974.

Although each organization may have its own definition of TQM, most definitions include the notion that *all* employees are responsible for *continuously* improving the quality of the organization's products and services. Thus, the word *total* is meant to signify that the quality of the organization's outputs is the concern of all employees. In general, TQM typically includes the following five steps:

1. Determining what the customers want.
2. Developing products and services that meet or exceed what the customers want (and even "delight" the customers).
3. Developing a production system that permits doing the job right the first time.
4. Monitoring the system and using the accumulated data to improve the system.
5. Including customers and suppliers in this process.

Today, many firms tie their TQM programs into their just-in-time (JIT) programs for enhanced effectiveness. (JIT will be discussed in detail in Chapter 14.) This approach to production focuses on eliminating waste and embraces several of the concepts discussed previously. When tied to JIT, total quality management becomes a powerful tool for achieving quality:

- ❖ Since inventories don't hide work-in-process, defective items can be spotted immediately.
- ❖ With JIT, there is less scrap and waste.
- ❖ JIT reduces the amount of rework, since good products have been made the first time.
- ❖ With JIT's mix of products, production rates are smoothed over time, resulting in less rushing and fewer errors.
- ❖ The JIT program naturally emphasizes quality at the source with, for example, immediate recognition of defects and smooth flows of materials.

If the responsibility for quality is taken from the quality control (QC) department and given to the workers, is there any need for maintaining a QC department? Certainly! In fact, the QC people can now concentrate on the real responsibilities of their jobs:

1. Training employees in how to control quality.
2. Conducting random quality audits within the firm and quality audits of suppliers.
3. Consulting on problems the employees are encountering regarding quality.
4. Overseeing the final test of finished goods.
5. Determining the cost of quality to help justify quality improvement programs and initiatives.
6. Helping implement ideas about quality control throughout the firm.

This last responsibility is related to another Japanese innovation that has gained acceptance in the United States—quality circles.

❖ Quality Circles

Traditionally, the Japanese tend to work together in teams for production, so team analysis was a natural way to attack production problems. These teams, known as quality circles, focus not solely on quality but on all problems facing the workers. In fact, no more than one-third of the ideas coming out of these circles are related to quality; most are actually related to productivity in the sense that a particular problem is slowing the production flow and its solution would speed up the flow.

The basic concept behind the movement is that the workers know most about problems in production, since they are the ones who face these problems every day. However, 95 percent of the problems are built into the system and are beyond the worker's control, thus requiring a larger group to address them. Frequently, a circle cannot solve a problem from within the group itself and must contact another group, or a higher level within the firm.

Circles are composed of natural work groups and range from a few employees to over a dozen. In some firms, the concept is not limited to shop workers but includes the clerical staff and even the managers. A trained facilitator usually leads the circle, perhaps the supervisor or even a coworker or team leader. The circle spends a couple of hours a week, usually on company time, analyzing and discussing its problems and brainstorming solutions. It then works on implementing the solutions on the job.

An important element of the problem analysis is a set of tools that are taught to the employees. These are illustrated in Figure 3.2 and described below.

- ❖ *Process analysis:* This is basically a flowchart of how a system or process works, showing inputs, operations, and outputs. By depicting the process visually, the workers can often spot the source of a problem they are facing, or identify where more information is needed to solve a problem.

- ❖ *Runs chart:* This graph shows how a variable has changed over time. By analyzing the data points, the circle's members can determine if the operation is doing what it is supposed to do. There may be excessive variation in the data, a disturbing trend, or random unacceptable points.

- ❖ *Control chart:* By putting control limits on a chart of sample data, the circle can determine if the operation or activity is out of control or experiencing natural variation. However, the natural variation may still not be acceptable, so that a better or improved operation may be needed to reduce variation to acceptable limits.

- ❖ *Pareto chart:* This chart, a type of bar chart, is based on a natural tendency for the *majority* of problems to be due to a *minority* of causes. Typically, 80 percent of the symptoms (problems) are due to 20 percent of the causes. By concentrating on the primary problems, most of the difficulties can be resolved.

- ❖ *Histogram:* This type of bar chart shows the statistical frequency distribution of a variable of interest. From this chart it can be determined how often some variable is "too low" or "too high" and whether further action is required.

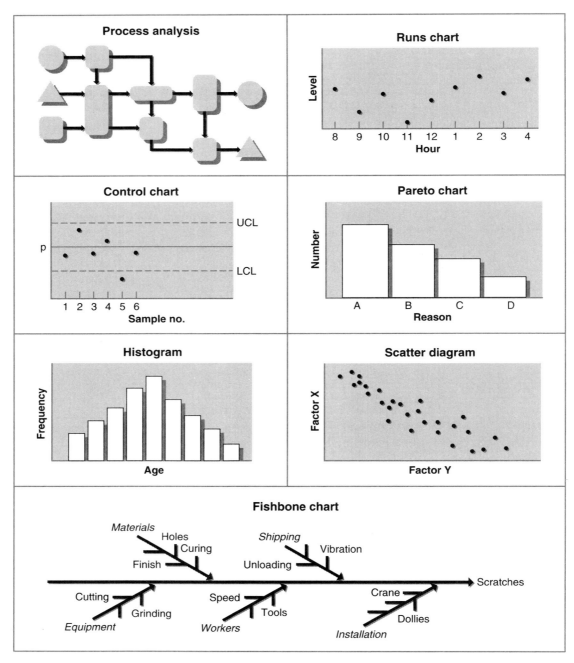

Figure 3.2 Tools for quality control.

OPERATIONS
IN PRACTICE

Analyzing a Problem in Education with a Fishbone Chart

In the West Babylon school district, it was widely perceived by the teachers that insufficient time was being spent covering the curriculum. To help understand and analyze the problem, a quality circle developed a fishbone chart. A simplified version of the fishbone chart developed by the team is shown below.

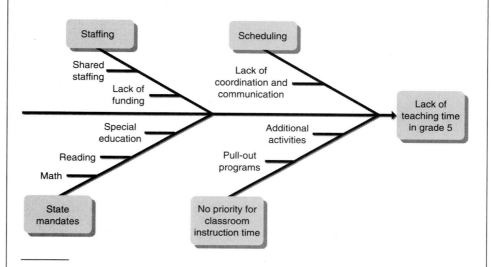

Source: Adapted from Manley, R. and J. Manley. "Sharing the Wealth: TQM Spreads from Business to Education." *Quality Progress* (June 1996): 51–55.

❖ *Scatter diagram:* These charts show the correlation between two variables and can be used to infer causality. If defects occur primarily on days when the temperature is over 50° C, for instance, the temperature-sensitive aspects of the operation (including the workers) should be looked into.

❖ *Fishbone chart:* A fishbone chart is also known as a cause-effect diagram. It lays out the process as a convergence of activities that result in the final product, or event. Major activity lines are plotted along the result line, and minor activities that make up the major activities are plotted as short lines along the major lines. The result looks like a fishbone. As with the process flow chart, the source of problems can often be identified on the basis of events and inputs in the diagram. The accompanying sidebar provides an example of how a fishbone chart was used to analyze a problem in a school district.

❖ *Presentation skills:* Not all the training for circles involves charts. Attention is also paid to facilitating good communication and presenting analyses clearly, both orally and in writing.

❖ *Analysis skills:* Time is also spent teaching the workers about the concepts of statistical quality control and the collection and analysis of data. Collecting invalid data, or making inferences on inappropriate information, can be more damaging than helpful.

❖ *Brainstorming:* Finally, time is spent training the employees how to brainstorm and use other methods of attacking problems.

❖ Taguchi Methods

Most of the quality of products and services is built in at the design stage, and the production system can have only a minor impact on it. Genichi Taguchi has focused on this fact to develop a new approach to designing quality into outputs. Rather than trying to constantly control machinery and workers to stay within specifications—sizes, finishes, times—he has devised a procedure for statistical testing to determine the best combination of product design and transformation system design to make the output relatively independent of normal fluctuations in the production system. This approach is called *design for manufacturability* (DFM) or, on occasion, *design for assembly* (DFA).

To do this, statistical experimentation is conducted to determine what product and transformation system designs produce outputs with the highest uniformity at lowest cost. Interestingly, the Japanese use the Taguchi method primarily in *product* design, whereas Americans use the method primarily in design of the production system. Obviously, this is more an engineering procedure than an operations approach, and we will not pursue it in detail here.

❖ Quality Function Deployment

As we noted earlier, the TQM approach involves developing products and production systems to meet customers' specific requirements. *Quality function deployment* (QFD) is a powerful tool for helping to translate customers' desires directly into attributes of products and services. It involves all functions of the firm in translating the customer's needs into specific technical requirements for each stage of output and production system design: from research and development to engineering to operations to marketing to distribution. In this manner, outputs are delivered to the customer faster, with better quality, and at lower cost. We discuss QFD in greater detail in Chapter 5.

❖ Benchmarking

In conjunction with their efforts to improve products and key processes, many organizations are engaging in a relatively new activity called **benchmarking**. Essentially, benchmarking involves comparing an organization's performance with the performance of other organizations. Benchmarking is used for a variety of purposes, including these:

❖ Comparing an organization's performance with the best organization's performance. When used in this way, benchmarking activities should not be restricted to other organizations in the same industry. Rather, the companies that are best in the world at performing a particular activity, regardless of industry, should be studied. For example, Xerox used L. L. Bean to benchmark the order fulfillment process.

❖ Comparing an organization's business processes with similar processes.

❖ Comparing an organization's products and services with those of other organizations.

❖ Identifying the best practices to implement.

❖ Projecting trends in order to be able to respond proactively to future challenges and opportunities.

Benchmarking generally involves three steps. The first step is concerned with preparing for the benchmarking study. In this phase it is important to get the support of senior management and its input on what should be benchmarked. Top management's support is particularly important because benchmarking studies can easily take six months or more to complete. Top management demonstrates its support for a benchmarking project by allocating the necessary resources and by eliminating organizational obstacles. Problem areas, activities related to serving the customer better, and activities related to the mission of the organization are all appropriate candidates for inclusion in the benchmarking study.

The second phase of benchmarking consists of collecting data. There are two general sources of benchmarking data. One source is *published data*. These are often available from universities, financial filings (e.g., 10k reports), consultants, periodicals, trade journals, and books. The other source of data is *original research* conducted by the organization itself. If this approach is employed, a list of organizations to benchmark must first be developed. Candidates for inclusion might be companies that have recently received quality awards or other business awards, are top-rated by industry analysts, have been the subject of recent business articles, or have a track record of superior financial performance. Once the companies have been identified, data can be collected in a variety of ways including interviews, site visits, and surveys. If site visits are to be used, it is important to arrive at an agreement with the participating organizations related to the length of the visit and the questions that will be asked. Regardless of how the data are collected, they should always be evaluated in terms of their reliability, accuracy, cost, timeliness, and availability.

The third and final phase of benchmarking involves using what has been learned to improve organizational performance. Benchmarking is primarily a tool for identifying best practices. Thus, completing a benchmarking study does not automatically translate into improved organizational performance. More specifically, some of the primary goals associated with benchmarking include:

❖ Helping an organization learn from the experiences of others.

❖ Determining how an organization is performing relative to the best.

❖ Helping an organization prioritize by identifying those areas most in need of improvement.

Once a benchmarking study has been completed, identified gaps in performance can be used to set challenging but realistic goals (often called *stretch goals*). Also, the results of the benchmarking study can be used to overcome and eliminate complacency within the organization.

❖ Quality in Services

Measuring the quality of a service is difficult for a variety of reasons. The thing we are trying to measure is often abstract rather than physical, transient rather than permanent, or psychological or subjective rather than objective. A hotel, for example, may be perceived as being of high quality because of its class, its superior service, and its reputation. All these attributes, however, may simply reflect its expensive decor, speed of service, amenities, location, cleanliness, spaciousness, or peacefulness. And these may, in turn, be measurable in terms such as the following:

- ❖ Dollars spent per room.
- ❖ Overall dollars spent on the hotel.
- ❖ Ratio of employees to patrons.
- ❖ Inches of insulation between rooms.
- ❖ Square footage per room.
- ❖ Number, size, and cost of amenities.
- ❖ Location.

Even a characteristic as subtle as reputation may be measured through the evaluations of groups that rate hotels and their dining facilities, regional write-ups in papers and magazines, and surveys of attitudes of upper-class people in the region.

In spite of the difficulty of measuring quality in services, it is known that the firms possessing it are also the most profitable. Thus, it behooves management to improve the quality of its services in whatever way it can.

A common approach to improving the quality of services is to methodically train the employees in standard procedures and to use equipment that reinforces this training. The ultimate example is McDonald's Hamburger University, where managers, in particular, are intensively trained in McDonald's system of food preparation and delivery. Not only is training intensive, but follow-up checkups are continuous, and incentives and rewards are given for continuing to pay attention to quality. Furthermore, the equipment is designed to reinforce the quality process taught to the employee, and to discourage sloppy habits that lead to lesser quality.

Quality as an aspect of services is an interesting subject to study because of the opportunities that are available to the creative and innovative start-up. As McDonald's shows, one good idea for putting quality into a drab existing service (the lunch-counter trade) can launch a million-dollar business. But quality can be successful in improving the competitiveness of existing service businesses too, as illustrated in the accompanying sidebar.

Service Defections

When a tangible product is produced, quality is often measured in terms of defects. In services, the analogy to a product defect is a defecting customer, i.e., a customer who takes his or her business elsewhere. Of course, the concept of a defecting customer is equally applicable to organizations that produce tangible outputs.

OPERATIONS IN PRACTICE

Quality at the Office

The value of better quality is becoming known in office processes as well as manufacturing. University Microfilms Inc. (UMI) of Ann Arbor, Michigan, was facing a growing backlog of requests for theses: 8000. Upon investigation, UMI found that the average thesis waits 150 days for processing but is processed only for a total time of two hours; much of the time is spent waiting for the author to reply to questions. By working on the quality of its editing and processing techniques, UMI cut the time in half within six months; it is now down to 60 days. As a result, customers' complaints were reduced by 17 percent and output increased by almost 50 percent with the same people.

Financial services can also benefit from better quality. Several years ago, First National Bank of Chicago noticed that its requests for letters of credit were handled by nine different employees who conducted dozens of steps, a process that consumed four days. By retraining its employees so that each would be able to process a customer's request through all the steps, First Chicago was able to let each customer deal with only one employee, who could complete the process within a day. Now each time a letter of credit is ordered, the customer is placed back with the same employee. As a result, the department involved has been able to double its output of letters of credit using the services of 49 percent fewer employees.

By paying attention to the quality delivered to customers, American Express was able to cut the processing time for new credit applications from 22 days to 11 days, thereby more than doubling the revenue per employee in its credit card division. It had previously tracked errors and processing time internally but had ignored the impacts on the customer. When it began focusing on the customer, it suddenly found that speed in the credit department was often immaterial in shortening the customer's waiting time for credit approval because four more departments still had to process every new application (Berstein, 1991).

Organizations should monitor their defecting customers for a number of reasons. First, research suggests that longtime customers offer organizations a number of benefits. For example, the longer a customer has a relationship with an organization, the more likely that customer is to purchase additional products and services. Also, long-term customers tend to be less price-sensitive; therefore, the organization can charge them more. In addition, no advertising is necessary to get the business of long-term customers. In fact, long-term customers may actually be a source of free advertising for the company. One study published in *Harvard Business Review* concluded that cutting defections in half more than doubles the average company's rate of growth. Likewise, improving customer retention rates by 5 percent can double profits.

Defections by customers can provide a variety of useful information. First, feedback obtained from defecting customers can be used to identify areas that need improvement. Also, the feedback can be used to determine what can be done to win these customers back. Finally, increases in the defection rate can be used as an early warning signal.

QUALITY AWARDS AND CERTIFICATIONS

One reflection of the importance quality has now assumed in business is that organizations can obtain a great deal of prestige and recognition by winning one of the major quality awards. In this section we overview the two most coveted quality awards: the Deming Prize and the Malcolm Baldrige National Quality Award. Because of its universal acceptance, we also discuss the ISO 9000 quality standard.

❖ The Deming Prize

The Deming Prize was established in 1950 and is still administered by the Japanese Union of Scientists and Engineers (JUSE). The prize is actually a medal and is used to recognize organizations that have excelled in TQM. It is open to all organizations regardless of their national origin.

The Deming Prize is based on the following 10 criteria:

1. *Policies and objectives.* This includes an evaluation of management and quality policies: the methods used to develop policies and objectives, the use of statistical methods, and the implementation and assessment of objectives.

2. *Operation of the organization.* Here, the organization is evaluated in terms of whether lines of responsibility are clearly defined, how well activities are delegated, the extent to which divisions cooperate with one another, and the use of quality circles.

3. *Education.* The education component is concerned with evaluating educational plans, the education of workers and suppliers in statistical methods, the activities of quality circles, and how well a suggestion system is used.

4. *Information management.* This factor focuses on information-gathering activities, the dissemination of information throughout the organization, the speed with which information is collected and used, and the use of statistical analysis.

5. *Analysis.* This factor is concerned with the methods that are used to select problems and the analytical tools used to solve these problems, the use of statistical tools, the use of quality and process analysis, and the organization's openness to suggestions for improvement.

6. *Standardization.* Standardization addresses the methods used to adopt and update standards, the actual content of the standards, the use of the standards, and the record keeping associated with maintaining standards.

7. *Control.* This factor is concerned with evaluating an organization's quality control systems, the use of statistical methods, the location of control points in the process, the items that are controlled, and activities of quality circles related to control.

8. *Quality assurance.* Included in quality assurance are procedures for developing new products, procedures for ensuring product safety, process de-

sign, use of statistical methods, and issues related to measurement and inspection.

9. *Results.* This part of the award focuses on both the visible and the invisible results obtained. Also, the gap between predicted and actual results is assessed.

10. *Future plans.* Included in this factor are the organization's plans for promoting TQM in the future and the relationship between short-range and long-range planning.

As you can see, the Deming Prize is quite comprehensive in its coverage of organizational activities. It is not surprising that so much emphasis is placed on statistical methods, given the person it was named after.

The Malcolm Baldrige Award.

President Ronald Reagan congratulates Motorola Chairman Robert W. Galvin at White House ceremonies honoring three recipients of the first Malcom Baldrige National Quality Award.

OPERATIONS
IN PRACTICE

Profiles of the Winners of the 1996 Malcolm Baldrige Award

ADAC Laboratories designs and manufactures products for the health care industry. The company was founded in 1970 and has 710 employees. In winning the award, the company was cited for its focus on customers. All its executives are expected to spend 25 percent of their time in direct contact with customers. Over the last five years ADAC's focus has paid off as customer retention has increased from 70 percent to 95 percent. The company has achieved impressive results in other areas as well. For example, since 1990 it has reduced the time needed to get a customer's system back in operation from 56 to 17 hours. One result of these improvements is that its market share has increased from 10 percent to 52 percent in the United States and from 5 percent to 28 percent in Europe.

Dana Commercial Credit Corporation (DCC) serves a variety of business niches through its leasing and financial services. It is committed to consistently meeting or exceeding its customers' key requirements. For example, DCC has reduced its transaction approval time from seven hours in 1992 to 1 hour or less in 1996. In addition to its focus on customers, DCC is committed to the development of its employees. On average, each employee receives 48 hours of education, and DCC emphasizes promoting from within. As a result of these initiatives, DCC has been able to consistently improve its financial performance. For example, its return on equity has increased by over 45 percent since 1991.

Custom Research Inc. (CRI) is a full-service marketing research firm. It is privately held and has 105 full-time employees. On the basis of customer feedback, CRI meets or exceeds its clients' expectations on 97 percent of its projects; and 92 percent of CRI's clients have indicated that it is better than the competition in terms of overall service. CRI has achieved excellent on-time delivery performance: 99 percent of its final reports are delivered on time. These improvements in service have translated into a number of organizational benefits. For example, revenue per full-time employee has increased 70 percent since 1988, and the client base increased from 67 to 138.

Trident Precision Manufacturing is a privately held company founded in 1979. Trident employs 167 people at its plant in Webster, New York. Its primary business is developing tools and processes to produce outputs designed by its customers. Trident has achieved a number of impressive improvements in quality. For example, it increased its on-time delivery from 87 percent in 1990 to 99.94 percent by 1995. In addition, from 1990 to 1995, the direct labor-hours needed for rework have been reduced from 8.7 percent to 1.1 percent. The company invests 4.6 percent of its payroll in training employees and has seen its employee turnover decrease from 41 percent to 5 percent. Trident's financial performance has also improved. For example, sales per employee increased from $67,000 in 1988 to $116,000 in 1995.

Source: http://www.quality.nist.gov/docs/winners/96win/adac.htm, December 18, 1996.

The Malcolm Baldrige National Quality Award

In response to Japan's Deming Award, in 1987 the United States established the Malcolm Baldrige National Quality Award. The award is given in three categories: manufacturing, service, and small business. Also, up to two organizations may receive the award in each category each year. The 1997 criteria for the award are summarized in Table 3.4 and the awardwinners through 1996 are summarized in Table 3.5.

*T*ABLE 3.4 ❖ Criteria for the Malcolm Baldrige Award of 1997

Category		Items	Point Values
1	**Leadership**		**110**
1.1		Leadership System	80
1.2		Company Responsibility and Citizenship	30
2	**Strategic Planning**		**80**
2.1		Strategy Development Process	40
2.2		Company Strategy	40
3	**Customer and Market Focus**		**80**
3.1		Customer and Market Knowledge	40
3.2		Customer Satisfaction and Relationship Enhancement	40
4	**Information and Analysis**		**80**
4.1		Selection and Use of Information and Data	25
4.2		Selection and Use of Comparative Information and Data	15
4.3		Analysis and Review of Company Performance	40
5	**Human Resource Development and Management**		**100**
5.1		Work Systems	40
5.2		Employee Education, Training, and Development	30
5.3		Employee Well-Being and Satisfaction	30
6	**Process Management**		**100**
6.1		Management of Product and Service Processes	60
6.2		Management of Support Processes	20
6.3		Management of Supplier and Partnering Processes	20
7	**Business Results**		**450**
7.1		Customer Satisfaction Results	130
7.2		Financial and Market Results	130
7.3		Human Resource Results	35
7.4		Supplier and Partner Results	25
7.5		Company-Specific Results	130
TOTAL POINTS			**1000**

Source: http://www.quality.nist.gov/docs/97_crit/itemlist.htm, December 18, 1996.

$\mathcal{T}$ABLE 3.5 ❖ Winners of the Baldrige Award

Year	Manufacturing	Services	Small Business
1996	ADAC Laboratories	Dana Commercial Credit Corporation	Custom Research Inc. Trident Precision Manufacturing Inc.
1995	Armstrong World Industries Inc.— Building Products Operations Corning Incorporated— Telecommunication Products Division		
1994		AT&T Computer Communications Services GTE Directories Corporation	Wainwright Industries, Inc.
1993	Eastman Chemical Company		Ames Rubber Corporation
1992	AT&T Network Systems Group—Transmission Systems Business Unit Texas Instruments Inc.— Defense Systems and Electronics Group	AT&T Universal Card Services The Ritz-Carlton Hotel Company	Granite Rock Company
1991	Solectron Corporation Zytec Corporation		Marlow Industries
1990	Cadillac Motor Car Company IBM Rochester	Federal Express Corporation	Wallace Company
1989	Milliken & Company Xerox Corporation— Business Products & Systems		
1988	Motorola, Inc. Westinghouse Electric Corp.—Commercial Nuclear Fuel Division		Globe Metallurgical Inc.

Source: http://www.quality.nist.gov/docs/winners/contact.htm, December 18, 1996.

❖ ISO 9000

Unlike the Deming Prize or the Baldrige Award, ISO 9000 is not an award for which companies must compete. Rather, ISO 9000 was developed as a guideline for designing, manufacturing, selling, and servicing products. In fact, in contrast to the Deming Prize and the Baldrige Award, which recognize organizations for excellent performance, ISO 9000 is intended as more of a checklist of good business practices.

$\mathscr{T}$ABLE 3.6 ❖ Elements of ISO 9000

1. Management responsibility
2. Quality system
3. Contract review
4. Design control
5. Document and data control
6. Purchasing
7. Control of customer-supplied product
8. Product identification and traceability
9. Process control
10. Inspection and testing
11. Control of inspection, measuring, and test equipment
12. Inspection and test status
13. Control of nonconforming product
14. Corrective and preventive action
15. Handling, storage, packaging, preservation, and delivery
16. Control of quality audits
17. Internal quality audits
18. Training
19. Servicing
20. Statistical techniques

Thus, the intent of the ISO 9000 standard is that, if an organization selects a supplier that is ISO 9000–certified, it has some assurance that the supplier follows accepted business practices in the areas specified in the standard. However, one criticism of ISO 9000 is that it does not require any specific actions, and therefore each organization determines how it can best meet the requirements of the standard.

ISO 9000 was developed by the International Organization for Standardization and first issued in March of 1987. Since that time, it has become the most widely recognized standard in the world. To illustrate its importance, in 1993 the European Community required that companies in several industries become certified as a condition of conducting business in Europe. The ISO 9000 standard consists of 20 elements (standards), which are summarized in Table 3.6.

$\mathscr{C}$HAPTER IN PERSPECTIVE

This has been the third chapter of Part One. Chapter 1 introduced the topic of operations. Chapter 2 then overviewed issues related to business strategy and international competitiveness. The present chapter built on these topics and discussed one of the most important ways operational activities support the business strategy and enhance competitiveness: through quality management. The chapter began with a discussion of quality costs and trade-offs. Next, the philosophies of three of the leading quality experts were presented. The following section then overviewed widely used quality programs. Finally, the last section addressed the topic of quality awards and certifications. In Chapter 4 we build on the *customer focus* established in this chapter, but we add the dimension of technology to address the topic of business process design. In Part Four, which focuses on the product supply process, we will return to the topic of quality and discuss how statistical procedures are used to help maintain the desired level of quality in the organization.

❖ CHECK YOUR UNDERSTANDING

1. List and briefly describe the four categories of quality costs. Explain how these costs can be traded off for one another.

2. What is meant by "Quality is free"?

3. List some of the primary factors in determining an appropriate level of quality.

4. Summarize and contrast the philosophies of Deming, Juran, and Crosby.

5. Contrast American and Japanese approaches to quality, identifying cultural, transferable, and nontransferable aspects.

6. What are the five steps associated with TQM?

7. Contrast quality control with TQM.

8. What is a quality circle?

9. List and briefly describe the tools that are often used by quality circles.

10. What is the Taguchi method?

11. What is benchmarking? What is it used for?

12. What are the steps involved in a benchmarking study? What are the sources of data?

13. List and briefly explain the criteria used in awarding the Deming Prize.

14. What are the major categories for the Malcolm Baldrige Award?

15. How does the ISO 9000 standard differ from the Deming Prize and the Baldrige Award?

❖ EXPAND YOUR UNDERSTANDING

1. Which of the reasons for inattention to quality in the United States might be the hardest to overcome?

2. Are all quality management programs aimed at improving quality in the same way? How do they differ in their focus?

3. If your firm has the top product in a market, is it always a good idea to try to make it obsolete by offering an even better product? When would or wouldn't it be a good idea?

4. Which of the problem-solving tools for quality circles might be hardest for employees to learn? Why?

5. Why do you think the Japanese use Taguchi methods in product design, whereas Americans use them in process design?

6. It is not uncommon for a firm to design a product in conjunction with one customer and then sell it to that customer's competitors. Is this unethical?

7. How is quality handled differently in service firms and product firms? Does quality mean something different in a service firm?

8. Frequently, a machine, with certain process capabilities, will be run by a human who has separate process capabilities. If the machine is barely capable of maintaining the tolerances specified for a part, what might the combination of machine and human do?

9. Contrast the discussion of inspection in the text with the current emphasis on building quality on the line rather than inspecting it in. Is there a contradiction here?

10. What role might advanced technology play in quality inspection, planning, or control?

11. Suppose a firm has identified the most cost-effective level of quality for its product, and any higher quality would make it unprofitable. Yet, it is occasionally unsafe at its current quality level. Discuss the ethical issues facing the firm.

12. If a plastic imitation cannot be distinguished from the real thing, what difference does it make?

13. How could a college control the quality of its graduates?

14. What types of outputs do not require high quality?

15. Why was the military the first to be concerned about quality?

16. Why is it important for an organization to go outside its industry in conducting a benchmarking study? What difficulties might occur if an organization tried to stay within its own industry?

❖ APPLY YOUR UNDERSTANDING
Officetech, Inc.

Officetech, Inc., produces office equipment for small businesses and home offices. Several months ago it launched its PFS 1000, a single unit that functions as a color printer, color scanner, color copier, and fax machine. The PFS 1000 won rave reviews for its functionality, affordable price, and innovative design. This, coupled with Officetech's reputation for producing highly reliable products, quickly lead to a severe backlog. Officetech's plant simply could not keep up with demand.

Initially, Officetech's CEO, Nancy Samuelson, was extremely concerned about the backlog and put a great deal of pressure on the plant manager, George Johnson, to increase production. However, she abruptly shifted gears when a new report indicated that returns and complaints for the PFS 1000 were running four times higher than the usual industry rate. Because Officetech's reputation was on the line, Nancy decided that the problem required immediate attention. She also decided that the quickest way to diagnose the problem and to avoid the usual mentality of "blaming it on the other department" would be to bring in an outside consultant with expertise in these matters.

Nancy hired Ken Cathey to investigate the problem. Nancy and Ken agreed that Ken should spend his first week interviewing key personnel in an effort to learn as much about the problem as possible. Because of the urgency of the problem, Nancy promised Ken that he would have complete access to—and the cooperation of—all employees. She would send out a memo immediately informing all employees that they were expected to cooperate and assist Ken in any way they could.

The next morning, Ken decided to begin his investigation by discussing the quality problem with several of the production supervisors. He began with the supervisor of the final assembly area, Todd Allision. Todd commented:

> I received Nancy's memo yesterday, and frankly, the problem with the PFS 1000 does not surprise me. One of the problems we've had in final assembly is with the casing. Basically, the case is composed of a top and a bottom. The problem that we are having is that these pieces rarely fit together, so we typically have to force them together. I'm sure this is adding a lot of extra stress on the cases. I haven't seen a breakdown on what the problems with quality are, but it wouldn't surprise me if one of the problems was cracked cases or cases that are coming apart. I should also mention that we never had this problem with our old supplier. However, when purchasing determined that we could save over $1 per unit, we switched to a new supplier for the cases.

The meeting with Todd lasted for about $1\frac{1}{2}$ hours, and Ken decided that rather than meet with someone else, he would be better off reviewing the notes he had taken and filling in any gaps while the conversation was still fresh in his mind. Then he would break for lunch and meet with one or two additional people in the afternoon.

After returning from lunch, Ken stopped by to talk with Steve Morgan, the production supervisor for the printed circuit boards. Ken found Steve and an equipment operator staring at one of the auto-insertion machines used to place components such as integrated circuits, capacitors, and resistors on the printed circuit board before wave soldering. Arriving, Ken introduced himself to Steve and asked, "What's up?" Steve responded:

> We are having an extremely difficult time making the printed circuit boards for the PFS 1000. The designers placed the components closer together than this generation of equipment was designed to handle. As a result, the leads of the components are constantly being bent. I doubt that more than 25 percent of the boards have all their components installed properly. As a result, we are spending a great deal of time inspecting all the boards and reworking the ones with problems. Also, because of the huge backlog for these boards and the large number that must be reworked, we have been trying to operate the equipment 20 percent faster than its normal operating rate. This has caused the machine to break down much more frequently. I estimate that on a given eight-hour shift, the machine is down one to two hours.

In terms of your job—to determine the cause of the problems with quality—faulty circuit boards are very likely a key contributor. We are doing our best to find and correct all the defects, but inspecting and reworking the boards is a very tedious process, and the employees are putting in a lot of extra hours. In addition, we are under enormous pressure to get the boards to final assembly. My biggest regret is that I didn't have more input when they were building the prototypes of the PFS 1000. The prototypes are all built by highly trained technicians using primarily a manual process. Unfortunately, the prototypes are built only to give the engineers feedback on their designs. Had they shown some people in production the prototypes, we could have made suggestions on changes that would have made the design easier to produce.

Ken decided to end the day by talking to the plant manager, Harvey Michaels. Harvey was in complete agreement with Todd and Steve and discussed at length the enormous pressure he was under to get product out the door: "The bottom line is that no one cooperates. Purchasing changes suppliers to save a few bucks, and we end up with components that can't be used. Then our own engineers design products that we can't produce. We need to work together."

On his second day, Ken decided to follow up on the information he had gathered the day before. He first visited the director of purchasing, Marilyn Reagan. When asked about the problem of the cases that did not fit together, Marilyn responded:

The fact of the matter is that switching suppliers for the cases saved $1.04 per unit. That may not sound like a lot, but multiply that by the 125,000 units we are expecting to sell this year, and it turns out to be pretty significant. Those guys in production think the world revolves around them. I am, however, sympathetic to their problems, and I plan on discussing the problem with the supplier the next time we meet. That should be some time next month.

After wrapping up the meeting with Marilyn, Ken decided he would next talk to the director of engineering. On the way, he recognized a person at a vending machine as the worker who had been standing next to Steve at the auto-insertion machine. Ken introduced himself and decided to talk with the worker for a few minutes. The worker introduced himself as Jim and discussed how he had been working in the shipping department just two weeks ago. The operator before Jim had quit because of the pressure. Jim hadn't received any formal training in operating the new equipment, but he said that Steve tried to check on him a couple of times a day to see how things were going. Jim appreciated Steve's efforts, but the quality inspectors made him nervous and he felt that they were always looking over his shoulder.

Ken thanked Jim for his input and then headed off to meet with the director of engineering, Jack Carel. After introducing himself, Ken took a seat in front of Jack's desk. Jack began:

So you are here to investigate our little quality snafu. The pressure that we are under here in engineering is the need to shrink things down. Two years ago fax machines, printers, scanners, and copiers were all separate pieces of equipment. Now, with the introduction of the PFS 1000, all this functionality is included in one piece of equipment not much larger than the original printer. That means design tolerances are going to be a lot tighter and the product is going to be more difficult to manufacture. But the fact of the matter is that manufacturing is going to have to get its act together if we are going to survive. The engineering department did its job. We designed a state-of-the-art piece of office equipment, and the prototypes we built proved that the design works. It's now up to the manufacturing guys to figure out how to produce it. We have done all that we can and should be expected to do.

To end his second day, Ken decided to meet with the director of quality assurance, Debbie Lynn. Debbie commented:

My biggest challenge as director of quality assurance is trying to convince the rest of the organization the importance quality plays. Sure everyone gives lip-service to the importance of quality, but as the end of the month approaches, getting the product out the door is always the highest priority. Also, while I am officially held accountable for quality, I have no formal authority over the production workers. The quality inspectors that report to me do little more than inspect product and tag it if it doesn't meet the specifications so that it is sent to the rework area. In all honesty, I am quite optimistic about Nancy's current concern for quality and very much welcome the opportunity to work closely with you to improve Officetech's quality initiatives.

Questions

1. Which departments at Officetech have the most impact on quality? What role should each department play in helping Officetech improve overall quality?

2. Draw a fishbone chart to help explain how the other functional areas are creating problems for manufacturing—which ultimately may be the causes of the excessive complaints and returns.

3. What recommendations would you make to Nancy concerning Officetech's problem with quality? What role should the quality assurance department play?

❖ EXERCISES

1. Many communities are seeing a rise in crime rates. Develop a fishbone chart to help city officials understand the causes and subcauses of rising crime rates.

2. Identify a problem you think needs to be addressed at your university, such as inadequate parking, excessive use of graduate teaching assistants, or lack of individual attention. Develop a fishbone chart to help university officials better understand the causes of the problem.

3. A principal at a high school was concerned about the writing skills of the students. Over a two-week period she took random samples of students' papers and tallied the errors by category. Develop a Pareto chart for the results of the study, summarized in the table below.

Type of Error	Number of Errors
Punctuation	43
Subject-verb agreement	29
Incomplete sentences	87
Capitalization	52
Spelling	195
Tense change	98

4. Develop a histogram for the data given in Exercise 3.

5. A gym monitors the number of memberships that are not renewed or are canceled each month. Develop a runs chart for last year's data. Should the manager of the gym be concerned?

Month	Number of Cancellations and Nonrenewals	Month	Number of Cancellations and Nonrenewals
January	5	July	7
February	3	August	8
March	2	September	10
April	7	October	14
May	6	November	10
June	7	December	17

Chapter 4

Business Process Design

$\mathscr{C}$HAPTER OVERVIEW

- ❖ The roots of the traditional functional organization date back to the late 1700s, when Adam Smith proposed his concept of the division of labor.

- ❖ Although there have been dramatic improvements in technology since Smith first proposed the division of labor, it is only recently that organizations have begun to challenge this concept and look for better ways to organize work activities.

- ❖ "Paving cow paths" refers to situations where companies simply adopt new technology without realizing that it allows work to be done in entirely new and better ways. This is often the explanation for why many organizations did not achieve the dramatic improvements in performance expected when new technologies were first adopted.

- ❖ Perhaps the most significant drawback associated with functional organizations is that work must be handed off from department to department, leading to delays and errors.

- ❖ A *process* may be defined as the entire set of activities that must be completed to produce a result valued by the customer.

- ❖ All organizations perform processes, but most are not organized on this basis. The term *process-centered* refers to organizations that have organized work on the basis of specific value-creating processes.

- ❖ Business process design (BPD) may be defined as the fundamental rethinking and radical redesign of business processes to bring about dramatic improvements in performance.

- ❖ Although BPD and total quality management (TQM) share the same objective—better meeting customers' requirements—the approaches taken are vastly different. Specifically, TQM seeks to continuously improve and tweak the existing system whereas BPD seeks to change the system in its entirety.

- ❖ A useful approach to facilitate starting with a clean slate in a BPD project is *idealized design*. Its goal is to think in terms of what the ideal or ultimate work system would be, rather than in terms of correcting the existing work system.

- ❖ BPD may have characteristics in common with downsizing, restructuring, and automation, but it is not equivalent to these approaches and should not be confused with them.

- ❖ Five generic business processes are (1) product and transformation design, (2) resource management, (3) product supply, (4) customer processes, and (5) support processes.

- ❖ In undertaking BPD, it is vital to identify assumptions and rules about work activities so that the opportunities created by eliminating them can be considered.

❖ The four primary roles in BPD are (1) leader, (2) process owner, (3) BPD team member, and (4) BPD specialist.

❖ Three approaches to BPD that have been used successfully in the past are the caseworker approach, reorganizing work so that it is performed in its natural order, and the case team approach.

❖ Two factors that have been found to be important to the long-term benefits achieved from BPD are breadth and depth. *Breadth* relates to the extent

that BPD cuts across functional boundaries. *Depth* refers to the extent that key elements of the organization are changed.

❖ Traditional functional departments may evolve into centers of excellence in process-centered organizations. These centers of excellence function as in-house versions of professional associations.

❖ Three useful tools for designing business processes are systems analysis, definition of relationships, and flow process charts.

INTRODUCTION

❖ In the early 1990s, Nynex released Robert Thrasher from his duties as chief operating officer and assigned him to lead an effort aiming to reinvent the company. From the very beginning, Thrasher chose not to examine the company in the traditional way in terms of its divisions, departments, and functions. Rather, he opted to analyze the company in terms of four core processes that cut across the entire organization. Thrasher defined these processes as customer operations, customer support, customer contact, and customer provisioning. With the processes defined, Thrasher next handpicked a captain to oversee the design of each process.

To learn more about what he was getting into, Thrasher spent a couple of days visiting GTE Corporation to learn about its experiences with business process design. On this basis, Thrasher decided to obtain the services of the Boston Consulting Group (BCG), as GTE had done, to help with the projects. Teams were formed from 80 Nynex employees and 20 BCG consultants with the charge of reducing operating expenses by 35 to 40 percent.

To stimulate their thinking and to learn from the best, team members visited 152 companies deemed to be "best practice" companies. The teams identified a number of major inefficiencies at Nynex. For example, it was learned that Nynex purchased 83 different brands of personal computers, that $500 per truck was being spent painting newly purchased trucks a different shade of white, and that $4.5 million was spent to identify and pursue $900,000 in unpaid bills. After identifying these problems, the teams developed a list of 85 "quick wins." For instance, Nynex will save $7 million a year in postage costs by printing on both sides of customers' bills and will save $25 million by standardizing on two personal computer models. Companywide, it is estimated that the changes suggested by the teams will reduce Nynex's $6 billion operating expenses by $1.5 to $1.7 billion dollars in 1997. Doing this would provide Nynex with an internal rate of return of 1025 percent and pay back its investment in two years. According to Thrasher, even if only 25 percent of these benefits are actually realized, Nynex would still achieve a 226 percent internal rate of return and pay back the investment in three years (*Business Week*, 1994).

❖ Recently, a number of companies have made improving their product supply process (i.e., the process by which materials, parts, and products are acquired, transformed, and delivered to customers) a top priority for obtaining a competitive advantage. With regard to the potential for improvement, for instance, Compaq Computer estimates that it lost revenues of $500 million to $1 billion in the first half of 1994 because its computers were not available at the time or place customers wanted them. As another example, consider that it takes a typical box of cereal 104 days to get from the factory to the supermarket because of the number of wholesalers, distributors, brokers, diverters, and consolidators it passes through in between. Indeed, as companies continue to define themselves in terms of their processes, they are also beginning to recognize that these processes extend beyond the boundaries of a single company. The implication is that competition is no longer company versus company, but rather product supply process versus product supply process.

One company that has streamlined its product supply process is National Semiconductor. Over a two-year period National Semiconductor closed six of its warehouses and began shipping its microchips to customers by air from a new 125,000-square-foot distribution center in Singapore. Using this approach, National Semiconductor was able to reduce its delivery time by 47 percent, lower its distribution costs by 2.5 percent, and increase sales by 34 percent. Another example is Saturn, which developed a state-of-the-art logistics system to link its suppliers, factories, and dealers. Using this system, Saturn has been able to turn its inventory over 300 times a year! Having so little inventory on hand would probably concern most inventory managers. However, Saturn manages its supply chain so well that it has had to halt production only once (for 18 minutes) over a four-year period because of a lack of parts. Saturn achieves these results by using a central computer to control deliveries of preinspected and presorted parts at precise times to the factory's 56 loading docks. Deliveries are received 21 hours per day, six days a week from 339 different suppliers in 39 states that are an average of 550 miles away from Saturn's Spring Hill plant (Henkoff, 1994).

❖ Pacific Telesis Group dispatches 20,000 trucks each day to fix problems with its customers' lines. However, since PacBell is responsible only for problems that occur outside a customer's home or office, it is a waste of time and money for PacBell to dispatch a truck when the problem is with an *inside* line. PacBell estimates that the cost of dispatching a truck is $140. To alleviate the problem, PacBell experimented with a new technology in a suburb north of Los Angeles. In the experimental homes and offices, a $10 circuit box was connected to the customer's *outside* lines. To test the line, a signal is sent from PacBell's computer to the circuit box. If the circuit box bounces the signal back, PacBell knows instantly that the problem is with the inside line. In the pilot program, PacBell reduced truck dispatches by 30 percent. If similar savings were achieved companywide, PacBell's daily savings would exceed $2 million.

In addition to saving PacBell a substantial amount of money, the circuit box offers customers a higher level of service. For example, customers can find out immediately if their problem is a broken inside or outside line. And by using the technology to continuously monitor lines, PacBell is able to respond to problems more quickly. In one instance, a phone line was shorted out after a child knocked over a fish tank. However, because PacBell was continuously monitoring the line with its new technology, it was able to dispatch a repair person to the house before the customer even became aware of the problem.

PacBell is using technology in other ways to improve the repair process. For example, PacBell repair workers now use portable computers and a new software program to obtain the information they need to fix a phone line. In the past, the repair worker would have to call another employee to get the information. Also, the computers are used to dispatch the workers to their next assignment, as opposed to having the workers call in for it. And when the workers do need to make phone calls, they use cellular phones installed in their vans instead of pulling over at phone booths (Rigdon, 1994).

Very few topics are creating as much interest and controversy in business today as *business process design* **(BPD).** It is perhaps most commonly referred to as *reengineering,* but a wide variety of other names are also frequently used, such as *business process reengineering, business process engineering, business process innovation,* and *business process design* or *redesign.* To compound the confusion, often managers incorrectly use terms such as *downsizing* and *restructuring* interchangeably with BPD. We rejected the term *reengineering* for this book, because the prefix "*re*" implies that the activity is being done over—which is not usually the case, since most organizations were not *engineered* in the first place. We use the term BPD to reflect the underlying principles and philosophy.

To illustrate the widespread interest in BPD, we can note that in a study of large industrial companies conducted by Pitney Bowes Management Services, 83 percent of the responding companies indicated that they had experience with reengineering. Furthermore, two independent studies conducted by "big six" firms found that 75 to 80 percent of large American companies had increased or would be increasing their commitment to BPD in the foreseeable future. Michael Hammer, who coined the term *reengineering,* found that the number of articles with this word in the title increased to over 800 in 1994 from 10 in 1990.

The examples that began this chapter provide a glimpse of several major themes associated with BPD. First, BPD's primary objective is improved customer service. This was clearly illustrated by the example of Nynex: each of its four core processes began with the word *customer.* Customer service also figured prominently in the other examples. For example, National Semiconductor's reduction of delivery times by 47 percent and PacBell's discovery of problems on phone lines before customers became aware of them both represent dramatic improvements in customer service.

This brings us to a second theme associated with BPD. Specifically, BPD is concerned with making *quantum* improvements in performance, not small *incremental* improvements. Nynex's goal to lower its operating expenses by 35 to 40 percent certainly represents a quantum improvement, as does its expected 1025 percent internal rate of return. Likewise, National Semiconductor's 47 percent reduction in delivery time (with no increase in delivery cost), Saturn's 300 inventory turns per year, and PacBell's opportunity to reduce its repair costs by $2 million per day all qualify as quantum improvements.

A third important theme of BPD is the central role of technology. For example, improvements in PacBell's repair operations were made possible by a $10 circuit box, portable computers, and cellular phones. At Saturn, the ability to manage the supply chain so effectively was based on advances in information technology.

The objective of this chapter is to introduce you to BPD. To begin, important background information, including a more formal definition of BPD, will be provided. The following section will then address issues related to the mechanics of BPD. Next, several tools to facilitate BPD will be discussed. Finally, the chapter will conclude with a discussion related to ensuring that BPD initiatives fulfill their objectives. In addition to presenting a very timely topic, this chapter is important for another reason. Namely, because the remainder of this book is organized around three business processes, this chapter provides the foundation on which the rest of the book is based.

BACKGROUND

Imagine an organization you are familiar with. Now consider how it is organized. For example, if you imagined a restaurant, you might have classified the workers as cooks, food servers, dishwashers, bartenders, and managers. Or, if you pictured a manufacturer of consumer goods, you might have imagined that it was organized into departments based on types of work, such as accounting, engineering, sales, finance, operations, human resource management, information processing, and so on.

In Chapter 1 we discussed the *functional* and the *process* view of organizations. In this discussion it was noted that, traditionally, companies have developed organizational structures based on the type of work performed. This type of organization is referred to as a functional organization because work is organized on the basis of the function it serves. A restaurant that classifies its workers as cooks, dishwashers, bartenders, and so on has classified them on the basis of the function they serve or the type of work they perform. Likewise, a manufacturer of consumer goods with accounting, finance, sales, and engineering departments has organized its employees on the basis of the tasks they perform.

❖ The Concept of the Division of Labor

The roots of the functional organization date back to the late 1700s, when Adam Smith proposed his concept of the division of labor in *An Inquiry into the Nature and Causes of the Wealth of Nations* (1776). Referring to the 17 operations required to produce a pin, Smith argued that assigning one task to each of 17 workers would be more efficient and would produce more pins than having 17 workers each autonomously perform all 17 tasks. According to Smith, dividing work into discrete tasks provides the following benefits:

- ❖ By repeatedly performing the same task, a worker would acquire greater skill at it.
- ❖ No time would be lost by switching workers from one task to another.
- ❖ Workers would be well positioned to develop improved tools and techniques as a result of focusing on a single task.

Although there have been dramatic advances in technology since Smith first proposed the division of labor, it is only recently that organizations have begun to challenge the concept and look for better ways to organize and integrate work. Indeed, if you were to compare how companies are organized today and how they were organized 20 or 30 years ago, you would find that little has changed in their organizational structures. This is true despite the advances in technology that have developed over this period, such as personal computers, fax machines, cellular phones, laser printers, the World Wide Web, compact disks, spreadsheets, word processors, client-server computing, groupware, E-mail, and cable modems, to name a few.

Initially, when these technologies were first adopted by organizations, the dramatic improvements in performance that were expected did not materialize. One popular explanation for this is that organizations were not taking advantage of the capabilities the new technologies offered. Rather, companies were simply using technology to speed up and automate existing practices. Clearly, if an activity or a set of activities is not effective to begin with, performing it faster and with less human intervention does not automatically make it effective. For instance, one major financial institution reported that more than 90 steps were required for an office worker to get office supplies. These steps mostly involved filling out forms and getting the required signatures. Given the capabilities of information technology, it is certainly true that these steps could be automated and speeded up. For example, a computer system could be developed to generate all the forms automatically and then automatically E-mail them to the appropriate person for authorization. However, is automating all these steps the best solution? Might it not make more sense to eliminate most of them? Consider that even if the forms are generated and dispatched faster, valuable managerial time is still being used to look over and approve these requests every time an employee needs a pad of paper or ballpoint pen. Indeed, when the cost of the controls is weighed against the benefits, it might be much more effective to give employees access to the supply cabinet to retrieve their own supplies as needed. Dr. Hammer uses the term *paving cow paths* to describe organizations that simply adopt a new technology without considering the capabilities it offers to perform work in entirely new and better ways.

❖ Processes

In addition to rapid advances in technology, there have been significant changes in the nature of competition. Two or three decades ago, the dominant concern of many businesses was controlling cost and increasing revenues. However, increased competition and a more global marketplace has led numerous organizations to shift their focus to producing high quality, providing value and service to customers, and making organizational innovations.

Given this shift in focus and the capabilities offered by new technology, companies also began questioning the way work was organized. In the traditional functional organization, work is broken down into narrowly defined "chunks" so that it can be efficiently completed by highly specialized workers. Of course, dividing work up in this fashion requires that the output be *handed off* from one worker to the next in order to complete a unit of output. And, although this arrangement may offer certain efficiencies, there are also a number of drawbacks when work must be passed between workers.

Perhaps the two most significant drawbacks associated with handing off work are the *delays* and *errors* that are introduced when the work must be passed from worker to worker. For example, consider the traditional approach to designing new products. The process typically begins when the marketing department collects information about customers' needs and desires. This information is then relayed to the research and development (R&D) department, which is responsible for designing the output to meet the customers' requirements. After the design is completed, it is then up to the manufacturing area to produce the output exactly as specified in the design. After the output is produced, it becomes the responsibility of the sales department to sell this product. Finally, after a customer purchases the output, the customer service department must provide after-sales services such as help with installation and warranty repairs.

As you can imagine, completing a set of activities sequentially, one at a time, will tend to maximize the time required to complete the activities in total. In addition, there can be significant delays in the discovery of important information, and this extends the completion time even further into the future. For example, assume that the engineers in R&D design a feature that manufacturing cannot produce, or that can be produced only at a very high cost. In the sequential approach, this problem will not be discovered until after the design is finalized and handed off to manufacturing. Upon discovering the problem, manufacturing will send the design back to R&D for modifications. Clearly, the more often a design has to go back and forth between R&D and manufacturing, the longer the delay will be in introducing the new output.

In addition, as the number of activities in the series increases or the interdependence among the activities increases (or both), the potential for delays increases. To illustrate this, let us continue with our earlier example. Let's assume that after several iterations, R&D finally develops a design that manufacturing can produce. Manufacturing begins producing the new output and sales begins selling it. After a couple of weeks, however, the first calls begin to come in for repair work. When the first couple of repairs are made, it is discovered that R&D has specified a component that the service personnel have no experience repairing. Management determines that it will be cheaper to redesign the product and use a component that the service personnel are familiar with than to train all service personnel in the repair of this one component. Thus, the design goes back to R&D. Of course, all design changes R&D makes create potential problems for manufacturing. And manufacturing changes to accommodate the new design may create new problems for service personnel. For example, after a replacement component is selected, it may be discovered that the manufacturing equipment is not properly adjusted and is, say, overtightening the screws that attach the new component, making it impossible for field technicians to repair.

In addition to extensive delays, every hand-off creates an opportunity for information to be miscommunicated and thus for an error to be introduced. You may recall playing the "telephone game" as a child. In this game, a group of people form a circle. One person in the circle is quietly read a message. This person whispers the message to the next person. The process is repeated, with each person hearing the message from the person on (say) the left and then repeating it to the person on the right. Finally, the last person in the circle repeats the message out loud, and this version is compared with the original message—which it usually resembles only vaguely. Since there are no mechanisms to correct changes that are made to the original message, these errors are propagated and amplified throughout the remainder of the chain.

In a similar way, information can be lost, or its meaning can be changed, each time it is handed off from one department to the next. Assume, for instance, that a market researcher goes to a retail store to personally interview consumers about their color preferences for small appliances. One customer points to a competitor's appliance and suggests that its color—maroon—is very appealing. Throughout the day, several other consumers also comment on the attractiveness of maroon. The next day at the office the market researcher tells the director that the company needs a line of "red" appliances. On the basis of the details provided by the market researcher, the director of market research E-mails the director of R&D, suggesting that R&D develop a line of red appliances. The R&D director then explains the need for a new line of red appliances to one of the designers. Unfortunately, as this requirement is being explained, the designer is imagining a bright cherry-red.

In the past when most companies were functionally organized, the delays and errors associated with hand-offs were considered a natural part of business. And since all companies experienced these same problems, no one company was at a competitive disadvantage. However, as soon as one company in a particular industry adopts an organizational structure that reduces or eliminates the delays and errors accompanying hand-offs, all remaining companies in the industry may be at a severe handicap.

Consider the automobile industry. In the early to middle 1980s, Japanese automobile manufacturers could design a new car in three to four years, compared with the five to six years needed by American automobile manufacturers. Now, consider the implications for organizational competitiveness. On one hand, a company that can design its new products in less time begins with a cost advantage. To put this another way, it costs more to fund a product development team for five or six years than it does for three or four years. Likewise, the organization with the shortest product development time can get innovative products to the market first. This is significant because organizations that are the first to the market with new products tend to be more profitable and have larger market shares than their slower counterparts. Finally, as product development time increases, risk and uncertainty also increase. For one thing, there is less uncertainty about how customers' preferences and the regulatory environment may change in three years than about such changes in six years. Thus, a company that takes six years to develop new products needs to be a much better predictor of the future than a company that takes three years.

With increasing competition and shorter product life cycles, the errors and delays that creep in when activities are performed sequentially are a luxury many organizations find they can no longer afford. Instead, as was discussed in Chapter 1, these companies are developing organizational structures on the basis of processes. A *process* may be defined as an entire set of activities that must be completed to produce a result valued by a customer. Note that the customer for a process may be *internal* (i.e., an entity inside the organization) or *external* (i.e., an entity outside the organization). For example, in a functional organization, the manufacturing department is the *internal customer* of the R&D department. On the other hand, the company or individual that actually purchases the products made by the manufacturing department is an *external customer*.

In contrast to a functional (or *vertical*) organization, in which similar activities are grouped together, process-based (or *horizontal*) structures bring together a number of *dis*similar activities that are required to produce the result of value. The rationale for organizing work on the basis of specific value-creating processes is to eliminate the need to hand off and coordinate work across numerous functional boundaries. For example, earlier we discussed potential problems that can occur when work must be handed off from R&D to manufacturing to customer service. As an alternative to performing these activities sequentially, a product development team could be created that has representatives from all areas affected by decisions made at the product design stage. With this approach, product designers could get immediate feedback on how alternative designs affect the product's manufacturability and repairability. In a functional organization, product designers do not typically get this kind of feedback until after the design is completed and a problem is discovered.

Furthermore, the idea of organizing activities on the basis of processes can be extended beyond a company's traditional boundaries. For example, many companies have found it beneficial to include key customers and suppliers on their product development teams. Including customers helps ensure that the new output will meet their needs, and suppliers can suggest alternatives based on their unique expertise that the company might not have otherwise considered.

Incidentally, it is important to point out that all companies perform processes; however, not all of them have chosen to organize work on this basis. We use the term *process-centered* to refer to companies that have organized their work activities on the basis of specific value-creating processes. Interestingly, employees of companies that have a functional structure, as opposed to a process-centered structure, are often unable to identify value-creating processes. Quite often, when asked to identify such processes, these employees simply list the functional departments. At other times, they may list a subprocess or subset of an actual process. For example, they may identify production scheduling as a process when in reality it is actually part of a larger process concerned with producing and distributing finished products to customers. Indeed, organizations have thought in terms of functions for so long that making the transition to thinking in terms of processes is often a very difficult adjustment. Thus, in addition to helping eliminate delays and errors, another important benefit associated with organizing work on the basis of processes is that it makes clear to all employees how the organization creates value for the customer and, equally important, how their work fits into the overall scheme.

Given the many potential benefits associated with adopting a process-centered organizational structure, we next discuss how companies make the transition from a functional to a process-centered organization.

❖ Business Process Design

As was mentioned earlier, when many of the new information technologies were initially adopted by companies, the expected improvements in organizational efficiency and effectiveness did not materialize. On closer examination, it was discovered that many companies were adapting new technology to fit current business practices rather than attempting to take advantage of the capabilities offered by the technology to perform activities in perhaps entirely different and better ways. The early 1990s marked the beginning of the reengineering movement—companies started to consider the capabilities that technology offered in relationship to the way work was performed and organized.

Michael Hammer and Steven Stanton, in their book *The Reengineering Revolution* (1995), define reengineering as "the fundamental rethinking and *radical redesign* of business *processes* to bring about *dramatic* improvements in performance" (p. 3). The keywords *radical, redesign, process,* and *dramatic* are particularly important to understanding the concept of reengineering or BPD.

The word *radical* is used to signify that the purpose of BPD is to *profoundly* change the way work is performed, not to make *superficial* changes. It has to do with understanding the foundation upon which work is based and eliminating old ways that no longer make sense. In other words, it refers to *reinventing* the way work is performed and organized, not simply improving it. Radically changing work is often best accomplished by starting with a clean slate and making no assumptions about how work activities are performed.

OPERATIONS IN PRACTICE

Software Dramatically Improves the Processing of Home Loan Applications

Traditionally, the process of approving a home loan requires 30 days or more. The process begins by having the applicant manually complete a loan application. Then, the application is transferred to and processed by a variety of specialists, including underwriters who compile credit reports to evaluate the application.

In an effort to streamline this process, both the Federal National Mortgage Association (Fannie Mae) and the Federal Home Loan Mortgage Corporation (Freddie Mac) have developed sophisticated software that makes getting a home loan as easy as getting a car loan. One key feature of the software is the inclusion of databases and statistical formulas to estimate the value of the property. Using this approach, a human appraiser needs only to drive by the property rather than conduct a complete inspection.

In effect, these programs reduce the loan approval process from several weeks to several hours or less. This reduction in time and human effort results in a saving of $1000 for the lender after the cost of the new software has been taken into account. Further, it is anticipated that real estate agents will be able to expand their role, using the software to handle the mortgage process as well (Blumenthal, 1995).

The second keyword, **redesign,** denotes the fact that BPD is concerned with the design of work. Typically people think of design as being primarily applicable to products. However, as is demonstrated in this chapter, the way work is accomplished can also be designed. In fact, Hammer and Stanton point out that having intelligent, capable, well-trained, motivated employees is of little value if work is badly designed to begin with. For example, at the beginning of a semester, college students frequently need to visit the registrar's office, the financial aid office, and the bursar's office. If each of these offices is located in a separate building and these buildings are on opposite sides of the campus, students are not going to be happy about having to walk so far between offices—especially during the winter and summer semesters—no matter how dedicated, talented, friendly, and so on the office staff is.

The third keyword is **process.** As was mentioned earlier, all organizations perform processes. However, it was not until recently that companies began organizing work on the basis of these processes. Partly as a result of total quality management (TQM, discussed in Chapter 3), companies began to focus more on meeting customers' needs. As they did this, they soon realized that customers are not particularly interested in the individual activities that are performed to create a product or service. Rather, they are more concerned about the final result of these activities. When you order a pizza for delivery, do you care about what temperature the pizza is baked at, how many phone lines the restaurant has, how your order is communicated to the cook, how often the pizza boxes are ordered, or how the workers' schedules are developed? Or are you more concerned with how quickly your pizza is delivered, whether you receive the pizza you ordered, and how it tastes?

Of course, since companies were not traditionally organized on the basis of their processes, they were not typically managed on the basis of processes either. Therefore, no one was assigned responsibility for the entire process that created the results of interest to the customer. Again, using the scenario of product design, a typical company would have departmental managers to oversee market research, manufacturing, and customer service. However, there was no manager responsible for ensuring that the results of all these activities were meeting customers' requirements.

To address this problem, companies have adopted a variety of approaches—

OPERATIONS IN PRACTICE

Faced with Significant Shifts in Customers' Requirements, the Supermarket Industry Is in Need of Radical Change

The challenges currently confronting the supermarket industry may turn out to be the greatest opportunity this industry has had in its 65-year history, or the reason for the extinction of the supermarket as we know it. The stakes are extremely high. In the United States alone, $800 billion is spent annually on food products and services.

One indicator of the challenge facing the food industry is the percent of a typical consumer's food budget that is spent on meals away from home. In 1980 approximately 36 percent of food dollars were spent on away-from-home meals. By 1995 this figure had increased to 44 percent.

The supermarket industry is being assaulted on a number of fronts. New competitors include discount chains such as Wal-Mart that compete on the basis of price, restaurant chains such as Boston Market and Chili's that compete on the basis of convenience and value, and new start-ups that offer a "virtual supermarket" which consumers can access with their home computers. Wal-Mart, for example, is annually adding 100 of its 180,000-square-foot supermarket–discount supercenters. In contrast, a typical supermarket has about 60,000 square feet. The problem is compounded because a large amount of overcapacity already exists in the food industry.

The bottom line for the supermarket industry is that consumers' requirements are shifting away from simply purchasing groceries. Rather, many consumers are now more concerned with purchasing "solutions" to their food problems. Some supermarket chains that have recognized this change have been able to capitalize on it. For example, Ukrop's Super Markets (located in Richmond) has added freshly made foods, take-out meal stations, and eat-in restaurants to its stores.

Other supermarket chains are betting on an approach called *efficient customer response* (ECR) to streamline the process of replenishing stock. Typically, it takes more than 100 days for a product to get from the factory to the shelf. The idea of ECR is to dramatically reduce this time by continuously replenishing products. It has been estimated that ECR will reduce costs by 10 percent, saving the industry $30 billion annually.

Rather than trying to improve the existing system, other grocery stores are using technology to completely overhaul the shopping process. For example, Peapod (located in Chicago and San Francisco) delivers groceries, liquor, prescriptions, and various other items that customers order using a personal computer. With this approach customers use their PCs to view "virtual aisles" of a Jewel or a Safeway store. The software allows customers to select from a number of different views. For example, the customer can view all specials or can request that the frozen food aisle be displayed. Customers' orders are delivered within three hours (Saporito, 1995).

from forming teams to adopting matrix organizations. In the team approach, representatives of a variety of functions and disciplines come together to accomplish an objective. Teams can be permanent or formed ad hoc. In a matrix organization, each employee has two supervisors: a functional supervisor and a results-oriented supervisor. For example an engineer assigned to a product development project would report to and be evaluated by both a functional engineering supervisor and the project manager.

The last keyword is ***dramatic.*** As the examples at the beginning of the chapter illustrate, BPD is concerned with making quantum improvements in performance, not small or incremental improvements. Thus, BPD focuses on achieving breakthroughs in performance. A company that lowers its lead time by 10 percent from the previous year does not exemplify a dramatic improvement. On the other hand, a company that reduces its lead time from three weeks to three days does.

Business Process Design versus Total Quality Management

In Chapter 3, it was noted that total quality management (TQM) is based on the notion that all employees are responsible for *continuously* improving the quality of the organization's products and services. In fact, the word *total* is included to signify that quality is the concern of all employees. On the basis of this definition, it may appear to the casual observer that BPD and TQM have more similarities than differences. However, although BPD and TQM share the objective of better meeting customers' requirements, the approaches taken to achieve this objective are quite different, as is summarized in Table 4.1.

In terms of the type of change effected, TQM is concerned with developing a large number of changes that improve the system incrementally. Often the source

$\mathscr{T}$ABLE 4.1 ❖ Characteristics of TQM and BPD

Characteristic	TQM	BPD
What type of change is being made?	Large number of small incremental changes.	Large radical change.
Where do we start?	Existing system.	Clean slate.
What is the frequency with which changes are made?	Changes are made continuously.	Major changes are made infrequently.
How much time is required to develop and implement the changes?	Short, perhaps as little as a day.	Long, at least several months and perhaps a year or more.
Who initiates the changes?	Change starts at the bottom of the organization.	Change starts at the top of the organization.
Who is affected by the changes?	Change affects workers in a single functional department.	Change affects workers across functional departments.
What is the primary enabler of the changes?	Statistical quality control techniques.	New technology.

Source: Adapted from Thomas H. Davenport, *Process Innovation: Reengineering Work Through Information Technology* (Boston: Harvard Business School Press, 1993), p. 11.

of these changes is a quality circle or a suggestion program. Frequently these changes focus on correcting specific problems that the employees themselves have identified. BPD, on the other hand, is concerned with making radical changes that fundamentally change the way work is performed and organized based on the capabilities offered by technology. Thus, TQM seeks to continuously tweak the existing system whereas BPD seeks to change the system in its entirety.

Another important distinction between TQM and BPD is the starting point. With TQM, the starting point is the existing system; in essence: What can we do to improve the system today? In contrast, the starting point with BPD is a clean slate. Starting with a clean slate requires *not* making assumptions and *not* having preconceived notions about how work is performed. This can be framed as a question: If I were starting this business today, how should the work be organized, given all the capabilities technology offers, to best meet the customers' needs?

One useful technique for facilitating the clean-slate approach is what Professor Russell Ackoff refers to as *idealized design*. The goal of idealized design is to think in terms of what the ideal or ultimate work system (or product) would be, rather than to think in terms of correcting problems associated with the existing work system or product. Ackoff suggests that the only constraint to be considered in idealized design is what is technologically feasible. No other constraints, such as economic, legal, political, and social considerations, should be included at this stage.

To illustrate this approach, Table 4.2 lists responses customers of a local phone company might give to two questions. The question on the left is meant to be representative of the type of questions market researchers commonly ask; the question on the right is based on idealized design. As a consumer, would you prefer a phone developed on the basis of the responses in the left column or the right column? Ini-

$\mathcal{T}$ABLE 4.2 ❖ **Conventional versus Idealized Design of Phone Service**

What are your major complaints about your current phone service?	How would you describe an ideal phone system?
I have too many phone numbers to remember (e.g., home, office, office fax, and cellular).	All phones would be wireless with batteries that never needed to be changed or recharged.
I have to pay for three lines at home (e.g., a line for me and my spouse, one for the kids, and one for the computer).	Only certain phones in my house would ring, depending on who the call was for.
Every time I move, we have to get all new The phone would automatically screen phone numbers.	I would be assigned one phone number for life, like a social security number, and no matter where I lived or worked, I would take the number with me.
The phone is constantly ringing—either somebody is trying to sell us something or somebody has gotten a wrong number.	The phone would automatically screen wrong numbers and people trying to sell me something.
Our friends have to remember our home number and our cellular number.	I could give out one phone number and people could reach me no matter if I was at home, at the office, in my car, or at my kid's soccer game.

tially, you might not think there would be much difference. But Table 4.3 shows how a phone company might respond to each set of responses. On the basis of Table 4.3, which phone system do you prefer?

Another difference between TQM and BPD is the frequency with which changes are made. With TQM, the approach is to strive continuously to improve the existing system. Each of the changes may lead to only marginal improvements, but the sum of a large number of such improvements can be quite significant. In contrast, BPD is concerned with making infrequent but large changes. Since BPD is primarily concerned with utilizing the capabilities of technology to organize work in order to better meet customers' needs, it needs to be done only when a major change occurs either in the capabilities offered by technology or in the customers' requirements.

In fact, as Figure 4.1 illustrates, TQM and BPD support each other. First, BPD develops work processes to meet customers' needs. Then a period of continuous improvement follows to continually tweak and improve the new processes. Eventually, when a major change occurs in either customers' requirements or technological capabilities, the company can redesign its processes accordingly.

TQM and BPD also differ in terms of the amount of time required to develop and implement changes. Since continuous improvement is concerned with improving the existing system, suggested changes typically come from employees' direct experiences with the system. Thus, no special effort is needed to identify these opportunities for improvement. On top of this, since the changes are usually small in scope and are directed toward improving the system, approval is often quick and routine. In contrast, BPD is concerned with starting from scratch and developing a work process that does not yet exist. Thus, the BPD team has no prior experience with the process. In order to carry out its mission, the BPD team must develop an understanding of the existing process, the customers' requirements, and the technology available. Then all this information must be assimilated. Finally, the task of actually designing the new process can be initiated.

Although the time needed to make incremental changes can be very short, perhaps even as little as a day, the time to complete a BPD project is at least several months and perhaps a year or more. Hammer and Stanton warn, however, that BPD should provide some tangible benefits within a year. According to these authors, BPD that stretches out more than a year without producing any tangible benefits runs the risk of losing support and momentum.

TQM and BPD also differ with regard to who initiates the change. With TQM, changes originate from the bottom, often in conjunction with suggestion programs or quality circles. In contrast, BPD seeks to eliminate boundaries that separate functional departments, and only a few top managers, or perhaps only the president, will have the authority to cross a number of departments. For example, a department manager in manufacturing cannot unilaterally decide to redesign the entire product design process. Simply put, this manager has no authority over the employees in the other key departments such as marketing and R&D.

A related matter is who is affected by the change. Given the source of the change and authority of the person approving the change, continuous improvement efforts are aimed at the functioning of a single department. In contrast, the purpose of BPD is to improve the functioning of workers across functional departments.

A final characteristic differentiating TQM and BPD is the primary enabler of the

$\mathcal{T}$ABLE 4.3 ❖ Phone Company's New Phone System Based on Customer Responses Given in Table 4.2

Phone Company's Approach to Addressing Problems	Phone Company's Approach to Developing an Ideal Phone
Phone company sets up a service whereby if the number a person calls is not answered, other phone numbers you supply are called in sequence.	All phones would be digital cellular phones. The phones would be solar-powered so that the batteries would never need recharging or replacing.
Phone company offers discounts to households with multiple lines.	All households would have a single digital phone line with enough bandwidth to carry several transmissions simultaneously. Also, each home would have a router to direct calls to the appropriate phone or fax in the house depending on the number dialed and the type of call (e.g., voice, fax, data).
Phone company offers a guarantee that if you move within certain radius, you can keep your current phone number.	Phone company assigns individuals one phone number for life. Number does not have to be activated. Phone number is unique and can be transferred anywhere in world.
Phone company no longer charges for having number unlisted. Also, phone customers to store up to 10 numbers to help cut down on dialing errors.	A call coming in from a source not in individual's database is first screened by a digital assistant before the individual's phone is rung. The digital assistant first identifies who is being called so that if an error was made, the caller can simply hang up. If an error was not made and the caller still wants the call to go through, the digital assistant will first ask for the caller's name and then for a short description of the purpose of the call. The digital assistant then rings the person, explains that a caller not in the database is trying to reach him or her, and then plays the caller's name and purpose. The digital assistant then asks if the call should be put through, terminated, or transferred to voice mail. If the individual specifies that the call should be put through, the digital assistant asks if the caller should be added to the database. Individuals can also add to their database all calls that should be terminated immediately by the digital assistant.
Phone company sets up service whereby if-the number a person calls is not answered, other phone numbers you supply are called in sequence.	Individual's unique phone number is linked to all phones individual specifies. At any time individual can specify which phones ring, what sequence the phones are to be tried in, and whether voice mail is to take calls. Users refer to the location of their phones using words such as *home, office, portable, car,* and *fax,* not numbers.

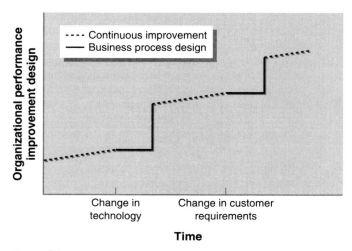

Figure 4.1 Organizations cycle between periods of continuous improvement and BPD.

change. Much of TQM is based on statistical quality control techniques that are used to help companies analyze and identify patterns in data. Here the intent is to uncover and even prevent problems on the basis of analysis of the data. In contrast, BPD is based on the capabilities offered by technology. Here the intent is to design entirely new work processes based on opportunities provided by technology.

What BPD Is Not

Another way to define BPD is to discuss what it is *not*. This is particularly important because the terms *BPD* and *reengineering* are often used incorrectly to describe a wide variety of organizational changes. As a result, the true meaning of BPD has been obscured, and a negative connotation has often been associated with it. To help clarify this, we note that although BPD may have elements in common with other types of organizational change, it is *not* equivalent to these other efforts, and therefore should not be used as an umbrella term to describe all types of organizational change. More specifically, BPD is

- ❖ *not* TQM or continuous improvement
- ❖ *not* downsizing
- ❖ *not* restructuring
- ❖ *not* automation
- ❖ *not* a fad

A number of researchers and practitioners have argued that BPD is not new and is actually just a fancy name for TQM or continuous improvement. However—to repeat—although it is true that TQM and BPD share the objective of improving the extent to which customers' requirements are satisfied, the approaches taken to achieve this objective are quite different: TQM seeks to improve the existing system; BPD seeks to design entirely new work systems based on new technologies.

Another term commonly confused with BPD is the term *downsizing*. Downsizing—or *right-sizing,* as it is sometimes called—is primarily concerned with reducing the head count. Perhaps the confusion between downsizing and BPD stems from the fact that BPD often does result in a need for fewer workers. However, even though BPD and downsizing may both result in fewer workers, the objectives are entirely different. Specifically, the objective of downsizing is to lower overall payroll expenses in an effort to improve organizational efficiency and profitability. In contrast, BPD is concerned with using technology to better satisfy customers' requirements. To put this another way, fewer employees are a possible by-product of BPD, not its objective.

Restructuring is another term frequently confused with BPD. Restructuring essentially involves moving boxes around the organizational chart or spinning off underperforming business units. Often, restructuring is based on the people occupying the boxes and is undertaken to reallocate authority. For example, instead of having the vice president of information technology report to the vice president of finance, the position may be moved up a level so that it reports directly to the president. This move increases the authority of the vice president of information technology. While it is true that BPD should result in changes to the organizational structure, its purpose is to serve customers better, not simply to change reporting relationships and authority.

Because so much emphasis is placed on technology, a common mistake is to equate *automation* and BPD. Thus, a popular misconception is that BPD essentially means using as much technology as possible to automate work. However, as we have discussed, the scope of BPD is much greater than simply throwing technology at problems. Rather, BPD is concerned with taking advantage of the *capabilities* offered by technology to better meet customers' requirements, not to automate work simply for the sake of using technology.

Finally, contrary to the opinions of many commentators, BPD is *not a fad.* Once again, as we have defined it, BPD is concerned with organizing work activities to meet customers' requirements, given the capabilities offered by technology. With customers becoming increasingly sophisticated and demanding, with their requirements constantly changing, with rapid advances in technology, and with increased global competition, it is clear that organizations will have to review their current business processes on an ongoing basis. Furthermore, regardless of what these efforts are called in the future—whether BPD, reengineering, or some other name—because competition is a moving target, companies will certainly be involved in BPD and continuous improvement for the foreseeable future.

❖ Generic Business Processes

In Chapter 1 it was noted that from the functional perspective, all organizations must perform three *core* functions: they must create valued outputs (operations), get the output to the customer (marketing), and raise capital to support their operations (finance). Analogously, from the process perspective it is possible to define five *generic* processes that are applicable to most organizations. These generic processes are composed of sets of functional activities that, taken together, produce a result of value to a customer:

1. *Product and transformation system design.* This process includes all the activities associated with developing new outputs. Also, because it is undesirable to isolate decisions about product design from decisions about designing transformation systems, these activities are best combined into a single business process. Part Two of this book focuses on how operations management supports this business process.

2. *Resource management.* The process of managing organizational resources includes activities such as obtaining and managing capital resources, managing human resources, locating and designing facilities, and managing technology. The operations management activities that support resource management processes are discussed in Part Three.

3. *Product supply.* The product supply process begins with the acquisition of raw materials and ends with delivering the finished output to the customer. Most of the traditional operations management activities support supplying the organization's outputs (including both products and services) to the customer. The operations management activities that support the product supply process are discussed in Part Four.

4. *Customer processes.* Customer processes include activities such as capturing market information, selecting markets, selling and advertising the product, providing customer service, and maintaining the product. Since operations management activities do not play a major role in supporting customer processes, there is no separate part dedicated to these processes.

5. *Support processes.* Organizations perform a number of support processes for stakeholders both within and outside the organization. Examples include legal processes, reporting financial information, developing and maintaining information systems, and managing innovation processes. This book will highlight only how these processes relate to and support the processes discussed in detail in Parts Two, Three, and Four.

The terms for the generic processes were purposely chosen to be broadly applicable to a wide variety of organizations. Of course, actual companies will most likely choose names for their specific business processes that better reflect and describe the actual results. For instance, in the example at the beginning of this chapter, Nynex named its processes *customer operations, customer support, customer contact,* and *customer provisioning.* Notice how the names of these processes reflect results or outputs.

Not all activities or employees need to be organized into processes. For one thing, it is usually prudent for a company to develop a process-centered organizational structure gradually. Thus, within a particular process, it is usually best to move employees to the process incrementally rather than all at once. For example, when a new business process is designed, it is common to test it by means of a pilot project. Once the kinks are worked out and the pilot project is running smoothly, additional workers can be incrementally added or new process teams can be formed.

In addition, some companies may decide to keep certain key areas organized functionally. When functional specialists are grouped together, workers have an opportunity to learn from one another and use their collective expertise to solve problems. Furthermore, grouping workers together on the basis of a single discipline increases the chances that new knowledge and techniques will be developed. For instance, consider a company that wants to adopt activity-based costing. Is it more likely that obstacles will be overcome by a group of accountants working together or by the same number of accountants each independently tackling these problems as they arise in the processes each account supports? Further, in which scenario would you expect the company to accumulate the greatest amount of knowledge about activity-based costing?

❖ Example: IBM Credit

To illustrate the concepts presented in this background section, we overview the experiences of IBM Credit Corporation. IBM Credit is in the business of financing purchases of IBM office equipment. Numerous companies including General Motors, Ford, Chrysler, and General Electric are in the lending business. These companies have found that operating financial units can be extremely profitable in addition to offering customers a higher level of service.

Originally, IBM Credit was organized into functional departments. The steps involved in processing a credit request are shown in Figure 4.2. The process began when an IBM sales rep closed a deal and the customer wanted to finance the purchase through IBM Credit. In this case the sales rep would relay the pertinent information to one of 14 order loggers at IBM Credit. The order loggers sat in a conference room and manually wrote down on pieces of paper the information supplied by the sales reps. Periodically during the day, the pieces of paper were carted upstairs to the credit department.

Employees in the credit department entered the pertinent information into a computer to check the borrower's creditworthiness. The results of this check were then recorded on another piece of paper.

Next, the documents would be transferred to the business practices department. This department would modify the standard loan covenant in response to specific requests by customers. The business practices department used its own computer system.

After being processed in the business practices department, the documents were transported to the pricing department, where pricers entered the data into a program running on a personal computer to determine the appropriate interest rate. Finally, the entire dossier was transported to an administrator who converted all the information into a "quote letter." The quote letter was then sent by Federal Express to the field sales rep.

The sales reps were extremely dissatisfied with this process. First of all, the entire process took an average of six days and sometimes as long as two weeks. What salesperson wants to give his or her customers two weeks to think over a purchase? On top of this, when a sales rep called to check on the status of a customer's credit request, often the request could not even be located.

As a result of complaints from the sales reps, a manager at IBM Credit decided to investigate the problem. The first thing this manager wanted to determine was how much work time actually went into processing a credit request. To determine this, the manager walked an actual request through the entire process. First, he recorded the time it took to log an actual order. Then, he took the order that was just called

Figure 4.2
Processing
credit requests
at IBM Credit.

Ford Organizes Its Customer Service Division into Four Key Processes

Ford employs 6200 people in its customer service division. After conducting a $2\frac{1}{2}$-year study, Ford decided to reorganize the division to focus on increasing customers' satisfaction. To achieve this objective, Ford announced that it was reorganizing the division on the basis of four customer processes:

❖ Fixing it right the first time, on time.

❖ Supporting dealers and handling customers.

❖ Engineering cars with ease of service in mind.

❖ Developing service "fixes" more quickly.

Notice how each of these processes describes a specific result as opposed to a particular activity (Jacob, 1995).

in and personally carried it to the credit department. Arriving at the credit department, he selected a worker at random and told the worker to stop what he or she was currently working on and perform the credit check. After repeating this in the other departments, the manager determined that the actual processing time of a credit request was about 90 minutes. Thus, out of an average of six days, each application was being processed only about 90 minutes, indicating a significant opportunity for improvement.

IBM Credit's approach to improving this process was to combine all these activities into one job called a *deal structurer*. Thus one worker handled all the activities required to process a credit request, from logging the information to writing the quote letter. As a result of using deal structurers, turnaround times were reduced to an average of four hours. Furthermore, with a small reduction in head count, the number of deals processed by IBM Credit increased 100 times (not 100 percent). Do these results qualify as dramatic?

Given these results, you may wonder why IBM Credit had ever adopted a functional organizational structure in the first place. To answer this, let's put ourselves in the shoes of a manager at IBM Credit. Suppose we were asked to develop an organization to process credit requests. One requirement that might occur to us is that the process should be able to handle *any* possible type of credit request. Given this requirement, if you look again at Figure 4.2, you will see that IBM Credit's original functional arrangement accomplishes this objective. For example, no matter how difficult checking a particular borrower's creditworthiness might be, the process could handle it, because everyone in the credit department was a highly trained specialist. The same is true of all the other departments. However, another important question is: How often will this specialized knowledge be needed? In other words, what percent of the credit requests are relatively routine and what percent require deep, specialized knowledge? As IBM found out, the vast majority of credit requests could be handled relatively routinely.

Another explanation for why IBM Credit originally created a functional organization relates to the technology that was available at the time. A key ingredient that allowed IBM Credit to move to the deal-structurer model was advances in technology. For example, spreadsheets, databases, and other decision support tools were adopted so that the deal structurers could quickly check interest rates, access standard clauses, and check the creditworthiness of the borrowers. In effect, the new technology allowed the deal structurers, who had only general knowledge, to function as though they had the specialized knowledge of an expert in a particular discipline.

MECHANICS OF BUSINESS PROCESS DESIGN

Having established a foundation in the previous section, we now turn our attention to the actual mechanics of designing business processes. We begin this section with an overview of the activities associated with BPD. Then, key roles in BPD are described. This is followed with a discussion of some common approaches to reorganizing work. Next, issues related to the depth and breadth of organizational changes are presented. Finally, the section concludes by overviewing the concept of *centers of excellence.*

❖ Primary BPD Activities

As shown in Figure 4.3, BPD typically begins when a leader in an organization recognizes a need, or formulates a vision, to dramatically improve the way customers are served. This vision may be based on a reaction to a competitor, on a specific idea of how activities need to be reorganized, or simply on a feeling that the organization can do a better job. Given the nature of BPD, it is essential that this leader be high enough in the organization to have authority across functional departments. Thus, for practical purposes the leader of BPD efforts tends to be the chief executive officer (CEO), the president, or a senior vice president.

In a traditional functional organization, a manager has responsibility for overseeing one functional activity. For example, a sales manager oversees sales associates, a plant manager oversees manufacturing activities, an MIS director oversees computer programmers, and so on. However, as discussed earlier, no one has authority for the entire business process that ultimately creates the valued results. Given this void, after a need to develop better business processes has been recognized, the next step is to appoint managers to oversee these processes. These *process owners,* as they are often called, perform two important functions. First, they select the members of the teams that will design the business process. Once a BPD team is selected, the process owners then become its customers. Second, after the new process has been designed, the process owner is responsible for implementing and running it on an ongoing basis.

The actual task of designing business processes is done by BPD teams. Given the nature of the task, teams consisting of five to twelve members appears to be ideal. As was seen in the example of Nynex at the beginning of the chapter, *team captains* can be appointed or elected to lead the teams.

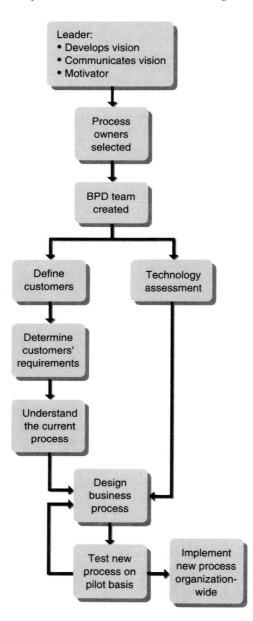

Figure 4.3 Sequence of major BPD activities.

Since the purpose of BPD is to devise new work processes based on capabilities offered by new technology, a key activity for the BPD teams is to identify and assess such capabilities. Because of its technical nature, this activity may best be performed by hiring consultants to serve on the BPD teams. Of course, organizations must be careful to choose outside consultants who are not locked into specific products. For example, a consultant from a particular software or hardware company could be biased.

In addition to identifying and assessing the technology available, the other major input into BPD is customers' requirements. As shown in Figure 4.3, before determining these requirements it is usually necessary to spend some time defining and categorizing the customers. Defining who the customer is can be more difficult than you might imagine. For example, consider Procter & Gamble. Is P&G's customer a retailer like Wal-Mart that purchases its products directly, or an individual who purchases a tube of Crest at Wal-Mart? Clearly, Wal-Mart and the individual shopper have entirely different needs. To illustrate, Wal-Mart's primary concern may be that items are delivered within three days of being ordered, in the exact quantities ordered. On the other hand, the shopper may be most concerned with how the toothpaste tastes, how well it prevents tooth and gum disease, and how much it costs. The point is, the way customers are defined and categorized significantly influences the identification of their requirements.

After the customers have been clearly defined and categorized, the specific requirements of each category of customers can be determined. An important source of information on customers' requirements may be existing data from market research. Also, personnel who have direct contact with the customers, such as sales reps and customer service agents, may be able to provide important insights. In addition, the BPD team can collect its own data by conducting focus groups and mail surveys and interviewing customers. One thing to be aware of when asking customers about their requirements is that the customers themselves may not be aware of what their true needs are; especially concerning what is possible given recent advances in technology. As an example, consider consumers' initial reaction to Sony's description of a tape recorder that could be worn on a belt and had headphones that were connected by a cord that ran up a person's body. Despite the negative reactions to this concept, Sony forged ahead and introduced its extremely successful Walkman.

Once the customers' requirements are identified, the next step is to gain an understanding of what process the organization is currently using to meet these needs. Of course, this will require a fair amount of investigative work if the company is not already organized on the basis of this process. For example, one or more team members may actually have to walk a job through the entire process to identify all the activities involved. This was the approach taken by the manager at IBM Credit in the example discussed earlier.

At this stage, it is important to emphasize that the objective of the BPD team is to *understand* the current process, not to *analyze* it. Understanding a process implies becoming familiar with it in a broad, general sense. Here the focus is on becoming aware of *what* is done and *why*, not on how it's done. Analysis, by contrast, is concerned with documenting the current process in detail; it focuses more on determining *how* work is done. Since BPD seeks to change how work is done, obtaining this level of comprehension is not necessary and is actually a waste of time. In fact, becoming too familiar with the existing process can actually inhibit the BPD team's creativity in designing the new process. Human nature suggests that the more familiar we are with an activity, the more difficult it becomes to imagine performing the activity in a different sort of way.

Thus, BPD teams have to guard against the temptation to spend too much time analyzing existing processes. There are a number of reasons why a team may fall into the trap of overanalysis. For one, analysis is a well-understood and widely accepted practice. In addition, generating lots of documentation seems to show that the team is making progress. As a rule of thumb, then, BPD teams should spend no more than four to six weeks analyzing a current process. Furthermore, the actual documentation of the process should not exceed ten pages and should consist primarily of diagrams.

When the team has assessed the capabilities of technology, identified customers' requirements, and understands the existing process, its next task is to assimilate this information and design the new business process. Thus, starting with a clean slate, the team's task is to design a business process based on the capabilities provided by technology. The only constraint imposed on the team at this point should be that the design be technologically feasible. All other considerations—such as economic, political, and social constraints—should be removed from the process so as not to stifle the team's creativity. The time to address these considerations is after the best process design has been identified.

OPERATIONS
IN PRACTICE

Technology Radically Alters
Emergency-Room Triage

It is estimated that over half the 90 million visits made annually to emergency rooms are unnecessary—and that the cost of these unnecessary visits exceeds $5 billion per year. To address this problem, many health maintenance organizations and physicians' group practices are using "phone triage lines." In early 1997, the number of Americans with access to phone triage lines had increased to 35 million, from less than 2 million in 1990.

To illustrate how phone triage works, consider Access Health in Denver. Access Health employs 90 nurses to staff its phone bank. When a person calls in to report a medical problem, the nurses use software that runs on a desktop computer to inquire about the caller's symptoms. On the basis of the answers, the computer program determines who should be rushed to the emergency room, who can safely wait for a doctor's appointment, and who needs only a simple home remedy.

The software was developed to mimic the thought processes of a good emergency-room doctor. The actual algorithms of the program are based on input provided by a team of 15 emergency-room doctors. The software seeks to rule out the worst possible reasons for the described symptoms, leaving the less serious and more common possibilities. In total, the program has been embedded with logic to diagnose 550 common ailments. Historically, only 2 percent of the callers have been advised to go to the emergency room.

Access Health handled 500,000 calls in 1996 and estimates that this number will double in 1997. An average call lasts $8^1/_2$ minutes, and the goal is to answer all calls within 20 seconds. Major clients include Humana and several state Blue Cross/Blue Shield plans.

Phone triage offers a number of benefits. First, it has been estimated that each $1 spent on a phone triage line saves $2 in use of the emergency room. Second, the computer programs are often more consistent than their human counterparts. For example, the computer program is not likely to be distracted by a recent squabble. Finally, the programs have been credited with saving several lives a year by identifying medical ailments that are hard to diagnose. For example, patients with severe hiccups are always asked questions to determine if they are having a heart attack, a rare but possible occurrence.

Not unlike other radical changes, phone triage has its critics. One key concern is that pressures to control costs will overshadow patient care (Anders, 1997).

A good way to begin the actual design of the new process is to list all the assumptions and rules that are being made about the way work is performed, both explicitly and implicitly. Once these assumptions and rules are listed, they can be checked against the capabilities offered by technology to see if they can be eliminated. Eliminating assumptions and rules is an extremely useful way to stimulate the development of ideas for improving work processes. For example, initially it was assumed at IBM Credit that workers needed highly specialized training to be able to assess a borrower's creditworthiness. However, after considering the capabilities offered by new decision support tools, IBM Credit determined that it was possible for a person with only general training to perform the work previously performed by highly trained experts. Had IBM Credit not identified and challenged this assumption, it would have never arrived at the idea of creating a new position: deal structurer. Table 4.4 provides some additional examples of how technology can be used to eliminate outdated assumptions and rules.

$\mathcal{T}$ABLE 4.4 ❖ Example Benefits of Using Technology to Eliminate Outdated Rules and Assumptions

Old Assumption or Rule	Technology	New Assumption or Rule	Benefit
Complex work can be performed only by experts.	Expert systems	A person with general skills can do the work of an expert.	Fewer hand-offs; organizational knowledge can be collected, centralized, and easily disseminated. Broader and more enriched jobs.
Managers make all the decisions.	Decision support systems and tools	Every employee is a decision maker.	Broader and more enriched jobs; decisions made by employees who are closer to the action; faster decision making.
Managers need secretaries to do typing.	Word processors, laser printers, spell-checkers, grammar-checkers	All employees can do their own typing.	Documents prepared faster, since people can type faster than they can write, and there are fewer iterations.
Humans are needed to answer phones.	Voice mail	Employees are responsible for their own voice messages.	Non–value-added activity eliminated. Can access voice mail system any time of day. More convenient way to leave brief messages than relying on human to write message down.

Figure 4.4 Cover all nine dots with four straight lines without lifting pen or pencil.

It is vital to identify the assumptions and rules being made about work activities so that the opportunities created by eliminating them can be considered. Also, it is important to recognize that the assumptions we make are often very subtle or so ingrained in the way we think that we are not even aware of making them. To illustrate this, redraw the nine dots shown in Figure 4.4 on a piece of paper. Next, place a pencil or pen on one of the dots and then draw four *straight* lines *without* lifting your pen or pencil from the paper so that all nine dots are covered by the four lines. Try it a few times before looking at the solution given in Figure 4.5.

If you were able to solve the exercise, well done! If you were not able to solve it, chances are you imposed *rules* on yourself or made *assumptions* that were not part of the problem. For example, quite often people *assume* that they cannot write outside of the area containing the nine dots, even though this is not specified. Notice that making this assumption precludes the solution shown in Figure 4.5. However, once you become *aware* of this assumption and *eliminate* it, a whole range of new options becomes available. What other assumptions did you make in trying to cover the dots? For example, did you assume that the paper could not be folded?

Once a process has been tentatively designed, the next step is to test it using a pilot program. We all know that it is rare for plans to go exactly as intended. This is especially true when it comes to implementing new technology. Often, what appears to work well on paper does not perform well in reality. Thus, just as product designers build prototypes to get feedback on how new products look and operate, BPD teams need to get similar feedback on the processes they are designing. For example, does the new database software respond to queries fast enough for customer service representatives to answer customers' questions over the phone? Does the new expert system for making credit checks make the right decisions? Are the notebook computers used by repair personnel running out of juice in the middle of jobs? Of course, it's much better to get this kind of feedback on a limited scale rather than after the process has been implemented organizationwide.

Once the BPD team is satisfied with the operation of the new process, it can then be implemented across the organization. Frequently, multiple versions of the process, each focusing on a different segment of customers, are added incrementally. For example, IBM Credit might have initially trained a handful of employees from various functional departments to become deal structurers. After receiving their training, the first group of deal structurers could be assigned to process all credit requests from retail customers in order to test the new process on a limited basis. After the bugs were worked out, another group of functional workers could be trained and assigned all credit requests coming from insurance companies. This process would be repeated until a process was created for all industries. Of course, to balance the workload it is possible to assign more workers to one instance of the process than another. Likewise, it is possible that one instance of the process might be assigned more industry groups than another.

❖ Roles in BPD

As a complement to the discussion of activities in BPD, we now turn our attention to the way these activities are actually accomplished. These activities are categorized into four primary roles.

Role 1: Leader

BPD begins when a top-level manager envisions a radically different organizational structure that allows the company to dramatically improve its performance and customer service. As discussed earlier, this *leader* of the BPD effort must be high enough in the organization to be able to make decisions that cut across functional boundaries. Thus, typically the leader is the CEO or president. The impetus for the leader's vision may be competitive necessity, with the firm's survival hanging in the balance, or it may be anticipation of future opportunities. The former approach is termed a *reactive* strategy; the latter approach is a *proactive* strategy.

Regardless of whether the leader's vision is a reaction to current circumstances or a desire to capitalize on potential opportunities, there are four primary tasks the leader must perform if BPD is to succeed. First, as we have already discussed, the leader must formulate a vision of the future. Second, this vision must be communicated throughout the organization. Simply formulating a vision is of little value if no one else in the organization knows about it. Indeed, one study found that when BPD fails, a primary reason is that the leader has greatly underestimated the amount of communication needed. We often think that if we say something once, the party receiving the message fully understands what we are trying to communicate. Adding the requirement that the listener must not only understand what is being communicated but also become committed to the vision further compounds the problem.

Third, in addition to developing and communicating a vision, the leader needs to ensure that everyone involved in the effort remains highly motivated and committed to the goals established. This is particularly true because of the risk and uncertainty associated with BPD. The very nature of BPD is to venture into uncharted territory. Thus, it is imperative that the leader continuously demonstrate his or her commitment and enthusiasm.

Jim Barksdale, CEO of Netscape Communications, serves as an excellent example of a leader who is an effective communicator and motivator (Hof, 1997). One approach he frequently takes is the use of metaphors. For instance, he once told a group of new employees that Microsoft was trying to lead customers "back into the cave," while "our job is to keep them in the sunlight." And to fire up a group of 120 Netscape recruits, Barksdale argued that every company needs a rival to inspire it to be its best: "We went out and found the best competitor in the world, and his name is Bill Gates. We got a killer. Enjoy it!"

Research indicates that for leaders to carry out their task properly, 20 to 50 percent of their time should be dedicated to BPD. While this may sound excessive, can you think of any other activities that are more critical to an organization than developing a vision and the organizational structure to achieve this vision?

The fourth task of the leader is to select the *process owners*—the people who will be responsible for the results created by an entire process.

Role 2: Process Owners

As was discussed earlier, in functional organizations no one has overall responsibility for the results created by a particular process. Therefore, the position of process owner must be created, and it represents a new way of thinking about managing work.

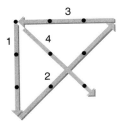

Figure 4.5   One four-line solution to the nine-dot exercise.

Process owners are responsible for both the design and the operation of the process created. In their capacity as designers, process owners select the BPD team. It is this team, not the process owner, that actually designs the new process. Also, the team should be self-managing, with the process owner viewed as its customer, not its manager. Additionally, the process owner is responsible for getting the team the organizational resources needed to complete its task and for sheltering the team from extraneous organizational pressures. Once the design for the new process is completed, the process owner's responsibility shifts to implementing the process and managing it on an ongoing basis.

Role 3: The BPD Team

The *BPD team* is the group of individuals whose actual task is to design the new process. The members of this team include both insiders and outsiders. *Insiders* are employees who work in the functions encompassed by the new process. These workers bring to the team their knowledge about the functioning of a portion of the entire process. *Outsiders* are people who have no direct involvement with the process and therefore may have a more objective view. Often, questions asked by outsiders, which on the surface appear naive to insiders, become an important source of breakthrough ideas. Outsiders may be employees of the company or hired consultants with specialized knowledge in a particular area such as uses of information technology. Outsiders are important because employees with too much familiarity with the existing process may initially have difficulty imagining different ways of accomplishing the work.

BPD team members should be assigned full-time to the project. Furthermore, the company's best employees should be assigned to the team. It may be more difficult to get functional managers to release their best performers, but what kind of results would you expect from a team made up of mediocre employees? Also, the team members should not think about returning to their old jobs. If their efforts succeed, their old jobs will no longer exist. Thus, the BPD team members will become a part of the process they design.

Role 4: The BPD Specialist

The fourth role is that of the *BPD specialist,* an expert in the tools and techniques used in designing business processes. In this role, the specialist consults with the BPD teams when they need assistance. Thus, the specialist serves as a resource for the teams, helping them obtain the information and tools they need to complete their task. It is important to point out, however, that the BPD specialist is only a resource to help the teams solve their own problems. It is not the specialist's role to help the teams actually design the new processes. Also, the process owners may consult with the BPD specialist in selecting team members. Likewise, the leader may seek the specialist's advice related to evaluating the progress of the BPD effort and identifying additional opportunities.

❖ Some Approaches to BPD

As a starting point to designing a new business process, it is helpful to review some of the approaches that have been used successfully in the past. One popular approach is to expand workers' roles from functional specialists into broader *caseworkers*. With the caseworker approach, several different jobs are combined into one. This is exactly the approach IBM Credit adopted in creating its position of deal structurer, as illustrated in Figure 4.6. In the case of IBM Credit, the jobs of logging orders, checking credit risk, determining interest rates, modifying the loan agreement, and writing the quote letter were combined into the position of deal structurer. As is illustrated in Figure 4.6, adopting the caseworker approach eliminates all hand-offs across departments.

There are situations, however, where not all the jobs required to complete a process can be combined into one job. For example, even with the best expert systems and computer-aided design tools, it is not likely that a person trained as a market researcher could design a new microwave oven, short of obtaining an engineering degree. One possibility in such a situation is to change what was previously a sequential process into a process where activities are processed in their natural order. To illustrate, let's assume that the knowledge required by the functional employees in the IBM Credit example is so specialized that it can be performed only by highly trained workers. In this case, substantial reductions in processing time may result if some of the activities are performed in parallel instead of sequentially, as shown in Figure 4.7. For example, since the activities performed in the credit department, the business practices department, and the pricing department do not depend on one another, why not perform these activities in parallel? In this scenario, once a credit request is logged, the information needed by each department can be distributed electronically to the three departments. After being processed in these departments, the results can be automatically forwarded and collected for the administrator to process.

Taking the resequencing of jobs one step further, another alternative is to use a *case team*. As shown in Figure 4.7, the case-team approach operates in a fashion

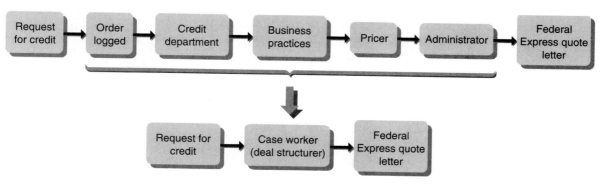

Figure 4.6   Functional jobs combined to create caseworker.

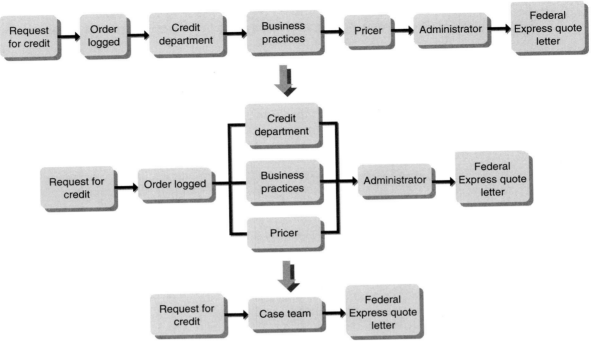

Figure 4.7 Jobs performed in natural order, then perhaps evolving to a case-team approach.

similar to the caseworker approach, except that a group of employees work together to complete the process. Thus, with the case-team approach, workers are re-
assigned from being members of a functional department to becoming members of
a case or process team.

Finally, as shown in Figure 4.8, organizations often find it beneficial to set up
multiple versions of the same process. This is particularly appropriate if the organization serves a variety of customer segments, each with different requirements. One
benefit of dedicating separate processes to the various customer segments is that it
provides the employees with the opportunity to increase their proficiency in serving a given segment. For example, in Figure 4.8, the employees who process credit
requests from the banking industry will gain a deeper understanding and apprecia-

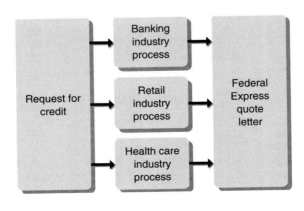

Figure 4.8 Multiple versions of
process.

tion of the unique requirements facing this industry than if they were involved in processing credit requests from all industries. Furthermore, it is often easier to manage several smaller processes than one large process.

❖ Breadth versus Depth

A study conducted by the management consulting firm McKinsey & Company identified two factors as critical determinants of the extent to which BPD efforts succeed in providing long-term benefits: breadth and depth. *Breadth* relates to the extent that BPD efforts cut across functional boundaries. Clearly, without sufficient breadth, important opportunities for eliminating hand-offs will not be identified.

Depth refers to the extent that key elements of the organization are changed by the new business process. Key elements include employees' roles and responsibilities, measurement and incentive systems, the organizational structure, the information technology used, shared values, and employees' skills. Table 4.5 provides some examples of how these key elements can be affected as a result of adopting a process-centered organizational structure.

❖ Centers of Excellence

One criticism often leveled against a process or horizontal organizational structure is that scattering functional specialists throughout the company hinders the development of discipline-specific knowledge and practitioners. For example, according

TABLE 4.5 ❖ **How Key Organizational Elements Change After Becoming Process Centered**

Key Element	Examples of Changes
Employees' roles and responsibilities	Jobs evolve from being narrowly defined and highly specialized to multidimensional.
	Managers focus more on coaching and less on supervising.
Measurement and incentive systems	Compensation depends more on results and value created than simply performing an activity well.
	Criteria for promotion shift from past performance to the ability to perform the new job.
Organizational structure	Process teams replace functional departments.
Information technology	Company implements a wide variety of new technology including notebook computers, client-server computing, cellular phones, groupware, videoconferencing, and so on.
Shared values	Employees care more about satisfying the customer than their direct supervisor.
Employee skills	Trend toward needing more employees with general skills and fewer with highly specialized skills.
	Job preparation will shift away from training (how to do it a particular way) to education (why it is done this way).

to this argument, splitting up a department of engineers by assigning them to different process teams would hamper their ability to learn from one another and to work together to advance the discipline. It could also impede the engineers' ability to stay current with advances in the field.

To address this concern, Michael Hammer and Steven Stanton proposed the concept of **centers of excellence.** As illustrated in Figure 4.9, process owners oversee the business processes that produce results desired by customers. Also, the processes are staffed by employees who are drawn from centers of excellence. In effect, the traditional functional departments evolve into centers of excellence in a process-centered organization. Thus, the centers of excellence facilitate the employees' continued development in their respective disciplines and the continued advancement of those disciplines within the organization. They offer employees the opportunity to network with other employees from the same discipline, to share war stories, and obtain discipline-specific training. Essentially, then, centers of excellence function as in-house versions of professional associations.

At the heart of each center of excellence is one or more *coaches*. The primary role of the coach is to work with the employees to help them develop the skills they will need to be effective members of the process team. Coaches also need to work closely with the process owners in order to anticipate future developmental needs.

Centers of excellence can be created for any number of disciplines the company desires. They can even be created to develop coaches and process owners. At a minimum, centers should be set up for all disciplines directly related to maintaining the organization's competitive advantage. For example, one of the keys to Procter & Gamble's ability to continuously develop new products is the understanding its scientists have developed over the years related to the chemistry of fats. Given the importance P&G places on continuously developing new products, it should certainly establish one or more centers of excellence for its chemists. Incidentally, centers of excellence do not necessarily require much in the way of physical resources. In fact, a center of excellence may consist of nothing more than the coach's office and perhaps a conference room.

$\mathscr{T}$OOLS OF BPD

With our overview of BPD complete, we now turn our attention to three tools that are useful in helping to identify and design business processes: (1) systems analysis, (2) definition of relationships, and (3) process flow charts. Then, in the last section of the chapter, we address issues related to ensuring that BPD is successful.

❖ Systems Analysis

One tool that is particularly useful in gaining an understanding of and defining business processes is systems analysis. A **system** is comprised of a set of components, each of which transforms inputs into outputs. Thus, in a sense, each component may be regarded as a sort of mini-process or subprocess. However, because these components *individually* do not create a result of value to the final customer,

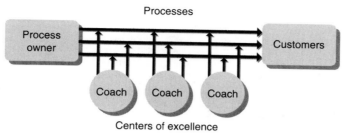

Figure 4.9 Process centered organization with centers of excellence. (Adapted from Hammer, M., *Beyond Reengineering*, Harper Business, 1996, p. 126.)

the components themselves are not considered to be a complete business process. Rather, it is the combination of the activities performed by a number of components that creates the desired result.

Systems analysis is a powerful tool for studying situations that are poorly defined and poorly structured. More specifically, systems analysis seeks to add a degree of structure to seemingly unstructured problems, mainly by identifying the relationships among the components of the system. As discussed in Chapter 1, focusing on the key components of a system, and the relationships among these components, provides a broad and complete picture of the situation. Furthermore, by recognizing the relationships among the various components, the tendency to *optimize* one part of the system to the *detriment* of the rest of the system can be avoided.

One approach to systems analysis is to construct a **system diagram.** The system diagram shows schematically the inputs and outputs of each component, as well as the relationships among the components.

Figure 4.10 shows the system diagram for IBM Credit, the example discussed earlier. One component of the system is logging orders. The input to this component is a phone call from a sales rep, and the output is a piece of paper with the relevant information. Also, the output of order logging becomes the input to the credit check, the modification of terms, and the determination of the interest rate. Finally, although these three components do not interact with one another, their output all becomes part of a dossier that is processed by an administrator in creating the actual quote letter.

An important decision in developing system diagrams is where the system boundary is drawn. The **system boundary** defines what components are to be included as part of the system, and therefore studied, and what components are to be considered part of the system's environment and therefore treated as givens. Stated another way, a system's **environment** is composed of all entities outside the system that interact with it in some way. Perhaps most important, the environment provides the inputs to the system and receives the system's outputs.

Related to defining the system's boundary is the issue of breadth. For BPD projects it is important for the system boundary to be defined broadly enough that hand-offs across various components are included in the study. For example, suppose that in response to the sales representative's complaints, the manager at IBM Credit defined the system as including only the order-logging function, as shown in

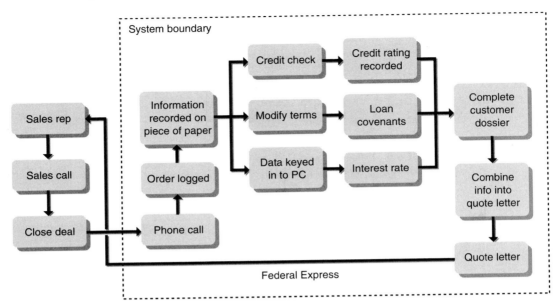

Figure 4.10   System diagram for IBM Credit.

Figure 4.11. Certainly, improvements could be made to this function. However, focusing on only this function does little to improve the entire process. In fact, had IBM Credit defined excessive processing time as a problem for the logging department to solve, or even asked each department to do what it could to process loan requests faster, it is highly unlikely that the solution—the deal structurer—would have been found. At the other extreme, the system boundary should not be defined so broadly that it includes components over which the decision makers have no control.

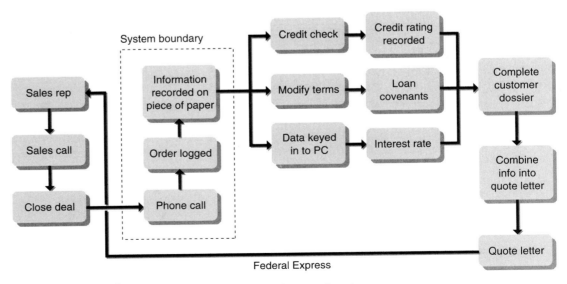

Figure 4.11   System diagram for order-logging function.

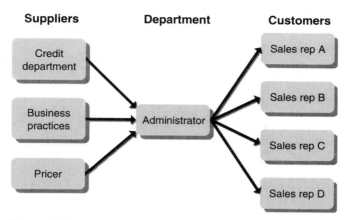

Figure 4.12 Administration department's customer-supplier relationships.

❖ Definition of Relationships

The ***definition of relationships*** is another useful approach in defining business processes. In a functional organization, as is illustrated in Figure 4.12, each department is supplied inputs which it in turn processes into outputs. Further, the outputs from one department typically become the inputs to another department. For example, in IBM Credit, the output of the credit department was one of the inputs used by the administration department. In effect, the departments become each other's suppliers and customers.

The first step in defining relationships is to have each departmental manager list the following:

- ❖ Suppliers to the department and what they supply.
- ❖ Customers of the department and the outputs supplied.
- ❖ Value each department contributes to the final product or service.

Once this information has been completed by all departmental managers, it can be linked together to create a ***customer-supplier relationship chain,*** as shown in Figure 4.13. Analysis of the chain should reveal key business processes. For example, in Figure 4.13 one process consists of activities performed in departments A, B, E, and G.

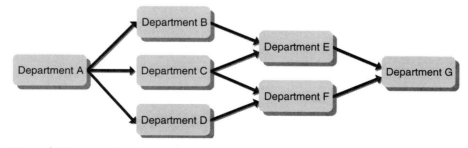

Figure 4.13 Example of a customer-supplier relationship chain.

❖ Flow Process Charts

Flow process charts are useful for studying a process in detail once it has been identified. These charts are particularly useful for identifying delays and hand-offs embedded in processes. With flow process charts, all steps of a process are documented using the standard set of symbols shown in Table 4.6. Once the entire process has been documented, the BPD team can study the chart to identify ways that delays, transports, and other non–value-adding steps can be eliminated. A flow process chart for IBM Credit is shown in Table 4.7. Even a casual examination of the chart reveals numerous delays and hand-offs.

$\mathcal{M}$AKING BPD WORK _____

According to Michael Hammer and Steven Stanton, BPD is now a *craft* that lies somewhere between an *art* and a *science*. The status of a craft implies that BPD techniques can be learned, studied, and improved. It is therefore appropriate to conclude our discussion of BPD with a brief overview of some of the general lessons learned to date related to ensuring that these efforts achieve the dramatic results intended.

One element that has been found crucial to the success of BPD is the role of top management. First, as we have discussed, BPD must begin at the top because of the need to make changes across a number of functional boundaries. Beyond initiating BPD, top management must actively support it. One way support can be demonstrated is by assigning the best people to BPD. Another way is by allocating 20 to 50 percent of the CEO's time to the effort. Also, top management must effectively deal with opposition to the changes. Perhaps this is best accomplished by having top management acknowledge that BPD is painful but emphasize that it is necessary.

$\mathcal{T}$ABLE 4.6 ❖ Symbols Used in Flow Process Charts

Symbol	Description
◯	Operation such as drilling a hole or cooking a pizza.
◎	Paperwork operation that creates a document such as writing a memo.
●	Paperwork operation that adds information to an existing document such as an account number added to an invoice.
⇒	Transport operation such as sending an invoice via interdepartmental mail.
▽	Storage operation such as filing a report or storing finished goods in a warehouse.
D	Delay such as waiting for an elevator.
☐	Inspection such as reading a report or counting the number of parts received in a shipment.

*T*ABLE 4.7 ❖ **Flow Process Chart for IBM Credit**

Activity	Description
◎	Log request for credit on piece of paper.
D	Wait for messenger.
⟹	Cart pieces of paper upstairs.
D	Wait for credit specialists.
◎	Enter information into computer.
☐	Check borrower's creditworthiness.
●	Record results on piece of paper.
D	Wait for messenger.
⟹	Dispatch paper to business practices department.
D	Wait for specialists in business practices department.
◎	Modify standard loan covenant.
○	Attach special terms to form.
D	Wait for messenger.
⟹	Deliver material to pricer.
D	Wait for pricer.
◎	Enter information into spreadsheet.
☐	Determine appropriate interest rate.
◎	Write interest rate on piece of paper.
D	Wait for messenger.
⟹	Deliver material to administrator.
D	Wait for administrator.
◎	Write quote letter.
⟹	Send quote letter to field sales rep by Federal Express.

Top management must also set aggressive performance targets, sometimes called **stretch goals.** However, setting appropriate performance goals requires balance. If the goals are too aggressive, the BPD team will perceive them as unrealistic and will not become committed to achieving them. On the other hand, goals that are not aggressive enough will not inspire or motivate team members.

The BPD team and the process owners also play a significant role in determining the success of BPD. At this level it is vital to ensure that a comprehensive review of customers' needs and market trends is conducted. Clearly, a prerequisite to designing new processes that better meet customers' needs is a thorough understanding of these needs. In fact, the BPD team may aim to understand customers' needs better than the customers themselves do.

Once a new process has been designed, research suggests that comprehensively testing it through a pilot program can greatly influence the success of the effort. Thus, it is important to guard against the temptation to try to roll out the new process too quickly.

As opposed to discussing what can be done to ensure that BPD will succeed, Hammer and Stanton developed the following list of the top *mistakes* organizations make in this regard:

- *Organizations say they are doing BPD when they are not.* Often organizations refer to downsizing, restructuring, and continuous improvement as BPD. The key to avoiding this mistake is to understand what BPD is.

- *Organizations attempt to apply BPD where it is not appropriate.* For example, an organization my attempt to apply BPD within a single functional department. However, as we have discussed, the focus of BPD is removing barriers between functional departments, not improving the performance of these departments. Of course, BPD requires understanding the concept of processes and being able to identify the processes within the organization.

- *BPD teams spend too much time analyzing existing processes.* As we have discussed, since BPD will change the existing process, obtaining a detailed understanding of the current process is a waste of time and may actually hinder the effort.

- *Organizations often attempt to do BPD without the requisite leadership.* Middle managers may be the first in the organization to discover BPD and see its potential. However, managers at this level lack the authority and broad view needed to direct BPD.

- *BPD teams are not aggressive enough.* BPD is concerned with making radical changes that provide dramatic improvements in performance. This is a new concept that may not be fully understood by team members. Also, it is human nature to resist such changes.

- *Organizations attempt to go from the new process design directly into full implementation.* Given the radical nature of the new process, it is highly unlikely that the new process will work flawlessly as planned on paper. Thus, it is important to experiment with the new process and have an opportunity to work the bugs out before full implementation.

- *Too much time is spent on the design phase.* BPD efforts that are allowed to drag on will lose momentum and lose the support of top management.

- *Organizations may place some departments or policies off limits.* For example, a company may not want to change the way performance is evaluated or the way employees are paid. Clearly, such restrictions constrain and jeopardize BPD.

- *Organizations often ignore the concerns of their people.* The success of any change depends on the people within the organization. Therefore it is important to address the concerns of employees head-on. Typically, employees are concerned about what's in it for them. One response to this may be "A more competitive company that offers better long-term job security."

CHAPTER IN PERSPECTIVE

This has been the final chapter of Part One. In Chapter 1, the topic of operations management was introduced. Chapter 2 then overviewed issues related to business strategy and international competitiveness. Chapter 3 followed with a discussion of how quality management activities support the business strategy and enhance competitiveness.

Because of the similarities and differences between quality management and BPD, Chapter 3 provides an excellent backdrop for Chapter 4. Indeed comparing the two philosophies may be the best way to understand them. The approaches share the objective of improving the organization's ability to meet its customers' needs. However, the approaches used to achieve this common objective are quite different. The approach of quality management, is to improve the existing system, whereas BPD seeks to use technology to develop entirely new systems.

This chapter is particularly important, as it lays the foundation for the rest of the book. Specifically, the remainder of the book is organized around three business processes. In each remaining part, the discussion centers on how operations management supports a particular process. Part Two is dedicated to the product and to transformation system design. Part Three focuses on how operations management supports resource management. Finally, Part Four focuses on product supply.

❖ CHECK YOUR UNDERSTANDING

1. Define BPD in your own words.
2. Contrast a functional organization with a process-centered one.
3. What is the relationship between division of labor and a functional organization?
4. What are the advantages and disadvantages of division of labor?
5. Provide an example of how a functional organization can lead to errors and delays in completing a process.
6. Define the term *process*.
7. List some of the internal and external customers for an organization that you are familiar with.
8. Contrast BPD with TQM.
9. Explain how the idealized design approach can be used to facilitate BPD.
10. Explain how TQM and BPD can support one another.
11. Contrast BPD with downsizing, restructuring, and automation.
12. List and briefly describe the five generic business processes.
13. List and briefly describe the major roles in BPD.
14. Briefly overview the major BPD activities.
15. Contrast understanding a process with analyzing a process. Why is it unnecessary to analyze a process in conjunction with a BPD project?
16. What is meant by the breadth and depth of organizational changes?
17. Explain the concept of centers of excellence.
18. Define the terms *system, system boundary,* and *environment.*

❖ EXPAND YOUR UNDERSTANDING

1. Do you think the technology available at the end of the 1700s influenced the concept of division of labor? Why or why not?

2. What impact have modern advances in technology had on the applicability and desirability of division of labor?

3. In your opinion, is BPD a fad?

4. A director of sales has recently attended a two-day seminar on BPD and is convinced that his company could benefit immensely from such efforts. The director reports to the vice president for marketing, who in turn reports to the executive vice president. The executive vice president reports to the CEO. What can the director of sales do to initiate BPD at his company?

5. Construct a table similar to Table 4.4 and fill it in with additional outdated assumptions and rules.

6. If you were the CEO of a company, what characteristics would you seek in the process owners you appointed?

7. As a process owner, what criteria would you use to select BPD team members?

8. Managers at a company are considering adopting a process-centered organization, but they are concerned about losing depth of knowledge in key specialties. Are they right to be concerned about this? Is there anything that can be done to mitigate this problem?

9. What advice would you offer a CEO related to ensuring that BPD will be successful?

10. Is BPD applicable to all organizations? If not, identify organizaitons to which it is not applicable and explain why it is not applicable.

❖ APPLY YOUR UNDERSTANDING
Valley State University's Medical Clinic

Valley State University operates a walk-in medical clinic to meet the acute medical needs of its 13,000 students, 1200 faculty and staff members, and covered relatives. Patients arriving at the clinic are served on a first-come-first-served basis.

As part of a new total quality management program, Valley State conducted an in-depth four-month study of its current operations. A key component of the study was a survey, distributed to all students, faculty, and staff. The purpose of the survey was to identify and prioritize areas most in need of improvement. An impressive 44 percent of the surveys were returned and deemed usable. Follow-up analysis indicated that the people who responded were representative of the population served by the clinic. After the results were tabulated, it was determined that the walk-in medical clinic was located at the bottom of the rankings, indicating a great deal of dissatisfaction with the clinic. Preliminary analysis of the respondents' comments indicated that people were reasonably satisfied with the treatment they received at the clinic but were very dissatisfied with the amount of time they had to wait to see a caregiver.

Upon arriving at the clinic, patients receive a form from the receptionist requesting basic biographical information and the nature of the medical condition for which treatment is being sought. Completing the form typically requires two to three minutes. After the form is returned to the receptionist, it is time-stamped and placed in a tray. Student workers collect the forms and retrieve the corresponding patients' files from the basement. The forms typically remain in the tray for about five minutes before being picked up, and it takes the student workers approximately 12 minutes to retrieve the files. After a patient's file is retrieved, the form describing the medical problem is attached to it with a paper clip, and it is placed in a stack with other files. The stack of files is ordered according to the time stamps on the forms.

When the nurse practitioners finish with their current patient, they select the next file from the stack and escort that patient to one of the treatment rooms. On average, files remain in the stack for 10 minutes, but this varies considerably depending on the time of day and the day of the week. On Monday mornings, for example, it is common for files to remain in the stack for 30 minutes or more.

Once in the treatment room, the nurse practitioner reads over the form describing the patient's ailment. Next, the nurse discusses the problem with the patient while taking some standard measurements such as blood pressure and temperature. The nurse practitioner then makes a rough diagnosis, based on the measurements and symptoms, to determine if the ailment is one of the 20 that state law permits nurse practitioners to treat. If the condition is treatable by the nurse practitioner, a more thorough diagnosis is undertaken and treatment is prescribed. It typically takes about 5 minutes for the nurse practitioners to make the rough diagnosis and another 20 minutes to complete the detailed diagnosis and discuss the treatment with the patient. If the condition (as roughly diagnosed) is not treatable by the nurse practitioner, the patient's file is placed in the stack for the on-duty MD. Because of the higher cost of MDs versus nurse practitioners, there is typically only one MD on duty at any time. Thus, patients wait an average of 25 minutes for the MD. On the other hand, because of their higher training and skill, the MDs are able to diagnose and treat the patients in 15 minutes, despite the fact that they deal with the more difficult and less routine cases. Incidentally, an expert system for nurse practitioners is being tested at another clinic that—if shown to be effective—would initially double the number of ailments treatable by nurse practitioners and over time would probably increase the list even more, as the tool continued to be improved.

Questions

1. Develop a flow chart for the medical clinic that shows the times of the various activities. Is the patients' dissatisfaction with the clinic justified?

2. What probably are the patients' key requirements for the clinic?

3. What assumptions are being made about the way work is performed and treatment administered at the clinic?

4. Redesign the process of treating patients at the clinic using technologies you are familiar with, to better meet the patients' needs as listed in question 2.

❖ EXERCISES

1. Complete the following tables.

What are your major complaints about your university?	How would you describe an ideal university?

List how your university's current administration would most likely respond to address your comments in the left column in the table above.	If you were president for a day, how would you respond to your comments in the right column in the table above?

2. Develop a system diagram for a fast-food restaurant you are familiar with.

3. Develop a process flow diagram for a fast-food restaurant you are familiar with.

4. Consider a specific fast-food restaurant you are familiar with.

   a. List the key requirements of the restaurant's customers.

   b. What are the primary processes performed by the restaurant?

   c. Develop a flow process chart for the process that prepares and delivers the food.

   d. Referring to the process selected in c, identify as many assumptions and rules associated with the process as you can.

   e. Redesign the process identified in c using the capabilities of technology to better meet the customers' needs you identified in a.

PART TWO

Product and Transformation System Design

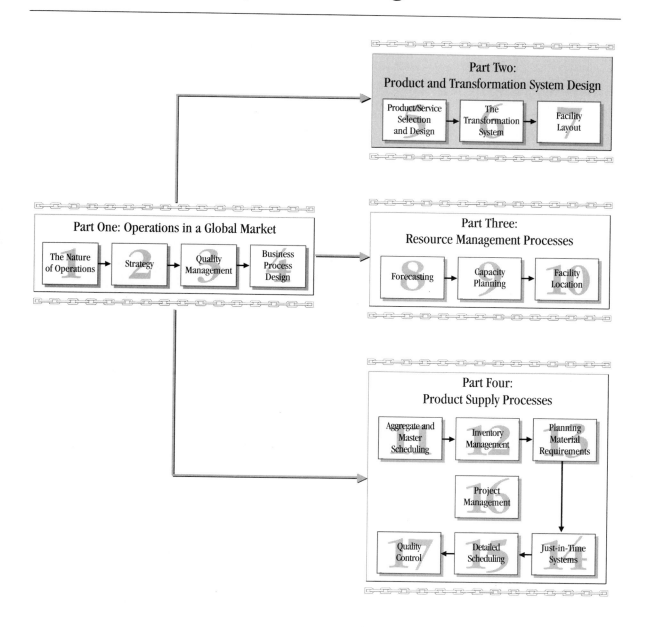

Chapter 5

Product/Service Selection and Design

*C*HAPTER OVERVIEW

- ❖ Product and service selection and design largely determine the resulting output life cycle and, more important, the profitability and cumulative profitability cycles as well as the breakeven point.

- ❖ The major stages of selection and design are selection, consisting of the generation, screening, and selection of ideas; design, which includes preliminary design, prototype testing, and final design; and production, which includes process design.

- ❖ The product-service development cycle begins near the applied end of the research cycle and involves improving the output, deriving variants of the output, and finding extensions to prolong its life.

- ❖ Ideas have a mortality rate on the order of 98 percent or more as they proceed through the design and commercialization cycle.

- ❖ Breakeven analysis is useful for screening new outputs to determine their financial and production viability as well as their cost-price-volume sensitivities.

- ❖ An analysis of organizational fit can help screen new outputs in terms of their match to the organization's current strengths, weaknesses, markets, outputs, and strategy.

- ❖ The design task involves trade-offs between a number of factors to arrive at the final design concept on which the prototype will be based.

- ❖ Standardization, with its advantages of mass production and interchangeability, and simplification, with its positive impacts on efficiency and effectiveness, are important tools in product-service design.

- ❖ Modularity allows the offering of extensive variety through combinations of available modules while holding production costs and complexity to reasonable levels.

- ❖ Computer-aided design (CAD) not only increases the productivity of design engineers but, when tied to testing, operation planning, and manufacturing software, also increases the efficiency of these tasks.

147

❖ Manufacturability, the simultaneous development of the production system with product design to expedite the introduction of new products and services, is a topic receiving major international attention.

❖ As the product-service design stabilizes, the number of operation innovations (particularly to reduce cost) tends to increase until maturity of the output.

❖ Quality function deployment (QFD) is used to help ensure that designs for new products and services simultaneously satisfy market requirements and are producible by the firm. With QFD, customers' attributes expressed in the customers' own language are sequentially translated into technical requirements, component requirements, and finally operation requirements.

❖ In the 1980s the key to competitive success was quality and manufacturing excellence. In the 1990s competitive success depends more on an organization's commercialization capabilities, i.e., its ability to rapidly move new products and services from the concept stage to the market.

❖ To improve its commercialization capabilities, organizations should make commercialization a priority, set goals and benchmarks, build cross-functional teams, and promote hands-on management to speed actions and decisions.

INTRODUCTION

❖ In the years before 1988, Progressive carved out a profitable niche in the automobile insurance industry by writing policies for high-risk drivers that its competitors weren't interested in and charging these customers high prices. In 1988 two events occurred that required Progressive to rethink its strategy: Allstate had overtaken it in the high-risk niche, and California, which accounted for 25 percent of Progressive's profits, passed Proposition 103, sharply curtailing insurance rates.

Progressive's response was the development of its round-the-clock "immediate response" program. With this program, claims adjusters are equipped with special vans complete with air-conditioning, comfortable chairs, a desk, and two cellular phones. Using the vans, the claims adjusters can travel to the scene of an accident and are often able to provide clients with a settlement check before the tow truck clears the scene.

Before adopting the immediate response program, claims adjusters spent the majority of their time on the phone and shuffling papers. With the immediate response program, contact is made with 80 percent of accident victims within nine hours of learning of the accidents. Further, 70 percent of the damaged vehicles are inspected within one day, and typically the claim is wrapped up within a week (Henkoff, 1994).

❖ In 1992 Thermos's 25 percent share of the $1-billion barbecue grill market accounted for a significant portion of its sales. However, the product was becoming a commodity, as numerous competitors were offering similar black gas boxes. The CEO of Thermos, Monte Peterson, believed that consumers were too intelligent and demanding to be tricked by clever advertising or slick packaging. According to Peterson, survival in this brutal environment requires that companies constantly innovate and create products that provide their customers with high quality at the right price—in other words, value.

To accomplish this objective, Peterson formed a flexible interdisciplinary team with representatives from marketing, manufacturing, engineering, and finance to develop a new grill that would stand out in the market. The interdisciplinary approach was used to reduce the time required to complete the project. For example, by including the manufacturing people in the design process from the beginning, the team avoided some costly mistakes later on. Initially, for instance, the designers opted for tapered legs on the grill. However, after manufacturing explained at an early meeting that tapered legs would have to be custom-made, the design engineers changed the design to straight legs. Under the previous system, manufacturing would not have known about the problem with the tapered legs until the design was completed. The output of this project was a revolutionary electric grill that uses a new technology to give food a barbecued taste. One major advantage of the electric grill is that it burns cleaner than gas or charcoal grills. Early indications are that the grill will be a huge success: it won four design awards in its first year (Dumaine, 1993).

❖ Faced with increased competition, automobile companies don't have the time, money, or people to design cars the way they used to. Given this pressure, the president of Chrysler, Robert Lutz, set strict guidelines for the development of a new sports car called the Viper. Specifically, it was mandated that the car be developed in three years (two years less than the typical time required to develop a car at Chrysler), and the development budget was set at $70 million (which was 45 percent less than the amount Mazda spent developing its Miata roadster).

To accomplish this objective, Chrysler formed small teams with representatives from engineering, manufacturing, marketing, and outside suppliers. These teams aided in identifying glitches early in the design process, such as having to redesign portions of the car because manufacturing couldn't produce what had been designed. Also, costs were reduced by delegating the design of major components (such as the transmission) to suppliers. Over 90 percent of the Viper's parts will be produced by suppliers, compared with 70 percent for a typical Chrysler car.

In many ways, the Viper project was an overwhelming success. For example, many innovative materials and production tricks were developed by the project team. The Viper is the first car produced by Chrysler with a body made entirely of plastic. One advantage of a plastic body is that the epoxy molds used for the panels cost 90 percent less than the steel molds used to form sheet-metal body parts. As a result of such cost reductions, Chrysler needs to sell only 2000 Vipers per year for a couple of years to break even. Chrysler used this development project as a laboratory for learning new, efficient development techniques, which will be transferred to future development projects (Woodruff, 1991).

❖ Designers at Caterpillar are using a virtual-reality system called *cave automatic virtual environment* (CAVE) to take their large earthmoving equipment for a test-drive before it is actually built. CAVE incorporates a surround-screen and surround-sound in a cube with 10-foot sides. A supercomputer is used to project 3D graphics onto the walls. Inside the CAVE, humans can walk around and operate imaginary controls. The system responds to such movements and adjusts the sights and sounds accordingly. The CAVE provides design engineers with a variety of perspectives on the machinery, ranging from sitting in the earthmover and operating its controls to standing outside the cab and looking up and walking around it. The CAVE has provided Caterpillar design engineers with numerous tangible benefits. For example, a backhoe and a wheel loader that were recently introduced incorporate improvements in visibility and performance based on data collected from virtual test-drives in the CAVE (Bylinsky, 1994).

These examples illustrate a number of important themes related to designing products and services. To begin, note that three of the examples are related to the design of a tangible product (the grill, the Viper, and earthmoving equipment) and one example (processing insurance claims) is related to the design of a service. It might not have occurred to you that design activities are as applicable to services as they are to a tangible product. This could be because many services are designed and developed rather informally, whereas product design is typically the result of a concerted, formalized effort.

A second important theme illustrated by the examples is the central role product and service design activities play in determining how competitive an organization is. In the case of Progressive and Thermos, increased competition was the major impetus for developing a new product or service; in the case of Chrysler, the competitive environment placed constraints on the resources that could be devoted to product development.

A third theme is the important role technology plays in product and service design. In the cases of Chrysler and Thermos, new technology was incorporated into the actual product (i.e., a new technology to give food a barbecued flavor and plastic body panels, respectively). In the case of Progressive, new technology, such as cellular phones, made the immediate response program possible. In Caterpillar's case, new technology was used to enhance the actual design process.

A final theme illustrated in the examples is the need to include people throughout the organization in design activities. At both Thermos and Chrysler, design teams were created with representatives from a variety of functional areas such as engineering, marketing, and manufacturing. In effect, firms that take such an approach are recognizing the advantages of organizing work on the basis of processes as opposed to functions, as we discussed in Chapter 4. Such design teams effectively become virtual process organizations. As more firms adopt process-centered organizational structures, there will be less need to form these teams ad hoc.

In Chapter 2 we identified four common business strategies: first-to-market, second-to-market, cost minimization, and market segmentation. To be successful, each of the different strategies involves many decisions about the timing, selection, and design of the firm's intended output. These decisions will have corresponding impacts on the resulting quality, response time, cost, and variety of the outputs, and thus, on the firm's success in the marketplace. Some examples of these decisions and their potential impacts are described in Table 5.1.

We will now look in more detail at how output selection and design occurs and the stages it progresses through. We begin with an overview of these stages.

$\mathcal{T}$HREE STAGES IN OUTPUT SELECTION AND DESIGN

In Chapter 4, product and transformation design was listed as a key business process. This process consists of three primary stages: selection, product and service design, and transformation system design, illustrated in Figure 5.1. We briefly describe each of these stages below and then elaborate on the first two stages. Also, this chapter describes a technique called *quality function deployment,* which is used to ensure that newly designed outputs satisfy market requirements and are ultimately producible by the firm. The chapter concludes with a discussion of how an organization's ability to commercialize its new offerings influences the extent to

$\mathscr{T}$ABLE 5.1 ❖ Impacts of Selection and Design Decisions

❖ *Fit*: How this product or service fits with existing offerings. If the new output matches the firm's existing focus and markets, then it may be synergistic with current products and services, thereby increasing their acceptability and exposure. If not, it may "defocus" the firm and impair the firm's existing competitive strengths.

❖ *Materials*: The types of materials chosen. Materials affect the strength, performance, durability, cost, producibility, and longevity of a product or a facilitating good. If the output is to be long-lasting and of particularly high quality, the materials will probably be different from those chosen if a cost minimization strategy, using cheaper materials, is pursued.

❖ *Labor*: The labor skills needed. For custom services and products, or highly varying, innovative ones, well-trained or educated labor is probably needed. For low-cost, high-volume production on very specialized, automated machines, the skill levels are significantly less.

❖ *Equipment*: The equipment that will be required. High-volume, automated equipment is more appropriate for a cost minimization strategy that offers a standard output, whereas more general-purpose, flexible equipment is appropriate when a skilled labor force produces customized outputs in conjunction with a market segmentation strategy.

❖ *Operations*: The production operations to be employed. The design of the product or service greatly affects the production operations required to produce the output. For example, robots are very unreliable at screwing nuts onto screws and bolts when attaching parts together. However, they are quite adept at snapping plastic parts together. Thus, when IBM redesigned the Proprinter for automated production, it used snap-together parts instead of nuts and screws.

❖ *Financing*: The capital financing required. If the output is designed for high-volume, low-cost production, then large, up-front capital outlays are normally required for the specialized machines needed. However, variable costs will be minimal, since the labor requirements are low. Profits will come from low margins with high volumes, if the strategy is successful. But if customized outputs are produced with highly skilled workers, then equipment costs can be low but wage and salary costs will be higher. Profit margins on the outputs will also be high, but unit volumes will be small. (As was discussed in Chapter 2, some of the flexible new technologies can alter this trade-off and allow organizations to pursue a mass customization strategy.)

which newly designed products and services succeed in the market. In Chapters 6 and 7 the last stage of product and transformation system design is discussed. Chapter 6 overviews alternative types of transformation systems, and Chapter 7 addresses the layout of facilities.

❖ Stage 1: Selection

❖ *Generation of ideas*: Ideas for promising potential products or services can come from a large number of sources: customers, market research, salespersons, internal research and development (R&D) laboratories, suppliers, and even competitors. Those that originate from an identified need, such as a need for high-speed connections to the Internet by people with home computers, are known as ***marketing pull.*** Those that come from R&D, such as lasers, plastics, and microwaves, are known as ***technology push.***

❖ *Screening and selection*: Ideas must pass a large variety of tests and screens before receiving the final go-ahead for full-scale production, and typically only 1 in 50 or so will pass them all. Screening includes market analysis and forecasts of customers' needs, assessments of the reaction of competitors, analyses of economic viability, studies of technical feasibility, and checklists for organizational fit. On the basis of these analyses and studies, one or a few ideas are selected for further study.

❖ **Stage 2: Product and Service Design**

❖ *Preliminary design*: The preliminary design focuses on decisions concerning major aspects of the product or service: Will the product be made out of metal or plastic? Will the service be performed by people or machines? Will

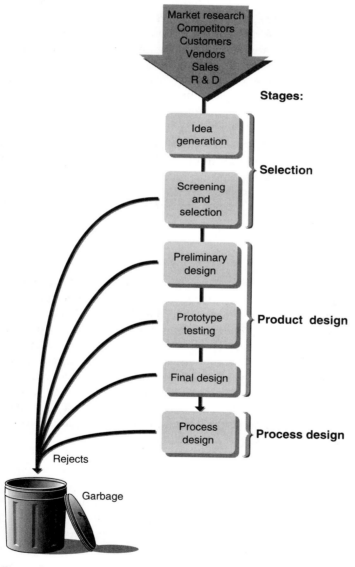

Figure 5.1 Steps in product-service selection and design.

the product be attached with screws or snapped together? And so on. Specific attributes of the product or service, such as cost, are first set as goals; various designs are then considered that may have the potential to achieve them. Basic but critical trade-offs (e.g., reliability versus price) are considered and made at this stage. These provide the information necessary for the construction of a prototype and lay the foundation for the final design that comes later.

❖ *Prototype testing*: For a *service*, a mock-up of the facility, servers, equipment, and other features may be put together and tested on volunteers typical of the target consumers. The efficiency and effectiveness of operation are also checked. For a *product*, a model or simplified representation of the final design is often built and tested. A clay or wooden model may be adequate to test appearance, or a limited version of operation may be sufficient to test technical performance and customers' reactions and tastes. Alternatively, the example of Caterpillar at the beginning of this chapter illustrates how organizations can use computer models in lieu of physical prototypes. Models based on computer technology can be developed to simulate a new production system or the operation of a product, and virtual-reality systems can be used to actually see and interact with new products and systems before they are created.

❖ *Final design*: On the basis of reactions to the prototype and any desirable changes or alterations in the preliminary design, a final design is developed, with full drawings, specifications, procedures, policies, and other information needed for the production system. If the changes from the preliminary design are extensive, a new prototype may be constructed and tested again.

❖ Stage 3: Process Design

❖ *Transformation system design*: Once the final design has been frozen, the production operations for making it must also be specified. As the examples at the beginning of the chapter illustrate, the limitations of producibility should be considered throughout the selection and design stages and may well alter the design substantially. This is exactly what happened at Thermos when its manufacturing people informed the designers that tapered legs were more difficult and more expensive to produce than straight legs. Nevertheless, a full operation plan is needed at this stage. The plan includes not only the product specifications, but also the quality required, capacity rates, technological needs, skill levels, materials required, production methods, and so on.

Although this is shown as a linear process in Figure 5.1, the use of product design teams allows many of these issues to be considered simultaneously. And whether or not design teams are used, often it is necessary to recycle back through the selection and design stages as ideas are tested, analyzed, evaluated, and rejected at all stages. For example, more realistic costs and market forecasts obtained late in the process can be reevaluated for continuing viability in the screening phase. Likewise, more realistic prototypes can be test-marketed for continued acceptability.

THE SELECTION STAGE

This section focuses on generation of ideas and on screening. As we will see, several marketing, R&D, and financial activities support the selection of products and services.

❖ Generation of Ideas

Clearly, because of their ties to customers, people who perform marketing activities play a key role in generating new ideas. These people can suggest new products or services for their customers, new regions, new types of customers for existing products and services, and even a change in the organization's focus, if needed.

R&D activities focus on creating and developing (but not producing) the organizational outputs. On occasion, R&D also creates new production methods by which outputs, either new or old, may be produced. *Research* itself is typically divided into two types: pure and applied. Pure research is simply working with basic technology to develop new knowledge. Applied research is attempting to develop new knowledge along particular lines. For example, pure research might focus on developing a material that conducts electricity with zero resistance, whereas applied research could focus on further developing this material to be used in cable products. *Development* is the attempt to utilize the findings of research and expand the possible applications, typically along the sponsor's line of interest (e.g., the development of cable to connect computers together in a local-area network).

The *development* end of R&D is more on the applications side and often consists of modifications or extensions to existing outputs. Figure 5.2 illustrates the range of applicability of development as the output becomes more clearly defined. In the early years of a new output, development is oriented toward removing "bugs," increasing performance, improving quality, and so on. In the middle years, options

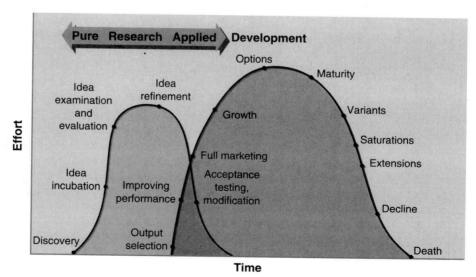

Figure 5.2 The development effort.

and variants of the output are developed. In the later years, development is oriented toward extensions of the output that will prolong its life.

Currently—as compared with 20 or 30 years ago—the development effort in R&D is much, much larger than the research effort. Some scholars of R&D attribute the shift away from research and toward the simple extension of existing outputs to the extensive influence of marketing on organizations. These scholars postulate that the marketing approach, "giving the customers what they want," is basically *wrong* because neither the customer nor the marketer has the vision to see what new technology can offer. By draining off funds from research and spending them on ever greater development of existing outputs, and on advertising those outputs, the organization leaves itself vulnerable to those competitors who are willing to invest in research to develop entire new generations of outputs.

Unfortunately, the returns from R&D are frequently meager, whereas the costs are great. Figure 5.3 illustrates the ***mortality curve*** (fallout rate) associated with the concurrent design, evaluation, and selection for a hypothetical group of 50 potential chemical products, assuming that the 50 candidate products are available for consideration in year 3. (The first three years, on the average, are required for the necessary research preceding each candidate product.) Initial evaluation and screening reduce the 50 to about 22, and economic analysis further reduces the number to about 9. Development reduces this number even more, to about 5, and design and testing reduce it to perhaps 3. By the time construction (for production), market development, and a year's commercialization are completed, there is only one successful product left. (Sometimes there are none!) A recent study found that, beyond this, only 64 percent of the new products brought to market were successful, or about two out of three.

Two alternatives to research frequently used by organizations are *imitation* of a proven new idea (i.e., employing a second-to-market strategy) or outright *purchase*

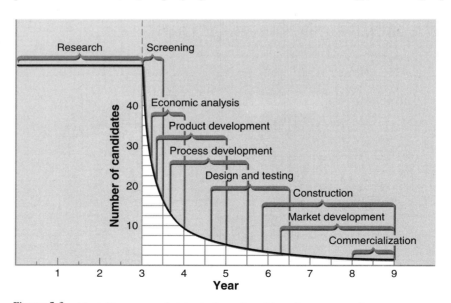

Figure 5.3 Mortality curve of chemical product ideas from research to commercialization. *Source:* Adapted from *This is DuPont 30.* Wilmington, DE, by permission of DuPont de Nemours and Co.

of someone else's invention. Although imitation does not put the organization first on the market with the new product or service, it does give an opportunity to study any possible defects in the original product or service and rapidly develop a better design, frequently at a better price. The second approach—purchasing an invention or the inventing company itself—eliminates the risks inherent in research, but it still requires the company to develop and market the product or service before knowing whether or not it will be successful. Either route spares the organization the risk and tremendous cost of conducting the actual research leading up to a new invention or improvement.

In addition to *product research* (as it is generally known), there is also *process research*, which involves the generation of new knowledge concerning *how to produce* outputs. Currently, the production of many familiar products out of plastic (toys, pipe, furniture, etc.) is an outstanding example of successful process research. Motorola, to take another example, extensively uses project teams that conduct process development at the same time as product development.

From the above discussion it is clear that there is a close relationship between the design of a product or service and the design of the production system. Actually, the link is even closer than it seems. Figure 5.4 illustrates the relationship between the changes throughout the life cycle of a product or service and changes throughout the life cycle of its production system. At the left, when the product or service is introduced, innovations and changes in its design are frequent. At this point, the production system is relatively uncoordinated and very general since the design is still changing (the number of *product* innovations is high). Toward the middle, the product design has largely stabilized, and cost competition is forcing innovations in the production process, particularly the substitution of machinery for labor (the number of *process* innovations is high). At the right, this phenomenon has subsided and innovations in production methods are primarily the result of competitors' actions, government regulations, and other external factors.

Although not typically involved on the research side of such innovations in production methods (a laboratory engineering function), the operations manager is intimately involved in *applying* these developments in day-to-day production. The possible trade-offs in such applications are many and complex. The new production system may be more expensive but may produce a higher-quality output (and

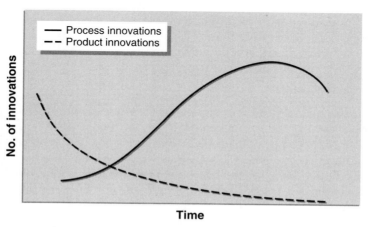

Figure 5.4 Product-process innovations over time.

thus the repeat volume may be higher or the price can be increased). Or the new production system may be more expensive and produce a *lower*-quality output but be simpler and easier to maintain, resulting in a lower total cost and, ultimately, higher profits. Clearly, many considerations—labor, maintenance, quality, materials, capital investment, and so on—are involved in the successful application of research to operations.

❖ Screening and Selection

The mortality rate shown in Figure 5.3 indicates the significant impact of screening and economic analysis, reducing research-derived ideas from 50 down to about 9, and then to just one or so by the end of the other evaluation activities. At this stage it is important to consider the consumer's needs and wants, as well as the typical consumer's reactions to the offerings of the firm's competitors. Considerations along these lines include expectations about promotion, sufficiency of demand, synergy with the current product or service line, current and potential competition, and adequacy of meeting customers' needs as regards price, performance, reliability, availability, and quality. Also, the possibility of segmenting the market by offering specially tailored outputs should be considered.

Operational activities include assessing the technical feasibility of the product or service—that is, the ability to produce it successfully. This would include the compatibility of the production system with existing equipment and methods, labor skills, facilities, and suppliers' abilities. The potential for patenting the product, as well as the possibility of patent infringements, also needs to be determined.

Financial activities at this stage are concerned with the up-front capital needs of the new product or service, as well as the returns. Here the possible risk of the project, the length of the life cycle, the anticipated profit margins, the initial investment required, the return on that investment, and the cash flows from the project are all evaluated.

To aid in this evaluation, payback period, return on investment (ROI), or net present value of the project may be calculated. These results offer a quick estimate of the opportunity the new product or service offers compared with other possible investments or choices the firm is facing. For example, many firms use a rule of thumb that to be acceptable an investment should have a payback (amount of time for profits to recover the investment) of two or three years, or a yearly ROI of 25 or 30 percent. Obviously, these rules are not absolute, but they do give managers a feel for the riskiness and profitability of the potential investment.

Breakeven Analysis

Management may also wish to conduct a **breakeven** analysis of the potential product or service. The introduction of a new output into the organization's existing output mix should be implemented only if a complete economic analysis has been conducted beforehand. This analysis would consider the fixed cost of existing capacity, the variable costs such as the materials and labor associated with producing the output, the return from the output, and the effect of different volumes of demand. Such an evaluation is called a **breakeven analysis.** (It is also known as *cost-volume-profit analysis*.) It was originally developed as an accounting technique used in the preparation of a profit budget for the firm. The analysis is based on a simplified income or profit-and-loss statement, which can be written as

revenue (unit selling price × units sold)
less   variable costs (variable cost per unit × units sold)
equals contribution margin
less   fixed costs
equals net profit

Clearly, there are many simplifications in these quantities that may not hold up in practice over a large range in output volume. For example, variable cost per unit may decrease, or increase, with larger volumes. Also, a company may be able to reduce its cost of materials if its suppliers offer discounts on large orders. And fixed costs will certainly jump if additional facilities are necessary to increase output capacity.

Nevertheless, within a limited range of volumes this basic income statement helps the operations manager to decide whether or not a new product or service should be produced. Consider, for example, a manufacturer of sporting goods who must decide whether or not to produce a new composite-alloy tennis racket.

Sharon Rigg, operations manager for King Sports Products, has made a sales forecast for the company's new composite-alloy tennis racket. The selling price assumed in preparing the forecast was $180; this price puts the racket somewhere in the middle price range for rackets of similar quality. To determine total revenue, she simply multiplies the selling price ($180) by the number of units (rackets) expected to be sold.

Variable costs are the "per racket" costs of manufacturing and selling. The costs that would vary with the number of rackets sold are the alloy and bonding materials used in the racket, the nylon used to string the racket, the leather grip, and the labor and energy used to mold, string, assemble, and package the racket. Since the company has been making sporting goods for some time and is familiar with the production methods, it estimates that the variable cost per racket will be $110.

Fixed costs are costs that do not vary with the volume of production or the number of rackets sold. In this case, the costs that would remain constant as production increased and decreased are building rent, insurance, property taxes, depreciation on equipment, administrative salaries, and interest on borrowed capital. Fixed costs are primarily determined by the selection of manufacturing equipment and the plant facility itself. The annual fixed costs associated with this new product have been determined to be $1.4 million. That is, the annual depreciation costs of the new molding equipment, the space rental, and other nonvariable costs total $1.4 million.

We can show each of the three factors bearing on net profit in a breakeven graph (Figure 5.5). Volume of sales (in units) is shown on the horizontal axis, and dollars (of revenue or cost) are measured on the vertical axis. The point at which the total revenue (TR) line and the total cost (TC) line intersect (i.e., $TR = TC$) is called the *breakeven point*, because the sales volume at this point is just enough to cover the fixed plus variable costs of operation without either earning a profit or suffering a loss. The firm just breaks even. For our sporting goods manufacturer we can see from the figure that the new tennis racket will break even, provided that sales are about 20,000 units.

For a more accurate analysis, we should use algebra. The income statement can be written algebraically as follows:

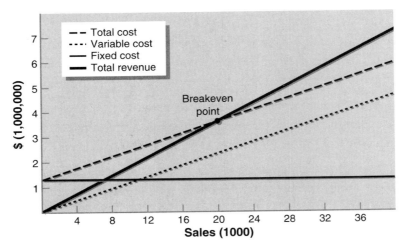

Figure 5.5 Breakeven graph for a tennis racket.

$$\text{revenue} - \text{variable costs} - \text{fixed costs} = \text{net profit}$$

where

$$\text{revenue} = \text{unit selling price} \times \text{volume of units sold}$$
$$\text{variable costs} = \text{variable cost/unit} \times \text{volume of units sold}.$$

If we let SP = selling price
U = volume in units sold
VC = variable cost/unit
FC = fixed cost
NP = net profit

then the income statement equation can be written as

$$(SP \times U) - (VC \times U) - FC = NP$$

and therefore the volume to meet a fixed net profit is

$$U = \frac{NP + FC}{SP - VC}$$

For example, to break even, and therefore earn zero net profit, the number of units that must be manufactured and sold is

$$U = \frac{0 + 1,400,000}{180 - 110} = \frac{1,400,000}{70} = 20,000 \text{ units}$$

as surmised from the graph.

Another way to find the breakeven point is to set total revenue equal to total cost:

$$TR = TC$$

or

$$U(SP) = FC + U(VC)$$

so

$$U = \frac{FC}{SP - VC} = 20,000 \text{ units}$$

as above. To earn a net profit of $100,000:

$$U = \frac{100,000 + 1,400,000}{180 - 110} = 21,429 \text{ units}$$

If the best estimate for sales in the next period is less than 21,429 units, then the company will not earn the desired profit of $100,000 and should decide not to produce the product. If the sales forecast is less than 20,000 units, the new racket will result in a net loss for the firm.

One of the most useful aspects of the breakeven model for operations managers is its ability to illustrate clearly the overall effect of different managerial and environmental actions. For example, if inflation increases the variable costs by 10 percent, what will the new breakeven volume be? What volume must be sold to maintain current profits? At current volumes, what price increase will maintain current profits?

The breakeven technique is particularly useful in the selection of products and services because it identifies information such as the following:

❖ At what volumes will the new output become profitable?
❖ Will the predicted sales volumes for the assumed prices be profitable?
❖ For the fixed costs, what must the variable costs be to make a profit?
❖ For the variable costs given, what must the fixed costs be to make a profit?
❖ How will the breakeven volume change as the price increases or decreases?

Analysis of Organizational Fit

Last, a general analysis of *organizational fit* is often conducted—that is, the fit between the new product or service and the existing organization is evaluated. Any new output should capitalize on an organization's core competencies and competitive advantage, complement the organization's existing outputs, and fit into the organization's structure, goals, and plans for the future.

General areas of strength (or weakness) are:

1. Experience with the particular output.
2. Experience with the production system required for the output.
3. Experience in providing an output to the same target recipients.
4. Experience with the distribution system for the output.

The organization must also consider the effect a new output will have on both the demand and the production methods used for existing outputs, a consideration of major importance to the operations manager. For example, introduction of inkjet printers reduced the demand for laser printers. Clearly, a new output may very well change the "best" production methods to be used for existing outputs in terms of labor skills, type of equipment, and possibly even the operations focus of the organization. It will certainly change scheduling, routing, and other aspects of production planning in the operations area.

Sometimes, of course, a new output totally changes the organization and its goals. On occasion, organizations do this on purpose to move into a new product or service area, especially if the old output is near the end of its life cycle.

One simple method for assessing the organizational fit of candidate outputs is to use a checklist, such as the one shown for *products* in Figure 5.6. Although such a list is not a substitute for analysis, it does provide a starting point for analysis. We can begin by concentrating attention on the areas of "poor" fit and analyzing their impact and the trade-offs available between "poor" and "excellent" areas.

Area of fit	Poor	Fair	Good	Excellent
I. General				
1. Fits long-term organizational goals				√
2. Capitalizes on organizational strengths			√	
3. Appealing to management				√
4. Utilizes organizational experience		√		
II. Market				
1. Adequate demand			√	
2. Existing or potential competition		√		
3. In line with market trend				√
4. Enhances existing line	√			
III. Economics				
1. Cost		√		
2. Price				√
IV. Production				
1. Capacity availability			√	
2. Material supply and price	√			
3. Engineering know-how			√	
Totals	2	3	4	4

Figure 5.6   Typical checklist for organizational fit.

Spreadsheet Analysis: Breakeven Number of Calls

Rancher's Vets provides veterinarian services to farmers and ranchers with dairy herds. Each service call brings an average of $300 in revenue. The cost for the vet's time, bovine feeds and medicines, disposable supplies, and transportation averages $100 per call. The fixed expenses of the office, trucks, and equipment are amortized at $60,000 per annum.

Spreadsheets offer capabilities that greatly facilitate breakeven analysis. For example, assume that we are interested in determining the breakeven number of calls for Rancher's Vets. The Excel spreadsheet below was developed to help answer this question.

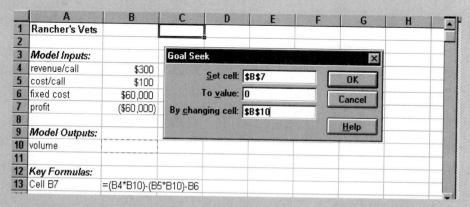

The spreadsheet is divided into three major sections: model inputs, model outputs, and key formulas. The model inputs section contains the parameters and other information that is given. In the case of Rancher's Vets this includes revenue/call, cost/call, and fixed cost. Also, a formula that calculates the profit for Rancher's Vets was entered in cell B7. As is shown in the key formulas section in cell B13, profit (cell B7) is calculated by subtracting total variable costs and fixed costs from total revenues. The model output section of the spreadsheet is reserved for the results that the decision maker is interested in. In the present case, the decision maker is interested in determining the volume of calls that will permit Rancher's Vets to break even.

To determine the breakeven number of calls for Rancher's Vets, Excel's *goal-seeking* feature was used. The goal-seeking feature will vary the value in a specified cell until a formula that depends on that cell returns the result you want. Thus, in many cases the goal-seeking feature makes it unnecessary to use trial and error. To find Rancher's Vets' breakeven point, we want to vary the volume of calls (cell B10) so that profit (cell B7) is zero. To do this, Tools was selected from the menu bar at the top of the screen and then Goal Seek was selected. After Goal Seek is selected, the Goal Seek dialog box is displayed in the spreadsheet, as shown above. The Set cell, To value, and By changing cell values were specified as shown. The cell addresses for Set cell and By changing cell can be specified either by typing the cell addresses in directly or by using the mouse and clicking on the desired cell. After the information was entered for Set cell, To value, and By changing cell, OK was selected, and the following results were obtained:

	A	B	C	D	E	F	G
1	Rancher's Vets						
2							
3	*Model Inputs:*						
4	revenue/call	$300					
5	cost/call	$100					
6	fixed cost	$60,000					
7	profit	$0					
8							
9	*Model Outputs:*						
10	volume	300.00					
11							
12	*Key Formulas:*						
13	Cell B7	=(B4*B10)-(B5*B10)-B6					

Goal Seek Status ☒

Goal Seeking with Cell B7 found a solution.

Target Value: 0
Current Value: $0

OK   Cancel   Step   Pause   Help

As is shown in this spreadsheet, a new dialog box with the title Goal Seek Status is displayed; this summarizes the results. The first piece of information in the window notes that cell B7 was the cell for which we specified a target value. The next piece of information tells us that a solution was found. The last two pieces of information tell us that the target value we specified for cell B7 was zero and currently cell B7 has a value of zero. Thus, the goal-seeking function found a value for volume (cell B10) so that the formula for profit (cell B7) returned a value of zero. Note that the values in the spreadsheet in both cells B7 and B10 have been updated. Cell B7 was originally −60,000, and cell B10 was initially left empty. After we used the goal-seeking routine, the values in these cells changed to zero and 300, respectively. Clicking on the OK button in the Goal Seek Status window clears this window from the screen.

Suppose that instead of determining the breakeven point, we would like to determine the number of calls required to generate a profit of $10,000. We can easily find this by using the spreadsheet we have already developed and making one minor change. Specifically, after selecting Goal Seek from the Tools menu, we enter 10,000 for the To value and enter all the other information exactly as we did when we were seeking the breakeven point, as shown below:

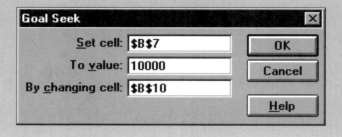

After clicking on the OK button in the Goal Seek dialog box, we obtain the following results:

	A	B	C	D	E	F	G
1	Rancher's Vets						
2							
3	*Model Inputs:*						
4	revenue/call	$300					
5	cost/call	$100					
6	fixed cost	$60,000					
7	profit	$10,000					
8							
9	*Model Outputs:*						
10	volume	350.00					
11							
12	*Key Formulas:*						
13	Cell B7	=(B4*B10)-(B5*B10)-B6					

Goal Seek Status ☒

Goal Seeking with Cell B7 found a solution.

Target Value: 10000
Current Value: $10,000

[OK] [Cancel] [Step] [Pause] [Help]

The results tell us that 350 calls are required to generate a profit of $10,000.

As a final example, the spreadsheet below was developed to investigate the effect of varying the volume of calls on profit. Thus, volume now becomes a model input and profit becomes the model output.

	A	B	C	D	E	F	G	H
1	Rancher's Vets							
2								
3	*Model Inputs:*							
4	revenue/call	$300						
5	cost/call	$100						
6	fixed cost	$60,000						
7	volume	400						
8								
9	*Model Outputs:*							
10	profit	$20,000.00						
11								
12	*Key Formulas:*							
13	Cell B10	=(B4*B7)-(B5*B7)-B6						

By changing the value entered for the volume of calls (cell B7), we are able to quickly determine the effect this will have on profit. In fact, we can use the above spreadsheet to quickly determine the effect on profit to changes made in any of the model inputs. Thus, we can investigate the effect of changing one model input at a time or we can change any number of model inputs in one step.

THE PRODUCT DESIGN STAGE

Because engineering activities dominate the product design stage, operations managers need to interact with a variety of engineering specialists during this stage. *Mechanical engineers* are typically concerned with designing products and other devices ranging from ballpoint pens to complex machinery. Operations managers should provide these engineers with information about the producibility of the products being designed. Also, the operations manager should be included in decisions about equipment design, since overseeing the day-to-day use of the machinery ultimately falls to the operations manager.

The functions of *industrial engineering* and operations management are frequently confused. Although there is considerable overlap between these functions, it should be noted that industrial engineering is *primarily* concerned with designing and implementing the production system whereas operations management is more concerned with overseeing it on an ongoing basis. Of course, industrial engineers may be involved in managing the system once it is designed, and operations managers should have input into the design of the system. It may be helpful to think about these functions as a sequence of activities: mechanical engineers design the products and equipment, industrial engineers combine the equipment into a production system, and operations management oversees the ongoing use of the production system. At any rate, regardless of which function dominates the completion of a particular activity, it is important that all affected areas be included in the decisions at each stage.

Operations managers also frequently interact with a number of other engineering specialists. For example, if a new facility needs to be constructed or an existing facility expanded, the planning, coordinating, and controlling of such construction projects is typically the responsibility of a *civil engineer*. If the output requires a new material that has special properties, a *materials engineer* may be called in. Materials engineering is concerned with developing materials that possess certain desired properties. Also, materials engineers are involved in the design of the production systems used to produce the materials. Finally, depending on the industry, the operations manager may interact with a variety of other engineering professionals including *chemical, electrical, metallurgical,* and *aeronautical engineers.*

A number of recent trends are having a profound impact on product design. One such trend is the emphasis being given to reducing the time required for product development. According to a study conducted by *Business Week* of 200 American companies, from 1991 to 1996 the average development time for breakthrough products was reduced by approximately 17 percent. Likewise, over this same period the average development time for new product lines, major product revisions, and minor product revisions was reduced 19 percent, 22 percent, and 25 percent, respectively.

Outsourcing product design is also becoming increasingly popular. By outsourcing the design of key components to suppliers, an organization can lower its cost of product development and tap the expertise of its suppliers. However, as was discussed in Chapter 2, a company must be careful not to outsource parts or activities that are strategically important to maintaining its competitive position. The sidebar on Johnson Controls provides an example of a company that has benefited considerably from the trend toward outsourcing in the automobile industry.

In the remainder of this section, we divide the product design stage into three chronological steps: preliminary design, prototype testing, and final design. In preliminary design, the design team considers various alternatives and makes early, basic trade-offs. The result is one or two preliminary designs for further consideration. Next, one or more prototypes are constructed to test the design or designs. The team then evaluates the results of various tests on the prototype and alters and improves the original design; this results in the final design.

❖ Preliminary Design

Preliminary design follows from the screening step in which various ideas and concepts were advanced and evaluated. Here, the team identifies the final specifications, describing how the product or service *should perform,* and then makes some basic trade-offs. That is, the team does *not* specify the item or service itself; rather, the team specifies how it should function when the customer uses it: how long it should last, what it should do, how fast it should execute its functions.

OPERATIONS IN PRACTICE

JOHNSON CONTROLS SURFS THE OUTSOURCING WAVE

Johnson Controls, headquartered in Milwaukee, has increased its sales to the automobile industry from $650 million in 1986 to a projected $7 billion for 1997. Initially, the company produced seating components for auto makers. However, it quickly enlarged its scope to the production of entire seat systems. Its share of the North American market is expected to increase from 36 percent in 1996 to 45 percent in 1998. Further, it is projected that Johnson Controls will gain 30 percent of the European market by 1998 and 20 percent of the Asian market by the year 2000.

One key to the success of Johnson Controls is its world-class manufacturing capabilities. Securing early contracts for its seating systems from Toyota Motor provided it with an opportunity to learn from one of the most highly regarded manufacturers in the world. One example of its manufacturing capability is that Johnson Controls has refined its production system so that completed seating systems can be delivered to an auto maker's assembly line within 90 minutes of receiving the order from the customer. To achieve this goal, Johnson Controls builds its seat factories near its customers' factories. As of early 1997, Johnson Controls operated more than 50 of these just-in-time factories.

Another key to its success is the expertise Johnson Controls has acquired in designing seat systems. Johnson Controls now employs 1000 product design engineers (10 years ago, it had none). It is awarded more patents for interior auto designs than General Motors, Ford, or Chrysler. In fact, Johnson Controls often comes up with new products before its customers request them (Rose, 1997).

Next, the team has to make some decisions regarding the trade-offs needed to achieve the desired performance. These basic trade-offs will narrow the many avenues for achieving this performance: Will it be made of cheaper plastic or more rugged metal? Will it be battery-driven or will it use household current? And so on. The result of these basic trade-offs is the design concept. Ideally, adequate decisions will be made at this stage so that the prototype based on this design concept will perform acceptably at the next stage. If poor decisions are made about the preliminary design and the prototype fails (as happens often), then the team must return to the preliminary design stage and repeat the entire process. The tasks involved in achieving the design concept are described below.

Trade-Off Analysis

Some of the basic factors to be considered in the initial trade-off analysis are listed in Table 5.2. The design task is to trade off these characteristics to best meet the demands of the marketplace. For example, gasoline stations and fast-food restaurants have become self-service to reduce the cost, as well as the service time, to the recipient. In return for the improvements in these two characteristics of the services, customers have had to give up such conveniences as checks of the battery, oil, and tire pressure; waiters and waitresses; full-line menus; and individual attention. For those people who still desire these features, standard full-service gas stations are available, as are numerous alternatives for dining.

In both product and service design, many alternatives usually exist that will meet the basic function of the output. The key to good design is a recognition of the major characteristics of the demand and a detailed analysis of the trade-offs available between and among the various attributes. Often, several different versions of the same output can be produced so that different market segments will find the output appealing. For example, Procter & Gamble offers a dazzling array of detergents, many of which even compete with each other. In the fast-food business, the major companies experimented with expanding their menus (at the risk of loss of focus) to broaden the appeal to new markets. For example, McDonald's has experimented with offering chili, pizzas, and sundaes at many locations.

Standardization

Many years ago the primary purpose of output design was to facilitate the production system. Since demand for goods was plentiful as long as the price was low, companies desired to minimize the unit cost of items. One method of reducing unit cost was increasing capacity through *mass production* or assembly-line manufacture. Thus, companies moved toward standardization and thereby interchangeability of parts to minimize both the costs and the difficulty of assembly. Standardization had the following cost-related advantages:

1. It minimized the number of different parts to stock.
2. It minimized the number of changes necessary in production equipment.
3. It simplified operations procedures and thus reduced the need for controls.
4. It allowed larger purchases with quantity discounts.
5. It minimized problems with repair and servicing.

𝒯ABLE 5.2 ❖ Trade-Off Analysis: Factors to Consider

❖ *Function:* The new design must properly perform the function (meet the recipient's need) for which it is required.

❖ *Cost:* The total cost (materials, labor, processing, etc.) cannot be excessive for the market under consideration.

❖ *Size and shape:* These must be compatible with the function and not distasteful or otherwise unacceptable to the market.

❖ *Appearance:* For some applications the appearance of the product or service is irrelevant; in other instances (e.g., art, sports cars) the appearance is equivalent to the function.

❖ *Quality:* The quality should be compatible with the purpose. Excessive quality may increase cost unnecessarily; insufficient quality leads to dissatisfied customers and decreased demand.

❖ *Reliability:* The output should function normally when used and should last the expected duration. Outputs with complex combinations of elements, all of which must work, will tend to have lower reliability unless this is allowed for in the design.

❖ *Environmental impact:* The output should not degrade the environment or pose a hazard to the recipient.

❖ *Producibility:* The output should be easily and speedily producible. The examples at the beginning of the chapter illustrate how organizations can use design teams with representatives from manufacturing to help ensure that the products being designed by the team are producible.

❖ *Timing:* The output should be available when desired. This characteristic is especially relevant to service outputs.

❖ *Accessibility:* The recipient should be able to obtain the output without difficulty.

❖ *Recipients' input requirements:* The amount and type of input required of the recipient should be considered in the design. "Do-it-yourself" projects are an example of product outputs and "self-service" is an example of service outputs.

Standardization is still an effective way to hold costs down. Beyond this, it provides many advantages for consumers too. For example, standardization lets us buy common items at the store such as lightbulbs, film, videotapes, and automobile tires without worrying about fit or proper function. In services, we depend on zip codes and area codes to direct our correspondence and phone calls correctly and efficiently. On the other hand, standardization has several drawbacks. For example, using standard parts rather than specially made parts sometimes means lower quality or reduced performance. The major disadvantage of standardization is the inflexibility of production; little variety is possible. For example, what happens when you order a Big Mac at a McDonald's drive-through and ask them to hold the pickles? The classic comment on this fact comes from Henry Ford, who reputedly declared that his customers could have any color Model T they desired, as long as it was black!

Modularity

One method used to obtain variety, or at least a semblance of variety, and still hold down cost is ***modularity***. This means producing the output in "modules" or subassemblies that are interchangeable, thus giving the customer some choice. For instance, the purchaser of a new car can specify engine size, type of transmission, upholstery, color, and numerous other aspects of the product. Such variety is achieved

OPERATIONS
IN PRACTICE

WHIRLPOOL'S GLOBAL PRODUCT LINE
BASED ON COMMON PLATFORMS

Whirlpool's European plant in Italy has what would appear to be an extremely difficult task. In this one plant a wide variety of ovens are produced, from boxy, expensive Bauknecht ovens to rounder, more modern Whirlpool-branded ovens to no-frills ovens bearing the Ingnis brand name. Interestingly, although each brand seems different on the basis of its outward appearance, the ovens all have a common interior. Building its new products around these common platforms has provided Whirlpool with a number of benefits. For example, operating margins for the first three quarters of 1994 were 6.5 percent compared with 3.6 percent in 1990. Also, over this same period, Whirlpool was able to increase its market share from 11.5 percent to 13 percent. Using common platforms has provided Whirlpool with a number of operating benefits as well. For example, it has reduced the number of suppliers of power cords for its refrigerators from 17 to 2. Across the board, similar reductions in its supplier base for other parts has contributed to Whirlpool's reducing its inventory by one-third (Oster and Rossant, 1994).

not by producing some number of every possible model but rather by producing modules (e.g., engines, transmission, bodies with varying colors, upholstery, tires and wheels, etc.) and then joining the appropriate modules together in final assembly according to the customer's order. An example of this was provided in the Operations in Practice "Mass Customization at Hewlett-Packard" in Chapter 2.

One example of modularization is an automobile that has three possible engines, two possible transmissions, five different exterior colors, and three different interiors available to the customer but requires only 13 modules for the operations manager to keep track of. However, these 13 modules can be combined to form $3 \times 2 \times 5 \times 3 = 90$ different versions of the same model.

This, of course, is what Whirlpool is striving for with its new common platforms, as described in the sidebar. By using a standard low-cost platform, Whirlpool is able to efficiently produce a wide range of appliances for a variety of different markets.

Computer-Aided Design

Engineers are making increasing use of the computer for product design and production planning. In ***computer-aided design*** (CAD), the engineer forms a drawing on the computer screen (see Figure 5.7) with the keyboard, a light pen, or a mouse and pad. Lines can be specified through coordinates, or the points can be "spotted" on the screen or pad and the computer will draw the line between the points.

CAD software provides the engineer with many of the same benefits word-77processing programs provide you. For instance, before graduating from college you may wish to send out your résumé and a cover letter to prospective employers.

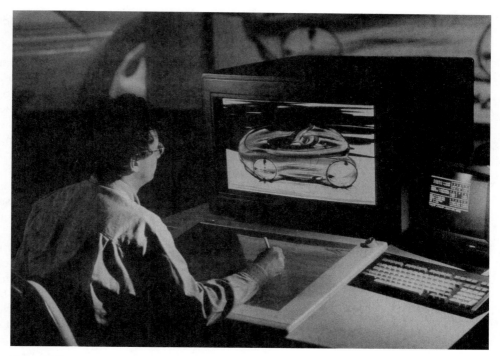

Figure 5.7 Computer-aided design.

Word-processing programs facilitate this task in that you can create a basic cover letter, retrieve this file as needed, and make minor changes to it for each prospective employer. In a similar fashion, when engineers need to design a new part, they can retrieve a design for a similar part and make changes to the design right on the computer screen. This saves considerable time, since the engineer doesn't have to develop each new design from scratch. In addition, just as word processing programs can check documents for spelling and grammatical errors, CAD software can often automatically check designs. For example, CAD software can be used to check the fit of parts that will be assembled together.

As the engineer designs the part, the CAD systems can be instructed to enlarge certain portions for a closer examination, rotate the design to show it from different angles, and so on. The capabilities of these systems have been growing tremendously in the last few years, while the prices of the software have fallen just as fast. Many excellent microcomputer CAD packages are now available. Productivity increases on the order of 300 and 400 percent are typical.

When the design is completed, it can be printed out on a graphics plotter or stored electronically to be used or changed later. As was mentioned before, most of the engineer's design work is initiated by retrieving a similar product or part from the system database—a similar wheel for another customer in the past, a recent factory layout—which cuts the design time by better than half. Rarely does the engineer draw a product totally from scratch. In addition, many marketing, R&D, and manufacturing activities are facilitated through the use of the electronic database on the parts. For example, the CAD database of parts can be used to obtain the bill of materials or the dimensions of critical parts.

CAD is being used for more and more purposes as the software becomes more user-friendly and prices drop. In addition to designing products and components of products as shown in Figure 5.7, architects use CAD to design buildings and bridges, designers to create new children's toys, automobile stylists to design futuristic cars, fire analysts to study the historical pattern of fires in a city and design new routes for fire engines and emergency vehicles, jewelers to design rings and other jewelry, and physicians to develop replacements for degenerated or irreparably injured bones.

Once an engineer has the product design on the CAD system, the database can be used for a number of other purposes. For example, computer-aided engineering (CAE) software uses CAD designs but then subjects them to stress, loads, and vibrations to determine their strength and reliability, as illustrated in Figure 5.8. Advanced engineering techniques such as finite element analysis are incorporated in the software to conduct the engineering analyses and save tremendous amounts of expensive skilled engineering time.

Computer-aided process planning (CAPP) is the technique of turning a part design into a manufacturing production plan, including routings, operations, inspections, times, and so on. Such a system is invaluable in overcoming problems that frequently occur at the interface between engineering and manufacturing.

Computer-aided manufacturing (CAM) was originally the specification by a computer of the machining instructions, based on a computer-aided design conducted beforehand. With CAM, the instructions to control the movement of machines are stored electronically and processed by computers. Before CAM was developed, the movement of machines was often controlled by instructions stored on a roll of paper with holes punched in it. The location of the holes triggered different machine

Figure 5.8   Computer-aided engineering of a robotic process.

functions. These types of machines are called numerical control machines. A player piano is an example of a numerical control machine: the location of the holes on the paper roll determines which note is struck. With the advent of microprocessor technology, microprocessors were added to machines, and machining instructions were stored magnetically on tapes and disks instead of being punched on paper. Equipping machines with microprocessors is called *computer numerical control*. An alternative to storing machining instructions on tapes and disks is to store these instructions on a central computer and download the instructions to the machines as needed. Using a central computer to control multiple machines in this fashion is called *direct numerical control*. CAM is applicable to a variety of manufacturing methods including turning, laser cutting (Figure 5.9), and other methods of fabrication or cutting.

❖ Prototype Testing

The concept developed in the preliminary design step is tested as a **prototype** in the next step. The prototype may take the form of a physical model, a computer simulation, or a real product or service. Examples of prototypes include the clay models of new car designs used in the 1960s as well as the computer simulations used in the 1990s. The Air Force uses actual first-off production units as prototypes of new fighters and bombers, such as the B–2 Stealth, to test original concepts such as radar invisibility and in-flight performance. Ray Kroc's original McDonald's restaurant in California was the service prototype for the thousands of franchised facilities that soon followed. Software prototypes (often referred to as *alpha* and *beta* versions) for new Web browsers and graphics programs are basic to the software industry. In fact, these prototypes can often be downloaded at no charge and

Figure 5.9   A computer-driven laser cutter.

evaluated by potential users to determine how they perform and to ensure they are free of bugs.

On the basis of these tests, the preliminary design may be accepted and extended, modified, or completely rejected. Inadequate prototype testing has frequently resulted in disasters for the firm's stock price—as when well-known software firms released packages that still included bugs or were not user-friendly. Hardware firms have made similar mistakes with computers, such as the widely publicized flaw in the Pentium. Most often, however, only minor changes are indicated to fine-tune the performance and achieve even better results on the critical variables. This fine-tuning is then incorporated into the final design.

❖ Final Design

Fine-tuning is based on the preliminary design, customers' reactions to the preliminary design, evaluation of the prototype tests, detailed financial analysis, and other relevant inputs. Although certain aspects are initiated somewhat before this stage, we also discuss them here: simplification, value analysis, safety and human factors, reliability, and manufacturability.

Simplification and Value Analysis

Simplification programs reduce the number of separate parts and operations required to produce an output. Fewer parts generally mean fewer materials, less labor, simplified assembly, easier service, and greater reliability. Often, the design team combines functions into one part so that two or three are not needed. Sometimes a molded plastic part will embody the function of two to six separate metal parts that previously needed to be welded or screwed together. For example, IBM redesigned its Proprinter for ease of robotic assembly, eliminating two-thirds of the former assembly operations.

The design team uses *value analysis* (sometimes called *value engineering*) to achieve the *function* of a product or service at less cost. The team considers cheaper methods, materials, and designs. Every element of the output that adds cost but not value is a candidate for examination. The procedure used in value analysis is a formalized approach that examines first the basic objective, second the basic function required, and then secondary functions. Team members propose ways to improve the secondary functions, such as combining, revising, or eliminating them. Ways to achieve the objective by using other basic functions are also considered.

Safety and Human Factors

During this final design step the team is also concerned with issues related to ease of use and the safety of the product or service. For example, the height or weight of a product and the location of its dials and switches can severely restrict its utility for many people. Buildings and facilities for the disabled (ramps, elevators, parking, lavatories) are a recent requirement that has assumed considerable importance in design.

Product liability is a major concern of firms, since civil lawsuits have severely restricted how firms operate, not to mention their profitability. We need only mention the hazards of asbestos, poisons, caustic chemicals, combustibles, and power tools to see the range of potential problems in the design stage. When hazards do exist, safety devices must be installed to eliminate the potential for an accident. Warning labels are also required in a number of situations.

Federal and state regulations concerning pollution, safety, disclosure of terms and conditions, drug prohibitions, and so forth also affect product design. Sometimes these prohibitions and regulations affect the design of the product or service itself (emission restrictions and mileage mandates on automobiles, for example), and sometimes they affect the production process (particulate discharges, water pollution, requirements for workers' safety).

Reliability

Reliability is one component of quality. There are two perspectives on calculating the reliability of a product or service. One is the likelihood that it will work on any given attempt to use it. The second is the likelihood that it will operate properly for a certain period of time.

One of the most important aspects of quality in the mind of the consumer is reliability. When we consider the reliability of a product, we generally separate items that are used or consumed only once, such as food and supplies (paper, bleach), from items that are reusable (a toaster, an automobile, or a stereo). The latter consist of a number of subcomponents that must all function properly for the product to work reliably.

Manufacturability

A major design consideration of current national interest is that of ***manufacturability,*** also called *simultaneous engineering, concurrent engineering, design for producibility, design for assembly*, and a variety of other, similar names. As the examples at the beginning of the chapter illustrate, the basic approach here is to form a team that includes the people responsible for *producing* an output as well as the people responsible for *designing* it.

These teams commonly include representatives of marketing, finance, R&D, suppliers, and other interested parties. Thus a complete product design is possible that does not hit any snags in the process of moving from concept to commercialization. Moreover, the product or service is generally brought to market much faster.

The major players on this team are the design engineers and manufacturing engineers. In the past, the typical American practice was for design engineers to design something and then "throw it over the wall" to the manufacturing engineers, almost with the challenge: "Let's see you make this one!" As noted earlier, the cost and even the success of a product are essentially *designed in* by the design engineers. There are typically many alternative ways to design a product to perform a particular function; if engineering chooses an unreliable, unsafe, or expensive way, no amount of efficiency in manufacture or advertising will make the product or service a success.

The design team can use a variety of tools and techniques to achieve manufacturability. These include quality approaches, techniques for enhancing productivity, computer integration, and faster responses, as well as the approaches described earlier such as standardization, simplification, and modularity. One tool that is particularly useful for ensuring that customers' requirements and manufacturing capabilities are met throughout the design is called *quality function deployment* (QFD). It is discussed in the next section.

Using design teams also has some disadvantages. For example, the design engineers are no longer unrestricted in how they design parts and products. They may not be allowed to use certain hole sizes, because drills in that size are not standard items for the firm; or certain materials or procedures may not be acceptable to other members on the team for reasons of safety or cost. In the team approach, everyone accepts more constraints on individual creativity in return for fewer hassles and problems in getting the product or service to market. In the process, better products and services are produced at less cost with much shorter lead times.

Global competitors are innovating faster and bringing out new products and services in about half the time that it takes in the United States. For example, American companies require about four to five years to bring new models of automobiles to market, but Japanese companies take only two to three years. In other industries, the Japanese maintain that the consumer research so commonly conducted by firms in the United States is a waste of time because they can bring to market and test actual new products in the same time it takes to do the consumer research.

The result is that American firms in all industries are now trying new methods for speeding the process of designing and introducing a product or service. Some of the new methods being evaluated are described in Table 5.3.

$\mathcal{Q}$UALITY FUNCTION DEPLOYMENT

The success of the design effort hinges on two criteria: the extent to which the new product or service meets customers' needs, and the extent to which the organization can produce or deliver it. Clearly, no amount of clever advertising and no degree of production efficiency will entice customers to purchase a product or service that does not meet their needs. Likewise, it serves no purpose for an organization to design new products or services when it does not have the capability to produce or deliver them. For instance, it would not make sense for a local phone company to design a new service that offers interactive cable television programming if it currently does not have the bandwidth necessary to deliver this type of service. Even if the phone company was able to work out the bugs for interactive programming in the lab, it would still take years to install the fiber-optic cable infrastructure that is necessary to deliver this type of service to the public. Of course, the development of new products and services can serve as the impetus for acquiring additional production capabilities; however, organizations typically seek to develop new products and services that capitalize on their existing capabilities.

Quality function deployment (QFD) is a useful tool for helping to ensure that designs for new products and services satisfy market requirements and are ultimately producible by the firm. As Figure 5.10 illustrates, QFD uses a series of matrices or tables to maintain the links between customers' attributes, technical requirements, component requirements, and operation requirements.

$\mathcal{T}$ABLE 5.3 ❖ Methods of Speeding the Introduction of New Outputs

❖ *Contract R&D:* Use external R&D laboratories to conduct the research work in your market.

❖ *Form product and process teams:* Use teamwork to develop the production system at the same time as the product or service.

❖ *Overlap developmental stages:* Proceed almost simultaneously on the stages described here, with only slight lags between them. That is, start the following stage when early returns from the prior stage start coming in.

❖ *Combine or eliminate stages:* Combine the design of product and production system. Eliminate final design. Use new technologies such as simulation and computer-aided engineering (CAE) to eliminate the need for testing a prototype.

❖ *Incremental emphasis:* Strive for incremental improvements rather than breakthrough innovations. Breakthroughs are harder to come up with in the first place, they take longer to design and test, and they result in more failures. Batching the incremental improvements will allow significantly improved products and services to be offered on a regular basis.

❖ *Use more extensive application:* Use the standard approaches and techniques such as standardization, modularization, part commonality, and simplification more extensively.

❖ *Use new technologies:* Employ CAD, CAE, and other technologies more widely and quickly. Be aggressive technologically.

With QFD, market requirements are specified in terms of customers' attributes. These attributes are often referred to as the "voice of the customer" because they are expressed in the customer's own terms. Examples of attributes for an electric guitar might include statements such as "It should have consistent action," "There should be no buzzing at the frets," and "The neck should not be bolted on."

After a comprehensive list of customers' attributes has been developed, the technical requirements for the product are specified and matched to the attributes, using the table shown in Figure 5.10. Technical requirements are expressed in the specialized language associated with engineering. Thus, technical requirements

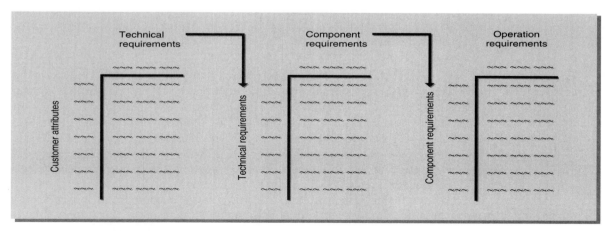

Figure 5.10 Using quality function deployment to link customers' attributes to technical, component, and operation requirements.

may be expressed in terms of dimensions, weights, performance, tensile strength, and compression. Two important outcomes result from using this table. First, it helps to ensure that each attribute noted by customers is addressed by the product designers. Second, it ensures that designers do not add technical requirements to the product that do not satisfy a particular requirement of customers. Designers who do not specifically consider customers' requirements run the risk of adding a number of "bells and whistles" that the customer may not be interested in. In these cases the designers are simply adding to the cost of the final product or service without proportionally increasing its value. For example, it might be an interesting challenge for an engineer to design a five-speed motor for garage doors. However, since customers would most likely operate it at only its fastest speed, adding the extra controls for additional speeds would not add value for the typical customer.

In the middle of Figure 5.10, the technical requirements for the product developed at the left are now linked to specific requirements for components or parts. Again, this table ensures two important outcomes: (1) each technical requirement is addressed by the components used to make the product and (2) component requirements that are not related to specific technical requirements are not added.

In the table shown at the right in Figure 5.10, the operation requirements necessary to produce the components are determined. Like the earlier tables, this table ensures that each component requirement is matched to specific operation requirements, and that each operation requirement is linked to specific component requirements. The former result ensures that the organization has the capability to produce the components; the latter result ensures that the organization does not attempt to develop production system capabilities that are not related to the component requirements.

Thus, we see that QFD provides a simple and straightforward approach for ensuring that product designs meet customers' requirements and are producible. This is accomplished by first translating the voice of the customer into the technical language of engineers. Next, these technical requirements are translated into specific requirements for the components of the new product. Finally, the component requirements are translated into specific requirements for the production system.

A more detailed example of the table on the left is shown in Figure 5.11 for a car door. This table is often called the *house of quality*. A triangular correlation table between the technical requirements at the top forms the roof of the house. This table identifies which requirements are synergistic with each other and which are in conflict.

On the right side of the house, opposite customers' attributes, are two sets of information. First is the importance rating (from 1 to 10) for that attribute. Next is the customers' evaluations (running from better to worse) of a product, based on each of the requirements. Thus, a producer can see how a particular product stacks up against the customer's wants or a competitor's offering. At the bottom of the house, opposite the technical requirements, are the specifications for each characteristic that will meet the customer's requirements and, beneath that, an engineering assessment (again running from better to worse) of the product in terms of its meeting those specifications.

By the use of the visual tool, a firm can analyze its outputs in terms of customers' desires, compare its outputs with competitors' outputs, determine what it takes to better meet the customer's requirements, and figure out how to do it. A number of Japanese and American firms such as Toyota and Hewlett-Packard have

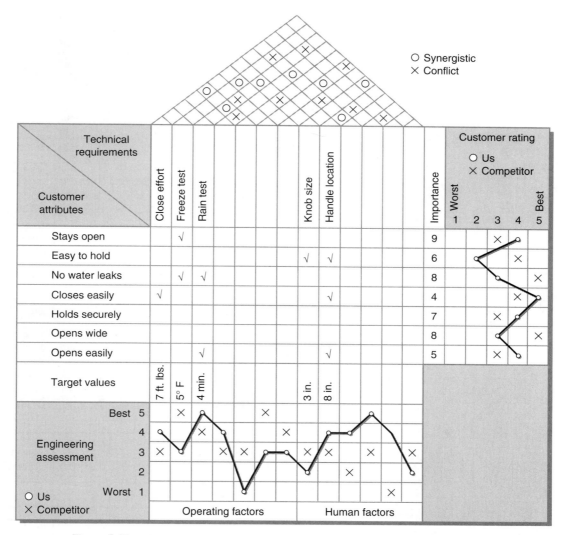

Figure 5.11 The house of quality for a car door.

taken this approach and found that it cut their product development time by one-third to one-half and their costs by up to 60 percent (while improving quality).

Spreadsheet Analysis: Setting Up QFD Tables in a Spreadsheet

United Door Locks has just completed extensive market research for a new line of door lock sets it will be developing. The results of the study indicate that purchasers of door lock sets have three major requirements: (1) they want the hardware to be easy to install; (2) they want the locks to provide security against break-ins; (3) they want a high-quality product. A spreadsheet was developed to link these three attributes to several technical requirements. In the spreadsheet below an X was used to indicate that a particular attribute is strongly related to a particular technical requirement. Likewise, the symbols O and * were used, respectively, if a particular attribute was strongly or weakly related to a technical requirement.

	A	B	C	D	E	F
1	customer attributes/technical requirements					
2						
3				heavy-duty	key cylinder	finish that
4		number of parts		ball bearings	resistant to	resists pitting
5		assembled by	strong	in lock	picking	flaking, and
6		customer < 4	cover	mechanism	and prying	tarnishing
7	ease of installation	X				
8	security	*	X	X	X	
9	quality	O	O	*	*	X
10						
11		X	very strongly related			
12		O	strongly related			
13		*	weakly related			

After the technical requirements were determined for each attribute, they were linked to specific component requirements, as shown in the following spreadsheet. This process was then repeated by creating a third table to link the component requirements to specific operation requirements. As this example illustrates, spreadsheets can be used as a quick way to set up QFD tables.

	A	B	C	D	E	F
16	technical requirements/component requirements					
17						
18		hands free clip		hardened		
19		for snap-	zinc	steel ball-	specially	use materials
20		together	die-cast	bearing lock	machined	that can be
21		assembly	cover	mechanism	key cylinder	electroplated
22	number of parts assembled					
23	by customer < 4	X				
24	strong cover		X			
25	heavy-duty ball bearings					
26	in lock mechanism			X		
27	key cylinder resistant					
28	to picking and prying				X	
29	finish that resists					
30	pitting, flaking, and					X
31	tarnishing					

COMMERCIALIZATION

In the previous section we discussed the importance of designing new products and services that meet customers' requirements and can be produced by the firm. The final ingredient in determining whether a new product or service will succeed is the organization's ability to commercialize its new offerings. *Commercialization* refers to the process of moving an idea for a new product or service from concept to market. It is frequently noted by top managers and academics alike that although quality and manufacturing excellence were the key to competitive success in the 1980s, commercialization of technology will be the key to competitive success in future decades.

Consider a common product such as the typewriter. The earliest modern typewriter was the mechanical typewriter, which dominated the market for 25 years. After the mechanical typewriter came the electromechanical typewriter, which dominated the market for 15 years. Then came the entirely electric typewriter, which dominated the market for the next 7 years. After the electric typewriter came the first generation of microprocessor-based machines, which dominated the market for another 5 years until the next generation of microprocessor-based machines became the market leader. Notice that the amount of time that each succeeding generation dominated the market decreased. The mechanical typewriter dominated the market for 25 years, but the first generation of microprocessor-based machines dominated the market for only 5 years. Couple significantly shorter product life cycles with a marketplace that is becoming increasingly competitive as a result of globalization, and you begin to get an idea of how important it is for organizations to be able to rapidly move ideas for new products and services from concept to market.

In the late 1980s McKinsey & Company conducted a study of the differences between leading and lagging companies with respect to commercialization (Nevens, Summe, and Uttal, 1990). The results of the study indicated that leading companies had the following four characteristics in common:

1. The leading companies commercialized two to three times as many new products and processes as their competitors (given equal sizes of firms).
2. The leading companies incorporated two to three times as many technologies in their products.
3. The leading companies were able to get their products to market in less than half the time than the laggards.
4. The leading companies tended to compete in twice as many product and geographic markets.

This study provided a number of other interesting insights related to commercialization. First, it was observed that the leading companies tended to view commercialization as a highly disciplined process. Also, not surprisingly, a strong relationship was observed between an organization's competitiveness and its commercialization capabilities. Further, the researchers observed that companies that are first-to-market with products based on new technologies tend to realize higher margins and increase their market shares. It is not uncommon for managers to dramatically underestimate the benefits of being first-to-market. For example, assume that you are leading a design team charged with designing a new laser printer. Assume that the market for laser printers is growing 20 percent annually, that prices for laser printers are declining by 12 percent per year, and that the life cycle for the printer is 5 years. As project leader, if you had to choose between incurring a 30 percent cost overrun to finish the project on schedule or miss the deadline by 6 months but meet the original budget, which would you choose? It turns out that under these circumstances incurring the 30 percent cost overrun will reduce cumulative profits by only 2.3 percent, whereas launching the printer six months late will reduce cumulative profits by approximately 33 percent!

The first step an organization should take to improve its commercialization capabilities is to begin to measure this capability. The McKinsey study suggested a number of measures of commercialization capability, including the following:

❖ *Time to market.* Earlier, we discussed the importance of getting products to the market as quickly as possible.

❖ *Range of markets.* As the cost of developing new technologies tends to be increasing, it is important for organizations to spread this development cost across multiple product and geographic markets.

❖ *Number of markets.* The McKinsey study found that the leading companies tended to serve more market segments than the laggards.

❖ *Breadth of technologies.* This refers to the number of different technologies a company has integrated into its new products and services.

Once appropriate measures for assessing commercialization capability have been established, organizations can begin working toward improving it. The McKinsey researchers recommend the following actions:

❖ *Make commercialization a priority.*

❖ *Set goals and benchmarks.*

❖ *Build cross-functional teams.*

❖ *Promote hands-on management to speed actions and decisions.*

$\mathscr{C}$HAPTER IN PERSPECTIVE _____

This has been the first chapter of three dealing with the business process associated with product and transformation system design. The design of products and services is strongly related to the material covered in Chapter 2 on business strategy and international competitiveness. For instance, the business strategy guides organizational efforts directed at selecting and designing new products and services. Furthermore, the ability to design and commercialize new products and services is a key determinant of an organization's overall competitive success.

In this chapter we saw that output selection and design consist of three stages: selection, design, and transformation system design. The importance of developing products and services that simultaneously meet customers' requirements and are producible, was discussed, as was the increasing importance of developing commercialization capabilities.

When the activities discussed in this chapter have been completed, new products and services have been selected and designed to enhance the organization's competitive position. Although production and delivery are considered to some extent in the design of a product, now the organization must focus its efforts on producing and delivering the output. Thus, in Chapter 6 we direct our attention to issues related to selecting an appropriate transformation system.

❖ CHECK YOUR UNDERSTANDING

1. Define the following terms: *mortality curve, breakeven, modularity, CAD, prototype, manufacturability,* and *reliability.*

2. Choose a product you are familiar with and discuss how the characteristics listed in Table 5.1 were probably chosen. How could some of these choices be modified to create new and perhaps improved versions of the product?

3. Briefly overview the three stages of output selection and design.

4. Contrast basic research, applied research, and development.

5. What are some alternatives to an organization conducting its own research?

6. Contrast product and process research.

7. Briefly list some of the key questions that the breakeven technique can help answer.

8. What trade-offs need to be considered in the preliminary design stage?

9. What are the key advantages of standardization? Of modularity?

10. What are the primary benefits of CAD?

11. What is quality function deployment? Why is it used?

12. What is meant by the term *commercialization?*

13. How can a computer test a product through CAE when the designer has just now dreamed it up and sketched it on the CAD screen? Can the computer test-drive a car? Can it test the appeal of a new line of furniture?

14. Describe how a service prototype might work.

15. What difficulties might develop during output design and development when each function "throws it over the wall" to the next function?

16. Contrast the two specific definitions of *reliability.* Provide examples of each measure.

17. In Figure 5.4, why do process innovations start increasing as the number of product innovations drops off, and then slow down and start decreasing with a further drop-off in product innovation?

18. Review the events that might occur in each of the steps of Figure 5.1 if a service was being selected and designed.

❖ EXPAND YOUR UNDERSTANDING

1. When might each of the factors in the *fit* checklist be important? What factors might be useful to add to the list?

2. As shown in the fit checklist, we add up the number of factors checked at each level of evaluation ("poor," "good," etc.) to determine how the factors spread across the levels. How might a total score be calculated if the factors varied in importance?

3. In what kind of organizations might new ideas have a low mortality rate? A high rate?

4. Has standardization hurt the service industry's image in any way?

5. For years, industry has tended to favor development over research, and product research over process research. How might this tendency be dangerous?

6. For what aspects of product and service design might new technologies be most important?

7. Managers like to use simple quantitative tools, such as breakeven, in spite of their simplistic, unrealistic treatment of costs and revenues compared with more sophisticated techniques, such as linear programming. Why do you think this is so?

8. Can you add any other trade-off factors to the list in Table 5.2? How might they trade off with the listed factors?

9. Is there any product or service you use that would be improved by greater industry standardization?

10. Consider a new product that comes in two battery sizes, three colors, two levels of performance, four weights, and two shapes. How many different combinations can be offered to customers? How many different modules will operations have to produce?

11. How ethical is it for a firm to imitate another firm's new idea instead of investing in its own research? Note that only the slightest change may be needed to avoid existing patent protection and lawsuits.

12. Many of the best-trained engineers and scientists of foreign competitors attended universities or

worked for firms in the United States. They now use their education and experience to compete against the same American firms. Is this ethical?

13. What might be the value of testing a prototype service in a foreign culture?

14. If technology is available, why bother with simplification or standardization?

15. What might be the advantages and disadvantages of using an international team to devise a new product or service?

16. Since the United States is a leader in advanced technology, how can foreign competitors develop new products and services in half the time it takes an American firm?

17. Since services are easier to compete in than products, why didn't foreign firms start with services when they invaded American markets?

18. Which is more profitable, product or process research? Which is likely to provide a more sustainable competitive advantage?

19. How might a service use the *house of quality?*

❖ APPLY YOUR UNDERSTANDING

Microstat, Inc.

After designing a highly innovative notebook computer as part of his senior engineering project at West Coast University, Patrick McKinsey founded Microstat to develop and market the computer. Having completed the initial design, Patrick decided that his first task was to find a company that could produce the computers. He searched a number of directories of the computer industry, discussed the matter with several of his former professors, and attended several industry trade shows in search of an appropriate company. As it turned out, several Korean electronics companies expressed an interest. After extensive follow-up discussions, Patrick decided to form a partnership with Leesung Electronics. As a relatively new company itself, Leesung had been particularly aggressive in trying to get Microstat's business.

With this decision made, Patrick spent his days designing a Web site that he planned to use to promote and sell the computer—and his nights working with Leesung's engineers to finalize the computer's design. Given that the primary selling point of his notebook computer was its highly innovative design, Patrick deemed it extremely important for the computer to incorporate the latest and most advanced technology and features. Leesung agreed to produce the computers as orders came in and to ship them to Microstat. Microstat would install the necessary software, test the computers, and then ship them directly to the customers. Patrick named his notebook computer the "2500 series," since he was 25 years old at the time.

Almost immediately, orders began to trickle in. Within a couple of months the volume of orders for the 2500 series exceeded even Patrick's most optimistic forecasts, despite its premium price. Much of this success was due to the praise the 2500 was receiving in computer magazines. Patrick quickly had to hire a number of employees to install the software, test the computers, and respond to E-mail from customers. During this time, Patrick preferred to spend his own time designing the next computer series (which he originally hoped would be the 2600 series but now seemed more likely to be the 2700). However, as the volume of business continued to grow, Patrick filled in wherever he was most needed, whether it was responding to E-mail inquiries, installing software, or packing up computers for shipment.

By the end of the first year, Microstat reached a landmark, selling 100 computers per day. If sales continued to grow at their current pace, Microstat would easily double its sales volume in the next year. However, even if the sales volume doubled, sales revenue would only show a slight increase and profits might actually decrease because price cuts had recently been forced on Microstat by new competitors. The importance of having a new follow-up product line quickly became apparent to Patrick.

During Microstat's second year, Patrick dedicated himself to the design of the 2700 series. His highest priority was to develop a new product that would enhance Microstat's reputation for highly innovative designs incorporating the latest technology. Because of its solid financial foundation, Patrick determined that Microstat would also produce the new 2700. Overall, Patrick was satisfied with Leesung's performance; however, he felt that the lead times resulting from using an overseas manufacturer were too long and could eventually become a competitive disadvantage.

The design for the 2700 series was becoming finalized midway through the second year, and Patrick found an electronics plant for sale in San Antonio that, with some minor modifications, could assemble it. Within a month, he purchased the plant and persuaded the plant manager and other key employees to stay on. By the end of the second year, the design for the 2700 was final, and it was in production at the plant in San Antonio.

Market acceptance of the 2700 series was extremely positive and all indications were that the 2700 would continue to fuel Microstat's growth. On the basis of this success, Patrick decided that Microstat would continue this strategy of introducing a new highly innovative model line incorporating the latest technology and features every two years. The two-year time frame would give Microstat $1\frac{1}{2}$ years to design the next computer series and six months to ramp-up the plant to produce it.

After the launch of the 2700 series, Patrick immediately formed a design team to begin work on the 2900 series. The design of the 2900 was proceeding on schedule and was to be handed off to production when a new cursor technology called a "touchpad" became available. Given Microstat's strategy of innovation, Patrick was adamant about incorporating a touchpad into the 2900. He argued that if the 2900 did not include a touchpad it would be another two years before Microstat had a computer that incorporated this technology, and that this would hurt Microstat's reputation. On the other hand, changing the design to incorporate the touchpad would require redesigning a significant portion of the computer and would add as much as four months to the design time, giving production only two months to ramp-up. Patrick immediately ruled out delaying the introduction of the 2900 series as inconsistent with Microstat's strategy. Microstat faced additional pressure because—unlike most of the other major notebook computer manufacturers, who changed their designs incrementally every six to nine months—Microstat modified its design only in conjunction with the launch of a new product line.

Ultimately, the 2900 was redesigned to incorporate the touchpad. The redesign delayed the project by $3\frac{1}{2}$ months, giving manufacturing less than half the time usually allocated for ramping-up production. By working numerous 15-hour days, six to seven days a week, the plant staff managed to get the new production line operational within the $2\frac{1}{2}$ months that remained.

Within a couple of months of the launch of the 2900 series, Microstat was experiencing an unusually large amount of returns for repairs. Extremely concerned that Microstat's image would be damaged, Patrick hired Amanda Jordan as Microstat's new director of quality. Amanda's first task was to identify the causes of the problem. She was to submit a report to Patrick detailing how the problem could be rectified and recommend ways to prevent such problems from occurring in the future.

Amanda began her investigation by interviewing the team leader in the rework area, Michael Scott. Michael commented:

> The majority of the computers are returned because of a missing resistor on one of the printed circuit boards or cracked casings where the display attaches to the base, or both. The casings are cracking because the plastic material we used simply cannot withstand the pressure the hinges place on the base when the computer is opened and closed.

On the basis of the information Michael provided, Amanda decided that she would follow up with the production manager, Bill Mitchell. After introducing herself to Bill, she explained that she was interested in determining the cause of the missing resistor and the cracked casings. Bill began:

In my opinion, the problem of the missing resistor is a result of our not having enough time to ramp-up production. To be perfectly honest, $2\frac{1}{2}$ months is not enough time to set up, test, and debug a new production line for a brand-new product. To me its actually amazing that we did get the line up and running in such a short time. But looking back, there is no way we could have done an adequate job of testing the product and working out the bugs in the process.

The problem with the casing is also related to not having enough time. I don't know how much you know about our product development process. The way it works is that the engineers begin designing a computer. At various times during the design, the engineers and some highly skilled technicians build a prototype to see how the design is progressing and to help them get a feel for the computer. Because only a few prototypes are constructed, different materials, suppliers, and production methods are used to make them. Thus, although the plastic casing material used in the prototypes held up fine, the production-grade material we selected does not. Had we had more time to test the computer, we would have most likely discovered this problem and been in a good position to change the material.

Questions

1. In what ways does Microstat's approach to developing new products contribute to its problems with quality?

2. In hindsight, do you think Patrick made the right decision when he incorporated the touchpad into the 2900, reduced the ramp-up time, and did not delay the 2900's introduction?

3. What would be the advantages of including production earlier in the product development process?

❖ EXERCISES

1. Given a fixed cost of $8000, a variable cost of $5, and a price of $8, what is the breakeven volume?

2. What is the net profit at a volume of 1000 units if the fixed cost is $5000, the variable cost is $2, and the price is $4? What is the net profit at a volume of 10,000?

3. What is the net profit at a volume of 2000 if the fixed cost is $0, the variable cost is $2, and the price is $4? What is the net profit at a volume of 2000 if the fixed cost is $5000, the variable cost is $0, and the price is $4?

4. What is the breakeven volume if the fixed cost is $3000, the variable cost is $0, and the price is $2?

5. What is the breakeven volume if the fixed cost is $3000 and the unit margin is $1.50?

6. What is the breakeven volume if the fixed cost is $3000, the variable cost is $4, and the price is set at 10 percent over variable cost?

7. The breakeven volume had to be revised for a particular component whose price was $3 per unit and whose unit variable cost was $1.50. Owing to an unforeseen escalation in material costs, there was a 10 percent increase in unit variable cost, and thus the breakeven volume had to be revised. By what percentage did the breakeven increase or decrease?

8. Given a fixed cost of $2000, a unit variable cost of $180, a price of $200, and a current sales volume of 120, how should $200 be invested if it can be used either to decrease variable cost by 10 percent or to increase sales volume by 15 percent? Find the net profitability of each alternative.

9. The controller of ABC Company arrived at the following cost structure relating to the introduction of a new product. Calculate the breakeven volume, assuming a price of 7.75 per unit.

	Production 10,000 Units	Volume 20,000 Units
Capital costs	60,000	60,000
Material at 1.50 per unit	15,000	30,000
Labor at 0.75 per unit	7500	15,000
Overhead		
Fixed	10,000	10,000
Variable at 0.25 per unit	2500	5000
Selling and administrative expense		
Fixed	5000	5000
Variable	7500	10,000
Total costs	107,500	135,000

10. Refer back to Exercise 1. Find the impact on the breakeven volume and profit of a 10 percent change in fixed cost; in variable cost; in price.

11. In the spreadsheet shown below, what formula should be entered into cell B7 to calculate the volume required given the model inputs that have been entered in cells B2:B5?

	A	B
1	Model inputs:	
2	revenue/unit	150
3	cost/unit	100
4	fixed cost	50,000
5	desired profit	$100,000
6	Model outputs:	
7	volume	

12. Develop a spreadsheet for Exercise 11. Note that the model inputs in column B are entered as constants, but a formula should be entered in cell B7. Use the spreadsheet to determine the volumes required to achieve a profit of $0, $10,000, and $100,000.

13. It cost ABC Sports $7 to restring a tennis racket (including both materials and labor). ABC's fixed costs are $75,000, and it restrings 25,000 rackets each year. Use Excel's Goal Seek function to find the amount ABC should charge per restrung racket if it desires to earn a $75,000 profit.

14. Develop the three QFD tables shown in Figure 5.10 for an introductory course on spreadsheets and word processors to be taken by first-year business students.

Chapter 6

The Transformation System

C HAPTER OVERVIEW

- ❖ The five basic forms of transformation systems are continuous process, flow shop, job shop, cellular, and project. Most organizations use combinations of these five forms to produce their outputs, considering the trade-offs with each form to devise the best production system.

- ❖ The continuous process industries use highly automated equipment to transform their fluid inputs into fluid outputs. Fixed costs are usually very high, and the input materials constitute the major variable cost.

- ❖ In flow shops, the process is also relatively continuous, with large investments in equipment. However, there may be multiple inputs to produce a single output or multiple discrete outputs. The primary advantages of the flow shop are its low cost and short lead times if the volumes are high. Disadvantages include low variety, labor boredom, vulnerability to a breakdown, and high initial cost of equipment.

- ❖ Job shops are divided into departments with relatively identical general-purpose equipment and highly skilled labor. Jobs must travel from department to department to obtain all the operations they need to be completed. The major advantage of the job shop is its ability to customize to suit the specific needs of a job or customer. However,

it achieves this ability at a high price. Usually, "batches" of outputs are produced instead. Managerial control of the job shop is also difficult because of the unique routing of each of the jobs and the need for constant monitoring.

- ❖ Cellular production is a relatively new form that combines the advantages of flow and job shops. In essence, the shop is divided into a number of discrete cells, each of which is a flow shop but produces, through a team of workers, a different "family" of outputs. Thus, some variety is available, as well as short lead times and low costs. The cells may be highly automated or manual; thus, up-front investment in equipment usually does not preclude adopting cellular production.

- ❖ Project operations are usually very large in scope, with a large number of different, sometimes simultaneous, activities requiring careful coordination to accomplish completion by a set time. Every job is different in some way. The materials are usually "staged" around the location where the output is to be performed, created, or produced, and the transformation is orchestrated by careful managerial planning and control. The major advantage of the project form is the ability to coordinate multiple activities to accomplish a goal within cost and time constraints.

❖ In general, as volumes increase and variety decreases, the most appropriate transformation form moves from project to job shop to cellular to flow shop to (if appropriate) continuous process. Accompanying this movement is an increasing percentage of make-to-stock production and a decreasing percentage of make-to-order production.

❖ Over its life cycle, as an output becomes standardized and more widely accepted, the transformation system also tends to change, from forms most appropriate for low volumes and high variety (project, and then job shop) to cellular form and then to forms appropriate for reduced variety but large volumes (flow shop and, if appropriate, continuous process).

❖ Because of the abstract nature of some services, training and education can be more important for these services than for product outputs. Designs for service transformation systems generally include an additional factor—the amount of customer contact. High-contact operations should employ workers with good social skills, whereas low-contact operations should use workers with good technical skills. If different operations in the service can be "decoupled" from the customer, thereby becoming low-contact or no-contact operations, they can be automated or made much more efficient through more technical labor and equipment.

❖ New service transformation technologies are based primarily on the power of the computer and include scanners, control systems, telecommunications, word processing systems, decision support systems, expert systems, artificial intelligence, the Internet, and the World Wide Web. The new manufacturing technologies are also largely computer-based. These technologies include numerical control, robots, and flexible manufacturing systems. Through the new technologies, the factory of the future will offer minimal lead times, unit batches, high quality, easy replicability, continuous operation, and integrated operation. However, it will require large fixed equipment costs and will be quite vulnerable to breakdowns.

❖ Fender's Custom Shop has produced guitars for many famous and gifted guitarists including Eric Clapton, John Deacon (Queen), David Gilmour (Pink Floyd), Yngwie Malmsteen, and Stevie Ray Vaughan, to name a few. The Custom Shop uses relatively new equipment and in some cases prototypical equipment.

To produce guitars, computer-controlled routers and lathes are first used to shape the bodies and necks to precise tolerances. Also, Fender has a state-of-the-art machine called a *neck duplicator,* which can produce a copy of the neck of any existing guitar. After the necks and bodies are fabricated, they are hand- and machine-sanded. Next, detailed inlay work is done with a Hegner precision scroll saw. Following this, paint and finishing operations are done in a special room where air is recirculated 10 times per minute to keep dust and impurities out of the finishes. After paint and finishing, the guitar parts are buffed and then hung up to be seasoned for two weeks. Next, they are moved to the final assembly area, where necks are attached to bodies, and the electronics and hardware are installed. Final assembly of the guitars is done by actual musicians (Bradley, 1988).

❖ Electronic Hardware Corp. (EHC) is a small manufacturer of plastic components, such as control knobs, for the aerospace, industrial, and consumer markets. At one time, as a result of reductions in defense spending, the company was struggling for survival. Its cash flow was poor, its accounts payable extended beyond 100 days, its credit line was exhausted, and on top of this, its suppliers were beginning to cut off shipments of raw materials. In an effort to turn this situation around, managers at EHC determined that a transition to cellular manufacturing was needed. Because EHC had no funds available to finance this transition, the cell project team needed to develop creative solutions so that existing machines and tooling could be used in the newly formed cells. The cell project team determined that seven cells were needed, each cell to be staffed with two operators. The cells were designed so that they could produce a complete product that would be ready for shipment to the customer.

The transition to cellular manufacturing was very successful at EHC. After one year of using the cells, work-in-process was reduced 55 percent, manufacturing lead time was reduced from five weeks to less than one week, customer returns were reduced from 4 percent to 1.5 percent, productivity increased from 39 to 60 pieces per hour, sales increased by 36 percent, and the morale of the operators improved considerably (Stone, 1996).

❖ The assembly line at IBM's plant in Charlotte, North Carolina, is unlike any other in the world. What makes it unique is that it was designed to produce 27 significantly different products. Indeed, the variety of products produced by the team of 40 workers who operate this line is astounding; these products include hand-held barcode scanners, portable medical computers, fiber-optic connectors, and satellite communications devices. The assembly line operates by delivering to each worker a "kit" of parts based on the production schedule. Since each product requires different assembly procedures, each worker has a computer screen at his or her station that displays updated assembly instructions for the current product (Bylinsky, 1994).

❖ Rickard Associates is an editorial production company that produces magazines and marketing materials. Interestingly, only two of its employees actually work at its headquarters in New Jersey. The art director works in Arizona; the editors are located in Florida, Georgia, Michigan, and the District of Columbia; and the freelancers are even more scattered. To coordinate work, the Internet and America Online are used. For example, art directors are able to submit electronic copies of finished pages to headquarters in a matter of minutes using these computer networks (Verity, 1994).

Chapter 5 discussed the degree to which outputs are customized or standardized. Among the examples above, Fender's Custom Shop produces highly customized guitars, but IBM uses an assembly line to mass-produce a variety of standard products. As we will see in the present chapter, the degree to which an organization's outputs are customized or standardized significantly influences the appropriateness of alternative transformation systems.

The above examples illustrate several transformation systems. The Fender Custom Shop is a job shop that has specialized departments for routing, and lathe operations, inlaying, paint and finishing, and final assembly. Likewise, because work is organized by the task performed, Rickard Associates is also a job shop—even though the work is not performed in one location. Actually, companies like Rickard, which rely on information technology to bring separated workers together, are beginning to be known as *virtual organizations.* EHC converted its job shop into another type of transformation process, cellular manufacturing. Assembly lines like the one IBM uses are referred to as flow shops.

This chapter continues the discussion of the design of the transformation system initially presented in Chapter 5. There, our discussion centered on the interdependence of developing a new product or service and developing the transformation system to produce and deliver it. Chapters 6 and 7 are devoted to the design of the transformation system for maximum competitiveness. The present chapter will cover selecting the form of a transformation system, describing the five basic forms. Continuing the discussion of the five forms, Chapter 7 will conclude Part Two by describing how the operations are laid out for each form.

The general procedure in designing a transformation system is to consider all alternative forms and combinations to devise the best strategy for obtaining the desired outputs. The major considerations in designing the transformation system— *efficiency, effectiveness, capacity, lead time, flexibility,* and so on—are so interdependent that changing the system to alter one will change the others as well.

Suppose, for example, that you decide to go into business for yourself to produce skateboards. Many options are open to you. In terms of the product, you could produce wooden, plastic, or metal skateboards. The wheels, too, could be steel or high-impact plastic, perhaps tinted or bright translucent red.

A wooden board might be easiest to make; you could even work out of your own garage. On the other hand, each board would take quite awhile to saw, laminate, glue, sand, and so on. Injection-molding a plastic board would be much faster. You could produce plastic boards by the thousands at very low cost. But because the molding dies would cost you about $30,000—exceeding your financial resources—you would probably have to outsource the work.

So far we have been talking about capacity and flexibility. That is, garage-produced wooden boards would be a low-capacity, high-flexibility operation appropriate for low volumes at high prices. But is there a market for wooden boards at high prices? If not, such an operation will not be very *effective*—at least, not in terms of making a profit. Perhaps a more effective process would be to invest in some semi-automatic equipment to produce a higher volume at a lower unit price.

As you can see from this simple example, the design of a transformation system is a rather complex, but crucially important, procedure. Numerous trade-offs are possible between different materials, labor and equipment, quality and volume, efficiency and flexibility; and every trade-off will affect the success of your business.

In a constantly changing environment, the transformation system may have to be constantly maintained and even redesigned to cope with new demands, new products and services, new government regulations, and new technology. Robots, microcomputers, increasing global competition, and shortages of materials and energy are only a few examples of changes in the past decade that have forced organizations to recognize the necessity of adapting their operations.

As noted, the five basic forms of transformation systems are (1) continuous process, (2) flow shop, (3) job shop, (4) cellular, and (5) project. The continuous process industries are in many ways the most advanced, moving fluid material continuously through vats and pipes until a final product is obtained. Flow shops produce discrete, usually standardized, outputs on a continuous basis by means of assembly lines or mass production, often using automated equipment. Cellular shops produce "families" of outputs within a variety of flow cells, but numerous cells within the plant can offer a range of families of outputs. Job shops offer a wide range of possible outputs, usually in batches, by individualized processing into and out of a number of functionally specialized departments. These departments typically consist of a set of largely identical equipment, as well as highly skilled workers. (Potentially, job shops could also produce unique—that is, one-of-a-kind—customized outputs, but job shops that do this are commonly called *model shops* or, in Europe, *jobbers*.) Finally, projects are one-of-a-kind endeavors on a massive scale when the labor and equipment are brought to a site rather than to a fixed production facility. In the following section we describe each of these forms in detail.

FORMS OF TRANSFORMATION SYSTEMS

❖ Continuous Process

The **continuous transformation process** is used to produce highly standardized products in extremely large volumes. In some cases these products have become so standardized that there are virtually no real differences between the products of different firms. Examples of such *commodities* include water, gases, chemicals, ores, rubber, flour, spirits, cements, petroleum, and milk. The name *continuous process* reflects the typical practice of running these operations 24 hours a day, seven days a week. One reason for running these systems continuously is to spread their enormous fixed cost over as large a volume as possible, thereby reducing unit costs. This is particularly important in commodity markets, where price can be the single most important factor in competing successfully. Another reason for operating these processes continuously is that stopping and starting them can be prohibitively expensive.

The operations in these industries are highly automated, with very specialized equipment and controls, often electronic and computerized. Such automation and the expense it entails are necessary because of strict processing requirements. Because of the highly specialized and automated nature of the equipment, changing the rate of output can be quite difficult. The facility is typically a maze of pipes, conveyors, tanks, valves, vats, and bins. The layout follows the *processing stages* of the product, and the output rate is controlled through equipment capacity and flow and mixture rates. Labor requirements are low and are devoted primarily to monitoring and maintaining the equipment.

The major characteristic of processing industries is that there is usually one primary, "fluid"-type input material (gas, wood, wheat, milk, etc.). This input is then often converted to multiple outputs, although there may be only one (e.g., water). In contrast, in discrete production many types of materials are made or purchased and combined to form the output.

In a processing industry we can visualize the process as having a singular input and many separate outputs. This is referred to as an *analytic process*. In *discrete* production, on the other hand, we visualize many materials coming together to form a singular (discrete) output; this is known as a *synthetic process*. (Synthetic fabrics require joining many inputs to make a single fiber, such as nylon.)

These descriptions are not definitive but are merely aids in visualizing and understanding the concept. Probably no organization uses a purely synthetic or analytic transformation system; rather, many combinations of the two are used. Our definition of "fluid" inputs is itself rather fluid, including granulated plastics, crushed ores, and powdered foods. Production specifications must include the order of adding various materials, the operations (including temperatures, times, etc.) to be conducted on the materials, where storage is to be located, what operations must be conducted simultaneously, and so on. Materials must come together in the proper amounts at the right time. Rates must be strictly regulated and operations carefully "balanced" to achieve perfect control over the production system.

Although human variation in continuous processing firms does not usually create the problems it creates in discrete manufacturing, the demands of processing are usually more critical. For example, chemical reactions must be accurately timed. The result is that initial setup of equipment and procedures is even more complex and critical than it is for flow shops. Fixed costs are extremely high; the major variable cost is materials. Variable labor (excluding distribution) is usually insignificant.

❖ Flow Shop

The ***flow shop*** is a transformation system very similar to the continuous process, the major difference being that in the flow shop there is a discrete product, whereas in continuous processes the end product is not naturally divisible. Thus, in continuous processes an additional step such as bottling or canning may be needed to get the product into discrete units. Like the continuous process, the flow shop treats all the outputs as basically the same, and the flow of work is thus relatively continuous. Organizations that use this form are heavily automated, with large, special-purpose equipment. The characteristics of the flow shop are a fixed set of inputs, constant throughput times, and a fixed set of outputs. Examples of the flow form are pencil manufacturing, steelmaking, automobile assembly, the car wash, and processing insurance claims.

An organization that produces, or plans to produce, a high volume of a small variety of outputs will thus probably organize its operations as a flow shop. In doing so, the organization will take advantage of the simplicity and the savings in variable costs that such an approach offers. Since outputs and operations are standardized, specialized equipment can be used to perform the necessary operations at low per

A paper mill—a good example of a process industry.

unit costs, and the relatively large fixed costs of the equipment are distributed over a large volume of outputs.

Continuous types of materials-handling equipment, such as conveyors—again operating at low per unit costs—can be used because the operations are standardized and, typically, all outputs follow the same path from one operation to the next. This standardization of treatment provides for a known, fixed throughput time, giving managers easier control of the system and more reliable delivery dates. The flow shop is easier to manage for other reasons as well: routing, scheduling, and control are all facilitated because each output does not have to be individually monitored and controlled. Standardization of operations means that less skilled workers can be used and each manager's span of control can increase.

The general form of the flow shop is illustrated in Figure 6.1, which shows a *production line*. (If only assembly operations were being performed, as in many automotive plants, the line would be called an *assembly line*.) This production line could represent new military inductees taking their physical exams, small appliances being assembled, or double-decker hamburgers being prepared.

Note that both services and products can be organized as flow shops and can capitalize on the many advantages of this form of processing.

Advantages of the Flow Shop

The primary advantage of a flow shop is the low per unit cost that is attainable owing to specialized high-volume equipment, bulk purchasing, lower labor rates, efficient utilization of the facility, low in-process inventories, and simplified managerial control. Because of the high rate of output, materials can often be bought in

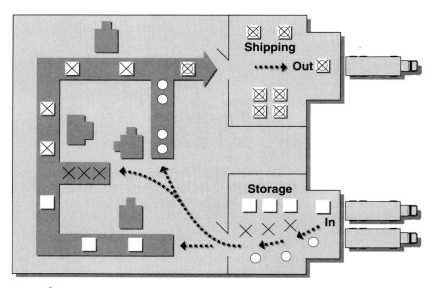

Figure 6.1 A generalized flow shop operation.

large quantities at a significant savings. Also, because operations are standardized, processing times tend to remain constant so that large in-process inventories are not required to queue up for processing. This minimizes investment in in-process inventory and queue (buffer) space. Also, because a standardized product is produced, inventory control and purchasing decisions are routine.

Because the machines are specialized, operators can be less skilled, and therefore lower wages can be paid. In addition, fewer supervisors are needed, further reducing costs. Since the flow shop is generally continuous, with materials handling often built into the system itself, the operations can be designed to perform compactly and efficiently with narrow aisles, thereby making maximum use of space.

The simplification in managerial control of a well-designed flow shop should not be overlooked. Constant operations problems requiring unending managerial attention penalize the organization by distracting managers from their normal duties—planning and decision making.

Disadvantages of the Flow Shop

In spite of the very important cost advantage of the flow shop, it can have some serious drawbacks. Not only is a variety of output difficult to obtain; even changes in the rate of output are hard to make. Changing the *rate* of output may require using overtime, laying off workers, adding additional shifts, or temporarily closing the plant. Also, because the equipment is so specialized, minor changes in the design of the product often require substantial changes in the equipment. Thus, important changes in product design are infrequent, and this weakens the organization's marketing position.

A well-known problem in flow manufacturing is boredom and absenteeism among the labor force. Since the equipment performs the skilled tasks, there is no challenge for the workers. And, of course, the constant, unending, repetitive nature of the manufacturing line can dehumanize the workers. Since the rate of work flow is generally set (*paced*) by the line speed, incentive pay and other output-based incentives are not possible.

The flow production line form has another important drawback. If the line should stop for any reason—a breakdown of a machine or conveyor, a shortage of supplies, and so forth—production may come to an immediate halt unless work-in-process (WIP) is stored at key points in the line. Such occurrences are prohibitively expensive.

Other requirements of the flow shop also add to its cost and its problems. For example, parts must be standardized so that they will fit together easily and quickly on the assembly line. And, since all machines and labor must work at the same repetitive pace in order to coordinate operations, the work loads along the entire line are generally *balanced* to the pace of the slowest element. To keep the line running smoothly, a large support staff is required, as well as large stocks of raw materials, all of which also add to the expense.

Last, in the flow shop, simplicity in *ongoing operation* is achieved at the cost of complexity in the initial *setup*. The planning, design, and installation of the typically complicated, special-purpose, high-volume equipment are mammoth tasks. The equipment is costly not only to set up originally but also to maintain and service. Furthermore, such special-purpose equipment is very susceptible to obsolescence and is difficult to dispose of or modify for other purposes.

❖ Job Shop

The *job shop* gets its name because unique jobs must be produced. In this form of transformation system each output, or each small batch of outputs, is processed differently. Therefore, the flow of work through the facility tends to be intermittent.

Conveyors complete the process flow at packaging.

The general characteristics of a job shop are *grouping* of staff and equipment according to function; a large *variety* of inputs; a considerable amount of *transport* of staff, materials, or recipients; and large *variations* in system flow times (the time it takes for a complete "job"). In general, each output takes a different route through the organization, requires different operations, uses different inputs, and takes a different amount of time.

This type of transformation system is common when the outputs differ significantly in form, structure, materials, or processing required. For example, an organization that has a wide variety of outputs or does custom work (e.g., custom skateboards) would probably be a job shop. Specific examples of product and service organizations of this form are tailor shops, general offices, machine shops, public parks, hospitals, universities, automobile repair shops, criminal justice systems, and department stores. By and large, the job shop is especially appropriate for service organizations because services are often customized, and hence each service requires different operations. This is illustrated in the following example.

Little People's Day Care

Suppose you have decided to open up a neighborhood day care service. As parents tend to find out after a while, every child is different. This means that your care for children will probably also have to be different. Some like to be read to, others like to be left alone; some like toys, others like television, still others want to play with children like themselves; and almost all like to eat (but they like to eat different things). As you can imagine, this makes for quite a mess.

You will need general-purpose equipment (television, play yards, bicycles, tables, chairs) that will appeal to general interests and varied ages. You cannot afford to buy equipment that only an 18-month-old is interested in—you may not even get an 18-month old. Similarly, your staff should be broadly skilled—equally at home keeping records and forms, playing the piano, and making mud pies. Again, you cannot afford someone who can only keep books and hates mud.

What you have started is an organization designed as a job shop. An organization that wants to produce a wide variety of individualized outputs (reading, eating, playing) will probably use this transformation form in order to gain the *flexibility* required to produce that large variety. General-purpose equipment and a broadly skilled staff are necessary. Also, because of the variety of outputs, there is usually a need for a variety of input materials.

Since only small volumes of any one output are produced, it is not worthwhile to form production lines for the outputs. (In a production line each child, one at a time, would first eat, then play with toys, then go to the restroom, then to the playground, then listen to music, etc.) Instead of organizing around standard *outputs*, the most efficient procedure for job-based production is to organize around standard *operations functions*. Thus, all similar types of operations are grouped together. For example, all the children have juice and crackers in one spot, play in the sandbox at another spot, watch television and play video games in yet another area, and so on. In a hospital, all X-ray functions are grouped together, as are the laboratory functions, the maternity wing, the psychiatric wing, and the burns unit.

The result of such a transformation system design is that each output or each small group of outputs follows a different processing route through the facility, from one location to another. As a result, this type of transformation system usually requires a considerable amount of transportation equipment: forklifts, pallet trucks, little legs, dumbwaiters, wheelchairs, and so forth. Also because all outputs are processed differently, large variations in throughput time result. (Some hospital patients may require only an overnight stay; others may require a much longer stay.) Each output may require different operations or sequences, thereby using different paths through the system. In some instances, all the outputs require one common operation (such as use of the restroom or, in manufacturing, inspection), and hence bottlenecks may occur.

Clearly, the efficient management of a job shop is a difficult task, since every output must be treated differently. In addition, the resources available for processing are limited. Furthermore, not only is it management's task to ensure the performance of the proper functions of each output, where considerations of quality and deadlines may vary, but management must also be sure that the available resources (staff, equipment, materials, supplies, capital) are being efficiently utilized. Often there is a difficult trade-off between efficiency and flexibility of operations. Job-based processes tend to emphasize flexibility over efficiency.

Figure 6.2 represents the flow through a job shop. This facility might be a library, an auto repair shop, or an office. Each particular "job" travels from one area to another, and so on, according to its unique routing, until it is fully processed. Temporary in-process storage may occur between various operations while jobs are waiting for subsequent processing (standing in line for the coffee machine).

Advantages of the Job Shop

The widespread use of the job shop form is due to its many advantages. The job shop is usually selected to provide the organization with the flexibility needed to respond to individual, small-volume demands (or even custom demands). The ability to produce a wide variety of outputs at reasonable cost is thus the primary advantage of this form. General-purpose equipment is used, and this is in greater

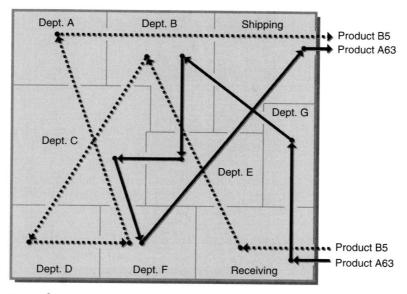

Figure 6.2   A generalized job shop operation.

demand and is usually available from more suppliers at a lower price than special-purpose equipment. In addition, used equipment is more likely to be available, further reducing the necessary investment. There is a larger base of experience with general-purpose equipment; therefore, problems with installation and maintenance are more predictable, and replacement parts are more widely available. Last, since general-purpose equipment is easier to modify or use elsewhere and disposal is much easier, the expense of obsolescence is minimized.

Because of the functional arrangement of the equipment, there are also other advantages. Resources for a function requiring special staff, materials, or facilities (e.g., painting or audiovisual equipment) may be centralized at the location of that function, and the organization can thus save expense through high utilization rates. Distracting or dangerous equipment, supplies, or activities may also be segregated from other operations in facilities that are soundproof, airtight, explosion-proof, and so forth.

One advantage to the staff is that with more highly skilled work involving constantly varying jobs, responsibility and pride in one's work are increased, and boredom is reduced. Other advantages to the staff are that concentrations of experience and expertise are available and morale increases when people with similar skills work together in centralized locations (all music teachers together). Because all workers who perform similar activities are grouped together, each worker has the opportunity to learn from others, and the workers can easily collaborate to solve difficult problems. Furthermore, because the pace of the work is not dictated by a moving "line," incentive arrangements may be set up. Last, because no line exists that must forever keep moving, the entire set of organizational operations does not halt whenever any one part of the operation stops working; other functional areas can continue operating, at least until in-process inventory is depleted. Also, other general-purpose resources can usually substitute for the nonfunctioning resource: one machine for another, one staff member for another, one material for another.

Disadvantages of the Job Shop

The general-purpose equipment of job shops is usually slower than special-purpose equipment, resulting in higher variable (per unit) costs. In addition, the cost of direct labor for the experienced staff necessary to operate general-purpose equipment further increases unit costs of production above what semi-skilled or unskilled workers would require. The result, in terms of costs of the outputs, is that the variable costs of production are higher for the general-purpose than for the special-purpose equipment, facilities, and staff, but the initial cost of the equipment and facilities is significantly less. For small-output volumes the job shop results in a lower total cost. As volume of output increases, however, the high variable costs begin to outweigh the savings in initial investment. The result is that, for high production volumes, the job shop is not the most economic approach (although its use may still be dictated by other considerations, as when particular equipment threatens workers' health or safety).

Inventories are also frequently a disadvantage in the job shop, especially in product organizations. Not only do many types of raw materials, parts, and supplies have to be kept for the wide variety of outputs anticipated, but *in-process inventories*, that is, jobs waiting for processing, typically become very large and thereby represent a sizable capital investment for the organization. It is not unusual for batches of parts in these environments to spend 90 to 95 percent of the time they are in the shop either waiting to be moved or waiting to be processed. Furthermore, because there are so many inventory items that must travel between operating departments in order to be processed, the cost of handling materials is also typically high. Since job routings between operations are not identical, inexpensive fixed materials-handling mechanisms like conveyor belts cannot be used. Instead, larger and more costly equipment is used; therefore, corridors and aisles must be large enough to accommodate it. This necessitates allocating even more space, beyond the extra space needed to store additional inventories.

Finally, managerial control of the job shop is extremely difficult, as mentioned earlier. Because the output varies in terms of function, processing, quality, and timing, the managerial tasks of routing, scheduling, cost accounting, and such become nearly impossible when demand for the output is high. Expediters must track down lost jobs and reorder priorities. In addition to watching the progress of individual jobs, management must continually strive to achieve the proper balance of materials, staff, and equipment; otherwise, highly expensive resources will sit idle while bottlenecks occur elsewhere. (In Chapter 15 we discuss some of the scheduling techniques available to help manage such problems.)

❖ Cellular Production

Cellular production is a relatively new type of transformation system that many firms have recently been adopting. It combines the advantages of the job shop and flow shop to obtain the high variety possible with the job form and the reduced costs and short response times available with the flow form. Figure 6.3 contrasts the

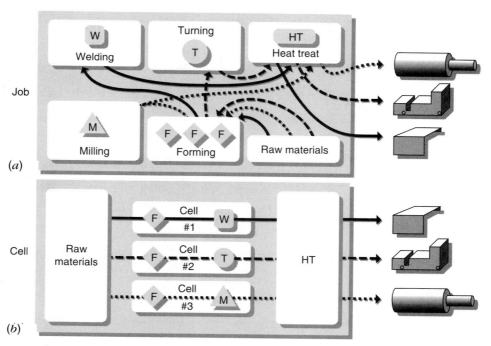

Figure 6.3   Conversion of (a) a job shop layout into (b) a cellular layout for part families.

job shop with cellular production. The job shop in Figure 6.3*a* has separate departments for welding, turning, heat treat, milling, and forming. This type of layout provides flexibility to produce a wide range of products simply by varying the sequence in which the products visit the five processing departments. Also, flexibility is enhanced, as machines are easily substituted for one another should a specified machine be busy or nonoperational.

Figure 6.3*b* shows cellular production. The cellular form is based on **group technology,** which seeks to achieve efficiency by exploiting similarities inherent in parts. In production, this is accomplished by identifying groups of parts that have similar processing requirements. Parts with similar processing requirements are called *part families.* Figure 6.4 provides an example of how a variety of parts can be organized into part families.

After the parts are divided into families, a **cell** is created that includes the human skills and all the equipment required to produce a family. Since the outputs are all similar, the equipment can be set up in one pattern to produce the entire family and does not need to be set up again for another type of output (as is necessary in a job shop). Some cells consist of just one machine producing a complete product or service. Other cells may have as many as 50 people working with dozens of machines.

A facility using cells is generally organized on the basis of *teams.* That is, a team is completely responsible for conducting the work within its cell. The team mem-

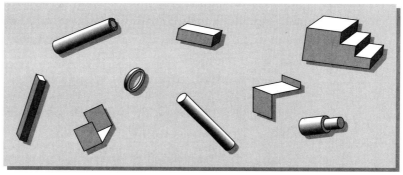

Unorganized parts

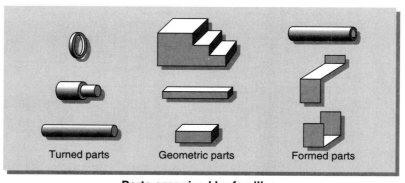

Turned parts   Geometric parts   Formed parts

Parts organized by families

Figure 6.4   Organization of miscellaneous parts into families.

bers usually schedule and inspect the work themselves, once they know when it is due. Occasionally, work must be taken outside a cell for a special treatment or process that is unavailable within the cell, but these operations are minimized whenever possible.

The families are derived from one of a number of different approaches. Sometimes the basis is the machines that are needed to produce the output, or the families may be based on the size of the equipment, the quality required, the skills needed, or any other overriding consideration. This is called the *classification stage*. Items are classified into families—sometimes by simple inspection and other times by complex analysis of their routing requirements, production requirements, part geometry, and the like. It is generally not feasible to classify all the outputs into one of a limited number of families, so at some point all the miscellaneous outputs are placed in a "remainder" cell, which is operated as a mini–job shop.

Advantages of Cellular Production

Organizations adopt the cellular form to achieve many of the efficiencies associated with products that are mass-produced using flow transformation systems in less repetitive job shop environments. However, not all the advantages of a full flow shop or a full job shop can be obtained, because not enough high-volume equipment can be purchased to obtain the economies of scale that flow shops enjoy. And because the equipment is dedicated to part families, some of the variety afforded by job shops is lost.

One of the most important advantages of the cellular form is reduced machine setup times. In the job shop, when a worker completes the processing of the batch being worked on, the machine is set up for the next batch. Because a wide variety of parts typically flow through each department in a job shop, there is a good chance that the next batch of parts processed by the worker will be very different from the one just completed. This means that the worker may have to spend several hours or more simply setting up and preparing the machine for the next batch of parts. In cellular production, machine setup times are minimized because each cell processes only parts that have similar (or identical) setup and processing requirements. It is extremely desirable to minimize machine setup times because setup time takes away from the amount of time machines can be used to produce the outputs.

Decreasing machine setup times provides several benefits. First, as we have just noted, when setup times decrease, the amount of time equipment is available to process parts increases. Second, increased capacity means that the company can produce at a given level with fewer machines. Reducing the number of machines used not only reduces the costs of equipment and maintenance, but also reduces the amount of floor space needed. Third, shorter setup times make it more economical to produce smaller batches. For instance, if the setup time is four hours, it would not be efficient to produce a small number of parts using a particular machine only to spend another four hours to set it up for the next batch. However, if the machine required only a few minutes of setup time, it might be practical to produce a few parts on the machine.

There are numerous benefits associated with producing parts in small batches. To begin, producing small batches enhances an organization's flexibility in responding to changes in product mix. Also, reducing the size of batches leads to reductions in work-in-process inventory. Less inventory means that less space is needed to store it and less capital is tied up in it. Also, product lead times are shorter, and shorter lead times facilitate more accurate forecasting and may also provide a competitive advantage.

Another major advantage of the cellular form is that parts are produced in one cell. Processing the parts in one cell simplifies control of the shop floor. To illustrate this, compare the amount of effort required to coordinate the production activities in the job shop and the cellular layout shown in Figure 6.3. Producing parts in a single cell also reduces the amount of labor and equipment needed to move materials because travel distances between successive operations are shorter. Additionally, producing the parts in one cell provides an opportunity to increase the workers' accountability, responsibility, and autonomy. Finally, reducing material handling and increasing the workers' accountability typically translates into reduced defects. In a job shop, it is difficult to hold the workers accountable for quality because the product is processed in several different departments and the workers in one department can always blame problems on another department.

A unique advantage of the cell form is that it maximizes the inherent benefits of the team approach. In a flow shop, there is little teamwork, because the equipment does most of the work; the labor primarily involves oversight and maintenance. Job shops are organized by department, and this allows for some teamwork—but not in terms of specific jobs, because everyone is working on a different job. In a cell, all the workers are totally responsible for completing every job. Thus, the effect is to enrich the work, provide challenges, encourage communication and teamwork, meet due dates, and maintain quality.

An additional advantage for manufacturers is the minimal cost required to move to cellular production. Although some cells may be highly automated, with expensive special-purpose equipment, it is not necessary to invest any additional capital in order to adopt the cellular form, as was illustrated at the beginning of this chapter by the example of EHC. It requires only the movement of equipment and labor into cells. Or, with even less trouble—though with some loss of efficiency—the firm can simply designate certain pieces of equipment as dedicated to a single part family, but not relocate them. The term used in this case is *virtual cell* or *logical cell*, since the equipment is not physically adjoining but is still reserved for production of only one part family.

Another form of cellular production is called a mini-plant. Here, the cell not only does the manufacturing but also has its own industrial engineer, quality manager, accountant, marketing representative, and salesperson, and almost all the other support services that a regular plant has. Only far-removed services, such as R&D and human resources, are not dedicated to the mini-plant. The entire facility of the firm is thus broken down into a number of mini-plants, each with its own general manager, production workers, and support services so that it can operate as an independent profit center.

Disadvantages of Cellular Production

Some disadvantages of the cellular form are those of the flow shop and the job shop, but they are not as serious. As in a flow shop, if a piece of equipment should break down, it can stop production in the cell; but in a cell form—unlike a flow shop, where that may be the only piece of equipment in the facility—there may be other machines in other cells that can be temporarily used to get a job out.

However, obtaining balance among the cells when demands for a product family keep changing is a problem that is less in both flow and job shops. Flow shops are relatively fixed in capacity and produce a standard output, so there is no question of balance. Job shops simply draw from a pool of skilled labor for whatever job comes in. With cells, by contrast, if demand for a family dries up, it may be necessary to break up that cell and redistribute the equipment, or reform the families. In the short run, though, labor can generally be assigned to whatever cell needs it, including the remainder cell.

Of course, volumes are too small in cellular production to allow the purchase of the high-volume, efficient equipment that flow shops use. The cellular form also does not allow for the extent of customization usually found in job shops, since the labor pool has largely been disbursed to independent cells (although the remainder cell may be able to do the work). Moreover, the fostering of specialized knowledge associated with various operational activities is reduced because the workers who perform these activities are spread out and therefore have limited opportunities to collaborate.

❖ Project Operations

Project operations are of large scale and finite duration; also, they are nonrepetitive, consisting of multiple, and often simultaneous, tasks that are highly interdependent. However, the primary characteristics of the tasks are their limited duration and, if the output is a physical product, their immobility during processing. Generally, staff, materials, and equipment are brought to the output and located in a nearby *staging area* until needed. Projects have particularly limited lives. Resources are brought together for the duration of the project: some are consumed, and others, such as equipment and personnel, are deployed to other uses at the conclusion of the project. Frequently, the output is unique (a dam, a park, firefighting, a presidential campaign) but it need not be (airplanes, buildings).

In designing a processing system, a number of considerations may indicate that the project form is appropriate. One of these is the rate of change in the organization's outputs. If one department must keep current on a number of markets that are rapidly changing, the typical organization would quickly fall behind its competition. The project form offers extremely short reaction times to environmental or internal changes and would thus be called for. In addition, if the tasks are for a limited duration only, the project form is indicated. Finally, the project form is chosen when the output is of a very large scale with multiple, interdependent activities requiring close coordination. During the project, coordination is achieved through frequent meetings of the representatives of the various functional areas on the project team.

Advantages and Disadvantages of the Project Form

One of the advantages of the project form, as noted earlier, is its ability to perform under time and cost constraints. Therefore, if performance time or cost is crucial for an output, the project form is most appropriate. However, in high-technology areas the project form, having a mixed personnel complement of different functional specialists (engineers, scientists, theoreticians, technicians, etc.), may be less capable than transformation systems in which operations are organized by specialty areas.

In these other designs, a number of specialists can be brought together to solve a problem. In addition, specialized resources (such as staff and equipment) often cannot be justified for a project because of their low utilization; hence, generalized resources must be used instead. The project form of transformation processes is discussed in more detail in Chapter 16.

$\mathscr{S}$ELECTION OF A TRANSFORMATION SYSTEM

This section addresses the issue of selecting the appropriate transformation system, or mix of systems, to produce an output. From the preceding discussion, it should be clear that the five transformation systems are somewhat simplified extremes of what is likely to be observed in practice. Few organizations use one of the five forms in a pure sense; most combine two or more forms. For example, in manufacturing computer keyboards, some parts and subassemblies are produced in job shops or cells but then feed into a flow shop at the final assembly line, where a batch of one model is produced. Then the line is modified to produce a batch of another model. Even in "custom" work, jobs are often handled in groups of generally common items throughout most of their processing, leaving minor finishing details such as the fabric on a couch or the facade of a house to give the impression of customizing.

Although services typically take the form of a job shop, the emphasis has recently been on trying to mass-produce them (using cells or flow shops) so as to increase volume and reduce unit costs. Some examples are fast-food outlets, multiphasic medical screening, and group life insurance. Even with services we often find combined forms of process design: McDonald's prepares batches of Big Macs but will accept individual custom orders. Burger King uses a conveyor assembly line for its Whoppers but advertises its ability to customize its burgers to suit any taste.

$\mathscr{T}$ABLE 6.1 ❖ Common Organizational Designs

Organization	Transformation System				
	Continuous process	Flow shop	Job shop	Cellular	Project
Utility	X				
Hospital			X	X	
Farm	X	X		X	X
Supermarket			X	X	
University		X	X	X	
Family		X	X		X
Construction					X
Girl Scouts		X	X	X	X
Charity					X
Distributor		X	X	X	
Chemical processor	X	X			

Some examples of transformation systems selected by various organizations are listed in Table 6.1. A few of these deserve special mention. The goals of the Girl Scouts—social benefits and building character—dictate a complex of activities such as trips and camp-outs (projects), training and counseling (job shop or cell), and production of cookies (flow shop). Similarly, the family has family *projects*, relatively *continuous* flow activities such as meal production and television viewing (assuming that children are present), and *intermittent* job activities such as baths, music lessons, and naps.

The problem for the operations manager is to decide what processing form is most appropriate for the organization, considering long-run efficiency, effectiveness, lead time, capacity, quality, and flexibility. Selection may be even more difficult because as mentioned previously, it is possible to combine processing forms to attain efficiency in some portions of the production process and flexibility in other portions. It is clear that the trade-offs must be well understood by the manager, and the expected benefits and costs well known.

❖ Considerations of Volume and Variety

One of the most important factors in the design of a transformation system is establishing the volume and variety of outputs the organization will produce. High volumes tend to indicate that highly automated mass production will be necessary. High variety, on the other hand, implies the use of skilled labor and general-purpose tools and facilities.

A related consideration here is whether the output will be make-to-stock or make-to-order. A **make-to-stock** item is produced in batches of some size that is economical (for the firm) and then stocked (in a warehouse, on shelves, etc.). As customers purchase them, the items are withdrawn from stock. A **make-to-order** item is usually produced in a batch of a size set by the customer (sometimes just one) and is delivered to the customer upon its completion. Generally, make-to-stock items are produced in large volumes with low variety, whereas make-to-order items are produced in low volumes with high variety. (Quite often, *every* item is different.)

Clearly, services will not normally be of a type that can be stocked, even if every service is identical (e.g., a physical examination). Also, exceptions to the above generalizations are abundant. Automobiles, for example, are made to order, but are produced in high volume and with high variety. (However, autos are really *assembled* to order; the assembly components are produced to stock.) And general-purpose machine shops often produce high volumes of low-variety items for specific customers.

Figure 6.5*a* illustrates these points as they relate to the various transformation systems. The horizontal axis shows volume, as measured by the batch size, and the left vertical axis shows the variety of outputs. Essentially, no organizations operate in the upper right or lower left segments of this grid. Organizations making a single unit of output that varies each time (such as dams and custom-built machines) use the project form or sometimes the job shop. Some services also fall into this region, as indicated by the upper left tip of the oval. Job shop and cellular systems, however, are mainly used when a considerable variety of outputs are required in relatively small batches. This is particularly characteristic of services. When the size of a batch increases significantly, with a corresponding decrease in variety, then a flow

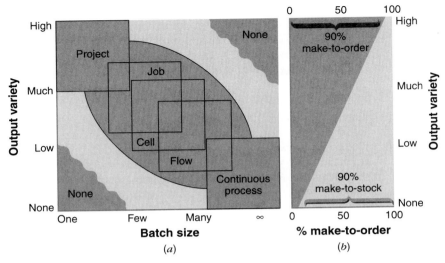

Figure 6.5   Effect of output characteristics on transformation systems.

shop is appropriate. Some services also fall into this category. Last, when all the output is the same and the batch is extremely large (or essentially infinite, as in the ore, petrochemical, and food and drink industries), the continuous process is appropriate. Very few services exist here.

Note the overlap in the different forms. This means for example, that on occasion some organizations will use a flow shop for outputs with smaller batches or larger variety, or both, than the outputs of organizations using a job shop. There are many possible reasons for this, including economic and historical factors. The organization may also simply be using an inappropriate transformation system. The point is that the categories are not rigid, and many variations do occur. Many organizations also use hybrids or combinations of systems, such as producing components to stock but assembling finished products to order, as in the auto industry.

Note in Figure 6.5*b* the general breakdown of make-to-order and make-to-stock with output variety and size of batch. Project forms (high variety, unit batch size) are almost always make-to-order, and continuous processing forms (no variety, infinite batch size) are almost always make-to-stock, though exceptions occasionally occur.

❖ Product and Process Life Cycles

In Chapter 2 we described the life cycle of an output: how long it takes to develop, bring to market, and catch on; how it quickly grows in popularity; how different versions are developed for different market segments; how the output reaches market saturation; how price competition emerges. A similar life cycle occurs in the production system for an output. As a result, a project form of transformation system may be used for the development of a new output, may evolve into a job shop or cellular layout as a market develops, and finally may evolve into a continuous flow shop as full standardization and high volumes develop. (We assume here that a continuous process is not appropriate for the output.) We briefly elaborate on this production life cycle below.

In the R&D stage, many variations are investigated during the development of a product. When a feasible output is taken to market, it is made in small volumes in a relatively inefficient, uncoordinated manner—as in a job shop—and sold at a high price. As demand grows and competitors enter the market, price competition begins and a cellular or flow system, with its high volume and low variable costs, becomes preferred. At the peak of the cycle, demand may increase to the point where such a system is justified.

This progress is illustrated in Figure 6.6, which presents a breakeven analysis for each of four transformation systems. The dark bold line illustrates the lowest-cost system for each stage of the life cycle. At the stage of project development and initiation (R&D and initial production), the cost of fixed equipment is nil, and labor is the predominant contributor to high variable costs. In the expansion stage, the job shop allows some trade-off of equipment for labor with a corresponding reduction in variable unit costs, thus leading, at these volumes, to a reduction in overall unit costs. Finally, at high volumes characterizing maturity, a nearly complete replacement of expensive labor with equipment is possible, using cellular form and the flow shop.

Be advised, however, that not all outputs can or should follow this sequence. The point is that the transformation system should evolve as the market and output evolve. But many organizations see their strength in operating a particular transformation system, such as R&D or low-cost production of large volumes. If their outputs evolve into another stage of the life cycle in which a different transformation system form is preferable, they drop the output (or license it to someone else) and switch to another output more appropriate to their strengths.

Failing to maintain this focus in the organization's production system can quickly result in a "white elephant"—a facility built to be efficient at one task but being inefficiently used for something else. This can also happen if the organization, in an

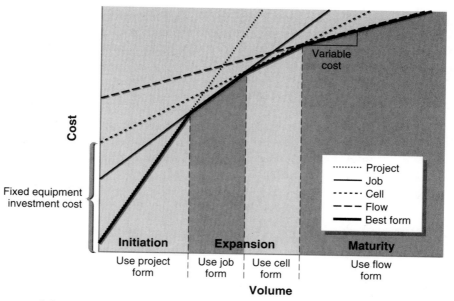

Figure 6.6 Selection of transformation systems by stage of life cycle.

attempt to please every customer, mixes the production of outputs that require different transformation systems. Japanese plants are very carefully planned to maintain one strong focus in each plant. If an output requiring a different process is to be produced, a new plant is acquired or built.

❖ Service Processes

As with the design of transformation systems for products, the design of transformation systems for services depends heavily on knowing exactly what characteristics of a service are important. Three main characteristics of a service that need to be considered are its *facilitating good,* its *explicit benefits,* and its *implicit, or psychological, benefits.* Knowing the importance of each of these allows the designer to make the necessary trade-offs in costs and benefits to offer an effective yet reasonably priced service.

Service transformation systems are frequently implemented with little development or pretesting. This is often the major reason why so many of them fail. Consider the extensive development and testing of the McDonald's fast-food production system, of airline reservations systems, and of many life insurance policies. Each of these examples also illustrates the many hours of training required to use equipment and procedures properly and efficiently. Yet most new service firms frequently fail to train their personnel adequately, once again inviting failure.

One very important element of a service system that is usually missing from product design is extensive customer contact during the delivery of the service. This presents both problems and opportunities. For one thing, the customer will often add new inputs to the delivery system or make new demands on it that were not anticipated when it was designed. In addition, customers do not arrive at smooth, even increments of time but instead tend to bunch up, as during lunch periods, and then complain when they have to wait for service. Furthermore, the customers' biased perception of the server, and the server's skills, can often influence their satisfaction with the quality of the service. Obviously, this can either be beneficial or harmful, depending on the circumstances.

On the other hand, having the customer involved in the delivery of a service can also present opportunities to improve it. Since customers know their own needs best, it is wise to let them aid in the preparation or delivery of the service—as with automatic teller machines and salad bars. In addition to improving the quality of the service, this can save the firm money by making it unnecessary to hire additional servers. However, the customer can also negligently—and quickly—ruin a machine or tool, and may even sue if injured by it, so the service firm must carefully consider how much self-service it is willing to let the customer perform.

Professor Richard Chase of the University of Southern California (Chase and Tansik, 1983) devised a helpful way to view this customer contact when designing service delivery systems. Chase's suggestion is to evaluate whether the service is, in general, high-contact or low-contact, and what portions of the service, in particular, are each. The value of this analysis is that the service can be made both more efficient and more effective by separating these two portions and designing them differently. For example, the high-contact portions of the service should be handled by workers who are skilled at social interaction, whereas the low-contact portion should employ more technical workers and take advantage of labor-saving equipment that may be available. For example, a bank may have a back office where checks are encoded separately from the front office, where customers deposit them. In this back office, equipment and efficiency are the critical job elements, whereas in the front office, social skills and friendliness are critical.

Whenever possible, the low-contact portion of a service should be decoupled from the high-contact portion so that it may be conducted with efficiency, whereas the high-contact portion is conducted with the grace and friendliness appropriate to the service. Close analysis of the service tasks may also reveal opportunities for decreasing contact with the customer—through, for example, automated teller machines, phone service, or the mail, if this is appropriate—with a concomitant opportunity for improving the efficiency of the service. Self-service, as mentioned earlier, may be very useful here also.

Similarly, there may be some opportunities for *increasing* the amount of customer contact, such as phone or mail follow-ups after service, that should be exploited to improve the overall service and its image. The service provider should thoroughly investigate these opportunities.

$\mathcal{N}$EW TRANSFORMATION TECHNOLOGIES

Many new technologies, materials, and production methods are revolutionizing service and manufacturing operations. We are constantly bombarded with terms and concepts related to the "factory of the future" and the "office of the future." Most of these systems (though not all) are, of course, due to the advent of the computer and its inexpensive power. Organizations must be careful, however, not to use this new tool simply to automate their existing manual procedures. One of the main advantages of computerization is its ability to aid in the execution of tasks that at one time could be done only inefficiently. If operations are not reorganized to use the computer's power and flexibility efficiently, most of that advantage will be lost. It is commonly said, "Simplify and systemize before you computerize."

Taking this concept one step further, many companies are formally designing their business processes. As was discussed in Chapter 4, with business process design (BPD), companies first determine their customers' needs. Then, on the basis of these needs and the capabilities offered by new technologies, the organization develops work processes to meet the needs. It is somewhat surprising that many organizations have never questioned the appropriateness of their processes, even though the technology available today is vastly different from the technology that was available when these processes were first developed.

A study by Battelle Laboratories of firms that achieve a return of over 50 percent on investment found that the primary tangible factor common to these firms was a significant technological advantage over their competitors. The importance of technology may come as a surprise, since all that we hear about success in business usually involves advertising or financial manipulation. In the next two sections we describe some of these technologies, first for services and then for products.

❖ Office and Service Technologies

The computer has had a dramatic effect on the service industries, probably even more than in the manufacturing industries. As general examples of this effect, consider the optical scanner at the grocery checkout counter, the CAT scanner in the hospital, the mail-sorting systems at the post office, or the energy control systems in buildings that regulate heat, water, and air conditioning.

Information Technology

As true as this may be for services in general, it is particularly true of services that are information-intensive. Here the computer has wrought a veritable revolution in the way of doing business. The impact of the computer has perhaps been greatest in the banking industry, with its automatic teller machines and electronic transfers of funds. However, the operations of other information-intense businesses have also been dramatically altered. Examples here would include reservations systems for hotels, airlines, rental cars, and so on; security systems; telecommunications; multiphasic screening; electronic classrooms; and on and on.

Typical of many of these situations is a person at a workstation interfacing with a terminal connected to a computer and a database. The person interfacing with the system is typically performing on-line data entry and retrieval, networking with other similar systems, processing information, and in some instances obtaining a printed output (such as a ticket).

One area that is receiving an enormous amount of attention is the Internet, especially its graphical component the World Wide Web or simply the Web. However, although the media have focused most of their attention on the Internet, a similar revolution is beginning within organizations as they develop similar private networks, called *intranets*. According to Forrester Research, in early 1996 22 percent of the Fortune 1000 companies used intranets—which is remarkable, given that virtually none of these organizations had intranets in 1994. Because intranets allow data to be exchanged freely among all users with access to the network, regardless of whether they are using Windows-based PCs, Apple Macintoshes, or UNIX workstations, intranets solve a number of problems for information managers.

There is little doubt that the Internet revolution will profoundly affect the way business is conducted. To illustrate this, consider the increasing number of "E" words that are becoming part of everyday language such as E-mail, E-cash, E-money, E-form, E-shops, E-Apps™, E-commerce, E-tickets, and E-trade. It is widely acknowledged that the Web offers organizations enormous opportunities to dramatically improve both efficiency and effectiveness. For example, organizations can update promotional and pricing materials instantaneously when these materials are stored electronically on a Web server. This is not typically possible with printed materials. Furthermore, providing access to promotional materials via the Web can greatly reduce the costs of distribution and printing while at the same time increasing international exposure. Finally, these promotional materials can be greatly enhanced by the inclusion of hypertext links and even audiovisual material.

Federal Express set up a Web server for its customers in late 1994. By early 1996 12,000 customers each day were using this service to access FedEx's package-tracking database. This provides the customer with a much higher level of service (they no longer have to wait for the next available customer service representative) and saves FedEx in the neighborhood of $2 million annually. On the basis of the success of its public Web site, FedEx decided to equip its 30,000 office personnel with Web browsers to access the company's intranet.

Here are further examples. An engineer at National Semiconductor developed a Web page for scheduling departmental meetings online. At Silicon Graphics, 7,200 employees can access 144,000 Web pages stored on 800 internal Web servers. One benefit of Silicon Graphics' intranet is that it gives employees immediate access to over two dozen corporate databases. In the past, employees requiring information had to submit a request to staff specialists, who then processed the request and returned the desired information within a couple of days.

Decision Support Systems, Artificial Intelligence, and Expert Systems

In more sophisticated applications, a manager may query a database through a *decision support system* (DSS) to obtain specific information or a printed report. The DSS may use *artificial intelligence* (AI) or an *expert system* (ES) to analyze preexisting data, collect and process external data, or network to another database through telecommunications.

Artificial intelligence is the part of the field of computer science that focuses on making computers behave like, or emulate, humans. To emulate humans, AI systems manipulate symbols rather than data. In addition, they use networks, rules, and processing procedures rather than algorithms. By using such relationships, AI systems can represent and manipulate abstract ideas and activities. With these abilities, AI systems can make assumptions when needed and can reason inductively, correcting their mistakes as they go by changing their rule systems. This makes them excellent for relatively straightforward decisions in which the data may change but the process is constant. AI will become especially useful in services where single decisions are relatively frequent but not extremely complex, such as repairing autos or handling paperwork. AI can also act as an interpreter between workers and other computerized systems, telling the human what the computerized system needs and acting as a general interface and facilitator.

Expert systems are one type of artificial intelligence and have, to date, received most of the attention in this area. These systems are individually designed to capture the expertise of particular individuals or groups with respect to one task or field, as illustrated in the sidebar on the loan expert system. Thus an expert system allows less experienced workers to have the expertise needed to help them make decisions. An ES consists of three main parts: a natural-language interface with the user, an inference engine to conduct the reasoning, and a knowledge base that includes rules, data, facts, and relationships. The inference engine determines which rules of thumb or reasoning to use as the situation progresses, and it will derive new rules or relationships as it goes. Quite a few expert systems have been devised for design, testing, repair, and automation.

Though only in the development stage, AI and ES offer considerable promise for the field of operations.

The "Office of the Future"

The office of the future will simply utilize information technology to support and enhance the usual office functions—filing, typing, taking messages, scheduling calendars, communicating, and the like. By the use of electronic mail, messages will be sent through computer networks and left for the recipient, who can then respond in the same manner. Typing will use word processing, of course, with its dramatic improvement over the electric typewriter in speed and quality. And records will be updated from computer files and returned to those files. If files

The Loan Expert at the Bank

In California, a computer software firm called Syntelligence Systems has developed an expert system to assess loan requests. It incorporates the rules and procedures that experienced bank loan officers use when evaluating companies requesting loans. The software package evaluates a host of financial data and information about the quality of management, emulating the activities of senior loan officials who have spent years learning to discriminate good risks from bad.

Through the use of this package, a junior loan officer can evaluate small and medium-sized loan applicants with the same expertise that senior officers would use, if they had the time to analyze all the loan applications. In the meantime, the junior official gains the experience of virtually working with a senior officer, and small applicants are guaranteed the attention and competence that a senior official would have spent on their applications (Galante, 1986).

need to be exchanged, networked computer transfer through telecommunication will be conducted. All personnel can maintain open calendars on a central database so that others can inquire about scheduling meetings and such.

During the 1980s the focus was on improving the productivity of individual office workers. Hence the term *personal computer* and the widespread use of spreadsheet and word processing programs. In the 1990s the focus seems to be shifting toward looking for methods to enhance teamwork. Thus we are witnessing the emergence of a new category of software called *groupware* and a transition from large centralized mainframe computers to client-server environments. Groupware supports three activities: communications (typically via E-mail), collaboration (via online discussion groups and access to shared data), and coordination (enabling individuals to jointly accomplish specific activities such as developing a strategic plan).

The impact of computerization on clerical, professional, and managerial workers will be significant. As with manufacturing, when the islands of automation (word processors, database systems, phone communications) begin to be linked, we will see considerable synergy. It is easier to think of this future as a paperless system than it is to try to determine how individual paper items will be replaced by the computer. For example, it is highly inefficient for a secretary to have a printout of a file in the corporate system mailed to him or her, only to turn around and type half the data back into the branch system. When *all* the systems are on the computer, then the manual interfacing can be eliminated.

What will be the effect of all this technology on jobs and the workforce? It is clear that the technology will eliminate the simpler rote jobs, just as it is now doing in manufacturing. A considerable number of jobs are nothing more than paper shuffling—taking information from one place and putting it someplace else. These jobs will be eliminated soon. Similar higher-level jobs will last longer, but eventually they will probably also be eliminated.

New technologies also open up new jobs, however. A hundred years ago, if we had told the farmers that, by 1990, only one person in a thousand would work on a farm, they too would have asked what the unemployed farmers would do. Obviously, the standard of living rose, new jobs opened up, the workweek was reduced, and other such changes accommodated the exodus from the farm. Undoubtedly, that will happen again.

❖ Manufacturing Technologies

Numerical Control

Numerical control (NC) is one of the oldest technologies available in manufacturing. As was briefly discussed in Chapter 5, NC allows a machine to operate automatically through coded numerical instructions. Until recently, these instructions were on punched paper tape, which directed the operations of a machine (e.g., a player piano) in the same way that an operator would. Numerical control of machines is considerably more flexible than simple automation because it can handle various operations, materials, speeds, and so forth.

The advantages of NC are many: better utilization of the machine, lower cost of labor, fewer setups, fewer manual operations, fewer fixtures, less machining time, optimal machining speeds and feeds, automatic tool selection, potential for development of a *machining center* that has multiple tools, fewer rejects, less scrap, consistent quality, easy modification of processes, reduced inspection costs. Some disadvantages are the initial cost ($20,000 to $500,000), higher maintenance costs, expensive programming costs, and time.

When the punched tape was replaced by a computer system attached to the machine, the operation—called *computer numerical control* (CNC)—was much more efficient. More recently, larger computers have been directing the activities of multiple machines through *direct numerical control* (DNC) and material-handling systems such as robots and carts as well, orchestrating their functions and movements to produce the desired parts and goods in much less time.

Clearly, such systems are very expensive. One might think that to justify the expense of these systems, relatively high volumes of standard products would need to be made on them. However, this is directly contrary to their purpose, which is to capitalize on their flexibility and produce *small* batches of a high variety of products. (Nevertheless, the net result of producing a large amount of goods to pay for the expensive equipment is still the goal; it is simply done in a different fashion.)

Robotics

Robots have come of age. Initially used for fairly simple tasks such as welding and spray-painting, these machines have increased tremendously in ability in the last few years. They have much more sophisticated sensors and can perform very complex and difficult tasks, not only in production but also in assembly. For its open house a few years ago, Cincinnati Milacron programmed one of its T³-model robots to cook an entire meal, including a roast turkey, and set a table for eight. The basic robot motions are shown in Figure 6.7.

A wide variety of robots have been developed to perform a number of highly varied tasks: painting, welding, positioning, lifting, assembly, handling materials,

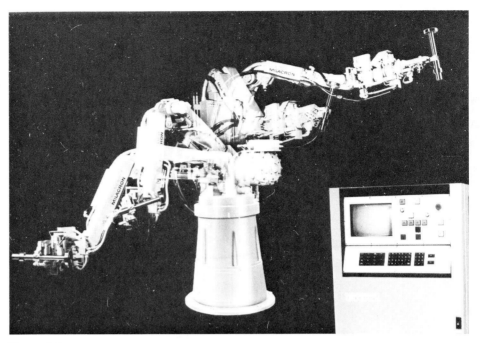

Figure 6.7   Basic robotic motions.

drilling. They are particularly valuable for jobs that are either uncomfortable for a human to perform (too hot, too dirty, and so forth) or too dangerous (because of nuclear contamination, corrosive chemicals, poisonous fumes, or the like).

A robot is usually composed of a base, a manipulator (its "arm"), and a form of gripper (its "hand," see Figure 6.8). The gripper can be pincers, suction cups, or any of a number of functional implements. The motive power originally was hydraulic or pneumatic, which is especially good for very heavy loads, but newer robots increasingly use electric control motors and are capable of finer coordination and positioning.

When augmented by a *vision* system, as is now happening more frequently, a robot can perform an even broader array of tasks. This would include sorting through parts to select the proper one, picking up a randomly oriented part without damaging it, inspecting a part for dimensional accuracy or flaws, and other such tasks. Clearly, when one technology is wedded to another, such as robots to vision, tremendous increases in capability are possible.

Flexible Manufacturing Systems

Flexible manufacturing systems (FMSs) are now in the limelight. Virtually unmanned, these systems include a series of identical machining centers; an automated, computer-controlled materials-handling system; and other possible peripherals such as a wash station, a coordinate measuring machine, a grinder, a storage rack, a robot, and loading and unloading stations. The materials management system is typically a series of automated guided vehicles (carts) for transporting pallets of materials, guided by a towline, rails, or an embedded wire in the floor. The carts,

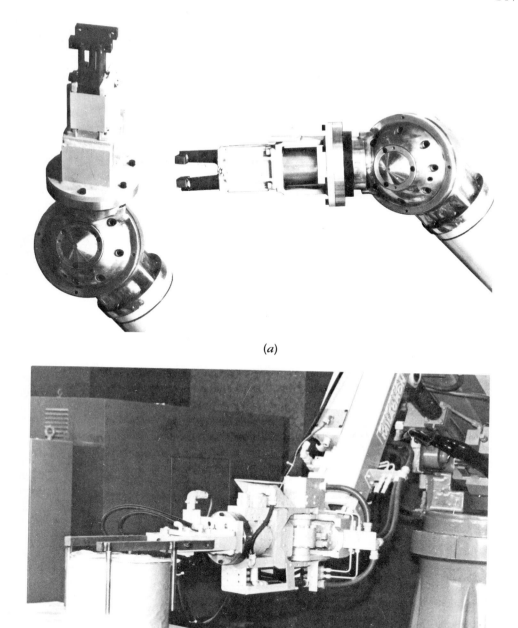

(a)

(b)

Figure 6.8 Robot grippers. (a) Gripper for small parts on universal wrist. (b) Special gripper for rolls of paper.

machines, cranes, and robots are programmed and supervised by a host computer, which interfaces with the plant computer when it needs additional data or is feeding data back.

The advantages of the FMS are those of cellular production (less space, faster response, low variable costs, and so on), as well as those of NC: consistency, quality, minimal labor expense, preprogrammed machining instructions (no blueprint reading). FMSs in Germany and Japan have given significant improvements in productivity, quality, space requirements, labor, and capacity, as shown in Table 6.2. The cost of these systems is extremely high, however—in the millions of dollars—and not all of them have been successful. Therefore, to make them productive in any firm, planning is essential.

In spite of their name, FMSs are "flexible" only in a limited sense. For example, most of them are machining systems. None of them could produce toasters or motorcycles. Thus, their flexibility is only relative to what is normally produced with such machines. This can also include various amounts of different types of flexibility such as flexibility of volume, product mix, materials, capacity, and other types.

The "Factory of the Future"

By integrating these technologies, the factory of the future is expected to take on certain characteristics that are unusual by today's standards:

❖ *Minimal lead times:* As mentioned before, the new technologies greatly reduce lead times for existing products and for designing and making new products. Not only does this provide better response to the customer, but it also aids in reducing costs through savings on inventory, reduction of scrap, higher capacity, greater throughput, less need for space, and so on.

❖ *Unit batch sizes:* Used to their fullest extent, the new technologies allow complete customization within their range of flexibility. That is, they offer high variety and small batches at the same time. Because there is no learning curve, there is no need for long runs. This again provides greater responsiveness to customers' needs, while maintaining high productivity on the expensive machinery.

𝒯ABLE 6.2 ❖ Reported Benefits of FMS

	As Percent of Conventional			
Area	MBB*	Mazak†	GE	Ingersoll
Labor required	60	8	40	70
WIP	—	25	—	50
Cycle time	60	10	13	—
Throughput	125	—	138	—
Floor space	70	—	25	50
Machine utilization	144	—	—	175
ROI	124	—	—	—

*German.

†Japanese.

❖ *High, consistent quality:* Because of the programmed repeatability of the technologies, their cuts are uniform and consistent. If there is an error, every unit will be in error until the fault is corrected. Thus, the typical variability of manual work is avoided. This provides better profit margins in the marketplace. For example, Litton Industries found that the cost of defects with automation was 1.7 percent of the cost of the capital assets, whereas manually it ran 14 percent.

❖ *Continuous operation:* Being programmed, the new technologies can operate continually and thereby utilize expensive facilities and equipment throughout three shifts. In addition, very few people—primarily maintenance workers—are needed to oversee the operations.

❖ *Vulnerability to breakdowns:* Since the process is virtually unmanned, with minimal buffers, the plant is very vulnerable to breakdowns. Maintenance, planning, and engineering will thus grow in importance.

❖ *Integrated operation:* All aspects of the firm are integrated in the same database. Sales information and orders drive the operations, and finance supports production with cash requirements as needed. Cash flows are tied to purchases and shipments; engineering designs for manufacturability; personnel obtains the human resources as forecast; operations is sequenced for the work flows in the plant; and so on throughout the firm.

❖ *Replicable plants:* Because all the knowledge of the process is built into the system and software, plants are easy to duplicate and build elsewhere. This allows adding plants closer to customers.

❖ *Largely fixed costs:* With the new technologies, almost all the costs are fixed costs. The equipment, the tooling, the software, and even the personnel (maintenance, supervisors) are fixed expenses. The primary variable cost is that of raw materials.

It has been said of the automated factory that variable costs will become fixed and fixed costs will become variable; the staff will become line and the line will become staff. In essence, the factory of the future seems to reverse many principles we thought were invariant.

𝒞HAPTER IN PERSPECTIVE _____

This chapter is the second of three chapters related to the design of products and transformation systems. Chapter 5 addressed the three stages associated with selecting and designing new products and services. Also, the highly interdependent nature of product design and the selection and design of new transformation systems were discussed. The present chapter has extended this discussion by providing additional information related to the selection of an appropriate transformation system. The chapter began with an overview of the five types of transformation systems and their respective advantages and disadvantages. Next, issues related to the selection of an appropriate transformation system—such as considerations of volume and variety and product life cycles—were discussed. The chapter concluded with a discussion of new transformation technologies. Building on this understanding of the various transformation systems, Chapter 7 will go a step further and address issues related to laying out a facility for each of the transformation systems.

❖ CHECK YOUR UNDERSTANDING

1. Define the following terms: *group technology, artificial intelligence, decision support system, expert system, robot.*

2. Briefly overview the five forms of transformation systems. Under what circumstances is each appropriate?

3. Contrast continuous processes, flow shops, job shops, and cellular production in terms of volume and variety.

4. What are the advantages and disadvantages of flow shops?

5. What are the advantages and disadvantages of job shops?

6. Contrast the five forms of transformation systems in terms of skills required of workers.

7. What are the advantages and disadvantages of cellular production?

8. What do cellular production and business process design (discussed in Chapter 4) have in common?

9. What are the advantages and disadvantages of the project form?

10. List some products and services that are make-to-stock and some that are make-to-order.

11. Contrast make-to-order with assemble-to-order.

12. Which transformation systems are more likely to be used in make-to-order situations, and which are more likely to be used in make-to-stock situations?

13. Explain the relationship between product life cycles and process life cycles.

14. Contrast NC, CNC, and DNC.

15. Contrast flexible manufacturing systems and cellular production.

16. What are the characteristics of the factory of the future?

17. What is the relationship between group technology and cellular production?

18. Is a logging mill an analytic processing operation or a synthetic operation?

19. Why is managing a high-volume continuous flow operation easier than, for example, managing a low-volume job shop?

20. Are there more or fewer inventories with a flow shop than with a job shop?

21. Why is the special-purpose equipment for a flow shop especially susceptible to obsolescence?

22. Distinguish cellular production from an FMS.

❖ EXPAND YOUR UNDERSTANDING

1. It is frequently said that in the factory of the future, the fixed costs will become variable and the variable costs will become fixed. What does this mean? Will this be true of the office of the future?

2. It is also said that in the factory of the future, the staff will become line workers and the line will become staff. What does this mean?

3. How might a service agency such as a state employment office use the cellular approach?

4. Can you think of some examples of synthetic transformations in a processing industry? Analytic transformations in a job shop?

5. Can you identify some examples of continuous job shops? Intermittent flow shops?

6. Cellular production is often conducted in a U-shaped (horseshoe-shaped) cell, rather than the rectangular cells shown in Figure 6.3b. What might be the advantages of this U shape?

7. It was noted that the cellular form has the advantage of teamwork. Do any of the other transformation forms also use teams?

8. The continuous process form is not included in Figure 6.6, since it is not appropriate. How, then, would small volumes of an output suitable for a process form be produced?

9. If efficiency, variety, and so on are the important measures of the low-contact, or no-contact portion of a service, what are the important measures of the high-contact portion?

10. How can expert systems and artificial intelligence be used in the manufacturing sector instead of the service sector?

11. In competitive situations, Japan has been very successful in the use of cellular and flow transformation systems, whereas the United States and Europe have typically used the job shop. Why do you think this is the case?

12. Foreign purchasers of American manufacturing firms tend to buy continuous process industries and to shun other transformation forms. Why?

13. Might the best transformation form for an output depend on the country in which the facility was built?

14. A common criticism of the job shop is that its workers hold such a strong allegiance to their department that they will work to make their department look particularly good, even if it hurts another department in the firm. How ethical is this?

15. How ethical is it for a worker to violate company policy in order to deliver an output as needed? What if a departmental policy rather than a company policy is violated?

16. The equipment of a job shop is less specialized than that of a flow shop. Is the labor also less skilled?

17. Why might it be preferable to implement group technology before the other new manufacturing technologies?

18. Contemporary responses to increasing labor costs have been aimed at increasing corporate operating leverage by utilizing automated machinery wherever feasible. What are the advantages and disadvantages of such a strategy?

19. Consider a typical grocery store. What type of transformation system would be best?

20. What transformation system would be best suited for processing college registration changes under a deadline?

21. As the process life cycle changes with the product life cycle, should a firm change along with it or move into new products more appropriate to its existing process? What factors must be considered in this decision?

22. In Figure 6.5, showing the five transformation systems, why don't firms operate in the regions marked "none"? Why don't the service industries extend all the way to the upper left corner?

❖ APPLY YOUR UNDERSTANDING
Paradise State University

Paradise State University (PSU) is a medium-sized private university offering both undergraduate and graduate degrees. Students typically choose Paradise State because of its emphasis on high levels of interaction and relatively small classes. University policy prohibits classes with more than 75 students (unless special permission is obtained from the provost), and the target class size is 25 students. All courses are taught by tenure-track faculty members with appropriate terminal degrees. Faculty members teach two courses each semester.

The Business School at PSU offers only an MBA degree in one of six areas of concentration: accounting, finance, general management, management information systems (MIS), marketing, and operations management (OM). The MBA program is a one-year (two-semester) lockstep program. Since the Business School does not offer undergraduate business courses, students entering the program are required to have completed all the undergraduate business prerequisites from an accredited university. The faculty is organized into six functional departments. The table below lists the number of faculty members in each department and the average number of students each year who choose a particular concentration. Students are not permitted to have double concentrations, and PSU does not offer minors at the graduate level.

Department	Faculty	Number of Students per Year
Accounting	8	100
Finance	6	40
General Management	7	70
MIS	10	150
Marketing	6	50
OM	10	30

The number of courses required by each concentration in each department are listed in the table below. For example, a student concentrating in accounting is required to take 4 accounting classes, 1 finance class, 1 management class, 1 MIS course, 1 marketing class, and 2 OM classes.

Number of Courses Taken in Respective Departments

Concentration	Accounting	Finance	Management	MIS	Marketing	OM
Accounting	4	1	1	1	1	2
Finance	1	4	1	1	1	2
General Management	1	1	4	1	1	2
MIS	1	1	1	4	1	2
Marketing	1	1	1	1	4	2
OM	1	1	1	1	1	5

Questions

1. How many students must each department teach each semester? Given the target class size—25 students—are there enough faculty members?

2. Conceptually, how could the cellular production approach be applied to the Business School?

3. What would be the advantages and disadvantages of adopting a cellular approach at the Business School? As a student, would you prefer a functional organization or a cellular organization? As a faculty member, what would you prefer?

4. On the basis of the information given, develop a rough plan detailing how the Business School faculty might be assigned to cells.

Facility Layout

𝒞 HAPTER OVERVIEW

❖ The main purpose of *layout analysis* is to maximize the efficiency or effectiveness of operations.

❖ Layout analyses are often based on some measure of efficiency. In a continuous process transformation system, it concerns the flow of materials; in the flow shop, it concerns the balance among operations; in the job shop, it concerns the cost of movement between operations; in the cellular form, it concerns the determination of part families; in the project form, it concerns the scheduling of staged materials.

❖ Line balancing in the flow shop involves the grouping of individual tasks, without violating requirements of precedence, into the minimum number of stations so that the sum of the task times assigned to each station doesn't exceed the overall cycle time. Sometimes it is impossible to aggregate the tasks into the theoretical minimum number of stations, and a greater number must be used at some loss of efficiency (or an increase in *balance delay*).

❖ To help clear up the confusion surrounding the word *cell*, a taxonomy is presented that classifies equipment groupings on two continuous dimensions: the purpose for grouping the equipment together into cells and the degree of interdependence between the cells.

❖ Cells and product/service families are formed, both in practice and in theory, in many different ways. One of the simplest and most common is based on the machine-component matrix derived from the product/service routings. *Production flow analysis* and the *rank order clustering algorithm* reorder the rows and columns of this matrix to form machine-component families along the diagonal.

❖ In laying out a job shop, the importance of the interrelations between departments can be directly specified qualitatively or quantitatively with the *cost-volume-distance model*. In either case, the layout is obtained by improving an arbitrary initial layout according to measures of importance.

❖ Given the number of combinations of possible job shop layouts, most procedures rely on heuristic approaches that locate high travel cost departments or important interrelated departments close together.

❖ *Operations sequence analysis* examines the routings of the outputs to ascertain the cost per foot of separation between departments.

❖ A wide variety of layout programs are available for both flow and job shops. The best-known is CRAFT, for job shops.

INTRODUCTION

❖ Martin Marietta's aerospace electronics manufacturing facility in Denver, Colorado, was initially set up as a job shop with numerous functional departments. As is typical of most job shops, the Marietta plant had high levels of work-in-process and long lead times, and parts had to travel long distances throughout the plant to complete their processing. Also, as is typical of functional organizations, departmental divisions created barriers to communication and often resulted in conflicting goals. To address these problems, Martin Marietta organized its plant into three focused factories. Each focused factory was completely responsible and accountable for building electronic assemblies for a particular application (e.g., flight, space, or ground use). The intent was to make each focused factory a separate business enterprise.

A factory manager was assigned to each focused factory. The factory managers then engaged in a sort of "NFL draft" to select employees for their teams. Workers not drafted had to find other positions either inside or outside the company. Within the focused factories, product families were identified; these were based on the technology and processing requirements of the products. Next, standardized routings and sequences were identified for each product family. The plant realized a number of improvements as a result of these and other changes, including seven consecutive months of production with no scrap, a 50 percent reduction in work-in-process, a 21 percent average reduction in lead times, and a 90 percent reduction in overtime (Ferras, 1994).

❖ Allsop, located in Bellingham, Washington, employs 120 people and focuses primarily on injection molding. Originally it was organized as a job shop. With this arrangement, products moved from the molding department to a warehouse, to final assembly, and on to shipping. Because of an excessive amount of material handling, Allsop decided to adopt cellular manufacturing.

The conversion to cellular manufacturing took six months and cost $60,000. The goal for moving to cells was to locate all secondary production and assembly activities next to the molding machines. Doing this would substantially reduce material handling and work-in-process inventory.

To develop the cells, management solicited employees' suggestions. This increased employees' comfort and lowered their resistance to the change. Allsop's approach to cellular manufacturing can best be described as "assembly on wheels." Because it is difficult to move the injection molding machines, the assembly line is constantly rearranged around the machines, depending on the product. Thus, once an order is completed, the assembly line and molds are changed for the next product. Also, workers are now cross-trained so that each worker is prepared to handle whatever tasks are required in a new assembly line configuration. With this "assembly on wheels," products are completely processed and ready to be shipped within 10 to 20 feet of the injection molding machines (Collett and Spicer, 1995).

❖ Steward, Inc., produces nickel-zinc-ferrite parts that are used to suppress electromagnetic interference, which creates problems in the transmission, reception, and processing of electronic data.

Steward's ferrite products begin as ferrite powder. The ferrite powder is pressed into the appropriate form and fired in kilns, and then the part is completed in a finishing area.

Recently, Steward completed a conversion from a job shop to cellular manufacturing. Because the kilns are the most important pieces of equipment, they were used as seeds for each cell. Then the parts that went to each kiln were listed and a spreadsheet was developed to determine which other machines were needed in each cell. This analysis resulted in the formation of four distinct, independent cells. Steward realized a number of benefits after converting to cells, including an 80 percent reduction in work-in-process inventory, an 86 percent reduction in lead times, a 96 percent reduction in late orders, and a 56 percent reduction in manufacturing space required (Levasseur, Helms, and Zink, 1995).

The above examples provide insight into the variety of ways organizations actually lay out their facilities. In the case of Martin Marietta, similarities in processing requirements and part routings were prime considerations in developing focused factories. In Allsop's case, no single layout would have achieved its goals, so it developed its "assembly on wheels." And in Steward's case, the prime consideration was use of a key type of equipment.

In Chapter 6, the five major transformation systems were described, and their major characteristics, advantages, and disadvantages were discussed. Now we take the design of the transformation system one step further and describe the different approaches to laying out the facility for each form.

The main purpose of *layout analysis* is to maximize the efficiency (cost-orientation) or effectiveness (e.g., quality, lead time, flexibility) of operations. In the examples at the beginning of the chapter, benefits realized by the companies after a new layout was adopted included reduced work-in-process inventory, shorter lead times, less scrap, shorter travel distances, and less need for manufacturing space. Other purposes also exist, such as reducing safety or health hazards, minimizing interference or noise between different operational areas (e.g., separating painting from sanding), facilitating crucial staff interactions, or maximizing customers' exposure to products or services.

In laying out service operations, the emphasis is often more on accommodating the customer than on operations per se. Moreover, capacity and layout analyses are frequently conducted simultaneously by analyzing service operations and the wait that the customer must endure. Thus, *waiting line* (or *queuing*) *theory* is heavily used in the design of a service delivery system. The layouts of parking lots, entry

Keying customer phone orders into the computer. Six-person carrousel work layouts provide optimum efficiency and flexibility.

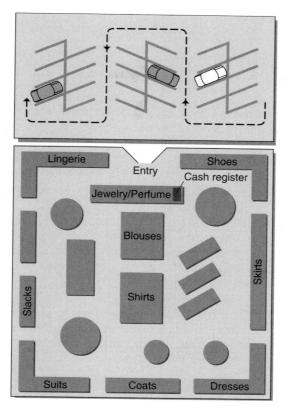

Figure 7.1 Layout of a department store.

zones, reception rooms, waiting areas, service facilities, and other areas of customer contact are of top priority in service-oriented firms such as nightclubs, restaurants, and banks.

For example, Figure 7.1 shows the layout of a department store. Notice that, even though an image of order and neatness prevails, the display racks, cabinets, and carousels are carefully arranged to break up any smooth flow of traffic. This is particularly the case at the entry-exit, where high-margin items (jewelry and perfume) are conspicuously displayed. An entering customer who successfully outflanks the jewelry counter is then distracted by high-visibility carousels and racks of merchandise, all seemingly aimed at him or her.

In general, most layouts are originally designed efficiently, but as the organization grows and changes to accommodate a changing environment, the operations layout becomes less efficient, until eventually a relayout is necessary. The following are some operations problems that might indicate the need for relayout:

❖ Congestion.

❖ Poor utilization of space.

❖ Excessive amounts of materials in processing.

❖ Excessive distances in the work flow.

❖ Bottlenecks occurring in one location simultaneously with idleness in another.

❖ Skilled workers doing excessive unskilled work.

❖ Long operation cycles and delays in delivery.

❖ Anxiety and strain among workers.

❖ Difficulty in maintaining operational control of work or staff.

When such special reasons exist for a relayout analysis, then, of course, the criteria for the new layout will be based on resolving a particular difficulty. Two- and three-dimensional scale models of the operation, such as an interior decorator might use with model furniture, are often used to aid in solving such problems. In general, however, the primary criterion for layout analyses is the efficiency of operations. Assuming that every potential layout satisfies any *required* constraints (the location of loading or shipping docks and restrooms, the shape of certain departments, etc.), we find that the criterion for efficiency usually reduces to a concern for the *interrelations* of operations. Examples of such interrelations are the cost of materials handling when the main flows between operations are materials, staff time when the major flows are people, or costs of lost or delayed information when the main flows are paperwork.

In a continuous process transformation system, the materials flows are the critical interrelations. For the correct final product to result, the materials must be in a certain form, held at certain temperatures for certain periods for chemical reactions to occur, screened at certain points in their transformation, and so on. If the interrelations are not precisely correct, the yield will be reduced or perhaps even completely lost.

With the *continuous process form,* the design of the layout and the specifications for equipment within the layout guarantee correct interrelations. Knowing what the specifications and layout should be requires unique expertise for the product under consideration. A chemical plant will be different from a food processor, which will in turn differ from a gold processor or a natural gas producer. Each industry uses specialists, such as petroleum engineers or chemical engineers, to design its layout. Thus, we will not further investigate the layout of continuous process industries.

In the *flow shop,* the critical aspect of the interrelations is the balance among the operations. Since the output moves directly from raw material to finished output, any bottleneck in the production system reduces efficiency, thereby increasing the cost of all the other operations that must wait out the bottleneck. The layout itself is relatively straightforward, since each operation is simply placed as close as possible to its predecessors. The details of layout and line balancing in the flow shop are discussed in the next section.

In *cellular production,* the difficult issue is to determine the most appropriate families of outputs. Once the families are identified, the required equipment can be determined and placed into convenient (often U-shaped) cells for the production of the outputs. Whenever possible, the cells are designed as flow cells rather than job cells to improve the speed and efficiency of each cell. This is usually possible for cells that handle a well-defined family of outputs; but it is not very feasible for the remainder cell, which handles all the miscellaneous jobs.

In the *job shop,* the primary relations between operations are identified, and it is determined whether or not these interrelatons require closeness. The reasons why closeness or separation is needed depend on the situation, but frequently they involve the job routings and the flow of materials between operations. Other reasons may involve safety, lead time, or interaction of workers.

In the *project transformation systems*, the layout primarily involves staging the materials around the project site and, more important, determining when each set of materials should arrive. Thus, the project layout is largely a matter of scheduling—an issue we address in considerably more detail in Chapter 16.

*F*LOW SHOP LAYOUT

The crux of the problem of realizing the advantages of a flow shop is whether the work flow can be subdivided sufficiently so that labor and equipment are utilized smoothly throughout the processing operations. If, for example, one operation takes longer than all the others, this will become a bottleneck, delaying all the operations following it and restricting the output rate to its low value.

Obtaining smooth utilization of workers and equipment across all operations involves assigning to groups tasks that take about the same amount of time to complete. This balancing applies to production lines where parts or outputs are produced, as well as to assembly lines where parts are assembled into final products.

Final assembly operations usually have more labor input and fewer fixed-equipment cycles and can therefore be subdivided more easily for smooth flow. Either of two types of lines can then be used. A ***paced line*** uses some sort of conveyor and moves the output along at a continuous rate, and operators do their work as the output passes by them. For longer operations the worker may walk or ride alongside the conveyor and then have to walk back to the starting workstation. The many disadvantages of this arrangement, such as boredom and monotony, are, of course, well known. An automobile assembly line is a common example of a paced line. Workers install doors, engines, hoods, and the like as the conveyor moves past them.

In unpaced lines, such as those described in the sidebar about Northern Telecom, the workers build up queues between workstations and can then vary their pace to meet the needs of the job or their personal desires; however, average daily output must remain the same. The advantage of an unpaced line is that a worker can spend longer on the more difficult outputs and balance this with the easier outputs. Similarly, workers can vary their pace to add variety to a boring task. For example, a worker may work fast to get ahead of the pace for a few seconds before returning to the task.

There are some disadvantages to unpaced lines, however. For one thing, they cannot be used with large, bulky products because too much in-process storage space is required. More important, minimum output rates are difficult to maintain because short durations in one operation usually do not dovetail with long durations in the next operation. When long durations coincide, operators downstream from these operations may run out of in-process inventory to work on and thus be forced to sit idle.

For operations that can be smoothed to obtain the benefits of a production line, there are two main elements in designing the most efficient line. The first is formulating the situation by determining the necessary output rate, the available work

Robotic welding line in automobile plant.

time per day, the times for operational tasks, and the order of precedence of the operations. The second element is actually to solve the balancing problem by sub-dividing and grouping the operations into balanced jobs.

❖ Balancing the Production Line

Formulation Stage

We illustrate the formulation of the **line balancing** situation with an example. Longform Credit receives 1200 credit applications a day, on the average. Longform's advertising touts its efficiency in responding to all applications within hours. Daily application processing tasks, average times, and required preceding tasks (tasks that must be completed before the next task) are listed in Table 7.1.

The *precedence graph* for these tasks is shown in Figure 7.2; it is constructed directly from Table 7.1. This graph is simply a picture of the operations (boxed) with arrows indicating which tasks must precede others. The number or letter of the operation is shown above the box, with its time inside.

In balancing a line, the intent is to find a **cycle time** in which each workstation can complete its tasks. A workstation is usually a single person, but it may include any number of people responsible for completing all the tasks associated with the job for that station. Conceptually, at the end of this time every workstation passes its part on to the next station. Task elements are thus grouped for each workstation

OPERATIONS IN PRACTICE

Northern Telecom Rebalances its Flow Lines

As a part of its efforts to become a world-class manufacturer, Northern Telecom's DMS-100 Switching Division reorganized its operations into a set of flow line cells. Each of these lines had to be designed and balanced to meet the requirements of throughput and cycle time. To help with the redesign and balancing, an animated simulation model, SIMAN/CINEMA of Systems Modeling, was used. The model not only helped determine the required number of assembly workstations but also helped size the between-station buffer inventories, identify the requisite capacity levels, and develop appropriate performance measures such as flow time, throughput, and inventory levels. Overall, the project affected more than 500 people in the process of rearranging 60,000 square feet of factory floor space.

The operations were divided into seven flow lines, handling seven primary families of products. The tasks along each line included, in order, machine insertion, prewave manual assembly, wave solder clean, postwave assembly, visual inspection, in-circuit test, functional test, module test, frame configuration, ambient test, and heat test. Following the final task, the product was sent to distribution. To understand how the new flow lines would operate, the supervisors and workers took a training course in which the simulation-animation model illustrated how the lines were expected to work and what benefits were anticipated.

In the redesign and rebalancing of the flow cells, some of the line flow tasks were combined, such as the functional test and the module test. In addition, some of the duplication between the in-circuit test and the functional test was eliminated. Moreover, the ambient and heat tests were taken out of the flow line cells and grouped into a separate, final task that would service all the flow lines together.

With the reorganization and rebalancing, Northern Telecom achieved several benefits. Work-in-process inventories were cut by 82 percent, and throughput volumes increased over 50 percent. Quality also increased, as is evidenced by a 70 percent reduction in visual inspection requirements and a composite increase in yield of 7 percent. In addition, the increased speed of throughput improved customer service, overhead was drastically cut, and workers' morale was raised significantly. The net result of the reductions in overhead and inventory alone was a savings of over $2 million in annual costs to the firm (Taheri, 1990).

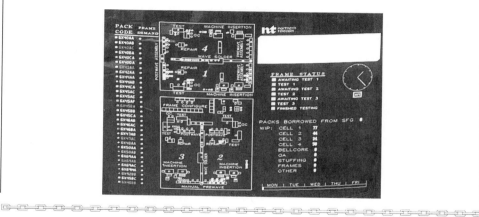

$\mathscr{T}$ABLE 7.1 ❖ Tasks in Credit Application Processing

Task	Average Time (Minutes)	Immediately Preceding Tasks
a. Open and stack applications	0.20	none
b. Process enclosed letter; make note of and handle any special requirements	0.37	*a*
c. Check off form 1 for page 1 of application	0.21	*a*
d. Check off form 2 for page 2 of application; file original copy of application	0.18	*a*
e. Calculate credit limit from standardized tables according to forms 1 and 2	0.19	*c, d*
f. Supervisor checks quotation in light of special processing of letter, notes type of form letter, address, and credit limit to return to applicant	0.39	*b, e*
g. Secretary types in details on form letter and mails	<u>0.36</u>	*f*
	Total 1.90	

so as to utilize as much of this cycle time as possible but not to exceed it. Each workstation will have a slightly different *idle time* within the cycle time.

The cycle time is determined from the required output rate. In this case, the average daily output rate must equal the average daily input rate, 1200. If it is less than this figure, a backlog of applications will accumulate. If it is more than this, unnecessary idle time will result. Assuming an 8-hour day, 1200 applications per 8 hours means completing 150 every hour or 1 every 0.4 minutes—this, then, is the cycle time.

$$\text{Cycle time} = \text{available work time/demand}$$

$$= \frac{(8 \text{ hr} \times 60 \text{ minutes/hour})}{1200 \text{ applications}} = 0.4 \text{ minute/application}$$

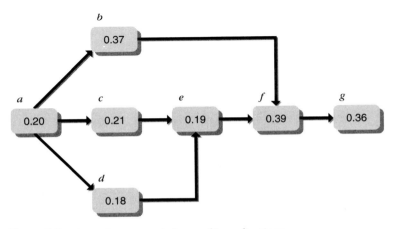

Figure 7.2   Precedence graph for credit applications.

Adding up the task times in Table 7.1, we can see that the total is 1.9 minutes. Since every workstation will do no more than 0.4 minute's worth of work during each cycle, it is clear that a minimum of 1.9/0.4 = 4.75 workstations are needed or, always rounding *up*, 5.

$$\text{Number of theoretical workstations, } N_T = \sum \text{task times/cycle time}$$

$$= \frac{1.9}{0.4} = 4.75 \text{ (i.e., 5)}$$

It may be, however, that the work cannot be divided and balanced in five stations—that six, or even seven, may be needed. For example, precedence relationships may interfere with assigning two tasks to the same workstation. This is why we referred to N_T as the *theoretical* number of workstations needed. If more workstations are actually needed than the theoretical number, the production line will be less efficient. The *efficiency* of the line with N_A actual stations may be computed from

$$\text{Efficiency} = \frac{\text{output}}{\text{input}} = \frac{\text{total task time}}{(N_A \text{ stations}) \times \text{cycle time}}$$

$$= \frac{1.9}{5 \times 0.4} = 95 \text{ percent if the line can be balanced with 5 stations}$$

$$= \frac{1.9}{6 \times 0.4} = 79 \text{ percent if 6 stations are required}$$

In the above formula for efficiency, input is represented by the amount of work required to produce one unit and output is represented by the amount of work that actually goes into producing one unit.

Keying in financial information for customer applications.

$\mathscr{S}$OLVED EXERCISE 7.1 ❖ Line Balancing: Formulation

Amity Products wishes to balance its line to meet a daily demand of 240 units. Amity works an eight-hour day on the following tasks:

Task	Time (minutes)	Preceding Tasks
1	0.4	none
2	0.3	1
3	1.1	1
4	0.2	3
5	0.5	2
6	0.3	3
7	0.6	5
8	0.6	4, 6, 7

Determine the cycle time and minimum number of stations.

Solution:

$$\text{Cycle time} = \frac{8 \times 60}{240} = 2.0 \text{ minutes/unit}$$

The sum of the task times is 4.0 minutes. Thus, the theoretical minimum number of work stations is:

$$N_T = \frac{4.0}{2.0} = 2.0$$

On occasion, the *inefficiency* of the line is calculated instead; this is called the **balance delay.**

$$\text{Balance delay} = 1.0 - \text{efficiency}$$
$$= 1.0 - 0.95 = 5 \text{ percent with 5 stations}$$

Solution Stage

Now that the problem has been formulated, we can attempt to balance the line by assigning tasks to stations. We begin by assuming that all workers can do any of the tasks and check back on this later. There are many heuristic[1] rules for which task to assign next. We will use the LOT rule; select the task with the *longest operation time* next.

---

[1]Heuristics are logically or experimentally derived rules of thumb.

The general procedure for line balancing is as follows:

Construct a list of the tasks whose predecessor tasks have already been completed. Consider each of these tasks, one at a time, in LOT order and place them within the station. As a task is tentatively placed in a station, new follower tasks can now be added to the list. Consider adding to the station any tasks in this list whose time fits within the remaining time for that station. Continue in this manner until as little idle time as possible remains for the station.

We will now demonstrate this procedure with reference to Longform, using the information in Table 7.1 and Figure 7.2. The first tasks to consider are those with no preceding tasks. Thus, task *a*, taking 0.2 of the 0.4 minute available, is assigned to station 1. This then makes tasks *b* (0.37 minute), *c* (0.21 minute), and *d* (0.18 minute) eligible for assignment. Trying the longest first, *b*, then *c*, and last *d*, we find that only *d* can be assigned to station 1 without exceeding the 0.4-minute cycle time; thus, station 1 will include tasks *a* and *d*. Since only 0.02 minute remains unassigned in station 1 and no task is that short, we then consider assignments to station 2.

Only *b* and *c* are eligible for assignment (since *e* requires that *c* be completed first), and *b* (0.37 minute) will clearly require a station by itself; *b* is, therefore, assigned to station 2. Only *c* is now eligible for assignment, since *f* requires that both *e* and *b* be completed and *e* is not yet completed. But when we assign *c* (0.21 minute) to station 3, task *e* (0.19 minute) becomes available and can also be just accommodated in station 3. Task *f* (0.39 minute), the next eligible task, requires its own station; this and leaves *g* (0.36 minute) to station 5. These assignments are illustrated in Figure 7.3 and Table 7.2.

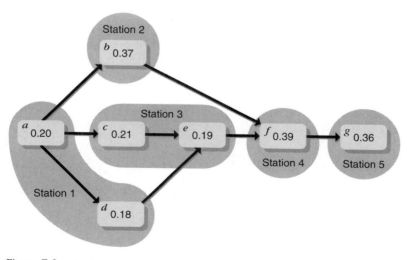

Figure 7.3   Station assignments.

$\mathcal{T}$ABLE 7.2 ✤ Station Task Assignments

Station	Time Available	Eligible Tasks	Task Assigned	Idle Time
1	.40	*a*	*a*	
	.20	*b, c, d*	*d*	
	.02	*b, c*	none will fit	.02
2	.40	*b, c*	*b*	
	.03	*c*	*c* will not fit	.03
3	.40	*c*	*c*	
	.19	*e*	*e*	0.00
4	.40	*f*	*f*	
	.01	*g*	*g* will not fit	.01
5	.40	*g*	*g*	.04

We now check the feasibility of these assignments. In many cases a number of aspects must be considered in this check (as discussed later), but here our only concern is that the clerk or the secretary does not do task *f* and that the supervisor does not do task *g* (or, we hope, much of *a–e*). As it happens, task *f* is a station by itself, so there is no problem.

$\mathcal{S}$OLVED EXERCISE 7.2 ✤ Line Balancing: Solution

Balance the line in Solved Exercise 7.1. Rebalance the line if task 8 required 0.7 minutes.

Solution:

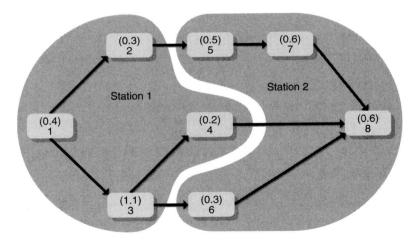

Station 1: Tasks 1, 2, 3, 4, taking 2.0 minutes
    2: Tasks 5, 6, 7, 8, taking 2.0 minutes

If task 8 takes 0.7 minutes, then 3 stations will be required. Station 2 will include tasks 5, 6, and 7 (idle time of 0.6), and station 3 will include task 8 (idle time of 1.4).

❖ Special Considerations

Longform is, of course, a highly simplified example. In realistic situations, many other difficulties and considerations are present, which complicate the problem even more. Some of these complications are listed here.

- ❖ Many, many tasks (hundreds, or even thousands) may be involved, with a large number of interactions and precedence relationships. Considerable research has been done on this problem, and numerous, heuristic techniques are available to aid in obtaining a solution (e.g., choose as the next task the one with the longest operation time).

- ❖ Some sets of tasks require the same skills, tools, parts, equipment, facilities, or positioning of workers, and might be more efficiently grouped together than is indicated from the pure line balancing solution. Thus, it is always worthwhile to inspect the initial solution for further possible efficiencies.

- ❖ In the spirit of job enrichment, it may be worthwhile to group some tasks together that normally would not be grouped, simply to ward off boredom and allow some variety, or to foster pride of workmanship.

- ❖ Potential task interference should be considered. For example, noisy, dangerous, or polluting tasks should be grouped and confined in facilities designed for them.

- ❖ Frequently, a task may by itself exceed the cycle time. If the task cannot be further broken down, the best alternative is to assign such tasks to two (or more) stations, each completing its task *every other* cycle. An approach to the opposite situation—in which one physically uncombinable task has a *low cycle* time—is to utilize two (or more) complete parallel lines with the one, short-cycle task in common.

*C*ELLULAR LAYOUT _____

Cellular production is the application of principles of group technology. As described in Chapter 6, it involves the formation of teams of workers and equipment to produce families of outputs. The workers are cross-trained so that they can operate any of the equipment in their cell, and they take full responsibility for the proper performance or result of the outputs. Whenever feasible, these outputs are final products or services. At other times, particularly in manufacturing, the outputs are parts that go into a final product. If the latter is the case, it is common to group the cells closely around the main production or assembly line so that they feed their output directly into the line as it is needed.

In some cases, a *nominal* (or *virtual*) *cell* is formed by identifying certain equipment and dedicating it to the production of families of outputs, but without moving the equipment into an actual, physical cell. In that case, no "layout" analysis is required at all; the organization simply keeps the layout it had. The essence of the problem, then, is the identification of the output families and the equipment to dedicate to each of them.

As the cases at the beginning of the chapter illustrate, it is more common for an organization to actually form physical cells. When physical cells are created, the layout of the cell may resemble a sort of mini–flow shop (e.g., Allsop's "assembly on wheels"), a job shop, or a mix of these, depending on the situation. Thus, we will direct our attention here to the formation of the part or product families and their associated equipment, leaving the issues of physical layout to be addressed in the discussions of the flow shop and job shop.

❖ A Taxonomy of Cells

In practice, organizations often use the term *cell* to include a wide range of very different situations: a functional department consisting of identical machines, a single machine that automatically performs a variety of operations, or even a dedicated assembly line. Earlier, we also referred to the portion of a shop that is not associated with a specific part family as a cell: a *remainder cell*. Nevertheless, we do not consider all these groups as part of what we are calling cellular production.

Organizations that formally plan their shop layouts typically choose to group their equipment on the basis of either the function it performs or the processing requirements of a product or group of products. As we discussed in Chapter 6, the purpose of grouping equipment on the basis of its function is to maximize flexibility, whereas the purpose of grouping it on the basis of processing requirements is to maximize efficiency.

To help clear up the confusion surrounding the word *cell,* a taxonomy of equipment groupings is presented in Figure 7.4. The taxonomy classifies equipment groupings on two continuous dimensions: the purpose of grouping the equipment together into cells and the degree of interdependence among the cells.

Although the two dimensions of the taxonomy are continuous, it is helpful to divide them into discrete categories. Thus, the dimension *purpose* has been divided into three categories: *functional cells, hybrid layouts,* and *product cells.* Similarly, the dimension *interdependence* has been divided into two categories: *multicell processing* and *cell-complete processing.* In Figure 7.4 a descriptive name is given for each category of shop layout.

Across the top of Figure 7.4 is a continuum ranging from shops where all the equipment is arranged into functional cells (departments) to shops where all the equipment is arranged into product cells. Plants falling into the category of functional cells have all or most of their equipment (e.g. more than 90 percent) arranged functionally. Plants beginning the conversion to product cells and perhaps experimenting with a pilot product cell also fall into this category. Plants with significant amounts of equipment arranged in both functional and product cells and those further along in their conversion are called *hybrid layouts.* Finally, plants where all or most of the equipment (e.g. more than 90 percent) is arranged in product cells are called product cells. Typically, any equipment not grouped into the product cells in these plants is what we referred to earlier as the remainder cell.

The left-hand side of Figure 7.4 considers the interdependence of cells by quan-

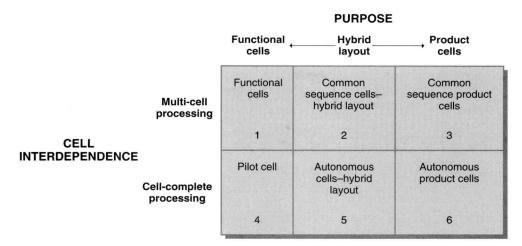

Figure 7.4   Taxonomy of equipment groupings.

tifying the number of cells required to complete the processing of a part. The bottom row is associated with autonomous machine cells that are capable of completely processing a part family. The top row is concerned with situations where the parts require processing in two or more different cells.

Category 1 in Figure 7.4 corresponds to the traditional functional layout or job shop. The equipment is grouped into functional departments, and none of the parts is completely processed within a single cell. Also included in category 1 are nominal or virtual product cell layouts where the equipment is kept in functional departments but dedicated to part families.

Categories 2 and 3 in Figure 7.4 are associated with situations where the arrangement of significant amounts of equipment is based on the processing requirements of the parts. The major difference between categories 2 and 3 is that in category 3 a smaller percentage of the equipment is in the remainder cell. The label *common sequence* is used to describe categories 2 and 3 because common machine sequences in the part routings are often used as the basis for forming these cells. However, because common machine sequences are used to create the cells, and not the complete processing requirements of the part families, parts processed in these layouts must travel to multiple cells to complete their processing.

In the bottom row of Figure 7.4, all parts are entirely processed within a single cell. Category 4 is called *pilot cell* because plants in this category are often just beginning to experiment with product cells and therefore most of the equipment in the shop is still arranged in functional departments. As firms operating in category 4 gain experience with the product cell and become convinced that it is beneficial, they begin a phase of implementing additional product cells. This is category 5, referred to as the *hybrid stage* because as the shop is incrementally converted to product cells, a significant portion of the facilities are still arranged in functional departments. At some point, the formation of additional product cells is terminated and the firm may or may not move to category 6, where the majority of the equipment is arranged in product cells. Often companies stop creating new product cells when the volume of the remaining parts is insufficient to justify forming additional product cells.

Next, we describe the problem of determining families and machine cells.

OPERATIONS
IN PRACTICE

Moving to Cells at Schlumberger

The Houston Downhole Sensors Division of Schlumberger Well Services produces sophisticated electromechanical equipment for oil-field boreholes. In late 1985 it produced 200 different products and maintained an inventory of 30,000 items. Average lead time for products was more than a year. The machine shop operated like a typical job shop: average throughput time was four months, completion schedules were unreliable, and defects at outgoing inspection were over 20 percent. Perhaps most important, to keep efficiency and utilization high, the firm produced the simple, high-volume parts in-house and subcontracted out (at premium prices) the difficult, low-volume, rush, and engineering prototype parts. This made its standard costs look good but prevented it from developing innovative production systems to gain a competitive edge.

At this point, Schlumberger decided that to remain competitive, it needed to slash its throughput times, greatly improve quality and reliability, simplify its shop operations, and start producing engineering prototype parts, rush parts, and more difficult and expensive parts in-house. To do so, it decided it would have to convert its job shop to a cellular operation.

The conversion was driven by the goals of slashing throughput times and machine setup times. Schlumberger started by canceling some previously approved ambitious plans: capital expenditures for automation, robots, sophisticated computer packages for shop floor scheduling, and flexible manufacturing systems. It returned a new robotic deburring station to the supplier and sold off a nearly new automated storage and retrieval system that had just been installed. It even turned off and sold its existing shop floor control computer, moving to a just-in-time "pull" scheduling approach. In general, rather than using expensive, automated, computerized equipment, the firm cross-trained its employees to use small, special-purpose, inexpensive machines, most of which it already had.

While dividing the job shop into 12 cells, Schlumberger also reorganized its employees into teams of three or four to operate the cells. This change improved employees' morale and motivation and also increased organizational teamwork, since each team had complete responsibility for the work within its cell. This included preventive maintenance, cross-training, improving quality, reducing cost, minimizing setup times, maintaining tools and gauges, and even assisting in developing production systems, designing fixtures, and modifying programs. Other changes included eliminating final inspections and tracking direct labor hours for each job.

With this movement to cellular production, Schlumberger was able to cut its average product lead time to less than six months, its shop throughput times to one week, and its defect rate to less than 2 percent. On-schedule order completion rose to about 90 percent, and orders that were late were less than five days overdue. Overall labor cost per part dropped about 50 percent as well. But most important, by moving to fast throughput the company was able to reverse its production philosophy and keep its prototype parts in-house, while outsourcing the simple, high-volume parts (at low cost). Thus, Schlumberger now controls its most difficult, and most expensive, parts and has been able to achieve significant cost reductions that its suppliers had no motivation even to attempt (Stoner, Tice, and Ashton, 1989).

❖ Methods of Forming Cells

There are a variety of ways available to determine what outputs should constitute a family and be produced in the same cell. Sometimes a family is dictated by the size or weight of the output; for example, huge pieces of steel may require an overhead crane to lift them onto the machines for processing. Sometimes electronic parts have special requirements for quality, such as being produced in a "clean room" or being welded in an inert gas environment. Sometimes it is obvious what family a part belongs in simply by looking at it and seeing how it was made.

Generally, procedures for cell formation can be classified into five categories:

1. Manual techniques

2. Classification and coding

3. Statistical cluster analysis

4. Mathematical programming techniques

5. Machine-component matrix techniques

Manual techniques are based on human judgment. One relatively simple approach involves taking photographs of a sample of the parts and then manually sorting these photographs into families based on the geometry, size, or other visual characteristics of the parts. A more sophisticated manual procedure is called ***production flow analysis*** (PFA). In this approach, families are determined by evaluating the equipment requirements for producing the outputs. Outputs that have the same complete set of equipment needs are grouped into a single family. It should then be possible to cluster a set of the necessary equipment together in a cell to produce that family. However, this is not always the case, because there may not be enough equipment to place one machine in each of the cells that needs it. Then some equipment must be shared between cells, or additional equipment must be purchased. Even if there is enough equipment to put it in each of the appropriate cells, two or three such machines may be needed in one cell to handle its capacity requirements while half a machine or less is needed in another cell. These difficulties are handled case by case.

The essence of PFA is to determine the *machine-component matrix* and then identify the components (parts or outputs) with common machine requirements. The matrix is based on information contained in the part routings. It is formed by listing all the components across the top and all the machines down the side. Then 1's are written in the matrix wherever a component uses a machine. For example, Table 7.3 shows a matrix with seven components that together require six machines. The objective is to *reorder* the components and machines so that "blocks" of 1's that identify the cells are formed along the diagonal, as shown in Table 7.4. Note that it is acceptable for a component not to use every machine in a group and for a machine not to process every component.

No component or machine should interact with a machine or component, respectively, *outside* of the cell. Thus, in Table 7.4, component 1 is listed as needing machine 3, but this is problematic. In this case, if we could duplicate machine 3, we could put it in both cell 1 and cell 2. Or we might consider putting machine 3 in cell 2 and sending component 1 to cell 2 after it is finished in cell 1 (but this violates our desire to produce cell-complete components). Or we could remove com-

$\mathcal{T}$ABLE 7.3 ❖ Original Machine-Component Matrix

	Components						
Machines	**1**	**2**	**3**	**4**	**5**	**6**	**7**
1		1			1		
2	1			1			1
3	1		1			1	
4		1					
5			1			1	
6	1						1

ponent 1 from the families and put it in a remainder cell (if there are other components and machines not listed in Table 7.3 within the facility).

The general guidelines for reordering the matrix by PFA are:

❖ Incompatible machines should be in separate cells.

❖ Each component should be produced in only one cell.

❖ Any investment in duplicate machinery should be minimized.

❖ The cells should be limited to a reasonable size.

The second category of cell formation is *classification and coding*. With classification and coding, an alphanumeric code is assigned to each part on the basis of design characteristics, processing requirements, or both. Parts with similar codes can be identified and grouped into families.

Statistical cluster analysis is the third category of cell formation. With this approach, a measure called a *similarity coefficient* is developed that quantifies how similar two parts are to one another. The similarity between *all* pairs of parts is

$\mathcal{T}$ABLE 7.4 ❖ Reordered Matrix

	Components						
Machines	**7**	**4**	**1**	**3**	**6**	**2**	**5**
6	1		1	Cell 1			
2	1	1	1				
3			1	1	1	Cell 2	
5				1	1		
1						1	1
4					Cell 3	1	

stored in a *similarity coefficient matrix*. Once developed, the similarity coefficient matrix is processed by a statistical clustering procedure such as the single-linkage clustering algorithm or the average-linkage clustering algorithm to identify part families.

Mathematical programming techniques use linear programming or goal programming to identify part families and their corresponding manufacturing cells. These approaches can consider a variety of objectives such as minimizing machine setup times, minimizing part transfers between cells, minimizing investments in new equipment, and maintaining acceptable levels of utilization. Likewise, these models can include a number of limitations on the size of a part family or a cell. Because these procedures require sophisticated algorithms to solve the mathematical models developed, they are not widely used.

Finally, *machine-component matrix procedures* rearrange the rows and columns of the matrix to form independent blocks of 1s along the diagonal. Thus, these approaches are similar to PFA, except that rather than relying on judgment to rearrange the matrix, they are based on specific algorithms—systematic step-by-step procedures for finding solutions to problems.

One popular machine-component matrix procedure is called the **rank order clustering** (ROC) algorithm. The ROC involves six steps:

1. Calculate the binary value of each row in the machine-component matrix.
2. If the rows are ordered from highest to lowest in terms of their binary value going from the top to the bottom, go to step 6. If the rows are not in this order, go to step 3.
3. Sort the rows of the machine-component matrix in decreasing order (i.e., highest to lowest). Calculate the binary value for each column.
4. If the columns are ordered from highest to lowest in terms of their binary value going from left to right, go to step 6. If the columns are not in this order, go to step 5.
5. Sort the columns of the machine-component matrix in decreasing order (i.e., highest to lowest) going from left to right. Go to step 1.
6. Stop.

Before presenting an example illustrating the ROC algorithm, we need to discuss how the binary value is calculated for the rows and columns of the machine-component matrix. If we let x_{ij} be the entry in row i and column j of the machine-component matrix, then the binary value for row i, BV_i, is calculated as follows:

$$BV_i = \sum_{j=1}^{N} x_{ij} \times 2^{N-j}$$

where N is the number of columns in the machine-component matrix. For instance, the binary value for machine 1 in Table 7.3 would be calculated as $0 \times 2^6 + 1 \times 2^5 + 0 \times 2^4 + 0 \times 2^3 + 1 \times 2^2 + 0 \times 2^1 + 0 \times 2^0 = 36$.

In a similar fashion, the binary value for column j, BV_j, is calculated as:

$$BV_j = \sum_{i=1}^{M} x_{ij} \times 2^{M-i}$$

where M is the number of rows in the machine-component matrix. To illustrate the calculation of the binary value for a column, the binary value for component 1 in Table 7.3 is calculated as $0 \times 2^5 + 1 \times 2^4 + 1 \times 2^3 + 0 \times 2^2 + 0 \times 2^1 + 1 \times 2^0 = 25$. We now illustrate how spreadsheets can be used to facilitate the task of reordering the rows and columns of a machine-component matrix in order to obtain a block diagonal pattern.

Spreadsheet Analysis: Rank Order Clustering Algorithm

Small Time produces 9 components using 10 machines. On the basis of the routing information shown below, it was determined that the components require from 2 to 4 operations on 2 to 3 different machines. The routing information indicates on which machine each operation is performed for the 9 components. Thus, component 1 is first processed on machine 2; then it is subsequently processed on machines 9 and 8.

Component	Operation 1	Operation 2	Operation 3	Operation 4
1	2	9	8	
2	2	6	8	9
3	9	8	4	8
4	3	5		
5	1	5		
6	7	4	7	
7	1	5		
8	4	7	10	
9	5	3	1	

The routing information was entered into a machine-component matrix in a spreadsheet, as shown below. In the machine-component matrix a 1 was entered if a particular component needed a particular machine; otherwise, a zero was entered.

	A	B	C	D	E	F	G	H	I	J	K	L
1					Components							
2	Machines	1	2	3	4	5	6	7	8	9	Rank Ord.	Prev Ord.
3	1	0	0	0	0	1	0	1	0	1	21	1
4	2	1	1	1	0	0	0	0	0	0	448	2
5	3	0	0	0	1	0	0	0	0	1	33	3
6	4	0	0	0	0	0	1	0	1	0	10	4
7	5	0	0	0	1	1	0	1	0	1	53	5
8	6	0	1	1	0	0	0	0	0	0	192	6
9	7	0	0	0	0	0	1	0	1	0	10	7
10	8	1	1	0	0	0	0	0	0	0	384	8
11	9	1	1	1	0	0	0	0	0	0	448	9
12	10	0	0	0	0	0	0	0	1	0	2	10
13	Rank Ord.	262	278	274	160	544	72	544	73	672		
14	Prev. Ord.	1	2	3	4	5	6	7	8	9		

In addition to entering the machine-component relationships into the spreadsheet, formulas were entered to calculate the binary value of each row (column K) and each column (row 13). For example, to calculate the binary value for the first machine (row 3), the following formula was entered into cell K3: = $(B3*2^8) + (C3*2^7) + (D3*2^6) + (E3*2^5) + (F3*2^4) + (G3*2^3) + (H3*2^2) + (I3*2^1) + (J3*2^0)$. Once this formula was entered into cell K3, it was copied to cells K4 to K12. In a similar fashion, to calculate the binary value for component 1, the following formula was entered into cell B13: $(B3*2^9) + (B4*2^8) + (B5*2^7) + (B6*2^6) + (B7*2^5) + (B8*2^4) + (B9*2^3) + (B10*2^2) + (B11*2^1) + (B12*2^0)$. This formula was then copied to cells C13 to J13.

Finally column L and row 14 were added to keep track of the previous order of the rows and columns—that is, their order before they were rearranged. If rearrangement of the rows and columns based on the binary value does not result in a new ordering of the rows or columns, the rank order clustering (ROC) algorithm terminates. The values for column L were obtained by simply copying the values in column A (rows 3 to 12), and the values for row 14 were obtained by copying the values from row 2 (columns B to J).

Entering the formulas to calculate the binary value for each row in the machine-component matrix completes step 1 of the ROC algorithm. In step 2 we need to sort the rows from highest to lowest in terms of their binary value (column K). To do this in Excel, highlight cells A2:K12. Then select Data from the menu bar at the top of the screen. Next select Sort. To sort the rows by their binary value, specify Rank Ord. for the Sort By field, select the Descending option (since we want the rows ordered from highest to lowest), and make sure the Header Row radio button is selected, since the header of the machine-component matrix was included in the highlighted range. After you enter this information, the Sort dialog box should look as follows:

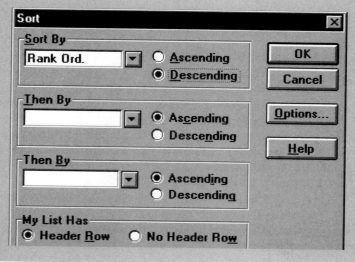

After this information has been entered, select OK, and the following re-arranged machine-component matrix wiil be displayed:

	A	B	C	D	E	F	G	H	I	J	K	L
1					Components							
2	Machines	1	2	3	4	5	6	7	8	9	Rank Ord.	Prev Ord.
3	2	1	1	1	0	0	0	0	0	0	448	1
4	9	1	1	1	0	0	0	0	0	0	448	2
5	8	1	1	0	0	0	0	0	0	0	384	3
6	6	0	1	1	0	0	0	0	0	0	192	4
7	5	0	0	0	1	1	0	1	0	1	53	5
8	3	0	0	0	1	0	0	0	0	1	33	6
9	1	0	0	0	0	1	0	1	0	1	21	7
10	4	0	0	0	0	0	1	0	1	0	10	8
11	7	0	0	0	0	0	1	0	1	0	10	9
12	10	0	0	0	0	0	0	0	1	0	2	10
13	Rank Ord.	896	960	832	48	40	6	40	7	56		
14	Prev. Ord.	1	2	3	4	5	6	7	8	9		

Comparing column A and column L, we note that the order of the rows has changed. (The values in column L were not affected by the sort, because this column was not included in the highlighted range before selecting the Data/Sort menu items.) Since the order of the rows has changed, we continue on with the ROC algorithm and calculate the binary value for each column in the machine-component matrix. Before moving on, however, we will first copy column A to column L. Now if we need to sort the rows again, we have their current order recorded and can use this to see if a change in their order occurs after another sort operation.

From the previous diagram of the spreadsheet, we can see that the columns are not ordered from highest to lowest in terms of their binary value going left to right (e.g., component 1 has a binary value of 896 and component 2 has a binary value of 960). Thus, in step 5 of the ROC algorithm we sort the columns in decreasing order from left to right. To sort the columns, we first highlight cells B2:J13. We then select Data and Sort as we did before. Now, however, we want to sort the columns, not the rows. To accomplish this we select Options from the Sort dialog box. Then, in the Orientation section of the Sort Options dialog box that appears, we select Sort Left to Right as shown below:

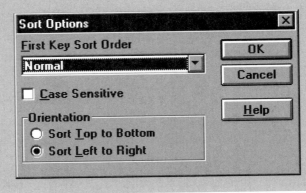

After Sort Left to Right has been selected, click the OK button to execute this change. After clicking on OK, we will see the Sort dialog box displayed on the screen.

Since we want to sort the columns on the basis of their binary value, we specify row 13 for the Sort By Field. Also, since we want the columns to be in decreasing order, we specify that we want to sort the columns in descending order, as shown below.

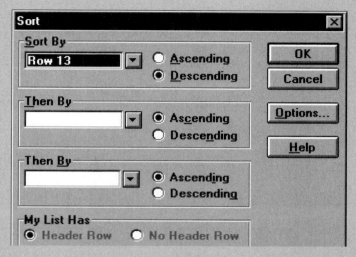

To sort the columns on the basis of their binary value, select OK in the Sort dialog box. Doing this results in the following machine-component matrix.

	A	B	C	D	E	F	G	H	I	J	K	L
1					Components							
2	Machines	2	1	3	9	4	5	7	8	6	Rank Ord.	Prev Ord.
3	2	1	1	1	0	0	0	0	0	0	448	2
4	9	1	1	1	0	0	0	0	0	0	448	9
5	8	1	1	0	0	0	0	0	0	0	384	8
6	6	1	0	1	0	0	0	0	0	0	320	6
7	5	0	0	0	1	1	1	1	0	0	60	5
8	3	0	0	0	1	1	0	0	0	0	48	3
9	1	0	0	0	1	0	1	1	0	0	44	1
10	4	0	0	0	0	0	0	0	1	1	3	4
11	7	0	0	0	0	0	0	0	1	1	3	7
12	10	0	0	0	0	0	0	0	1	0	2	10
13	Rank Ord.	960	896	832	56	48	40	40	7	6		
14	Prev. Ord.	1	2	3	4	5	6	7	8	9		

Comparing row 2 and row 14, we see that the order of the columns has changed. Thus, we return to step 1 of the ROC algorithm. Before doing so, however, we will copy row 2 to row 14 to record the current order of the columns.

Step 1 is automatically done for us as the formulas in column K calculate each row's binary value. A quick check of the rows indicates that they are already ordered from highest to lowest in terms of their binary value. Thus according to step 2, we now go to step 6, which terminates the procedure. In this example, the ROC algorithm terminates with the following solution:

	A	B	C	D	E	F	G	H	I	J	K	L
1					Components							
2	Machines	2	1	3	9	4	5	7	8	6	Rank Ord.	Prev Ord.
3	2	1	1	1	0	0	0	0	0	0	448	2
4	9	1	1	1	0	0	0	0	0	0	448	9
5	8	1	1	0	0	0	0	0	0	0	384	8
6	6	1	0	1	0	0	0	0	0	0	320	6
7	5	0	0	0	1	1	1	1	0	0	60	5
8	3	0	0	0	1	1	0	0	0	0	48	3
9	1	0	0	0	1	0	1	1	0	0	44	1
10	4	0	0	0	0	0	0	0	1	1	3	4
11	7	0	0	0	0	0	0	0	1	1	3	7
12	10	0	0	0	0	0	0	0	1	0	2	10
13	Rank Ord.	960	896	832	56	48	40	40	7	6		
14	Prev. Ord.	1	2	3	4	5	6	7	8	9		

According to our solution, three cells should be created. Cell 1 would consist of machines 2, 9, 8 and 6 and would process parts 2, 1, and 3. Cell 2 would consist of machines 5, 3, and 1 and would process parts 9, 4, 5, and 7. Finally, Cell 3 would consist of machines 4, 7, and 10 and would process parts 8 and 6. These cells are completely independent, as no part needs to be processed in more than one cell.

JOB SHOP LAYOUT

Because of its relative permanence, the layout of the operations is probably one of the most crucial elements affecting the efficiency of a job shop. In general, the problem of laying out operations in a job shop is quite complex. The difficulty stems from the variety of outputs and the constant changes in outputs that are characteristic of organizations with an intermittent transformation system. The optimal layout for the existing set of outputs may be relatively inefficient for the outputs to be produced six months from now. This is particularly true of job shops where there is no proprietary product and only outside customers are served. One week such a shop may produce 1000 ashtrays and the next week an 8000-gallon vat. Therefore, a job-shop layout is based on the historically stable output pattern of the organization and expected changes in that pattern rather than on current operations or outputs.

A variety of factors can be important in the interrelations among the operations of a job shop. If all the qualitative and quantitative factors can be analyzed and combined, the relative importance of locating each department close to or far from each of the other departments may be used to determine a layout. This approach, described next, is particularly useful for service operations where movements of materials are not particularly significant.

❖ Directly Specified Closeness Preferences

As a simplified example, consider Table 7.5, where six departments have been analyzed for the desirability of closeness to each other. It is standard, for this type of analysis, to specify *closeness preferences* by the letters A, E, I, O, U, and X, with the meanings given in the table. In general, the desirability of closeness decreases along the alphabet until U, which is "immaterial," and then jumps to "undesirable" with X; there is no range of undesirability.

One way of starting the layout process is simply to draw boxes representing the departments in the order given in the table and show closeness preferences on the arcs (line segments) joining them. This is illustrated, for Table 7.5, in Figure 7.5. The next step is to shift the departments with A on their arcs nearer each other and those with X away from each other. When these have been shifted as much as possible, the E arcs, then the I arcs, and finally the O arcs will be considered for relocation. The process of incrementally shifting departments to improve their relative locations will be deferred until a later section, where a more precise measure of closeness is used.

$\mathcal{T}$ABLE 7.5 ❖ Directly Specified Closeness Preferences*

Department	Department					
	1	2	3	4	5	6
1		E	A	U	U	U
2			U	I	I	U
3				U	U	A
4					I	U
5						I
6						

*Note:

A = Absolutely necessary   O = Ordinary closeness OK
E = Especially important   U = Unimportant
I = Important   X = Undesirable

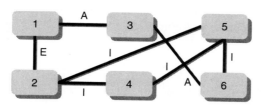

Figure 7.5   Initial layout.

*S*OLVED EXERCISE 7.3 ❖ Layout by Preferences

Determine a layout for six departments, 1–6, where the preferences are as follows (if no preference is noted, it is unimportant): 1–4 A, 3–2 A, 3–6 A, 4–5 X, 2–4 X, and 5–6 E.

Solution:

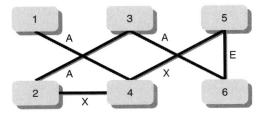

Initial preferences

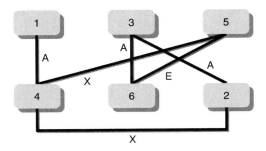

First iteration: Move 2, 4, 6

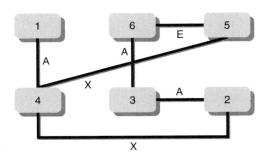

Second iteration: Interchange 3 and 6

The second iteration is about optimal. All the As and even the E are adjacent, while the two Xs are as far apart as possible.

❖ Cost–Volume–Distance Model

In the cost–volume–distance (CVD) approach, the desirability of closeness is based on the cost of moving materials or people between departments. Clearly, a layout can never be completely reduced to just one such objective, but where the cost of movement is significant, this approach produces reasonable first approximations. The objective is to minimize the costs of interrelations among operations by locating those operations that interrelate extensively close to one another. If we label one of the departments i and another department j, then the cost of moving materials between departments i and j depends on the distance between i and j, D_{ij}.

In addition, the cost will usually depend on the amount or volume moving from i to j, such as trips, cases, volume, weight, or some other such measure, which we will denote by V_{ij}. Then, if the cost of the flow from i to j per unit amount per unit distance is C_{ij}, the total cost of i relating with j is $C_{ij}V_{ij}D_{ij}$. Note that C, V, and D may have different values for different types of flows and that they need not have the same values from j to i as from i to j, since the flow in opposite directions may be of an entirely different nature. For example, information may be flowing from i to j, following a certain paperwork path; but sheet steel may flow from j to i, following a lift truck or conveyor belt path.

Adding the flows from i to every one of N possible departments, we find that the total cost of department i interrelating with all other departments is

$$\sum_{j=1}^{N} C_{ij}V_{ij}D_{ij}$$

(It is normally assumed that $C_{ii}V_{ii}D_{ii} = 0$, since the distance from i to itself is zero.) Adding together the costs for all the departments results in the total cost.

$$TC = \sum_{i=1}^{N}\sum_{j=1}^{N} C_{ij}V_{ij}D_{ij}$$

Our goal is to find the layout that minimizes this total cost. This may be done by evaluating the cost of promising layouts or, as in the following simplified example, by evaluating *all possible* layouts.

The section of a business school containing the administrative offices of the operations management department is illustrated in Figure 7.6. Each office is approximately 10 by 10 feet, so the walking distance (D) between adjacent offices (i.e., offices 1 and 2, and offices 2 and 3) is 10 feet, whereas that between diagonal offices (offices 1 and 3) is 15 feet.

The average number of interpersonal trips made each day is given in a travel or **load matrix** (Table 7.6). According to Table 7.6, each day the assistant makes 5 trips to the chair's office and 17 trips to the secretary's office. Thus, the assistant would travel 305 feet (10 feet × 5 trips + 15 feet × 17 trips) each day. Assuming that the chair is paid approximately twice as much as the secretary and the junior administrative assistant, determine if the present arrangement is best (i.e., least costly) in terms of transit time and, if not, what arrangement would be better.

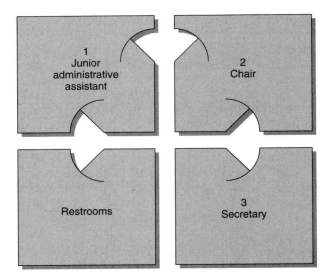

Figure 7.6   Office layout.

$\mathscr{T}_{ABLE}$ 7.6 ❖ Load Matrix, V_{ij} (Trips)

	To		
From	1 Assistant	2 Chair	3 Secretary
1 Assistant	—	5	17
2 Chair	10	—	5
3 Secretary	13	25	—

For convenience, the offices are numbered in Figure 7.6. Before calculating total costs of all possible arrangements, some preliminary analysis is worthwhile. First, because of special utility connections, restrooms are usually not considered relocatable. In addition, the relocation of the restrooms in this example would not achieve any result that could not be achieved by moving the other offices instead.

Second, many arrangements are mirror images of other arrangements and thus need not be evaluated, since their cost will be the same. For example, interchanging offices 1 and 3 will result in the same costs as the current layout. The essence of the problem, then, is to *determine which office should be located diagonally across from the restrooms*. There are three alternatives: chair, assistant, or secretary.

Now, let us evaluate each of the three possibilities as the "diagonal office"—first the chair, then the assistant, and last the secretary. The costs will simply be denoted as 1 for the assistant and the secretary or 2 for the chair (who earns twice as much as the others). As noted, the V_{ij} "volumes" will be the number of trips from i to j taken from the load matrix, and the distances will depend on who has the diagonal office across from the restrooms. The calculations for each arrangement are shown below.

1. *Chair:* TC $= 1(5)10 + 1(17)15 + 2(10)10 + 2(5)10 + 1(13)15$
$+ 1(25)10 = 1050$

2. *Assistant:* $TC = 1(5)10 + 1(17)10 + 2(10)10 + 2(5)15 + 1(13)10$
$+ 1(25)15 = 1070$

3. *Secretary:* $TC = 1(5)15 + 1(17)10 + 2(10)15 + 2(5)10 + 1(13)10$
$+ 1(25)10 = 1025$ (lowest)

To better understand these calculations, consider the current arrangement, in which the chair has the office diagonal to the restrooms. In this case, the assistant must travel 305 feet each day, as was explained earlier. Each day the chair would have to travel 150 feet: (10 feet × 10 trips to the assistant) + (10 feet × 5 trips to the secretary). Finally, the secretary would have to travel 445 feet each day: (15 feet × 13 trips to the assistant) + (10 feet × 25 trips to the chair). Since the chair is paid twice as much as the secretary and assistant, we weight the chair's travel distance as twice that of the other two workers. Using this weighting scheme provides a total cost of the current office arrangement of 1050: that is, 305 + (2 × 150) + 445.

The best arrangement is to put the secretary in the office diagonal to the restrooms for a relative cost of 1025. In the next section, we consider a more complex situation using operations sequence analysis.

*S*OLVED EXERCISE 7.4 ❖ CVD Approach

Given the following trips, in either direction, find a least-cost layout.

	To			
From	1	2	3	4
1	—	7	2	5
2		—	8	3
3			—	6
4				—

Solution:

There are four departments, with the largest number of trips being 2–3, 1–2, 3–4, and then 1–4. Thus:

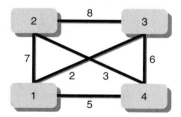

This arrangement places the departments with the fewest trips diagonally across from each other.

❖ Operations Sequence Analysis

With ***operations sequence analysis***, we follow a prescribed methodology for determining the CVD total cost. First, we choose two departments to determine if there are any materials flows between them. We determine this by checking the sequence of processing operations for *each* of the outputs. For each output that does have such flows, we multiply the annual unit production requirements for that output by its transport cost per unit per foot; then we add the results for all the identified outputs. This gives us the total annual cost per foot of separation between those departments. Repeating this procedure for every combination of departments results in a set of CV values that can be entered in a convenient matrix.

Next, an arbitrary arrangement of departments is sketched, and the cost per foot of separation between each set of departments is entered on the diagram. Then the departments are rearranged to bring those with higher costs between them closer together. Then the CVD cost can be calculated for each arrangement by using department centroids and measuring or calculating interdepartmental distances. Note again, however, that we are considering the cost of transportation as the sole basis for the job shop layout, when in reality there may be many other considerations. We illustrate the procedure with an example based on a three-product manufacturing firm: Topstar Company.

Table 7.7 shows the three products made by Topstar Company, the departmental processing sequence each requires, the transport cost per unit per foot moved, and the annual number of units of each product. Table 7.8 gives the required size of each of the six departments. To begin the layout analysis, we calculate the costs per foot of moving products between departments and enter them on a grid, as in Table 7.9. For example, tops and star tops both move from department 1 to 2. The annual cost per foot of separation between these departments is the annual production rate times the transportation cost:

$$\text{Tops: } 1000 \text{ units} \times \$0.20/\text{unit/foot} = \$200/\text{foot}$$
$$\text{Star tops: } 500 \text{ units} \times \$0.40/\text{unit/foot} = \underline{\$200/\text{foot}}$$
$$\text{Total} = \$400/\text{foot}$$

Thus, the annual cost of materials handling will be $400 *for every foot* separating departments 1 and 2. Similar calculations result in the remaining values given in Table 7.9. Note from the values that it is not important to have some departments (such as 3 and 5) close together. On the other hand, it is extremely important that department 3 be near 1 and 6.

To initiate the layout analysis, we make an arbitrary diagram of the six departments, as in Figure 7.7, and label the total annual costs of flow per foot between them directly on the diagram. (Note that this diagram is the same example we dis-

𝒯ABLE 7.7 ❖ Topstar Product Operations Sequence

Product	Annual Production	Transport Cost	Department Processing Sequence
Tops	1000	$0.20	1–2–5–6
Deluxe tops	2000	0.25	1–3–6
Star tops	500	0.40	1–2–4–5–6

$\mathcal{T}$ABLE 7.8 ❖ Department Size

Department	Size (ft²)
1	100
2	200
3	200
4	200
5	400
6	100

$\mathcal{T}$ABLE 7.9 ❖ Annual Cost per Foot of Separation Between Departments

	Department					
Department	1	2	3	4	5	6
1		400	500			
2				200	200	
3						500
4					200	
5						200
6						

cussed at the beginning of this section; see Figure 7.5.) Next, we analyze the diagram to ascertain if the departments can be better arranged to shorten the distances, particularly the high-cost distances. One final result of this approach is shown in Figure 7.8 (though there may be better—i.e., less costly—layouts).

Last, we must consider the departmental sizes in Table 7.8. To fit a typically rectangular building may require relocating the arrangement of Figure 7.8. The initial and final results are shown in Figure 7.9.

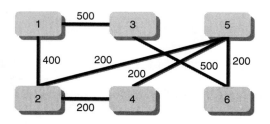

Figure 7.7   Initial department layout.

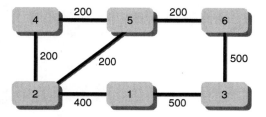

Figure 7.8   Final department layout.

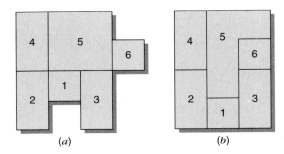

Figure 7.9 Allocating space to the layout. *(a)* Initial. *(b)* Adjusted final.

Let us now consider a realistic complication in the above process; there may be many such complications in practice. Suppose that the transport cost depended on the departments between which products were moved rather than on the product. How would this be handled? This is shown in Table 7.10, where the interdepartmental transport cost (in dollars/unit/foot) is given in *b*. Multiplying the production units in Table *a* by the rates in Table *b* results in the cost-per-foot-of-separation grid, *c*.

❖ Computer Layout Programs

One difficulty with all the approaches to laying out a job shop is that for larger problems the number of calculations and arrangements quickly becomes unmanageable. In general, the number of arrangements of N facilities is $N!$ (N factorial). For our earlier example of an arrangement with three offices, $N!$ was $3 \times 2 \times 1 = 6$. Because of symmetry, we were able to eliminate half of these, reducing the number of arrangements to three, each of which we rigorously analyzed. In our Topstar example $N!$ was $6 \times 5 \times 4 \times 3 \times 2 \times 1 = 720$. However, we did not bother to investigate all of these. For that matter, we did not calculate the cost of *any* of them, not even the "final" layout in Figure 7.9. Instead, we used the heuristic of locating higher-cost interrelating departments close together and hoped that the result would be "good enough," as a heuristic solution is meant to be.

𝒯ABLE 7.10 ❖ Cost of Separation with Interdepartmental Rates

						Department												
Department	1	2	3	4	5	6	1	2	3	4	5	6	1	2	3	4	5	6
1		1500	2000	X	X	X		$.20	.30	X	X	X		300	600	X	X	X
2			X	500	1000	X			X	.20	.20	X			X	100	200	X
3				X	X	2000				X	X	.40				X	X	800
4					500	X					.50	X					250	X
5						1500						.40						600
6																		
	(a) Units of flow						*(b)* Interdepartmental rate						*(c)* Cost of separation					

ℐOLVED EXERCISE 7.5 ❖ Operations Sequence Analysis

Find the best layout, given the following information. Assume rectangular (not diagonal) travel distances. Thus, distance is calculated as the sum of horizontal and vertical distances.

Product	Annual Units	Transport Cost ($/unit/foot)	Sequence
A	1500	2	1–3–4
B	800	3	2–3–4
C	1050	1	1–4

Solution:

Department	A	B	C	Total ($/foot)
1–2	0	0	0	0
1–3	2 × 1500 = 3000	0	0	3000
1–4	0	0	1050	1050
2–3	0	2400	0	2400
2–4	0	0	0	0
3–4	3000	2400	0	5400

Thus, 3 and 4 must be adjacent. Then 1 and 3, and 2 and 3, Last, 1 and 4.

First trial:

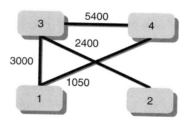

Second trial:

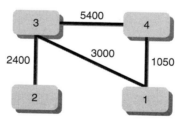

First trial: Cost (using unit rectangular distance; e.g.,1 → 4 is 2 units):
5400(1) + 3000(1) + 1050(2) + 2400(2) = 15,300

Second trial: Cost: 5400(1) + 1050(1) + 2400(1) + 3000(2) = 14,850

Thus, the second layout is less expensive.

A better approach is to use a computer to analyze layout situations. However, even with the speed and power of a computer, many problems are still too large to be evaluated economically. Thus, even computer packages employ heuristic routines to generate "good" initial solutions and then evaluate these solutions economically.

Typical of such computer approaches is an early package called Computerized Relative Allocation of Facilities Technique (CRAFT). This program assumes that the cost of interrelations between departments is the product of a rate matrix (such as cost per unit volume per unit distance) and a load matrix (such as volume of trips), both of which are inputs. Interdepartmental distances are obtained from an initial floor plan (existing or preliminary), which is read into the program. The computer routine itself then calculates distances between operational areas from the floor plan. A version of this program for personal computers is called Micro-CRAFT (see the Bibliography for Chapter 7).

The program's relayout heuristic is to interchange two areas at a time (more recent versions of CRAFT use three), recompute the total costs, and save the identity of the best switch. After all possible interchanges are evaluated, the best switch is then substituted for the original layout (if less costly), and the entire process is repeated. Common results with CRAFT are 20 percent savings over initial layout costs. CRAFT can handle up to 40 separate departments.

Even though CRAFT does not guarantee the lowest-cost layout, the nature of the problem is such that usually only trivially better solutions may exist. Although limited to single-story buildings, CRAFT does have the flexibility of allowing certain areas to be specified as fixed. A minor drawback of CRAFT is that the solution found is not allowed to alter the shape of the building. This is appropriate when the building is already in existence but perhaps inappropriate if a new building is being designed. Last, the realities of a particular situation may violate CRAFT's assumptions. For example, straight-line distances between operations areas may be inaccurate when there is only limited access to some areas (such as by forklift); CRAFT-designed shapes may not be appropriate for areas needing specialized shapes (such as L or T patterns); and certain areas may require other specific areas to locate (or not locate) near to them (e.g., inspection near shipping; painting away from welding). Nevertheless, these difficulties can be resolved with slight manual modifications to the final CRAFT solution, quick relayouts on CRAFT using higher costs between areas to bring them closer together (or lower costs to space them farther apart), or relayouts with fixed locations for certain areas.

Other computerized layout routines also exist in which departmental closeness preferences are specified directly (e.g., "very important to be close to department A") and used as the criterion variable, which may or may not be more appropriate than interoperation cost. Buildings of more than one story may also may be analyzed.

$\mathcal{C}$HAPTER IN PERSPECTIVE

This chapter is the last of three chapters related to product and transformation system design. Chapter 5 began this part with an overview of the three stages associated with selecting and designing new products and services. Chapter 6 then provided additional information related to the selection of an appropriate transformation system. The present chapter went one step further and addressed issues related to laying out the facility for each transformation system. For flow shops, assembly line balancing was discussed. For cellular layouts, five generic procedures for cell formation were briefly overviewed and the rank order clustering (ROC) algorithm was discussed in detail. Finally, closeness preferences, the cost-volume-distance (CVD) model, and operations sequence analysis were presented as methods for laying out job shops. In Chapter 8, our discussion turns to how operations management activities support resource management processes.

❖ CHECK YOUR UNDERSTANDING

1. Define the following terms: *load matrix, operations sequence analysis, line balancing, paced line, production flow analysis, balance delay, cycle time, machine-component matrix.*

2. What are the key considerations in laying out a continuous process, a flow shop, a job shop, and cellular production?

3. What are some operations problems that might indicate a need for a new shop layout?

4. In calculating the number of stations in line balancing, why do we round *up?*

5. Compare the layout task for continuous process industries with that for flow shops in terms of balance and cost of materials transportation.

6. What is the relationship between an assembly line's cycle time and its rate of output?

7. Why might the actual number of workstations needed to balance an assembly line differ from the theoretical number?

8. In balancing an assembly line, how might a task that takes longer than the cycle time and cannot be broken down further be handled? What about an uncombinable task that uses very little of the allotted cycle time?

9. Describe how the layout procedures for job shops might be applied to an appropriate service facility.

10. Describe how the layout procedures for cellular shops might be applied to an appropriate service facility.

11. Describe how the layout procedures for flow shops might be applied to an appropriate service facility.

12. Why do we not worry about "balance" in a job shop layout or cost of materials movement in a flow shop layout?

13. Referring to Figure 7.4, explain the evolution from functional cells to product cells.

14. Briefly list and overview the major categories of methods of cell formation. Which techniques are most likely to be used in industry? Why?

15. List the steps in the rank order clustering (ROC) algorithm.

16. How is a machine-component matrix constructed from part routings?

17. How are job shop layouts developed using closeness preferences?

18. How is operations sequence analysis different from the CVD model?

❖ EXPAND YOUR UNDERSTANDING

1. In addition to considering the longest operation time, can you think of other heuristic rules that might be useful in balancing an assembly line?

2. When a line cannot be perfectly balanced, some people will have more work time than others within each cycle. What might be a solution for this situation?

3. What might be the advantages of closeness preferences compared with CRAFT's criterion for closeness?

4. How does the layout of a retail establishment satisfy the needs for both efficiency and maximizing customers' exposure?

5. A current sociological trend is to move away from paced lines. Yet increasing automation is pushing workers to match their work pace to that of machines and computers. How can both of these trends be happening at the same time?

6. How should cells be laid out internally, as a job shop or a flow shop? Why?

7. What benefits would a nominal cell obtain, and not obtain, compared with a physical cell?

8. If a remainder cell is just the residual job shop, then aren't all job shops cellular facilities?

9. What form of layout do the new technologies described in Chapter 6 favor? Why?

10. A number of firms are moving toward mini-factories. What advantages might this offer over straight cellular production?

11. Where does the problem come in for forming production cells if a family has been identified?

12. One approach that mathematical methods frequently take when faced with the exceptional component 1–machine 3 element in Table 7.4 is to group cell 1 and cell 2 into a single cell. What is the problem with doing this?

13. In the job shop layout technique of directly specifying closeness preferences, why is there no range for "undesirable"?

14. What other complications might there be in the operations sequence analysis besides those described in Table 7.10?

15. If a job shop was being laid out in a third world country, how might the procedure be different? What other factors might enter in that would not exist in an industrialized country? Might the layout also differ among industrialized countries such as Europe and Japan? How about a flow shop?

16. In highly automated facilities, firms frequently increase the job responsibilities of the skilled workers who remain after automation has replaced the manual laborers, although there is less potential for applying their skills. Workers complain that they are under increased pressure to perform but have less control over the automated equipment. Is this ethical on the part of the companies involved? What approach would be better?

❖ APPLY YOUR UNDERSTANDING ———————————————
X-Opoly, Inc.

X-Opoly, Inc., was founded by two first-year college students to produce a knockoff real estate board game similar to the popular Parker Brothers' game Monopoly®. Initially, the partners started the company just to produce a board game based on popular local landmarks in their small college town, as a way to help pay for their college expenses. However, the game was a big success and because they enjoyed running their own business, they decided to pursue the business full-time after graduation.

X-Opoly has grown rapidly over the last couple of years, designing and producing custom real estate trading games for universities, municipalities, chambers of commerce, and lately even some businesses. Orders range from a couple of hundred games to an occasional order for several thousand. This year X-Opoly expects to sell 50,000 units and projects that its sales will grow 25 percent annually for the next five years.

X-Opoly's orders are either for a new game board that has not been produced before, or repeat orders for a game that was previously produced. If the order is for a new game, the client first meets with a graphic designer from X-Opoly's art department and the actual game board is designed. The design of the board can take anywhere from a few hours to several weeks, depending on how much the client has thought about the game before the meeting. All design work is done on personal computers.

After the design is approved by the client, a copy of the computer file containing the design is transferred electronically to the printing department. Workers in the printing department load the file onto their own personal computers and print out the board design on special decals, 19.25 inches by 19.25 inches, using high-quality color inkjet printers. The side of the decal that is printed on is usually light-gray, and the other side contains an adhesive that is covered by a removable backing.

The printing department is also responsible for printing the property cards, game cards, and money. The money is printed on colored paper using standard laser printers. Ten copies of a particular denomination are printed on each 8.5-inch by 11-inch piece of paper. The money is then moved to the cutting department, where it is cut into individual bills. The property cards and game cards are produced similarly, the major difference being that they are printed on material resembling posterboard.

In addition to cutting the money, game cards, and property cards, the cutting department also cuts the cardboard that serves as the substrate for the actual game board. The game board consists of two boards created by cutting a single 19-inch by 19.25-inch piece of cardboard in half, yielding two boards each measuring 19.25 inches by 9.5 inches. After being cut, game boards, money, and cards are stored in totes in a work-in-process area and delivered to the appropriate station on the assembly line as needed.

Because of its explosive growth, X-Opoly's assembly line was never formally planned. It simply evolved into the 19 stations shown in the table below.

Station Number	Task(s) Performed at Station	Time to Perform Task
1	Place plastic money tray in box bottom. Take two dice from bin and place in box bottom in area not taken up by tray.	10 seconds
2	Count out 35 plastic houses and place in box bottom.	35 seconds
3	Count out 15 plastic hotels and place in box bottom.	15 seconds
4	Take one game piece from each of eight bins and place them in box bottom.	15 seconds
5	Take one property card from each of 28 bins. Place rubber band around property cards and place cards in box bottom.	40 seconds
6	Take one orange card from each of 15 bins. Place rubber band around cards and place cards in box bottom.	20 seconds
7	Take one yellow card from each of 15 bins. Take orange cards from box and remove rubber band. Place yellow cards on top of orange cards. Place rubber band around yellow and orange cards and place cards in box bottom.	35 seconds
8	Count out 25 $500 bills and attach to cardboard strip with rubber band. Place money in box bottom.	30 seconds
9	Count out 25 $100 bills. Take $500 bills from box bottom and remove rubber band. Place $100 bills on top of $500 bills. Attach rubber band around money and place in box bottom.	40 seconds
10	Count out 25 $50 bills. Take $500 and $100 bills from box bottom and remove rubber band. Place $50 bills on top. Attach rubber band around money and place in box bottom.	40 seconds
11	Count out 50 $20 bills. Take money in box and remove rubber band. Place $20 bills on top. Attach rubber band around money and place in box bottom.	55 seconds
12	Count out 40 $10 bills. Take money in box and remove rubber band. Place $10 bills on top. Attach rubber band around money and place in box bottom.	45 seconds
13	Count out 40 $5 bills. Take money in box and remove rubber band. Place $5 bills on top. Attach rubber band around money and place in box bottom.	45 seconds
14	Count out 40 $1 bills. Take money in box and remove rubber band. Place $1 bills on top. Attach rubber band around money and place in box bottom.	45 seconds

Station Number	Task(s) Performed at Station	Time to Perform Task
15	Take money and remove rubber band. Shrink wrap money and place back in box bottom.	20 seconds
16	Take houses, hotels, dice, and game pieces and place in bag. Seal bag and place bag in box.	30 seconds
17	Place two cardboard game board halves in fixture so that they are separated by 1/4-inch. Peel backing off of printed game board decal. Align decal over board halves and lower it down. Remove board from fixture and flip it over. Attach solid blue backing decal. Flip game board over again and fold blue backing over front of game board, creating a 1/4-inch border. Fold game board in half and place in box covering money tray, game pieces, and cards.	90 seconds
18	Place game instructions in box. Place box top on box bottom. Shrink-wrap entire box.	30 seconds
19	Place completed box in carton.	10 seconds

Questions

1. What kind(s) of transformation system(s) does X-Opoly use?

2. What would be involved in switching the assembly line over from the production of one game to the production of another?

3. What is the cycle time of the 19-station line? What is its efficiency?

4. What is the line's maximum capacity per day, assuming that it is operated for one 8-hour shift less two 15-minute breaks? Assuming that X-Opoly operates 200 days per year, what is its annual capacity? How does its capacity compare with its projected demand?

5. On the basis of the task descriptions, develop a precedence graph for the assembly tasks. (Assume that tasks performed in the 19 stations cannot be further divided.) Using these precedence relationships, develop a list of recommendations for rebalancing the line in order to improve its performance.

6. What would be the impact on the line's capacity and efficiency if your recommendations were implemented?

❖ EXERCISES

1. Given the following machine-component matrix, form cells using the rank order clustering (ROC) algorithm.

	Components				
Machines	1	2	3	4	5
1	1			1	
2			1		1
3		1			1
4	1				

2. Given the following machine-component matrix, form cells using the ROC algorithm.

	Components						
Machines	1	2	3	4	5	6	7
1		1			1		
2			1			1	
3			1	1			
4		1			1		1
5	1						1

3. Given the following machine-component matrix, form cells using the ROC algorithm.

	Components				
Machines	1	2	3	4	5
1				1	1
2			1		
3	1	1			
4			1		1
5			1	1	
6					1
7		1			
8	1				

4. Given the following machine-component matrix, form cells using the ROC algorithm.

	Components						
Machines	1	2	3	4	5	6	7
1				1	1		
2		1	1				
3		1				1	1
4	1			1	1		
5	1						
6	1					1	
7	1			1			
8			1			1	1

5. a. Given the following load matrix, find the best layout.

	Department					
Department	1	2	3	4	5	6
1	—	4	6	2	0	7
2		—	3	5	1	3
3			—	2	6	5
4				—	5	2
5					—	3

b. Resolve part *a* if the rates are $4 from odd to even departments, $5 from even to odd, $6 from odd to odd, and $7 from even to even.

6. a. PVT Company makes three products, as listed in the following table. It is moving into a 40- by 60-foot building and has five departments with space needs as indicated. Suggest a layout for the building.

Product	Annual Volume	Cost/Unit/Foot	Processing Sequence
Peas	300	$0.05	1–2–4–5
Vees	700	0.03	1–2–3–5
Teas	600	0.05	1–2–3–4–5

Department	1	2	3	4	5
Size (ft²):	400	400	600	500	500

b. Solve the exercise in **a** if the cost in cents to transport units between departments is as shown here for all products:

From Department	To Department				
	1	2	3	4	5
1	x	3	x	x	x
2		x	4	5	x
3			x	3	4
4				x	4
5					x

7. An office is laid out as in the following table. The office manager is considering switching departments 2 and 6 to reduce transport costs. Should this be done? (Use rectangular distances. Assume that offices are 10 feet on a side.) What is the difference in annual cost, assuming a 250-day work year?

1	2	3
4	5	6

Daily Trip Matrix

From	To					
	1	2	3	4	5	6
1	x	40	x	x	x	40
2	30	x	20	30	60	0
3	x	70	x	x	x	20
4	x	0	x	x	x	30
5	x	10	x	x	x	0
6	40	50	20	0	10	x

Trip Cost (to any department) per Foot From

1	2	3	4	5	6
$0.02	$0.03	$0.01	$0.03	$0.02	$0.02

8. a. Relayout PVT's new building in Exercise 6 if the desired closeness ratings are as given below.

Department	1	2	3	4	5
1		E	O	U	X
2			I	I	U
3				E	I
4					E
5					

b. Solve Exercise **a** given the following ratings and compare the new solutions with the previous solutions.

Department	1	2	3	4	5
1		U	O	I	A
2			X	U	I
3				U	U
4					X
5					

9. Relayout the office in Exercise 7 given the following desired closeness ratings.

Department	1	2	3	4	5	6
1		I	A	X	O	U
2			X	E	I	O
3				O	X	I
4					I	E
5						A
6						

10. Demand for a certain subassembly in a toy manufacturing facility is 96 items per eight-hour shift. The following six tasks are required to produce one subassembly.

Task	Time Required (minutes)	Predecessor tasks
a	4	—
b	5	a
c	3	a
d	2	b
e	1	b, c
f	5	d, e

What is the required cycle time? Theoretically, how many stations will be required? Balance the line. What is the line's efficiency? What is the balance delay?

11. An assembly line has the following tasks (times shown in minutes).

   a. Six assemblies are required per hour. Balance the line.
   b. What is the efficiency of the line?

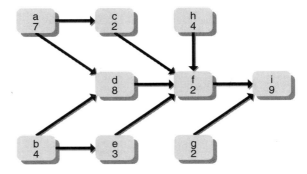

12. Balance the following line (times are given in minutes) to a cycle time of 10 minutes using the LOT rule and determine:

   a. Theoretical minimum number of workstations.
   b. Practical minimum number of workstations.
   c. Balance delay.
   d. How many units will be produced in a day if the line runs 7 hours 20 minutes.
   e. What the balance delay is if the cycle time is 20 minutes and if the cycle time is 7 minutes.

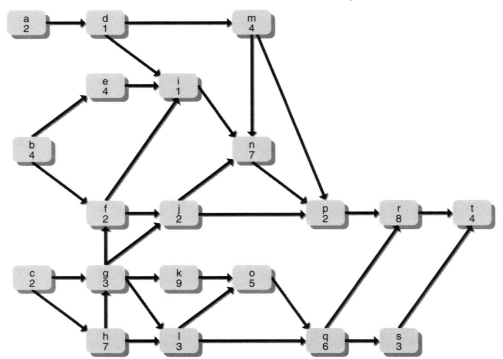

PART THREE

❖ ❖ ❖

Resource Management Processes

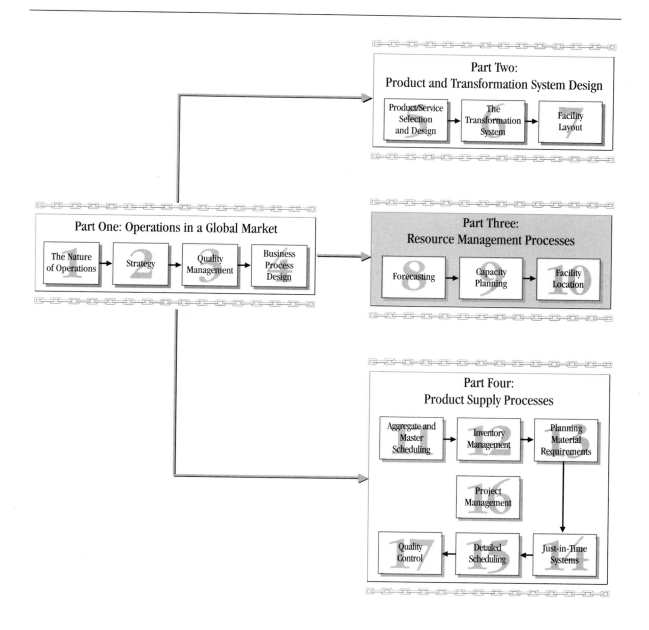

$\mathscr{C}$HAPTER OVERVIEW

❖ Forecasts are used in organizations for four primary purposes: (1) to determine if demand is sufficient when evaluating a new output; (2) to determine how much long-term capacity is needed; (3) to determine medium-term demand, for the purpose of aggregate scheduling; and (4) to ascertain short-term fluctuations in demand, for the purpose of production planning and workforce scheduling.

❖ Forecasting techniques can generally be divided into formal and informal. Formal techniques include quantitative and qualitative approaches. Quantitative techniques can be further classified as causal and autoprojection.

❖ Factors that influence the choice of a forecasting method include the availability of historical data, limitations on time and money, and the degree of accuracy required.

❖ A *time series* is a set of values collected at regular points in time or over sequential intervals of time. A time series can be considered as composed of four parts: trend, seasonality, cycles, and random fluctuations.

❖ *Autoprojection* techniques assume that past behavior exhibited in a time series can be used to predict future behavior of the time series.

❖ *Moving averages* is an autoprojection technique that develops a forecast by averaging the most recent demand values.

❖ The *weighted moving average* approach is a refinement of the moving average approach and pro-

vides flexibility regarding which data in the average are emphasized. For example, it is common to weight the newer data more heavily, since they may be more representative of the current environment.

❖ *Exponential smoothing,* another autoprojection technique, develops a forecast by correcting the previous forecast depending on the forecast error from the prior period. One advantage of exponential smoothing is that minimal data storage is required.

❖ Two methods of measuring forecast errors are *mean absolute deviation* (MAD) and *bias*. MAD provides an indication of the average error (i.e., the accuracy) of the forecasting model; bias provides an indication of the direction of the errors (i.e., whether the model consistently underestimates or overestimates demand).

❖ In the *multiplicative model,* forecasts are generated by multiplying the trend and seasonal components. Regression analysis is often used to estimate the trend component. The seasonal component for a particular period can be calculated by dividing actual demand by the trend estimate for the period.

❖ *Causal* forecasting methods are based on relationships between one or more variables and demand. Regression analysis can be used to quantify the relationship between these variables and demand.

INTRODUCTION

- ❖ Many technology companies were not sorry to see the 1980s come to an end. In January 1989, Apple Computer announced that its quarterly profit would decline more than 40 percent because it had built up excessive inventories of costly memory chips. To make matters worse, Apple tried to offset these costs by raising prices on some of its computers, only to drive customers away. Earlier—in October 1988—Seagate Technology had a quarterly loss of more than $50 million because it had miscalculated demand for a disk drive that a newer, more advanced version was replacing. And by Intel's own admission, its growth was stalled by large inventories of 80386 microprocessors (Schlender, 1989).

- ❖ IBM began 1994 with a $700 million inventory of obsolete PCs that took six months to unload. Because of this experience, the company was too conservative when it released its new Aptiva home PCs, and its new models sold out before the holiday season had even begun (Sager and Cortese, 1995).

- ❖ In industries, such as fashion, that are characterized by highly volatile demand, the combined costs of stockouts and markdowns can be greater than total manufacturing costs. One approach to forecasting in these highly volatile industries is to determine what can and cannot be predicted well. Products in the "predictable" category are made farthest in advance, saving manufacturing capacity for the "unpredictable" products so that they can be produced closer to their actual selling season. Using this approach, Sport Obermeyer, a producer of fashionable skiwear, increased its profits between 50 percent and 100 percent over a three-year period in the early 1990s (Fisher, Hammond, Obermeyer, and Raman, 1994).

The examples above illustrate the relationship between competing successfully and being able to predict key aspects of the future accurately. Clearly, it is not practical to try to plan anything without some prediction of the future. Even planning a simple party requires predicting how many people will show up, how much they will eat and drink, what kind of snacks and beverages they will enjoy, and how long they will stay. A business introducing a new product needs to predict the demand for the product, how prices and advertising will affect this demand, how competitors will respond, and so on. The severe consequences of misjudging the future are illustrated by the cases of Apple, Seagate, Intel, and IBM. On the other hand, the potential rewards of being able to predict the future accurately are illustrated by Sport Obermeyer.

In Part Two of this book, our focus was on business processes associated with designing and selecting products and their transformation systems. We now focus our attention on business processes associated with managing resources. Management of organizational resources includes obtaining and managing capital resources, human resources, and technology; and locating and designing facilities. In Chapter 5 we discussed the selection and design of the organization's outputs. Here we consider what the demand for those outputs may be. If insufficient demand exists, pursuing those markets may not be an effective strategy for the organization. Furthermore, at some demand levels the requirements placed on the production system may be beyond the skills of the organization. Or the organization may not have the equipment or materials necessary to produce the output at that demand level. Thus, we see that an accurate estimate of demand for the output is crucial to the efficient operation of the production system and, hence, to managing the organization's resources.

For example, a supermarket chain that is contemplating the addition of a new store must have a reasonable estimate of demand in order to determine how big the store and the parking lot should be, what ancillary departments (such as a bakery, pharmacy, deli, and bank) should be included, and how many shopping carts and checkout lanes should be specified in the plans. Once the facility is constructed, a more specific, perhaps weekly, forecast of demand will be needed so that the manager will be able to schedule workers and order merchandise. The same is true for decisions about capacity, scheduling, and staffing in a product organization. Capacity (obtaining the proper level of resources) and scheduling (the timing of resource usage) both require forecasting, whether or not it be a formal procedure.

But it is not only demand for the output that can be forecast. The tools of forecasting can also be used to predict the development of new technology, national and international economic conditions, and even many factors internal to the organization such as changes in lead time, scrap rates, cost trends, personnel growth, and departmental productivity.

FORECASTING IN USE

Forecasts are used in organizations for four primary purposes.

1. To decide whether demand is sufficient to justify entering the market. If demand exists but at too low a price to cover the costs that an organization

will incur in producing an output, then the organization should reject the opportunity.

2. To determine long-term (2- to 5-year) capacity needed, in order to design facilities. An overall projection of demand for a number of years in the future serves as the basis for decisions related to expanding, or contracting, capacity to meet the demand. Since there is competition, even in the not-for-profit sector, an organization is courting disaster if it produces inefficiently, because of excess idle capacity, or insufficiently to meet demand, because of too little capacity.

3. To determine midterm (3-month to 18-month) fluctuations in demand, in order to avoid shortsighted decisions that will hurt the company in the long run. To illustrate, if a company planned its staffing solely on the basis of its weekly forecast, each week it might adjust the level on the basis of a forecast for the coming week. Thus, in some weeks it might lay off workers only to rehire them in the following week. Such weekly adjustments would most likely lower morale and productivity. A better approach is to base staffing on a longer-term perspective.

4. To ascertain short-term (1-week to 3-month) fluctuations in demand for the purposes of production planning, workforce scheduling, materials planning, and other such needs. These forecasts support a number of operational activities and can have a significant effect on organizational productivity, bottlenecks, master schedules, meeting promised delivery dates, and other such issues of concern to top management and to the organization as a whole.

❖ Forecasting Methods

Forecasting methods can be grouped in several ways. One classification, illustrated in Figure 8.1, distinguishes between formally recognized forecasting techniques and informal approaches such as intuition, spur-of-the-moment guesses, and seat-of-the-pants predictions. Our attention here will obviously be directed to the formal methods.

In general, qualitative forecasting methods are often used for long-range forecasts, especially when external factors (e.g., the Gulf war of 1991) may play a significant role. They are also of use when historical data are very limited or nonexistent, as in the introduction of a new product or service.

Some of the most significant decisions made by organizations, frequently strategic decisions, are made on the basis of *qualitative* forecasts. These often concern either a new product or service or long-range changes in the nature of the organization's outputs. In both cases, relevant historical data on demand are typically not available. Qualitative demand forecasts for a new output will help managers determine the most efficient method of producing it and whether the organization will gain or lose.

Qualitative forecasts are made using information such as telephone or mail *surveys* of consumers' attitudes and intentions, consumer panels, test marketing in limited areas, expert opinion and panels, and analyses of historical demand for similar products or services—a method known as *historical analogy*. One example of historical analogy was the use of demand data for black-and-white television sets to predict the demand curve for color TV sets.

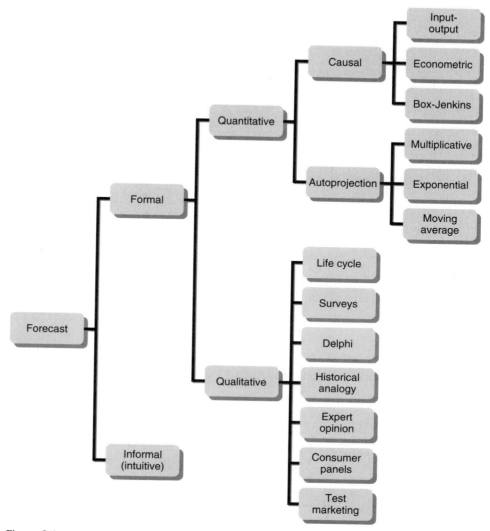

Figure 8.1 A classification of forecasting methods.

A special type of expert panel is called *Delphi*. The RAND Corporation developed the Delphi method as a group technique for forecasting the demand for new or contemplated products or services. The intent was to eliminate the undesirable effects of interaction between members of the group (such as loud and dominating individuals) while retaining the benefits of their broad experience and knowledge. The method begins by having each member provide individual written forecasts along with any supporting arguments and assumptions. These forecasts are submitted to a Delphi researcher, who edits, clarifies, and summarizes the data. These data are then provided as feedback to the members, along with a second round of questions. This procedure continues, usually for about four rounds, when a consensus among panel members can often be reached on some of the issues.

Another qualitative device often used in forecasting is called *life-cycle analysis.* Experienced managers who have introduced several new products are often able to estimate how long a product will remain in each stage of its life cycle. This forecast, coupled with other market information, can produce reasonably accurate estimates of demand in the medium to long range.

Quantitative forecasting methods are generally divided between methods that simply project the past history or behavior of the variable into the future (*autoprojection*) and those that also include external data (*causal*). Autoprojection is the simpler of the two and ranges from just using an average of the past data to using regression analysis corrected for cycles in the data. Simple projection techniques are obviously limited to, and primarily used for, very short-term forecasting. Such approaches often work well in a stable environment but cannot react to changing industry factors or changes in the national economy. These approaches are described in the following sections.

Causal methods, which are usually quite complex, include histories of external factors and employ sophisticated statistical techniques. These approaches, most appropriate for midterm forecasting, are briefly overviewed at the end of the chapter, but for more specific information the reader should consult the Bibliography.

Many "canned" computerized forecasting packages are available for the quantitative techniques, both autoprojection and causal. Also, as we will demonstrate throughout the chapter, spreadsheets are particularly useful for developing forecasts.

❖ Factors Influencing the Choice of Forecasting Method

What method is chosen to prepare a demand forecast depends on a number of factors. First, if the data are available, one of the quantitative forecasting methods just mentioned can be used. Otherwise, nonquantitative techniques are required. Attempting to forecast without a demand history is almost as hard as using a crystal ball. The demand history need not be long or complete, but some historical data should be used if at all possible.

Second, the greater the limitation on time or money available for forecasting, the more likely it is that an unsophisticated method will have to be used. In general, management wants to use a forecasting method that minimizes not only the cost of making the forecast but also the cost of an *inaccurate* forecast; that is, management's goal is to minimize the total forecasting costs. Costs of inaccurate forecasting include the cost of over- or understocking an item (e.g., Apple's overstocking of memory chips), the costs of under- or overstaffing, and the intangible and opportunity costs associated with loss of goodwill because a demanded item is not available.

Third, with the advent of computers, the cost of statistical forecasts based on historical data and the time required to make such forecasts have been reduced significantly. It has therefore become more cost-effective for organizations to conduct sophisticated forecasts.

Fourth, if the forecast must be very accurate, highly sophisticated methods are usually called for. Typically, long-range (two- to five-year) forecasts require the least accuracy and are only for general (or aggregate) planning, whereas short-range forecasts require great accuracy and are for detailed operations.

AUTOPROJECTION: TIME SERIES ANALYSIS

For autoprojection forecasting, a time series analysis is conducted. A *time series* is simply a set of values of some variable measured either at regular points in time or over sequential intervals of time. We measure the number of items of inventory at specific points in time and the number of units sold over specific intervals of time. If, for example, we recorded the number of automobiles sold each month of the previous year at Schroeder Oldsmobile Company and kept those data points in the order in which they were recorded, the 12 numbers would constitute a *12-period time series*. Time series data can be collected over very short intervals (such as hourly sales at a fast-food restaurant) or very long intervals (such as the census data collected every 10 years).

We analyze a time series because we believe that knowledge of its past behavior might help us understand (and therefore help us predict) its behavior in the future. In some instances, such as the stock market, this assumption may be unjustified, but in planning many operational activities history does (to some extent, at least) repeat itself and past tendencies continue. Autoprojection concludes with the development of a *time series forecasting model* that can be used to predict future demand. To begin our discussion of time series analysis, let us consider the component parts of any time series.

Time series analysis assumes that historical demand data have four components:

1. *Trend, T.*
2. *Seasonal* variation, *S.*
3. *Cyclical* variation, *C.*
4. *Random* variation, *R.*

❖ The Trend

The *trend* is the long-run direction of the series, including any constant amount of demand in the data. Figure 8.2 illustrates three fairly common trend lines showing changes in demand; a horizontal trend line would indicate a constant level of demand.

A straight-line or linear trend (showing a constant amount of change, as in Figure 8.2*a*) could be an accurate fit to the historical data over some limited range of time, even though it might provide a rather poor fit over an entire time series. For example, the curve in Figure 8.2*c* could be approximated by three separate straight trend lines, as shown in Figure 8.3. Over each of these shorter ranges, a straight line provides a good approximation to the actual curve. Figure 8.2*b* illustrates the situation of a constant *percentage* change. Here, changes in demand depend on the current size of demand (rather than being constant each period as in Figure 8.2*a*). The trend line shown in Figure 8.2*c* resembles the life cycle or "stretched-S" growth curve referred to in Chapters 2 and 5.

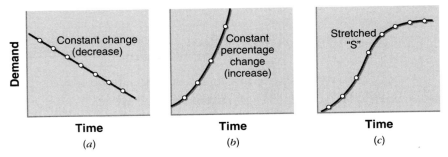

Figure 8.2   Three common trends.

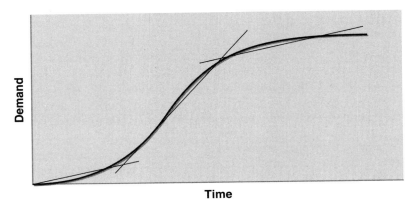

Figure 8.3   Straight trend approximation of the life cycle curve.

❖ Seasonal Variation

Seasonal fluctuations are fairly regular fluctuations that repeat within one year's time. Seasonal fluctuations result primarily from nature, but they are also brought about by human behavior. Sales of heart-shaped boxes of candy and Christmas trees are brought about by events that are controlled by humans. Snow tires and antifreeze enjoy a brisk demand during the winter months, whereas sales of golf balls and bikinis peak in the spring and summer months. Of course, seasonal demand often *leads* or *lags behind* the actual season. For example, the production season for meeting retailers' demand for Christmas goods is August through September. Also, seasonal variation in events need not be related to the seasons of the year. For example, fire alarms in New York City reach a "seasonal" peak at 7 P.M. and a seasonal low at 7 A.M. every day. And restaurants reach three seasonal peaks every day at 7:30 A.M., 12:30 P.M., and 8 P.M.

❖ Cyclical Variation

The cycle or *cyclical* component is obvious only in time series that span several years or more. A cycle can be defined as a *long-term oscillation,* or a swing of the

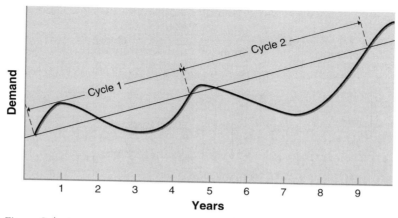

Figure 8.4   Typical cycles.

data points about the trend line over a period of at least three complete seasonals. National economic cycles of booms and depressions and periods of war and peace are examples of such cycles. Figure 8.4 presents two complete cycles and the underlying straight-line trend of a time series where no yearly seasonal is assumed to exist. Note that the oscillations around the trend line are *not* symmetrical, because they seldom are symmetrical in actual time series.

Cycles, particularly business cycles, are often difficult to explain, and economists have devoted considerable research and speculation to their causes. Identification of a cyclic pattern in a time series requires the analysis of a long period of data. For example, only two cycles were completed in nine years for the time series shown in Figure 8.4. For most operational activities, forecasting the cyclic component is not considered, since data are typically unavailable to determine the cycle. In addition, cycles are not likely to repeat in similar amplitude and duration; hence, the assumption of repeating history does not hold.

❖ Random Variation

Random variations are, as the name implies, without a specific assignable cause and without a pattern. Random variations are the fluctuations left in the time series after the trend, seasonality, and cyclical behaviors have been accounted for. Random fluctuations can sometimes be explained after the fact, such as an increase in consumption of energy owing to abnormally harsh weather, but cannot be systematically predicted and, hence, are not included in forecasting models.

The objective of time series analysis is to determine the magnitude of one or more of these components and to use that knowledge for the purpose of forecasting. Time series forecasts are often found to support operational activities better than qualitative forecasts do. For example, time series analysis is useful in planning annual production and inventory schedules based on previous demand patterns.

In the next two sections we will consider three models of time series analysis:

1. Moving averages (trend component of the time series).
2. Exponential smoothing (trend component of the time series).
3. Linear trend, multiplicative model (trend and seasonal components).

These models will be presented within the context of two example situations.

$\mathscr{D}$EMAND FORECASTING FOR THE INNER CITY HEALTH CLINIC: MOVING AVERAGES AND EXPONENTIAL SMOOTHING

Inner City Health Clinic is a federally funded health clinic that serves the needs of the urban poor. Currently the clinic is in its fourth year of operation and is preparing its staffing plan for the upcoming quarter. The federal government requires the clinic to prepare a budget request each quarter for the coming quarter. The request is based largely on the forecast of demand for specific services during the next quarter.

Demand data for emergency services at the clinic are available for each of the four quarters of the preceding three years and for the first two quarters of the current year. The data were entered into an Excel spreadsheet as shown in Figure 8.5 and plotted using Excel in Figure 8.6. The first step in forecasting is *always* to plot the data. Given a plot of the data, the analyst can begin to rule out forecasting models whose assumptions are not met by the pattern revealed in the plot. For example, if the data exhibit a nonlinear pattern, then the linear trend model could be ruled out as a forecasting model.

	A	B	C	D	E	F	G
1	Year Since		Period	Number of			
2	Opening	Quarter	Number	Patient Visits			
3	1	1	1	3,500			
4		2	2	8,000			
5		3	3	5,500			
6		4	4	10,000			
7	2	1	5	4,500			
8		2	6	6,000			
9		3	7	3,000			
10		4	8	5,500			
11	3	1	9	5,000			
12		2	10	9,500			
13		3	11	7,500			
14		4	12	15,000			
15	4	1	13	13,500			
16		2	14	17,500			

Figure 8.5   Spreadsheet with data on demand for emergency services for the Inner City Health Clinic.

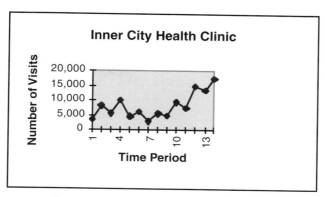

Figure 8.6 Plot of quarterly demand for emergency services at Inner City Health Clinic.

ChartWizard button

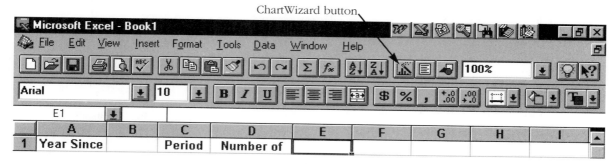

Figure 8.7 Using Excel's ChartWizard.

The graph shown in Figure 8.6 was developed using Excel's ChartWizard. To use this feature, select the ChartWizard button from the toolbar at the top of the screen (see Figure 8.7). Next highlight the range in the spreadsheet where you want the chart to be placed. In the spreadsheet shown in Figure 8.5, the range E5 to I5 was highlighted. (The range highlighted at this stage is not very important, as the size of the chart can be easily changed at a later time.)

Next the ChartWizard–Step 1 of 5 dialog box appears, as shown in Figure 8.8. In this step we specify the data we want to plot in our chart. In our case we want to

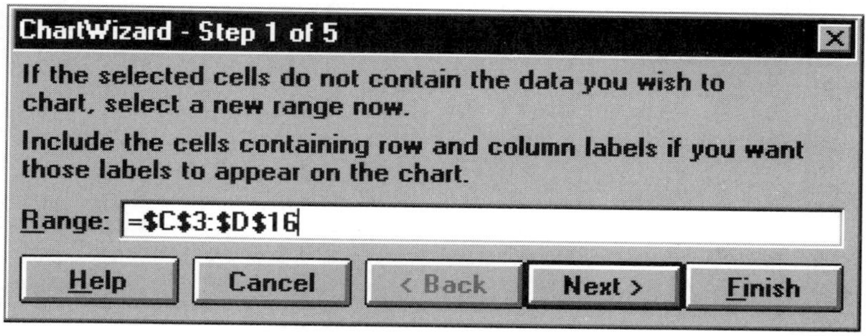

ChartWizard - Step 1 of 5

If the selected cells do not contain the data you wish to chart, select a new range now.

Include the cells containing row and column labels if you want those labels to appear on the chart.

Range: =$C$3:$D$16

| Help | Cancel | < Back | Next > | Finish |

Figure 8.8 First step in using ChartWizard.

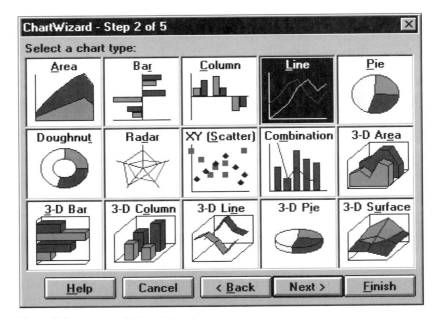

Figure 8.9   Step 2 of ChartWizard.

plot the number of visits to the clinic over time. Thus, referring to Figure 8.5, for the Range we specify cells C3:D16, as shown in Figure 8.8. After the range has been specified we select the Next button.

Now the ChartWizard–Step 2 of 5 dialog box appears, as shown in Figure 8.9. In this step we specify the type of chart or graph we would like. In our case we select the Line option as shown in Figure 8.9 and then select Next to move on to step 3.

In step 3, we have a variety of different line graphs to choose from, as shown in Figure 8.10. For our purposes, the first line chart is fine and is selected. To advance to step 4, we select the Next button.

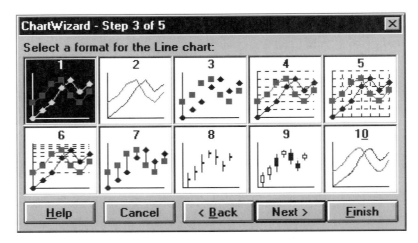

Figure 8.10   Step 3 of ChartWizard.

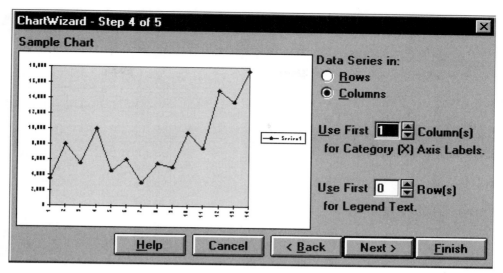

Figure 8.11 Step 4 of ChartWizard.

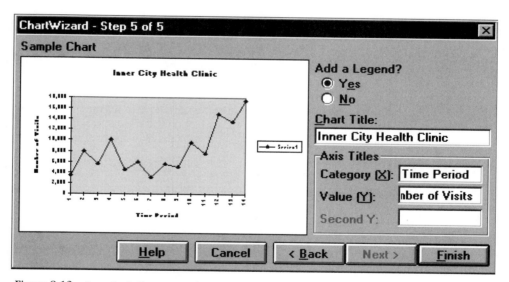

Figure 8.12 Step 5 of ChartWizard.

In step 4, we indicate that the data are organized in columns, and we specify that the first column should be used as the values for the *X*-axis (see Figure 8.11). Finally, in step 5 we add a legend and labels for the *X*- and *Y*-axes, as shown in Figure 8.12. When we have finished entering the information in the ChartWizard–Step 5 of 5 dialog box (Figure 8.12), we select the Finish button and our newly created line graph appears next to the data, as shown in Figure 8.13.

In the past, the administrator of the clinic has tried using the last period's demand and has also tried using the average of all past demand to predict the next period's demand for the center. Neither of these two techniques has proved satisfactory. Using the last period's demand as a predictor of the next period's demand

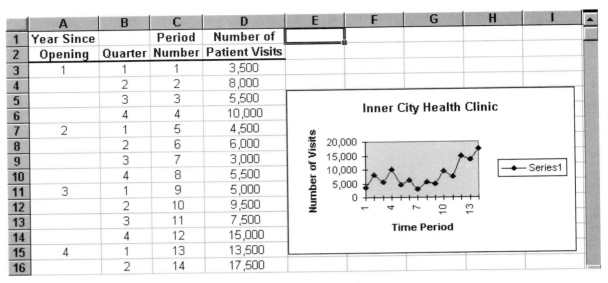

	A	B	C	D
1	Year Since		Period	Number of
2	Opening	Quarter	Number	Patient Visits
3	1	1	1	3,500
4		2	2	8,000
5		3	3	5,500
6		4	4	10,000
7	2	1	5	4,500
8		2	6	6,000
9		3	7	3,000
10		4	8	5,500
11	3	1	9	5,000
12		2	10	9,500
13		3	11	7,500
14		4	12	15,000
15	4	1	13	13,500
16		2	14	17,500

Figure 8.13   Line plot shown next to actual data.

produced erratic forecasts. For example, using this method the administrator predicted (and staffed, scheduled, and purchased for) a demand of 3500 visits for the second quarter of year 1, but there were actually 8000 visits. (Overtime and rush orders reached a peak during this quarter.) The administrator then predicted 8000 visits for the third quarter, but only 5500 visits materialized. Clearly, this method could not sort out the fluctuations in the demand data, and it was therefore deemed unsatisfactory.

The administrator then turned to the average of all demand data to predict the next period's demand. For the fourth quarter of year 1 the administrator predicted 5667 visits [i.e., (3500 + 8000 + 5500)/3], but 10,000 actually occurred. For the tenth period he forecast 5666 visits (i.e., the sum of the first nine periods' demand divided by 9) and 9500 occurred. The administrator recognized that this averaging method produced forecasts that smoothed out the fluctuations but did not adequately respond to any growth or reduction in the demand trend. As a matter of fact, the averaging method performed progressively worse as the amount of data increased. This was because each new piece of demand data had to be averaged with *all* the old data from period 1 to the present, and therefore each new element of data had less overall impact on the average. In fact, if the administrator were to use the averaging method to forecast the third-quarter demand for year 4, the forecast would be 8143, clearly a poor forecast when compared with demand in the past few periods.

After evaluating these two simple methods, the administrator decided to consider the three time series methods mentioned earlier, each of which is capable of producing the needed forecasts. The remainder of this section will be devoted to an analysis of the first two methods: moving averages and exponential smoothing. The third method (linear trend, multiplicative) is discussed in the next section.

❖ Moving Averages

To overcome the problem of using a simple average, the *moving average* technique generates the next period's forecast by averaging the actual demand for only the last n time periods (n is often in the range of 4 to 7). Any data older than n are thus ignored. The value of n is usually based on the expected seasonality in the data, such as four quarters or 12 months in a year. If n must be chosen arbitrarily, then it should be based on experimentation; that is, the value selected for n should be the one that works best for the available historical data.

Mathematically, a forecast using the moving average method is computed as

$$F_{t+1} = \frac{1}{n} \sum_{i=(t-n+1)}^{t} A_i$$

where

t = period number for the *current* period

F_{t+1} = forecast of demand for the next period

A_i = actual demand in period i

n = number of periods of demand to be included in the moving average (known as the *order* of the moving average)

For example, to forecast demand for the next quarter of this year (i.e., quarter 3 of year 4, or period 15, in Figure 8.5) using a moving average of order 4 (that is, $n = 4$), the administrator of the clinic would compute

$$F_{14+1} = \frac{1}{4} \sum_{i=14-4+1}^{14} A_i$$

or

$$F_{15} = \frac{1}{4} \sum_{i=11}^{14} A_i$$
$$F_{15} = .25\left(A_{11} + A_{12} + A_{13} + A_{14}\right)$$
$$F_{15} = .25\left(7500 + 15,000 + 13,500 + 17,500\right) = 13,375$$

The forecast for the next quarter using a moving average forecast of order 4 would therefore be 13,375 emergency services.

The moving average is a *compromise* between using the last period's demand as the forecast and using the simple average, both of which the administrator has rejected as unsatisfactory. The number of periods to be averaged in the moving average depends on the specific situation. If too few periods are included in the average, the forecast will be similar to that obtained when only the last period's demand had been used. Using too many periods in the moving average will result in a forecast similar to that obtained when the simple average was used.

	A	B	C	D	E	F
1	Year Since		Period	Number of	4 Period	
2	Opening	Quarter	Number	Patient Visits	Moving Average	
3	1	1	1	3,500		
4		2	2	8,000		
5		3	3	5,500		
6		4	4	10,000		
7	2	1	5	4,500	6,750	
8		2	6	6,000	7,000	
9		3	7	3,000	6,500	
10		4	8	5,500	5,875	
11	3	1	9	5,000	4,750	
12		2	10	9,500	4,875	
13		3	11	7,500	5,750	
14		4	12	15,000	6,875	
15	4	1	13	13,500	9,250	
16		2	14	17,500	11,375	
17			15		13,375	

Figure 8.14   Using a spreadsheet to calculate moving averages.

Spreadsheets can be used to facilitate the task of developing forecasts based on moving averages. In Figure 8.14, formulas were entered in column E of the spreadsheet shown in Figure 8.5 to calculate a four-period moving average. Specifically, the formula = AVERAGE(D3:D6) was entered in cell E7. Then this formula was "copied" to cells E8 to E17. With spreadsheets, moving averages with different orders could be easily investigated. For example, if we wanted to use a three-period moving average, the formula = AVERAGE(D3:D5) could be entered in cell E6 and "copied" to cells E7 to E17. (*Note:* Excel has an add-in function to generate moving average formulas. To access this feature select Tools from the menu at the top of the screen. If the Data Analysis Add-In has been installed, select it, and then select Moving Average.)

❖ Weighted Moving Averages

A refinement of the moving average approach is to weight the older or, more commonly, the newer data more heavily, rather than use equal weights. For example, we might believe that the newest data point is the best indicator of where the data are headed, but to guard against a random fluctuation we also include the three prior data points, each with a decreasing level of importance. Thus, rather than using weights of 1/4, or 0.25, in a four-period moving average, we might use 0.10, 0.20, 0.30, and 0.40. (Note that they still sum to 1.0.) This would give the third-oldest data point only half the importance, or weight, of the most recent data point. Other weights might be 0.20, 0.20, 0.25, 0.35 or 0.05, 0.10, 0.25, 0.60.

Applying the first set of weights—.10, .20, .30, .40—to the past four periods of data, we obtain the period 15 forecast:

$$F_{15} = 0.10A_{11} + 0.20A_{12} + 0.30A_{13} + 0.40A_{14}$$
$$= 0.10(7500) + 0.20(15,000) + 0.30(13,500) + 0.40(17,500)$$
$$= 14,800$$

This compares with the equally weighted moving averages forecast of 13,375. As with regular moving averages, a longer or shorter order may be used and the weights adjusted appropriately.

As with simple moving averages, spreadsheets can be used to facilitate the task of developing a forecast using weighted moving averages. The spreadsheet shown in Figure 8.15 provides a four-period weighted moving average with weights 0.10, 0.20, 0.25, and 0.40, as is indicated in cells B1 to B4. If we enter the weights in separate cells (not as constants within the formulas that actually calculate the weighted moving average) and then refer to these cells in our weighted moving average formula, we can quickly investigate how our forecast is affected by changing these weights. If we used constants in our formulas, we would have to change all the formulas whenever we wanted to change the weights; also, the weights used would not be as clear to someone using the spreadsheet.

The data for the first year were deleted in the spreadsheet shown in Figure 8.15 so that the entire model would be visible on the screen. In cell E11 the following formula was entered to calculate the weighted moving average for period 9:

$$= (D7*B\$1) + (D8*B\$2) + (D9*B\$3) + (D10*B\$4)$$

This formula contains a combination of relative and absolute cell references. Normally in spreadsheets we use relative cell addresses because we want the formula to change as it is copied. In the formula that was entered in cell E11, D7 is a

	A	B	C	D	E	F
1	w(1)	0.10				
2	w(2)	0.20				
3	w(3)	0.30				
4	w(4)	0.40				
5	Year Since		Period	Number of	Weighted	
6	Opening	Quarter	Number	Patient Visits	Moving Average	
7	2	1	5	4,500		
8		2	6	6,000		
9		3	7	3,000		
10		4	8	5,500		
11	3	1	9	5,000	4,750	
12		2	10	9,500	4,850	
13		3	11	7,500	6,700	
14		4	12	15,000	7,400	
15	4	1	13	13,500	10,650	
16		2	14	17,500	12,350	
17			15		14,800	

Figure 8.15   Spreadsheet for calculating weighted moving averages.

relative cell address. Entering D7 as part of the formula in cell E11 tells the spreadsheet to use the value in the cell over one column to the left and up four rows. Thus, when the formula is copied down a row to cell E12, the D7 is automatically changed to D8 (cell D8 is over one column to the left and up four rows *relative* to cell E12). However, there are times when we want a formula not to update itself automatically but rather always to refer to a particular cell. This is the case with the weights entered in cells B1 to B4. We always want the fourth-oldest data point to refer to cell B1, the third-oldest data point to cell B2, and so on. If we don't want a formula to change the cell reference when it is copied, we use absolute cell references. To indicate that a reference is absolute, we put a dollar sign ($) in front of the row number or column letter (or both) that we don't want to change when a formula is copied. In cell E11, we don't want the row numbers for the weights to change as the formula is copied down the spreadsheet. Thus, the references to the weights were entered as B$1, B$2, B$3, and B$4. This allows us to enter the formula just one time in cell E11 and then copy it to cells E12 to E17. To illustrate how the absolute and relative cell addresses work, the formula entered in cell E11 appears as follows when it is "copied" to cell E12:

$$= (D8*B\$1) + (D9*B\$2) + (D10*B\$3) + (D11*B\$4)$$

Note that the forecast for period 15 shown in Figure 8.15 (14,800) is the same as what we calculated manually earlier.

Finally to investigate the effect of changing the weights, we simply change the weights entered in cells B1 to B4. For example, Figure 8.16 shows that changing the weights to 0.20, 0.20, 0.25, and 0.35 reduces the forecast from 14,800 to 14,000.

	A	B	C	D	E	F
1	w(1)	0.20				
2	w(2)	0.20				
3	w(3)	0.25				
4	w(4)	0.35				
5	Year Since		Period	Number of	Weighted	
6	Opening	Quarter	Number	Patient Visits	Moving Average	
7	2	1	5	4,500		
8		2	6	6,000		
9		3	7	3,000		
10		4	8	5,500		
11	3	1	9	5,000	4,775	
12		2	10	9,500	4,925	
13		3	11	7,500	6,275	
14		4	12	15,000	7,100	
15	4	1	13	13,500	10,025	
16		2	14	17,500	11,875	
17			15		14,000	

Figure 8.16 Spreadsheets permit quick analysis of different weights.

*S*OLVED EXERCISE 8.1 ❖ Moving Averages

Consider the following data:

Period:	1	2	3	4	5	6
Data:	24	22	26	23	25	19

a. Forecast period 7 using the average of the data.

b. Forecast period 7 using a moving average of order 3.

c. Forecast period 7 using a weighted moving average of order 3 with weights of 0.2, 0.3, 0.5.

d. Repeat (c) with weights of 0.5, 0.3, 0.2.

e. Repeat (c) with weights of 0.33, 0.33, 0.33 and compare with (b).

f. If the "periods" above represented weeks (assume exactly 4 weeks per month), what order would you suggest using instead of 3? What if the periods were months?

Solution:

a. $(24 + 22 + 26 + 23 + 25 + 19)/6 = 23.17$

b. $(23 + 25 + 19)/3 = 22.3$

c. $0.2(23) + 0.3(25) + 0.5(19) = 21.6$

d. $0.5(23) + 0.3(25) + 0.2(19) = 22.8$

e. $0.33(23) + 0.33(25) + 0.33(19) = 22.3$, the same as (b), of course.

f. The natural cycle is 4 weeks per month, so the order should be 4. Since there are 12 months per year, the natural order would be 12.

❖ Difficulties in Forecasting

Autoprojection involves two inherent difficulties, and a compromise solution that addresses both must be sought. The first problem is producing as good a forecast as is possible with the available data. Usually, this can be interpreted as using the most current data because those data are more representative of the present behavior of the time series. In this sense, we are looking for an approach that is responsive to recent changes in the data.

The second problem is to smooth the random behavior of the data. That is, we do not want a forecasting system that forecasts increases in demand simply because the last period's demand suddenly increased, nor do we want a system that indicates a downturn just because demand in the last period decreased. All time series data contain a certain amount of this erratic or random movement. It is impossible for a manager to predict this random movement of a time series, and it is folly to attempt it. The only reasonable conclusion is to avoid overreaction to a fluctuation that is simply random. The general interpretation of this objective is that several periods of data should be included in the forecast so as to "smooth" the random fluctuations that typically exist. Thus, we are also looking for an approach that is stable, even with erratic data.

Clearly, methods used to attain both responsiveness and stability will be somewhat contradictory. If we use the most recent data so as to be responsive, only a few periods will be included in the forecast; but if we want stability, large numbers of periods will be included. The only approach to deciding how many periods to include is to experiment with several different numbers and evaluate each on the basis of its ability to produce good forecasts and to smooth out random fluctuations. *Mean absolute deviation* (MAD) is one measure often used to evaluate a forecasting model. MAD, which is discussed in the next section, is generally *lowest* for the best model.

❖ Exponential Smoothing

As noted above, we generally want to use the most current data and, at the same time, use enough observations of the time series to smooth out random fluctuations. One technique perfectly adapted to meeting these two objectives is *exponential smoothing*.

Exponential smoothing has an advantage over moving averages in that the computations required are much simpler and less data storage is required, particularly in situations that need data from a large number of past time periods.

Forecasting with Exponential Smoothing

The computation of a demand forecast using exponential smoothing is carried out with the following equation:

$$\text{New demand forecast} = (\alpha)\text{current actual demand}$$
$$+ (1 - \alpha)\text{previous demand forecast}$$

or

$$F_{t+1} = \alpha A_t + (1 - \alpha)F_t$$

where α is a smoothing constant that must be between zero and 1, F_t is the exponential forecast for period t, and A_t is the actual demand in period t.

The smoothing constant α can be interpreted as the *weight* assigned to the last (i.e., the current) data point. The remainder of the weight $(1 - \alpha)$ is applied to the last forecast. However, the last forecast was a function of the previous weighted data point and the forecast before that. To see this, note that the forecast in period t is calculated as

$$F_t = \alpha A_{t-1} + (1 - \alpha)F_{t-1}$$

Substituting the right-hand side in our original formula yields

$$F_{t+1} = \alpha A_t + (1 - \alpha)[\alpha A_{t-1} + (1 - \alpha)F_{t-1}]$$

Thus the data point A_{t-1} receives a weight of $(1-\alpha)\alpha$, which, of course, is less than α. Since this process is iterative, we see that exponential smoothing automatically applies a set of diminishing weights to each of the previous data points and is therefore a form of weighted averages. Exponential smoothing derives its name from the fact that the weights decline exponentially as the data points get older and older. In general, the weight of the nth most recent data point can be computed as follows:

Weight of nth most recent data point in an exponential average $= \alpha(1 - \alpha)^{n-1}$

Using this formula, the most recent data point, A_t, has a weight of $\alpha(1 - \alpha)^{1-1}$ or simply α. Similarly, the second most recent data point, A_{t-1}, would have a weight of $\alpha(1 - \alpha)^{2-1}$ or simply $\alpha(1 - \alpha)$. As a final example, the third most recent data point, A_{t-2}, would have a weight of $\alpha(1 - \alpha)^{3-1}$ or $\alpha(1 - \alpha)^2$.

The higher the weight assigned to the current demand, the greater the influence this point has on the forecast. For example, if α is equal to 1, the demand forecast for the next period will be equal to the value of the current demand, the approach used earlier by the Inner City Health Clinic's administrator. The closer the value of α is to 0, the closer the forecast will be to the previous period's *forecast* for the current period. (Check these results by using the equation.)

Rearranging the terms of the original formula provides additional insights into exponential smoothing, as follows:

$$F_{t+1} = \alpha A_t + (1 - \alpha)F_t$$
$$= \alpha A_t + F_t - \alpha F_t$$
$$= F_t + \alpha A_t - \alpha F_t$$
$$= F_t + \alpha(A_t - F_t)$$

In this formula $A_t - F_t$ represents the forecast error made in period t. Thus, the formula shows that the new forecast developed for period $t + 1$ is equal to the old forecast plus some percentage of the error (since α is between 0 and 1). Notice that when the forecast in period t exceeds the actual demand in period t, we have a negative error term for period t and the new forecast will be reduced. On the other hand, when the forecast in period t is less than the actual demand in period t, the error term in period t is positive and the new forecast will be adjusted higher.

Selecting the Appropriate Value of α

Our objective in exponential forecasting is to choose the value of α that results in the best forecasts. Forecasts that tend always to be too high or too low are said to be *biased*—positively if too high and negatively if too low. When forecasts are in error, then operations costs will be unnecessarily high, owing to idle capacity if the forecasts are high (positive bias) and insufficient capacity (overtime, etc.) if the forecasts are low (negative bias). The value of α is critical in producing good forecasts, and if a large value of α is selected, the forecast will be very sensitive to the current demand value. With a large α, exponential smoothing will produce forecasts that react quickly to fluctuations in demand. This, however, is irritating to those who have to constantly change plans and activities on the basis of the latest forecasts. Conversely, a small value of α weights historical data more heavily than current demand and therefore will produce forecasts that do not react as quickly to changes in the data; that is, the forecasting model will be somewhat *insensitive* to fluctuations in the current data.

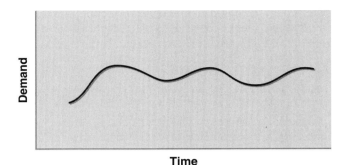

Figure 8.17   Data exhibiting low variability (use a high α).

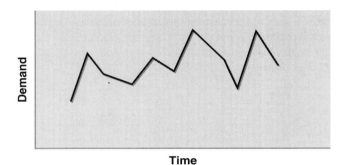

Figure 8.18   Data exhibiting high variability (use a low α).

Generally speaking, larger values of α are used in situations in which the data can be plotted as a rather smooth curve, such as Figure 8.17. The data in this figure are said to exhibit *low variability*. If, on the other hand, the data look more like Figure 8.18, a lower value of α should be used. These data are subject to a high degree of variability. Using a high value of α in a situation like Figure 8.18 would result in a forecast that constantly overreacted to changes in the most current demand.

As with *n,* the appropriate value of α is usually determined by trial and error; values typically lie in the range of 0.01 to 0.30. One method of selecting the best value is to try several values of α with the existing historical data (or a portion of the data) and choose the value of α that minimizes the average forecast errors. As we will see, spreadsheets can greatly speed the evaluation of potential smoothing constants and the determination of the best value of α.

❖ Errors in Forecasting

Up to this point we have indirectly mentioned two methods of measuring forecast error: mean absolute deviation (MAD) and bias. Although there are others (such as standard deviation, mean square error, and the running sum of errors), these two are commonly, and easily, calculated. Algebraically,

$$\text{MAD} = \frac{1}{n} \sum_{i=1}^{n} |F_i - A_i|$$

$$\text{Bias} = \frac{1}{n} \sum_{i=1}^{n} (F_i - A_i)$$

where

F_i = forecast of demand in period i

A_i = actual demand in period i

n = number of periods of data

Though very similar in appearance, these two variables measure extremely different forecasting effects. Since MAD sums only absolute values of errors, both positive and negative errors add to the sum and the average size of the *error* is determined. This gives the manager a sense of the *accuracy* of the forecasting model. A manager might use this knowledge by saying, "Our forecasts are typically accurate only within 10 percent; we had better maintain an extra stock of 10 percent or so to hedge against this potential error."

Bias, on the other hand, indicates whether the forecast is typically too low or too high, and by how much. A manager knowing this might say, "On average, we are forecasting 10 percent too high; we can safely make 5 to 10 percent less to hedge against this potential error." That is, MAD shows only the average size of the error, whereas bias shows the average total error and its direction.

As mentioned earlier, the best forecast methods will exhibit the least error. However, because MAD and bias each provide a different view of forecast errors, it is often desirable to use both measures to evaluate alternative forecasting methods. To illustrate this, suppose that two methods of forecasting are tested against demand data for a four-month period. Method A gives forecasts for January through April of 105, 107, 109, and 109, respectively; Method B gives 108, 107, 105, 106; and the actual demands are 103, 106, 106, and 111. MAD for method A would be $(|105 - 103| + |107 - 106| + |109 - 106| + |109 - 111|)/4 = 2$, and bias would be $[(105 - 103) + \ldots]/4 = 1$. Thus, MAD indicates that the average forecast error using method A is 2, and the bias of +1 indicates that the forecast tends to exceed demand. For method B, MAD is 3 but bias is 0 (check the data). With method B, positive and negative forecast errors cancel out, resulting in no bias. However, examining MAD indicates that even though there is no bias, the actual forecasts developed using method B are less accurate than those generated using method A. Thus, with method B the average forecast is off by 3; however, method B is as likely to overestimate as to underestimate demand.

The ratio of bias to MAD is also sometimes used as a "tracking signal" in certain adaptive forecasting models. Briefly, adaptive forecasting models *self-adjust* by increasing or decreasing the smoothing constant α when the tracking signal becomes too large. Since this ratio can range only from -1 to $+1$, its absolute value is used as the smoothing constant, α. Ratios approaching -1 indicate that all or most of the forecast errors tend to be negative (i.e., the forecasts are too low). Ratios approaching $+1$ indicate that all or most of the forecast errors tend to be positive. Regardless, as the tracking signal gets closer to -1 or $+1$, α automatically increases, making the model more responsive and (it is hoped) leading to smaller forecast errors.

	A	B	C	D	E	F	G
	Year Since		**Period**	**A**	**Forecast**	**Forecast**	
1					**0.1**	**0.3**	
2	**Opening**	**Quarter**	**Number**	**Acutal**			
3	1	1	1	3,500	3,500	3,500	
4		2	2	8,000	3,500	3,500	
5		3	3	5,500	3,950	4,850	
6		4	4	10,000	4,105	5,045	
7	2	1	5	4,500	4,695	6,532	
8		2	6	6,000	4,675	5,922	
9		3	7	3,000	4,808	5,945	
10		4	8	5,500	4,627	5,062	
11	3	1	9	5,000	4,714	5,193	
12		2	10	9,500	4,743	5,135	
13		3	11	7,500	5,218	6,445	
14		4	12	15,000	5,447	6,761	
15	4	1	13	13,500	6,402	9,233	
16		2	14	17,500	7,112	10,513	
17			15		8,151	12,609	

Figure 8.19   Actual and exponentially forecast values of quarterly demand for Inner City Health Clinic.

Let us now use exponential smoothing to forecast demand for the Inner City Health Clinic. We will use two different smoothing constants and calculate MAD and bias to determine which forecast is best, as well as the tracking signal. Figure 8.19 shows a spreadsheet with the actual historical data for emergency services provided by the Inner City Health Clinic and the exponentially smoothed forecasts for the corresponding periods using α values of 0.1 and 0.3., entered in cells E2 and F2, respectively. Since there were no data on which to base a forecast for period 1, F_1 (the forecast that would have been made in period 0), some value must be selected. We let F_1 be equal to A_1, the actual value of the series in period 1. Thus the formula =D3 was entered into cells E3 and F3. F_2 is computed (using $\alpha = 0.1$) as

$$F_2 = \alpha A_1 + (1 - \alpha)F_1$$
$$= 0.1 \times 3500 + (1 - 0.1) \times 3500$$
$$= 3500 + 0.9(3500)$$
$$= 3500$$

In the same manner, we compute F_3 as

$$F_3 = 0.1(8000) + 0.9(3500)$$
$$= 3950$$

The formula entered into cell E4 to calculate F_2 using $\alpha = .1$ was

$$= (E\$2*\$D3) + ((1 - E\$2)*E3)$$

E\$2 was used so that the value of α entered in row 2 would always be used. Likewise, \$D3 was used so that when this formula was copied over to column F, the actual data values in column D would still be used. Once the formula was entered into cell E4, it was copied to cells E5 to E17. Then the formulas contained in cells E4 to E17 were copied to cells F4 to F17 to complete the spreadsheet shown in Figure 8.19. As can be seen, F_{15}, the forecasts for the next quarter using each of the two α values, are 8151 and 12,609 emergency services, a considerable difference.

The spreadsheet shown in Figure 8.20 was developed to calculate the quarterly errors needed for the computation of the final MAD, bias, and tracking signal (TS) for the two forecasts. To calculate the MAD, Excel's absolute-value function ABS was used. Thus, to calculate the absolute value of the forecast error made in period 2 for the forecast developed using $\alpha = 0.10$, the following formula was entered in cell G4:

$$= ABS(E4 - \$D4)$$

The formula entered in cell G4 was then copied to cell H4. Next, the formulas in cells G4:H4 were copied to cells G5:H16.

To calculate the actual forecast error made in period 2 for the forecast developed using $\alpha = 0.10$, the following formula was entered in cell I4:

$$= E4 - \$D4$$

This formula was then copied to cell J4. Next, the formulas in cells I4:J4 were copied to cells I5:J16.

To calculate MAD and bias, the averages of columns G through I were computed. Thus, to calculate MAD for the forecast using $\alpha = 0.10$, the following formula was entered in cell G17:

$$= AVERAGE(G4:G16)$$

	A	B	C	D	E	F	G	H	I	J	K	L
1			Period	A	Forecast	Forecast	MAD	MAD	Bias	Bias	TS	TS
2	Year	Quarter	Number	Acutal	0.1	0.3	0.1	0.3	0.1	0.3	0.1	0.3
3	1	1	1	3,500	3,500	3,500						
											-0.92	-0.75
4		2	2	8,000	3,500	3,500	4500	4500	-4,500	-4,500		
5		3	3	5,500	3,950	4,850	1550	650	-1550	-650		
6		4	4	10,000	4,105	5,045	5895	4955	-5895	-4955		
7	2	1	5	4,500	4,695	6,532	195	2032	195	2032		
8		2	6	6,000	4,675	5,922	1325	78	-1325	-78		
9		3	7	3,000	4,808	5,945	1808	2945	1808	2945		
10		4	8	5,500	4,627	5,062	873	438	-873	-438		
11	3	1	9	5,000	4,714	5,193	286	193	-286	193		
12		2	10	9,500	4,743	5,135	4757	4365	-4757	-4365		
13		3	11	7,500	5,218	6,445	2282	1055	-2282	-1055		
14		4	12	15,000	5,447	6,761	9553	8239	-9553	-8239		
15	4	1	13	13,500	6,402	9,233	7098	4267	-7098	-4267		
16		2	14	17,500	7,112	10,513	10388	6987	-10388	-6987		
17	Average						3885	3131	-3577	-2336		

Figure 8.20 Calculation of forecast errors.

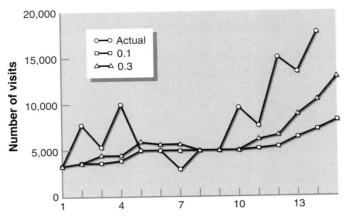

Figure 8.21   Plot of actual data and exponential forecasts.

This formula was then copied to cells H17:J17.

Finally, recall that the tracking signal is the ratio of bias to MAD. Thus, to calculate the tracking signal for the forecast using $\alpha = 0.10$, =I17/G17 was entered in cell K3. This formula was then copied to cell L3.

As indicated by the calculations of MAD, the error is quite high with either value of α, though 0.3 seems the better of the two. The large negative value of the bias indicates that most of the error is due to negative bias in the model, in this case consistently forecasting too low or "lagging" the demand (a characteristic of simple exponential forecasting models such as this one). The tracking signals are both quite high (i.e., close to +1 or −1), indicating that a problem exists.

This result is also seen in Figure 8.21, which shows the actual demand data and the forecast values using $\alpha = 0.1$ and $\alpha = 0.3$. Notice, for example, that the downturn after quarter 4 and the upturn after quarter 9 are detected more quickly by the $\alpha = 0.3$ model, as we have indicated should be the case. You may notice that both models lag behind the upward trend after quarter 9. In general, if values of α greater than 0.3 seem to give the best results, exponential forecasting should probably not be used. A simple smoothing model is best used in situations where demand fluctuates around an overall level trend. If the trend is increasing or decreasing, other models are usually more appropriate. In the next section, we consider a time series model more appropriate for data with an upward or downward trend than the models presented so far.

Spreadsheet Analysis: Choosing a Smoothing Constant

In this example, we will use data from the Inner City Health Clinic to demonstrate how spreadsheets can greatly facilitate the task of selecting a smoothing constant. A spreadsheet to help select the smoothing constant was developed and is shown below.

	A	B	C	D	E	F	G	H	I	J
1			Period	A						
2	Year	Quarter	Number	Acutal	Forecast	|error|	error			
3	1	1	1	3,500	3,500					
4		2	2	8,000	3,500	4,500	-4,500		Alpha	0.1
5		3	3	5,500	3,950	1,550	-1,550		TS	-0.92
6		4	4	10,000	4,105	5,895	-5,895			
7	2	1	5	4,500	4,695	195	195			
8		2	6	6,000	4,675	1,325	-1,325			
9		3	7	3,000	4,808	1,808	1,808			
10		4	8	5,500	4,627	873	-873			
11	3	1	9	5,000	4,714	286	-286			
12		2	10	9,500	4,743	4,757	-4,757			
13		3	11	7,500	5,218	2,282	-2,282			
14		4	12	15,000	5,447	9,553	-9,553			
15	4	1	13	13,500	6,402	7,098	-7,098			
16		2	14	17,500	7,112	10,388	-10,388			
17	Average					3,885	-3,577			

The exponential smoothing forecast is calculated in column E and is based on the smoothing constant α entered in cell J4. In cell E3 the formula =D3 was entered, since $F_1 = A_1$. In cell E4 the following formula was entered:

$$=(J\$4*D3)+((1-J\$4)*E3)$$

This formula was then copied to cells E5 to E16.

The absolute value of the forecast error is calculated in column F. For example, to calculate the absolute value of the forecast error for period 2, =ABS(E4–D4) was entered in cell F4. This formula was then copied to cells F5 to F16. Similarly, the actual forecast errors are calculated in column G. To calculate the forecast error in period 2, =E4–D4 was entered in cell G4. This formula was then copied to cells G5 to G16. The spreadsheet above shows that for α = 0.10, MAD is 3885.

To quickly investigate how alternative values of α affect the accuracy of a forecast, we simply need to enter new values for α into cell J4 and observe the effect on MAD, bias, and the tracking signal. For example, the spreadsheet below shows that increasing α from 0.10 to 0.20 leads to a reduction in MAD from 3885 to 3409.

	A	B	C	D	E	F	G	H	I	J
1			Period	A						
2	Year	Quarter	Number	Actual	Forecast	|error|	error			
3	1	1	1	3,500	3,500					
4		2	2	8,000	3,500	4,500	-4,500		Alpha	0.20
5		3	3	5,500	4,400	1,100	-1,100		TS	-0.82
6		4	4	10,000	4,620	5,380	-5,380			
7	2	1	5	4,500	5,696	1,196	1,196			
8		2	6	6,000	5,457	543	-543			
9		3	7	3,000	5,565	2,565	2,565			
10		4	8	5,500	5,052	448	-448			
11	3	1	9	5,000	5,142	142	142			
12		2	10	9,500	5,114	4,386	-4,386			
13		3	11	7,500	5,991	1,509	-1,509			
14		4	12	15,000	6,293	8,707	-8,707			
15	4	1	13	13,500	8,034	5,466	-5,466			
16		2	14	17,500	9,127	8,373	-8,373			
17	Average					3,409	-2,808			

This trial-and-error approach allows us to quickly investigate the effect of alternative smoothing constants, since an infinite number of smoothing constants are available; however, it is not possible to guarantee that the best smoothing constant is being used. Fortunately, Excel offers a solution. Specifically, Excel's Solver can find the optimal smoothing constant, subject to criteria and constraints we specify. In the remainder of this example we will demonstrate how Excel can be used to select a smoothing constant such that the value of MAD is minimized.

To access Excel's Solver, select Solver from the Tools menu item at the top of the screen. The Solver Parameters dialog box is then displayed as shown below.

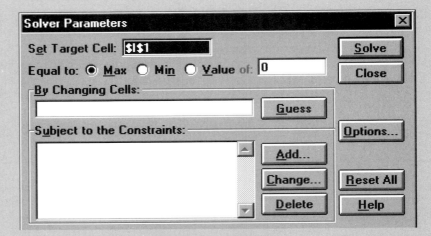

Target Cell refers to the cell in the spreadsheet that contains the criteria we wish to maximize or minimize. In our case we wish to minimize the value of MAD. Thus, in the Set Target Cell box we specify cell F17 by clicking on this cell with the mouse. Since we want to find a value of α that minimizes the value of MAD, we select Min for the Equal to choices. The By Changing Cells refers to the cells Excel's Solver can change to arrive at a minimum value for MAD. In our case there is only one variable we can change: the value of α entered in cell J4. Next we specify any constraints or limitations in the Subject to Constraints section. Here our only constraint is that α should be between 0.01 and 0.30. After we select Add, the Add Constraint dialog box appears as shown below.

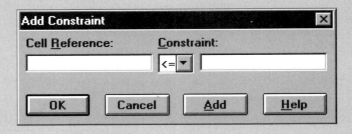

For Cell Reference we click on cell J4 (i.e., the cell that contains α). Next, in the Constraint box we specify the type of constraint (i.e., $\leq$, $\geq$, or =). We specify $\leq$ and then enter 0.3 in the last box. After we add this information, the Add Constraint dialog box appears, as follows.

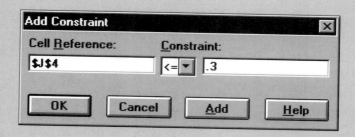

This constraint says that the value of cell J4 must be less than or equal to 0.30. Next we select Add to add this constraint to our constraint set. After Add is selected a blank Add Constraint dialog box appears so that we can add additional constraints. Now we want to add a constraint to ensure that α is greater than or equal to 0.01. Thus, we select cell J4 for the Cell Reference, $\geq$ for the Constraint box, and enter 0.01 in the last box. Since this is the last constraint we need to enter, we select OK. Then the Solver Parameter dialog box appears, as follows.

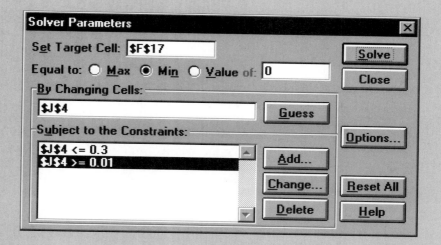

As this window shows, our two constraints have been added. We next select Solve. After selecting Solve, the following message is displayed telling us that Excel found a solution.

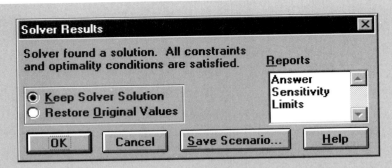

Select OK to keep the solution. As shown in the spreadsheet below, the value in cell J4 has been changed to .30. Thus, given the constraints that α must be between .01 and .30, a value of α = .30 provides the lowest possible MAD.

	A	B	C	D	E	F	G	H	I	J
1			Period	A						
2	Year	Quarter	Number	Acutal	Forecast	|error|	error			
3	1	1	1	3,500	3,500					
4		2	2	8,000	3,500	4,500	-4,500		Alpha	0.3
5		3	3	5,500	4,850	650	-650		TS	-0.75
6		4	4	10,000	5,045	4,955	-4,955			
7	2	1	5	4,500	6,532	2,032	2,032			
8		2	6	6,000	5,922	78	-78			
9		3	7	3,000	5,945	2,945	2,945			
10		4	8	5,500	5,062	438	-438			
11	3	1	9	5,000	5,193	193	193			
12		2	10	9,500	5,135	4,365	-4,365			
13		3	11	7,500	6,445	1,055	-1,055			
14		4	12	15,000	6,761	8,239	-8,239			
15	4	1	13	13,500	9,233	4,267	-4,267			
16		2	14	17,500	10,513	6,987	-6,987			
17	Average					3,131	-2,336			

Since our optimal solution bumped up against the upper limit for α, we might want to investigate what the effect would be if we relaxed this constraint. In other words, suppose that we wanted to see what the optimal value of α would be if it could take on values from 0.01 to 1.0. To investigate this, we again select Solver from the Tools menu. In the Solver Parameters dialog box we select the constraint we want to change by clicking on it. In our case we want to change the first constraint entered. After selecting the first constraint, we select Change and then change the 0.3 in the last box to 1.0 as shown below.

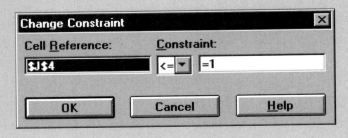

After we select OK, the constraint is changed in the Solver Parameters dialog box as shown below.

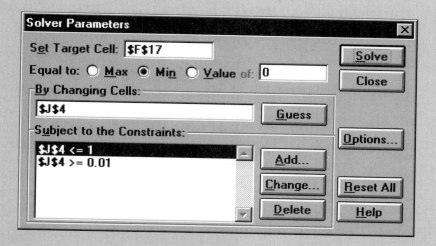

Next, we select Solve and obtain the solution shown in the spreadsheet below.

	A	B	C	D	E	F	G	H	I	J
2	Year	Quarter	Number	Acutal	Forecast	|error|	error			
3	1	1	1	3,500	3,500					
4		2	2	8,000	3,500	4,500	-4,500		Alpha	0.61
5		3	3	5,500	6,255	755	755		TS	0.56
6		4	4	10,000	5,793	4,207	-4,207			
7	2	1	5	4,500	8,369	3,869	3,869			
8		2	6	6,000	6,000	0	0			
9		3	7	3,000	6,000	3,000	3,000			
10		4	8	5,500	4,163	1,337	-1,337			
11	3	1	9	5,000	4,982	18	-18			
12		2	10	9,500	4,993	4,507	-4,507			
13		3	11	7,500	7,753	253	253			
14		4	12	15,000	7,598	7,402	-7,402			
15	4	1	13	13,500	12,130	1,370	-1,370			
16		2	14	17,500	12,969	4,531	-4,531			
17	Average					2,750	-1,538		1,538	

As a result of relaxing the constraint, the optimal value of α increased from 0.30 to 0.61. An optimal value of α above 0.30 indicates that there is some type of behavior in the time series—such as an upward trend or seasonality—that simple exponential smoothing wasn't meant to handle. Thus, the Inner City Health Clinic would be advised to use a different model or a more sophisticated type of exponential smoothing that can account for upward trends, seasonality, or both.

This example demonstrates the power spreadsheets provide in terms of identifying good smoothing constants. Furthermore, they offer a high degree of flexibility to include other criteria and other constraints.

$\mathscr{D}$EMAND FORECASTING FOR INNER CITY MASS TRANSIT: LINEAR TREND, MULTIPLICATIVE MODEL

Figure 8.22 presents the quarterly ridership for the new Inner City Mass Transit. Demand is seen to be generally increasing. To forecast future ridership, the city manager has decided to try a linear trend time series model, which is based on the belief that demand follows both a fairly constant trend from quarter to quarter and a quarterly seasonal pattern. Just from observing the time series plot of the demand data, it is clear that demand is above average during the second and fourth quarters and below average during the first and third quarters, probably because of the weather.

Excel's ChartWizard was used to create the graph shown in Figure 8.22. Since we have discussed ChartWizard earlier in this chapter, we will only briefly summarize the steps here. First, cells A3:B17 were highlighted, and then the ChartWizard button was selected. Next, the range for the chart within the spreadsheet was specified as C2:I18 by dragging the mouse over this range. In step 1, the suggested range was accepted by selecting the Next button. In the next step it was specified that the data series was in columns, that the first column should be used for the X-axis and that the first row should be used for the legend, and labels were entered for both the X- and the Y-axis.

After the graph was created for just the ridership volume over time, a built-in Excel feature was used to add the trend line. To add the trend line, first select the graph. Once the graph has been selected, select the actual line of ridership volume by clicking on it with the mouse. Then select Insert from the menu at the top of the screen. From the next menu select Trendline. Finally, select Linear and then OK. Af-

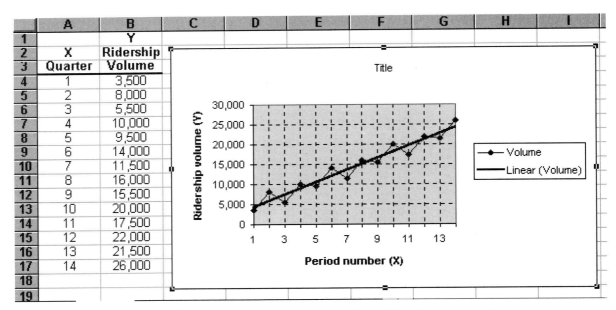

Figure 8.22   Quarterly ridership volume and trend line for mass transit.

ter you click OK, Excel adds to the original ridership data a linear trend line based on regression analysis.

This example demonstrates the power of spreadsheets. With just a few keystrokes and mouse clicks, we were able to fit a regression line to a time series. Although logarithmic, polynomial, power, and exponential curves are much more complex mathematically, we could have fitted them to the data just as easily as the linear trend line.

There are several versions of the linear trend time series model (for example, there are additive and multiplicative versions) and also many different approaches to determining the components of these forecasting models. We will present one method for determining the two demand components of a simple multiplicative model. Conceptually, the model is presented as

$$\text{Forecast} = \text{trend component (or } T\text{)} \times \text{seasonal component (or } S\text{)}$$

In order to develop this model, we must first analyze the available historical data and attempt to break down the original data into their trend and seasonal components.

❖ Trend Component

As indicated earlier, a *trend* is a long-run direction of a series of data. In our example the trend in demand appears to follow a straight line—that is, to be a trend with respect to time. In order to project this linear trend into the future, we must first estimate the parameters of the trend line. The parameters of the straight line that must be estimated are the Y-axis intercept and the slope of the line. The *Y-axis intercept* is the value of Y where the trend line crosses the Y-axis (at $X = 0$). The *slope* is the amount of change in Y for a one-period change in X.

The Regression Equation

There are several procedures for estimating the slope and intercept of a straight line from the observed value of X and Y, but a method known as *least squares regression* is the most widely used.* We will not attempt to derive the equations used in estimating the slope and the intercept but will simply state them and explain their use. The equation we will use to forecast the trend into the future is known as the *regression equation:*

$$T_X = a + bX$$

where

$T_X =$ trend forecast value of ridership volume Y for period number X

$a =$ estimate of Y-axis intercept

---

*The method derives its name from the way in which the parameters of the line are estimated. That is, the method minimizes the sum of the squares of the vertical deviations between the trend line and the original data points.

b = estimate of slope of the demand line

X = period number

The two equations used to determine a and b are

$$b = \frac{\sum XY - n\overline{X}\,\overline{Y}}{\sum X^2 - n\overline{X}^2}$$

$$a = \overline{Y} - b\overline{X}$$

where

$\Sigma XY = X$ times Y for each period, summed over all periods

$\Sigma X^2 = X$ squared for each period, summed over all periods

$\overline{X}$ = average of X values

$\overline{Y}$ = average of Y values

n = number of periods of data used in the regression

Using Least Squares Regression for the Inner City Mass Transit

Using the data for Inner City Mass Transit, we can estimate the slope and the intercept of the trend forecasting equation for quarterly ridership. To simplify the computations we will arrange the data in four columns, as shown in Figure 8.23. The numbers in column C are simply the numbers in column A squared, and the num-

	A	B	C	D	E	F	G
1		Y					
2	X	Ridership					
3	Quarter	Volume	X^2	XY			
4	1	3,500	1	3500			
5	2	8,000	4	16000			
6	3	5,500	9	16500			
7	4	10,000	16	40000			
8	5	9,500	25	47500			
9	6	14,000	36	84000			
10	7	11,500	49	80500			
11	8	16,000	64	128000			
12	9	15,500	81	139500			
13	10	20,000	100	200000			
14	11	17,500	121	192500			
15	12	22,000	144	264000			
16	13	21,500	169	279500			
17	14	26,000	196	364000			
18	105	200,500	1,015	1,855,500			

Figure 8.23   Quarterly ridership volume and least squares data for Inner City Mass Transit.

bers in column D are computed by multiplying each number in column A by the corresponding number in column B. Thus, in cell C4 the formula =A4^2 was entered, and in cell D4 the formula =A4*B4 was entered. These formulas were then copied to cells C5:D17.

To compute the slope of the regression line *(b)* we need the average of column A, which is

$$\overline{X} = \frac{\sum X}{n} = \frac{105}{14} = 7.5$$

and the average of column B, which is

$$\overline{Y} = \frac{200,500}{14} = 14,321.4$$

Note that in the spreadsheet shown in Figure 8.23, a formula that summed each column was entered in row 18. Thus the formula =SUM(A4:A17) was entered in cell A18 and then copied to cells B18 to D18. Additionally, a formula could have been added that calculated the average of columns A and B. For example, =AVERAGE(A4:A17) could have been entered in cell A19.

Also, we need the total of columns C and D. In our algebraic notation, ΣX^2 is the sum of column C and ΣXY is the sum of column D.

The slope can then be computed by using the above equation.

$$b = \frac{1,855,500 - 14(7.5)(14,321.4)}{1015 - 14(7.5)^2}$$
$$= \frac{351,753}{227.5} = 1546.2$$

which means that volume is, on the average, increasing by 1546 riders every quarter.

The Y-axis intercept is computed from the equation for *a* as follows:

$$a = 14{,}321.4 - 1546.2(7.5) = 2725$$

which means that the initial volume at $X = 0$ would have been 2725 riders.

The forecasting equation for the trend in ridership volume is therefore

$$T_X = 2725 + 1546.2X$$

Figure 8.22 shows the regression trend line and the original data.

Although the formula for *a* and *b* could be easily entered into a spreadsheet, Excel offers some advanced functions that make it much easier to calculate these parameters. The spreadsheet shown in Figure 8.24 will be used to explain two of these built-in functions.

	A	B	C	D	E	F	G
1		Y					
2	X	Ridership			b	a	
3	Quarter	Volume	Trend		1546.15	2725.27	
4	1	3,500	4271.43				
5	2	8,000	5817.58				
6	3	5,500	7363.74				
7	4	10,000	8909.89				
8	5	9,500	10456.04				
9	6	14,000	12002.20				
10	7	11,500	13548.35				
11	8	16,000	15094.51				
12	9	15,500	16640.66				
13	10	20,000	18186.81				
14	11	17,500	19732.97				
15	12	22,000	21279.12				
16	13	21,500	22825.27				
17	14	26,000	24371.43				

Figure 8.24   Using Excel's LINEST and TREND functions.

The LINEST function uses the least squares method to calculate the parameters a and b of a trend line, just as we did before. The syntax of the LINEST function is:

$$= \text{LINEST(range of } Y \text{ values, range of } X \text{ values)}$$

To illustrate the use of this function, we first enter the labels b and a in cells E2 and F2, as shown in Figure 8.24. Next we highlight cells E3 and F3 and enter the following formula:

$$= \text{LINEST((B4:B17),(A4:A17))}$$

Because we are using LINEST as an *array function* (i.e., using it to return multiple values, not a single value), when we finish entering the above formula we must press and hold down the Ctrl key and the Shift key as we press the Enter key. After we press Ctrl+Shift+Enter, the values of b and a are calculated and displayed in cells E3 and F3, respectively. Note that the LINEST function returns the value for b first and then the value for a—just as we calculated b first and then used it to calculate a. Array functions are always enclosed in brackets. Thus, if you look at cell E3 or F3, you will see the following formula displayed:

$$\{=\text{LINEST((B4:B17),(A4:A17))}\}$$

When using array-based functions, you do not enter the squiggly brackets (Excel does this automatically).

A second useful function is TREND. The TREND function fits a straight line to a column of X and Y values and then returns the values that would appear on the trend line for each value of X. Column C in Figure 8.24 provides these trend line values. The syntax for the TREND function is as follows:

$$\text{=TREND(range of } Y \text{ values, range of } X \text{ values)}$$

To calculate the trend values in column C, cells C4:C17 were first highlighted. Then the following formula was entered:

$$\text{=TREND((B4:B17),(A4:A17))}$$

After this formula was entered, the Enter key was pressed while the Ctrl and Shift keys were being held down. These trend values are the values that you would get if the actual values for X were substituted in the trend equation.

❖ Seasonal Component: Ratio-to-Trend Method

As was noted earlier, and made even clearer in Figure 8.22, the data are above the trend line for all of the second and fourth quarters and below the trend line for all of the first and third quarters. Recognizing this distinct seasonal pattern in the data should allow us to estimate the amount of seasonal variation around the trend line (i.e., the seasonal component, S).

The trend line is the long-run direction of the data and does not include any seasonal variation. We can compute, for each available quarter of data, a measure of the "seasonality" in that quarter by *dividing actual ridership by the computed value of the trend* for that quarter. This method is known as the *ratio-to-trend method.* Using the notation developed thus far, we can write the seasonal component for any quarter X as

$$\frac{Y_X}{T_X}$$

Consider the second and third quarters of the first year. The computed trend value for each of these two quarters is

$$T_2 = 2725 + 1546.2(2) = 5817$$

and

$$T_3 = 2725 + 1546.2(3) = 7364$$

The actual volumes (in thousands) in quarters 2 and 3 were

$$Y_2 = 8000$$
$$Y_3 = 5500$$

Dividing Y_2 by T_2 and Y_3 by T_3 gives us an indication of the seasonal pattern in each of these quarters.

$$\frac{Y_2}{T_2} = \frac{8000}{5817} = 1.38$$

$$\frac{Y_3}{T_3} = \frac{5500}{7364} = 0.75$$

In quarter 2 the actual volume was 138 percent of the expected volume (i.e., the ridership predicted on the basis of a linear trend), but in quarter 3 the volume was only 75 percent of that expected. Note that over the 14 periods of available data we have four observations of volume for first and second quarters and three observations of volume for third and fourth quarters. We can compute the average of each of these sets of quarterly data and use the averages as the seasonal components for our time series forecasting model.

The spreadsheet shown in Figure 8.25 was developed to simplify our computation of the seasonal values for each of the 14 quarters. Column B was added to Figure 8.24 to keep track of the quarter each period is associated with. The trend calculations in column D were developed using Excel's TREND function. Finally, the seasonal values shown in column E were calculated as the ratio of column C to column D. Thus, in cell E4, =C4/D4 was entered. This formula was then copied to cells E5:E17.

Once Figure 8.25 is complete, the seasonal factors for each of the four seasons or quarters are averaged as in Figure 8.26. The seasonal components for each of the four quarters are found in row 7 (columns B–E) of Figure 8.26. In row 6 of Figure 8.26 the SUM function was used; in row 7 the AVERAGE function was used.

Using both the trend component and the seasonal component, the city manager now can forecast ridership for any quarter in the future. First, the trend value for

	A	B	C	D	E	F	G
1			Y				
2	X		Ridership				
3	Period	Quarter	Volume	Trend	Y/T		
4	1	1	3,500	4271.43	0.82		
5	2	2	8,000	5817.58	1.38		
6	3	3	5,500	7363.74	0.75		
7	4	4	10,000	8909.89	1.12		
8	5	1	9,500	10456.04	0.91		
9	6	2	14,000	12002.20	1.17		
10	7	3	11,500	13548.35	0.85		
11	8	4	16,000	15094.51	1.06		
12	9	1	15,500	16640.66	0.93		
13	10	2	20,000	18186.81	1.10		
14	11	3	17,500	19732.97	0.89		
15	12	4	22,000	21279.12	1.03		
16	13	1	21,500	22825.27	0.94		
17	14	2	26,000	24371.43	1.07		

Figure 8.25 Computations of quarterly seasonal factors.

	A	B	C	D	E	F	G
1	Year	Quarter 1	Quarter 1	Quarter 1	Quarter 1		
2	1	0.82	1.38	0.75	1.12		
3	2	0.91	1.17	0.85	1.06		
4	3	0.93	1.10	0.89	1.03		
5	4	0.94	1.07				
6	Total	3.60	4.72	2.49	3.21		
7	Average	0.90	1.18	0.83	1.07		
8							
9							
10							
11							

Figure 8.26 Computations of seasonal component (S) for quarters 1 through 4.

the forecast quarter is computed and is, in turn, multiplied by the appropriate seasonal factor. For example, to forecast for the last quarter of the fourth year (quarter 16) and the first quarter of the fifth year (quarter 17), the city manager would first compute the trend values.

$$T_{16} = 2725 + 1546.2(16) = 27,464$$
$$T_{17} = 2725 + 1546.2(17) = 29,010$$

Next, the forecast is computed by multiplying the trend value by the appropriate seasonal factor. For the fourth quarter S_4 is 1.07, so the forecast F is

$$F_{16} = 27,464 \times 1.07 = 29,386$$

The seasonal factor for the first quarter is 0.90; therefore, the forecast for quarter 17 is

$$F_{17} = 29,010 \times 0.90 = 26,109$$

These two forecasts correspond to the previous results for fourth and first quarters in that the fourth-quarter forecast is above the trend and the first-quarter forecast is below the trend. Seasonal indexes can be used in a similar way with exponential smoothing or moving averages. Again, simple ratios are calculated, averaged out, and then applied to the exponential smoothing or moving average forecasts.

This linear trend model can be useful in planning and scheduling of operations for Inner City Mass Transit. Procuring new vehicles, scheduling maintenance and overhaul during slack seasons, and scheduling staff are all possible using this model. If data were available regarding ridership by route or area of the city, the operations staff could plan for new or modified routes and determine the number of buses to run on each route to produce acceptable waiting times for riders.

❖ Cautions

Although a simple linear trend model should be tried before more complex models, in many forecasting situations it is simply not appropriate. The student is cautioned that a forecasting procedure produces useful results only if the input data conform to the assumptions of the model. Data that follow an obviously nonlinear pattern should not be subjected to a linear analysis. Also, models, for all their power in analyzing data, cannot think and reason intelligently about environmental changes that might affect demand, and external effects such as political events and recessions can clearly overwhelm a simple projection of past data.

For instance, in our earlier example of demand for emergency services, there was a sudden upsurge after period 9, to which the exponential forecasting models could only react. But suppose that the administrator knew that a local hospital was closing an evening clinic that had not proved to be self-supporting. If the only medical services otherwise available in the community during the evening hours are those provided by the center's emergency services division, the administrator could predict that demand would increase. This may, in fact, have been the cause of the observed increases.

To clarify the point of using a linear model to predict demand in an inherently nonlinear situation, consider again the demand data for emergency services (Figure 8.6). Demand first increases, then decreases, and then appears to be increasing at an accelerating rate. But if the administrator were to use the least squares model on these data, the regression line would look like the line in Figure 8.27 superimposed on the plot of the original data. Note that a forecast for period 15 will be well under that which would be expected if demand continues to grow as it has over the past five quarters. Use of a nonlinear regression model would be appropriate in this case, whereas the use of a linear model would not. If a tracking signal were used in this situation, it would quickly indicate that the model needed to be altered.

𝒞AUSAL FORECASTING METHODS

In the previous section we saw that demand for an organization's output could be related to time, that is, demand changed as time changed. Although a relationship existed, we could not say that time *caused* the demand. But factors other than time are often related to demand, and these factors often do cause, or at least precede, demand.

For example, increases in the demand for single-family housing during a given quarter might be highly related to the number of new marriages during the previous quarter. Marriages do not directly *cause* new houses to be purchased, but it is logical to argue that marriages (which cause new households to form) are a major precondition of new housing starts. Figure 8.28 illustrates the probable relationship between new marriages (the independent variable) and single-family housing starts (the dependent variable). This figure indicates a rather close relationship between the two variables. The variables are thus said to be *highly correlated*. The relationship between housing starts in one quarter and marriages in a previous quarter is an example of a *logical* relationship. Many causal models use such leading indica-

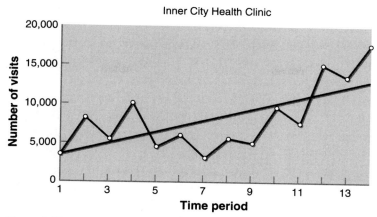

Figure 8.27 Plot of quarterly demand for emergency services at Inner City Health Clinic.

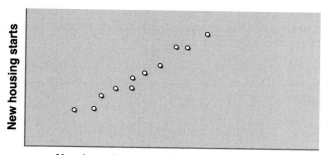

Figure 8.28 Plot of marriages versus housing starts, showing a close relationship.

tors to predict upcoming demand, or to *forecast* the indicator, as with time series analysis, to predict demand.

❖ Calculations

The least squares regression method used in the preceding section to determine the linear time series trend can also be used to estimate a predicting equation for new housing starts. The linear equation

$$Y'_X = a + bX$$

would be interpreted as

Y'_X = the predicted number of new housing starts

a = the Y-axis intercept

b = the slope

X = the number of new marriages in the previous quarter

and the two parameters a and b are estimated in the same manner as before, that is

$$b = \frac{\sum XY - n\overline{X}\,\overline{Y}}{\sum X^2 - n\overline{X}^2}$$

$$a = \overline{Y} - b\overline{X}$$

❖ Extensions

This linear regression methodology can be extended to situations in which more than one variable is used. Called multiple regression, it explains the behavior of the dependent variable Y. For example, in addition to the number of marriages, the

𝒮olved Exercise 8.2 ❖ Causal Regression

Predict the number of new housing starts for Buckeye County in the summer of 1998 when the number of marriages that spring is forecast as 12,000 and the following data are available for the county:

	Fall 1993	Spring 1994	Winter 1995	Winter 1996
Marriages, previous quarter (000s), X:	8.7	9.4	10.1	10.2
Housing starts (000s), Y:	6.5	6.9	7.3	7.1

Solution:

	X	Y	XY	X^2
	8.7	6.5	56.55	75.69
	9.4	6.9	64.86	88.36
	10.1	7.3	73.73	102.01
	10.2	7.1	72.42	104.04
Sum:	38.4	27.8	267.56	370.10

$\overline{X} = 38.4/4 = 9.60$

$\overline{Y} = 27.8/4 = 6.95$

$b = [267.56 - 4(9.60)6.95]/[370.10 - 4(9.60)^2] = 0.466$

$a = 6.95 - 0.466(9.60) = 2.476$

Thus, $Y'_X = 2.476 + 0.466X$

Forecast for $X = 12$ (thousand marriages):

$Y'_X = 2.476 + 0.466(12) = 8.068$ or 8,068 housing starts

employment rate in the previous quarter might also explain a great deal of the change in housing starts. The regression equation would be of the form

$$Y'_{X1X2} = a + b_1X_1 + b_2X_2$$

where

Y'_{X1X2} = predicted number of housing starts based on new marriages *and* the employment rate

a = Y-axis intercept

b_1 and b_2 = slopes (rates of change in Y') with respect to X_1 and X_2

X_1 and X_2 = number of marriages and employment rate, respectively, in the previous quarter

Generally, a computer is used to solve multiple regression models. Most spreadsheets have built-in functions for sophisticated analysis, including multiple regression and even fitting nonlinear models.

A number of extensions of regression methodology are used in causal forecasting. One is the econometric model. In many cases the dependent and independent variables used in forecasting models are interdependent. That is, for instance, demand may be a function of personal income and personal income a function of demand. Econometric models take these interrelationships into consideration by formulating not one regression equation but a series of simultaneous regression equations that relate the demand data to all the interdependent factors, many of which are also predicted by the model.

Another extension is the *Box-Jenkins* approach. This complex statistical method optimally fits time series models to the data and frequently gives quite accurate forecasts. However, it is a costly and time-consuming process.

A different type of causal model is the *input-output* approach. Here interindustry demands are analyzed to determine the net effect on each industry of all the other industries combined. A forecast of total demands on each and all of the industries is then computed in one overall solution. The model is particularly useful for determining expected *changes* in demand owing to changes in other industries.

Managers can use causal forecasting methods to help predict the impact on production costs of increases or decreases in volume and changes in the product mix. In addition, production time can be estimated on the basis of a number of independent factors. For example, the time required to design, program, and implement a new computer system has been estimated on the basis of such factors as number of files required, number of reports produced, number of individual programs, and subjective factors relating to the level of complexity of various portions of the system.

Nevertheless, the complexity of causal models and the corresponding time and data required for their construction are impediments to their use in operations. Most commonly, a highly skilled statistician—a person not commonly available in many organizations—is required to design and validate these models.

CHAPTER IN PERSPECTIVE

This chapter is the first of three chapters in Part Three of this textbook related to the business process of managing resources. In Part Two our focus was on processes associated with designing and selecting products and their transformation systems. Now our attention has turned to the processes of managing the organizational resources that are used to produce outputs.

In Chapter 5 we discussed the selection and design of an organization's outputs. In the present chapter we have focused on forecasting the demand for these outputs. In Chapter 9 we translate the forecast into capacity requirements to facilitate capacity planning. Then, in Chapter 10—the final chapter in this part—with capacity requirements determined, we discuss issues related to where capacity should be located.

❖ CHECK YOUR UNDERSTANDING

1. List the four primary purposes of forecasting.

2. How does the Delphi method work? What are its advantages and disadvantages?

3. Contrast historical analogy and life cycle analysis.

4. Contrast autoprojection forecasting techniques and causal techniques.

5. What is a time series? Provide some examples.

6. How does changing the order of a moving average affect the responsiveness of the forecast?

7. How does changing the smoothing constant affect the responsiveness of the forecast?

8. Why is it generally preferable to use a less responsive forecast when the demand data exhibit a high level of variability?

9. What are the factors that influence the choice of a forecasting model?

10. List and briefly define the four components of a time series.

11. Why is plotting the data always the first step in forecasting?

12. How is exponential smoothing like a weighted moving average?

13. Explain in English how exponential smoothing works.

14. How does one go about selecting an appropriate value of the smoothing constant, the order of a moving average, or the weights to be used in a weighted moving average?

15. Contrast MAD and bias.

16. Explain how a spreadsheet can be use to help find the optimal smoothing constant.

17. The seasonal index for quarter 1 has been calculated to be 1.25. Explain what this means to a manager.

❖ EXPAND YOUR UNDERSTANDING

1. Provide examples of how the four primary purposes of forecasting apply to a university and to a manufacturer of consumer goods.

2. What impact do the Internet, the World Wide Web, and intranets have on the Delphi method?

3. Are there any products or services that can be used as a historical analogy to direct satellite broadcasting? Personal communication systems?

4. In what situations would exponential smoothing, moving average, and weighted moving average be most appropriate?

5. Why might a decision maker choose a qualitative forecasting method when extensive historical demand data are available?

6. Are there any dangers related to having sophisticated forecasting techniques readily accessible such as built-in features of spreadsheets?

7. To help pay their college expenses, two of your

friends have purchased a hot dog concession stand that they plan to operate during sporting events and to meet daily lunch demand on campus. They have asked for your help in forecasting the demand for hot dogs. How would you develop a forecast for demand, assuming that no historical data are available? What are the consequences of overestimating versus underestimating demand?

8. Explain how a spreadsheet could be used to deter-

mine the optimal weights in a weighted moving average.

9. Show that exponential smoothing includes all past demand data.

10. What independent variables would you include in a multiple regression model to predict industry sales for automobiles?

❖ APPLY YOUR UNDERSTANDING
Bardstown Box Company

Bardstown Box Company is a small, closely held corporation in Bardstown, Kentucky. Its stock is divided among three brothers, with the principal shareholder being the founding brother, Bob Wilson. Bob formed the company 20 years ago when he resigned as a salesman for a large manufacturer of corrugated boxes.

Bob attributes his success to the fact that he can serve the five-state area he considers "his territory" better than any of his large competitors. Bardstown Box supplies corrugated cartons to many regional distilleries and to several breweries. Also, it prints standard-size boxes to order for many small manufacturing firms in the region. Bob feels that the large box manufacturers cannot economically provide this personal service to his accounts.

Bob recognizes the danger of becoming too dependent upon any one client and has enforced the policy that no single customer can account for over 20 percent of sales. Two of the distilleries account for 20 percent of sales each, and hence are limited in their purchases. Bob has persuaded the purchasing agents of these two companies to add other suppliers, since this alternative supply protects them against problems Bardstown might have—shipping delays, paper shortages, or labor problems.

Bardstown currently has over 600 customers with orders ranging from a low of 100 boxes to blanket orders for 50,000 boxes per year. Boxes are produced in 16 standard sizes with special printing to customers' specifications. Bardstown's printing equipment limits the print to two colors. The standardization and limited printing allow Bardstown to be price-competitive with the big producers while also providing service for small orders and "emergency" orders that large box manufacturers cannot provide.

Such personal service, however, requires tight inventory control and close production scheduling. So far, Bob has always forecast demand and prepared production schedules on the basis of experience, but because of the ever-growing number of accounts and changes in personnel in customer purchasing departments, the accuracy of his forecasts has been rapidly declining. The number of back orders is on the increase, late orders are more common, and inventory levels of finished boxes are also on the increase. A second warehouse has recently been leased because of overcrowding in the main warehouse. Plans are to shift some of the slower-moving boxes to the leased space.

There has always been an increase in demand for boxes just before the holiday season, when customers begin stocking up. This seasonality in demand has always substantially increased the difficulty of making a reliable forecast.

Bob feels that it is now important to develop an improved forecasting method to help smooth production and warehousing volume. He has compiled the following demand data.

Month	Sales (in number of boxes)				
	1993	1994	1995	1996	1997
January	12,000	8,000	12,000	15,000	15,000
February	8,000	14,000	8,000	12,000	22,000
March	10,000	18,000	18,000	14,000	18,000
April	18,000	15,000	13,000	18,000	18,000
May	14,000	16,000	14,000	15,000	16,000
June	10,000	18,000	18,000	18,000	20,000
July	16,000	14,000	17,000	20,000	28,000
August	18,000	28,000	20,000	22,000	28,000
September	20,000	22,000	25,000	26,000	20,000
October	27,000	27,000	28,000	28,000	30,000
November	24,000	26,000	18,000	20,000	22,000
December	18,000	10,000	18,000	22,000	28,000

Questions

1. Develop a forecasting method for Bardstown and forecast total demand for 1998.

2. Should Bob's experience with the market be factored into the forecast? How?

❖ EXERCISES

1. How many periods n should be included in a moving average for each of the following sets of data?

    a. Hourly fire alarms.

    b. Daily output from a 40-hour-per-week manufacturer.

    c. Monthly sales.

    d. Quarterly earnings.

    e. Daily sales from a 24-hour convenience food store.

    f. Weekly bank deposits.

*2. Plot the following data and then calculate and plot a moving average of order 3. Then plot a moving average of order 4. Then order 5.

Period	1	2	3	4	5	6	7	8	9	10
Data	6	5	5	4	5	3	2	4	3	3

*3. Use a weighted moving average of order 3 with weights 0.2, 0.3, and 0.5 with the data in exercise 2. Compare the results with the unweighted moving average of order 3.

*4. Use the data in exercise 2 to make an exponential forecast for period 11. Try three values of smoothing constants, α: 0.05, 0.30, and 0.90. Compare these with the moving average forecasts obtained from the answers to exercise 2.

*5. Make an exponential forecast for period 5 with two values of α, 0.05 and 0.60, given the following data. Compare the results.

Period	1	2	3	4
Data	32	14	41	10

*6. Calculate MAD and bias solely on the basis of periods 3 through 10 of the six forecasts in Exercises 2 and 4 to determine the best forecast method.

*7. Referring to Exercise 2, use Excel's Solver to choose an optimal value for α such that MAD is minimized. Restrict α to between 0.05 and 0.30.

*8. Use the data in Exercise 5 to calculate MAD, bias, and the tracking signal for the two sets of forecasts based on periods 2 through 4. How do they compare?

9. Referring to the spreadsheet below:

	A	B	C
1	Period	Demand	Forecast
2	1	25	
3	2	22	
4	3	27	
5	4	23	
6	5		

    a. What formula would you enter in cell C6 to calculate a forecast for period 5 based on a three-period moving average?

    b. What formula would you enter in cell C6 to calculate a forecast for period 5 based on ex-

---

Note: Exercises marked with asterisk (*) are best solved using a spreadsheet package.

ponential smoothing? Assume that cell C5 contains the forecast for period 4.

*10. Develop a linear regression equation to predict demand in the future from the following data:

Demand	23	24	31	28	29
Year	1993	1994	1995	1996	1997

*11. Determine the linear regression trend equation and seasonals for the following:

Units	5	4	3	5	6	5	4	6
Quarter	1	2	3	4	5	6	7	8

*12. Plot the data in Exercise 11 using a spreadsheet. Add a trend line to the plotted data.

13. Determine in Exercise 10 if odd-numbered years are different from even-numbered years by calculating seasonals for each.

14. Predict quarter 10 in Exercise 11 by linear regression and seasonals and calculate current MAD and bias.

*15. Develop a demand regression equation for the following data and predict demand at a price of $4 and $9:

Price, dollars	7	6	8	5
Demand	1050	1100	1020	1130

*16. a. Demand for snow tires in Toronto depends on snowfall. The history for the last ten years is given in the following table. Use the data to develop a linear regression equation for demand. Calculate MAD and bias and predict demand in 1997, if weather forecasters predict 22 inches of snowfall.

Year	Snowfall (inches)	Demand
1987	25.0	2050
1988	27.6	1944
1989	22.4	2250
1990	24.0	1700
1991	28.2	1842
1992	22.2	2404
1993	23.4	1756
1994	25.2	1780
1995	23.8	2144
1996	24.6	1862

b. A friend in the used auto business thinks you might get a better forecast by considering the possibility that demand lags snowfall by a year. That is, consider the possibility that demand is related to the snowfall of the previous year and develop a new regression equation, MAD, bias, and prediction for 1997. Is the result better or worse?

*17. Consider the following data on a toy for children:

Month	J	F	M	A	M	J	J	A	S	O
Demand (in thousands)	0.2	0.5	1.0	2	4	8	25	45	59	66

a. Forecast November demand by a three-month moving average.

b. Forecast November demand by exponential forecasting with an α of 0.3.

c. Forecast November demand by linear regression.

d. Plot the data and the linear trend line from c. What appears to be happening? Can you intuitively forecast November?

e. Use Excel's TREND function to determine the expected demand for the years 1987 to 1996.

*18. Calculate the linear regression trend line for the data on Inner City Health Clinic in Figure 8.5 and determine MAD and bias on the basis of the past data. Also, calculate MAD and bias of the moving average of order 4. Compare these with the MAD and bias of exponential smoothing for an α of 0.3 found in Figure 8.20. Which method appears to be best? Is it "fair" to compare modeling errors on past data when one model was derived from those data? What should be compared?

19. Economists have calculated that sales of new homes (H) are related to the number of new families formed (F), average annual income (I), average interest rate (R), and cost of construction (C) through the following equation:

$$H = 62{,}731 + 0.74F + 5.1I - 4126R - 0.9C$$

where I and C are in dollars and R is a percentage. If it is predicted that, in 1998, F will be 100,000 new families, I will be $50,000, R will be 26 percent, and C will be $200,000, how many new homes will be sold? How sensitive are sales to a 1 percent increase in the interest rate; to a $1000 increase in the cost of construction; to a $1000 increase in average annual income? Do you think there may be any relationship between average annual income and formation of new families? Or between average annual income and the cost of construction? If so, what effect might this have on your results?

*20. Use a weighted moving average of order 4 with weights 0.1, 0.2, 0.3, and 0.4 for the data on Inner City Health Clinic in Figure 8.19, plot the result on Figure 8.21, and compare it with the two series of exponential forecasts. How does it compare?

*21. Recompute the expo'nential forecast for Inner City Health Clinic using an α of 0.3, but use MAD as a tracking signal. That is, whenever MAD exceeds

3.0, switch to an α of 0.8. When MAD drops to less than 3.0, return to an α of 0.3. Plot the result on Figure 8.21. Is this method of adaptive smoothing better than simple exponential smoothing for these data?

*22. A conceptually simple method of adaptive smoothing is known as *Chow's method*. With this approach, after the actual demand is known for the forecast period, one recalculates the forecast two times, using an α 0.05 larger and 0.05 smaller than what was previously used. Using the best result of the three, one then forecasts the next period using the value that performed best in the last period. Starting with an α of 0.3, try this approach on the data for Inner City Health Clinic in Figure 8.19 and plot the results on Figure 8.21. How does this method compare with the others?

*23. Given the demand data below:

   a. Plot the data using a spreadsheet. Then fit a linear trend line to the plotted data. What do the plot of the data and the trend line tell you?

   b. Use a spreadsheet to develop a linear trend, multiplicative model of the data, including

seasonality, and forecast box demand for each month of 1997.

   c. Use exponential forecasting with an α of 0.3 and forecast each month of 1997, assuming after each forecast that the value calculated in (*a*) above then occurs. For F_1, use December 1996 sales.

   d. Calculate MAD and bias resulting from the calculations in (*b*). What do they indicate?

Demand (in number of boxes)

Month	1994	1995	1996
January	12,000	15,000	15,000
February	8,000	12,000	22,000
March	18,000	14,000	18,000
April	13,000	18,000	18,000
May	14,000	15,000	16,000
June	18,000	18,000	20,000
July	17,000	20,000	28,000
August	20,000	22,000	28,000
September	25,000	26,000	20,000
October	28,000	28,000	30,000
November	18,000	20,000	22,000
December	18,000	22,000	28,000
Total	209,000	230,000	265,000

Capacity Planning

❖ Capacity is usually measured in aggregate units of some standard output—except for services, which often measure their capacity in terms of inputs because the output is intangible.

❖ Capacity is often defined in three ways. *Design capacity* is the maximum rate of producing output under ideal conditions. *Effective capacity* is the rate of production given normal operating conditions. *Actual output* is the rate of output actually achieved.

❖ Three performance measures related to capacity are *utilization, efficacy,* and *yield.*

❖ There is a close relationship between capacity and scheduling. In fact, what seems to be a limitation on capacity may in fact be a problem stemming from inefficient scheduling, particularly if multiple outputs are involved. The difference between capacity and scheduling is that capacity is oriented primarily toward the *acquisition* of productive resources, whereas scheduling concerns the *timing* of their use.

❖ Some short-term alternatives regarding capacity are to increase resources (overtime, part-time workers, subcontracting), to improve existing resource use (appointments, staggered shifts, stocking inventory), to modify the output (standardize, have the customer do some of the work), to modify the demand (change the price or advertising), and simply not to meet the demand.

❖ For services, the primary issue regarding capacity is how to meet peak demand with appropriate skills and resources at the right time. In addition to the standard approaches, services also employ duty tours, overbook, use on-call help, share capacity with other services, and shift part of the peak demand to other periods.

❖ The *cycle time* in a production system consisting of a fixed sequence of operations is the slowest time on any one of the operations, and this determines the capacity of the system.

❖ Long-term capacity relates primarily to expansion and contraction of major production facilities.

315

These facilities can be added in small increments, with little risk of a major error; or in a single large increment, with an opportunity to build a state-of-the-art production facility. In addition, capacity can be added before or after the demand has materialized or while demand is materializing—each of which entails its own costs and risks.

❖ Both products and services often have some seasonality in their demand, on an hourly, daily, weekly, monthly, or quarterly basis. By adding counterseasonal outputs to a firm's offerings, the capacity requirements can be smoothed out somewhat for more efficient operation of the production system.

❖ Products and services have their own life cycles, which can greatly affect capacity requirements. By evaluating expected life cycles, a firm can see where smoothing is required and act to improve its efficient use of capacity.

❖ When various alternatives for capacity are being compared, the breakeven model can be useful for making a choice.

❖ Economies of scale arise from sharing fixed expenses, but diseconomies of scale may also arise, from poor communication, loss of focus, and increased bureaucracy. Another form of economy of scale is called *economies of scope,* in which scale is derived from a family of similar products rather than a standard product produced in volume.

❖ An important aspect of capacity planning is the ability of humans to increase their productive capacity through learning. The learning curve is based on the empirical evidence that every time the cumulative amount of units produced doubles, the per unit time required decreases by a fixed percentage.

INTRODUCTION

❖ As is typical of a service business, fast-food chains such as Burger King must respond to sharp increases in demand but still keep costs low. Building up inventory to handle surges in demand is barely helpful, since the maximum allowed shelf life of its products is 10 minutes. And during the lunchtime rush, hamburger production may have to jump from 40 an hour to 800 an hour. To accommodate this high variability, Burger King has designed its facilities and processes for flexible capacity. For example, the drive-through, which accounts for almost half of its business, may be staffed by only one person during slow periods. This person takes the order, assembles it, and makes change. But during high-demand periods the production space is large enough to accommodate five people, who divide up the duties.

A number of other techniques are employed to speed up the process. For example, opening a second drive-through window allows customers with special orders to pull forward if their order isn't ready at the first window, thereby permitting following customers to proceed with their service. By this and other techniques designed to reduce the average transaction time from 45 to 30 seconds, sales during peak demand periods have been increased 50 percent.

Similar efforts are being directed at the counter area, where the goal is to reduce the average time from entering the store to picking up the completed tray and looking for a table to under 3 minutes.

Payroll costs these days are just as large as food costs in the operation of a typical Burger King. Thus, keeping costs low while meeting highly variable demand requires attention to staffing costs as well as transaction times. Clearly, part-time workers are one part of the solution for fast-food restaurants, but detailed planning and management are also crucial. Burger King's award-winning restaurant design, the "BK-50," is 32 percent smaller and costs 27 percent less to build than the previous design, yet it can handle 40 percent more sales with less labor (Filley, 1983).

317

❖ You might be surprised to learn that the semiconductor industry is taking a lesson from the steel industry. After all, the semiconductor industry is on the leading edge of technology, whereas the steel industry is decidedly more mature. However, these industries have one important characteristic in common: both tend to require factories that are large and expensive (i.e., in excess of $1 billion).

However, in the late 1980s steelmakers began to abandon economies of scale as a rationale for building large factories and began to develop smaller production facilities called *minimills*. Now chip makers are adopting a similar approach: they are constructing smaller and more automated wafer fabrication factories. One reason for this is that shorter product life cycles will make it virtually impossible to recoup the estimated $2 billion it will cost to build a conventional wafer fab in 1998. It takes 22 to 30 months to recapture the investment in a conventional wafer fabrication facility, but it is projected that it will take only 10 months to recoup the development costs of a so-called *minifab*. Another important benefit associated with the minifabs is that because equipment can be grouped in clusters, the time required to complete the 200 processing steps can be reduced from the current 60 to 90 days to 7 days. This is particularly important because studies indicate that getting a new chip to market a few months earlier can result in as much as $1 billion in added revenues (Port, 1994).

❖ General Motors (GM) recently began experimenting with operating some of its assembly plants 24 hours per day in an effort to turn these inefficient plants around. Of course, trying to operate a plant 24 hours a day can create additional problems, such as how to schedule maintenance. Also, new workers may need to be hired and trained, and adjusting to the new schedule can be a problem for workers. GM's plant in Oshawa (Ontario) faced an additional obstacle related to traffic. Specifically, as its 700 third-shift employees were leaving, 3500 first-shift employees were arriving. GM overcame these hurdles through careful planning. For example, GM operates its third shift at half the rate it runs its other two shifts to allow workers time to perform maintenance functions. Also, traffic jams outside the plant have been avoided by adjusting the traffic lights. The results at the Oshawa plant have been impressive. For example, it produces 48,000 extra units a year, representing an 18 percent increase in output with no capital investment. GM is now turning its attention to changing its design process so that multiple models can be processed using the same tools in each plant. GM estimates that doing this will allow it to reduce its plants from 29 to 22–24 (Templin, 1993).

As we will discuss in more detail throughout this chapter, *capacity* represents the rate at which a transformation system can create outputs. As is illustrated by the example of Burger King, capacity planning is as important to service organizations as it is to traditional manufacturing organizations such as GM and semiconductor manufacturers. Options for altering an organization's capacity are categorized as either *short-term* or *long-term* alternatives. In GM's case, adding a third shift would fall into the short-term category, whereas building a new minifab facility would be in the long-term category.

These examples illustrate a number of other important aspects associated with capacity planning. In Burger King's case, the transformation system was designed so that capacity could be quickly adjusted to match a highly variable demand rate throughout the day. The case of the semiconductor industry demonstrates the enormous cost often associated with expanding capacity. To further complicate matters, shorter product life cycles mean that organizations have less time to recoup their investment, especially when the next generation of products makes the current production system obsolete. Finally, GM illustrates the substantial gains an organization can achieve by using its current capacity more efficiently.

It is clear from these examples that successful businesses pay at least as much attention to the design of their production systems as they do to the design of their outputs. In Part Two, you learned about the process of designing a product or service and, to some extent, the production system as well. Now, in Part Three, we consider the production system from the perspective of managing it as a resource. In the present chapter, we are interested in setting the level of production capacity required, based on the forecast of demand we developed in Chapter 8. Of course, there may be more than one facility; if so, capacity must be determined for each of them. We will discuss this issue in more detail in Chapter 10.

We begin this chapter with a discussion of the many meanings of capacity and how each is measured. We then describe the most economical manner of obtaining capacity, for both the short term and the long term. That is, in addition to worrying about the form and amount of capacity needed, we must also consider its timing. Next, we discuss an important aspect related to capacity planning: the ability of humans to increase their productive capacity through learning. Finally, our attention turns to discussing some of the unique aspects of planning capacity for services.

CAPACITY: TERMINOLOGY AND MEASURES

Capacity may be taken to mean the maximum rate at which a transformation system produces outputs or processes inputs. Table 9.1 lists measures of capacity for a number of production systems. Notice that since capacity is defined as a *rate*, measures should include a *time dimension*. For instance, how meaningful it is to know that a hospital can perform 25 surgeries? Without knowing whether this is per day, per week, or possibly per month, the number is relatively meaningless.

As illustrated in Table 9.1, airlines often measure their capacity in *available seat miles* (ASMs) per year. One ASM is 1 seat available for 1 passenger for 1 mile. Clearly, the number of planes an airline has, their size, how often they are flown, and the route structure of the airline all affect its ASMs, or capacity. An elementary

$\mathscr{T}_{ABLE}$ 9.1 ❖ Examples of Measures of Capacity

Production System	Measure of Capacity in Terms of Outputs Produced	Measure of Capacity in Terms of Inputs Processed
airline	available seat miles per year	reservation calls handled per day
hospital	babies delivered per month	patients admitted per week
supermarket	customers checked out per hour	cartons unloaded per hour
post office	packages delivered per day	letters sorted per hour
university	graduates per quarter	students admitted per year
automobile assembly plant	autos assembled per year	deliveries of parts per day

measure of a hospital's capacity is often simply the number of beds. Thus, a 50-bed hospital is "small" and a 1000-bed hospital is "large." Similarly, a restaurant may measure its capacity in tables, a hotel in rooms, a public service agency in family contacts, a durable goods manufacturer in appliances produced per year, a consumer goods manufacturer in units produced per week, a chemical producer in barrels or tons produced per quarter, and so on.

Notice that these measures of capacity do not recognize the multiple types of outputs an organization may, in reality, be concerned with. ASMs say nothing about the freight capacity of an airline, but freight may be a major contributor to profits. Similarly, number of beds says nothing about outpatient treatment, ambulance rescues, and other services provided by a hospital. Thus capacity planning must often consider the capacity to produce multiple outputs. Unfortunately, some of the outputs may require the same organizational resources, as well as some very specialized resources.

The provision of adequate capacity is clearly a generic problem, common to all types of organizations, but in pure service organizations capacity is a special problem because the output cannot normally be stored for later use. A utility, for example, must have capacity available to meet peak power demands, yet the *average* power demand may be much, much lower. Where the provision of the service is by human labor, low productivity is a danger when staffing is provided to meet the demand peaks.

Another characteristic of capacity is that, frequently, a variety of restrictions can limit it. For example, the capacity of a fast-food restaurant may be limited not only by the number of order-takers on duty but also by the number of cooks, the number of machines to prepare the food, the amount of food in stock, the space in the restaurant, and even the number of parking spaces outside. Any one of these factors can become a ***bottleneck*** that limits the restaurant's actual capacity to something less than its theoretical capacity.

Clearly, the capacity of each of these potential bottlenecks must be adequate for the restaurant's target capacity of customers, but an excess of any one when the bottleneck becomes something else is a waste of the organization's resources (e.g., having 100 parking spaces when the restaurant seats only 75 people). Unfortunately, the bottleneck resource doesn't usually remain the same over time and depends on the random characteristics of customers: what they decide to order, when they come, and so on.

❖ Capacity-Related Measures

A variety of measures and interpretations of capacity must be sorted out. We will describe and illustrate the major ones here.

Design Capacity

A facility's *design capacity* (also referred to as its *theoretical capacity*) is the target output rate at which it was designed to run. For instance, a manufacturing plant may have been designed to produce a maximum of 500 appliances per week. This goal may or may not have been actually attained. When a contractor is employed to build or install a new plant or piece of equipment, there is usually an agreed-upon percentage (e.g., 95 percent) of design capacity that the contractor must attain in running the plant or machine before the customer will accept the work (this is called the *handoff*) and pay the final invoice.

Effective Capacity

Effective capacity is the rate of output given normal operating conditions. Thus, it is a working output rate for currently existing conditions: machines need to be maintained, workers need breaks, equipment must be switched over from the production of one product to another; and so on. For instance, the effective capacity of the 500-appliance plant may be practically restricted to 450 appliances in any given week, under normal operating conditions.

Actual Output

Actual output is the actual level of capacity achieved. To illustrate the distinction between design capacity, effective capacity, and actual output, assume that you own an automobile with a top speed of 100 miles per hour, and that you live 10 miles from where you work. Further, we will assume that the travel time to get to the freeway and the travel time to get off the freeway are negligible. The design capacity of your automobile is 100 miles per hour, and theoretically you should be able to commute to work in 6 minutes (or 0.1 hour). However, you live in the real world, and the real world has laws that limit your speed to 55 miles per hour. Thus, your effective capacity is 55 miles per hour, and realistically you should be able to commute to work in 10.9 minutes. If there was a traffic jam on your way to work and it actually took you 45 minutes to get to work, then your actual output would have been 13.3 miles per hour. Effective capacity and actual output are always less than design capacity; however, actual output may exceed effective capacity. For example, it is possible for you to drive to work at a speed of greater than 55 mile per hour.

Performance Measures

The alternative definitions of capacity can be used to measure the effectiveness of a system. For example, the *efficacy* of an organization can be measured as the ratio of actual output to effective capacity, and *utilization* as the ratio of actual output to design capacity.

$$\text{Efficacy} = \frac{\text{actual output}}{\text{effective capacity}}$$

$$\text{Utilization} = \frac{\text{actual output}}{\text{design capacity}}$$

Another, similar measure is **yield.** This measure is often used to indicate the output of a good emerging from a production system compared with the amount of actual (total) output or the amount of product that entered it. For example, some microelectronic products are highly susceptible to minor flaws, and so the yield from the large number of production steps may be as low as 40 percent. This was the case in the early days of integrated circuits and still is for many new products just off the drawing board. Similarly, chemical products often involve spillage, pipe and vat residue, sampling losses, and other such normal reductions in volume, resulting in a yield of, at best, only 90 or 95 percent. Another consideration is that in cutting circles of material out of sheets of steel (or cookies out of rolled-out dough), scrap is large but unavoidable. Thus, the concept of yield is meant to include natural losses, waste (avoidable), scrap (unavoidable), and defects or errors, all combined.

Note that all these expressions are various forms of productivity measures: output divided by input. The only difference involves how the outputs and inputs are measured. In calculating the capacity requirements for a system given the yield, a common error is to multiply by 1 plus the yield instead of dividing by the yield. For example, suppose that a system in which one machine can produce 1 unit has only a 40 percent yield. Then, if customers demand 100 units, a frequent mistake is to calculate that 100(1.4) = 140 machines are needed. This is wrong, because 40 percent (the yield) of the 140 results in only 56 good units (0.40 × 140), rather than the desired 100. Instead, the calculation is 100/0.40 = 250 machines. Now, 250(0.40) = 100.

$\mathscr{S}$OLVED EXERCISE 9.1 ❖ Yield and Utilization

A delicate laser cutter is used to produce silicon wafers for computer memory chips. The cutter was designed to produce 30 chips an hour. Considering maintenance on the machine, required setup time, and other such factors, the resulting utilization is 90 percent and the yield is 82 percent. If this shop works a 40-hour week and 1 million chips are needed over the next year, how many laser cutters will the shop need?

Solution:

One machine is designed to produce:

$$(30 \times 40 \text{ hours/week}) \times (52 \text{ weeks/year}) = 62,400 \text{ chips/year}$$

Therefore:

$$1,000,000/(62,400 \times 0.82 \times 0.90) = 21.7 \text{ (or 22 machines)}$$

❖ Bottlenecks in a Sequential Process

A major concept in operations is *efficiency versus output capacity.* Normally, we expect that the amount of productive capacity and the capital investment to gain this capacity will be proportional. In the case of one worker, or one machine that produces the output, this is generally true. But when many workers or machines, or both, are required to produce the output (as is usually the case), such a simple correspondence may not exist.

Thus, if rubber balls are molded in one machine run by one worker (and both machine and worker are constantly busy with this task) at the rate of 100 per hour, and a capacity of 1000 per hour is required, then the resource investment translates directly—10 machines and 10 workers will be needed. If two more workers are doing the same job but one produces 90 per hour and the other produces 143 per hour, the total output will be 333 per hour. If these workers are typical, then the average hourly production is 333/3 = 111 per hour, and to obtain 1000 balls per hour will require 1000/111 = 9 workers and machines.

If a **sequential** process is involved, however, the resource investment does not translate so directly into the required output. For example, assume that King Sports Products produces a variety of tennis rackets *sequentially* on four machines, and the **cycle times** required on each machine for one typical racket are as shown in the illustration.

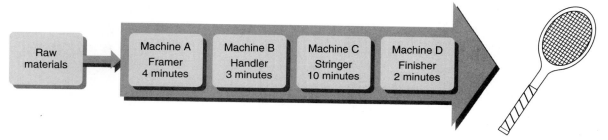

To minimize the cost of equipment, King could use one of each machine and have a resulting output rate (based on the *slowest* machine cycle, 10 minutes) of 6 units per hour. That is, since *every* item must go through *each* of the machines, in order, every racket must wait for machine C, the bottleneck, to finish before it can proceed. During this wait, the first, second, and fourth machines will be idle 6, 7, and 8 minutes, respectively, out of every 10-minute cycle. This gives an overall efficiency of only 47.5 percent:

$$\text{Efficiency} = \frac{\text{output}}{\text{input}} = \frac{4 + 3 + 10 + 2}{4(10)} = \frac{19}{40} = 47.5 \text{ percent}$$

Note that it does not matter whether the bottleneck is at the end of the sequence, at the beginning, or in the middle. The process is still slowed to the output rate of the slowest machine.

If King is willing to invest in another, fifth machine, it should purchase another machine of type C, since that is the bottleneck. Then it could run machines C_1 and C_2 concurrently and put out two units every 10 minutes, obtaining an "effective" cycle time of 5 minutes for the machines by staggering the output.

The effect of this single investment would be to *double* the output rate to 12 units per hour and increase the system efficiency to

$$\frac{4+3+5+2+5}{5(5)} = \frac{19}{25} = 76 \text{ percent}$$

Note, in this efficiency calculation, that the output per racket is *always* 19 minutes regardless of the number of machines; only the input changes. Continuing in this manner results in the data shown in Table 9.2 and sketched in Figure 9.1. In developing Table 9.2, the next machine added was always the machine that currently had the longest machine time. For example, when there were six machines, machine A had the largest machine time. Thus, the seventh machine added was a machine A.

Note from the table and figure that efficiency of production does not always increase when machines are added, although the general trend is upward. This is be-

𝒯ABLE 9.2 ❖ Return to King for Using More Machines

Number of Machines	Type of Next Machine	Machine Times (minutes)				Total Cycle Time	Hourly Output	Utilization Efficiency (percent)
		A	B	C	D			
4	—	4	3	10	2	10	6	47.5
5	C	4	3	5	2	5	12	76.0
6	C	4	3	3.33	2	4	15	79.2
7	A	2	3	3.33	2	3.33	18	81.4
8	C	2	3	2.5	2	3	20	79.2
9	B	2	1.5	2.5	2	2.5	24	84.4
10	C	2	1.5	2	2	2	30	95.0
11	D	2	1.5	2	1	2	30	86.0
12	A	1.33	1.5	2	1	2	30	79.2
13	C	1.33	1.5	1.67	1	1.67	36	87.5
14	C	1.33	1.5	1.43	1	1.5	40	90.5

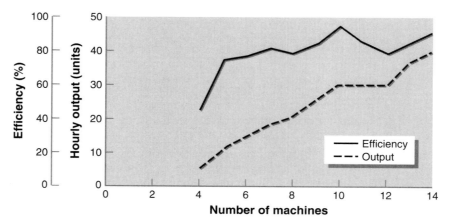

Figure 9.1   Efficiency and output increase when machines are being added.

cause some systems are fairly well "balanced" to begin with. (For example, the cycles are quite even with 7 machines, 2, 3, 3.33, 2; and more so at 10 machines; and the addition of only one extra machine at such points does not pay for itself.) If points of high efficiency are reached "early" (as machines are added), these points will tend to be natural operating solutions. For example, a tremendous gain in efficiency (and in output percentage) is reaped by adding a fifth machine to the system. Further additions do not gain much. The next largest gain occurs when the tenth machine is added to the system.

Although this analysis describes the general trade-offs of the system, no mention has been made of demand. Suppose that demand is 14 units per hour. Then, to minimize risk but still keep an efficient system, King might use five machines and either work overtime, undersupply the market, or use a number of other strategies, as will be discussed later. Similarly, for a demand of 25 to 35 per hour, the use of 10 machines would be appropriate.

*S*OLVED EXERCISE 9.2 ❖ Bottlenecks

A team of three skilled assemblers—Bill, Mandy, and Todd—are fully assembling compact disk (CD) players. Bill's tasks require 8 minutes, Mandy's take 6 minutes, and Todd's takes 10 minutes. What will their hourly output and efficiency be? If they each completely assemble the CD player by themselves (assume they are all equally proficient in all the tasks), what will their output and efficiency be?

Solution:

Todd takes the longest at 10 minutes, resulting in 60/10 = 6 units/hour. So the team's combined efficiency is (8 + 6 + 10)/(3 × 10) = 80 percent.

Working separately, they will each produce 1 unit every 8 + 6 + 10 = 24 minutes, or on average, 60/24 = 2.5 units/hour. Since three of them are working, the combined output will be 2.5 × 3 = 7.5 units/hour. Their efficiency will be 3(8 + 6 + 10)/(3 × 24) = 100 percent. This is *better* than before.*

---

*Note that the concept of division of labor as a production method is appropriate only if the workers can become sufficiently proficient to reduce task times enough to overcome the inherent inefficiency of a sequential process.

❖ Relationship between Capacity and Scheduling

Another aspect of capacity worth noting is its close tie to scheduling. That is, poor scheduling may result in what appears to be a capacity problem, and a shortage of capacity may lead to constant scheduling difficulties. Thus, capacity planning is very closely related to the scheduling function, a topic to be discussed in Chapters 11 and 15. The difference is that capacity is oriented primarily toward the *acquisition* of productive resources, whereas scheduling concerns the *timing* of their use. However, it is often difficult to separate the two, especially where human resources are involved, such as in the use of overtime or the overlapping of shifts.

As a simple example, suppose that an organization has to complete within two weeks the two customers' jobs shown in Table 9.3. The table shows the sequential processing operations still to be completed and the times required. (The operations

Table 9.3 ❖ Sequential Operations Required for Two Jobs

Job	Operations Resource Needed	Time Required (hours)
1	A	10
	C	10
	A	30
	B	20
	C	5
2	B	15
	A	10
	C	10
	A	10
	B	10

resources may be of any form—a facility, a piece of equipment, or a specially skilled worker.) In total, 60 hours of resource A are needed, 45 hours of B, and 25 hours of C. It would appear that two weeks (80 hours) of capacity on each of these three resources would be sufficient, and additional capacity would, therefore, be unnecessary.

Figure 9.2 shows the resource requirements of the two jobs plotted along a time scale. Such a chart (discussed further in Chapter 15) is called a ***Gantt chart*** and can be used to show time schedules and capacities of facilities, workers, jobs, activities, machines, and so forth. In Figure 9.2*a* each job was scheduled on the required resource as soon as it finished on the previous resource, whether or not the new resource was occupied with the other job. This infeasible schedule is called ***infinite loading*** because work is scheduled on the resource as if it had infinite capacity to handle any and all jobs. Note that in this way capacity conflicts and possible resolutions can be easily visualized. Shifting the jobs to avoid such conflicts—this is called ***finite loading***—gives the longer but feasible schedule shown in Figure 9.2*b*.

The first resource conflict in Figure 9.2*a* occurs at 20 hours, when job 1 finishes on resource C and next requires resource A, which is still working on job 2. The second conflict, again at A, occurs at 35 hours, and the third, on B, at 50 hours. It is quickly seen that deferring one job for the other has drastic consequences for conflicts of resources later on as well as for job completion times. Another consideration, not specified here, is whether an operation can be stopped to let another job pass through (this is called *operation splitting*) or, once started, must be worked on until completion.

*S*HORT-TERM AND LONG-TERM CONSIDERATIONS

❖ Long-Term Capacity Planning

Issues of capacity planning over the long run relate primarily to the expansion and contraction of major facilities used in producing the output. This is clearly a strategic issue rather than a tactical issue, as with short-term capacity planning.

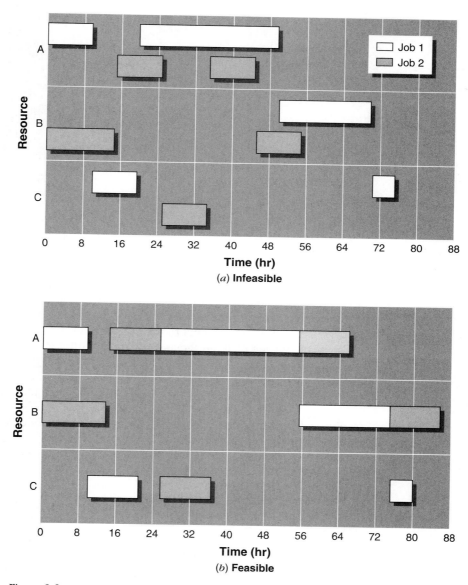

Figure 9.2   Gantt charts for capacity planning and scheduling.

Figure 9.3 illustrates the issue of facilities in terms of capacity and unit cost. Product cost curves are shown for five sizes of production facilities. When plants are operated at their lowest-cost production level (*A, B,* or *C*), the larger facilities will generally have the lowest costs, a phenomenon known as *economies of scale.* However, if nonoptimal production levels must be set, the advantage of a larger facility may be lost. For example, point *D* is characterized by congestion and excessive overtime, and point *E* by idle labor and low equipment utilization. Points *F* and *G* illustrate some of the diseconomies of scale, as described next.

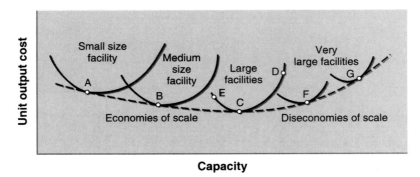

Figure 9.3   Envelope of lowest unit output costs with facility size.

❖ Economies of Scale and Scope

Obtaining lower unit costs through the use of larger facilities is known as **economies of scale.** In essence, the economy comes from spreading the required fixed costs—land, administration, sales force, facilities, and such other factors— over a larger volume of products or services. However, as illustrated by points *F* and *G* in Figure 9.3, there is a limit to the benefits that can be obtained, because the inherent inefficiencies of large facilities begin to counter their economic benefits. This occurs through increased bureaucracy, poor communication, long lines of responsibility and authority, and the like. Many manufacturers now have a corporate policy that no plant will be larger than 200 to 250 workers, often considered an optimum size.

Managers frequently think in terms of economies of scale when making decisions about where to produce new products or services, or whether or not to extend their line of products and services. However, the focus lost through adding

---

𝒮OLVED EXERCISE 9.3   ❖ Economies of Scale

Taylor Products uses $1 million of fixed costs (land, administration, equipment utilities, and so on) each year to produce 100,000 desk telephone sets. It is considering adding cellular telephones to its line. Taylor estimates that it can produce and sell 10,000 of these phones by using available slack in its fixed expenses and thus not increase fixed costs at all. If fixed costs are allocated equally by accounting to all products, what impact will adding cellular phones have on the profitability of Taylor's desk telephones?

Solution:

Current fixed-cost allocation: $1,000,000/100,000 = $10 per set

Proposed fixed-cost allocation $1,000,000/110,000 = $9.09 per set

Thus, profitability would increase by $0.91 per set.

---

these new production requirements can jeopardize the competitive strength of a firm. Managers would be well advised to examine more closely where the economies are expected to come from: sometimes it is from higher volumes, sometimes from the use of common technology, sometimes from availability of off-peak capacity. If the source of the economy results in offsetting diseconomies of scale, as a result of loss of focus or for other reasons, the firm should not proceed.

An allied concept related to the use of many of the advanced, flexible technologies such as programmable robots is called *economies of scope.* The phrase implies that economies can also be obtained with flexibility by offering variety instead of volume. However, upon closer examination it is not clear why being flexible offers any particular economies. The real reason for economies of scope derives from the same economies as those of scale—spreading fixed costs among more products or services—but the scale is now obtained over many small batches of a wide variety of outputs rather than large batches of only a few standard outputs.

❖ Short-Term Capacity Alternatives

The problem of short-term capacity is to handle unexpected but imminent actual demand, either less than or more than expected, in an economic manner. It is known, of course, that the forecast will not be perfect; thus, managers of resources must plan what short-term capacity alternatives to use in either case. Such considerations are usually limited to, at most, the next six months, and usually much less, such as the next few days or hours.

Some alternatives for obtaining short-run capacity are categorized in Table 9.4. Each of the techniques in the table has advantages and disadvantages. The use of overtime is expensive (time and a half), and productivity after eight hours of work is typically poor. It is a simple and easily invoked approach, however, that does not require additional investment and is one of the most common alternatives. As the GM example at the beginning of the chapter illustrated, the use of extra shifts requires hiring but no extra facilities. However, productivity on second and third shifts is often lower than that of the first shift. Part-time hiring can be expensive and is usually feasible for only low or unskilled work. Floating workers are flexible and very useful, but of course also cost extra. Leasing facilities and workers is often a good approach, but the extra cost reduces the profit, and these external resources may not be available during the high-demand periods when they are needed. Subcontracting may require a long lead time, is considerable trouble to implement, and may leave little, if any, profit.

For daily demand peaks, shifts can be overlapped to provide extra capacity at peak times, or staggered to adjust to changes in demand loads. Appointment systems, if feasible, can also help smooth out daily demand peaks. If the output can be stocked ahead of time, as with a product, this is an excellent and very common approach to meeting capacity needs. If recipients are willing, the backlogging of demand to be met later during slack periods is an excellent strategy; a less accurate forecast is needed and investment in finished goods is nil. However, this may be an open invitation to competition.

Modifying the output is a creative approach. Doing less customization, allowing fewer variants, and encouraging recipients to do some assembly or finishing tasks themselves, perhaps with a small price incentive, are infrequently employed yet good alternatives.

*T*ABLE 9.4 ❖ Techniques for Increasing Short-Run Capacity

I. Increase resources
   1. Use overtime.
   2. Add shifts.
   3. Employ part-time workers.
   4. Use floating workers.
   5. Lease workers and facilities.
   6. Subcontract.

II. Improve resource use
   7. Overlap or stagger shifts.
   8. Schedule appointments.
   9. Inventory output (if feasible) ahead of demand.
   10. Backlog or queue demand.

III. Modify the output
   11. Standardize the output.
   12. Have the recipient do part of the work.
   13. Transform service operations into inventoriable product operations.
   14. Cut back on quality.

IV. Modify the demand
   15. Change the price.
   16. Change the promotion.

V. Do not meet demand
   17. Do not supply all the demand.

Attempting to alter or shift the demand to a different period is another creative approach. Running promotions or price differentials, or both, for slack periods is an excellent method for leveling out demand, especially in utilities, telephones, and similar services. Prices are not easily increased above normal in high-demand periods, however. Last, the manager may simply decide not to meet the market demand—again, however, at the cost of inviting competition.

In actuality, many of these alternatives are not feasible except in certain types of organizations or in particular circumstances. For example, when demand is high, subcontractors are full, outside facilities and staff are already overbooked, second-shift workers are employed elsewhere, and marketing promotion is already low-key. Thus, of the many possible alternatives, most firms tend to rely on only a few, such as overtime and stocking up ahead of demand.

So far we have primarily discussed increasing capacity in the short run, but firms also have a need to *decrease* short-run capacity. This is more difficult, however, and most such capacity simply goes unused. If the output involves a product, some inventory buildup may be allowed in order to make use of the available capacity; otherwise, system maintenance may be done (cleaning, fixing, preprocessing, and so on).

❖ Demand and Life Cycles for Multiple Outputs

Realistically, organizations are not always expanding their capacity. We usually focus on this issue because we are studying firms in the process of growth, but even successful organizations often reduce their capacity. Major ways of contracting capacity are to divest the firm of operations, lay off workers, and sell or lease equipment and facilities. Most organizations, however, try to contract only capacity that is inefficient or inappropriate for their circumstances, owing in part to a felt responsibility to the community. If it appears that organizational resources are going to be excessively idle in the future, organizations often attempt to add new outputs to their current output mix rather than contracting capacity (the latter frequently being done at a loss). This entails an analysis of the candidate output's life and seasonal demand cycles.

Demand Seasonality

It is traditional in fire departments to use the slack months for building inspections, conducting fire prevention programs, giving talks on safety, and other such activities. The large investment in labor and equipment is thus more effectively utilized throughout the year by adoption of an *anticyclic* output (an output counter to the fire cycle)—fire prevention. For much the same reasons, many fire departments have been given the responsibility for the city or county's medical rescue service (although rescue alarms are not entirely anticyclic to fire alarms).

Clearly, many organizations, such as the makers of Christmas ornaments, fur coats, swimming pool equipment, and fireworks, face this cyclic difficulty. A classic case of ***seasonality*** is that of furnace dealers. For the last 100 years all their business typically was in the late autumn and winter, as illustrated in Figure 9.4. With the rapid acceptance of air conditioning in the 1950s and 1960s, many furnace dealers eagerly added this product to their output mix. Not only was it conceptually along the same lines (environmental comfort) and often physically interconnected with the home furnace but, most important, it was almost completely anticyclic to the seasonal heating cycle. As shown in Figure 9.4, the addition of air conditioning considerably leveled dealers' sales throughout the year in comparison with furnace sales alone.

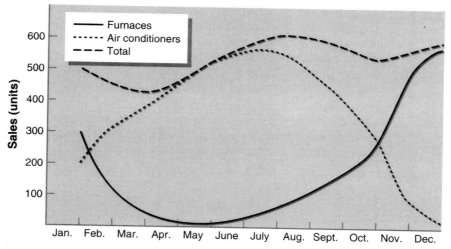

Figure 9.4 Anticyclic product sales.

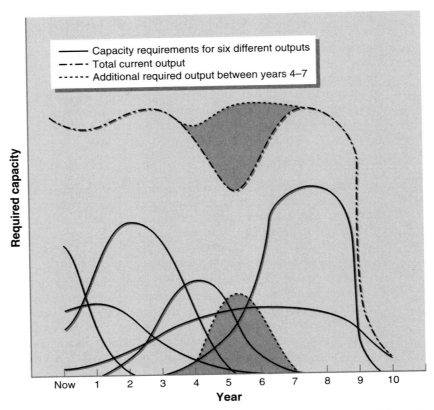

Figure 9.5   Forecast of required organizational capacity from multiple life cycles.

Output Life Cycles

In a similar manner, and for much the same reasons, organizations add to their mix outputs that are anticyclic to existing output *life cycles.* Figure 9.5 illustrates the expected life cycles of an organization's current and projected outputs. Total required capacity is found by adding together the separate capacities of each of the required outputs. Note the projected dip in required capacity five years in the future, and, of course, beyond the eight-year R&D planning horizon.

The message of Figure 9.5 should be clear to the organization—an output with a three-year life cycle (appearing similar to the shaded area) is needed between years 4 and 7 in order to maintain efficient utilization of the organization's available capacity. A priority output development program will have to be instituted immediately. At this point it is probably too late to develop something through R&D; a more effective strategy, especially in light of the relatively low volume and short life cycle, might be an extension of an existing output.

❖ Capacity Strategies

Breakeven Analysis

Another important application of the breakeven concept, introduced in Chapter 5, for managers of resources is the comparison of alternative methods of achieving capacity. For example, Figure 9.6 shows three different methods of producing an output. (Only the total cost functions are depicted.) Method A is an almost all-labor approach ($VC = \$160$) with very little equipment ($FC = \$20,000$) and hence is good for small volumes but very expensive for large volumes. On the other hand, method C is a mass-production automated factory with high fixed costs ($\$400,000$) but low variable costs ($\$10$) and hence is best for large volumes. Method B ($FC = \$160,000$; $VC = \$85$) is a compromise between A and C.

Depending on the forecast of demand, now and in the not-too-distant future, method A, B, or C may be the wisest choice regarding capacity. For example, for volumes in excess of 3200 units, method C is best. This value can be determined by equating the costs of methods B and C to find the intersection: $160,000 + 85U = 400,000 + 10U$ or $U = 3200$. But even though method C can produce parts for much less than A or B, production volume must be quite high before C becomes the optimal alternative. Fixed costs add significantly to the total cost of operations, yet too often operations managers are attracted to investments solely on the basis of low *variable* costs. Then, after production has begun, they realize that their volume is not sufficient to reap the rewards of low variable costs.

Application of Breakeven Analysis in the Public Sector

Because public-sector organizations are not profit-oriented, breakeven analysis is not directly applicable to them. But minor modification of the approach will make it a useful aid for the manager of a public operation.

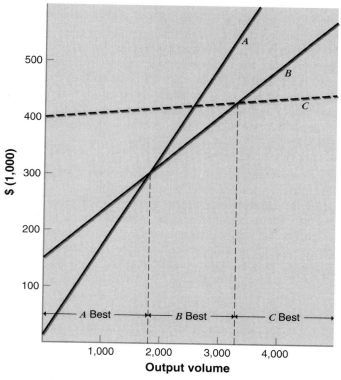

Figure 9.6 Comparison of capacity alternatives.

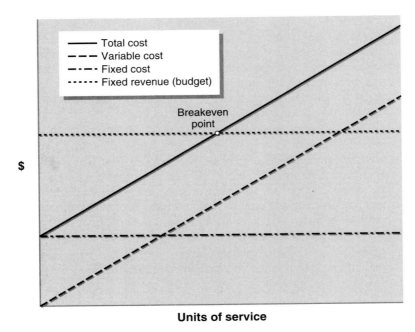

Figure 9.7 Fixed annual budget for public-sector operations.

Although no profits are involved in the operation of a public organization (e.g., a police department), there are revenues that are often fixed by the annual budget. This situation is shown in Figure 9.7. As with traditional breakeven analysis, the breakeven point is the point at which the total cost line and the revenue line intersect. But the interpretation here is somewhat different. To the right of the breakeven volume, the organization exceeds its budgeted revenue—a situation analogous to a loss for a profit-oriented firm. To the left of the breakeven volume, the organization is not using up all its budget and therefore has resources available to provide additional services. The *ideal volume* for the public-sector organization is the *breakeven volume*. Of course, this assumes that the resources are not better spent by another public-sector organization.

Once the best alternative for obtaining the desired capacity has been determined, the timing and manner must still be chosen. The importance of these decisions is illustrated by the sidebar on Cathay Pacific. A number of approaches are illustrated in Figure 9.8. Sometimes there is an opportunity to add capacity in small increments (Figure 9.8*a*) rather than as one large chunk (Figure 9.8*b*), such as an entire plant. Clearly, small increments are less risky, but they do not offer an opportunity to upgrade the entire production system at one time, as a single chunk does. Other choices are to add capacity before the demand has arisen (Figure 9.8*c*) or after (Figure 9.8*d*). Adding capacity before demand occurs upstages the competition and enhances customers' loyalty but risks the cost of the capacity if the expected demand never materializes. Adding capacity after demand arises will encourage the competition to move into the market and take away part of your share. Clearly, the most appropriate strategy must be carefully evaluated for the situation at hand.

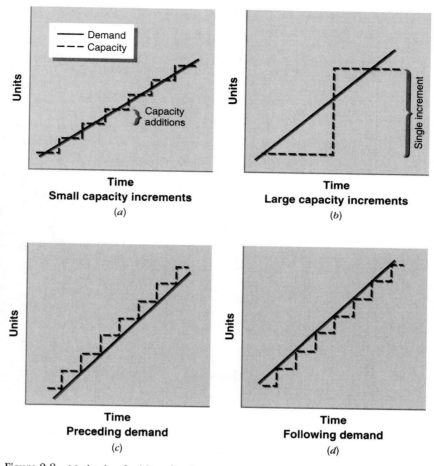

Figure 9.8 Methods of adding fixed capacity.

OPERATIONS IN PRACTICE

Airport Curfew Limits Cathay Pacific Capacity Growth

Asian air travel is forecast to grow faster than any other region in the next two decades and this has made Cathay Pacific, headquartered in Hong Kong, one of the fastest-growing and most successful airlines in the world. Cathay Pacific currently operates 59 wide-body aircraft to 48 destinations on five continents.

With a 1996 average load factor of 72.6 percent, compared to a regional average of 68 percent (Association of Asia Pacific Airlines), Cathay Pacific added 12 percent more capacity in 1996. Furthermore, this rapid capacity growth is expected to continue as Cathay Pacific has more than $4 billion worth of aircraft on order, including Boeing

777-300s, and Airbus A330s and A340s. The airline also holds options to add to its fleet of 19 Boeing 747-400 aircraft.

The reasons behind this continued growth include the need to capture market share as routes develop, and to take advantage of the opening at the new 24-hour, two-runway airport at Chak Lap Kok, secheduled for April 1998. Currently, all airlines operating into Hong Kong face severe restrictions on capacity growth due to the lack of available landing and takeoff slots resulting from an overnight curfew.

Cathay Pacific is spending more than $1 billion on new headquarters and associated facilities at the new airport to demonstrate its commitment to further develop the Hong Kong Special Administrative Region (Cathay Pacific, August 1997).

Solved Exercise 9.4 ❖ Breakeven Approach to Capacity Analysis

Given the capacity alternatives below, for what range of volumes would alternative D be best? Alternative C? Alternative E?

Alternative:	A	B	C	D	E
Fixed cost:	0	100	130	140	150
Variable cost:	5	4	3	4	2

Solution:

The alternatives are drawn in the accompanying figure. Note from the table that *B*, *C*, and *E* have a variable cost less than or equal to that of *D*. *B* and *C* also have a lower fixed cost than alternative *D* and hence dominate *D*. Thus, as seen in the figure, there is *no* range of volumes for which *D* is best.

Conducting the same inspection of the table for *C* (and *E* as well), we see that neither alternative is dominated by one of the other alternatives. For example, *A* and *B* have lower fixed costs than *C* but higher variable costs, and *E* has a lower variable cost than *C* but a higher fixed cost. Nevertheless, that does not guarantee that some combination of the other alternatives may not be better than *C*.

We can tell from the table that *A*, with no fixed costs, will be the best of all the

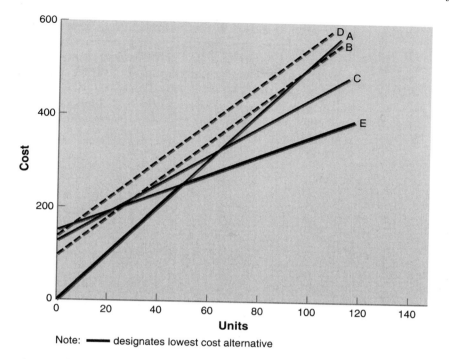

Note: ━━━ designates lowest cost alternative

alternatives at the lowest volumes and *E,* with the lowest variable costs, will be the best at the highest volumes. The only question, then, is whether *B* or *C* may be better at some of the midrange volumes. The easiest way to quickly determine this is to graph the alternatives. Attempting to solve the equations for all the intersections becomes a very big job when there are many intersections (10 in this problem), and the comparisons become confusing.

Inspecting the graph of the alternatives, we see that neither *B* nor *C* is best for any range of volumes. At the lower volumes *A* is better than both of them, and at the higher volumes *E* is better than both of them. The point where *E* is preferred to *A* is at their intersection, found by setting their equations equal to each other:

$$0 + 5X = 150 + 2X \quad \text{or } X = 50$$

$\mathcal{S}$OLVED EXERCISE 9.5 ❖ Breakeven in City Government

---

The Lincoln City Fire Department has a labor budget of $5 million for 1999. The fixed cost of its firehouses, engines, utilities, administrators, and so on is $2 million. If the average cost of a firefighter is $3000 a month, how many firefighters can the department afford?

Solution:

At $3000 a month, a firefighter costs $36,000 a year. The money remaining in the budget for labor expense is $5,000,000 − 2,000,000 = $3,000,000. Dividing the 3 million by 36,000 results in 83.33, or 83 firefighters.

ℐOLVED EXERCISE 9.6 ❖ Breakeven with Capacity Limits

Juenger Toys produces plastic baby toys on injection molding machines. Juenger is considering producing a new product whose variable cost would be $5 per toy. It could be produced on either of two different types of machines: medium-capacity machines with a fixed annual cost, per machine, of $20,000, and a capacity limit of 9000 toys per machine per year; or large machines ($30,000 and 12,000 toys per year). Which machine or machines should Juenger select if it forecasts annual demand to be 10,000 toys? 13,000 toys? Draw the cost chart.

Solution:

At 10,000 units:

$$\text{Total cost, medium} = \$5(10,000) + 2(20,000) = \$90,000$$
$$\text{Total cost, large} = \$5(10,000) + 1(30,000) = \$80,000 \text{ (best)}$$

At 13,000 units:

$$\text{Total cost, medium} = \$5(13,000) + 2(20,000) = \$105,000 \text{ (best)}$$
$$\text{Total cost, large and medium} = \$5(13,000) + 30,000 + 20,000 = \$115,000$$

These results can be seen in the accompanying chart. Clearly, the identification of good alternatives is not obvious.

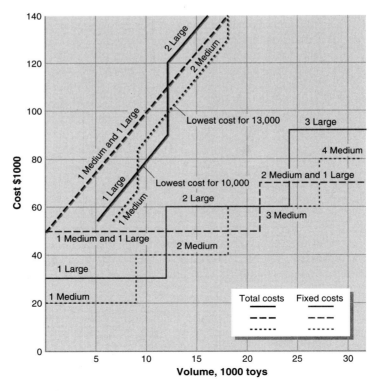

Spreadsheet Analysis: Breakeven with Capacity Limits

Referring to the information given in Solved Exercise 9.6 for Juenger Toys, we now demonstrate how spreadsheets can be used to solve this problem. After further discussing the problem, managers at Juenger have indicated that if multiple machines are purchased, they should all be of the same type, to minimize maintenance and training costs and the costs associated with carrying spare parts. The spreadsheet shown below was created to help Juenger analyze its capacity.

	A	B	C	D	E
1	Juenger Toys				
2					
3	*Model Inputs:*				
4		**Medium**	**Large**		
5		**Machine**	**Machine**		
6	variable cost	$5	$5		
7	fixed cost	$20,000	$30,000		
8	capacity	9,000	12,000		
9					
10	forecast	10,000			
11					
12	*Model Outputs:*				
13	total cost	90,000	80,000		
14					
15	*Key Formula:*				
16	Cell B13	=(B6*$B10)+(ROUNDUP($B10/B8,0)*B7)			

The spreadsheet is divided into three major sections. The first section contains the inputs to the decision about capacity. In Juenger's case these inputs correspond to the variable costs, fixed costs, and capacities of the machines. Also, Juenger wishes to be able to determine the total costs associated with the two machines on the basis of alternative forecasts of demand. The second section contains the output that managers at Juenger are interested in. In this case, they are interested in determining the costs of operating the two machines at various output levels. The final section of the spreadsheet contains the key formula used in the spreadsheet.

Total cost (cells B13 and C13) is calculated as follows:

Total cost = total variable cost + total fixed cost = (unit variable cost × forecast) + (number of machines required × fixed cost/machine)

The number of machines required is equal to the forecast divided by the machine's capacity rounded up to the nearest integer. Excel's ROUNDUP function rounds a number up (i.e., away from zero). The syntax of the ROUNDUP function is:

ROUNDUP(number, number of digits to the right of the decimal point)

Referring to the spreadsheet above, the formula to calculate the number of medium machines needed on the basis of the capacity of the machine entered in cell B8 and the forecast entered in cell B10 would be:

ROUNDUP(B10/B8,0)

This formula specifies that the result of dividing cell B10 by cell B8 should be rounded up to the nearest integer (i.e., 0 decimal places to the right of the decimal point).

Extending this logic, the following formula·was entered into cell B13 to calculate the total cost of using medium machines:

=(B6*$B10)+(ROUNDUP($B10/B8,0)*B7)

The dollar sign ($) was entered in front of the B when referring to cell B10 so that when this formula was copied to cell C13, the forecast in cell B10 would still be referred to.

The spreadsheet above indicates that at a volume of 10,000 toys, buying one large machine is the least costly alternative. In the next spreadsheet, the forecast was changed by entering 13,000 in cell B10. With a volume of 13,000 units, 2 machines are now required regardless of whether a medium or large machine is purchased first. The results indicate that at a volume of 13,000 toys, buying two medium machines is less costly than buying two large machines (and referring to Solved Exercise 9.6, less costly than buying one large and one medium machine).

	A	B	C	D	E
1	Juenger Toys				
2					
3	Model Inputs:				
4		Medium	Large		
5		Machine	Machine		
6	variable cost	$5	$5		
7	fixed cost	$20,000	$30,000		
8	capacity	9,000	12,000		
9					
10	forecast	13,000			
11					
12	Model Outputs:				
13	total cost	105,000	125,000		
14					
15	Key Formula:				
16	Cell B13	=(B6*$B10)+(ROUNDUP($B10/B8,0)*B7)			

$\mathscr{T}$HE LEARNING CURVE _____

An important aspect of capacity planning is the ability of humans to increase their productive capacity through "learning." This issue is particularly important in the short-term start-up of new and unfamiliar processes such as those involving new technologies like automation and word processing. This improvement, generally called the **_learning curve_** effect, is not necessarily due to learning alone, however. Better tools, improvements in work methods, upgraded output designs, and other such factors also help increase productivity. Hence, such curves are also known as _improvement curves, production progress functions, performance curves,_ and _experience curves._

The learning curve effect, from this viewpoint, also becomes a matter of long-term capacity and is often factored into five- and ten-year planning processes. The Japanese, in particular, count on increasing the long-term capacity of a facility through the workers' development of better work methods and improvements in tools.

The derivation of the learning curve began in the airframe manufacturing industry during the 1930s, when it was found that the labor-hours needed to build each successive airplane decreased relatively smoothly. In particular, _each time the output doubled, the labor hours per plane decreased to a fixed percentage of their previous value_—in this case, 80 percent. Thus, when the first plane of a series required 100,000 labor-hours to produce, the _second_ took 80,000 labor hours, the _fourth_ took $80,000 \times 0.80 = 64,000$, the _eighth_ $64,000 \times 0.80 = 51,200$, and so on. This type of mathematical relationship is described by the _negative exponential function_

$$M = mN^r$$

where

M = labor-hours for the Nth unit*

m = labor hours for first unit

N = number of units produced

r = exponent of curve corresponding to learning rate

= log(learning rate)/0.693†

The plot of this function for airplanes is shown in Figure 9.9‡.

To illustrate the equation, let us find the time that the second airplane will take to build in the example.

$$M = (100,000)2^{\log_e(0.8)/0.693}$$

$$\xi = (100,000)2^{-0.322}$$

$$= 80,000 \text{ labor-hours}$$

_____

*Two forms of the learning curve relationship are used in the literature. In one form M corresponds to the cumulative _average_ labor-hours of all N units, and in the other form M corresponds to the _actual_ labor-hours to produce the Nth unit. The second interpretation is more useful for capacity planning and will be used here. For example, then, a learning rate of 90 percent would mean that each time production doubled from, say, N_1 to N_2, unit N_2 would require 90 percent of the labor hours that N_1 required.

†The log here is the "natural" log (the base e), and 0.693 is the natural log of 2.0. But base 10, or any other base, may be used if divided by the log of 2.0 to the same base. That is, $r = \log [\text{rate}]/\log 2.0$.

‡Using Excel's ChartWizard to create similar plots will be explained later in this section.

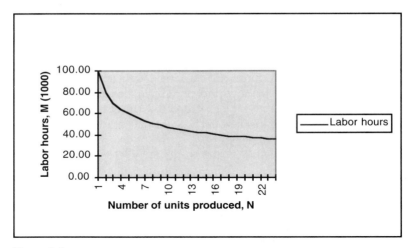

Figure 9.9   Eighty-percent learning curve for airplane production.

A number of factors affect the learning curve rate, but the most important are the complexity of the task and the percentage of human, compared with mechanical, input. The greatest learning—sometimes at a rate as high as 60 percent—occurs for highly complex tasks consisting primarily of human inputs. A task that is highly machine-automated clearly leaves little opportunity for learning. (Thus a rate close to 100 percent would apply, because only the human can learn; the machine generally cannot.) In airframe manufacturing the proportion of human effort is about 75 percent, and an 80 percent learning rate applies. For similar work of the same complexity and ratio of human-to-machine input, approximately the same rate will apply.

But learning curves are not limited to manufacturing, or even to product-oriented organizations. These curves apply just as well to hairdressing, selling, finding a parking space, and preparing pizza. As indicated, they also apply to *groups* of individuals, and *systems* that include people and machines, as well as to individuals.

The primary question, of course, is what learning rate to apply. If previous experience is available, this may give some indication; if not, a close watch of the time it takes to produce the first few units should give a good indication. Let us illustrate the use of the learning curve, and some learning curve tables, with a simple example.

❖ Learning Curve Tables

The solution to the equation for various learning rates, assuming that the first item took 1 time unit, has been calculated; it is tabulated in Tables 9.5 and 9.6. These tables provide the percentage of time the Nth unit will require relative to what the first unit required, or N^r (Table 9.5) and the cumulative amount of time that the first N units will take relative to what the first unit took, or ΣN^r (Table 9.6). Thus, to use Tables 9.5 and 9.6, you multiply the values given in these tables by the labor-hours required for the first unit to get the time for the Nth unit or the cumulative time for units 1 through N, respectively. Returning to our example—the 80 percent learning curve for airplanes—we see in Table 9.5 that unit 2 (left-hand column) under "80%" will require 0.8 of what unit 1 required (100,000 labor-hours), that unit 4 will require 0.64, that unit 8 will take 0.512, and so forth. In addition, we also see that unit

3 will take 0.7021 and unit 6, for example, 0.5617 (i.e., 0.5617 × 100,000 or 56,170 labor-hours). The *total* labor-hours to produce two, four, or eight planes can be found by adding the necessary values together, or by looking at Table 9.6, where this has already been done. Again, reading under "80%" for 2, 4, and 8 units, we get 1.8, 3.142, and 5.346 × 100,000 respectively, for 180,000, 314,200, and 534,600 labor-hours, cumulative.

We will illustrate the use of the learning curve tables with a simple example, followed by a more complex example.

Following the engineering specifications for the assembly of a new motor, a production team was able to assemble the first (prototype) motor in 3.6 hours. After more practice on the second and third motors, the team was able to assemble the fourth motor in 1.76 hours. What is the team's learning rate, and how long will the next motor probably take?

Here the actual individual assembly times are given, so we can use Table 9.5, which tabulates the *ratio of what the Nth unit took relative to the first unit*. First, we need to find the ratio from the given data and then locate that value somewhere in the table. Our ratio for the fourth motor would be: 1.76/3.6 = 0.49. Next, we turn to Table 9.5 and scan across row "4" under the column "Units". We find the value 0.49 under "70%," so this is our learning rate for the team (which is pretty good, by the way).

To find out how long the next (fifth) motor will take, we drop down the column "70%" to the next row that corresponds to the fifth unit. (Note: The rows are not always in increments of 1. For example, at 10 they jump by 2, and at 100 by 20.) At the fifth row the value is 0.4368, which, when multiplied by what the first unit took (3.6 hours), gives: 0.4368 × 3.6 = 1.57 hours. Remember: The tabulated values assume that the first unit took only 1 hour (or minute, or day, or whatever the measure is), so if the first unit took something other than "1," you need to multiply the table value by the actual time it took to produce the first unit.

Next, let us consider a more complex, real-life problem that also requires the use of the cumulative table, Table 9.6.

$\mathcal{T}$ABLE 9.5 ❖ Unit Values of the Learning Curve

Example: Unit 1 took 10 hours. 80% learning rate. What will unit 5 require?
Solution: Unit 5 row, 80% column value = 0.5956. Thus, unit 5 will take 10 (0.5956) = 5.956 hours.

| | Improvement Ratios | | | | | | | |
Units	60%	65%	70%	75%	80%	85%	90%	95%
1	1.0000	1.0000	1.0000	1.0000	1.0000	1.0000	1.0000	1.0000
2	0.6000	0.6500	0.7000	0.7500	0.8000	0.8500	0.9000	0.9500
3	0.4450	0.5052	0.5682	0.6338	0.7021	0.7729	0.8462	0.9219
4	0.3600	0.4225	0.4900	0.5625	0.6400	0.7225	0.8100	0.9025
5	0.3054	0.3678	0.4368	0.5127	0.5956	0.6857	0.7830	0.8877
6	0.2670	0.3284	0.3977	0.4754	0.5617	0.6570	0.7616	0.8758
7	0.2383	0.2984	0.3674	0.4459	0.5345	0.6337	0.7439	0.8659
8	0.2160	0.2746	0.3430	0.4219	0.5120	0.6141	0.7290	0.8574
9	0.1980	0.2552	0.3228	0.4017	0.4930	0.5974	0.7161	0.8499
10	0.1832	0.2391	0.3058	0.3846	0.4765	0.5828	0.7047	0.8433
12	0.1602	0.2135	0.2784	0.3565	0.4493	0.5584	0.6854	0.8320

$\mathcal{T}$ABLE 9.5 ❖ Unit Values of the Learning Curve (continued)

Units	\multicolumn{8}{c}{Improvement Ratios}							
	60%	65%	70%	75%	80%	85%	90%	95%
14	0.1430	0.1940	0.2572	0.3344	0.4276	0.5386	0.6696	0.8226
16	0.1296	0.1785	0.2401	0.3164	0.4096	0.5220	0.6561	0.8145
18	0.1188	0.1659	0.2260	0.3013	0.3944	0.5078	0.6445	0.8074
20	0.1099	0.1554	0.2141	0.2884	0.3812	0.4954	0.6342	0.8012
22	0.1025	0.1465	0.2038	0.2772	0.3697	0.4844	0.6251	0.7955
24	0.0961	0.1387	0.1949	0.2674	0.3595	0.4747	0.6169	0.7904
25	0.0933	0.1353	0.1908	0.2629	0.3548	0.4701	0.6131	0.7880
30	0.0815	0.1208	0.1737	0.2437	0.3346	0.4505	0.5963	0.7775
35	0.0728	0.1097	0.1605	0.2286	0.3184	0.4345	0.5825	0.7687
40	0.0660	0.1010	0.1498	0.2163	0.3050	0.4211	0.5708	0.7611
45	0.0605	0.0939	0.1410	0.2060	0.2936	0.4096	0.5607	0.7545
50	0.0560	0.0879	0.1336	0.1972	0.2838	0.3996	0.5518	0.7486
60	0.0489	0.0785	0.1216	0.1828	0.2676	0.3829	0.5367	0.7386
70	0.0437	0.0713	0.1123	0.1715	0.2547	0.3693	0.5243	0.7302
80	0.0396	0.0657	0.1049	0.1622	0.2440	0.3579	0.5137	0.7231
90	0.0363	0.0610	0.0987	0.1545	0.2349	0.3482	0.5046	0.7168
100	0.0336	0.0572	0.0935	0.1479	0.2271	0.3397	0.4966	0.7112
120	0.0294	0.0510	0.0851	0.1371	0.2141	0.3255	0.4830	0.7017
140	0.0262	0.0464	0.0786	0.1287	0.2038	0.3139	0.4718	0.6937
160	0.0237	0.0427	0.0734	0.1217	0.1952	0.3042	0.4623	0.6869
180	0.0218	0.0397	0.0691	0.1159	0.1879	0.2959	0.4541	0.6809
200	0.0201	0.0371	0.0655	0.1109	0.1816	0.2887	0.4469	0.6757
250	0.0171	0.0323	0.0584	0.1011	0.1691	0.2740	0.4320	0.6646
300	0.0149	0.0289	0.0531	0.0937	0.1594	0.2625	0.4202	0.6557
350	0.0133	0.0262	0.0491	0.0879	0.1517	0.2532	0.4105	0.6482
400	0.0121	0.0241	0.0458	0.0832	0.1453	0.2454	0.4022	0.6419
450	0.0111	0.0224	0.0431	0.0792	0.1399	0.2387	0.3951	0.6363
500	0.0103	0.0210	0.0408	0.0758	0.1352	0.2329	0.3888	0.6314
600	0.0090	0.0188	0.0372	0.0703	0.1275	0.2232	0.3782	0.6229
700	0.0080	0.0171	0.0344	0.0659	0.1214	0.2152	0.3694	0.6158
800	0.0073	0.0157	0.0321	0.0624	0.1163	0.2086	0.3620	0.6098
900	0.0067	0.0146	0.0302	0.0594	0.1119	0.2029	0.3556	0.6045
1000	0.0062	0.0137	0.0286	0.0569	0.1082	0.1980	0.3499	0.5998
1200	0.0054	0.0122	0.0260	0.0527	0.1020	0.1897	0.3404	0.5918
1400	0.0048	0.0111	0.0240	0.0495	0.0971	0.1830	0.3325	0.5850
1600	0.0044	0.0102	0.0225	0.0468	0.0930	0.1773	0.3258	0.5793
1800	0.0040	0.0095	0.0211	0.0466	0.0895	0.1725	0.3200	0.5743
2000	0.0037	0.0089	0.0200	0.0427	0.0866	0.1683	0.3149	0.5698
2500	0.0031	0.0077	0.0178	0.0389	0.0806	0.1597	0.3044	0.5605
3000	0.0027	0.0069	0.0162	0.0360	0.0760	0.1530	0.2961	0.5330

Source: Albert N. Schreiber, Richard A. Johnson, Robert C. Meier, William T. Newell, and Henry C. Fischer, *Cases in Manufacturing Management* (New York: McGraw-Hill, 1965), p. 464. Reprinted by permission of McGraw-Hill, © 1965.

$\mathscr{T}_{ABLE}$ 9.6 ❖ Cumulative Values of the Learning Curve

Example: Unit 1 took 10 hours. 80% learning rate. What will be the total hours required to produce the first five units?

Solution: Unit 5 row, 80% column: value = 3.738. Thus, the first five units will require 10 (3.738) = 37.38 hours.

	Improvement Ratios							
Units	60%	65%	70%	75%	80%	85%	90%	95%
1	1.000	1.000	1.000	1.000	1.000	1.000	1.000	1.000
2	1.600	1.650	1.700	1.750	1.800	1.850	1.900	1.950
3	2.045	2.155	2.268	2.384	2.502	2.623	2.746	2.872
4	2.405	2.578	2.758	2.946	3.142	3.345	3.556	3.774
5	2.710	2.946	3.195	3.459	3.738	4.031	4.339	4.662
6	2.977	3.274	3.593	3.934	4.299	4.688	5.101	5.538
7	3.216	3.572	3.960	4.380	4.834	5.322	5.845	6.404
8	3.432	3.847	4.303	4.802	5.346	5.936	6.574	7.261
9	3.630	4.102	4.626	5.204	5.839	6.533	7.290	8.111
10	3.813	4.341	4.931	5.589	6.315	7.116	7.994	8.955
12	4.144	4.780	5.501	6.315	7.227	8.244	9.374	10.62
14	4.438	5.177	6.026	6.994	8.092	9.331	10.72	12.27
16	4.704	5.541	6.514	7.635	8.920	10.38	12.04	13.91
18	4.946	5.879	6.972	8.245	9.716	11.41	13.33	15.52
20	5.171	6.195	7.407	8.828	10.48	12.40	14.61	17.13
22	5.379	6.492	7.819	9.388	11.23	13.38	15.86	18.72
24	5.574	6.773	8.213	9.928	11.95	14.33	17.10	20.31
25	5.668	6.909	8.404	10.19	12.31	14.80	17.71	21.10
30	6.097	7.540	9.305	11.45	14.02	17.09	20.73	25.00
35	6.478	8.109	10.13	12.72	15.64	19.29	23.67	28.86
40	6.821	8.631	10.90	13.72	17.19	21.43	26.54	32.68
45	7.134	9.114	11.62	14.77	18.68	23.50	29.37	36.47
50	7.422	9.565	12.31	15.78	20.12	25.51	32.14	40.22
60	7.941	10.39	13.57	17.67	22.87	29.41	37.57	47.65
70	8.401	11.13	14.74	19.43	25.47	33.17	42.87	54.99
80	8.814	11.82	15.82	21.09	27.96	36.80	48.05	62.25
90	9.191	12.45	16.83	22.67	30.35	40.32	53.14	69.45
100	9.539	13.03	17.79	24.18	32.65	43.75	58.14	76.59
120	10.16	14.11	19.57	27.02	37.05	50.39	67.93	90.71
140	10.72	15.08	21.20	29.67	41.22	56.78	77.46	104.7
160	11.21	15.97	22.72	32.17	45.20	62.95	86.80	118.5
180	11.67	16.79	24.14	34.54	49.03	68.95	95.96	132.1
200	12.09	17.55	25.48	36.80	52.72	74.79	105.0	145.7
250	13.01	19.28	28.56	42.08	61.47	88.83	126.9	179.2
300	13.81	20.81	31.34	46.94	69.66	102.2	148.2	212.2
350	14.51	22.18	33.89	51.48	77.43	115.1	169.0	244.8
400	15.14	23.44	36.26	55.75	84.85	127.6	189.3	277.0
450	15.72	24.60	38.48	59.80	91.97	139.7	209.2	309.0
500	16.26	25.68	40.58	63.68	98.85	151.5	228.8	340.6

$\mathcal{T}$ABLE 9.6 ❖ Cumulative Values of the Learning Curve (continued)

| | Improvement Ratios | | | | | | | |
Units	60%	65%	70%	75%	80%	85%	90%	95%
600	17.21	27.67	44.47	70.97	112.0	174.2	267.1	403.3
700	18.06	29.45	48.04	77.77	124.4	196.1	304.5	465.3
800	18.82	31.09	51.36	84.18	136.3	217.3	341.0	526.5
900	19.51	32.60	54.46	90.26	147.7	237.9	376.9	587.2
1000	20.15	34.01	57.40	96.07	158.7	257.9	412.2	647.4
1200	21.30	36.59	62.85	107.0	179.7	296.6	481.2	766.6
1400	22.32	38.92	67.85	117.2	199.6	333.9	548.4	884.2
1600	23.23	41.04	72.49	126.8	218.6	369.9	614.2	1001
1800	24.06	43.00	76.85	135.9	236.8	404.9	678.8	1116
2000	24.83	44.84	80.96	144.7	254.4	438.9	742.3	1230
2500	26.53	48.97	90.39	165.0	296.1	520.8	897.0	1513
3000	27.99	52.62	98.90	183.7	335.2	598.9	1047	1791

Source: Albert N. Schreiber, Richard A. Johnson, Robert C. Meier, William T. Newell, and Henry C. Fischer, *Cases in Manufacturing Management* (New York: McGraw-Hill, 1965), p. 465. Reprinted by permission of McGraw-Hill, © 1965.

❖ Spreadsheet, Inc.

Spreadsheet, Inc., has just entered the growing software training market with a contract from a financial organization to teach spreadsheet modeling techniques to the organizaton's 10 managers, for purposes of financial and pension planning. The lesson for the last manager has just ended, and the organization, considering the first 10 lessons highly successful, has engaged Spreadsheet to give the same lessons to its staff of 150 agents. The lesson for the first manager was highly experimental, requiring 100 hours in all, but careful analysis and refinement of the techniques have gradually decreased this time to the point where the average time for all 10 initial lessons was just under half that value, 49 hours each. To properly staff, schedule, plan, and cost out the work for the 150 lessons, Spreadsheet needs to know how many hours of lessons will be required.

To begin, we can use Table 9.6 to determine the learning rate: the average of 49 hours each, times 10 managers, gives 490 hours, cumulative. This is 4.9 times what the first manager required (490 hours/100 hours). Finding the value 4.9 in Table 9.6 for 10 units will then give the learning curve rate applying to these complex lessons. Reading across the 10-unit row, we find 4.931 (close enough) under the column "70%". (On occasion, interpolation between columns may be necessary.)

Assuming that the lessons are continuous and the teaching techniques are not forgotten (an important assumption), we can look further down the "70%" column in Table 9.6 to find the value corresponding to the *total* number of lessons to be given: 10 + 150 = 160. This value, 22.72, is then multiplied by the amount of time required for the first lesson (100 hours) to give a grand total of 2272 hours for the 160 lessons. Since the initial 10 managers required a total of 490 hours by themselves, the second group, consisting of the agents, will require 2272 − 490 = 1782 hours. The time phasing of this 1782 hours is also available, if desired, from Table 9.5.

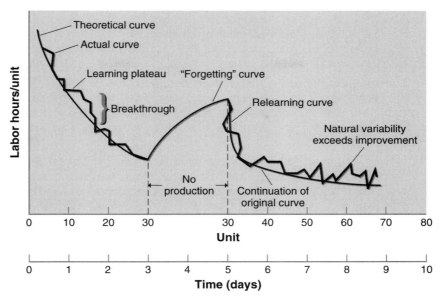

Figure 9.10 Typical pattern of learning and forgetting.

The learning curve is only a theoretical construct, of course, and therefore it only approximates actual learning. A more realistic, and typical, learning pattern is illustrated in Figure 9.10. Initially, actual labor hours per unit vary around the theoretical curve until a "learning plateau" is reached at, perhaps, the tenth unit. At this plateau no significant learning appears to occur, until there is a breakthrough. Learning typically involves a number of such plateaus and breakthroughs. At about 30 units, production is halted for a period of time and "forgetting" occurs, rapidly at first but then trailing off. When production is resumed, relearning occurs very quickly (as when someone relearns to ride a bicycle after 40 years) until the original efficiency is reached (at about 33 units). If the conditions are the same at this time as for the initial part of the curve, the original learning curve rate will then hold. After sufficient time passes, the improvement due to learning becomes trivial in comparison with natural variability in efficiency, and at that point we say that learning has ceased.

ꞗolved Exercise 9.7 ❖ Learning Curve

A work team produced a first prototype electronic appliance in 6 hours and a second in 5 hours. What will be the production time after a (40-hour) week of experience? How many appliances will the team have produced by then?

Solution:

Unit 1 to 2 is a doubling, so we may use the ratio to determine the learning rate: $5/6 = 83$ percent; thus, interpolation in the tables will be required. In general, the time to produce units 1 through N is

$$T_{1-N} = m \times TV_{9.6}$$

where T_{1-N} = cumulative time to produce units 1 through N

m = labor-hours to produce unit 1

$TV_{9.6}$ = appropriate value from Table 9.6.

In this example T_{1-N} is given as 40 hours and m is given as 6 hours. Thus, substituting these values in the above formula yields:

$$40 = 6 \times TV_{9.6}$$

or $TV_{9.6} = 6.7$. Scanning the columns in Table 9.6, associated with an 80% improvement ratio and an 85% ratio (because 83% is between these two columns), we see that 6.7 is between the values associated with 10 units. Thus, after 40 hours, the team will have produced 10 units. The production time at that point (unit 10) will be (interpolating in Table 9.5):

$$0.54 \times 6 = 3.24 \text{ hours}$$

Spreadsheet Analysis: Learning Curves

Spreadsheets can facilitate learning curve analysis in a number of ways. First, as Solved Exercise 9.7 illustrates, learning curve tables provide information only for a limited number of improvement ratios, and for a limited number of units. Using a spreadsheet, tables similar to Tables 9.5 and 9.6 can be quickly developed for any improvement ratio and for any number of units. Also, once the information is entered into a spreadsheet, it can be easily plotted. Finally, spreadsheets with projected time estimates based on learning can be easily enhanced to calculate budgets and schedules.

To illustrate the use of spreadsheets, we return to Solved Exercise 9.7. The spreadsheet below was developed to analyze this problem.

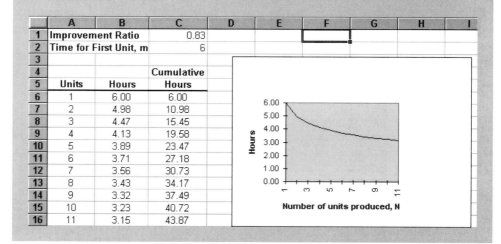

In this spreadsheet, the improvement ratio is entered in cell C1, and the time for the first unit in cell C2. Column A is used to keep track of the unit number, column B to track individual unit times, and column C to track cumulative times. To calculate the unit time, the following formula was entered into cell B6:

$$=\$C\$2*(A6^{\wedge}(LN(\$C\$1)/LN(2)))$$

This formula was then copied to cells B7:B16. (Note that absolute cell references are used for cells C1 and C2.) Since cumulative time and unit time are the same for the first unit, the formula =B6 was entered in cell C6. To calculate the cumulative time for the second unit, the following formula was entered in cell C7:

$$=B7+C6$$

This formula was then copied to cells C8:C16. Note that you can easily extend this spreadsheet to give unit and cumulative times for any number of units simply by copying the formulas in columns B and C down additional rows. Excel has 16,384 rows, and if this is not enough you can continue the calculations in another column. Using such a spreadsheet allows us to assess a situation more accurately than we can with simple interpolation. In fact, the spreadsheet contradicts our previous estimate and indicates that only 9 units will be completed within 40 hours (completing 10 units will require 40.72 hours).

The graph in the above spreadsheet was created using Excel's ChartWizard. First, the range A5:B16 is highlighted. Then, the ChartWizard button is selected. After selecting the ChartWizard button, use the mouse to highlight the area in the spreadsheet where you want the graph to be displayed. In the spreadsheet above, the range D3:I16 was specified. After you specify where the graph should be displayed, ChartWizard will lead you through five steps to gather the information needed to create the graph.

As shown in the figure below, in step 1 the range in the spreadsheet that contains the data to be plotted is specified. Here, before the ChartWizard button was selected, the range A5:B16 was highlighted. Thus, this range is suggested as the range to plot in step 1. We accept this range by selecting the Next button to move on to step 2.

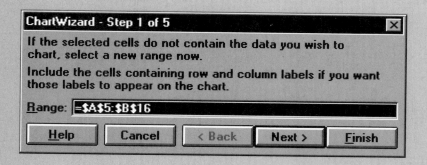

In step 2, the type of graph to be created is specified. From the choices provided, the Line graph was chosen by clicking in it.

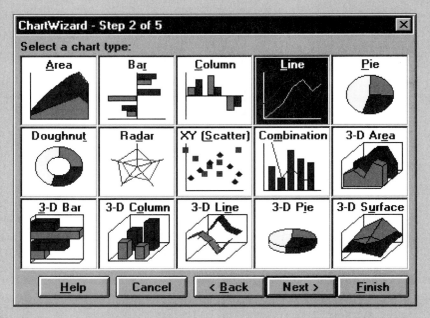

After selecting the Line graph, the Next button was selected to move on to step 3.

In step 3, the specific type of line graph is selected. As shown below, the second line graph was specified in this example.

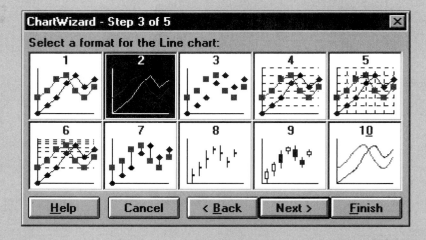

After the second line graph was selected, the Next button was selected to move on to step 4. As shown below, in step 4 we tell ChartWizard that the data are entered in columns, the first column should be used for the X-axis, and the first row contains the labels to be used for the legend. After we specify this information, we select the Next button once again to take us to step 5.

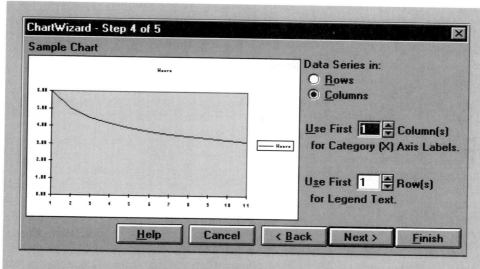

In step 5 we specify whether or not we want a legend. Also, we enter the labels for the *X*- and *Y*-axes. For the *X*-axis the label "Number of units produced, *N*" was entered, and for the *Y*-axis "Hours" was entered.

Finally, the Finish button is selected and the chart shown in the original spreadsheet is displayed in the range specified.

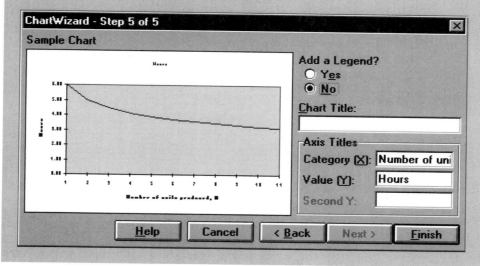

CAPACITY PLANNING FOR SERVICES

Capacity planning is much more difficult for pure service operations than for products, and with a service there is a clearer distinction between long- and short-run capacity planning. For services, the more difficult aspects of providing capacity occur in the short run, usually because the demand for a service is subject to daily peaks and valleys, and the output cannot be stored ahead of time to buffer this fluctuation. For example, doctors' offices see demand peaks at 9 A.M. and 1 P.M., and college classes at 10 A.M. Or there may be weekly peaks, monthly peaks, or yearly peaks such as Friday's demand on banks to deposit (or cash) paychecks, and the first-of-the-month demand on restaurants when social security checks arrive in the mail. Some services, such as fire departments, experience multiple peaks, as illustrated in Figure 9.11*a*, which shows the regular *daily* cycle of fire alarms, with a peak from 3 to 7 P.M.; and Figure 9.11*b*, which shows the *yearly* cycle of fire alarms, with a peak in April.

❖ Capacity Alternatives in Services

As noted earlier with regard to products, frequently it is not clear whether a problem is a matter of scheduling or capacity; this is particularly true with services. The primary problem is matching availability of staff to demand in terms of timing and skills, both on a daily basis and over the longer term (such as weekly and monthly). Service organizations have developed many novel approaches to this problem, such as split shifts, overlapping shifts, duty tours (e.g., 48 or 72 hours for firefighters), part-time help, overbooking, appointment systems, and on-call staff. These approaches will be considered again in Chapter 11 (on aggregate scheduling) and Chapter 15 (on detailed scheduling).

Another alternative is to share capacity with neighboring units by pooling resources such as generators, police patrols, or hotel rooms. As one organization is temporarily overloaded, the neighbor absorbs the excess demand.

Yet another approach is to attempt to shift the demand to off-peak periods by offering, say, lower phone rates after 5 P.M., and then again after 11 P.M. As a matter of fact, the telephone company was so successful at doing this that it had to raise the Sunday-night 5–11 P.M. rate owing to excessive shifted demand.

In certain cases, the customers can provide some of the services themselves, as at self-service gasoline stations and fast-food restaurants. This effectively adds capacity to the organization's ability to serve more customers. As another example of the alternatives available for restaurants, consider a typical 1940s lunchroom during the noon rush hour:

> As the customers started filling all the tables, a receptionist came on duty and attended to the parties queuing (waiting in line) for a table. More waitresses, busboys, and an extra cook also showed up and started working. As customers got to a table and opened the menu they noticed the statement "No substitutions between 11 A.M. and 2 P.M." Waitresses were a long time in coming to take orders and service in general seemed slow. Hamburgers and other sandwiches were served plain with lettuce and tomato on the side, regardless of how they were ordered. Pre-prepared relish cups were included on every plate whether ordered or not. At the conclusion of the meal, signs on the table implored the customers to do their part to leave the table clean. (based on Whyte, 1948)

We are more sophisticated in queuing for tables these days, of course. The receptionist takes our name and the size of our party and tells us there will be a 20-minute wait (he or she must never tell a customer the wait will be longer than 20 minutes) and then motions us to a bar. This serves three purposes.

1. It gets us out of the receptionist's hair and into more comfortable surroundings where we are less likely to leave.

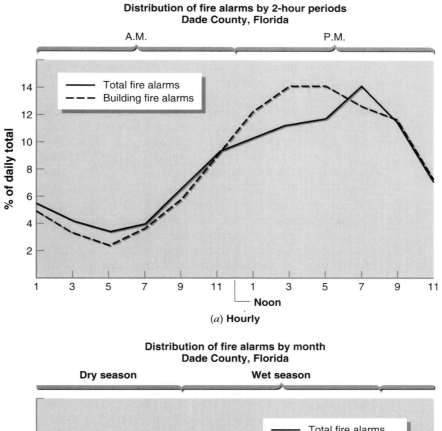

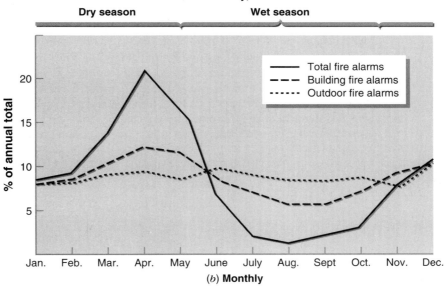

Figure 9.11   Fire alarm histories: (a) hourly and (b) monthly.

2. It makes money for the restaurant, whose greatest profits come from drinks, not food.

3. It deadens our senses so that when we finally do receive our meal it does not really taste too bad and the service does not seem as terrible as it really is.

❖ Measuring Service Capacity Through Inputs

In many situations, it is almost impossible to measure an organization's capacity to produce a service, because the service is so abstract. Thus, a more common approach is to measure *inputs* rather than outputs, and assume (perhaps with regular checkups) that the production system is successful at transforming the inputs into acceptable services (outputs). For example, organizations that offer plays, art exhibits, and other such intangible services do not measure their patrons' pleasure or relaxation; rather, they measure number of performances, number of actors and actresses, and number of paintings (or painting-days, since many exhibits have a rotating travel schedule). Even fire departments do not attempt to measure their capacity by the number of fires they can extinguish; instead, they use the number of engines or companies they can offer in response to a call, the service or response time, or the number of firefighters responding.

Clearly, this manner of measuring service capacity can leave a lot to be desired. Do more paintings give greater satisfaction? Do higher-quality paintings give greater satisfaction? Might there be other factors that are equally or more important, such as the crowd, the parking facilities, or the lighting on the paintings? Is a hospital where more deaths occur providing worse service? Is a hospital with more physicians on staff providing better service?

𝒞HAPTER IN PERSPECTIVE _____

This chapter is the second of three chapters in Part Three related to the process of managing resources. In Chapter 8 our focus was on forecasting demand. In the present chapter our attention turned to translating the forecast of demand into capacity requirements for the organization's various resources.

The chapter began with a discussion of various measures of capacity. Next, issues related to short-term and long-term capacity planning were presented. This was followed by a discussion of how humans' ability to learn affects capacity planning. The chapter concluded with a discussion of some unique aspects of planning capacity for services. With capacity requirements now determined, in Chapter 10 we turn to issues related to where capacity should be located.

❖ CHECK YOUR UNDERSTANDING

1. Briefly define the following terms: *capacity, bottleneck, infinite loading, economies of scale, economies of scope, sequential processes,* and *seasonality.*

2. Suppose per unit variable costs decrease as volume increases. Draw the breakeven chart. What happens to per unit profit above and below the breakeven point?

3. What are the dangers for a not-for-profit organization in operating below the breakeven point? Above the breakeven point?

4. How does the existence of multiple outputs complicate capacity planning?

5. List several measures of capacity (in terms of both output produced and inputs processed) for a police department, a furniture manufacturer, and a law firm.

6. Contrast design capacity, effective capacity, and actual output.

7. Develop a formula for yield.

8. Why is capacity planning more difficult for services than for products? Are there more or fewer alternatives available for services?

9. How is cycle time determined in a sequential process? What is the relationship of cycle time to capacity?

10. Contrast capacity planning and scheduling.

11. List the primary advantages and disadvantages associated with each of the alternatives listed in Table 9.4 for short-term capacity.

12. Explain how the bottleneck in a production system might shift over time and conditions. Give an example.

13. How are the numerators and denominators of the efficiency measures *yield, utilization,* and *effective capacity* different?

14. Explain how demand seasonality and output life cycles are related to capacity planning.

15. Explain the learning curve.

16. Would you expect to find greater learning in a highly automated production system or one that required mostly human labor? Why?

❖ EXPAND YOUR UNDERSTANDING

1. Frequently, simple models such as breakeven are much more appealing to management than more sophisticated models (such as linear programming). Why might this be so?

2. Exactly what decreases in unit cost occur with larger facilities as a result of economies of scale. Might any costs increase with size of a facility?

3. What other types of businesses besides heating and air conditioning firms produce anticyclic products?

4. Why has the concept of economies of scope never arisen before? What does advanced technology have to do with it?

5. Might not computerized technology be able to offset some of the disadvantages of increasing scale so that economies of scale might continue far longer than otherwise? What diseconomies might be reduced? What role should information systems analysts play in this problem?

6. What ethical issues might arise when a firm, to enjoy countercyclic demand, offers both inspection and repair services?

7. In terms of a breakeven chart, such as Figure 9.6, how would manufacturing overseas compare with domestic production?

8. Under what conditions would it be best to precede an expected demand with additional capacity increments? When would it be best to follow expected demand?

9. How ethical is it for airlines, hotels, and other service providers to overbook their limited-capacity facilities intentionally, knowing that at some point they will have to turn away a customer with a "guaranteed" reservation?

10. Does the concept of bottlenecks apply to services as well as products?

11. What elements would be measured if a product firm were to measure its capacity by its inputs, as some service firms do?

12. Does the learning curve continue downward forever?

❖ APPLY YOUR UNDERSTANDING
Exit Manufacturing Company

The planning committee of Exit Manufacturing Company (made up of the vice presidents of marketing, finance, and production) was discussing the plans for a new factory to be located outside of Atlanta, Georgia. The factory would produce exterior doors consisting of prehung metal over Styrofoam insulation. The doors would be made in a standard format, with 15 different insert panels that could be added by retailers after manufacture. The standardization of construction was expected to create numerous production efficiencies over competitors' factories that produced multidimensional doors. Atlanta was felt to be an ideal site because of its location—in the heart of the sunbelt, with its growing construction industry. By locating close to these growing sunbelt states, Exit would minimize distribution costs.

The capital cost for the factory was expected to be $14,000,000. Annual maintenance expenses were projected to total 5 percent of capital. Fuel and utility costs were expected to be $500,000 per year. An analysis of the area's labor market indicated that a wage rate of $10 per hour could be expected. It was estimated that producing a door in the new facility would require 1.5 labor-hours. Fringe benefits paid to the operating labor were expected to equal 15 percent of direct labor costs. Supervisory, clerical, technical, and managerial salaries were forecast to total $350,000 per year. Taxes and insurance would cost $200,000 per year. Other miscellaneous expenses were expected to total $250,000 per year. Depreciation was based on a 30-year life with use of the straight-line method and a $4 million salvage value. Sheet metal, Styrofoam, adhesive for the doors, and frames were projected to cost $12 per door. Paint, hinges, doorknobs, and accessories were estimated to total $7.80 per door. Crating and shipping supplies were expected to cost $2.50 per door.

Exit's marketing manager prepared the following price-demand chart for the distribution area of the new plant. Through analysis of this data, the committee members felt that they could verify their expectation of an increase from 15 to 25 percent in the current market share, owing to the cost advantage of standardization.

Average Sales Price ($/door)	Area Sales (in units)
$90	40,000
$103	38,000
$115	31,000
$135	22,000

Questions

Develop a breakeven capacity analysis for Exit's new door and determine:

a. Best price, production rate, and profit.
b. Breakeven production rate with the price in *a*.
c. Breakeven price with the production rate in *a*.
d. Sensitivity of profits to variable cost, price, and production rate.

❖ EXERCISES

1. Three professors are grading a combined final exam. Each is grading different questions on the test. One professor requires 3 minutes to finish his or her portion, another takes 6 minutes, and the third takes 2 minutes. Assume there is no learning curve effect.

a. What will their hourly output be?
b. If there are 45 tests to grade, how long will the grading take?
c. If each professor were to grade the exams separately in 18 minutes, how long would it take to grade the 45 tests? How long if another professor (who also required 18 minutes) joined them?
d. If another professor pitches in just to help the second professor, how long will it take the four of them to grade the tests?

e. If a fifth professor offers to help, what might happen?

2. A bank consists of four departments with average service times of 7, 5, 8, and 6 minutes. What will the average output rate be during the noon rush hour if a typical customer visits two departments? State your assumptions.

3. A toy firm produces drums sequentially on three machines A, B, and C with cycle times of 3, 4, and 6 minutes, respectively.

a. Determine the optimum efficiency and output rates for adding one, two, . . . , six more machines.
b. Assume now that two identical lines are operating, each with machines A, B, and C. If new ma-

chines can be shared between the lines, how should one, two, and then three new machines be added? What are the resulting efficiencies and outputs of the two lines? Is it always best to equally share extra machines between the two lines?

4. If the production system for a good has a utilization of 80 percent and a yield of 75 percent, what capacity is needed to produce 1000 units a year?

5. What was the design capacity of a production system that produces 753 good units a year with a utilization of 90 percent and yield of 85 percent?

6. If each machine has an effective capacity of 34 units a month but can attain only a 60 percent yield, how many machines will be needed to produce 1 million units a year?

7. Assume that two jobs, I and II, require 3 hours on machine A, 2 hours on B, and 4 hours on C. Assume that job I flows in the sequence A, B, and C.

   a. What sequence would be best for job II to minimize interference?
   b. What sequence would be worst for job II?

8. a. If a firm produces a set of 130 XR products a year with a fixed cost of $780,000 a year and a variable cost of $5000 each, what would be the economies of scale of producing another 20 YR products using slack time on the fixed resources? Assume the same variable cost and a price on all products of $13,000.
   b. Assume that there are three other products, XB, YC, and ZA, with a total additional volume of 5, that could also be squeezed into the slack on the fixed resources. What considerations would be important in deciding whether to add these products to the production schedule?

9. Two methods are available for producing artistic renderings of commercial buildings. One method, electography, requires a complex piece of machinery but can produce the renderings quickly on any kind of paper at minimal cost. The other method, copiest, uses a simple operation on an inexpensive machine but requires special paper and takes quite a while per copy. If Commercial Renderings is just breaking into the business and anticipates low volumes for a while, which method should it choose?

10. Given four alternatives, which one(s) are dominated?

Alternative:	1	2	3	4
Fixed cost:	100	250	175	225
Variable cost:	15	16	17	15

11. The breakeven point between method A, with a fixed cost of $200, and method B, with a fixed cost of $190, is 433 units. Which method should be used for a volume of 679 units?

12. If the variable cost in Solved Exercise 9.6 for the more expensive machine were $4, would that change the answers?

13. Develop a spreadsheet similar to the one shown in Spreadsheet Analysis: Breakeven with Capacity Limits and determine how changing the variable cost for the large machine to $4 per toy would affect the previous results.

14. Given a service that sells for $11, has a variable and fixed machine cost of $9 per service and $277 respectively, and has a capacity limit of 200 services per machine, what demand volumes would you avoid?

15. Assume that in Figure 9.2a, job 1 sequentially requires 10 hours on A, 10 hours on C, 29 hours on A, 20 hours on B, and 7 hours on C. Job 2 requires 15 hours on B, 10 hours on A, 8 hours on C, 11 hours on A, and 10 hours on B. How soon can both jobs realistically be completed? Does it help to split operations—that is, to take a job off a resource for a few hours to let the other job pass through?

16. Given the following four capacity alternatives, find the best production method for every production volume.

Method	Fixed Cost, Dollars	Variable Cost, Dollars/Unit
A	200	5
B	100	10
C	150	4
D	250	2

17. River City operates a Senior Services Department for senior citizens. One program, Meals on Wheels, is partially funded by the federal government and partially funded by collections from recipients who can afford to pay. The fixed cost of operating the program is $60,000 per year, and the variable cost is $0.80 per meal. The federal contribution to the program is $140,000. If, on average, $0.35 of the cost of each meal is covered by recipients' contributions, how many meals can be served annually?

18. A total of 1200 units of a product are made per year at a fixed cost of $1 each, allocated evenly across the units. If the same facilities are used to

double the volume the following year (owing to slack capacity), how much will the fixed-cost allocation decrease? If additional fixed costs of $600 are required instead, to double the volume, how much will the fixed costs per unit decrease?

19. Ace Machinery is forecasting a major increase in demand for its product next year: 70,000 units. It is currently producing 50,000 units a year on the equipment it has. By employing a third shift it could reach 75,000 units, but the per unit variable cost would rise from $1.10 each (currently) to $1.50 each for the extra units. By adding capital equipment, this cost could be cut to as low as $1 each.

    Two alternatives are available: (1) buy $100,000 worth of new equipment (20,000-unit capacity) and attain a unit variable cost of $1.20 for the extra units; or (2) buy $120,000 worth of new equipment and attain a unit cost of $1 for the extra units. In both cases the equipment would last 10 years, and the capacity of the equipment would be the same. Management is strongly leaning toward the second alternative as being worth the extra $20,000. Construct a breakeven-type chart and recommend a decision.

20. Find the learning rate without using the tables:
    a. Unit 1: 15 labor hours; unit 2: 9
    b. Unit 1: 128; unit 2: 109
    c. Unit 2: 60; unit 4: 42
    d. Unit 6: 40; unit 12: 36
    e. Find, in (c), what unit 8 will require and what unit 16 will require.
    f. Find what unit 48 will require in part (d).

21. If unit 1 requires 6 labor hours and unit 5 requires 1.8324, what is the learning rate? What will unit 6 require? What have the first five units required in total?

22. A production lot of 25 units required 103.6 hours of effort. Accounting records show that the first unit took 7 hours. What was the learning rate?

23. If unit 1 required 200 hours to produce and the labor records for an Air Force contract of 50 units indicate an average labor content of 63.1 hours per unit, what was the learning rate? What total additional number of labor-hours would be required for another Air Force contract of 50 units? What would be the average labor content of this second contract? Of both contracts combined? If labor costs the vendor $10 per hour on this second Air Force

contract and the price to the Air Force is fixed at $550 each, what can you say about the profitability of the first and second contracts, and hence the bidding process in general?

24. All the reports you wrote for one class had three sections: introduction, analysis, conclusion. The times required to complete these sections (including typing, etc.) are shown below in hours.

Report	Introduction	Analysis	Conclusion
1	1.5	6	2
2	—	(lost data)	—
3	1	3	0.8

The class requires 5 reports in all. You are now starting report 4 and, although you are working faster, you can afford to spend only 1 hour a day on these reports. Report 5 is due in one week (7 days). Will you be done in time?

25. A defense contractor is bidding on a military contract for 100 radar units. The contractor employs 30 machine operators who work 165 hours a month each. The first radar unit required 1145 operator-hours, and the learning curve for this type of work is known to be 75 percent. It takes a month to order and receive raw material components, which cost $500 per radar unit. The material is then paid for in the month it is received. Fixed costs include a month to tool up, which costs $10,000, and then $5000 per month for every month of production. Direct labor and variable overhead are $8 per hour. The contractor can deliver only completed units and is paid the following month. Profit is set at 10 percent of the bid price. Find the bid price, derive the production schedule, and calculate the cash flow schedule.

26. Poolside, Inc., hires a team of five workers each summer to install pools during the months of May through August. There are 18 weeks available to install pools during this period, and the team works 40 hours per week. Since the members of the team are different each year, and since the workers typically have little past experience with pool installation, past experience has shown that a team's ability to install pools improves substantially over the summer. For example, last year the second pool installed required a total of 350 labor hours whereas the fourth pool required 252 hours. (The time required to install the first pool was not used because one of the workers on the team was replaced after the first pool was completed.)

Given this information, develop a spreadsheet to determine how many pools Poolside will be able to install in the 18-week period. Also, develop a schedule for when each pool will be completed, so that each customer can be informed of projected start and completion time. Add a formula to the spreadsheet that calculates the average labor cost for the installation of a pool, given that the workers are paid $10/hour. If two workers each week work one day of overtime, how will that affect the number of pools produced in the 18-week period? How would it affect the labor cost of the pools, given that the workers are paid time and half for overtime?

Chapter *9* SUPPLEMENT

Linear Programming

Throughout our discussion of capacity planning in Chapter 9, we referred to the complications that multiple outputs create for both capacity planning and scheduling. The objective, of course, is to maximize the returns to the organization by selecting the best mix of outputs that do not exceed the limitations of its resource capacity. This is known as the *output mix problem*. To determine this best mix of outputs requires considering three factors simultaneously:

1. Demand forecast for each output.

2. Resource requirements for each output.

3. Relative return of each output.

The *expected demand* for each output provides an upper limit on the number of each that will be provided. There is no reason why an organization would want to produce more of a product or service than could be expected to be consumed. The *resource requirements* for each output determine the maximum number that can be produced. For example, if a social worker can make only five visits per day and the municipal social services department employs seven social workers, then we cannot expect to "produce" more than 35 visits per day. The *return* to the organization from the production of each type of output does not limit or constrain the organization in the amounts it can produce or sell but rather guides management in maximizing returns to the organization. The contribution of each of the different outputs to the objective of maximizing total return to the organization is measured by the *contribution margin*, as it is called, which tells management the increase in return for providing one more unit of a given output.

Some products and services have higher marginal returns than others. For example, in a restaurant the marginal profit on wines and liquors is higher than the return on the same dollar amount of food. And automobile dealers earn a higher contribution for each dollar in sales from accessory items than they do from basic automobiles.

If both demand and resources were unlimited, then the obvious conclusion regarding optimal output mix would be to make and sell "*everything*," that is, everything that has a positive contribution margin. But demand is seldom unlimited, even though it may appear to be for short periods of time, and resources are *never* unlimited. The question then becomes: How do we simultaneously consider all three sets of factors to arrive at the best combination of outputs? One answer to this question is provided by *linear programming*, a mathematical tool demonstrated in the following example.

*E*XAMPLE: LINEAR PROGRAMMING

Addemup, Inc., is a relatively new firm making small calculators. Addemup entered the business with the production of an inexpensive handheld calculator, the A-

1000, which sells for $15. It has recently added a more powerful version of the A-1000, called the A-2000. The A-2000 sells for $25.

The variable costs of producing an A-1000 and an A-2000 are given in Table 9S.1.

Addemup produces its own circuits boards and purchases all other materials from other firms. Manufacturing of circuit boards is a complex operation, which requires precision equipment. Addemup has the capacity to produce, at most, 61,000 basic circuit boards per month. One of these circuit boards is used in each A-1000 calculator. To manufacture the advanced circuit board for the A-2000 calculator takes three times as long on this precision equipment as the A-1000. Therefore, if Addemup made no basic circuits at all, it could produce no more than 20,333 (i.e., 61,000/3) of the A-2000 boards. Addemup can manufacture any combination of A-1000 and A-2000 circuit boards, as long as the combined production time does not exceed the available capacity.

Assembly time of the two calculators is:

❖ A-1000: 0.2 hour

❖ A-2000: 0.25 hour

If the company maintains its current two-shift operation, it has available 8000 hours of assembly time per month.

The marketing manager has undertaken a detailed study of the calculator market and foresees a monthly demand of 40,000 units for the A-1000 calculator and 18,000 units for the A-2000.

❖ Objective Function

If we assume that Addemup is interested in maximizing its monthly profit, we can begin to structure this problem in a way that will lead to a relatively simple solution. Total monthly profit for next year will be equal to the marginal profit of each calculator times the number of each produced and sold.

We define the following decision variables:

$$A1 = \text{number of A-1000s produced and sold}$$
$$A2 = \text{number of A-2000s produced and sold}$$

Then we can write an equation for the monthly profit, as follows:

$$\text{Profit} = (15 - 11)A1 + (25 - 19)A2$$
$$= 4A1 + 6A2$$

$\mathcal{T}_{ABLE}$ 9S.1 ❖ Variable Costs of Producing Calculators

	A-1000	A-2000
Labor	$3.00	$5.00
Material	6.00	12.00
Factory overhead	2.00	2.00
Total	$11.00	$19.00

Since we wish to maximize the monthly profit, our "objective function" is:

$$\text{maximize } 4A1 + 6A2$$

If the capacity were available and if the marketing manager's demand forecasts are correct, the company could expect to earn

$$\text{Monthly profit} = 4(40{,}000) + 6(18{,}000)$$
$$= \$268{,}000$$

❖ Constraints

But there is only limited manufacturing capacity for the circuit board, so even though Addemup may be able to *sell* 40,000 A-1000s and 18,000 A-2000s, the capacity is not available to produce these quantities. The capacity to produce circuit boards thus limits the number of calculators that can be manufactured and sold. Using the same notation as before, we can express this capacity limitation or constraint algebraically as

$$1(A1) + 3(A2) \leq 61{,}000$$

This inequality states that Addemup can produce either 61,000 A-1000s and no A-2000s, or 20,333 A-2000s and no A-1000s, or any combination of A-1000s and A-2000s that does not exceed the capacity constraint of 61,000 equivalent circuit boards.

But manufacturing is not the only limited resource. Assembly time is limited to 8000 hours per month. This capacity restriction can be written as

$$0.2(A1) + 0.25(A2) \leq 8000$$

This inequality states that the hours used to assemble A-1000s (0.2 hour/unit × number of units) plus the hours to assemble A-2000s (0.25 hour/unit × number of units) must not exceed the available assembly time (8000 hours).

Furthermore, the restrictions on demand for the two models must be considered. The marketing manager expects to be able to sell 40,000 A-1000s and 18,000 A-2000s. Since we do not want to produce any more than we can sell, the following two constraints must also be included.

$$A1 \leq 40{,}000$$
$$A2 \leq 18{,}000$$

Under the first constraint, the number of A-1000s produced cannot exceed 40,000 units; and under the second constraint, the number of A-2000s cannot exceed 18,000.

Finally, since it is not possible to produce and sell a negative number of circuit boards, the following two *nonnegativity constraints* are also needed:

$$A1 \geq 0$$
$$A2 \geq 0$$

❖ Format and Solution

Bringing together all the previous equations and inequalities, we have the following mathematical formulation of the problem:

$$\text{maximize profit} = 4A1 + 6A2 \text{ (objective)}$$

subject to the following limitations:

$$A1 + 3A2 \leq 61{,}000 \text{ (circuit board manufacturing capacity)}$$
$$0.2A1 + 0.25A2 \leq 8000 \text{ (assembly time capacity)}$$
$$A1 \leq 40{,}000 \text{ (maximum demand for A-1000s)}$$
$$A2 \leq 18{,}000 \text{ (maximum demand for A-2000s)}$$
$$A1 \geq 0 \text{ (cannot produce and sell fewer than zero A-1000s)}$$
$$A2 \geq 0 \text{ (cannot produce and sell fewer than zero A-2000s)}$$

Again, our objective is to find the combination of A–1000s and A–2000s that can be produced and sold, within the limitations of capacity and demand, to maximize profit.

This output mix problem is in a form that can be solved by *linear programming*. Linear programming is a mathematical technique that can solve management problems characterized by:

1. A single objective (e.g., maximize profit) that can be stated algebraically as a linear equation.

2. A set of constraints (e.g., capacities) that can be stated algebraically as linear equalities or inequalities.

3. One or more variables representing management decisions (e.g., how much to produce of each output) that can have only nonnegative values.

In this highly simplified example, only two products and a few limited organizational resources were considered, but linear programming can be and has been used to solve much larger, more realistic product mix problems. In the lumber and petroleum refining industries it is not uncommon to see computer solutions to linear programs with hundreds of constraints and thousands of variables.

It is beyond the scope of this text to teach linear programming solution techniques such as the simplex method. However, to illustrate the process, we do present a simple graphical solution procedure for linear programming problems and demonstrate it with the example of Addemup. Also, we demonstrate how a spreadsheet's built-in optimization capabilities can be used to solve linear programming problems. For large and complex problems there are a wide variety of special-purpose software programs that can be run on microcomputers as well.

The solution to Addemup's output mix problem, obtained with a software program for microcomputers, is to produce 25,000 A-1000s and 12,000 A-2000s for a total profit of $172,000. This solution uses all the assembly-time capacity

$$0.2(25{,}000) + 0.25(12{,}000) = 8000 \text{ hours}$$

and all the circuit board manufacturing capacity

$$1(25,000) + 3(12,000) = 61,000 \text{ equivalent boards}$$

One advantage of solving linear programming problems with a computer software program is the additional information it provides. For example, standard outputs will also include the values of *slack, surplus,* and *dual* variables for the six constraints. Slack represents the amount of unused resource for less-than-or-equal-to constraints; surplus represents the amount the lower limit is exceeded by for greater-than-or-equal-to constraints. For our problem, surplus variables are associated with the last two constraints (i.e., the nonnegativity constraints) and slack variables are associated with the first four constraints. The slacks on the constraints would be, in order, 0, 0, 15,000, and 6000. These values indicate the residual amount of each resource or the amount that was *not* used. We saw in the solution that *all* the circuit board manufacturing and assembly time capacities were used, so there was no slack for these resources. However, we did not reach the maximum demand for either A-1000 or A-2000 model calculators, so slack existed here. The surpluses on the last two constraints are 25,000 and 12,000, since these are the quantities produced above the lower limit of zero. In other words, we could reduce the production quantity of the A-1000s by 25,000 units and still satisfy the nonnegativity requirement.

The dual variables for each constraint represent the incremental value to us of *one* more unit of that resource. Since there was slack in meeting the demand for A-1000 and A-2000 models, their dual variables are zero. That is, another unit of *demand* for either of these two models would not help our profit, because we are already at the limit of our resources—we cannot even supply the existing demand! However, more circuit board manufacturing capacity or assembly-time capacity would have value for us. The dual variable is $0.60 for the former and $18 for the latter. This means that another hour of circuit board manufacturing capacity would increase our profit by $0.60, but another hour of assembly-time capacity would be worth 30 times as much.

GRAPHICAL SOLUTION TO A LINEAR PROGRAM

If a linear program has only two decision variables, as in the example of Addemup, a simple solution procedure is the graphical method. The method begins by developing a graph that can be used to display the possible solutions (values of $A1$ and $A2$). We will show the solution to our linear program to be the most profitable number of A-1000s and A-2000s.

❖ Plotting the Constraints

By using a graph to plot the constraints and objective, we can begin to limit the set of solution points to only those that satisfy the constraints in the problem. Consider, first, the constraint on circuit manufacturing capacity, which was of the form

$$A1 + 3A2 \leq 61{,}000$$

We want to locate all the solution points that satisfy this relationship, and therefore we start by plotting the line corresponding to the equation

$$A1 + 3A2 = 61{,}000$$

To plot this line, we need find only two points on the line and then draw a straight line through them. The simplest way of finding two points on the line is first to set $A1$ equal to zero and solve for $A2$, and then set $A2$ equal to zero and solve for $A1$.

If $A1 = 0$, then $3A2 = 61{,}000$ or $A2 = 20{,}333$

Therefore, $(0; 20{,}333)$ is on the line.

If $A2 = 0$, then $A1 = 61{,}000$

Therefore, $(61{,}000; 0)$ is on the line. With these two points we can plot the equation

$$A1 + 3A2 = 61{,}000$$

which is called the *circuit board capacity constraint*. The line is shown in Figure 9S.1. We know that for any ≤ constraints the solution points that satisfy the constraint are

1. All points on the constraint line itself.
2. All points below the constraint line. Verify this for yourself by selecting points on both sides of the line. You will see that only the points below the line satisfy the inequality.

All points that satisfy the circuit board capacity constraint are shown by the shaded area in Figure 9S.1.

Next, we can identify all points satisfying the assembly-time capacity constraint:

$$0.2A1 + 0.25A2 \leq 8000$$

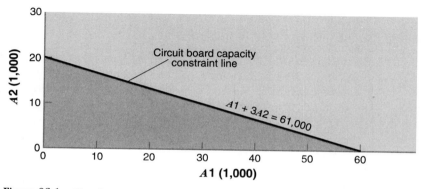

Figure 9S.1 Circuit capacity constraint.

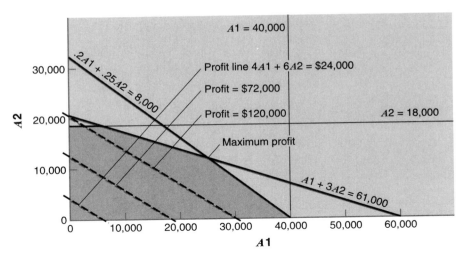

Figure 9S.2   Feasible region with isoprofit lines.

Again, we draw the line corresponding to the equation:

$$0.2A1 + 0.25A2 = 8000$$

as shown in Figure 9S.2.

Our third constraint, the maximum demand for A-1000s, is given by $A1 \leq 40,000$. The feasible region for this constraint corresponds to all points to the left of the vertical line $A1 = 40,000$ in Figure 9S.2.

The next constraint is the limitation on demand for A-2000s, which is $A2 \leq 18,000$ and is also shown in Figure 9S.2. Finally, the nonnegativity constraints limit the feasible region to all points above the $A1$ axis and to the right of the $A2$ axis.

Since our original intention was to determine all the points that satisfied the six constraints, we must locate all the points that satisfy the six constraints simultaneously. These points are shown by the shaded area in Figure 9S.2. Any point on the border of this area or within the area is a *feasible solution* to the linear program. The whole set of points is called the *feasible region*. Any *one* of these points is a potential solution point, but only one of them (in this case) will be the *optimal solution point*.

❖ Finding the Maximum Profit Solution Point

Because there are such a great number of feasible solution points, it is virtually impossible to determine by trial and error the solution point that maximizes profit. A less time-consuming method than this is to continue with our graphical analysis of the problem. The objective that we want to maximize is given by the equation

$$\text{Profit} = 4A1 + 6A2$$

If we arbitrarily select some value of profit, we can then plot a profit line just as we plotted the constraint lines. For example, the set of points that yield a profit of $24,000 is given by

$$4A1 + 6A2 = 24,000$$

This profit line is superimposed on the feasible region in Figure 9S.2.

Clearly, an infinite number of points will yield a profit of $24,000—that is, all the points on the line "profit = $24,000" that are in the feasible region. Since our objective is to maximize profit, we select larger and larger values for profit and plot the lines as shown in Figure 9S.2.

What you should recognize by now is that

1. The profit lines are parallel to one another.
2. The farther the line moves to the upper right, the higher the profit.

Given this, a logical solution procedure is simply to move the profit line *parallel* to the lines already determined and to the *upper right*. As we do this, we are moving in the direction of higher and higher profits, but eventually we will not be able to move the profit line any farther without moving outside the feasible region. The point at which the profit line is farthest to the upper right and just touches the feasible region is the point of maximum profit.

Reading from the graph, this point is (25,000; 12,000). That is, to maximize profit, Addemup should produce and sell 25,000 A-1000 calculators and 12,000 A-2000 calculators, resulting in a net profit of $172,000 [4(25,000) + 6(12,000)].

$\mathcal{S}$OLVING LINEAR PROGRAMMING PROBLEMS WITH SPREADSHEETS

A significant limitation associated with the graphical method of solving linear programs is that it can be applied only to problems with two variables. Thus, problems with more than two variables are typically solved with the aid of a computer. In this section, we illustrate how a spreadsheet's built-in optimization capabilities can be used to solve linear programs.

❖ Spreadsheet Formulation

To illustrate the use of spreadsheets for solving linear programs, the relevant data for Addemup were entered into the spreadsheet shown in Figure 9S.3. As you can see, the spreadsheet has been organized into three main areas. "Input Data" contains all the *parameters* or information given. The second section is "Decision Variables." In the case of Addemup, there are two decision variables: how many A-1000s to produce ($A1$) and how many A-2000s to produce ($A2$). In the spreadsheet, cell B12 corresponds to $A1$ and cell B13 corresponds to $A2$. The last section of the spreadsheet is "Model Outputs." This section contains formulas that calculate various quantities based on the chosen values of the decision variables. The formulas that were entered in column B are displayed in column C.

There are two ways the spreadsheet shown in Figure 9S.3 can be used to find the optimal values for the decision variables. One approach would be to use trial

	A	B	C	D
1	**Addemup Capacity Planning**			
2				
3	**Input Data:**			
4		A-1000s	A-2000s	Available
5	Unit Profit	4	6	
6	Circuit Board Manufacturing Time	1	3	61000
7	Assembly Time	0.2	0.25	8000
8	Demand	40000	18000	
9				
10	**Decision Variables:**			
11				
12	A-1000s to Produce			
13	A-2000s to Produce			
14				
15	**Model Outputs:**			
16		Value	Formula	
17	Profit	0	=(B12*B5)+(B13*C5)	
18	Circuit Board Manf. Capacity	0	=(B12*B6)+(B13*C6)	
19	Assembly Time Capacity	0	=(B12*B7)+(B13*C7)	

Figure 9S.3   Capacity planning spreadsheet for Addemup.

and error by systematically entering values in cells B12 and B13 and observing the values in "Model Outputs." Given that there are an infinite number of possible values for the decision variables, a better alternative is to use the spreadsheet's built-in optimization capabilities to find the optimal values.

❖ Using Excel's Solver

Solving a linear program with a spreadsheet is quite similar to the formulation presented earlier. The major difference is that instead of using constants and parameters in the formulation, references to cells are used. Also, the terminology is a little different. For example, in Excel a formula corresponding to the objective function is entered in a cell and this cell is referred to as the "Target Cell." Likewise, the cells corresponding to the decision variables are referred to as the "Changing Cells." Referring to Figure 9S.3, the target cell (objective) is cell B17, where a formula that calculates profit was entered; and the changing cells (decision variables) are cells B12 and B13.

Excel's built-in optimization routine is called Solver. To access Excel's Solver, select Solver from the Tools menu item at the top of the screen. After we select Solver, the Solver Parameters dialog box is displayed as shown in Figure 9S.4.

In Figure 9S.4, the box labeled "Set Target Cell:" refers to the cell we wish to maximize or minimize. In Addemup's case, the objective is to maximize profits. Thus, in the Set Target Cell box we specify cell B17 by first clicking on the box with the mouse and then either entering the cell reference directly or clicking on cell B17 with the mouse. Since our objective is to find values for our decision variables that provide the maximum level of profit, we next select the Max radio button. The other

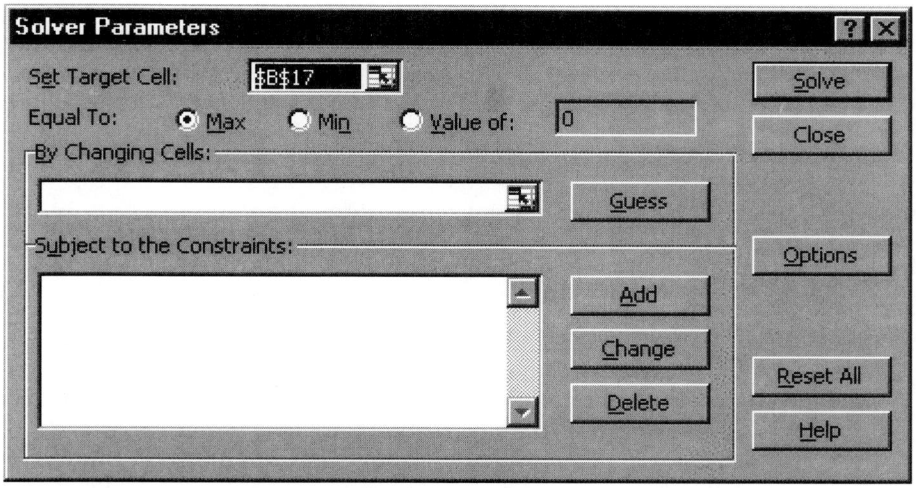

Figure 9S.4   A new Solver Parameters dialog box.

two radio buttons are used for solving minimization problems or to select values for the decision variables such that a specific value of the objective function is found (e.g., to find the values for *A*1 and *A*2 that provide a profit of exactly $10,000).

As mentioned earlier, the <u>B</u>y Changing Cells are the cells Excel's Solver is permitted to change to arrive at the maximum value of profit. In Addemup's case, there are two variables that can be changed: *A*1 (cell B12) and *A*2 (cell B13). To enter this information, click on the box directly below the label "<u>B</u>y Changing Cells:" and then enter the cell range B12:B13, using either the keyboard or the mouse.

The final step is to enter the six constraints of the linear program. To enter constraints, click on the <u>A</u>dd button in the "S<u>u</u>bject to Constraints:" section of the Solver Parameters dialog box. After we click on this button, the Add Constraint dialog box is displayed as shown in Figure 9S.5.

The first constraint in our linear program is that the circuit board capacity must be less than or equal to 61,000 equivalent boards. In the spreadsheet shown in Figure 9S.3, the required capacity is calculated in cell B18. Therefore, in the spreadsheet, this constraint is equivalent to specifying that cell B18 must be less than or equal to 61,000. This information is entered into the Add Constraint dialog box as shown in Figure 9S.6. Note that the cell reference D6 could have been entered instead of 61,000 in the <u>C</u>onstraint: box shown in Figure 9S.6. In fact, entering cell

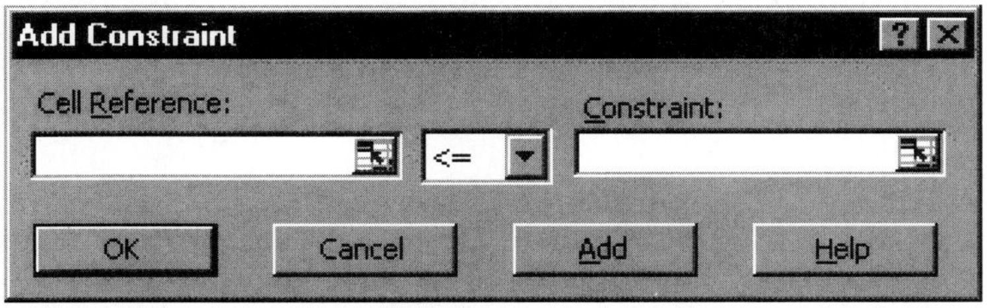

Figure 9S.5   A new Add Constraint dialog box.

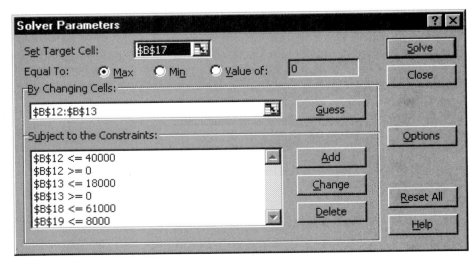

Figure 9S.6   Entering manufacturing circuit board capacity constraint.

references instead of the constants makes it easier to make changes to the linear program and is considered a good modeling practice.

Once the information has been entered in the Add Constraint dialog box as shown in Figure 9S.6, the Add button is selected and a new Add Constraint dialog box is displayed. The remaining constraints are entered similarly. When the last constraint has been entered, select the OK button in the Add Constraint dialog box to redisplay the Solver Parameters dialog box. Next, select the Options button, select the Assume Linear Models check box, and then click OK. After entering the information for Addemup, the Solver Parameters dialog box appears as shown in Figure 9S.7.

Once the information has been entered as shown in Figure 9S.7, select the Solve button in the upper right-hand corner of the Solver Parameter dialog box to solve the linear program. When Excel finds its best solution, the Solver Results dialog box is displayed as shown in Figure 9S.8. Select the OK button to keep the solution found by Excel. According to the results shown in Figure 9S.9, Excel found the same optimal solution that we found earlier using the graphical method. Also, notice in the Solver Results dialog box shown in Figure 9S.8 that Excel provides a variety of reports, including a sensitivity report that includes values for the dual variables.

Figure 9S.7   Excel's Solver Parameters dialog box for Addemup.

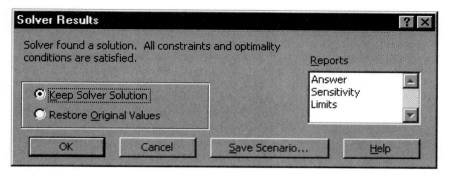

Figure 9S.8 Excel's Solver Results dialog box.

	A	B	C	D
1	**Addemup Capacity Planning**			
2				
3	**Input Data:**			
4		A-1000s	A-2000s	Available
5	Unit Profit	4	6	
6	Circuit Board Manufacturing Time	1	3	61000
7	Assembly Time	0.2	0.25	8000
8	Demand	40000	18000	
9				
10	**Decision Variables:**			
11				
12	A-1000s to Produce	25000		
13	A-2000s to Produce	12000		
14				
15	**Model Outputs:**			
16		Value	Formula	
17	Profit	172000	=(B12*B5)+(B13*C5)	
18	Circuit Board Manf. Capacity	61000	=(B12*B6)+(B13*C6)	
19	Assembly Time Capacity	8000	=(B12*B7)+(B13*C7)	

Figure 9S.9 Optimal solution found by Excel's Solver.

❖ EXERCISES

1. Shootemup, Inc., makes fireworks for the holiday season. The company has two skyrocket lines available to fill an order of 2000 skyrockets. Line "Wan," as it is called, can produce skyrockets at four per hour and is available for 600 hours at a cost of $10 per hour. Line "Tuo" is newer and can produce a skyrocket every 12 minutes but is available for only 340 hours at a cost of $8 per hour. Formulate a linear program to find the best production plan. What seems like a logical solution? Compare it with your formulation.

2. In another department, Shootemup makes both firecrackers and small Roman candles (RCs) on one automated line followed by hand assemblers. The line can handle either 1000 RCs or 2000 firecrackers (or any linear combination) per day. The assemblers can produce either 1500 RCs and 1700 firecrackers (or any combination) per day. The company has contracted to produce at least 800 firecrackers and 400 RCs a day. If the profit of firecrackers is $0.02 each and RCs is $0.03 each, formulate a linear program to determine the best production plan.

3. Sherwood Acres, a farm in central Kentucky, grows tobacco and soybeans on 350 acres. An acre of soybeans brings $150 profit and an acre of tobacco brings $500 profit. Because of state agricultural regulations, no more than 150 acres can be planted in tobacco. Each acre of tobacco requires 100 labor-hours over the growing season, and each acre of soybeans requires 20 labor-hours. There are 16,000 hours of labor available during the growing season. How many acres should be planted in tobacco and how many in soybeans to maximize profit?

4. Robin, Inc., produces two different concrete products with the price and input data shown in table titled Exercise 4.

Labor costs $5 per hour, materials cost $0.05 per pound, and power costs $1.000 per kWh. If the company is limited to 100,000 pounds of material, 9000 kilowatt-hours of power, and 1200 hours of labor and if demand for decorative blocks is at most 3500 units, what quantity of each block should be produced to maximize profit?

5. A manufacturer of guitars makes three models: acoustic, classical, and electric. Producing the guitars requires six major operations: (1) cutting and crafting the wood, (2) assembling the wood components, (3) applying the finish to the guitars, (4) installing the hardware, (5) testing and adjusting, and (6) packaging. Additional information for this manufacturer is given in the table titled Exercise 5.

The cutting and crafting department has 800 hours of labor available. The assembly, finishing, hardware installation, testing, and packaging departments have 640, 500, 500, 340, and 200 hours available, respectively.

a. Formulate a linear program model to help management determine how many guitars of each type should be made, given its desire to maximize profits.

b. Use a spreadsheet to find the optimal mix of guitars to make.

Exercise 4

| | Input Requirements | | | |
	Selling Price ($)	Material (pounds)	Power Consumed (kWh)	Labor (hours)
Construction blocks	0.75	4	0.1	0.04
Decorative blocks	1.75	3	0.2	0.10

Exercise 5

	Acoustic Guitar	Classical Guitar	Electric Guitar
Profit per guitar	$25	$55	$75
Time to cut and craft	2 hours	3 hours	1 hour
Time to assemble	3 hours	3 hours	1 hour
Time to finish1 hour	1.5 hours	0.5 hours	
Hardware installation	1 hour	1 hour	2 hours
Testing and adjusting	1.5 hours	1 hour	2 hours
Packaging	0.5 hours	0.75 hours	0.25 hours
Demand forecast	175 guitars	30 guitars	100 guitars

Facility Location

$\mathscr{C}$HAPTER OVERVIEW

* *Supply chain* management concerns the internal and external supply, storage, and movement of materials. This includes the functions of purchasing, materials management, maintenance, and distribution.

* Generally, a decision about location is closely tied to the method of distribution of the firm's outputs. In some cases—as with many pure services, where the recipient must travel to the facility—the location must be able to fulfill all the organization's distribution requirements. With product firms, transportation can fulfill much of the distribution requirements, and location can be based on other criteria.

* In two particular situations, choice of location is extremely limited. First, when a firm is processing natural resources and a large amount of weight is lost during processing or when the raw material is perishable, the firm will locate near the source of natural resources. Second, for a large construction project the firm must locate temporarily at the construction site.

* Usually the location decision involves locating several facilities and this is known as the multifacility location problem. In these circumstances, the analysis is complicated by several factors, including the need to simultaneously locate multiple facilities, the existence of multiple stages in the distribution chain, not knowing in advance the number of facilities to locate, not knowing what sites are available for the facilities, and the existence of multiple outputs that may need to be distributed differently.

* The four major modes of transport are water, rail, truck, and air. Water and rail handle most of the volume and long hauls, whereas trucks handle most of the short hauls. Air is best for small, high-value items where speed is critical.

* The routing problem involves determining how many vehicles of what capacities will be needed to handle the daily volume and what the best routes should be.

❖ Normally, a decision about location is made in three stages: regional or international, community, and site. The four major considerations at the regional-international stage are proximity to customers and suppliers, labor supply, availability of inputs, and environment.

❖ The cost of distribution—rate times volume times distance—summed over all distribution sites provides the primary measure for decisions about location. This factor can be used to determine a good site through incremental analysis or through the center-of-gravity (*weighted mean*) technique.

❖ The breakeven model can be used to select among sites where fixed costs and volume-related variable costs are specified. The costs of distribution can be included as either fixed or variable.

❖ The *weighted score* model is a generic approach that can include both qualitative and quantitative factors. Each factor is weighted by its importance, and standardized scores are calculated for each site on each of the factors.

❖ For the location of pure service facilities, we often rely on more individualized approaches. For situations where the recipient comes to the facility, we can use measures of facility utilization and average travel distance. For retail locations, equations to predict drawing power have been derived that relate to the facility's size and travel time. For situations where the facility goes to the recipient, the critical questions usually relate to the number of facilities needed and their locations.

INTRODUCTION

* In the early 1990s Mercedes-Benz began investigating the feasibility of producing a luxury sports-utility vehicle, referred to as the Multi-Purpose Vehicle (MPV). Faced with increasing international competition, Mercedes deviated from its established procedures and staffed the project team with young product planners, engineers, and marketers.

  The team was charged with finding a site outside of Germany to build the MPV (up to this time, all Mercedes automobiles had been built in Germany). The team initially narrowed the search for the new facility to North America, believing that the combined costs of labor, shipping, and components would be lowest in this region. Costs were particularly important to the team, since the MPV was to be priced about the same as a fully loaded Jeep Grand Cherokee, yet Mercedes would operate its plant at a much lower volume than producers such as Chrysler. Plans for the plant were based on producing 65,000 vehicles per year and breaking even at a volume of 40,000.

  After further analysis, the team decided to limit the search to sites in the United States in order to be close to the primary market and to avoid the penalties associated with currency fluctuations. The team identified 100 possible sites in 35 states. As it began analyzing the sites, its primary concern was the cost of transportation. Since the MPV was going to be built only in the United States and half of its output would be exported, the team focused on sites near Atlantic or Gulf seaports, major highways, and rail lines. Also, workers' ages and mix of skills were considered. Eventually, the original list of sites was pared down to three sites in North Carolina, South Carolina, and Alabama. All three finalists were evaluated as relatively equal in terms of business climate, education levels, transportation, and long-term operating costs. According to the managing director, the decision to locate the new facility in Alabama came down to a perception on the part of Mercedes that Alabama was dedicated to the project (Woodruff and Templeman, 1993).

❖ *A geographic information system* (GIS) is used to view and analyze data on digital maps as opposed to analyzing the same data printed out in massive tables that require reams of paper. One upscale clothing retailer with stores in Eau Claire and Green Bay, Wisconsin, analyzed its sales data on a map of the central part of the state. The map showed that each store drew the majority of its customers from a 20-mile radius. The map also highlighted an area between Eau Claire and Green Bay where only 15 percent of the potential customers had actually visited either store. Management's conclusion was that a new store in Wausau was needed to reach this untapped market. To take another example, at Super Valu (the nation's largest supermarket wholesaler), analysts would spread out paper maps and compare them with demographic data. Now, using a GIS, the same information is displayed on the screen of a personal computer, making it much easier to read and analyze (Tetzeli, 1993).

❖ In the mind of many Americans, Saturn is GM's last chance to prove itself to buyers. Needing to demonstrate top quality at a reasonable price, Saturn planning focused on doing things differently, starting with the location. As one spokesman said: "The bottom line for us is that we are looking for a site where we can produce a small car inexpensively and do it on a long-term basis." After examining over 1000 potential sites in two dozen states, GM selected Spring Hill, Tennessee. Among the 60 different factors examined, the deciding features included Spring Hill's proximity to three major interstate highways and rail, its distance from existing GM plants and their antimanagement attitudes, its stable economy, its low-cost power, its abundance of water, the high quality of life in Tennessee horse country, its proximity to Nashville (only 30 miles), and its universities and cultural attractions. In addition, Tennessee is historically an antiunion state, although the plant is run by a UAW workforce under a highly innovative and flexible contract (Treece, 1990).

The example of Mercedes-Benz illustrates two important characteristics of decisions about location: they are often done in stages, and multiple criteria are often considered. Related to the stages, decisions typically start off very broadly and, as additional information is collected, become narrower and more specific. In the case of Mercedes, the location for the new facility was specified broadly as someplace in North America. Then it was sequentially narrowed to the United States, to 100 sites within the United States, to three states, and finally to a site in Alabama that was chosen. As regards to the criteria used to compare locations, Mercedes considered factors such as labor cost, shipping cost, accessibility to transportation, the age and skill of the workforce, and the state government's dedication to the project. In Saturn's case, 60 factors were considered in selecting a site in Tennessee.

Up to this point in our discussion of resource management, we have developed a forecast of demand and sized the production facility for sufficient capacity to meet the demand. Knowing the size of the facility and the characteristics of the output (e.g., its weight, materials), we can next determine the most economical way to obtain the inputs we need to produce and deliver it to the customers. This includes considerations regarding the location of the facility relative to suppliers and potential customers and, if the output includes a facilitating good, what means of transportation might be possible. An important aspect of the decision, as seen with Mercedes-Benz and Saturn, is the skill and cost of local labor, as well as other costs and risks.

Our discussion of resource management concludes with this chapter. In Part Four, beginning with Chapter 11, we turn to the final business process discussed in this book: product supply. Thus, having identified, acquired, and located the necessary organizational resources in the resource management process (Part Three), our focus in Part Four is on the daily operation of these resources to supply customers with outputs that meet their needs.

$\mathcal{T}$HE SUPPLY-DISTRIBUTION SYSTEM

The term *supply chain management* as currently used in organizations typically includes the supply, storage, and movement of materials, information, personnel, equipment, and finished goods within the organization and between it and its environment. This all-encompassing interpretation would include purchasing, materials management, distribution, maintenance, and a number of other functions. In this chapter, however, we will concentrate on supply and distribution as aspects of locating a facility. Part Four will then address in detail other aspects of the product supply process.

How an output is distributed is of special concern to managers. First, the location of the production facility will affect the supply of labor, the cost of shipping materials, the timeliness of repair services, and numerous other aspects of the product supply process. Second, transportation of the output will place certain additional constraints on the product supply process regarding weight, throughput time, sturdiness, and so forth. In addition, intermediate distribution points will have an impact on inventory control, materials handling, warehousing, routing, and the like.

In these days of intense worldwide competition, supply chain management is taking on significantly more importance, as it accounts for a greater and greater proportion of the total cost of all products. Labor cost is dropping as a proportion of total output cost, as are manufacturing costs in general, but the costs of acquisition and distribution have remained about the same. For example, the cost of *physical distribution*—that is, getting the product or service to the consumer—ranges from about 10 percent of sales in the mechanical equipment industry to 30 percent in the food industries.

❖ Tradeoffs between Transportation and Location

Outputs can be distributed to customers by transporting them, if there is a facilitating good, or by locating where the customers can easily obtain them. Since service outputs without a facilitating good are generally difficult, expensive, or even impossible to transport, service organizations distribute their output by locating in the vicinity of their recipients. Examples of this approach are medical clinics, churches, parks and playgrounds, dry cleaners, and beauty shops. Of course, there are exceptions to this general practice when the recipients transport themselves to the service location. These situations usually occur when a service is of exceptional quality, scarce, or famous—such as the Mayo Clinic, to which people come from all over the world; or Yosemite National Park, which delights thousands of visitors every year.

Advances in information and telecommunications technology have allowed some pure service organizations (i.e., those without a facilitating good) to reach their recipients through phone, cable, the Internet, or microwave links. Thus, stockbrokers, banks, and other such service providers may locate in areas removed from their customers or recipients but more economical in other respects, such as proximity to the stock exchange or the downtown business district.

Some pure service organizations, however, do attempt to transport their services, although frequently with a great deal of trouble. These instances occur when the nature of the service makes it (a traveling carnival, a home show), impractical to remain in one fixed location for an extended duration or, more commonly, when the service (mobile X-ray, blood donor vehicle, bookmobile) is deemed very important to the public but may otherwise be inaccessible.

Product organizations, on the other hand, can generally trade transportation costs for location costs more easily and, therefore, can usually minimize their logistics costs. In some instances, however, even product organizations are forced into fixed locations. One of these instances concerns the nature of the firm's inputs, and the other concerns its outputs.

Processing Natural Resources

Organizations that process natural or basic resources as raw materials or other essential inputs to obtain their outputs will locate near their resource if one of the following conditions holds:

1. There is a large loss in size or weight during processing.
2. High economies of scale exist for the product. That is, the operating cost of one large plant with the same total capacity as two smaller plants is significantly less than the combined operating costs of the two small plants.
3. The raw material is perishable (as in fish processing and canning) and cannot be shipped long distances before being processed.

One of the distribution centers that helps process 1.5 million shipments a day. Federal Express was the 1990 Malcolm Baldrige National Quality Award Winner.

Examples of these types of industries are mining, canning, beer production, and lumber. In these cases the natural inputs (raw materials) are either voluminous or perishable, and the final product is much reduced in size, thus greatly reducing the cost of transportation to the recipients (either final users or further processors).

Immobile Outputs

The outputs of some organizations may be relatively immobile, such as dams, roads, buildings, and bridges. In these cases (referred to as *projects*) the organization locates itself at the construction site and transports all required inputs to that location. The home office is frequently little more than one room with a phone, secretary, files, and billing and record-keeping facilities.

Product organizations may also locate close to their market, not necessarily to minimize transportation costs of distribution, but to improve customer service. Being in close proximity to the market makes it easier for the recipient to contact the organization and also allows the organization to respond to changes in demand (involving both quantity and variety) from current and new recipients. As in war, the people on the front line are closest to the action and are able to respond to changing situations faster than those far away, simply because information about changes is available sooner and is generally more accurate.

❖ Multifacility Distribution

Up to this point in our discussion of the trade-off between transportation and location, we have restricted our discussion to the single-facility situation in which, for example, one facility services a set of geographically dispersed recipients (Figure

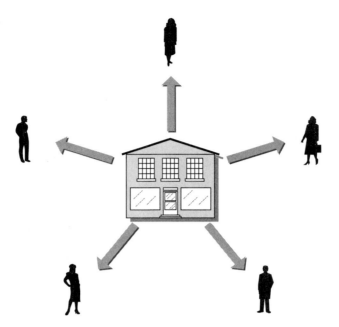

Figure 10.1   The problem of location with a single source and multiple recipients.

10.1). The next level of complexity is multiple facilities. Determining the best locations for multiple facilities is known as the ***multifacility location problem.*** Franchises are a specialized form of branch facilities, as are warehouses, branch banks, and adult evening classes offered at local high schools and colleges.

The multifacility situation also involves issues of channel selection discussed in the marketing literature, such as the use of wholesalers, retailers, and factory representatives. These channels often have additional locations that must be considered in the overall distribution analysis.

The analysis is complex because the best location-distribution pattern for each facility depends on the location-distribution patterns for each of the other facilities. Some of the major complications associated with multifacility distribution are described below.

1. *Multiple facilities*: First, more than one facility may produce the output for multiple recipients. That is, there may be a southeastern plant, a midwestern plant, and a western plant among which the output can be divided up to supply the customers. Three situations often arise in this case: locating one additional facility with N existing facilities already situated; locating (or relocating) all N facilities at once; and, last, once facilities are situated, determining the new allocation of outputs from them to the recipients.

   A special point about the location of all N facilities is that the problem cannot be solved by locating them one at a time. Rather, they must all be located at once, since changing the distribution pattern of any one facility will change the distribution patterns of some or all of the other facilities as well.

2. *Multiple stages*: There may also be multiple intervening staging points between the production facility and the recipients, such as factory warehouses,

distribution centers, wholesalers, and retailers. This can be the case with either a single production facility or, as shown in Figure 10.2, with multiple production facilities.

3. *Unspecified sites*: Sometimes possible sites are identified beforehand, and the problem becomes one of selecting the best set of N sites from M locations. This may even be the case in the single-facility problem. If the sites are not determined in advance, the problem is clearly more complex.

4. *Unknown quantities*: The number of production facilities may also be unknown, and the problem is to determine not only *where* they should be located and *which recipients* they should serve but also *how many* facilities there should be. Obviously, this problem is very complicated. In addition, the number of intervening facilities at any stage (e.g., warehouses) may be unknown, as well as the *number* of stages, making for a significantly more complex problem.

5. *Multiple outputs*: So far, we have assumed that there is only one output; in fact, though, there may be any number. The problem arises when the distribution of demand among the recipients for the different outputs varies considerably, necessitating different solutions in the situations above.

In the remainder of this chapter we consider only the most elementary problem: locating one facility to serve multiple recipients. This situation includes the basic difficulties of location versus transportation that are encountered in all the above situations, without their added complexity. Some techniques are also given for addressing this simple problem. For approaches to the more complex situations, consult the Bibliography for this chapter at the end of the text.

❖ Modes of Transportation and Routing

The four major ***modes of transportation*** are, historically, water, rail, truck, and air. Water is the least expensive mode and is good for long trips with bulky, nonperishable items. But it is very slow and of limited accessibility. It handles the majority of ton-miles of traffic. However, railroads handle the most total tons of traffic and are thus used for shorter hauls than water. They have many advantages: ability to handle small as well as large items, good accessibility, specialized services (e.g., refrigeration, liquids, cattle), and still a relatively low cost.

Trucking holds more advantages for short hauls with small volumes to specialized locations. Truck transport has grown at the expense of rail because of a number of factors, such as the national highway system, better equipment, and liberalized regulations.

Air transport is used for small, high-value, or perishable items such as electronic components, lobsters, optical instruments, and important paperwork. Its main advantage is speed of delivery over long distances. Thus, for the appropriate products, it can significantly reduce inventory and warehousing costs, with a corresponding improvement in customer service.

Taking all the pros and cons of each mode of transportation into consideration in planning is a complex task. The major considerations that should be factored

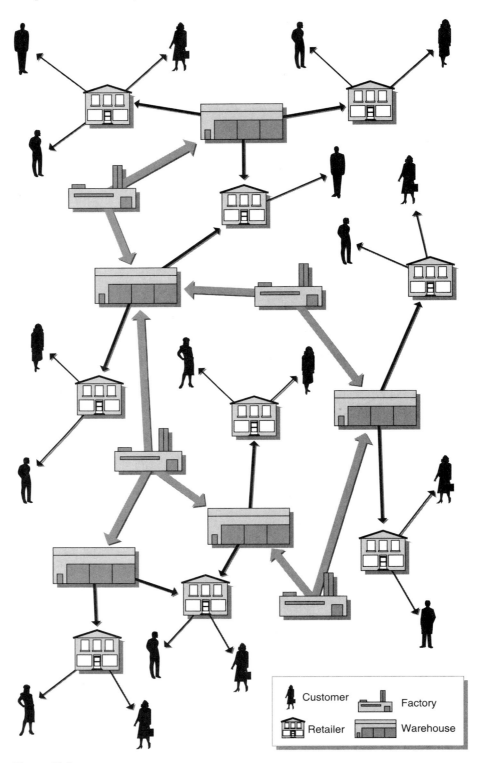

Figure 10.2   The multifacility problem.

$\mathscr{T}$ABLE 10.1 ❖ Factors to Consider in Transportation Decisions

❖ Cost per unit shipped.
❖ Ability to fill the transporting vehicle.
❖ Total shipment cost.
❖ Protection of contents from theft, weather, and the like.
❖ Shipping time.
❖ Availability of insurance on contents, delivery, and so forth.
❖ Difficulty of arranging shipment (governmental regulations, transportation to shipment site, and so on).
❖ Delivery accommodations (to customer's site, transfer to another transportation mode, extra charges).
❖ Seasonal considerations: weather, holidays, and so on.
❖ Consolidation possibilities (among multiple products).
❖ Risk: to contents, to delivery promises, to cost, and the like.
❖ Size of product being shipped.
❖ Perishability of product during shipment.

into the decision are listed in Table 10.1. Each particular situation may have additional factors that need to be considered as well.

Independent of the specific mode of transport are additional transportation problems involving such considerations as the *number* of transporting vehicles, their *capacities*, and the *routes* that each vehicle will take. In general, these interrelated problems are frequently included as part of the *routing problem*.

Solving the routing problem involves finding the best number of vehicles and their routes to deliver the organization's output to a group of geographically dispersed recipients. When only one vehicle is serving all the recipients, the problem is known as the *traveling salesman problem*. In this problem a number of possible routes exist between the organization and all the recipients, but only a few or perhaps just one of these routes will minimize the total cost of delivery.

In the routing and traveling salesman problems, certain procedures are available to minimize either the distance traveled or the cost, but quite often there are other considerations, such as balancing workloads among vehicles or minimizing idle or delay time. For approaches to such problems, see the Bibliography.

❖ Three-Stage Location Process

In general, the decision about location is divided into three stages: regional (including international), community, and site. Sources of information for these stages are chambers of commerce, realtors, utilities, banks, suppliers, transportation companies, savings and loan associations, government agencies, and management consultants who specialize in relocation. For some pure service organizations (e.g., physicians), only the site selection stage may be relevant because they are already focused on a specific region and community.

Stage 1: Regional-International

In the regional-international stage, an organization focuses on what part of the world (e.g., North America, Europe, Pacific rim) or perhaps what region of a country (e.g., southwest, midwest, northeast) it wants to locate its new facility in. In the example at the beginning of the chapter, Mercedes-Benz initially decided that its new facility should be located in North America and subsequently further narrowed the region to sites in the United States. There are four major considerations in selecting a national or overseas region for a facility: *proximity, labor supply, availability of inputs,* and *environment.* We discuss each in turn.

To minimize transportation costs and provide acceptable service to customers, the facility should be located in a region in close *proximity* to customers and suppliers. Although methods of finding the location with the minimum transportation cost will be presented later in this chapter, a common rule of thumb within the United States is that the facility should be within 200 miles of major industrial and commercial customers and suppliers. Beyond this range, transportation costs begin to rise quickly.

For example, a major appliance firm found that annual distribution costs were $100,000 more if its plant was located even 50 miles from the geographically optimal center of national distribution to its customers. However, the same figure also held for not locating at the geographically optimal center for incoming supplies. Since the two centers were not at the same spot, the firm was forced to trade off between these two points to obtain the best overall location.

The region should have the proper *supply of labor* available and in the correct proportions of required skills. One important reason for the past expansion of American firms abroad was the availability of labor at wage rates much lower than rates at home. Currently, this disparity has been reduced significantly because of increased wages abroad. However, the real consideration should be, not wage rates, but the productivity of domestic labor relative to productivity abroad. This comparison would thus involve level of skills, use of equipment, wage rates, and even work ethics (which differ even between regions within the United States) to determine the most favorable labor supply in terms of output per dollar of wages and capital investment.

In addition to regional wage rates, the organization of the labor pool should also be given consideration—that is, whether all the skills are unionized or whether there is an open shop. Some states have passed *right-to-work laws* that forbid any requirement that all employees join a union in order to work in an organization. Often, these laws result in significantly lower wage rates in these states.

The region selected for location of the facility should have the necessary *inputs* available. For example, supplies that are difficult, expensive, or time-consuming to ship and those that are necessary to the organization (i.e., no reasonable substitutes exist) should be readily available. The proper type (rail, water, highway, air) and supply of transportation; sufficient quantities of basic resources such as water, electricity, gas, coal, and oil; and appropriate communication facilities should also be available. Obviously, many American industries are located abroad in order to use raw materials (oil, copper, etc.) available there.

The regional *environment* should be conducive to the work of the organization. Not only should the weather be appropriate, but the political, legal, and social climate should also be favorable. The following matters should be considered:

1. Regional taxes.
2. Regional regulations on operations (pollution, hiring, etc.).
3. Barriers to imports or exports.
4. Political stability (nationalization policies, kidnappings).
5. Cultural and economic peculiarities (e.g., restrictions on workingwomen).

These factors are especially critical in locating in a foreign country, particularly an underdeveloped country. Firms locating in such regions should not be surprised to find large differences in the way things are done. For example, in some countries governmental decisions tend to move slowly, with extreme centralization of authority. Very little planning seems to occur. Events appear to occur by "God's will" or by default. The pace of work is unhurried, and at times discipline, especially among managers, seems totally absent. Corruption and payoffs often seem to be normal ways of doing business, and accounting systems are highly suspect. Living conditions for the workers, especially in urbanized areas, are depressing. Transportation and communication systems (roads, ports, phone service) can be incomplete and notoriously unreliable. Attempting to achieve something under such conditions can, understandably, be very discouraging. When locating in such countries, a firm should allow for such difficulties and unexpected problems. In such an environment, Murphy's law thrives.

Not all international decisions involve firms locating outside the United States—many are concerned with foreign firms locating in this country. In the emerging global marketplace it is becoming more common to see foreign firms locating in the United States to minimize transportation charges, import tariffs, and ill will. Japan, in particular, has placed many plants in the United States. Nissan at Smyrna, Tennessee; Kawasaki at Lincoln, Nebraska; and Sony at San Diego, California, are just three of many examples.

OPERATIONS IN PRACTICE

Mercedes Locates in Vance, Alabama

In the case of Mercedes at the beginning of the chapter, the general sequence of events in establishing the plant were:

January 1993: Regional site-selection process begins.

April 1993: Mercedes decides that the new plant will be located in the United States.

May 1993: One hundred sites in 35 states are identified.

August 1993: Candidate sites are narrowed down to three finalists in North Carolina, South Carolina, and Alabama.

September 1993: Site in Alabama is selected for the new plant (Woodruff and Templeman, 1993).

Stage 2: Community

After the region of a new facility has been decided on, candidate communities within the region are identified for further analysis. Many of the considerations made at the regional-international stage should also be considered at this next stage. For example, the availability of acceptable sites, attitudes of the local government, regulations, zoning, taxes, labor supply, the size and characteristics of the market, and the weather would again be considered. In addition, pollution peculiar to a community, the availability of local financing, monetary inducements (such as tax incentives) for establishing operations there, and the community's attitude toward the organization itself would be additional factors of interest to the organization. Taxes and monetary inducements may, by themselves, require a comprehensive financial analysis, including a cash flow statement.

Last, the preferences of the organization's staff should play a role in selecting a community. These would probably be influenced by the amenities available in the community such as homes, religious congregations, shopping centers, schools and universities, medical care, fire and police protection, and entertainment, as well as

---

OPERATIONS
IN PRACTICE

Selecting Audit Offices for the State of Texas

The comptroller of Public Accounts heads the agency that collects taxes for the state of Texas. One of the tasks facing this agency is collecting sales, corporate franchise, and oil and gas taxes from out-of-state corporations that conduct business in Texas. These taxes represent about 7 percent of the total tax collections of the agency, approximately $180 million in the case of sales taxes.

At one time, collection was coordinated through the main office in Austin, with tax collectors commuting to the headquarters of the firms that owed taxes to Texas. But when this became very expensive and increased turnover among tax collectors, it was decided to open regional offices around the country. However, it was not known where to locate these offices, how many people should operate out of each office, or what states should be served by which office.

On the basis of historical concentrations of out-of-state taxpaying corporations, a list of 12 potential cities was drawn up and the data were entered into a software package for warehouse location (LOCATE/ALLOCATE User's Guide, Analysis, Research, and Computation Inc., Austin, Texas, 1980). The problem was modeled as analogous to warehouse location, as follows:

Warehouses	Audit Offices
Warehouse	Audit office
Storage capacity	Audit worker-hours
Facility fixed cost	Office rent and overhead
Customer demand zone	State
Commodity demand	Audit trips
Transportation cost	Airfare plus per diem to largest city in the state

The software package, using a network optimization algorithm, found that the cheapest solution was to locate offices in New York City, Chicago, Los Angeles, and Tulsa (Oklahoma), for a total cost of slightly over $3 million. But this required 11 collectors in New York City and 16 in Chicago, whereas the agency preferred to limit the office staff to 10 in any one office. A second run, limiting the staff to a maximum of 10 and including the site preferences of the staff, resulted in locating offices in New York City, Chicago, Los Angeles–San Francisco (combined), Atlanta, and Tulsa, with a total cost only 0.4 percent ($12,566) greater than the first, optimal run.

The agency then moved to adopt this solution, with one modification: putting offices in both Los Angeles and San Francisco to avoid excessive commuting. The regional offices not only reduced the cost to Texas, but also increased payment compliance and improved service at the same time (Fitzsimmons and Allen, 1983).

local tax rates and other costs. Upper-level educational institutions may also be of interest to the organization in terms of opportunity for relevant research and development. For example, it is no coincidence that major IBM plants are located in Lexington, Kentucky; Denver, Colorado; and Austin, Texas, which are also sites of major state universities.

Stage 3: Site

After a list of candidate communities is developed, specific sites within them are identified. The *site*—the actual location of the facility—should be appropriate to the nature of the operation. Such matters as size; adjoining land; zoning; community attitudes; drainage; soil; the availability of water, sewers, and utilities; waste disposal; transportation; the size of the local market; and the costs of development are considered. The development of industrial parks in some communities has alleviated many of the difficulties involved in choosing a site, since the developer automatically takes care of most of these matters. Before any final decision is made, a cash flow analysis is conducted for each of the candidate sites; this includes the cost of labor, land, taxes, utilities, transportation, and so on.

$\mathcal{L}$ OCATION MODELS

In this section we investigate some approaches that have been useful to firms in locating their facilities. Some of the techniques are more appropriate to the regional stage and others to the site stage, but all of them can be used for any of the stages. We will illustrate each technique with a specific situation in one of the stages described earlier.

❖ Transportation Cost Model: Rate-Volume-Distance

A number of approaches, such as the one described in the sidebar about Texas, are based on a simple measure of total distribution costs, supply costs, or both. The procedure is to sum the products of the transportation rate (T), the volume (V), and the distance (D) over all the locations—hence the abbreviation for this approach: TVD. The usual method of calculating total transportation cost is as follows:

$$C = T_1V_1D_1 + T_2V_2D_2 + T_3V_3D_3 + \ldots + T_nV_nD_n = \sum_i T_iV_iD_i$$

where

T = cost of transportation needed, in dollars per unit volume (or weight) per unit distance (e.g., \$/pound/mile)

V = volume (or weight) being transported

D = distance from facility to recipients' demand locations

C = total cost

i = 1, 2, 3, ..., n (subscripts) = first, second, third, . . . nth recipients

This is the total cost of shipping the desired quantities to all n recipients.

Thus, we can simply place the facility in one site and determine what it will cost to supply the recipients, move it to another site and see if the cost is less, and so on. If all the sites are prespecified, then the site with the lowest cost is deemed best (at least on this one measure).

The basic concept of a cost measure applies in other situations as well. For example, if cost is independent of weight or volume, or weight or volume simply is not relevant, ignore V in the formula. If no "rate" is given, perhaps time spent is an adequate surrogate measure of cost ("time is money") and the product of travel time (minutes per mile) times distance (miles) will give an adequate measure. In other cases, some creativity may be needed to determine the most appropriate measure.

In the example below, the potential sites are not prespecified, but (it is hoped) a good initial site is selected intuitively. The first step is to calculate the total transportation cost to supply all the geographically dispersed demands. Then the facility is moved slightly north, east, south, and west of the initial site, and the total trans-

$\mathcal{S}$OLVED EXERCISE 10.1 ❖ TVD Calculations

Select the best location, A or B, for a warehouse with the following site demands.

Location	Site	Rate ($/ton/mile)	Volume (tons)	Distance (miles)
A	1	10	2	30
	2	12	4	22
	3	10	5	9
B	1	10	2	25
	2	13	4	26
	3	10	5	7

Solution:

$$C_A = 10 \times 2 \times 30 + 12 \times 4 \times 22 + 10 \times 5 \times 9 = 2106$$

$$C_B = 10 \times 2 \times 25 + 13 \times 4 \times 26 + 10 \times 5 \times 7 = 2202$$

Location A has the lower cost.

---

portation cost is calculated for each of these changes, in turn. This is a simple variant of a technique known as *incremental analysis*. If all four changes result in higher costs, then the initial site is best* and the problem is solved. However, if some movement results in a lower cost, the facility should be moved in that direction and the entire process repeated until a final location is found where none of the directional changes produces an improvement.

The example demonstrates both the calculation of the cost measure TVD and the incremental analysis and its interpretation.

Brandex Medical Supplies

A new firm, Brandex, is entering the acetaminophen (aspirin substitute) market and plans to compete directly with Tylenol, the major acetaminophen supplier, by offering retailers a generic drug that could be sold as a house brand at a reduced price. Brandex has made contact with two large wholesalers in the Dallas (D) and Seattle (S) areas and has established two manufacturing representatives in Los Angeles (L) and Chicago (C) who would then further distribute the product as a house brand (Figure 10.3).

Denver, Colorado, has been suggested as a possible site at which to locate the production facilities. Trucking rates, T, for the product to the four demand cities and the mileages, D, from Denver (obtained from a truck routing map) are given in

---

*At least among sites in that region. Although this does not happen frequently, there is occasionally a somewhat better site much farther away.

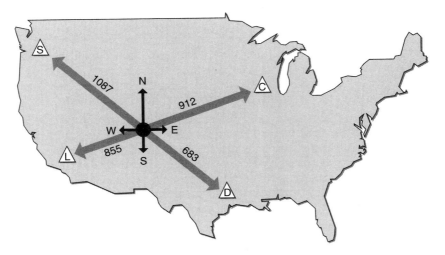

Figure 10.3   Nationwide distribution map.

Table 10.2. (Note that rates among the four different trucking firms differ slightly.) Included in the table are the levels, *V*, of demand (in cartons) expected in the first year and the product of *T* times *V*, which (we assume here) is independent of the location.

The last row of Table 10.2 shows total annual transportation cost. The first figure, $13,064, represents the cost from Denver. The next figure $13,074, is the cost due to changing the distances involved simply by moving the facility 10 miles north. As can be seen, the effect of this move, D(N), is to increase the distance, and thus costs, to Los Angeles (L); an expensive, high-demand area) and Dallas (D) for a cost increase of 4133 − 4104 = 29 for L and 690 − 683 = 7 for D, thus totaling 36. But this move also *decreases* the cost for Seattle (S) and Chicago (C) for a decrease of 21 + 5 or 26. The net effect of this location shift is thus a total *increase* in cost of 36 − 26, or $10.

Comparing the total costs of next moving the facility 10 miles east, then south, and then west, we see that the lowest cost is obtained by moving south. Moving west also reduces the cost somewhat, though not nearly as much as moving south, so the next step is to look for an acceptable location somewhat south of Denver

$\mathcal{T}$ABLE 10.2 ❖ **Data and Calculations for Denver**

Destination	T ($/carton mile)	V (cartons)	TV ($/mile)	D (miles)	C = TVD ($)	D(N) (miles)	C(N) ($)	C(E) ($)	C(S) ($)	C(W) ($)
S	0.0015	2000	3	1087	3261	1080	3240	3282	3282	3240
L	0.0012	4000	4.8	855	4104	861	4133	4142	4075	4066
D	0.0010	1000	1	683	683	690	690	676	676	690
C	0.0011	5000	5.5	912	5016	911	5011	4967	5022	5066
	Total cost:				13,064		13,074	13,067	13,055	13,062

and perhaps a bit west and then repeat the entire process. A natural question, for which there is no single answer, is, "How far should the facility be moved for the next test?" Clearly, we would not move farther south than Dallas, because then the facility would be farther away from *all* the demand points. It is best to be conservative in this process and locate a city, or site, that is generally acceptable with regard to other factors and is not very far from the previously tested location. In this case, Colorado Springs would be a logical next choice for Brandex, and it is only 75 miles away.

$\mathcal{S}$OLVED EXERCISE 10.2 ❖ Incremental Analysis

Evaluate whether a wholesaler is currently located in the best position.

Retailer	Rate ($/cubic foot/mile)	Volume (cubic feet)	Distance (miles east/west)
1	5	88	130 E
2	4	34	244 W
3	4	125	67 E
4	5	56	102 W

Solution:

Current cost, C:

$$= 5 \times 88 \times 130 + 4 \times 34 \times 244 + 4 \times 125 \times 67 + 5 \times 56 \times 102$$
$$= 152{,}444$$

Move 1 mile west:

$$C = 5 \times 88 \times 131 + 4 \times 34 \times 243 + 4 \times 125 \times 68 + 5 \times 56 \times 101$$
$$= 152{,}968 \text{ (worse)}$$

Move 1 mile east:

$$C = 5 \times 88 \times 129 + 4 \times 34 \times 245 + 4 \times 125 \times 66 + 5 \times 56 \times 103$$
$$= 151{,}920 \text{ (better)}$$

Since the cost decreases by moving east, the current location is not best.
Note: An abbreviated way to make the calculation is to use just the change; for example:

$$\text{Move 1 mile east: } 5 \times 88 \times (-1) + 4 \times 34 \times (+1)$$
$$+ 4 \times 125 \times (-1) + 5 \times 56 \times (+1)$$
$$= -524 \text{ (a decrease)}$$

Finding the Best Location: Center-of-Gravity Method

The TVD measure can also be used to find the location that will minimize distribution costs. The technique is simply to find the weighted average distance from some base point, such as an arbitrarily chosen origin. The weighted average distance can be found for one-, two-, or three-dimensional situations. In one-dimensional situations, distances are measured along only one axis, such as east to west. In a two-dimensional situation, distances are measured along two axes such as north-south and east-west. If there are no rate or volume weights, then the **center of gravity** is just the average distance for the set of locations from the origin. If the volumes, or rates, vary among locations, then a mean is calculated based on the volume or rate-weighted distances. If both the volumes and the rates vary with location, then the product of volume and rate becomes the weight. The mean is found, as always, by dividing by the sum of the weights. For example, suppose a warehouse is to be located to receive goods from plants and to then supply customers. For simplicity, assume that only three plants or customers are to be considered:

- ❖ A, who supplies 10 tons at a cost of $5/ton/mile.
- ❖ B, who desires 2 tons at a cost of $8/ton/mile.
- ❖ C, who desires 8 tons at a cost of $4/ton/mile.

If A, B, and C are located as in Figure 10.4, where should the warehouse be built? The weighted mean distance in any direction Z is

$$\bar{Z} = \sum_i T_i V_i Z_i \Big/ \sum_i T_i V_i$$

where $\sum_i$ is the sum over all points i

T_i = transportation cost per unit volume (or weight) per mile for each point i

V_i = volume (or weight) to be transported to or from each location i

Z_i = distance in miles from any arbitrary origin to each point i

Hence, in the easterly direction X

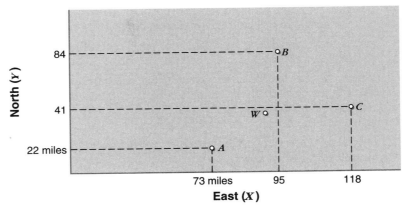

Figure 10.4   Location by center-of-gravity method.

$$\bar{X} = (T_A V_A X_A + T_B V_B X_B + T_C V_C X_C)/(T_A V_A + T_B V_B + T_C V_C)$$
$$= [(5 \times 10 \times 73) + (8 \times 2 \times 95) + (4 \times 8 \times 118)]/[(5 \times 10) + (8 \times 2) + (4 \times 8)]$$
$$= 8946/98$$
$$= 91.3 \text{ miles east}$$

Similar calculations for the northerly direction Y yield $\bar{Y} = 38.3$ miles. This point is shown as W in Figure 10.4.

$\mathcal{S}$OLVED EXERCISE 10.3 ❖ Center of Gravity

Find the center-of-gravity location in Solved Exercise 10.2.

Solution:

Let west be the negative X direction; then:

$$\bar{X} = [(5 \times 88 \times 130) - (4 \times 34 \times 244) + (4 \times 125 \times 67) - (5 \times 56 \times 102)]/$$
$$[(5 \times 88) + (4 \times 34) + (4 \times 125) + (5 \times 56)]$$
$$= 28{,}956/1356$$
$$= 21.35 \text{ (miles east)}$$

Spreadsheet Analysis: Center-of-Gravity Method

In the example at the beginning of this section, the following information was given:

Plant	Transportation Cost/Unit Volume/Mile	Volume To Be Transported	Distance of Plant East of Origin	Distance of Plant North of Origin
A	$5.00	10	73	22
B	$8.00	2	95	84
C	$4.00	8	118	41

The spreadsheet shown below was developed to calculate the center-of-gravity location for a new warehouse to serve these three plants.

	A	B	C	D	E	F	G	H
1	Center of Gravity for New Warehouse							
2								
3		T	V	X	Y			
4		Transportation		Miles East	Miles North			
5	Plant	Cost/Unit/Mile	Volume	of Origin	of Origin	T*V*X	T*V*Y	T*V
6	A	5	10	73	22	3650	1100	50
7	B	8	2	95	84	1520	1344	16
8	C	4	8	118	41	3776	1312	32
9	Sum					8946	3756	98
10	Simple Avg.			95.33	49.00			
11	Center of							
12	Gravity			91.29	38.33			

Columns A through E are self-explanatory. In column F, the $\sum_i T_i V_i Z_i$ is calculated for the X (east) directions, and in column G this formula is calculated for the north direction. Specifically, the following formula was entered in cell F6:

$$=B6*C6*D6$$

Similarly, the following formula was entered in cell G6:

$$=B6*C6*E6$$

In column H, $\sum_i T_i V_i$ is calculated. Thus, the following formula was entered in cell H6:

$$=B6*C6$$

Once the formulas were entered in cells F6:H6, they were copied to cell F7:H8.

To calculate the sum of column F, =SUM(F6:F8) was entered in cell F9 and then copied to cells G9 and H9. The average of column D was calculated by entering =AVERAGE(D6:D8) in cell D10 and then copying this formula to cell E10. Finally, the center of gravity in the X (east) direction was calculated by entering =F9/$H9 in cell D12 and then copying this formula to cell E12.

In comparing the center-of-gravity location to a location based on simply averaging the X and Y coordinates (and thus not accounting for differences in transportation costs or volumes across the three plants), the results indicate that the center of gravity is shifted down and to the left toward plant A. Given plant A's high volume and relatively high transportation costs, it makes sense to shift the location of the warehouse toward plant A. The location of the three plants, the simple average location, and the center of gravity are shown in the figure below.

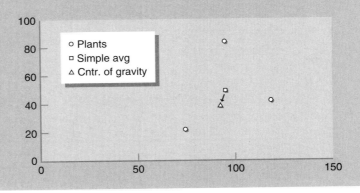

❖ Breakeven Model: Comparing Fixed and Variable Costs

The breakeven model assumes that the problem is to choose from among a set of predetermined sites, on the basis of a range of fixed and variable costs rather than just distribution cost. That is, distribution cost may be considered, but it is only one factor (perhaps fixed, perhaps variable with output volume) among many that need to be considered to make a decision. Although the relevant factors for comparison may be known, their values may be uncertain. This is particularly true of factors that are a function of the output rate of the facility being located: utility costs, labor charges, materials usage, and so on.

A useful technique for handling this uncertainty is the breakeven technique for comparing the costs of different alternatives (presented in Chapters 5 and 9). Various alternatives for location and distribution may be compared by graphing total operating costs for each alternative at different levels of demand, as in Figure 10.5.

This is accomplished by dividing the total operating cost into two components—fixed costs that do not vary with the demand for the output (e.g., land, buildings, equipment, property taxes, insurance) and variable costs such as labor, materials, and transportation—and plotting them on the axes of a graph. At the demand point E (the intersection of the two lines) the costs for the two alternatives are the same; for demand levels in excess of E, community 2 is best, and for levels less than E, community 1 is best. Thus, if the range of uncertainty concerning the output volume is entirely *above* point E, the manager need not be concerned about which community to choose—community 2 is best. Similar reasoning holds for any uncertainty existing entirely *below* point E—community 1 is best. If the uncertainty encompasses point E, then two additional situations must be considered:

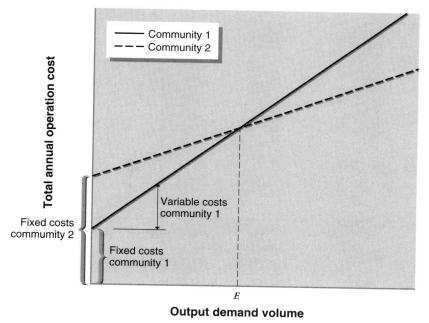

Figure 10.5 Breakeven location model.

1. If the range of uncertainty is closely restricted to point E, then either community may be selected because the costs will be approximately the same in either case.

2. If the range of uncertainty is broad and varies considerably from point E in both directions, then the breakeven chart will indicate to the manager the extra costs that will be incurred by choosing the wrong community. Before selecting either community, the manager should probably try to gather more information, to reduce the range of uncertainty in demand.

We will demonstrate with the following example.

Upp and Adam Elevators

Figure 10.6 shows the annual costs, calculated in Table 10.3, for four candidate locations for Upp and Adam. Note from the figure that communities 1, 2, and 3 all have approximately the same fixed costs and the same variable costs compared with community 4, which has a very high fixed cost but a low variable cost—beyond a demand volume of 11 (thousand units), community 4 is clearly the best. Note also that community 2 should never be considered because community 3 is *always* better than community 2; its fixed cost and its variable cost are *both* lower. Community 3 appears to be optimal between volumes (in thousands) of 6.5 and 11. Below 6.5, community 1 is best; and above 11, community 4 is best.

Suppose uncertainty in demand for Upp and Adam is relatively high because the product is new and may catch on quickly or, just as likely, languish for years at

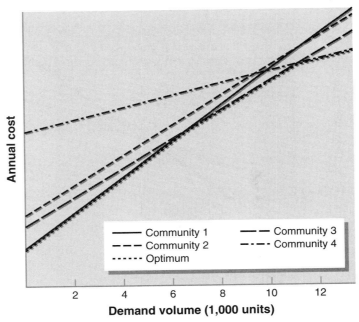

Figure 10.6   Comparison of costs for four potential communities.

TABLE 10.3 ❖ Annual Costs for Four Community Locations

Annual Costs (thousands of dollars)	Community			
	1	2	3	4
Fixed				
Interest	4	8	7	19
Rent	30	45	40	100
Insurance	6	10	9	15
Taxes	7	8	8	16
G and A	5	9	5	16
Marketing	5	8	7	17
Other	3	2	4	17
Total	60	90	80	200
Variable				
Material	6	6	5	2
Transportation	3	3	3	1
Labor	7	6	6	3
Sales	5	4	4	2
Utilities	3	2	2	1
Other	1	1	1	1
Total	25	22	21	10

fairly low sales before any significant growth. Ms. Smyth, the operations manager, believes, under these circumstances, that the demand could range anywhere from 4000 to 12,000 units.

For such a situation, can the breakeven chart be helpful? Most certainly! For most of this range, community 3 is best. At a demand of 4000, although community 1 is best, community 3 is only slightly worse, whereas community 4 is very poor. And at a demand of 12,000, although community 4 is best, community 3 is not much worse. Thus, community 3, assuming that its other factors are acceptable, appears to be a safe bet. Of course, for considerably higher volumes only community 4 would be economically acceptable; but according to Ms. Smyth's estimate, such volumes are not expected.

SOLVED EXERCISE 10.4 ❖ Breakeven Location

Given three locations below, which one is best for a production volume of 5000 barrels a year? Suppose demand increases to 6000 barrels? Or drops to 4000 barrels?

Location	Annualized Fixed Costs	Variable Cost/Barrel
Centerville	$2,450,000	$239
Madison	$2,360,000	$255
Williamstown	$2,680,000	$223

Solution:

$$\text{Centerville cost, } C = 2,450,000 + 239(5000) = 3,645,000$$

$$\text{Madison cost} = 2,360,000 + 255(5000) = 3,635,000 \text{ (best)}$$

$$\text{Williamstown cost} = 2,680,000 + 223(5000) = 3,795,000$$

Madison has the lowest cost at 5000 barrels. At the other volumes, we could just re-calculate the equations for each, but instead we will find the relevant "breakeven" intersections:

$$\text{Madison and Centerville: } 2,360,000 + 255X = 2,450,000 + 239X$$

$$X = 5,625$$

$$\text{Madison and Williamstown: } 2,360,000 + 255X = 2,680,000 + 223X$$

$$X = 10,000$$

$$\text{Centerville and Williamstown: } 2,450,000 + 239X = 2,680,000 + 223X$$

$$X = 14,375$$

Since Madison has the lowest fixed cost, it will be best for all volumes up to 5625. This certainly includes 4000 barrels. Centerville will be best at 6000 barrels and will continue to be best until 14,375 barrels, after which Williamstown will be best.

Spreadsheet Analysis: Breakeven Location

The spreadsheet below was developed to analyze the problem discussed in Solved Exercise 10.4.

	A	B	C	D	E	F
2						
3	*Model Inputs:*					
4		Centerville	Madison	Williamstown		
5	Fixed Costs	$2,450,000	$2,360,000	$2,680,000		
6	Variable Costs	$239	$255	$223		
7						
8	Volume	5000				
9						
10	*Model Outputs:*					
11						
12	Total Cost	$3,645,000	$3,635,000	$3,795,000		
13						
14	*Key Formula:*					
15	cell B12	=B5+(B6*$B8)				
16	cells C12 and D12	formula entered in cell B12 copied to cells C12 and D12				

In Model Inputs, the fixed costs and variable costs for the three locations were entered in rows 5 and 6 respectively. Cell B8 contains the volume.

The total costs for the three locations, based on the model inputs, are calculated in row 12. In cell B12 the following formula was entered:

$$=B5+(B6*\$B8)$$

This formula was then copied to cells C12 and D12. On the basis of the results obtained, at a volume of 5000 barrels, Madison has the lowest total costs (which is exactly the same result obtained in Solved Exercise 10.4.) To determine the effect of increasing the volume to 6000 barrels, 6000 was entered in cell B8, with the following results.

	A	B	C	D	E	F
2						
3	**Model Inputs:**					
4		Centerville	Madison	Williamstown		
5	Fixed Costs	$2,450,000	$2,360,000	$2,680,000		
6	Variable Costs	$239	$255	$223		
7						
8	Volume	6000				
9						
10	**Model Outputs:**					
11						
12	Total Cost	$3,884,000	$3,890,000	$4,018,000		
13						
14	**Key Formula:**					
15	cell B12	=B5+(B6*$B8)				
16	cells C12 and D12	formula entered in cell B12 copied to cells C12 and D12				

This spreadsheet indicates that Centerville has the lowest total costs at an annual volume of 6000 barrels. By changing the value of cell B8, any number of other annual volumes can be quickly investigated.

❖ Weighted Score Models

The most general approach of all is the **weighted score model**. This approach can combine cost measures, profit measures, other quantitative measures, and qualitative measures to help analyze locations, and many other situations.

Deciding on a location, whether for products or services, is complicated by the existence of multiple criteria such as executives' preferences, maximization of facility use, and customers' attitudes. These and other criteria may be very difficult to quantify, or even measure qualitatively; if they are important to the decision, however, they must be included in the location analysis.

Locations can be compared in a number of ways. The most common is probably just managerial intuition: which location best satisfies the important criteria? The weighted score model is a simple formalization of this intuitive process that is useful as a rough screening tool for locating a single facility. In this model a weight is assigned to each factor (*criterion*), depending on its importance to the manager. The most important factors receive proportionately higher weights. Then a score is assigned to each of the alternative locations on each factor, again with higher scores representing better results. The product of the weights and the scores then gives a set of weighted scores, which are added up for each location. The location with the highest weighted score is considered best. In quantitative terms:

$$\text{Total weighted score} = \sum_i W_i S_i$$

where

i = index for factors

Wi = weight of factor i

Si = score of the location being evaluated on factor i

Quebec City used the weighted score model in relocating its blood bank, as described in the accompanying sidebar. The following example illustrates the method.

Communicable Disease Center

A county health department is investigating three possible locations for a specialized control clinic that will monitor acquired immune deficiency syndrome (AIDS) and other sexually transmitted diseases (STDs). The county director of public health is particularly concerned with four factors.

1. The most important consideration in the treatment of STDs is ease of access for those infected. Since they are generally disinclined to recognize and seek treatment, it is foolish to locate a clinic where it is not easily accessible to as many patients as possible. This aspect of location is probably as much as 50 percent more important than the lease cost of the building.

2. Still, the annual cost of the lease is not a minor consideration. Unfortunately, the health department is limited to a very tight budget, and any extra cost for the lease will mean that less equipment and staff are available to the clinic.

3. For some patients it is of the utmost importance that confidentiality be maintained. Thus, although the clinic must be easily accessible, it must also be relatively inconspicuous. This factor is probably just as important as the cost of the lease.

4. The director also wants to consider the convenience of the location for the staff, since many of the physicians will be donating their time to the clinic. This consideration is the least important of all, perhaps only half as important as the cost of the lease.

The three locations being considered are a relatively accessible building on Adams Avenue, an inconspicuous office complex near the downtown bus terminal, and a group of public offices in the Civic Center, which would be almost rent-free.

$\mathcal{T}_{\text{ABLE}}$ 10.4 ❖ Potential Clinic Sites

W: Weight	F: Factor	Potential Locations		
		A: Adams Avenue	B: Bus Terminal Complex	C: Civic Center
2	1. Annual lease cost	1	3	4
3	2. Accessibility for patients	3	3	2
2	3. Inconspicuousness	2	4	2
1	4. Accessibility for personnel	4	1	2

Note: Factor scoring scale: 1, poor; 2, acceptable; 3, good; 4, excellent.

$\mathcal{T}_{\text{ABLE}}$ 10.5 ❖ Comparison of Site Factors by the Weighted Score Method

Factor	Weight	Sites:		
		A	B	C
1	2	$2 \times 1 = 2$	$2 \times 3 = 6$	$2 \times 4 = 8$
2	3	$3 \times 3 = 9$	$3 \times 3 = 9$	$3 \times 2 = 6$
3	2	$2 \times 2 = 4$	$2 \times 4 = 8$	$2 \times 2 = 4$
4	1	$1 \times 4 = 4$	$1 \times 1 = 1$	$1 \times 2 = 2$
Total		19	24	20

The director has decided to evaluate (score) each of these alternative locations on each of the four factors. He has decided to use a 4-point scale on which 1 represents "poor" and 4 represents "excellent." His scores and the weights (derived from the relative importance of the four factors) are shown in Table 10.4. The problem now is somehow to use this information to determine the best location for the clinic.

To determine the weighted score for each location, we multiply each score by the weight for that factor and then the sum over all factors for each location, as illustrated in Table 10.5. Since higher scores indicate better ratings, the location with the largest score—B, the office near the bus terminal—is best, followed by C, the Civic Center.

$\mathcal{S}_{\text{OLVED}}$ EXERCISE 10.5 ❖ Selection by Weighted Scores

Sue is trying to buy a used car and has narrowed her choices to two possibilities: Rabbit and Mustang. Her criteria are economy (30 percent importance), reliability (25 percent), and price (45 percent). She estimates the economy of the Rabbit to be good (28 MPG) and the Mustang to be OK (18 MPG). She considers the reliability of the Rabbit good (about twice that of the Mustang). But the price of the Rabbit is $1500 (OK), while that of the Mustang is only $1100 (good). Identify a way to score these factors for Sue and evaluate the choice by each of the methods.

Solution:

One way to score the factors is by ranking the two cars on each factor, for example, with 2 as "good" and 1 as "OK."

Importance	Factor	Rabbit	Mustang
0.30	Economy	× 2 = 0.60	× 1 = 0.30
0.25	Reliability	× 2 = 0.50	× 1 = 0.25
0.45	Price	× 1 = 0.45	× 2 = 0.90
		Total: 1.55	1.45

On the basis of these rankings, the Rabbit is preferred.

Spreadsheet Analysis: Weighted Score Method

As we have seen in this section, the weighted score method is a useful tool when a decision maker needs to consider multiple criteria simultaneously. This approach can be applied to a variety of situations and can include both subjective and objective criteria. In this example, we illustrate how the ability of spreadsheets to perform sensitivity or "what if" analyses significantly extends the usefulness of the weighted score method.

Because purchasing a car is something most people are familiar with, we will stick with this scenario. In fact, as graduation gets closer, many of you may already be thinking of what car you will purchase upon graduating. For the purpose of this example we will assume that your candidates are the sports car listed below and you have collected the information given.

Car	Price	Acceleration 0 to 60 mph (seconds)	MPG	Appearance
Integra	$19,300	6.8	24	OK
325i	$29,900	6.9	18	more of sedan
Corvette	$34,000	5.3	17	very sporty
Stealth Turbo	$30,100	5.2	17	very sporty
RX–7	$34,000	5.0	17	very sporty
300 ZX Turbo	$38,200	5.0	18	very sporty

To score these cars we will use a 3-point scale. It is important to scale all criteria with the same number of points, or the weighting scheme will be thrown off. Thus, if you score the cars on price using a 3-point scale, you must also use a 3-point scale for acceleration, MPG, and appearance. After looking over the data you collected on the cars, you have decided on the following 3-point scales for each of the criteria:

Criteria	1 point	2 points	3 points
Price	> $32,000	$25,000 to $32,000	< $25,000
Acceleration	≥ 6 seconds	> 5 and < 6	≤ 5
MPG	≤ 17 MPG	> 17 and < 20	≥ 20
Appearance	more of a sedan	OK	very sporty

In defining how you are going to score the options, it is more important that an approximately even number of options fall into each category than that intervals are even. This is to ensure that your model does a good job of discriminating between the options. A model with evenly defined intervals where all the options fell into one category would not help you distinguish one option from another.

Also, in defining the scales for your criteria, make sure that the higher points are assigned to the more favorable outcomes. In our example, a common mistake is to assign more points to a higher price; however, since we prefer to spend less on a car, the lower the price, the higher the score assigned. On the other hand, since we prefer higher levels of MPG, the higher the MPG, the higher the score assigned. Finally, note that both objective criteria (price, acceleration, and MPG) and subjective criteria (appearance) are included in our model.

The last thing we need to do is decide on weights for the criteria. Let's assume that after careful thought, you have arrived at the following weighting scheme:

Factor	Weight
Price	40
Acceleration	30
MPG	10
Appearance	20

The spreadsheet shown below was developed to help analyze your decision.

	A	B	C	D	E	F
1	Weighted Score Model for Car Purchase Decision					
2						
3	Criteria:	Price	Acceleration	MPG	Appearance	
4	Weights:	40	30	10	20	
5						
6	**Options**	**Price**	**Acceleration**	**MPG**	**Appearance**	**Score**
7	Integra	3	1	3	2	220
8	325i	2	1	2	1	150
9	Corvette	1	2	1	3	170
10	Stealth Turbo	2	2	1	3	210
11	RX-7	1	3	1	3	200
12	300 ZX Turbo	1	3	2	3	210
13						
14	**Key Formula:**					
15	cell F7:	=(B$4*B7)+(C$4*C7)+(D$4*D7)+(E$4*E7)				
16	cells F8 to F12	formula in cell F7 copied to cells F8:F12				

The criteria are listed in row 3 and the weights for each criteria in row 4. Rows 7–12 list the cars being considered and the score for each car, based on the scale points defined above for each criterion. In column F, a formula calculates the score for each car, given its score on each criterion and the weight of the criterion in row 4. To illustrate, the following formula was entered in cell F7:

$$= (B\$4*B7)+(C\$4*C7)+(D\$4*D7)+(E\$4*E7)$$

The formula entered in cell F7 was then copied to cells F8:F12. The total scores range from 150 to 220, with the Integra earning the highest total score: 220.

To illustrate how spreadsheets can be used to facilitate sensitivity analysis, assume that this weighted score model was developed by General Motors (GM). Thus, GM conducted some market research and identified the cars that most commonly compete with the Corvette. Further, GM identified the criteria car buyers use and the weights they give to these criteria. After collecting all this information, managers at GM developed the model. Seeing that the Corvette is ranked next to last, the managers would like to know what actions they could take to boost the Corvette's overall score. One obvious focus would be the Corvette's low score on the most important criterion (price). Suppose, for example, GM was able to lower the Corvette's price from $34,000 to $32,000. Making this change would increase the Corvette's score on price from 1 to 2. Thus, to determine how this change would effect the Corvette's total score, cell B9 was changed from 1 to 2, as shown in the spreadsheet below. As you can see, making this change would boost the Corvette's score from 170 to 210, putting it into a three-way tie for second place.

	A	B	C	D	E	F
1	Weighted Score Model for Car Purchase Decision					
2						
3	Criteria:	Price	Acceleration	MPG	Appearance	
4	Weights:	40	30	10	20	
5						
6	**Options**	**Price**	**Acceleration**	**MPG**	**Appearance**	**Score**
7	Integra	3	1	3	2	220
8	325i	2	1	2	1	150
9	Corvette	2	2	1	3	210
10	Stealth Turbo	2	2	1	3	210
11	RX-7	1	3	1	3	200
12	300 ZX Turbo	1	3	2	3	210
13						
14	**Key Formula:**					
15	cell F7:	=(B$4*B7)+(C$4*C7)+(D$4*D7)+(E$4*E7)				
16	cells F8 to F12	formula in cell F7 copied to cells F8:F12				

As another example, suppose that since the Corvette does well on appearance, the managers would like to know what the effect would be if they undertook an advertising campaign to change the way the consumers value price and appearance. In other words, suppose that an advertising campaign could successfully lead consumers to switch their values (and thus their weights) for price and appearance. To determine the effect of this change, the weight for price was changed from 40 to 20 and the weight for appearance was changed from 20 to 40, yielding the following results.

	A	B	C	D	E	F
1	Weighted Score Model for Car Purchase Decision					
2						
3	Criteria:	Price	Acceleration	MPG	Appearance	
4	Weights:	20	30	10	40	
5						
6	**Options**	**Price**	**Acceleration**	**MPG**	**Appearance**	**Score**
7	Integra	3	1	3	2	200
8	325i	2	1	2	1	130
9	Corvette	1	2	1	3	210
10	Stealth Turbo	2	2	1	3	230
11	RX-7	1	3	1	3	240
12	300 ZX Turbo	1	3	2	3	250
13						
14	**Key Formula:**					
15	cell F7:	=(B$4*B7)+(C$4*C7)+(D$4*D7)+(E$4*E7)				
16	cells F8 to F12	formula in cell F7 copied to cells F8:F12				

The result of this change increases the Corvette's total score from 170 to 210 and moves it up one spot in the rankings. However, this change also increases the total scores of the 300 ZX and the RX-7 as much as the Corvette's and thus does not reduce the substantial lead these cars have over the Corvette.

Making a number of similar changes to the scores of individual options and to the weighting scheme will provide you with a great deal of information and insight into the nature of a decision. Indeed, performing such sensitivity or "what if" analysis is often of greater value to decision makers than simply using the model once to choose the option with the highest total score.

OPERATIONS
IN PRACTICE

Relocating Quebec City's Blood Bank

The Red Cross Blood Donor Clinic and Transfusion Center of Quebec City in Canada was located in a confined spot in the downtown area and wanted to expand in another location. The center's main activities affecting the choice of a new location were receiving donors, delivering blood and blood products throughout the community and the province of Quebec, and holding blood donor clinics over the same region.

Accordingly, the criteria for a site were identified as:

❖ Highway access for both clinics and blood deliveries.

❖ Ability to attract more donors as a result of improved accessibility and visibility.

❖ Convenience to both public and private transportation.

❖ A continuingly favorable location even with shifts and changes in population and transportation networks.

❖ Ease of travel for employees.

❖ Internal floor space.

❖ Lot size.

❖ Acceptability of the site to management and governmental authorities involved in the decision.

The analysis of the problem was very complicated, owing to conflicting requirements and the unavailability of data. Nevertheless, by using center-of-gravity methods, five sites were finally identified and evaluated on the basis of four final criteria: accessibility to roads, accessibility to public transit, proximity to the previously determined centers of gravity, and availability of a lot or suitable building.

The five sites were then ranked on each of these criteria, and a scoring model was constructed to help management determine the best location. The weights were to be determined by management, and they could be modified to determine if changing them would have any effect on the best location.

The final scores and rankings, assuming equal weights across the four criteria, are shown below (Price and Turcotte, 1986).

Site	Road Access	Bus Access	Proximity	Availability	Rank
1	0.4	0	0.4	0.7	1
2	0.2	0.2	0.3	0.7	2
3	0.3	0.3	0.2	0	4
4	0	0.4	0.1	0	5
5	0.1	0.1	0	0.7	3

$\mathscr{L}$ OCATING PURE SERVICE ORGANIZATIONS

Although all the material presented so far applies relatively equally to services and product firms, some situations unique to service organizations are worth noting. Two that we will look at in detail here involve the recipient coming to the facility, as in retailing, and the facility going to the recipient, as with "alarm" services.

❖ Recipient to Facility

In recipient-to-facility situations, the facility draws customers or recipients from an area surrounding it, possibly in competition with other, similar facilities. Research has found that under these circumstances the drawing power of retail facilities is proportional to the size of the facility and inversely proportional to the square (or cube, in some cases) of the average recipient's travel time. This assumes that all other factors—such as price and quality—are equivalent or insignificant. Again, this type of relationship is known as a *gravity* method because, like gravity, it operates by drawing nearby objects in.

Next, consider the situation of public services such as health clinics, libraries, and colleges. Apart from the difficulty of framing a location model is the probably more significant problem of choosing a measure, or measures, of service: number of recipients served (a "surrogate" measure), change in the recipient's condition (a direct measure of benefit), quantity of services offered (another surrogate), and so on. Some measures recommended in the literature on health clinics, which can be used for trial-and-error procedures, are:

1. *Facility utilization:* Maximize the number of visits to the facilities.
2. *Travel distance per citizen:* Minimize the average distance per person in the region to the nearest clinic.
3. *Travel distance per visit:* Minimize the average distance per visit to the nearest clinic.

No one measure has been found to work best for all cases of deciding on a location.

❖ Facility to Recipient

Facility-to-recipient situations are common among the urban "alarm" services: fire, police, and ambulance. Again, the problem of measuring a service appropriately involves such factors as number of recipients served, average waiting time for service, value of property saved, and number of service facilities. Two general cases are encountered in this problem, whether a single- or multiple-facility service is being located:

1. High-density demand for services where multiple vehicles are located in the same facility and vehicles are often dispatched from one alarm directly to another.
2. Widely distributed demand for services where extreme travel distances require additional facilities.

Typical of situation 1 are fire companies in New York City and ambulances in Los Angeles (see the Bibliography). Queuing (waiting line) theory is also applicable in these situations (see Chapter 15 Supplement).

Results in these cases have been basically the same. There is a significant dropoff in the returns to scale as more units are added to the system. Typically, the first three or four will improve all measures by up to 80 percent of the maximum improvement. Each additional unit gains less and less. A second common finding is that optimally located facilities yield only about a 15 percent improvement over existing or evenly dispersed facilities. Last, incremental approaches to selecting additional locations provide slightly poorer service than a total relocation analysis of all the facilities.

CHAPTER IN PERSPECTIVE

This chapter concludes Part Three, which has covered the business processes associated with managing resources. In Chapter 8 we focused on developing forecasts of demand. In Chapter 9, we turned our attention to determining the amount of organizational resources that would be needed to meet the demand forecast. Finally, in the present chapter, having determined how much capacity was needed, we discussed issues related to locating the organization's resources. Having identified, acquired, and located the necessary organizational resources, in Part Four we focus on the daily business processes of operating these resources to supply customers with outputs that meet their needs.

❖ CHECK YOUR UNDERSTANDING

1. Define the following terms: *supply chain management, multifacility problem, center of gravity, incremental analysis, weighted score model.*

2. How can organizations trade off transportation costs for location costs?

3. List the conditions for locating near a natural resource.

4. Where do organizations that produce immobile outputs tend to locate? Why?

5. Briefly explain the factors that complicate the multifacility location problem.

6. List the key advantages and disadvantages of the four modes of transportation.

7. Can an organization combine the modes of transportation to distribute its products?

8. What are the factors that should be considered in decisions about transportation?

9. Briefly explain the three-stage location process. List key criteria considered at each stage.

10. How does the center-of-gravity model work?

11. Interpret the routing problem for garbage trucks; for U-Haul trucks; for prescription deliveries from a drugstore.

❖ EXPAND YOUR UNDERSTANDING

1. Describe the complications that can occur with multiple outputs in a single facility and in multiple facilities.

2. How might air transport save inventory and warehousing costs?

3. City governments give tax rebates and other financial inducements to large firms to locate in their community. However, small firms and existing firms do not usually receive such breaks. What ethical problems can arise in this process? To prevent violations of ethical standards, what should be the guidelines on such inducements?

4. Are there any overriding situations other than the two given in the chapter for processing natural resources and locating immobile outputs whose characteristics might largely determine their location?

5. How might distribution costs be represented as a fixed cost in a breakeven model? How might they be represented as variable costs?

6. In the discussion regarding the location of pure services, it was noted that "incremental approaches to selecting additional locations provide slightly poorer service than a total relocation analysis of all the facilities." What does this suggest as a possible way to solve the multiple-facility location problem?

7. What trade-offs are involved between locating near recipients and transporting to them?

8. How has technology changed the costs and benefits of location and transportation? Consider banking and express mail.

9. Which measures used to locate pure service organizations are direct measures of benefit and which are surrogate measures of benefit? Can you think of better direct measures? Why aren't they used?

10. The text pointed out a number of risks involved in locating in a foreign country. What might be some offsetting advantages?

11. Might the weighted score model be used to select a region or a community? Might the breakeven model be used to select a region or site? How?

12. For what service organizations is transportation a feasible method of distribution?

13. When would an organization *not* use the three stages of decision making described in this chapter?

14. What factors would be considered in locating an airport in a metropolitan area?

❖ APPLY YOUR UNDERSTANDING
Stafford Chemical, Inc.

Stafford Chemical, Inc., is a privately held company that produces a range of specialty chemicals. Currently, its most important product line is paint pigments used by the automobile industry. Stafford Chemical was founded over 60 years ago by Phillip Stafford in a small town north of Cincinnati, Ohio, and is currently run by Phillip's grandson, George Stafford. Stafford has over 150 employees, and approximately three-quarters of them work on the shop floor. Stafford Chemical operates out of the same plant Phillip built when he founded the company; however, it has undergone several expansions over the years.

Recently, a Japanese competitor of Stafford Chemical by the name of Ozawa Industries announced plans to expand its operations to the United States. Ozawa, a subsidiary of a large industrial Japanese company, decided to locate a new facility in the United States to better serve some of its customers: automobile manufacturers who have built assembly plants there.

The governor of the state in which Stafford Chemical operates has been particularly aggressive in trying to persuade Ozawa Industries to locate in a new industrial park located about 30 miles from Stafford's current plant. She has expressed a willingness to negotiate special tax rates, to subsidize workers' training, and to expand the existing highway to meet Ozawa's needs. In a recent newspaper article, she was quoted as saying:

Making the concessions I have proposed to get Ozawa to locate within our state is a good business decision and a good investment in our state. The plant will provide high-paying jobs for 400 of our citizens. Furthermore, over the long run, the income taxes that these 400 individuals will pay will more than offset the concessions I have proposed. Since several other states have indicated a willingness to make similar concessions, it is unlikely that Ozawa would choose our state without them.

George Stafford was outraged after being shown the governor's comments.

I can't believe this. Stafford Chemical has operated in this state for over 60 years. I am the third generation of Staffords to run this business. Many of our employees' parents and grandparents worked here. We have taken pride in being an exemplary corporate citizen. And now our governor wants to help one of our major competitors drive us out of business. How are we supposed to compete with such a large industrial giant? We should be the ones who are getting the tax break and help with workers' training. Doesn't 60 years of paying taxes and employing workers count for something? Where is this governor's loyalty? It seems to me that the state should be loyal to its long-term citizens, the ones who care about the state and community they operate in—not some large industrial giant looking to save a buck.

Questions

1. How valid is George Stafford's argument? How valid is the governor's argument? Is Stafford Chemical being punished because it was already located within the state?

2. How ethical is it for states and local governments to offer incentives to attract new businesses to their localities? Are federal laws needed to keep states from competing with one another?

3. Does the fact that Ozawa is a foreign company alter the ethical nature of the governor's actions? What about Ozawa's size?

4. What are George's options?

❖ EXERCISES

1. Evaluate the following three locations in terms of access to five destinations. Site I is located 313, 245, 188, 36, and 89 feet, respectively, from the five destinations; site II, 221, 376, 92, 124, and 22 feet; and site III, 78, 102, 445, 123, and 208 feet.

2. Reevaluate Exercise 1 if the number of trips to each of the destinations is, respectively, 15, 6, 12, 33, and 21.

3. Reevaluate Exercise 2 if the first destination requires an expert who is paid three times what the courier is paid to the rest of the destinations.

4. Elevators are frequently programmed to "home" to a centrally located floor. If the elevator in a seven-story building has its home at the fourth (middle) floor, is it optimally located if the following calls are typical of a day? First floor: 77; second: 18; third: 33; fourth: 21; fifth: 27; sixth: 23; seventh: 46.

5. Calculate the center of gravity in Exercise 4. Which floor is closest to this center?

6. An automated stacking crane in a warehouse picks and stores pallets from and to cells in storage racks up to 4 levels high and 20 columns wide. If all the picks-stores can be approximated by the following four points, is level 3, column 10 the optimal location for the loading-unloading cell? 1200 picks at level 2, column 4; 860 picks at level 4, column 8; 1560 picks at level 3, column 13; 1030 picks at level 1, column 18. (Assume that the crane moves only vertically and horizontally, not diagonally. How would you solve the problem if it did move diagonally?)

7. Find the center of gravity in Exercise 6.

8. Is Clarton or Uppingham the best location for a production volume of 600 services? The fixed costs

of Clarton total £6000 (pounds, United Kingdom) per year, while those of Uppingham total only £4500. However, the variable costs of Clarton are £8, while those of Uppingham are £10.

9. Reconsider Exercise 8 adding fixed bridge tolls: £500 for Clarton and £1000 for Uppingham.

10. Resolve Exercise 9 if the transportation cost is £2 per unit from Clarton and £1.5 from Uppingham.

11. Choose the best coat on the basis of two equally important factors: price and quality. Only the rankings are available for each factor (where 1 is best).

Coat:	1	2	3	4	5	6	7	8	9
Cost (rupees):	2	5	3	1	7	8	9	4	6
Quality:	6	3	4	8	1	7	9	5	2

12. Resolve Exercise 11 if price is 50 percent more important than quality. Repeat if the situation is the opposite.

13. A large waterproof container is used to store supplies for four underwater laboratories, as follows. Find the best location for the container.

Lab No.	Location (feet)			Supply Weight (pounds)	Resupply Cost (cents/ pound/ foot)
	Depth	East	North		
1	240	560	320	40	1
2	130	425	270	120	3
3	405	190	485	60	2
4	340	851	70	80	1

14. A supply depot is located at $x = 3$, $y = 4$ to supply stores 1, 2, and 3 as indicated. Use incremental analysis to determine a better location and then test it to verify that it is indeed better.

Store	x	y	Trips
1	5	4	7
2	3	5	4
3	3	3	3

15. The head of the Campus Computing Center is faced with locating a new centralized computer center at one of three possible locations on the campus. The decision is to be based on the number of users in each department and the distance of the various departments from each possible location. Which location should be chosen?

Department	Number of Users	Distance by Location		
		1	2	3
1	25	0	3	5
2	30	5	4	3
3	10	2	0	1
4	5	3	2	0
5	14	6	2	3

16. A new product involves the following costs associated with three possible locations. If demand is forecast to be 3900 units a year, which location should be selected?

	Location		
	A	B	C
Annual cost	$10,000	40,000	25,000
Unit variable cost	$10.00	2.50	6.30

17. a. Find the best point location for an inspection-repair station to service five valves (1, 2, 3, 4, 5) on a straight pipeline. The valves' locations and their weekly number of required inspections are as follows:

Valve	Miles East of Town	Inspections/Week
1	5	3
2	3	6
3	1	2
4	10	2
5	8	4

b. A politician has suggested locating the inspection-repair station at valve 2, since that valve requires the most inspections per week. Show by incremental analysis whether this is the best location and, if not, in which direction the station should be located.

18. The location subcommittee's final report to the board has focused on three acceptable communities. Table 15b in the appendix to the report indi-

cates that the cost of locating in communities 1, 2, and 3 is approximately $400,000, $500,000 and $600,000 per year (respectively), mortgaged over 30 years. Paragraph 2 on page 39 of the report indicates that the variable cost per unit of product will increase 15 percent in community 1 but decrease 15 percent in community 3, owing to differences in labor rates. As plant manager, you know that variable costs to date have averaged about $3.05 per unit and sales for the next decade are expected to average 20 percent more than the last 10 years, during which annual sales varied between 40,000 and 80,000 units. Which location would you recommend?

19. Use a weighted score model to choose between three locations (A, B, C) for setting up a factory. The weights for each criterion are shown in the following table. A score of 1 represents unfavorable, 2 satisfactory, and 3 favorable.

Category	Weight	Location		
		A	B	C
Labor costs	20	1	2	3
Labor productivity	20	2	3	1
Labor supply	10	2	1	3
Union relations	10	3	3	2
Material supply	10	2	1	1
Transport costs	25	1	2	3
Infrastructure	10	2	2	2

20. Use a modified center-of-gravity method to locate two warehouses to service the following retail outlets (1–7).

Outlet	Miles North	Miles West
1	50	20
2	10	40
3	60	40
4	40	30
5	0	30
6	50	40
7	10	20

21. a. Use a map of the United States to optimally decide between Chicago and Saint Louis for a single facility to serve the following cities. (a) Portland, Oregon—5 carloads per week. (b) Des Moines, Iowa—2 carloads per week. (c) New York, New York—1 carload per week. (d) Saint Louis, Missouri—7 carloads per week. (e) Chicago, Illinois—10 carloads per week. (f) New Orleans, Louisiana—5 carloads per week. Assume the same transportation rate per carload to all destinations and zero cost for same-city delivery (e.g., Chicago to Chicago). Use straight-line distances measured by a ruler.

b. Assume that two small warehouses can be built and operated for 50 percent more than a single ($175,000/year) warehouse. What per mile cost results in the same expense as the best answer above if the two warehouses are located in Chicago and Saint Louis?

22. The Nuclear Energy Commission (NEC) is attempting to locate a nuclear waste dump in a region that is surrounded by three cities, as described in the following table. Derive a method for locating the dump and find the best location. State your assumptions.

City	Population (thousands)	Miles East	Miles North
A	40	0	0
B	110	70	20
C	70	30	60

23. A manufacturer is considering three possible locations for its new factory. The choice depends not only on the operating costs at each location but also on the cost of shipping the product to its three major marketing regions. Given in the following table are operating costs and distribution costs. Which location would you recommend for a production volume of 80,000 units per year?

	Location		
	A	**B**	**C**
Construction cost (amortize over 10 years)	$1,000,000	$1,800,000	$950,000
Material cost per unit	2.46	2.17	2.64
Labor cost per unit	0.65	0.62	0.67
Overhead: Fixed	100,000	150,000	125,000
Variable per unit	0.15	0.18	0.12

Total Distribution Costs

To	From Location		
Region	**A**	**B**	**C**
1	$10,000	$20,000	$26,000
2	17,000	10,000	15,000
3	12,000	18,000	10,000

24. Nina is trying to decide in which of four shopping centers to locate her new boutique. Some cater to a higher class of clientele than others, some are in an indoor mall, some have a much greater volume than others, and, of course, rent varies considerably. Because of the nature of her store, she has decided that the class of clientele is the most important consideration. Following this, however, she must pay attention to her expenses; and rent is a major item—probably 90 percent as important as clientele. An indoor, temperature-controlled mall is a big help, however, for stores such as hers, where 70 percent of sales are from passersby slowly strolling and window-shopping. Thus, she rates this as about 95 percent as important as rent. Last, a higher volume of shoppers means more potential sales; she thus rates this factor as 80 percent as important as rent.

As an aid in visualizing her location alternatives, she has constructed the following table. "Good" is scored as 3, "fair" as 2, and "poor" as 1. Use a weighted score model to help Nina come to a decision.

	Location			
	1	**2**	**3**	**4**
Class of clientele	Fair	Good	Poor	Good
Rent	Good	Fair	Poor	Good
Indoor mall	Good	Poor	Good	Poor
Volume	Good	Fair	Good	Poor

25. Develop a spreadsheet for Exercise 11. Which coat would you recommend if cost and quality are ranked equally? If cost is 50 percent more important than quality?

26. Referring to Exercise 13, develop a spreadsheet to find the best location for the container. What is the best location for the container if the resupply costs of lab 1 increase to $0.03/pound/foot?

27. Develop a spreadsheet for Exercise 16. What is the best location if the demand forecast is 3900 units a year? 5000 a year?

28. Develop a spreadsheet for Exercise 19.

a. What would your recommendation be if the weight for the transport cost went down to 10 and the weight of union relations went up to 25?

b. Suppose location A received a score of 3 for transport cost and location C received a score of 2 for transport cost. Would your recommendation change under these circumstances?

c. The vice president of finance has looked at your scoring model and feels that tax considerations should be included in the model with a weight of 15. In addition, the VP has scored the locations on tax considerations as follows: location A received a score of 3, location B received a score of 2, and location C received a score of 1. How would this additional information affect your recommendation?

d. What changes in location B's scores are required to make it the recommended location?

29. Referring to Exercise 24, develop a spreadsheet to help Nina select a location for her boutique. Suppose Nina is able to negotiate a lower rent at location 3 and thus raise its ranking to "good." How does this affect the overall rankings of the four locations?

❖ ❖ ❖

Product
Supply Processes

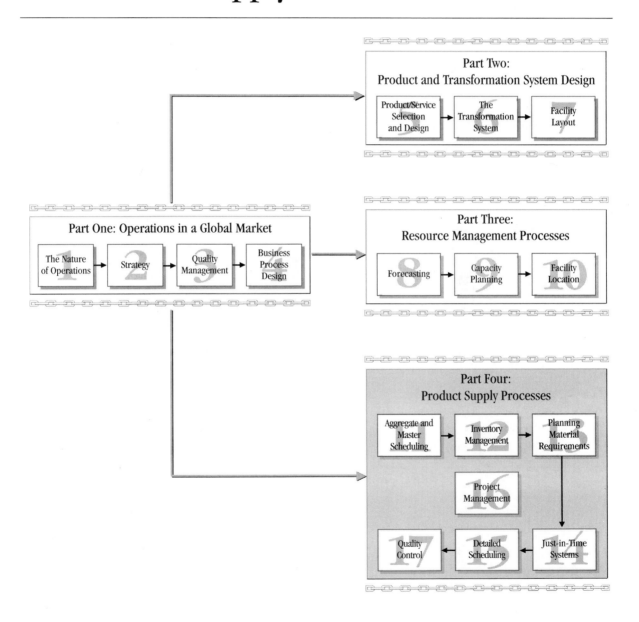

Aggregate and Master Scheduling

CHAPTER OVERVIEW

❖ The sequence of scheduling activities starts with the demand forecast, moves through aggregate planning to the creation of a production plan for the acquisition of labor and equipment, and then involves the creation of a master schedule.

❖ Following the creation of an initial master schedule, an evaluation is conducted in terms of capacity planning, lead times, availability of materials, and so on to check its feasibility. Once a feasible and satisfactory master schedule is approved, planning for loading the work on workstations, sequencing it, and detailed scheduling may be conducted.

❖ All these are planning activities. The actual work begins with the release of a work order, called *dispatching*. As work flows through the shop, it is expedited to meet its promised delivery date.

❖ *Aggregate planning* is the process of using various capacity strategies (e.g., regular time, overtime, inventory storage, back-ordering, hiring and layoffs, subcontracting) to meet overall (aggregate) demand for an organization's outputs.

❖ Two pure aggregate planning strategies are *level production,* producing the same amount each period; and *chase demand,* producing the demanded amount each period. The advantage of the first is stable employment levels and no need for overtime. The advantage of the second is the reduction, or avoidance, of inventories and their costs.

❖ The aggregate planning process consists of attempting to meet period demand rates at minimal cost or disruption. Thus, the planner must trade off advantages and disadvantages among strategies by mixing them in different amounts at different periods in the production *horizon.*

❖ A helpful way to see the interplay between some of the costs is on a cumulative graph of demand and production. In general, bends in the production line as well as large spaces between the production and demand lines are to be avoided.

❖ The master schedule is the final "build" schedule for the firm and is upper management's primary handle on the business, since it says what in fact is actually going to be made, on the basis of both the forecast and actual orders from customers.

❖ The master schedule horizon is about a year and is made up of four periods: (1) *frozen,* in which nothing can be changed without great expense and trouble; (2) *firm,* in which changes can still be made; (3) *full,* in which no capacity is left; and (4) *open,* in which orders can still be taken. The difference between the forecast and existing orders in the open period is called *available to promise.*

❖ Sometimes the master schedule stops with assemblies or modules, which are then assembled to order as customer orders come in. In this case, there will be a separate final assembly schedule.

❖ The master schedule is constructed by applying historical ratios to the aggregate schedule for each of the products or services the firm offers. The process considers initial inventories of final goods on hand, safety stocks desired, and batching to avoid frequent but expensive setup costs.

❖ The master schedule is checked in rough-cut capacity planning by applying historical ratios for each workstation to each unit to be produced, in order to determine workstation loads in hours per week. These loads are then matched against capacity to identify potential problems.

$\mathcal{J}$NTRODUCTION _____

❖ American Olean Tile Company (AO) manufactures a wide variety of ceramic tiles at eight factories across the United States to supply about 120 sales distribution points (SDPs). Growth in AO's distribution network forced its management to develop a computer modeling program to assist in manual planning of production and distribution. A crucial element of the situation was the need to coordinate plans at the factory level with sales forecasts and inventories at the SDPs, and to allocate capacities at the factories to the SDPs. A hierarchical production planning system based first on making an aggregate plan and then on disaggregating it, was developed to facilitate the integration of several forecasts, the annual plan, short-term scheduling, and inventory control.

The planning process begins with an annual sales forecast for total factory sales. These forecasts, plant capacities, production costs, and transportation costs are then input to a computer model that assigns annual demands for SDPs to plants. Each plant then develops a monthly production plan based on these assignments, as well as seasonal inventory targets and demand patterns. The master production schedule for each plant is then derived from these plans, scheduled orders already received from customers, and short-term demand forecasts from each SDP. The master schedule horizon is one quarter, broken down into weeks.

The benefits of this hierarchical production planning system have been many. In addition to saving about half a million dollars a year in reduced distribution costs, the system helps AO better coordinate its production plans and thereby position itself more competitively in the marketplace (Liberatore and Miller, 1985).

❖ At the Henry Ford Hospital, the aggregate planning problem is to match available capital, workers, and supplies to a highly variable pattern of demand. The hospital has 903 beds arranged into 30 nursing units, with each nursing unit containing 8 to 44 beds. For purposes of planning, each of the nursing units is treated as an independent production facility.

A number of factors complicate the aggregate planning process at the hospital. First, as noted, demand exhibits a high degree of variability. For example, while the average number of occupied beds in 1991 was 770, in one eight-week period the average was 861 occupied beds each day and in another eight-week period the average number of occupied beds was 660. Further analysis showed that the number of occupied beds could change by as many as 146 in less than two weeks!

A second complicating factor is the large penalty incurred by the hospital for HMO patients who require care but cannot be admitted because a bed is not available. In these cases, not only does the hospital lose the revenue from the patient, but it must also pay another hospital for the patient's stay. For a simple obstetrics case, the cost to the Henry Ford Hospital is approximately $5000 for each HMO patient who must be turned away.

A third complication is the tight labor market for registered nurses, making it difficult and expensive to change the rate of production. On average, it takes the hospital 12 to 16 weeks to recruit and train each nurse, at a cost of approximately $7600 per nurse.

A final complication is the high costs associated with idle facilities. The hospital estimates that the cost of one eight-bed patient module exceeds $35,000 per month (Schramm and Freund, 1993).

These examples illustrate factors, considerations, and complications associated with developing aggregate production plans. Developing an aggregate production plan is important because without taking a sufficiently long-term view of the organization, we may end up making short-run decisions that adversely affect the organization in the long run. For example, during one period at the Henry Ford Hospital, a decision was made to reduce the staff. However, shortly after the staff was reduced, it was determined that the staff was needed and thus new staff members were recruited. The net result was that the hospital incurred both the costs associated with reducing its staff and the costs associated with recruiting and training a new staff a short time later. A better approach would have been to compare the costs of reducing and hiring staff with the costs of having too large a staff during this time period. Of course, the only way to accomplish this is to look far enough into the future to estimate if and when demand will pick up again.

Our point here is not to single out the Henry Ford Hospital as an example of poor forecasting. Indeed, we all know that hindsight is 20/20. Rather, our intent is to highlight the importance and complexity of aggregate planning. Put yourself in the shoes of the administrator at Henry Ford Hospital. First, you are faced with a highly variable demand rate: the capacity needed can shift by more than 16 percent (146/903) in a two-week period. Now consider the options available to you to respond to these shifts. One option is to hire more nurses. Unfortunately, it takes 12 to 16 weeks and costs $7600 apiece to hire new nurses. Thus, by the time you have hired and trained the new nurses, demand may have dropped again. And if you have more nurses than you need, the cost of one idle eight-bed patient module is $35,000 per month or $420,000 per year. On the other hand, if you don't have enough staff to serve HMO patients, the cost is $5000 per patient for simple cases and much more than this for patients requiring more extensive treatment!

In Part Two we dealt with designing the output and transformation system. Then in Part Three we dealt with identifying and managing the resources needed to produce the outputs. But both of these processes were discussed as a snapshot of the operations system, with workers, machines, and materials all frozen in space and time. Now, in Part Four, we add the dimension of *time* to this static picture, transforming it into a running, operating set of activities that are producing and supplying outputs to live, demanding people and organizations. More specifically, our focus in Part Four is on how a variety of operational activities support the process of supplying a product or service. In this first chapter of Part Four, we are concerned with ensuring that the *right* tasks are conducted at the *right* time on the *right* items to produce the output—which is, in a sense, a matter of "orchestration," more generally known as *scheduling.*

Problems with productivity are often attributable, in large part, to poor management of the schedule: *not* having the right items when they are needed, *not* having equipment available when it is needed, and so on. Scheduling is an important component of the overall product supply process that addresses issues managers must face on a daily basis: where each input (material, machine, worker) must be, when it must be there, what form it must be in, how many must be available, and other such details.

Scheduling for continuous process and flow organizations is not anywhere near the problem that it is for job shops. This is because scheduling is largely *built into* the transformation process when the facility is designed and therefore need not (in fact *cannot*) be constantly changed. To reschedule these facilities, beyond just increasing or decreasing the rate of input, requires a rebalancing of the entire flow through the production system.

At the other extreme, the scheduling of project operations is probably the most important single planning activity in the successful management of projects. Because of the extent of this topic, we will defer its treatment to Chapter 16.

In the present chapter we will primarily treat scheduling in job shops, for services as well as products. We begin, however, with a look at the generic sequence of the scheduling activities in product firms, since these functions are better developed and more common in product firms than in service organizations.

Following this general view of scheduling, we look at the first major activity in the sequence of activities: aggregate planning. As illustrated by American Olean, the aggregate plan forms the foundation for all other scheduling and materials management. Two pure strategies—level production and chase demand—are described and illustrated, with two examples. Next, we consider the major task of master scheduling and discuss its purpose, procedures, and results. Finally, we briefly note the role of rough-cut capacity planning in validating the feasibility of the master production schedule.

$\mathcal{T}$HE SEQUENCE OF SCHEDULING ACTIVITIES

In most organizations a department (or an individual) is specifically responsible for scheduling operations. In product organizations this function is frequently called *production planning and control* or some similar name. The breadth of this department's responsibility varies considerably; for example, it may consist only of planning gross output levels or may include all the scheduling activities illustrated in Figure 11.1.

This figure does not describe a *standardized* scheduling system, such as might exist in an available computer package; rather, it shows a complex of activities and terms that are often grouped under *scheduling*. Many of these have become major activities only since the advent of computerized scheduling. Before that, they were simply a matter of individual judgment (as some of them still are). Let us look at the scheduling activities on the chart and their interrelationships; in the following sections of the chapter we will then look more intensively at some of the major activities and describe some approaches to dealing with them.

❖ The Demand Forecast

The foundation that supports scheduling is, in most cases, the forecast of demand for the upcoming planning horizon. In some industries, however, only minimal forecasting is needed because customers place orders a year or more ahead of the time when the output will be needed. For example, in the airframe industry, airlines may place orders years ahead of time because of long lead times and backlogs of orders. In these situations, organizational operations are scheduled on the basis of actual orders instead of forecasted demand.

Most organizations do not operate in such a favorable environment, however, and their success often hinges on the accuracy of their forecasts of demand. In these cases the concepts and techniques of forecasting illustrated in Chapter 8 are especially relevant for scheduling.

It might be noted that forecasts over different periods are used for different purposes. For example, long-range forecasts (i.e., 2 to 10 years) are used more for facility and capacity planning than for any scheduling function. In the range of 9 to 18 months, forecasts are used for aggregate planning, as described later, and detailed forecasts for the next few months are particularly crucial in near-term scheduling such as loading and sequencing.

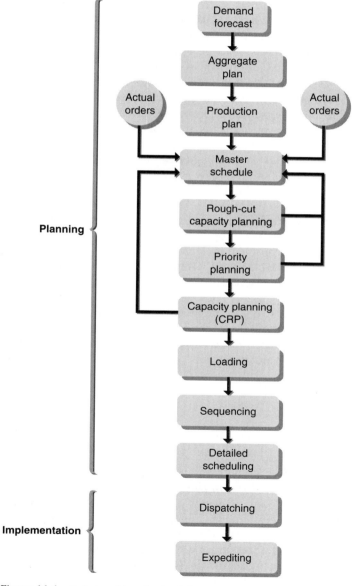

Figure 11.1 Relationship of scheduling activities.

❖ The Aggregate Plan

The **aggregate plan** is a preliminary, approximate schedule of an organization's overall operations that will satisfy the demand forecast at minimum cost. The *planning horizon,* the period over which changes and demands are taken into consideration, is often one year or more and is broken into monthly or quarterly periods. This is because one of the purposes of aggregate planning is to minimize the effects of shortsighted day-to-day scheduling, in which small amounts of material may be ordered from a supplier and workers laid off one week, only to be followed by re-ordering more material and rehiring the workers the next week. By taking a longer-term perspective on use of resources, short-term changes in requirements can be minimized with a considerable saving in costs.

In minimizing short-term variations, the basic approach is to work only with "aggregate" units (that is, units grouped or bunched together). Aggregate resources are used, such as total number of workers, hours of machine time, and tons of raw materials, as well as aggregate units of output—gallons of product, hours of service delivered, number of patients seen, and so on—totally ignoring the fact that some are blue and others are red, some soft and some hard, and so forth. In other words, neither resources nor outputs are broken down into more specific categories; that occurs at a later stage.

On occasion, the units of aggregation are somewhat difficult to determine, especially if the variation in output is extreme (as when a manufacturer produces dishwashers, clothes washers, and dryers). In such cases, *equivalent units* are usually determined; these are based on value, cost, worker-hours, or some similar measure. For the appliance manufacturer, the aggregate plan might be: January, 5000 "appliances"; February, 4000 "appliances"; and so on.

The resulting problem in aggregate planning is to minimize the long-run costs of meeting forecasted demand. The relevant costs include hiring and laying off workers, storing finished goods (if a product is involved), paying wages and overtime, covering the expense of shortages and *backorders,* and subcontracting. As it turns out, the use of inventory to buffer production against variations in demand is an extremely important managerial option. In service organizations this option is usually not available, since services—such as plane trips—cannot be inventoried. The result is an increased cost of producing the service, with an increase in its price. Aggregate planning is discussed in considerably more detail later in this chapter.

❖ The Production Plan

The result of managerial iteration and changes to the aggregate plan is the organization's formal **production plan** for the planning horizon used by the organization (e.g., one year). Sometimes this plan is broken down (i.e., *disaggregated*) one level into major output groups (still aggregated)—for example, by models but not by colors. In either case, the production plan shows the resources required and changes in output over the future: requirements for hiring, limitations on capacity, relative increases and decreases in inventories of materials, and output rate of goods or services.

❖ The Master Schedule

The driving force behind scheduling is the master schedule, also known in industry as the **master production schedule** (MPS). There are two reasons for this:

1. It is at this point that *actual* orders are incorporated into the scheduling system.
2. This is also the stage where aggregate planned outputs are broken down into individual scheduled items that customers actually want (called **level zero items**). These items are then checked for feasibility against lead time (time to produce or ship the items) and operational capacity (if there is enough equipment, labor, etc.).

The actual scheduling is usually iterative, with a preliminary schedule being drawn up, checked for problems, and then revised. After a schedule has been determined, the following points are checked:

- ❖ Does the schedule meet the production plan?
- ❖ Does the schedule meet the end item demand forecasts?
- ❖ Are there conflicts in the schedule involving priority or capacity? (See the next two scheduling activities.) "Rough-cut capacity planning" (discussed next), based on the MPS, derives weekly work-center loads and compares them with capacities available.
- ❖ Does the schedule violate any other constraints regarding equipment, lead times, supplies, facilities, and so forth?
- ❖ Does the schedule conform to organizational policy?
- ❖ Does the schedule violate any legal regulations or organizational or union rules?
- ❖ Does the schedule provide for flexibility and backups?

Problems in any one of these areas may force a revision of the schedule and a repeat of the previous steps. The result is that the master schedule then specifies *what end items* are to be *produced in what periods* to *minimize costs* and gives some measure of assurance that such a plan is *feasible*. Clearly, such a document is of major importance to any organization—it is, in a sense, a blueprint for future operations. Master scheduling is discussed in more detail later in this chapter.

❖ Rough-Cut Capacity Planning

As a part of checking the feasibility of the master schedule, a simple type of **rough-cut capacity planning** is conducted. Historical ratios of workloads per unit of each type of product are used to determine the loads placed on the work centers by all the products being made in any one period. Then the loads are assumed to fall on the work centers in the same period as the demands; that is, the lead times are not used to offset the loads. If a work center's capacities are not overloaded (underloads are also checked), it is assumed that sufficient capacity exists to handle the master schedule, and it is accepted for production. Capacity planning is discussed in more detail in Chapter 13.

❖ Priority Planning

The term *priority planning* relates not to giving priorities to jobs (a topic included under *sequencing*), but rather to determining *what material* is needed *when*. For a master production schedule to be feasible, the proper raw materials, purchased materials, and manufactured or purchased subassemblies must be available when needed, top priority going to immediate needs. The key to production planning is the "needed" date. Years ago, scheduling concentrated on *launching orders*, that is, on when to *place* the order. Priority planning concentrates on when the order is actually needed and schedules *backward* from that date. For example, if an item is needed on June 18 and requires a two-week lead time, then the order is released on June 4 and not before. Why store inventory needlessly?

The systems that have been devised for accomplishing this task are inventory control systems based on lead times and expected demands. The classic order-point inventory systems are most appropriate for organizations *producing to stock* (e.g., flow shops). These are called *order-point systems* because new orders for materials are sent out when the inventory on hand reaches a certain low point. For organizations that *produce to order* (e.g., many job shops), requirements for materials are known with near-certainty because they are tied to specified outputs. For example, every car requires four wheel covers—the number of wheel covers depends only on the number of cars. Computerized **materials requirements planning** (MRP) systems (discussed in Chapter 13) anticipate needs, consider lead times, release purchase orders, and schedule production in accord with the master schedule. If insufficient lead time exists to produce or obtain the necessary materials, or other problems arise, the master schedule must be revised or other arrangements made. These inventory systems are discussed in greater detail in Chapters 12 and 13.

❖ Capacity Planning

The inventory control system and master schedule drive the **capacity requirements planning** (CRP) system, described in detail in Chapter 13. This system projects job orders and demands for materials into requirements for equipment, workforce, and facility and finds the total required capacity of each over the planning horizon. That is, during a given week, how many nurses will be required, how many hours of a kidney machine, how many hours in operating rooms?

This may or may not exceed *available* capacity. If it is within the limits of capacity, then the master schedule is finalized, work orders are released according to schedule, orders for materials are released by the priority planning system, and *load reports* are sent to work centers, listing the work facing each area on the basis of the CRP system. Note that external lead times (usually longer than internal lead times) from suppliers have already been checked at the stage of priority planning, so the master schedule can indeed now be finalized.

If the limits of capacity are exceeded, however, something must be changed.

Some jobs must be delayed, or a less demanding schedule must be devised, or extra capacity must be obtained elsewhere (e.g., by hiring more workers or using overtime). It is the task of production planning and control to solve this problem.

❖ Loading

Loading means deciding which jobs to assign to which work centers. Although the capacity planning system determines that sufficient gross capacity exists to meet the master schedule, *no actual* assignment of jobs to work centers is made. Some equipment will generally be superior for certain jobs, and some equipment will be less heavily loaded than other equipment. Thus, there is often a "best" (fastest or least costly) assignment of jobs to work centers. The problem of loading is considered in more detail in the supplement to this chapter.

❖ Sequencing

Even after jobs have been assigned to work centers, the *order* in which to process the jobs—their *sequencing*—must still be determined. Unfortunately, even this seemingly small final step can have major repercussions on the organization's workload capacity and on whether or not jobs are completed on time. A number of priority rules have been researched and some interesting results are available which will be discussed in Chapter 15.

❖ Detailed (Short-Term) Scheduling

Once all this has been specified, detailed schedules itemizing specific jobs, times, materials, and workers can be drawn up. This is usually done only a few days in advance, however, since changes are always occurring and detailed schedules become outdated quickly. It is the responsibility of production planning and control to ensure that when a job is ready to be worked on, all the items, equipment, facilities, and information (blueprints, operations sheets, etc.) are available as scheduled. This topic is the essence of Chapter 15.

❖ Dispatching

All the previous activities constitute schedule *planning*; no production per se has taken place yet. **Dispatching** is the physical *release* of a work order from the production planning and control department to operations. The release may be manual—from the *dead load file*, as it is called—or through a computerized master scheduling system.

❖ Expediting

Once production planning and control has released a job to operations (or the *shop floor*, as it is sometimes called), the department usually has no more responsibility for it, and it is the production manager's task to get the job done on time. This task is known as **expediting.** When jobs fall behind schedule, managers have historically tended to use expediters to help push these "hot" jobs through the operations. Of course, expediting can be done more proactively, by monitoring the progress of jobs to ensure that they stay on schedule.

Before computerized scheduling techniques were available, extensive use of expediters was common (and it still is in many organizations). The problem was the impossibility of the scheduling task facing production planning and control. Not only could it not determine a good production schedule; it often could not even tell when insufficient capacity existed. Production managers thus relied heavily on expediters to gather all the necessary materials together (often cannibalizing parts from other jobs) in order to get important jobs completed. Of course, this further delayed the remaining jobs, so that more and more jobs tended to become "hot."

Commonly, yellow tags were used to label "hot" jobs until, pretty soon, all the jobs had yellow tags. To identify "especially hot" jobs, then, red tags were used. After a while the operations area resembled a rainbow, whereupon no new orders were accepted, the backlog was worked off, and the cycle started from scratch.

It may be presumed that a clear indication of the failure of a scheduling system is the existence of a great many expediters. One problem with the informal scheduling system, of course, was a lack of *deexpediting* (delaying jobs that had dropped in priority) to reflect changes in required due dates and thus in priorities and schedules. Deexpediting has now been built into the computerized manufacturing resource planning (MRP II) and scheduling systems that are becoming so common in industry.

AGGREGATE PLANNING

The problem of aggregate planning arises in the following context. Managers have a month-to-month forecast of total demand for all outputs (combined) for the next year or so. They are expected to capitalize on this demand by supplying whatever portion of it will maximize long-run profitability. That is, not all the demand need be satisfied if attempting to fill it will result in lower overall profits. But a loss of market share might result, which, in turn, may reduce long-run profitability.

The managers have a set of productive facilities and workers with some maximum capacity to supply demand. There may also be some finished output available in inventory to help meet the demand, but there may, as well, be backorders of unsatisfied demand. They must decide how to employ the resources at their disposal to best meet the demand. If excess capacity is available, they may lease it out, sell it, or lay off workers. If insufficient capacity is available, but only for a short time in the future, they may employ overtime or part-time workers, subcontract work, or simply not meet the demand.

As discussed in Chapter 9, there are a number of ways of changing the capacity available to a manager to meet demand at minimum cost, such as:

1. Overtime.
2. Additional or fewer shifts.
3. Hiring or laying off workers (including part-time).
4. Subcontracting.
5. Building up inventories during slack periods.
6. Leasing facilities or workers, or both.
7. Backlogging demand.
8. Changing demand through marketing promotions or pricing.
9. Undersupplying the market.

Each of these strategies has advantages and disadvantages and perhaps certain restrictions on its use (such as legal or union regulations, or limitations on a public facility, as described in the sidebar about airline scheduling). The managers must plan their strategy carefully, because a shortsighted strategy, such as laying off workers when they will be needed again later, can be very expensive to rectify. However, an excessively long-range perspective may also be incorrect: a worker may be kept idle for a year when it would be much cheaper to lay off and then re-hire the worker. Note that some of these alternatives (e.g., overtime, hiring, and lay-offs) assume that equipment and facilities are already available and that there are not three shifts working seven days a week. If this is not the case, then additional facilities and equipment may also need to be acquired.

❖ Pure Strategies

There are two aggregate planning strategies, known as *pure strategies*, which, though rarely used in practice because of their expense, give managers a starting point to improve upon and also a feel for some upper limits on cost:

1. *Level production.* With a level production strategy, the same amount of out-put is produced each period. Inventories of finished goods (or backlogged demand) are used to meet variations in demand, at the cost of investment in inventory or the expense of a shortage (stockout). The advantage is steady employment with no workforce expenses. Since service outputs cannot gen-erally be inventoried, this strategy, for a service firm, normally results in a constant but poorly utilized workforce (e.g., repair crews, firefighters) of a size large enough to meet peak demand. If the service firm uses a smaller workforce, it risks losing some demand to a competitor.

2. *Chase demand.* In this strategy, production is identical to the expected de-mand for the period in question. This is typically obtained either through overtime or hiring and laying off. (Again, this assumes sufficient equipment and facilities.) The advantage of this policy is that there are no costs entailed by inventories of finished goods, except perhaps for buffer stock (also called *safety stock,* as discussed in Chapter 12), and no shortage costs, including

---

OPERATIONS IN PRACTICE

Small Shifts in Airline Schedules Avoid Costs and Crises

An airline schedules flights in two stages. First, an aggregate base schedule is produced for an entire year, giving flight personnel and others an idea of their expected schedules. As this base or target schedule is initiated, delays, maintenance problems, and other events conspire to alter it in some regions, with some planes, and with some crews. Thus, the real schedule is always attempting to catch up to the original base schedule. If the base schedule is well planned and includes flexibility in critical areas, last-minute crises can be avoided with the real schedules. Following are two examples of the alteration of base schedules to avoid crises in the real schedules.

Delays at Atlanta's Hartsfield International Airport used to be legendary. The cause was that perhaps 50 planes were all trying to land within the same 20-minute period, when at best 30 planes could be handled. The resulting delays approached an hour in some cases. Finally, the two major users of the airport got together and staggered their arrivals and takeoffs throughout the day. As a result, the number of planes trying to use the runways at any given period was cut by up to 75 percent, thereby eliminating the worst congestion and delays.

Similarly, American Airlines flights from Puerto Plata in the Dominican Republic to San Juan, Puerto Rico, were always late. Investigation showed that it was because the pilots' contract with the company required 11.5 hours of rest between flights and the incoming flight to Puerto Plata was arriving too late to take off on time the next morning. There were two alternatives: bring in another crew at an additional cost of over $1 million a year, or reschedule the flight from Puerto Plata to depart 10 minutes later and arrive in San Juan 10 minutes later. The second solution was adopted, although it meant also shifting the schedules of 9 other flights out of San Juan by 10 minutes (Kilman, 1984; *Wall Street Journal,* 1988).

---

loss of goodwill. Service firms use this strategy by making use of overtime, split shifts, overlapping shifts, call-in workers, part-time workers, and so on.

The vast majority of firms, as noted in the sidebar on a hospital food service, often achieve lower costs than the costs of these two pure strategies by using hybrid (mixed) strategies that include overtime, hiring and layoffs, subcontracting, and the like. Product firms also have the option of trading off investment in inventories of finished goods for changes in capacity level or vice versa. (For example, a product firm can build up inventory ahead of demand rather than acquiring all the capacity needed to meet peak demand.) We demonstrate with some examples.

❖ Example: Aggregate Planning at Rap-X-Press

Rap-X-Press is a new local express pickup and delivery business. Sarah Primes is responsible for determining and acquiring the personnel Rap-X-Press will need in the coming year. Sarah has determined the firm's needs for each quarter in each of

Aggregate Planning of Hospital Food Services

Hospital food-service systems are expected to meet the daily needs of patients, employees, and visitors every day of the year. Monthly staffing and plans for food production are usually determined by the hospital administration on the basis of anticipated demands and its own experience and judgment. Generally, accounting for future staffing and demand is not considered in the monthly staffing and production plan.

A midwestern hospital affiliated with a university was selected to test the advantage of an aggregate planning procedure instead of the usual manual scheduling. Two different techniques for arriving at aggregate plans were also tested. The test was conducted through a computer simulation of daily demands for a period of one year, and the hospital's normal staffing and food costs were used.

The results of the simulation showed that an aggregate planning procedure would result in approximately 15 percent lower costs than the manual procedure. In the case being simulated, this would have reduced costs by $182,487 over the year (Connell, Adam, and Moore, 1984).

the three major personnel categories shown in Figure 11.2. The sum of the three categories gives the aggregate personnel needs.

In trying to determine a hiring schedule for next year, Sarah must make a judgment concerning whether the increased need for personnel is simply seasonal or, instead, represents permanent growth in the market. Essentially, will the number of drivers needed in the first quarter of the year following that shown in Figure 11.2 drop back to 10, or will it remain at 15? If the need will decrease, Sarah might want to use overtime, or temporary drivers and sorters, in quarters 3 and 4, for example. However, if the growth in demand is permanent, she may decide to hire permanent workers.

Suppose the average salary for Rap-X-Press is $5000 per quarter per employee, but the cost of lost sales, including goodwill, when there are insufficient employees is estimated to be $6000 per quarter per employee. The cost of using overtime in place of hiring a worker is $8000 per quarter. What would be the total annual cost for a level production strategy of 40 workers? What would be the cost for a chase demand strategy employing 30 workers? 40 workers?

Solution for Level Production

The analysis for the level production strategy at 40 workers is given in Figure 11.3. Two sets of costs are incurred: the cost of having excess workers in the first two periods (totaling $60,000), and the cost of being short in the last two periods (totaling $66,000), for a grand total over the year of $126,000. Note that if the level of starting workers is raised (to, say, 45) or lowered (to, say, 35), the two costs will change, giving a different total annual cost. Thus, with a level production strategy in a simplistic setting such as this, there may be an optimal number of employees to keep on the payroll.

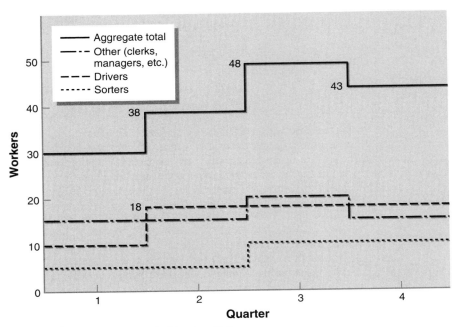

Figure 11.2   Personnel needed by Rap-X-Press.

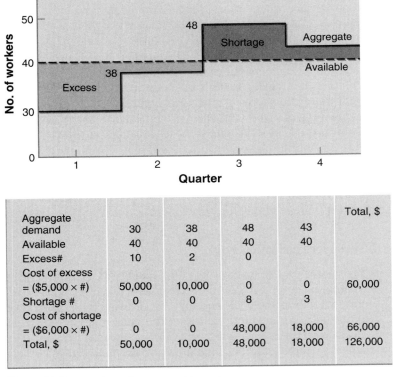

					Total, $
Aggregate demand	30	38	48	43	
Available	40	40	40	40	
Excess#	10	2	0		
Cost of excess = ($5,000 × #)	50,000	10,000	0	0	60,000
Shortage #	0	0	8	3	
Cost of shortage = ($6,000 × #)	0	0	48,000	18,000	66,000
Total, $	50,000	10,000	48,000	18,000	126,000

Figure 11.3   Level production at 40 workers.

Solution for Chase Demand

Table 11.1 gives the cost calculations for the chase demand strategy using overtime with 30 workers. As can be seen, there is no excess employee cost, but the overtime cost is overwhelming: $312,000 total for the year. In Table 11.2, overtime is used, assuming a starting workforce of 40. In this case, an excess employee cost is incurred, but the required overtime is so much less that the total cost for the year drops to $148,000. Although chase demand is a much better strategy with 40 workers than with 30, it is not as cheap as level production.

The point of all these calculations is to show the potential complexity of the problem. The best solution for any firm depends on the costs of overtime, shortage, ill will, excess staffing, hiring and layoffs (which were not considered here), and the other alternatives open to the firm (such as subcontracting). But the best solu-

$\mathcal{T}$ABLE 11.1 ❖ Cost of Chase Demand with 30 Workers

Quarter	1	2	3	4	Total $
Aggregate demand	30	38	48	43	
Available	30	30	30	30	
Overtime #	0	8	18	13	
Overtime cost = ($8,000 × #)	0	64,000	144,000	104,000	312,000

$\mathcal{T}$ABLE 11.2 ❖ Cost of Chase Demand with 40 Workers

Quarter	1	2	3	4	Total $
Aggregate demand	30	38	48	43	
Available	40	40	40	40	
Overtime #	0	0	8	3	
Overtime cost = ($8,000 × #)	0	0	64,000	24,000	88,000
Excess #	10	2	0	0	
Cost of excess = ($5,000 × #)	50,000	10,000	0	0	60,000
					148,000

tion depends not only on the set of costs facing a firm, but also on the expected (and actual) demand rates over the year, as illustrated in the sidebar on Ohio National Bank. Given the risk that demand forecasts may be in error, managers may choose a staffing strategy that is more expensive relative to the forecast in order to protect themselves against the risk of being in error (such as having inadequate staff to handle a potential explosion in demand).

OPERATIONS IN PRACTICE

Shift Scheduling at Ohio National Bank

In 1980, Ohio National Bank (ONB) was one of the largest banks in Ohio, employing 1800 people who provided a full range of banking services. (ONB is now integrated into BancOhio National Bank.) The management of ONB was seeking ways to better schedule its full and part-time encoders while reducing the number of unencoded checks at the end of each day. Existing methods of scheduling were unable to give an accurate estimate of either the number of encoders needed at any given time or the time when a set of encoders would finish the day's work. As a result, some checks went unencoded at the end of the workday, increasing the bank's float costs, or last-minute overtime was required to complete the encoding, which irritated the encoders, increased turnover and personnel costs, and reduced productivity and morale.

ONB's existing schedule consisted of 33 full-time encoders from 11 A.M. to 8 P.M., 2 part-time encoders from 12 noon to 5 P.M., and 2 more part-time encoders from 5 P.M. to 10 P.M. every day of the week. This fixed schedule did not accommodate variability in the volume of checks arriving, and the full-time encoders frequently had to work overtime to complete all the work. It was clearly necessary to do a better job of matching the workforce to the expected volumes.

This was done by designing a computer program to schedule the encoders' shifts. It consisted of two primary models. The first model used simple linear regression to predict expected hourly volumes on the basis of past data about arrivals by hour of the day, day of the week, day of the month, and month of the year. The second model used linear programming to determine the optimal number of full- and part-time encoders to schedule for each shift to minimize the sum of weekly regular-time wages, overtime wages, and float costs. The major data required for this second model are definitions of shifts, volumes of checks, encoder productivities, costs, number of encoding machines, and any limits on the number of encoders and the amount of overtime. The output consisted of three reports: shift assignments, hourly clerks on hand, and the costs of the schedule.

The general solution for ONB was to use 2 full-time encoders from 11 A.M. to 8 P.M. and 33 part-time encoders from 1 to 6 P.M. all week, plus 27 part-time encoders from 6 to 10 P.M. on Mondays, Tuesdays, and Fridays. This schedule was estimated to save ONB almost $80,000 per year. Regular use of the program indicated that the encoding was completed by 10 P.M. about 98 percent of the time, whereas it had rarely been achieved in the past. Moreover, unexpected overtime and poorly defined work schedules ceased to be a significant cause of turnover (Krajewski and Ritzman, 1980).

❖ Aggregate Planning for Product Firms

The major difference between aggregate planning for a product firm and a service firm is that the product firm can stock inventory ahead of anticipated demand, thereby allowing production at a constant, or near-constant, rate with a level workforce. As a result, the costs of producing for a seasonal market with a given strategy, such as a level workforce, may also depend on when a product firm enters the market. That is, if the firm enters a seasonal market during the off-season, when demand is low, it can store inventories (at a cost) to meet the later, peak-demand season. But if it enters the market in the peak-demand season, it may have to backlog the demand (at the cost of ill will, expediting, or lost market share) and make it up later during the off-season. The best strategy to use in such a case will depend on the costs of storing inventory compared with the costs of back-ordering or lost sales.

𝒮OLVED EXERCISE 11.1 ❖ Aggregate Labor Force Planning

A service firm faces demands of 40, 50, 30, and 20 services per quarter and costs of $4000 in wages per quarter per employee (each of whom can produce 5 services a quarter), $1000 per lost service, and $800 per service produced on overtime. Determine the annual cost of a level production strategy based on average demand and a chase demand strategy with the same number of employees.

Solution:

Construct a table of demand, production, and costs as shown below. The level strategy must provide $(40 + 50 + 30 + 20)/4 = 35$ services a quarter, requiring $35/5 = 7$ employees. The result is shown in the table. However, since the services cannot be stored, they are lost when demand exceeds capacity. And when demand doesn't meet capacity, the resources sit idle. The lost demand could be captured with more workers (3), but they would cost another $12,000 per quarter. The chase strategy is also shown and, in this case, is cheaper.

Quarter	1	2	3	4	Total, $
Demand	40	50	30	20	
Level production: 7 *workers*					
Available	35	35	35	35	
Lost demand	5	15	0	0	
Cost, $	5000	15,000	0	0	20,000
Wages, $	28,000	28,000	28,000	28,000	112,000
Sum:					132,000
Chase demand: 7 *workers*					
Regular available	35	35	35	35	
Overtime	5	15	0	0	
Overtime cost,	$4000	12,000	0	0	16,000
Wages,	$28,000	28,000	28,000	28,000	112,000
Sum:					128,000

Another possible strategy for a product firm is to use one strategy to move the firm to another point in the seasonal cycle, where it can use a different strategy. For example, a firm may use overtime or subcontracting if it enters a market during the peak season, and then move to a level production strategy of storing inventories beginning with the off-season.

❖ Example: Aggregate Planning at Precision Products

Precision Products makes a variety of complex, highly engineered wastewater pumps. Sales forecasts for individual models have been aggregated and are given, along with other important data, as follows.

Quarterly demand forecasts are 400, 600, 300, and 100, with this pattern repeating itself in the future as far as can be foreseen. The current workforce is 30, and each worker can produce 10 units per quarter, which is typical of this industry. Inventory costs are $100 per unit per quarter, whereas shortage costs for expediting backorders are $130 per unit per quarter. Hiring and layoff have each been estimated to cost $1000 per worker, but idle workers effectively cost $1500 per quarter. The cost of producing units on overtime is an additional $150 each.

Find the best aggregate plan if all demand must be met, either immediately or through back orders. Assume that no initial inventory exists, and consider only the incremental costs listed here. (Note that idle time is charged as a cost, since no revenues or wages are considered.)

Solution for Level Production

Figure 11.4, top, shows the aggregate demand not just over this coming year but, for illustrative purposes, for two years (eight quarters). If Precision Products wants to use a level production strategy and this demand cycle is expected to keep repeating, it should produce at a quarterly rate of one-fourth the total annual demand:

$$(400 + 600 + 300 + 100)/4 = 350 \text{ units}$$

Producing more than this amount would continue to build up unneeded inventory; producing less would lead to a continuing shortage and backlog.

This production rate of 350 units per quarter is also shown in Figure 11.4, top. The portions above 350 are demand backlogs, and the portions below 350 are periods when the backlog is being worked off. Figure 11.4, middle, shows the inventory or backlog situation (backlog, in this case) for Precision Products. The calculations below this chart show what the cost of the strategy would be if overtime (rather than hiring) was used to make up the 50-unit difference between what the workers can normally produce (30 × 10 = 300 units) and the 350 units that the level production strategy calls for. As can be seen, the total annual cost of this strategy for Precision Products is $108,000.

To see the effect of entering the market at a different time, consider Figure 11.5, in which Precision Products is assumed to enter at the start of quarter 3. Now, rather than always running with a backlog situation (as in Figure 11.4, except for quarters 4 and 8, when it finally caught up), it is running with inventories. The total cost of this strategy is also different: $90,000, which is considerably less than the previous costs.

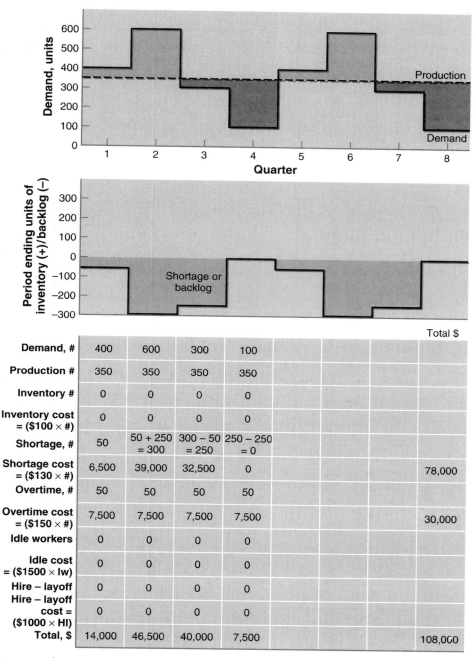

Figure 11.4   Level production starting in quarter 1.

Solution for Chase Production

Let us next consider the pure strategy of chase demand. In this case the production rate is identical to the demand rate, as shown in Figure 11.6, and there are neither shortages nor inventories. But how Precision Products attains the production schedule shown has not yet been determined. Figure 11.6 shows the costs if it uses over-

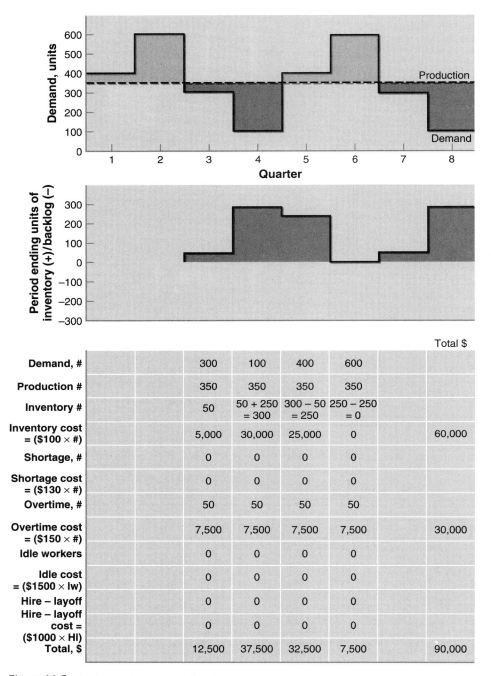

			Demand, #	300	100	400	600		Total $
			Production #	350	350	350	350		
			Inventory #	50	50 + 250 = 300	300 − 50 = 250	250 − 250 = 0		
			Inventory cost = ($100 × #)	5,000	30,000	25,000	0		60,000
			Shortage, #	0	0	0	0		
			Shortage cost = ($130 × #)	0	0	0	0		
			Overtime, #	50	50	50	50		
			Overtime cost = ($150 × #)	7,500	7,500	7,500	7,500		30,000
			Idle workers	0	0	0	0		
			Idle cost = ($1500 × Iw)	0	0	0	0		
			Hire − layoff	0	0	0	0		
			Hire − layoff cost = ($1000 × HI)	0	0	0	0		
			Total, $	12,500	37,500	32,500	7,500		90,000

Figure 11.5   Level production starting in quarter 3.

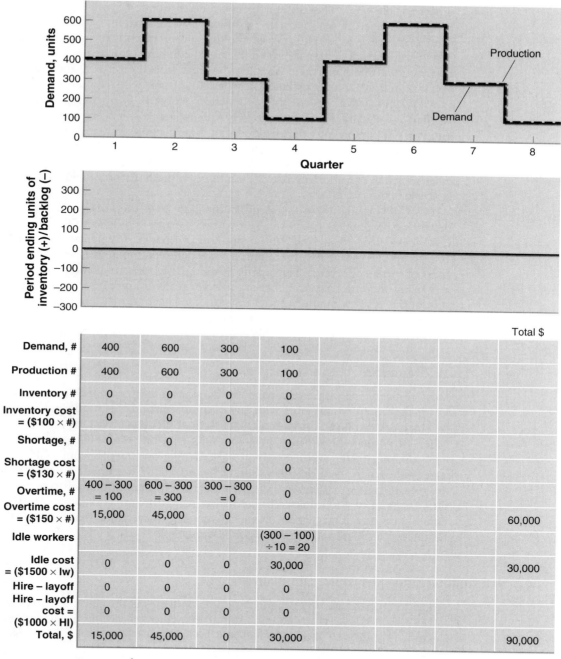

Figure 11.6 Chase demand with overtime and idle time.

time and idle time. The amount of overtime in quarter 1 will be 400 units actual production less the 300 normally produced, for an overtime amount of 100 units, each at a cost of $150. The cost of idle time in quarter 4 is the usual production of 300 less the actual of 100, for 200 units not needed. At 10 units per worker, this represents 20 workers who will be idle. The total annual cost is $90,000, which is no better than the last level production schedule, but no worse either.

Another way to achieve this production schedule is by hiring and laying off workers seasonally. (This alternative is uncommon in countries where job security and workers' involvement are valued, but it is still used in many places.) The costs of this production schedule are shown in Figure 11.7. Summing the first four quarters results in a total cost of $10,000 + 20,000 + 30,000 + 20,000 = 80,000 for the first year, which is considerably better than the two previous production schedules that cost $90,000.

But is this really a good strategy, particularly over the long term? Look again at the hiring program in quarter 1. Ten workers are to be added to the current 30, to reach a level of 40 in total. But at the end of quarter 4, when production is only 100, there are only 10 workers left, a very different situation going into quarter 5 (start of the second year). For quarter 5, then, 30 workers must be hired, not 10. On a regular, ongoing basis the annual costs are really going to be represented by the sum of the costs of quarters 2 to 5 instead of 1 to 4, and this sum totals $100,000, or $10,000 worse than the two previous production schedules and fully $20,000 worse than we first calculated. Thus, this is probably not the best production strategy.

Mixed Strategies

Most firms use a combination of production strategies to achieve considerably lower costs than are possible with any of the pure strategies used singly. In the case of Precision Products, a better strategy than any considered thus far is to hire another 10 permanent workers, which results in a one-time charge of $10,000 and adds nothing to the normal annual cost. (Hiring and layoffs contribute to annual costs only when used on a continuing basis.) Then, 400 units of level production are run for three quarters, and 200 units are run in the last quarter to match the annual demand of 1400 units. The annual costs of this mixed strategy are shown in Figure 11.8 and total $69,000, which is considerably better than any of the pure strategies. Yet there may be even better strategies.

❖ Determining Strategies with a Cumulative Graph

One way to help identify potentially good strategies is through the use of a cumulative graph. Unlike a bar chart, a cumulative graph shows total demand and production to date and thus automatically identifies any accumulated inventories as well as accumulated shortages.

Figure 11.9 shows an example for the earlier level production strategy of producing 350 units per quarter (Figure 11.4). Actual demand is plotted as the top line and the level production strategy as the straight line. Notice that the annual cycle starts and finishes the year with no inventories or backlogs. (This *must* be the case, since we determined the quarterly production rate of 350 units by totaling annual demand and dividing by 4.) If a chase demand production plan were to be plotted on the cumulative graph, it would of course fall directly on top of actual demand.

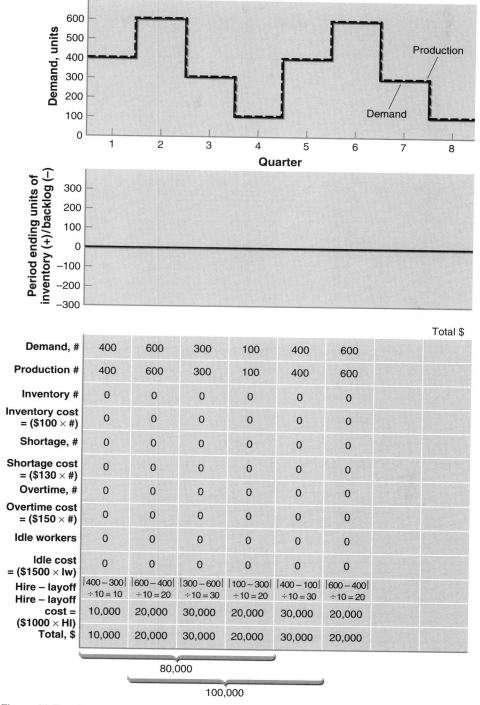

Figure 11.7   Chase demand with hiring and layoffs.

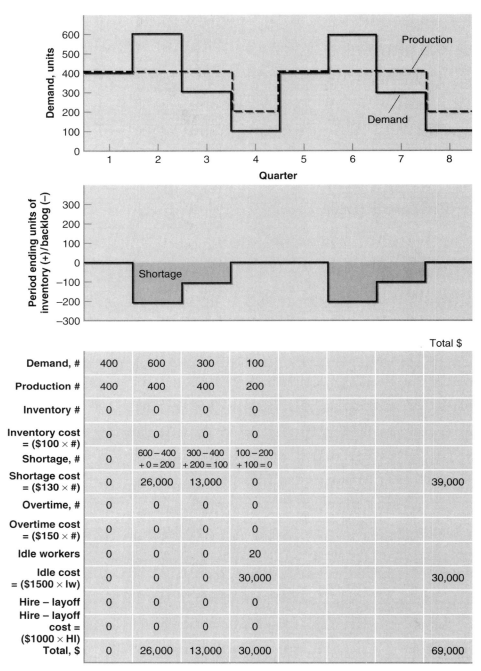

									Total $
Demand, #	400	600	300	100					
Production #	400	400	400	200					
Inventory #	0	0	0	0					
Inventory cost = ($100 × #)	0	0	0	0					
Shortage, #	0	600 − 400 + 0 = 200	300 − 400 + 200 = 100	100 − 200 + 100 = 0					
Shortage cost = ($130 × #)	0	26,000	13,000	0					39,000
Overtime, #	0	0	0	0					
Overtime cost = ($150 × #)	0	0	0	0					
Idle workers	0	0	0	20					
Idle cost = ($1500 × lw)	0	0	0	30,000					30,000
Hire − layoff	0	0	0	0					
Hire − layoff cost = ($1000 × HI)	0	0	0	0					
Total, $	0	26,000	13,000	30,000					69,000

Figure 11.8   Aggregate scheduling with a mixed strategy.

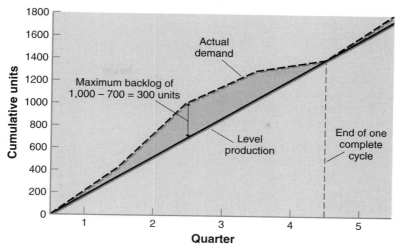

Figure 11.9 Cumulative demand and production for level production of 350 units per quarter.

$\mathscr{S}$OLVED EXERCISE 11.2 ❖ Aggregate Planning for Products

Use the same data as in Solved Exercise 11.1 but assume that *parts* are being produced instead of services, shortage costs are per quarter until filled, storage cost is $500 per quarter, and the cost of hiring and layoffs is $1000 per person. Find the cost of a level production strategy that exactly meets demand (start with the first quarter), a chase demand strategy through hiring and layoffs, and a mixed strategy with one change in production level and hiring during the year.

Solution:

The three strategies are shown in the table below. For the mixed strategy, we chose two levels of workers, augmented by storage and shortages.

Quarter	1	2	3	4	Total, $
Demand	40	50	30	20	
Level production: 7 workers					
Production	35	35	35	35	
Shortage	5	5 + 15 = 20	20 − 5 = 15	15 − 15 = 0	
Shortage cost, $	5000	20,000	15,000	0	40,000
Wages, $	28,000	28,000	28,000	28,000	112,000
Sum:					152,000
Chase demand: Hiring and layoffs					
Production	40	50	30	20	
Workers	8	10	6	4	
Hire-layoff cost					
(start with 4), $1000	|8 − 4| = 4	|10 − 8| = 2	|6 − 10| = 4	|4 − 6| = 2	12,000
Wages, $	32,000	40,000	24,000	16,000	112,000
Sum:					124,000

Quarter	1	2	3	4	Total, $
Mixed strategy					
Production	45	45	25	25	
Workers	9	9	5	5	
Wages, $	36,000	36,000	20,000	20,000	112,000
Hire-layoff cost (start with 5), $1000	$\lvert 5-9 \rvert = 4$	$\lvert 9-9 \rvert = 0$	$\lvert 9-5 \rvert = 4$	$\lvert 5-5 \rvert = 0$	8,000
Storage, $	$5 \times 500 = 2500$	0	0	0	2,500
Shortage, $	0	0	$5 \times 1000 = 5000$	0	5,000
Sum:					127,000

$\mathscr{S}$OLVED EXERCISE 11.3 ❖ Using the Cumulative Graph

Use the same data as in Solved Exercise 11.2. Graph the mixed-strategy solution found in that problem. Find and graph a level production strategy that starts with an inventory of 10 parts but ends with no inventory or backorders. Do the same for a strategy that starts with no inventory but ends with 20 parts.

Solution:

The mixed strategy is shown in the graph. Level production with an initial inventory of 10 parts would be $(40 + 50 + 30 + 20 - 10)/4 = 32.5$. Level production that ends with 20 parts would be $(40 + 50 + 30 + 20 + 20)/4 = 40$. All these strategies are shown in the graph.

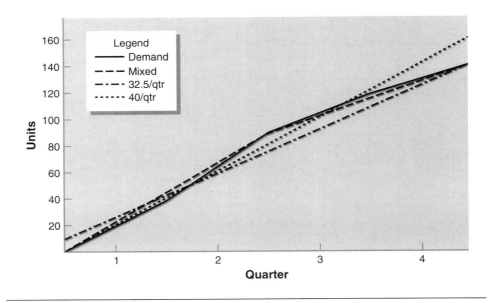

Figure 11.10 illustrates the fact that every level production strategy will be a straight line on the cumulative graph. If production is *above* actual demand, then the space between these two lines represents inventories; if it is *below* the actual demand, then the space between the lines represents shortages. The production plan shown by the upper line is too high and will continue to accumulate excess inventory; the plan shown by the lower line will continue to accumulate shortages.

Both level production plans shown in Figure 11.10 started at the origin (no beginning inventories or shortages). But if there had been some initial inventory—say, 200 units—the level production lines would have started at 200 instead of 0. To end the cycle with no inventories or shortages, the lines would have to just touch the actual demand curve at the end of quarter 4, as in Figure 11.9. And, of course, if an ending inventory or shortage is desired, the straight production line should end above the actual demand line or below it, respectively, by the appropriate amount.

Figure 11.11 illustrates the mixed strategy of Figure 11.8. Notice the straight line for the level production strategy (produce 400 units per quarter) used for the first three quarters and then the bend as the plan changes to 200 units in quarter 4. By using a cumulative graph, it is possible to see the costs of inventory and shortage and thereby look for solutions that might minimize them. Bends in the production curves usually indicate costs of idle time, overtime, or hiring and layoffs and should generally be avoided, if possible.

Note the difficulty of even this simple problem: constant demands (from year to year), clear-cut costs, and limited strategies—and all for only a single aggregate product. Obviously, real aggregate production planning is much more complex. Note also that the layout of Figures 11.3 to 11.8 makes the analysis of aggregate scheduling particularly amenable to being modeled with spreadsheets, as will be demonstrated. With spreadsheets, long-range forecasts can be easily input, and different policies can be tested. Changes in costs can also be quickly tested to see their effect.

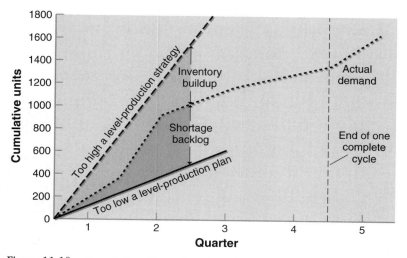

Figure 11.10   Cumulative demand and production for two level-production strategies.

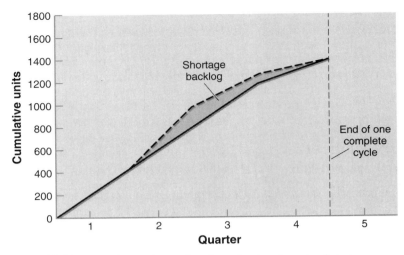

Figure 11.11   Cumulative demand and production for mixed strategy.

Spreadsheet Analysis: Aggregate Planning

In this example, we refer again to Precision Products to illustrate how spreadsheets can be used to facilitate aggregate planning. Specifically, we will demonstrate how the ability of a spreadsheet to quickly update itself greatly facilitates the task of developing aggregate plans using the familiar trial-and-error approach. We will also demonstrate how built-in spreadsheet capabilities can be used to find the optimal aggregate plan subject to the criteria and constraints we specify. Finally, we will show how spreadsheets can be used to quickly develop the cumulative graphs of demand and production as additional aids in evaluating the aggregate plan being developed.

Recall that the demand forecasts for Precision Products for the next four quarters are 400, 500, 300, and 100. The current workforce consists of 30 workers, and each worker can produce 10 units per quarter. Inventory costs are $100/unit/quarter and backorder costs are $130/unit/quarter. The cost of hiring or laying off a worker is $1000. Finally, producing a unit on overtime adds an additional $150 to the cost. In this discussion, we will ignore costs of idle time.

The spreadsheet shown below was developed to help Precision formulate and evaluate alternative aggregate plans. A level strategy is shown, with 30 workers and 50 units produced on overtime. The cost of this aggregate plan is $108,000 (the same as Figure 11.4).

	A	B	C	D	E	F	G
1	**Level production with 30 workers and 50 units of overtime**						
2	Quarter	0	1	2	3	4	Total
3	Demand		400	600	300	100	1400
4	Workers	30	30	30	30	30	
5	Regular production		300	300	300	300	1200
6	Overtime production		50	50	50	50	200
7	Total production		350	350	350	350	
8	Total prod. - demand		-50	-250	50	250	0
9	Inventory	0	0	0	0	0	
10	Backorders	0	50	300	250	0	
11	Hired workers		0	0	0	0	
12	Fired workers		0	0	0	0	
13	Overtime cost		$7,500	$7,500	$7,500	$7,500	$30,000
14	Inventory cost		$0	$0	$0	$0	$0
15	Backorder cost		$6,500	$39,000	$32,500	$0	$78,000
16	Hire/fire cost		$0	$0	$0	$0	$0
17	**Total cost**		**$14,000**	**$46,500**	**$40,000**	**$7,500**	**$108,000**

Row 2 of the spreadsheet has labels (numbers) for the quarters. Note that column B corresponds to quarter zero to keep track of initial conditions such as the beginning number of workers and the initial levels of inventory and backorders.

The demand for each quarter is entered in row 3. Row 4 is filled in by the aggregate planner and corresponds to the number of workers who will be used in a given quarter. Row 5 contains a formula that calculates the amount of regular-time production based on the number of workers entered in row 4. Since each worker produces 10 units per quarter, the following formula was entered in cell C5:

$$=C4*10$$

This formula was then copied to cells D5:F5. (*Note:* In the ensuing discussion all formulas entered in column C can be copied to columns D, E, and F. Thus we will discuss only the formula in column C and assume that once entered, it is copied to columns D–F unless something else is indicated.)

The values for overtime production (in units) are entered by the aggregate planner in row 6. Thus the development of an aggregate plan requires that only the values for rows 4 and 6 be entered by the planner. As you will see, all the other information in the spreadsheet is calculated on the basis of the values entered in rows 4 and 6.

In row 7, total production for a particular quarter (i.e., the sum of regular time and overtime production) is computed. To illustrate, in cell C7 the following formula was entered:

$$=C5+C6$$

In row 8, the amount that total production in a given quarter exceeds or falls below the demand for the quarter is calculated. In cell C8, =C7–C3 was entered.

In row 9 the ending inventory level for each quarter is computed. Note that ending inventory cannot be negative (i.e., it is not possible to have negative inventory). Therefore, the logic used to calculate ending inventory is as follows: If the amount of total production plus beginning inventory less demand and beginning backorders is greater than zero, then ending inventory equals total production plus beginning inventory less demand and beginning backorders. Otherwise, ending inventory equals zero. One way to include this logic in a formula is to use Excel's IF function. The syntax of the IF function is: =IF(condition, value returned if the condition is true, value returned if the condition is false). Thus, the IF function requires three parameters: (1) a condition that can be either true or false, (2) the result returned by the function if the condition is true, and (3) the result returned by the function if the condition is false. On the basis of this logic, the following formula was entered in cell C9:

$$=IF(C8+B9-B10>0,C8+B9-B10,0)$$

In English, this formula says that if the amount that total production exceeds or falls below demand (C8) plus the beginning inventory (B9) minus beginning backorders (B10) is greater than zero, then ending inventory is equal to the amount that total production exceeds or falls below demand (C8) plus the beginning inventory (B9) minus beginning backorders (B10). If the condition is false, then ending inventory is equal to zero. An alternative way to capture this same logic is to enter the following formula in cell C9:

$$=MAX(C8+B9-B10,0)$$

This formula returns the maximum of two values: C8+B9−B10 or zero.

Ending backorders are calculated in row 10. Like ending inventory, this cannot be negative. Since backorders are kind of the reverse of inventory (i.e., a negative inventory would represent positive backorders and vice versa), the formula for calculating the ending backorders is the reverse of the formula used to calculate ending inventory. Specifically, to calculate the ending level of backorders in quarter 1, the following formula was entered in cell C10:

$$=IF(B10-C8-B9>0,B10-C8-B9,0)$$

Equivalently, the formula =MAX(B10−C8−B9,0) could have been entered in cell C10.

In cell C11, the number of workers hired in quarter 1 is calculated as follows:

$$=IF(C4>B4,C4-B4,0)$$

Equivalently, =MAX(C4−B4,0) could have been entered in cell C11. Likewise, in cell C12 the number of workers fired in quarter 1 is calculated. Either of the following formulas could be entered in cell C12:

$$=IF(B4>C4,B4-C4,0)$$
$$=MAX(B4-C4,0)$$

In rows 13 through 16, respectively, the costs of overtime, inventory, back-orders, and hiring or layoffs are calculated. Since each unit produced using overtime costs an extra $150, =C6*150 was entered in cell C13. The inventory carrying cost is $100/unit/quarter and the backorder cost is $130/unit/quarter. Thus, the following formulas were entered in cells C14 and C15, respectively:

$$C14: = C9*100$$
$$C15: = C10*130$$

The cost of hiring or laying off was given as $1000 per worker. Thus, =(C11+C12)*1000 was entered in cell C16. Finally, to compute the total cost for quarter 1, the following formula was entered in cell C17:

$$=SUM(C13:C16)$$

Two other cells are worth pointing out. Cell G8 contains the amount that total production exceeds or falls below demand over the entire 4 quarters. In cell G8, =SUM(C8:F8) was entered. Cell G17 calculates the total cost of the aggregate plan over the 4 quarters. In cell G17, =SUM(C17:F17) was entered.

Once this spreadsheet is developed, it can be used to quickly develop and test other aggregate plans. For example, in the aggregate plan we originally developed, 50 units are produced each quarter, using overtime. Since overtime is more expensive than both inventory and backorders, it might be worthwhile investigating other aggregate plans that use less overtime. For example, instead of using overtime, suppose we hire 5 workers in the first quarter. To investigate this, we simply change the values in cells C4:F4 from 30 to 35 and the values in cells C6:F6 from 50 to 0. The results of making these changes are shown in the spreadsheet below.

	A	B	C	D	E	F	G	H
1	Level production with 35 workers and no overtime							
2	Quarter	0	1	2	3	4	Total	
3	Demand		400	600	300	100	1400	
4	Workers	30	35	35	35	35		
5	Regular production		350	350	350	350	1400	
6	Overtime production		0	0	0	0	0	
7	Total production		350	350	350	350		
8	Total prod. - demand		-50	-250	50	250	0	
9	Inventory	0	0	0	0	0		
10	Backorders	0	50	300	250	0		
11	Hired workers		5	0	0	0		
12	Fired workers		0	0	0	0		
13	Overtime cost		$0	$0	$0	$0	$0	
14	Inventory cost		$0	$0	$0	$0	$0	
15	Backorder cost		$6,500	$39,000	$32,500	$0	$78,000	
16	Hire/fire cost		$5,000	$0	$0	$0	$5,000	
17	Total cost		$11,500	$39,000	$32,500	$0	$83,000	

Making this change proved to be advantageous. In this case, total costs were reduced from $108,000 to $83,000.

Now let's investigate a chase strategy by hiring and laying off workers. As the spreadsheet below shows, this approach yields a total cost of $80,000, making it the lowest-cost aggregate plan developed so far. Note also that this is the same cost we computed in Figure 11.7.

	A	B	C	D	E	F	G
1	Chase production with hiring and layoff						
2	Quarter	0	1	2	3	4	Total
3	Demand		400	600	300	100	1400
4	Workers	30	40	60	30	10	
5	Regular production		400	600	300	100	1400
6	Overtime production		0	0	0	0	0
7	Total production		400	600	300	100	
8	Total prod. - demand		0	0	0	0	0
9	Inventory	0	0	0	0	0	
10	Backorders	0	0	0	0	0	
11	Hired workers		10	20	0	0	
12	Fired workers		0	0	30	20	
13	Overtime cost		$0	$0	$0	$0	$0
14	Inventory cost		$0	$0	$0	$0	$0
15	Backorder cost		$0	$0	$0	$0	$0
16	Hire/fire cost		$10,000	$20,000	$30,000	$20,000	$80,000
17	Total cost		$10,000	$20,000	$30,000	$20,000	$80,000

Similarly, we can investigate a wide variety of alternative aggregate plans simply by changing the values we enter in rows 4 and 6. Furthermore, we could include other options for meeting demand in the model, such as part-time workers or subcontracting. However, including additional options increases the complexity of the model. As the complexity of the model increases, finding good solutions based on the trial-and-error approach also becomes more difficult. One option is to use Excel's built-in optimization capabilities to find an optimal (i.e., lowest-cost) aggregate plan subject to the criteria and limitations we specify. Even if we don't like everything about the "optimal" solution, at least it provides a good starting point and provides an indication of the penalty (in terms of increased cost) of adopting some other aggregate plan.

In this example, our objective is to choose the number of workers and the amount of overtime production for each quarter so that the total cost over the four quarters is minimized. The most important constraint is that by the end of the fourth quarter, all demand must be met. Also, we want to ensure that the number of workers and the amount of overtime in all periods are greater than or equal to zero. A solution with a negative number of workers or a negative amount of overtime does not make sense. Finally, we are interested only in solutions with integer values for the number of workers and the amount of overtime, since we cannot hire or lay off a fraction of a worker, nor can we produce a fraction of a unit on overtime.

To find the optimal aggregate plan, we will use Excel's Solver by selecting Tools from the menu bar at the top of the screen and then selecting Solver from the Tools menu. After we select Solver, the Solver Parameters' dialog box is displayed. In the Set Target Cell box, we enter the address of the cell that contains the formula we want to optimize. In this case we want to minimize the value of cell G17. Thus, we enter G17 in the Set Target Cell box (either by typing it in directly or by clicking on cell G17 with the mouse) and then click on the Min radio button, since we want to minimize the value of cell G17. Next, we tell Excel which values it can change to minimize total costs (cell G17). The cells that can be changed are C4:F4 and C6:F6. Thus we enter C4:F4,C6:F6 in the By Changing Cells: box.

Next we click on the Add . . . button in the Subject to the Constraints: section, to begin adding the constraints. We will first add the constraint that all demand is met by the fourth quarter. Recall that cell G8 calculates the amount that total production exceeds or falls below total demand over the four quarters. To ensure that we produce exactly the amount demanded, we need the constraint: G8=0. We enter this constraint in the Add Constraint dialog box as shown below.

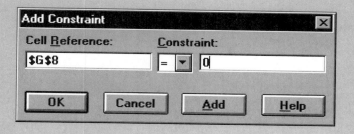

After this information is entered, select the Add button to add additional constraints. The constraints that you need to enter are listed below. The constraints to ensure that the number of workers in any quarter is greater than or equal to zero are as follows:

$$C4 \geq 0$$
$$D4 \geq 0$$
$$E4 \geq 0$$
$$F4 \geq 0$$

Alternatively, as a shortcut we could simply enter these constraints as: C4:F4$\geq$0.

The constraints to ensure that overtime production in any quarter is greater than or equal to zero are as follows:

$$C6 \geq 0$$
$$D6 \geq 0$$
$$E6 \geq 0$$
$$F6 \geq 0$$

or, equivalently, C6:F6$\geq$0.

Finally, to ensure that the solution contains only integer values for number of workers and amount of overtime, add constraints for each of the above cells by selecting "int" in the middle box. Note that when "int" is selected in the middle box, "integer" is automatically entered in the last box. Thus, you want to add the following constraints:

C4 int integer
D4 int integer
E4 int integer
F4 int integer
C6 int integer
D6 int integer
E6 int integer
F6 int integer

or C4:F4 int integer and C6:F6 int integer.

After entering F6 int integer, select OK instead of Add to tell Excel this is the last constraint you wish to enter. The Solver Parameters dialog box now looks as follows:

Note that in the Solver Parameters dialog box all cell addresses are shown as absolute cell references even if you entered them as relative cell references. From the Solver Parameters dialog box, select Solve to find the optimal solution. When Excel finishes its calculations and has found the optimal solution, the Solver Results dialog box is displayed.

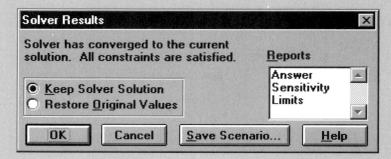

Select OK from the Solver Results dialog box to keep and display the solution found by Excel's Solver. The solution found using Excel's Solver is shown below:

	A	B	C	D	E	F	G
1	Hybrid solution developed using Excel's Solver						
2	Quarter	0	1	2	3	4	Total
3	Demand		400	600	300	100	1400
4	Workers	30	40	40	40	20	
5	Regular production		400	400	400	200	1400
6	Overtime production		0	0	0	0	0
7	Total production		400	400	400	200	
8	Total prod. - demand		0	-200	100	100	0
9	Inventory	0	0	0	0	0	
10	Backorders	0	0	200	100	0	
11	Hired workers		10	0	0	0	
12	Fired workers		0	0	0	20	
13	Overtime cost		$0	$0	$0	$0	$0
14	Inventory cost		$0	$0	$0	$0	$0
15	Backorder cost		$0	$26,000	$13,000	$0	$39,000
16	Hire/fire cost		$10,000	$0	$0	$20,000	$30,000
17	Total cost		$10,000	$26,000	$13,000	$20,000	$69,000

Excel's Solver solution has the lowest total cost of any solution found thus far. The table below summarizes the solutions evaluated in this example.

Costs	First Level Schedule	Second Level Schedule	Chase Schedule	Excel Solver Schedule
Overtime	30,000	0	0	0
Inventory	0	0	0	0
Backorder	78,000	78,000	0	39,000
Hire/fire	0	5,000	80,000	30,000
Total	108,000	83,000	80,000	69,000

Finally, note that spreadsheets can be used to quickly develop plots of cumulative demand and cumulative production. The plot shown below was developed using Excel's ChartWizard for the first level strategy evaluated.

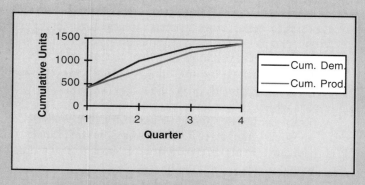

Note that plots developed from data in a spreadsheet are automatically updated as the spreadsheet is updated. Thus, once the ranges for the data lines are specified, new plots corresponding to new aggregate plans are automatically developed.

M ASTER SCHEDULING _____

As briefly described earlier, aggregate planning leads to the firm's production plan. Disaggregating the production plan into individual end items results in the master production schedule (MPS), as illustrated in the sidebar on Dow Corning. The master production schedule shows how many of what end items (or assemblies, in the case of a make-to-order firm) to produce when. If the production plan is stated, as it sometimes is, in dollars or pounds or some other such measure, it will have to be converted into units of production in the MPS.

Because it is the final word about what the company will actually build and when, the MPS also acts as upper management's "handle" on the production system. By altering the MPS, management can alter inventory levels, lead times, capacity demands, and so on. Such power is a two-edged sword, however. If management attempts to overload the MPS in order to produce more output than can realistically be made (this is called "lying to the master schedule"), the shop will jam up with work to be done and will not get anything out. In creating the MPS, limits on capacity must be carefully observed; they cannot be ignored by using a master schedule that is only top management's "wish list."

In the traditional functional organization, the main players in creating the master schedule are sales and operations, each representing one of two primary objectives of master scheduling:

1. ***Sales:*** To schedule finished goods to meet delivery needs.
2. ***Operations:*** To maintain efficient utilization of work centers by not overloading or underloading them.

If these objectives cannot be met—because of, say, a capacity limitation in a work center—then the production plan may have to be revised.

In addition to limiting work to what can realistically be done, the MPS also includes other functions. First, it buffers the forecast by "smoothing" demand over time, reducing capacity-constrained peaks, and raising low-demand idle periods. It also subtracts existing inventories of products from the forecasts so that the shop doesn't make products that already exist in inventory. And it "batches" demands over time into convenient and economical groups for production so that scarce facilities and equipment aren't wasted.

As noted earlier, the MPS is based both on firm orders, received through salespersons or directly from the customer, and on end item forecasts of future demand for which orders have not yet been received. In addition to the forecast demands, extra demands, such as demand for spares and parts, are added to the MPS. Then these requirements are all summed by the delivery time period to make up the total demand facing the organization over the planning horizon. As more firm orders come in, they continue to replace or "consume" the forecasted orders, as shown in Figure 11.12. The items still remaining in the forecast that have not been replaced by firm orders are considered *available to promise* by sales.

The MPS is usually stated in terms of weekly periods, or *buckets,* as they are called. Some firms use days, and some even use hours. Nevertheless, the disaggregation of the quarterly, or monthly, production plan into MPS buckets is still the same. The planning horizon may extend for a year or more, but it must extend at least as long as the longest lead time item in the product. Otherwise, the demands

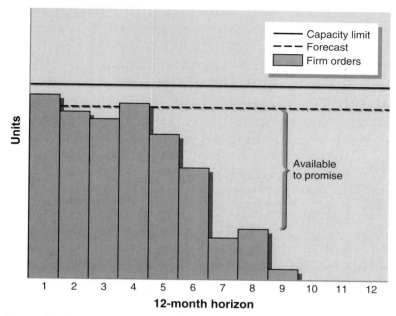

Figure 11.12 Orders replacing the forecast in the master schedule.

cannot be placed on the schedule. For example, if you maintained a 12-month MPS and had a component that took 15 months to obtain, you wouldn't be able to schedule the delivery of orders taken today (and due to be delivered in 16 months or so).

In some situations (such as make-to-order firms), final products are assembled to order from existing components, modules, or assemblies that have been produced at some earlier time. That is, the assemblies are produced to stock and scheduled on the MPS, but the final products are produced to order and scheduled on a separate final assembly schedule. This is shown in Figure 11.13. Note that the final demands total to the MPS, but the specific *combination* of components was unknown until the actual orders arrived. Automobiles, some computers, and prefabricated homes are made this way. And some restaurants prepare meals in this way, to meet peak demand periods with only one cook or only a few workers.

An MPS is needed for both job shops and flow shops, although the detailed issues of scheduling are different (see Chapter 15). That is, both require a production schedule that satisfies customers' demands but doesn't exceed the limits of capacity. Nevertheless, just because aggregate capacity may be satisfied for a workstation or facility, certain scheduling aspects may limit the use of that capacity and thereby pose another problem for the MPS, if not the entire production plan. We will discuss these kinds of problems in Chapter 15.

Although we appear to discuss master scheduling as a static process, in reality it is very dynamic, changing continually and being reworked weekly. It is best visualized as a rolling schedule that is replanned every week, the previous week being deleted and a new week being added at the end of the planning horizon.

The MPS itself includes four separate periods in the planning horizon that serve four unique purposes, as shown in Figure 11.14. First, there is usually an immediately upcoming *frozen* period, delineated by a *time fence,* during which orders can

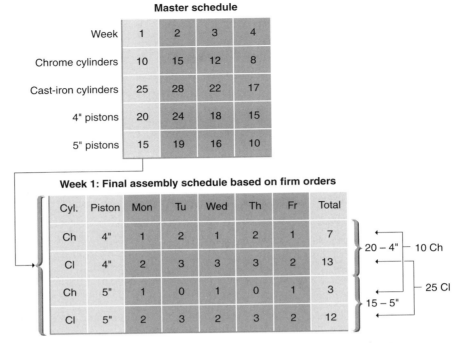

Figure 11.13   Master and final assembly schedules: custom pumps division.

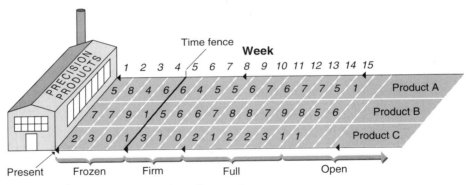

Figure 11.14   Four periods in the rolling MPS.

no longer be changed because critical subcomponents have already been ordered, produced, or installed. This frozen period is usually stated as one month because many products are assembled in the last two or three weeks before delivery. Up until assembly, the components are still being made in the shop, and changes may still be possible in their manufacture or assembly.

Following this time is a *firm* period of just a few weeks when changes may be taken, but only if they are exceptional. These changes may require approval from a senior manager. The next period is called *full* because the forecast has been fully consumed, so no more orders can be taken. However, changes may be taken in existing orders. Last is the *open* period, when there are still items available to promise.

Master Scheduling at Dow Corning

Dow Corning is a large multinational chemical company headquartered in Michigan, with sales of more than $2.2 billion. It ranked 500th on 1994's *Fortune 500*, 458th in net income, and 460th in return on sales. Dow Corning manufactures more than 4000 silicone-based products.

Corning's production planning is initiated from both short- and long-range forecasts of 23 separate entities, which are disaggregated into about 200 separate families that include the 4000-plus products. The production plans for the families are then developed jointly by the corresponding marketing managers, the director of materials management, and the appropriate plant managers. These production plans, however, are only by quarters and extend for the next five quarters into the future.

The master schedule then disaggregates the production plan into weekly time periods for each of the products, but it is limited to only the next 26 weeks. From this detailed schedule of what the plants are to actually make, 12 master schedulers are responsible for implementing the schedule. Of course, the schedule is always subject to change, owing to cancellations and changes by the customers, so these must also be accommodated (Walter, 1986).

❖ Constructing a Master Production Schedule

The data needed to construct an MPS are the production plan (items, quantities, due dates) and production capacities (by period, less planned downtime for maintenance). As an example of the process, let us continue with our earlier example: Precision Products. The production plan that produced a low cost was a mixed strategy of producing 400, 400, 400, and 200 in the four quarters. This plan is shown in Figure 11.15, with a breakdown into Precision Products' three models of wastewater pumps: hazardous (HZ), high-capacity (HC), and regular (R).

Typically, Precision Products sells these pumps in the ratio of 10 percent HZ, 35 percent HC, and 55 percent R; thus, the production plan is disaggregated by these

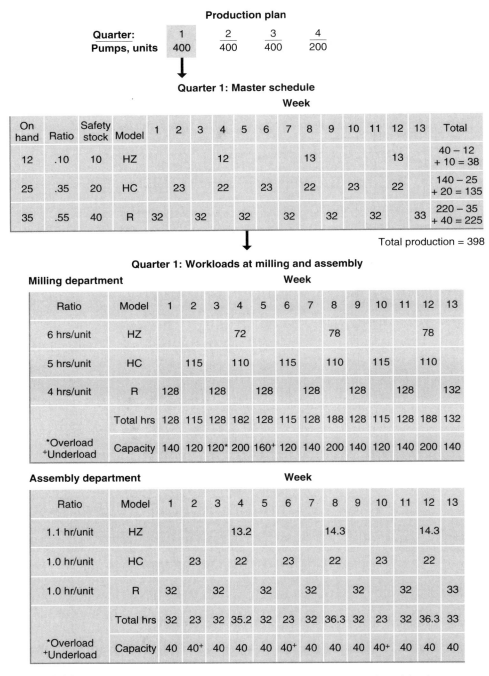

Figure 11.15   Precision Pump's production plan, master schedule, and workloads.

*S*OLVED EXERCISE 11.4 ❖ Master Scheduling

Use the chase demand solution for Solved Exercise 11.2 to produce a monthly master schedule for the two products: A units (10 units already exist in inventory) and B units (5 units are on hand). Historical records indicate that these units sell in the ratio of two A's for every B. Then calculate the resulting workloads for the assembly department, which has 1200 hours of capacity available, at most, per quarter. Each A unit takes 35 hours to assemble, and each B takes 45 hours.

Solution:

The calculations are shown in the table.

Quarter			1	2	3	4
Production, Units			40	50	30	20
On-Hand	Ratio	Model	Units			
10	0.67	A	27 − 10 = 17	33	20	13
5	0.33	B	13 − 5 = 8	17	10	7
Assembly Department			Hours			
Ratio		Model				
35 hours/unit		A	595	1155	700	455
45 hours/unit		B	360	765	450	315
Total hrs.			955	1920	1150	770
Capacity			1200	1200*	1200	1200

*Overload

ratios. For example, 0.10 × 400 units in quarter 1 = 40 HZ pumps required. Note that inventories of finished goods of 12, 25, and 35 units, respectively, are already in stock and that Precision Products tries to maintain a safety stock of 10 HZ, 20 HC, and 40 R. Thus, production requirements for the first quarter are reduced or increased by the appropriate amounts, as shown.

To create an initial master schedule, the resulting production requirements for the first quarter of 13 weeks could be spread evenly over the weeks by dividing the entire production amount by 13. However, that would mean setting up the equipment for all these products each week. If unique equipment were used to produce these pumps, this would probably be acceptable, since it would have to be set up only once. But many firms use the same equipment for all their products, and the equipment must be torn down after one model and set up again for the next one. When this setup time is long—and sometimes it takes hours or even days—it is more efficient to produce a large batch (or *lot*) of one model and then run a large batch of another model. Of course, the large batch must be stored in inventory until it is needed, costing money all the while.

Thus a trade-off exists in terms of finding the best lot size for producing the pumps. We will treat this subject further in Chapters 12 (Inventory Management) and 15 (Detailed Scheduling). At this point, let us just note that the Japanese have adopted a philosophy of minimizing the cost of equipment changeovers so that they are able to produce some amount of each product every period.

Here, we will assume that the best lot size is a two-week batch for R and HC pumps and a four-week batch for the less common HZ pumps. The result is the master schedule shown in the figure. However, this schedule may be excessive in terms of capacity requirements for some of the workstations, and that must be checked next. The process of checking individual workstations against production requirements is called *rough-cut capacity planning*.

❖ Rough-Cut Capacity Planning

Again, historical ratios are used to distribute a load of products across the various workstations (or work centers). The ratios give the number of work hours needed in each station to produce one of each of the pumps required. These data, and the resulting calculations, are shown in Figure 11.15 for two of the many workstations involved in producing the pumps.

After the workloads are distributed, on the basis of the initial master schedule, they are totaled and compared against the capacity available at each of the workstations. If a workstation is overloaded, some action must be taken; either additional capacity must be found (e.g., overtime or subcontracting) or the master schedule must be changed. Underloads are also checked in order to keep the workstations well utilized. If an underload exists, more work may be added through changes in the master schedule, or capacity (e.g., workers) may be shifted out of that workstation.

Spreadsheet Analysis: Master Scheduling

The spreadsheet shown below was developed to facilitate rough-cut capacity planning for the master schedule presented in Solved Exercise 11.4.

	A	B	C	D	E
1	*Model Inputs:*				
2		Model A	Model B		
3	On-Hand	10	5		
4	% of Production	0.67	0.33		
5	Assembly Time	35	45		
6					
7	Assembly Capacity	1200			
8	Quarter	1	2	3	4
9	Total Production	40	50	30	20
10	*Model Outputs:*				
11	Production of A	17	34	20	13
12	Production of B	8	17	10	7
13	Assembly Hours, A	595	1190	700	455
14	Assembly Hours, B	360	765	450	315
15	Total Assembly Hrs.	955	1955	1150	770
16	Capacity	1200	1200	1200	1200
17	Excess Capacity	245	-755	50	430

The top half of the spreadsheet contains the model inputs. In this case the model inputs are on-hand inventory (row 3), the percent of production each model accounts for (row 4), and assembly time (row 5). This information is entered in column B for model A and column C for model B. The available assembly capacity (in hours/quarter) is entered in cell B7. Finally, rows 8 and 9 contain the master schedule for the next four quarters.

The bottom half of the spreadsheet contains the model outputs. In row 11 the number of units of A that are to be produced is calculated. Given that on-hand inventory for Model A is entered in cell B3, and percent of total production that model A accounts for is entered in cell B4, the number of units to produce of A in the first quarter is calculated as follows in cell B11:

$$=ROUND(B9*\$B\$4,0)–B3$$

In English, this formula says that the total production for quarter 1 (cell B9) is multiplied by the percent of total production model A accounts for (B4) and this result is rounded to zero decimal places. Then the on-hand inventory of model A is subtracted from this result to determine exactly how many units need to be produced in the first quarter. Since all of the on-hand inventory is used in the first quarter, the formula to calculate the number of units to produce in the second quarter is entered as follows in cell C11:

$$=ROUND(C9*\$B\$4,0)$$

The formula entered in cell C11 can be copied to cells D11 and E11.

Similarly in row 12 the number of units of model B to produce is calculated. In cells B12 and C12 the following formulas are entered, respectively:

$$=ROUND(B9*\$C\$4,0)–C3$$
$$=ROUND(C9*\$C\$4,0)$$

The formula entered in cell C12 can be copied to cells D12 and E12.

In cell B13 the hours required to assemble the model As in the first quarter are calculated as follows:

$$=B11*\$B\$5$$

This formula can then be copied to cells C13 to E13. Similarly, the hours required to assemble the model Bs are calculated in cell B14 as follows:

$$=B12*\$C\$5$$

The formula entered in cell B14 can be copied to cells C14 to E14.

In cell B15 the total assembly hours required in the first quarter are calculated as follows:

$$=B13+B14$$

This formula can then be copied to cells C15 to E15. The assembly hours available each quarter are entered in the Model Inputs section in cell B7. Thus, =$B$7 is entered in cell B16 and then copied to cells C16 to E16.

Finally, to calculate the excess capacity in the first quarter, the following formula is entered in cell B17:

$$=B16-B15$$

There are two things to note in this spreadsheet. First, the solution is slightly different from that obtained in Solved Exercise 11.4 because production of model A in the second quarter was rounded up to 34 in the spreadsheet and rounded to 33 in Solved Exercise 11.4. Second, note that in quarter 2 there is a shortage of 755 hours of assembly time. With the spreadsheet developed, the scheduler can easily investigate alternative master schedules by changing the numbers entered in row 9 in an effort to eliminate this capacity shortage. The scheduler can alleviate the shortage by reducing the amount produced in the second quarter, either by moving production from quarter 2 to the other quarters (since they have extra capacity) or simply by producing less in the second quarter and leaving the other quarters as is.

CHAPTER IN PERSPECTIVE

In Part Two we discussed the business process of designing the output and transformation system. Then in Part Three we dealt with identifying and managing the resources needed to produce outputs. As noted earlier, our focus here in Part Four is on how a variety of operational activities support the product-service supply process. Thus, we add the dimension of *time* to our previously static picture of the organization, transforming it into a running, operating set of activities that are producing and supplying outputs to live, demanding customers.

In this opening chapter of Part Four, we have been concerned with ensuring that the *right* tasks are conducted at the *right* time on the *right* items to produce the output—that is, we have been concerned with *scheduling*. We began this chapter with a broad overview of the sequence of scheduling activities. We then discussed the topics of aggregate planning and master scheduling in more detail. In Chapters 12, 13, and 14, we turn to issues related to planning and managing inventory. After this, our discussion shifts to detailed scheduling for traditional transformation systems and then for projects. Finally, we conclude Part Four with a discussion of quality control.

❖ CHECK YOUR UNDERSTANDING

1. Define the following terms: *scheduling, aggregate plan, level production, sequencing, production plan, master production schedule, loading, rough-cut capacity planning, chase demand, dispatching,* and *expediting.*

2. In what sense is chase demand a pure aggregate planning strategy?

3. Briefly overview the sequence of scheduling activities.

4. In what way is the master production schedule the driving force behind scheduling?

5. What is the objective of aggregate planning?

6. List some ways an aggregate planner can change the amount of capacity available.

7. Contrast aggregate planning with production planning. Does every firm do both?

8. Contrast a level production plan with a chase demand approach. What are the advantages and disadvantages of each?

9. Explain how an aggregate schedule can be developed using a cumulative graph.

10. Why does using the same aggregate planning strategy but starting at different points in the demand cycle result in different costs?

11. Describe how you would use a cumulative graph (e.g., Figure 11.10) to derive a good initial aggregate plan.

12. What is the difficulty of using a 12-month master schedule with some products that have a 13-month lead time? Where in scheduling will difficulties appear?

13. Why do loading and sequencing not apply to continuous and flow transformation systems?

❖ EXPAND YOUR UNDERSTANDING

1. Since an assemble-to-order firm waits for customers' orders before setting its schedule, why doesn't it just produce the whole product to order and not worry about the forecast or aggregate planning?

2. Why go through the process of aggregating forecasts to produce an aggregate plan, which is then disaggregated into the actual product or service master schedule? Why not just use the individual forecasts to produce the master schedule?

3. Why is a capacity check done twice in the scheduling process? Why not just do it once in detail?

4. Top management usually wants to get as much production out of its facility as possible and thus is usually optimistic about putting orders into its master production schedule. Is it ethical for upper management to set a production schedule that is virtually impossible for the workers to achieve—say, one chance in a hundred? What about one chance in ten? One in two? When does it stop being unethical, and why?

5. Describe the role of sales in setting the master schedule. Is its only concern to get as much pro-

duced as possible? What else may sales be concerned about when it helps set the schedule?

6. A lot of scheduling seems to be the straightforward manipulation of data, applying ratios, batching lots, meeting deadlines, converting pounds to units, and so on. Couldn't all this be done by computer? What would be hard to do by computer?

7. Describe any of your experiences with level production or chase demand. Do these concepts apply only to businesses? Where else might you see them?

8. Suppose you are a production scheduler and receive a notice from sales that a customer has canceled an order that was in the frozen portion of the master schedule. Would you go ahead and build the product anyway because the schedule is frozen? Or would you immediately stop work on the order? If you stopped work, what good is having a frozen schedule that really is not frozen?

9. In what way is rough-cut capacity planning actually "rough"? What does it ignore?

❖ APPLY YOUR UNDERSTANDING
Grassboy, Inc.

Grassboy, Inc., produces a line of lawn mowers in a variety of engine sizes and cutting widths. In an effort to deal with the highly seasonal nature of its demand, Grassboy forecasts demand for the next eight quarters. The forecast for the next eight quarters is given in the table below.

Quarter	Demand Forecast
1	5000
2	7500
3	15,000
4	5000
5	6000
6	8000
7	16000
8	5500

Grassboy has a single production line that can assemble 7000 units per quarter per shift using regular time and can assemble an additional 25 percent using overtime. The assembly line can be operated for either one or two shifts; however, the union contract permits making changes to the number of shifts only at the beginning of a quarter. The company is permitted to send the workers home early without pay if its plans call for producing less than 7000 units in a given quarter. The cost of adding a shift is $7500, and the cost of eliminating a shift is $14,000. Grassboy also has identified several overseas manufacturers that can produce as many of its lawn mowers as needed as subcontractors.

On average, the cost of producing a single lawn mower is $25 per mower using regular time and $33 using overtime. The delivered cost of mowers produced by subcontractors is $49. Grassboy's cost of holding a lawn mower in inventory for one quarter is $4, and the cost of backordering a unit is $12 per quarter. Inventory costs are calculated on the basis of average inventory held during the quarter (i.e., the average of the quarter's beginning and ending inventory). Backorder costs are calculated on the basis of the ending backorder position in a given quarter.

Grassboy was operating with one shift in the quarter just ending and expects to end the quarter with 750 units in inventory.

Questions

1. Develop an aggregate plan that calls for a constant level of employment that meets the fluctuations in demand by using inventory, backorders, overtime, subcontracting, or some combination of these. Assume that all demand must be met by the eighth quarter.

2. Develop an aggregate plan that meets the fluctuations in demand by adjusting the number of shifts.

3. What are the advantages and disadvantages of the aggregate schedules you developed? Which one would you recommend to Grassboy's management?

❖ EXERCISES

1. How many workers are needed with level production to meet quarterly demands of 45, 65, 50, and 40 if each worker can produce 5 units a quarter? Recalculate your answer if there are already 20 units in inventory. Recalculate again assuming that there are 20 inventory units but also that 10 units are required as safety stock.

2. Currently, 2 workers can each produce 10 units a quarter. Find the long-run average annual cost of using overtime (at $20/unit) and undertime (at $10/unit) to chase quarterly demands of 40, 60, 30, and 20.

3. Use the same data as in Exercise 2 but use hiring and layoffs, at a cost of $30 each, to chase demand.

4. Find the costs of inventory and backordering with level production to meet quarterly demands of 20, 50, 30, and 40. Inventory costs $10/unit/quarter, and backordering costs $15/unit/quarter.

5. Quarterly demand for the next four quarters is 140, 215, 80, and 20. Holding inventory costs $10/unit/quarter, and backordering costs $12/unit/quarter. All demand must be met by the end of the fourth quarter.

   a. Devise a level production strategy, a beginning inventory level, and an ending inventory level that minimize costs over the four quarters.
   b. Devise a level production strategy and a beginning inventory level to minimize total costs if the ending inventory level must be zero.
   c. Devise a level production strategy and an ending inventory level to minimize total costs if the beginning inventory level is zero.
   d. Devise a two-level production strategy (i.e., nonlevel) that begins and ends the four quarters with no inventory. The level of production can change at any quarter.

6. Use Excel's Solver to find the lowest-cost strategy for Exercise 5. Assume that there is no beginning inventory and that all demand must be met by the end of the fourth quarter.

7. Demand forecasts of the year for your product for each quarter are 120, 140, 110, and 90, with this pattern repeating in the future as far as can be told. The current workforce is 11, and each worker can produce 10 units in a quarter. Inventory costs are $10 per unit per quarter, whereas shortage costs with backordering are $13 per unit per quarter. Hiring and layoff costs $100 per worker, but idle workers cost $150 a quarter. Cost to produce units on overtime is an additional $15 each. Find the best long-term production plan if all demand must be met.

8. Find the best long-term production plan for Exercise 7 using Excel's Solver if all demand must be met. Use Excel to plot the cumulative production and demand of your solution.

9. Can you find a better aggregate plan than that in Solved Exercise 11.2?

10. Refer to Spreadsheet Analysis: Master Scheduling. Use the spreadsheet to produce as much of the current master schedule as possible without exceeding the hours available for assembly time in any quarter. Alternatively, use the spreadsheet to determine how many extra hours of assembly time are needed to meet the current master schedule.

11. Allocate an aggregate quarterly production of 30, 60, 90, and 60 to four products in the ratio of 20 percent A, 40 percent B, 30 percent C, and 10 percent D. Create a monthly master schedule that distributes production as evenly as possible. Create another master schedule that minimizes setups, given that existing inventory includes 5 of each item and capacity is 20 items of any type per month.

12. Develop a spreadsheet to solve Exercise 11.

13. The master monthly schedule for a firm's AZW product is: 4, 7, 3, 3, 2, 3, 4, 4, 6, 7, 8, 6. Distribute the workload on this product to department II, which requires 60 labor hours per AZW item. If the existing workload in department II is 800 hours a month and there are 170 hours per worker per month, find how many workers are needed in the department each month.

14. If the idle workers in Exercise 13 are used to produce AZZ items, which require 5 hours each, what will the master production schedule for these items be?

Chapter 11 SUPPLEMENT

Loading and the Assignment Model

For continuous process systems such as assembly-line operations and chemical processors, loading is a moot problem because all output goes through essentially the same operations. Moreover, the load on each facility is fairly constant. But for many intermittent transformation systems, there is considerable choice in determining which facilities should handle which jobs. Some choices are much better than others, however, because particular resources are more efficient for some jobs than for other jobs. It is desirable to process the operations as quickly as possible to minimize late jobs and the use of facilities.

When the problem involves deciding which of a number of jobs to allocate among a number of facilities on a one-to-one basis, the assignment model, a special type of linear program, is useful. This model results in an optimal allocation and is described in the second section. If the facilities can receive more than one job each, then a heuristic approach, the index method, is helpful. This technique is illustrated first.

THE INDEX METHOD

A simple model can be used when more than one job is assigned to each work center. The approach, called the *index method,* is to calculate an "efficiency" index for each job on each work center and then to load each center with those jobs that have the best indices for it. Simply put, this method assigns jobs to the centers best able to do them. Let us demonstrate with a simple example.

❖ Example: Stereo Re-Pairs, Inc.

Bill, owner-manager of Stereo Re-Pairs, employs three part-time electrical engineering students—John, Mary, and Bo—to service the stereos customers bring to the shop. Bill knows that the three students have different experience with the various brands of stereos and also knows on which stereo each of the students works best. Bill can usually estimate their repair times fairly accurately. On this particular Monday, six stereos, brought in on Saturday, are awaiting repair. Table 11S.1 shows Bill's estimate of the repair times for each unit, depending on who services it, and the weekly hours each student works for him.

Assuming that the students are all paid the same hourly rate, it is desirable to load any tasks on the student who is expected to be fastest on it. Letting the shortest repair time take an index value of 1.00 and giving other times an index equal to the ratio of repair time to the minimum repair time will give the results shown in Table 11S.2.

We now attempt to load the tasks on those facilities where the index is 1.00. Notice, however, that if Bo is loaded first, total hours will exceed the 5 hours available, so the procedure is initiated with John, who has the most hours available. John then gets the Panasonic, Juliette, and Heathkit, as indicated by the boxes, for a total

$\mathscr{T}$ABLE 11S.1 ❖ Stereo Repair Times in Hours

	John	Mary	Bo
Total Hours Available	20	15	5
Stereo			
Lloyds	4	3	3
Panasonic	2	3	2
Sound Design	5	(?)	3
Juliette	1	1	1
Heathkit	3	4	5
Realistic	2	3	1

$\mathscr{T}$ABLE 11S.2 ❖ Index Loading Procedure

	John		Mary		Bo	
Stereo	Hours	Index	Hours	Index	Hours	Index
Lloyds	4	(4/3=)1.33	3	1.00	3	1.00
Panasonic	2	1.00	3	1.50	2	1.00
Sound Design	5	1.67	(?)	—	3	1.00
Juliette	1	1.00	1	1.00	1	1.00
Heathkit	3	1.00	4	1.33	5	1.67
Realistic	2	2.00	3	3.00	1	1.00
Hours remaining	14		12		1	

of 6 hours, leaving 20 − 6 = 14 hours available for the rest of the week. Mary next takes the Lloyds (3 hours), leaving the Sound Design and Realistic to Bo (4 hours total).

In case a facility with the lowest index becomes overloaded, jobs are simply shifted to the facility with the next lower index that is not already overloaded. In some situations the work may have to be split between facilities. For example, if Mary had only 1 hour available to spend on the Lloyds and then was to leave the rest of the job to John, he would *not* spend (Mary's remaining) 2 hours on it. Rather, he would have two-thirds of the job left to finish, which would take him ⅔ × 4 = 2.67 hours.

The model is simple enough that pay rates can also be easily included. This is done by deriving indices based on Bill's *labor* cost (rate × hours) rather than just on hours. The hours available would still constrain the allocations, however, not the labor cost per student.

$\mathscr{T}$HE ASSIGNMENT MODEL _____

For a loading problem that consists of deciding which of a number of jobs to allocate among a number of facilities on a one-to-one basis, the *assignment model* is useful. For example, suppose the costs of producing five jobs at each of five differ-

$\mathcal{T}$ABLE 11S.3 ❖ Costs of Assigning Jobs to Various Work Centers

Work Centers	Jobs				
	1	2	3	4	5
R	$30	$50	$40	$80	$20
S	90	40	30	50	70
T	110	60	80	100	90
D	60	100	40	120	50
F	30	50	60	40	90

ent work centers are as shown in Table 11S.3. The assignment method will indicate which job should be allocated to which work center in order to minimize costs.

❖ Solution Procedure

Although the problem appears simple enough, the solution is not always easy. For example, in Table 11S.3 it appears by inspection that job 3 should go to center S. It costs less to assign job 3 to center S than any of the other jobs, *and* assigning job 3 to center S is cheaper than assigning it to any other center. Nevertheless, this would be a poor assignment, as we will soon see. Overall, it is less expensive to assign job 4 to center S, even though it costs $20 more initially. A better procedure than simple inspection is derived from the following logic.

Since the assignments are on a one-to-one basis, then adding (or subtracting) a *constant* to every cost in the same row, or the same column, will not alter the relative costs of the assignments. For example, adding $10 to all the costs in column 1 still leaves the cost of assigning job 1 to center S $20 cheaper than assigning it to center T. Therefore, the least-cost solution (which job to which center) will be unchanged by this process, even though the *values* will be different.

One way, then, to identify good assignments is to subtract amounts from the rows and the columns so as to generate zeros in some of the cells, being careful not to generate negative numbers in the process. Then, if a feasible assignment can be made to only zero-valued cells, this will result in the lowest possible cost. The assignment method uses the essence of this approach in a five-step procedure. We will illustrate it with the example.

❖ *Step 1.* Subtract the lowest cost in each row from all the other costs in that row (Table 11S.4).

$\mathcal{T}$ABLE 11S.4 ❖ Row Reduction

	1	2	3	4	5
R	30 − 20 = 10	50 − 20 = 30	40 − 20 = 20	80 − 20 = 60	20 − 20 = 0
S	90 − 30 = 60	40 − 30 = 10	30 − 30 = 0	50 − 30 = 20	70 − 30 = 40
T	110 − 60 = 50	60 − 60 = 0	80 − 60 = 20	100 − 60 = 40	90 − 60 = 30
D	60 − 40 = 20	100 − 40 = 60	40 − 40 = 0	120 − 40 = 80	50 − 40 = 10
F	30 − 30 = 0	50 − 30 = 20	60 − 30 = 30	40 − 30 = 10	90 − 30 = 60

❖ *Step 2.* Next, subtract the lowest remaining cost in each column from all the other costs in that column. (Steps 1 and 2 may be reversed.) See Table 11S.5.

❖ *Step 3.* Since all costs at this point are nonnegative, the minimum possible assignment cost using these "new" cost elements will be zero. *If* a one-to-one assignment can be made to only cells with zero costs, this will be an optimal assignment. Rather than attempting to make an optimal assignment by trial and error, we follow a special procedure: cover all the zeros in the matrix with the *lowest* possible number of straight horizontal and vertical lines. If the number of lines is equal to the number of rows (or columns) in the table, an assignment can be made. (The *minimum* number of lines never exceeds the number of rows or columns.) If not, then it is possible to improve the solution. (In Table 11S.6 all the zeros can be covered with only four lines; hence, it is possible to improve the solution.)

❖ *Step 4.* If an assignment can be made, go to Step 5. Otherwise, inspect the values *not* covered by lines and select the lowest one (10 in Table 11S.6). *Subtract* this value from all the *uncovered* values and *add* it to the values where two lines *intersect.* Return to Step 3. (See Tables 11S.7 and 11S.8. We find that, following the first improvement, it requires five lines to completely cover all the zeros in Table 11S.8. An optimal assignment can therefore be made.)

𝒯ABLE 11S.5 ❖ Column Reduction

	1	2	3	4	5
R	10	30	20	60 − 10 = 50	0
S	60	10	0	20 − 10 = 10	40
T	50	0	20	40 − 10 = 30	30
D	20	60	0	80 − 10 = 70	10
F	0	20	30	10 − 10 = 0	60

𝒯ABLE 11S.6 ❖ Optimality Test

10	30	20	50	0
60	10	0	10	40
50	0	20	30	30
20	60	0	70	10
0	20	30	0	60

𝒯ABLE 11S.7 ❖ First Improvement

10 − 10 = 0	30 − 10 = 20	20	50 − 10 = 40	0
60 − 10 = 50	10 − 10 = 0	0	10 − 10 = 0	40
50	0	20 + 10 = 30	30	30 + 10 = 40
20 − 10 = 10	60 − 10 = 50	0	70 − 10 = 60	10
0	20	30 + 10 = 40	0	60 + 10 = 70

$\mathscr{T}$ABLE 11S.8 ❖ Second Optimality Test

0	20	20	40	0
50	0	0	0	40
50	0	30	30	40
10	50	0	60	10
0	20	40	0	70

$\mathscr{T}$ABLE 11S.9 ❖ Optimal Solution

	1	2	3	4	5
R	0	20	20	40	[0]
S	50	0	0	[0]	40
T	50	[0]	30	30	40
D	10	50	[0]	60	10
F	[0]	20	40	0	70

❖ *Step 5.* To identify the optimal assignment, make the first assignment, if possible, to a row or column with only one zero in it. Delete that row and column and then continue the procedure. If more than one optimal solution exists, this process will quickly indicate that. (Table 11S.9 illustrates the procedure. Assignments R-5, T-2, or D-3 are identified first. In this case there is only one solution: R-5, S-4, T-2, D-3, F-1, with minimum cost, from Table 11S.3, of 20 + 50 + 60 + 40 + 30 = $200.)

The most economical assignment of jobs to centers will therefore cost $200. The assignment method is quite flexible in handling special conditions. Prohibited assignments, for example, can simply be marked out with an X without disrupting the solution process. The *maximization* problem can be treated simply by converting it to a minimization problem. This is accomplished by subtracting every entry in the original table from the largest entry. Once the optimal assignment is found, the original values (to be maximized) are used to determine the value (profit) of the solution.

❖ Linear Programming Formulation of the Assignment Model

By following the five-step solution procedure for the assignment model, you are actually solving a linear programming problem. To show this, we will use the following notation:

$$c_{ij} = \text{cost of assigning job } i \text{ to work center } j$$
$$X_{ij} = 1 \text{ if job } i \text{ is assigned to work center } j, 0 \text{ otherwise}$$

The objective of the assignment method is to minimize the costs of assigning the jobs to the work centers. Mathematically, we can express this objective as follows:

$$\text{minimize } z = \sum_i \sum_j c_{ij} X_{ij}$$

Next, we consider the constraints. One constraint is that each work center should be assigned exactly one job. We can express this constraint mathematically as follows:

$$\sum_i X_{ij} = 1, \text{ for all } j$$

"For all j" means that we have a constraint like this for each available work center.

We also have to make sure that each job gets assigned to exactly one work center. This constraint is expressed mathematically as:

$$\sum_j X_{ij} = 1, \text{ for all } i$$

The complete linear programming formulation for the assignment model is:

$$\text{minimize } z = \sum_i \sum_j c_{ij} X_{ij}$$

subject to:

$$\sum_i X_{ij} = 1, \text{ for all } j$$

$$\sum_j X_{ij} = 1, \text{ for all } i$$

$$X_{ij} = 0,1 \text{ for all } i, j$$

Spreadsheet Analysis: The Assignment Model

Rather than using a specialized software package to solve the linear programming formulation of the assignment model, this example will demonstrate how Excel's built-in optimization capabilities can be used. The spreadsheet below was developed to solve the assignment problem.

	A	B	C	D	E	F	G	H
1	**Model Inputs:**							
2								
3	Work Center	1	2	Jobs 3	4	5		
4	R	30	50	40	80	20		
5	S	90	40	30	50	70		
6	T	110	60	80	100	90		
7	D	60	100	40	120	50		
8	F	30	50	60	40	90		
9	**Decision Variables and Model Outputs:**							
10		1	2	3	4	5	Row Sum	Cost
11	R						0	0
12	S						0	0
13	T						0	0
14	D						0	0
15	F						0	0
16	Column Sum	0	0	0	0	0		
17	Total Cost							0

The model inputs are entered in the top portion of the spreadsheet. In the assignment model, the inputs are the c_{ij} values. These values were entered in cells B4:F8 in the spreadsheet. For example, cell D7 corresponds to c_{34} or the cost of assigning job 3 to work center 4. (Note that R, S, T, D, and F correspond to work centers 1, 2, 3, 4, and 5, respectively.)

The bottom of the spreadsheet contains the decision variables and model outputs. The decision variables in the assignment model are the X_{ij} variables. In general, decision variables are variables the decision maker has control over. In this case the decision maker has control over assigning the jobs to the work centers. The X_{ij} variables correspond to cells B11:F15. For example, cell B15 corresponds to X_{15}. Recall that the X_{ij} variables can take on values of only 0 or 1.

When we discussed the linear programming formulation for the assignment model, we noted that constraints were needed to ensure that each work center is assigned exactly one job. Mathematically, we expressed this constraint as follows:

$$\sum_i X_{ij} = 1, \text{ for all } j$$

In column G, rows 11–15 contain formulas that sum X_{ij} over i for each work center. For example, in cell G11: =SUM(B11:F11) was entered. This formula was then copied to cells G12 to G15. According to the above constraint, we will need to add constraints that require the values in cells G11:G15 to be equal to 1.

We add the other set of constraints to ensure that each job is assigned to exactly one work center. This constraint was expressed mathematically as:

$$\sum_j X_{ij} = 1, \text{ for all } i$$

In row 16, columns B to F contain formulas that sum X_{ij} over j for each job. Thus, in cell B16: =SUM(B11:B15) was entered and then copied to cells C16 to F16. Again, according to the constraint, we have to ensure that the values in these cells are equal to 1.

Column H contains the model outputs. In cells H11 to H15 the cost of assigning a job to a particular work center is calculated. For example, in cell H11, the following formula was entered:

=(B11*B4)+(C11*C4)+(D11*D4)+(E11*E4)+(F11*F4)

This formula was then copied to cells H12 to H15. Finally, to calculate the total cost of assigning the jobs to the work centers, H17 contains the formula: =SUM(H11:H15).

Having developed the spreadsheet as described above, we are now ready to use Excel's Solver to find the optimal solution. We begin by selecting Tools from the menu bar displayed at the top of the screen, and then Solver . . . from the new menu displayed. After we select Solver, the Solver Parameters dialog box is displayed. The target cell we wish to optimize is the cell that calculates the total cost of assigning the jobs to the work centers, cell H17. Thus, for the Set Target Cell: enter cell H17 and then select the Min radio button, since we wish to minimize this value.

Next, we tell Excel which cells it can change to minimize the target cell. In our case, the cells in the range of B11:F15 can be changed. Therefore, for the By Changing Cells: box, enter the range B11:F15.

The last thing we need to do is add the constraints. To begin adding the constraints, click on the Add . . . button in the Subject to the Constraints section of the Solver Parameters window. Let's first add the constraints to ensure that each job is assigned to exactly one work center. For job 1 we specify this by entering the constraint B16=1 in the Add Constraint window as shown below.

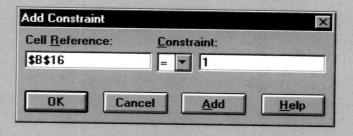

After this information has been entered, select Add. For the other jobs, enter the following constraints:

$$C16 = 1$$
$$D16 = 1$$
$$E16 = 1$$
$$F16 = 1$$

Equivalently, these constraints could be entered as B16:F16 = 1.

Next we add the constraints to ensure that each work center is assigned exactly one job. For work center 1 (i.e., work center R) this constraint is entered as: G11 = 1. Add similar constraints for the other work centers as follows:

$$G12 = 1$$
$$G13 = 1$$
$$G14 = 1$$
$$G15 = 1$$

Or, using the shortcut approach, you could enter these with one constraint: G11:G15 = 1.

The last thing we have to do is to make sure that the X_{ij} values in cells B11:F15 take on only values of 0 or 1. To do this we need to add 3 constraints for each cell in this range: (1) the value is greater than or equal to 0, (2) the value is less than or equal to 1, and (3) the value is an integer. For example, we would add the following constraints for cell B11:

$$B11 >= 0$$
$$B11 <= 1$$
$$B11 \text{ int integer}$$

Add these three constraints for cells B12 to B15, C11 to C15, D11 to D15, E11 to E15, and F11 to F15. After you enter F15 int integer, select OK instead of Add to tell Excel you are finished entering constraints. (Alternatively, you could enter the following three constraints: B11:F15 >=0, B11:F15 <= 1, and B11:F15 int integer.) After you select OK, the Solver Parameters dialog box looks as follows:

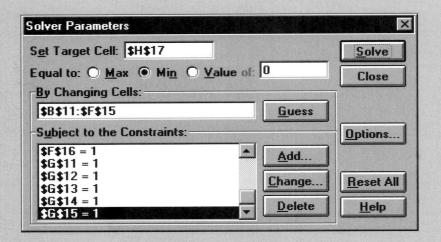

Select Solve in the Solver Parameters dialog box to have Excel find the optimal assignment. After Excel has found the optimal solution, the Solver Results dialog box is displayed.

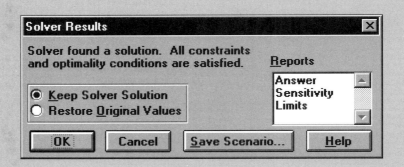

Selecting OK in the Solver Results dialog box displays the following solution:

	A	B	C	D	E	F	G	H
1	Model Inputs:							
2				Jobs				
3	Work Center	1	2	3	4	5		
4	R	30	50	40	80	20		
5	S	90	40	30	50	70		
6	T	110	60	80	100	90		
7	D	60	100	40	120	50		
8	F	30	50	60	40	90		
9	Decision Variables and Model Outputs:							
10		1	2	3	4	5	Row Sum	Cost
11	R	0	0	0	0	1	1	20
12	S	0	0	0	1	0	1	50
13	T	0	1	0	0	0	1	60
14	D	0	0	1	0	0	1	40
15	F	1	0	0	0	0	1	30
16	Column Sum	1	1	1	1	1		
17	Total Cost							200

The Excel solution assigns job 5 to work center R at a cost of ($20), 4 to S ($50), 2 to T ($60), 3 to D ($40), and 1 to F ($30) for a total cost of $200. This is the same solution shown in Table 11S.9.

❖ EXERCISES

1. John, Mary, and Henry have been asked to work this Saturday morning, but the union contract calls for double-time pay on Saturday. Since the work must get out, the production supervisor has decided to load the three jobs so as to minimize the total cost of overtime. The jobs and the time required for each person are shown below. John earns $12 per hour, Mary $16 per hour, and Henry $20 per hour on overtime. Who should do which job if one job is assigned to each worker?

	John	Mary	Henry
Job 1	2	1.5	1.5
Job 2	1.5	1.5	1
Job 3	1	2	1

2. Solve exercise 1 using the index method. Note that none of the employees is willing to work more than 4 hours on Saturday morning. More than one job can be assigned to a worker.

3. The following table gives the hours to run each job on each machine, machine costs per hour, and machine hours available. If jobs can be split, what jobs should go on which machines for how many hours?

	Machine		
Job	A	B	C
1	50	40	75
2	25	40	50
3	27	30	54
4	40	100	80
5	20	100	50
Cost, $/hr	4	2	3
Hours available	75	75	75

4. Solve the following minimization assignment problem.

Job	A	B	C	D	E
1	3	9	11	6	3
2	5	4	6	10	5
3	4	3	8	4	6
4	8	6	10	12	4
5	2	7	9	5	9

5. The following table shows the profits to a company from assigning salespersons to different regions. Find the best overall assignment if only one salesperson can be assigned to one region.

	Salesperson		
Region	A	B	C
I	5	6	8
II	4	7	11
III	7	3	2

6. In the Sunset Nursing Home, the director is attempting to assign nine practical nurses to nine patients. Six of the patients are difficult and three are easy. The nurses' experience with such patients also varies: three have only one year of experience, four have two years, and two have three years. On the basis of her experience, the director expects the following number of complaints from each type of assignment. How should she assign the nurses to the patients?

	Years of Experience		
Type of Patient	1	2	3
Hard	24	28	20
Easy	10	9	12

7. Develop the linear programming formulation of the assignment model for Exercise 1.

8. Develop a linear programming formulation for Exercise 1 that minimizes the cost of assigning the jobs to the workers, assuming that each worker can be assigned more than one job but that no worker can be assigned more than 4 hours of work.

9. Solve Exercise 1 as an assignment problem, using the optimization capabilities of a spreadsheet.

Inventory Management

$\mathscr{C}$ HAPTER OVERVIEW

* In terms of *function,* there are five basic kinds of inventories: (1) transit or pipeline inventories, (2) buffer or safety stocks to protect against uncertainty, (3) anticipation inventories to protect against periods of high demand, (4) decoupling inventories to smooth flows between operations with different production rates, and (5) cycle inventories to reduce the overall costs of ordering, setting up, and holding stocks.

* There are four *forms* of inventories. Three represent the final product in various states of completion: (1) raw materials, (2) work-in-process, and (3) finished goods. The last, (4) maintenance, repair, and operating (MRO) supplies, includes items that are used as spare parts and supplies used to facilitate the production of a product or service.

* There are five broad categories of *costs* involved with inventories: (1) costs of ordering or setting up to get the items, (2) costs of holding or carrying the inventory, (3) extra costs incurred if the organization stocks out of the inventory, (4) costs associated with obtaining the capacity to produce the items, and (5) costs of buying or producing the items.

* With regard to inventories, the two major decisions facing a manager are when to order inventory and how much to order.

* The three major types of inventory management systems are (1) reorder point and (2) periodic review systems, for items that are independently demanded; and (3) material requirements planning systems, for items subject to dependent demand.

* Inventories are classified according to the value of controlling them. The 15 to 20 percent of the items that represent 75 to 80 percent of inventory value (cost times usage) are called A items and are subject to very tight control. B items represent perhaps 30 to 40 percent of the items and are subject to normal inventory controls. The 40 to 50 percent of the items that represent only 10 to 15 percent of the inventory value are the C items and are subject to very loose controls.

477

❖ The *economic order quantity* (EOQ) is the "best" amount to order (under certain restrictive assumptions) in the sense that it minimizes the sum of two inventory costs: the cost of ordering (or setting up to produce) and the cost of holding the resulting inventory.

❖ The "newsboy" problem is a one-period situation (owing to perishability of the product or service) with demand uncertainty. Given this uncertainty, two mistakes can be made: overordering and having outputs left that cannot be sold; or underordering and not having outputs that could have been sold. Given the probability distribution of demand, the best amount to order can be determined from the expected value of the possible outcomes—which in turn are determined through either a decision table or incremental analysis.

❖ When the inventory is a multiple-period situation with uncertainty in demand or lead time or both, some protection against stockouts can be obtained by using safety stock and prespecifying the desired level of service to the customer (the chance of not having a stockout). The analysis to determine the best level of safety stock is based on the probability of demand during the lead time, when a stockout is most likely to occur.

*J*NTRODUCTION _____

❖ Blue Bell is one of the largest apparel manufacturers, with sales of over $1 billion and 27,000 employees worldwide. It includes Wrangler brand sports and casual apparel, Red Kap industrial garments, and Jantzen sports and casual clothing. In the 1980s, management became concerned about the rapidly escalating cost of inventories—exceeding 50 percent of the total asset base, with an annual maintenance cost of 25 percent of the cost of the goods inventoried. This increase in inventories derived from increased demands by retailers—higher availability, more on-time shipments, and more complete orders—and reduced lead times in order to reduce the retailers' own inventory costs. The number of stock-keeping units (SKUs) increased dramatically along with the interest expense, which increased from $1 million to $22 million in a three-year period. Yet supplying the products to retailers was a complex process involving 80 domestic and 15 foreign plants and 32 domestic and 17 foreign distribution centers. Reducing inventories had to be done carefully, with close attention to plant capacities, retailers' needs, and economic production lots, all the while maintaining a stable workforce throughout the year.

It was determined that two key tasks were required to effectively reduce inventories. The first was to determine a better way to manage plant capacity and allocate it to the production of specific lots. The second task was to find a better balance between carrying inventory and risking shortages. Initially, some SKUs had months of supply while others were constantly out of stock. To address these problems, a team constructed seven computer models: (1) forecasting sales, (2) planning safety stock, (3) planning product lines, (4) planning lots, (5) planning sizes, (6) planning net requirements, and, finally, (7) pattern design and selection. These models take forecasts, plant capacities, needs of distribution centers, and costs into account to determine gross needs of line production and disaggregate them into weekly SKU requirements by plant. Use of these models resulted in inventory reductions of 31 percent within two years, in turn reducing the need for working capital by more than 50 percent, or $64 million. Another significant benefit was reduced costs of raw materials—on the order of $1 million, where no reduction, or even an increase, had been expected. The indirect benefits included a significant improvement in service, particularly more on-time shipments and fewer canceled orders (Edwards, Wagner, and Wood, 1985).

479

❖ A custom-designed inventory management system has helped transform Mothers Work, Inc., from a small mail-order company to the dominant retailer of maternity clothes. The inventory system provides details down to level of individual garments and gives managers a comprehensive picture of the entire inventory pipeline. The system provides daily reports on what is and what isn't selling, and how long before more product can be purchased or made. Also, Mothers Work uses the system to test market fashions in stores before committing itself to large production runs.

Monitoring daily sales figures allows the company to produce more of hot-selling styles in two weeks or less and to speed new ideas from the design table to stores in a month. Other retail stores are often restricted to selling styles selected six months in advance. Having the ability to wait until the last possible moment before ordering or producing garments greatly minimizes the need to mark down slow-selling styles and helps maintain sufficient inventory levels of styles the customers desire (Bird, 1996).

❖ Electronic commerce (E-commerce) is no longer simply a management buzzword; it is fundamentally changing the way products are bought and sold. Over the last decade large companies such as Wal-Mart, General Motors, Eastman Kodak, and Baxter International have been developing private computer networks for controlling the flow of goods across the value chain. Still evolving, these private networks are moving to the public Internet. One major advantage of these networks is that less time and money is spent reentering information into different computer systems.

Campbell Soup, for example, estimates that 60 percent of the orders it receives contain mistakes. As a result, salespeople spend 40 percent of their time fixing these problems instead of selling. With these and other savings, it is estimated that E-commerce will reduce the costs of processing a purchase order from $150 to $25. As another example, Fruit of the Loom developed a system to link its 50 wholesalers to its central warehouse. With the system, its central inventory becomes virtual inventory for the wholesalers. For example, if a silk-screener needs black T-shirts for a coming concert and the wholesaler is low, Fruit of the Loom's central warehouse is notified and the T-shirts are shipped from there directly to the customer (Verity, 1996).

In Chapter 11, we discussed the dynamics of scheduling operations. As part of this, stocks of inventories were also considered because holding unneeded inventory, within or outside the production system, is expensive, as is well illustrated by the case of Blue Bell. In the present chapter we continue our discussion of the product supply process by looking at the uses of inventories, and the means of determining the best levels of inventories to hold.

Our time frame is shorter in this chapter than in Chapter 11—days or weeks rather than a quarter or year. In addition, the chapter considers both purchased and internally produced inventories. Although we describe various functions of inventories, the material in the chapter focuses largely on cycle inventories that are replenished on a regular basis in "lots" or batches—that is, where the production of the materials is not produced by a continuous or flow process (which is considered in Chapter 15).

We start with a discussion of the different purposes of holding inventories and the various forms of inventories—from raw materials to finished goods. The costs involved in any inventory system are then identified, and the critical questions that inventory managers must address are spelled out. The overview ends with a general discussion of the three different types of inventory management systems that are in common use.

Following this introduction, we present a method for identifying which inventories need close control and a way of determining the best amount of inventory to hold. We then introduce the special situation of the single-period inventory and how demand uncertainty complicates decisions regarding it. We extend the idea of uncertainty in the last section to the multiperiod case and describe the use of safety stock for dealing with it. Simulation—a technique described in the supplement to this chapter—is also very useful for dealing with situations involving uncertainty.

$\mathcal{G}$ENERAL CONSIDERATIONS

Although inventory is inanimate, the topic of inventory and inventory control can arouse completely different sentiments in the minds of people in various departments within an organization. The salespeople generally prefer large quantities of inventory to be on hand. In this way they can meet customers' requests without having to wait. Customer service is their primary concern. The accounting and financial personnel see inventory in a different light. High inventories do not translate into high customer service in the accountant's language; rather, they translate into large amounts of tied-up capital that could otherwise be used to reduce debt or for other more economically advantageous purposes. From the viewpoint of the operations manager, inventories are a tool that can be used to promote efficient operation of the production facilities. Neither high inventories nor low inventories, per se, are desirable; inventories are simply allowed to fluctuate so that production can be adjusted to its most efficient level. And top management's concern is with the "bottom line"—what advantages the inventories are providing versus their costs.

❖ Functions of Inventories

There are many purposes for holding inventory but, in general, inventories have only five basic functions. Be aware that inventories will not generally be identified and segregated within the organization by these functions and that not all functions will be represented in all organizations.

1. *Transit inventories:* **Transit inventories** exist because materials must be moved from one location to another. (These are also known as **pipeline inventories.**) Five hundred tons of coal moving slowly on a coal train from the mines of southeastern Kentucky to an industrial northeastern city cannot provide customer service by powering furnaces or generators. This inventory results because of the transportation time required.

2. *Buffer inventories:* Another purpose of inventories is to protect against the uncertainties of supply and demand. **Buffer inventories**—or, as they are sometimes called, **safety stocks**—serve to cushion the effect of unpredictable events. The amount of inventory over and above the *average* demand requirement is considered to be buffer stock held to meet any demand in excess of the average. The higher the level of inventory, the better the customer service—that is, the fewer the **stockouts** and **backorders.** A stockout exists when a customer's order for an item cannot be filled because the inventory of that item has run out. If there is a stockout, the firm will usually backorder the materials immediately, rather than wait until the next regular ordering period.

3. *Anticipation inventories:* An anticipated future event such as a price increase, a strike, or a seasonal increase in demand is the reason for holding **anticipation inventories.** For example, rather than operating with excessive overtime in one period and then allowing the productive system to be idle or shut down because of insufficient demand in another period, inventories can be allowed to build up before an event and consumed during or after the event. Manufacturers, wholesalers, and retailers build anticipation inventories before occasions such as Christmas and Halloween, when demand for specialized products will be high.

4. *Decoupling inventories:* It would be a rare production system in which all equipment and personnel operated at exactly the same rate. Yet if you were to take an inspection tour through a production facility, you would notice that most of the equipment and people were producing. Products move smoothly even though one machine can process parts five times as fast as the one before or after it. An inventory of parts between machines, or fluid in a vat, known as **decoupling inventory,** acts to disengage the production system. That is, inventories act as shock absorbers, or cushions, increasing and decreasing in size as parts are added to and used up from the stock. Even if a preceding machine were to break down, the following machines could still produce (at least for a while), since an in-process inventory of parts would be waiting for production. The more inventories management carries between stages in the manufacturing and distribution system, the less coordination is needed to keep the system running smoothly. Clearly, there is an optimum balance between inventory level and coordination in the operations system. Without decoupling inventories, each operation in the plant

would have to produce at an identical rate (a *paced line*) to keep the production flowing smoothly, and when one operation broke down, the entire plant would come to a standstill.

5. *Cycle inventories:* **Cycle inventories**—or, as they are sometimes referred to, *lot-size* inventories—exist for a different reason from the others just discussed. Each of the previous types of inventories serves one of the major purposes for holding inventory. Cycle inventories, on the other hand, result from management's attempt to minimize the total cost of carrying and ordering inventory. If the annual demand for a particular part is 12,000 units, management could decide to place one order for 12,000 units and maintain a rather large inventory throughout the year or place 12 orders of 1000 each and maintain a lower level of inventory. But the costs associated with ordering and receiving would increase. Cycle inventories are the inventories that result from ordering in batches or "lots" rather than as needed.

❖ Forms of Inventories

Inventories are usually classified into four forms, some of which correspond directly with the previous inventory functions but some of which do not.

1. *Raw materials:* Raw materials are objects, commodities, elements, and items that are received (usually purchased) from outside the organization to be used directly in the production of the final output. When we think of raw materials, we think of such things as sheet metal, flour, paint, structural steel, chemicals, and other basic materials. But nuts and bolts, hydraulic cylinders, engines, frames, integrated circuits, and other assemblies purchased from outside the organization would also be considered part of the raw materials inventory.

2. *Maintenance, repair, and operating supplies:* Maintenance, repair, and operating (MRO) supplies are items used to support and maintain the production system, including spares, supplies, and stores. Spares are sometimes produced by the organization itself rather than purchased. These are usually machine parts or supplies that are crucial to production. The term *supplies* is often used synonymously with *inventories.* The general convention, and the one that we will adopt in this book, is that supplies are stocks of items used (consumed) in the production of goods or services but are not directly a part of the finished product. Examples are copier paper, staples, pencils, and packing material. *Stores* commonly include both supplies and raw materials that are kept in stock or on shelves in a special location.

3. *Work-in-process:* **Work-in-process (WIP)** inventory consists of all the materials, parts, and assemblies that are being worked on or are waiting to be processed within the operations system. Decoupling inventories are an example of work-in-process. That is, they are all the items that have left the raw materials inventory but have not yet been converted or assembled into a final product.

4. *Finished goods:* The **finished goods** inventory is the stock of completed products. Goods, once completed, are transferred out of work-in-process in-

ventory and into the finished goods inventory. From here they can be sent to distribution centers, sold to wholesalers, or sold directly to retailers or final customers.

As you can see from this discussion, the inventory system and the operations system within an organization are strongly interrelated. Inventories affect customer service, utilization of facilities and equipment, capacity, and efficiency of labor. Therefore, the plans concerning the acquisition and storage of materials, or "inventories," are vital to the production system.

The ultimate objective of any inventory system is to make decisions regarding the level of inventory that will result in a good balance between the purposes for holding inventories and the costs associated with them. Typically, we hear inventory management practitioners and researchers speaking of *total cost minimization* as the objective of an inventory system. If we were able to place dollar costs on interruptions in the smooth flow of goods through the operations system, on not meeting customers' demands, or on failures to provide the other purposes for which inventories exist, then minimization of total costs would be a reasonable objective. But, since we are unable to assign costs to many of these subjective factors, we must be satisfied with obtaining a good balance between the costs and the functions of inventories.

❖ Costs Involved in Decisions about Inventories

There are essentially five broad categories of costs associated with inventory systems:

1. Ordering or Setup Costs

Ordering costs are costs associated with outside procurement of material, and ***setup costs*** are costs associated with internal procurement (i.e., internal manufacture) of parts of material. Ordering costs include writing the order, processing the order through the purchasing system, postage, processing invoices, processing accounts payable, and the work of the receiving department, such as handling, testing, inspection, and transporting. Setup costs also include writing orders and processing for the internal production system, setup labor, machine downtime due to a new setup (i.e., cost of an idle, nonproducing machine), parts damaged during setup (e.g., actual parts are often used for tests during setup), and costs associated with employees' learning curve (i.e., the cost of early production spoilage and low productivity immediately after a new production run is started).

2. Inventory Carrying or Holding Costs

Inventory ***carrying*** or ***holding*** costs have the following major components:

- ❖ Capital costs.
- ❖ Storage costs.
- ❖ Risk costs.

Capital costs include interest on money invested in inventory and in the land, buildings, and equipment necessary to hold and maintain the inventory. These rates often exceed 20 percent. If these investments were not required, the organization could invest the capital in an alternative that would earn some return on investment.

Storage costs include rent, taxes, and insurance on buildings; depreciation of buildings; maintenance and repairs; heat, power, and light; salaries of security personnel; taxes on the inventory; labor costs for handling inventory; clerical costs for keeping records; taxes and insurance on equipment; depreciation of equipment; fuel and energy for equipment; and repairs and maintenance. Some of these costs are variable, some fixed, and some "semifixed."

Risk costs include the costs of obsolete inventory, insurance on inventory, physical deterioration of the inventory, and losses from pilferage. Even though some of these costs are relatively small, the total costs of carrying items in inventory can be quite large. Studies have found that for a typical manufacturing firm, the cost is frequently as large as 35 percent of the cost of the inventoried items. A large portion of this is the cost of the invested capital.

3. Stockout Costs

If inventory is unavailable when customers request it, or when it is needed for production, a stockout occurs. Several costs are associated with each type of stockout. A stockout of an item demanded by a customer or client can result in lost sales or demand, lost goodwill (which is very difficult to estimate), and costs associated with processing back orders (such as extra paperwork, expediting, special handling, and higher shipping costs). A stockout of an item needed for production results in costs for rescheduling production, costs of downtime and delays caused by the shortage, the cost of "rush" shipping of needed parts, and possibly the cost of substituting a more expensive part or materials.

4. Capacity-Associated Costs

Capacity-associated costs are incurred because a change in productive capacity is necessary or because there is a temporary shortage of or excess in capacity. Why would capacity be too great or too small? If, for example, a company tried to meet seasonal demand (or any fluctuations in demand) by changing the level of production rather than by allowing the level of inventory to rise or fall, capacity would have to be increased during high-demand periods and lie idle during low-demand periods. Also, capacity problems are often due to scheduling conflicts. These commonly arise when multiple products have to be produced on the same set of facilities.

Capacity-associated costs include the overtime required to increase capacity; the costs of hiring, training, and terminating employees; the cost of using less skilled workers during peak periods; and the cost of idle time if capacity is *not* reduced during periods when demand decreases. The trade-offs in these costs were considered earlier, in Chapter 11, with regard to aggregate planning.

5. Cost of Goods

Last, the goods themselves must be paid for. Although they must be acquired sooner or later anyway, *when* they are acquired can influence their cost considerably, as through quantity discounts.

❖ Decisions in Inventory Management

The objective of an inventory management system is to make decisions regarding the appropriate level of inventory and changes in the level of inventory. To maintain the appropriate level of inventory, decision rules are needed to answer two basic questions:

1. When should an order be placed to replenish the inventory?
2. How much should be ordered?

The decision rules guide the inventory manager in evaluating the current state of the inventory and deciding if some action, such as replenishment, is required. Various types of inventory management systems incorporate different rules to decide "when" and "how much." Some depend on time and others on the level of inventory, but the essential decisions are the same. Even when complexities, such as uncertainty in demand and delivery times, are introduced, deciding "how many" and "when to order" still remains the basis of sound inventory management.

❖ Types of Inventory Management Systems

All inventory systems can be classified as one of three varieties, based on the approach taken to deciding "when to order":

1. Reorder point systems.
2. Periodic review systems.
3. Materials requirements planning (MRP) systems, described in detail in Chapter 13.

Before we discuss these three systems, let us consider a simplified inventory management situation, to provide a background.

Consider the Charger Corporation, a wholesaler that sells 1000 generators per month to automobile parts retailers in the southeast. Demand for generators is constant throughout the year. Suppose that Charger has a policy of ordering 2000 generators per order and that it has just received a shipment of 2000, bringing its inventory level to 2000.

Charger sells 1000 generators per month, and therefore the beginning inventory of 2000 units will be depleted by the end of the second month. To avoid "stocking out," an order must be placed and shipment received before the end of the second month. To keep the costs of carrying inventory as low as possible, it is desirable to schedule receipt of the order at the time that the previous inventory is exhausted. Assuming this perfect scheduling and "instantaneous replenishment" (the entire order quantity is received when the inventory level reaches zero), we can graph the inventory level as it changes over time as in Figure 12.1.

Inventory is used at the rate of 1000 per month, and orders are received so that the inventory level is replenished before a stockout can occur. No stockouts occur, and the inventory level never exceeds the order quantity of 2000. As we progress through this chapter, we will eliminate the unrealistic assumptions of constant demand and instantaneous replenishment and introduce other, more "realistic" as-

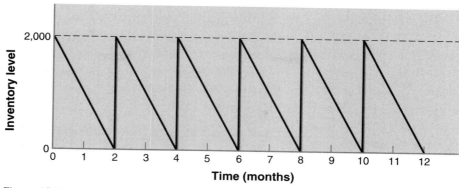

Figure 12.1   Fluctuations in inventory.

sumptions. For now, let us turn to a discussion of the three types of inventory control systems.

Reorder Point Systems

In reorder point systems an inventory *level* is specified at which a replenishment order for a fixed quantity of the inventory item is to be placed. Whenever the inventory on hand reaches the predetermined inventory level—the ***reorder point***—an order is placed for a prespecified amount, as illustrated in Figure 12.2. The reorder point is established so that the inventory on hand at the time an order is placed is sufficient to meet demand during the ***lead time*** (i.e., the time between placement of an order and receipt of the shipment). The quantity of inventory to be ordered is often based on the ***economic order quantity (EOQ)*** (one answer to the question "how much to order"), an approach illustrated later in this chapter. But other rules

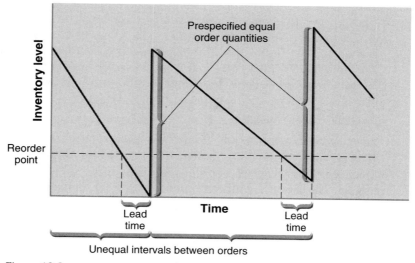

Figure 12.2   A reorder point system.

for deciding "how much," such as ordering a "six-week supply," are also used in reorder point systems.

A simplified and much used variation of the reorder point system is the **two-bin** system, in which parts are stored in two bins—one large and one small. The small bin usually holds sufficient parts to satisfy demand during the replenishment lead time. Parts are used from only the large bin, until it is empty. At that time, a replenishment order is placed, and parts from the small bin are used until the replenishment order is received.

Many variations of two-bin systems have been developed. In some systems it is simply the responsibility of the employee who removes the last item from the large bin to place a requisition for materials with the purchasing department or with the supervisor. In others, a completed requisition is placed at the bottom of the larger bin and needs to be picked up and submitted only when the last item is removed. In others, a card is affixed to a wrapped quantity of items in the small bin. When these items are opened, the card is removed and sent to data processing to generate an order. The advantage of the two-bin system is that no detailed real-time records of inventory use (a **perpetual inventory system**) must be kept, and inventory need not be continually recounted to determine whether or not a reorder should be placed.

This latter point is important. A perpetual inventory system requires either a manual card system or a computerized system to keep track of daily usage and daily stock levels. Also, each day the cards or the computer file must be "searched" to find all items that have fallen to or below the reorder point. Note that these are clerical functions, which remove the burden of assessing proper inventory levels from the people who use the inventory. Perpetual systems run into problems when those who use the inventory fail to report its use. Management controls over the inventory system must be fairly rigid, to ensure that perpetual records remain accurate and, in turn, result in the proper placement of orders for inventory. This also requires a regular physical check of the inventory to be sure that the records are accurate. A reorder point system could not perform adequately without either a two-bin system or perpetual inventory control. Without one of these, someone would have to record the inventory balances for all items each day in order to have accurate counts and, therefore, to know when to order. The recent development of real-time inventory control systems that include computerized order entry and invoicing has greatly eased difficulties of the perpetual system and reduced the need for two-bin systems. For example, inventory records at grocery stores can be instantaneously updated as items are scanned at the cash registers.

Periodic Review Systems

In **periodic review systems** the inventory level is reviewed at equal time intervals, and at each review a reorder may be placed to bring the level up to a desired quantity. Such a system is especially appropriate for retailers ordering families of goods. The amount of the reorder is based on a maximum level established for each inventory item. The quantity that should be reordered is the amount necessary to bring the *on-hand* inventory, plus the *on-order* quantity, less the expected demand over the lead time, to the maximum level:

$$\text{Reorder quantity} = \text{maximum level} - \text{on-hand inventory}$$
$$- \text{on-order quantity} + \text{demand over lead time}$$

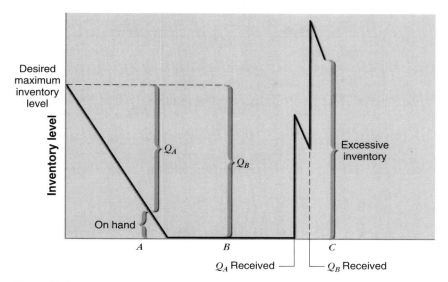

Figure 12.3   Periodic review system without considering on-order quantity.

The on-hand inventory is the amount actually in stock. If the system allows backorders, then on-hand could be negative, at least in theory. If backorders are not used, then a stockout simply results in a zero on-hand quantity.

The on-order amount is the quantity for which purchase orders have been issued, but delivery has not yet been made. We deduct the on-order quantity to ensure that an order is not placed for the same goods. Figure 12.3 illustrates such an occurrence. Suppose that at review point A an order is simply placed for Q_A. At review point B, the first order has not arrived, so an order for Q_B is placed. No attention was paid to the on-order quantity. Now, some time later, Q_A is received, and then Q_B. At review point C, inventory exceeds the desired maximum.

In periodic review systems the *review period* (and therefore the *reorder period*) *is fixed,* and the *order quantity varies* (see Figure 12.4) according to the above rule. This system is more appropriate when it is difficult to keep track of inventory levels

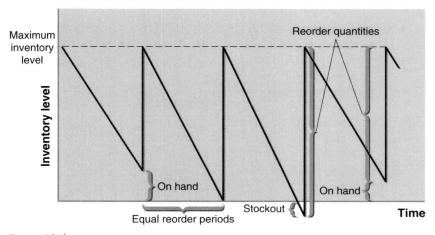

Figure 12.4   Periodic review system (assumes none on order at time of reorder).

*S*OLVED EXERCISE 12.1 ❖ Reorder Point and Periodic Review Systems

A small firm uses the two-bin system. Its average demand is 3 units a day; it uses an order quantity of 27 units; and its lead time is two days. How many units should be placed in the small bin? If the firm switches to a periodic review system, how often should it review? If, in using the periodic system, the firm finds at one of its review points that there are 2 units on hand and 22 units on order, what should it do?

Solution:

We draw the inventory graph as below.

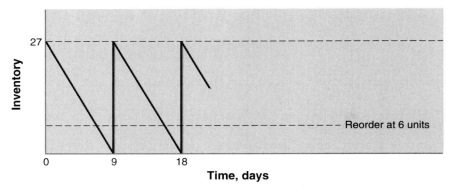

One cycle requires 27/3 = 9 days. In two days, demand will be 2 × 3 = 6 units. Therefore, the small bin should hold 6 units.

The periodic reviews should be the same as the cycle time: 9 days.

Reorder quantity = 27 − 2 − 22 + 6 = 9 units should be ordered.

and the cost of stockouts or safety stock is not excessive. Since inventory is not continuously tracked, there is a significant chance of stocking out. This possibility can be avoided by using safety stock, as described later in this chapter.

In reorder point systems the *order quantity is fixed,* and the *reorder period varies* (see Figure 12.2). This system is best where a continuing watch of inventory levels is feasible and stockouts or safety stock would be expensive. If demand increases during the period, the reorder point system would simply place an order sooner than normal. The periodic review system would review and place an order at the regularly scheduled time but for a quantity larger than normal. However, in both systems there is a risk of a stockout because the demand during the lead time may be greater than the amount on hand at the time the order is placed. As we will see, there are ways to compensate for this risk.

Materials Requirements Planning (MRP) Systems

The two systems discussed so far are appropriate for inventory items with fairly constant, and independent, demand. **Independent demand** means simply that demand for an item is not based on demand for some other item. Examples include clothing, furniture, automobiles, retail items, and supply-type items (paper, pencils) in a manufacturing or office environment. The most likely applications for the two previous systems are inventories of finished goods.

Conversely, **dependent demand** items are components, assemblies, and subassemblies of the finished item (called the *end item*), such as the bicycle tires on a bike, the lampshades, or any raw materials. These materials and parts are not usually subject to random demands from customers; they are subject primarily to the demands placed on them from the end items or assemblies they go into. Since demand for them depends on the demand for the end item, they do not require separate forecasts. For instance, a manufacturer of bikes does not need to forecast the demand for both bikes and tires, since the demand for tires depends on the demand for bikes (i.e., each bike requires two tires). Thus, we derive the demand for dependent demand items from the demand of end items, and control their inventory levels through materials requirements planning (MRP, described in detail in Chapter 13). As we will see, the MRP system considers how the product is made and how long it takes to make each of the items.

As with the perpetual and periodic inventory systems, MRP time-phases orders on the basis of lead times and minimum stocking levels also. The size of an order can be based on an economic order quantity, six weeks' worth of stock, or any other such rule. In this regard it is not much different from the other inventory systems. However, in MRP it is not the stock level that is monitored but rather the demands of the parent product for the part. These expected future demands are updated continuously as the demands of the final product change, thus giving a better forecast.

In the remaining sections of this chapter, we will address the issues of determining which inventory items to monitor most closely, how to determine economic order sizes, and how to take uncertainty into account when reordering stock.

$\mathscr{P}$RIORITIES FOR INVENTORY MANAGEMENT: THE ABC CONCEPT

In practice, not all inventories need be controlled with equal attention. Some inventories are simply too small or too unimportant to warrant intensive monitoring and control. In addition, in implementing new inventory management systems, priorities must be developed to allow management to decide the order in which to include the inventoried items in the control system. One simple procedure that has been widely and successfully used is the ABC classification system, as is illustrated in the accompanying sidebar about Johnson & Johnson.

OPERATIONS IN PRACTICE

Johnson & Johnson Cuts Costs of Spare Parts

Johnson & Johnson's Devro Division uses very expensive, complex machinery in a 24-hour, 7-day continuous process to produce sausage casings for food processors in the United States, England, Australia, Canada, and Germany. To keep the equipment working and quickly repair any breakdowns, Devro maintains a large, expensive stock of over 1000 spare parts. Previously, parts were ordered from a routine check of the stockroom, which resulted in excesses of some parts and shortages of others. For the shortages, air freight was used to expedite the deliveries, since normal lead times were too long.

To gain better control over these parts, Devro implemented a more formal inventory control, based on the ABC approach. To initiate the study, data were collected on each of the 1337 spare parts and a standard ABC analysis was conducted. The result was that 33 items were identified as class A (representing about 50 percent of total annual usage), 330 items as class B (representing 35 percent of usage), and the remaining 974 items as class C.

The A and B items were placed on perpetual inventory cards, and traveling requisitions were prepared for them beforehand. For traveling requisitions, departmental approval was required only once a year, so the requisition could go directly to purchasing for ordering.

The result has been a reduction in air freight charges of 46 percent and item-ordering time from three days to one day. The frequency of ordering the wrong part has also been reduced, and since all the necessary information is on the requisition, the crib room attendant is saving an hour a day. Last, owing to the consolidation of information, parts are now being ordered from the lowest-cost supplier and competitive bids are being sought on the items most frequently used (Flowers and O'Neill, 1978).

$\mathscr{T}$ABLE 12.1 ❖ Inventory Value by Item

Annual Quantity Used	Percentage of Total Items	Annual Dollar Purchases	Percentage of Total Purchases
521	4.8	$15,400,000	50.7
574	5.3	6,200,000	20.4
1023	9.4	3,600,000	11.8
1145	10.5	2,300,000	7.6
3754	34.0	1,800,000	5.9
3906	36.0	1,100,000	3.6
10,923	100.0	$30,400,000	100.0

The **ABC classification system** is based on the annual dollar purchases of an inventoried item. As can be seen from Table 12.1, a relatively small proportion of the total items in an inventory account for a relatively large proportion of the total annual dollar volume, and a large proportion of the items account for a small proportion of the dollars. This phenomenon is often found in systems in which large numbers of different items are maintained. It is also in evidence in marketing, where a small number of customers represent the bulk of the sales; in complaint departments, where a large volume of complaints come from a relatively small group; and so forth.

The three classifications used in the ABC system are:

❖ **A.** *High-value items:* The 15 to 20 percent or so* of the items that account for 75 to 80 percent of the total annual inventory value.

---

*The percentages are somewhat arbitrary and vary to suit individual needs.

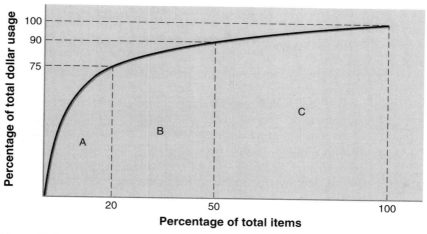

Figure 12.5   ABC inventory categories.

❖ **B.** *Medium-value items:* The 30 to 40 percent of the items that account for approximately 15 percent of the total annual inventory value.

❖ **C.** *Low-value items:* The 40 to 50 percent of the items that account for 10 to 15 percent of the annual inventory value.

The classification is shown in Figure 12.5, which gives the cumulative distribution of the dollar value of inventory items. In practice, the A items are identified first, then the C items, and what is left is usually considered to represent the B items. Of course, at times it may be appropriate to reclassify an item classification on the basis of other criteria. For example, a B item that has especially long lead times or is considered critical can be elevated to category A.

A common misconception is that the ABC classification is based on the dollar value of the individual items. In actuality, relatively costly items can still be classified as C if annual usage is low enough. Table 12.2 is a simple table of cost-volume combinations and the inventory class likely to result from them.

𝒯ABLE 12.2 ❖ Classification of Inventory Items

Dollar Value/Unit	Volume/Year	Category
High	High	A
High	Medium	A
Medium	High	A
High	Low	B
Medium	Medium	B
Low	High	B
Medium	Low	C
Low	Medium	C
Low	Low	C

The ABC classification is management's guide to the priorities of inventory items, as described in the accompanying sidebar on hospital inventories. The A items should be subject to the tightest control, with detailed inventory records and accurate, updated values of order quantities and reorder points. B items are subject to normal control, with order quantities set by EOQ (as shown in the next section) but with less frequent updating of records and review of order quantities and reorder points. C items are subject to little control; orders are placed for a six-month to one-year supply so that relatively little control must be exercised and inventory records can be kept simple. Essentially, the time and effort saved by not controlling C items is used to tighten control of A items.

The ABC concept is not only used for inventory control but is also frequently used to determine priorities for customer service and to decide on levels of safety stock, a subject we will address later in this chapter. The concept is also known by other names, such as the *80-20 rule* and the *Pareto principle* (after the economist who discovered the effect).

OPERATIONS
IN PRACTICE

Using ABC to Control Hospital Inventories

Cost containment in hospitals has taken on renewed importance in recent years, in light of the ever-increasing cost of medical care. Since inventories represent a major investment of a hospital's assets, many hospital administrators are seeking more systematic methods of controlling these inventories. The objective is both to lower investment costs and thus to improve service.

In one study, the ABC inventory classification method was applied to a group of 47 disposable stock-keeping units (SKUs) in the respiratory unit of a regional hospital. These items were entered into a spreadsheet and rank-ordered in accordance with their annual dollar usage. There was a large break in annual usage between the tenth and eleventh items on the list, which represented 21 percent of all SKUs but 74 percent of the total annual usage value of $51,685. Thus, these first 10 SKUs were deemed class A items.

The next class, B, was determined by both natural breaks in the annual value and informed judgment regarding the importance of individual SKUs to the goals of the hospital. The 13 items in the B class thus represented 28 percent of the items and 18 percent of the annual usage value. The remainder of the SKUs—24 in total—represented 51 percent of the items, but only 8 percent of the annual value.

The management of these classes was then differentiated to provide better control at less cost. The class A items were monitored closely, and forecasts were updated monthly. Stocks were counted and replenished weekly, or more often if the reorder point was passed. Minimum stock levels were established for these items relative to their lead times, the availability of substitute SKUs, and their criticality. The B items were replenished biweekly, and price discounts were negotiated through blanket order commitments with suppliers. The ordering of C items was automated for replenishment to a preestablished maximum every two to three months. A two-bin system was implemented to trigger purchases between replenishments, if necessary.

This system gave the hospital better control over its inventories, with reduced inventory costs. It also offered a cost-effective inventory control policy. The ABC procedure offers a simple yet powerful approach to managing assets such as inventories for a reasonable investment of managerial time and energy, particularly in designing control procedures (Reid, 1987).

Spreadsheet Analysis: ABC Analysis

Spreadsheets can be used to quickly sort data on part usage. The parts can then be classified as A, B, or C items by identifying natural breaks in the data. The spreadsheet below contains data for 12 parts.

	A	B	C	D	E
1	Item Number	Annual Usage	Unit Cost	Annual Cost	% Total Annual Cost
2	320X	1000	$1.25	$1,250.00	0.97%
3	320Y	2500	$11.52	$28,800.00	22.24%
4	500SC	900	$3.75	$3,375.00	2.61%
5	250TY	450	$10.35	$4,657.50	3.60%
6	900QT	7500	$8.01	$60,075.00	46.39%
7	275G	400	$12.65	$5,060.00	3.91%
8	925PR	150	$9.05	$1,357.50	1.05%
9	712MP	1200	$2.75	$3,300.00	2.55%
10	212MY	500	$3.76	$1,880.00	1.45%
11	780CY	200	$9.12	$1,824.00	1.41%
12	600DT	350	$21.00	$7,350.00	5.68%
13	400LM	500	$21.12	$10,560.00	8.16%
14	Total			$129,489.00	

Columns A, B, and C respectively contain the part item numbers, annual usage, and unit costs for the 12 parts. In column D the annual usage cost for the parts is calculated by multiplying a part's annual usage by its unit cost. For example, in cell D2: =B2*C2 was entered and then copied to cells D3:D13. Cell D14 contains the formula: = SUM(D2:D13) and thus provides the total annual usage costs of all 12 parts.

In column E, the percent an item's annual cost is of the total annual cost of all items is calculated. In cell E2: =D2/$D$14 was entered and then copied to cells E3:E13.

To identify natural breaks in the annual usage of the parts, we will sort column E from highest to lowest. First, highlight the range A2:E13 and with this range highlighted, select Data from the menu bar at the top of the screen. Next, select the Sort menu item. After you select Sort, the Sort dialog box is displayed as shown below. In the "Sort By" box we tell Excel which column to sort on. Since we want to sort the data from highest to lowest on the basis of each part's percent of total annual cost (column E), we specify this in the "Sort By" box and then click on the Descending radio button.

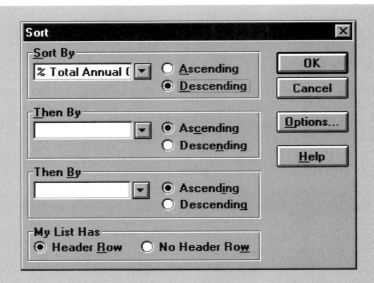

Select OK in the Sort dialog box to sort the data. After you select OK, the rows are sorted as shown below.

	A	B	C	D	E
1	Item Number	Annual Usage	Unit Cost	Annual Cost	% Total Annual Cost
2	900QT	7500	$8.01	$60,075.00	46.39%
3	320Y	2500	$11.52	$28,800.00	22.24%
4	400LM	500	$21.12	$10,560.00	8.16%
5	600DT	350	$21.00	$7,350.00	5.68%
6	275G	400	$12.65	$5,060.00	3.91%
7	250TY	450	$10.35	$4,657.50	3.60%
8	500SC	900	$3.75	$3,375.00	2.61%
9	712MP	1200	$2.75	$3,300.00	2.55%
10	212MY	500	$3.76	$1,880.00	1.45%
11	780CY	200	$9.12	$1,824.00	1.41%
12	925PR	150	$9.05	$1,357.50	1.05%
13	320X	1000	$1.25	$1,250.00	0.97%
14	Total			$129,489.00	

According to this spreadsheet, one break point occurs after part 320Y. Classifying parts 900QT and 320Y as A items represents 68.6 percent of the annual dollar value and 17 percent of the part volume. Another break could be drawn after part 250TY. Thus, the B items would be 400LM, 600DT, 275G, and 250TY. The B items represent 21.34 percent of the annual dollar value and 34 percent of the volume. The remaining parts would be classified as C items and would represent 50 percent of the volume of parts but only 10 percent of the dollar value.

$\mathcal{T}$HE ECONOMIC ORDER QUANTITY (EOQ)

The concept of ***economic order quantity*** (EOQ) applies to inventory items that are replenished in *batches* or *orders* and are not produced and delivered continuously. Although we have identified a number of costs associated with inventory decisions, only two categories, carrying cost and ordering cost, are considered in the basic EOQ model. Shortage costs and capacity-associated costs are not relevant, because shortages and changes in capacity should not occur if demand is constant, as we assume in this basic case. The cost of the goods is considered to be fixed and, hence, does not alter the decisions as to *when* inventory should be reordered or *how much* should be ordered.

More specifically, we assume the following in the EOQ model:

1. Rate of demand is constant (e.g., 50 units per day).
2. Shortages are not allowed.
3. Stock replenishment can be scheduled to arrive exactly when the inventory drops to zero.
4. Purchase price, ordering cost, and per unit holding cost are independent of quantity ordered.
5. Items are ordered independently of each other.

❖ Charger Corporation

Let us again consider the Charger Corporation, which sells 1000 generators per month (30 days) and purchases in quantities of 2000 per order. Lead time for the receipt of an order is six days. The cost accounting department has analyzed inventory costs and has determined that the cost of placing an order is $60 and the annual cost of holding one generator in inventory is $10.* Under its present policy of ordering 2000 per order, what is Charger's total annual inventory cost?

Charger's inventory pattern is represented by the "sawtooth" curve of Figure 12.6. For simplicity, let

$$Q = \text{order quantity}$$
$$U = \text{annual usage}$$
$$C_O = \text{order cost per order}$$
$$C_H = \text{annual holding cost per unit}$$

To determine the total annual incremental cost of Charger's current inventory policy, we must determine two separate annual costs: total annual holding cost and total annual ordering cost.

---

*Sometimes holding cost is given as fixed value per year and other times as a percentage of the value of the inventory, especially when interest charges represent the major holding cost. Then $C_H = iC$ where C is the cost of the inventory item and i is the interest rate.

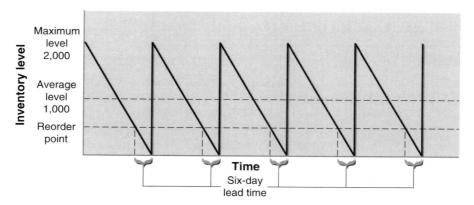

Figure 12.6   Charger Corporation's inventory pattern.

The *ordering cost* is determined by C_O, the cost to place one order ($60), and the number of orders placed per year. Since Charger sells 12,000 generators per year and orders 2000 per order, it must place 6 (that is, 12,000/2000) orders per year for a total ordering cost of $360 (6 orders per year × $60 per order). Using our notation, we write the annual ordering cost as

$$\text{annual ordering cost} = \frac{U}{Q} \times C_O$$

The annual holding cost is determined by C_H, the cost of holding one generator for one year ($10) and the number of generators held as "cycle stock." Notice that the inventory level is constantly changing and that no single generator ever remains in inventory for an entire year. On average, however, there are 1000 generators in the inventory. Consider one cycle of Charger's inventory graph, as shown in Figure 12.7.

The inventory level begins at 2000 units and falls to 0 units before the next cycle begins. Since the rate of decline in inventory is constant (i.e., 1000 per month), the average level is 1000 units or simply the arithmetic average of the two levels: (2000 + 0)/2 = 1000.

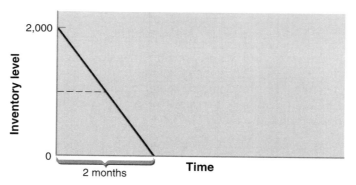

Figure 12.7   Charger's inventory graph.

If, on the average, there are 1000 generators in inventory over the entire year, then the annual inventory holding cost is $10,000 ($10 per unit 1000 units). Or, in our general notation,

$$\text{annual holding cost} = \frac{Q}{2} \times C_H$$

Adding annual ordering cost and annual holding cost gives the following equation for total annual cost (TAC):

$$\text{TAC} = \left(\frac{Q}{2}\right)C_H + \left(\frac{U}{Q}\right)C_O$$

For Charger, TAC is $360 + $10,000 = $10,360.

❖ Improving Charger's Inventory Policy

Charger's current inventory policy of ordering quantities of 2000 generators is costing $10,360 per year. Is this the best policy, or can it be improved? Using a simple trial-and-error approach, we can answer this question.

First, let us see what happens if we increase the order quantity to 5000 units:

$$\begin{aligned}
\text{TAC} &= \left(\frac{5000}{2}\right)10 + \left(\frac{12,000}{5000}\right)60 \\
&= 2500 \times 10 + 2.4 \times 60 \\
&= 25,000 + 144 \\
&= \$25,144
\end{aligned}$$

Annual holding cost increases, and ordering cost decreases; but the overall result is a significant increase in the total annual inventory cost. This is clearly an uneconomical choice. Let us try some other values. The resulting costs are given in Table 12.3.

We see from the table that 100 units is too small and the costs are beginning to increase again. But we have bounded the range of solutions. The best order quantity is somewhere between 100 and 1000 items.

𝒯ABLE 12.3 ❖ Costs of Various Order Quantities

Order Quantity	Annual Holding Cost	Annual Ordering Cost	Total Annual Cost
2000	$10,000	$360	$10,360
5000	25,000	144	25,144
1000	5000	720	5720
500	2500	1440	3940
100	500	7200	7700

❖ Finding an Optimal Policy

As you can imagine, the trial-and-error approach used above could go on for quite some time before an optimal policy (based on the previous five assumptions) is determined. A more straightforward approach to finding an optimal policy is to use graphing or an algebraic solution.

We can graph annual holding cost and annual ordering cost as a function of the order quantity, as shown in Figure 12.8. Since the annual holding cost is $(Q/2)C_H$, which can be written $(C_H/2)Q$, we see that holding cost is linear and increasing with respect to Q. Annual order cost is $(U/Q)C_O$, which can be rewritten as $(UC_O)/Q$. We can see that ordering cost is nonlinear with respect to Q and decreases as Q increases.

Now, if we add the two graphed quantities for all values of Q, we have the TAC curve shown in Figure 12.8. Note that TAC first decreases as ordering cost decreases but then starts to increase quickly. The point at which TAC is minimized is the optimal order quantity; that is, it gives the quantity Q which provides the least total annual inventory cost. This point is called the *economic order quantity* (EOQ), and for this inventory problem it happens to occur where the order cost curve intersects the holding cost curve. (The minimum point is not *always* where two curves intersect; it just happens to be so in the case of EOQ.) From Figure 12.8 we can see that EOQ is approximately 400 generators per order.

We can compute an accurate value algebraically by noting that the value of Q at the point of intersection of the two cost lines is the EOQ.* We can find an equation for EOQ by setting the two costs equal to one another and solving for the value of

---

*For students with an understanding of calculus: We could find the minimum of the TAC equation by taking the first derivative and setting it equal to zero as follows.

$$\text{TAC} = \left(\frac{Q}{2}\right)C_H + \left(\frac{U}{Q}\right)C_O$$

$$\frac{\partial \text{TAC}}{\partial Q} = \frac{C_H}{2} - \left(\frac{U}{Q^2}\right)C_O$$

Setting this equal to zero, we have,

$$0 = \frac{C_H}{2} - \left(\frac{U}{Q^2}\right)C_O$$

or:

$$\left(\frac{U}{Q^2}\right)C_O = \frac{C_H}{2}$$

$$UC_O = \frac{Q^2 C_H}{2}$$

$$\frac{2UC_O}{C_H} = Q^2$$

$$\sqrt{\frac{2UC_O}{C_H}} = Q$$

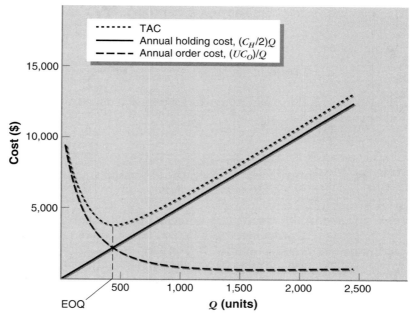

Figure 12.8   Graph of annual inventory costs.

Q that satisfies the equality:

$$\left(\frac{Q}{2}\right)C_H = \left(\frac{U}{Q}\right)C_O$$

Multiplying both sides by Q gives

$$\left(\frac{Q^2}{2}\right)C_H = UC_O$$

and dividing both sides by $C_H/2$ gives

$$Q^2 = \frac{2UC_O}{C_H}$$

Finally, taking the square root of both sides gives

$$Q = \sqrt{\frac{2UC_O}{C_H}}$$

Since Q is the economic order quantity, it is most often written as

$$EOQ = \sqrt{\frac{2UC_O}{C_H}}$$

For the Charger Corporation, we can compute EOQ as

$$EOQ = \sqrt{\frac{2(12,000)60}{10}} = \sqrt{144,000} = 379.5$$

Obviously, since we cannot order half a generator, the order quantity would be rounded to 380 units.

The total annual cost (TAC) of this policy would be:

$$TAC = \left(\frac{380}{2}\right)10 + \left(\frac{12,000}{380}\right)60 = 1900 + 1894.74 = \$3794.74$$

Note that this is an improvement in total annual cost of $6565.26 over the present policy of ordering 2000. But also note that the optimal policy of ordering 380 per order provides only a saving of $145.26 over the "order 500" policy, which we considered in our trial-and-error procedure. Actual inventory situations often exhibit this relative "insensitivity" to changes in quantity in the vicinity of EOQ. To the inventory manager what this means is added flexibility in order quantities. If, for example, shipping and handling was more convenient or economical in quantities of 500 (perhaps the items are wrapped in quantities of 250), the additional 120 units per order would cost the organization only an extra $145.26 per year.

❖ Cautions Regarding EOQ

The EOQ is a computed minimum-cost order quantity. As with any model or formula, the GIGO rule (garbage in, garbage out) applies. If the values used in computing EOQ are inaccurate, then EOQ will be inaccurate—though, as mentioned previously, a slight error will not increase costs significantly. EOQ relies heavily on two variables that are subject to considerable misinterpretation. These are the two cost elements: holding cost (C_H) and order cost (C_O). In the derivation of EOQ, we assumed that by ordering fewer units per order the cost of holding inventory would be reduced. Similarly, it was assumed that by reducing the number of orders placed each year the cost of ordering could be proportionately reduced. Both assumptions must be thoroughly questioned in looking at each cost element that is included in both C_H and C_O.

For example, if a single purchasing agent is employed by the firm, and orders are reduced from 3000 per year to 2000 per year, does it stand to reason that the purchasing expense will be reduced by one-third? Unless the person is paid on a piecework basis, the answer is clearly no. Similarly, suppose we rent a warehouse that will hold 100,000 items and that we currently keep it full. If the order sizes are reduced so that the warehouse is only 65 percent occupied, can we persuade the owners to charge us only 65 percent of the rental price? Again, the answer is no. Clearly, then, when costs are determined for computations, only real, out-of-pocket costs should be used. Costs that are committed or "sunk," no matter what the inventory level or number of orders is, should be excluded because they violate the assumptions of the EOQ model.

Note also that C_H and C_O are *controllable* costs. That is, they can be reduced, if this is advantageous. This is exactly what the Japanese recognized. The problems they saw with holding inventory were:

- Product defects becomes hidden in the inventory, thereby increasing scrap and rework later in the production system, when defects are harder to repair. Just as important, the problem in the system that led to the defective part cannot be tracked down so easily later on.
- Storage space takes up precious room and separates all the company's functions and equipment, thereby increasing problems with communication. Space itself is extremely expensive in Japan (directly increasing the variable C_H).
- More inventory in the plant means that more control is needed, more planning is required, larger systems are required to move all that stock, and in general more "hassle" is created, which leads to errors, defects, missed deliveries, long lead times, and more difficulty in product changeovers.

Rarely do American firms consider these real costs in the EOQ formula. More typically, these costs are considered part of the indirect, overhead, or "burden" costs that are assumed to be uncontrollable. Again, the message is: Be very careful about the values used in the EOQ formula.

Also, it should be noted that very small EOQ values (e.g., 2) will not usually be valid, because the cost functions are questionable for such small orders. Last, EOQ reorder sizes should not be followed blindly. There may not be enough cash just now to pay for an EOQ, or storage space may be insufficient. We will illustrate how spreadsheet analysis can be used to cope with these obstacles.

$\mathcal{S}$OLVED EXERCISE 12.2 ❖ Economic Order Quantity and Costs

Given annual demand of 33,000 items, order cost of $150, and carrying cost of $4 per item per month, what are the EOQ, annual ordering cost, and monthly carrying cost?

Solution:

$$EOQ = \sqrt{\frac{2(33,000)(150)}{4 \times 12}} = 454$$

$$\text{Annual ordering cost} = \frac{(33,000) \times 150}{454} = \$10,903$$

$$\text{Monthly carrying cost} = \frac{454}{2} \times 4 = \$908$$

Spreadsheet Analysis: Determining Order Quantities in Multiple-Product Situations

A basic assumption of the EOQ model is that items are independent of one another. However, this assumption rarely reflects actual situations. In this example we demonstrate how spreadsheet analysis can be used to overcome the problems created when multiple items share a common warehouse and are therefore not independent of one another. These items are dependent in the sense that if the warehouse is filled with one of them, there is no place to store the rest.

Fiveco purchases and then resells five products. The table below provides information related to the annual demand or usage of these products (U), the cost of placing an order (C_O), the cost of holding one unit in inventory for one year (C_H), and the storage space (in square feet) one unit takes up when stored in the warehouse.

Part	U	C_O	C_H	Square feet
A	1000	20	1.25	1.50
B	1500	20	1.75	2.10
C	750	20	2.55	3.00
D	1200	20	1.35	1.60
E	1600	20	1.65	2.00

Fiveco has 650 square feet of space available in its warehouse to store these five products. It has determined that using the average inventory level of each item provides an accurate estimate of the total space required when these averages are summed across all five products.

This information was entered into the spreadsheet shown below.

	A	B	C	D	E	F	G	H	I
1		Annual	Order	Holding	Storage			Storage	
2		Usage	Cost	Cost	Space		Average	Space	Total
3	Part	U	C_O	C_H	(ft²)	EOQ	Inventory	Required	Cost
4	A	1000	20	1.25	1.50	179	89.44	134.16	$223.61
5	B	1500	20	1.75	2.10	185	92.58	194.42	$324.04
6	C	750	20	2.55	3.00	108	54.23	162.70	$276.59
7	D	1200	20	1.35	1.60	189	94.28	150.85	$254.56
8	E	1600	20	1.65	2.00	197	98.47	196.95	$324.96
9	Total							839.08	$1,403.75
10									

Columns A to E contain the data. In column F, the EOQ is calculated for each item, independent of the other items. For example, in cell F4, the following formula was entered:

$$=SQRT((2*B4*C4)/D4)$$

This formula was then copied to cells F5:F8.

In column G, the average inventory is calculated by dividing the EOQ by 2. Thus, =F4/2 was entered in cell G4 and then copied to cells G5:G8.

The storage space required for each item is calculated in column H by multiplying the average inventory of each item by the space that item requires, as given in column E. Thus, the formula =G4*E4 was entered in cell H4 and then copied to cells H5:H8. In cell H9, the total space required for all five products is calculated by summing the values in cells H4:H8. Specifically, =SUM(H4:H8) was entered in cell H9.

Finally, the annual cost of ordering and carrying each item is calculated in column I. For example, in cell I4

$$=(G4*D4)+((B4/F4)*C4)$$

was entered and then copied to cells I5:I8. The first part of this formula computes the annual holding cost, and the second part computes the annual ordering cost. In cell I9 the total cost over the five products is calculated by summing the values in cells I4:I8. Rather than entering a new formula, the formula in cell H9 was copied to cell I9.

The total annual cost of using the individual EOQs is $1,403.75. Unfortunately, this is not a feasible solution, since the space required exceeds the 650 square feet available. One approach to this problem is to use trial and error and enter new order quantities in cells F4:F8 until the amount of space needed no longer exceeds what is available. However, using Excel's optimization capabilities, we can arrive at a better solution in less time.

To begin, our goal is to minimize total annual costs associated with ordering and carrying the five items (i.e., cell I9). However, we need to make sure that the solution we arrive at does not require more storage space than we have available. In this example, this means that the value in cell H9 must be less than or equal to 650. In order to arrive at a solution that minimizes total annual costs and does not exceed the storage space available, we can choose the values of the order quantities for the five items (e.g., cells F4:F8), subject to two restrictions. First, we cannot place an order for a negative number of units; second, we can't order a fraction of a unit.

To use Excel's optimization capability, select Tools from the menu bar at the top of the screen and then select Solver from the new menu that is displayed. We tell Excel we wish to minimize the value in cell I9 (total annual cost) by entering I9 in the "Set Target Cell" box and then selecting the Min radio button. Next, we tell Excel that it can change the values in cells F4:F8 in order to find the lowest total annual cost by entering the range F4:F8 in the "By Changing Cells" box.

Last, we enter constraints and limitations. In this problem we have three constraints: (1) Total space required (cell H9) must be less than or equal to 650 square feet. (2) The values chosen for the order quantities cannot be negative. (3) The values chosen for the order quantities must be whole numbers. To add these constraints, select the Add button in "Subject to the Constraints" section. Doing this displays the Add Constraint dialog box as shown below.

To enter the constraint: H9 ≤ 650, fill in the dialog box as shown below. Then select the Add button to enter the next constraint.

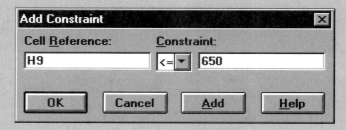

Continue adding constraints until all the following constraints have been added. After entering the last constraint, select the OK button in the Add Constraint dialog box instead of Add to tell Excel that this is the last constraint. The constraints you need to enter include:

F4 ≥ 0
F5 ≥ 0
F6 ≥ 0
F7 ≥ 0
F8 ≥ 0
F4 int integer
F5 int integer
F6 int integer
F7 int integer
F8 int integer

A quicker way to enter these constraints involves using ranges as a sort of shorthand. For example, these constraints could be entered as: F4:F8 ≥ 0 and F4:F8 int integer. After entering these constraints using either longhand or shorthand, select the OK button. The Solver Parameters dialog box is then displayed as shown below.

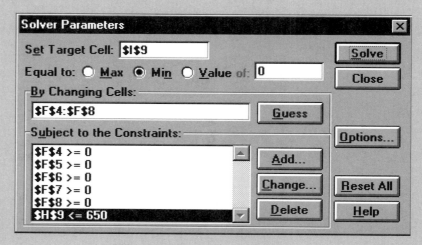

After returning to the Solver Parameters dialog box, select the Solve button. Once Excel has found a solution, the Solver Results dialog box is displayed. Select the OK button in the Solver Results dialog box to keep and display the current solution. The solution found by Excel is shown below.

	A	B	C	D	E	F	G	H	I
1		Annual	Order	Holding	Storage			Storage	
2		Usage	Cost	Cost	Space		Average	Space	Total
3	Part	U	C_o	C_H	(ft²)	EOQ	Inventory	Required	Cost
4	A	1000	20	1.25	1.50	139	69.50	104.25	$230.76
5	B	1500	20	1.75	2.10	143	71.50	150.15	$334.92
6	C	750	20	2.55	3.00	84	42.00	126.00	$285.67
7	D	1200	20	1.35	1.60	147	73.50	117.60	$262.49
8	E	1600	20	1.65	2.00	152	76.00	152.00	$335.93
9	Total							650.00	$1,449.76

The cost of the new solution increased from $1,403.75 to $1,449.76. However, the space required, based on the new order quantities, is now acceptable.

❖ Using the EOQ in Reorder Point and Periodic Review Inventory Systems

As we mentioned in the previous section, both reorder point systems and periodic review systems rely on the EOQ for reorder level and review interval. Consider first the graph for the optimal "order 380" policy, shown in Figure 12.9.

Charger's maximum inventory level will be 380 units. Selling at the rate of 1000 per month, or 33.34 per day, the firm will sell the beginning supply of 380 in 11.4 days. An order must be placed 6 days prior to the time the original supply will be exhausted (this is the *lead time*, LT) so that an order will be received in time to avoid stockouts. In order to avoid stockouts, therefore, Charger must reorder when

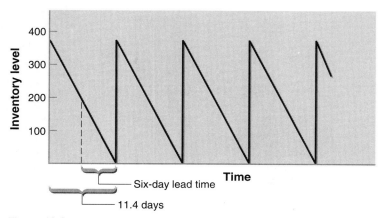

Figure 12.9   Optimal inventory pattern for Charger Corporation.

OPERATIONS
IN PRACTICE

Weyerhaeuser's Inventory Model Saves $2 Million a Year

To produce paper and pulp, modern manufacturers store thousands of tons of wood in chip form in outside storage facilities with sophisticated bulk-handling equipment. These inventories serve as a buffer against differences between mill supply and demand and thereby reduce the risk of a stockout owing to weather, strikes, or transportation problems. A stockout is a catastrophic situation, since it involves lost sales and perhaps lost customers, layoffs, and extremely expensive shutdowns and restartups. The inventories also act as a hedge against abrupt changes in the price of wood and allow purchases when prices are low.

Aging the wood outside can lead to deterioration, however, with a resulting increase in cost and loss of quality. Even more important, this inventory is expensive, running $50 per ton. If a mill keeps 100,000 tons in inventory, the wood is worth $5 million. And if interest on capital is 15 percent a year, this means the firm is paying $750,000 per year just to hold this inventory.

Precisely these considerations led Weyerhaeuser to initiate an inventory analysis study. A computer model called SPRINT (Springfield Target Inventory) was developed to project chip inflows, outflows, and resultant inventory levels for any time period. Each source and use can be modeled as probability distributions, and SPRINT will derive the resulting probability distribution of a stockout for various inventory policies. SPRINT also calculates all the relevant costs involved in the situation: wood losses, by-product losses, pulping losses, and the cost of capital associated with the inventory.

This model has led to reduced chip inventories in several regions totaling 190,000 dry tons, representing an annual savings to Weyerhaeuser of $2 million. Side benefits have been the demonstration that uncertainty and risk can be rigorously considered in the choice of an inventory level and that mill management and wood procurement managers can share this risk successfully (Finke, 1984).

the inventory level falls to 200 units (6 days 33.34 per day). We can also see this result from Figure 12.9. If the inventory is used at a constant rate (this is one of the assumptions we have made), then 6 days before the inventory level falls to zero, the inventory level will be 200 units and 33.34 units will be sold (on average) in each of the days remaining before the order is received.

For the periodic review system our concern is not with the optimal order quantity but with the *time interval* for review and reordering. Using information provided by the EOQ model, we can derive an effective period review policy. If Charger orders 380 generators per order, then, on the average, it will place 31.6 orders per year. That is, since the number of orders is given by U/Q, Charger will place $12,000/380 = 31.6$ orders. The review period in a periodic review inventory system is constant; only the order quantity changes. Therefore, to space 31.6 orders equally throughout the year Charger should order every 7.91 working days. (Practically, this would be rounded to 8 for convenience.) That is, 250 working days per year/31.6 orders per year = 7.91.

$\mathscr{E}$ XTENSIONS TO THE BASIC EOQ MODEL

In the previous section, it was noted that the EOQ model is based on five assumptions. Often, however, these assumptions may not be representative of the actual situation facing an organization. For example, an optimization approach using spreadsheets was presented for dealing with situations where the assumption that items are independent of one another is not valid. In this section we relax two of the other assumptions. First, we present a model for dealing with situations in which the replenishment does not arrive exactly as the inventory level drops to zero. Then, we discuss how to handle situations in which the purchase price is not independent of the quantity ordered.

❖ The Economic Production Quantity (EPQ) Model

The **economic production quantity** (EPQ) model is used when the replenishment does not arrive exactly as the inventory drops to zero. Rather, in these cases the inventory level is built up gradually as the product is produced internally. Thus, with its assumption of instantaneous replenishment, the EOQ model is more appropriate for situations in which the product is purchased, whereas the EPQ model is appropriate for situations in which the product is made in-house. With internal products, the inventory level is gradually increased as additional units of the product are completed. Also, with internally produced items, an equipment setup cost (C_S) is incurred as opposed to an ordering cost (C_O). The inventory pattern is shown in Figure 12.10.

Notice, in Figure 12.10, that in the EPQ model the maximum level of inventory (I_{max}) is less than the production quantity, because the product is being used to meet customers' demand as it is being produced. In the basic EOQ model, I_{max} is equal to the EOQ, since the order arrives all at once just as the inventory level drops to zero.

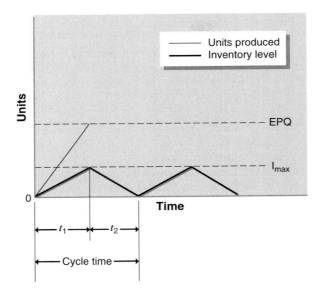

Figure 12.10   Inventory pattern for internally produced items.

In Figure 12.10, one inventory cycle takes $t_1 + t_2$ time units. This cycle consists of two parts: the period when the product is being made (i.e., from time 0 to time t_1), and the period from time t_1 to time $t_1 + t_2$ when production has ceased and inventory is being used to meet demand. The length of t_1 and t_2 depends on the production rate (P) and usage rate (U). In the formulas below we use Q_{EPQ} to distinguish the EPQ from the economic order quantity Q.

$$t_1 = \frac{Q_{EPQ}}{P}$$

$$t_2 = \frac{I_{max}}{U}$$

$$\text{Cycle time} = t_1 + t_2 = \frac{Q_{EPQ}}{U}$$

In summary, t_1 is the time required to produce Q_{EPQ} units given a production rate of P; t_2 is the time it takes to use up the accumulated inventory given a usage rate U; and cycle time ($t_1 + t_2$) is the time it takes to use up the Q_{EPQ} units produced. Note that t_1 is often referred to as the *run time*.

To use these formulas, we need Q_{EPQ} and I_{max}. Here we simply present the formulas for the EPQ and I_{max} and note that they can be derived using elementary calculus and geometry.

$$Q_{EPQ} = \sqrt{\frac{2UC_S}{C_H}} \sqrt{\frac{P}{P-U}}, \text{ and}$$

$$I_{max} = \frac{Q_{EPQ}}{P}\left(P - U\right)$$

The first term in the formula for Q_{EPQ} is the formula used to calculate the EOQ. Also, note that in calculating Q_{EPQ}, it is assumed that the production rate (P) is greater than the usage rate (U). If this were not true, the product would have to be produced nonstop and there would be no need to decide how much should be produced once the equipment was set up. Since P is greater than U, the second term in the formula for Q_{EPQ} will always be greater than 1. Thus the economic production quantity (Q_{EPQ}) will always be greater than the economic order quantity (Q). The reason why the batch is larger when the product is made, as opposed to being purchased, is that less inventory is held, since some of the product is being used to meet demand as it is being made. Thus it is less expensive to produce more.

For products made internally, total annual cost is calculated as

$$\text{TAC} = \left(\frac{I_{max}}{2}\right)C_H + \left(\frac{U}{Q_{EPQ}}\right)C_S$$

✐ SOLVED EXERCISE 12.3 ❖ Economic Production Quantity

The annual demand for a certain printed circuit board (PCB) is 15,000 units per year. The production line used for this PCB can make 75,000 boards per year. The cost to hold a PCB in inventory for one year is $2.50, and the cost to set up the production line for the board is $100. How many PCBs should be produced each time the line is set up? What is the length of one inventory cycle? What is the run time? What is the maximum quantity of boards that will need to be stored?

Solution:

The number of PCBs to produce each time the line is set up is calculated as:

$$Q_{EPQ} = \sqrt{\frac{2UC_S}{C_H}}\sqrt{\frac{P}{P-U}}$$

$$= \sqrt{\frac{2(15,000)(100)}{2.50}}\sqrt{\frac{75,000}{75,000-15,000}} \approx 1225 \text{ PCBs}$$

Given the EPQ as calculated above, the length of one inventory cycle and the run time can be computed as:

$$\text{Cycle time} = \frac{Q_{EPQ}}{U} = \frac{1225}{15,000} = 0.082 \text{ year}$$

$$\text{Run time} = \frac{Q_{EPQ}}{P} = \frac{1225}{75,000} = 0.016 \text{ year}$$

Usually, it is more intuitive to think in terms of days or weeks as opposed to fractions of a year. If we assume that the company operates 250 days per year, then 0.082 year is equivalent to 20.5 days (0.082 × 250), and 0.016 year is equivalent to 4 days (0.016 × 250).

Finally, the maximum inventory level is calculated as follows:

$$I_{\max} = \frac{Q_{EPQ}}{P}(P - U)$$

$$= \frac{1225}{75,000}(75,000 - 15,000) = 980 \ \text{PCBs}$$

The resulting inventory pattern for this company is shown below.

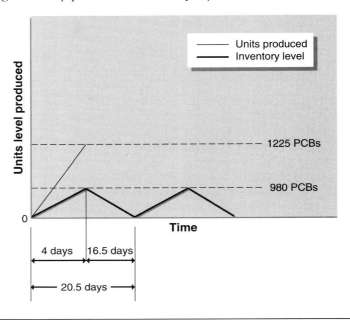

❖ The EOQ Model with Quantity Discounts

In the basic EOQ model, the unit purchase price is assumed to be independent of the quantity ordered. However, in many situations suppliers offer discounts to encourage their customers to purchase in larger quantities. In these cases, the order quantity affects the annual purchase cost in addition to the annual ordering and annual carrying cost. Letting C_P represent the unit price (which now depends on the quantity ordered), the total annual cost is computed as

$$\text{TAC} = \left(\frac{Q}{2}\right)C_H + \left(\frac{U}{Q}\right)C_O + UC_P$$

Unfortunately, we cannot develop a simple formula to determine the optimal order quantity in this situation. Instead, we use the following four-step procedure:

1. Calculate the EOQ, ignoring quantity discounts for the time being.

2. If the calculated EOQ qualifies for the lowest unit price, this is the optimal order quantity. If the calculated EOQ does not qualify for the lowest unit price, go to step 3.

3. Calculate TAC for the EOQ quantity. Also, calculate TAC for all order quantities that occur at price breaks offering a lower unit price.

4. Select the order quantity that has the lowest TAC.

The best way to illustrate this procedure is with an example.

$\mathcal{S}$OLVED EXERCISE 12.4 ❖ EOQ Model with Quantity Discounts

We Train, Inc. (WT), gives seminars for executives on basic computer skills. Each attendee at one of its seminars is provided with a notebook containing course material. WT orders its notebooks from a company that prints the WT logo and course title on the notebook. The price schedule for ordering notebooks is as follows:

Number of Notebooks Ordered	Unit Price
25 or less	$5.00
26–99	$4.75
100–199	$4.50
200 or more	$4.10

WT uses about 3000 notebooks per year. The cost of storing notebooks in its supply room is $1.75 per notebook per year. The cost of placing an order for notebooks is $4. How many notebooks should WT order each time it places an order?

Solution:

In step 1 we calculate the EOQ, ignoring quantity discounts, as follows:

$$\text{EOQ} = \sqrt{\frac{2UC_O}{C_H}} = \sqrt{\frac{2(3,000)4.00}{1.75}} = 95.6 \approx 96$$

In step 2 we assess whether the EOQ calculated qualifies for the lowest unit price. In this case, an order quantity of 200 or more is needed to qualify for the lowest unit price. Since ordering 96 notebooks does not qualify WT for the lowest unit price, we move on to step 3.

In step 3 we calculate the TAC for the EOQ and for all order quantities that occur at price breaks offering a lower unit price. In this example, ordering 96 notebooks qualifies WT for a unit price of $4.75. To qualify, for a price of $4.50 per notebook, WT would need to increase its order to 100 notebooks; and to qualify for a unit price of $4.10, it would have to order 200 notebooks. Thus, we must check the TAC for three order quantities: 96 notebooks (the EOQ), 100 notebooks (the first price break), and 200 notebooks (the second price break).

$$\text{TAC}_{96} = \left(\frac{96}{2}\right)1.75 + \left(\frac{2000}{96}\right)4 + 2000(4.75) = \$9667.33$$

$$\text{TAC}_{100} = \left(\frac{100}{2}\right)1.75 + \left(\frac{2000}{100}\right)4 + 2000(4.50) = \$9167.50$$

$$\text{TAC}_{200} = \left(\frac{200}{2}\right)1.75 + \left(\frac{2000}{200}\right)4 + 2000(4.10) = \$8415$$

In step 4, we select the order quantity that offers the lowest TAC. In this example an order quantity of 200 notebooks should be used.

You might be wondering why only price breaks need to be checked and not other order quantities. The reason is that the EOQ makes the optimal trade-off between annual ordering and carrying cost. By investigating larger order quantities that offer a lower unit price, we are essentially determining whether the saving in price across all units offsets the higher carrying cost that will result from the higher order quantity. Since we get all the benefits at the price break order quantity, increasing the order quantity beyond the price break only further increases the holding cost and provides no additional saving in the total annual purchase cost.

$\mathscr{S}$INGLE-PERIOD, UNCERTAIN DEMAND: THE "NEWSBOY" PROBLEM

In the previous sections we discussed the fundamental concepts and terminology of inventory management. The systems we described assumed an absolute knowledge of the parameters that determine optimal order quantities. We also discussed the notion of an order point based on a known demand and a known lead time. Now it is appropriate to relax these assumptions so as to consider more realistic inventory situations. That is, we will introduce uncertainty into the inventory environment.

First, we will consider a problem that has traditionally been referred to as the **newsboy problem** but is applicable in numerous situations in which a perishable commodity is purchased in some order size (before demand is known) and is then either sold or scrapped, depending on the demand level. The following example will clarify the problem.

For three years, Clark has sold newspapers each morning at the corner of First and Banker Streets. He purchases the morning edition of the *Daily* at 6:00 A.M. and stands on the corner from 6:30 to 8:30 each morning before walking two blocks to school. Clark buys the newspapers for $0.10 each and sells them for $0.15. Even though he is making a good profit on each newspaper sold and has developed quite a sizable bank account for a lad his age, he knows that he can do better.

It seems that Clark is either running out of newspapers before 8:30 A.M. and therefore missing potential sales, *or* having several papers left over that cannot be sold or returned to the publisher. He reasons that there must be some "best" order quantity to stock each day that will produce the largest average profit over the long run. Clark knows that he cannot perfectly predict daily demand and that he is

TABLE 12.4 ❖ Clark's Newspaper Demand

Demand (Newspapers)	Frequency (Days)	Relative Frequency
28	10	0.10
29	20	0.20
30	35	0.35
31	25	0.25
32	10	0.10
	100	1.00

TABLE 12.5 ❖ Payoff Table for the Newsboy Problem

Order Quantity	Demand				
	28	29	30	31	32
28	$1.40	$1.40	$1.40	$1.40	$1.40
29	1.30	1.45	1.45	1.45	1.45
30	1.20	1.35	1.50	1.50	1.50
31	1.10	1.25	1.40	1.55	1.55
32	1.00	1.15	1.30	1.45	1.60

bound to run out on some days and to overstock on others. But he is sure that a consistent policy will maximize his expected profit over the long run. How many newspapers should Clark stock each day?

To answer this question we must first consider the demand for newspapers on Clark's corner. Suppose that Clark has kept a record of the number of papers demanded each day for 100 days. That is, even when he ran out of papers, Clark remained on the corner until 8:30 A.M. to count the number of people who asked for a paper, even though he had to tell them he had none left. His summary of the 100 days' demand is presented in Table 12.4.

Clark's lowest demand was for 28 newspapers, and his highest demand was for 32. Therefore, he at least knows that he should never order more than 32 or less than 28.* But Clark could order any of the five quantities in between on any given day. Which number will maximize profits? Table 12.5, which is called a **_payoff table,_** presents the daily profit for each combination of order quantity and demand.

❖ Decision Table Analysis

The rows of Table 12.5 are the five potential order quantities, and the columns are the five potential demands. Each combination of order quantity and demand will result in a different payoff.

---

*We are making the assumption here that 100 days' history is enough to predict the future. Obviously, demand can change; Clark must simply be aware of the possibility and monitor for it.

Each entry in the payoff table is computed as follows. If Clark orders enough to equal or exceed demand, then

$$\text{Profit} = \text{number demanded} \times \$0.15 - \text{number ordered} \times \$0.10$$

For example, if he orders 30 and 28 were demanded,

$$\text{Profit} = 28 \times \$0.15 - 30 \times \$0.10$$
$$= 4.20 - \$3.00$$
$$= \$1.20$$

If Clark orders less than is demanded on a given day, then he can sell only what he has in stock. Therefore,

$$\text{Profit} = \$0.05 \times \text{number ordered}$$

If 32 were demanded and he had ordered only 30,

$$\text{Profit} = \$0.05 \times 30$$
$$= \$1.50$$

With the information provided in the payoff table, Clark now knows the profit that will be earned for each of the potential order quantities and each of the possible daily demands. He can now determine the best order quantity by determining the expected profit to be earned using each order quantity.

Clark knows the relative frequency of occurrence of each level of demand. On the average, 28 newspapers are demanded 10 percent of the time, 29 newspapers are demanded 20 percent of the time, 30 newspapers are demanded 35 percent of the time, and so on. If Clark plays it safe and orders 28 newspapers each day, then the expected daily profit will be

$$E(P_{28}) = 0.1(1.40) + 0.2(1.40) + 0.35(1.40) + 0.25(1.40) + 0.1(1.40) = \$1.40$$

That is, his expected daily profit is $1.40 if he orders 28 newspapers each day and the relative frequency of the demand levels remains as it was for the 100-day data collection period. This result is obvious, since he is sure of selling at least 28 papers at $0.05 profit each.

If Clark orders 30 newspapers each day, his expected daily profit is

$$E(P_{30}) = 0.1(1.20) + 0.2(1.35) + 0.35(1.50) + 0.25(1.50) + 0.1(1.50) = \$1.44$$

Therefore, even though he will not sell all of the 30 newspapers each day (in fact, he will not sell all of them 30 percent of the time), his expected long-run daily profit is greater than the more conservative approach.

Table 12.6 contains the expected profits for each of the five possible order quantities. Since the expected profit is greatest for "order 30," the optimal policy is to order 30 newspapers each day.

TABLE 12.6 ❖ Clark's Expected Profits

Order Quantity	Expected Daily Profit
28	$1.400
29	$1.435
30	$1.440 (best)
31	$1.392
32	$1.307

Does this mean that Clark will never run out of newspapers, or that he will never have bought more than he can sell? The obvious answer is no. In fact, Clark can expect to *run out* 35 percent of the time (that is, the times when demand is 31 or 32), and to stock *more* than he needs 30 percent of the time (the times when demand is 28 or 29). This policy, though, produces the greatest long-run profit.

SOLVED EXERCISE 12.5 ❖ Newsboy's Decision Table

A perishable product that costs $5 and sells for $7 faces a period demand of 8 with a probability p of .4, 9 with .4, and 10 with .2. What amount should be ordered per period to maximize profit?

Solution:

| Order Quantity | Demand | | | Expected Profit |
	8 ($p=.4$)	9 ($p=.4$)	10 ($p=.2$)	
8	$2 \times 8 = 16$	16	16	16 (best)
9	$16 - 5 = 11$	18	18	$0.4(11) + 0.4(18) + 0.2(18) = 15.2$
10	$8 \times 7 - 10 \times 5 = 6$	13	20	11.6

❖ Marginal (Incremental) Analysis

There is another, more flexible, method for solving Clark's problem, called *incremental* (or *marginal*) *analysis*. The idea here is to start with a very small order for items and compare the advantages and disadvantages of *ordering one more* item. The advantage, of course, is the potential profit the unit might bring. The disadvantage is that the item may not be sold (or needed), and then a loss might be sustained. Of course, for very small initial orders, the probability that one more unit will be sold is quite high, so it usually makes sense to order at least one more. For example, in Clark's case, if he is at an initial order size of 27 or less, it certainly makes sense to order at least one more paper because the probability of selling it is 100 percent.

The next step is to consider adding still another unit to the order. Is the expected gain greater than (or equal to) the expected loss? This process is continued until ordering one additional unit cannot be justified on the basis of the expected return for that unit.

To frame this process mathematically, let

p = probability of selling (or using) *at least* one more unit

$1 - p$ = probability of *not* selling or using the unit

MCO = marginal cost of ordering one more unit

MPU = marginal profit of selling one more unit

Then the expected gain from ordering one more unit is the probability of selling the unit times the profit to be gained. Mathematically,

$$\text{Expected gain} = p(\text{MPU})$$

Similarly, the expected loss from ordering the unit is the probability that it will not sell (or will not be needed) times the loss incurred (usually its price, or price less salvage value):

$$\text{Expected loss} = (1 - p)\text{MCO}$$

Now, it is logical to keep increasing the order size as long as the expected marginal profit from ordering one more unit exceeds the marginal cost of ordering one more unit. Expressing this logic mathematically will allow us to identify that critical value of p *below which* it is not worthwhile to order another unit. Thus, as more units are added to the order, p (the probability of selling one more unit) keeps falling until it reaches this critical value.

$$p(\text{MPU}) \geq (1 - p)\text{MCO}$$

or

$$p \geq \frac{\text{MCO}}{\text{MCO} + \text{MPU}}$$

In Clark's problem MCO = \$0.10 (the cost of the papers; there is no salvage value) and MPU = \$0.05 (the profit; there are no losses of goodwill or penalties). Thus:

$$p \geq \frac{0.10}{0.10 + 0.05} = 0.67$$

Therefore, Clark should increase the number of papers he stocks as long as the probability of selling the last paper stocked is at least 67 percent. Now we need a table showing the probability of selling N or more units as a function of order size, N. This is shown in Table 12.7.

$\mathcal{T}$ABLE 12.7 ❖ Probability Table for Newsboy Problem

Order Size, N	Probability of Selling N Units	Cumulative Probability of Selling More Than N Units
28	.10	.90
29	.20	.70
30	.35	.35
31	.25	.10
32	.10	0

For example, if Clark goes from stocking 28 to 29 papers, he has a 90 percent probability of selling the twenty-ninth paper. Notice that our value for $p = .67$ falls between $N = 29$ and $N = 30$. That is, if our current order size was 29, the probability is .70 of selling 30, 31, or 32 units, which is *greater* than the critical probability of .67, so 30 is acceptable. But at $N = 30$ the value of 0.35 is less than 0.67, so 31 cannot be justified. Thus, our process is to go down the table of N values until we reach the first cumulative probability that is *less* than p. Notice that we arrive at the same solution—to stock 30 papers—with the decision table and marginal analysis.

This is a common problem. Retailers purchase seasonal clothing, perishable foods, and other items such as Christmas trees, Valentine candy and cards, pumpkins, and fruit and vegetables in anticipation of demand. If too little demand is realized, then the remaining goods are scrapped if not salable or "reduced for clearance," either at a loss or at a reduced profit.

$\mathcal{S}$OLVED EXERCISE 12.6 ❖ Incremental Analysis for the Newsboy Problem

Reconsider Solved Exercise 12.5 and solve by incremental analysis.

Solution:

$$p \geq \frac{5}{5+2} = .714$$

Order Size	Probability of N	Cumulative Probability of $> N$
8	0.4	0.6 (0.714 before here)
9	0.4	0.2
10	0.2	0

Since the probability of selling the ninth unit when going from an order size of 8 to 9 units is less than .714, an order size of 8 should be used.

$\mathscr{R}$EORDER POINT (ROP) MODELS

EOQ, EPQ, and the newsboy problem all address the first fundamental question about inventory: *how much* to order. The second fundamental question that all inventory management systems must address is *when* to order. In this section we discuss reorder point (ROP) models that address the issue of when to order. In the newsboy problem, the concern was with ordering quantities of a perishable commodity that experienced uncertain demand over a *single* period. The ROP model, on the other hand, is concerned with uncertain demand over *multiple* periods, but the commodities are not perishable.

Before we present the reorder point model, the concepts of **safety stock** and **service level** must be addressed. Safety stocks are inventories maintained to reduce the chances of a stockout. Safety stocks are needed because *demand during lead time* (DDLT) can vary, as can the lead time itself.

Service level is the portion of demand that is met with on-hand inventory. Service level can be measured in a variety of ways, such as the percentage of orders that can be filled with on-hand inventory or the percentage of demanded items that are shipped from on-hand inventory.

There is an important relationship between safety stock and service level: safety stock is held to achieve the desired service level set by management. This is illustrated in the sidebar describing safety stocks at navy supply centers.

Figure 12.11 illustrates the ROP model. The expected demand during lead time is Q_1 units. At time A, on-hand inventory is equal to Q_1 plus the safety stock. The safety stock is carried only as an insurance policy against unexpected demand during lead time or unexpected delays in lead time. Thus, we don't expect to use any of it. Since we are not expecting to use any of the safety stock, point A represents

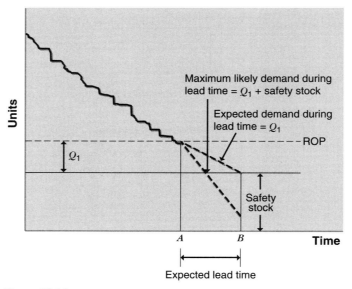

Figure 12.11   Reorder point (ROP) model.

the ROP because the amount of inventory on-hand is equal to the expected demand during lead time. In other words, if we place a replenishment order when the on-hand inventory reaches Q_1 plus the safety stock, then the replenishment order should arrive just as Q_1 units are used up and only the safety stock remains. In Figure 12.11, the replenishment order arrives at time B. The expected lead time is the amount of time between points A and B.

For the purpose of discussing ROP models, it is helpful to distinguish four scenarios as follows:

	Constant lead time	Variable lead time
Constant demand	scenario 1	scenario 3
Variable demand	scenario 2	scenario 4

The following notation will be used:

u = demand rate when demand is constant

$\bar{u}$ = average demand rate when demand can vary

σ_u = standard deviation of demand when demand varies

LT = lead time when lead time is constant

$\overline{LT}$ = average lead time when lead time can vary

σ_{LT} = standard deviation of lead time when lead time varies

In general, ROP is calculated as

$$\text{ROP} = \text{expected demand during lead time} + \text{safety stock}$$

$$= \text{usage rate} \times \text{lead time} + \text{safety stock}$$

OPERATIONS IN PRACTICE

Cutting Safety Stocks at Navy Supply Centers

The navy maintains eight supply centers in the United States, and each holds about 80,000 line items valued at approximately $25 million. The EOQ for each line is used to set order quantities, and about 840,000 total orders are placed each year. To minimize the likelihood of stockouts, safety stocks are maintained with a service goal of filling 85 percent of all requisitions from stock.

By law, a 2.5-month stockage is required for each line, although there is no specification for how much of this should be safety stock versus cycle stock. Current policy is to maintain 1.5 months of safety stock and 1 month of cycle stock, the cycle stock being half the EOQ on average.

The navy initiated a study to see if these policies were best, or if better service or reduced cost could be obtained by using other policies. Service was found to be a function of two factors: the likelihood of a shortage on each reorder cycle and the number of cycles. At extremes of either of these factors, service deteriorates. At the current level of 1.5 month's safety stock, the service level was 85 percent. However, this service level was still maintained with only 1.0 month's safety stock.

By analyzing each of the supply centers separately, the navy found that the 85 percent level could be maintained with safety stocks ranging from 0.8 to 1.1 months. The policy was thus changed to keeping a safety stock of just 1 month instead of 1.5 months. This reduced the total number of annual work orders from 840,000 to 670,000, thereby saving an estimated $2 million in annual costs (Gardner, 1987).

❖ Constant Demand and Constant Lead Time

In situations where both demand and lead time are constant, there is no uncertainty and therefore no need to carry safety stock. Thus, ROP is calculated as

$$\text{ROP} = \text{usage rate} \times \text{lead time} = u(LT)$$

ℐolved Exercise 12.7 ❖ ROP Calculations for Scenario 1

A gas station sells 1000 gallons of gasoline per day. The time from the placement to the actual receipt of the replenishment order is 3 days. At what point should the replenishment order be placed?

Solution:

$$\text{ROP} = 1000 \text{ gallons/day} \times 3 \text{ days} = 3000 \text{ gallons}$$

Thus, the gas station should place its replenishment order when the on-hand level of gas reaches 3000 gallons.

❖ Variable Demand and Constant Lead Time

In situations where the demand rate varies, inventory can be carried over and above the expected demand during lead time to guard against unexpectedly high demand during this period. As we discussed earlier, such inventory is referred to as *safety stock*. Often, the demand during lead time is assumed to be normally distributed, as shown in Figure 12.12. Given this distribution of demand, management must determine a desired service level. The service level represents the probability of meeting all demand during lead time. Since the area under the normal curve sums up to 1, the probability of stockout is represented by 1 minus the service level.

Once the desired service level is specified, an appropriate value of z can be found from a standard normal table such as the one given in Appendix A. For example, suppose management desires a 97 percent service level. Using the table in Appendix A, we find a value as close as possible to 0.97 and then determine the z-value for it. The number closest to 0.97 is 0.9699, which corresponds to a z-value of 1.88. In essence, a z-value of 1.88 means that to provide a 97 percent service level, we must carry an extra 1.88 standard deviations of demand in safety stock.

On the basis of this intuition, the ROP for situations with variable demand and constant lead time is calculated as

$$\text{ROP} = \overline{u}LT + z\sqrt{LT}\left(\sigma_u\right)$$

In this equation, the first term represents the expected demand during lead time. The second represents the safety stock. Note that $\sqrt{LT}(\sigma_u)$ is the standard deviation of demand during lead time. Thus, when this quantity is multiplied by the appropriate z-value, the safety stock represents z standard deviations of demand during lead time.

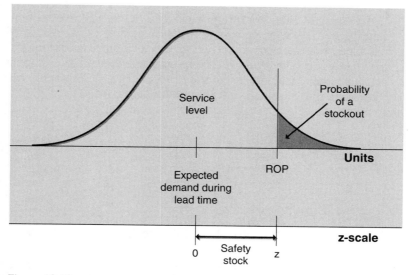

Figure 12.12   Determining ROP assuming normal distribution for demand during lead time.

$\mathscr{S}$OLVED EXERCISE 12.8 ❖ ROP Calculations for Scenario 2

A gas stations sells an average of 1000 gallons of gas per day with a standard deviation of 10 gallons. The time from the placement to the actual receipt of replenishment orders is 3 days. At what point should the replenishment order be placed if management desires a 99 percent service level?

Solution:

First we must determine the appropriate z-value. From Appendix A, the value closest to 0.99 is 0.9901, corresponding to a z-value of 2.33. Using this and the other information provided, we calculate the ROP for the gas station as:

$$\begin{aligned} \text{ROP} &= 1000(3) + 2.33\sqrt{3}(10) \\ &= 3000 + 40.36 \\ &= 3040.36 \text{ gallons} \end{aligned}$$

Thus, when the on-hand level of gas reaches 3040.36 gallons, the gas station should place its replenishment order. Note that while our best estimate is that the demand during the lead time will be 3000 gallons, an extra 40.36 gallons is held in safety stock in case demand is unexpectedly high during the 3-day lead time.

❖ Constant Demand and Variable Lead Time

In scenario 2, demand varied while lead time was assumed to be constant. In these cases safety stock can be held to guard against unexpectedly high demand during the lead time. In scenario 3, we reverse our previous assumptions and assume that demand is constant and lead time varies. Here, safety stock can be held to guard against unexpected delays in the receipt of a replenishment order. When demand is constant and lead time varies, the ROP is calculated as

$$\text{ROP} = u(\overline{LT}) + z(u)\sigma_{LT}$$

$\mathscr{S}$OLVED EXERCISE 12.9 ❖ ROP Calculations for Scenario 3

A gas station sells 1000 gallons per day. The time from the placement to the actual receipt of replenishment orders averages 3 days, with a standard deviation of 1 day. Management desires a 99 percent service level. At what point should the replenishment order be placed?

Solution:

In Solved Exercise 12.8 we determined that a z-value of 2.33 corresponds to a service level of 99 percent. Thus, the ROP for the gas station in this example is

$$\text{ROP} = 1000(3) + 2.33(1000)(1)$$
$$= 3000 + 2330$$
$$= 5330 \text{ gallons}$$

Therefore, the gas station should place its replenishment order when the on-hand level of gas reaches 5330 gallons. While demand during lead time is expected to be 3000 gallons, an extra 2330 gallons will be held as safety stock to guard against late deliveries.

❖ Variable Demand and Lead Time

Perhaps most realistic are situations were both demand and lead time can vary. In these cases both sources of variation have to be "pooled" together to get a single measure of overall variation in demand during lead time (DDLT). Without going into detail, we simply note that the formula for calculating the overall variation of demand during lead time in this situation is based on the product of two independent variables (demand and lead time). The overall standard deviation of demand during lead time is calculated as

$$\sigma_{\text{DDLT}} = \sqrt{\overline{LT}^2 \sigma_u^2 + \overline{u}^2 \sigma_{LT}^2 + \sigma_\mu^2 \sigma_{LT}^2}$$

On this basis, the ROP for situations where both demand and lead time vary is calculated as

$$\text{ROP} = \overline{u}\left(\overline{LT}\right) + z\left(\sigma_{\text{DDLT}}\right)$$

𝒮OLVED EXERCISE 12.10 ❖ ROP Calculation for Scenario 4

Demand at a gas station averages 1000 gallons per day, with a standard deviation of 10 gallons. The lead time for replenishment orders averages 3 days, with a standard deviation of 1 day. If management desires a 99 percent service level, at what point should replenishment orders be placed?

Solution:

First, we calculate the overall standard deviation of demand during lead time as follows:

$$\sigma_{DDLT} = \sqrt{3^2\left(10^2\right) + 1000^2\left(1^2\right) + 10^2\left(1^2\right)}$$
$$= \sqrt{900 + 1,000,000 + 100}$$
$$= 1000.5$$

Next, the ROP can be calculated as

$$ROP = 1000\left(3\right) + 2.33\left(1000.5\right)$$
$$= 3000 + 2331.17$$
$$= 5331.17 \text{ gallons}$$

Thus, a replenishment order should be placed when the on-hand level of gas reaches 5331.17 gallons. The expected demand during lead time is 3000 gallons, and 2331.17 gallons will be held to guard against unexpectedly high demand during the lead time, unexpected late deliveries, or both.

*C*HAPTER IN PERSPECTIVE

This second chapter of Part Four has dealt with the product supply process. With the aggregate and master production schedules developed in Chapter 11, our focus in this chapter was on determining how much and when to order independent demand items to support these schedules. In terms of how much to order, the EOQ, EPQ, EOQ with quantity discounts, and the "newsboy problem" were discussed. To address the issue of when to order, reorder point models based on the nature of demand and lead time were presented. In Chapter 13, we continue our discussion of the product supply process and consider managing the inventory of dependent demand items.

❖ CHECK YOUR UNDERSTANDING

1. Define the following terms: *newsboy problem, safety* or *buffer stocks, reorder point, lead time, two-bin system, independent demand, ordering cost, setup cost, work-in-process, periodic review system, economic order quantity, economic production quantity, perpetual inventory system, ABC classification system, stockouts, holding cost, service level, dependent demand.*

2. List and briefly describe the five functions of inventory.

3. List and briefly describe the four forms of inventory.

4. List and briefly explain the five categories of cost associated with inventory systems.

5. What are the two basic inventory questions?

6. List and briefly explain the three types of inventory management systems.

7. Contrast independent and dependent demand.

8. Briefly explain the ABC concept.

9. List the assumptions associated with the EOQ model.

10. Contrast setup costs with capacity-associated costs. What is the critical difference between them?

11. What is the relationship of annual holding cost to annual carrying cost at the economic order quantity?

12. When is it appropriate to use the EOQ model? When is it appropriate to use the EPQ model?

13. Show schematically the inventory patterns for both externally purchased items and internally produced items.

14. With periodic review systems, what inventory decisions are fixed and what decisions are variable? With reorder point systems?

15. Why is the maximum inventory level different in the EOQ and EPQ models?

16. Why are only price break points investigated in the EOQ model with quantity discounts?

17. State the critical test of whether a cost should be included in the EOQ equation.

18. In general, how is the reorder point determined?

19. Contrast and compare the single with the multi-period inventory situation when demand is uncertain. Note that there are no reorders in the former, and uncertainty during the demand period in the latter is of no concern.

20. Describe the relationship between safety stock and the reorder point.

21. Discuss why the reorder period will vary in a reorder point system.

22. What happens to total annual inventory cost as lead time uncertainty increases? As demand uncertainty increases?

23. What other inventory situations are similar to the "newsboy problem" discussed in this chapter?

❖ EXPAND YOUR UNDERSTANDING

1. What inflexibilities are forced on service organizations as a result of their inability to inventory their output? Which of the five inventory costs are avoided?

2. Do any of the five functions and four forms of inventories still exist in service firms? If so, which ones, and why? If not, how are the functions served?

3. What effects on the functions of inventories would "beaming" à la *Star Trek* produce?

4. Contrast the functions and forms of inventories. Does every form exist for each function and vice versa, or are some more common?

5. Contrast two of the newest inventory-oriented technologies facing managers: automated warehouses that quickly store and retrieve any item desired, and the Japanese just-in-time system, which produces the items so fast that inventories are not needed. What factors should a manager consider in choosing one or the other?

6. What costs go up if buffer and decoupling inventories (and their costs) are eliminated? What steps can be taken to control these additional costs?

7. Why is the largest cost in inventory—the cost of the goods themselves—not considered in the EOQ model?

8. How do you make the actual decision about identifying A and B items when you have the list of total annual inventory values? How do you decide where to draw the line? Is the process different from deciding between grades of A or B in a university class?

9. How realistic are each of the assumptions of the EOQ model?

10. Suppose you determine an EOQ for a situation but you know the value is too low to last until the next time supplies arrive. What should you do? Should you order two EOQs?

11. In making reservations for services, a common approach to single-period, uncertain demand is to "overbook" (and confirm), just to avoid the costs of no-shows. How ethical is this practice?

12. Why is incremental analysis a more useful approach to the newsboy problem than the more straightforward decision table?

13. Discuss the use of EOQ-type models in such places as hospitals (blood banking, gauze, pacemakers, etc.) and pharmacies. What service level is appropriate?

14. Grocery stores have traditionally used periodic review for inventory control. What type of system

can be maintained with the automatic sensing equipment at checkout counters?

15. Discuss the limitations of the EOQ model. Is certainty in demand and lead time a reasonable assumption?

❖ APPLY YOUR UNDERSTANDING _____
Delta Products Inc.

Delta Products makes a line of door hardware including doorknob sets and deadbolts. Its product line is particularly well known for excellent quality, a high level of security, and ease of installation.

Delta hired Nikki Scott, a college senior majoring in operations management, for one of its summer internships. Her task was to spend the summer analyzing the operation and usage of the large transfer press, the plant's current bottleneck machine. The transfer press stamps out the doorknobs used in Delta's door hardware and is available 2000 hours per year for this task. At the end of the summer, in a report to the department manager and plant manager, Nikki was to submit her recommendations for improving the operation of the transfer press.

Nikki spent the first week familiarizing herself with the operation of the transfer press by observing and questioning the machine operator. By the end of the first week, she determined that Delta uses six unique doorknobs in its door hardware.

She decided that her next task was to get an estimate of the annual demand for the knobs. She studied Delta's product catalogs and determined which products each knob was used in. Next, she got from the sales manager a copy of a spreadsheet that contained the complete sales figures for each product over the last three years. After casually looking over the data, she observed that the sales were remarkably stable over the three-year period. Nikki added formulas to the spreadsheet to average the sales data over the three-year period and to calculate the number of knobs of each type that were used.

With her analysis of the demand for knobs completed, Nikki turned her attention to the actual production of the knobs. She spent the next couple of weeks collecting data on the individual processing times of the knobs on the transfer press, the time required to set up the press to produce a new batch of knobs, and the production batch sizes currently being used. She also worked closely with the cost accountant to determine the cost of holding knobs in inventory, and she found that machine operators are paid $15 per hour, including fringe benefits. Nikki summarized the information for her report in the spreadsheet shown below.

	A	B	C	D	E	F
1			Unit	Setup	Annual	Current
2		Annual	Processing	Time	Holding Cost	Batch
3	Item	Demand	Time (hours)	(hours)	($/unit)	Size
4	Knob A	6000	0.0500	6.2	3.25	1500
5	Knob B	3000	0.0420	4.6	3.85	1500
6	Knob C	7000	0.0400	7.2	2.75	1500
7	Knob D	10000	0.0380	5.4	3.70	2000
8	Knob E	8400	0.0375	3.8	4.20	1500
9	Knob F	9400	0.0480	6.8	2.25	2000

Her next task was to analyze the information she had compiled and look for ways to improve the operation. Given the information she had available, she began by developing a spreadsheet to calculate the economic production quantity. She then developed another spreadsheet to compare the total annual cost (TAC) of using the current batch sizes with the economic production quantities she calculated. Nikki was extremely pleased when she realized she could save Delta over $5400 per year in just one department if it adopted her recommended economic production quantities. After rechecking her calculations, she was convinced of the validity of her analysis and couldn't wait to see the plant manager's reaction to her report. She was actually hoping that the plant manager would be impressed enough with her work to offer her a full-time position upon graduation. The final spreadsheet she developed to summarize the potential savings to Delta is shown below.

	A	B	C	D	E
1				TAC	
2		Current	Economic	Current	
3		Batch	Production	Batch	TAC
4	Item	Size	Quantity	Size	EPQ
5	Knob A	1500	636	2444	1756
6	Knob B	1500	339	2844	1222
7	Knob C	1500	800	2278	1891
8	Knob D	2000	735	3402	2203
9	Knob E	1500	520	2973	1841
10	Knob F	2000	1049	2222	1828
11					
12	Total			16162.09	10741.03
13					
14	Annual Savings			5421.05	

On the Monday of her last week, Nikki met with the plant manager, Joe Thomas, and the press department manager, Mike Willis. After complimenting Nikki on a very thorough and well written report, Joe asked Mike what his reaction was. Mike commented:

I also was very impressed with the thoroughness of Nikki's analysis. The data that she collected on setup times, production times, and holding costs are the best data we have ever had about our operations. Unfortunately, while I have not had a chance to thoroughly run the numbers, I think there is a problem with Nikki's analysis. Her analysis requires significant reductions in our batch sizes. While I agree that we could save money by cutting the batch sizes, the fact of the matter is that the transfer press she analyzed is one of our major bottlenecks. We are currently using every second of the 2000 hours we have available on the machine. Cutting the lot sizes as Nikki has suggested will require more setups, and we simply don't have the time for additional setups.

Nikki was quite distraught by the outcome of the meeting. She still had a week left in her internship, and she desperately wanted to salvage the work she had spent an entire summer working on. She was determined to spend her final week finding a way to save Delta money while at the same time not exceeding its available capacity.

Questions

1. Verify Nikki's calculations of the economic production quantity and total annual cost.

2. Is Mike's intuition correct—that using Nikki's economic production quantities will exceed the 2000 hours of capacity available on the transfer press?

3. Are there any opportunities for Delta to save money without exceeding its available capacity?

❖ EXERCISES

1. A firm maintains a maximum inventory level of 55 units, has a reorder point of 35 units, and is currently at 15 units with an outstanding order of 30 units. How many units should it order? Suppose its current inventory was 30 units? Assume that demand over the lead time is 5 units.

2. Grants Tools orders EOQs of 1000 at a time, faces an annual demand of 45,000, and has an ordering cost of $10. What is the annual carrying cost and average inventory level?

3. Categorize the following inventory items as type A, B, or C.

Unit Cost ($)	Annual Usage (Units)
10,000	4
7000	1
4000	13
1200	5
700	500
300	20
250	45
60	5,000
25	400
17	4,000
9	1,000
7	8,000
3	750
2	4,000
1	12,000

4. Frame-Up, a self-service picture framing shop, orders 3000 feet of a certain molding every month. The order cost is $40 and the holding cost is $0.05 per foot per year. What is the current annual inventory cost? What is the maximum inventory level? What is the EOQ?

5. Wing Computer Corporation uses 15,000 keyboards each year in the production of computer terminals. Order cost for the keyboards is $50, and holding cost for one keyboard is $1.50 per unit per year. What is the EOQ? If Wing orders 1250 per month, what will the total annual cost be? What is the average inventory level?

6. The Corner Convenient Store (CCS) receives orders from its distributor in three days from the time an order is placed. Light Cola sells at the rate of 860 cans per day. (It can sell 250 days of the year.) A six-pack of Light Cola costs CCS $1.20. Annual holding cost is 10 percent of the cost of the cola. Order cost is $25.00. What is CCS's EOQ, and what is the reorder point?

7. Refer to Spreadsheet Analysis: Determining Order Quantities in Multiple-Product Situations. How much is an extra square foot of storage space worth to Fiveco? What is the maximum amount of additional storage space Fiveco would be willing to acquire? (Hint: Resolve the problem but increase the amount of space available. Then determine how much the extra space reduces total costs.)

8. Gaming, Inc., has the capacity to produce 25,000 slot machines per year. Demand has been stable over the last few years at about 10,000 slot machines per year. It costs the company $250 to set up its production line to produce the slot machines and $35 to hold one slot machine in inventory for a year. What batch size should be used to produce the slot machines?

9. In Exercise 8, how much would Gaming save annually if it used your batch quantity versus a batch quantity of 750 slot machines?

10. In Exercise 8, what is the maximum inventory level of slot machines that Gaming would accumulate? What are the run and cycle times? Plot the inventory pattern for Gaming.

11. A company produces four products. Annual demands, production rates, setup times, and holding costs are given in the table below. Workers who perform the setup operations are paid $15 per hour.

Item	Annual Demand	Annual Production Rate	Setup Time (hours)	Annual Holding Cost per Unit
A	3000	10,000	3	6
B	1500	7000	2	10
C	3500	8000	3	8
D	5000	13,000	2	12

Assuming that the products are independent of one another, what batch sizes would you recommend for each product? What would the total annual cost be across all four products?

12. Refer to Exercise 11. Find the optimal batch sizes for the four products such that total annual costs are minimized and the number of setup hours does not exceed 125. How does the cost of the new solution compare with the cost calculated in Exercise 11? How much should the company be willing to pay to get additional setup hours? What is the maximum number of additional setup hours the company should consider acquiring?

13. A consulting company buys special shirts with its logo to give to employees and clients. The company buys about 1200 shirts per year. The cost of holding a shirt in inventory for one year is $4.50. The cost of placing an order is $40. Given the price schedule of the shirts listed below, what' order quantity should the company use?

Order Quantity	Unit Price
less than 100	$12.50
100 to 149	$12.25
150 to 199	$12.00
200 or more	$11.75

14. Demand for strawberries at McDonald's Berry Patch has been recorded as follows:

Demand (Quarts)	Probability
13,000	.1
15,000	.5
18,000	.3
20,000	.1

McDonald's orders berries on Monday morning from a large wholesaler and pays $0.40 per quart. Any berries not sold at the retail price of $0.95 per quart are sold for $0.30 per quart to a local family that makes strawberry jelly for sale at a flea market. How many quarts of berries should McDonald's purchase to maximize profits? Solve two different ways.

15. Mario's Pizza, across from the main gate of the campus, serves pizza by the slice and does a substantial lunch business. The following table provides demand information based on an analysis of the last six months' activity. Mario's direct cost in a pizza is $2. He sells each pizza for a total revenue of $5. If Mario wants to maximize profits, how many pizzas should he make each day?

Pizza Demand	Probability
45	.15
46	.15
47	.25
48	.20
49	.15
50	.10

16. Given: yearly demand = 12,000; carrying cost/unit/year = $1; ordering cost = $15; lead time = 5 days; safety stock = 200; price = $0.10 each. Find the total annual cost of the inventory system under an optimal ordering policy.

17. Given: annual demand of 12,000 units; monthly carrying cost of $1 per unit; ordering cost of $5. Find the EOQ, annual ordering cost, annual holding cost, and average inventory level.

18. Categorize the following inventory-related expenses as to cost type and probable relevance in an inventory model to determine the best order size: postage, warehouse rent, purchase order forms, secretarial labor (writing orders), warehouse guard, interest cost of money, costs of the goods, distribution cost per unit, receiving cost for raw materials, ill will for lost sales, warehouse heating, advertising, expediting costs to meet due dates, president's salary, fire insurance on finished goods.

19. It is time to consider reordering material in a periodic review inventory system. The inventory on hand is 100 units, maximum desired level of inventory is 250 units, usage rate is 10 units a day, reorder period is every two weeks (10 working days), lead time for resupply is 15 days, and amount on order is 250 units. How much should be ordered?

20. Quarry Company places orders for blasting caps once each month. The order quantity is 500 per month. The purchasing agent has just learned of the EOQ model and wants to try it out. He or she determines that order costs are $1.50 and that holding cost is $8 per cap per year. What is the EOQ? Should the company change its order quantity to the EOQ? Base your answer on economic and practical grounds.

21. A wholesaler purchases $1 million worth of equipment a year. It costs $100 to place and receive an order, and the annual holding cost per item is 20 percent of the item's value.

  a. What is the dollar value of the EOQ?
  b. How many months' supply is the EOQ?
  c. How often should orders be placed?
  d. How much will the annual holding cost change if the company orders monthly? How much will the annual ordering cost change?
  e. What should the dollar value of the EOQ be if the wholesaler doubles its annual purchases? What should it be if (instead) the ordering cost doubles? What should it be if the holding cost drops to 10 percent?

22. A book publisher prints softcover manuals for $10 each. If the publisher stocks out and must produce extras, they will cost $30 each. If demand for the manuals is considered equally probable for all values between 1 and 100, how many should be produced? If demand is normally distributed around 100 with a standard deviation of 20, how many should be produced?

23. Kidney machines cost $100,000 apiece. The chance of needing two such machines in a large midwestern city is exactly 1 in 100, and the chance of needing 3 is 1 in 1000. If the city hospital buys three such machines, what is the implied cost of ill will due to the unavailability of such a machine?

24. A law office purchases copier paper from a local office supply company. The lead time is always one day. The law office uses an average of 10 reams of paper a day, with a standard deviation of 1.5 reams. What reorder point should the law office use if it is willing to accept only a 2.5 percent chance of a stockout?

25. An electronic instruments maker has a contract to supply a governmental agency with 25 units of a particular piece a equipment each month. The lead time for the display units averages 5 days, with a standard deviation of 0.72 day. What reorder point should be used for the display units?

26. Sales of a particular calculator at a university bookstore average 35 per month, with a standard deviation of 1.3 units. The lead time for replenishment orders averages 4 days, with a standard deviation of 0.8 day. What reorder point should the bookstore use for the calculators?

Chapter 12 SUPPLEMENT
Simulation

The problem of determining the proper amount of safety stock can be approached from two directions: attempting to determine a solution *analytically* (as was done in all the inventory control situations in this chapter) or through *simulation*. We will use the following example to demonstrate both approaches.

GREAT GUSHER OIL AND GAS EXPLORATION COMPANY

Great Gusher Oil and Gas Exploration Company has been drilling oil and gas wells, working at one site at a time, for the past three years. Weekly use of diamond-tipped drill bits over the past year has been between 0 and 3 units per week, as shown in Table 12S.1. The supplier is located several hundred miles from Great Gusher's primary drill site, and the drilling foreman has tabulated lead times for bit delivery to the site. From these data, he has developed the probability distribution shown in Table 12S.2.

Over the past three years Great Gusher has never stocked out of the required drill bit, primarily because an excessively high inventory of the units has always been maintained. The foreman wants to reduce the investment in the inventory by reducing the safety stock currently being held. He reasons that some number of stockouts is acceptable, since, in an emergency, he could "borrow" a bit from any of six other drilling companies working in adjacent areas. Because of the number of personnel and the investment in equipment, shutdowns of the drilling rig must be avoided.

ANALYTICAL APPROACH

The foreman initially needs to know the probability distribution for demand during lead time (DDLT). As was illustrated in the chapter, the distribution of DDLT is essential in determining the risk of a stockout associated with each of the various lev-

TABLE 12S.1 ❖ Probability Distribution for Weekly Use of Drill Bits

Number Required	Probability
0	.10
1	.40
2	.30
3	.20
	1.00

TABLE 12S.2 ❖ Probability Distribution for Lead Time for Drill Bits

Number of Weeks from Order to Delivery	Probability
0	.20
1	.50
2	.30
	1.00

els of safety stock that could be maintained. In the chapter, we assumed that DDLT was normally distributed, but here we will assume that it has discrete probability distribution. Because both weekly usage and lead time are uncertain, the distribution of demand (usage) during lead time is a function of the probability distributions of both lead time and demand. This DDLT distribution is known as a joint probability distribution. For relatively simple problems like the case of Great Gusher, it can be computed using a simple tree diagram.

Figure 12S.1 presents the tree diagram used to compute Great Gusher's DDLT distribution for drill bits. To illustrate the computations involved in the tree, consider the branch "LT = 2 weeks." The probability that lead time will be 2 weeks is .3. If lead time is 2 weeks, then there will be 2 weeks during which demand can be either 0, 1, 2, or 3 units each week. Hence, there are two levels or sets of branches after the branch "LT = 2 weeks." That is, demand can be 0, 1, 2, or 3 units in week 1 and 0, 1, 2, or 3 units in week 2, each weekly demand being determined by the probability distribution shown in Table 12S.2. For example, if lead time is 2 weeks, the probability that demand will be 3 units the first week and 1 unit the second week is .2 × .4 = .08. The probability of the joint occurrence of LT = 2 weeks and 3 units demanded in the first week and 1 unit demanded in the second is .3 × .2 × .4 = .024. The probabilities of each of the other branches of the tree are computed in an identical manner.

The last two columns, labeled "DDLT" and "Probability," provide the data necessary for constructing the DDLT probability distribution. You will notice that there are several ways to get a total demand during lead time equal to a specific number

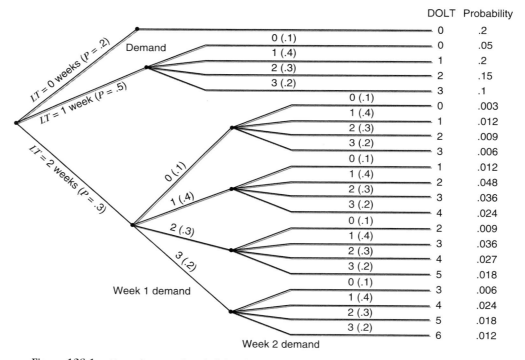

Figure 12S.1   Tree diagram for drill bit demand over lead time distribution.

of units. For example, to get a DDLT of 4 drill bits, lead time must be 2 weeks, and demand for weeks 1 and 2 could be either 1 and 3, 2 and 2, or 3 and 1, respectively. Since the end result of each of these demand patterns is the same (i.e., DDLT = 4 drill bits), we simply add the probabilities for all like DDLTs to find that the probability of DDLT equaling 4 is .075 (i.e., .024 + .027 + .024). The final result of these calculations is shown in the DDLT probability distribution (Table 12S.3).

We can now use this DDLT probability distribution. First, we construct the cumulative probability distribution for demand during lead time, as shown in Table 12S.4. We can now use this distribution to determine safety stocks and reorder points given the foreman's desired maximum risk of stockout—that is, his service level.

For example, if the foreman wanted no more than a 10 percent chance of stockout (that is, at least a 90 percent service level), the reorder point should be set at 4 units (see Table 12S.4). Since average demand (computed from Table 12S.1 as $0 \times 0.10 + 1 \times 0.40 + 2 \times 0.30 + 3 \times 0.20 = 1.6$) is 1.6 drill bits per week, the safety stock is thus 2.4 units (4 − 1.6). To have a 99 percent service level requires a reorder point of 6 units; and if a service level of 87.7 percent is acceptable (stockouts are expected to occur on 12.3 percent of exposures), the reorder point can drop to 3 units.

𝒯ABLE 12S.3 ❖ Demand During Lead Time Distribution

Demand During Lead Time	Probability
0	.253
1	.224
2	.216
3	.184
4	.075
5	.036
6	.012
	1.000

𝒯ABLE 12S.4 ❖ Cumulative Probability Distribution for DDLT

Demand, D	Service Level or Probability (DDLT ≤ D)
0	.253
1	.477
2	.693
3	.877
4	.952
5	.988
6	1.000

$\mathscr{S}$IMULATION APPROACH _____

The second approach to inventory problems with uncertainty in both demand and lead time is simulation. Clearly, the tree diagram would become quite cumbersome if lead time exceeded 3 or 4 weeks (e.g., adding a lead time of 3 weeks to Great Gusher's problem would add 64 branches to the tree). Also, if the distribution of demand and lead time were continuous probability distributions rather than discrete distributions, such as we have used here, the tree would be impossible and the mathematics required to form the joint distribution for DDLT would be quite complex.

Simulation is a technique for experimenting with a real situation through an artificial model that represents it. The three-dimensional models that architects and car designers frequently use are forms of simulation. In these cases, the models are physical, small-scale versions of the real object. However, the simulations we are concerned with here are *mathematical-logical* models, which are usually programmed on a computer. The purpose of the simulation is to discover how various policies affect the performance of a system.

Simulation has a number of inherent advantages that other evaluation methods frequently do not have.

❖ The simulation can begin very simply and grow with the addition of more and more realistic processing complexity as the manager gradually understands the dynamics of what is happening in the system.

❖ The mathematics and logic of simulation are relatively simple.

❖ Each component in the model corresponds to some real-life element.

❖ A considerable amount of "what if" experimentation can be conducted on the model to test new and creative designs or policies, without altering an existing actual design.

❖ Considerable time compression is possible, especially if the simulation is computerized. Years of experience can be obtained in seconds.

❖ Simulation can handle an extremely large variety of situations and problems.

The primary disadvantage of simulation is that time and money are needed to construct the model, especially if a complex system is being simulated. Also, simulation will not *find* an optimal design—it will only describe the results of those designs identified by the manager.

The type of mathematical simulation we will consider here is called *Monte Carlo*, after the famous gambling principality. The procedure is used when events follow patterns that can be described by probability distributions. The steps in building a Monte Carlo simulation are shown in Figure 12S.2. As an example, we will manually simulate the Great Gusher problem for several periods. For more details, consult the Bibliography.

1. The supply and demand process for Great Gusher drill bits was described earlier by Tables 12S.1 and 12S.2. In addition to this information, we will now need to specify the managerial policies that describe a service level. Recall that simulation does not itself *find* optimal policies; it only *describes* the

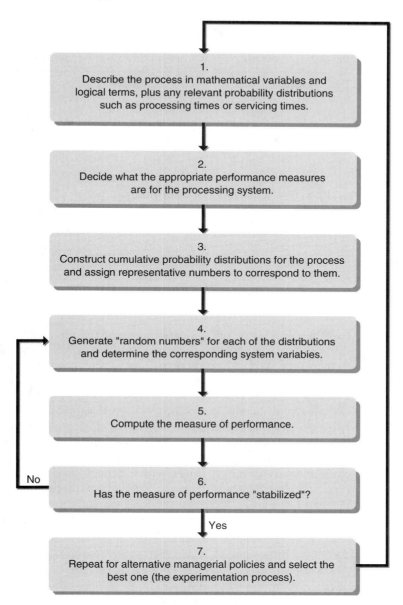

Figure 12S.2   Steps in Monte Carlo simulation.

result of *given* policies. Let us assume that the economic order quantity of drill bits is 15 and that this amount is currently in inventory. In addition, let us for the moment try a policy of reordering whenever the weekly ending inventory level falls to 2 units or less. Alternative policies regarding order quantities and reorder levels may also be simulated later.

2. The important variables here are the inventory level, which the foreman wishes to reduce, and the frequency of stockouts. We will "track" the average weekly value of these two variables as our "measures of performance."

*T*ABLE 12S.5 ❖ Simulation for Weekly Demand

Demand Equals	Probability	Cumulative Probability	Representative Numbers
0	.10	.10	00–09
1	.40	.50	10–49
2	.30	.80	50–79
3	.20	1.00	80–99

*T*ABLE 12S.6 ❖ Simulation for Lead Time

Lead Time Equals	Probability	Cumulative Probability	Representative Numbers
0	.2	.20	00–19
1	.5	.70	20–69
2	.3	1.00	70–99

3. In Tables 12S.5 and 12S.6 we have constructed the cumulative probability distributions and assigned two-digit "representative numbers" in proportion to their probabilities to represent these probabilities. Note that of the 100 digits used (00–99), 10 percent represent 0 demand, 40 percent a demand of 1 unit, and so on. A simple way of assigning these 100 digits is to follow the cumulative probability distribution—each assignment *begins* with the cumulative probability from the previous category. It actually does not matter *how* the digits are assigned, or even how many there are, as long as 10 percent of them represent a demand of 0, and so on. For example, we could just as easily have used only 10 digits, with 0 demand being represented by 3; 1 unit by 4, 2, 0, 8; 2 by 7, 9, 1; and 3 by 5, 6. If more precise probability values had been given such as 0.103 for 0 demand, then 3-digit representative numbers would have been required; for example, the first set might then have run from 000 to 102.

4. To conduct the simulation, we first create a table to enter the data, Table 12S.7. We will represent weekly demand by choosing two-digit random numbers from the table in Appendix B, starting at the top left and working across the row. Generally speaking, random numbers for different parameters should start at different places in the table and work in different directions: for example, middle of the table and working up, bottom right and working left, and so on. For lead time random numbers we will arbitrarily select a number by closing our eyes and picking from the table. As we obtain random numbers for demand, we will enter Table 12S.5 and see which set of representative numbers the random number falls in and then select the corresponding demand.

The first random number is 39, which falls between 10 and 49 in Table 12S.5. Therefore, the demand for week 1 is 1 unit. Ending inventory for the week is therefore 14 units (15 − 1), and since it is not less than or equal to the reorder point of 2, no order is placed. Demand for week 2 is 2 units,

$\mathcal{T}_{ABLE}$ 12S.7 ❖ Great Gusher Simulation

(1) Week	(2) Receipts	(3) Beginning Inventory	(4) Random Number (RN)	(5) Demand	(6) Ending Inventory	(7) Stockout	(8) Order Placed	(9) RN	(10) Weeks to Arrive	(11) Average of (6)	(12) Average of (7)
0					15						
1	0	15	39	1	14					14.0	0
2	0	14	73	2	12					13.0	0
3	0	12	72	2	10					12.0	0
4	0	10	75	2	8					11.0	0
5	0	8	37	1	7					10.2	0
6	0	7	02	0	7					9.7	0
7	0	7	87	3	4					8.6	0
8	0	4	98	3	1		15	76		7.9	0
9	0	1	10	1	0					7.0	0
10	0	0	47	1	0	1			2	6.3	.100
11	15	15	93	3	12					6.8	.091
12	0	12	21	1	11					7.2	.083
13	0	11	95	3	8					7.2	.077
14	0	8	97	3	5					7.1	.071
15	0	5	69	2	3					6.8	.066
16	0	3	41	1	2		15	23		6.5	.063
17	0	2	91	3	0	1				6.1	.118
18	15	15	80	3	12				1	6.4	.111
19	0	12	67	2	10					6.6	.105
20	0	10	59	2	8					6.7	.100

found by using the second random number. Ending inventory is 12, which is still not below the reorder point. Table 12S.7 presents the results of the simulation for 20 weeks. At the end of the eighth week the ending inventory has fallen to 1 unit; therefore, an order for 15 drill bits is placed between weeks 8 and 9. The lead time random number (column 9) 76 generates (Table 12S.6) a lead time of 2 weeks; therefore, receipt of the order is scheduled in weeks 10 and 11.

5. The measures of performance are listed in the last two columns of Table 12S.7, average weekly ending inventory and average weekly number of stockouts.

6. The two measures are plotted in Figure 12S.3 to determine if they have stabilized over the 20-week simulation; such simulations are typically run for 100 or 1000 trials. From the figure, it appears that neither measure has stabilized but that "inventory" is stabilizing faster than "stockouts" and will end up between 6 and 7 units. It appears that the "stockouts" measure will converge to around 0.08 or 0.09 per week (equivalent to 12 or 11 weeks between stockouts).

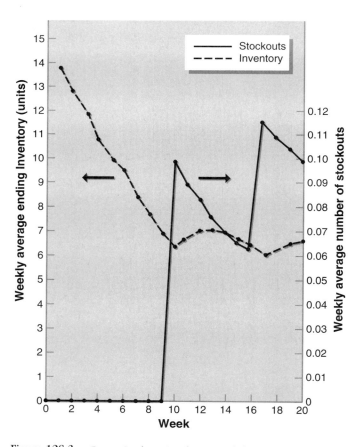

Figure 12S.3   Great Gusher simulation stabilization.

"Stabilization" is normally determined by the average absolute rate of change in the parameter and the cost to run the simulation for a longer period. If the expense represented by a weekly inventory of 6 compared with 7 units is not especially significant, then the 20 runs in Table 12S.7 may be sufficient. Stabilization generally occurs faster for variables that occur often. In our example, replenishments and stockouts occurred only about every 10 weeks, so the stockout graph jumped excessively every time a stockout occurred. With 100 weeks of simulation, the jumps in the graph would have been much subdued.

7. The managerial decision policy simulated, "order 15 when ending inventory reaches 2 units," resulted in a relatively poor service level—in both cases of reordering, a stockout occurred. This could possibly be avoided by ordering sooner, for example, when inventory reaches 3 or 4 units. For that matter, ordering fewer units more frequently may give much better service without a significant increase in cost. By varying the two parameters and simulating them in a short computer program (a minimal programming effort), the foreman could quickly find the best policy without disrupting his current inventory process.

This example has illustrated the use of simulation in analyzing alternative inventory policies. Although the example was highly simplified, simulation can also handle exceedingly complex systems. Simulation is particularly appropriate for problems that do not satisfy the assumptions of some of the optimizing models of management science, or where human behavior is concerned. Of course, simulation is not limited to inventory analysis but has been used throughout the field of operations management for logistics analysis, quality control, maintenance, layout, scheduling, and so on. And, of course, simulation is so general and so powerful that it is used in physics (to study atomic interactions), chemistry (for analyzing molecular behavior), biology (to study metabolism), and many other fields as well.

Spreadsheet Analysis: Simulating Reordering Policies

Mario's Pizza is located close to a college campus and does a substantial lunch business. Mario has collected data over the past month for the number of pizzas sold during the lunch period on weekdays, as summarized below.

Demand	Probability
45	.15
46	.15
47	.25
48	.20
49	.15
50	.10

Mario receives 48 unbaked pizza crusts each morning. The quantity of demand that exceeds the 48 crusts delivered plus any leftover crusts from the previous day is lost and cannot be made up. Unused crusts can be saved and used the next day. Assume that Mario's has no beginning pizza crust inventory. Develop a spreadsheet to simulate 2 weeks (excluding weekends) of operation and determine the average and maximum level of inventory. Also, have the model calculate the average and maximum number of stockouts during the week.

Solution:

The first step in performing a Monte Carlo simulation by hand is defining how the random numbers are to be assigned to the various outcomes. In performing these types of simulation with Excel, however, only the outcomes (demand in our case) and their probabilities need to be specified. The spreadsheet below was developed to simulate Mario's operations.

	A	B	C	D	E	F	G	H	I
1	Day		Beginning	Generated	Ending				
2	Number	Receipts	Inventory	Demand	Inventory	Stockouts			
3	1	48	0	45	3	0			
4	2	48	3	47	4	0			
5	3	48	4	46	6	0		Demand	Probability
6	4	48	6	47	7	0		45	0.15
7	5	48	7	45	10	0		46	0.15
8	6	48	10	47	11	0		47	0.25
9	7	48	11	48	11	0		48	0.20
10	8	48	11	49	10	0		49	0.15
11	9	48	10	50	8	0		50	0.10
12	10	48	8	46	10	0			
13	Average				8	0			
14	Maximum				11	0			

Column A is used to keep track of the day. Column B contains daily receipts of pizza crusts. Currently, Mario's orders and receives 48 crusts each morning. Column C contains the beginning inventory level of pizza crusts for each day. We start the simulation with no beginning inventory of pizza crusts, so 0 is entered in cell C3. Because the ending inventory on day 1 becomes the beginning inventory on day 2, =E3 was entered in cell C4. Since this logic applies over the 2-week simulation model, the formula in cell C4 can be copied to cells C5:C12.

Column D contains the randomly generated demand based on the probability distribution entered in cells H6:I11. Specifically to generate the random demand based on the distribution of demand entered in cells H6:I11, Excel's Random Number Generation feature was used. To do this, Tools was selected from the menu bar at the top of the screen. Next, Data Analysis was selected; this in turn displays the Data Analysis dialog box. In the Data Analysis dialog box, the Random Number Generation option was selected; this then displays the Random Number Generation dialog box as shown below.

In our situation there is only one variable (demand) for which we need to generate random numbers. Thus, in the "Number of Variables:" box enter the number 1. Next, since we need to generate 10 random numbers (one for each of the 10 days we are simulating, or cells D3:D12), enter the number 10 in the "Number of Random Numbers:" box. The type of distribution we have is discrete, so we leave the "Distribution:" box unchanged. Note that Excel can generate random numbers for a variety of distributions, including uniform, normal, poisson, and binomial.

For the "Value and Probability Input Range" box, we specify the range that contains the outcomes and the probabilities for these outcomes. In the spreadsheet shown above, these values are contained in cells H6:I11.

A seed value is used to start the simulation. The advantage of specifying a seed value is that each time the simulation is run using a particular seed value, the same sequence of random numbers is returned. Thus, specifying a seed value permits you to repeat the simulation with the same sequence of random numbers. This is particularly useful for debugging the simulation model. It is also used to reduce variation in simulating different scenarios. In other words, if different seeds are used to test different policies, the decision maker may not know whether the results depend on the random numbers used or on actual differences between the policies. To specify a seed value, enter the seed value in the "Random Seed:" box. If a seed value is not specified, Excel will automatically choose one for you. For this example, we will let Excel choose the seed value.

Finally, in the Output options section, select the Output Range: radio button and enter the range D3:D12 in the corresponding box to tell Excel where to place the 10 randomly generated numbers. The Random Number Generator dialog box appears as follows.

Select the OK button in this window to generate a batch of 10 random numbers based on the distribution entered in cells H6:I11, to be placed in cells D3:D12.

In column E the ending inventory for the day is calculated. In column F the number of pizzas that were demanded but could not be supplied owing to insufficient supplies of crusts is calculated. Note that for a given day, only one of these quantities can be positive. That is, it is not possible to have ending inventory and stockouts on the same day. The logic for calculating the ending inventory is as follows:

1. If the sum of receipts plus beginning inventory is greater than the demand for a day, then ending inventory equals receipts plus beginning inventory minus demand.
2. Otherwise the ending inventory is zero (i.e., demand was equal to or greater than the supply of pizza crusts).

To capture this logic, the IF function is used. The IF function has three arguments separated by commas, with the following syntax:

=IF(condition, value returned if condition is true, value returned if condition is false)

If the condition is true, the second argument of the function is returned. If the condition is false, the third argument of the function is returned. The second and third arguments can be constants or formulas.

To calculate the ending inventory for the first day, the following formula was entered in cell E3:

$$=IF(B3+C3>D3,B3+C3-D3,0)$$

The formula entered in cell E3 can then be copied to cells E4:E12.

Similar logic is used to calculate the number of stocks for a given day, as follows:

1. If demand on a given day is greater than or equal to the beginning inventory plus the receipts, then stockouts for the day equal demand minus the receipts minus the beginning inventory.
2. Otherwise stockouts equal zero.

To calculate the stockouts for the first day, the following formula was entered in cell F3:

$$=IF(D3>B3+C3,D3-B3-C3,0)$$

This formula can be copied to cells F4:F12.

The performance measures for the simulation model are entered in cells E13:F14. Cell E13 calculates the average inventory level over the 10 days simulated with the formula: =AVERAGE(E3:E12). Similarly, the maximum inventory carried on any given day is calculated in cell E14 as: =MAX(E3:E12). These formulas can be copied to cells F13 and F14 to compute the average and maximum number of stockouts, respectively.

The real value of simulation models is not in using them once but in running them many times to see how they perform under a wide variety of situations. Generating multiple runs of a simulation model that was developed in a spreadsheet is quite easy. For example, to get another run of the simulation model we developed in this example, simply select Tools from the main menu, Data Analysis, Random Number Generation, and the OK button in the Random Number Generation dialog box. The spreadsheet shown below was generated in this fashion.

	A	B	C	D	E	F	G	H	I
1	Day		Beginning	Generated	Ending				
2	Number	Receipts	Inventory	Demand	Inventory	Stockouts			
3	1	48	0	49	0	1			
4	2	48	0	47	1	0			
5	3	48	1	50	0	1		Demand	Probability
6	4	48	0	49	0	1		45	0.15
7	5	48	0	48	0	0		46	0.15
8	6	48	0	49	0	1		47	0.25
9	7	48	0	47	1	0		48	0.20
10	8	48	1	46	3	0		49	0.15
11	9	48	3	50	1	0		50	0.10
12	10	48	1	47	2	0			
13	Average				0.8	0.4			
14	Maximum				3	1			

As you can see, the results obtained in the second run are quite different from the results obtained in the first run, yet both sets of results were generated from the same distribution of demand. For example, in the first run, ending inventory averaged 8 crusts and reached a maximum level of 11 crusts. In the second run, the average inventory was only 0.8 crusts and the maximum number of crusts in inventory on any given day was 3. The point is that simulation models should be replicated (repeated) numerous times and that it is the *distribution* of the performance measures which should be evaluated and compared, not the results of a single run of the model.

Spreadsheet Analysis: Generating Random Numbers

In addition to being used to develop complete simulation models, spreadsheets can also be used simply to generate random numbers. These random numbers can be used like tables of random numbers. The advantage of using a spreadsheet to generate random numbers is that it can generate these numbers from a variety of probability distributions. Also, it can generate as many random numbers as you need.

To illustrate, let's assume we would like to generate 10 random numbers from a uniform distribution between 0 and 99. To display the Random Number Generation dialog box, select the menu items Tools, Data Analysis, and then Random Number Generation. Then, to generate the 10 random numbers and store them in cells A1:A10, enter the information as shown below in the Random Number Generation dialog box.

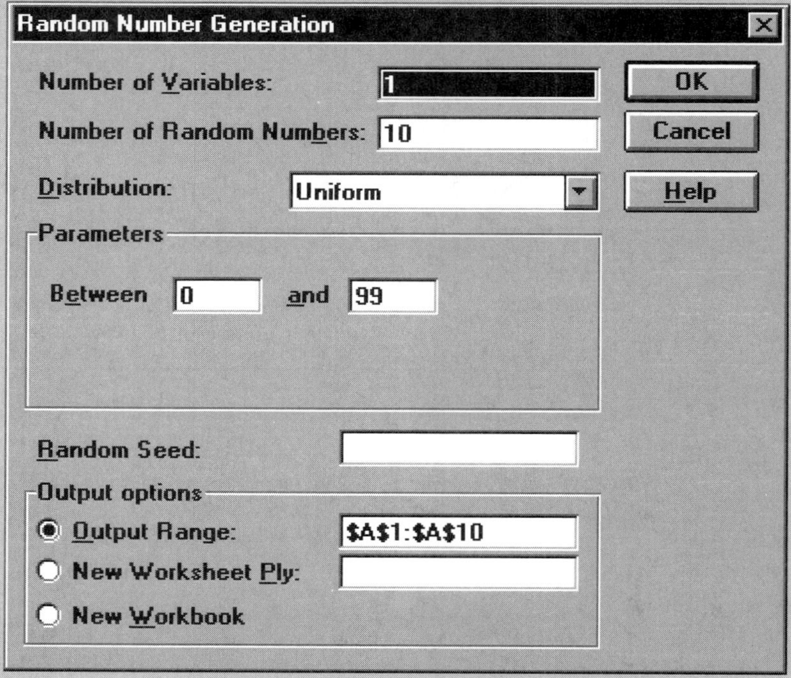

After formatting cells A1:A10 to display no digits to the left of the decimal point, the spreadsheet with the 10 randomly generated numbers appears as follows.

	A	B
1	1	
2	35	
3	45	
4	44	
5	85	
6	15	
7	5	
8	41	
9	47	
10	42	
11		

Note that if you followed these steps, your random numbers will be different from those displayed, since a different seed value was used.

As another example, suppose we would like to generate 10 random numbers from a normal distribution with a mean of 0 and standard deviation of 1. To place these random numbers in cells B1:B10, fill in the Random Number Generation dialog box as follows:

After we select the OK button, the spreadsheet appears as follows.

	A	B
1	1	1.65
2	35	0.02
3	45	1.88
4	44	-0.26
5	85	0.53
6	15	1.63
7	5	-0.28
8	41	0.89
9	47	-0.50
10	42	-0.93
11		

❖ EXERCISES

1. For the following distributions, determine the DDLT distribution. What service level will a reorder point of 7 generate? What reorder point is needed to give an 80 percent service level?

Lead Time (weeks)	Probability
1	.7
2	.3

Demand/Week	Probability
3	.6
4	.4

2. If, in Exercise 1, a stockout costs $10/unit a week and holding stock costs $8/unit a week, find the best reorder point by simulation. Use the following random digits:
45642610749842015501470327195486.

3. Use a spreadsheet to find the best reorder point for Exercise 1, assuming that stockout costs $10/unit a week and holding costs $8/unit/week. Have the spreadsheet generate the random numbers.

4. Refer to the Spreadsheet Analysis for Mario's Pizza. Assume that a pizza costs a total of $2, sells for $5, costs $1/day to hold in inventory, and effectively costs $3.50 per stockout. Enter formulas that calculate total revenue, the costs of the pizzas, the inventory holding costs, the cost associated with stockouts, and the profit earned at the end of the 10-day simulation period. Assume that 48 pizza crusts are delivered each day. Run this model 15 times and calculate the average, maximum, and minimum profit earned over a 10-day period.

5. Repeat Exercise 4, but assume that the delivery for a given day is equal to the previous day's demand.

6. Repeat Exercise 4, but add a formula providing a delivery quantity that is the average demand of the previous 2 days. Assume that 48 pizza crusts are to be delivered for the first two days of the simulation.

7. Repeat Exercise 4, but develop your own ordering policy. How do the results of Exercises 4–7 compare with one another in terms of profit, costs, stockouts, etc.?

8. Repeat Exercise 4, but assume that leftover crusts cannot be saved and used the next day. The crusts cost $0.50 each.

9. Lead time for delivery of frozen hamburgers to a fast-food restaurant is one day. Daily demand had been charted as follows:

Daily Demand	Probability
1200	.3
1300	.2
1400	.5

Assume that 1300 hamburgers are delivered each day. Develop a spreadsheet that will simulate this situation for 30 days. Assume that hamburgers not used on a given day can be used on the following day.

10. Refer to Exercise 9. Assume that the cost of a hamburger is $1.50, selling price is $2.25, holding cost is $0.25 per day per hamburger, and stockout cost is lost profit plus $0.50 in ill will. Develop formulas similar to those specified in Exercise 4 to calculate the profit earned over the 30-day simulation.

11. Experiment with different ordering policies in an effort to find the best ordering policy for Exercise 9. For each policy investigated, run the model at least 10 times.

12. Repeat the manual simulation for Great Gusher Oil using a reorder point of 4.

13. Repeat the manual simulation for Great Gusher Oil with a reorder point of 2, using a spreadsheet to generate the random numbers. Have the spreadsheet generate random numbers between 0 and 99 based on a uniform distribution.

Chapter 13

Planning Material Requirements

❖ Materials requirements planning (MRP) is appropriate only for items whose demand is dependent on another item whose demand has been specified or is known. Thus, it is primarily appropriate for the components of finished goods that have been master-scheduled.

❖ The basic operation of MRP is to use the product tree or bill of materials, plus the lead times, and explode the parts requirements with the lead time offsets to determine when the work on individual items needs to begin and how many items need to be made or purchased.

❖ MRP inputs include the *master production schedule,* the *inventory master file,* and the *bill of materials file.* The most important MRP outputs are the planned order releases.

❖ *Net requirements* is simply gross requirements less the planned on-hand inventory.

❖ Safety stock is generally discouraged in the MRP system.

❖ Lot sizing can be conducted in a number of different ways: lot-for-lot, by the Wagner-Whitin algorithm, by trial and error, and by part period balancing.

❖ *Capacity requirements planning* (CRP) and *distribution requirements planning* (DRP) are direct extensions of MRP. CRP uses the MRP output plus routings, lead times, and other information to determine the workloads on each of the workstations. DRP is analogous to MRP but front-ends the process by accumulating demands from the warehouses and distribution centers.

❖ MRP II ties the MRP system into a number of other areas in the firm, including engineering, purchasing, finance, sales, accounting, maintenance, and distribution.

❖ The latest stage in the evolution of information systems has been integrating all business activities and processes throughout an entire organization. The objective for these enterprise resource planning systems is to provide seamless real-time information to all employees throughout the entire organization (or enterprise) who need it.

INTRODUCTION

❖ Courtaulds Films produces plastic films used to package food products, such as candy bars and potato chips. Its plants, located in England and France, are operated 24 hours a day 7 days a week and supply food manufacturers worldwide. The company uses 60 types of raw material to produce 40 types of film and offers a total of 12,500 make-to-order end products. At the end of the 1980s, 25 percent of its deliveries were shipped late, because its production planning and scheduling system was unable to handle the complexity inherent in this situation. In an effort to reach a goal of 95 percent on-time shipments, managers at Courtaulds visited the Formica Company and learned about its manufacturing resource planning (MRP II) system. By the early 1990s, Courtaulds had implemented its own MRP II system and distinguished itself as a class A user. The employees now take a great deal of pride in their excellent on-time performance (Goddard, 1992).

❖ It is not unusual for a particular assembly line in IBM's plant in Charlotte, North Carolina, to produce 27 different products on a given morning. Before a particular product is made, a group of workers assemble "kits" of parts based on the needs of each work station. These kits are matched to the production orders and are delivered to the assembly-line workers. Computer terminals hooked up to the factory network are installed at each assembly station. The computer screen provides the workers with a list of parts they will need to complete their portion of the job. Workers match this list with the actual parts in the kit. The computer screen can also display step-by-step assembly instructions if a worker needs this information. Once a worker completes his or her tasks, a button is pressed and the completed assembly is moved on to the next station. Then a new product is delivered to the worker, and a new parts list that matches the next product is displayed on the computer screen (Bylinsky, 1994).

❖ Recording for the Blind & Dyslexic (RFB&D) is the only national nonprofit organization that loans textbooks in recorded or computerized formats to individuals who cannot read standard print because of a visual, perceptual, or other physical disability. When RFB&D was about to move from its existing facility in New York to a new facility in New Jersey, it took the opportunity to design and implement a new, integrated production system utilizing high technology materials-handling automation. RFB&D faces the difficult situation of having to satisfy, with extremely limited resources, an annual increase in demand for its books of three to five percent. Moreover, fast response is critical because many requests are for class textbooks needed for classes that are soon to begin.

With limited space, only limited inventories of recordings can be maintained and access must be swift and reliable. RFB&D's goals were to achieve a lead time of no more than two working days for at least 95 percent of all requests and to reduce the production cost per book served. Before the move and installation of the system, performance was 333 books per day. This had to be increased 28 percent, at the same cost per book or less. Thus, RFB&D turned to a version of MRP known as resource requirements planning (RRP).

This new software was teamed with new or upgraded hardware to achieve RFB&D's goals. Specifically, automated carousels were obtained for fast storage and retrieval of the 45,000 most active titles. Six hundred feet of overhead conveyors were added to connect all workstations. The speed of the machines that copied master recordings to cassettes was doubled. An automated sorting system was added for returned cassettes, and a bar code reader was installed for computer processing of mailed and returned cassettes. The results were gratifying: 27 percent more books could be produced, unit costs were reduced 16 percent (representing nearly $500,000, or 13 percent of RFB&D's annual budget), and 97 percent of the orders were mailed within five working days. (Almost half of those were mailed within 24 hours.) The next goal was to mail 95 percent of the orders within two working days (Jarkon and Nanda, 1985; RFB&D, 1997).

Chapter 12 focused on managing the inventory of independent-demand items. In the present chapter, our focus shifts to managing the inventory of dependent-demand items. *Dependent-demand* items are so named because their demand is derived from (depends on) the demand for independent-demand items. Although the calculations involved in managing dependent-demand items are not very complicated, as the examples above illustrate, the quantity of data can be overwhelming. Therefore, materials management systems for dependent-demand items typically require a computer.

The examples illustrate a number of important issues related to managing dependent-demand items. First, IBM and Courtaulds Films illustrate how computers can help an organization cope with the complexity of managing a large number of materials. Recording for the Blind & Dyslexic and Courtaulds illustrate a second important issue—the increasing emphasis many organizations are placing on reducing lead times and meeting delivery schedules. Finally, Recording for the Blind & Dyslexic and Courtaulds demonstrate the importance of integrating the materials management system with the rest of the organization, and especially with the production scheduling system.

From Chapters 11 and 12, as well as the examples above, it is clear that the materials management systems must fit closely with the scheduling systems. In fact, such systems are typically known as *production and inventory control systems*. This tie has become closer with the development of computerized production planning and control systems, since the management of tremendous quantities and varieties of materials is not the problem for computers that it was for manual systems. This has allowed the two systems to be joined, for both substantial savings in costs and significant improvement in the control of materials and operations, thereby resulting in higher productivity, adherence to promised due dates, and other such benefits.

Figure 13.1 shows how these topics relate to each other in the organization. The materials inputs from suppliers are initiated by purchase orders and scrap recycling requisitions from procurement. (A description of the purchasing and procurement is included in the supplement to Chapter 14.) Receiving confirms the quality and amount of the shipments from suppliers and sends the goods to storage, from which they are withdrawn, as needed, by operations. In the transformation system, goods are temporarily stored as work-in-process (WIP) and, as they become finished products, as finished goods inventory. From there they are distributed to various outlets—for example, directly to customers, manufacturing representatives, and wholesalers.

$\mathcal{M}$RP FOR DEPENDENT DEMAND

Many items, particularly *finished products* such as automobiles, televisions, and cartons of ice cream, are said to experience independent demand. That is, the demand for these items is unrelated to the demand for other items. For instance, in general there is no product that creates a demand for an automobile. However, every time an automobile is demanded, a demand for one steering wheel is created. Thus, the demand for steering wheels depends on and is derived from the demand for automobiles.

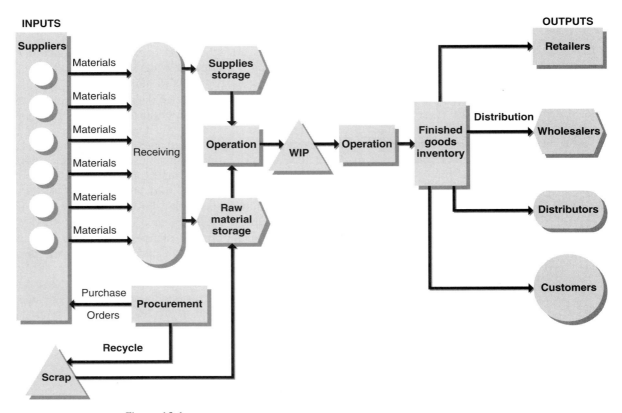

Figure 13.1   The materials management system.

Independent demand appears to be random—that is, caused by chance events. Most *raw materials, components,* and *subassemblies* are dependent on demands for these finished goods and other assemblies and subassemblies. Furthermore, as we illustrated in Chapter 12, independent demand may occur at a constant rate over an inventory cycle. However, these items are usually produced or ordered in batches based on the economic order quantity model or the economic production quantity model. Therefore, when a lot is ordered for production in the factory, all materials and components needed for production are ordered at the same time, creating a "lump" in demand for the dependent-demand items.

Examples of constant and lumpy demands are shown in Figure 13.2. In the case of constant demand, demand varies around the average (shown by the dashed line). Materials requirements planning (MRP) is a system designed specifically for the situation when "lumps" in demand are known about beforehand, typically because the demands are "dependent." For example, in a facility that produces wooden doors, reorders of (finished) doors may be based on a reorder point system. When the number of finished doors on hand reaches a prespecified reorder point, then an order is placed into production on the shop floor. Figure 13.3*a* illustrates this inventory time pattern where the demand for finished doors is relatively constant.

If a reorder point system similar to the one used in managing the inventory of finished doors was used in managing the inventory of lumber used to produce the

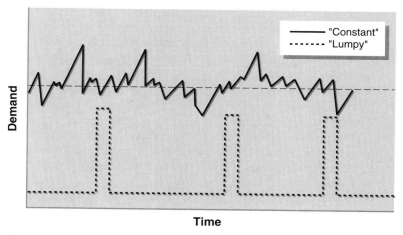

Figure 13.2   Constant and lumpy demands.

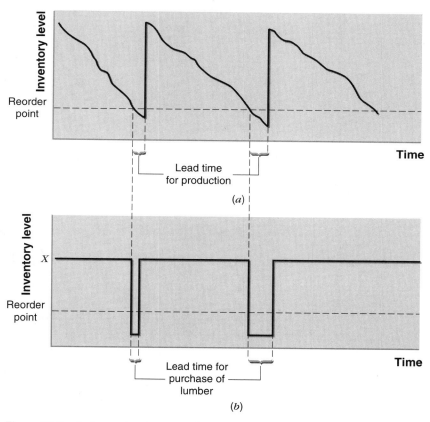

Figure 13.3   Relationship between finished item inventory and raw material/subassembly item inventory—reorder point approach. (*a*) Finished doors. (*b*) Lumber.

doors, the pattern shown in Figure 13.3*b* would result. Notice that in Figure 13.3*b* the normal inventory level is *X* units; when the inventory of finished doors in Figure 13.3*a* reaches its reorder point and a production order is released to the shop, a requisition for the required quantity of lumber is made against that inventory. The inventory level will drop by the quantity used in producing the lot, thus causing the raw materials inventory to fall below *its* reorder point. This triggers a reorder for a quantity of lumber, resulting in replenishment of the inventory after its purchase lead time.

As you can see, the average inventory level for the lumber is quite high, and most of this inventory is being held for long periods of time without being used. A logical approach to help lower this level is to anticipate the timing and quantities of demands on the lumber inventory and then schedule purchases to meet this requirement. Figure 13.4 illustrates the results of this anticipation of demand. Figure 13.4*a* illustrates the same pattern of finished-product inventory as Figure 13.3*a*. Figure 13.4*b* depicts the scheduling of receipts of lumber just before the time when it is needed. The impact on average inventory level is obvious.

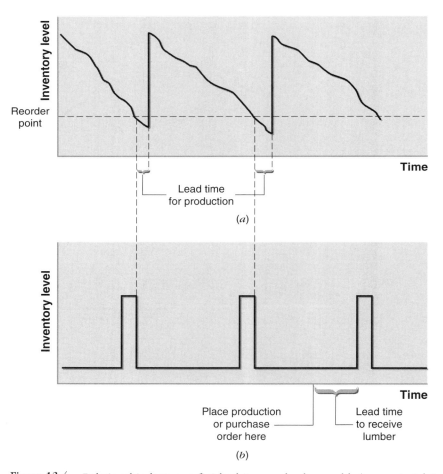

Figure 13.4   Relationship between finished item and subassembly/raw material item inventories—a requirements planning approach. (*a*) Finished doors. (*b*) Lumber.

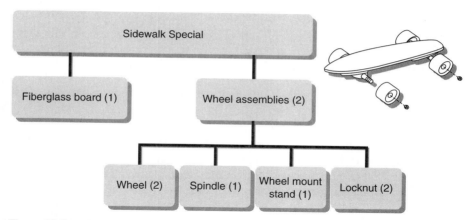

Figure 13.5 Skateboard product tree.

All reorder point systems assume (even though implicitly) that demand for each item in inventory is independent of the demand of other items in the inventory. These systems work well when the assumption holds but rather poorly for items whose demand is dependent on higher-level items. Materials requirements planning is one method used for dependent inventory items.

However, dependent demand is not the only cause of lumpy demand. Demand can appear in lumps if only a small number of customers exist for the item and their purchasing habits are discontinuous. MRP is not a solution to the general problem of lumpy demand, since no basis exists for developing the materials plan unless the demand is *dependent* on something that a planner can either measure or forecast.

The availability and practicality of MRP systems are directly related to the advent of relatively inexpensive computer power. Without the computer, inventory professionals would simply be unable to perform all the calculations and maintain all the schedules necessary for requirements planning. A simple example will illustrate this point.

❖ The Boardsports Company

The Boardsports Company produces a skateboard known as the Sidewalk Special. Its major components are one fiberglass board and two wheel assemblies. The lead time to assemble a Special from its two major components is one week. The first component, the board, is purchased and has a three-week delivery lead time. The second component, the wheel assembly, is assembled by Boardsports. Each wheel assembly is made up (with a one-week lead time) of one wheel mounting stand (manufactured by Boardsports with a four-week lead time), two wheels (purchased with a one-week lead time), one spindle (manufactured by Boardsports with a two-week lead time), and two chrome-plated locknuts (purchased with a one-week lead time). The product structure (or ***product tree***) is shown in Figure 13.5.

To produce an order for 50 Specials, the material requirements are computed as follows.

Fiberglass boards: 1 × number (no.) of specials = 1 × 50   =   50

Wheel assemblies: 2 × no. of specials = 2 × 50   = 100

Wheels: 2 × no. of wheel assemblies = 2 × 100 = 200

Spindles: 1 × no. of wheel assemblies = 1 × 100 = 100

Wheel mount stand: 1 × no. of wheel assemblies = 1 × 100 = 100

Locknut: 2 × no. of wheel assemblies = 2 × 100 = 200

Assume that according to the master schedule, an order for 50 Specials is due to be delivered in 10 weeks. The calendar in Table 13.1 illustrates the timing of due dates and the necessary order dates (assuming the lead times stated earlier) that must be met in order to deliver in the tenth week.

Note that MRP is a highly *logical* system. Knowing that 50 Specials must be shipped at the end of week 10 means that 50 boards must be placed on order for outside procurement at the end of week 6, that an order for 100 mounting stands must be placed in the shop at the end of week 4, and so forth. This is illustrated in the time-scaled assembly chart in Figure 13.6. (In essence, this is the product tree of Figure 13.5 laid on its side, with its components time-scaled to show their lead times.)

Ordering later than these dates would result in late shipment (or working overtime and otherwise expediting the order), and ordering earlier would result in having inventory available (and occupying space, requiring paperwork, and incurring other holding costs) before it is needed. MRP looks at each end product and the dates when each is needed. From these due dates, needed dates for all lower-level items are computed, and from these due dates starting or order dates are determined.

The overall idea is simple, but consider the extreme complexity of operating an MRP system manually. In this simple example, with only one end product, the calculations and record keeping are straightforward. But for a large firm that manufactures

𝒯ABLE 13.1 ✧ Demand for Sidewalk Specials

		Week								
		1	2	4	5	6	7	8	9	10
Sidewalk Specials										50
Boards	Date needed				3 week lead time				50	
	Order date					50				
Wheel assembly	Date needed							100		
	Order date						100			
Wheels	Date needed							200		
	Order date					200				
Spindles	Date needed							100		
	Order date					100				
Mounting stands	Date needed							100		
	Order date			100						
Locknuts	Date needed							200		
	Order date					200				

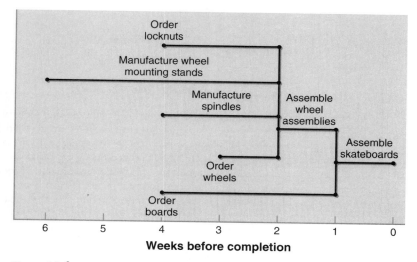

Figure 13.6   Time-scaled assembly chart for skateboard.

hundreds of end items with thousands of intermediate components, only a computer can keep up with the processing volume, as illustrated in the sidebar about Corning.

This is an important point, for MRP is not a revolutionary idea. The basic idea has been around for some time. It is and has been practiced for construction projects (from a single house to a mammoth skyscraper) that are scheduled according to a philosophy of having "the right materials to the right place at the right time." MRP has come of age in manufacturing and assembly operations because large-scale and relatively inexpensive computer power is available.

❖ The Implementation Problem

Unfortunately, the gains in productivity promised by computerized scheduling systems are more difficult to achieve than might be thought. Recent studies point out some of the pitfalls. Three separate sets of factors constitute significant impediments to implementation.

Technical Factors

Technical factors constitute a set of minimum criteria for implementation and relate primarily to the *mechanics* of the process. That is, although these are not by themselves sufficient, probably no system will work without them. They include the following:

- ❖ Valid data.
- ❖ Simple, transparent system (understandable to all).
- ❖ Adaptable system (as the organization changes).
- ❖ Low-cost system (both to install and run).
- ❖ Complete training of users.
- ❖ Representative project team (of all users).
- ❖ Implementation as a major goal.

OPERATIONS IN PRACTICE

Corning Adopts MRP

Corning Incorporated employs 29,000 people in 63 plants around the world and exports to over 90 nations. Sales—not just in cookware but also in technical, scientific, medical, and industrial products—top $1 billion. Some years ago, Corning's customers were displeased with its inability to deliver—only 50 percent of its orders were being delivered on time.

To get a better handle on its multiple production systems for various products at a wide range of plants, Corning decided to implement an MRP system that managers at all levels would use across plants. It was time, Corning decided, that Fred in finance should communicate about production with Mike in manufacturing, Mark in marketing, and Peter in purchasing. The initial investment to install MRP in 12 of Corning's domestic plants exceeded $1 million over a four-year period. But three of these—in Greencastle, Pennsylvania; Harrodsburg, Kentucky; and Martinsburg, West Virginia— were quickly implemented and began receiving the benefits of Corning's investment.

Corning's Greencastle facility is the largest and is its packaging, storage, and distribution center. The cost to adapt its existing computer system to MRP was $250,000, but it was able to reduce its inventory by $2 million. Moreover, inventory accuracy over the implementation period climbed from a disappointing 69 percent to 86 percent. Inventory turns also improved, from 5.4 to 6.6. Scheduling aspects also improved significantly: compliance with schedules jumped from 71 percent to 90 percent, and on-time deliveries leaped from 64 to 91 percent. Best of all, crisis management at Greencastle has all but disappeared.

Corning's prescription glasses, in 65 different types, are manufactured at its Harrodsburg plant. The MRP investment for hardware and software ran about $400,000 but has already paid for itself, saving Corning about $500,000 a year. In addition, the plant manager, Dick Sphon, believes the system has been a major labor-saver. For example, it has eliminated the need for taking physical inventory, a task that required about 800 labor-hours a year. Inventory accuracy exceeds 90 percent, in general. In maintenance, where 8000 items must be tracked, accuracy is 99 percent.

At Martinsburg, the 456,000-square-foot plant is equipped with state-of-the-art machinery to make saucepans, baking dishes, skillets, teapots, coffeepots, and platters. Before MRP, its inventory accuracy was only about 81 percent; now, accuracy runs 95 percent, meaning that there are far fewer crises about shipments. It also means a large reduction in inventory—$4 million—representing a direct annual saving of $400,000 in carrying costs. One department head feels that Corning couldn't compete without MRP (Horovitz, 1982).

✐OLVED EXERCISE 13.1 ❖ PRODUCING SCISSORS

Children's school scissors are made from four items: two identical blades, a 6–32 screw, and a nut. The blades are manufactured internally with a two-week lead time, and the screw and nut are purchased from a hardware supplier with a one-week lead time. The assembly process for 10 dozen scissors (120) is a week. Construct a product tree, an assembly chart, and an MRP table for an order of 10 dozen in week 7.

Solution:

PRODUCT TREE:

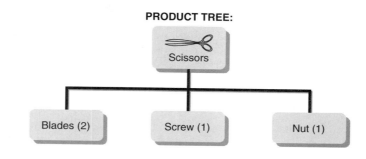

ASSEMBLY CHART:

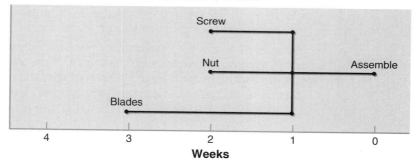

MRP TABLE:

		1	2	3	4	5	6	7
					Week			
Scissors								120
Blades:	Need						240	
	Order				240			
Screws:	Need						120	
	Order					120		
Nuts:	Need						120	
	Order					120		

Process Factors

Process factors are concerned with supporting the initiation and use of the system and are more complex and less well understood than technical factors. Process factors include the following:

❖ *Support from top management:* This support must be broad-based and knowledgeable. Managers would rather keep a problem they understand than employ a solution they don't. An MRP system, for example, commonly requires an investment of $240,000, takes 10 hours a month of a vice president's time, and takes 16 months to implement successfully. Managers must be prepared for at least this much time, money, and effort.

❖ *Support from users:* Those who will eventually use the system in their jobs— the users—should help design and implement it. In fact, they should fund and "own" the system.

Inner-Environmental Factors

These two factors may well provide the foundation for all the preceding factors:

❖ *A crucial situation:* If a problem or an opportunity is not of crucial importance to the organization, with significant resources already committed or about to be, the cost and difficulty of a computerized system will militate against successful implementation.

❖ *Willingness to change:* Management must be willing to change the way it operates the firm. These systems *demand* it! If the VP still plans to have old Joe run the "hot" jobs through the shop for them, the computerized system is doomed to failure, because two systems cannot ever both be in use. One will always be the "real" system, and the other will be a phony. Management must be willing to make changes and give up some power to the system. More than that, management must use this new system and *stop using* (and thereby *stop rewarding*) the old system.

These impediments are very difficult to remove, and they require a major commitment from management. For those who are successful, however, the rewards can be significant: much lower inventory investment, shorter lead times, fewer missed deliveries, and higher productivity.

But a warning is in order. To gain these benefits, MRP must be used as an ongoing system to operate the business. Many firms have "installed" MRP but have failed to realize significant benefits. That has happened either because they are not using it to run their operations or because they have not tied it into the surrounding systems. That is, they may be getting reports out of MRP, but actual schedules and work orders are derived from some other process—often the process that was used to operate the production system before MRP came in.

This relates to a second cause of failure: not tying MRP into the interfacing systems. Unless MRP is tied into the system for purchasing raw materials, for scheduling work at work centers, for conducting quality checks, and so on, it will not yield its full benefits. Any new system that is used in a business must be tied into the interfacing systems through its inputs and its outputs. If it is not, conflicts will occur and other systems will be devised to handle the inevitable problems.

$\mathcal{T}$HE MECHANICS OF MRP

Materials requirements planning is a management system for production and inventory. As such, it requires information about both production and inventory in order to produce its primary output—a schedule or plan for orders, both released and pending, which specifies actions to be taken now and in the future. Figure 13.7 illustrates the flows of information within an MRP system and indicates three primary inputs to the MRP system:

1. Master production schedule.
2. Bill of materials file.
3. Inventory master file.

A major output from the MRP computer system is the planned order release report, although other reports—on changes, exceptions, and deexpediting—are also outputs.

Figure 13.7 shows in detail a portion of Figure 11.1. Here we are not concerned with the aggregate plan or the production plan, and the demand forecast is passed right through the master production schedule, which feeds the MRP system. However, MRP also requires other inputs that are not related to the major scheduling functions shown in Figure 11.1, such as current inventory levels and bills of material for the products. The MRP output reports shown in Figure 13.7 are, then, the inputs to the capacity planning function shown in Figure 11.1.

The relationship between materials planning and operations scheduling is, of necessity, intimate. Any attempts to design these two systems so that they operate independently will either fail outright or, at best, be grossly inefficient.

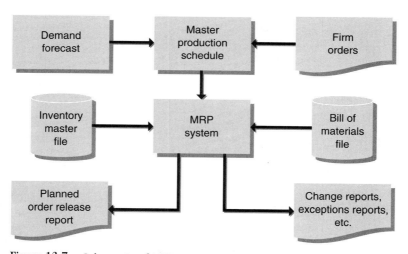

Figure 13.7   Schematic of MRP system.

❖ MRP Inputs

As indicated above, the MRP inputs are the master production schedule, the bill of materials file, and the inventory master file.

Master Production Schedule

As discussed in Chapter 11, the master production schedule is based on actual customer orders and predicted demand. This schedule indicates exactly when each ordered item will be produced to meet the firm and predicted demand. That is, it is a time-phased production plan: "Tuesday we make 100 S-3s for Smith; Wednesday 200 R-1s for Jones," and so on.

Bill of Materials

For each item in the master production schedule, there is a **_bill of materials_** (**BOM**). The bill of materials file indicates all the raw materials, components, subassemblies, and assemblies required to produce an item. The MRP computer system accesses the bill of materials file to determine exactly what items, and in what quantities, are required to complete an order for a given item.

Rather than simply listing all the parts necessary to produce one finished product, the BOM shows the way a finished product is put together from individual items, components, and subassemblies. For example, the product structure illustrated in Figure 13.8 would generate the BOM illustrated in Figure 13.9.

This BOM shows the finished product (sometimes called the **_parent item_**) at the highest, or _zero,_ level. Subassemblies and parts that go directly into the assembly of the finished product are called level 1 components, parts and subassemblies that go into level 1 components are shown as level 2, and so on. Thus, when a master pro-

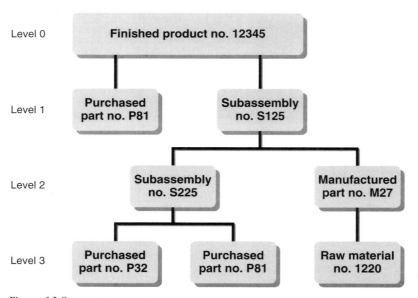

Figure 13.8   Product structure tree.

Level 1 Parts	Level 2 Parts	Level 3 Parts	Description	Quantity	Source
No. P81				1	Purchased
No. S125				1	Manufactured
	No. S225			1	Manufactured
		No. P32		1	Purchased
		No. P81		2	Purchased
	No. M27			1	Manufactured
		No. 1220		3 lb	Purchased

Figure 13.9   Bill of materials (BOM) for a three-level product.

duction schedule shows a requirement for a given quantity of finished products for a certain due date, production planners can **explode** the BOM for that finished product to determine the number, due dates, and necessary order dates of subcomponents.

Exploding a BOM simply means stepping down through all its levels and determining the quantity and lead time for each item required to make up the item at that level. Note that if some items are manufactured internally, their lead time will be a function of the number of items to be produced rather than a fixed period. The result of exploding a BOM for a given product is a time-phased requirement for specific quantities of each item necessary to make the finished product. We exploded an order for skateboards earlier, although we had not formally introduced the notion of a bill of materials. A great deal of the time required to implement an MRP system is spent restructuring BOMs (so that they can be exploded properly) and verifying their accuracy. Clearly, exploding incorrect BOMs will only cause trouble further downstream.

Note in Figures 13.8 and 13.9 that purchased part No. P81 is used as both a level 1 and a level 3 component and is specifically identified in both locations in the product tree and bill of materials. Purchased part No. P81 could perhaps be a stainless steel nut and bolt assembly used to produce subassembly No. S225 and to complete the assembly of the finished product 12345 by being put together with subassembly No. S125. We do not aggregate the number of P81s used to produce a single finished product (that is, we do not show part No. P81 as requiring 3 to produce finished product No. 12345), because aggregating would not allow us to identify the specific number of P81s necessary to produce a lot of S225 subassemblies. It would also preclude knowing how many P81s would be necessary to complete final assembly of S125 subassemblies into finished products.

Inventory Master File

The inventory master file contains detailed information regarding the number or quantity of each item on hand, on order, and committed to use in various time periods. The MRP system accesses the inventory master computer file to determine the quantity available for use in a given time period, and if enough are available to meet the needs of the order, it commits these for use during the time period by updating the inventory record. If sufficient items are not available, the system includes this item, as well as the usual lot size, on the planned order release report.

Low-Level Coding

In exploding the BOM, the requirements for the components are determined level by level. Thus, the requirements for the level 1 items are determined first. Next, the requirements for the level 2 items are computed, and so on. According to this logic, a problem can arise when a given component occurs on more than one level. The best-case scenario is that only the computational time increases, because the calculation is repeated several times. The worst-case scenario is that an error is made in determining the component requirements. To illustrate this, consider the product tree structure shown in Figure 13.10. The numbers in parentheses represent the number of components required. If we determine the requirements level by level, at level 1 we calculate that three B's are needed for each end item P. However, when we get to level 2 we calculate that six B's are needed (ignoring the three needed at level 1). One of two things can happen at level 2. Either we completely ignore the requirements at level 1 and conclude that only six B's are needed, or the program is smart enough to know that component B is also used in level 1. If the program is able to figure this out, then it can recalculate the number of B's needed at level 1 and add this to the number of B's needed at level 2.

An alternative approach is to use low-level coding in constructing the BOM. With low-level coding, the lowest level at which a component occurs is determined. Then, any other occurrences of this component are shifted down to this level. For example, in Figure 13.10, component B occurs on levels 1 and 2. Since level 2 is the lowest level at which component B occurs, all occurrences of component B are shifted down to level 2, as shown in Figure 13.11. Now, with the product tree structure shown in Figure 13.11, the requirements for component B need be calculated only one time at level 2. Note that low-level coding is often an iterative process because the product tree structure is constantly changing as various components are shifted to lower levels.

❖ MRP System Outputs

Three specific outputs of the MRP system constitute the plan of action for released and pending orders:

1. Order action report.
2. Open orders report.
3. Planned order release report.

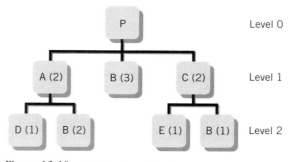

Figure 13.10   Original product tree structure.

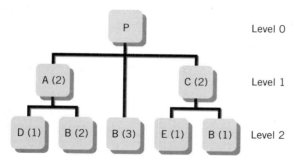

Figure 13.11 Low-level-coded product tree structure.

The *order action report* indicates which orders are to be released during the current time period and which orders are to be canceled. The *open orders report* shows which orders are to be expedited or deexpedited. This report is an exception report, listing only those open orders for which action is necessary. The *planned order release report* is the time-phased plan for orders to be released in future time periods. It is this report that determines whether or not a master production schedule is feasible.

❖ MRP Computations

An order for 100 of a finished product due 12 weeks from today may or may not be cause for action in the production-inventory system. If 1000 are currently on hand and planned order deliveries for 350 are scheduled between now and 12 weeks from now, 650 will be available from which the order for 100 can be shipped. But if 400 are available now and 350 will be shipped between now and the due date for the order of 100, action is necessary. The resulting MRP calculations are relatively straightforward:

  ❖ Process all items in the bill of materials level by level.
    ❖ For each item at a level:
      ❖ Determine the time-phased gross requirements by summing planned order releases of its parent items multiplied by the quantity usage rate per parent item, for each period of the planning horizon.
      ❖ Subtract on-hand and on-order amounts from gross requirements to determine the net requirements.
      ❖ Apply the lot-sizing rule assumed to determine the lot size.
      ❖ Offset the order release for lead time, yielding time-phased planned order releases.

MRP computations are based, in large part, on gross and net requirements. The order for 100 to be shipped in 12 weeks is a gross requirement. Actions, however, should be based on net requirements. In the first instance, the net requirement is −550 (i.e., 100 − 650); thus, there is no production requirement. But in the second case, the net requirement in the twelfth week is 50 (i.e., 100 − 50). Since there is a net requirement for 50 units, at least that quantity will have to be produced to meet the shipping requirement for 50. These quantities are based on the following two formulas:

$$\text{Net requirements for planning period} = \text{gross requirements}$$
$$\text{for the planning period} - \text{planned on hand at planning period}$$

and

$$\text{Planned } on \text{ hand at planning period} = \text{current on hand} +$$
$$\text{scheduled receipts prior to planning period} - \text{scheduled}$$
$$\text{requirements prior to planning period}$$

Using the lead times available in the inventory file, we can calculate order release dates by backscheduling or time phasing from the due date by the amount of the lead time. Orders are scheduled to be received when needed to meet the due date or dates. If the net requirements for the planning period are positive, then an order must be scheduled to be received in time for use in the planning period. MRP answers the question of when to order by first determining when items are needed, and then scheduling an order release so that the items will be received just before that date. On the other hand, if the net requirements are negative or zero, no order is necessary.

Each component that goes into the production of the 100 parent items is scheduled in an analogous fashion. A planned order release at one level generates requirements at the level below it. The differences in on-hand inventory at each level, the order quantities used at different levels, and the number of different finished products that use a particular component result in different order cycles for items at the various levels.

For example, suppose that in the order for 100 items in week 12, the planned on-hand quantity is 50 and the lead time for production (assembly) of level 1 items is three weeks. Then, an order for at least 50 (and possibly more, depending on the company's policy of ordering in standard reorder or lot sizes) would be placed in week 9. On the next MRP table, this order will show up in the row "Planned order receipts." The materials requirements plan at level 0 of the product is shown in Table 13.2.

At level 1, a purchased hose may be required, and therefore a requirement plan must be developed for this item as well. But the same hose may be used on an-

$\mathcal{T}$ABLE 13.2 ❖ Zero-Level MRP

Week	1	2	3	4	5	6	7	8	9	10	11	12
Gross requirements		50			150			50	100			100
On hand 400	400	400	350	350	350	200	200	200	150	50	50	50
Net requirements	—	—	—	—	—	—	—	—	—	—	—	50
Planned order receipts												50
Planned order releases									50			
Lead time = 3 weeks												

$\mathcal{T}$ABLE 13.3 ❖ Level 1 MRP

Week	1	2	3	4	5	6	7	8	9	10	11	12
Gross requirements									50	200		
On hand 50	50	50	100	100	100	100	100	100	100	50	100	
Net requirements		—	—	—	—	—	—	—	—	150		
Planned order receipts		50										
Planned order releases						250						

Lead time = 4 weeks

other product. Therefore, the requirements plan for the hose must incorporate the requirements generated from all items in which it is used. The materials requirements plan for the purchased hose is shown in Table 13.3. Lead time is four weeks. Notice the planned order receipt of 50 units in week 2, resulting from a planned order release some weeks previously.

But also notice the demand in week 10 for 200 of the hoses. Assume that these are required to produce subassemblies used in an entirely different end product. The requirements for both uses are aggregated, and an order is planned in week $10 - 4 = 6$ for 250. The order of 250 is for a standard reorder quantity.

This same procedure is followed at each level. All requirements from higher levels generate needs at lower levels. These needs are aggregated at each level for each item, and a requirements plan is established using the formulas and tables outlined above.

$\mathcal{S}$OLVED EXERCISE 13.2 ❖ MRP EXPLOSION

Construct the MRP table for Solved Exercise 13.1, assuming that there is another order for 360 in week 9 and there are 360 blades currently available in inventory, 500 screws, and 100 nuts.

Solution:

	Week								
	1	2	3	4	5	6	7	8	9
Scissors: Lead time 1 week									
Gross requirements							120		360
On hand 0	0	0	0	0	0	0	0	0	0
Net requirements							120		360
Planned receipts							120		360
Planned releases						120		360	
Blades: Lead time 2 weeks									
Gross requirements						240		720	
On hand 360	360	360	360	360	360	360	120	120	0

					Week				
	1	2	3	4	5	6	7	8	9
Net requirements						0		600	
Planned receipts								600	
Planned releases						600			
Screws: Lead time 1 week									
Gross requirements						120		360	
On hand 500	500	500	500	500	500	500	380	380	20
Net requirements						0		0	
Planned receipts									
Planned releases									
Nuts: Lead time 1 week									
Gross requirements						120		360	
On hand 100	100	100	100	100	100	100	0	0	0
Net requirements						20		360	
Planned receipts						20		360	
Planned releases					20		360		

Spreadsheet Analysis: MRP Explosion for Multiple Products

PaddlePong produces two models of its best-selling table tennis paddles. The company cuts the paddles out of wood and then glues the rubber padding and the wood handle grips to the wood paddle. The bill of materials for these two paddles is as follows:

Level 0	Level 1	Quantity	Source
Standard paddle			
	Wood paddle	1	Manufacturing
	Wood handle grips	2	Manufacturing
	1/4-inch rubber pad	2	Purchasing
Pro paddle			
	Wood paddle	1	Manufacturing
	Wood handle grips	2	Manufacturing
	3/8-inch rubber pad	2	Purchasing

The company has orders for 50 Standard paddles to be delivered in week 4, 75 Standard paddles in week 6, 100 Pro paddles in week 5, and 50 Pro paddles in week 6. On-hand inventory and lead times are given in the table below.

Item	Beginning On-hand Inventory	Lead Time
Pro paddles	30	1 week
Standard paddles	10	1 week
Wood paddles	0	1 week
Wood handle grips	0	1 week
1/4-inch rubber pads	0	2 weeks
3/8-inch rubber pads	0	2 weeks

PaddlePong uses lot-for-lot ordering and thus orders or produces exactly what is needed to meet net requirements.

The spreadsheet below was developed to help PaddlePong plan its purchasing and production to meet its delivery requirements.

	A	B	C	D	E	F	G
1		Master Production Schedule					
2	Week	1	2	3	4	5	6
3	Pro paddle				50		75
4	Standard paddle					100	20
5							
6	**Pro paddle (lead time = 1 week)**						
7	Gross requirements	0	0	0	50	0	75
8	On hand (30)	30	30	30	30	0	0
9	Net requirements	0	0	0	20	0	75
10	Planned order receipts	0	0	0	20	0	75
11	Planned order releases	0	0	20	0	75	0
12							
13	**Standard paddle (lead time = 1 week)**						
14	Gross requirements	0	0	0	0	100	20
15	On hand (10)	10	10	10	10	10	0
16	Net requirements	0	0	0	0	90	20
17	Planned order receipts	0	0	0	0	90	20
18	Planned order releases	0	0	0	90	20	0
19							
20	**Wood paddle (lead time = 1 week)**						
21	Gross requirements	0	0	20	90	95	0
22	On hand	0	0	0	0	0	0
23	Net requirements	0	0	20	90	95	0
24	Planned order receipts	0	0	20	90	95	0
25	Planned order releases	0	20	90	95	0	0
26							
27	**Wood handle grip (lead time = 1 week)**						
28	Gross requirements	0	0	40	180	190	0
29	On hand	0	0	0	0	0	0
30	Net requirements	0	0	40	180	190	0
31	Planned order receipts	0	0	40	180	190	0
32	Planned order releases	0	40	180	190	0	0
33							
34	**1/4 inch rubber pads (lead time = 2 weeks)**						
35	Gross requirements	0	0	0	180	40	0
36	On hand	0	0	0	0	0	0
37	Net requirements	0	0	0	180	40	0
38	Planned order receipts	0	0	0	180	40	0
39	Planned order releases	0	180	40	0	0	0
40							
41	**3/8 inch rubber pads (lead time = 2 weeks)**						
42	Gross requirements	0	0	40	0	150	0
43	On hand	0	0	0	0	0	0
44	Net requirements	0	0	40	0	150	0
45	Planned order receipts	0	0	40	0	150	0
46	Planned order releases	40	0	150	0	0	0

The master production schedule for PaddlePong is contained in rows 2 through 4. In row 2 the week number is tracked. Row 3 contains the quantities of Pro paddles needed each week over the six-week planning horizon. Row 4 contains the quantities of Standard paddles needed.

Rows 6 through 11 contain the MRP table for the Pro paddle. In row 7, the gross requirements for the Pro paddle are calculated. Since the gross requirements for an end item (or level 0 item) come directly from the master production schedule, to calculate the gross requirements for the Pro paddle in week 1, =B3 was entered in cell B7 and then copied to cells C3:G3.

On-hand is defined as the inventory available at the beginning of the week. In general, on-hand inventory for a period is calculated as the on-hand from the prior period plus planned order receipts in the prior period minus gross requirements in the prior period. Since it was given that the beginning on-hand balance was 30 Pro paddles, 30 was entered in cell B8. To calculate the on-hand balance in week 2, we add to the on-hand in period 1 any planned order receipts in week 1 and subtract any gross requirements in week 1. Thus, the week 2 on-hand (cell C8) was calculated as: MAX((B8+B10−B7),0). The MAX function was used because it is not possible to have a negative amount of inventory. The formula entered in cell C8 can be copied to cells D8:G8.

There is a positive net requirement in a particular period only if the gross requirement in that period is greater than the on-hand inventory of the period. To capture this logic, the net requirement in week 1 for the Pro paddle was calculated in cell B9 as: =IF(B7>B8,B7−B8,0). This formula can then be copied to cells C9:G9.

With the lot-for-lot lot sizing rule, the amount that we plan to receive in any period is equal to the net requirements for that period. Thus, to calculate the planned order receipts in week 1 for the Pro paddle, =B9 was entered in cell B10 and then copied to cells C10:G10. In a similar fashion, associated with each planned order receipt there has to be a planned order release. For the Pro paddle there is a one-week lead time. Thus, it takes one week from the time an order for more Pro paddles is released until the paddles are completed and ready for shipment. In the present case this one-week lead time corresponds to the time it takes to glue the rubber pads and completed wood handle grips to the completed wood paddles. Given the one-week lead time, there will be a planned order release one week before each planned order receipt. For example, to be able to plan on receiving completed Pro paddles in week 2, we must plan on releasing an order for more paddles in week 1. Therefore, the formula to calculate the planned order releases in week 1 for the Pro paddles (cell B11) is: =C10. The formula entered in cell B11 can be copied to cells C11:G11.

The same logic, with some minor modifications, was used to enter the formulas in the five other MRP tables shown in the spreadsheet above. For example, the MRP table for the Standard paddle (rows 13–18) was created by copying the MRP table for the Pro paddle and changing only the "Gross requirements" row. Specifically, the gross requirements for the Standard paddle come from row 4. Thus, to calculate the gross requirements for the Standard paddle in week 1, =B4 was entered in cell B14 and then copied to cells C14:G14.

Likewise, only the gross requirements row (row 21) required modification in the table created for the wood paddles (rows 20–25). Since planned order releases for both the Pro and the Standard paddles create a gross requirement for wood paddles, we need to aggregate these requirements in each week to determine the gross requirements for the wood paddles. For example, to calculate the gross requirements for wood paddles in week 1, =B11+B18 was entered in cell B21 and then copied to cells C21:G21. Cell B11 contains the planned order releases for Pro paddles in week 1 and cell B18 contains the planned order releases for Standard paddles in week 1.

Rows 27–32 correspond to the MRP table for the wood handle grips. Since each complete Pro and Standard paddle needs two wood handle grips, the gross requirements of the wood handle grips were calculated in week 1 (cell B28) as: =2*(B11+B18). This formula was then copied to cells C28:G28.

Finally, in addition to modifying gross requirements, the MRP tables for the 1/4-inch and 3/8-inch rubber pads require one more modidfication. Specifically, both of these items have a two-week lead time. Thus, the planned order releases for these items have to be placed two weeks prior to the corresponding planned order receipt. To illustrate, the planned order release in week 1 for 1/4-inch rubber pads will result in a planned order receipt in week 3. Therefore, in cell B39 (planned order releases for 1/4-inch rubber pads in week 1): =D38 was entered and then copied to cells C39:G39.

A few notes are in order with respect to using spreadsheets for material requirements planning. To begin, as this example illustrates, spreadsheets can be quickly set up to handle the materials explosion process. Futhermore, a spreadsheet's ability to quickly update itself when changes are made to one or more cells can greatly facilitate the development of a feasible master production schedule and identify the operational impact of a variety of changes, such as late orders. In addition, the ability to delete columns, add new ones, and copy formulas to the new columns facilitates maintaining a rolling planning horizon. On the other hand, as the complexity of the situation increases—as measured by the number of items to track, the extent of common components, and the frequency of changes to the bill of materials—the complexity of setting up and maintaining an MRP system in a spreadsheet increases to the point where a specialized MRP software package may be more appropriate.

❖ Safety Stock

As discussed in Chapter 12, safety stock is used to guard against uncertantities in demand and lead time. Demand for dependent-demand items—since it is derived from demand for independent-demand items—involves no uncertainty. Thus, because MRP exerts better control over materials, safety stock is usually discouraged for dependent-demand items. The only exceptions may be if supply of critical items is at risk or if production yields are uncertain. The demand for other parts in the bill of materials is derived from the level-zero items and includes adequate lead time, so that safety stocks are unnecessary. Note also that safety stock of dependent-demand items is contained in the safety stock of the end items, which are made up of the dependent-demand items.

If safety stock is going to be held for a parent item or a critical part, it is not usually included in the on-hand count, or else an "available" row is added to the MRP table to show that the on-hand quantity differs from the available quantity, owing to safety stock or prior allocations.

❖ Lot Sizing

In conjunction with scheduling orders to be released (i.e., deciding "when to order"), the second major question of inventory management—"how many to order"—must be answered. A simple approach, called **lot-for-lot,** is to order only what is needed. However, this **lot size** may not be the most appropriate. Determining the appropriate lot size for the production of intermittently demanded products is complex, but the general objective is to balance the cost of ordering or setup with the cost of holding inventory.

One approach is to determine, the best quantity through trial and error, by trying all possible order quantities that meet the master schedule and comparing their costs. This is obviously a large and tedious problem, since there are so many possibilities.

A second method, known as the *Wagner-Whitin algorithm,* determines optimal lot sizes systematically by evaluating all possible ways of ordering to meet the master schedule. Note that this procedure is an optimizing technique. Its major drawback is the complexity of the computations, particularly as the number of ordering alternatives increases.

A third approach is simply to try the lot sizes determined by accumulating the time-phased requirements. For example, suppose that requirements of 100, 40, and 75 units were scheduled for weeks 13, 18, and 21, respectively. This approach would simply evaluate the three order quantities 100, 140 (100 + 40), and 215 (100 + 40 + 75). The evaluation would compare the costs of ordering three times (quantities of 100, 40, 75), two times (quantities of 140, 75), and one time (quantity of 215) with the costs of holding the extra inventory above the first 100 units until weeks 13 and 18. Although this approach appears to be logical and is certainly better than performing no evaluation at all, it does not consider all alternatives (e.g., 40 + 75) and therefore does not guarantee an optimal solution.

Part period balancing uses the same general approach but provides a more systematic procedure. Part period balancing attempts to equate the cost of placing a single order with the cost of holding the inventory produced by that order, since—as shown in Chapter 12—the optimal order quantity is that quantity for which order cost equals holding cost. This method recognizes that relationship and attempts to use it to find an order quantity, from those available, for which the order cost and the holding cost associated with that order are approximately the same. Although this method is not guaranteed to produce optimal order quantities, it does produce satisfactory approximations, with much less computational difficulty than is entailed by the methods that produce optimal solutions. For example, one study compared the Wagner-Whitin algorithm (which does produce optimal results) with part period balancing and found that the cost of the optimal solution was only 7 percent lower than the solution developed with part period balancing. We will demonstrate this approach with an example.

❖ Auto-Spring Company

The Auto-Spring Company manufactures a variety of compression springs for use in automobile rocker arm assemblies. Current orders for model x-250 used in several V6 engines, are as follows:

Week 28   10,000
Week 31   18,000
Week 40   12,000

Setup of the spring winding equipment for a production run costs approximately $700. The cost of holding an x-250 spring in inventory for 1 week is considered to be $0.0025.

Under part period balancing, the alternative three lot size available before week 28 are as follows:

Alternative	1	2	3
Produce in week 28	10,000	28,000	40,000

Part period balancing selects the alternative for which the holding cost is closest to the setup cost of $700. The three holding costs are:

$$C_H(10,000) = 0$$
$$C_H(28,000) = 3 \text{ weeks} \times 18,000 \text{ excess units} \times \$0.0025/\text{unit/week} = \$135$$
$$C_H(40,000) = 3 \times 18,000 \times 0.0025 + 12 \times 12,000 \times 0.0025 = \$495$$

Because producing all 40,000 springs in one lot results in the closest match between order cost and holding cost, the third alternative should be chosen.

To summarize, the MRP system follows these steps:

1. Determine requirements of finished products, the master production schedule, from firm orders and sales forecasts.

2. Using the bill of materials, calculate the gross requirements for each item, beginning with the item at level zero.

3. Using the bill of materials file and the inventory master file, determine the order release dates and the order quantities for each item necessary to meet the master production schedule.

4. Regenerate the MRP on the basis of changes in the master production schedule or in order priorities.

ᏚOLVED EXERCISE 13.3 ❖ PART PERIOD BALANCING

Use part period balancing for the nuts in Solved Exercise 13.2, assuming that it costs $2 for the order and that the holding cost of 1 nut is $0.002 per week.

Solution:

The two alternatives are to order 20 nuts in week 5 (holding cost = 0) or 380 nuts.

$$C_H(380) = 2 \text{ weeks} \times 360 \text{ excess} \times \$0.002 = \$1.44.$$

Ordering 380 results in a holding cost that comes closest to the ordering cost of $2.

Spreadsheet Analysis: Lot Sizing

A spreadsheet's ability to quickly recalculate itself makes it an ideal tool for investigating alternative lot sizes. To illustrate this, we will use the MRP table for wood paddles from the previous Spreadsheet Analysis.

After a discussion of the situation with the managers at PaddlePong, it was determined that it costs $0.25 to hold 1 wood paddle in inventory for 1 week and $35 to set up the equipment used to cut the paddles from wood boards. The spreadsheet previously developed for PaddlePong was modified as shown below to help evaluate alternative lot sizes for the wood paddles.

	A	B	C	D	E	F	G	H
1	Per Unit Holding Cost	$0.30						
2	Setup Cost	$35						
3								
4	Week	1	2	3	4	5	6	
5								
6	Wood paddle (lead time = 1 week)							
7	Gross requirements	0	0	20	90	95	0	
8	On hand	0	0	0	0	0	0	
9	Net requirements	0	0	20	90	95	0	
10	Planned order receipts	0	0	20	90	95	0	
11	Planned order releases	0	20	90	95	0	0	
12								
13	Weekly Holding Cost	$0.00	$0.00	$0.00	$0.00	$0.00	$0.00	$0.00
14	Weekly Setup Cost	$0.00	$35.00	$35.00	$35.00	$0.00	$0.00	$105.00
15	Total Weekly Cost	$0.00	$35.00	$35.00	$35.00	$0.00	$0.00	$105.00

In the spreadsheet above, the weekly holding cost per unit was entered in cell B1, and the equipment setup cost in cell B2. Rows 6–11 contain the MRP table for the wood paddle and are identical to rows 20–25 in the previous Spreadsheet Analysis.

The total cost of holding wood paddles in each week is calculated in row 13. Thus, the weekly holding cost in week 1 was calculated in cell B13 as: =B8*$B$1. This formula was then copied to cells C13:F13. Weekly setup cost (row 14) is $35 in any week that has a planned order release. Otherwise, the setup cost for the week is zero. To capture this logic the IF function was used. For example, to calculate the setup cost in week 1: =IF(B11>0,$B$2,0) was entered in cell B14 and then copied to cells C14:G14. In row 15 the total weekly cost is calculated by adding each week's holding and setup cost. Finally, in column H (rows 13 to 15) the weekly holding, setup, and total costs are summed over the six-week planning horizon. In this spreadsheet, the lot-for-lot lot sizing rule was used, resulting in a total cost over the six weeks of $105.

In the next spreadsheet, the batches for weeks 3 and 4 are combined by entering 110 in cell D10. As a result, total cost decreases from $105 to $97.

	A	B	C	D	E	F	G	H
1	Per Unit Holding Cost	$0.30						
2	Setup Cost	$35						
3								
4	Week	1	2	3	4	5	6	
5								
6	Wood paddle (lead time = 1 week)							
7	Gross requirements	0	0	20	90	95	0	
8	On hand	0	0	0	90	0	0	
9	Net requirements	0	0	20	0	95	0	
10	Planned order receipts	0	0	110	0	95	0	
11	Planned order releases	0	110	0	95	0	0	
12								
13	Weekly Holding Cost	$0.00	$0.00	$0.00	$27.00	$0.00	$0.00	$27.00
14	Weekly Setup Cost	$0.00	$35.00	$0.00	$35.00	$0.00	$0.00	$70.00
15	Total Weekly Cost	$0.00	$35.00	$0.00	$62.00	$0.00	$0.00	$97.00

As a third alternative, we investigate combining the requirements for weeks 3, 4, and 5. As the next spreadsheet shows, this alternative increases total cost to $119.

	A	B	C	D	E	F	G	H
1	Per Unit Holding Cost	$0.30						
2	Setup Cost	$35						
3								
4	Week	1	2	3	4	5	6	
5								
6	Wood paddle (lead time = 1 week)							
7	Gross requirements	0	0	20	90	95	0	
8	On hand	0	0	0	185	95	0	
9	Net requirements	0	0	20	0	0	0	
10	Planned order receipts	0	0	205	0	0	0	
11	Planned order releases	0	205	0	0	0	0	
12								
13	Weekly Holding Cost	$0.00	$0.00	$0.00	$55.50	$28.50	$0.00	$84.00
14	Weekly Setup Cost	$0.00	$35.00	$0.00	$0.00	$0.00	$0.00	$35.00
15	Total Weekly Cost	$0.00	$35.00	$0.00	$55.50	$28.50	$0.00	$119.00

As a final example, the net requirements of weeks 4 and 5 are combined in the spreadsheet below.

	A	B	C	D	E	F	G	H
1	Per Unit Holding Cost	$0.30						
2	Setup Cost	$35						
3								
4	Week	1	2	3	4	5	6	
5								
6	Wood paddle (lead time = 1 week)							
7	Gross requirements	0	0	20	90	95	0	
8	On hand	0	0	0	0	95	0	
9	Net requirements	0	0	20	90	0	0	
10	Planned order receipts	0	0	20	185	0	0	
11	Planned order releases	0	20	185	0	0	0	
12								
13	Weekly Holding Cost	$0.00	$0.00	$0.00	$0.00	$28.50	$0.00	$28.50
14	Weekly Setup Cost	$0.00	$35.00	$35.00	$0.00	$0.00	$0.00	$70.00
15	Total Weekly Cost	$0.00	$35.00	$35.00	$0.00	$28.50	$0.00	$98.50

As these examples demonstrate, a variety of alternative lot sizes can be investigated quickly and easily with spreadsheets. Futhermore, the entire spreadsheet originally developed for PaddlePong could be modified to include similar information so that policies regarding lot sizes for the entire production system could be investigated with a single spreadsheet model.

$\mathcal{Q}$UALITY VALVE COMPANY

To illustrate the MRP procedure in more detail, consider Quality Valve Company (QVC), which manufactures industrial valves and fittings. QVC has decided to implement an MRP system throughout its production facilities and is planning first to test the operation of the system using one finished product, the No. 3303 check valve. Table 13.4 shows the master production schedule for this valve. It is based on existing orders and promised shipping dates as well as anticipated sales.

This schedule indicates the number of valves required to be shipped by the end of each of the indicated weeks. The master production schedule is prepared every week for the current week and the next 10 weeks. The "Past Due" column indicates the number of valves that are currently backordered (in this example, none). Suppose that the current inventory of No. 3303 check valves is 800 units. Table 13.5 shows a partially completed MRP for the valve. The MRP will be completed when lot sizes are determined.

❖ Determining Lot Sizes

Because this is a relatively simple situation in which only one item is being considered, all three possible order quantities can be evaluated to determine the best lot size. Suppose that QVC's accounting department has found setup cost to be $90 and holding cost per unit per week to be $0.08. If QVC produced one batch for each required shipment, there would be no excess inventory, but the total setup cost over the next 10 weeks would be $270 (3 × $90). Producing 3200 for week 21 plus the 3000 required for week 24 in one batch would result in a saving of one setup ($90) but would increase the holding cost by $720 (3 weeks × 3000 units × $0.08 per unit per week). Combining all three shipping requirements results in a

$\mathcal{T}$ABLE 13.4 ❖ No. 3303 Check Valve: Master Production Schedule

Item no.: 3303
Description: check valve
Current inventory level: 800

Week	Past Due	18	19	20	21	22	23	24	25	26	27	28	29
Gross requirements	0	0	0	0	4000	0	0	3000	0	0	0	6000	0

$\mathscr{T}$ABLE 13.5 ❖ No. 3303 Check Valve: Partially Completed MRP

Week	Past Due	18	19	20	21	22	23	24	25	26	27	28	29
Gross requirements	0	0	0	0	4000	0	0	3000	0	0	0	6000	0
On hand: 800		800	800	800	800								
Net requirement					3200								
Planned order receipts													
Planned order releases													

Lead time = 3 weeks

saving of $180 ($2 × $90) in setup costs, but it incurs additional holding costs of $4080 (3 weeks × 3000 × 0.08 + 7 × 6000 × 0.08). Clearly, for this situation the best policy is to order in lot sizes equal to the requirements of each period, for this results in the lowest total cost.

Part period balancing, which attempts to equate the cost of placing a single order and the cost of holding the inventory produced in that order, requires computation of the holding cost of each of the three possible lot sizes:

$$3,200$$
$$6,200$$
$$12,200$$

The decision rule in part period balancing is that QVC select the lot size for which holding cost is closest to order cost, $90. The computations are:

$$C_H(3200) = 0$$
$$C_H(6200) = 3 \text{ weeks} \times 3000 \text{ excess units} \times \$0.08/\text{unit/week} = \$720$$
$$C_H(12,200) = 3 \times 3000 \times 0.08 + 7 \times 6000 \times 0.08 = \$4080$$

Clearly, the holding cost of zero is closest to $90, and therefore the order size of 3200 (as recommended previously) would also be selected by part period balancing.

Assuming a lead time of three weeks for assembly of the No. 3303 check valve, orders should be released in weeks 18, 21, and 25 for order quantities of 3200, 3000, and 6000, respectively. Table 13.6 illustrates the completed MRP for the No. 3303 check valve.

❖ Parts Explosion for Scheduling

QVC, having determined the order quantities and release dates of finished No. 3303 valves, must now determine the quantities and timing of orders for the component parts and subassemblies. This determination begins with a *bill of materials,* which

$\mathscr{T}$ABLE 13.6 ❖ No. 3303 Check Valve: Completed MRP

Week	Past Due	18	19	20	21	22	23	24	25	26	27	28	29
Gross requirements	0	0	0	0	4000	0	0	3000	0	0	0	6000	0
On hand: 800		800	800	800	800	0	0	0	0	0	0	0	0
Net requirement					3200			3000				6000	
Planned order receipts													
Planned order releases		3200			3000			6000					

Lead time = 3 weeks

is the structured list of all required parts needed to produce one No. 3303 valve. Table 13.7 illustrates the multilevel bill of materials. (In this case there are two levels of items.) Figure 13.12 shows the same bill of materials as a product tree. Note in Table 13.7 the column labeled "Quantity." This column indicates the number of that item required to produce 1 of the next higher level of items. For example, 2 locknuts are required to produce 1 poppet assembly, and 2 poppet assemblies are necessary for 1 No. 3303 check valve. Therefore, 4 locknuts are required for 1 No. 3303 valve. The parts in the second level are used to produce a subassembly (e.g., 1 valve body and 1 valve seat are assembled to produce 1 valve body assembly), and the subassemblies in turn are coupled with other first-level parts to make the finished product.

In addition to the bill of materials, two pieces of information are required from the inventory master file for each item in the production of the No. 3303 check valve: quantity on hand and lead time (for assembly, manufacture, or purchase, as appropriate). This information is summarized in Table 13.8.

Now that the three sources of information are available (i.e., master production

$\mathscr{T}$ABLE 13.7 ❖ No. 3303 Check Valve: Bill of Materials

First Level Part No.	Second Level Part No.	Description	Quantity	Source
79221		Valve body assembly	1	Manufacturing
	82392	Valve body	1	Manufacturing
	64103	Valve seat	2	Manufacturing
30468		Spring	2	Purchasing
84987		Poppet assembly	2	Manufacturing
	29208	Stem	1	Manufacturing
	91182	Facing	1	Purchasing
	73919	Locknut	2	Purchasing

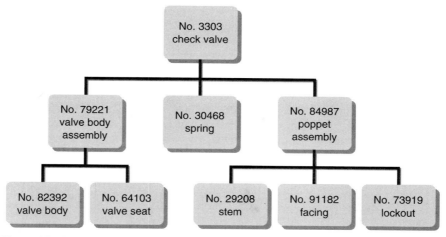

Figure 13.12 Product tree for No. 3303 check valve.

𝒯ABLE 13.8 ❖ Inventory Master File Information For MRP

Final Product: No. 3303 Description: Check valve	Quantity on Hand: 800 Lead Time for Assembly: 3 weeks	
Item No.	**Quantity on Hand**	**Lead Time (Weeks)**
79221	1000	1
82392	2200	2
64103	500	1
30468	800	2
84987	1000	3
29208	500	1
91182	1200	2
73919	2000	2

schedule, bill of materials file, and inventory master file), the MRP system can produce a requirements plan. Assume, for this example, that all order quantities will be exactly the quantity necessary to meet net requirements. Table 13.9 shows the MRP for a complete No. 3303 check valve, including all items at all levels. The entire MRP is developed by doing the following:

1. The bill of materials is referenced to determine the number of each level of item necessary to produce 3200, 3000, and 6000 check valves, respectively.

2. For each item the inventory record is accessed, and both current inventory level and lead time are determined.

3. On the basis of current inventory level, gross and net requirements are calculated.

4. On the basis of lead time, the order release date is determined by back-scheduling the amount of the lead time from the needed date.

*T*ABLE 13.9 ❖ Check Valve Requirements Plan

a. No. 3303 Check Valve

Week	Past Due	13	14	15	16	17	18	19	20	21	22	23	24	25	26	27	28	29
Gross requirement										4000			3000				6000	
On Hand 800							800	800	800	800								
Net requirement										3200			3000				6000	
Planned order receipts																		
Planned order releases							(3200)			3000				6000				
Lead time = 3 weeks																		

b. No. 79221 Valve Body Assembly

Week	Past Due	13	14	15	16	17	18	19	20	21	22	23	24	25	26	27	28	29
Gross requirement							(3200)			3000				6000				
On Hand 1000						1000	1000											
Net requirement							2200			3000				6000				
Planned order receipts																		
Planned order releases						(2200)			3000				6000					
Lead time = 1 week																		

c. No. 30468 Spring

Week	Past Due	13	14	15	16	17	18	19	20	21	22	23	24	25	26	27	28	29
Gross requirement							(6400)			6000			12000					
On Hand 800					800	800	800											
Net requirement							5600			6000			12000					
Planned order receipts																		
Planned order releases					5600		6000					12000						
Lead time = 2 weeks																		

TABLE 13.9 ❖ (continued)

d. No. 84987 Poppet Assembly

Week	Past Due	13	14	15	16	17	18	19	20	21	22	23	24	25	26	27	28	29
Gross requirement							6400			6000				12000				
On Hand 1000				1000	1000	1000	1000											
Net requirement							5400			6000				12000				
Planned order receipts																		
Planned order releases				5400			6000				12000							
Lead time = 3 weeks																		

e. No. 82392 Valve Body

Week	Past Due	13	14	15	16	17	18	19	20	21	22	23	24	25	26	27	28	29
Gross requirement						2200			3000				6000					
On Hand 2200				2200	2200	2200												
Net requirement									3000				6000					
Planned order receipts																		
Planned order releases							3000				6000							
Lead time = 2 week																		

f. No. 64103 Valve Seat

Week	Past Due	13	14	15	16	17	18	19	20	21	22	23	24	25	26	27	28	29
Gross requirement						4400			6000				12000					
On Hand 500					500	500												
Net requirement						3900			6000				12000					
Planned order receipts																		
Planned order releases					3900		6000					12000						
Lead time = 1 week																		

$\mathcal{T}$ABLE 13.9 ❖ (continued)

g. No. 29208 Stem

Week	Past Due	13	14	15	16	17	18	19	20	21	22	23	24	25	26	27	28	29
Gross requirement				5400			6000				12000							
On Hand 500			500	500														
Net requirement				4900			6000				12000							
Planned order receipts																		
Planned order releases		4900				6000				12000								

Lead time = 1 week

h. No. 91182 Facing

Week	Past Due	13	14	15	16	17	18	19	20	21	22	23	24	25	26	27	28	29
Gross requirement				5400			6000				12000							
On Hand 1200		1200	1200	1200														
Net requirement				4200			6000				12000							
Planned order receipts																		
Planned order releases		4200			6000				12000									

Lead time = 2 week

i. No. 73919 Locknut

Week	Past Due	13	14	15	16	17	18	19	20	21	22	23	24	25	26	27	28	29
Gross requirement				10800			12000				24000							
On Hand 2000		2000	2000	2000														
Net requirement				8800			12000				24000							
Planned order receipts																		
Planned order releases		8800			12000				24000									

Lead time = 2 weeks

The MRP for the finished No. 3303 check valve is shown in Table 13.9*a*. The MRP for all items is developed from this requirement plan by first generating requirement plans for level 1 items, and then, from each of these, generating the level 2 items. Table 13.9*b* through *i* lists the requirements plans generated from this finished item plan. The arrows indicate the order of plans and the relationship of one plan to the other.

To clarify the development of these plans, let us consider the plan for valve seats. To meet the shipping requirements for 4000 check valves (Table 13.9*a*) in week 21, component parts to assemble 3200 must enter production in week 18 (a three-week lead time). In order to release an order for 3200 in week 18, 2200 additional valve body assemblies (Table 13.9*b*) must be produced by that time. To do this, an order for 2200 must be placed in week 17 (a one-week lead time). Finally, to produce 2200 *additional* valve body assemblies, 4400 valve seats (2 × 2200) must be available. Since 500 are currently on hand (Table 13.9*f*), 3900 must be produced by week 17. With a one-week lead time, this means that an order for 3900 must be released in week 16. Required order releases for each level 1 and level 2 component are planned in exactly the same manner.

We began this example by assuming that QVC was experimenting with the use of MRP on its No. 3303 check valve. As with Park Plaza Hospital, described in the sidebar, when a firm decides to include all products in the system, the situation is further complicated. The major difference is that some subassemblies and components will be used in more than one end product. Therefore, for example, the MRP for an item such as the 73919 locknut would include in the "Net requirement" row all the requirements from all final products. Orders would be scheduled simultaneously to meet all the requirements rather than being scheduled product by product. The necessity of using a computer becomes obvious when one considers a situation in which there are over 1000 finished products with perhaps as many as 30,000 purchased and manufactured components. The need for rapid computation and summarization of requirements, as well as handling of massive bills of materials and inventory master files, is obvious.

OPERATIONS IN PRACTICE

Park Plaza Hospital Cuts Costs With MRP

Park Plaza Hospital in Houston, Texas, is a privately owned 374-bed facility with a surgical suite of 9 operating rooms. Like most hospitals, Park Plaza is under heavy pressure to contain the cost of its operations. One area investigated by Park Plaza was waste, excessive inventory, and obsolescence of the more than 2000 items of equipment, materials, and supplies used in the operating rooms.

Park Plaza's administration therefore initiated a study to design a requirements planning system that could accomplish three tasks, while better controlling materials and cutting costs:

1. Identify the net needs for equipment, material, and supplies to meet the ongoing demands of the surgical rooms.

2. Automate purchase orders for required materials and supplies.

3. Determine a schedule for surgical supplies that require sterilization.

Physicians reserve the operating rooms at Park Plaza at least one week in advance; therefore, the schedule of planned operations for the next seven days is known with some certainty. There are some complications, however. Sterilization requires up to 16 hours for some instruments, and the hospital may have only one unit of some high-technology surgical equipment (such as a heart-lung machine).

The required materials, equipment, and supplies needed for each operation differ both with the particular operation and with the physician scheduled for the procedure. The seven-day surgical schedule represents the master schedule in the process, with each operation being the "end product" (of only 1 unit). The bill of materials is represented by the specified materials, equipment, and supplies need for the operation. If some pieces of equipment must be sterilized, these are considered level 2 subassemblies with lead times as specified by the sterilization time.

The master schedule is then exploded through the surgical requirements file to generate the gross requirements for all materials and supplies. Net requirements are then determined by subtracting out the projected on-hand inventory for all required items. A time fence at 48 hours before each operation represents a "frozen" period and cannot be changed except under dire circumstances.

For Park Plaza Hospital, the above system offers improved availability of required materials, supplies, and equipment for operations while cutting the costs of waste, obsolescence, and excessive inventory. More accurate inventory records and more reliable schedules are another advantage of the system (Steinberg, Khumawala, and Scamell, 1982).

$\mathcal{M}$RP EXTENSIONS FOR CAPACITY AND DISTRIBUTION

Next, let us look at some derivatives of the MRP procedure for the downstream activities of capacity planning and distribution.

❖ Capacity Requirements Planning

Capacity requirements planning (CRP) is the process of determining workloads on each of the work centers due to the master schedule of final products. The workloads are typically stated in production-hours (or labor-hours, machine-hours, or both) required for each week in the future. In terms of complexity, this is at the other extreme from comparing the aggregate plan (discussed in Chapter 11) with existing capacity to see if there is a potential problem (*rough-cut capacity planning*).

There, the aggregate plan, or perhaps the master production schedule (MPS), was converted from units into equivalent workers, machine hours, or other critical dimensions of capacity, and overall capacity demands were compared with capacity limits. If the demands were close to, or higher than, the limits, overtime was scheduled, another shift (or partial shift) was added, subcontracting was initiated, and so on.

But this rough-cut planning ignored a number of factors: existing inventories, lead times, loads on individual work centers, and so on. In actuality, four different procedures are in common use for capacity planning. In increasing order of complexity, they are:

❖ *Capacity using overall factors:* This is the basic rough-cut approach, based on the MPS and production standards that convert required units of finished goods into historical loads on each work center. The loads are assumed to fall into the same period as the finished goods in the MPS.

❖ *Bills of capacity:* This procedure again uses the MPS, but instead of historical ratios, it uses the bill of materials and the routing sheet. The routing sheet shows each work center, in order, needed to work on a part, the setup time required, and the run time required. With this information, all the work centers and their times needed to produce each required component to support the MPS can be identified. Then, multiplying by the number of units specified in the MPS gives the workloads at each work center for those periods.

❖ *Resource profiles:* This procedure is the same as bills of capacity, except lead times are included so the workloads fall in the correct periods.

❖ *Capacity requirements planning:* Finally, CRP uses the preceding information plus the MRP outputs to take the existing inventories and lot sizing into consideration as well. It also considers partially completed work, demands for service parts that are not usually included in the MPS, scrap adjustments, and so on.

The result of capacity planning is a tabular load report for each work center and each week in the future (as shown in Table 13.10) or a graphical load profile (as in Figure 13.13), which the manager can use to help plan for production requirements. The report or profile will indicate where capacity is inadequate for certain work centers and idle for others.

The imbalances may be corrected by a simple shift of personnel or equipment from one work center to another. Or perhaps work can be shifted in the schedule to smooth out the loads and balance the capacity demands. If not, overtime or another shift may be needed. Or it may be possible to alter the MPS, shifting some customers' orders earlier, to reduce excessive capacity demands. Of course, if none

$\mathcal{T}$ABLE 13.10 ❖ Tabular Load Report

Week	Work Center 021	Work Center 055	Work Center 122
11	32 hr	74 hr	17
12	15	80	8
13	21	32	6
14	5	51	12
15	8	24	10
•	•	•	•
•	•	•	•
•	•	•	•

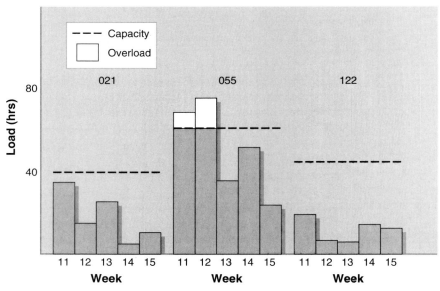

Figure 13.13   Work center load profiles.

of these strategies are possible, it may be necessary to contact some customers to determine if a delay in their orders is acceptable.

❖ Distribution Requirements Planning

The concept of distribution requirements planning (DRP) follows naturally from MRP and "front-ends" the whole process in the forecasting portion of the procedure. The distribution process is illustrated in Figure 13.14, where retailers order from local warehouses, the warehouses are supplied from regional centers, and the regional centers draw from the central distribution facility, which gets its inventory directly from the factory.

Clearly, there are time lags in each chain of this process. Also, each distribution point has its own standard reorder quantity, "trigger" inventory level (ROP), storage capacity, safety stock level, and so on. Without planning by the factory or central distribution facility, orders can often bunch up, requiring high stocking levels to avoid shortages or stockouts. This is, of course, true throughout the system, so high inventory levels are held by each of the distribution points in the entire system.

By applying MRP to the distribution function, such demands are anticipated and orders are released ahead of time to avoid stockouts and their resultant high follow-on inventories. This process is shown in Table 13.11. In the appropriate distribution environment, factory orders are built up from lower levels in the distribution network and provide significant advantages in scheduling and coordination. The DRP process is, however, vulnerable to poor forecasts at the lower levels. If local forecasts are incorrect, then demands placed on the factory will also be incorrect, and either excess stock, at an unnecessary cost, or shortages will result.

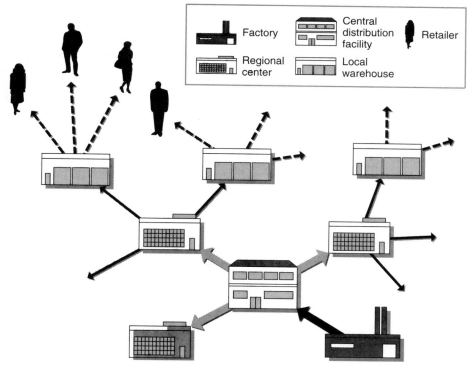

Figure 13.14   Distribution requirements planning situation.

$\mathcal{S}$OLVED EXERCISE 13.4 ❖ DISTRIBUTION REQUIREMENTS PLANNING

Assume that two warehouses stock children's school scissors. Warehouse A has 1500 cartons on hand and orders for 400 cartons in week 34, 1000 cartons in week 36, 700 cartons in week 37, and 1200 cartons in week 39. Warehouse B is out of stock and has orders for 500 cartons in week 35, 300 cartons in week 36, and 200 cartons in week 39. Delivery time from the factory is 3 weeks. Construct the distribution requirements plan.

Solution:

					Week				
	32	33	34	35	36	37	38	39	40
Warehouse A: Lead time 3 weeks									
Carton requirements			400		1000	700		1200	
On hand 1500	1500	1500	1500	1100	1100	100	0	0	0
Net requirements			0		0	600		1200	
Planned receipts									
Planned releases			600		1200				

					Week				
	32	33	34	35	36	37	38	39	40
Warehouse B: Lead time 3 weeks									
Carton requirements				500	300			200	
On hand 0	0	0	0	0	0	0	0	0	0
Net requirements				500	300			200	
Planned receipts									
Planned releases	500	300			200				
Factory									
Carton requirements	500	300	600		1400				

$\mathcal{T}$ABLE 13.11 ❖ The DRP Process

Local warehouse A				Local warehouse B					
Week	11	12	13	14	15	16	17	18	19
Carton requirements			83	16		17			
On hand	90	90	90	7	21	21	4	4	4
Net requirement				9					
Planned receipts									
Planned releases			30						

Regional center I (1 week lead time Order size: 30)

Regional center II

Week	11	12	13	14	15	16	17	18	19
Carton requirements			30			60			
On hand	10	10	10	30	30	30	20	20	20
Net requirement			20			30			
Planned receipts									
Planned releases		50			50				

Central distribution facility (1 week lead time Order size: 50)

Week	11	12	13	14	15	16	17	18	19
Carton requirements		50			50				
On hand	90	90	40	40	40	190	190	190	190
Net requirements					10				
Planned receipts									
Planned releases			200						

Factory (2 week lead time Order size: 200)

MANUFACTURING RESOURCE PLANNING (MRP II)

When the scheduling activities illustrated in Figure 11.1 are computerized and tied in with purchasing, accounting, sales, engineering, and other such functional areas, the result is known as ***manufacturing resource planning (MRP II).*** A typical MRP II system is illustrated in Figure 13.15. The forecast and actual customer orders come into the master schedule, which drives the production system. Another major input to the production system is the engineering database, which includes bills of materials, engineering designs, drawings, and other such information required to manufacture and assemble the product.

At the right side of Figure 13.15 is the actual build stage, where plant monitoring and control operates. This function receives additional information and gives information to plant maintenance. Cost accounting data are also collected at this stage. The process is completed with distribution requirements planning.

Clearly, all other company functions can also be tied to this system. Finance, knowing when items will be purchased and when products will be delivered, can properly project cash flows. Human resources (personnel) can similarly project re-

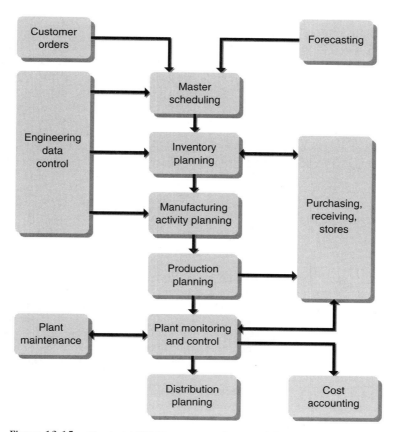

Figure 13.15 Typical MRP II system and as modules.

quirements for hiring (and layoffs). And marketing can determine up-to-date customer delivery times, lead times, and so on.

A number of MRP II software packages are available, for all sizes of computers. Many, such as Micro-MRP, now run on microcomputers. Each of these packages operates in basically the same manner. First, it takes the sales forecast and basic engineering data for each product and, using an MRP subsystem, develops the time-phased materials requirements. Once this information is available, the purchasing, capacity planning, and operations scheduling components take over to produce purchase order requirements, route the product through operations, generate capacity requirements by individual operations, and load and schedule operations for production.

Requirements-based scheduling systems, such as MRP II and the NASA flight operations planning schedule (described in the sidebar), require a computer system for implementation because of their relatively large scale and complexity. The role of the computer is extremely important here. Again, the concept of requirements-based scheduling is not novel; it simply was previously too cumbersome to pursue in a clerically oriented system. Construction management has for years recognized the need for detailed requirements planning and scheduling. If material, labor, or equipment was at the job site in the wrong sequence or at the wrong time, not only would bottlenecks be unending, but wasted time and material losses from weather damage and theft would raise the cost of construction to unreasonable levels.

The computer has simply allowed all this clerical data processing and file handling to be accomplished more efficiently. Hence, what once was conceptually feasible but technically infeasible is now both technically and conceptually possible. And because of the speed of the computer, managers can perform as many simulations and "what if" experiments as they wish, in order to determine the best decision. The system simulates the impacts of the decision throughout the organization, and the results in terms of customer orders and due dates.

OPERATIONS IN PRACTICE

Applying MRP to Plan Nasa's Space Shuttle Missions

When NASA was planning on perhaps as many as 30 shuttle launches a year, it became aware that many scheduling conflicts were possible, given its limited, and expensive, resources. To handle the extensive demands of each launch, it had to design a *flight operations planning schedule* (FOPS), or calendar of *resource readiness*. The resource demands of different flights, of which there are eight varieties, had to be coordinated with the perhaps self-conflicting demands of individual flights. The approach taken to address this problem was a variant of MRP, called *requirements planning*.

To use the requirements planning approach for FOPS, a bill of requirements based on component activities needed for each flight was identified. Since some activities cannot proceed until other activities have been completed, there is a dependent-demand element that is directly analogous to MRP, even though there are no inventories of materials to consider. It is also necessary to check how much "load" each activity places on the different departments in NASA in each time period. The schedule can be constructed either through infinite loading (not worrying about exceeding departmental capacities) or through finite loading, where excessive loads are shifted either earlier or later in time to remain within departmental capacities.

The *flight schedule file* represents the master production schedule in MRP because it identifies final "products" (launches) that must be completed without delays. Activities are scheduled backward from the flight schedule file as each is required. This gives the resulting schedule for all activities to support each flight. If there is a conflict for scarce resources, the earliest scheduled flight takes priority. Two primary resources are checked: labor and equipment. Each department must identify whether it is labor-constrained or equipment-constrained for the system to check. Each department then receives a weekly load profile summary that indicates its planned activities to support each launch. It also receives a summary of the required activities over the coming weeks.

Through the use of the FOPS system, NASA has been able to effectively manage multiple, simultaneous schedules for its space shuttle launches (Steinberg, Lee, and Khumawala, 1980).

$\mathscr{E}$ NTERPRISE RESOURCE PLANNING (ERP)

As discussed above, MRP II extends MRP systems to share information with a variety of other functional departments outside the operations area including engineering, purchasing, customer order entry, plant maintenance, and cost accounting. Thus, a key component of MRP II is storing operational information centrally and providing access to those departments that need it. Before MRP II systems, it was not uncommon for each functional department to maintain its own computer system. With these separate systems, the same information would be stored in several different databases throughout an organization. One problem with this approach is that it is difficult to update information consistently when it is stored in multiple locations. Indeed, it was frequently not even known how many different databases a particular piece of information was stored in. Thus, it was common for the same information to have different values in each database. For example, the cost to produce a particular item would often have different values in the engineering, production, sales, and accounting databases.

The next stage in the evolution of information systems has been directed toward integrating all the business activities and processes throughout an entire organization. These information systems are commonly referred to as ***enterprise resource planning (ERP)*** systems. As the name suggests, the objective of these systems is to provide seamless, real-time information to all employees who need it, throughout the entire organization (or enterprise). In many cases, business process design (BPD, discussed in Chapter 4) has served as the impetus for developing and implementing these ERP systems.

Figure 13.16 illustrates a typical ERP system. As shown, ERP extends the idea of a central shared database to all areas within an organization. Using ERP, each area interacts with a centralized database and servers. With this approach, information is entered once at the source and made available to all employees needing it. Clearly, this approach eliminates the incompatibility created when different functional departments use different systems, and it also eliminates the need for people in different parts of the organization to reenter the same information over and over again into separate computer systems.

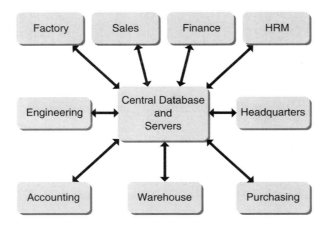

Figure 13.16   Typical ERP system.

OPERATIONS
IN PRACTICE

SAP's ERP System Is Taking the Corporate World by Storm

One of the most popular ERP systems is SAP AG's R/3 system. As of March 1997, over 7000 companies had adopted it, and SAP's share of the ERP market was estimated to be 26 percent. Indeed, with sales of $2.4 billion in 1996, SAP is the world's fourth-largest software company, trailing only Microsoft, Oracle, and Computer Associates International.

Examples of companies that use R/3 include Microsoft, Owens-Corning, IBM, Chevron, Colgate-Palmolive, Compaq Computer, and Analog Devices. Owens-Corning spent two years installing R/3 at a cost of $100 million. Chevron estimated that it also spent $100 million installing R/3 and expects the system to save it $50 million annually. Microsoft spent 10 months and $25 million installing R/3. In Microsoft's case, R/3 was used to replace 33 different financial tracking systems that were used in 26 of its subsidiaries. It expects to save $18 million annually.

A primary consideration in Owens-Corning's case was the need to provide buyers of its building products—including insulation, pipes, and roofing material—with one-stop shopping. R/3 facilitated this task by allowing the sales representatives to quickly see what products were available at any plant or warehouse.

Analog Devices uses R/3 to integrate its international operations. For example, Analog uses R/3 to consolidate the products stored at its warehouses, thereby creating a worldwide order-processing system. Furthermore, the system calculates exchange rates automatically (Lieber, 1995; White, Clark, and Ascarelli, 1997).

CHAPTER IN PERSPECTIVE

This is the third chapter of Part Four, dealing with the product supply process. In Chapter 11 we addressed issues related to developing the aggregate and master production schedules. Following this, in Chapter 12 our focus was on determining when and in what quantities to order independent-demand items to support these schedules. In the present chapter we discussed how MRP can be used to manage the inventory of dependent-demand items. We described the mechanics of MRP, the three primary inputs to MRP, and issues related to lot sizing and exploding the BOM. In Chapter 14 we continue our discussion of materials management and present the just-in-time approach to inventory.

❖ CHECK YOUR UNDERSTANDING

1. Define the following terms: *lot size, parent item, explode, bill of materials, part period balancing, MRP II, ERP, lot-for-lot, product tree,* and *low-level coding.*

2. What are the various sources of "demands" coming to MRP?

3. In your own terms, distinguish between dependent and independent demand.

4. Is MRP or EOQ best for smooth, dependent demand? For lumpy, independent demand?

5. What actually is a planned order release? What happens with one?

6. Since MRP is such a logical and straightforward idea, why has it taken so long to develop?

7. Summarize the technical, process and inner-environmental factors, that influence the success of MRP.

8. Contrast MRP, MRP II, and ERP.

9. Describe how MRP uses each set of data provided by the MPS, the inventory master file, and the bill of materials file.

10. Describe the four methods of capacity planning and the increasing amount of data used with each method.

❖ EXPAND YOUR UNDERSTANDING

1. Why are accurate records, particularly regarding bills of material and inventories, important for MRP?

2. Comparing Figures 13.4 and 13.3, what percentage of inventory reduction would you estimate has occurred? If this firm holds $1 million worth of lumber before MRP and values its capital at 20 percent, how much is the MRP conversion worth to it?

3. In Table 13.3, the planned order release is for 250 items, not the 150 net requirement. Why?

4. Another way to do lot sizing is to use the EOQ as calculated in Chapter 12. Why not just do this, since it gives an optimal answer?

5. How might MRP be applied to services? Are the same inputs required? Will the outputs be the same?

6. MRP II and ERP are relatively new applications of computer technology. How difficult do you think each would be to implement in the typical firm? What aspects of these technologies might make them difficult? How long might each take to implement?

7. In many of today's firms, the customer's computer is tied to the supplier's computer over phone lines, so that purchase orders go directly into the supplier's planning system. What are the implications of this close relationship?

8. Since MRP II is meant to be an integrated planning process, where do top management's control and influence come in? Shouldn't there be some direction to such an integrated plan?

❖ APPLY YOUR UNDERSTANDING
Andrew Jacobs and Company

Andrew Jacobs and Company employs approximately 280 people in the manufacture of a number of add-on appliances for residential heating and air conditioning units. The company began 15 years ago, producing a home humidifier, and has since expanded into dehumidifiers and air purifiers. It currently produces 30 different models, but because of heavy competition, engineering changes are constantly taking place and the product line is often changing. Each model is made up of between 40 and several hundred different parts, which range from purchased nuts and bolts and prefabricated subassemblies to internally manufactured components.

Andrew Jacobs purchases over 2500 parts and manufactures over 1000 parts and assemblies of its own. Many of the parts are used in several different models, and some parts—such as nuts and bolts—are used in over 75 percent of the finished products.

The finished goods inventory is kept relatively small. Sales are forecast on a month-to-month basis, and production is scheduled according to actual sales orders and the sales forecast. For this reason, production lots placed in the final assembly line are usually for relatively small quantities.

Rather than producing manufactured parts and subcomponents and purchasing other parts according to the sales forecast, parts, subassemblies, and purchased items are ordered on the basis of reorder point and economic order quantity. Since it is imperative to maintain accurate control of these raw materials and subassembly items, all parts and materials stored in the main supply area are controlled with the use of perpetual inventory cards, which are maintained by the scheduling department. Each card contains the reorder point, the economic order quantity, and the lead time for outside procurement or internal manufacture.

Both receipt of new inventory into the main supply room and use of items from the supply room are recorded on the inventory card.

The scheduling department is responsible for checking the availability of inventory on the inventory cards. Approximately three weeks before a final assembly order is to be placed on the floor, the scheduler checks all the cards for parts needed in that assembly to determine whether issuing the number required to complete the assembly will reduce the inventory below the reorder point. If the scheduler determines that the projected final assembly order will result in hitting the reorder point, a production order or a purchase order is issued.

Physical inventories are taken every quarter, and usually a substantial number of small adjustments must be made. The quarterly physical inventory was suggested after a series of major inventory shortages occurred several years ago. The company's current policy allows any worker to enter the main supply area to remove needed parts. The workers are to fill out materials requisitions and to sign for all parts removed, but they are frequently in a rush and fail to complete the inventory requisitions accurately. There have been several cases where parts staged for final assembly of one product were removed and used on the assembly of another item.

To adjust for many of these problems, the production schedulers often add a safety factor to the reorder point when placing orders, and they have typically increased the order quantity from 10 to 25 percent over the economic order quantity. Their justification is that "it is less expensive to carry a little extra inventory than to shut down the production facility waiting for a rush order."

Questions

1. Evaluate and critique the existing system used by Andrew Jacobs and Company.
2. How might MRP work in a situation like this?
3. Beyond implementing a computerized MRP system, what other suggestions would you make to help alleviate Andrew Jacobs's problems?

❖ EXERCISES

1. Wooden pencils are made in 1 week out of 4 parts: 2 wooden halves, the graphite, the metal cap, and the rubber eraser. Construct an MRP explosion for orders of 10 dozen in week 2, 30 dozen in week 3, and 15 dozen in week 5. There are currently 500 wooden halves on hand, 300 graphite rods, and 1500 metal caps, but no rubber erasers. All items are purchased with a 1-week lead time except the graphite, which takes 2 weeks. Use lot-for-lot sizing.

2. Use part period balancing for the erasers in exercise 1. It costs $1 to place an order and $0.002 to hold one in inventory for 1 week. Find the best lot sizing.

3. Product 101 consists of three 202 subassemblies and one 204 subassembly. The 202 subassembly consists of one 617, one 324 subassembly, and one 401. A 204 subassembly consists of one 500 and one 401. The 324 subassembly consists of one 617 and one 515.

   a. Prepare a product tree.
   b. Prepare an indented bill of materials.
   c. Determine the number of each subassembly or component required to produce fifty 101s.

4. Complete the MRP for item No. 6606 below.

Week	5	6	7	8	9	10	11	12	13	14	15	16	17
Gross requirement			100				50	30			80		
On hand 100													
Net requirement													
Planned order receipts													
Planned order releases													
Lead time = 3 weeks													

5. Suppose that in exercise 4 the company wishes to maintain a safety stock of 50 No. 6606s. Complete the MRP.

6. Conduct a part period lot sizing for part 1098, given the following demand schedule and these facts: holding a 1098 part in inventory for 1 week costs $1, and ordering and shipment (0 lead time) cost a total of $100 for an order of any size.

Week	16	17	18	19	20	21	22
1098 demand	85	40	25	40	105	75	80

7. Conduct a lot sizing by part period balancing for the following item, which has a $190 ordering cost and a holding cost of $0.10 per unit per month.

Month	1	2	3	4	5	6	7	8	9	10	11	12
Demand	700	400	200	300	400	500	560	400	800	400	200	300

8. Develop the MRP for Quality Valve Company, assuming that lead time for the valve body assemblies increases to 4 weeks.

9. Picture Frame Company sells two 8- by 10-inch picture frames complete with backs and glass. The standard model uses a thin black frame, and the deluxe model uses a gold-trim frame. The backs and glass are the same for both. Assembly lead time for the complete process from frame material, glass, and back is 2 weeks for either model. Frame material (2.5 feet for each frame) is ordered from a local supplier and has a 1-week lead time. The glass is purchased, is cut to size, and has a 3-week lead time. Backs are purchased finished from a hardboard manufacturer with a 2-week lead time. The master production schedule for the two models is shown in the following table.

Week	8	9	10	11	12	13	14
Standard frame				100	150		300
Deluxe frame			200		200		150

The on-hand inventory is as follows:

Deluxe frame material	300 ft	Backs	50
Standard frame material	150 ft	Standard frames (complete)	75
Glass plates	150	Deluxe frames (complete)	100

Prepare the MRP to exactly meet the demand schedule.

10. End item A is made up of 1 B, 1 C, and 1 D. Each B is made up of 1 C and 1 E. C's are made from 1 G. E's are made from 1 C and 1 I. D's consist of 1 F and 1 H. Each F is made from 1 I and 1 J. Each H is made from 1 J and 1 K.

a. Develop a product tree for end item A.
b. Low-level-code the product tree.
c. How many of each component are required to complete 80 A's?

11. Solve Exercise 7 by ordering in EOQ batches and compare the cost with the part period method.

12. Another lot-sizing technique is called *period order quantity* (POQ). This approach converts the EOQ into an integer number of periods, and then sizes lots for whatever demand occurs in the next POQ number of periods. Solve Exercise 7 by POQ and compare the costs with those in Exercise 11.

13. Solve Exercise 7 by ordering in every period the amount needed the next period (lot-for-lot) and compare it with the previous costs.

14. Another lot-sizing method similar to part period balancing is called *least unit cost*. In this method part period holding costs are accumulated, but the ordering cost is added to the total, and this entire sum is divided by the total number of units ordered. The ordering policy with the smallest per unit total cost is then followed. Solve Exercise 7 using least unit cost and compare the results with the previous costs.

15. Assume that there is another warehouse—say, C—in Solved Exercise 13.4 that has demands of 400 gross in week 34 and 500 gross in week 37. Reconstruct the distribution requirements plan.

16. A product is made up of 2 XYs, 1 CK, and 1 DX. Each XY is assembled from 2 DXs and 1 CK. Each DX is made up 1 CK and 1 RT.

a. Develop a product tree for the product.
b. Low-level-code the product tree.
c. How many of each component are required to complete 150 end items?

17. Given the following, how many No. 1342 items should be purchased and when?

	Lead Times		Demand in Week				
Item	(Weeks)	On Hand	11	12	13	14	15
19	1	100	100	0	100	200	0
1342	2	200	0	500	0	0	0
102	1	0	50	0	0	0	0
312	2	0	5	0	0	10	0

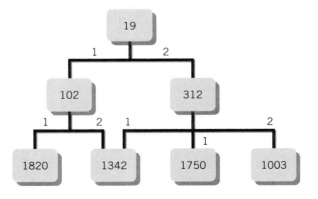

Just-in-Time Systems

*C*HAPTER OVERVIEW

* *Just-in-time* (JIT) was developed by Toyota in Japan in the mid–1970s but is used in various ways and is given different names in the United States.

* The three primary tenets of JIT are minimizing waste in all forms, maintaining respect for all workers, and continually improving all processes and systems.

* The basic idea behind JIT is to make goods flow like water through the shop and not build up, or arrive either early or late.

* JIT is based on repetitive, standardized outputs rather than customized products. With standardized outputs, low costs and high quality can be achieved.

* Engineering works from previous designs and incrementally simplifies, alters, and improves them for both product attributes and manufacturability.

* Buffers are largely eliminated in the JIT production system through better design and control of the system itself.

* Production systems are converted to cellular manufacturing and product line flow shops, rather than job shops. Throughout the conversion, work flows are smoothed, lead times are shortened, mixed-model sequencing is employed, and pull systems such as *kanban* are installed.

* The JIT layout uses much less space because the equipment is much closer together and the materials are passed manually from workstation to workstation.

* The workforce is used to uncover and solve problems. Workers are broadly skilled and flexible and are typically organized into teams responsible for entire families of products.

* The pace of work in JIT is fast but steady and can proceed only when the downstream worker needs more parts.

* Scheduling under JIT is simple and visible, rarely computerized. When JIT and MRP are combined, MRP is generally used to bring material into the

plant and JIT to run the plant once the material has arrived.

❖ A major focus of JIT is reducing setup time. This can be accomplished by adopting cellular manufacturing, advanced automation, or simple techniques such as transferring internal activities to external activities or using Lazy Susans.

❖ Under JIT, inventory is an evil that hides problems and defects. As much as possible, inventory is reduced or totally eliminated and the space saved is used to move equipment closer together.

❖ Suppliers are invited to cooperate with the firm on project teams and become certified single-source suppliers. Incoming inspection is then canceled, and schedules and needs are closely coordinated to meet the firm's JIT schedule. The firm helps the supplier become a JIT firm itself.

❖ JIT focuses on control rather than planning, since plans often go astray but better control can adjust for such changes. Simple visual systems are preferred to complex computerized systems that cannot be seen.

❖ Quality is ensured at the source—the worker or supplier—rather than by inspection, with the goal of zero defects.

❖ Maintenance is preventive rather than corrective, with the workers primarily responsible for attending to their own equipment. This includes operating the equipment at rates far below their stated capacity but over long durations.

❖ JIT produces benefits in four primary ways: cost savings, increased revenues, investment savings, and improvements in the workforce.

❖ The difficulties in using JIT concern identifying a repetitive situation for application; taking the appropriate preliminary steps such as reducing setup times, inventories, and lot sizes; placing suppliers on project teams and moving to single-source contracts; and fostering an atmosphere of trust and cooperation among all the firm's employees.

❖ JIT can also be used to advantage in services, particularly where repetitive operations are conducted or materials are used extensively.

$\mathscr{I}$ NTRODUCTION _____

❖ Setex, Inc., located in Saint Marys, Ohio, produces and delivers seats to Honda's assembly plant in Marysville, Ohio, on a just-in-time basis. Under this arrangement, Honda requires shipments from Setex be delivered to the installation point on the assembly line within 2 hours of the time a ship order is placed. Initially, this created somewhat of a problem for Setex, given the 55 miles that separate the two plants. Specifically, it takes Setex approximately 30 minutes to load a trailer after receiving a new order from Honda. Then, getting the seats off the trailer and to the installation point requires another 45 minutes. This leaves only 45 minutes for all the other activities that need to be accomplished, including actually transporting the seats the required 55 miles.

Setex's solution to this problem was to construct a 30,000-square-foot warehouse $1\frac{1}{2}$ miles from Honda's plant. With this warehouse, the Saint Marys plant produces seats using Honda's 4-hour production forecast. Completed seats are palletized, coded, and moved to shipping. In the shipping area a two-tier conveyor system automatically loads the seats into custom trailers that transport the seats to the warehouse. After a trailer arrives at the warehouse, a computer cable is connected to the trailer, and it is automatically unloaded. As the seats are being unloaded, bar code labels are scanned and a transfer car automatically moves the seats to their assigned location. To load and deliver the seats to the Honda plant, this process is reversed. Amazingly, 800 seats are moved through the warehouse each day with only two employees staffing the warehouse per shift (Gould, 1994).

❖ Although Hewlett Packard's inkjet printer assembly plant near Camas, Washington, had more than a decade of experience with just-in-time manufacturing techniques, 50 percent yearly increases in production rates and a plant expansion resulted in substantial inventory overflows. One manager at Hewlett Packard (HP) commented, "We were storing more parts in trailers than in the warehouse." To address these problems, HP formed a project team to upgrade its existing materials handling system. Typically, suppliers ship their parts in tote boxes. These totes are automatically unloaded from trailers, and bar code labels on the totes are used to route them to a system of 24 double-stacked carousels. The carousels were designed to hold enough materials to support one day of production. Automatic inserter-extractor devices are used to load and unload the carousels. The inserter-extractor devices need to be able to unload 1000 totes per hour in order to adequately support the six manual assembly lines and four robotic subassembly cells.

In the new system, HP uses a "pull" strategy whereby parts and assemblies are moved from the carousels to the assembly line only when requested. To request parts from the carousel system, an operator on the assembly line scans the bar code on a tote. Then, an overhead conveyor transports the requested materials from the carousel to a drop-off location. This system has reduced delivery times to the line from 30 minutes to 3–5 minutes (Auguston, 1995a).

❖ Rio Bravo Electroicos' plant in Juárez, Mexico, assembles wiring harnesses for Delphi Packard Electric Systems, located in the United States. Rio Bravo is what is known as a *maquiladora* facility. Maquiladora facilities receive components from suppliers in the United States duty-free, perform assembly operations, and then export the products back to the United States or to other countries.

Rio Bravo employs a pull production system. With this system, material needed to support the plant's 36 subassembly and assembly lines is replenished every 2 hours from materials stocked in the main storage area. The main storage area contains a 15-day supply of materials.

One problem with operating a just-in-time delivery system across international boundaries is the possibility that a shipment will be stopped at customs. To eliminate this problem, Rio Bravo participates in a bilateral security program. With this program, products shipped to the United States do not require inspection as long as the shipments have been properly sealed at the Mexican plant. Participation in the bilateral security program requires that Rio Bravo establish its shipping area as a secured area. Furthermore, it must allow United States customs officials regular access to its facilities to review its operations (Auguston, 1995b).

❖ "Buick City" is the name General Motors has applied to the transformation of its automobile assembly facility in Flint, Michigan. This extensive 1.8-million-square-foot assembly plant is based on JIT and automation. A major part of the JIT program is a sophisticated computerized production control system that ties all the production robots and equipment to the material requirements planning and inventory control systems. This system continuously recalculates and submits orders to the production system.

With this system, in-plant inventories have been reduced to less than an hour's supply in some cases, and they never exceed more than 16 hours' worth. There are separate delivery schedules for over 600 suppliers providing more than 4000 parts. Each part has only a 20-minute window for delivery. The Woodbridge Group, for example, delivers car seats in assembly order within 3½ hours of receiving an order. A continuous broadcast every 54 seconds from the assembly factory tells Woodbridge the sequence and specifications of the seats needed in the next 3 hours. Eighty-five separate point-of-use receiving dock doors have reduced dock-to-line delivery distances to less than 300 feet. Seven types of standard, bar-coded, returnable containers are used for all parts processed in the plant. Both the supplier and the factory's automatic receiving and dispatch equipment use the bar codes. Furthermore the plant uses state-of-the-art materials handling equipment, including automated guided vehicles and over 200 robots. The robots load and unload trucks and perform other manufacturing operations. In one application, a robot unloads car seats from a truck and passes them to an overhead conveyor. When they reach the end of the conveyor line, another robot takes them off and places them at their point-of-use on the assembly line. The robot that unloads also places the empty boxes returning on the conveyor back in the delivery truck.

The primary benefits of this program include major reductions in the costs of labor, materials, damage to parts, and repairs. Even more significant are the improvements in the quality of the product (Sepehri, 1988).

As these examples illustrate, ***just-in-time (JIT)*** has taken on the nature of a crusade in American industry. Chapter 13 discussed the MRP approach to planning the ordering and production of materials. JIT is another approach for managing the delivery of materials. However, as we will see, JIT is much more than simply planning and scheduling the delivery of materials. Perhaps it is best described as a philosophy that seeks to eliminate all types of waste, including carrying excessive levels of inventory and long lead times. Let us look closer at the history and philosophy of this intriguing approach to production.

HISTORY AND PHILOSOPHY OF JUST-IN-TIME

The concept of JIT was originally developed by the Toyota Motor Company in Japan in the mid-1970s, and it is still called the *Toyota system* by Japanese firms. To understand why JIT was developed, it is important to understand a little about the history and culture of Japan.

Japan is a small country with minimal resources and a large population. Thus, the Japanese have always been careful not to waste resources, including space (especially land) as well as time and labor. Waste is abhorrent because the country has so little space and so few natural resources to begin with. Always, then, the Japanese have been motivated to maximize the gain or yield from the few resources available. It has also been necessary for them to maintain their respect for each other in order to work and live together smoothly and effectively in such a densely populated space. As a result, their work habits tend to reflect this philosophy of minimizing waste and maintaining respect. JIT, an example of this philosophy, is based on three primary tenets:

1. Minimizing waste in all forms.
2. Continually improving processes and systems.
3. Maintaining respect for all workers.

During production, the Japanese studiously avoid waste of materials, space, and labor. They therefore pay significant attention to identifying and correcting problems that could potentially lead to such waste. Moreover, operation and procedures are constantly being improved and fine-tuned so as to increase productivity and yield, further eliminating waste. Equal respect is paid to all workers, and the trappings of status are minimized so that respect among all can be maintained.

JIT takes its name from the idea of replenishing material buffers just when they are needed and not before or after. This eliminates the waste of having expensive materials sit idle while awaiting processing, as well as the waste of having expensive resources wait for late materials. However, JIT is much broader than its name suggests: it seeks to eliminate all types of waste, including scrap, defective products, unneeded space, unnecessary inventories, and idle facilities.

Translated into actions for operations, JIT means keeping work flows moving all the time from receipt in the plant to delivery to the customer, eliminating inventories, reducing travel distances, eliminating defects and scrap, making maximum use of precious space, and so forth. This philosophy is applied however and wherever it can be. Thus, JIT cannot be reduced to a "formula"; every firm may apply the philosophy differently.

By using JIT, Toyota was able to reduce the time needed to produce a car from 15 days to 1 day. In fact, JIT is best applied to a production system, such as automobile assembly, that would be considered repetitive, such as a flow shop. Although automobile assembly is not a flow shop in the sense that every item is identical, it is closer to a flow shop than to a job shop where every item, or lot, is completely different. The Japanese perception of JIT is to attempt to make the goods "flow like water" through the shop. Although this is more difficult for a job shop, the approach can still be used there with significant benefits.

Because of its broad nature and wide range of benefits—from increased market share to better quality to lower costs—JIT has become, for many companies, a major element in competitive strategy. The firms may adopt only particular or especially relevant elements of JIT, or add certain other aspects or programs to it, but it still plays a major role in their overall strategy. For instance, the inventory philosophy in many firms goes by the name *zero inventories*. At IBM, JIT is known as *continuous flow*, whereas at Hewlett-Packard it is called *stockless production*. In some plants it is even called *repetitive manufacturing*.

More recent adoptions of JIT have also stressed its second aspect: continuous improvements. That is, JIT is considered not simply a means of converting the transformation system from a sloppy, wasteful form (sarcastically referred to as *just-in-case*) to an efficient, competitive form, but also as producing continuing improvements throughout the system to keep the firm competitive and profitable in the future.

Yet to be seen in any significant form is the third aspect of JIT: "respect for people." This is probably the most basic and important of the three tenets. American industry seems to be moving slowly in this direction, particularly with the adoption of production teams, quality circles (Chapter 3), and cellular manufacturing. Nonetheless, American firms and industries seem far behind the Japanese in obtaining contributions, respect, and loyalty from their workers. This is probably because these firms and industries do not show respect for and loyalty to their employees in the first place.

Initially, in the early 1980s, JIT was greeted with a great deal of ambivalence in the United States. Typical of the sentiment at this time was "It will never work here." However, this view abruptly changed when a number of domestic companies such as Hewlett Packard and Harley Davidson began demonstrating the significant benefits of JIT.

Next, we describe the most common characteristics of JIT systems and compare them with the more traditional just-in-case systems.

$\mathcal{T}$RADITIONAL SYSTEMS COMPARED WITH JUST-IN-TIME

Table 14.1 presents a dozen characteristics of JIT systems that tend to distinguish them from the more traditional systems historically used in American industry. These characteristics range from philosophy and culture to standard operating procedures. The contrasts summarized in the table are described in the following subsections.

$\mathcal{T}$ABLE 14.1 ❖ Comparison of Traditional Systems and JIT

Characteristic	Traditional	JIT
Priorities	Accept all orders Many options	Limited market Few options Low cost, high quality
Engineering	Customized outputs Design from scratch	Standardized outputs Incremental design Simplify, design for manufacturing
Capacity	Highly utilized Inflexible	Moderately utilized Flexible
Transformation system	Job shop	Flow shops, cellular manufacturing
Layout	Large space Materials handling equipment	Small space Close, manual transfer
Workforce	Narrow skills Specialized Individualized Competitive attitude Change by edict Easy pace Status: symbols, pay, privilege	Broad skills Flexible Work teams Cooperative attitude Change by consensus Hard pace No status differentials
Scheduling	Long setups Long runs	Quick changeovers Mixed-model runs
Inventories	Large WIP buffers Stores, cribs, stockrooms	Small WIP buffers Floor stock
Suppliers	Many Competitive Deliveries to central receiving area Indepedent forecasts	Few or single-source Cooperative, network Deliveries directly to assembly line Shared forecasts
Planning and control	Planning-oriented Complex Computerized	Control-oriented Simple Visual
Quality	Via inspection Critical points Acceptance sampling	At the source Continuous Statistical process control
Maintenance	Corrective By experts Run equipment fast Run one shift	Preventive By operator Run equipment slowly Run 24 hours

❖ Priorities

Traditionally, most firms want to accept all customer orders, or at least provide a large number of options from which customers may order. However, this confuses the production task, increases the chance of errors, and increases costs. With JIT, the target market is usually limited and the options are also limited. A wise JIT firm knows which customers it does *not* want.

In JIT firms the emphasis is on low cost but high quality within that limited market. This does not mean, however, that high performance or comfort is unavailable. For example, a car may have many accessories that would be considered luxury options on traditional cars, such as air conditioning, but are included as standard. By including these features as standard equipment, the production task is simplified and the product can be produced at lower cost. The primary options, if offered, would usually include mutually exclusive aspects such as color.

Thus, we see that right from the start the overall priorities of JIT firms are different from those of the traditional firm. This perspective is reflected in the approach JIT firms take to each of the other production characteristics as well. In one sense, their "strategy" for competing is different from that of the traditional firm, and this strategy permeates their production system.

❖ Engineering

In line with the priorities, engineering in the JIT firm designs standard outputs and incrementally improves each design. The parts and subassemblies that make up each output are also standardized; over time they are further simplified and improved. More traditionally, engineers attempt to design custom outputs to satisfy unique customers, starting from scratch each time and designing new parts and subassemblies. The reason for the new parts and subassemblies is often that the engineers change and do not know what their predecessors have already designed. Yet even if the same engineers are doing the design work, they often design new parts when a previously designed, tested, and proven part would do—because they cannot afford the time to find the previous design.

Last, JIT designs usually include considerations about the manufacturability of the part or product. This is called ***design for manufacturability (DFM)*** or ***ease of assembly (design for assembly, DFA).*** Too often, the traditional firm whips up an engineering design as quickly as it can (since it has had to start from scratch) and then passes the design on to manufacturing without giving a thought to how it can be made (sometimes it cannot). With this approach, poor quality and high costs often result and cannot be improved on the shop floor, since they were designed in from the start. If the product or part absolutely cannot be made, or perhaps cannot be assembled, then the design is sent back to engineering to modify, taking more time and costing more in engineering hours.

❖ Capacity

In the traditional firm, excess capacities of all kinds are usually designed into the system ***just-in-case*** a problem arises and they are needed. These capacities may consist of extra equipment, overtime, partial shifts, and frequently, large work-in-process (WIP) inventories. All of them cost extra money to acquire and maintain, which eventually increases the cost of the product.

In the JIT firm, excess capacities are kept to a minimum to avoid inherent waste, particularly the WIP inventories, as will be noted later. In place of the excess capacities, tighter control is exerted over the production system so that conditions do not arise where significant additional capacity is needed in the first place.

❖ Transformation System

Although JIT can be used profitably in the continuous process and project industries, it offers the most benefit in repetitive production. If the true market situation consists of unique products, then JIT may not have a lot to offer (although its three basic tenets and the various characteristics described earlier may still be of value). In these less repetitive cases, an MRP system may be most appropriate. However, in the common batch situation where the United States typically uses job shops, JIT can be used by smoothing flows, converting to mixed-model assembly and sequencing, minimizing lead times, and employing cellular manufacturing and product line–based flow shops. Cellular manufacturing and flow shops were discussed in earlier chapters; the other concepts are described here.

Smoothing Work Flows

The Japanese have noticed that erratic flows in one part of a production system often become magnified in other parts of the system, not only further down the line but, because of scheduling, further *up* the line as well. This is due to the formation of queues in the production system, the batching of parts for processing on machines, the lot-sizing rules we use to initiate production, and many other similar policies. These disruptions to the smooth flow of goods are costly to the production system and waste time, materials, and human energy.

Another different aspect of JIT production is that the parts flow so quickly through the production system that the typical disposable packaging can become a major nuisance. Thus, manufacturers are turning to reusable, and generic, packages, totes, cartons, pallets, carriers, and other approaches that will perform a number of tasks such as protection and identification, as well as being carriers.

Note that early production or delivery is just as inappropriate as late delivery. The goal is *perfect* adherence to schedule—without this, erratic flows are introduced throughout the plant. With continuous, smooth flows of parts come continuous, level flows of work so there are no peak demands on workers, machines, or other resources. Then, once adequate capacity has been attained it will always be sufficient.

The Japanese therefore attempt to make the goods "flow like water," as they describe it. The first step in achieving this smooth flow is to master-schedule small lots of final products, but frequently. Every product will be produced at least once in a day, and often many times throughout the day. With many small lots master-scheduled for final assembly, multiple small lots of components must also be produced. This is achieved by mixed-model sequencing.

Converting to Mixed-Model Assembly and Sequencing

The mixed-model approach to assembly and sequencing is basically a matter of even production. With even production, items are produced smoothly throughout the day rather than in large batches of one item, followed by long shutdowns and setups and then by another large batch of another item. Let us demonstrate with an example.

Suppose three different models are being produced in a plant that operates two shifts, and the monthly demands are as given in Table 14.2. Dividing the monthly demand by 20 working days per month and then again by two shifts per day gives the daily production requirements per shift. A common divisor of the required production per shift of 20 A's, 15 B's, and 10 C's is 5. Using 5 as the common divisor means that we would produce 5 batches of each of these models each shift. Dividing the required production per shift of each model by 5 batches indicates that on each production cycle 4 units of A, 3 units of B, and 2 units of C will be produced. Assuming two 15-minute breaks per 8-hour shift (480 minutes), the production rate must be 45 units per 450 minute shift (480 − 15 − 15 = 450), or 10 minutes per unit (450 minutes per shift/45 units per shift). Since 1 cycle consists of 9 units (4 A's, 3 B's, and 2 C's), the entire cycle will take 90 minutes, or $1\frac{1}{2}$ hours. Thus, each production cycle of 4 A's, 3 B's, and 2 C's will be repeated 5 times each shift to produce the required 45 units.

One possible production cycle would be to produce the three models in batches using a sequence such as A—A—A—A—B—B—B—C—C. Alternatively, to smooth the production of the nine units throughout the production cycle, a sequence such as A—B—A—B—C—A—B—A—C might be used. Clearly, numerous other sequences are also possible. With daily production of all models, no erratic changes are introduced into the plant through customer demand, because some of every product is always available. When models are produced in traditional batches (such as producing 1000 A's, then 750 B's, followed by 500 C's), one or more batches may well be depleted before the other batches are finished. This then necessitates putting a "rush" order through the plant (in order not to lose a customer for the models that are out of stock), disrupting ongoing work, and adding to the cost of all products—not to mention the frustration involved.

Minimizing Lead Times

In the traditional firm, long lead times are often thought to allow more time to make decisions and get work performed. But in the JIT firm, short lead times mean easier, more accurate forecasting and planning. Moreover, a way to capitalize on

$\mathcal{T}$ABLE 14.2 ❖ Mixed-Model Assembly Cycle

Model	Monthly Demand	Required/Shift	Units/Cycle
A	800	800/(20 × 2) = 20	4
B	600	15	3
C	400	10	2
Total	1800	45	9

the increasing strategic importance of fast response to the customer is to minimize all the lead times. If lead times are reduced, there is less time for things to go awry, to get lost, or to be changed. For example, it is not at all uncommon for an order placed two months ago to be changed every three weeks until it is delivered: leave a bracket off, produce 10 more than requested, and so on. However, if the delivery time is one week, the customers get exactly what they need and can delay ordering until the week before they need it (when they know best what they will actually need).

Sometimes this concept of short lead times and fast responsiveness is captured by the phrase, "Don't let the parts touch the floor." In order not to touch the floor, the parts have to be kept on the machines and thus be worked on until completed. A way to help keep the parts off the floor and cut lead times is to move workstations closer together. This facilitates passing the parts from station to station and making small amounts of each part.

Smaller batches result in shorter lead times and less inventory, at the same time. With smaller batches, engineering changes get to the customer sooner, problems with quality are corrected more quickly, rework is reduced, there is less obsolete inventory, and new products get to market more promptly. Thus, although reduced inventory is an important benefit of short lead times and small batches, there are other benefits that are equally valuable, if not more so.

OPERATIONS IN PRACTICE

Gateway and Dell Slash Prices by Reducing Inventory and Lead Times

The approach used by Gateway 2000 and Dell Computer to assemble personal computers illustrates the benefits of shorter lead times. Specifically, both Gateway and Dell build computers to order rather than producing large inventories of finished computers. Building to order allows these companies to substantially reduce their inventory level—Dell carries 35 days of inventory, compared with Compaq, which carries a 110-day supply. Maintaining less inventory enhances Gateway's and Dell's ability to respond rapidly to changes in technology, such as advances in microprocessors or storage devices. For instance, because Gateway and Dell had substantially less inventory, both companies were able to introduce higher-margin computers featuring the Pentium chip earlier than their competition. In early January 1995, approximately 50 percent of Gateway's computers had the Pentium chip, compared with less than 10 percent for Compaq and IBM. Furthermore, having less inventory better positioned Gateway and Dell to respond effectively to the flaw in the Pentium chip by being among the first in the industry to announce the shipment of computers with replacement chips. Finally, because Gateway and Dell sell directly to the customer, both companies are able to reduce operating costs—Gateway's operating costs are 5.4 percent of revenues compared with Compaq's 13 percent—as well as reduce the selling price (Burrows, 1995).

Using Kanban

As opposed to the MRP approach of "pushing" materials through a plant, there are **pull systems** based on signals indicating need. Push systems are planning-based systems that determine when workstations will probably need parts if everything goes according to plan. However, operations rarely go according to plan, and as a result, materials may be either too late or too early. To safeguard against being too late and to make sure that people always have enough work to keep busy, safety stocks are used, even with MRP; these may not even be needed, but they further increase the stocks of materials in the plant. Thus, in a push system we see workers always busy making items and lots of material in the plant.

In comparison, a pull system is a control-based system that signals the requirement for parts as they are needed in reality. The result is that workers may occasionally (and sometimes frequently) be idle because more materials are not needed. This keeps material from being produced when it is not needed (waste). The appearance of a plant using a pull system is quiet and slow, with not much material around.

To further contrast the differences between push and pull systems, consider the production system shown in Figure 14.1. The system consists of one machine of type A and one machine of type B. Machine A has the capacity to produce 75 units per day, and machine B has the capacity to produce 50 units per day. All products are first produced on machine A and then processed on machine B. Daily demand for the organization is 50 units.

In a push system each work center would work as fast as it could and *push* the product on to work centers downstream, regardless of whether or not they needed additional materials. In Figure 14.1, after the first day of operation, machine A would produce 75 units, machine B would process 50 of the 75 units it received from machine A, and 25 units would be added to work-in-process inventory. Each day the system operates in this fashion, 25 more units will be added to the work-in-process inventory in front of machine B. This might seem irrational to you, but the only way for inventory not to be built up is for machine A to produce less than it is capable of producing. In this example, we could idle machine A 33 percent of the day and produce and transport only 50 units to machine B. However, if you were the plant manager and you noticed that the worker assigned to machine A was working only 67 percent of the time, what would you think? You might think the worker was goofing off and order him or her to run the machine. Of course, doing this only increases the amount of money tied up in inventory and does nothing to increase the amount of product completed and shipped to the customer.

In a pull system, the worker at machine A would produce only in response to requests for more materials made by the worker at machine B. Furthermore, the worker at machine B is authorized to make additional product only to replenish

Figure 14.1 Sequential production system with two machines.

product that is used to meet actual customer demand. If there is no customer demand, machine B will sit idle. And if machine B sits idle, machine A will be idle. In this way, the production of the entire operation is matched to actual demand.

The signals used in a pull system to authorize production may be of various kinds. Dover Corporation's OPW Division makes gasoline nozzles for gas pumps and uses wire bins as signals. Each bin holds 500 nozzles, and two are used at any time. Raw material is taken out of one bin until it is empty, and then material is drawn from the second bin. A bin collector constantly scouts the plant, looking for empty bins, and returns them to the stockroom where they are refilled and returned to the workstations. In this manner, no more than two bins' worth of material (1000 units) is ever in process.

Hewlett-Packard uses yellow tape to make squares about 1 foot on a side as the signals for its assembly lines. One square lies between every two workers. When workers finish an item, they draw the next unit to work on from the square between them and the previous worker. When the square is empty, this is the signal that another item is needed from the previous worker. Thus there are never more than two items in process per worker.

These two examples are actually modifications of Toyota's original JIT system. Toyota's materials management system is known as ***kanban,*** which means "card" in Japanese. The idea behind this system is to authorize materials for production only if there is a need for them. Through the use of *kanban* authorization cards, production is "pulled" through the system, instead of pushed out before it is needed and then stored. Thus, the MPS authorizes final assembly, which in turn authorizes subassembly production, which in its turn authorizes parts assembly, and so on. If production stops at some point in the system, immediately all downstream production also stops, and soon thereafter all upstream production as well.

Typically, two cards are used—a withdrawal *kanban* and a production *kanban.* The cards are very simple, showing only the part number and name, the work centers involved, a storage location, and the container capacity. The approach is illustrated in Figure 14.2.

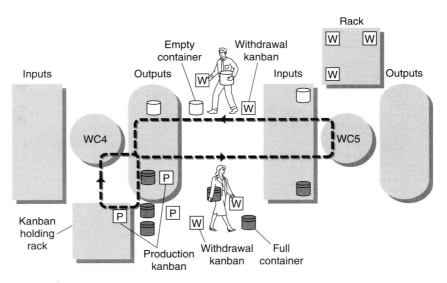

Figure 14.2 Kanban process.

Assume that work flows from work center (WC) 4 to WC5, and containers are used to transport the output from WC4 to WC5, where they are used as inputs. When WC5 sees that it will be needing more input parts, it takes an empty container and a withdrawal *kanban* back to WC4. There it leaves the empty container and locates a full one, which has a production *kanban* with it. WC5 replaces the production *kanban* with its withdrawal *kanban,* which authorizes it to remove the full container and the withdrawal *kanban.* It puts the production *kanban* in a rack at WC4, thereby authorizing the production of another container of parts. Back at WC5, the withdrawal *kanban* is placed back in its rack. WC4 cannot initiate production and fill an empty container until it has a production *kanban* authorizing additional production. Thus, withdrawal *kanbans* authorize the acquisition of additional materials from a supplying work center and production *kanbans* authorize a work center to make additional product.

The advantage of such a system is its simplicity. Being entirely visual in nature, it facilitates smooth production flow, quality inspection, minimization of inventory, and clear control of the production system.

The sidebar illustrates how Toyota is using *kanban* for shop floor control in its motor manufacturing facility in Long Beach, California. Some of the benefits are also described.

❖ Layout

The traditional method of layout follows the job-shop approach of using widely spread-out equipment with space for stockrooms, tool cribs, and work-in-process inventories between the equipment. To handle and move all this inventory, automated or semiautomated equipment such as conveyors, carousels, and forklifts is also required, which takes even more space.

With JIT, equipment is moved as close together as possible so that parts can be actually handed from one worker or machine to the next. The use of cells and flow lines dictates small lots of parts with minimal work-in-process and material-moving equipment. The cells are often U-shaped so that one worker can easily access all the machines without moving very far, and finished products will exit at the same point where raw materials enter the cell.

It is not unusual for the work flows in a traditional job shop to look like a plate of spaghetti when traced on a diagram of the shop. With JIT, however, the work flows are short and direct, with only a few major flow streams, because each part family has the same flows.

❖ Workforce

One of the key elements of JIT is the role of the workforce as a means of uncovering and solving problems. Rather than considering the workers as the traditional cogs in the great plant machine, each with its own tasks, skills, and narrow responsibilities, JIT strives for a broadly skilled, flexible worker who will look for and solve production problems wherever they appear.

A means to help achieve this with JIT is the use of work teams, whereby each team has the entire responsibility for a set of parts or products. Moreover, to keep JIT working properly, the workers must coordinate themselves, filling in for each

OPERATIONS
IN PRACTICE

Using Kanban at Toyota Motor Manufacturing, Long Beach

The Long Beach, California, plant of Toyota Motor Manufacturing (TMM) fabricates, assembles, and paints four models of truck beds for Toyota light trucks. Initially producing only 25,000 beds per year, the facility has grown to produce 150,000 a year, employing 375 people in a 300,000-square-foot facility. As part of its JIT program, TMM added *kanban* to control the production and movement of work-in-process. *Kanban* was pioneered by Toyota Motor Company in Japan as a practical pull system for minimizing inventory and simplifying production.

Although MRP is used for overall production planning, *kanban* is the primary means of shop floor control. At TMM, the *kanbans* are embedded with much more information and used for many more purposes than at other firms. For example, the *kanbans* are traveling paper tickets containing detailed information sufficient to satisfy the needs of accounting and the IRS. In some instances, the *kanbans* include bar coding to facilitate rapid access to inventory information and cycle counting. The *kanbans* travel widely as well, circulating between suppliers, the warehouse, and the production departments. All in all, TMM employs upward of 5000 *kanbans* a day.

Among the benefits to TMM was a reduction of WIP inventory by about 45 percent, raw material inventory by about 24 percent, and the warehousing cost of material by about 30 percent. As the inventory was reduced, the warehouse space was used for other productive purposes, and about 30 percent of the forklifts were eliminated. In production, about 30 percent of the presses were eliminated, about 20 percent less labor was required for the same tasks, and the production volume per shift increased by 40 percent. Nevertheless, the tangible improvements in workers' attitudes and awareness have been the most noticeable improvement (Sepehri, 1985; Monden, 1983).

other and solving each problem as it arises, since there is no inventory to use as a cover. Broadly skilled, flexible workers who do their own quality inspections and maintain their own equipment also facilitate this goal.

In the traditional approach, a competitive attitude is assumed, not only among workers but also between workers and managers. The manager has the authority and responsibility for the workers' performance. Changes are made according to managerial planning and decisions, with the worker adapting as needed. In JIT systems, everyone in the firm assumes a cooperative attitude, and plans and decisions are made by consensus.

In the traditional shop, much of the employees' time is nonworking time: looking for parts, moving materials, setting up machines, getting instructions, and so on. Thus, when actually working, the employees tend to work fast, producing parts at a rapid pace whether or not the parts are needed. (This, of course, results in errors, scrap, and machine breakdowns, which again provide a reason to stop working.) The outcome is a stop-and-go situation that, overall, results in a relatively inefficient, ineffective pace for most workers.

Conversely, with JIT, the workers produce only when the next worker is ready. The pace is steady and fast, although never frantic. In spite of the built-in rule that workers should be idle if work is not needed, the focus on smooth flows, short setups, and other such simplifications means that workers are rarely idle. (Of course, if they *are* idle, that is an immediate signal to the system designers that work is not progressing smoothly through the plant and adjustments need to be made.) The result is that with JIT the pace is considerably harder, though smoother and less frenetic.

Managerial treatment is different under JIT as well. In the traditional shop, managers are distinguished with a variety of symbols and privileges, most significant of which may be much higher pay rates, which at times approach the ridiculous. The special parking spaces, suits and ties, bonuses, freedom from time clocks, executive cafeterias, and other trappings of status tend to alienate the workers and produce a competitive rather than a cooperative attitude.

In the JIT shop, the managers share the same facilities as the workers and are expected to work longer hours. There are no particular status differentials. If a pay cut comes, it is taken out of the managers' salaries first and the workers' last. Everyone pitches in to do extra work when hard times roll around, but the managers are expected to do more than the floor workers.

❖ Scheduling

We have already contrasted the traditional scheduling, with its long setups and long runs, and the JIT approach: mixed models and smooth flows. However, it might be of interest to present a more specific contrast of JIT and MRP in terms of their characteristics. For example, JIT is clearly much simpler, more transparent in its operation, and less data- (and computer-) intensive. There are also major differences regarding inventory that have been noted already and will be detailed in the next subsection.

But is there no way to combine the advantages of JIT and MRP? Yes, there is a way. It consists of using MRP to pull the long-lead-time items and purchases *into* the shop, and it then employs JIT once the parts and raw materials have entered the shop. Dover's OPW Division uses this approach, for example. It employs MRP's explosion and lead-time offsetting to identify and order the external parts and raw materials and JIT's procedures to run a smooth, efficient plant once the parts and materials arrive. In other cases MRP is used as a planning tool for order releases and final assembly schedules, while JIT is used to execute and implement the plan.

One element of scheduling that we have not yet focused on is how JIT reduces setup times so that mixed-model production and smooth work flows are possible. In the traditional plant, machine setups take a long time, and this has resulted in long runs of items that are subsequently made. It is easy to understand why workers get upset if a five-hour setup has to be "broken" and set up again for a special customer's rush order.

But if small lots of every product must be produced at least once each day, five-hour setups must be reduced. In fact, such setups usually can be reduced fairly easily because so little attention has been paid to reducing setup time in the past. It is common for firms to reduce setups from n hours to n minutes—for example, reducing a setup that took all day (eight hours) to just eight minutes.

As was discussed in Chapter 6, one approach to reducing setup times is to adopt cellular manufacturing. Another approach, if the equipment is available and utilization rates are not a problem, is to use multiple machines that have already been set up for the new task. Alternatively, some of the more advanced and automated equipment will automatically reset itself. In the remaining cases, the setup task can be made much more efficient through a number of techniques that have been largely identified and catalogued by the Japanese. Some of these are described next.

The Japanese distinguish between internal setup time, which requires that the machine be turned off, and external setup time, which can be conducted while the machine is still working on the previous part. First, a major effort is directed toward converting internal to external setup time, which is easier to reduce. This is largely done by identifying all the previously internal setup tasks that can either be conducted just as easily as external setup work or, with some changes in the operation, be done externally. Then, the external task times are reduced by such techniques as staging dies, using duplicate fixtures, employing shuttles, and installing roller supports. Last, internal time is reduced by such creative approaches as using hinged bolts, folding brackets, guide pins, or lazy Susans.

Once the setup times are reduced to reasonable periods, the firm gains not only in smoother work flows and shorter lead times but also in flexibility to any changes in production schedules stemming from accidents, unexpected breakages, customers' problems, and so on. Clearly, this flexibility is immensely valuable.

❖ Inventories

In Chapter 12, the economic order quantity was presented as the optimal order quantity, given the trade-off between inventory carrying cost and setup or ordering cost. The formula for calculating economic order quantity (EOQ) was given as

$$EOQ = \sqrt{\frac{2UC_O}{C_H}}$$

where:

$$U = \text{annual usage}$$
$$C_O = \text{order cost or setup cost per order}$$
$$C_H = \text{annual holding cost per unit}$$

This model demonstrates the relationship between setup cost and average inventory levels. Specifically, the model demonstrates that order quantities, and consequently average inventory levels, increase as setup time and cost increase. Knowing that the EOQ minimized total costs, managers in the United States simply plugged values into the EOQ formula to determine optimal order quantities. However, use of the EOQ model assumes that its inputs are fixed. In contrast to their American counterparts, managers in Japan did not assume that these inputs were fixed. In fact, they invested significant amounts of time and other resources in finding ways to reduce equipment setup times. These efforts led to substantial reductions in setup times and therefore in setup costs, and ultimately to much smaller batch sizes, which became the basis of the JIT system.

The sidebar on Omark Industries describes how this corporation focused on inventory reduction through a program named ZIPS, and the benefits it achieved.

In Japan, inventory is seen as an evil in itself. It is a resource sitting idle, wasting money. But, more important, inventory tends to hide problems. In the traditional plant, inventories are used to buffer operations so that problems at one stage don't have an impact at the next stage. However, inventories also hide problems, such as defective parts, until the inventory is needed and then is found to be defective. For example, in a plant with lots of work-in-process inventory, a worker who discovers a batch of defective parts can simply put them aside and work on something else. By the time the worker returns to the defective batch, if ever, so much time has elapsed since the batch was processed upstream that the cause of the problem is unlikely to be discovered and corrected to prevent a recurrence. In contrast, in an environment where there is little or no buffer inventory, a worker who discovers a defective batch has no choice but to work on the batch. Furthermore, the worker is in a good position to notify upstream operations of the problem so that they can correct it and ensure that it does not occur in the future.

The Japanese liken inventory, and the money it represents, to the water in a lake. They see problems as boulders and obstacles under the water, as shown in Figure 14.3. To expose the problems, they reduce the inventories, as shown in Fig-

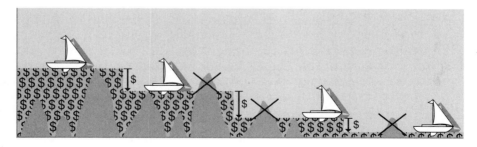

Figure 14.3 Lowering inventory investment to expose problems.

ure 14.3, and then solve the problems. Then they lower the inventory some more, exposing more problems, and solve those too. They continue this until all the problems are solved and the inventory investment is practically gone. The result is a greatly improved and smoother production system.

OPERATIONS
IN PRACTICE

Omark Industries' ZIPS Program

Omark is a $300 million a year corporation. It has 21 plants, with headquarters in Portland, Oregon. Several years ago it saved approximately $7 million in inventory carrying costs by installing its own version of just-in-time production, called ZIPS: zero inventory production system.

When Omark started its ZIPS program, each plant was asked to evaluate the relevance of ZIPS to its operation and proceed with its own program if it wished. Smaller plants, being more flexible, were the first to launch pilot projects, but the program spread quickly, with the following results.

❖ In a log-loader plant, parts that once traveled almost half a mile between machines now move only 18 inches. Lead times dropped from 30 days to minutes, inventories fell by 45 percent, and work-in-process was cut from 60 pieces to 1.

❖ At a firearms parts plant, 70 percent of all products were ZIPSed within a year. This reduced lead time from 6 weeks to 2 days, cut inventories by 50 percent, and reduced lot sizes from 500 to 30.

❖ In another plant, inventory was cut 92 percent, productivity increased 30 percent, scrap and rework fell 20 percent, and lead time was slashed from 3 weeks to 3 days.

At Omark's largest division, Oregon Saw Chain, a task force was set up to identify initial programs for ZIPS. The goals were modest but significant: to reduce lead time from 6 weeks to 1 and cut inventory by 40 percent within 3 years. Within 5 months, the division achieved these goals, and better: inventory was reduced by 55 percent. Because of these tremendous reductions in inventory, Omark has been able to increase its inventory turns from two times a year to seven. Inventory costs Omark 3 percent of a product's value each month—thus, inventory kept for a year has lost all potential profit.

There were many other benefits also. The massive reductions in inventory freed up large blocks of time so that other inefficiencies could be examined. For example, relationships with suppliers were examined for the possibility of greater efficiency. One result was that, although Oregon Saw Chain had plenty of room for staging inventory, it realized that handling this twice was foolish. Deliveries are now made directly to their point of use. Another result was better screening of incoming materials for quality. Costly defects in raw materials that had been a major source of problems in the past were thereby uncovered.

In its first year, Omark invested $200,000 in ZIPS. On the basis of these results, it planned to invest $800,000 in the second year (Waters, 1984).

In the traditional plant, almost the opposite happens. Because managers know that their plant produces, say, 15 percent defective products, they produce 15 percent extra, which goes into inventory. That's the wrong way to handle the problem—they should fix the problem in the first place, not cover it up with expensive inventory.

All types of inventories are considered liabilities: work-in-process, raw materials, finished goods, component parts, and so on. By eliminating storage space, not only do we save space, but we also disallow inventories where defectives can be hidden until no one knows who made them. And by eliminating queues of work waiting for machines, we facilitate automatic inspection by workers of hand-passed parts, thereby identifying problems when they begin rather than after 1000 units have been made incorrectly.

If the space saved when operations are moved closer to each other—frequently 33 percent of the original space—is immediately used for something else, then inventory can't be dumped there. This facilitates reducing the lead time, smoothing the workload, and reducing the inventory, all at the same time.

Last, with minimal or no inventory, control of materials is much easier and less expensive. Parts don't get lost, don't have to be moved, don't have to be labeled, and don't have to be held in computer memory or inventory records. Basically, discipline and quality are much improved and cost is reduced, simultaneously.

❖ Suppliers

Traditional practice has been to treat suppliers as adversaries and play them off against each other. Multiple sourcing purportedly keeps prices down and ensures a wide supply of parts. However, multiple sourcing also means that no supplier is getting an important fraction of the order; thus, there is no incentive to work with the firm to meet specifications for quality and delivery.

With JIT and the desire for frequent, smooth deliveries of small lots, the supplier must be considered part of the team. As part of the team, the supplier is even expected to help plan and design the purchased parts to be supplied. Schedules must be closely coordinated, and many small deliveries are expected every day. Thus it is in the supplier's interest to locate a plant or warehouse close to the customer. Clearly then, the supplier must have a large enough order to make this trouble worthwhile; thus, *single-sourcing* for 100 percent of the requirements is common. But with such large orders, the customer can expect the supplier to become more efficient in producing the larger quantities of items, so quantity discounts become available. Moreover, having just one source is also more convenient for a firm that must interact and coordinate closely with the supplier. Companies that develop single-sourcing relationships recognize the mutual dependency of the supplier-customer relationship. Specifically, for the customer to prosper in the marketplace, the supplier must supply high-quality items in the right quantities on time. On the other hand, the more successful the customer, the more business is generated for the supplier.

Perhaps equally significant, there is no incoming inspection of the materials to check their quality—all parts must be of specified quality and guaranteed by the supplier. Again, this requires a cooperative rather than an adversarial approach, with the supplier working with the team. Many JIT firms are now establishing a list of "certified" suppliers that they can count on to deliver perfect quality and thus become members of their production teams. In fact, many organizations implementing such programs will purchase products only from suppliers that pass their certification criteria. Often companies that set up certification programs work with their suppliers to help them become certified.

Single-sourcing also has some disadvantages, however. The largest, of course, is the risk of being totally dependent on one supplier. If the supplier, perhaps through no fault on the its part, cannot deliver as needed, the firm is stuck. With the minimal buffers typical of JIT, this could mean expensive idled production and large shortages. There is also some question about the supplier's incentive to become more creative in terms of producing higher quality or less expensive parts, since it already has the single-source contract. Yet the Japanese constantly pressure their suppliers to continue reducing prices, expecting that, at the least, the effect of increased learning with higher volumes will result in lower prices.

In many early and unsuccessful applications of JIT in the automobile industry, rather than change their internal procedures, firms simply required their suppliers to stock finished goods for quick, small deliveries to the firm. However, this added significant costs to the suppliers' operations, and the approach failed. The JIT firm must work with its suppliers and teach them the JIT procedures it is itself employing internally that will reduce costs and increase quality, thereby allowing suppliers also to deliver small lots more frequently.

With the adoption of JIT, the role and importance of purchasing are increasing significantly, while the size of the function is decreasing, owing to a reduced supplier base. Given the opportunities, many of the best managers are now moving into this area. Tremendous cost savings are possible with JIT, and this translates into larger profits and improved competitiveness for the firm, as illustrated in the sidebar on Harley-Davidson. The supplement to this chapter discusses purchasing and procurement in more detail.

❖ Planning and Control

In the traditional firm, planning is the focus, and it is typically complex and computerized. MRP is a good example of the level of planning and analysis that goes into the traditional production system. Unfortunately, plans often go astray, but since the firm is focused on planning rather than control, the result is to try to improve planning the next time, and this in turn results in ever more complex plans. Thus, these firms spend most of their time planning and replanning and very little time actually executing the plans.

In the JIT approach, the focus is on control. Thus, procedures are kept simple and visual. Rather than planning and forecasting for an uncertain future, the firm attempts to respond to what actually happens in real time with flexible, quick operations. Some planning is certainly conducted, but to be even more effective and efficient in responding to actual events, the planning is directed to simple expectations and improvements in the control system.

❖ Quality

The traditional approach to quality is to inspect the goods at critical points in the production system to weed out bad items and correct the system. At the least, final inspection on a sample should be conducted before a lot is sent to a customer. If

OPERATIONS
IN PRACTICE

Harley-Davidson Recovers with the Help of JIT

In the process of attempting to compete with stiff Japanese competition in motorcycles, Harley became one of the first American firms to implement JIT. It discovered that three Japanese practices largely accounted for the ability to produce at costs 30 percent lower than its own: quality circles, statistical process control to maintain high quality, and just-in-time manufacturing. It embarked on projects to install all three.

Harley's initial efforts at JIT were not particularly successful, since it perceived the program as placing a greater burden on suppliers. As one supplier noted: "Harley was notorious for juggling production schedules and was one of the worst customers when it came to last-minute panic calls for parts." Nevertheless, Harley pressed on and started working with its suppliers to simplify their designs, reduce their setup times, and improve their quality. Harley even gave courses in statistics to help its suppliers use statistical process control. Harley also started shifting its business to fewer and closer suppliers; about three-quarters of the suppliers for its Milwaukee engine plant are located within 175 miles. This allows the firm to reduce the safety stocks it previously kept as protection against transportation delays.

The JIT program has been successful, reducing Harley's costs for warranty repairs, scrap, and rework by 60 percent. The resulting higher-quality product has boosted its reputation with customers. From its earlier low market share of less than 4 percent, Harley has now moved up to almost 20 percent (Boyer, 1989; Hutchins, 1986; Conway, 1987).

too many defectives are found, the entire lot is inspected and the bad items are replaced with good ones. Scrap rates are tracked so that the firm knows how many to initiate through the production system in order to yield the number of good items desired by the customer.

With JIT, the goal is zero defects and perfect quality. A number of approaches are used for this purpose, as described in Chapters 3 and 17. But the most important elements are the workers themselves—who check the parts as they hand them to the next worker—and the small lot sizes produced, as described earlier. If a part is bad, it is caught at the time of production, and the error in the production system is corrected immediately.

❖ Maintenance

In the traditional approach to production, maintenance has been what is termed *corrective maintenance,* although *preventive maintenance* is also common. Corrective maintenance is repairing a machine when it breaks down, whereas preventive maintenance is conducting maintenance before the machine is expected to fail, or at regular intervals. Corrective maintenance is more acceptable in the traditional firm, because there are queues of material sitting in front of the machines to be worked on so that production can continue undisturbed, at least until the queues are gone.

But in the JIT shop, if a machine breaks down it will eventually stop all the following *downstream* equipment for lack of work. (It will almost immediately stop all *upstream* equipment as well, through the pull system.) Thus, the JIT shop tends to use preventive maintenance extensively so that stoppages do not occur. JIT firms operate in other ways to minimize the chance of stoppages; for example, they run the equipment at much slower and steadier rates to prevent overloads that lead to failures. (Recall the frenetic pace of traditional shops when they were in a work mode.) Running the machines slowly, at less than their rated capacity, and steadily, throughout 24 hours a day, minimizes their chance of breakdown while maximizing their output.

But a more significant difference between the traditional firm and the JIT firm lies in their approach to maintenance and repair. The traditional shop uses a "crew" of experts who do nothing but repair broken equipment, whereas the JIT shop relies much more heavily on the operator for most maintenance tasks, especially simple preventive maintenance.

$\mathcal{J}$IT: BENEFITS, PROBLEMS, AND APPLICATIONS

In this section we discuss JIT in terms of both its potential benefits and it problems. Full implementation of JIT is not required to obtain some of the benefits; partial implementation can also provide many benefits. We then address the issue of services and how JIT might be applied in this sector of the economy.

❖ Typical Benefits of JIT

As we have seen, JIT offers a variety of possible benefits: reduced inventories and space, faster response to customers due to shorter lead times, less scrap, higher quality, increased communication and teamwork, and greater emphasis on identifying and solving problems. In general, there are four primary types of benefits: (1) cost savings, (2) revenue increases, (3) investment savings, and (4) workforce improvements.

1. *Cost savings:* Costs are saved a number of ways: inventory reductions, reduced scrap, fewer defects, fewer changes due to both customers and engineering, less space, decreased labor hours, less rework, reduced overhead, and other such effects. Total savings range in the neighborhood of 20 to 25 percent, with significantly higher savings on individual categories such as inventory and defects.

2. *Revenue increases:* Revenues are increased primarily through better service and quality to the customer. Short lead times and faster response to customers' needs result in better margins and higher sales. In addition, revenues will be coming in faster on newer products and services.

3. *Investment savings:* Investment is saved through three primary effects. First, less space (about a third) is needed for the same capacity. Second, inventory is reduced to the point that turns run about 50 to 100 a year (compared with 3 or 4 in American industry). Third, the volume of work produced in the same facility is significantly increased, frequently by as much as 100 percent.

4. *Workforce improvements:* The employees of JIT firms are much more satisfied with their work. They prefer the teamwork it demands, and they like the fact that fewer problems arise. They are also better trained for the flexibility and skills needed with JIT (inspection, maintenance), and they enjoy the growth they experience in their jobs. All this translates into better, more productive work.

Figure 14.4 illustrates how these benefits are derived from JIT and which elements interact and support other elements. The synergies throughout the JIT system are clear. For example, reduced scrap and better quality lead to faster feedback on remaining scrap and defects, leading in turn to better awareness of these problems in the team and a focus on ideas for further reducing scrap and defects. Similarly, smaller lot sizes lead to better quality, which leads to a focus on remaining defects, which in turn leads to ideas for further cuts in lot sizes. All the synergistic aspects of JIT eventually result in lower costs, higher productivity, and better customer response (higher revenues and market shares).

❖ Potential Problems in Implementing JIT

Nevertheless, the use of JIT involves some difficulties and potential problems that should be noted. First, JIT is applicable primarily to repetitive production situations involving relatively standard products—rather than to custom, continuous flow, or project situations. It also means moving toward identical daily mixed-model sched-

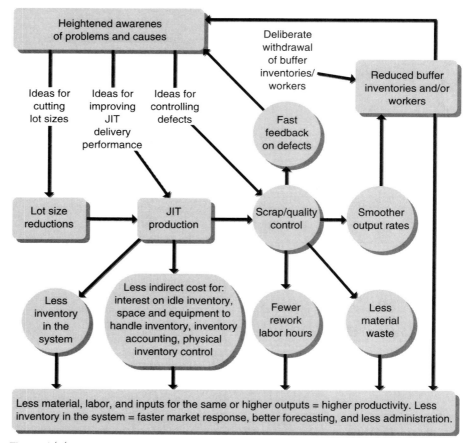

Figure 14.4   Interaction of elements of JIT. *Source:* R. J. Schonberger, "Japanese Manufacturing Techniques," *Operations Management Review,* Spring 1983.

ules rather than long runs, so if setups take a long time, JIT will not work. Not only are there frequent setups but there are also frequent shipments and receipts, so the firm must be prepared for this as well.

JIT also demands discipline. If products don't arrive on time, or if defects occur, production will stop. Again, there are no buffers of inventory or time to absorb mistakes, sloppy work, or bad management. The production system must operate correctly and employees must do their job right, or else JIT will fail.

Moreover, JIT is based on cooperation and trust between people: workers, managers, suppliers, customers, and so on. If the current environment is one of suspicion, distrust, and competition, JIT will not operate. Trust and cooperation must extend outside the plant to suppliers and customers as well. With suppliers, this means moving to risky, single-source contracts and bringing an outsider into the project team, where there may be proprietary secrets.

The major reason for not implementing JIT has little to do with these problems, however. Instead, the primary difficulty seems to involve philosophy, or a worldview, as evidenced through the measures used to assess the organization. Most frequently, managers cannot bring themselves to let utilization levels of either capital

OPERATIONS
IN PRACTICE

Smart Practice Uses JIT to Improve Customer Service

Smart Practice is a national direct marketer to dentists. Its catalogs list a variety of products, but one of its lines—personalized printed materials—was creating a larger-than-normal number of complaints from customers, resulting in an increasing number of calls, up to 26,000, to the customer service department. Analysis of the calls indicated that two questions accounted for 64 percent of all the calls: "What is this charge on my statement?" and "Where is my order?"

Investigation of the order process for these materials indicated that the long lead times to order (4 to 6 days), produce (7 days), and deliver (up to 10 days) the products resulted in charges on the customer's account statement for orders invoiced but not yet received. It was concluded that the problem could be solved by turning to the concepts of JIT to reduce the lead time for these materials.

One major problem was that the orders were "batched" by day as they progressed through the process. Frequent inspections, verifications, new account setup, invoicing, order printing, proofreading, and other activities were all slowed by the need to handle the orders in these batch sizes. To address this problem, the orders are now "batched" every 15 minutes so there is a continuous work flow. At the same time, the process itself was analyzed and improved by eliminating unnecessary, or redundant, steps, integrating multiple steps into single steps, and generally improving the efficiency of the overall process.

The result of the JIT project was to reduce the average time from order taking to typesetting from 4 days to 1 to 2 hours. Delivering the orders to typesetting in smaller batches has helped reduce the backlog in typesetting and printing and has also improved the productivity and lead times in these areas. Eighty percent of orders are now being processed, printed, and shipped the same day, with the customers receiving the order within 4 business days. After the first month of using the JIT system, service calls relating to the two problem categories fell by 20 percent (Levis, 1997).

assets (equipment and machines) or people fall—that is, to let these resources sit idle. They see this low utilization as increasing unit costs, and they are too frequently reinforced in this belief by accounting reports that value inventories as assets rather than liabilities. If this basic mind-set cannot be changed, it may be best not to attempt JIT in the first place.

❖ JIT in Services

Of course many services, and especially pure services, have no choice but to provide their service exactly when it is demanded. For example, a hair stylist cannot build up inventories of haircuts before the actual customers arrive. Now JIT is being adopted in other services that use materials rather extensively, as illustrated in the sidebar about Smart Practice. The JIT philosophy applies primarily to repetitive operations where the same activities are continually being done, or services, where the same materials are being produced. The volume need not be high, however. In cases where the end products vary, there may still be significant repeatability among the components further down the parts ladder. In addition, the output mix must remain relatively stable, within a month's time, for example. JIT will not work in an environment where the schedule keeps changing.

In summary, it appears that JIT is not one of the annual fads of American management but rather a philosophy for efficiently using the resources industry already has at its disposal. As such, it will not soon disappear from the scene, though the name may fade as its tenets are embraced by a wider and wider following in both manufacturing and service firms. Not to adopt JIT will probably mean failure in the marketplace for the majority of American firms.

*C*HAPTER IN PERSPECTIVE _____

This is the fourth chapter of Part Four, dealing with the product supply process. In Chapter 11 we addressed issues related to developing the aggregate and master production schedules. Following this, in Chapter 12 our focus was on determining when to order independent-demand items to support these schedules, and how much to order. Then in Chapter 13 we discussed how MRP can be used to manage the inventory of dependent demand items. In the present chapter we continued our discussion of the product supply process in general and materials management in particular and overviewed the just-in-time (JIT) philosophy. Major topics included the history and philosophy of JIT, a comparison between traditional systems and JIT, and benefits and problems associated with JIT. In Chapter 15 we continue our discussion of the product supply process and focus on developing detailed schedules.

❖ CHECK YOUR UNDERSTANDING _____

1. Define the following terms: *preventive maintenance, corrective maintenance, single-sourcing, just-in case, downstream, just-in-time, kanban, upstream, pull system,* and *mixed-model assembly.*

2. What are the three primary tenets of JIT?

3. Contrast the traditional approach with the JIT approach.

4. What elements of JIT are being emphasized under the alternative names *zero inventories, stockless production, continuous flow,* and *repetitive manufacturing?*

5. How do the Japanese use water as an analogy in their production systems?

6. What aspects of the traditional production system are "just-in-case"?

7. Explain how the two-card *kanban* system works.

8. What are the typical benefits of JIT?

9. Contrast JIT and MRP. How can these two approaches be used together by a single organization?

10. Describe the sequence of events in a JIT production system if a machine breaks down. What happens upstream and downstream?

11. Contrast push and pull systems. Isn't MRP pulling materials into the plant on the basis of forecasts and firm orders? How can it be a push system?

12. Accounting treats inventory as an asset. How does JIT treat inventory?

13. Identify the elements that bins, taped squares, and *kanban* cards have in common.

❖ EXPAND YOUR UNDERSTANDING

1. Which of the three tenets of JIT do you imagine the Japanese consider to be the most important? Which have Americans adopted? Which would Europeans consider most important? Which would apply best to services?

2. Although the Japanese espouse respect for the worker, they employ a great deal of part-time workers, mostly women, who are quickly laid off if demand slackens. Moreover, foreign workers such as Chinese and Koreans also are quickly released when times get tough. Is this ethical, in view of JIT's tenet that all workers should be respected?

3. How does JIT apply to production systems that are not repetitive?

4. Describe how trying to please every customer turns into a "trap" for traditional production. Aren't customization and multiple options the way of the future, particularly for differing national tastes and preferences?

5. Why might traditional engineers prefer to start a product design from scratch instead of incrementally improving an existing design? What role might technology play here in helping engineers?

6. Why do engineers not design products that can be easily made?

7. The Japanese say that "a defect is a treasure." What way do they mean, and how does this relate to JIT?

8. How smooth is a production flow where every item requires a setup? Wouldn't flows be smoother with long runs where no setups were required for days?

9. How do you think the Japanese would handle, say, adding a model D to Table 14.2 if it had a very

small production requirement of perhaps only 50 units a month?

10. How do parts that are too heavy to be passed manually between workstations get passed along? Besides the minimization of inventories, What are some other advantages of manually passing along parts?

11. Contrast the American desire for long lead times with the Japanese desire for short lead times. Don't the Japanese also need time to make decisions and get the work performed?

12. American managers hate to see high-paid workers sitting idle, even maintenance employees. What is the alternative, according to JIT?

13. Many of JIT's elements are synergistic. What aspects of layout, as described in this chapter, are synergistic?

14. If workers in a JIT system are broadly skilled and highly flexible, why organize them into teams responsible for, say, one product line? Why not let them solve problems and work anywhere in the shop?

15. Given American attitudes toward status and pay for managers, will JIT ever be feasible in the United States? Postulate arguments, either pro or con, about the treatment of managers in the traditional system compared with the JIT system.

16. In the United States, optimal lot sizes are determined from the EOQ equations. Why don't the Japanese also do this? Why are our optimal lots so much bigger than those of JIT?

17. One JIT consultant suggests that managers implement JIT by just removing inventories from the

floor. What is likely to happen if they do this? What would the Japanese do?

18. With single-sourcing, how does the firm protect itself from price gouging? From strikes or interruptions to supply?

19. Why does the supplier's stockpiling of finished goods for just-in-time delivery not work? Won't the items arrive just in time as needed by the customer?

20. What is the problem with the traditional firm's use of quality experts to inspect products? Why doesn't JIT do this?

21. In changing to a better way of manufacturing, it frequently happens that things get worse before they get better. Is this likely with JIT? If so, why?

22. How might JIT apply to a service like a hospital? A department store? A university?

❖ APPLY YOUR UNDERSTANDING _____

J. Galt Lock Company

The J. Galt Lock Company produces a line of door locksets and hardware for the residential, light commercial, and retail markets. The company's single plant, located in a small southern town, is just over 200,000 square feet and is organized into the following functional departments: screw machines, presses, machining, maintenance, tool and dies, latches, plating, buffing, subassembly, and final assembly. The company is not unionized and employs approximately 375 people, 290 of whom are hourly workers. The largest category of employees—assemblers—accounts for two-thirds of the workforce.

The company uses a proprietary planning and scheduling system that uses both an AS/400 minicomputer and spreadsheet analysis performed on a microcomputer to determine production and purchasing requirements. At any given time there are 1500 to 3000 open work orders on the shop floor. The average lot size is 50,000 parts, but for some products the size is as high as 250,000 parts.

The planning system creates work orders for each part number in the bills of materials, which are delivered to the various departments. Department supervisors determine the order in which to process the jobs, since the system does not prioritize the work orders. A variety of scheduling methods are used throughout the plant, including *kanbans*, work orders, and expediters; however, the use of these different methods often creates problems. For example, one production manager commented that although a "*kanban* pull scheduling system is being used between subassembly and final assembly, frequently the right card is not used at the right time, the correct quantity is not always produced, and there are no predetermined schedules and paths for the pickup and delivery of parts." In fact, it was discovered that work orders were often being superseded by expediters and supervisors, that large lag times existed between the decision to produce a batch and the start of actual production, and that suppliers were not being included in the "information pipeline." One production supervisor commented:

> We routinely abort the plans generated by our formal planning system because we figure out other ways of pushing product. Although we use Kanban systems in two areas of the plant, in reality everything here is a push system. Everything is based on inventory levels and/or incoming customer orders. We push not just the customer order but all the raw materials and everything that is associated with the product being assembled.

In an effort to improve its operations, J. Galt Lock hired a consulting company. The consultant determined that 36 percent of the floor space was being used to hold inventory, 25 percent was for work centers, 14 percent for aisles, 7 percent for offices, and 18 percent for nonvalue-adding activities. The production manager commented:

> We have an entire department that is dedicated to inventory storage consisting of 10 to 11 aisles of parts. What is bad is that we have all these parts, and none of them are the right ones. Lots of parts, and we still can't build.

The consultants also determined that supplying work centers were often far from the downstream work center, material flows were discontinuous as the parts were picked up and set down numerous times, and workers and supervisors often spent a considerable amount of time hunting for parts. The production manager commented:

> Work-in-process is everywhere. You can find work-in-process at every one of the stations on the shop floor. It is extremely difficult to find materials on the shop floor because of the tremendous amount of inventory on the shop floor. It is also very difficult to tell at what state a customer order is in or the material necessary to make that customer order, because we have such long runs of components and subassemblies.

The plant manager commented:

> My biggest concern is consistent delivery to customers. We just started monitoring on-time delivery performance, and it was the first time that measurement had ever been used at this operation. We found out actually how poorly we are doing. It is a matter of routinely trying to chase things down in the factory that will complete customer orders. The challenge of more consistent delivery is compounded by the fact that we have to respond much faster. Our customers used to give us three to six weeks of lead time, but now the big retailers we are starting to deal with give us only two or three days. And if we don't get it out in that small period of time, we lose the customer.

Questions

1. Evaluate and critique the existing operation and the J. Galt Lock Company.
2. How applicable is JIT to a situation like this? Would converting from a functional layout to a cellular layout facilitate the implementation of JIT?
3. What problems would JIT alleviate at the J. Galt Lock Company?

❖ EXERCISES

1. A manufacturer of door hardware uses a large transfer press to stamp out doorknobs. Demand for the company's doorknobs is 1 million per year. Setting up the press requires 16 hours (two employees working 8 hours each). The employees are paid $20 per hour including benefits. The cost to hold 1 knob in inventory for 1 year is $1.

   a. What is the economic order quantity (EOQ) for the manufacturer?
   b. On the basis of the EOQ, what is the average inventory level of knobs, and what is the annual carrying cost?
   c. How many times a year is the transfer press set up, and what is the annual cost of setting up the press?
   d. If the company reduced setup time by 50 percent, what would the new EOQ be?
   e. What would be the effect of a 50 percent reduction in setup times on annual carrying cost, annual setup cost, number of setups per year, and total annual cost?
   f. Is it logical that annual carrying cost and annual setup cost *both* decline owing to a reduction in setup cost?

2. Refer to Exercise 1. How much money should the company be willing to invest to achieve a 75 percent reduction in setup time? Assume that the company requires a three-year payback on investments in these types of projects.

3. Refer to Exercise 1. What percent reduction in setup time is needed to economically produce batches of 5000 knobs?

4. Refer to Exercise 1. What size batch would be appropriate if the company was able to reduce the 16-hour setup time to 16 minutes? What are the implications for the organization's flexibility?

Chapter 14 SUPPLEMENT

Purchasing/Procurement

An organization depends heavily on purchasing activities to reliably obtain materials by the time they are needed in the product supply process. Purchasing must make some important trade-offs in this process. Particularly because of the current fierce price competition from abroad, purchasing activities—matching varying prices, qualities, quantities, and lead time to meet the needs of production; inventory control; quality control; and other operations activities—are crucial.

Manufacturing organizations spend on average 55 percent of their revenues for outside materials and services (Tully, 1995). It is perhaps somewhat surprising that, on average, these companies spend only 6 percent of revenues on labor and 3 percent on overhead. And with factory automation increasing, the percentage of expenditures on purchases is increasing even more. In addition, with JIT programs at so many firms, "just-in-time purchasing" is even further increasing the importance of the purchasing and procurement, since delays in the receipt of materials, or receiving the wrong materials, will stop a JIT program dead in its tracks.

Thus, the purchasing system has a major potential for lowering costs and increasing profits—perhaps the most powerful within the organization. Consider the following data concerning a simple manufacturing organization.

$$
\begin{aligned}
\text{Total sales} &= \$10,000,000 \\
\text{Purchased materials} &= 7,000,000 \\
\text{Labor and salaries} &= 2,000,000 \\
\text{Overhead} &= 500,000 \\
\text{Profit} &= 500,000
\end{aligned}
$$

To double profits to $1 million, one or a combination of the following five actions could be taken.

1. Increase sales by 100 percent.
2. Increase selling price by 5 percent (same volume).
3. Decrease labor and salaries by 25 percent.
4. Decrease overhead by 100 percent.
5. Decrease purchase costs by 7.1 percent.

Although action 2 looks best, it may well be impossible, since raising prices almost always reduces the sales volume. In fact, raising prices often decreases the total profit (through lower volume). Alternative 5 is thus particularly appealing.

Decreasing the cost of purchased material provides significant profit leverage. In the example above, every 1 percent decrease in the cost of purchases results in a 14 percent increase in profits. This potential is often neglected in both business and public organizations. Indeed, a recent study found that a 5 percent reduction in total purchasing cost at a typical manufacturing organization increases net profit by 3 percent. The same manufacturer would have to cut payroll in half to achieve this same increase in profit. Furthermore, this logic is equally applicable to more service-oriented organizations. For example, investment firms typically spend 15 percent of their revenues on purchases.

Another common term for the purchasing function is *procurement*. Whereas "purchasing" implies a *monetary* transaction, "procurement" is simply the responsibility for acquiring the goods and services the organization needs and thus may include, for example, scrap, as well as purchased materials.

Procurement by an organization is similar to purchasing by an individual consumer, except for the following differences:

1. The volume and dollar amounts are much larger.
2. The buyer may be larger than the supplier, whereas in consumer purchases the buyer is typically smaller than the supplier.
3. Very few suppliers exist for certain organizational goods, whereas many typically exist for consumer goods.
4. Certain discounts are available for organizations (discussed later).

PURCHASING FORMS AND PROCEDURES

Purchasing forms and procedures in most organizations have become relatively standardized. *Purchase requisitions* are the forms sent to the purchasing department from another department within the organization authorizing it to obtain needed materials, supplies, or equipment. The standard purchase requisition usually includes the items indicated in Table 14S.1. On occasion, a *traveling requisition* is used when a standard item must constantly be resupplied. This form is simply a heavy-duty card with the standard information listed on it, which can just be pulled and sent to purchasing when new items are needed.

TABLE 14S.1 ❖ Standard Purchase Forms Information

Standard Purchase Requisition	Standard Purchase Order
* Identification number	* P.O. number
* Date of request	* Date of issuance
* Originator	* Supplier's name and address
* Billing account and authorization	* Item description and amount
* Item description and amount	* Delivery date
* Date needed	* Carrier
* Supplier information: Name P.O. number Carrier Promised delivery	* Price, terms, conditions

INSTRUCTIONS TO DEPARTMENT: COMPLETE FORM IN FULL. USE TYPEWRITER ONLY. THIS FORM CAN BE USED ONLY WHEN THE TOTAL AMOUNT OF GOODS OR SERVICES BEING REQUESTED IS $25.00 OR LESS. MULTIPLE ORDERS MUST NEVER BE USED AS A MEANS OF CIRCUMVENTING THE $25.00 LIMITATION. THIS FORM MUST BE AUTHORIZED (SIGNED) BY THE DEPARTMENT HEAD BEFORE SEPARATING AND DISTRIBUTING ALL COPIES. MAIL ORIGINAL COPY TO VENDOR, SEND THIRD COPY TO PURCHASING DEPARTMENT, AND RETAIN SECOND AND FOURTH COPIES. IMMEDIATELY UPON RECEIPT OF INVOICE, DEPARTMENT MUST COMPLETE SECOND COPY (RECEIVING REPORT AND RECOMMENDATION FOR PAYMENT) AND FORWARD THIS COPY ALONG WITH THE INVOICE TO OFFICE OF CONTROLLER FOR PAYMENT. FOURTH COPY SHOULD BE RETAINED FOR DEPARTMENTAL FILES.

A-116 20M 7-75

UNIVERSITY OF CINCINNATI

DEPARTMENTAL PURCHASE ORDER

Cincinnati, Ohio 45221

No. D 38374

DATE _____

TO: _____   DELIVER & _____
        VENDOR NAME   INVOICE   NAME OF ORIGINATING DEPARTMENT
                                    TO:

_____   _____
        ADDRESS   ADDRESS

_____   _____
CITY   STATE   ZIP CODE   DEPARTMENTAL TELEPHONE NUMBER

QUANTITY	DESCRIPTION	PRICE	AMOUNT

1. Invoice in duplicate to Department issuing order. Do not invoice for partial shipments; send one invoice only upon completion of order.
2. The articles specified herein are to be used exclusively by the University of Cincinnati and are not subject to Ohio State Sales Tax or Federal Excise Tax.
3. This order is valid only if the total amount of purchase is twenty five dollars ($25.00) or less.
4. PLEASE READ DIRECTIONS on reverse side.

VENDOR CAUTION!

Do not accept this order 1) unless it has been signed, 2) unless you know its bearer, 3) unless you have been paid for all previous shipments made to the department shown above. Contact the originating department concerning any overdue payments or the validity of this order.

DO NOT WRITE IN THIS SPACE

Authorized By:

_____
Department Head Signature
(Order Valid Only When Signed)

Figure 14S.1   Typical purchase order.

In some computerized production systems, such as materials requirements planning (MRP) systems, the supplier's lead time, dependability, price, and so forth are stored internally, and when an item is determined to be needed a computerized *purchase order* is automatically generated. In manual systems, purchasing will draw up the purchase orders authorizing a supplier to ship items directly from the requisitions (see Figure 14S.1). The required information is similar to that for the purchase requisition and is also shown in Table 14S.1. However, a purchase order is considered a legally binding contract in the Uniform Commercial Code, whereas a purchase requisition is not. For items that are constantly needed, there is a *blanket purchase order* (corresponding to the traveling requisition) through which the originator in an organization can order without having to go through purchasing. This order system is usually negotiated by purchasing with individual suppliers for a year at a time. Blanket purchase orders are also used for small-value purchases where the cost of ordering might even exceed the cost of the item.

AlliedSignal refers to its blanket purchase orders as *presourcing*. With presourcing, AlliedSignal negotiates contracts with one to six suppliers for a particular product each year. The company's plants and offices then order supplies directly from the suppliers as needed, on the basis of the negotiated low price.

For high-cost and high-volume items, an intensive analysis is usually conducted before a decision is made as to which supplier will receive the purchase order. Bids are usually solicited from suppliers, and an analysis of all bidding suppliers is conducted. The considerations in such an analysis will be discussed next.

$\mathcal{S}$ELECTING A SUPPLIER

Some of the general characteristics of a good supplier are as follows.

1. Deliveries are made on time and are of the quality and in the quantity specified. This maintains the consistent flow of processing operations for the purchasing organization.

2. Prices are fair, and efforts are made to hold or reduce the price.

3. Supplier is able to react to unforeseen changes such as an increase or decrease in demand, quality, specifications, or delivery schedules—all frequent occurrences in operations.

4. Supplier continually improves products and services.

Suppliers with all these characteristics are difficult to find. The purchasing function must recognize these criteria and not be swayed by considerations of cost or price alone.

Evaluating sources of supply can be divided into four major areas:

1. Technical and engineering capability.
2. Manufacturing strengths.
3. Financial strengths.
4. Management capability.

Each of these four areas can be evaluated through generally available information and through meetings with the potential supplier. The supplier's technical and manufacturing capability can often be evaluated by meeting with engineering and manufacturing personnel, evaluating bids, touring plants, and using a trial order.

Financial strength is an important consideration, for even if a company is technically competent, it may not be financially sound enough to meet deliveries. An analysis of financial statements—including financial ratio analysis of ability to repay short- and long-term debt, profitability, and the general trend of the capitalization structure of the firm—should also be undertaken.

Management strength is paramount in long-term and high-dollar contracts. For example, the management of construction contractors for buildings, bridges, and highways or airframe manufacturers for aircraft must be evaluated to determine its ability to successfully complete the project. The technical capability may well exist, but managerial talent and organization may not be available to guide the project. Even for short-term arrangements, the ability of the supplier's management to control its own operations will lead to better prices, delivery and quality.

Last, in these days of intense global competition, just-in-time, and six-sigma quality, the relationship between customers and their suppliers has changed significantly. More and more, customers are seeking a closer, more cooperative relationship with suppliers. They are cutting back the number of suppliers they do business with by a factor of 10 or 20, with those remaining getting the overwhelming volume of their business.

These single-sourcing arrangements are becoming close to partnerships, with the customer asking the supplier to become more involved even at the design stage, and asking for smaller, more frequent deliveries of higher-quality items. In some cases, suppliers are being certified or qualified so that their shipments do not need to be inspected by the customer—the items go directly to the production line.

In the not-too-distant past, when JIT was still novel, customers were using single-sourcing as a way to put pressure on their suppliers, forcing the supplier to stock inventories of items for immediate delivery rather than holding the stock themselves. Singing the praises of JIT—and insisting that the supplier implement JIT so that its deliveries could be made in smaller, more frequent batches—was often just a ploy to accommodate the customers' own sloppy schedules, because they never knew from week to week what they were going to need the following week. Although some firms may still be doing this, the majority are moving to JIT and quality first, and then bringing their suppliers along with them. In many cases, the customer is teaching the supplier how to implement effective JIT and quality programs.

$\mathscr{C}$OST-PRICE ANALYSIS

Price is an important element in any purchase. Whether the item being purchased is a new pair of jeans or a ton of coal, the purchasers are expected to search for the best value possible for themselves or their organization. However, lowering purchasing price does not mean browbeating suppliers into lowering their costs. A better approach is for organizations to work with and help key suppliers increase their manufacturing efficiency, and then to share the savings. Both AT&T and Chrysler seek to reduce the *total cost* of items purchased and consider price only one component of total cost. Along these lines, these companies work closely with their suppliers to help them reduce inventories and other wastes. As another example, the sidebar overviews how AlliedSignal works in partnership with its suppliers to reduce total cost.

In the process of establishing a price, the purchasing agent or buyer will expect the supplier's costs to come down in accordance with the learning curve, a concept discussed in Chapter 9. As the volume increases, the supplier can make the items with less expense, and the buyers expect that saving to be passed on to their firms. Frequently, there will be a good deal of argument concerning the *rate* of learning (the supplier saying it is slow and the buyer trying to prove that it should be fast).

Price is not the only consideration, however. A large price cut is meaningless if the material purchased is of insufficient quality or is not delivered on time to meet operations schedules.

DISCOUNTS

There are four standard types of discounts that purchasing managers should take advantage of.

1. *Trade discounts:* These are discounts to the retailer from the distributor, or to the wholesaler from the manufacturer. Only the final customer ever buys at the "manufacturer's suggested price."
2. *Quantity discounts:* These discounts are available for buying in large quantity and thus should be especially important to purchasing.

3. *Seasonal discounts:* These discounts are available to purchasers for buying in the off-season and help the supplier or manufacturer level out its production. If storage is available, excellent discounts can be obtained in this fashion.

4. *Cash discounts:* These are cash and "near cash" purchases (prompt payment). The most common is "2/10, net 30" which means a 2 percent discount if the bill is paid within 10 days; otherwise, the entire amount is due in 30 days. Such discounts represent a significant saving to organizations and should rarely be passed up.

Purchasing managers are also concerned with determining the price that will ensure a reliable source of supply in the right quantities, quality, and timing. They must be able to enter negotiations with suppliers with a reasonable estimate of the price the organization is willing to pay and must be aware of both prices that are excessive and prices that cannot possibly earn the supplier a profit.

While discussing materials pricing, mention should be made of the Robinson-Patman Act and other federal legislation affecting pricing in interstate commerce. Although it was originally intended to curb discriminatory practices by large retailers, the Robinson-Patman Act has also become applicable to manufacturers. The effect of the act has been to make it illegal, in most circumstances, for sellers to offer different customers different prices for the identical material in the same quantities. In addition to the Robinson-Patman Act, the operations manager should be acquainted with many others, including Miller-Tydings, Clayton, and Sherman.

Last, it is commonly said that buyers are underpaid, underappreciated, and under temptation. Ethical considerations are a major problem in purchasing, and companies' policies regarding what gifts and services employees accept from suppliers, and potential suppliers, vary considerably. Since it is so difficult to draw the line, wise purchasing personnel refuse *all* gifts, services, and meals from outside sources. It is best to avoid any situation in which your judgment could even be *challenged* because of something you accepted from someone.

$\mathcal{K}$EY ELEMENTS OF EFFECTIVE PURCHASING

Organizations that are highly effective in purchasing follow three practices:

1. *They leverage their buying power.* The advantages associated with decentralization are typically not achieved when it comes to purchasing. For example, Columbia/HCA combines the purchases of its 200-plus hospitals to increase its overall purchasing power. By combining all of its purchases for supplies ranging from cotton swabs to IV solution, for instance, it was able to reduce purchasing costs by $200 million and boost profits by 15 percent.

2. *They commit to a small number of dependable suppliers.* Leading suppliers are invited to compete for an organization's business, on the basis of set requirements such as state-of-the-art products, financial condition, reliable delivery, and commitment to continuous improvement. The best one to three suppliers are selected from the field of bidders on the basis of the specified requirements. Typically, one- to five-year contracts are awarded to the selected suppliers. These contracts provide the supplier with the opportunity to demonstrate its commitment to the partnership. If a supplier is able to consistently improve its performance, the organization should reciprocate by increasing the volume of business awarded to that supplier and extending the contract.

3. *They work with and help their suppliers reduce total cost.* Often, organizations will send their own production people to a supplier's plant to help the supplier improve its operating efficiency, improve its quality, and reduce waste. Additionally, an organization may benchmark key aspects of a supplier's operation such as prices, costs, and technologies. If it is discovered that a supplier has slipped relative to the competition, the organization can try to help the supplier regain its lead. If the supplier is unable or unwilling to take the steps necessary to regain its leadership position, the organization may need to find a new partner.

Detailed Scheduling

$\mathscr{C}$ HAPTER OVERVIEW

❖ Priority rules for job shop workstations address the problem of sequencing by trying to minimize inventory, maximize throughput, and meet due dates simultaneously. *Shortest operation time* (SOT) is a rule that tends to minimize average delays and maximize throughput, but results in a high degree of lateness for long jobs. *Due date* is usually a better rule for meeting all due dates.

❖ *Gantt charts,* in a variety of formats, are in common use in all industries because they so clearly present information about loads and scheduling.

❖ *Forward scheduling* consists of placing jobs on workstations up to their capacity limits as early as possible. *Backward scheduling* consists of scheduling on the final workstations first so that jobs meet due dates and then working backward through the workstations to the present. A problem with forward scheduling is that due dates may

be missed; a problem with backward scheduling is that it may violate capacity constraints.

❖ The *theory of constraints* is a scheduling procedure that attempts to schedule job shops by keeping the bottleneck workstations fully utilized.

❖ No other approach does better at minimizing the makespan of a group of jobs than *Johnson's rule* when the jobs must pass sequentially through two workstations. This rule works by scheduling the fastest jobs on the first station first so that jobs can be started on the second station as early as possible.

❖ The *runout* method of scheduling a flow line is simply to produce next the item whose inventory will run out next. The *critical ratio* method is to produce next the item that, including the processing time for the next batch, will stock out next.

❖ When multiple items must be produced on the same facility, economic lot sizes may not be feasible because their timing may conflict. If the overall capacity is adequate, another scheduling method that will avoid conflicts is to produce batch sizes that will last equal amounts of time.

❖ In scheduling services, it is more common (and feasible) to schedule resources than outputs, to the extent that demand cannot be shifted. Thus, a number of approaches to adjusting capacity have been derived.

❖ *Overbooking* is a technique that trades off the opportunity cost of unused capacity with the costs of undercapacity, including ill will. Risk is the major concern in this situation, and the *newsboy approach* to the single-period inventory problem gives a theoretically optimal amount to overbook.

INTRODUCTION

❖ A wide variety of companies such as Ford Motor, Blistex, Texas Instruments, and Octel Communications are using a new type of software to help them control their shop floors. This new software is called *manufacturing execution systems* (MES) and provides managers with real-time information about their manufacturing operations. MES was not developed to replace existing manufacturing systems; rather, it is used to link and integrate the schedules developed by manufacturing resource planning (MRP II) systems and the machine-control systems that manage production. Thus, these systems help managers control work-in-process, production activities, and workers on the shop floor.

Benefits of using MES include reduced cycle times, shorter lead times, less work-in-process, and improved on-time delivery. After developing its MES, for example, Blistex reduced its inventories of raw materials and finished goods while simultaneously increasing plant throughput. Blistex increased its planning accuracy, thereby reducing rescheduling. To take another example, Waterloo Industries uses its MES to control the sequence of jobs and track the status of 3000 parts used in the production of its toolboxes. It was able to increase its plant utilization by 20 percent, reduce work-in-process by 50 percent, and shorten lead times from 14 days to 8 days. At Texas Instruments, cycle time was reduced by 65 percent, and much of the paperwork was removed from the shop floor (Forger, 1995).

❖ Package Products, in Pittsburgh, Pennsylvania, produces folding carton packing for the bakery and deli industries. A key aspect of Package Products' strategy is to be recognized by its customers for quality, reliability, and service. Significant growth during the 1990s greatly complicated the task of managing the company's operations. In addition, its customers were becoming more demanding, and the marketplace was becoming more competitive.

Producing folding cartons requires 4 to 11 steps. Typically, the product starts as rolls of pulpboard. The pulpboard is initially cut into sheets. Then, print presses are used to add four-color images to the sheets. Next, the printed sheets are dried and die-cut. Finally, cellophane windows are added, the folding cartons are glued, and the product is prepared for shipping. To gain better control over its operations, Package Products implemented a finite capacity scheduling (FCS) software package. Before it acquired the FCS system, a Gantt chart was maintained manually to schedule jobs. With the Gantt chart, each machine was placed on a board and magnetic strips of varying lengths (depending on job processing times) were used to schedule jobs on the machines. Problems with the manual system included chronic capacity shortages and the fact that key data resided in the heads of people who were scattered throughout the organization. Two criteria used for selecting the FCS software package were that it should work with the company's existing business system and that it should not be a "black box," claiming to provide optimal schedules that no one could really understand.

A project team consisting of the information systems manager, the scheduling manager, and the shop floor supervisors was formed to evaluate alternative scheduling software. Ultimately a PC-based program was selected. With the program, the scheduler updates the previous day's production, enters any new orders, and makes any necessary changes to due dates and order quantities for existing orders. Also, the program allows the scheduler to perform "what-if" analysis to determine the impact of changes such as adding overtime or additional shifts, or reducing setup times. Finally, the computerized scheduling system is used to generate schedules for the next three to six months, to better plan future capacity requirements.

Through the use of the FCS program, overtime has been substantially reduced, on-time delivery has been improved by 32 percent, and backorders have been reduced by 53 percent. Additionally, customer service can now respond to customers' inquiries in an average of 22 seconds—versus taking overnight to respond to the same types of inquires before the new system was implemented (Trail, 1996).

❖ Hill Parts, located in Atlanta, Georgia, produces replacement parts for poultry processing machines. Over its 40-year history, the company's product line has increased from two items to more than 1000. Furthermore, since the early 1980s, the company's compound growth rate has exceeded 25 percent. To manage this growth, the company recognized the strategic importance of planning and scheduling. Given its focus on customer service, the company determined that being able to deliver on demand required reliable forecasts, visibility of jobs released to the shop floor, and an ability to quote reliable completion dates on backorders.

Hill develops monthly forecasts and produces to stock on the basis of these forecasts. To keep production on track, a PC-based finite scheduling system was recently acquired. With this software, schedules need be developed only once or twice a week. A major benefit of the finite scheduling system is that up-to-date production schedules can be displayed on terminals throughout the factory. Also, the scheduling system has reduced the amount of material on the shop floor and has increased the flexibility of responding to backorders. Additionally, the inventory of raw materials has been significantly reduced. Finally, the scheduling system provides more detailed costing information than the existing accounting system. Thus, the scheduling system has allowed Hill to do a better job of tracking budget versus actual expenditures, and units and labor hours as well. Using this information, Hill was able to determine which parts were losing money and then adjust its prices accordingly (Wymann, 1996).

In Chapter 11 we described the sequence of scheduling activities and explained aggregate and master scheduling. Then in Chapters 13 and 14 we moved into the tactical issue of scheduling the materials on the basis of deliveries set in the master schedule.

We are now ready to look at the detailed operations involved in the transformation system and how work is actually scheduled. It is at this level that plans so often go awry and productivity is lost—a machine breaks down, an employee gets sick, or other such problems arise to invalidate our carefully worked-out plans. Therefore, tremendous benefits can be attained by paying careful attention to scheduling activities, as illustrated in the examples above.

In the sequence of scheduling activities presented in Chapter 11, loading—the assignment of jobs to workstations—was the last task described. Loading is usually relatively straightforward, and it was described in detail in the Supplement to Chapter 11.

Here we move to the issue of scheduling work at the detailed level. This is usually concerned with the problem of sequencing jobs so as to achieve some goal, such as minimizing lateness or maximizing throughput. We look at this problem first for job shops and then for flow shops. Finally, we consider the problem of detailed scheduling for services and the common procedure of overbooking to reduce the opportunity costs of the expensive resources.

$\mathscr{S}$CHEDULING OF
JOB SHOPS

In this section we examine a number of approaches to the scheduling of job shops under a variety of conditions. In general, the work in a job shop is made-to-order, rather than made-to-stock, and thus has critical customers' due dates associated with it. First, we describe a few priority rules that are generally used to find the "best" sequence for a stack of jobs sitting in front of a single workstation. The data available concern when the jobs are due, when they arrived at the workstation, and how long each job will take. The objectives are usually to minimize the lateness of the jobs and maximize the throughput, both of which can be measured in different ways.

One useful tool for evaluating and understanding the ramifications of schedules is the Gantt chart. This chart can be developed for any number of workstations and is simply a way of charting three variables: a set of stations, a set of jobs, and time. Gantt charts can be found with all variations of arrangements of these three variables on two axes. The relevant data are the number of stations, the number of jobs, the sequence and times of each job on each station, and perhaps the due dates of the jobs. Other information can also be added, but the chart does not solve anything; it is just a physical description of what will happen with a given sequence of jobs.

Next follows a discussion of two common ways of scheduling jobs on multiple workstations: forward or backward. The available data are the sequence and times of each job on each of the work centers, the capacities of each work center, and the due dates of the jobs. Forward scheduling loads to capacity but may violate due dates; backward scheduling meets due dates but may violate workstation capacity limits.

Last, the theory of constraints is an approach to scheduling multiple jobs through a number of workstations without violating capacity limits but minimizing inventory and attempting to meet due dates. It uses all the information specified above, and more, such as bills of materials, inventories of raw materials, and purchases.

❖ Priority Rules for Single Workstations

An ideal sequencing rule would result in the completion of all jobs on time, with maximum facility utilization and minimal in-process inventory. Since no rule is perfect, the task is to identify the rule that minimizes the sum of these interrelated costs, as the sidebar on BancOhio illustrates. In some organizations (e.g., ambulance services) the cost of lateness will far overshadow the other costs while in other organizations (e.g., machine shops), utilization of workers will be the largest cost. In still others (e.g., retailers), inventories will be the largest cost. It may also be that at different times in an organization's life, different factors will be of first importance, and so the best rule will change. Such rules are known more generally as *decision rules*. When applied to sequencing, they are known as ***priority rules.***

OPERATIONS IN PRACTICE

Using Priority Rules at BancOhio

A major element of cost to banks is the amount of "float" they have not been able to present for claim. This is the amount of funds to which they are entitled by checks written on another institution, called *transit checks*. The faster a bank can process checks, the lower its float. For a large bank, typical values of float run as much as $30 million a day, which at 7 percent interest represents an annual loss of $2.1 million.

Float can be minimized by providing sufficient capacity to handle all checks that might come in during a day's activities, but this requires considerable expense in equipment and clerical idle time. A better strategy is first to balance work flow and capacity and then use the capacity to maximum advantage. Most banks do not use their capacity to maximum advantage, however; they simply process checks in first-come, first-served (FCFS) order. Checks left unprocessed at the end of the day under this system may well represent major amounts of funds.

This study investigated the use of prioritizing the checks for processing purposes at BancOhio and several other banks. Nine priority rules were devised that considered factors such as the volume in the bundles of checks (weight or number of items), the value in the bundles, the average unit value of the items in the bundles, and the source of the checks (residential or metropolitan branches—metropolitan branches usually receive larger checks). Also considered was the capacity of the processing facility.

The results of the study clearly showed that FCFS priority rules were the least effective. Among the most effective were those rules that used the available information concerning the value of each bundle and its source. The difference between FCFS and the better rules amounted to a reduction in float of from 50 to 90 percent.

The results of this study show that prioritizing check processing can reduce float costs for banks by millions of dollars each year (Mabert and Showalter, 1980).

Let us look at some of these priority rules, how they are used, and what costs they tend to minimize. The situation is this: There is a workstation with a number of jobs waiting to be run. Which job should be selected next? Table 15.1 illustrates such a situation, in which five jobs are awaiting processing. The due date (assuming that the current time is zero) and expected operation (processing) time for each job are given, plus a calculation of the "dynamic slack" for each job: its due date less its expected operation time.

Table 15.2 presents the results of invoking four different priority rules for these jobs. Let us follow the analysis conducted using priority *rule 1: first-come* (to the work center), *first-served* (FCFS). We assume the jobs arrived in the order listed in Table 15.1. First, we repeat the operation times given in Table 15.1, and from this we calculate the ***flow time*** for each job—the time it takes for the job to get through this operation, that is, the job's operation time plus its ***queue time*** while waiting for other jobs to finish on the facilities. For example, PDQ's queue time waiting for ABC is 1 day. The derivation of these flow times is illustrated for rule 1 in Figure 15.1.

Next is listed the due date, again from Table 15.1. The setting of this due date, typically by sales, has a significant impact on *lateness*. Lateness is calculated as simply the flow time less the due date, which is shown in the next column. The last column gives what is called *tardiness* which is the same as lateness, if the job is late, or else 0 (i.e., there are no negative values). Again, tardiness is also significantly affected by the setting of the due dates. Finally, we calculate the average (per job) flow time, lateness, and tardiness.

Rule 2 orders jobs by when they are *due,* thereby trying to minimize lateness but not being concerned with how long jobs take to get through operations (thus ignoring the cost of materials-in-process). Yet we see that this rule lowered flow time while significantly lowering lateness.

Rule 3 considers *slack,* applying the logic that those jobs that cannot "afford" to be delayed should be processed first. Thus, jobs that have more slack (Table 15.1) are all held back, and the slack is used up, while more critical jobs are worked on. We see from the average flow time that jobs are, on average, held longer with rule 3 than with either rule 1 or rule 2 (for this particular situation); yet the average lateness is worse.

Rule 4 orders those jobs with the *shortest operation times* (probably the easiest) first. We see that this rule minimizes the average flow time of the jobs, as would be expected. But, perhaps surprisingly, it also seems to give good results on lateness and tardiness, running second only to rule 2 on tardiness. This is no accident; the shortest operation time (SOT) usually gives good results.

$\mathscr{T}$ABLE 15.1 ❖ Characteristics of Five Jobs

Job	Due Date	Operation Time	"Dynamic Slack"
ABC	4	1	3
PDQ	7	5	2
XYZ	2	2	0
Z11	10	6	4
Z12	9	3	6

$\mathcal{T}$ABLE 15.2 ❖ Priority Rule Results

Job Order	Operation Time	Flow Time	Due Date	Days Late	Days Tardy
RULE 1: FCFS					
ABC	1	1	4	−3	0
PDQ	5	6	7	−1	0
XYZ	2	8	2	6	6
Z11	6	14	10	4	4
Z12	3	17	9	8	8
Average:		9.2		2.8	3.6
RULE 2: Due date					
XYZ	2	2	2	0	0
ABC	1	3	4	−1	0
PDQ	5	8	7	1	1
Z12	3	11	9	2	2
Z11	6	17	10	7	7
Average:		8.2		1.8	2.0
RULE 3: Minimum slack					
XYZ	2	2	2	0	0
PDQ	5	7	7	0	0
ABC	1	8	4	4	4
Z11	6	14	10	4	4
Z12	3	17	9	8	8
Average:		9.6		3.2	3.2
RULE 4: SOT					
ABC	1	1	4	−3	0
XYZ	2	3	2	1	1
Z12	3	6	9	−3	0
PDQ	5	11	7	4	4
Z11	6	17	10	7	7
Average:		7.6		1.2	2.4

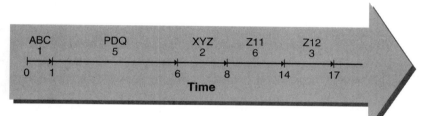

Figure 15.1   Rule 1 flow times.

There are over 100 priority rules, and they can be classified in a number of different ways, such as on the basis of the costs they most often minimize. Another basis is whether they are static (based on situations existing at the time the job came in, such as order of acceptance) or dynamic (taking into account current events such as delays and rush orders).

A number of researchers have investigated the characteristics of many of the more common priority sequencing rules and have come to some interesting conclusions. The following rules are in most common use:

❖ FCFS. *First come, first served.* The first job to arrive at a work center (not at the organization) is processed first. This rule is based on "fairness" to all jobs waiting at the same work center and is probably the most common rule used in processing people for service.

❖ *Due date.* With this rule, the earlier a job is due, the higher its priority. Often, due dates are based on when the order was placed. In these instances, a job entering the organization first will usually be given an earlier due date, independent of the length of the job.

❖ SOT. *Shortest operation time.* Do the short, easy jobs first and get them out of the way. This maximizes throughput and, thus, billings.

❖ LOT. *Longest operation time.* The longer jobs are often bigger and more important (and more profitable) and should be done first.

❖ SS. *Static slack.* Slack here equals the due date minus the time of arrival at the work center. Jobs with the smallest slack are done first.

❖ SS/RO. *Static slack per remaining operation.* A job with more operations remaining to be completed should have a higher priority.

❖ DS/RO. *Dynamic slack per remaining operation.* The dynamic slack is defined as the remaining time until the due date *less* the remaining expected processing time; this is then divided by the number of remaining operations.

❖ COVERT. Priority is given to the job with the *highest* ratio of cost of delay c over processing time t (c over t). This rule attempts to operate like the SOT rule but also to consider the cost of delays.

❖ RAND. *Random order.*

In terms of maximizing work flow through the operations, maximizing facility utilization, and minimizing lateness, the SOT rule was often found to do very well. In general, with the SOT rule jobs finish early, with low average flow times and low, in-queue waiting times, but high utilization of labor and equipment. In addition, the SOT rule generally ranks second only to the DS/RO and due-date rules in minimizing the percentage of jobs completed late. However, it is this one characteristic of the SOT rule that hampers its use—when short jobs are always taken before long jobs, there will invariably be some *very* long jobs that just *never* seem to get done. Perhaps this is a legitimate justification for expediting.

Researchers have attempted to devise SOT-type rules that would negate this one drawback of SOT. And that, of course, was the basis for devising the COVERT rule. However, the determination of the "cost" of delay is a difficult matter and not easily identified with a particular job once it is in processing. Also, such modifications to the SOT rule destroy one of its most important characteristics—its simplicity. Any worker can usually tell which job among those available is going to be easiest, thereby eliminating the sequencing task and freeing the operations manager to handle bottlenecks, overdue jobs, and so forth.

In addition to these formal priority rules, there are also informal priority systems. Examples are *most important customer first, most profitable item first,* and *most crucial subassembly first.* Indeed, well justified priority rules are sometimes not used at all in organizations. Instead, "chaos" rules. That is, a worker may be told to start on one job and 15 minutes after a customer's call, may be told to work now on that customer's job instead. This "hat switching" often consumes more of a day than actual productive work.

Solved Exercise 15.1 ❖ Priority Rules

Given the three jobs below, find their average flow times, lateness, and tardiness using these rules: due date, SOT, LOT, and DS/RO.

Job	Due Date	Operation Time	Number of Remaining Operations
S—1	17	13	5
S—6	11	10	7
S—8	22	16	3

Solution:

1. Due date

Job	Operation Time	Flow Time	Due Date	Lateness	Tardiness
S–6	10	10	11	−1	0
S–1	13	23	17	6	6
S–8	16	39	22	17	17
	Sum:	72		22	23
	Average:	24		7.33	7.67

2. SOT: This rule orders the jobs identically to the due-date rule.

3. LOT

S—8	16	16	22	−6	0
S—1	13	29	17	12	12
S—6	10	39	11	28	28
	Sum:	84		34	40
	Average:	28		11.33	15.33

4. DS/RO: First, we must calculate the values of DS/RO. For job S—1: (17 − 13)/5 = 0.80; for job S—6: (11 − 10)/7 = 0.14; for job S—8: (22 − 16)/3 = 2.0. Thus, the order is S—6, S—1, S—8. This is the same as with due date, above.

Spreadsheet Analysis: Priority Rules

Spreadsheets' built-in sorting capability can be used to rearrange the processing order of jobs on the basis of the priority rules discussed here. To illustrate this, the information from Solved Exercise 15.1 was entered into the spreadsheet below.

	A	B	C	D	E	F
1						
2						
3		**Operation**				
4	**Job**	**Time**	**Due Date**	**Flow Time**	**Lateness**	**Tardiness**
5	S-1	13	17	13	-4	0
6	S-6	10	11	23	12	12
7	S-8	16	22	39	17	17
8		Average		25.00	8.33	9.67
9						
10	**Key Formulas:**					
11	Cell D5: =B5					
12	Cell D6: =D5+B6 [copy to cell D7]					
13	Cell E5: =D5-C5 [copy to cells E6:E7]					
14	Cell F5: =MAX(E5,0) [copy to cells F6:F7]					
15	Cell D8: =AVERAGE(D5:D7) [copy to cells E8:F8]					

Cells A5:A7 contain labels that identify the three jobs waiting for processing. The operation times and due dates of the three jobs were entered in cells B5:B7 and C5:C7, respectively. In column D, the flow time is calculated. If we assume the first job is started at time zero, then the flow time for this job is simply its processing time. Thus, in cell D5 the formula: =B5 was entered. Likewise, if we assume that the second job is started immediately after the first job is completed, then the flow time for the second job is its completion time plus the flow time for the first job. To capture this logic, =D5+B6 was entered in cell D6 and then copied to cell D7.

Lateness is calculated in column E. Lateness is defined as due date minus flow time. Thus, in cell E5: =C5-D5 was entered and then copied to cells E6:E7. On the other hand, tardiness is the same as lateness, except that tardiness never drops below zero. In other words, jobs that are finished early are considered zero time units tardy, not negative time units tardy. To reflect this logic, =MAX(E5,0) was entered in cell F5 and then copied to cells F6:F7. Finally, three performance measures are calculated in row 8: average flow time, average lateness, and average tardiness. In cell D8, the formula to calculate average flow time was entered as: =AVERAGE(D5:D7). This formula was then copied to cells E8:F8 to compute average lateness and average tardiness, respectively.

We can now use the spreadsheet's built-in sorting capability to determine the order in which the jobs should be processed using a number of priority rules, and to automatically update the three performance measures for the new job sequence. First, we illustrate this for the due-date rule.

To sort the jobs on the basis of their due dates, we begin by highlighting the range of cells we want to sort. In the spreadsheet above, the cells we want to sort are A5:C7. We don't want to highlight the cells in columns D-F, since these cells contain formulas based on the information contained in cells A–C.

After highlighting the range A5:C7, select <u>D</u>ata from Excel's menu bar and <u>S</u>ort from the menu that appears after selecting <u>D</u>ata. After we select <u>S</u>ort, the Sort dialog box appears as shown below.

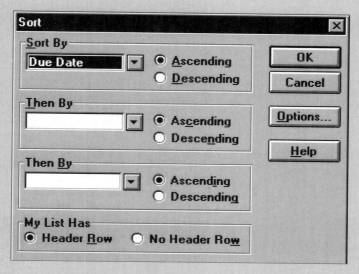

Since we want to sort the jobs by due date, we specify that the column labeled "Due Date" in the spreadsheet be used to sort the jobs. Furthermore, since jobs with earlier due dates should be processed first, we specify the <u>As</u>cending radio button. Next, we select the OK button to actually sort the jobs as shown below.

	A	B	C	D	E	F
1	Priority Rule: Due Date					
2						
3		Operation				
4	Job	Time	Due Date	Flow Time	Lateness	Tardiness
5	S-6	10	11	10	-1	0
6	S-1	13	17	23	6	6
7	S-8	16	22	39	17	17
8		Average		24.00	7.33	7.67
9						
10	Key Formulas:					
11	Cell D5: =B5					
12	Cell D6: =D5+B6 [copy to cell D7]					
13	Cell E5: =D5-C5 [copy to cells E6:E7]					
14	Cell F5: =MAX(E5,0) [copy to cells F6:F7]					
15	Cell D8: =AVERAGE(D5:D7) [copy to cells E8:F8]					

The jobs have now been rearranged according to their due dates. Note that the performance measures calculated are exactly the same as what was calculated in Solved Exercise 15.1.

Next, we illustrate the LOT priority rule. As we did previously, we begin by highlighting the range A5:C7. Then we select the menu items Data and Sort. The Sort dialog box is then filled in as shown below.

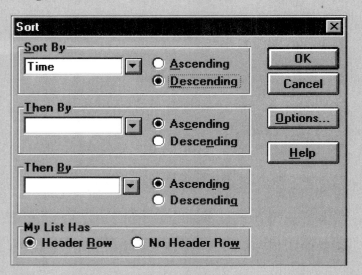

Since Operation Time was entered on two lines, only the word Time is used to identify column B as the column we wish to use as the basis for sorting the jobs. Also, since we are using the LOT rule, we specify the Descending radio button. After we select the OK button in the Sort dialog box, the spreadsheet appears as follows:

	A	B	C	D	E	F
1	Priority Rule: LOT					
2						
3		Operation				
4	Job	Time	Due Date	Flow Time	Lateness	Tardiness
5	S-8	16	22	16	-6	0
6	S-1	13	17	29	12	12
7	S-6	10	11	39	28	28
8		Average		28.00	11.33	13.33
9						
10	Key Formulas:					
11	Cell D5: =B5					
12	Cell D6: =D5+B6 [copy to cell D7]					
13	Cell E5: =D5-C5 [copy to cells E6:E7]					
14	Cell F5: =MAX(E5,0) [copy to cells F6:F7]					
15	Cell D8: =AVERAGE(D5:D7) [copy to cells E8:F8]					

Finally, we illustrate the use of the DS/RO priority rule. To use this rule we need to add the remaining number of operations for each job, and we also need to enter formulas that calculate the DS/RO for each job. To incorporate this information into our spreadsheet, two columns were inserted into the spreadsheet right before the Flow Time column, as shown below. In the first new column, column D, the number of remaining operations was entered for each job. In the second new column, column E, the dynamic slack per remaining number of operations was calculated.

	A	B	C	D	E	F	G	H
1	Priority Rule: DS/RO							
2								
3		Operation		# Remaining				
4	Job	Time	Due Date	Operations	DS/RO	Flow Time	Lateness	Tardiness
5	S-1	13	17	5	0.80	13	-4	0
6	S-6	10	11	7	0.14	23	12	12
7	S-8	16	22	3	2.00	39	17	17
8		Average				25.00	8.33	9.67
9								
10	Key Formulas:							
11		cell E5: =(C5-B5)/D5 [copy to cells E6:E7]						
12								

To sort the jobs on the basis of the DS/RO priority rule, the range A5:E7 was initially highlighted. Then the Data and Sort menu items were selected. In the Sort By box, DS/RO was specified and the Ascending radio button was selected. After we select the OK button in the Sort dialog box, the spreadsheet appears as follows.

	A	B	C	D	E	F	G	H
1	Priority Rule: DS/RO							
2								
3		Operation		# Remaining				
4	Job	Time	Due Date	Operations	DS/RO	Flow Time	Lateness	Tardiness
5	S-6	10	11	7	0.14	10	-1	0
6	S-1	13	17	5	0.80	23	6	6
7	S-8	16	22	3	2.00	39	17	17
8		Average				24.00	7.33	7.67
9								
10	Key Formulas:							
11		cell E5: =(C5-B5)/D5 [copy to cells E6:E7]						

As this example illustrates, the ease with which spreadsheets can sort data greatly facilitates the task of determining job processing sequences. A wide variety of priority rules can be investigated with spreadsheets, and new jobs can be easily added to and completed jobs deleted from the spreadsheet.

❖ Gantt Charts for Visualizing Multiple Workstations

Probably the oldest, most useful, and yet most easily understood graphical aid for conveying the sequencing and status of operations is the **_Gantt chart,_** developed by Henry L. Gantt, a pioneer in scientific management, around 1917. The Gantt chart usually shows planned _and_ actual progress on a number of items displayed against a horizontal time scale. The items may be jobs, machines, departments, parts, staff, and so forth. A variety of symbols may be added to the chart, depending on the activity being charted. Some common symbols are given in Figure 15.2. Their use is illustrated in Figure 15.3, which shows job loadings for three facilities. As of July 15, 5 P.M., job 481 was completed as planned, even with the shutdown of facility A-2 on July 9; job 502, though completed, took half a day longer than expected. Job 563 was delayed one day, owing to lack of materials, and is still incomplete; job 459, besides starting late, was delayed for repairs. Last, job 496 is half a day ahead of schedule.

The use of a Gantt chart for sequencing is illustrated in Figure 15.4. In this situation the jobs to be considered over the next two weeks with their facility and time requirements, in order, are as shown.

Figure 15.4 shows only one possible sequencing; a better one might have been to delay job 607 and put job 703 on facility A-2 first at day 6½ and then job 717 on A-5 so facility A-5 would be better utilized over the two-week duration. What is "best" depends on a number of factors, such as the importance and due dates of the jobs and the relative expense of the facilities. If the objective is to meet due dates, _backward scheduling_, as described next, is particularly useful. This is also the basic approach of materials requirements planning (MRP), which we discussed in detail in Chapter 13.

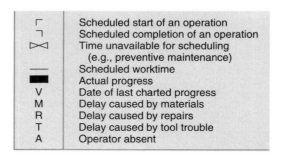

⌐ ⌐	Scheduled start of an operation
⌐	Scheduled completion of an operation
⋈	Time unavailable for scheduling (e.g., preventive maintenance)
—	Scheduled worktime
■	Actual progress
V	Date of last charted progress
M	Delay caused by materials
R	Delay caused by repairs
T	Delay caused by tool trouble
A	Operator absent

Figure 15.2   Gantt chart symbols.

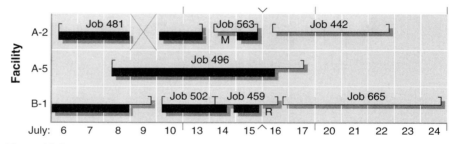

Figure 15.3   Typical Gantt status chart.

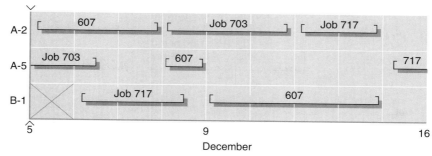

Job 607: Facility A-2 (3 days); A-5 (1 day); Facility B-1 (4 days)
703: Facility A-5 ($1\frac{1}{2}$ days left); Facility A-2 (3 days)
717: Facility B-1 ($2\frac{1}{2}$ days); Facility A-2 (2 days); Facility A-5 (6 days)

Figure 15.4   Sequencing by Gantt chart.

A number of variations of the basic Gantt chart have been developed, using pegs, colored string, colored tape, and so forth. Nevertheless, the purpose remains the same: to clearly communicate the current status of operations, facilities, and jobs for purposes of expediting, sequencing, allocating resources between idle and bottleneck facilities, and so on.

Although the Gantt chart communicates job and facility status quite well, it is not a scheduling technique per se, but it can be helpful for determining the best sequence of activities or for rescheduling activities. Other approaches, described in the following subsection, have been found to be more useful.

❖ Forward and Backward Scheduling of Multiple Workstations

Forward and backward scheduling of multiple workstations are used for a somewhat different situation from priority rules. Those rules are meant to determine the best sequence for working on a group of jobs sitting in front of a workstation of some sort. Here we are interested in trying to schedule a group of jobs through a *variety* of workstations. With the priority rules, we always used forward scheduling: we first ordered the jobs and then took whatever time was needed on the workstation to finish one job before starting on the next job.

A common situation in which forward and backward scheduling may be used is as follows: Marketing usually promises customers delivery dates based on some fixed lead time specified by operations. As new jobs come in, operations then attempts to slot processing times for the new jobs between those for existing jobs already scheduled on the equipment. **Backward scheduling,** in which due dates are used to determine the *latest* possible time a job can be started, is often used in this situation because starting at the latest acceptable time for each task will indicate where bottlenecks exist. **Forward scheduling,** in which jobs are scheduled in the order they come in, is usually conducted when a delivery date is to be *directly* set for the job by operations rather than by marketing on the basis of fixed lead times. The job is then simply scheduled into each facility as the facilities are expected to become available, and the resulting expected completion date is transmitted to the customer.

The difference between forward and backward scheduling is illustrated in the following example. Table 15.3 describes three jobs in terms of when they are due and their processing requirements. Requirements are shown as the first processing

$\mathscr{T}$ABLE 15.3 ❖ Jobs to Be Scheduled

Job	Hour Due	Facility, Hours Required (in Order of Processing)
A	8	III (1), II (3), I (2)
B	6	II (2), III (1), I (1)
C	4	I (2), III (1)

facility required and, in parentheses, the hours required on that facility; the second facility and hours; and, for jobs A and B, the third facility and hours. Job A, for example, requires using facility III first for 1 hour, then facility II for 3 hours, and, last, facility I for 2 hours. We assume in this situation that job tasks can be split. That is, a job can be started on a facility, taken off so that a higher-priority job can use the facility, and then put back on to continue its processing. To simplify the illustration we will assume that there are no existing jobs on the facilities.

Figure 15.5*a* shows the forward scheduling for the three jobs. Job A comes in first and thus is scheduled first. Its first processing task is on facility III for 1 hour only, so it is scheduled there for hour 1, as shown circled in Figure 15.5*a*. Following this, job A requires 3 hours on facility II, so it is scheduled there for hours 2, 3, and 4, also shown circled. Last, it spends 2 hours on facility I, so hours 5 and 6 are scheduled there.

Next, job B is scheduled when it comes in sometime later. It first requires 2 hours on facility II, so it is started there in hour 1; but because job A has been previously scheduled on facility II for hours 2, 3, and 4, job B must be removed to let job A "pass through," and B is finished up on facility II in hour 5. (If job B could *not* be split, we would have to delay its processing on facility II until hour 5, when it could be scheduled for hours 5 and 6.) Next it spends 1 hour—hour 6—on facility III; last, it spends hour 7 on facility I. But it was due at the end of hour 6 and hence is an hour late. Last, job C is scheduled with no difficulty.

Backward scheduling for the same three jobs is illustrated in Figure 15.5*b*. Again, job A is scheduled first; but since it is due in hour 8, it is scheduled for its last hour of processing on the last facility, I, at hour 8. Since 2 hours of processing are required on facility I in the final stage, job A is also scheduled there for hour 7. Then 3 hours are required on facility II: hours 6, 5, and 4. Last, 1 hour is required on facility 3: hour 3.

Job B is then scheduled backward from hour 6 on its last processing facility, I. Since only 1 hour is required there, it is scheduled next on facility III for hour 5 (no

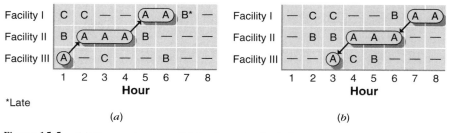

*Late

(a)   (b)

Figure 15.5   (a) Forward versus (b) backward scheduling.

$\mathcal{S}$OLVED EXERCISE 15.2 ❖ Forward and Backward Scheduling

a. Use forward and backward scheduling to schedule the following two jobs on two facilities. Job S13 (due at hour 10): 3 hours on facility A, 2 hours on B, 1 hour on A, 2 hours on B. Job X10 (due at hour 12): 1 hour on A, 1 hour on B, 2 hours on A, 3 hours on B.

b. Then see if job Z04 can also be accommodated. It is due at hour 15 and requires 2 hours on A, 2 on B, 1 on A, and 1 on B.

Solution:

a. Forward (starting with S13): Acceptable.

Hour

Facility	1	2	3	4	5	6	7	8	9	10	11	12	13	14	15	16
A	S13	S13	S13	X10		S13	X10	X10								
B				S13	S13	X10	S13	S13	X10	X10	X10					

Backward (starting with S13): Unacceptable.

	1	2	3	4	5	6	7	8	9	10	11	12	13	14	15	16
A		X10	S13	S13	S13	X10	X10	S13								
B						X10	S13	S13	X10*	S13	S13	X10	X10			

*We are forced either to split job X10 or to make it late.

Backward (starting with X10): Acceptable.

	1	2	3	4	5	6	7	8	9	10	11	12	13	14	15	16
A		S13	S13	S13		X10	S13	X10	X10							
B						S13	S13	X10	S13	S13*	X10	X10	X10			

*We cannot start S13 from hour 10, but hour 9 is acceptable.

b. Use the acceptable forward and backward solutions above: Forward.

	1	2	3	4	5	6	7	8	9	10	11	12	13	14	15	16
A	X	X	X	X	Z04	X	X	X	Z04					Z04		
B		X	X	X	X	X	X	X	X	Z04	Z04		Z04			

Backward (starting with X10):

	1	2	3	4	5	6	7	8	9	10	11	12	13	14	15	16
A	Z04	X	X	X	Z04	X	X	X	X					Z04		
B						X	X	X	X	X	X	X	X	Z04	Z04	Z04

We see that it is necessary to split job Z04; it will meet its due date with the forward schedule but not with the backward schedule.

---

conflict appears), and last on facility II for 2 hours. But it cannot be scheduled there for hour 4, because Job A is there. The next available backward hour is 3, so it is scheduled there for hours 3 and 2. (Note that another job might have totally occupied facility II, and job B could not have been successfully scheduled to be completed by hour 6 *at all.* Backward scheduling *may not* result in a successful schedule; but *if it is possible,* one will usually be found. Forward scheduling, on the other hand, never results in such a conflict, but it may not meet desired due dates either.) Last, job C is scheduled on its final facility, III, for its due hour, hour 4, and then on facility I for 2 hours, hours 3 and 2.

Of interest here is the fact that not only did we successfully schedule all the jobs to meet their due hours, but in the process we also saved 1 complete hour on the three facilities (hour 1). Either this hour could now be used for later oncoming jobs to be slotted in earlier, or the entire set of jobs A, B, and C could be run and delivered 1 hour earlier than promised. This is why backward scheduling is used for situations in which due dates are set externally. The problem with backward scheduling, of course, is that the shop sometimes simply cannot meet the promised due date.

❖ The Theory of Constraints

The **theory of constraints** was originally used in a proprietary package called *optimized production technology* (OPT), which uses an alternative way of scheduling a job shop. The basic procedure is first to identify bottleneck workstations in the shop, schedule them forward with the jobs in the shop to keep them fully utilized, and then schedule the nonbottleneck workstations backward to keep the bottlenecks busy so that they are never waiting for work.

The theory of constraints can be compared with MRP in the following way. Basically, candidate schedules are tested through simulation, with the objective of increasing throughput and decreasing inventories but not overloading any workstations (this is called *finite loading*). In the process, however, due dates may be missed. MRP works from the due dates and explodes the bill of materials backward through the shop, loading work centers as much as necessary (this is called *infinite loading*) to meet the specified lead times of the component parts. MRP uses a lot of data and requires a computer to execute it, but the theory of constraints requires even more information (such as purchases, current orders, stores of raw materials, workstation capacities, and routings) as well as more computer power.

The following nine guidelines capture the essence of the theory:

1. *Flows rather than capacities should be balanced throughout the shop*. The objective is to move material quickly and smoothly through the production system, not to balance capacities or utilization of equipment or human resources.

2. *Utilization of a nonbottleneck is determined by other constraints in the system, such as bottlenecks*. Nonbottleneck resources do not restrict the amount of output that a production system can create. Thus, these resources should be managed to support the operations of those resources (i.e., the bottlenecks) that do constrain the amount of output. Clearly, operating a nonbottleneck resource at a higher rate of output than the bottleneck resource does nothing to increase the output produced of the entire production system.

3. *Utilization of a workstation is not the same as activation (producing when material is not yet needed)*. Traditionally, managers have not made a distinction between using a resource and activating it. However, according to the theory of constraints, a resource is considered activated only if it is helping the entire system create more output. If a machine is independently producing more output than the rest of the system, the time the machine is operated to produce outputs over and above what the overall system is producing is considered utilization, not activation.

4. *An hour lost at a bottleneck is an hour lost for the whole shop.* Since the bottleneck resource limits the amount of output the entire system can create, time when this resource is not producing output is a loss to the entire system that cannot be made up. Lost time at a bottleneck resource can result because of downtime for maintenance or because the resource was starved for work. For example, if a hair stylist is idle for an hour because no customers arrive, this hour of lost haircuts cannot be made up even if twice as many customers as usual arrive in the next hour.

5. *An hour saved at a nonbottleneck is a mirage.* Since nonbottlenecks have plenty of capacity and do not limit the output of the production system, saving time at these resources does not increase total output. The implication for managers is that timesaving improvements to the system should be directed at bottleneck resources.

6. *Bottlenecks govern shop throughput and work-in-process inventories.*

7. *The transfer batch need not be the same size as the process batch.* The size of the *process batch* is the size of the batch produced each time a job is run. Often, this size is determined by trading off various costs, as is done with the economic order quantity (EOQ) model. On the other hand, the size of the *transfer batch* is the size of the batch of parts moved from one work center to another work center. Clearly, parts can be moved in smaller batches than they are produced in. Indeed, considerable reductions in flow times can often be obtained by using a transfer batch that is smaller than the process batch. For example, assume that a manufacturer produces a part in batches of 10. This part requires three operations, each performed on a different machine. The operation time is 5 minutes per part per operation. Figure 15.6 demonstrates the effect on flow time when a process batch of 10 units is reduced to a transfer batch of 1 unit. Specifically, in Figure 15.6a the transfer batch is the same size as the process batch, and a flow time of 150 minutes results. In Figure 15.6b the 1-unit transfer batch reduces flow time to 60 minutes. The reason for long flow time with a large transfer batch is that in any batch the first part must always wait for all the other parts to complete their processing before it is started on the next machine. In Figure 15.6a, the first part in the batch has to wait 45 minutes for the other nine parts. When the transfer batch is reduced to 1 unit, the parts in the batch do not have to wait for the other parts in the process batch.

8. *The size of the process batch should be variable, not fixed.* Because the economics of different resources can vary, the process batch does not need to be the same size at all stages of production. For example, consider an item that is produced on an injection molding machine and then visits a trimming department. Since the time and cost to set up injection molding equipment are likely to be very different from the time and cost to set up the trimming equipment, there is no reason why the batch size should be the same at each of these stages. Thus, batch size at each stage should be determined by the specific economics of that stage.

9. *A shop schedule should be set by examining all the shop constraints simultaneously.* Traditionally, schedules are determined sequentially. First the batch size is determined. Next lead times are calculated and priorities set. Finally, schedules are adjusted on the basis of capacity constraints. The theory of

Time	5	10	15	20	25	30	35	40	45	50	55	60	65	70	75	80	85	90	95	100	105	110	115	120	125	130	135	140	145	150
Opn 1	P1	P2	P3	P4	P5	P6	P7	P8	P9	P10																				
Opn 2											P1	P2	P3	P4	P5	P6	P7	P8	P9	P10										
Opn 3																					P1	P2	P3	P4	P5	P6	P7	P8	P9	P10

(a)

Time	5	10	15	20	25	30	35	40	45	50	55	60
Opn 1	P1	P2	P3	P4	P5	P6	P7	P8	P9	P10		
Opn 2		P1	P2	P3	P4	P5	P6	P7	P8	P9	P10	
Opn 3			P1	P2	P3	P4	P5	P6	P7	P8	P9	P10

(b)

Figure 15.6   Transfer batch size and its effect on flow time. (*a*) Transfer batch size equals process batch size. (*b*) Transfer batch size equals one part.

constraints advocates considering all constraints simultaneously in developing schedules. The theory also argues that lead times are the result of the schedules and therefore cannot be determined beforehand.

The critical aspect of these guidelines is the focus on bottleneck workstations, finite loading, and the splitting of batches in order to move items along to the next workstation when desirable. Quite a few manufacturing firms have adopted the theory of constraints. Some appear to have reaped significant benefits, but in other cases the results are not as clear. More time and testing should help determine the value of this new approach.

SCHEDULING OF FLOW SHOPS

In this section, we again consider a variety of approaches for scheduling under different conditions and with different sets of information. However, a flow shop usually involves a make-to-stock rather than a make-to-order situation. Thus, there are usually no customer due dates to meet; rather, there are different objectives related to utilizing equipment or replacing stocks of finished goods before they run out. In addition, a flow shop is often a single, though complex, facility rather than a set of workstations.

First, we examine a technique called *Johnson's rule*, after its originator. This technique involves two workstations that process all jobs sequentially and in the same order; what comes off the first station goes next to the second station. The information available is the operation time on each of the workstations, and the objective is to minimize the total span of time on the two workstations together (so that both can be used for some other set of jobs), commonly called the *makespan*. Johnson's rule finds an optimal sequence of jobs to minimize the makespan, although equally good sequences are possible. Note that no due dates or arrival times are explicitly considered here.

Next, we describe some sequencing heuristics that are somewhat similar to priority rules in terms of the objective. The *runout method* and the *critical ratio method* both address the situation in which inventories or stocks of different items or materials are being depleted, and new batches (with specified processing times) need to be run (all on one fixed facility). The focus here, however, is not on maximizing throughput rate or meeting due dates but on avoiding a stockout of the existing inventories. The information available includes the amount of each material remaining in stock, the demand for each material, and, in the case of the critical ratio, the processing time for each batch. Runout and critical ratio heuristics simply give us the "best" order in which to process the materials; they do not specify batch size, which is assumed to be fixed.

Last, we consider the situation of determining individual batch sizes for this situation. Costs are not considered. An entire cycle of production for all batches is derived here, as compared with simply determining which batch to run next (as with the heuristic rules).

❖ Johnson's Rule for Dual Workstations

The general problem of sequencing usually involves getting jobs through operations as quickly as possible. The dual objectives are (1) to maximize facility utilization by smoothly processing a large number of jobs, and (2) to avoid delaying any one job excessively. As a simple motivating example, consider the situation of two jobs, J_1 and J_2, going through two facilities in the *same order*, F_1 and then F_2. Suppose one of the jobs (say, J_1) requires 4 hours on F_1 and 5 hours on F_2, and the other job (J_2) requires 7 hours on F_1 and 4 hours on F_2. In what order should the jobs be run to minimize the total facility time?

This problem is simple enough that we may enumerate both possible solutions: start J_1 first or J_2 first. Figure 15.7 shows the Gantt charts for each solution. In the case of J_1 first, Figure 15.7*a*, we see that, owing to our scheduling, there exists some delay on facility 2 before the second job can begin. We hope that scheduling job 2 first will eliminate this delay. We see in Figure 15.7*b* that indeed it does; however, even with the delay eliminated, it takes *longer* to process both jobs: 16 hours with J_2 scheduled first, compared with 15 hours with J_1 first.

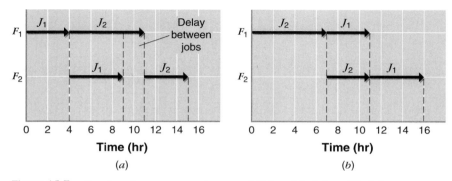

Figure 15.7   Results of two sequencing possibilities: (*a*) J_1 first; (*b*) J_2 first.

Upon further examination we can see why. No matter which job is scheduled first, the two jobs complete work on facility 1 in 11 hours. Therefore, if the job with the longer time on facility 2 is scheduled last, the overall duration for completion of both jobs will be greatest. The message is clear: schedule the job with the *shorter* time on facility 2 *last.*

By the same token, it would be well to get jobs *started* on facility 2 as soon as possible. Hence, the *short* jobs on facility 1 should be scheduled as *early* as possible. These intuitive conclusions have been formalized by S. M. Johnson, a scheduling researcher, in a form now referred to as ***Johnson's rule,*** which deals with the task of optimally sequencing N jobs through two facilities in the same order:

> If the shortest time for a job is on the *first* facility, schedule the job as *early* as possible. If the shortest time is on the *second* facility, schedule it as *late* as possible. Delete that job and repeat the procedure.

Let us next consider an example from the field of health. Screening for sickle-cell anemia is a common medical process that uses an inexpensive, but not definitive, test called a *sickledex.* Five patients who have tested positive on the sickledex are to be scheduled for definitive testing by electrophoresis and then consultation with a physician, for genetic education. A mobile laboratory is to be used, starting at 8 A.M. Naturally, it is desirable to conclude the screening and education as quickly as possible, so that the mobile lab may be used elsewhere. On the basis of the sickledex results, the nurse estimates that the times (in minutes) listed in Table 15.4 will be required for screening and education. In what order should the patients be scheduled, and when can we expect the work to be completed?

$\mathcal{T}$ABLE 15.4 ❖ Sickle-Cell Screening Time: Estimates in Minutes

	Patient				
	1	2	3	4	5
Lab (electrophoresis)	120	30	20	40	60
Genetic education	10	60	120	30	60

Analysis

Applying Johnson's rule, we find that the shortest time is 10 minutes in the second task with patient 1 (P_1). Thus, this patient should be scheduled last. The problem now appears as

$$
\begin{array}{ccccc}
P_1 & P_2 & P_3 & P_4 & P_5 \\
120 & 30 & 20 & 40 & 60 \\
10 & 60 & 120 & 30 & 60
\end{array}
\qquad
\boxed{\ \ \ |\ \ \ |\ \ \ |\ \ \ |\ P_1\ }
$$

The next-shortest time is for P_3 on task 1 (20 minutes), so it is scheduled first. Deleting this patient, the next-shortest time is 30, but this appears twice. In general,

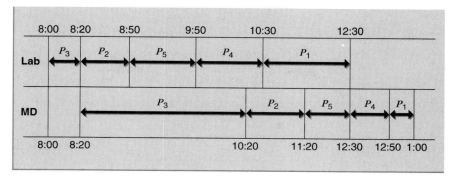

Figure 15.8   Mobile lab schedule.

ties may be broken arbitrarily; but here there really is no problem, since for P_2 the 30 is on the first task and for P_4 it is on the second. Hence, P_2 is scheduled right after P_3 (see below) and P_4 just before P_1, leaving P_5 in the middle. The resulting schedule is illustrated in Figure 15.8; it appears that the mobile lab will be able to leave by about 1 P.M.

P_3	P_2	P_5	P_4	P_1

Although Johnson's rule will find an optimal schedule, it is not necessarily the *only* optimal schedule—there may be also others, but none will finish *sooner*. It should also be noted that there are extensions to Johnson's rule concerning the case of two jobs and N facilities—and for certain N-jobs, 3-facility situations—but there is no solution to the general sequencing problem, although Johnson's approach usually gives good results even in these cases. However, the general sequencing problem is not limited to jobs undergoing the same sequence of operations.

❖ Runout and Critical Ratio Heuristics for Sequencing

The *runout* and *critical ratio* approaches to sequencing extend our analysis to entire production lines when only one job can use the facilities at any given time. In a sense, this situation is similar to the N-job, 1-machine problem for which we used priority rules. This situation is actually quite different, however, in that we are not trying to minimize flow times or meet due dates. Instead, we are producing to stock and are trying to replenish existing stocks of goods before they are depleted.

In the **runout** method, we simply produce the item next that we will run out of first.

$$\text{Runout time} = \frac{\text{inventory remaining}}{\text{demand rate}}$$

In the **critical ratio** (CR) method, this logic is carried one step further, and the remaining processing time is also factored in, so that jobs with longer processing times are viewed as more important. The equation is

$$\text{Critical ratio} = \frac{\text{runout time}}{\text{processing time}}$$

◯OLVED EXERCISE 15.3 ❖ Johnson's Rule

Sequence the following tasks on two facilities, A first and then B, to minimize their makespan.

Tasks:	1	2	3	4	5	6
A:	3	6	2	7	4	5
B:	8	1	4	3	8	6

Solution:

The shortest time is 1 for task 2 on B, so we place it *last.* After we delete task 2, the next-shortest is 2—task 3 on A, so we put it *first.* Deleting task 3, we find that the next is 3—task 4 on B (last) *and* task 1 on A (first). Finally, 4 is next—task 5 on A (first), leaving task 6 for the remaining spot.

3	1	5	6	4	2

For critical ratios above or near 1.0, we are not usually concerned, because stock is being used up more slowly than or at about the same rate as processing time. But for values near 0.8 or less, the stock is being used significantly faster than the remaining processing time, and there is a good chance of a shortage. Clearly, the lower the critical ratio, the greater the priority, and the greater the need for management intervention.

Table 15.5 illustrates these rules. As can be seen, the runout rule sequences the jobs in the order R3S, X17, and 27Y because this is the order in which they will be depleted. It should be noted, however, that the runout method is used only to select the *next* job. After R3S has completed processing, a new runout analysis should be conducted. There are two reasons for this: (1) conditions may have changed the urgency of the other jobs, or (2) a recently completed job may now again be more urgent than one of the other jobs. For example, if X17 is run next, following its completion job R3S may again be due to run out and job 27Y still has quite a while before it will run out. That is, not every job may need to be run in every "cycle" of processing, or, to state it another way, some jobs may need to be run more often than others.

The calculation of the critical ratio in Table 15.5 totally reorders the sequencing of the jobs: X17, 27Y, and R3S. This rule operates much like the minimum slack pri-

◯ABLE 15.5 ❖ Runout and Critical Ratio Sequencing Heuristics

Job	Units of Inventory Remaining	Daily Demand (units)	Runout Time (RT) (days)	Sequence by Runout	Batch Process Time (PT) (days)	CR = RT/PT	Sequence by CR
X17	12	4	3	2nd	4	0.75	1st
R3S	8	4	2	1st	2	1.00	3rd
27Y	20	2	10	3rd	12	0.83	2nd

ority rule and says that even though job R3S is due to run out soon, a new batch can also be run very quickly, so we should not worry about it. Though responsive to considerations of lateness, the critical ratio rule often delays the processing of items until the need is more critical. This may, then, significantly decrease the in-process inventory investment, but if the jobs are run in the new sequence derived, R3S will be *extremely* late. Again, the message is to use this approach only for the *next* job and reevaluate when that job is completed.

ᏚOLVED EXERCISE 15.4 ❖ Sequencing Heuristics

Sequence the following jobs according to the runout and critical ratio rules.

Job	Inventory Remaining	Daily Demand	Batch Processing Time
1	12	2	4 days
2	28	5	10 days
3	8	1	5 days

Solution:

Job	Inventory	Demand	Runout	Sequence	Processing Time	Critical Ratio	Sequence
1	12	2	6.0	2	4	1.50	2
2	28	5	5.6	1	10	0.56	1
3	8	1	8.0	3	5	1.60	3

Both techniques result in the same sequence.

Spreadsheet Analysis: Sequencing Heuristics

In a fashion similar to sorting jobs using priority rules, spreadsheets can also be used to sort jobs using sequencing heuristics. To illustrate this, the spreadsheet shown below was developed for the data given in Solved Exercise 15.4.

	A	B	C	D	E	F
1				**Batch**		
2		**Inventory**	**Daily**	**Processing**		**Critical**
3	**Job**	**Remaining**	**Demand**	**Time**	**Runout**	**Ratio**
4	1	12	2	4	6.00	1.50
5	2	28	5	10	5.60	0.56
6	3	8	1	5	8.00	1.60
7						
8						
9	**Key Formulas:**					
10		cell E4: =B4/C4 [copy to cells E5:E6]				
11		cell F4: =E4/D4 [copy to cells F5:F6]				

Column A contains labels to identify the jobs. Inventory remaining, daily demand, and batch processing times were entered for each job, in columns B, C, and D respectively. In column E the runout time was calculated for each job as the ratio of remaining inventory to the daily demand rate. Thus, in cell E4, the formula: =B4/C4 was entered and then copied to cells E5:E6. Finally, the critical ratio (runout time/processing time) is calculated in column F for each job. In cell F4: =E4/D4 was entered and copied to cells F5:F6.

To sort the jobs on the basis of runout time, first the range A4:F6 was highlighted. Next, Data was selected from Excel's menu bar, and then Sort was selected from the next menu. In the Sort dialog box, Runout was specified in the Sort By box, and the Ascending radio button was selected as shown below.

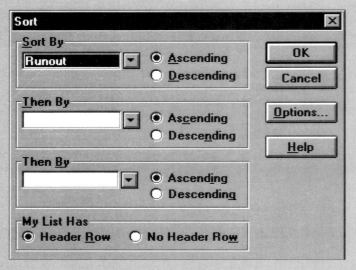

After we select the OK button in the Sort dialog box, the sorted spreadsheet appears as follows.

	A	B	C	D	E	F
1				Batch		
2		Inventory	Daily	Processing		Critical
3	Job	Remaining	Demand	Time	Runout	Ratio
4	2	28	5	10	5.60	0.56
5	1	12	2	4	6.00	1.50
6	3	8	1	5	8.00	1.60
7						
8						
9	Key Formulas:					
10		cell E4: =B4/C4 [copy to cells E5:E6]				
11		cell F4: =E4/D4 [copy to cells F5:F6]				

To sort the jobs on the basis of the critical ratio, all the previous steps are repeated except that Ratio is specified in the Sort By box. In this case, the critical ratio method and the runout method yield the same job sequence.

OPERATIONS IN PRACTICE

A New Scheduling System for LTV Steel's New Caster

At LTV's Cleveland Works, a continuous slab caster was installed to convert molten steel into solid steel slabs, which are later rolled into coils of sheet steel at a hot-strip mill. Along with the new caster, LTV installed a sophisticated, minicomputer–based scheduling system to select the best slab casting sequences on the basis of a wide variety of considerations. These included the types of steel needed to fill customer orders, the number of slabs produced from a 250-ton batch of molten steel, metallurgical limits on changes from one batch to the next, physical limits on changes in slab width, required maintenance intervals, and wastage in changing the grades, quality, or shape of the slabs.

The goal of the scheduling system is to select and batch customer orders for particular grades and quantities of steel so as to maximize on-time deliveries and caster productivity while minimizing semifinished inventory. These goals often conflict because scheduling for on-time delivery tends to produce schedules with short, inefficient, stop-and-go runs, whereas scheduling for efficient, productive runs tends to produce schedules with long runs that produce output too early, so that it must then be inventoried. In addition, long runs do not allow the flexibility of adding small, recent orders, or changes, to a run.

The benefits of this scheduling system for LTV have been many, especially the high productivity of the caster while producing steel to customers' orders. Although the caster was designed for a capacity of 150,000 tons of steel a month, tonnage has often exceeded this, reaching a record-breaking 222,145 tons at one point. The system is estimated to save LTV $1.95 million per year in combined personnel savings and increased production. Other benefits have been the ability to produce reasonable schedules from very unreasonable casting orders; quick response to unexpected situations; continual and unrelenting adherence, day in and day out, to the rules, restrictions, and complexities of evaluating sequences and building schedules; and avoidance of the long-term penalties of short-term errors in scheduling (Box and Herbe, 1988).

❖ Scheduling Multiple Recurring Batches

As illustrated in the sidebar on LTV, the two basic problems of multiple-batch production are to determine (1) what size batches to produce and (2) how the batches should be sequenced and scheduled. These two problems are highly interrelated, however—specifying the batch size to a large extent fixes the schedule, and vice versa.

For multiple batches, more than one output is competing for the *same* facilities. Inventories of the various outputs are used up (demanded) at different rates, can be produced at other rates, and undoubtedly have different economic lot sizes. Given that production capacity is limited, what is the "best" batch size for each of the products?

Consider the following very simple situation. A manufacturer has limited equipment available to make two products, A and B, for which demand, production rate,

*T*ABLE 15.6 ❖ Demand and Production Rates for
Two Products

	Product	
	A	B
Monthly demand, units	100	200
Production rate, units/month	200	500
Economic lot size, units	20	180

and economic lot size are shown in Table 15.6. Note that the manufacturer can produce all the monthly demand for A in half a month (demand rate/production rate =
100/200 = 0.5) and all the demand for B in 2/5 (or 0.4) month. In total, production
of both A and B requires only 0.9 month; therefore, productive capacity seems
quite adequate. The economic lot size for A is only 20 units, which take 20/200 =
0.1 month to produce and will last for 0.2 month. The economic lot size for B is 180
units, so this requires 180/500 = 0.36 month to produce. Assuming that A is scheduled on the equipment first, A finishes at 0.1 month and B at 0.46 month (0.1 for A
+ 0.36). In the meantime, however, product A will suffer a stockout (at 0.1 + 20/100
= 0.3 month). This situation is illustrated in Figure 15.9, for greater clarity.

The conclusion is that economic lot sizes computed for products on a single-
item basis are not at all economic when other products compete for the same production equipment. One way to avoid this problem is by producing in lots other
than the economic lot size—for example, in lots for each product that last an equal
length of time. This approach is called *equalization of runout time*.

In the previous two-product case, this would mean producing A for some fraction of a month and then B for the remainder of the month so that the units of A
and B produced would each last X months. The amount to be produced within the
month would thus be

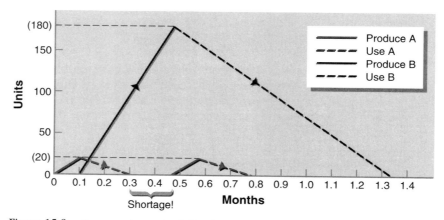

Figure 15.9   Two-product scheduling by economic lot size.

100X units of product A + 200X units of product B

The amount of time to make product A would be 100X/200 months, and the amount of time to make B would be 200X/500 months. Considering a one-month production plan:

$$\frac{100X}{200} + \frac{200X}{500} = 1$$

or

$$0.5X + 0.4X = 1$$

and therefore

$$X = \frac{1}{0.9} = 1.11 \text{ months}$$

100X = 111 units of A taking 111/200 = 0.555 month to produce
200X = 222 units of B taking 222/500 = 0.444 month to produce

This schedule is shown in Figure 15.10. Because of the extra capacity of the equipment, it can be shut down (for maintenance, etc.) for 0.11 month every cycle. Although shown as following the production of B, this shutdown could be divided between the two runs or allocated in any other manner. Figure 15.10 represents a *feasible* schedule, but it is not very efficient (although the ease of scheduling may outweigh any loss in cost efficiency). More complex techniques do exist for determining economic lot sizes for multiple-product batch operations, however (see the Bibliography).

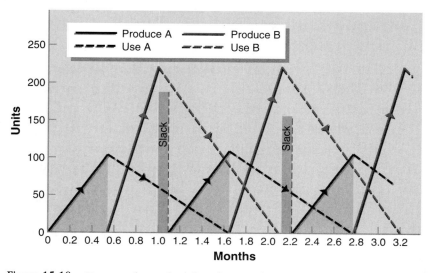

Figure 15.10   Two-product scheduling for equal usage periods.

$\mathcal{S}$OLVED EXERCISE 15.5 ❖ Batch Scheduling

a. Determine batch sizes and a scheduling sequence for the following items so that stocks are not depleted.

Products:	A	B	C
Annual demand, units:	1500	2500	100
Production rate, units/month:	280	400	80

b. Solve the problem again, assuming that demand for A drops to 1000 a year.

Solution:

a. First, check the capacity. To produce a month's demand of:

$$A \text{ will require } \frac{1500}{12(280)} = 0.446 \text{ month}$$

$$B \text{ will require } \frac{2500}{12(400)} = 0.521 \text{ month}$$

$$C \text{ will require } \frac{100}{12(80)} = \underline{0.104 \text{ month}}$$

$$\text{Total}: \quad 1.071 \text{ months}$$

Thus, there is insufficient capacity.

b. Now there is sufficient capacity (check it). Produce enough of each product to last X months:

$$\frac{1000X}{12(280)} + \frac{2500X}{12(400)} + \frac{100X}{12(80)} = 1 \text{ (month of production)}$$

or

$$0.298X + 0.521X + 0.104X = 1$$

$$X = 1.08\text{-month supply}$$

Thus, produce:

$$A: \frac{1000}{12}(1.08) = 90 \text{ units, requiring } \frac{90}{280} = 0.32 \text{ month}$$

$$B: \frac{2500}{12}(1.08) = 225 \text{ units, requiring } \frac{225}{400} = 0.56 \text{ month}$$

$$C: \frac{100}{12}(1.08) = 9 \text{ units, requiring } \frac{9}{80} = \underline{0.12 \text{ month}}$$

$$\text{Total} = 1.00 \text{ month}$$

Another alternative would be to produce all of C's annual demand at once, thereby saving the monthly setup cost for C. If we produced, each month, a month's worth of A, it would require (see above) 0.298 month, and a month's worth of B would take 0.521 month, for a total of 0.819 month. This leaves 1 − 0.819 = 0.181 month's worth of time to aggregate toward making C. A year's supply of C would take 100/80 = 1.25 months total. Thus, 1.25/0.181 = 6.9 months, or in 7 months we could produce a year's supply of C (if we had 7 months' inventory of C available). Then we could wait for a year before producing C again.

$\mathscr{S}$CHEDULING SERVICES

In this section we consider the scheduling of pure services. Much of what was said previously applies to the scheduling of services as well as products, but here we consider some scheduling issues of particular relevance to services.

Up to now we have dealt primarily with situations where the jobs (or recipients) were the items to be loaded, sequenced, or scheduled. There are, however, many operations for which scheduling of the jobs themselves is either inappropriate or impossible, and it is necessary to concentrate instead on scheduling one or more of the input resources. Therefore, the staff, the materials, or the facilities are scheduled to correspond, as closely as possible, with the expected arrival of the jobs. Such situations are common in service systems such as libraries, supermarkets, hospitals, urban alarm services, colleges, restaurants, and airlines.

In the scheduling of jobs we were primarily interested in minimizing the number of late jobs, minimizing the rejects, maximizing the throughput, and maximizing the utilization of available resources. In the scheduling of resources, however, there may be considerably more criteria of interest, especially when one of the resources being scheduled is staff. The desires of the staff regarding shifts, holidays, and work schedules become critically important when work schedules are variable and not all employees are on the same schedule. In these situations there usually exist schedules that will displease everyone and schedules that will satisfy most of the staff's more important priorities—and it is crucial that one of the latter be chosen rather than one of the former.

❖ Approaches to Resource Scheduling

The primary approach to the scheduling of resources is to match availability to demand (e.g., 7 P.M.–12 A.M. is the high period for fire alarms). By so doing, we are not required to provide a continuing high level of resources that are poorly utilized the great majority of the time. However, this requires that a good forecast of demand be available for the proper scheduling of resources. If demand cannot be accurately predicted, the resulting service with variable resources might be worse than using a constant level of resources.

Methods of increasing resources for peak demand include using overtime and part-time help and leasing equipment and facilities. Also, if multiple areas within an organization tend to experience varying demand, it is often helpful to use *floating workers* or combine departments to minimize variability. On occasion, new technologies, such as 24-hour computerized tellers and paying bills by telephone, can aid the organization.

As mentioned previously, the use of promotion and advertising to shift *demand* for resources is highly practical in many situations. Thus, we see *off-peak pricing* in the utilities and communication industries, summer sales of snowblowers in retailing, and cut rates for transportation and tours both in off-peak seasons (fall, winter) and at off-peak times (weekends, nights). Let us now consider how some specific service organizations approach their scheduling problems.

Hospitals

There are multiple needs for scheduling in hospitals. Although arrivals of patients (the jobs) are in part uncontrollable (e.g., emergencies), they are to some extent controllable through selective admissions for hernia operations, some maternity cases, in-hospital observation, and so on. With selective admissions, the hospital administrator can smooth the demand faced by the hospital and thereby improve service and increase the utilization of the hospital's limited resources.

Very specialized, expensive equipment such as a kidney machine is also carefully scheduled to allow other hospitals access to it, thus maximizing its utilization. Two-stage scheduling may exist in some cases: the availability of equipment may be scheduled for a hospital only during certain periods on certain days of the week (such as 7–11 A.M. Monday; 9 P.M.–4 A.M. Thursday to Friday; and 2–6 P.M. Sunday), and the scheduling of jobs (patients) for those periods of availability may be conducted by the hospitals (Mr. R. from 2 to 2:30 Sunday the sixth; Miss S. from 2:30 to 5). By sharing such expensive equipment among a number of hospitals, more hospitals have access to modern technology for their patients at a reasonable level of investment.

Of all the scheduling in hospitals, the most crucial is probably the scheduling of nurses, as illustrated in the sidebar describing Harper Hospital. This is because (1) it is mandatory, given the nature of hospitals, that nurses always be available; (2) nursing resources are a large expense for a hospital; and (3) there are a number of constraints on the scheduling of nurses, such as number of days per week, hours per day, weeks per year, and hours during the day.

OPERATIONS
IN PRACTICE

Scheduling Nurses' Staffing Levels
at Harper Hospital

Like many other hospitals, Harper Hospital of Detroit was under heavy pressure from Blue Cross, Medicare, and Medicaid to provide more health care at less cost. In addition, it needed to achieve more economies of scale from a merger that had taken place some years before. It also desired to improve its patient care. One target to help achieve these goals was a better system for scheduling nurses.

Previously, nurses were scheduled on the basis of strict bed counts, problems with inadequate staffing during the prior day, and requests for extra help. What was developed was a *patient classification system* (PCS) that incorporated labor standards to determine what levels of nursing were needed. At the end of each shift, designated nurses evaluated each area's patients by their condition and assigned them to a "care level" ranging from minimal to intensive. An hour before the next shift begins, the patients' needs for care are added up—accounting for new admissions, checkouts, and returns from surgery—to determine the total levels of care required. Given the levels in each area, nursing labor standards are used to determine how many nurses are needed on the next shift.

As a result of the new system, both the quality of patient care and the nurses' satisfaction went up. Annual labor savings from the new system were estimated as exceeding $600,000. Harper has further fine-tuned the PCS system and now recalibrates its standards every 2 years (Filley, 1983).

Urban Alarm Services

In urban services that respond to alarms—such as police, fire, and rescue services—the jobs (alarms) appear randomly and must be quickly serviced with sufficient resources, or extreme loss of life or property may result. In many ways this problem is similar to that of a hospital, since the cost of staffing personnel is a major expense, but floating fire companies and police SWAT units may be utilized where needed, and some services (such as fire inspection) can be scheduled to help *smooth* demand.

There is sometimes a major difference that vastly complicates some of these services (particularly fire): **duty tours** of extended duration, as opposed to regular shifts, which run over multiple days. These tours vary from 24 to 48 hours in teams of two to four members. Common schedules for such services are "two (days) on and three off" and "one on and two off," with every fifth tour or so off as well (for a running time off, every 3 weeks, of perhaps $3 + 2 + 3 = 8$ days). Because living and sleeping-in are considered part of the job requirements, the standard work-week is in excess of 40 hours—common values are 50 and 54 hours. Clearly, the scheduling of such duty tours is a complex problem, not only because of the unusual duration of the tours but also because of the implications concerning overtime, temptations of "moonlighting," and other such issues. For further discussion of such problems, consult the Bibliography.

Educational Services

Colleges and universities have scheduling requirements for all types of transformations: intermittent (such as counseling), continuous (English 1), batch (committee meetings), and project (regional conferences). In some of these situations the jobs (students) are scheduled, in some the staff (faculty administrators) are scheduled, and in others the facilities (classrooms, convention centers) are scheduled.

The primary problem, however, involves the scheduling of classes, assignment of students, and allocation of facilities and faculty resources to these classes. To obtain a manageable schedule, three difficult elements must be coordinated in this process:

1. Accurate forecast of students' demand for classes.
2. Limitations on available classroom space.
3. Multiple needs and desires of the faculty, such as
   ❖ Number of "preparations."
   ❖ Number of classes.
   ❖ Timing of classes.
   ❖ Level of classes.
   ❖ Leave requirements (sabbatical, without pay, etc.).
   ❖ Release requirements (research, projects, administration).

Because of the number of objectives in such scheduling problems, a variety of multicriteria approaches have been used to aid in finding acceptable schedules, including simulation, goal programming, and interactive modeling.

In summary, the approach to scheduling services is usually to match resources and forecasted demand. Since demand cannot be controlled, it is impossible to build up inventory ahead of time, and backordering is usually not feasible. Careful scheduling of staff, facilities, and materials is done instead, with (limited) flexibility achieved through floating part-time and overtime labor and off-peak rates to encourage leveling of demand.

Scheduling techniques for resources are similar to those for scheduling jobs: the use of indexes, weights, priorities, programming, simulation, and so forth. Simulation appears to be an especially useful approach, since it can handle multiple criteria in highly varied situations. The main advantage of simulation is that actual operational conditions—equipment breakdowns, emergencies, and so forth—can be easily included to determine their effect. Various schedules can be tested, and their impact on resource utilization and level of service under varying distributions of demand can be found with ease. The best schedule is often not the one that optimizes the use of resources or minimizes lateness for the expected demand, but rather the one that gives acceptable results under all likely operating conditions.

An important element in the scheduling of operations to produce either products or services concerns the waiting lines, or *queues*, that tend to build up in front of the operations. With an unpaced production line, for example, buffer inventory between operations builds up at some times and disappears at other times, owing to natural variability in the difficulty of the operations.

In the production of services, this variability is even greater because of both the amount of highly variable human *input* and the variable *requirements* for services. What is more, the "items" in queue are often people, who tend to complain and make trouble if kept waiting too long. Thus, it behooves the operations manager to provide adequate service to keep long queues from forming. This costs more money for service facilities and staffs. But long queues cost money also, in the form of in-process inventory, unfinished orders, lost sales, and ill will. Figure 15.11 conceptually illustrates, as a function of the capacity of the service facility, the trade-offs in these two costs.

1. *Cost of waiting:* In-process inventory, ill will, lost sales. This cost decreases with service capacity.
2. *Cost of service facilities:* Equipment, supplies, and staff. This cost increases with service capacity.

At some point the total of the two costs is minimized, and it is at this point that managers typically wish to operate. *Queuing* (or *waiting line*) theory has been developed to address exactly these kinds of situations. (It is addressed in more detail in the supplement to this chapter.)

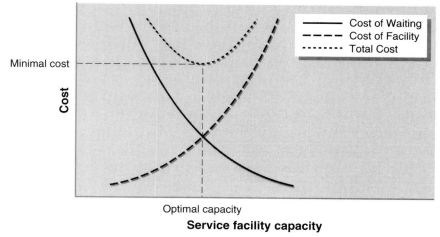

Figure 15.11   Relevant costs of queuing.

❖ Overbooking

Overbooking in services is an attempt to reduce costs through better schedule management, as illustrated in the sidebar on Scandinavian Airlines. This technique is based on the inventory solution for the "newsboy problem"—the single-period, uncertain-demand situation discussed in Chapter 12. (You may wish to read or reread that section.) Recall that two approaches to the problem gave the same result: using a decision table to calculate the expected outcomes of each possible policy, and using marginal-incremental analysis to find the "critical" probability where the expected gain from stocking one more item is not worth the expected loss.

To understand the situation in a service, let us use an example from Chapter 12 in two very different ways. First, consider a situation in which overbooking is not an alternative but a variable number of resources can be supplied, as in the newsboy's situation. Let us assume that an airline can quickly install between 25 and 35 seats on a plane at a cost per seat of $100 and that at the gate it sells tickets for $150 to all who show up. Given the flight history in Table 15.7, how many seats should the airline install to maximize its profit? Assume that an unfilled seat represents a loss for that flight of $100 and that the plane is refitted for every new flight.

Using either decision analysis (similar to Tables 12.5 and 12.6, but with the results in thousands) or the incremental approach (Table 12.7), we find that the best number of seats to install is 30. The logic is the same as for the newsboy problem.

In fact, airlines do change the number of seats on planes much as described here. But an example that better illustrates overbooking is to assume that the number of seats on the plane is fixed at 28 and to ask how many reservations the airline should accept, given the chances described in Table 15.7 of no-shows when 32 reservations have been accepted. (If a smaller number of reservations are accepted, then the probabilities just move down correspondingly; if more are accepted, they move up, but the distribution remains the same as in the table.)

Suppose that a profit of $50 is made for each passenger carried, but a cost is incurred if a passenger with a reservation has to be turned away. This cost could be a free ticket, ill will, passage on another airline, or whatever. If the cost is low—say, less than the profit—then it will be to the airline's advantage to overbook quite a bit (although possibly not all the way to 32, since there would then be a 90 percent chance of having an overbooking cost). On the other hand, suppose that the cost is very high—much more than the profit. Then the airline would be very reluctant to overbook much at all, out of fear of having to pay one or more costs of overbook-

𝒯ABLE 15.7 ❖ Demand for Flights

Demand	Relative Frequency
28	0.10
29	0.20
30	0.35
31	0.25
32	0.10
	1.00

OPERATIONS IN PRACTICE

Overbooking for Scandinavian Airlines

Scandinavian Airlines (SAS) operates a fleet of DC–9 aircraft with 110 seats each. If SAS accepts reservations for only these 110 seats, "no-shows" (passengers who fail to show up for a flight) will refuse to pay for their reservations and SAS can lose from 5 to 30 percent of the available seats. If there are 100 flights every day, these no-shows can cost the airline as much as $50 million a year. To avoid this loss, all airlines overbook flights by accepting a fixed percentage of reservations in excess of what is actually available.

The management of SAS decided to develop an automated overbooking system to include such factors as class, destination, days before departure, current reservations, and existing cancellations. The objective of the system was to determine an optimal overbooking policy for the different classes on each flight, considering the costs of ill will, alternative flight arrangements, empty seats, and upgrading or downgrading a passenger's reserved class.

A number of interesting findings were made in the process of conducting the study. For example, an early finding was that the probability that a reservation would be canceled was independent of the time the reservation was made. When the system was completed, it was tested against the heuristics used by experienced employees who had a good "feel" for what the overbooking rate should be. It was found that the automated system would increase SAS's net revenue by about $2 million a year (Alstrup, 1989).

ing. Table 15.8 gives the probabilities of demand for each set of overbookings accepted, as specified in the previous paragraph. Assume that turning a passenger away costs the airline $20, how many reservations should be accepted? Suppose the cost is $100?

Using the probabilities with accepting 32 reservations (shown in Table 15.7), we can calculate the costs and profits according to Table 15.9. (There is no sense in accepting more than 32 reservations, because this will definitely fill the plane.) Here we see that the total profit is $1359. The process is repeated for 31 reservations, and

$\mathcal{T}$ABLE 15.8 ❖ Demand Probabilities with Reservations

	Reservations				
Relative Frequency	28	29	30	31	32
0.10	24	25	26	27	28
0.20	25	26	27	28	29
0.35	26	27	28	29	30
0.25	27	28	29	30	31
0.10	28	29	30	31	32
1.00					

$\mathcal{T}$ABLE 15.9 ❖ Expected Profit with 32 Reservations

	Demand					
	28	29	30	31	32	Total
Probabilities	0.10	0.20	0.35	0.25	0.10	
Seats filled (S)	28	28	28	28	28	
Profit: $50 S	1400	1400	1400	1400	1400	
Turnaways (T)	0	1	2	3	4	
Cost: $20 T	0	20	40	60	80	
Net profit	1400	1380	1360	1340	1320	
Expected net profit	140	276	476	335	132	$1359

the calculations are given in Table 15.10. Continuing with 30, 29, and 28 reservations (it makes no sense to accept fewer than 28 reservations), we get the values shown in Table 15.11. Clearly, the maximum profit is obtained with 31 reservations.

If the turnaway cost is raised to $100, the results are shown in Table 15.12. Now the highest profit is obtained with 29 reservations. It is interesting that the answer in this situation is different from the earlier example. We have used the simpler decision table in this demonstration, but marginal-incremental analysis can be used just as well.

$\mathcal{T}$ABLE 15.10 ❖ Expected Profit with 31 Reservations

	Demand					
	27	28	29	30	31	Total
Probabilities	0.10	0.20	0.35	0.25	0.10	
Seats filled (S)	27	28	28	28	28	
Profit: $50 S	1350	1400	1400	1400	1400	
Turnaways (T)	0	0	1	2	3	
Cost: $20 T	0	0	20	40	60	
Net profit	1350	1400	1380	1360	1340	
Expected net profit	135	280	483	340	134	$1372

$\mathcal{T}$ABLE 15.11 ❖ Expected Profit at $20 Turnaway Cost

Reservations	Expected Profits
32	$1359
31	$1372 (best)
30	$1371
29	$1345.5
28	$1302.5

$\mathcal{T}$ABLE 15.12 ❖ Expected Profit at $100 Turnaway Cost

Reservations	Expected Profits
32	$1195
31	$1280
30	$1335
29	$1337.5 (best)
28	$1302.5

$\mathcal{S}$OLVED EXERCISE 15.6 ❖ Overbooking

The Arms Hotel has 56 rooms. An unfilled room represents $50 a night in lost profit, whereas every turnaway due to a filled room costs $30 in ill will. If N reservations are accepted, the probability that N, $N-1$, and $N-2$ guests will actually show is 0.2, 0.5, or 0.3, respectively. How many reservations should be accepted?

Solution:

Calculate the expected cost for each alternative: 56, 57, 58.

	Reservations Accepted								
	56			**57**			**58**		
Demand	56	55	54	57	56	55	58	57	56
Probability	0.2	0.5	0.3	0.2	0.5	0.3	0.2	0.5	0.3
Unfilled rooms	0	1	2	0	0	1	0	0	0
Lost profit	0	50	100	0	0	50	0	0	0
Turnaways (T)	0	0	0	1	0	0	2	1	0
Cost, $30T$	0	0	0	30	0	0	60	30	0
Total cost	0	50	100	30	0	50	60	30	0
Expected cost	0	25	30	6	0	15	12	15	0
Total		$55			$21			$27	

The best alternative is 57, for an expected cost of $21.

$\mathcal{C}$HAPTER IN PERSPECTIVE

This chapter is the fifth addressing the product supply process. Chapter 11 began our discussion of this process, overviewing aggregate and master scheduling. Chapter 12 continued the discussion and addressed determining when to order independent-demand items, and how much to order, to support the plans developed in Chapter 11. Then in Chapter 13 and 14 we turned our attention to the management of dependent-demand items with MRP and JIT systems, respectively. In the present chapter we have focused on the development of detailed schedules. Major topics covered in this chapter included using priority rules for job-shop scheduling, the distinction between forward and backward scheduling, the theory of constraints, flow-shop scheduling, and detailed scheduling for services.

❖ CHECK YOUR UNDERSTANDING

1. Briefly define: *flow time, queue time, Gantt chart, priority rules, overbooking, theory of constraints, duty tours.*

2. Contrast forward and backward scheduling.

3. Review the purposes for and results of each priority rule. What are the advantages and disadvantages of each?

4. Contrast the use of priority rules in job shops with the use of runout and critical ratio heuristics in flow shops.

5. Briefly explain the nine guidelines in the theory of constraint.

6. What is the difference between SOT and Johnson's rule? Aren't they about the same thing?

7. What is the difference between job shop and flow shop scheduling?

8. How might the Gantt chart help in scheduling, since it is not a technique in itself?

9. According to the guidelines of the theory of constraints, the utilization of a nonbottleneck is determined by the bottlenecks. Why is this so?

10. Is flow time the same as customer waiting time? Explain.

11. What are the critical ratio and runout methods actually minimizing in order to determine priorities? Which is better?

12. Explain how reducing the size of a transfer batch affects the total flow time for that batch. Are any additional costs incurred as a result of reducing the transfer batch?

13. Explain why an hour lost at a bottleneck resource is an hour lost to the entire shop. Why is an hour saved at a nonbottleneck resource a mirage?

❖ EXPAND YOUR UNDERSTANDING

1. How ethical is it to overbook (and guarantee) limited service capacity in a restaurant? What about a hospital, where lack of service could have serious, perhaps fatal, consequences?

2. Might other nations or cultures have a different opinion about the acceptability, or morality, of overbooking certain service facilities? Can you give some examples?

3. With the availability of computers to simulate and test all possible variations of schedules, why do we have to rely on priority rules or other nonoptimal approaches to scheduling?

4. Would the priority rules and flow shop heuristics be appropriate for services? If so, when?

5. Figure 15.3 shows one way of arranging three sets of data among two axes. How else might a Gantt-type chart be arranged?

6. For what situations is backward scheduling best? Forward scheduling? Which would you use if a salesperson wanted to add a rush job to the shop's current load?

7. What other approach might be used for scheduling multiple recurring batches? Might any optimization be possible? How?

8. Many services, such as airlines, conduct their scheduling in two stages. First, an overall macro schedule is constructed and optimized for costs and service to the customer. This schedule is then considered to be the baseline for detailed scheduling to attempt to achieve. The second, detailed stage is then a real-time schedule to adjust the macro schedule for any necessary changes, emergencies, and so on. Describe how this might work for airlines, hospitals, schools, and urban alarm services. What serious problems might arise with this approach?

❖ APPLY YOUR UNDERSTANDING
Data Tronics

Data Tronics assembles custom-printed circuit boards (PCBs) in small quantities. To process a particular order, the assembly line must first be set up for the order. This involves loading the PCB components (e.g., chips, resistors, and capacitors) into the auto-insertion equipment and loading the correct software that controls the automated equipment. Once the line is set up, a customer order is processed and then the line is set up for the next customer order. Data Tronics runs three shifts per day, five days per week. Occasionally, overtime is scheduled during weekends.

Rebecca Wilson was intensely studying the figures (Exhibits I and II) on her desk related to the most recently accepted orders for Data Tronics. She had graduated from Purdue University in industrial engineering the previous June and had been hired to improve Data Tronics's production flow in its shop. The managers were particularly interested in getting jobs out faster so that they could be paid, thereby improving the firm's cash flow.

In the past, Data Tronics's approach to scheduling was to simply work on jobs in order of receipt. Rebecca had been considering some other possibilities, however, such as SOT and due date. She wondered what each of these rules would do for Data Tronics's cash flow. She decided to analyze these four jobs and consider them typical of all the jobs received by Data Tronics. In order not to bias the results by the particular terms of the negotiated prices, she planned to assume that they all had the same profitability.

$\mathcal{E}$XHIBIT I ❖ Recent Customer Orders Listed in Order Received

Customer	Days Left Prior to Promised Delivery Date	Processing Time per Board (hours)	Order Size (number of PCBs)
IBX	3	0.15	100
ESI	2	0.25	150
QBS	4	0.20	200
X-Pro	6	0.10	125

$\mathcal{E}$XHIBIT II ❖ Time (in hours) to set up the assembly line for a new job on the basis of the previous job.

For example, if QBS is the first job of the four processed after the job currently being processed, the time to set up the line would be 2.2 hours. Likewise, if X-Pro's order is processed right after IBX's, the time to set up the line for X-Pro's order would be 6.6 hours.

Switch Line From Job	To Job			
	IBX	ESI	QBS	X-Pro
Current Job	2.5	3.6	2.2	4.6
IBX	—	5.1	6.3	6.6
ESI	4.4	—	4.1	6.6
QBS	6.3	3.4	—	2.4
X-Pro	4.2	3.2	4.1	—

Questions

1. The time needed to set up an assembly line varies with the sequence in which the jobs are processed. How does this affect the FCFS, due date, and SOT priority rules?
2. Compare the performance of the FCFS, due date, and SOT rules in terms of average flow time and lateness. In terms of cash flow, which rule is best?
3. Determine the average flow time and lateness for all possible job sequences. How does the best sequence compare with the ones you found in question 2? How much more work would there have been if there were six jobs instead of four?
4. How valid is Rebecca's assumption about the equal profitability of each job? Might this lead her to an incorrect conclusion concerning the best priority rule for Data Tronics? Consider the fact that profitability is not the same as revenue; should Rebecca change her assumption?

❖ EXERCISES

1. Sequence the following jobs by due date, SOT, LOT, and dynamic slack.

Job	Due Date	Operation Time
R	6	4
S	4	1
T	5	3
V	2	2

2. Calculate the average flow time, lateness, and tardiness for each of the priority rules in Exercise 1.

3. More information is given below about the five jobs in Table 15.1. Continue Table 15.2 for rules LOT, SS, SS/RO, and DS/RO.

Job	Days Ago Arrived*	Remaining Operations
ABC	6	2
PDQ	2	6
XYZ	1	1
Z11	3	4
Z12	5	3

*Today is date 0.

4. Sequence the following jobs by Johnson's rule.

	Job									
Machines	A	B	C	D	E	F	G	H	I	J
1	33	37	31	38	35	36	43	34	32	30
2	41	35	30	39	32	40	38	43	31	34

5. Chippo Bakery Company has five cakes that must be produced today for pickup this evening. Each cake must go through the bakery department and then the decorating department. Each department can process only one cake at a time. If the following estimates are available for production in each department, in what order should the cakes be scheduled?

	Baking (minutes)	Decorating (minutes)
Cake 1	30	30
Cake 2	20	15
Cake 3	20	45
Cake 4	15	35
Cake 5	17	25

6. Calculate when each cake will be completed in Exercise 5. What is the total idle time of the two departments while the cakes are being made? Draw a Gantt chart for your solution.

7. Use the runout and critical ratio rules to derive a processing sequence for the following jobs.

Job	Inventory	Daily Demand	Processing Time (days)
1	30	5	4
2	110	7	10
3	70	3	12
4	50	10	3
5	20	2	1
6	90	8	8

8. a. Draw a Gantt chart to depict the schedule for four jobs on two machines, A and B. Today is Wednesday, August 5. The firm is closed on Saturday and Sunday.

   Job

   1: Two days on A, one on B, one on A.

   2: One day on B, one day on A.

   3: One day on B, two on A.

   4: One day on A, two on B.

   Machine

   A: Preventive maintenance August 12.

   B: Operator called in with a toothache this morning; will be in at noon for half a day today.

   Material

   Job 2: Materials delay for work on machine A, will arrive August 10.

   b. Show the actual progress as of August 11, 8 A.M.

   August 6: Machine B is down all day for repairs.

   August 10: Materials for Job 2 on A did not arrive.

   Job 3 finished (or is) a day ahead of schedule.

   Job 4 delayed a day on A owing to defective materials.

9. Johnson's rule can be extended to three machines under certain circumstances. Using the following rule, solve the problem in the table and find the completion times for each job: If the minimum time on the first machine is greater than or equal to the maximum on the second machine, or if the minimum time on the third machine is greater than or equal to the maximum on the second, add the time on the second to both the time on the first and the time on the third, and solve as a two-machine problem.

Machine	Job				
	J_1	J_2	J_3	J_4	J_5
M_1	2	3	0	1	3
M_2	1	2	2	1	2
M_3	3	2	3	3	4

10. Assume that the process times in Table 15.5 are 2, 1, and 6, respectively (instead of 4, 2, and 12). Track the inventories of the three jobs under each of the two processing sequences given in Table 15.5. What happens? Solve the problem again by resequencing the orders as the facilities complete a job. Use both sequencing methods. What sequence do you now get with each method? Are there still problems?

11. Two products, W and Z, have to be produced on the same facilities. Annual demands (and production capacity) for W and Z are 1800 units (3000 units capacity) and 1000 units (2500 units capacity), respectively. Design a feasible production schedule for these products.

12. Use both forward and backward scheduling to add another job, D, to the schedules in Figure 15.5a and b. D is due in hour 8 and has the following facility processing requirements: III (2), I (1), II (2).

13. Schedule the following jobs on two shifts to best meet their due hours.

Job	Hour Due	Facility, Hours Required (in order)
A	10	3 (2), 1 (2), 2 (2), 1 (1)
B	3	2 (1), 3 (2)
C	7	1 (3), 2 (2), 3 (1)
D	12	2 (1), 3 (2), 2 (2), 1 (2), 3 (1)
E	15	3 (1), 2 (3), 1 (3), 3 (3), 2 (1)

14. Accept as many of the following jobs as possible on the loaded (with jobs W, Y, and Z) facilities below and set promised delivery hours, as early as possible, for them. All the jobs must be completed, if accepted, within the 8-hour period.

Job	Facility, Hours (in order)
A	2 (1), 1 (2), 2 (1)
B	1 (2), 2 (1), 1 (1)
C	1 (1), 2 (1), 1 (2), 2 (1)
D	2 (1), 1 (1)

Hour	Facility 1	Facility 2
1	W	Y
2	W	—
3	—	W
4	Z	—
5	—	Z
6	—	—
7	—	—
8	—	—

15. A restaurant has 30 tables. If it accepts N reservations, the probability that N will arrive is 0.1; $N-1$ is 0.2; $N-2$ is 0.3; and $N-3$ is 0.4. If each unfilled table costs $20 but a customer turned away costs $10, find how many reservations to accept. Solve again, assuming that a customer turned away costs $25.

16. Referring to Exercises 1 and 2, develop a spreadsheet to sort the four jobs using the specified priority rules. Include formulas that calculate average flow time, lateness, and tardiness for each job sequence.

17. Develop a spreadsheet to sort the jobs listed in Exercise 3 for rules LOT, SS, SS/RO, and DS/RO.

18. Develop a spreadsheet to calculate runout and critical ratio for the 6 jobs listed in Exercise 7. Use the spreadsheet to determine the sequence the jobs would be processed in using the runout and critical ratio.

Chapter 15 SUPPLEMENT _____
Waiting-Line Analysis

The formation of waiting lines, also known as *queues,* is a very common phenomenon in operations. People wait for service, items wait for repair, products wait for processing, and so on. Managers often desire to know how long the wait will be and how much the wait will be decreased if they add resources to the service process such as additional servers or productivity-enhancing equipment. The basic problem facing the manager is to find the best trade-off between the cost of service facilities and the cost of waiting, usually ill will.

The analysis of queues to determine waiting time and other characteristics can sometimes involve sophisticated mathematical techniques. This is particularly true for unusual situations such as a service facility with a limited waiting area or multiple servers. In this supplement we will consider only the most basic queuing situations and derive the characteristics for these queues through fairly simple graphs and equations.

The pioneer in queuing theory was a Danish telephone engineer named A. K. Erlang, who developed the theory in the 1920s to predict telephone call service. Given an arriving population and a service facility (or facilities) with a certain speed of service, the theory will determine, given certain assumptions, the expected (average) length of the queue, the number of people or items in the queue, the idle time of the facility, and other such criteria for the performance of a service facility.

The structure of the queuing system to be considered here is illustrated in Figure 15S.1. It is assumed that the arrivals wait in *one* queue (or take a number for service or add their names to a list) and, as they come to the front of the line, go to the next available service facility. This system is called first-come, first-served (FCFS), and is commonly adopted for reasons of fairness. The arrivals are assumed to come at random, with average rate λ (arrivals per unit time). Service is also assumed to be random, with the average μ (services per unit time when there is a queue). Note in Figure 15S.1 that the queue, as normally interpreted, does *not* include the arrival or arrivals currently being serviced at the service facility or facilities.

$\mathcal{T}$HE FORMATION OF QUEUES _____

If a service can be performed *before* the recipient arrives and then stored until his or her arrival (and the demand rate is less than the service rate), a continuing queue will not form. For example, if punch is being served at a party where people arrive for refreshments, on the average, every 4 seconds and it takes 4 seconds to pour a drink, there will never be a permanent queue. This is because even when people are not coming for a drink, the server keeps on pouring drinks; then, when a batch of people all come at once, the drinks are ready.

However, if mixed drinks are being served so that the mix cannot be poured *until the person gives his or her order,* a queue will tend to form under exactly the same conditions. To see this, let us assume that people arrive consecutively 2 and then 6 seconds apart (thereby averaging 4). The results are tabulated in Table 15S.1.

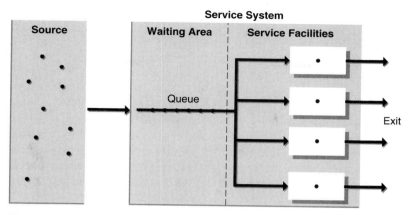

Figure 15S.1 Queuing system structure.

$\mathcal{T}_{ABLE}$ 15S.1 ❖ Formation of a Queue

Time (seconds)	Waiting	Time (seconds)	Waiting
1	—	26	G, F
2	A	27	G, F
3	A	28	G
4	A	29	G
5	A	30	G
6	—	31	G
7	—	32	H
8	B	33	H
9	B	34	I, H
10	C, B	35	I, H
11	C, B	36	I
12	C	37	I
13	C	38	I
14	C	39	I
15	C	40	J
16	D	41	J
17	D	42	K, J
18	E, D	43	K, J
19	E, D	44	K
20	E	45	K
21	E	46	K
22	E	47	K
23	E	48	L
24	F	49	L
25	F	50	M, L

As seen in the table, following the arrival of person B there is never a time when someone is not waiting for a drink, either being served or in a queue. On many occasions there is a queue of one person waiting to be served (while another is being served). Starting from the arrival of B at 8 seconds, there are 11 seconds (out of 50 − 7 = 43 seconds or 11/43 = 26 percent of the time) when a person is waiting to be served. The *expected queue length* in this case is thus said to be 0.26 × 1 = 0.26 persons.

In some situations, as in medicine and dentistry, the recipients do *not* arrive randomly but are *scheduled*. If possible, in such a case appointments should be scheduled so that the first recipient has the most *definite* required service time and the last recipient the most *variable* service time. For similar needs, variability is often proportional to the expected length of service. That is, a 10-minute appointment may run 5–15 minutes, but a 4-hour appointment may run $3^1/_2$ to $4^1/_2$ hours. Scheduling in this manner then minimizes the potential wait for all *subsequent* recipients.

SSUMPTIONS OF QUEUING THEORY

Queuing theory can determine the expected length of a queue, and many other such variables, for situations much more realistic than this—as for variable service and arrival rates and for more than one server. There are, however, some basic assumptions that must be satisfied.

- ❖ **The system is in "steady state."** Note in the example above that we ignored the 7-second "start-up transient" in Table 15S.1. This time to reach steady state is usually a small fraction of an ongoing service system and may be ignored. (However, some systems, such as banks, may always be in transient states such as 9:00 A.M. start-up, 10:00 A.M. coffee break, 11:30 A.M.–1:30 P.M. noon rush, 2:00 P.M. break, 2:30 P.M. closing rush. In these cases queuing theory is inappropriate, and simulation must be used.)

- ❖ **First-come, first-served "priority discipline."** We assume that people (items) are served in the order they join the queue and that only one queue exists, even if there are multiple service facilities.

- ❖ **An unlimited source exists.** We assume that we never run out of recipients from the source.

- ❖ **Unlimited queue space is available.** We assume that there is sufficient space in the (single) queue to hold any recipient who desires service.

- ❖ **Standard queue behavior, which prohibits:**

  Balking—refusing to join the queue.

  Reneging—leaving the queue before being served.

  Jockeying—switching between multiple queues as their lengths vary.

  Cycling—returning to the queue following service (e.g., children with playground equipment).

❖ ***Random arrivals and service.*** As stated earlier, the random arrivals occur at the average rate λ and the services at the average rate μ when this system is busy.

Although limited results have been obtained for situations that relax some of the above restrictions, we will not consider them here.

$\mathscr{C}$ALCULATION OF QUEUING CHARACTERISTICS _____

The assumption of random arrivals and services results in a particular distribution of arrival and service rates known as the *Poisson distribution*. With the assumptions given above, these distributions allow us to find a number of useful characteristics that describe the queue and the service process. The most important characteristic of a queue is its expected (average) length, L_q. This characteristic is presented in Figure 15S.2 as a function of two parameters of the queuing situation.

❖ *K*—Number of servers or service facilities, known as *channels* (four are shown in Figure 15S.1) in the service system.
❖ λ/μ—"Utilization" of the facility. If the arrival rate λ exceeds the service rate of a single server μ, the queue will grow indefinitely unless more than one server is available.

Note in Figure 15S.2 that as curves of constant *K* reach values $\lambda/\mu = K$ (near the top of the chart), the length of the queue, L_q gets larger and larger. This is because the arrivals tend to fully utilize the capacity of the system. For example, if the arrival rate is twice that of the service rate, this will keep two servers busy full time. When there is only one service facility (i.e., $K = 1$), L_q can be calculated as

$$L_q = \frac{\lambda^2}{\mu(\mu - \lambda)}$$

Once a value for L_q is found using either Figure 15S.2 or the above formula, many other interesting characteristics describing the system can be derived from it.

1. *Average number of items in the system,* both in the queue and in service combined, *L.* The number being served, on the average, is simply the utilization of the service facility, λ/μ. Thus,

$$L = L_q + \frac{\lambda}{\mu}$$

2. *Expected waiting time in the queue,* W_q. This is *not,* as might be expected, simply the average length of the queue times the service time. Rather, another relationship is used: average *length* of the queue will equal average *waiting time* multiplied by average *arrival rate:* $L_q = W_q \lambda$. Rearranging terms,

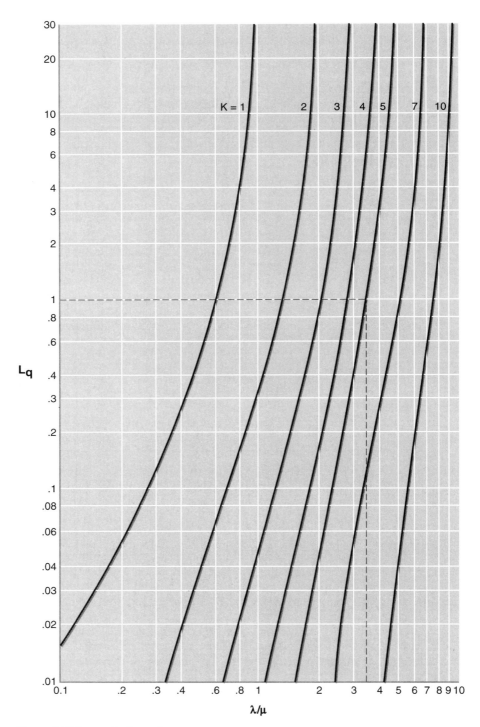

Figure 15S.2   Multichannel queue.

$$W_q = \frac{L_q}{\lambda}$$

3. *Expected total time in the system, W.* This will be queuing time plus service time, $1/\mu$.

$$W = W_q + \frac{1}{\mu}$$

4. For service systems composed of a *single server* (channel) we can determine the *probability P_n of n items occupying the system* (both queuing and in service).

$$P_n = \left(\frac{\lambda}{\mu}\right)^n \left(1 - \frac{\lambda}{\mu}\right) \text{ for } K = 1$$

Note that when $n = 0$ this reduces to the *probability P_0 that the system is empty.*

$$P_0 = 1 - \frac{\lambda}{\mu} \text{ for } K = 1$$

The *probability that the system is busy,* otherwise known as the *utilization* of the facility, is thus $1 - P_0$ or

$$P_{\text{busy}} = \frac{\lambda}{\mu} \text{ for } K = 1$$

❖ Example

One of the most confounding aspects of waiting-line analysis is that it defies normal expectations. For example, if a service system with one server results in an average queue length of 12 recipients, then most people expect that adding a second server will cut the queue in half, to 6 recipients. But consider the following situation. A one-person service facility can serve, on the average, 10 customers per hour and customers arrive, on the average, every 7.5 minutes. What will happen if a second server is added?

Analysis

$$\lambda = \frac{60}{7.5} = 8 / \text{hour}, \quad \mu = 10 / \text{hour}, \quad \frac{\lambda}{\mu} = 0.8, \quad K = 1$$

From Figure 15S.2, $L_q = 3$, approximately. If a second server is added, then reading from Figure 15S.2 at $K = 2$ and $\lambda/\mu = 0.8$, we find $L_q = 0.14$. That is, the expected line length reduces by

$$\frac{3.0 - 0.14}{3.0} = 0.95$$

or 95 percent. This is much greater than just one-half (50 percent). The reasons stem from the randomness of the arrivals and the fact that services cannot be produced during idle periods and stored for use in busy periods. A second server is no help when the facility is idle or only one customer is being served, but when *groups of people* arrive, the second server is a *great* help.

Let us now consider an example of a more complex managerial situation.

❖ Gupta Trucking

Mr. R. Gupta is trying to estimate the best number of work crews to employ in a local excavating job in India. The crews can each load, on the average, four trucks per hour but cost 100 rupees (Rs 100) per hour in total wages. (Only one crew can work on a truck at one time.) On the other hand, the idle time of trucks is charged at Rs 160 per hour. If the trucks arrive every 20 minutes, on the average, how many crews should Mr. Gupta hire? (Assume that loading and arrival rates are random.)

Analysis

$$\lambda = 60/20 = 3/\text{hour}$$

$$\mu = 4/\text{hour}$$

$$\frac{\lambda}{\mu} = 0.75$$

One crew.   From Figure 15S.2 at the intersection of $\lambda/\mu = 0.75$ and $K = 1$, we find $L_q = 2.3$. Hence: $W_q = 2.3/3 = 0.77$ hours per truck. At three trucks per hour, the total hourly waiting cost of the trucks is

$$0.77 \times 3 \times \text{Rs } 160 = \text{Rs } 370$$
$$+ \underline{\text{Rs } 100} \text{ (cost of one crew)}$$

Total   Rs 470/hour

Two crews.   From Figure 15S.2 at $K = 2$: $L_q = 0.12$

$$W_q = \frac{0.12}{3} = 0.04$$

waiting cost of trucks: $0.04 \times 3 \times \text{Rs } 160 = \text{Rs } 20$

cost of two crews: Rs 200

Total   Rs 220/hour

Three or more crews.   The most that can now be saved from the cost of waiting trucks is Rs 20, so clearly it is not worthwhile to add another Rs 100 crew. The best answer is, therefore, *two* crews.

Spreadsheet Analysis

The formulas for calculating the characteristics of a queue can be easily entered into a spreadsheet. Once it is created, decision makers can use the spreadsheet to quickly investigate a variety of scenarios. To illustrate this, the spreadsheet shown below was developed for single-channel queuing situations.

	A	B	C
1	**Queuing Analysis (K=1)**		
2			
3	**Model Inputs:**		
4	Mean Arrival Rate (lambda) per Hour	8	
5	Mean Service Rate (mu) per Hour	10	
6	Number of Items in System (n)	3	
7			
8	**Model Outputs:**		*Formulas:*
9	Utilization	0.80	=B4/B5
10	Average Number of Items in the Queue (L_q)	3.20	=(B4^2)/B5*(B5-B4))
11	Average Number of Items in the System (L)	4.00	=B10+B9
12	Expected Waiting Time in the Queue (W_q)	0.40	=B10/B4
13	Expected Total Time in the System (W)	0.50	=B12+(1/B5)
14	Probability of n Items Occupying the System (P_n)	0.10	=B9^B6)*(1-B9)
15	Probability System is Idle (P_0)	0.20	=1-B9
16	Probability System is Busy (P_{busy})	0.80	=1-B15

The spreadsheet is divided into two major sections: model inputs and model outputs. The mean arrival rate (λ), and the mean service rate (μ) are required inputs. Optionally, the number of items in the system (n) can be entered in cases where the decision maker is interested in calculating the probability that n items are in the system.

Given the information entered in model inputs, formulas were entered in cells B9:B16 to calculate the information about model outputs. The formulas entered in cells B9:B16 are listed in cells C9:C16.

To illustrate the use of the spreadsheet, the arrival rate and service rate used in the earlier example were entered into cells B4 and B5, respectively. Also, for illustrative purposes, we assume that the decision maker is interested in determining the probability that there are exactly three items in the system.

According to the results, the single server would be utilized 80 percent of the time. Note that the utilization (cell B9) and the probability that the system is busy (cell B16) will always be the same for single-channel queues (i.e., $K = 1$).

In this situation, the average number of items in the queue is 3.2 and the average number of items in the system is 4.00. The time an item will wait in the queue is 0.40 hour (or 24 minutes) and the expected total time an item will spend in the system is 0.50 hour (or 30 minutes). Finally, there is a 10 percent probability that there will be three items in the system and a 20 percent probability that there will be no items, resulting in an idle system.

Suppose that the company expects the arrival rate to increase to 9 arrivals per hour because of a special promotion. What will the effect of the promotion be? To investigate this, we simply enter 9 in cell B4. The results of making this change are shown in the spreadsheet below.

	A	B	C
1	**Queuing Analysis (K=1)**		
2			
3	**Model Inputs:**		
4	Mean Arrival Rate (lambda) per Hour	9	
5	Mean Service Rate (mu) per Hour	10	
6	Number of Items in System (n)	3	
7			
8	**Model Outputs:**		Formulas:
9	Utilization	0.90	=B4/B5
10	Average Number of Items in the Queue (L_q)	8.10	=(B4^2)/(B5*(B5-B4))
11	Average Number of Items in the System (L)	9.00	=B10+B9
12	Expected Waiting Time in the Queue (W_q)	0.90	=B10/B4
13	Expected Total Time in the System (W)	1.00	=B12+(1/B5)
14	Probability of n Items Occupying the System (P_n)	0.07	=(B9^B6)*(1-B9)
15	Probability System is Idle (P_0)	0.10	=1-B9
16	Probability System is Busy (P_{busy})	0.90	=1-B15

Initially, you might not have expected the arrival of one more customer an hour to make that big a difference. However, as the results above indicate, the promotion would have a significant impact on the performance of the system. For example, utilization of the system would increase from 80 percent to 90 percent. Management's reaction to this might be quite positive. However, accompanying this increase in utilization are large increases in waiting times. The average time an item would have to wait in the queue would more than double, from 24 minutes to 54 minutes (0.9×60); and the total time an item spent in the system would double, from 30 minutes to 60 minutes. Likewise, the average number of items in the queue would almost triple, from 3.2 to 8.1; and the average number of items in the system would increase from 4 to 9.

❖ EXERCISES

1. The emergency room of a local hospital employs three doctors. Emergency patients arrive randomly at an average rate of 3.5 per hour. Service is good and averages about $1/2$ hour per patient, so the hospital is considering reducing the number of doctors to two. What effect would this have on waiting time?

2. Jim sells tickets at a counter where the customers arrive randomly, on the average, every 2 minutes. He finds that he can service no more than 10 customers per hour. For management to maintain an average

queue length of no more than one customer, how many more ticket sellers must it provide to help Jim?

3. City Bank is trying to determine how to staff its teller windows so that the average number of customers waiting for service in the single-line queue ("cattle stall") does not exceed eight. On average, one customer arrives every minute, and one teller can service 20 customers an hour. On the average, how long will a customer have to wait in the cattle stall? Find the utilization of the facility. How many square

feet of space will be required if every teller needs 50 square feet and every waiting customer requires 15 square feet?

4. On average, 35 customers arrive at an ATM located on Bank Street every hour. It takes a customer an average of 72 seconds to complete his or her transaction at the machine. Develop a spreadsheet similar to the one discussed in the Spreadsheet Analysis to determine all the relevant queue characteristics. The bank is considering eliminating its ATM located on College Street and expects the number of arrivals at the Bank Street ATM to increase by 4 per hour. Explain to management what the effect will be on the Bank Street ATM if the one located at College Street is eliminated.

5. Another useful measure of performance is the probability that an item will be in the system longer than some specified time. This is calculated as:

$$P\{T > t\} = e^{(\lambda - \mu)t}$$

where,

T = actual time in system

t = specified time

Modify the spreadsheet developed in Exercise 4 to calculate $P\{T > t\}$. Specifically, in model inputs, add a row for the decision maker to enter a specified time t. Then, in model outputs, enter a formula to calculate the probability that an item will be in the system longer than the time specified. What is the probability that a customer will be in the system 5 minutes or more? (Assume that the ATM at College Street has not been eliminated.) What is the probability that a customer will be in the system 10 minutes or more? (Hint: Convert times to hours.)

Project Management

$\mathscr{C}$ HAPTER OVERVIEW

❖ The major reasons for the growth in project operations include more sophisticated technology, better-educated citizens, more leisure time, increased accountability, higher productivity, and faster response to customers.

❖ A project is based on a work breakdown structure that defines all tasks for costing and scheduling and is the basis for the project master schedule. The project tends to follow a standard life cycle: a slow start, accelerating progress, and a slow finish.

❖ PERT and CPM are the primary techniques used for scheduling projects. A project is made up of activities that take time and must be followed according to precedence. The longest path through the network is called the *critical path*. Each of the

activities has associated with it an earliest start and finish time, and a latest start and finish time so that the entire project will not be delayed.

❖ If optimistic, most likely, and pessimistic times are given for activities, the probabilities of project completion by various times can be calculated from the normal distribution.

❖ If it is possible to expedite activities, a cost-completion time curve can be derived by economically crashing the activities.

❖ Projects are often controlled through cost-schedule reconciliation charts or an earned value chart. These charts illustrate spending, schedule, time, and total variances from expected values.

INTRODUCTION

❖ Numerous examples of projects have already been discussed in this book. For example, in Chapter 1 a project for transporting the Olympic Flame to Atlanta was described. You may recall that two years of planning went into this project and completing it required coordinating 10,000 runners who carried the Olympic Torch 15,000 miles in 84 days. In Chapter 5, two product development projects were discussed: Thermos's revolutionary electric grill and Chrysler's new roadster, called the Viper. In another example from the automobile industry, Mercedes-Benz formed a project team to find a location for its new manufacturing facility, as was described in Chapter 10. And, as a final example, Chapter 14 mentioned that Hewlett Packard formed a project team to upgrade its materials handling system at its inkjet assembly plant.

❖ At a more detailed level, consider that the team formed to develop the Chrysler Viper had only three years to complete the development project from concept to roadster. This included developing an entirely new 8.0-liter V-10 aluminum engine and a high-performance six-speed transmission. Typically, such development projects required five years at Chrysler. Thus, from the very beginning of the project, managers at Chrysler recognized the importance of consistent end-to-end project management.

Team members for the project were hand-picked, and a project management system called *Artemis Prestige* was selected as a tool to help manage the project. According to managers at Chrysler, the project management system required the ability to track multiple projects concurrently, allow users to use it interactively, provide project personnel with a broad picture of the entire project, and help identify the impact of each activity on the ultimate completion of the project. These capabilities could then be used to perform "what if" analyses to access the impact of changes in resource allocations and other engineering changes. With these capabilities, personnel could determine the effect of a proposed change before making a commitment to the change. In general, the Artemis software package provided a vital communications network and helped ensure that critical links between different parts of the project were completed according to the plan.

By most accounts, the Viper project was an overwhelming success and yielded several significant innovations. For example, the first test engine required less than a year to develop. This was particularly important because several other major components including the transmission depended on the engine. The transmission was developed in $1^{1}/_{2}$ years, down from the usual 5 to 6 years. Additionally, many important innovations in the frame, body, and brakes were incorporated into the Viper (O'Keeffe, 1994).

❖ Zeneca Pharmaceuticals U.S. is a unit of the research-intensive pharmaceutical business of Zeneca Group PLC, headquartered in the U.K. The Zeneca Pharmaceuticals mission is to develop new drugs for the medical community. The development of a new drug is a complex project requiring extensive management and guidance over a long duration, typically 10 years.

Basically, drug development is the process by which a new chemical entity is synthesized, is found to have therapeutic pharmacologic "activity" in living animals, is tested in more animals and in humans, and is approved by the Food and Drug Administration (FDA) as a "new drug." After approval, the drug is sold to patients, usually by prescription. Unfortunately, in the process that begins with research and ends with approval for market, only about one drug in 10,000 meets with success, due to the many hurdles that must be overcome.

The major steps that the project manager must follow in the development process are as follows. (1) *Preclinical testing* is done in the lab and with animals to determine if the compound is biologically active and safe. (2) *Investigational new drug* (IND). Before tests with human subjects can be conducted, an IND application giving the test results and describing how the drug is made must be filed. (3) *Human clinical testing, phase I:* Pharmacological profile of a drug's actions; safe dosages; patterns of absorption, distribution, metabolism, and excretion; duration of action from tests on a small sample of healthy subjects. *Phase II:* Pilot efficacy studies in 200 to 300 volunteer patients to assess effectiveness, which may last two years. *Phase III:* Extensive clinical trials (in 1000 to 3000 patients) to confirm efficacy and identify low-incidence adverse reactions; this phase may last three years. (4) *New drug application* (NDA): The results of the previous testing must be reported, typically in thousands of pages, in an NDA filed with the FDA. Additional information includes the structure of the drug, its scientific rationale, details of its formulation and production, and the proposed labeling. (5) *Approval:* Following approval of the NDA, the company must submit periodic reports to FDA concerning adverse reactions and production, quality control, and distribution data.

There are some major differences between project management of pharmaceutical R&D and that in other industries. For one thing, the final result here is not a physical product such as a dam or a computer, but rather information—reams of paper giving proof that the drug is safe and efficacious. Because of the abstract nature of this "proof," the result may be sufficient at one point in time, or for one drug, but not at another time or for another drug.

In addition, the long duration, extreme costs (averaging $250 million per drug), and high chances for failure anywhere along the route to development are generally rare in other projects. Moreover, failure can come from diverse causes, including the success of competing drugs, adverse patient reactions, escalating costs, or insufficient efficacy. The extensive and sophisticated use of project management techniques is the main tool that pharmaceutical R&D firms like Zeneca Pharmaceuticals can use to improve their chances of success.

Project management is concerned with managing organizational activities. As the examples above illustrate, many organizations use project management techniques to integrate and coordinate diverse activities. For example, in the traditional functional organization, a product development team with representatives from production, finance, marketing, and engineering can be assembled to ensure that new product designs simultaneously meet the requirements of each area. Ensuring that each area's requirements are being met as the new design is developed reduces the likelihood that costly changes will have to be made later in the process. The result is that new products can be developed faster and less expensively, thereby enhancing the firm's overall responsiveness. Perhaps a better product is developed as well, owing to the synergy of including a variety of different perspectives earlier in the design process.

Up to this point, you might not have realized that projects are actually a special type of process. As you know, in this book the term *process* has been used to refer to a set of activities that taken together create something of value to customers. Typically, the term *process* is used to refer to a set of activities that are routinely repeated, such as processing insurance forms, handling customers' complaints, and assembling a VCR. The term *project* also refers to a set of activities that taken together produce a valued output. However, unlike a typical process, each project is unique and has a clear beginning and end. Therefore, projects are processes that are performed infrequently and ad hoc.

In Chapter 6, the project form of the transformation process was briefly described. The choice of the project form usually indicates the importance of the project objective to the organization. Thus, top-grade resources, including staff, are often made available for project operations. As a result, project organizations become very professionalized and are often managed on that basis. That is, minimal supervision is exercised, administrative routine is minimized, and the professional is given the problem and the required results (cost, performance, deadline). The individual is then given the privacy and freedom to decide *how* to solve his or her portion of the problem.

A great many projects require varying emphases during their life cycle. For example, technical performance may be crucial at the beginning, cost overruns in the middle, and on-time completion at the end. The flexibility of making spur-of-the-moment changes in emphasis by trading off one criterion for another is basic to the project design form. This ability results from the close contact of the project manager with the technical staff—there are few, if any, "middle managers."

Following are some examples of projects:

Constructing highways, bridges, tunnels, and dams.

Building ships, planes, and rockets.

Erecting skyscrapers, steel mills, homes, and processing plants.

Locating and laying out amusement parks, camping grounds, and refuges.

Organizing conferences, banquets, and conventions.

Managing R&D projects such as the Manhattan Project (which developed the atomic bomb).

Running political campaigns, war operations, advertising campaigns, or firefighting operations.

Chairing ad hoc task forces, overseeing planning for government agencies, or conducting corporate audits.

Converting from one computer system to another.

As may be noticed in this list, the number of project operations is growing in our economy, probably at about the same rate as services (which many of them are). Some of the reasons for this growth in project operations are as follows:

1. *More sophisticated technology.* An outgrowth of our space age, and its technology, has been increased public awareness of project operations (e.g., Project Apollo) and interest in using the project form to achieve society's goals (Project Head Start).

2. *Better-educated citizens.* People are more aware of the world around them, and of techniques (such as project management) for achieving their objectives.

3. *More leisure time.* People have the time available to follow, and even participate in, projects.

4. *Increased accountability.* Society as a whole has increased its emphasis on the attainment of objectives (affirmative action, environmental protection, better fuel economy) and the evaluation of activities leading toward those objectives.

5. *Higher productivity.* People and organizations are involved in more activities, and are more productive in those activities, than ever before.

6. *Faster response to customers.* Today's intense competition has escalated the importance of quick response to customers' needs, and projects are many times more responsive and flexible than bureaucracies or functionally organized firms.

In physical project operations, such as bridge construction, most of the *production* per se is completed elsewhere and brought to the project area at the proper time. As a result, a great many project activities are *assembly* operations. The project design form concentrates resources on the achievement of specific objectives primarily through proper *scheduling* and *control* of activities, many of which are simultaneous. Some of the *scheduling* considerations in project management are knowing what activities must be completed and in what order, how long they will take, when to increase and decrease the labor force, and when to order materials so that they will not arrive too early (thus requiring storage and being in the way) or too late (thus delaying the project). The *control* activities include anticipating what can and might go wrong, knowing what resources can be shifted among activities to keep the project on schedule, and so forth.

In the remaining sections of this chapter we will discuss project planning, scheduling, expediting, and control.

𝒫LANNING THE PROJECT

In this section we focus in some detail on the planning of projects. In the area of project management, planning is probably the single most important element in the success of the project, and considerable research has been done on the topic.

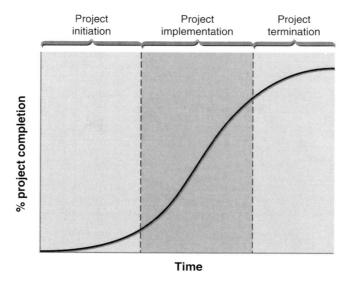

Figure 16.1 Life cycle of a project.

It has been found, for example, that progress in a project is not at all uniform but instead follows the life cycle curve shown in Figure 16.1. When the project is initiated, progress is slow as responsibilities are assigned and organization takes place. But the project gathers speed during the implementation stage, and much progress is made. As the end of the project draws near, the more difficult tasks that were postponed earlier must now be completed, yet people are being drawn off the project and activity is "winding down," so the end keeps slipping out of reach.

One of the project manager's major responsibilities during the initiation stage is to define all the tasks in as much detail as possible so that they can be scheduled and costed out, and responsibility can be assigned. This set of task descriptions is

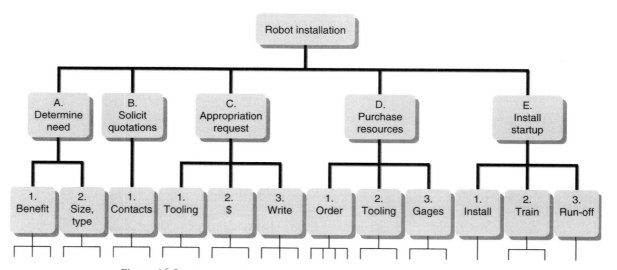

Figure 16.2 Work breakdown structure.

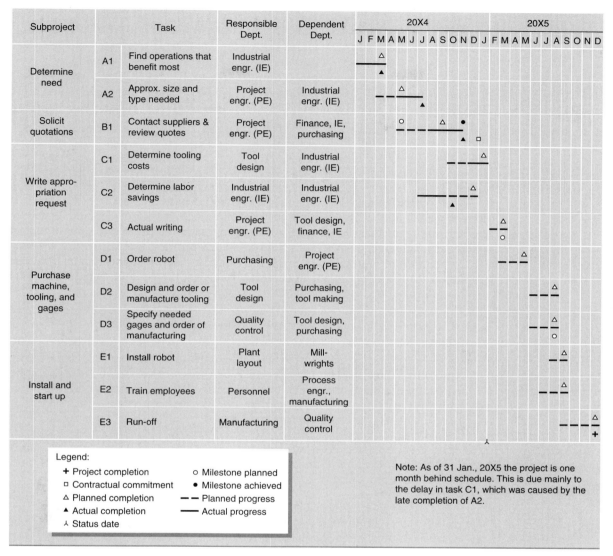

Figure 16.3 Project master schedule. Reprinted from J. Meredith and S. J. Mantel, Jr., *Project Management: A Managerial Approach,* 2nd ed., Wiley, 1989. Used with permission.

called the ***work breakdown structure*** (WBS) and provides the basis for the project master schedule.

A typical WBS and master schedule are illustrated in Figures 16.2 and 16.3 for a project installing assembly-line robots. Milestone, commitment, and completion points are shown, and actual progress is graphed. The last status update shows that the project is a month behind schedule.

The scheduling of project activities is highly complex because of (1) the number of activities required, (2) the precedence relationships among the activities, and (3) the limited time of the project. Project scheduling is similar to the scheduling discussed earlier in some ways but still differs significantly. For example, the basic network approaches, ***program evaluation and review technique (PERT)*** and ***critical path method (CPM)**** are based on variations of the Gantt chart. Figure 16.3 is, in a sense, a type of Gantt chart but is inadequate for scheduling the multitude of subtasks that compose, for example, task A1. That is, a project schedule has to handle an enormous number of different operations and materials, which must be coordinated in such a way that the subsequent activities can take place and the entire project (job) can be completed by the due date. For example, the use of a shortest-operation-time (SOT) priority rule would be entirely inappropriate here, since some activities must be completed before others can be started. Rather, the *critical operation*, which must precede all the remaining operations, should be performed next.

The scheduling procedure for project operations must be able not only to identify and handle the variety of tasks that must be done but also to handle their time sequencing. In addition, it must be able to integrate the performance and timing of all the tasks with the project as a whole so that control can be exercised, for example, by shifting resources from operations with *slack* (permissible slippage) to other operations whose delay might threaten the project's timely completion. The tasks involved in planning and scheduling project operations are:

❖ *Planning.* Determining *what* must be done and which tasks must *precede* others.

❖ *Scheduling.* Determining *when* the tasks must be completed; when they *can* and when they *must* be started; which tasks are *critical* to the timely completion of the project; and which tasks have *slack* in their timing and how much.

$\mathscr{S}$CHEDULING THE PROJECT: PERT AND CPM

The project scheduling process is based on the activities that must be conducted to achieve the project's goals, the length of time each requires, and the order in which they must be completed. If a number of similar projects must be conducted, sometimes these activities can be structured generically to apply equally well to all the projects, as illustrated by the sidebar on Cincinnati Milacron.

Two primary techniques have been developed to plan projects consisting of ordered activities: PERT and CPM. Although PERT and CPM originally had some differences in the way activities were determined and laid out, many current approaches to project scheduling minimize these differences and present an integrated view, as we will see here. It will be helpful to define some terms first.

---

*PERT was developed by the U.S. Navy with Booz-Allen Hamilton and Lockheed Corporation in the late 1950s to manage the Polaris missile project. CPM was developed independently at about the same time by Du Pont, Inc.

OPERATIONS
IN PRACTICE

Cincinnati Milacron Uses Project Management for Planning Automation

In the process of installing its Mount Orab flexible manufacturing system, Cincinnati Milacron developed a project management process not only for carrying out the implementation of advanced technological systems but also for planning them. That is, although installing a new automated process is a project in itself, the project planning process, the strategic concept planning, and the after-installation routinization and integration of the automation are also projects in their own right. The entire automation undertaking is thus a "megaproject" and needs to be managed as one if it is to be successful.

Cincinnati Milacron's automation philosophy is to plan from the top down and to implement from the bottom up. The commitment of top management is crucial to these megaprojects because they inevitably require extensive change in an organization over the years involved in their planning and implementation; without backing from the top, this degree of change will not occur.

The steps involved in these automation megaprojects are detailed below. The first six steps are concerned with the strategic, conceptual, and planning stages of the megaproject and, for an automation undertaking such as the one at Mount Orab, they may easily require 5000 or more labor-hours. Steps 7–11 are then concerned with the installation and implementation process, projects in themselves that often take another two to four years. The entire 11 steps may be viewed as constituting the *work breakdown structure* for the megaproject, leading to a more detailed network plan. This megaproject plan was used in the successful implementation of the Mount Orab flexible manufacturing system (Meredith, 1986, 1988).

Project Steps	Percent of Total Time	Preceding Tasks
1. Define current performance	5	—
2. Identify goals	2	1
3. Conduct an "as is" study	13	1
4. Define the "to be" situation	12	2
5. Research existing technologies	4	—
6. Define system specifications	17	4
7. Conduct equipment analyses	26	3, 5, 6
8. Identify and schedule implementation activities	5	3, 7
9. Identify organization impacts	8	3, 4, 8
10. Prepare justification report	4	3, 4, 7
11. Establish audit procedure	4	1, 4, 6, 8

❖ *Activity.* One of the project operations, or tasks. An activity requires resources and takes some amount of time to complete.

❖ *Event.* Completion of an activity, or series of activities, at a particular point in time.

❖ *Network.* Set of all project activities graphically interrelated through precedence relationships. In this text, network lines (or *arcs*) represent activities, connections between the lines (called *nodes*) represent events, and arrows on the arcs represent precedence. (This is typical of the PERT approach; in CPM the nodes represent activities.)

❖ *Path.* Series of connected activities from the start to the finish of the project.

❖ *Critical path.* Any path that if delayed will delay the completion of the entire project.

❖ *Critical activities.* Activities on the critical path or paths.

❖ Project Planning When Activity Times Are Known

The primary inputs to project planning are a list of the activities that must be completed, the *activity completion times* (also called *activity durations*), and precedence relationships among the activities (i.e., what activities must be completed before another activity can be started). In this section we assume that activity completion times are known with certainty. Later, we relax this assumption and consider situations in which activity completion times are not known with certainty.

Important outputs of project planning include:

❖ Graphical representation of the entire project, showing all precedence relationships among the activities.

❖ Time it will take to complete the project.

❖ Identification of critical path or paths.

❖ Identification of critical activities.

❖ Slack times for all activities and paths.

❖ Earliest and latest time each activity can be started.

❖ Earliest and latest time each activity can be completed.

Project Completion and Critical Paths

Table 16.1 shows the activity times and precedence for seven activities that must all be finished to complete a project. According to the table, activities A and B can be started at any time. Activities C and D can be started once activity A is completed. Activity E cannot be started until both activities B and C are finished, and so on. The network diagram for this project is shown in Figure 16.4, in which nodes (circles) represent events (i.e., the start or completion of an activity) and arcs (lines) correspond to activities. Each arc is labeled with a letter to identify the corresponding activity. Activity durations are shown in parentheses next to the activity labels. Finally, arrows are used to show precedence relationships among activities.

From Figure 16.4, it can be seen that there are three paths from node 1 to node

$\mathscr{T}$ABLE 16.1 ❖ Data for a Seven-Activity Project

Activity	Time (days)	Preceded By
A	10	—
B	7	—
C	5	A
D	13	A
E	4	B, C
F	12	D
G	14	E

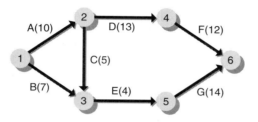

Figure 16.4   Network diagram for project.

6: A–D–F (or 1–2–4–6), A–C–E–G (or 1–2–3–5–6), and B–E–G (or 1–3–5–6). Summing the activity times on a particular path provides the path completion time. For example, the time to complete path A–D–F is 35 (10 + 13 + 12).

To determine the expected completion time of the entire project, *early start times* T_{ES} and *early finish times* T_{EF} can be calculated for each activity as shown in Figure 16.5. The values of T_{ES} and T_{EF} are calculated moving left to right through the network. Thus, we begin with the leftmost node (node 1) and work our way to the rightmost node (node 6). To illustrate, if the project is started at time zero, then activities A and B can be started as early as time zero, since neither of them is preceded by another activity. Since activity A requires 10 days, if it is started as early as time zero, it can be completed on day 10. Likewise, if activity B is started at time zero, it can be completed as early as day 7. Continuing on, since activity A can be finished as early as day 10, activity C can start as early as day 10 and finish as early as day 15. Now consider activity E. Activity E cannot be started until activities B and C are both completed. Since activity B can be finished as early as day 7 and C can

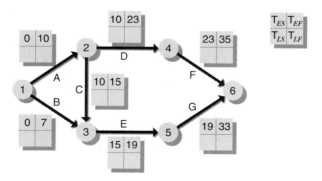

Figure 16.5   Early start and finish times.

be finished as early as day 15, activity E can be started only as early as day 15 (remember E cannot start until *both* activities B and C are completed). If activity E is started as early as day 15, it can finish as early as day 19. The remaining earliest start and finish times are calculated in a similar fashion. After T_{ES} and T_{EF} are calculated for all the activities, we can determine the earliest time that the project can be completed. Since this project cannot be completed until all paths are completed, the earliest it could be completed is day 35.

Once T_{ES} and T_{EF} have been calculated for each activity, the latest times each activity can be started and finished without delaying the completion of the project can be determined. In contrast to T_{ES} and T_{EF}, latest start time (T_{LS}) and latest finish time (T_{LF}) are calculated by moving backward through the network, from right to left. Times T_{LS} and T_{LF} for this example are shown in Figure 16.6.

In calculating T_{ES} and T_{EF}, we determined that the project could be completed by day 35. If the project is to be completed by day 35, then activities F and G can be completed as late as day 35 without delaying completion of the project. Thus, the latest finish time for activities F and G is 35. Since activity F requires 12 days, it can start as late as 23 (35 − 12) and still finish by day 35. Likewise, activity G can start as late as 21 (35 − 14) and still finish by day 35. Continuing on, since activity F can start as late as day 23, activity D can finish as late as day 23. Since activity D requires 13 days, it can start as late as day 10 (23 − 13) without delaying the entire project. Activity E must finish by 21 so as not to delay activity G and thus can start as late as day 17. To permit activity E to start by day 17, activities B and C must finish by day 17. Activity C can start as late as day 12 and still finish by day 17. Activity A precedes both C and D. Activity C can start as late as day 12 and D as late as day 10. Since activity A must be finished before either of these activities is started, A must be finished by day 10. (If A finished later than day 10, then activity D would start later than its latest start time and the entire project would be delayed.)

Slack Time

Times T_{ES}, T_{EF}, T_{LS}, and T_{LF} can be used by the project manager to help plan and develop schedules for the project. For example, if an activity requires a key resource or individual, its earliest and latest start times provide a window during which that resource can be acquired or assigned to the project. Alternatively, if an activity falls behind schedule, the latest completion time provides an indication of whether the slippage will delay the entire project or can simply be absorbed.

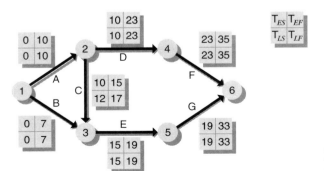

Figure 16.6   Latest start and finish times.

*S*OLVED EXERCISE 16.1 ❖ Critical Path

Draw the network diagram for the project activities listed below. Determine completion time and critical path. What is the effect on the project if CD slips to 6 days? 7 days? 8 days?

Activity	Time
AB	6
AC	4
CB	3
CD	3
CE	3
BD	1
BE	5
DF	5
DE	1
EF	4

Solution:

Note that the manner of designating the activities, from event to event, makes it unnecessary to give precedence.

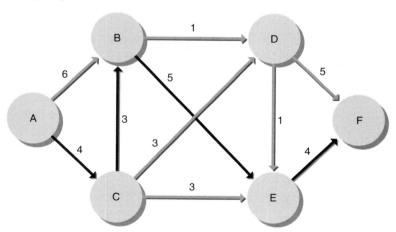

Path	Duration
A–C–B–E–F	16 (critical path)
A–B–E–F	15
A–B–D–E–F	12
A–B–D–F	12
A–C–B–D–F	13
A–C–B–D–E–F	13
A–C–D–F	12
A–C–D–E–F	12
A–C–E–F	11

If CD becomes 6: No effect on project or critical path.

If CD becomes 7: Three critical paths but same completion time—16.

$$A–C–B–E–F$$
$$A–C–D–E–F$$
$$A–C–D–F$$

If CD becomes 8: Two new critical paths ($A–C–D–E–F$ and $A–C–D–F$) and a new completion time of 17.

Notice in Figure 16.6 that for some activities T_{ES} is equal to T_{LS} and T_{EF} is equal to T_{LF}. For these activities, there is no flexibility in terms of when they can be started and completed. In other cases, an activity's T_{ES} is less than its T_{LS} and its T_{EF} is less than its T_{LF}. In these cases the project manager can exercise some discretion in terms of when the activity is started and when it is completed. The amount of flexibility the project manager has in terms of starting and completing an activity is referred to as its **slack** (or **float**) and is calculated as:

$$\text{Activity slack} = T_{LS} - T_{ES} = T_{LF} - T_{EF}$$

All activities on the critical path have zero slack—that is, there is no room for delay in any activity on the critical path without delaying the entire project. Activities off the critical path may delay up to a point where further delay would delay the entire project. Table 16.2 shows T_{ES}, T_{EF}, T_{LS}, T_{LF}, and slack for our seven-activity project shown earlier in Figure 16.6.

In addition to calculating slack times for individual activities, slack times can be calculated for entire paths. Since all paths must be finished to complete the project, the time to complete the project is the time to complete the path with the longest duration. Thus, the path with the longest duration is critical in the sense that any delay in completing it will delay the completion of the entire project. Path slacks are calculated as:

$$\text{Path slack} = \text{duration of critical path} - \text{path duration}$$

TABLE 16.2 ❖ Event Early and Late Times

Activity	T_{ES}	T_{EF}	T_{LS}	T_{LF}	Slack
A	0	10	0	10	0
B	0	7	10	17	10
C	10	15	12	17	2
D	10	23	10	23	0
E	15	19	17	21	2
F	23	35	23	35	0
G	19	33	21	35	2

TABLE 16.3 ❖ Calculation of Path Slacks

Path	Duration	Slack	Critical?
A–D–F	35	0 (35–35)	Yes
A–C–E–G	33	2 (35–33)	No
B–E–G	25	10 (35–25)	No

Table 16.3 contains the slack times for the three paths in our example project. Path A–D–F has the longest duration, and therefore its completion determines when the project is completed. The other paths require less than 35 days and therefore have slack. For example, path B–E–G has a slack of 10 days, implying that its completion can be delayed by 10 days without delaying the completion of the entire project.

Before leaving the topic of slack, it is important to point out that the slack times computed for individual activities are not additive. To illustrate, when the slack times were calculated for the individual activities, slack times of 10, 2, and 2 were computed for activities B, E, and G, respectively (see Table 16.2). If these slack times were additive, then path B–E–G would have a slack of 14 days. However, from Table 16.3 we observe that the slack for path B–E–G is only 10 days. The point is that slack times for individual activities are computed on the assumption that only a particular activity is delayed and all the other activities on the path begin at their earliest start time. As an example, activity B's slack of 10 days means that it can be delayed by up to 10 days without delaying the entire project, as long as the other activities on the path (activities E and G) are not delayed beyond their earliest start time. However if activity B is delayed by 10 days and either activity E or G is delayed by even 1 day beyond its early start time, the entire project will be delayed.

SOLVED EXERCISE 16.2 ❖ Slack Times

Find the slack times for all the activities in Solved Exercise 16.1.

Solution:

All activities on the critical path have 0 slack.

Activity	T_{ES}	T_{EF}	T_{LS}	T_{LF}	Slack
AB	0	6	1	7	1
AC	0	4	0	4	0
CB	4	7	4	7	0
CD	4	7	8	11	4
CE	4	7	9	12	5
BD	7	8	10	11	3
BE	7	12	7	12	0
DF	8	13	11	16	3
DE	8	9	11	12	3
EF	12	16	12	16	0

❖ Project Planning When Activity Times Are Not Known with Certainty

The previous section discussed project planning in situations where the activity completion times were known with certainty before the project was actually started. In reality, however, project activity times are frequently not known with certainty beforehand. In these cases project managers often develop three estimates for each activity: an optimistic time t_o, a pessimistic time t_p, and a most likely time t_m. The *optimistic time* is the amount of time the project manager estimates it will take to complete the activity under ideal conditions. The *pessimistic time* refers to how long the activity will take to complete under the worst-case scenario. The *most likely* time is the project manager's best estimate of how long the activity will take to complete. In addition to these three time estimates, the precedence relationships among the activities are also needed as inputs to the project planning process.

The primary outputs of project planning when activity times are not known with certainty include:

- ❖ Graphical representation of the entire project, showing all precedence relationships among the activities.
- ❖ Expected activity and path completion times.
- ❖ Variance of activity and path completion times.
- ❖ Probability that the project will be completed by a specified time.

We now illustrate project planning in a situation where activity durations are not known with certainty before the project starts.

❖ Black Cross Plan E

Black Cross is a volunteer organization recently formed in California to prepare for and respond to "the big one," a major earthquake that has been expected for a decade. Black Cross has developed a single, efficient, uniform response plan (plan E) consisting of 10 major activities for all cities where the earthquake causes major damage. Clearly, completing the project activities as quickly as possible is crucial to saving lives and property and aiding victims in distress. The staff of Black Cross has determined not only the most likely times for each activity but also the fastest time in which each could probably be done (i.e., the *optimistic time*), as well as the slowest time (i.e., *pessimistic time*) that might be encountered by a project team out in the field (if everything went wrong). The project operations and the optimistic, most likely, and pessimistic times, in hours, are listed in Table 16.4, along with the activities that must precede them.

Construction of the Network: Ordering the Activities

The project network illustrating the activities and their interdependence is constructed by first examining Table 16.4 for those activities that have no activities preceding them. These activities—a, b, and c,—are all drawn out of a starting node, which, for convenience in Figure 16.7, we have labeled **1**.

Next, the activity list is scanned for activities that require only that activities a, b, or c be completed. Thus, activities d through h can be drawn in the network next.

$\mathcal{T}$ABLE 16.4 ❖ Plan E Activity Times (Hours)

Project Activity	Optimistic Time t_o	Most Likely Time t_m	Pessimistic Time t_p	Required Preceding Activities
a	5	11	11	none
b	10	10	10	none
c	2	5	8	none
d	1	7	13	a
e	4	4	10	b, c
f	4	7	10	b, c
g	2	2	2	b, c
h	0	6	6	c
i	2	8	14	g, h
j	1	4	7	d, e

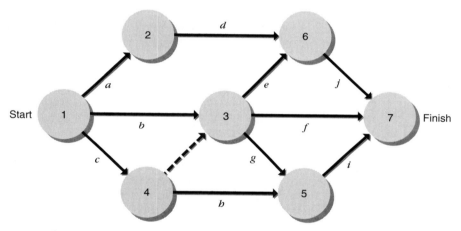

Figure 16.7 Plan E project operations network.

Activity *d* can be drawn directly out of node **2**, and activity *h* can be drawn out of node **4**. But if node **3** indicates the completion of activity *b*, how can activities *e*, *f*, and *g* be drawn, since they also depend on the completion of activity *c*? This is accomplished by the use of a ***dummy activity*** from event **4** to event **3**, which indicates that event **3** depends on the accomplishment of activity *c* (event **4**) as well as activity *b*. The dummy activity, shown as a dashed line in Figure 16.7, requires no time to accomplish, but the link is necessary, so that activities *e*, *f*, and *g* cannot start before both activities *b* and *c* are completed.

What if activity *e* did *not* require that activity *c* be completed whereas *f* and *g* did? If this was the case, the diagram would be drawn as shown in Figure 16.8. Care must be taken to ensure that the *proper* precedence relations are drawn; otherwise, the project might be unnecessarily delayed.

The remainder of the diagram is drawn in the same manner. Activity *i*, which depends on activities *g* and *h*, comes out of node **5**, which represents the completion

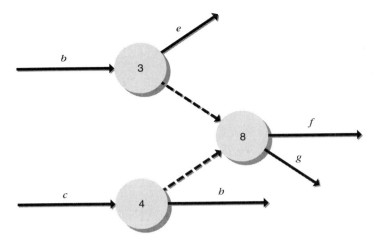

Figure 16.8   Proper use of dummy activities.

of g and h. A similar situation occurs with activity j. All of the remaining activities without completion nodes (f, i, and j) are then directed to the project completion node **7.**

Calculating Activity Durations

We have now completed a *graphic* network representation of the information about precedence shown in Table 16.4. Next we can place the expected activity times on the network to get an indication of which activities should be scheduled first and when they should be completed, in order for the project not to be delayed.

The estimation of the three activity times in Table 16.4 is based on the assumption that the activities are independent of one another. Therefore an activity that goes wrong will not necessarily affect the other activities, which can still go right. Additionally, it is assumed that the difference between t_o and t_m need *not* be the same as the difference between t_p and t_m. For example, a critical piece of equipment may be wearing out. If it is working well, this equipment can do a task in 2 hours that normally takes 3 hours; but if the equipment is performing poorly, the task may require 10 hours. Thus, we may see nonsymmetrical optimistic and pessimistic task times for project activities, as for activities e and h in Table 16.4. Note also that for some activities, such as b, the durations are known with certainty.

The general form of nonsymmetrical or skewed distribution used in approximating PERT activity times is called the *beta* distribution and has a mean (expected completion time t_e) and a variance, or uncertainty in this time, σ^2, as given below. The results of these calculations are listed in Table 16.5 and indicated on the networks of Figures 16.7 and 16.9 in parentheses.

$$t_e = \frac{t_o + 4t_m + t_p}{6}$$

$$\sigma^2 = \left(\frac{t_p - t_o}{6}\right)^2$$

$\mathscr{T}$ABLE 16.5 ❖ Expected Times and Variances of Activities

Activity	Expected Time, t_e	Variance, σ^2
a	10	1
b	10	0
c	5	1
d	7	4
e	5	1
f	7	1
g	2	0
h	5	1
i	8	4
j	4	1

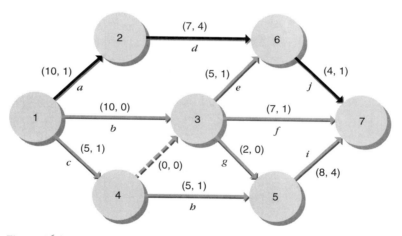

Figure 16.9 Early start times, latest allowable times, and critical path.

The discussion of project management with known activity times included critical paths, critical activities, and slack. In situations where activity times are not known with certainty, these concepts are not particularly useful. To demonstrate this we will use Table 16.6, where the paths and their expected completion times, earliest completion times, and latest completion times are listed for the network diagram shown in Figure 16.7. To calculate a path's expected completion time, the activity expected times t_e were summed up for all activities on the path. Similarly, times t_o and t_p were summed up for all activities on a given path to determine the path's earliest completion time and latest completion time, respectively.

Referring to Table 16.6, path a–d–j is most likely to take the longest (i.e., 22 hours). However, to see why this path is not considered the critical path, observe that if all the activities go exceptionally well on this path it can be completed in as few as 7 hours. Referring to the last column in Table 16.6, we can see that it is possible for any of the other paths to take longer than 7 hours. Therefore, without knowing the activity times with certainty we see that any of the paths has the po-

$\mathcal{T}$ABLE 16.6 ❖ Expected, Earliest, and Latest Completion Times of Paths

Path	Most Likely Completion Time (hours)	Earliest Completion Time (hours)	Latest Completion Time (hours)
a–d–j	22	7	31
b–e–j	18	15	27
b–f	17	14	20
b–g-i	20	14	26
c–e–j	13	7	25
c–f	12	6	18
c–g–i	15	6	24
c–h–i	19	4	28

$\mathcal{S}$OLVED EXERCISE 16.3 ❖ Activity Durations

Find the expected times and variances of the following activities; times are stated in days.

Activity	Optimistic Time	Most Likely Time	Pessimistic Time
AB	3	6	9
AC	1	4	7
CB	0	3	6
CD	3	3	3
CE	2	2	8
BD	0	0	6
BE	2	5	8
DF	4	4	10
DE	1	1	1
EF	1	4	7

Solution:

	t_e		σ^2
AB: $[3 + 4(6) + 9]/6 =$	6	$[(9 - 3)/6]^2 =$	1
AC	4		1
CB	3		1
CD	3		0
CE	3		1
BD	1		1
BE	5		1
DF	5		1
DE	1		0
EF	4		1

tential to be the longest path. Furthermore, we will not know which of the paths will take longest to complete until the project is actually completed. And since we cannot determine before the start of the project which path will be critical, we cannot determine how much slack the other paths have.

Probabilities of Completion

When activity times are not known with certainty, we cannot determine how long it will actually take to complete the project. However, using the variance of each activity (the variances in Table 16.5), we can compute the likelihood or probability of completing the project in a given time period, assuming that the activity durations are independent of each other. The distribution of a path's completion time will be approximately normally distributed if the path has a large number of activities on it. For example, the mean time along path a–d–j was found to be 21 hours. The variance is found by summing the variances of each of the activities on the path. In our example, this would be

$$V_{\text{path a-d-j}} = \sigma_a^2 + \sigma_d^2 + \sigma_j^2$$
$$= 1 + 4 + 1$$
$$= 6$$

The probability of completing this path in, say, 23 hours is then found by calculating the standard normal deviate of the desired completion time less the expected completion time, and using the table of the standard normal probability distribution (Appendix A) to find the corresponding probability:

$$Z = \frac{\text{desired completion time} - \text{expected completion time}}{\sqrt{V}}$$
$$= \frac{23 - 21}{\sqrt{6}}$$
$$= 0.818$$

which results in a probability (see Figure 16.10) of 79 percent.

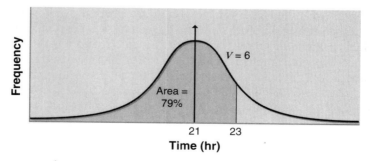

Figure 16.10 Probability distribution of project completion times.

So far, we have determined only that there is a 79 percent chance that path a–d–j will be completed in 23 hours or less. If we were interested in calculating the probability that the entire project will be completed in 23 hours, we would need to calculate the probability that all paths will be finished within 23 hours. To calculate the probability that all paths will be finished in 23 hours or less, we first calculate the probability that each path will be finished in 23 hours or less, as we just did for path a–d–j. Then we multiply these probabilities together to determine the probability that all paths will be completed by the specified time. The reason we multiply these probabilities together is that we are assuming that path completion times are independent of one another. Of course, if the paths have activities in common, they are not truly independent of one another. However, if a project has a sufficiently large number of activities, the assumption of path independence is acceptable.

To simplify the number of calculations required to compute the probability that a project will be completed by some specified time, for practical purposes it is reasonable to include only those paths whose expected time plus 2.33 standard deviations is more than the specified time. The reason for doing this is that if the sum of a path's expected time and 2.33 of its standard deviations is less than the specified time, then the probability that this path will take *longer* than the specified time is very small (i.e., less than 1 percent), and therefore we assume that the probability that it will be completed by the specified time is 100 percent. Finally, note that to calculate the probability that a project will take longer than some specified time, we must first calculate the probability that it will take less than the specified time. Then we subtract from 1 this probability that it will take less than the specified time.

$\mathcal{S}$olved Exercise 16.4 ❖ Completion Probabilities

Find the probability of completing the project in Solved Exercise 16.3 in 18 days.

Solution:

All the paths, along with their expected completion times, variances, standard deviations, are shown in the spreadsheet below. Also, in column E the expected time of each path plus 2.33 of its standard deviations was computed in order to determine which paths need to be considered in determining the probability that the entire project will be completed in 18 days or less. According to these calculations, only paths A–B–E–F and A–C–B–E–F are likely to take more than 18 days. Thus only these two paths need be considered in our calculations. To see why the other paths need not be included in our calculations, consider path A–B–D–F. This path has an expected time of 12 days, and therefore the probability that it will take longer than 18 days is very small (less than 1 percent). Therefore, we assume that the probability that this path will be completed in 18 days or less is 100 percent.

	A	B	C	D	E
1		Path		Path	Path Expected
2		Expected	Path	Standard	Time + 2.33
3	Path	Time	Variance	Deviation	Standard Deviations
4	A-B-D-F	12	3	1.73	16.04
5	A-B-E-F	15	3	1.73	19.04
6	A-B-D-E-F	12	3	1.73	16.04
7	A-C-B-D-F	13	4	2.00	17.66
8	A-C-B-D-E-F	13	4	2.00	17.66
9	A-C-B-E-F	16	4	2.00	20.66
10	A-C-D-F	12	2	1.41	15.30
11	A-C-D-E-F	12	3	1.73	16.04
12	A-C-E-F	11	3	1.73	15.04
13					
14	Key Formulas:				
15	cell D4: =SQRT(C4) [copy formula in cell D4 to D5:D12]				
16	cell E4: =B4+(2.33*D4) [copy formula in cell E4 to E5:E12]				

The probability distribution for path A–B–E–F is shown below.

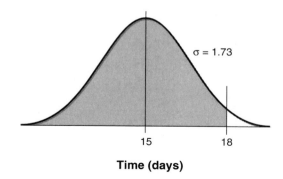

Time (days)

The probability that this path will be completed by day 18 is calculated as

$$Z = \frac{18 - 15}{1.73} = 1.73$$

Checking the normal distribution table in Appendix A:

$$\text{Probability}\,(Z \le 1.73) = 0.9582$$

The probability distribution for path A–C–B–E–F is

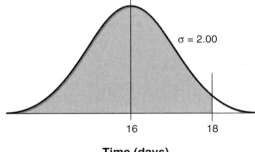

Time (days)

The probability that path A–C–B–E–F will be completed by day 18 is

$$Z = \frac{18 - 16}{2} = 1.00$$

Checking the normal distribution table in Appendix A:

$$\text{Probability } (Z \le 1.00) = 0.8413$$

The probability that the entire project will be completed within 18 days is the probability that paths A–B–E–F and A–C–B–E–F will both be completed within 18 days. Thus, to find the probability that the entire project will be completed in 18 days, we multiply the individual probabilities of the paths' being completed in 18 days:

Probability that project will be finished by day 18 = 0.9582 × 0.8413 = 0.81

Spreadsheet Analysis: Simulating Project Completion Times

When activity times are uncertain, it is usually not possible to know before the project is actually completed which path will be the critical path. In these situations, simulation analysis can provide some insights into the range and distribution of project completion times. To illustrate this, we use the following network diagram, consisting of six activities A through F.

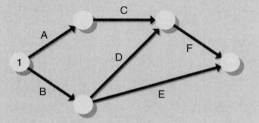

From historical data it has been determined that all the activity times are approximately normally distributed, with the means and standard deviations given in the following table.

Activity	Mean (days)	Standard Deviation
A	32.1	1.2
B	24.6	3.1
C	22.2	2.2
D	26.1	5.2
E	34.4	6.2
F	34.5	4.1

Inspection of the network diagram reveals three paths: A–C-F, B–D-F, and B–E.

To simulate the completion of this project, the spreadsheet shown below was developed. Completing the project is simulated by generating random numbers for the six activities and then adding up the activity times that make up each path to determine how long the paths take to complete. The longest path determines the project completion time. The spreadsheet was created to simulate 25 replications of the project (rows 3 to 27).

	A	B	C	D	E	F	G	H	I	J
1	Activity	Activity	Activity	Activity	Activity	Activity	Path1	Path 2	Path 3	Project
2	A	B	C	D	E	F	(A-C-F)	(B-D-F)	(B-E)	Finish Time
3							0.00	0.00	0.00	0.00
4							0.00	0.00	0.00	0.00
5							0.00	0.00	0.00	0.00
6							0.00	0.00	0.00	0.00
7							0.00	0.00	0.00	0.00
8							0.00	0.00	0.00	0.00
9							0.00	0.00	0.00	0.00
10							0.00	0.00	0.00	0.00
11							0.00	0.00	0.00	0.00
12							0.00	0.00	0.00	0.00
13							0.00	0.00	0.00	0.00
14							0.00	0.00	0.00	0.00
15							0.00	0.00	0.00	0.00
16							0.00	0.00	0.00	0.00
17							0.00	0.00	0.00	0.00
18							0.00	0.00	0.00	0.00
19							0.00	0.00	0.00	0.00
20							0.00	0.00	0.00	0.00
21							0.00	0.00	0.00	0.00
22							0.00	0.00	0.00	0.00
23							0.00	0.00	0.00	0.00
24							0.00	0.00	0.00	0.00
25							0.00	0.00	0.00	0.00
26							0.00	0.00	0.00	0.00
27							0.00	0.00	0.00	0.00
28						Minimum	0.00	0.00	0.00	0.00
29						Maximum	0.00	0.00	0.00	0.00

In the spreadsheet, columns A to F are used to store the randomly generated activity times for activities A to F, respectively. In column G the time to complete path A–C-F is calculated on the basis of the activity times generated in columns A to F. For example, in cell G3, the formula =A3+C3+F3 was entered. Similarly, columns H and I are used to calculate the time to complete paths B–D-F and B–E, respectively. Thus, the formula =B3+D3+F3 was entered in cell H3, and =B3+E3 was entered in cell I3. The formulas entered in cells G3:I3 were then copied to cells G4:I27.

Column J keeps track of when the project is actually completed on a given replication. Since the longest path determines the time when the project is completed, =MAX(G3:I3) was entered in cell J3 and then copied to cells J4:J27.

Finally, in rows 28 and 29 (columns G − J) the minimum and maximum path and project completion times are calculated. For example, in cell G28, =MIN(G3:G27) was entered and in cell G29, =MAX(G3:G27) was entered. The formulas in cells G28:G29 were then copied to H28:J29.

To generate the random numbers for activities A to F, first select Tools from Excel's menu bar. Next, select Data Analysis and then select Random Number Generation in the Data Analysis dialog box as shown below.

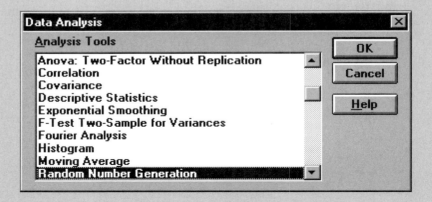

After we select Random Number Generation, the Random Number Generation dialog box is displayed. First, we will generate 25 random numbers for activity A (cells A3:A27). Recall that activity A is approximately normally distributed, with a mean of 32.1 and a standard deviation of 1.2.

To generate 25 random numbers for activity A, we specify 1 for the Number of Variables and 25 for the Number of Random Numbers. Next, we tell Excel that the random numbers should be generated from a normal distribution. Finally, we tell Excel to place the random numbers in cells A3:A27 by specifying this range in the Output Range box. After we enter this information, the Random Number Generation dialog box appears as follows:

Random Number Generation ☒

Number of Variables:	1		**OK**
Number of Random Numbers:	25		**Cancel**
Distribution:	Normal ▼		**Help**

Parameters

Mean = 32.1

Standard Deviation = 1.2

Random Seed: [ ]

Output options

◉ Output Range: $A$3:$A$27

○ New Worksheet Ply: [ ]

○ New Workbook

After we select OK in the Random Number Generation window, 25 random numbers from a normal distribution with a mean of 32.1 and a standard deviation of 1.2 are entered in cells A3:A27 as shown below.

	A	B	C	D	E	F	G	H	I	J
1	Activity	Activity	Activity	Activity	Activity	Activity	Path1	Path 2	Path 3	Project
2	A	B	C	D	E	F	(A-C-F)	(B-D-F)	(B-E)	Finish Time
3	30.80						30.80	0.00	0.00	30.80
4	31.91						31.91	0.00	0.00	31.91
5	32.21						32.21	0.00	0.00	32.21
6	32.65						32.65	0.00	0.00	32.65
7	31.91						31.91	0.00	0.00	31.91
8	34.78						34.78	0.00	0.00	34.78
9	32.07						32.07	0.00	0.00	32.07
10	29.27						29.27	0.00	0.00	29.27
11	30.26						30.26	0.00	0.00	30.26
12	30.55						30.55	0.00	0.00	30.55
13	32.17						32.17	0.00	0.00	32.17
14	31.74						31.74	0.00	0.00	31.74
15	32.15						32.15	0.00	0.00	32.15
16	33.23						33.23	0.00	0.00	33.23
17	31.05						31.05	0.00	0.00	31.05
18	34.07						34.07	0.00	0.00	34.07
19	32.81						32.81	0.00	0.00	32.81
20	30.39						30.39	0.00	0.00	30.39
21	33.99						33.99	0.00	0.00	33.99
22	31.18						31.18	0.00	0.00	31.18
23	32.17						32.17	0.00	0.00	32.17
24	32.94						32.94	0.00	0.00	32.94
25	30.94						30.94	0.00	0.00	30.94
26	31.15						31.15	0.00	0.00	31.15
27	32.25						32.25	0.00	0.00	32.25
28						Minimum	29.27	0.00	0.00	29.27
29						Maximum	34.78	0.00	0.00	34.78

This procedure is repeated to generate activity times for activities B to F. For example, to generate activity times for activity B, change the mean to 24.6, the standard deviation to 3.1, and the output range to B3:B27 in the Random Number Generation dialog box. After random numbers have been generated for all six activities, the spreadsheet appears as follows:

	A	B	C	D	E	F	G	H	I	J
1	Activity	Activity	Activity	Activity	Activity	Activity	Path1	Path 2	Path 3	Project
2	A	B	C	D	E	F	(A-C-F)	(B-D-F)	(B-E)	Finish Time
3	30.80	18.57	23.00	30.58	39.13	28.68	82.48	77.83	57.70	82.48
4	31.91	25.65	25.00	26.64	39.65	35.16	92.06	87.45	65.30	92.06
5	32.21	23.30	20.97	33.93	29.43	34.91	88.09	92.14	52.73	92.14
6	32.65	19.35	16.53	31.36	24.52	35.08	84.26	85.79	43.87	85.79
7	31.91	20.69	23.51	27.48	28.52	29.13	84.55	77.30	49.21	84.55
8	34.78	21.48	20.99	24.39	38.38	33.23	89.00	79.10	59.86	89.00
9	32.07	28.65	20.76	30.02	35.64	34.28	87.11	92.95	64.29	92.95
10	29.27	27.70	20.93	21.12	42.70	40.94	91.15	89.75	70.40	91.15
11	30.26	19.01	25.00	19.11	44.07	33.54	88.80	71.66	63.09	88.80
12	30.55	22.83	18.65	11.08	33.58	30.46	79.66	64.36	56.40	79.66
13	32.17	21.70	24.19	21.25	35.78	34.60	90.96	77.55	57.47	90.96
14	31.74	19.48	22.75	28.11	28.60	28.96	83.45	76.56	48.08	83.45
15	32.15	26.80	20.63	19.65	37.05	35.27	88.06	81.72	63.85	88.06
16	33.23	21.96	22.69	17.70	50.66	26.21	82.13	65.86	72.62	82.13
17	31.05	23.12	21.86	31.91	32.60	32.37	85.29	87.40	55.72	87.40
18	34.07	28.74	20.97	25.75	38.23	31.79	86.82	86.28	66.97	86.82
19	32.81	26.78	20.64	24.36	31.34	41.62	95.07	92.76	58.12	95.07
20	30.39	25.52	21.09	28.20	40.22	39.79	91.28	93.51	65.74	93.51
21	33.99	23.37	21.29	30.02	30.31	38.59	93.87	91.98	53.68	93.87
22	31.18	23.37	21.19	23.66	30.58	45.35	97.72	92.39	53.95	97.72
23	32.17	16.62	22.20	25.22	35.10	32.37	86.74	74.21	51.72	86.74
24	32.94	24.57	20.54	26.38	14.15	34.34	87.82	85.29	38.72	87.82
25	30.94	23.71	26.54	22.24	35.23	32.73	90.20	78.68	58.94	90.20
26	31.15	28.24	22.96	33.34	37.54	30.14	84.25	91.71	65.78	91.71
27	32.25	28.28	24.06	29.06	31.22	31.98	88.29	89.32	59.50	89.32
28						Minimum	79.66	64.36	38.72	79.66
29						Maximum	97.72	93.51	72.62	97.72

Several insights emerge as a result of this simulation analysis. First, in the 25 replications of the project shown above, the fastest project completion time was 79.66 days and the longest was 97.72 days. Furthermore, 72 percent (18/25) of the time path A–C-F was the critical path, whereas 28 percent (7/25) of the time path B–D-F was the critical path. Of course, the more times the project is replicated, the more confidence we have in the results.

EXPEDITING THE PROJECT: TRADE-OFFS BETWEEN COST AND TIME

When activities run late, it is necessary to expedite them to keep on schedule. This process is well illustrated in the sidebar about Florida Power and Light's St. Lucie No. 2 nuclear power plant. The comparison of the planned completion of activities from the PERT chart and actual performance allows managers to adjust schedules through additional resource reallocations so as to keep the project on course when delays have been experienced. The speeding up of critical activities is known as **crashing** and is derived from the original concepts employed in the critical path method (CPM). The technique works as follows.

Activities can be *expedited* (or *crashed*) up to a limit, at some increase in cost. The assumption is usually made that the relationship between activity duration and cost is linear between the normal schedule and the crash schedule. For example, a normal 3-week activity may cost $2000, and a crash 2-week schedule may cost $3000. Then a 2.5-week duration is assumed to cost $2500. Each activity usually has its own minimum duration and expediting cost, some activities being more efficient than others.

As the more efficient *critical* activities are expedited (there is no point in crashing noncritical activities—they will not speed up the delayed project), more and more activities and paths become critical and must be expedited simultaneously to further reduce the project duration. Thus, the cost of expediting the project increases faster and faster until the point is reached where the project can be expedited no further: all activities on one (or more) critical path are at their crash point. An example of this concept is provided in the next subsection.

OPERATIONS IN PRACTICE

Project Management at Florida Power and Light

An amazing event occurred at Florida Power and Light (FP&L)—the St. Lucie No. 2 nuclear power plant in Florida was completed almost on schedule! This was a stunning event in an industry that is known for running up to 10 years late in completing nuclear projects. One plant in Michigan had been nearly 15 years in progress and may still be uncompleted. It takes 10 to 12 years on average to build these plants, twice the time originally envisioned for most of the 48 projects under construction. St. Lucie No. 2 was finished in 6 years and ran only 4 months over schedule.

Late projects mean increased expenditures, since financing and other construction costs must be met over the extended period and alternative power must be supplied to customers. A 10-years-late plant in New York, for example, ran 15 times more costly than originally proposed. With these kinds of delays and costs, utilities can no longer afford to build nuclear power plants. As with all such plants, FP&L used highly sophisticated project management techniques to keep the 20,000 tasks of St. Lucie No. 2 on schedule. It used a lot of unusual techniques, too. For instance, it pressured its suppliers (who were inclined to dawdle), as well as federal safety regulators (who scheduled inspections on the assumption that construction would be years late), and it appointed a squadron of crisis managers, nicknamed "mothers," to give motherly care to critical activities that had to be kept on schedule. These project management techniques allowed St. Lucie No. 2 to weather a hurricane, two strikes, and hundreds of federally mandated design changes without significant delay.

Other examples of innovative techniques included handing out 2000 desk calendars that highlighted construction milestones at St. Lucie, initiating the debugging of the plant's 500 systems three years before physical plant completion, and adopting advanced construction techniques such as "slipform" concrete pouring. Keeping suppliers and subcontractors on schedule was a major element of FP&L's success; the project manager and the "mothers" flew note than half a million miles to prod suppliers. One supervisor flew from Florida to California just to pick up a critical valve.

In spite of its success, FP&L wished to avoid the uncertainties and hassles of another nuclear power plant. Its next facility is to be coal-fired (Winslow, 1984).

❖ The Bonfire Boys

Fathers and their sons in Brood 22 of the Bonfire Boys are planning a special Biannual Bonfire Blast, beginning in three days. However, there are a number of expensive and time-consuming project activities remaining before the Blast can get under way, as shown in Table 16.7. Every day the Blast is delayed will be discouraging to the fathers. What is the minimum cost of expediting the remaining activities for various project durations?

The network and critical path are shown in Figure 16.11; note the *dummy activity*. Activity c is shown for its actual two-day duration to the arrowhead, and then the line is continued (shown thinner) to node **5** to indicate project completion.

Inspecting the critical activities a, d, and e in Table 16.7 for the most efficient activity to crash in order to gain 1 day in completion time, we see that activity e is best. The six-day schedule from expediting activity e by 1 day is shown in Figure 16.12. Note that there are now two critical paths: a–d–e and a–b–dummy.

To expedite completion by another day will require expediting *both* critical paths. This can be done in this case by expediting activities *common* to both paths (such as activity a, for $20) or separate activities on the two paths (b and d, for $10 + $30 = $40; or b and e, for $10 + $10 = $20). Either way, a reduction of 1 day (5 days total) will cost at least $20 and then $20 again for another day (4 days total). The final result of both $20 reductions is shown in Figure 16.13.

One more day's reduction can come about only by expediting activities b and d; activities a and e are already fully crashed. The cost of this reduction, to 3 days' project duration, is $10 + $30 = $40. The result, shown in Figure 16.14, is the maxi-

𝒯ABLE 16.7 ❖ Trade-Offs Between Network Time and Cost

Activity	Precedence	Normal		Crash		Cost/Time "Slope" ($/Day)
		Duration (Days)	Cost ($)	Duration (Days)	Cost ($)	
a	—	2	20	1	40	20
b	a	4	30	1	60	10
c	a	2	10	2	10	—
d	a	2	10	1	40	30
e	d	3	10	1	30	10
			Total = 80		Total = 180	

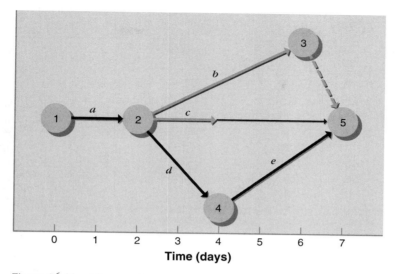

Figure 16.11 All-normal seven-day schedule.

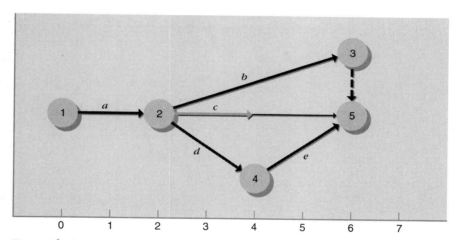

Figure 16.12 Two-critical-path six-day schedule.

mum reduction possible because all activities along critical path *a–d–e* have been crashed. In addition, path *a–c* is now also critical and cannot be further reduced. Figure 16.15 shows the cost increases as a function of the shortened project duration.

For use as a feedback control technique the crashing of activity *a* would probably not be applicable, since it is the *first* activity that might be delayed. That is, by the time control was necessary, activity *a* would probably already be completed. Of more use for control purposes would be the reduction possible in activities *b* and *e* and the initial slack in activities *b* and *c*. Thus, for example, a 1-day delay in activity *d* could be negated by expediting activity *e*.

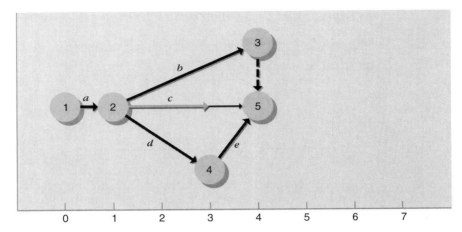

Figure 16.13 Second and third reduction, four-day schedule.

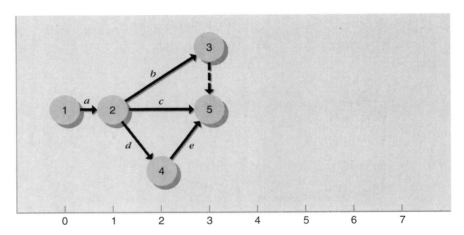

Figure 16.14 Final reduction, three-day schedule.

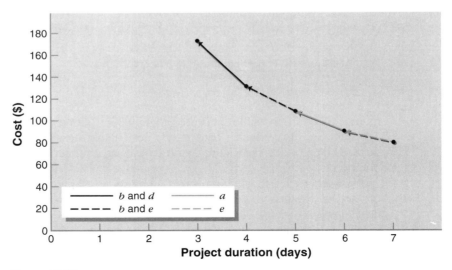

Figure 16.15 Project cost duration.

SOLVED EXERCISE 16.5 ❖ Critical Path Method

Given the following information, find which activities to crash to meet a project deadline of 10 days at minimum cost. What is the cost?

Activity	Normal Time	Crash Time	Normal Cost	Total Crash Cost	Precedence
A	7	4	$500	$800	—
B	3	2	200	350	A
C	6	4	500	900	—
D	3	1	200	500	C
E	2	1	300	550	B, D

Solution:

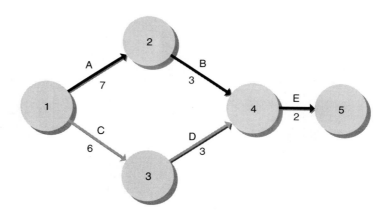

Crash cost per day:
  A*: (800–500)/(7–4) = $100 ← lowest
  B*: 150/1   = $150
  C: 400/2   = 200
  D: 300/2   = 150
  E*: 250/1   = 250

If we crash *A* by 1 day, then project completion is 11 days. But two critical paths A–B–E and C–D–E are formed.

Next, we could either crash *E*, common to both paths for $250, or crash *A* for $100 *and D* for $150, for the same total of $250.

Thus, we crash either *A* and *E* by 1 day each, or *A* by 2 days and *D* by 1 day. In either case the cost will be $100 + $250 + normal cost ($1700) for a total of $2050.

---

*On critical path

Spreadsheet Analysis: Crashing a Project

In this example we demonstrate how spreadsheets can greatly facilitate the task of choosing activities to crash so that a project will be completed by some specified time. To illustrate this, the spreadsheet below was developed for Solved Exercise 16.5.

	A	B	C	D	E	F	G	H	I	J
1					Total	Crash	Amount	Cost of		Maximum
2		Normal	Crash	Normal	Crash	Cost	To Crash	Crashing	Actual	Crash
3	Activity	Time	Time	Cost	Cost	Per Day	Activity	Activity	Time	Days
4	A	7	4	$500	$800	$100	0	$0	7	3
5	B	3	2	$200	$350	$150	0	$0	3	1
6	C	6	4	$500	$900	$200	0	$0	6	2
7	D	3	1	$200	$500	$150	0	$0	3	2
8	E	2	1	$300	$550	$250	0	$0	2	1
9	Total							$0		
10										
11		Event								
12	Node	Time								
13	2									
14	3									
15	4									
16	5									
17										
18										
19	Key Formulas:									
20	Cell F4: =(E4-D4)/(B4-C4) [copy formula to cells F5:F8]									
21	Cell H4: =G4*F4 [copy formula to cells H5:H8]									
22	Cell H9: =SUM(H4:H8)									
23	Cell I4: =B4-G4 [copy formula to cells I5:I8]									
24	Cell J4: =B4-C4 [copy to J5:J8]									

At the top of the spreadsheet, columns A to E contain the information given in Solved Exercise 16.5 pertaining to the activities, their normal times, their crash times, the normal cost, and the total crash cost, respectively. In column F, the crash cost per day is calculated by dividing the incremental cost of crashing the activity as much as possible (by the maximum number of days the activity can be shortened). For example, =(E4–D4)/(B4–C4) was entered in cell F4 and then copied to cells F5:F8.

Column G corresponds to one of our decision variables: the amount to crash each activity. In column H, the cost of partially crashing an activity is calculated on basis of the amount of time the activity is actually crashed. To illustrate, in cell H4 the formula =G4*F4 was entered and then copied to cells H5:H8. In cell H9 the total crash cost is computed by summing the values in cells H4:H8.

In column I the actual time to complete the activity is calculated by subtracting the activity's normal time (column B) from the amount the activity is crashed (column G). Thus, in cell I4 the formula =B4–G4 was entered and then copied to cells I5:I8.

Column J contains a formula that calculates the maximum number of days an activity can be crashed, by subtracting the crash time from the normal time. For example, in cell J4 the formula =B4–C4 was entered and copied to cells J5:J8.

The middle of the spreadsheet (cells B13:B16) contains the other decision variables needed. More specifically, cells B13:B16 correspond to the event times for each of the nodes in the network diagram. (Node 1 is excluded because we assume that this node occurs at time zero.) As you will see, we need these decision variables to preserve the precedence relationships specified in the network diagram. For example, we need to make sure that node 5 does not occur until after node 4 occurs, plus the time it takes to complete activity E.

We now demonstrate how Excel's Solver can be used to help determine which activities to crash so that the entire project is completed within 10 days at the minimum cost. To begin, we select Tools from the menu bar and then Solver from the next menu that appears. The Solver Parameters dialog box is now displayed. The cell we wish to minimize is the total crash cost, cell H9. To specify this we enter H9 in the Target Cell box and then select the Min radio button. Next, we tell Excel what cells it can change in order to find the solution with the least total crashing cost. In our spreadsheet the values that can be changed are the amount of time each activity is crashed (cells G4:G8) and the time when each event occurs (cells B13:B16). Thus, these ranges are entered in the By Changing Cells box.

Now we are ready to enter the constraints for this problem. Perhaps the most obvious constraint is that we want to complete the project within 10 days. Since node 5 (cell B16) corresponds to the event of the project being completed, we can specify this constraint as follows:

$$B16 <= 10$$

Another important set of constraints is needed to make sure we don't crash an activity more than the maximum number of days that it can be crashed. Constraints to ensure this could be entered as follows:

$$G4 <= J4$$
$$G5 <= J5$$
$$G6 <= J6$$
$$G7 <= J7$$
$$G8 <= J8$$

Another set of constraints is needed to make sure that the precedence relationships specified in the network diagram are not violated. We do this by keeping track of the event times of the nodes. For example, the event time of node 2 cannot occur until after activity A has been completed (assuming that the project begins at time zero). The time to complete activity A is its normal time less the amount of time it is crashed. Since cell B13 corresponds to the event time for node 2, mathematically we could enter this constraint as follows:

$$B13 >= B4-G4$$

This constraint says that the event corresponding to node 2 cannot occur until after activity A has been completed.

Constraints for the other nodes could be created in a similar fashion. For example, the constraint for node 3 would be:

$$B14 >= B6-G6$$

Moving on to node 4, note that this node has 2 arrows pointing to it. A node with more than one arrow pointing to it will need a separate constraint for each such arrow. Thus, we need the following two constraints for node 4:

$$B15 >= B13+B5-G5$$
$$B15 >= B14+B7-G7$$

The first constraint says that node 4 cannot occur until after node 2 has occurred, plus the amount of time it takes to complete activity B. The second constraint says that node 4 cannot occur until after node 3 has occurred, plus the amount of time it takes to complete activity C.

Node 5 has only one arrow pointing to it and therefore will require only one constraint. More specifically, node 5 cannot occur until after node 4 has been completed, plus the amount of time it takes to complete activity E, or

$$B16 >=B15+B8-G8$$

Finally, we need to add constraints to ensure that all decision variables are greater than or equal to zero:

$$G4:G8 >= 0$$
$$B13:B16 >= 0$$

In this example we assume that the activities can be crashed a fraction of a day, so we do not need to add constraints that restrict the decision variables to integers.

To enter these constraints, select the Add button in the Subject to the Constraints section of the Parameters dialog box. The entire set of constraints needed is as follows:

$$B16 <= 10$$
$$G4 <= J4$$
$$G5 <= J5$$
$$G6 <= J6$$
$$G7 <= J7$$
$$G8 <= J8$$

$$B13 >= B4-G4$$
$$B14 >= B6-G6$$
$$B15 >= B13+B5-G5$$

$$B15 >= B14+B7-G7$$
$$B16 >= B15+B8-G8$$
$$G4:G8 >= 0$$
$$B13:B16 >= 0$$

After we enter these constraints, the Solver Parameters dialog box appears as:

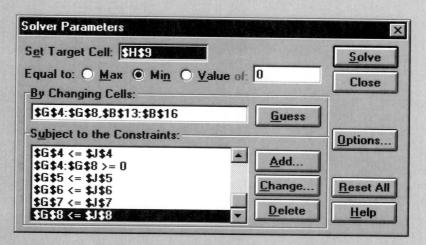

To find the least costly way to crash the project down to 10 days, select the Solve button. As is shown below, the solution Solver found is to crash activity A by 2 days and activity D by 1 day for a total cost of $350. This is the same solution that we found in Solved Exercise 16.5.

	A	B	C	D	E	F	G	H	I	J
1					Total	Crash	Amount	Cost of		Maximum
2		Normal	Crash	Normal	Crash	Cost	To Crash	Crashing	Actual	Crash
3	Activity	Time	Time	Cost	Cost	Per Day	Activity	Activity	Time	Days
4	A	7	4	$500	$800	$100	2	$200	5	3
5	B	3	2	$200	$350	$150	0	$0	3	1
6	C	6	4	$500	$900	$200	0	$0	6	2
7	D	3	1	$200	$500	$150	1	$150	2	2
8	E	2	1	$300	$550	$250	0	$0	2	1
9	Total							$350		
10										
11		Event								
12	Node	Time								
13	2	5								
14	3	6								
15	4	8								
16	5	10								
17										
18										
19	Key Formulas:									
20	Cell F4: =(E4-D4)/(B4-C4) [copy formula to cells F5:F8]									
21	Cell H4: =G4*F4 [copy formula to cells H5:H8]									
22	Cell H9: =SUM(H4:H8)									
23	Cell I4: =B4-G4 [copy formula to cells I5:I8]									
24	Cell J4: =B4-C4 [copy to J5:J8]									

CONTROLLING THE PROJECT: COST AND PERFORMANCE

One of the control systems most widely used in projects is the *cost variance report*. Cost standards are determined through engineering estimates or through analysis of past performance and become the target costs for the project. The actual costs are then monitored by the organization's cost accounting system and compared with the cost standard. Feedback is provided to the project manager, who can exert any necessary control if the difference between standard and actual (called a *variance*) is considered significant.

As an example, consider the cost-schedule charts in Figure 16.16. In Figure 16.16*a*, actual progress is plotted alongside planned progress, and the "effective" progress time (TE) is noted. Because progress is less than planned, TE is less than the actual time (TA). On the cost chart (Figure 16.16*b*) we see that the apparent variance (SC − AC) from the planned cost at this time is quite small, despite the lack of progress. But this is misleading; the variance should be much more given the lack of progress.

These two graphs are combined for project managers into an ***earned value*** chart—Figure 16.17—where the planned (scheduled) cost (SC), actual cost (AC), and value completed (actual earned dollars of progress or effective cost, EC) are plotted. In this situation (which is different from that in Figure 16.16), the actual cost is *greater* than the plan, even though progress lags behind the plan (thus, the huge spending variance). Plotted in this manner, one chart will serve to monitor both progress and cost. We can then define three variances: (1) a *spending variance* equal to the value completed less the actual cost (EC − AC), where a cost overrun is negative; (2) a *schedule variance* equal to the effective cost or value completed less the scheduled cost (EC − SC), where "behind" is negative; and (3) a

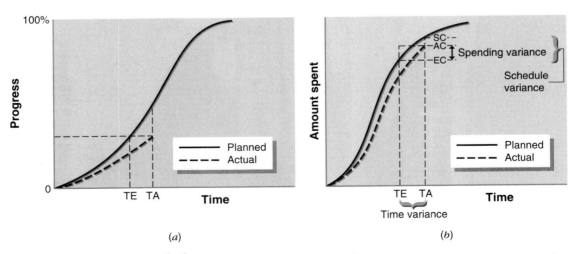

Figure 16.16   Cost-schedule reconciliation charts.

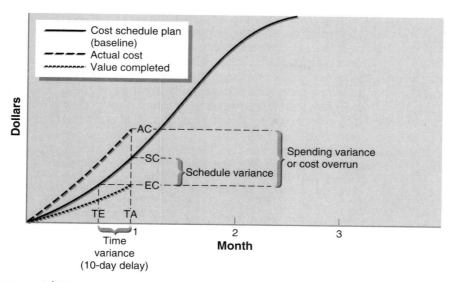

Figure 16.17 Earned value chart.

time variance equal to the effective time less the actual time (TE − TA), where a delay is negative.

When these variances are significant, the project manager must identify (or at least attempt to identify) an *assignable cause* for the variance. That is, he or she must study the project to determine why the variance occurred. This is so that the proper remedy can be used to keep the variance from recurring. A corrective action is called for if some inefficiency or change in the prescribed process caused the variance.

Variances can be both favorable and unfavorable. A significant *favorable variance* (for example, a variance resulting from a large quantity discount on material) will usually not require corrective action, though investigation is still worthwhile so that this better-than-expected performance can be repeated.

The accompanying sidebar describes how Heublein was having trouble with capital project costs that went over budget and what it did to address the problem.

OPERATIONS IN PRACTICE

Heublein's Capital Project Management System

Some years ago, Heublein, a large manufacturer of food and beverage products, was facing difficulties with its capital project process in its four major business groups (Spirits, Wines, Food Service/Franchising, and Grocery Products). Major projects were going significantly over budget, and inflationary costs were dictating that better utilization of capital funds was required.

Heublein thus instituted the development of a project management and control system (PM&C) that could be tailored to the specific needs of each of its separate groups. The directors of the engineering department of each group were assigned responsibility to help the PM&C program manager both design the system and implement it, not only within their own groups but throughout Heublein.

A four-phase project ensued to develop the PM&C system. Phase I constituted an educational overview for the participants; phase II focused on the design of PM&C; phase III consisted of the development of a project plan; and phase IV was implementation and final evaluation.

During phase II, it was decided that PM&C would consist of a number of subsystems that could be individually called up from a "menu." This would allow each group to use only those portions of the system that it needed, without forcing it to include functions that were a hindrance. This menu consisted of the following 10 subsystems.

1. Executive summary and justification
2. Project objectives
3. Project structure
4. Project costs
5. Network
6. Schedule
7. Resource allocation
8. Organization and accountability
9. Control system
10. Milestones and project subdivisions

Heublein allowed a year and $200,000 ($60,000 out of pocket) to design and implement PM&C. The system has had a major impact throughout the company. Typical was one manager's comment: "Its value has been immeasurable. Since its inception, 15 new products have gone through the [system]" (Spirer and Hulvey, 1981).

$\mathcal{S}$OLVED EXERCISE 16.6 ❖ Earned Value

A project at week 35 has an actual cost of $235,000; a schedule (planned) cost of $250,000; and a value completed of $220,000. Find the spending and schedule variances.

Solution:

Spending variance = value completed − actual cost = $220,000 − $235,000 = −$15,000.
Schedule variance = value completed − scheduled cost = $220,000 − $250,000 = −$30,000.

CHAPTER IN PERSPECTIVE

This is the sixth chapter of seven addressing the product supply process. Our discussion of the product supply process began with aggregate and master scheduling in Chapter 11. Chapter 12 continued the discussion and addressed issues related to determining when to order independent demand items and how much to order, in support of the schedules developed in Chapter 11. Next, in Chapters 13 and 14, we focused on managing dependent demand items with MRP and JIT systems, respectively. In Chapter 15 our planning horizon was shortened and detailed scheduling for job shops and flow shops was discussed.

In the present chapter we continued our discussion of detailed scheduling but shifted our attention to the scheduling of projects. Projects are actually processes that are performed infrequently or ad hoc. The majority of this chapter focused on project scheduling techniques. In general, project planning techniques have been developed for cases when activity times are known and cases when activity times are not known with certainty. The chapter also briefly discussed crashing projects and controlling project cost and performance.

❖ CHECK YOUR UNDERSTANDING

1. Briefly define: *work breakdown structure, critical path, crashing, slack,* and *dummy activity.*

2. What is the overriding advantage of a project, particularly in comparison with the other forms of transformation systems?

3. Describe the construction of the work breakdown structure and the project master schedule. Where should this information come from?

4. How is the project master schedule different from a Gantt chart? How is it the same?

5. What are some reasons for the growth in project operations?

6. It is sometimes given as a rule of thumb that optimistic and pessimistic times should be values that would occur only once in 100 repetitions of an activity. Why, then, are these times not symmetrical about the most likely time or even the mean time?

7. Define the four variances: spending, schedule, time, and total. What do negative variances mean for each one of them?

8. Could there ever be negative slack?

9. How does the earned value chart monitor both cost and performance?

10. Why can the SOT rule not be used for projects?

❖ EXPAND YOUR UNDERSTANDING

1. Frequently, the project's tasks are not well defined, and there is an urge to "get on with the work," since time is critical. How serious is it to minimize the planning effort and get on with the project?

2. Another way to get a cost-time graph for expediting a project is to begin with the all-crash project instead of the all-normal project and proceed to "relax" the crash activities one at a time. Will this procedure give the same cost-time graph as the all-normal method?

3. Contrast the cost-schedule reconciliation charts with the earned value chart. Which one would a project manager prefer?

4. How would a manager calculate the value completed for an earned value chart?

5. Some texts define *free slack* along a path. What might this be?

6. Do you think people's estimates are more accurate for optimistic or pessimistic activity times?

7. Of the reasons discussed for the growth in project operations, which do you think are contributing most?

8. Why doesn't it make sense to think in terms of a critical path when activity times are not known with certainty?

9. For situations with uncertain activity times, provide some intuition into why t_e and σ^2 are calculated using the formulas given in this chapter.

10. For situations with uncertain activity times, why must the probability that all paths finish by the specified time be calculated, rather than just the probability for the path with the longest expected time?

11. In calculating the probability that a project will be finished by some specified time, the probabilities of each path are multiplied together, on the assumption that the paths are independent of one another. How reasonable is this assumption?

❖ APPLY YOUR UNDERSTANDING

Nutri-Sam

Nutri-Sam produces a line of vitamins and nutritional supplements. It recently introduced its Nutri-Sports Energy Bar, which is based on new scientific findings about the proper balance of macronutrients. The energy bar has become extremely popular among elite athletes and other people who follow the diet. One distinguishing feature of the Nutri-Sports Energy Bar is that each bar contains 50 milligrams of eicosapentaenoic acid (EPA), a substance strongly linked to reducing the risk of cancer but found in only a few foods, such as salmon. Nutri-Sam was able to include EPA in its sports bars because it had previously developed and patented a process to refine EPA for its line of fish-oil capsules.

Because of the success of the Nutri-Sports Energy Bar in the United States, Nutri-Sam is considering offering it in Latin America. With its domestic facility currently operating at capacity, the president of Nutri-Sam has decided to investigate the option of adding approximately 10,000 square feet of production space to its facility in Latin America at a cost of $5 million.

The project to expand the Latin American facility involves four major phases: (1) concept development, (2) definition of the plan, (3) design and construction, and (4) start-up and turnover. During the *concept development* phase, a program manager is chosen who will oversee all four phases of the project and the manager is given a budget to develop a plan. The outcome of the concept development phase is a rough plan, feasibility estimates for the project, and a rough schedule. Also, a justification for the project and a budget for the next phase are developed.

In the *plan definition* phase, the program manager selects a project manager to oversee the activities associated with this phase. Plan definition consists of four major activities that are completed more or less concurrently: defining the project scope, developing a broad schedule of activities, developing detailed cost estimates, and developing a plan for staffing. The output of this phase is a detailed plan and proposal for management specifying how much the project will cost, how long it will take, and what the deliverables are.

If the project gets management's approval and management provides the appropriations, the project progresses to the third phase, *design and construction*. This phase consists of four major activities: detailed engineering, mobilization of the construction employees, procurement of production equipment, and construction of the facility. Typically, the detailed engineering and the mobilization of the construction employees are done concurrently. Once these activities are completed, construction of the facility and procurement of the production equipment are done concurrently. The outcome of this phase is the physical construction of the facility.

The final phase, *start-up and turnover,* consists of four major activities: pre-start-up inspection of the facility, recruiting and training the workforce, solving start-up problems, and determining optimal operating parameters (called *centerlining*). Once the pre-start-up inspection is completed, the workforce is recruited and trained at the same time that start-up problems are solved. Centerlining is initiated upon the completion of these activities. The desired outcome of this phase is a facility operating at design requirements.

The table below provides optimistic, most likely, and pessimistic time estimates for the major activities.

Activity	Optimistic Time (months)	Most Likely Time (months)	Pessimistic Time (months)
Concept Development	3	12	24
Plan Definition			
Define project scope	1	2	12
Develop broad schedule	0.25	0.5	1
Detailed cost estimates	0.2	0.3	0.5
Develop staffing plan	0.2	0.3	0.6
Design and Construction			
Detailed engineering	2	3	6
Facility construction	8	12	24
Mobilization of employees	0.5	2	4
Procurement of equipment	1	3	12
Start-up and Turnover			
Pre-start-up inspection	0.25	0.5	1
Recruiting and training	0.25	0.5	1
Solving start-up problems	0	1	2
Centerlining	0	1	4

Questions

1. Draw a network diagram for this project. Identify all the paths through the network diagram.

2. Simulate the completion of this project 100 times assuming that activity times follow a normal distribution. Estimate the mean and standard deviation of the project completion time.

3. Develop a histogram to summarize the results of your simulation.

4. Calculate the probability that the project can be completed within 30 months. What is the probability that the project will take longer than 40 months? What is the probability that the project will take between 30 and 40 months?

❖ EXERCISES

1. The following PERT chart was prepared at the beginning of a small construction project.

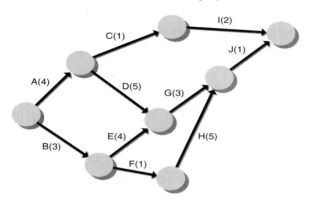

C(1), I(2), J(1), A(4), D(5), G(3), E(4), H(5), B(3), F(1)

The duration, in days, follows the letter of each activity. What is the critical path? Which activities should be monitored most closely?

At the end of the first week of construction, it was noted that activity A was completed in 2.5 days, but activity B required 4.5 days. What impact does this have on the project? Are the same activities critical?

2. Refer to Exercise 1. Compute the earliest start and finish times, the latest start and finish times, and the slack times for each activity. Also, calculate the slack for each path.

3. Consider Exercise 1 again. Suppose that the duration of both activity A and activity D can be re-

duced to 1 day, at a cost of $15 per day of reduction. Also, activities E, G, and H can be reduced in duration by 1 day at a cost of $25 per day of reduction. What is the least-cost approach to crash the project 2 days? What is the shortest "crashed" duration, the new critical path, and the cost of crashing?

4. Consider Exercise 1 again. Suppose that the duration of both activity A and activity D can be reduced to 1 day, at a cost of $15 per day of reduction. Also, activities E, G, and H can be reduced in duration by 1 day at a cost of $25 per day of reduction. Use a spreadsheet to find the least-cost approach to crash the project so that it is finished within 9 days.

5. Given the following project, find the probability of completion by 17 weeks; by 24 weeks.

Times (Weeks)

Activity	Optimistic	Most Likely	Pessimistic
1–2	5	11	11
1–3	10	10	10
1–4	2	5	8
2–6	1	7	13
3–6	4	4	10
3–7	4	7	10
3–5	2	2	2
4–5	0	6	6
5–7	2	8	14
6–7	1	4	7

If the firm can complete the project within 18 weeks, it will receive a bonus of $10,000. But if the project is delayed beyond 22 weeks, it must pay a penalty of $5000. If the firm can choose whether or not to bid on this project, what should its decision be if this is normally only a breakeven project?

6. Construct a network for the project below and find its expected completion time.

Activity	t_e (Weeks)	Preceding Activities
a	3	None
b	5	a
c	3	a
d	1	c
e	3	b
f	4	b, d
g	2	c
h	3	g, f
i	1	e, h

7. In the project network shown in the following figure, the number alongside each activity designates its known duration in weeks. Determine:

a. Earliest and latest start and finish times for each activity.

b. Earliest time that the project can be completed.

c. Slack for all activities.

d. Critical events and activities.

e. Critical path.

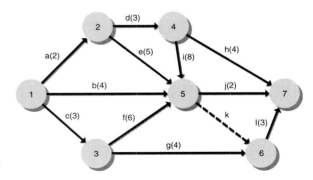

8. Given the following information regarding a project:

Activity	Duration (Weeks)	Preceding Activities
a	3	none
b	1	none
c	3	a
d	4	a
e	4	b
f	5	b
g	2	c, e
h	3	f

a. Draw the PERT network.

b. What is the critical path?

c. What will the scheduled (earliest completion) time for the entire project be?

d. What is the effect on the project if activity *e* takes an extra week? Two extra weeks? Three extra weeks?

9. Given the following schedule for a liability work package done as part of an accounting audit in a corporation:

Activity	Duration (Days)	Preceding Activities
a. Obtain schedule of liabilities	3	None
b. Mail confirmation	15	a
c. Test pension plan	5	a
d. Vouch selected liabilities	60	a
e. Test accruals and amortization	6	d
f. Process confirmations	40	b
g. Reconcile interest expense to debt	10	c, e
h. Verify debt restriction compliance	7	f
i. Investigate debit balances	6	g
j. Review subsequent payments	12	h, i

Find:

a. Critical path.

b. Slack time on "process confirmations."

c. Slack time on "test pension plan."

d. Slack time on "verify debt restriction compliance."

10. Given a PERT network:

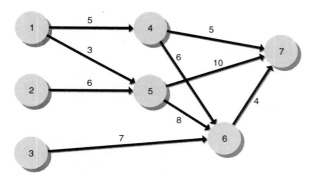

Note that three activities can start immediately.

Find:

a. Critical path.

b. Earliest time to complete the project.

c. Slack on activities 4–6, 5–6, and 4–7.

11. Given the following network:

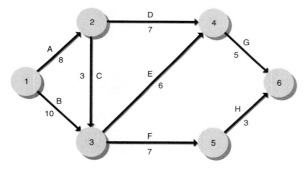

a. What is the critical path?

b. How long will it take to complete this project?

c. Can activity B be delayed without delaying the completion of the project? If so, by how many days?

12. Given the estimated activity times below and the network in Exercise 11:

Activity	t_o	t_m	t_p
A	6	7	14
B	8	10	12
C	2	3	4
D	6	7	8
E	5	5.5	9
F	5	7	9
G	4	6	8
H	2.5	3	3.5

What is the probability that the project will be completed within:

a. 21 days?

b. 22 days?

c. 25 days?

13. The events of the project below are designated 1, 2, and so on.

a. Draw the PERT network.

b. Find the critical path.

c. Find the slacks on all activities.

Activity	Preceding Event	Succeeding Event	t_e (weeks)	Preceding Activities
a	1	2	3	none
b	1	3	6	none
c	1	4	8	none
d	2	5	7	a
e	3	5	5	b
f	4	5	10	c
g	4	6	4	c
h	5	7	5	d, e, f
i	6	7	6	g

14. From historical data, it has been determined that the activity times for an upcoming project are approximately normally distributed, with the means and standard deviations given in the following table. Develop a spreadsheet that simulates the completion of this project 30 times. What is your estimate of the completion time of the project? What is a reasonable range of project completion times?

Activity	Mean (days)	Standard Deviation
1–2	10	1.6
2–3	13	1.2
2–4	20	5.2
3–4	10	2.3
3–5	6	1.5
4–5	5	1.0

15.

Activity	Duration
A–B	1
A–C	2
A–D	3
D–C	4
C–B	3
D–E	8
C–F	2
B–F	4
I–J	2
C–E	6
E–F	5
F–G	10
F–H	11
E–H	1
G–H	9
E–J	3
G–I	8
H–J	6

a. Draw the PERT diagram.

b. Find the critical path.

c. Find the completion time.

16. Denver Iron and Steel Company is expanding its operations to include a new drive-in weigh station. The weigh station will be a heated, air-conditioned building with a large floor and a small office. The large room will have the scales, a 15-foot counter, and several display cases for its equipment.

Before erection of the building, the project manager evaluated the project using PERT/CPM analysis. The following activities with their corresponding times were recorded:

# Activity	Optimistic	Most Likely	Pessimistic	Preceding Tasks
1 Lay foundation	8	10	13	—
2 Dig hole for scale	5	6	8	—
3 Insert scale bases	13	15	21	2
4 Erect frame	10	12	14	1, 3
5 Complete building	11	20	30	4
6 Insert scales	4	5	8	5
7 Insert display cases	2	3	4	5
8 Put in office equipment	4	6	10	7
9 Give finishing touches	2	3	4	8, 6

Using PERT/CPM analysis, find the expected completion time.

17. The network shown in the following table has a fixed cost of $90 per day, but money can be saved by shortening the project duration. Find the least-cost schedule.

Activity	Normal Time	Crash Time	Cost Increase ($) (1st, 2nd, 3rd day)
1–2	7	4	30, 50, 70
2–3	9	6	40, 45, 65
1–3	12	10	60, 60
2–4	11	9	35, 60
3–4	3	3	—

18. Given a network with normal times and crash time (in parentheses), find the least-cost solution to completing the project in the shortest time.

Activity	Time Reduction Direct Cost Per Day
1–2	$30 first, $50 second
2–3	$80 each
3–4	$25 first, $60 second
2–4	$30 first, $70 second, $90 third

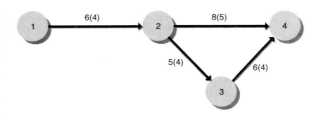

19. The following data were obtained from a study of the times required to overhaul a chemical plant:

Activity	Crash Schedule Time	Cost	Normal Schedule Time	Cost
1–2	3	$6	5	$4
1–3	1	5	5	3
2–4	5	7	10	4
3–4	2	6	7	4
2–6	2	5	6	3
4–6	5	9	11	6
4–5	4	6	6	3
6–7	1	4	5	2
5–7	1	5	4	2

Note: Costs are given in thousands of dollars; time is given in weeks.
a. Find the all-normal schedule and cost.
b. Find the all-crash schedule and cost.
c. Find the total cost required to expedite all activities from all-normal (case *a*) to all-crash (case *b*).
d. Find the *least-cost* plan for the all-crash time schedule. Start from the all-crash problem (*b*).

20. Consider Exercise 19 again. Use Excel to find the *least-cost* plan to finish the project in 10 weeks; in 8 weeks.

21. As in the situation illustrated in Figure 16.16, a project at day 70 exhibits only 35 percent progress when 40 percent was planned, for an effective date of 55. Planned cost was $17,000 at day 55 and $24,000 at day 70, and actual cost was $20,000 at day 55 and $30,000 at day 70. Find time variance, spending cost variance, and schedule variance.

22. As in the situation shown in Figure 16.17, a project at month 2 exhibited an actual cost of $78,000, a scheduled (planned) cost of $84,000, and a value completed of $81,000. Find the spending and schedule variances. Estimate time variance.

23. A project at month 5 had an actual cost of $34,000, a planned cost of $42,000, and a value completed of $39,000. Find the spending and schedule variances.

Quality Control

$\mathscr{C}$ HAPTER OVERVIEW

❖ Quality control techniques can be applied to an organization's inputs, transformation system, and outputs. Quality control applied to inputs and outputs is called *acceptance sampling*. Quality control applied to the transformation system is called *process control*.

❖ Every productive system generates variability in its output. At some times, the system will exhibit only chance (or random) variation. At other times, the variation in the transformation system may be due to a specific cause; this is called *assignable variation*.

❖ Control charts are used to identify when assignable variation is present and therefore when corrective action is needed. The upper and lower control limits of control charts are usually set at the mean plus and minus 3 standard deviations.

❖ Rules to indicate that a situation is out of control, besides a point exceeding the upper or lower control limits, include 2 consecutive points very near the same limit, 5 consecutively increasing or decreasing points, 7 points on the same side of the mean, and worsening erratic behavior.

❖ Control charts can be developed on the basis of variable data or attribute data. *Variable data* are measurable characteristics, such as weight, temperature, and diameter. *Attribute data* are descriptive characteristics of an output such as acceptable and defective or good and bad.

❖ Two control charts are used simultaneously when variable data are collected: a means chart and a range chart. The control limits for both can be found from tables based on sample size and average range.

❖ The two major charts for attributes are the *fraction defective* (p) chart and the *number of defects* (c) chart. The p chart is based on the binomial distribution and the c chart is based on the Poisson distribution.

❖ *Acceptance sampling* involves the selection of a sampling plan for a "lot" of items that specifies how many items to sample (n) and the maximum number of defectives (c) beyond which the lot will be rejected. The probabilities of acceptance and rejection are given by the operating characteristic curve for that sampling plan.

❖ *Process capability* measures the extent to which an organization's production system can meet design specifications. It depends on the location of the process mean, the natural variability inherent in the production system, the stability of the system, and the product's design requirements.

$\mathscr{I}$ NTRODUCTION _____

❖ Chapter 3 concluded with an overview of major quality awards and certifications, including the Malcolm Baldrige National Quality Award. One characteristic that many of the Baldrige winners share is a commitment to the statistical measurement of their progress. More specifically, these companies collect data for a wide variety of performance measures and use statistical tools to identify and correct problems. For example, Westinghouse Electric collects and monitors data daily on 60 key performance measures. Similarly, Wallace Company monitors 72 processes that affect on-time delivery and accuracy of invoices. And AT&T's Universal Card Services unit collects over 100 quality measurements divisionwide each day (Nadkarni, 1995).

❖ NCR's plant in West Columbia, South Carolina, produces business information processing systems. With competition increasing, NCR recognized the necessity of continuously improving its products. A major component of NCR's continuous improvement program is the use of statistical techniques.

   The NCR plant began using statistical process control techniques in 1985 to monitor its autoinsertion operation on its assembly line for printed circuit boards. At the time, the autoinsertion operation was producing an unacceptable number of defective boards because parts were misinserted or broken, the wrong parts were used, and so on. As part of the quality assurance program, the quality engineering department established process averages, control limits, and guidelines for action for "out-of-control" conditions. The guidelines specified that production should stop when an out-of-control condition was detected until the cause was identified. Random samples of 1000 insertions were collected each hour, and the results of the sample were plotted on a *c* chart. Out-of-control situations were investigated to identify the assignable cause. NCR learned a great deal about the autoinsertion operation from using the control charts. For example, the problem of broken parts was traced to a specific supplier. Because this experiment was a success, statistical process control was implemented across the entire assembly line. NCR has since changed its approach "from inspect and repair" to "prevent and design for quality" (Dobbins and Padgett, 1993).

❖ As a result of environmental restrictions and reduced quantities of high-quality large-diameter trees, timber companies have used a number of statistical quality control techniques to maximize the quality and quantity of finished lumber produced from each tree. There are seven basic steps required to covert a log into finished lumber. First, the log is debarked. Second, the debarked log is split down the middle in the primary sawing stage. Third, the split log is resawed to create boards of various sizes. Fourth, the ends of the boards are trimmed. Fifth, the boards are stacked. Sixth, after being stacked, the boards are dried in a kiln for 2 to 30 days. Seventh, the boards are planed.

The stacking operation provides a good illustration of how sawmills are using statistical quality control. This operation is particularly important because the way the boards are stacked determines the straightness of the finished lumber. The lumber is actually stacked in layers. Separators are placed between the layers to form an air channel that carries heat to the wood and allows moisture to move away from it. Also, the separators are used to transfer the weight of the wood.

Because automated equipment is used to stack the lumber, it is important to monitor the alignment of the separators. To illustrate, it is estimated that each misplaced separator increases costs $31.50, owing to board warping. Because an average sawmill handles upward of 30,000 separators each day, if just 1 percent of the separators are misplaced, the daily cost to the company would be $9450. If we assume that the sawmill operates 250 days per year, the annual cost of misplacing just 1 percent of the separators would exceed $2.3 million.

To monitor separator alignment, a measuring board is placed in front of each column of separators in a stack of lumber. Each stack of lumber typically has 15 columns of separators and approximately 360 separators. All separators that are not hidden by the board are considered misplaced. The total number of misplaced separators is divided by the total number of separators in the stack of lumber, and this result is plotted on a p chart. Using the p chart, workers can monitor the stacking equipment and identify problems before an out-of-control situation arises so that corrective action can be initiated (Maki and Milota, 1993).

This final chapter presents the classic techniques for controlling outputs created by the product supply process, known as *quality control.* As we will see, quality control can be applied to an organization's inputs, transformation system, and outputs. Quality control applied at the input stage and the output stage is called *acceptance sampling.* Quality control applied to the transformation system is called *process control,* or sometimes *statistical process control* (SPC).

Quality control is typically carried out in one of two ways: control of variables (characteristics that can be measured on a scale) and control of attributes (descriptive characteristics such as defective or not defective, good or bad, and yes or no). Each of these two areas has its own set of control charts and its own approaches to data collection.

We begin our discussion with an overview of statistical quality control. Next, we address process control. In the following sections, control charts for variables and control charts for attributes are discussed in more detail. The chapter concludes with discussions of acceptance sampling and the ability of a production system to meet design specifications.

$\mathcal{S}$ TATISTICAL QUALITY CONTROL

To maintain the quality of their output, organizations must inspect and test throughout their operations. Both machines and humans can start to deteriorate and begin producing defects. As a machine wears out, for example, its process capability may degrade to the point that it cannot hold the **tolerances** specified by engineering design. Figure 17.1 illustrates this situation. Humans degrade with fatigue, boredom, age, and many other factors. Through continuous testing and inspection, we can monitor this problem and correct it before poor-quality outputs are produced.

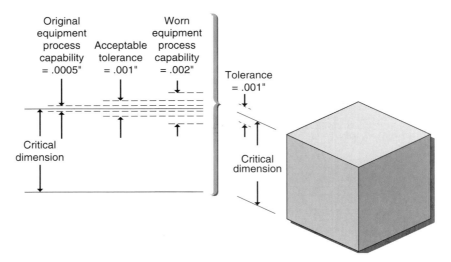

Figure 17.1   Engineering tolerance versus process capability.

❖ Inspection

Inspection is an important part, although only *one* part, of a quality control program. Inspection involves determining, sometimes by testing, whether or not an input or output conforms to organizational standards of quality. However, the role of inspection is not to *correct* the system deficiencies that produced the defective items or, for that matter, even to decide *what* to inspect or *when*.

Inspection is a very commonplace activity. It is prominent not only in manufacturing organizations but also in processing, distributing, and service organizations. Wine tasters and coffee tasters inspect their outputs for many different quality criteria. Order pickers in warehouses inspect the packaging and age of the goods they send out. And bank examiners, federal Occupational Safety and Health Administration (OSHA) inspectors, and Food and Drug Administration (FDA) agents may interrupt the activities of organizations at any time to test conformance to regulations and standards. We often hear about licensing boards that have closed local businesses such as restaurants because their facilities could not pass inspection. Even at home, we regularly inspect the food we eat, the cars we drive, and the clothes we wear.

Because of the extent and difficulty of inspection, it can occupy a considerable amount of time. For simple, repetitive, automated production it may require only a small fraction of a direct worker's time. But in complex, technical, or manual work, such as the development of computer software, it may occupy nearly half the direct labor-hours.

In spite of the time dedicated to the function, it is still not uncommon for inspectors to miss half of all defects passing by them. About two-thirds of defects are caught, but, depending on the situation, this rate may vary from one in five to four in five. For example, spend a minute with Figure 17.2.

"Don't look for coupons or premiums in this pack. The cost of the tobaccos blended in HORSE cigarettes prohibits the use of them."

Figure 17.2 Counting-the-defects exercise. During World War II, soldiers used to bet a new recruit $50 that he could not count all the "e"s on the back of a pack of a certain brand of cigarettes in one reading. Here is an approximate rendition of what that package stated in the 1940's; try it yourself for about 15 seconds.

Bear in mind that most inspectors are probably tired, not quite as enthusiastic about their work as they once were, and not as young as they used to be. To produce approximately the equivalent conditions, the exercise in Figure 17.2 should be completed during the last quarter or semester of your schooling, on a Friday night, at about one o'clock in the morning. The correct number of *e*'s on the pack of cigarettes is 12. The number typically reported by a class of undergraduates is from 8 to 12, with an average of 11. From this it should be clear that inserting inspectors into the end of a production system is not going to miraculously improve the quality of an organization's output.

Better quality will be obtained through inspection if the inspectors know what to look for, have been given proper training (including training in human relations), and have the physical and psychological makeup required for the job. But many organizations use inspectors who are not properly qualified simply because they never checked to see if these people *were* qualified. Instances exist, for example, when inspection jobs demanding high visual acuity were given to workers who were partially blind.

There are a number of particularly important points in the transformation system where inspection is more valuable than at other times. Some of these are the following:

1. *Upon receipt of resources*—checking the quality of raw materials and purchased parts and supplies, testing equipment for ability to meet specifications, verifying the skills of the staff.

2. *Before transformation operations by the worker*—if an operation is expensive, irreversible (such as mixing food ingredients), or of a concealing nature (such as assemblies, coatings, platings).

3. *Immediately before any bottleneck operation*—There is no advantage in feeding a scarce resource defective items that simply consume more of its time.

4. *When the first few items come out of an automatic operation.*

5. *After transformation operations.*

6. *In final inspection.*

7. *When customers complain, return goods, or require service.*

After inspection has revealed a defective item or defective material, what should be done with it? Typically, it is not discarded. It may be reworked and repaired or refashioned into another output if doing so is worthwhile. If not, it may be sold as a "second," as is done with clothing and "second pressings" of wine. If even sale as a second is not feasible, it may be recycled (e.g., shredded, remelted), if possible, and used as new raw material. Last, it may be sold as scrap.

In some instances, it is possible to take a number of defective outputs and combine them to form an acceptable output. This "magic" is common in processing-type industries. Grain in silos and mined coal are both tested for a number of characteristics, any one of which may be either exceeded or insufficient. For example, the corn in one silo may have a moisture content too high to qualify as top-grade corn, while the sugar content of corn in another silo may be too low. By *mixing* the contents of these two silos, however, a combined product is achieved that is now within *both* moisture and sugar requirements for classification as top-grade corn—an interesting example of synergism, in which the whole is equal to more than the sum of the parts.

❖ Sampling

In some processes 100 percent of the output is machine-tested, but many others require manual inspection by a human. Fortunately, it is not usually necessary to inspect *all* the items or material during an inspection; only a *sample* need be tested. This is fortunate, since there are a number of reasons for not conducting 100 percent manual inspection:

1. *Infinite population.* To inspect all the paper clips coming out of a factory, or all the oil from a refinery, would be virtually impossible. In the first situation, the inspection would fall far behind the production rate and go on forever, and in the second, the output is not in discrete form but is infinitely divisible.

2. *Lack of time.* The time needed to adequately test each item may preclude inspecting all the items, as with the paper clips. Answers are needed very quickly for management decisions, and late answers are worthless.

3. *Excessive cost.* Even if time were no problem, the cost of 100 percent inspection and testing is typically prohibitive.

4. *Destructive testing.* In some cases, so-called destructive testing is performed. This involves testing an output until it fails, as is sometimes done with fuses, structural beams, and lightbulbs. If this testing were applied to the entire output, there would be nothing left to sell.

5. *Inaccuracy.* As pointed out earlier, inspection does not catch all defects. As an inspector becomes fatigued or bored, more defects slip by. With 100 percent inspection, this would occur rather quickly. Therefore, better accuracy is often obtained by inspecting and testing only a representative sample rather than the entire output, even with the inherent sampling error.

In some instances, however, 100 percent manual inspection may still be called for. These infrequent cases usually fall among the following situations:

1. *Extreme cost of defects.* If, failure of an output will incur an extremely high cost (such as a loss of human life in a shuttle launch), complete inspection is necessary.

2. *High variability.* In cases where the variability of the output may be extreme (typically with human inputs, as in education) but consistency is desired (thus excluding artworks, musical compositions, novels, etc.), 100 percent inspection may be desirable, if it is not too expensive or time-consuming.

3. *Operating unit assemblies.* When an assembled item is dispensed to recipients a unit at a time and is always expected to operate initially (as with a television set, an automobile, or a clothes dryer), it is desirable to check the gross performance of 100 percent of the output if it can be done quickly and cheaply. For example, whether a dryer heats up and spins when turned on can be checked in seconds. But checking all the various cycles of the dryer could entail a major, time-consuming test.

4. *Rejected lots.* If a lot (a binful, a gross, a filled railroad car) has been sampled and rejected, it may be desirable to check the entire lot, not to determine the defect rate of the lot, but to locate and *remove* the defective items so that those remaining can be used or sold.

❖ Type I and II Errors

Inspection is identical in concept to our society's procedure in criminal trials. We assume that a defendant is innocent until proven guilty. Similarly, we assume that a batch of output is of acceptable quality until proven otherwise. The information obtained by sampling then constitutes the evidence on which a "verdict" is reached.

As in the legal process, two types of errors can be made (Figure 17.3). A ***type I error*** is committed when an innocent defendant (a good-quality lot) is found guilty (declared "defective"). A ***type II error*** is made when a guilty defendant (a "defective" lot) is found innocent (declared of good quality). The seriousness of these two types of errors depends on the organization and the type of output. Our society considers a type I error in the legal process extremely serious and goes to great lengths to prevent it. Organizations producing goods and services, on the other hand, do not need to worry about the "rights" of their outputs. Hence, they have more concern with the harm that may be done by passing a lot off as good when it actually is defective. Thus they are more concerned about type II errors. In medicine, where a disease has no "rights" and the patient suffers the consequences of an error in inspection, type II errors are of even more concern. The result has therefore been to utilize more and more sophisticated (and expensive) testing equipment to reduce the possibility that a patient who *has* a particular disease will be found *disease-free* by a test—a type II error.

In the terminology of quality control, the probability of a type I error is known as ***producer's risk,*** since this is the chance that the producer's output will be incorrectly declared defective or unacceptable. The probability of a type II error is known as ***consumer's risk.*** The consumer will sometimes, because of the sampling plan, accept a lot as acceptable when it is actually defective. As we will see later in this chapter, one objective of a sampling plan is to balance these two risks.

Every productive system generates variability in its output. One goal of quality control is to ensure that this variability is small enough that the output as a whole may be deemed of acceptable quality. This natural variability is seen as emanating primarily from two sources: *chance (random) variation* and *assignable (nonrandom) variation.*

Chance variation is the variability that is built into (actually, allowed to remain in) the system. There is "play" between the gears and mechanical parts of machines; there is variation in the inputs; processing conditions are variable; and human performance is particularly variable. When the productive operations are designed, the allowable chance variability *(tolerance)* is accounted for, and the most economical system that can produce within those limits is constructed. If it later turns out that this chance variation is too great, the entire system may have to be reworked.

Assignable variation occurs because some element of the system or some operating condition is out of control. A machine may be excessively worn, a part may be broken, a worker may be mistrained, inspection gages or instruments may be

Lot (defendant) is actually	Inspection decision (verdict)	
	Good (innocent)	Defective (guilty)
Good (innocent)	Correct	Type I error
Defective (guilty)	Type II error	Correct

Figure 17.3 Possibilities for errors in inspection.

faulty, and so forth. Quality control must identify this variation so as to correct the faulty element or condition (or refuse shipment of the goods).

If we consider the simplest model of an organization's operations—the *input–transformation system–output* model (Figure 1.1 in Chapter 1)—we see that two elements must be controlled in order to control the quality variation of the output: (1) the transformation system and (2) the inputs. Two separate types of control have been developed for these two elements: ***process control*** for the transformation system and ***acceptance sampling*** for the inputs. Acceptance sampling may also be performed on outputs to ensure the quality of products being delivered to customers.

1. *Process control.* Control of the productive operations of an organization. With regular examination of an output, quality control can determine if a system element is malfunctioning. A blood test, for example, can detect many anomalies in the functioning of the human body.

2. *Acceptance sampling.* Determination of acceptable and unacceptable products and services. This function is important to the organization in its acquisition of appropriate resources, especially materials, for producing its output. Although every organization must certify the acceptability of its resources, *quality control* performs this function for physical materials (parts, raw materials), *personnel* performs it for human resources, *engineering* performs it for plant and equipment, and so on. Since most of nonmaterials purchases are single-unit acquisitions, sampling is not usually done; each item is inspected by itself.

When quality control is performing an inspection, it will either *measure* something or simply determine the existence of a characteristic. Measuring, called *inspection for variables,* usually relates to weight, length, temperature, diameter, or some other variable that can be *scaled*. Identifying a characteristic, called *inspection of attributes,* can also examine scaled variables but usually considers *dichotomous* variables such as right-wrong, acceptable-defective, black-white, timely-late, and other such characteristics that either cannot be measured or do not *need* to be measured with any more precision than yes-no. Both types of inspection—for variables or for attributes—can be used for either process control or acceptance sampling.

PROCESS CONTROL

One of management's most difficult decisions in quality control centers on whether or not an activity is out of control and needs adjustment. Consider the management of a large city library. To manage such an organization would require monitoring and controlling the flow and inventories of library materials (books, periodicals, records, cassettes, etc.); the condition of facilities and equipment (building, chairs, shelves, tables, utilities, duplicating machines, computers); the hours and performance of employees (payroll, personnel records, interview forms); information about users (requests, reference calls, monthly borrowing, returns); and so on.

CONTROL CHARTS

Walter A. Shewhart, a researcher at Bell Telephone Laboratories, developed the concept of statistical **control charts** in the 1920s to distinguish between *chance variation* in a system and variation caused by the system's being out of control—*assignable variation*. Should a process go out of control, that must first be detected, then the assignable cause must be identified, and finally the appropriate action or adjustment must be performed. The control chart is used to detect when a process has gone out of control.

One example of a general control chart, used to detect loss of control over cost and schedule, is illustrated in Figure 17.4, which is monitoring a project's *critical ratio (CR)*, defined here for projects as

$$\frac{\text{actual progress}}{\text{scheduled progress}} \times \frac{\text{budgeted cost}}{\text{actual cost}}$$

The standard of performance is 1.0, where everything is on schedule or else the deviation in cost exactly counterbalances the deviation in progress. Above 1.0, progress is ahead of cost for that point or cost is below progress—in either case, a welcome situation unless the ratio gets very large. Then the project manager should investigate to find out why things are going so well. Are data really being reported accurately? Has someone made a breakthrough the project manager has not heard about?

Ratios less than 1.0 indicate trouble. As noted in Figure 17.4, slight deviations from 1.0 may be safely ignored, but larger deviations warrant investigation, the extent and promptness of investigation increasing with the size of the deviation. The heavy line indicates actual plotted critical ratio values to date. The critical ratio looked as if trouble were coming, but things seem to have been corrected.

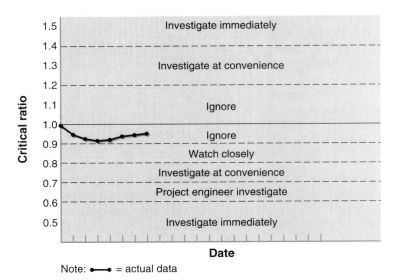

Note: •—• = actual data

Figure 17.4 Critical ratio (CR) control chart.

Applications of ratio analysis, as in this example, are particularly useful in pure service operations, where control is still critical but hard physical measurements of outputs or progress are unavailable. Many other ratios can then be monitored as well.

A repetitive operation will seldom produce *exactly* the same quality or size, or so on; rather, with each repetition the operation will generate variation around some average. Because this variation usually has a large number of small, uncontrollable sources, the pattern of variability is often well described by a standard frequency distribution such as the *normal distribution,* shown plotted against the vertical scale in Figure 17.5.

The succession of measures that result from the continued repetition of the operation can thus be thought of as a *population* of numbers, normally distributed, with some mean and standard deviation. As long as the distribution remains the same, the process is considered to be in control and simply exhibiting chance variation. One way to determine if the distribution is staying the same is to keep checking the mean of the distribution—if it changes to some other value, the operation may be considered to be out of control. The problem, however, is that it is too expensive for organizations to keep constantly checking operations. Therefore, *samples* of the output are checked instead.

In sampling output for inspection, it is imperative that the sample fully *represent* the population being checked; therefore, a *random sample* should be used. But when checks are made only of sample averages, rather than 100 percent of the output, there is always a chance of selecting a sample with an unusually high or low mean. The problem facing the operations manager is thus to decide what is *too high* or *too low* and therefore should be considered out of control. Also, the manager must consider the fact that the more samples are eventually taken, the higher the likelihood of accidentally selecting a sample that has too high (or too low) a mean *when the process is actually still under control.*

The values of the mean selected by the manager as too high or low are called the ***upper control limit*** (UCL) and the ***lower control limit*** (LCL), respectively. These limits generally allow an approach to control known as *management by exception,* since, theoretically, the manager need take no action unless a *sample*

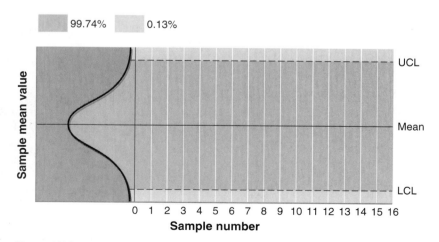

Figure 17.5 Control chart with the limits set at three standard deviations.

mean exceeds the control limits. The control limits most commonly used in organizations are plus and minus 3 *standard deviations*. We know from statistics that the chance that a sample mean will exceed 3 standard deviations, in either direction, due simply to chance variation, is less than 0.3 percent (i.e., 3 times per 1000 samples). Thus, the chance that a sample will fall above the UCL or below the LCL because of natural random causes is so small that this occurrence is strong evidence of assignable variation. Figure 17.5 illustrates the use of control limits set at 3 standard deviations. Of course, using the higher limit values (3 or more) increases the risk of not detecting a process that is only slightly out of control.

An even better approach is to use control charts to predict when an out-of-control situation is likely to occur rather than waiting for a process to actually go out of control. If only chance variation is present in the process, the points plotted on a control chart will not typically exhibit any pattern. On the other hand, if the points exhibit some systematic pattern, this is an indication that assignable variation may be present and corrective action should be taken.

In addition to simply finding a data point outside the control limits, there are rules that should warn a manager of a potential out-of-control condition. These are listed in Figure 17.6. We will call them the **2—5—7 *rules*.** Note in Figure 17.6*a* and *b* that *improvement* in a chart, not just loss of control, should be investigated. Perhaps a worker has discovered a new method or tool that could be applied to other, similar operations. (Or maybe the worker is throwing away defective items.) In Figure 17.6*c*, it appears that there has been a definite, and permanent, change in the process, which should clearly be investigated.

Since the probability is quite low that 2 consecutive points will occur near a control limit by random chance alone, the *2*-rule suggests that corrective action be taken immediately rather than waiting for a future point to actually fall outside the limit. Likewise, the probability is quite low that 5 consecutive points will move in the same direction when only chance variation is present. Thus, rather than waiting

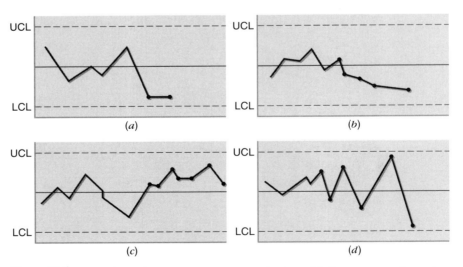

Figure 17.6 Special conditions warranting investigation. (*a*) Two consecutive points, near a control limit. (*b*) Five consecutive decreasing (or increasing) points. (*c*) Seven consecutive points on one side of central line. (*d*) Worsening erratic behavior.

for a trend to move beyond the control limit, the 5-rule suggests taking action as soon as the trend is identified. Finally, there is only a 1.56 percent probability that 7 consecutive points will occur on one side of the central line when only chance variation is present, so this is a strong indication that assignable variation may be present.

The control chart, though originally developed for quality control in manufacturing, is applicable to all sorts of repetitive activities in any kind of organization. Thus, it can be used for services as well as products, for people or machines, for cost or quality, and so on. We look further at the control chart, and particularly the setting of control limits, in the following material.

CONTROL CHARTS
FOR VARIABLES

For the control of variables—that is, measured characteristics—two control charts are commonly used:

1. Chart of the *sample means* ($\overline{X}$).

2. Chart of the *range* (R) of values in each sample (largest value in sample minus smallest value in sample).

It is important to use two control charts for variables because of the way in which control of process quality can be lost. To illustrate this we will use the data supplied in Table 17.1, which correspond to weights of tacos made at a fast-food restaurant. Three samples are taken each day: one during the lunch-hour rush, one during the dinner-hour rush, and one a couple of hours before the restaurant is closed. Each sample consists of three tacos randomly selected from a bin that stores completed tacos waiting to be sold to customers.

Referring to scenario 1, we can easily determine that the average of sample 1 is 5 ounces and the range is 2 ounces ($\overline{X}_1 = 5$, $R_1 = 2$). Similarly, $\overline{X}_2 = 7$, $R_2 = 2$, $\overline{X}_3 = 8$, and $R_3 = 2$. If we consider only the ranges of the samples, no problem is indicated, because all three samples have a range of 2 (assuming that a range of 2 ounces is acceptable to management). On the other hand, the behavior of the process means shows evidence of a problem. Specifically, the process means (weights) have increased throughout the day from an average of 5 ounces to an average of 8 ounces. Thus, for the data listed in scenario 1, the sample ranges indicate acceptable process performance while the sample means indicate unacceptable process performance.

TABLE 17.1 ❖ Sample Data of Weights of Tacos (Ounces)

Sample	Scenario 1	Scenario 2
1	4, 5, 6	4, 5, 6
2	6, 7, 8	3, 5, 7
3	7, 8, 9	2, 5, 8

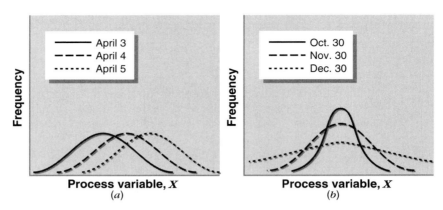

Figure 17.7   Patterns of change in process distributions.

The sample statistics can be calculated in the same way for scenario 2: $\overline{X}_1 = 5$, $R_1 = 2$, $\overline{X}_2 = 5$, $R_2 = 4$, $\overline{X}_3 = 5$, and $R_3 = 6$. In contrast to scenario 1, the sample means show acceptable performance while the sample ranges show unacceptable performance. Thus, we see the necessity of monitoring *both* the mean and the variability of a process.

Figure 17.7 illustrates these two patterns of change in the distribution of process values more formally. These changes might be due to boredom, tool wear, the weather, fatigue, or any other such influence. In Figure 17.7*a* the variability in the process remains the same but the mean changes (scenario 1 above); this effect would be seen in the means ($\overline{X}$) chart but not in the range (R) chart. In Figure 17.7*b* the mean remains the same, but the variability tends to increase (scenario 2 above); this would be seen in the range (R) chart but not the means ($\overline{X}$) chart.

In terms of quality of the output, either type of change could result in lower quality, depending on the situation. Regarding control limits, the lower control limit (LCL) for the means chart *may* be negative, depending on the variable being measured. For example, variables such as profit and temperature can be negative, but variables such as length, diameter, and weight cannot. Since (by definition) the range R can *never* be negative, if calculations indicate a negative LCL for the range chart, it should simply be set to zero.

As indicated earlier, control limits for the means chart are usually set at plus and minus three standard deviations. But if a range chart is also being used, these limits for the means chart can be found by using the average range, which is directly related to the standard deviation,* in the following equations (where $\overline{\overline{X}}$ is the average of the sample means):

$$\mathrm{UCL}_{\overline{X}} = \overline{\overline{X}} + A_2\overline{R}$$

$$\mathrm{LCL}_{\overline{X}} = \overline{\overline{X}} - A_2\overline{R}$$

Similarly, control limits for the range chart are found from:

$$\mathrm{UCL}_R = D_4\overline{R}$$

$$\mathrm{LCL}_R = D_3\overline{R}$$

---

*$A_2\overline{R} = 3\sigma_{\overline{X}}$; $D_4\overline{R} = \overline{R} + 3\sigma_R$; $D_3\overline{R} = \overline{R} - 3\sigma_R$

$\mathscr{T}_{ABLE}$ 17.2 ❖ Control Chart Factors to Determine Control Limits

Sample Size, n	A_2	D_3	D_4
2	1.880	0	3.267
3	1.023	0	2.575
4	0.729	0	2.282
5	0.577	0	2.115
6	0.483	0	2.004
7	0.419	0.076	1.924
8	0.373	0.136	1.864
9	0.337	0.184	1.816
10	0.308	0.223	1.777
12	0.266	0.284	1.716
14	0.235	0.329	1.671
16	0.212	0.364	1.636
18	0.194	0.392	1.608
20	0.180	0.414	1.586
22	0.167	0.434	1.566
24	0.157	0.452	1.548

The factors A_2, D_3, and D_4 vary with the sample size and are tabulated in Table 17.2. We illustrate the construction of means and range charts in the following example.

❖ Sweet 'n' Cold, Inc.

Sweet 'n' Cold is a chain of 10 fountain ice cream stores in southern Texas. Management is keenly concerned over the age of the ice cream, since the chain's ads stress that the ice cream is "jes' like homemade"—in contrast to that of its competitors. To maintain a continuing check on this quality, for the last three weeks management has been selecting four stores at random from the chain each day and noting the age of the ice cream being served. Management believes that, because of the trouble of sampling, a sample of $n = 4$ of the 10 stores each day will give the best control for the trouble involved (see Figure 3.1).

The mean age and range in ages for each sample were entered into the spreadsheet shown in Table 17.3. The grand mean ($\overline{\overline{X}}$), and the average range ($\overline{R}$) are also calculated (cells B23 and C23, respectively). For example, the calculations for June 1 were

Main Street store:	7 days	
Southside store:	2 days	
Bayfront store:	20 days	
West Mall store:	11 days	
Total	40 days	

$$\text{Mean: } \overline{X} = \frac{40}{4} = 10 \text{ days}$$

$$\text{Range: } R = 20 - 2 = 18 \text{ days}$$

$\mathcal{T}$ABLE 17.3 ❖ Mean and Range of Ages of Ice Cream

	A	B	C
1		**Sample**	**Sample**
2	**Date**	**Mean**	**Range**
3	June 1	10	18
4	June 2	13	13
5	June 3	11	15
6	June 4	14	14
7	June 5	9	14
8	June 6	11	10
9	June 7	8	15
10	June 8	12	17
11	June 9	13	9
12	June 10	10	16
13	June 11	13	12
14	June 12	12	14
15	June 13	8	13
16	June 14	11	15
17	June 15	11	11
18	June 16	9	14
19	June 17	10	13
20	June 18	9	19
21	June 19	12	14
22	June 20	14	14
23	**Average**	**11**	**14**

The grand mean $\overline{\overline{X}}$ is then simply the average of all the daily means:

$$\overline{\overline{X}} = \frac{\sum \overline{X}}{N}$$

where N is 20 days of samples and the average range is:

$$\overline{R} = \frac{\sum R}{N}$$

The data in Table 17.3 can now be used to construct control charts that will indicate to management any sudden change, for better or worse, in the quality (age) of the ice cream. Management will use both a chart of means, to check the age of the ice cream being served; and a chart of ranges, to check consistency among stores. The grand mean and average range will give the center line on these charts. The values of A_2, D_3, and D_4 are obtained from Table 17.2 for $n = 4$, resulting in the following control limits:

Ice cream bars in production at Ben & Jerry's, Springfield, Vermont. Ben & Jerry's is the second-largest vendor of super-premium ice cream in the United States.

$$\text{UCL}_{\bar{X}} = 11 + 0.729(14) = 21.206$$
$$\text{LCL}_{\bar{X}} = 11 - 0.729(14) = 0.794$$
$$\text{UCL}_R = 2.282(14) = 31.948$$
$$\text{LCL}_R = 0(14) = 0$$

The control charts for this example were developed using a spreadsheet and are shown in Figures 17.8 and 17.9. In addition, the data in Table 17.3 are graphed on the charts. As seen in Figure 17.8, none of the $\bar{X}$ points exceeds the control limits. Furthermore, no pattern is apparent; the points appear to fall randomly around the grand mean (centerline).

The range chart, Figure 17.9, again shows that the variability of the process is well within the limits. Of course, whether or not this normal range of variability (of 10 days) is acceptable to management is another question.

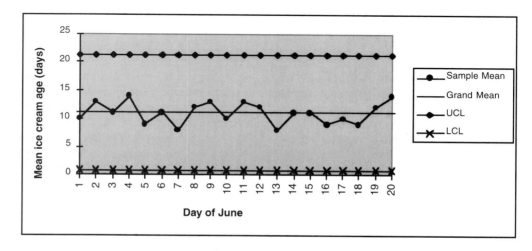

Figure 17.8   Mean age of ice cream.

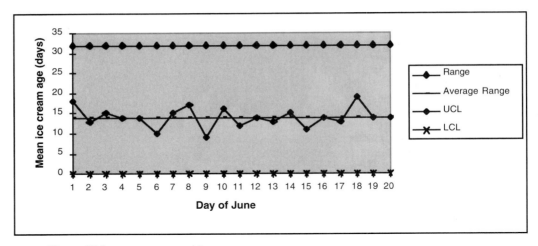

Figure 17.9   Range in age of ice cream.

Each day, as a new sample is taken, $\overline{X}$ and R are calculated and plotted on the two charts. If either $\overline{X}$ or R is outside the LCL or UCL, management must then undertake to find the assignable cause for the variation. Also, management should monitor the charts for any nonrandom patterns such as those suggested in the 2—5—7 rules.

As described in the accompanying sidebar, statistical process control executed through control charts is helping Whirlpool improve its quality significantly. Although process control charts were originally confined to manufacturing, it should be clear that they represent a significant tool for the control of *services* as well. Furthermore, because a control chart is simple to use, workers can use it to monitor their own performance. Thus, a positive behavioral effect can also be achieved.

CONTROL CHARTS
FOR ATTRIBUTES _____

The control chart is also valuable for controlling attributes of the output, as illustrated in the sidebar about IBM's errors in purchase orders and problems with moving. The most common of these charts are the *fraction-defective (p) chart* and the *number-of-defects (c) chart*. These names were used because the charts emerged in a manufacturing context, but they apply to a number of other situations as well. As with the range chart, the lower control limit for attribute charts can never be negative.

❖ Fraction-Defective (p) Charts

The fraction-defective (p) chart can be used for any two-state (*dichotomous*) process such as heavy versus light or acceptable versus unacceptable. The control chart for p is constructed in much the same way as the control chart for $\overline{X}$. First, a large sample of historical data is gathered, and the fraction (percent) having the characteristic

OPERATIONS
IN PRACTICE

Statistical Process Control Helps
Whirlpool Improve Quality

Whirlpool, the leader in laundry equipment, invested $150 million in its washing machine plant in Clyde, Ohio, to produce newly designed machines. The new designs, by reducing the number of parts, simplifying assembly, and eliminating major amounts of machining, have improved Whirlpool's quality to the point that it can promise customers it will replace any machine free of charge within a year of purchase if the buyer isn't completely satisfied.

New production methods have also had a major impact on quality. The workers are being trained in statistical process control, so that they can measure critical product dimensions and adjust their machinery before it goes out of tolerance. The workers now have a major say in determining what production equipment to purchase and how to assemble the laundry machines. Moreover, engineers now spend a week on the production line so that they will be familiar with what it takes to produce their new designs.

Such attention to quality, both in engineering and in production, has paid off. To take one example, service calls were reduced by 68 percent over a five-year period (Schiller, 1987; Bowles, 1986; and Vasilash, 1991).

$\mathscr{S}$OLVED EXERCISE 17.1 ❖ Control of Variables

Find the mean and control limits for the means and range chart given the following data.

Day 1: 34, 36, 41
Day 2: 33, 33, 38
Day 3: 37, 36, 40
Day 4: 35, 33, 35

Solution:

	A	B	C	D	E	F	G	H
1		Item 1	Item 2	Item 3	Mean	Range		
2	Day 1	34	36	41	37.0	7		
3	Day 2	33	33	38	34.7	5		
4	Day 3	37	36	40	37.7	4		
5	Day 4	35	33	35	34.3	2		
6	Sum				143.7	18.0		
7	Average				35.92	4.50		
8								
9	Key Formulas:							
10	Cell E2:	=AVERAGE(B2:D2) [cell E2 copied to E3:E5]						
11	Cell F2:	=MAX(B2:D2)-MIN(B2:D2) [cell F2 copied to F3:F5]						
12	Cell E6:	=SUM(E2:E5) [copied to cell F6]						
13	Cell E7:	=AVERAGE(E2:E5) [copied to cell F7]						

$$\overline{\overline{X}} = \frac{143.7}{4} = 35.92$$

$$\overline{R} = \frac{18}{4} = 4.5$$

$$\text{UCL}_{\overline{X}} = 35.92 + 1.023^*(4.5) = 40.52$$

$$\text{LCL}_{\overline{X}} = 35.92 - 1.023^*(4.5) = 31.32$$

$$\text{UCL}_R = 2.575^*(4.5) = 11.59$$

$$\text{LCL}_R = 0^*(4.5) = 0$$

*From Table 17.2.

in question (e.g., too light, defective, too old), $\overline{p}$, is computed on the entire set of data as a whole.

Large samples are usually taken because the fraction of interest is typically small and the number of items in the samples should be large enough to include *some* of the defectives. For example, a fraction defective may be 3 percent or less. Therefore, a sample size of 33 would have to be taken (i.e., 1/0.03 = 33) to expect to include even 1 defective item.

Since the fraction defective follows a *binomial* distribution (*bi* means "two": either an item is or it is not) rather than a normal distribution, the standard deviation may be calculated directly from $\bar{p}$ as

$$\sigma_p = \sqrt{\frac{\bar{p}(1-\bar{p})}{n}}$$

where n is the uniform sample size to be used for controlling quality. Although the fraction defective follows the binomial distribution, if $\bar{p}$ is near 0.5, or n is "large" (greater than 30 or so), the normal distribution is a good approximation and the control limits of $3\sigma_p$ will again represent 99.7 percent of the sample observations. Again, the LCL cannot be negative. An example is given next.

❖ Downtown Library

Downtown Library has decided to monitor the number of lost books, as a fraction of books requested, by checking daily samples of 50 books requested by its patrons. Through the procedures described previously, the library staff has developed a control chart, shown in Figure 17.10, based on three typical days of requests (Table 17.4). No assignable variations in lost books appear to have occurred in the four days of April plotted so far in Figure 17.10.

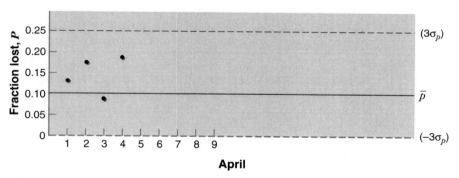

Figure 17.10 Control chart for percentage of lost books.

𝒯ABLE 17.4 ❖ Data on Lost Books for p Chart

Date	Books Requested	Books That Could Not Be Located (Lost)
Feb. 7	122	15
Feb. 8	91	12
Feb. 9	137	13
Total	350	40

$$\bar{p} = \frac{40}{350} = 0.114$$

$$\sigma_p = \sqrt{0.114(0.886)/50} = 0.045$$

OPERATIONS
IN PRACTICE

IBM, Kingston Tracks Key Attributes

IBM's site services department (SSD) in Kingston, New York, is responsible for providing support services such as purchasing, security, administration, maintenance, and personnel for a growing facility, while at the same time reducing personnel resources and operating expenses. To achieve these goals, SSD relied on a quality program and used measurement as its key.

SSD found that simply tracking accidents or complaints wasn't sufficient to reduce them. Better measures were required that analyzed processes at an earlier stage. The SSD team identified 200 key processes used to provide services for customers and quizzed managers about the critical measures for these processes: response times, error rates, defects, and so on. These measures were then plotted on control charts to observe their variation. Four programs illustrate this:

Speak up! This program is a communication channel between employees and management. Timely responses from management that address the issues raised by the employees are critical to the success of the program. Response time was tracked and plotted for all departments, and the results were made public. Workshops were held for managers concerning what was required to properly respond to a letter from an employee. Response times improved significantly.

Preemployment medical exams: These exams were taking too long and taxed the staff assigned to conduct them. Charting the exam times indicated that the average time was 74 minutes, but the range varied greatly. Newer equipment and extensive training on both old and new equipment reduced the average to 40 minutes, with a much more acceptable range: less than 70 percent of its former value.

Purchase orders: Errors in purchase orders were causing considerable expense and trouble. Tracking the errors on a control chart indicated that vacation replacements were a major cause of the trouble. Better training of replacements and better scheduling of vacations were instituted.

Rearrangements: With so much growth at the Kingston facility, office moves, transfers, and relocations were common. Problems with moving on the part of the office workers were tracked, and limits were set. If an upper control limit was exceeded, the contract mover was given a warning. If the limit was exceeded twice, the mover's name was removed from the bidding list. One contractor had to be put on notice. In more than 20 subsequent moves, problems virtually disappeared.

The above process has worked extremely well—managers and other employees are very encouraged by the results. Understanding requirements, setting targets, and measuring performance are basic to any control process. Taking such an organized approach to the provision of services is paying exceptional dividends (McCabe, 1985).

Note in this example that the data used to *derive* the control chart did not use the same size sample as was used to determine $\bar{p}$. *Any* set of data could have been used to determine $\bar{p}$. In this case three samples were used from two months previously, one of 122 books, the second of 91, and the third of 137. All the data were *combined,* and then $\bar{p}$ was found. However, to set control limits, the actual size of the sample to be monitored (n) was used in the calculation of σ_p. If, on a particular day, fewer than 50 books—say, 40—are requested, then a new value of σ_p, and new control limits based on the value $n = 40$, should be determined.

$\mathcal{S}$OLVED EXERCISE 17.2 ❖ Controlling the Fraction Defective

Use the following data based on samples of 20 to determine the mean and control limits for a fraction-defective chart. Number of defects: 1, 0, 2, 0, 0, 1, 0, 1.

Solution:

Sum of defects = 5 out of 8 samples of 20 or 160 items.

$$\bar{p} = \frac{5}{160} = 0.03125$$

$$\sigma_p = \sqrt{0.03125(0.96875)/20} = 0.0389$$

$$UCL = 0.03125 + 3(0.0389) = 0.1480$$
$$LCL = 0.03125 - 3(0.0389 = 0$$

❖ Number-of-Defects *(c)* Charts

The number-of-defects (*c*) chart is used for a single situation in which any number of incidents may occur, each with a small probability. Typical of such incidents are scratches in tables, fire alarms in a city, and typesetting errors in a newspaper. An average number of incidents, $\bar{c}$, is determined from combined past data. The distribution of such incidents is known to follow the *Poisson distribution* with a standard deviation of

$$\sigma_c = \sqrt{\bar{c}}$$

Again, the normal distribution is used as an approximation to derive control limits with a minimum LCL of zero.

❖ Brit Bank

To better monitor the quality of its 24-hour teller services, Brit Bank has instituted a charting procedure for the number of customers' complaints. A quick review of the previous week's complaints gave the following information.

Number of Complaints

Monday	5
Tuesday	0
Wednesday	3
Thursday	(data missing)
Friday	8
Total	16

Calculating the mean and standard deviation:

$$\bar{c} = \frac{16}{4} = 4/\text{day}$$

$$\sigma_c = \sqrt{4} = 2$$

The control chart based on this one-week sample of daily complaints is shown in Figure 17.11. Tuesday's data point (at $-3\sigma_c$) tends to imply that the bank's quality of services is not under control. An investigation should be conducted and additional data collected.

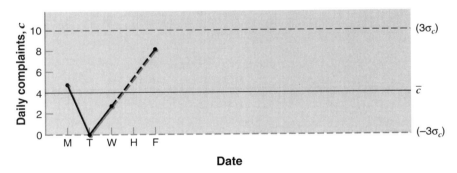

Figure 17.11 Control chart for complaints.

$\mathscr{S}$OLVED EXERCISE 17.3 ❖ Controlling the Number of Defects

The number of returns from a mail-order catalog for each day of a recent week was 8, 5, 3, 12, 4. Determine the mean and control limits for a number-of-defects chart.

Solution:

$$\bar{c} = \frac{8 + 5 + 3 + 12 + 4}{5} = 6.4$$

$$\sigma_c = \sqrt{6.4} = 2.53$$

$$\text{UCL} = 6.4 + 3(2.53) = 13.99$$

$$\text{LCL} = 6.4 - 3(2.53) = 0$$

❖ Acceptance Sampling

Acceptance sampling was developed in the 1940s and has been used since then by manufacturers as an efficient way to decide whether to accept or reject a shipment of incoming material. It was widely used during World War II to help ensure the quality of goods produced in support of the war effort and later became a key component of quality control programs. Whereas process quality control is a dynamic technique, acceptance sampling is a *static* technique for computing incoming and outgoing quality of lots.

With acceptance sampling (as opposed to control charts), it is not necessary for the organization to construct its own charts or tables. Two men, again from Bell Telephone Laboratories—H. F. Dodge and H. G. Romig—applied the theory of statistics to acceptance sampling and derived the necessary data in a form now known as the *Dodge-Romig Sampling Inspection Tables.*

Given certain information, these tables will provide an inspector with a ***sampling plan*** consisting of the size of the sample *n,* and the maximum acceptable number *c* of defectives in the sample. (This is not to be confused with the *c* used in control charts.) The ability of this plan to discriminate between good lots and bad lots is then checked and revised if it is found to be unacceptable. To check a sampling plan, an ***operating characteristic*** (OC) curve based on the binomial distribution is constructed for the plan. The OC curve shows the chance of accepting lots versus the percentage of defects in the lot. Clearly, the greater the percentage of defects in the lot, the smaller the chance that it will be accepted.

Ideally, such a plan would have the curve shown in Figure 17.12. In this case, the stated quality of the lot is 1 percent or less defective. The ideal sampling plan would accept the lot if the actual number of defectives was 1 percent or less but reject it if it was more than 1 percent. This result, however, could come about only by very careful inspection of the *entire lot!* Only then (and quite possibly not even then) could its *true* percentage of defectives be known and the lot accepted or rejected according to the 1 percent rule. However, such a process would undoubtedly prove extremely expensive to the organization and very inefficient. To minimize the total cost of both accepting defective items (cost of errors) and paying for inspection (cost of quality), a much better approach would probably be to *sample* the lot and make a decision on the basis of the sample.

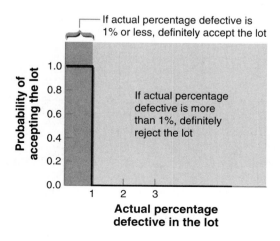

Figure 17.12 Ideal operating characteristic (OC) curve where stated quality is 1 percent or less defective.

The result of implementing such a strategy is to increase the chance of making type I and type II errors, as discussed earlier, especially very near the 1 percent point in the example above. This increased chance of error is illustrated in Figure 17.13, showing a plan that rejects lots having samples with more than 1 percent defectives. In this case, the plan is to sample 100 items ($n = 100$) and reject the lot if more than 1 defect ($1/100 = 1$ percent) is found ($c = 1$). The figure also illustrates what the chances of accepting the lot are, depending on the actual percentage of defectives. As can be seen, if the actual defect rate $p = 1$ percent, there is about a 74 percent chance of accepting the lot, P_a. If the actual defect rate $p = 0.5$ percent, the probability of acceptance $P_a = 91$ percent. (There is a 9 percent chance of rejecting the lot, even though only 0.5 percent are defective, the type I error called *producer's risk*). Similarly, $p = 2$ percent (2 percent are actually defective), the probability of accepting the lot decreases to about 41 percent (the type II error called *consumer's risk*). Thus, a batch that contains 2 percent defectives and should be rejected given the 1 percent rule will have a 41 percent chance of being accepted using the sampling plan $n = 100$ and $c = 1$. This may or may not be acceptable to management, depending on the cost of inspection.

Figure 17.14 illustrates the effect of changing various parameters in the plan. Note that those plans based on 1 percent are either more or less discriminating (steep) between good and bad batches than the plan in Figure 17.13, depending on whether n is greater or less than 100. For example, the plan $n = 200$, $c = 2$ is very discriminating but requires twice as much sampling. In general, as the sample size n is increased or the maximum number of defects in the sample c is decreased (or both), the sampling plan becomes more discriminating. Thus, for a given lot size N, the specification (by management) of the two probabilities of making a type I and type II error determines, through the use of the Dodge-Romig tables, a sampling plan.

With the increasing popularity of total quality management (TQM) programs, many organizations are placing much less emphasis on acceptance sampling. One reason is that acceptance sampling identifies poor quality only after the fact and therefore does little to prevent these expensive problems from occurring in the first place. Second, in conjunction with their TQM programs, many organizations have

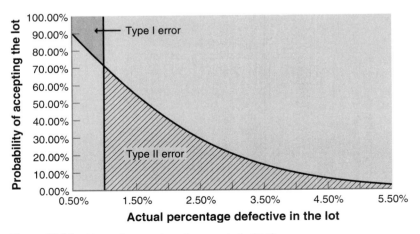

Figure 17.13   Typical operating characteristic (OC) curve.

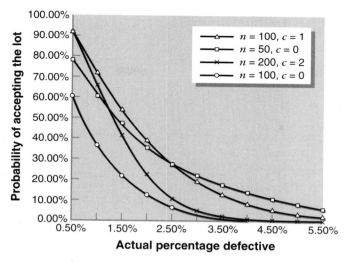

Figure 17.14 OC curves of other sampling plans.

improved their production systems to the point where acceptance sampling is no longer needed. For example, in 1987 Motorola set a goal to produce fewer than 3.4 defective parts per million (this is referred to as *six sigma capability*) by 1992. Third, the trend toward supplier certification programs and long-term relationships between organizations and their suppliers has greatly reduced the need to inspect incoming batches of materials.

$\mathcal{P}$ROCESS CAPABILITY

With the advent of total quality management programs and their emphasis on "making it right the first time," organizations are becoming increasingly concerned with the ability of a production system to meet design specifications rather than evaluating the quality of products after the fact with acceptance sampling. **Process capability** measures the extent to which an organization's production system can meet design specifications. As shown in Figure 17.15, process capability depends on:

1. Location of the process mean.
2. Natural variability inherent in the process.
3. Stability of the process.
4. Product's design requirements.

In Figure 17.15*a* the natural variation inherent in the process and the product's design specifications are well matched, resulting in a production system that is consistently capable of meeting the design requirements. However, in Figure 17.15*b* the natural variation in the production system is greater than the product's design requirements. This will lead to the production of a large amount of product that

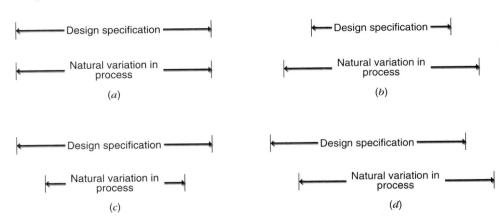

Figure 17.15 Natural variation in a production system versus product design specifications.

does not meet the requirements: the production system simply does not have the necessary ability. Options in this situation include improving the production system, relaxing the design requirements, and producing a large quantity of product that is unfit for use.

In Figure 17.15*c* the situation is reversed: the product has wider design specifications than the natural variation inherent in the production system. In this case the production system is easily able to meet the design specifications, and the organization may choose to investigate more economical production systems in order to lower costs. Finally, although the widths of design specifications and process variation are equal in Figure 17.15*d*, their means are out of sync. Thus, this system will produce a fair amount of output above the upper specification limit (USL). In this situation the solution would be to shift the process mean to the left so that it is better aligned with the design specifications.

More formally, the relationship between the natural variation in the production system and the product's design specifications can be quantified using a ***process capability index.*** The process capability index C_p is typically defined as the ratio of the width of the product's design specification to 6 standard deviations of the production system. Six standard deviations for the production system is used because 3 standard deviations above and below the production system's process mean will include 99.7 percent of the possible production outcomes, assuming that the output of the production system can be approximated with a normal distribution. Mathematically, the process capability index is calculated as

$$C_p = \frac{\text{product's design specification range}}{6 \text{ standard deviations of the production system}} = \frac{USL - LSL}{6\sigma}$$

where *LSL* and *USL* are a product's lower and upper design specification limits, respectively, and σ is the standard deviation of the production system.

According to this index, a C_p of less than 1 indicates that a particular process is not capable of consistently meeting design specifications; a C_p greater than 1 indicates that the production process is capable of consistently meeting the requirements. As a rule of thumb, many organizations desire a C_p index of at least 1.5.

However, a recent trend is the pursuit of *six sigma quality,* providing a C_p index of 2.0 and yielding only 3.4 defective parts per million.

Figure 17.16 illustrates the impact that changes in the natural variation of the production system have on the C_p index for fixed product design specifications. In Figure 17.16*a* the natural variation in the process is much less than the product's design specification range, yielding a C_p index greater than 1. In contrast, in Figure

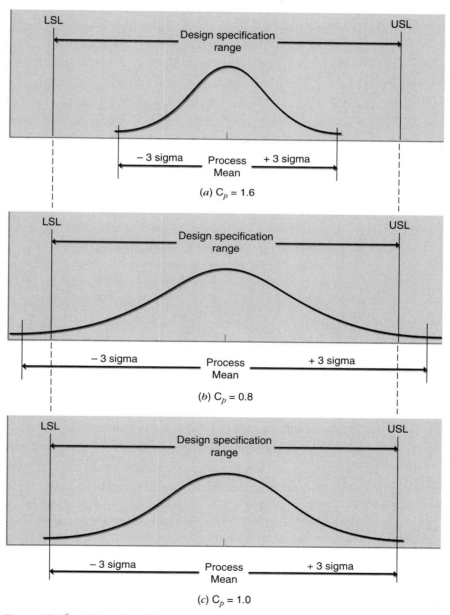

Figure 17.16 Effect of production system variability on process capability index. (a) $C_p = 1.6$; (b) $C_p = 0.8$; (c) $C_p = 1.0$.

17.16*b* the natural variation in the process is larger than the product's design specifications, yielding a C_p index less than 1. Finally, in Figure 17.16*c* the natural process variation and the design specifications are equal, yielding a C_p index equal to 1.

One limitation of the process capability index is that it only compares the magnitudes of the product's design specification range and the process's natural variation. It does not consider the degree to which these ranges are actually aligned. For example, the situations shown in Figure 17.15*a* and Figure 17.15*d* both yield a C_p index of 1.0. However, as was pointed out earlier, a considerable amount of defective product would be produced in the situation shown in Figure 17.15*d*, owing to the lack of alignment between the design specifications and the process mean. One way to evaluate the extent to which the process mean is centered within the product's design specifications is to calculate a one-sided process capability index C_{pk} as follows:

$$C_{pu} = \frac{USL - \text{process mean}}{3\sigma}$$

$$C_{pl} = \frac{\text{process mean} - LSL}{3\sigma}$$

$$C_{pk} = \min(C_{pl},\ C_{pu})$$

$\mathscr{S}$OLVED EXERCISE 17.4 ❖ Process Capability

A company's engineers designed a new lighting product to provide 900 to 1100 hours of use. From a pilot study of the manufacturing process that will produce the product, it was determined that the product had an average life of 1000 hours with a standard deviation of 75 hours. Compute the process capability index for this product. What does this index tell you?

Solution:

Given the description of the situation, we have:

Upper specification limit *(USL)*	=	1100 hours
Lower specification limit *(LSL)*	=	900 hours
Process mean (μ)	=	1000 hours
Process standard deviation (σ)	=	75 hours

Thus, the process capability index C_p calculated as:

$$C_p = \frac{1100 - 900}{6(75)} = 0.44$$

Since the C_p index is less than 1, the current process does not have the capability to consistently meet the engineering design specifications.

CHAPTER IN PERSPECTIVE

As the last of seven chapters addressing the product supply process, this chapter focused on controlling the quality of the outputs. Our discussion of the product supply process began with the development of aggregate and master production schedules. Following this, we moved on to the topic of managing inventory items to support these schedules. Then, before our discussion of quality control in the present chapter, we discussed detailed scheduling in job shops, flow shops, and projects.

The emphasis in this chapter was on using statistical quality control techniques to control the quality of outputs. As we discussed, these techniques can be applied to an organization's inputs, its transformation system, and its outputs. Also, quality control can be carried out on the basis of either variables or attributes.

The chapter began with an overview of issues related to inspection, sampling, and types of sampling errors. Then process control was discussed in more detail, including a general discussion of control charts. In the following sections, control charts for variables and control charts for attributes were expanded on. Finally, the chapter concluded with a discussion of acceptance sampling and process capability.

❖ CHECK YOUR UNDERSTANDING

1. Define the following terms: *sampling plan, 2—5—7 rules, control chart, control limit, tolerance, type I error, type II error.*

2. Contrast acceptance sampling with the process capability approach.

3. List points in the transformation system where inspection may be particularly appropriate.

4. What are the reasons for not conducting 100 percent manual inspection? In what cases would 100 percent manual inspection be appropriate?

5. Why is a type I error referred to as *producer's risk* and a type II error referred to as *consumer's risk?*

6. Contrast chance variation and assignable variation. How can control charts be used to distinguish between them?

7. How do control charts based on variables differ from control charts based on attributes?

8. Why must the sample means chart and the range chart both be used when control charts based on variables are used?

9. Contrast *p* charts and *c* charts. When should each be used?

10. How is the operating characteristic (OC) curve used in the development of a sampling plan?

11. For a given sampling plan, what is the effect of changing the sample size n and the maximum number of defectives in the sample c?

12. What are the factors that affect process capability?

13. Explain how design specifications and a process's natural variation affect process capability.

14. What problems can be uncovered by using the process capability index C_p? What problems cannot be uncovered using this index?

15. Why is a one-sided process capability index used?

❖ EXPAND YOUR UNDERSTANDING

1. Why does the control chart in Figure 17.4 not have symmetrical control limits? Might this approach also apply to regular control charts?

2. Under what kinds of circumstances might an organization wish to use control limits of 2 standard deviations or even 1 standard deviation? What should it bear in mind when using these lower limits?

3. Why are two control charts not necessary in controlling for attributes? Might not the variability of the fraction defective or the number of defects also be going out of control?

4. It is generally not appropriate to apply control charts to the same data that were used to derive the mean and limits. Why? What are the two possi-

ble outcomes if this is done, how likely is each, and what are the appropriate interpretations?

5. Since both attribute charts concern defects, why is the p chart based on the binomial when the c chart is based on the Poisson?

6. Isn't it possible to convert the p chart into a number-of-defectives chart just by multiplying by n? How does this chart differ from the c chart?

7. In deriving the p chart, why can the sample size vary? What must be remembered if the p chart is applied to a different sample size each time?

8. In a firm that is largely automated, how might quality control operate? What might be the role of technology in such a firm?

9. Firms regularly employ a taster for drinkable food products. What is the purpose of this taster?

10. Most of the quality control procedures described in this chapter were devised for manufacturing firms. How can the concepts be applied to services?

11. How would you describe the sample size for the c chart?

12. How would you respond to the statement that a drawback associated with rules such as the 2—5—7 rule is that they require managers to jump the gun and take corrective action before an out-of-control situation actually develops?

13. Is it equally important to investigate situations when sample statistics fall below the lower control limit?

14. Which control charts can have a negative lower control limit? Which ones cannot?

15. In what ways is process capability more consistent with total quality management than acceptance sampling?

16. What is meant by *six sigma quality*?

❖ APPLY YOUR UNDERSTANDING _____

Paint Tint

Late last month, Jim Runnels, a sales representative for the Paint Tint Corporation, was called to the plant of Townhouse Paint Company, one of his largest accounts. The purchasing agent for Townhouse Paint was complaining that the tubes of paint tint it had received over the last couple of weeks were not within the specified range of 4.9 to 5.1 ounces.

The off-weight tubes had not been detected by Townhouse's receiving clerks and had not been weighed or otherwise checked by their quality control staff. The problem arose when Townhouse began to use the tubes of tinting agent and found that the paint colors were not matching the specifications. The mixing charts used by the salespeople in Townhouse's retail stores were based on 5-ounce tubes of tinting agent. Overfilled or underfilled tubes would result in improper paint mixes, and therefore in colors that did not meet customers' expectations.

In consequence, Townhouse had to issue special instructions to all its retail people that would allow them to compensate for the off-weight tubes. The Townhouse purchasing agent made it clear that a new supplier would be sought if this problem recurred. Paint Tint's quality control department was immediately summoned to assist in determining the cause of the problem.

Paint Tint's quality manager, Ronald Wilson, speculated that the cause of the problem was with the second shift. To analyze the problem, he entered into a spreadsheet the data from all the previous samples taken over the last two months. As it turned out, 15 random samples had been taken over the two-month period for both the first and the second shifts. Samples always consisted of 10 randomly selected tubes of paint tint. Also, separate sampling schedules were used for the first and second shifts so that the second shift would not automatically assume that it would be subject to a random sample just because the first shift had been earlier in the day.

After entering the sample weight data of the tubes into the spreadsheet below and calculating the sample means, Ronald was quite puzzled. There did not seem to be any noticeable difference in the average weights across the two shifts. Furthermore, although the lines were running at less than full capacity during the first six samples, there still did not seem to be any change in either line after reaching full production.

Questions

1. Can you identify any difference between the first and second shifts that explains the weight problem? If so, when is this difference first detectable?
2. How would you rate the ability of Paint Tint's production process to meet Townhouse Paint's requirements? What are the implications of your evaluation?

	A	B	C	D	E	F	G	H	I	J	K	L	M	N	O	P
1	**First Shift**															
2							**Sample Number**									
3	**Observation**	**1**	**2**	**3**	**4**	**5**	**6**	**7**	**8**	**9**	**10**	**11**	**12**	**13**	**14**	**15**
4	1	4.90	5.05	4.96	4.92	4.96	5.03	4.99	5.00	5.02	5.03	5.01	4.95	5.02	4.96	5.06
5	2	5.03	5.04	4.96	5.00	5.00	4.99	5.03	5.01	5.05	4.90	4.94	4.95	4.95	4.97	4.97
6	3	5.00	5.00	4.92	5.05	5.03	4.98	5.01	4.95	5.00	4.95	5.00	5.06	5.00	4.93	5.00
7	4	5.03	5.11	5.01	5.03	4.98	4.99	5.02	5.01	5.01	5.01	5.00	5.02	4.98	5.01	5.00
8	5	5.02	4.94	4.98	5.01	5.00	4.98	5.01	4.99	5.03	5.01	4.96	4.94	5.04	5.00	5.03
9	6	4.92	5.02	5.00	5.02	5.02	5.01	4.99	4.98	5.00	4.94	4.98	4.99	5.02	5.04	5.08
10	7	5.04	5.03	4.98	5.02	5.00	4.99	5.06	4.96	5.01	4.98	5.01	4.97	4.99	4.98	4.97
11	8	4.92	5.00	5.00	4.96	5.01	5.01	5.05	5.00	4.97	4.98	4.97	4.97	5.05	5.08	4.98
12	9	4.95	4.95	4.94	5.02	4.95	4.98	4.97	4.94	5.07	5.00	5.00	4.96	5.02	4.94	5.00
13	10	5.02	4.99	5.08	4.94	5.00	4.95	5.04	4.98	5.02	5.01	4.98	5.02	5.06	5.02	4.97
14	**Average**	**4.98**	**5.01**	**4.98**	**5.00**	**5.00**	**4.99**	**5.02**	**4.98**	**5.02**	**4.98**	**4.99**	**4.98**	**5.01**	**4.99**	**5.01**
15																
16																
17	**Second Shift**															
18							**Sample Number**									
19	**Observation**	**1**	**2**	**3**	**4**	**5**	**6**	**7**	**8**	**9**	**10**	**11**	**12**	**13**	**14**	**15**
20	1	5.03	5.02	4.99	4.96	5.03	5.02	5.08	5.10	5.16	5.00	4.97	5.11	5.11	4.90	5.02
21	2	4.90	4.95	4.97	4.97	4.98	5.03	4.97	4.93	4.92	4.97	4.91	5.05	4.98	4.92	4.98
22	3	5.02	4.94	5.04	4.98	5.00	4.98	4.93	4.92	4.99	5.08	5.15	4.93	5.13	4.97	4.86
23	4	4.98	5.05	5.02	5.00	4.97	5.06	4.84	4.93	5.00	5.07	4.96	5.15	5.15	4.92	4.94
24	5	5.01	4.95	5.02	5.02	4.98	5.04	5.07	5.03	4.98	4.94	4.91	4.98	5.10	5.04	4.93
25	6	4.99	4.99	4.99	5.03	5.00	5.04	4.95	4.96	4.99	4.96	5.07	4.88	5.12	5.03	4.97
26	7	4.99	4.97	5.00	4.98	4.99	4.99	4.93	4.86	5.01	5.13	5.15	4.74	5.01	4.91	5.05
27	8	5.02	5.00	5.00	4.96	4.98	4.98	4.99	5.08	5.07	4.93	4.95	4.90	4.93	4.95	4.97
28	9	5.01	5.00	5.05	5.02	5.03	4.97	4.82	4.96	4.93	4.96	4.91	5.03	5.04	4.98	5.03
29	10	4.97	4.99	4.95	5.03	5.00	4.99	5.05	5.14	5.03	4.91	5.11	5.04	5.03	5.08	4.92
30	**Average**	**4.99**	**4.99**	**5.00**	**5.00**	**5.00**	**5.01**	**4.96**	**4.99**	**5.01**	**5.00**	**5.01**	**4.98**	**5.06**	**4.97**	**4.97**

❖ EXERCISES

1. Top management of the Security National Bank monitors the volume of activity at 38 branch banks with control charts. If deposit volume (or any of perhaps a dozen other volume indicators) at a branch falls below the LCL, there is apparently some problem with the branch's market share. If, on the other hand, the volume exceeds the UCL, this is an indication that the branch should be con-sidered for expansion or that a new branch might be opened in an adjacent neighborhood.

Given the 10-day samples for each of the six months below, prepare an $\bar{X}$ chart for monthly deposit volume (in hundreds of thousands of dollars) for the Transurban branch. Use control limits of $\pm 3\sigma$. The average range of the six samples was found to be \$85,260.

	Average of 10-Day Deposits ($\bar{X}$) ($100,000)
June	0.93
July	1.05
August	1.21
September	0.91
October	0.89
November	1.13

2. Using the following weekly demand data for a new soft drink, determine the upper and lower control limits that can be used in recognizing a change in demand patterns. Use ±3σ control limits.

Week	Demand (6-packs)
1	3500
2	4100
3	3750
4	4300
5	4000
6	3650

3. Where should the UCL and LCL be set for a control chart of defect rates if the mean is 18 and the standard deviation is 5? Use control limits of +3σ and −2σ.

4. The average cost of processing a computer run at a local service bureau is $38, with an upper control limit of $46 and a lower control limit of $30. Consider the following four sets of observations:
  a. $35, $42, $45, $38, $46
  b. $39, $38, $41, $45, $31
  c. $31, $33, $41, $42, $46
  d. $42, $41, $40, $46, $45

  Are they all in control? On what rule would you base your decision?

5. A control chart has a mean of 50 and two-sigma control limits of 40 and 60. The following data are plotted on the chart: 38, 55, 58, 42, 64, 49, 51, 58, 61, 46, 44, 50. Should action be taken?

6. Given the following data, construct a 3σ range control chart.

Day of Sample	Sample Values
Saturday	22, 19, 20
Sunday	21, 20, 17
Monday	16, 17, 18
Tuesday	20, 16, 21
Wednesday	23, 20, 20
Thursday	19, 16, 21

  a. If Friday's results are 15, 14, and 21, is the process in control?

b. Construct a 3σ means control chart and determine if the process is still in control on Friday.

7. Construct a *p* chart using 2σ limits based on the following results of 20 samples of size 400.

Sample Number	Number of Defects
1	2
2	0
3	8
4	5
5	8
6	4
7	4
8	2
9	9
10	2
11	3
12	0
13	5
14	6
15	7
16	1
17	5
18	8
19	2
20	1

8. Twenty samples of 100 were taken, with the following number of defectives: 8, 5, 3, 9, 4, 5, 8, 5, 3, 6, 4, 3, 5, 6, 2, 5, 0, 3, 4, 2. Construct a 3σ *p* chart.

9. Sheets of Styrofoam are being inspected for flaws. The first day's results from a new machine that produced five sheets are 17, 28, 9, 21, 14. Design a control chart for future production.

10. Customers of Dough Boy Inc. have specified that pizza crusts they order should be 28 to 32 centimeters in diameter. Sample data recently collected indicate that Dough Boy's crusts average 30 centimeters in diameter, with a standard deviation of 1.1 centimeters. Is Dough Boy's pizza crust production system capable of meeting its customers' requirements? If not, what options does Dough Boy have to rectify this situation?

11. Design specifications for a bottled product are that it should contain 350 to 363 milliliters. Sample data indicate that the bottles contain an average of 355 milliliters, with a standard deviation of 2 milliliters. Is the filling operation capable of meeting the design specifications? Why or why not?

12. a. Using the following data, prepare a *p* chart for the control of picking accuracy in a wholesale food warehouse. Sample size is 100 cases.

Day	Number of Cases Picked	Number of Incorrect Picks
1	4700	38
2	5100	49
3	3800	27
4	4100	31
5	4500	42
6	5200	48

b. Determine if days 7, 8, and 9 are under control.

Day	Cases Picked	Incorrect
7	4600	53
8	6100	57
9	3900	48

13. A new machine for making nails produced 25 defective nails on Monday, 36 on Tuesday, 17 on Wednesday, and 47 on Thursday. Construct an $\bar{X}$ chart, p chart, and c chart based on the results for Monday through Wednesday and determine if Thursday's production was in control. The machine produces 1 million or so nails a day. Which is the proper chart to use?

Chapter 17 SUPPLEMENT

Reliability and Maintenance

This supplement includes two other areas of control: controlling the system's design to ensure its reliable functioning, and maintaining or repairing the system to keep it functioning. Reliability is generally designed into the system up front, and maintenance typically is conducted after the system is operational. Yet systems and equipment can also be designed up front for easy and inexpensive maintenance.

RELIABILITY

In Chapter 3, we noted that *reliability* can be defined in one of two ways:

1. As the probability that a product or service will perform as intended for a stated period under specific operating conditions.
2. As the probability that a product will work on any given attempt to use it.

The probability that a personal computer will operate without failure for three years is an example of the first definition; the probability that your car will start on any given morning is an example of the second definition.

Often a distinction is made between outputs that are used once as opposed to those that are used either over some period of time or many times in succession. Although the concept of reliability can also apply to one-time use, we do not usually think about the "reliability" of a piece of paper or a potato chip.

Reliability is usually concerned with products and services, or groups of products and services, that consist of multiple interacting elements. This includes products such as machines, toasters, and even hinges; services such as banking, medical treatment, and legal counsel (which can also be unreliable); and major groups of both, such as production systems, organizations, assembly lines, product development teams, and computer systems. Therefore, in our discussion of reliability we will use the term *system* rather than product, service, output, or groups.

Given that systems, as defined in Chapter 1, are composed of multiple interacting elements, any of which can fail in one or more ways, it should come as no surprise that a system's reliability can be very poor unless special precautions are taken. And, of course, this is especially true of systems composed of elements with a wide range of variability in their functioning, such as people. Since many services are labor-intensive, it would be expected that the reliability of services, at least in terms of a standard output, would not be as high as for machine-produced products. Although this is often the case, there are also many services in which the human element of the system can modify its performance so as to increase reliability. (This, for example, is the function of the staff in a final inspection operation.)

Through experience, a number of ways have been developed to enhance the reliability of a system. Table 17S.1 describes several alternatives available to management.

$\mathscr{T}$ABLE 17S.1 ❖ Typical Methods of Enhancing a System's Reliability

❖ *Build redundant elements into the system.* This approach results in a dramatic improvement in reliability but often significantly increases the cost of the system. In situations where the same element is used many times, one backup may suffice (e.g., *one* spare tire). Or, as in the human body, the system may be designed so that the backup is used in part of the normal functioning of the system as well (kidneys, eyes).

❖ *Increase element reliabilities.* The reliability of the system may be enhanced through special design features. For example, special high-quality materials may be used, such as self-lubricating bearings, or elements may be "overdesigned" to handle higher-than-expected loads—e.g., using thick-skinned customer relations (complaints) personnel. Two considerations exist here: increasing the reliability of the *weakest* "link" in the system (the one most likely to fail), and increasing the reliability of the *most critical* link in the system (the one with the highest expected cost). These may not be the same elements, and proper consideration should be given to each. In a vacuum cleaner, for example, the belt is the weakest link, whereas the motor is the most critical. In some models, the vacuum cleaner will continue to draw air and dirt when the belt is broken, but the brushes won't turn. With a motor failure, however, *nothing* works.

❖ *Improve working conditions.* On occasion, it is possible to increase the reliability of a system by improving the conditions under which it must perform. Reducing the load on a system, giving more frequent breaks, improving the quality of the environment (new oil for an engine, carpeting for an office, air conditioning for a plant), and other, similar interventions may considerably extend the working life of the system's elements.

❖ *Conduct preventive maintenance.* It may be worthwhile to plan, ahead of time, on shutting down the system at off-peak hours to conduct maintenance on elements that are at high risk (especially bottleneck machines). Such maintenance could consist of inspection, repair, or replacement. The costs of such programs vary considerably, and their utility depends, in part, on the seriousness of a system breakdown.

❖ *Provide a standby system.* Another alternative—an extreme version of redundancy—is to make a complete replacement system available as a backup for a failed system ("pair and a spare" stockings). Many two-car families operate on this basis, owning one dependable (or new) car and using a second, unreliable jalopy for transportation to and from work. If the jalopy fails, the good car is used until the old one can be fixed. To minimize the effective cost of such an expensive backup, it is typically used for other miscellaneous duties as well, such as around-town shopping, and chauffeuring children.

❖ *Speed the repair process.* The seriousness of a system failure may be minimized by providing sufficient facilities to repair it in case of a breakdown (extra buttons for clothes, extra needles for sewing machines). This approach is especially useful when the inherent reliability of the system is hard to increase. The speed of repair can sometimes be increased by providing a larger or higher-quality repair crew or better facilities. It may also be possible to design the system for speed of repair by using, for example, modules that can be replaced quickly (computer circuit boards) all at one time instead of having to identify the individual element that failed.

❖ *Isolate system elements.* At times it is possible to isolate critical or high-risk elements from the rest of the system, at least for some period of time. In a production system, for example, it may be possible to provide storage between operations for the items being processed so that the failure of one operation in the system does not stop the functioning of all the operations downstream of it. Although providing such in-process storage is expensive, it may well be worthwhile from the standpoint of reliability.

❖ *Accept the risk.* The final alternative we consider here is for the manager simply to accept the risk of failure. It may well be that all other alternatives appear too expensive in light of the effects of system failure. A particularly relevant topic in this regard is the safety of consumer products. The manager *must* decide at what point sufficient precautions have been taken in view of legal regulations and possible damage claims a consumer may bring against the organization.

Our discussion of reliability is divided into two sections. The first deals with the likelihood that a system will operate properly on every attempt to use it, which we call *instantaneous reliability*. The second deals with the chance that a system will continue to perform properly over a period of time T, which we term *continuous reliability*.

❖ Instantaneous Reliability

Instantaneous reliability involves two different sets of calculations, depending on whether the system's elements are connected in series (if any one element fails, the system fails), or parallel (one element acts as a backup for another element). After this introductory discussion, we consider the calculation of reliability in each of these two cases separately.

If a system consists of two elements, of which one works 60 percent of the time (has a reliability of 60 percent) and the other 40 percent of the time, then the reliability of the system is $0.60 \times 0.40 = 0.24$ or 24 percent if both elements must perform properly for the system to operate. Thus, a system consisting of *interdependent* (or *series*) elements has a combined *system reliability* worse than any of its individual *element reliabilities*. Furthermore, if there are many elements, even of high reliability, the system reliability may still be poor. For example, a seven-element system with element reliabilities of 0.9 will have a system reliability of $(0.9)^7 = 0.48$.

Certainly, then, any common household item such as a sewing machine or radio consisting of at least 50 interdependent parts must have an extremely high part (element) reliability, say 99.99 percent, in order for the device to operate most of the time. To an extent, the same holds true for organizations and process activities, but these situations are more complex. For instance, in operations such as final assembly or check processing there are a number of elements involved (people, machines, etc.), each with different reliabilities, and a number of ways (modes) the system can fail.

How, then, can an automobile, with many thousands of parts, function so reliably? There are three answers to that. For one thing, it may, indeed, not be so reliable. If you have ever owned an old car, you have probably experienced the irritation of needing to fix something every time you drive it. Second, the car will "run" even if the radio does not work, or the lights, or even third gear. That is, not all the elements are in series, per se. So the failure of one part does not necessarily lead to a failure of the whole system—just a portion of the system (perhaps critical, perhaps not). Third, intelligent designers often build *redundancy* (parallel elements) into a system to increase its reliability. For example, our bodies contain numerous redundancies: redundant kidneys, eyes, hands, and so on. That is, with two eyes, seeing is easier, the field of vision is enlarged, and depth perception is possible. The loss of one eye reduces these advantages but does not render the system blind. The cardiovascular system contains even more complex redundancy, since it has the ability to rebuild substitutes for some injured and destroyed sections.

Redundancy in an automobile is illustrated by multiple cylinders, dual headlights and taillights, spare tires, and dual brake systems (hydraulic and mechanical). Furthermore, in emergency situations there are usually even more backup systems available, at a cost. For example, if the brakes fail on your car while you are coming down a long, steep hill, the mechanical (parking) brakes can be used. If these also fail, the transmission can be shifted into "low" to slow the car down. If this is insufficient, the ignition can be turned off (on some cars) to further slow the car. And if the emergency is serious enough, the car can be shifted into "reverse" or "park" to lock (and probably destroy) the transmission so the wheels will not turn. And in the advent that all these measures fail, the automobile's air bag and seat belt systems come into play. Dual circuitry in computers is another common example of redundancy.

Reliability of Elements in Series

We can illustrate the effect on system reliability of multiple, interacting elements with the systems in Figure 17S.1. In Figure 17S.1*a* are two separate elements in series, *A* and *B*. In order for the system to work, both elements must operate properly (e.g., the car must start and the transmission must function). If the operations of the two elements, *A* and *B*, are independent of each other and the reliabilities (the probability of proper operation) of *A* and *B* are $R(A)$ and $R(B)$, then

$$\text{Reliability } R \text{ of the system} = R(A \text{ and } B) = R(A)R(B)$$

In the special case where $R(A) = R(B) = r$ the reliability of the system will be r^2.

In Figure 17S.1*b* are seven identical elements in, we shall assume, a semiseries configuration. That is, *all* the elements must function properly in order for the system to function properly. In this case the reliability of the system will be r^7.

If, for example, r is 90 percent, then the reliability R of the two-element system as a whole (Figure 17S.1*a*) would be $(0.9)(0.9) = 0.81$ and the reliability of the seven-element system (Figure 17S.1*b*) would be $(0.9)^7 = 0.48$, both considerably less than 0.9. Figure 17S.2 shows this degradation in reliability R as the number of interdependent (series-type) elements n increases for a number of typical values of r. At the top of the figure is the curve for a 1-element system whose reliability R is

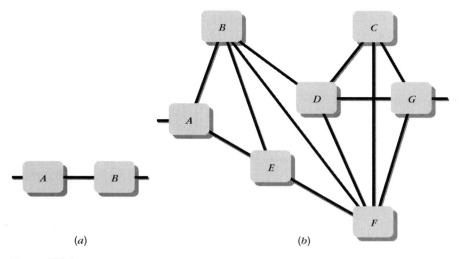

(*a*)   (*b*)

Figure 17S.1 Multiple-element series systems. (*a*) Two elements. (*b*) Multiple, interdependent elements.

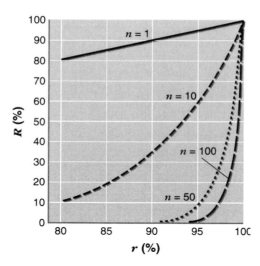

Figure 17S.2   Series system reliability.

equal to the reliability *r* of the element itself. Thus, at the far right where $r = 100$ percent, $R = 100$ percent; and at the far left where $r = 80$ percent, *R* also is 80 percent. The next curve down represents a 10-element (series or semiseries) system. Again at the right, if every element has a reliability *r* of 100 percent, the reliability *R* of the system will also be 100 percent. But if the reliability *r* of each element is only 90 percent, then *R* is $(0.9)^{10} = 35$ percent. And for element reliabilities of 80 percent, *R* is only 11 percent.

Reliability of Elements in Parallel

The effect of parallel elements (redundancy) on a system's reliability is illustrated in Figure 17S.3. Here, if *A* fails to work, *B* can take over, and vice versa. For the system as a whole to fail, both *A and B* must fail, which is unlikely. The reliability *R* of the system—in this case of (again) independent elements—is

$$R = R(A \text{ or } B) = R(A) + R(B) - R(A \text{ and } B)$$

In calculating *R(A)*, we have included those times when *B* is also working—*R(A* and *B)*. In calculating *R(B)*, we have included those times when *A* is also working—*R(A* and *B)*. We have therefore included those times when both are properly

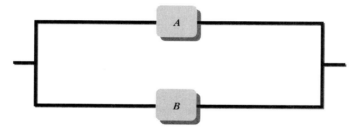

Figure 17S.3   Parallel redundant system.

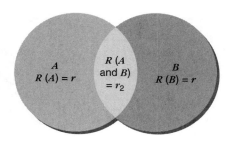

Figure 17S.4   Reliability of a two-element system.

functioning twice. To avoid this double count, we must subtract one $R(A$ and $B)$. This is shown in the Venn diagram in Figure 17S.4.

The reliability of element A is given by the left circle, $R(A)$, and the reliability of element B by the right circle, $R(B)$. If (as with elements in series) *both* A and B must operate properly for the system to work, this reliability is given by the area of overlap, $R(A$ and $B)$ or, for independent elements with identical reliabilities r, as simply r^2 (as explained earlier).

But if the system will work when *either* A or B is operating properly, then $R(A$ or $B)$ is given by the total area enclosed by circles A and B. This area would normally be $R(A) + R(B)$ but, because A and B are not mutually exclusive (i.e., A's working does not keep B from working, and vice versa), there is some overlap in their areas and this area is counted twice in the term $R(A) + R(B)$ and thus must be subtracted out once. The overall resulting reliability of the redundant parallel system is then

$$R(A) + R(B) - R(A \text{ and } B) = r + r - r^2 = 2r - r^2$$

Another, easier, way to obtain this result uses the following logic. The reliability of the system is

$$1 - \text{Probability } (A \text{ and } B \text{ both fail})$$

The probability that A will fail is $1 - R(A)$ or $1 - r$, and the probability for B is $1 - R(B)$ or $1 - r$ again. The resulting reliability of the system is therefore

$$1 - (1 - r)^2 = 1 - 1 + 2r - r^2 = 2r - r^2$$

This simple approach can easily be extended to any number of elements. For example, with n elements in parallel, all with the same reliability r, we have

$$R = 1 - (1 - r)^n$$

The resulting reliability figures for various values of n and r are plotted, in a fashion similar to Figure 17S.2, in Figure 17S.5. Note that for three elements in parallel with reliabilities of only 0.9 each, the system reliability is enhanced to

$$R = 1 - (1 - 0.9)^3 = 1 - 0.1^3 = 1 - 0.001 = 0.999$$

or only one expected failure in 1000 trials.

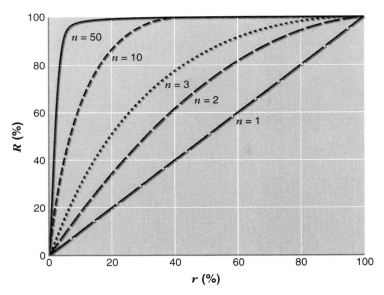

Figure 17S.5   Parallel system reliability.

More generally, where there are n components in parallel with reliabilities r_i (for $i = 1, 2, 3, \ldots, n$), the reliability of the system is calculated as

$$R = 1 - (1 - r_1)(1 - r_2)(1 - r_3) \ldots (1 - r_n)$$

❖ Continuous Reliability

We now turn to the likelihood that a system will function properly over some given period of time. This concept is frequently used in product warranties such as a five-year guarantee, or a television manufacturer's parts and labor guarantee.

Infant Mortality and Wear-out Failures

The typical failure rate of a system is illustrated in Figure 17S.6. The initial failure rate of the system, called *infant mortality,* may actually be quite high because of errors in the construction of the system. If the system is subject to repair on a regular basis, early failures after repair can even be due to something a repairperson did (like forgetting to replace a critical part that needed to come off to get to the failed item). Not all systems exhibit an infant mortality period, but many do. Sometimes the rate here is very low, or negligible, and sometimes it is high.

The infant mortality period is usually quite short because if something has been done wrong, it will usually show up right away. Sometimes a producer, as a regular part of production, tests every system by operating it throughout this period (referred to as the *burn-in period*) to ensure that the customer will not receive a product or service that may experience infant mortality. For example, manufacturers of personal computers often run their computers through a battery of operations and tests for an extended time before shipping.

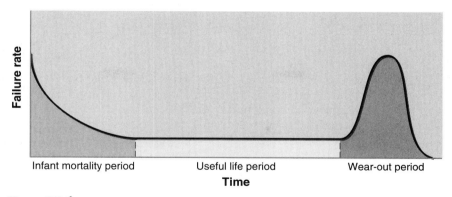

Figure 17S.6 Typical system failure rate distribution.

Following the infant mortality period is a period of very few failures that extends for some duration during the system's useful life. Major design issues are how low this rate should be, how long the duration should be, and, of course, how to obtain this reliability. This period may continue until ultimate product failure, or there may be a final *wear-out* period, as shown in Figure 17S.6. This wear-out period may be quite pronounced, as in this figure, or more gentle. Given the shape of the curve in Figure 17S.6, it is clear why this is called a *bathtub curve*.

The result of applying the failure rate distribution of Figure 17S.6 to a group of, say, 1000 items and graphing how many are left over time is shown in Figure 17S.7. As a result of the initial failures due to infant mortality, the number of items left from the original group of 1000 decreases quickly at first but then levels off when the failure rate falls and the period of useful life begins. Toward the end of this period, the curve starts dropping again as the wear-out peak is approached, hitting the maximum falloff at the top of the wear-out peak, and then tapering off to zero as the failure rate slows down.

Reliability over the Usage Period

If the infant mortality and wear-out failures are relatively insignificant compared with the "useful life" failures, we can determine the reliability of a system lasting for some period of time T before failing. (Equivalently, we can consider just those

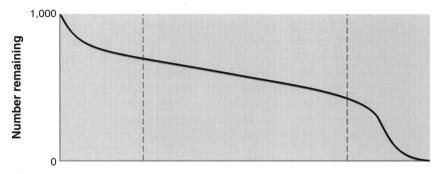

Figure 17S.7 Mortality history.

items that fail during the useful life period, excluding those that fail in infant mortality and wear-out.) Note that in this definition of *continuous reliability,* in contrast to the definition *of instantaneous reliability,* the time period *T* must be specified for a reliability value to be calculated. If *T* is very short, we find that the system has very high reliability; that is, the likelihood is quite high that it will last at least a little while. Conversely, if *T* is very long, the system's reliability is rather low because it will most likely fail before then.

In the useful life period in Figure 17S.6, we find that the failures are relatively random and that the time between failures follows the negative exponential distribution. That is, there are a lot of failures with a short period of time between them, some with a moderate amount of time between them, and very few with a long, long period between them. From these data we can calculate the *average* time between failures, known as the *mean time between failures* (MTBF) and thereby derive the reliability of the system for any time *T.*

$$\text{Reliability for time } T = e^{-T/\text{MTBF}}$$

where *e* is the natural logarithm (2.7183), *T* is the time duration of interest, and MTBF is the mean time between failures. The reliability is the chance that the system will last this long. The probability the system will fail *before* time *T* is simply 1.0 − reliability. The values of $e^{-T/\text{MTBF}}$ are given in Table 17S.2. These values can also be easily calculated using a calculator's e^x function.

For example, suppose we want to find the reliability of a system lasting 20 days (480 hours). Earlier tests on the system found that of four units tested, one failed at 120 hours, one failed at 900 hours, and one failed at 1380 hours, and the last one kept running until the test period was over at 100 days (2400 hours). The average is thus

$$\text{MTBF} = (120 + 900 + 1380 + 2400)/4 = 1200$$

and

$$\text{Reliability} = e^{-480/1200} = e^{-0.40}$$

From Table 17S.2, looking up a value of *T*/MTBF equal to 0.4, we find that the reliability $e^{-0.4}$ is 0.67032, or about 67 percent. Thus, about two out of three will last the full 20 days. For the reliability corresponding to 40 days, we can look up in the table the value for twice that, 0.8, and find that the reliability has dropped to 0.44933, or less than 50 percent.

Using another procedure, we can calculate the reliability of a system during the wear-out period. For example, the infant mortality and useful life periods may have a relatively minor amount of failures, and most failures may occur during the wear-out period. Or, equivalently, we can calculate the *likelihood that any system entering the wear-out period* will last longer than time *T.*

In this case, the distribution of failures can be approximated by the normal distribution (see Appendix A). Again, we need data on the failure rate to approximate the mean and standard deviation of the wear-out distribution. Using the values from the test data plotted in Figure 17S.8, we calculate

$$Z = \frac{T = \text{mean wear-out time}}{\text{standard deviation of wear-out time}} = \frac{50 - 36}{7} = 2.0$$

$\mathcal{T}_{ABLE}$ 17S.2 ❖ Reliability Values of $e^{-T/MTBF}$

T/MTBF	$e^{-T/MTBF}$	T/MTBF	$e^{-T/MTBF}$	T/MTBF	$e^{-T/MTBF}$	T/MTBF	$e^{-T/MTBF}$
0.1	0.90484	2.6	0.07427	5.1	0.00610	7.6	0.00050
0.2	0.81873	2.7	0.06721	5.2	0.00552	7.7	0.00045
0.3	0.74082	2.8	0.06081	5.3	0.00499	7.8	0.00041
0.4	0.67032	2.9	0.05502	5.4	0.00452	7.9	0.00037
0.5	0.60653	3.0	0.04979	5.5	0.00409	8.0	0.00034
0.6	0.54881	3.1	0.04505	5.6	0.00370	8.1	0.00030
0.7	0.49659	3.2	0.04076	5.7	0.00335	8.2	0.00027
0.8	0.44933	3.3	0.03688	5.8	0.00303	8.3	0.00025
0.9	0.40657	3.4	0.03337	5.9	0.00274	8.4	0.00022
1.0	0.36788	3.5	0.03020	6.0	0.00248	8.5	0.00020
1.1	0.33287	3.6	0.02732	6.1	0.00224	8.6	0.00018
1.2	0.30119	3.7	0.02472	6.2	0.00203	8.7	0.00017
1.3	0.27253	3.8	0.02237	6.3	0.00184	8.8	0.00015
1.4	0.24660	3.9	0.02024	6.4	0.00166	8.9	0.00014
1.5	0.22313	4.0	0.01832	6.5	0.00150	9.0	0.00012
1.6	0.20190	4.1	0.01657	6.6	0.00136	9.1	0.00011
1.7	0.18268	4.2	0.01500	6.7	0.00123	9.2	0.00010
1.8	0.16530	4.3	0.01357	6.8	0.00111	9.3	0.00009
1.9	0.14957	4.4	0.01228	6.9	0.00101	9.4	0.00008
2.0	0.13534	4.5	0.01111	7.0	0.00091	9.5	0.00007
2.1	0.12246	4.6	0.01005	7.1	0.00083	9.6	0.00007
2.2	0.11080	4.7	0.00910	7.2	0.00075	9.7	0.00006
2.3	0.10026	4.8	0.00823	7.3	0.00068	9.8	0.00006
2.4	0.09072	4.9	0.00745	7.4	0.00061	9.9	0.00005
2.5	0.08208	5.0	0.00674	7.5	0.00055	10.0	0.00005

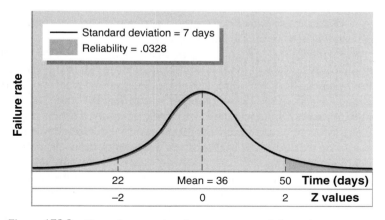

Figure 17S.8   Normal approximation to wear-out failure data.

From the table in Appendix A, we find for $Z = 2.0$ that the area to the left of Z is 0.9772. Thus, the area to the right, which represents the reliability of lasting as long as 50 days or more, is 0.0328, or a little more than 3 percent. Clearly, this is fairly poor reliability. For a value of T equal to the mean, 36 days, the reliability is obviously 50 percent. In terms of application, if a firm were to warrant this product for 50 days, it should expect to replace about 97 percent; if for 36 days, then 50 percent; and if for just 22 days ($Z = -2$), then 3 percent.

AINTENANCE

❖ The Maintenance Function

Although the design and installation of an organization's operating system, consisting of facilities, equipment, materials, supplies, and staff, is a large and expensive undertaking, the trouble and expense do not end there. To keep these resources productive and reliable, constant maintenance must be performed: repair, rest, lubrication, replacement, inspection, and so forth. Belts wear down, grease wears thin, valves tighten up, corrosion sets in, parts crack and break, people get bored and tired, paint peels, pipes leak, and on and on. All these items must be repaired or replaced if they are allowed to reach a point of failure, or failure must be prevented or retarded through certain activities if the system is to remain reliable. This is the general role of maintenance.

In a factory there is usually a maintenance engineer or manager whose job it is to keep the buildings and equipment in proper working order. In other organizations the maintenance function may be performed at random (as things break down) or by contract to an external party, or in a number of other ways.

Regardless of whether the maintenance task is performed formally or informally, the function is essential. The proper role of maintenance is not only to *repair* disabled resources when they fail—this is called *corrective maintenance* (CM)—but also to prevent breakdown or poor performance. This idea of prevention, similar to our concept of preventive control, is called *preventive maintenance* (PM) and is accomplished through inspection, service, and replacement of parts before they fail (all topics to be discussed in more detail later). When equipment is designed and built so that it tends to remain trouble-free and can be easily repaired when necessary, the system is said to have *good maintainability*.

High reliability and good maintainability are especially important in the implementation of JIT systems where any failure can shut the entire production system down, since there are minimal buffers between elements. Preventive maintenance should be scheduled on work centers just like any other job and should have a significant priority so that it isn't constantly postponed when capacity gets tight. Moreover, preventive maintenance on bottleneck work centers is particularly critical and should be treated as more important than nonbottleneck maintenance. Firms where reliability and maintainability are especially important are those that operate 24 hours a day, leaving no slack time for maintenance jobs or additions to capacity.

Maintainability is sometimes measured by the *mean time to repair* (MTTR) a product, where a smaller value is better. A similar measure can be defined for a product's reliability where mean time before (or between) failures (MTBF) is measured rather than the probability of failure within a given period. By combining these measures, an overall measure of a product's "availability" for service may be obtained:

$$\text{Availability} = \frac{\text{MTBF}}{\text{MTBF} + \text{MTTR}}$$

For example, if a computer terminal has a mean time between failures of 1000 hours and a mean time to repair of four days (96 hours), then its availability will be 1000/1096 = 91 percent. If the repair time can be cut in half (to 48 hours), the terminal's availability will increase to 1000/1048 = 95 percent.

❖ The Maintenance Problem

The problem facing the operations manager concerned about maintenance is, as always, how to minimize the total costs to the organization. Idled production due to an unanticipated breakdown can be very expensive, but so can a large maintenance crew that frequently sits idle, as well as downtime due to extensive preventive maintenance. The general cost curves facing the manager are shown in Figure 17S.9. The axis labeled *quality of maintenance* refers to a combination of elements such as the size and ability of the repair crew, the frequency of inspection, and the frequency of replacing critical system elements through PM. As this quality goes up, the cost goes up even faster, while the cost of breakdowns, in terms of both number of failures and duration of idled equipment due to failure, decreases. At some point, as illustrated in the *total cost* curve, a minimum is reached. This is the point the manager is trying to locate.

Another way of interpreting the *quality of maintenance* axis is as a scale of frequency of PM, with less frequent PM (annually) on the left and more frequent PM (monthly) on the right. Then the breakdown cost will be high and the PM cost low

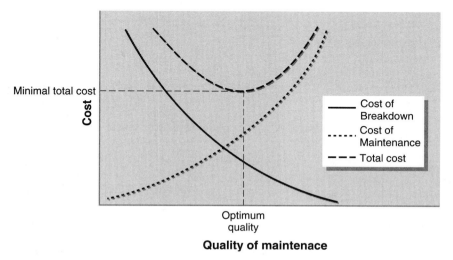

Figure 17S.9 Cost factors in maintenance.

on the left and vice versa on the right. In the midrange PM periods (quarterly) the total costs may tend to be minimal.

In many cases only a subjective estimate of this point is ever attempted, and even that is typically based on having recently experienced, or not experienced, a breakdown. Of necessity, some elements of the cost of a breakdown are subjective (such as the cost of ill will), but many other aspects of the costs can be obtained and analyzed fairly accurately.

Standbys for Corrective Maintenance

If the investment cost is not excessive and standby equipment can be quickly moved in to take over when regular equipment breaks down, then using standbys may be the most economical way of handling corrective maintenance. Let us demonstrate with an example.

Bill Beauty and Bob Beast own and manage Beauty and Beast's Hair Salon near the upper-middle-class suburb of a large city. The salon has a dozen relatively new "Kurl-n-Dri" machines, which provide the majority of the salon's income. Bob has kept track of the number of these curler-dryers out of order every day since the salon opened. Forty percent of the time, none was out of order; 30 percent of the time, one was out; 20 percent, two were out; and 10 percent, three. Considering this history, Bob has wondered if it might be worthwhile to keep one or even two or three spare curler-dryers on hand to recoup the inevitable $20 daily loss of income when a regular machine is out of order. The curler-dryers cost $5 a day, on the average, over their short lifetimes.

ANALYSIS

By using the following expected value formula, we may analyze each of Bob's possible operations alternatives.

$$E(L) = \sum_{n=0}^{3} p_n(n - s)c$$

where

$E(L)$ = expected loss

p_n = probability that n curler-dryers are out of order

s = number of spares available *and used* as replacements

c = loss per unavailable curler-dryer

Current situation (0 spares): The current expected loss per day is

$$0.4(0) + 0.3(1)(\$20) + 0.2(2)\$20 + 0.1(3)\$20 = \$20$$

One spare: The expected revenue loss is

$$0.4(0) + 0.3(1 - 1)\$20 + 0.2(2 - 1)\$20 + 0.1(3 - 1)\$20 = \$8$$
$$\text{Cost of the spare} = \underline{\$5}$$
$$\text{Total daily cost} = \$13$$

Two spares: The expected revenue loss is

$$0.4(0) + 0.3(1 - 1)\$20 + 0.2(2 - 2)\$20 + 0.1(3 - 2)\$20 = \$2$$

$$\text{Cost of spares} = \underline{\$10}$$

$$\text{Total daily cost} = \$12 \text{ (best)}$$

Three spares: The expected revenue loss is

$$0.4(0) + 0.3(1 - 1)\$20 + 0.2(2 - 2)\$20 + 0.1(3 - 3)\$20 = \quad 0$$

$$\text{Cost of spares} = \underline{\$15}$$

$$\text{Total daily cost} = \$15$$

It is clear that four or more spares would be unnecessary. Thus, the best policy is to keep two spares handy and reduce current losses from $20 a day to $12, for a saving of $8 per day.

Preventive Versus Corrective Maintenance

As noted earlier, repairing systems *before* they fail is called *preventive maintenance* (PM), and repairing them after they fail is *corrective maintenance* (CM). Preventive maintenance is an expensive undertaking. The commitment to regularly incurring the high costs of skilled labor, deliberately shutting down a productive system, and replacing parts that still have some life in them is not to be made lightly. Besides, there will *still* be breakdowns when the system is needed—in some cases possibly even due to something that was done during PM! Let us consider the advantages.

PM repairs are much cheaper than breakdown repairs. When a system fails, many other elements of the system besides the failed element, if there is one, are usually damaged in the process. For example, if a $50 motor freezes up, it may destroy a $1000 pump that it powers. Even if a part does not completely fail, as one element in a system begins to deteriorate it puts more of a load on other elements in the system—a load that they were not designed to bear. If alcoholism begins to affect the comptroller of a business, purchasing will start having more trouble getting materials, finance will have problems with its credit, and so forth.

In addition to the costs of repair, there are often the much greater costs of idled production. In some cases this loss must be made up by overtime—perhaps at time and a half or possibly even double time. As *Murphy's law* states: "What *can* go wrong *will* go wrong." And it will go wrong in the worst possible way, at the worst possible time, and in the worst possible place. PM, on the other hand, can be scheduled for a convenient time, such as at night or during lunch.

PM is not, of course, always desirable. If breakdown repairs are hardly more costly overall than PM repairs, then there is probably not a sufficient reason for PM. Or if other alternatives are easily available when a breakdown occurs, such as standby equipment, then PM is unnecessary for continuity of production.

❖ The Replacement Problem

When a system's critical element is easily reached and a breakdown is no great inconvenience, replacement is simply a problem of economics and usually arises in either of the following forms (both of which are discussed in more detail later):

1. *Optimum life*. The situation here is anticipating the most economic future time to replace a current asset (typically, a machine) with another that is identical but new.

2. *Value of a "challenger."* In this situation a new asset has become available that can more efficiently perform a task that a current asset is performing. Should the old asset be replaced?

When it is difficult or expensive to reach the critical system element, replacement is a more complex decision. "Since we've got the tires off, maybe we should reline those worn brakes, too. Save you a lot of trouble and expense later on." "While I'm here, Sam, why don't you replace the filter, too?" As can be seen from these examples, early replacements derive from a situation in which either the labor involved in *getting to* the critical element is significant, thereby justifying premature replacement, or the inconvenience or cost of a later breakdown justifies the early replacement.

A common example of this situation occurs when a larger number of typically low-priced items are more and more likely to fail with age. This decision is called *group replacement*, and it relies heavily on knowledge of the item's lifetime distribution. Somewhat later we will investigate the problem of item replacement versus group replacement, but first let us consider the simpler economic policies.

Optimum Life

The analysis needed to determine the optimum life of an asset involves finding the replacement cycle that minimizes the average annual cost of the asset. Typically, the asset deteriorates over its life, resulting in higher operating costs and loss of resale value. The behavior of these costs with age of the asset is shown in Figure 17S.10. As the age of the asset increases, the operating cost increases, owing to wear, maintenance, and reduced efficiency. For much the same reasons, the salvage value of the asset decreases, but by a steadily lessening amount, year by year. In some particular year the annual cost of the asset will be a minimum—if possible, we would like to use the asset only for *that* particular year, but we generally cannot. Following that year the costs start rising, and after a few years we have gotten the "best years" (in terms of average annual cost) out of the asset. It is uneconomical to hold the asset beyond that point.

The simplest way to find the optimum life is to *accumulate* the total annual costs and find the year for which the average cost (cumulative total annual cost divided by number of years) the lowest. This calculation procedure is illustrated in the following example.

The costs of a CD player used for background music in retail stores are listed in Table 17S.3. We see that the lowest total annual cost for the CD player, $150, occurs in year 3. However, the *average* annual cost through year 3 (years 1, 2, and 3 combined) is $176, higher than the average annual cost through year 4, $172. But by year 5 the average annual cost has again risen to $176, and since this is an increase, the CD player is not worth holding through this year.

If desired, interest and present value corrections can also be incorporated into the figures. We might also note that expected future occurrences should be factored in. For example, if a retailer planned to terminate business after three years and sell the CD players, then the $172 average cost would not be the appropriate figure for selecting the *most economical* CD players to purchase. Rather, a three-year horizon

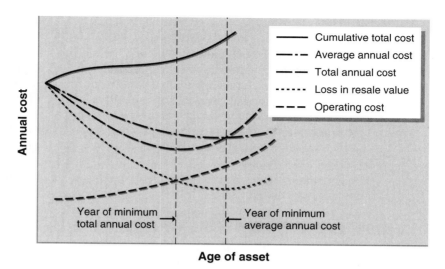

Figure 17S.10 Determination of optimum life of a single asset.

$\mathscr{T}$ABLE 17S.3 ❖ Establishing the Optimum Life of a CD Player

Year	0	1	2	3	4	5	6
Resale value	600	450	370	320	290	270	260
Loss in resale value	—	150	80	50	30	20	10
Repair cost	—	70	80	100	130	170	220
Total annual cost	—	220	160	150	160	190	230
Cumulative total cost	—	220	380	530	690	880	1110
Average annual cost	—	220	190	176	172	176	185

should be used, resulting in $176. In general, costs should be minimized only over the horizon of expected need for the asset. Similarly, if a much more efficient asset is expected to enter the market in the following year, perhaps the best strategy would be to delay the purchase one year and lease an acceptable asset in the interim.

The problem of optimum life exists for all operations investments where the asset, unlike an antique, loses value with age and wear. On occasion, such assets may be replaced prematurely if a new type of asset becomes available, as discussed below.

Value of a Challenger

We now deal with the arrival of a new type of asset (called a *challenger*), which could replace the existing asset (called the *defender*) with a (typically) lower operating cost. The problem is that the challenger is expensive. Also, a considerable amount may have been paid for the defender, and its book value may still be high. Managers are reluctant to part with a like-new asset unless they can obtain a good resale price for it on the used asset market. To the extent that they *cannot,* the difference is called a *sunk cost*. It is important to realize that sunk costs should not enter the replacement decision; only expected future costs are relevant.

For example, suppose you bought a labor-saving machine and paid a considerable amount for it, but felt the machine was well worth it. Then a month later, a new type of machine becomes available that can do the same job at almost no operating cost and overnight makes your machine worthless. If the cost to do the job with the new machine, considering all costs of acquisition, resale, and operating, is less than the operating cost alone of the old machine, then the new machine should be bought. What about the money you poured into the purchase of the original machine? That is a sunk cost and should be ignored. There is no point in using the original machine if another one will have less overall costs for the duration of need. The general approach to such problems is to compare the present values of the costs and revenues of the defender and the challenger in order to make the replacement decision.

Group Versus Individual Replacement

The problem of *group replacement,* one form of preventive maintenance, arises in situations where the cost or trouble associated with a replacement upon failure is very high. A number of policies may be considered: replace only defective items; replace defectives plus all those exceeding x hours of service; replace all the items. The most important set of data needed to address the problem is the failure rate distribution of the item in question, which may resemble Figure 17S.6. Consider the following example.

Nimble Fingers Typing Service

Jane Nimble operates a word processing service that employs 50 typists, each using an identical personal computer and inkjet printer. The printers are older models, so replacing the ink cartridge is a fairly time-consuming procedure. Because many of the typists cannot replace the ink cartridges, Jane, as operations manager, personally replaces all of them when they run out. Jane's typists vary in typing speeds and accuracy; hence, cartridges are used up at varying rates, as shown in Table 17S.4.

Jane estimates that the cost of interruption of her work and the idle time of the typist while a cartridge is being replaced is $10. The cartridge costs $2. One of Jane's typists has suggested that, rather than use only corrective maintenance and change the cartridges when they run out, perhaps preventive maintenance should also be used in the evening, replacing all the cartridges every week, or every other week. Someone could be trained to do the job at a cost of $1 per change, since the machines would be idle anyway. Does the additional policy—replace each week or replace every other week—make sense?

ANALYSIS

The *cost of the current policy* can be computed by first calculating the expected life of a cartridge. This is

ᴛᴀʙʟᴇ 17S.4 ❖ Failure Rate Distribution of Ink Cartridges

Cartridge life, weeks	1*	2	3	4	5	6	7
Probability of "failure" during the week	.15	.05	.10	.15	.20	.30	.05

*Early failure due to defective cartridge.

$$E(\text{life}) = 0.15(1) + 0.05(2) + 0.10(3) + 0.15(4) + 0.20(5) + 0.3(6) + 0.05(7)$$
$$= 0.15 + 0.1 + 0.3 + 0.6 + 1.0 + 1.8 + 0.35$$
$$= 4.3 \text{ weeks}$$

The current policy therefore calls for, on the average, replacement of all cartridges at $12 each ($10 + $2 cartridge cost) every 4.3 weeks for a cost of

$$\$12 \times 50 = \$600$$

or, per week,

$$\frac{\$600}{4.3} = \underline{\underline{\$139.53}} \text{ per week}$$

Replacing at the end of each week would result in costs of

Failures during week $= 0.15 \times 50 \times \$12 = \$\ 90$
Plus end-of-week replacement of all $= 50 \times \$3 \qquad = \underline{\$150}$
$$\text{Total} = \$240$$

or

$$\text{Weekly cost} = \underline{\underline{\$240}}$$

Replacing at the end of every other week would result in costs of

Failures during week 1 $= 0.15 \times 50 \times \$12 \qquad = \ \$90.00$
Failures during week 2 $= 0.05 \times 50 \times \$12 \qquad = \ \ \ 30.00$
Week 1 replacements failing in week 2 $= 0.15 \times (0.15 \times 50) \times \$12 = \ \ \ 13.50$
End-of-week-2 replacement of all $= 50 \times \$3 \qquad = \underline{\ 150.00}$
$$\text{Total} = \$283.50$$

or

$$\text{Weekly cost} = \frac{\$283.50}{2} = \underline{\underline{141.75}} \text{ per week}$$

Therefore, for this problem, neither replacement every week nor replacement every other week is a better policy. (As an exercise, what would be the average weekly cost of replacing the cartridges every *third* week?)

The policies considered in the example of Nimble Fingers were only three of several. Jane could also have used a policy of replacing each week those cartridges that appeared more than half used, or any other plan. Because the calculations become unmanageable very quickly, this problem is very amenable to solution by simulation (see Chapter 12 Supplement). Through simulation, exact times until "failure" may be used rather than "nearest week" times. Once a model has been developed for a replacement problem, any number of potential policies can be tested.

The replacement problem occurs in a number of operations settings, but always where the cost of group replacement is much less than that of individual replacement. This is usually because the items are hard to get to, require special tools or equipment, or idle other productive resources. Examples that are seen frequently are the replacement of lightbulbs; supplies such as paper, ink, and toner in machines; products in vending machines; fast-wearing parts in certain equipment; and so forth.

❖ EXERCISES

1. Determine the reliability of the following system:

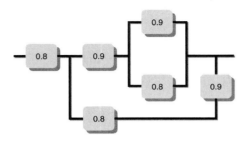

2. For a new clock radio that you purchased, the clock, the alarm switch, and the radio must all work in order for you to be awakened in the morning.

   a. If the reliabilities of the three independent components are 0.95, 0.90, and 0.92, what is the probability that the alarm clock will perform as expected in the morning?

   b. If there is a backup switch (with the same reliability as the first) that will function if the primary switch fails, what is the chance of your being awakened in time?

3. Use Figure 17S.2 to determine the requisite increase in *element* reliability of a series of 50 identical items that are 95 percent reliable to reach a *system* reliability of 40 percent.

4. According to Figure 17S.5, what is the increase in system reliability of a network of 10 identical, parallel items that are 10 percent reliable if their element reliabilities are increased to 20 percent? What would have been the decrease in reliability if, instead, 7 items were removed from the network?

5. A machine is needed that will, on average, be available 35 hours a week, out of a 40-hour-weekly shift. Two machines are being considered. One can be repaired in 90 minutes but has an average time between failures of only 20 hours. The other machine has an MTBF of 30 hours with an average repair time of 3 hours. Which machine, if either, will meet the need?

6. A firm has a machine with an MTBF of 100 hours and an MTTR of 10 hours. It is considering two ways of raising the availability of this machine. One way is to invest in improving the working environment. For every $10 invested, the MTBF will increase by 2 hours. The second alternative is to hire a part-time helper for the repairperson. Every hour of help will cost $5 but will reduce MTTR by 10 minutes. Which alternative is best for the firm?

7. a. Corrective maintenance costs $50 each for repairing the following dozen machines whenever they fail. Is this the best policy, or is additional nightly preventive maintenance at a cost of $10 per machine better?

Days	1	2	3	4
Probability of failure	.2	.1	.3	.4

   b. Evaluate the cost of additional preventive maintenance every other night and compare it with the previous answers.

8. Solve Exercise 7 again, with each of the following two lifetime distributions.

Days	1	2	3	4
(*a*) P(failure)	.25	.25	.25	.25
(*b*) P(failure)	.4	.3	.2	.1

9. Ray Gordon, owner-operator of a single 18-wheeler tractor-trailer, has had trouble with flat tires over the past year. Ray is considering the possibility of using additional spare tires. His rig currently carries one spare. On any given trip, the probability of zero or more flat tires is given as follows.

Flats	Probability
0	.3
1	.5
2	.1
3	.1

   If Ray has more than one flat tire, a new tire must be purchased on the road and a special "road service" fee paid to the tire company. The cost to Ray is $600. The cost per trip of each extra spare is based on the expected life of the tire (even if it is not used, it is subject to dry rot, so its life is not indefinite) and is anticipated to be $20 per trip. How many spares would you recommend that Ray carry?

10. Solve Nimble Fingers's group replacement problem for replacements every third night. Can you derive an equation for the cost of PM at any arbitrary interval?

11. Resolve the Beauty and Beast's problem if:

   a. The cost of one curler-dryer out of order is $20, of two is $50, and of three is $90.

   b. The cost of one curler-dryer out of order is $20, of two is $35, and of three is $45.

   c. The curler-dryers cost $5 for one, $12 for two, and $20 for three.

   d. The curler-dryers cost $5 for one, $8 for two, and $9 for three.

12. The Last National Bank of Pleasantville uses a magnetic ink character reader (MICR) to process checks. The machine loses 20 percent each year in resale value (its original purchase price was $80,000) and has the following maintenance cost schedule over its 10-year useful life.

Year	1	2	3	4	5	6	7	8	9	10
Cost, $	8000	9000	10,200	12,000	15,000	16,500	17,000	17,400	17,750	18,000

When should the machine be replaced?

13. A machine costing $4000 with a five-year life loses 30 percent of its value every year. Maintenance is free the first year but thereafter increases $600 every year. When is the best time to replace the machine?

Area Under the Normal Distribution

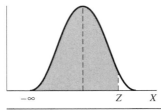

Example: the area to the left of $Z = 1.34$ is found by following the left Z column down to 1.3 and moving right to the 0.04 column. At the intersection read 0.9099. The area to the right of $Z = 1.34$ is $1 - 0.9099 = 0.0901$. The area between the mean (dashed line) and $Z = 1.34 = 0.9099 - 0.5 = 0.4099$.

Z	0.00	0.01	0.02	0.03	0.04	0.05	0.06	0.07	0.08	0.09
0.0	0.5000	0.5040	0.5080	0.5120	0.5160	0.5199	0.5239	0.5279	0.5319	0.5359
0.1	0.5398	0.5438	0.5478	0.5517	0.5557	0.5596	0.5636	0.5675	0.5714	0.5753
0.2	0.5793	0.5832	0.5871	0.5910	0.5948	0.5987	0.6026	0.6064	0.6103	0.6141
0.3	0.6179	0.6217	0.6255	0.6293	0.6331	0.6368	0.6406	0.6443	0.6480	0.6517
0.4	0.6554	0.6591	0.6628	0.6664	0.6700	0.6736	0.6772	0.6808	0.6844	0.6879
0.5	0.6915	0.6950	0.6985	0.7019	0.7054	0.7088	0.7123	0.7157	0.7190	0.7224
0.6	0.7257	0.7291	0.7324	0.7357	0.7389	0.7422	0.7454	0.7486	0.7517	0.7549
0.7	0.7580	0.7611	0.7642	0.7673	0.7704	0.7734	0.7764	0.7794	0.7823	0.7852
0.8	0.7881	0.7910	0.7939	0.7967	0.7995	0.8023	0.8051	0.8078	0.8106	0.8133
0.9	0.8159	0.8186	0.8212	0.8238	0.8264	0.8289	0.8315	0.8340	0.8365	0.8389
1.0	0.8413	0.8438	0.8461	0.8485	0.8508	0.8531	0.8554	0.8577	0.8599	0.8621
1.1	0.8643	0.8665	0.8686	0.8708	0.8729	0.8749	0.8770	0.8790	0.8810	0.8830
1.2	0.8849	0.8869	0.8888	0.8907	0.8925	0.8944	0.8962	0.8980	0.8997	0.9015
1.3	0.9032	0.9049	0.9066	0.9082	0.9099	0.9115	0.9131	0.9147	0.9162	0.9177
1.4	0.9192	0.9207	0.9222	0.9236	0.9251	0.9265	0.9279	0.9292	0.9306	0.9319
1.5	0.9332	0.9345	0.9357	0.9370	0.9382	0.9394	0.9406	0.9418	0.9429	0.9441
1.6	0.9452	0.9463	0.9474	0.9484	0.9495	0.9505	0.9515	0.9525	0.9535	0.9549
1.7	0.9554	0.9564	0.9573	0.9582	0.9591	0.9599	0.9608	0.9616	0.9625	0.9633
1.8	0.9641	0.9649	0.9656	0.9664	0.9671	0.9678	0.9686	0.9693	0.9696	0.9706
1.9	0.9713	0.9719	0.9726	0.9732	0.9738	0.9744	0.9750	0.9756	0.9761	0.9767
2.0	0.9772	0.9778	0.9783	0.9788	0.9793	0.9798	0.9803	0.9808	0.9812	0.9817
2.1	0.9821	0.9826	0.9830	0.9834	0.9838	0.9842	0.9846	0.9850	0.9854	0.9857
2.2	0.9861	0.9864	0.9868	0.9871	0.9875	0.9878	0.9881	0.9884	0.9887	0.9890
2.3	0.9893	0.9896	0.9898	0.9901	0.9904	0.9906	0.9909	0.9911	0.9913	0.9916
2.4	0.9918	0.9920	0.9922	0.9925	0.9927	0.9929	0.9931	0.9932	0.9934	0.9936
2.5	0.9938	0.9940	0.9941	0.9943	0.9945	0.9946	0.9948	0.9949	0.9951	0.9952
2.6	0.9953	0.9955	0.9956	0.9957	0.9959	0.9960	0.9961	0.9962	0.9963	0.9964
2.7	0.9965	0.9966	0.9967	0.9968	0.9969	0.9970	0.9971	0.9972	0.9973	0.9974
2.8	0.9974	0.9975	0.9976	0.9977	0.9977	0.9978	0.9979	0.9979	0.9980	0.9981
2.9	0.9981	0.9982	0.9982	0.9983	0.9984	0.9984	0.9985	0.9985	0.9986	0.9986
3.0	0.9987	0.9987	0.9987	0.9988	0.9988	0.9989	0.9989	0.9989	0.9990	0.9990
3.1	0.9990	0.9991	0.9991	0.9991	0.9992	0.9992	0.9992	0.9992	0.9993	0.9993
3.2	0.9993	0.9993	0.9994	0.9994	0.9994	0.9994	0.9994	0.9995	0.9995	0.9995
3.3	0.9995	0.9995	0.9995	0.9996	0.9996	0.9996	0.9996	0.9996	0.9996	0.9997
3.4	0.9997	0.9997	0.9997	0.9997	0.9997	0.9997	0.9997	0.9997	0.9997	0.9998

Random Numbers

39	73	72	75	37		02	87	98	10	47		93	21	95	97	69		41	91	80	67	59		34	18	04	52	35
79	57	92	36	59		89	74	39	82	15		08	58	94	34	74		21	89	11	47	99		11	20	99	45	18
22	45	44	84	11		87	80	61	65	31		09	71	91	74	25		95	18	94	06	97		27	37	83	28	71
80	45	67	93	82		59	73	19	85	23		53	33	65	97	21		97	08	31	55	73		10	65	81	92	59
53	58	47	70	93		66	56	45	65	79		45	56	20	19	47		69	26	88	86	13		59	71	74	17	32
26	72	39	27	67		53	77	57	68	93		60	61	97	22	61		41	47	10	25	03		87	63	93	95	17
43	00	65	98	50		45	60	33	01	07		98	99	46	50	47		91	94	14	63	62		08	61	74	51	69
52	70	05	48	34		56	65	05	61	86		90	92	10	70	80		80	06	54	18	47		08	52	85	08	40
15	33	59	05	28		22	87	26	07	47		86	96	98	29	06		67	72	77	63	99		89	85	84	46	06
85	13	99	24	44		49	18	09	79	49		74	16	32	23	02		59	40	24	13	75		42	29	72	23	19
87	03	04	79	88		08	13	13	85	51		55	34	57	72	69		02	89	08	16	94		85	53	83	29	95
52	06	79	79	45		82	63	18	27	44		69	66	92	19	09		87	18	15	70	07		37	79	49	12	38
46	72	60	18	77		55	66	12	62	11		08	99	55	64	57		98	83	71	70	15		89	09	39	59	24
47	21	61	88	32		27	80	30	21	60		10	92	35	36	12		10	08	58	07	04		76	62	16	48	68
12	73	73	99	12		49	99	57	94	82		96	88	57	17	91		47	90	56	37	31		71	82	13	50	41
63	62	06	34	41		79	53	36	02	95		20	26	36	31	62		58	24	97	14	97		95	06	70	99	00
78	47	23	53	90		79	93	96	38	63		31	56	34	19	19		47	83	75	51	33		30	62	38	20	46
87	68	62	15	43		97	48	72	66	48		98	40	07	17	66		23	05	09	51	80		59	78	11	52	49
47	60	92	10	77		26	97	05	73	51		24	33	45	77	48		69	81	84	09	29		93	22	70	45	80
56	88	87	59	41		06	87	37	78	48		01	31	60	10	27		35	07	79	71	53		28	99	52	01	41
22	17	68	65	84		87	02	22	57	51		56	27	09	24	43		21	78	55	09	82		72	61	88	73	61
19	36	27	59	46		39	77	32	77	09		48	13	93	55	96		41	92	45	71	51		09	18	25	58	94
16	77	23	02	77		28	06	24	25	93		00	06	41	41	20		14	36	59	25	47		54	45	17	24	89
78	43	76	71	61		97	67	63	99	61		58	76	17	14	86		59	53	11	52	21		66	04	18	72	87
03	28	28	26	08		69	30	16	09	05		27	55	10	24	92		28	04	67	53	44		95	23	00	84	47
04	31	17	21	56		33	73	99	19	87		74	13	39	35	22		68	95	23	92	35		36	63	70	35	33
61	06	98	03	91		87	14	77	43	96		76	51	94	84	86		13	79	93	37	55		98	16	04	41	67
23	68	35	26	00		99	53	93	61	28		79	57	95	13	91		09	61	87	25	21		56	20	11	32	44
15	39	25	70	99		93	86	52	77	65		77	31	61	95	46		20	44	90	32	64		26	99	76	75	63
58	71	96	30	24		18	46	23	34	27		48	38	75	93	29		73	37	32	04	05		60	82	29	20	25
93	22	53	64	39		07	10	63	76	35		81	83	83	04	49		77	45	85	50	51		79	88	01	97	30
78	76	58	54	74		92	38	70	96	92		92	79	43	89	79		29	18	94	51	23		14	85	11	47	23
61	81	31	96	82		00	57	25	60	59		48	40	35	94	22		72	65	71	08	86		50	03	42	99	36
42	88	07	10	05		24	98	65	63	21		64	71	06	21	66		89	37	20	70	01		61	65	70	22	12
77	94	30	05	39		28	10	99	00	27		06	94	76	10	08		81	30	15	39	14		81	83	17	16	33
39	65	76	45	45		19	90	69	64	61		94	61	09	43	62		20	21	14	68	86		84	95	48	46	45
73	71	23	70	90		65	97	60	12	11		34	85	52	05	09		21	43	01	72	73		14	93	87	81	40
72	20	47	33	84		51	67	47	97	19		53	16	71	13	81		59	97	50	99	52		24	62	20	42	31
75	17	25	69	17		17	95	21	78	58		88	46	38	03	58		72	68	49	29	31		75	70	16	08	24
37	48	79	88	74		63	52	06	34	30		65	88	69	58	39		07	29	73	72	38		51	28	84	89	47

Bibliography

CHAPTER 1

1. Albrecht, K., and R. Zemke. *Service America: Doing Business in the New Economy*. Homewood, Ill.: Dow Jones–Irwin, 1985.
2. Andrew, C. G., et al. "The Critical Importance of Production and Operations Management." *Academy of Management Review* 7 (1982): 143–147.
3. Avishai, B. "A CEO's Common Sense of CIM: An Interview with J. Tracy O'Rourke." *Harvard Business Review* (January–February 1989): 110–117.
4. Buffa, E. S. *Meeting the Competitive Challenge*. Homewood, Ill.: Dow Jones–Irwin, 1984.
5. Bylinsky, G. "The Race to the Automatic Factory." *Fortune* (February 21, 1983): 52–64.
6. Chase, R. B., and E. L. Prentis. "Operations Management: A Field Rediscovered." *Journal of Management* 13, No. 2 (October 1987): 351–366.
7. Cohen, S. S., and J. Zysman. *Manufacturing Matters: The Myth of the Post-Industrial Economy*. New York: Basic, 1987.
8. Collier, D. A. *Service Management: The Automation of Services*. Reston, Va.: Reston, 1985.
9. Drucker, P. *The Practice of Management*. New York: Harper, 1954.
10. Duff, C., and B. Ortega. "How Wal-Mart Outdid a Once-Touted K-Mart In Discount-Store Race." *Wall Street Journal* (March 24, 1995): A1, A4.
11. Gibson, R. "At McDonald's, New Recipes for Buns, Eggs." *Wall Street Journal,* (June 13, 1995): B1, B6.
12. Hall, R. W. *Attaining Manufacturing Excellence*. Homewood, Ill.: Dow Jones–Irwin, 1987.
13. Hammer, M., and J. Champy. *Reengineering the Corporation*. New York: Harper Business, 1993.
14. Hayes, R. H., and W. J. Abernathy. "Managing Our Way to Economic Decline." *Harvard Business Review* 58 (July–August 1980): 67–77.
15. Hayes, R. H., and S. C. Wheelwright. *Restoring Our Competitive Edge: Competing Through Manufacturing*. New York: Wiley, 1984.
16. Heskett, J. L. *Managing in the Service Economy*. Boston: Harvard Business School Press, 1986.
17. Ingrassia, P., and J. B. White. "With Its Market Share Sliding, GM Scrambles to Avoid a Calamity." *Wall Street Journal,* (December 14, 1997): A1, A10.
18. Lovelock, C. *Managing Services*. New York: Prentice-Hall, 1985.
19. Maremont, M. "The Times of Your Life—As Many Times as You Want." *Business Week* (January 30, 1995): 68.
20. Nadler, D. A., and M. L. Tushman. "Strategic Linking: Designing Formal Coordination Mechanisms," in Michael L. Tushman and William L. Moore, *Readings in the Management of Innovation,* 2nd ed., New York: Harper Business, 1988, pp. 469–486.
21. O'Rourke, J. T. Speech given at 1989 Annual Conference of the Operations Management Association, Columbus, Ohio.

22. Porter, M. E. *Competitive Advantage*. New York: Free Press, 1985.

23. Ruffenach, G. "Getting the Olympic Flame to Atlanta Won't Be a Simple Cross-Country Run." *Wall Street Journal* (February 29, 1996): B1.

24. Schoenberger, R. J. *World Class Manufacturing: The Lessons of Simplicity Applied*. New York: Free Press, 1986.

25. Shafer, S. M., and Oswald, S. L. "Product Focused Manufacturing for Strategic Advantage." *Business Horizons* (November–December 1996): 24–29.

26. Shafer, S. M. *Operations Management Primer*. Burr Ridge, Ill.: Irwin, 1994.

27. Smith, A. *An Inquiry into the Nature and Causes of the Wealth of Nations*. London: Stranham & T. Cadell, 1776.

28. Taylor, F. W. *The Principles of Scientific Management*. New York: Harper & Row, 1911.

29. Waterman, R. H., Jr. *The Renewal Factor: How to Get and Keep the Competitive Edge*. Toronto: Bantam, 1987.

CHAPTER 2

1. American Productivity Center. *Productivity Perspectives*. Houston, Tex.: December 1987, p. 12.

2. Berger, J. "Productivity: Why It's the Number 1 Underachiever." *Business Week* (April, 20, 1987): 54–55.

3. Blauchard, K., and N. V. Peale. *The Power of Ethical Management*. New York: Morrow, 1988.

4. Borrus, A. "This Trade Gap Ain't What it Used to Be." *Business Week* (March 18, 1996): 50.

5. Bowles, J. G. "The Quality Imperative: Banking on Quality at First Chicago." *Fortune* (September 29, 1986): 61–96.

6. Buffa, E. S. *Meeting the Competitive Challenge: Manufacturing Strategy for U.S. Companies*. Homewood, Ill.: Dow Jones–Irwin, 1984.

7. Buzzell, R. D., and B. T. Gale. *The PIMS Principles: Linking Strategy to Performance*. New York: Free Press, 1987.

8. Crosby, P. B. *Quality Is Free: The Art of Making Quality Certain*. New York: McGraw-Hill, 1979.

9. Demeyer, A., J. Nakane, J. G. Miller, and K. Ferdows. "Flexibility: The Next Competitive Battle." Manufacturing Roundtable Research Report Series, School of Management (February 1987). Reprinted in *Strategic Management Journal* 10 (1989): 135–144.

10. Eklund, C. S. "Why Black & Decker Is Cutting Itself Down to Size." *Business Week* (November 25, 1985): 42–43.

11. Feitzinger, E., and H. L. Lee. "Mass Customization at Hewlett-Packard: The Power of Postponement." *Harvard Business Review* (January–February 1997): 116–121.

12. Ferdows, K., ed. *Managing International Manufacturing*. New York: North-Holland, 1989.

13. Garvin, D. A. "Competing on the Eight Dimensions of Quality." *Harvard Business Review* (November–December 1987): 101–109.

14. Garvin, D. A. "What Does 'Product Quality' Really Mean?" *Sloan Management Review* (Fall 1984): 25–43.

15. Gilmore, J. H., and B. J. Pine II. "The Four Faces of Mass Customization." *Harvard Business Review* (January–February 1997): 91–101.

16. Groover, M. P., and E. W. Zimmers, Jr. *CAD/CAM: Computer-Aided Design and Manufacturing*. Englewood Cliffs, N.J.: Prentice-Hall, 1984.

17. Hayes, R. H., and G. P. Pisano. "Beyond World-Class: The New Manufacturing Strategy." *Harvard Business Review* (January–February 1994): 77–86.

18. Hellriegel, D., and J. W. Slocum, Jr. *Management,* 7th ed. South-Western College Publishing, 1996.

19. Hill, T. *Manufacturing Strategy: Text and Cases*. Homewood, Ill.: Irwin, 1989.

20. Jonas, N. "The Hollow Corporation." *Business Week* (March 3, 1986): 57–85.

21. Juran, J. M., F. M. Gryna, Jr., and R. S. Bingham, Jr., eds. *Quality Control Handbook,* 4th ed. New York: McGraw-Hill, 1988.

22. Kantrow, A. M. "The Strategy-Technology Connection." *Harvard Business Review* (July–August 1980): 6–8, 12.

23. Kendrick, J. W. *Improving Company Productivity*. Baltimore: Johns Hopkins University Press, 1984.

24. Maidique, M. A., and Patch, P. "Corporate Strategy and Technological Policy," in M. L. Tushman and W. L. Moore, eds., *Readings in the Management of Innovation,* 2nd ed. Harper Business, 1988, pp. 236–248.

25. Mehl, W. "Strategic Management of Operations: A Top Management Perspective." *Operations Management Review* (Fall 1983): 29–40.

26. Meredith, J. R., and D. M. McCutcheon. "Responsiveness: The Next Strategic Imperative," working paper. Cincinnati, Ohio: University of Cincinnati, 1989.

27. Pare, T. "The Big Threat to Big Steel's Future." *Fortune* (July 15, 1991): 104–108.

28. Pine, B. J., II, B. Victor, and A. C. Boynton. "Making Mass Customization Work." *Harvard Business Review* (September–October 1993): 108–119.

29. Porter, M. E. *Competitive Advantage: Creating and Sustaining Superior Performance*. New York: Free Press, 1985.

30. Porter, M. E., ed. *Competition in Global Industries*. Boston: Harvard Business School Press, 1986.

31. Prahalad, C. K., and G. Hamel. "The Core Competence of the Corporation." *Harvard Business Review* (May–June 1990): 79–91.

32. "Putting Excellence into Management." *Business Week* (July 21, 1980): 196–205.

33. Richardson, P. R., A. J. Taylor, and J. R. M. Gordon. "A Strategic Approach to Evaluating Manufacturing Performance." *Interfaces* (November–December 1985): 15–27.

34. Rosegger, G. *The Economics of Production and Innovation: An Industrial Perspective*. Oxford: Pergamon, 1986.

35. Schonberger, R. J. *Building a Chain of Customers*. New York: Free Press, 1990.

36. Shafer, S. M., *Operations Management Primer*. Burr Ridge, Ill.: Irwin, 1994.

37. Shostack, G. L. "Designing Services That Deliver." *Harvard Business Review* (January–February 1984): 133–139.

38. Skinner, W. "Operations Technology: Blind Spot in Strategic Management." *Interfaces* (January–February 1984): 116–125.

39. Skinner, W. *Manufacturing: The Formidable Competitive Weapon*. New York: Wiley, 1985.

40. Skinner, W. "The Productivity Paradox." *Harvard Business Review* (July–August 1986): 55–59.

41. Starr, M. K. *Global Competitiveness: Getting the U.S. Back on Track*. New York: Norton, 1988.

42. Stevenson, W. J. *Production/Operations Management,* 4th ed. Homewood, Ill.: Irwin, 1993.

43. Stobaugh, R., and P. Telesio. "Match Manufacturing Policies and Product Strategies." *Harvard Business Review* (March–April 1983): 113–120.

44. Thomas, D. R. E. "Strategy Is Different in Service Businesses." *Harvard Business Review* (July–August 1978): 158–165.

45. Venkatesan, R. "Strategic Sourcing: to Make or Not to Make." *Harvard Business Review* (November–December 1992): 98–107.

46. Wall Street Journal. "Black & Decker Meets Japan's Push Head-On in Power-Tool Market" (February 18, 1983).

47. Wessel, D. "With Labor Scarce, Service Firms Strive to Raise Productivity." *Wall Street Journal* (June 1, 1989): A1, A16.

48. Wheelwright, S. C. "Japan—Where Operations Really Are Strategic." *Harvard Business Review* (July–August 1981): 67–74.

49. Wheelwright, S. C. "Reflecting Corporate Strategy in Manufacturing Decisions." *Business Horizons* (February 1978): 57–66.

50. Wheelwright, S. C., and R. H. Hayes. "Competing Through Manufacturing." *Harvard Business Review* (January–February 1985): 99–109.

51. Whitford, D. "Sale of the Century." *Fortune* (February 17, 1997): 92–100.

52. Zachary, G. P. "Service Productivity Is Rising Fast—and So Is the Fear of Lost Jobs." *Wall Street Journal* (July 8, 1995): A1, A10.

CHAPTER 3

1. Berstein, A. "Quality Is Becoming Job One in the Office, Too." *Business Week* (April 29, 1991): 52–54.

2. Berry, L. L., V. A. Zeithmal, and A. Parasuraman. "Quality Counts in Services, Too." *Business Horizons* 28, No. 3 (May–June 1985): 44–52.

3. Blodgett, N. "Law Firm Pioneers Explore New Territory." *Quality Progress* (August 1996): 90–94.

4. Bowles, J. G. "The Quality Imperative." *Fortune* (September 29, 1986): 61–96.

5. Crosby, P. B. *Quality Without Tears.* New York: McGraw-Hill, 1984.

6. Deming, W. E. *Out of Crisis.* Cambridge, Mass.: MIT Press, 1986.

7. Deming, W. E. *Quality, Productivity and Competitive Position.* Cambridge, Mass.: MIT Press, 1982.

8. DiPrimio, A. *Quality Assurance in Service Organizations.* Radnor, Pa.: Chilton, 1987.

9. Feigenbaum, A. V. *Total Quality Control: Engineering and Management,* 3rd ed. New York: McGraw-Hill, 1983.

10. Gale, B. T. *Quality as a Strategic Weapon.* Cambridge, Mass.: Strategic Planning Institute, 1985.

11. Garvin, D. A. "Competing on the Eight Dimensions of Quality." *Harvard Business Review* (November–December 1987): 101–109.

12. Garvin, D. A. *Managing Quality: The Strategic and Competitive Edge.* New York: Free Press, 1988.

13. Garvin, D. A. "Quality on the Line." *Harvard Business Review* (September–October 1983): 64–75.

14. Gitlow, H. S., and S. J. Gitlow. *The Deming Guide to Quality and Competitive Position.* Englewood Cliffs, N.J.: Prentice-Hall, 1987.

15. George, S., and A. Weimerskirch. *Total Quality Management*. New York: Wiley, 1994.
16. Greising, D. "Quality: How to Make it Pay." *Business Week* (August 8, 1994): 54–59.
17. Harrington, H. J., and J. S. Harrington. *High Performance Benchmarking*. New York: McGraw-Hill, 1996.
18. Hoffherr, G. D., J. W. Moran, and F. Nadler. *Breakthrough Thinking in Total Quality Management*. Englewood Cliffs, N.J.: Prentice-Hall, 1994.
19. Ingle, S. *In Search of Perfection: How to Create/Maintain/Improve Quality*. Englewood Cliffs, N.J.: Prentice-Hall, 1985.
20. Juran, J. M., and F. M. Gryna, Jr. *Quality Planning and Analysis*. New York: McGraw-Hill, 1980.
21. King, C. A. "Service Quality Assurance Is Different." *Quality Progress* 18, No. 6 (1985): 14–18.
22. Lawler, E. E., III, and S. Mohrman. "Quality Circles After the Fad." *Harvard Business Review* (January–February 1985): 65–71.
23. Leonard, F. S., and W. E. Sasser. "The Incline of Quality." *Harvard Business Review* (September–October 1982): 163–171.
24. Manley, R., and J. Manley. "Sharing the Wealth: TQM Spreads from Business to Education." *Quality Progress* (June 1996): 51–55.
25. Port, O. "The Push for Quality." *Business Week* (June 8, 1987): 135–137.
26. Rau, H. "15 Years and Still Going . . ." *Quality Progress* (July 1995): 57–59.
27. Reddy, J., and A. Berger. "Three Essentials of Product Quality." *Harvard Business Review* (July–August 1983): 153–159.
28. Reichheld, F. F., and Sasser, W. E., Jr. "Zero Defections: Quality Comes to Services." *Harvard Business Review* (September–October 1990): 105–111.
29. Sager, I. "How IBM Became a Growth Company Again." *Business Week* (December 9, 1996): 154–162.
30. Sinha, M. N., and W. O. Wilborn. *The Management of Quality Assurance*. New York: Wiley, 1985.
31. Townsend, P. L. *Commit to Quality*. New York: Wiley, 1986.

CHAPTER 4

1. Ackoff, R. L. *The Art of Problem Solving*. New York: Wiley, 1978.
2. Anders, G. "Triage by Phone: How Nurses Take Calls and Control Care of Patients from Afar." *Wall Street Journal* (February 4, 1997): A1, A6.
3. Blumenthal, K. "Systems Slicing Home Loan's Cost, Times Are Set by Fannie Mae and Freddie Mac." *Wall Street Journal* (April 4, 1995): A2, A8.
4. Business Week. "He's Gutsy, Brilliant, and Carries an Ax." Cover story May 9, 1994): 62–66.
5. Davenport, T. H. *Process Innovation*. Boston, Mass.: Harvard Business School Press, 1993.
6. Hall, G., J. Rosenthal, and J. Wade. "How to Make Reengineering Really Work." *Harvard Business Review* (November–December 1993): 119–131.
7. Hammer, M. "Reengineering Work: Don't Automate, Obliterate." *Harvard Business Review* (July–August 1990): 104–112.
8. Hammer, M. *Beyond Reengineering*. New York: Harper Business, 1996.
9. Hammer, M., and J. Champy. *Reengineering the Corporation*. New York: Harper Business, 1993.

10. Hammer, M., and S. A. Stanton. *The Reengineering Revolution*. New York: Harper Business, 1995.
11. Henkoff, R. "Delivering the Goods." *Fortune* (November 28, 1994): 64–78.
12. Hof, R. D. "Netspeed at NetScape." *Business Week* (February 10, 1997): 78–86.
13. Jacob, R. "The Struggle to Create an Organization for the 21st Century." *Fortune* (April 3, 1995): 90–99.
14. Martin, P. K. *Leading Project Management into the 21st Century*. Flemington, N.J.: Renaissance Educational Services, 1995.
15. Niebel, B. W. *Motion and Time Study,* 7th ed. Homewood, Ill.: Irwin, 1982.
16. Rigdon, J. E. "Retooling Lives: Technological Gains Are Cutting Costs, and Jobs, in Services." *Wall Street Journal* (February 4, 1994): A1, A7.
17. Saporito, B. "What's for Dinner?" *Fortune* (May 15, 1995): 50–60.
18. Smith, A. *An Inquiry into the Nature and Causes of the Wealth of Nations*. London: Stranham & T. Cadell, 1776.

CHAPTER 5

1. Albrecht, K., and R. Zemke. *Service America*. Homewood, Ill.: Dow Jones–Irwin, 1985.
2. Ben-Arieh, D., C. A. Fritsch, and K. Mandel. "Competitive Product Realization in Today's Electronic Industries." *Industrial Engineering* (February 1986): 34–42.
3. Bylinsky, G. "The Digital Factory." *Fortune* (November 14, 1994): 92–110.
4. Business Week. "Development Time Is Money" (January 27, 1997): 6.
5. Chase, R. B. "Where Does the Customer Fit in a Service Operation?" *Harvard Business Review* (November–December 1978): 137–142.
6. Collier, D. A. *Service Management: The Automation of Services*. Reston, Va.: Reston, 1985.
7. Dean, J. H., Jr., and G. I. Susman. "Organizing for Manufacturable Design." *Harvard Business Review* (January–February 1989): 28–36.
8. Dumaine, B. "Payoff from the New Management." *Fortune* (December 13, 1993): 103–110.
9. Evans, J. R., and W. M. Lindsay. *The Management and Control of Quality,* 2nd ed. New York: West, 1993.
10. Groover, M. P., and E. W. Zimmers, Jr. *CAD/CAM: Computer-Aided Design and Manufacturing*. Englewood Cliffs, N.J.: Prentice-Hall, 1984.
11. Henkoff, R. "Service Is Everybody's Business." *Fortune* (June 27, 1994): 48–60.
12. Malott, R. H. "Let's Restore Balance to Product Liability Law." *Harvard Business Review* (May–June 1983): 66–74.
13. Meredith, J. R., and S. J. Mantel, Jr. *Project Management: A Managerial Approach,* 2nd ed. New York: Wiley, 1989.
14. Mitchell, R. "How Ford Hit the Bull's-Eye with Taurus." *Business Week* (June 30, 1986): 69–70.
15. Nevens, T. M., G. L. Summe, and B. Uttal. "Commercializing Technology: What the Best Companies Do." *Harvard Business Review* (May–June 1990): 60–69.
16. Normann, R. *Service Management: Strategy and Leadership in Service Businesses*. New York: Wiley, 1984.
17. Oster, P., and J. Rossant. "Call it Worldpool." *Business Week* (November 28, 1994): 98–99.
18. Rose, R. L. "Johnson Controls Gets a Big Boost from the Bottom." *Wall Street Journal* (February 3, 1997): B4.

19. Scarpello, V., W. R. Boulton, and C. R. Hofer. "Reintegrating R&D into Business Strategy." *Journal of Business Strategy* (Spring 1986): 49–56.
20. Schmenner, R. W. "How Can Service Businesses Survive and Prosper?" *Sloan Management Review* (Spring 1986): 21–32.
21. Shostack, G. L. "Designing Services That Deliver." *Harvard Business Review* (January–February 1984): 133–139.
22. Uttal, B. "Speeding New Ideas to Market." *Fortune* (March 2, 1987): 62–66.
23. Utterback, J. M., and W. J. Abernathy. "A Dynamic Model of Process and Product Innovation by Firms." *Omega* 3 (1975): 639–656.
24. Whitney, D. E. "Manufacturing by Design." *Harvard Business Review* (July–August 1988): 83–91.
25. Woodruff, D. "The Racy Viper Is Already a Winner for Chrysler." *Business Week* (November 4, 1991): 36–38.

CHAPTER 6

1. Bradley, T. "Fender Blenders." *1988–1989 Guitar Buyers' Guide:* 129–133.
2. Bylinski, G. "The Race to the Automatic Factory." *Fortune* (February 21, 1983): 52–60.
3. Bylinski, G. "The Digital Factory." *Fortune* (November 14, 1994): 92–107.
4. Chase, R. B., and W. K. Erikson. "The Service Factory." *Academy of Management Executive* (August 1988): 191–196.
5. Chase, R. B., and D. A. Tansik. "The Customer Contact Model for Organization Design." *Management Science* 29, No. 9 (September 1983): 1037–1050.
6. Cincinnati Enquirer. "Robert Store Believed World's First" (November 21, 1989).
7. Collier, D. A. *Service Management: The Automation of Services.* Reston, Va.: Reston, 1985.
8. Cortese, A., "Here Comes the Intranet." *Business Week* (February 26, 1996): 76–84.
9. Galante, S. P. "Your Loan Officer Next Time May Be an 'Expert' on a Disk." *Wall Street Journal* (December 8, 1986): 23.
10. Gerwin, D. "Do's and Don'ts of Computerized Manufacturing." *Harvard Business Review* (March–April 1982): 107–116.
11. Groover, M. P. *Automation, Production Systems, and Computer Integrated Manufacturing.* Englewood Cliffs, N.J.: Prentice-Hall, 1987.
12. Haas, E. "Breakthrough Manufacturing." *Harvard Business Review* (March–April 1987): 75–81.
13. Hayes, R. H., and S. C. Wheelwright. "Link Manufacturing Process and Product Life Cycles." *Harvard Business Review* (January–February 1979): 133–140.
14. Hyer, N. L., and U. Wemmerlov. "Group Technology and Productivity." *Harvard Business Review* (July–August 1984): 140–149.
15. Kilpatrick, D. "Riding the Real Trends in Technology." *Fortune* (February 19, 1996): 57.
16. Kirkpatrick, D. "The Internet Saga Continues . . . IBM and Lotus: Not So Dumb After All." *Fortune* (July 8, 1996): 63–70.
17. Miller, J. G., and T. E. Vollmann. "The Hidden Factory." *Harvard Business Review* (September–October 1985): 142–150.
18. Poppel, H. L. "Who Needs the Office of the Future?" *Harvard Business Review* (November–December 1982): 146–155.

19. Schmenner, R. W. "Every Factory Has a Cycle." *Harvard Business Review* (March–April 1983): 121–129.

20. Shafer, S. M., J. R. Meredith, and R. F. Marsh. "A Taxonomy for Alternative Equipment Groupings in Batch Environments." *Omega* 23, No. 4 (1995): 361–376.

21. Shostack, G. L. "Designing Services That Deliver." *Harvard Business Review* (January–February 1984): 133–139.

22. Skinner, W. "Operations Technology: Blind Spot in Strategic Management." *Interfaces* 14, No. 1 (January–February 1984): 116–125.

23. Stone, S. D. "Cellular Manufacturing for Small Manufacturers." *APICS: The Performance Advantage* (May 1996): 34–38.

24. Verity, J. W. "A Company That's 100% Virtual." *Business Week* (November 21, 1994): 85.

CHAPTER 7

1. Collett, S., and R. J. Spicer. "Improving Productivity Through Cellular Manufacturing." *Production and Inventory Management Journal* (First Quarter 1995): 71–75.

2. Ferras, L. "Continuous Improvements in Electronics Manufacturing." *Production and Inventory Management Journal* (Second Quarter 1994): 1–5.

3. Francis, R. L., and J. A. White. *Facility Layout and Location: An Analytical Approach*. Englewood Cliffs, N.J.: Prentice-Hall, 1987.

4. Green, T. J., and R. P. Sadowski. "A Review of Cellular Manufacturing Assumptions, Advantages, and Design Techniques." *Journal of Operations Management* 4, No. 2 (February 1984): 85–97.

5. Gunther, R. E., G. D. Johnson, and R. S. Peterson. "Currently Practiced Formulations of the Assembly Line Balance Problem." *Journal of Operations Management* 3, No. 3 (August 1983): 209–221.

6. Ham, I., K. Hitomi, and T. Yoshida. *Group Technology: Application to Production Management*. Boston: Kluwer-Nijhoff, 1985.

7. Jacobs, F. R., J. W. Bradford, and L. P. Ritzman. "Computerized Layout: An Integrated Approach to Spatial Planning and Communication Requirements." *Industrial Engineering* (July 1980): 56–61.

8. Johnson, R. "SPACECRAFT for Multi-Floor Layout Planning." *Management Science* 28, No. 4 (April 1982): 407–417.

9. King, J. R. "Machine-Component Grouping in Production Flow Analysis: An Approach Using a Rank Order Clustering Algorithm." *International Journal of Production Research* 18, No. 2 (1980): 213–232.

10. Kinney, H. D., Jr., and L. F. McGinnis. "Design and Control of Manufacturing Cells." *Industrial Engineering* (October 1987): 28–38.

11. Konz, S. *Facility Design*. New York: Wiley, 1985.

12. Levasseur, G. A., M. M. Helms, and A. A. Zink. "A Conversion to a Cellular Manufacturing Layout at Steward, Inc." *Production and Inventory Management Journal,* (Third Quarter 1995): 37–42.

13. Lewis, W. P., and T. E. Block. "On the Application of Computer Aids to Plant Layout." *International Journal of Production Research* 18, No. 1 (1980): 11–20.

14. Manivannan, S., and D. Chudhuri. "Computer-Aided Facility Layout Algorithm Generates Alternatives to Increase Firm's Productivity." *Industrial Engineering* (May 1984): 81–84.

15. "Micro-Craft." (Plant layout Software.) Atlanta, Ga.: Industrial Engineering and Management Press, IIE, 1986.

16. Moore, J. M. "The Zone of Compromise for Evaluating Layout Arrangements." *International Journal of Production Research* 18, No. 1 (1980): 1–10.

17. Schonberger, R. J. *World Class Manufacturing: The Lessons of Simplicity Applied.* New York: Free Press, 1986.

18. Schuler, R. S., L. P. Ritzman, and V. L. Davis. "Merging Prescriptive and Behavioral Approaches for Office Layout." *Journal of Operations Management* 1, No. 3 (February 1981): 131–142.

19. Shafer, S. M., J. R. Meredith, and R. F. Marsh. "A Taxonomy for Alternative Equipment Groupings in Batch Environments." *Omega, International Journal of Management Science,* 23, No. 4 (1995): 361–376.

20. Stone, P. J., and R. Luchetti. "Your Office Is Where You Are." *Harvard Business Review* (March–April 1985): 102–117.

21. Stoner, D. L., K. J. Tice, and J. E. Ashton. "Simple and Effective Cellular Approach to a Job Machine Shop." *Manufacturing Review* 2, No. 2 (June 1989): 119–128.

22. Taheri, J. "Northern Telecom Tackles Successful Implementatation of Cellular Manufacturing." *Industrial Engineering* (October 1990): 38–43.

23. Tompkins, J. A., and J. A. White. *Facilities Planning.* New York: Wiley, 1984.

CHAPTER 8

1. Armstrong, J. S. "Forecasting by Extrapolation: Conclusions from 25 Years of Research." *Interfaces* (November–December 1984): 52–66.

2. Dalrymple, D. J. "Sales Forecasting Methods and Accuracy." *Business Horizons* (December 1984): 69–73.

3. Fisher, M. L., J. H. Hammond, W. R. Obermeyer, and A. Raman. "Making Supply Meet Demand in an Uncertain World." *Harvard Business Review* 72 (May–June 1994): 83–93.

4. Gardner, E. S. "Exponential Smoothing: The State of the Art." *Journal of Forecasting* 4 (March 1985): 1–28.

5. Georgoff, D. M., and R. G. Murdick. "Manager's Guide to Forecasting." *Harvard Business Review* 64 (January–February 1986): 110–120.

6. Hogarth, R. M., and S. G. Makridakis. "Forecasting and Planning: An Evaluation." *Management Science* 27 (February 1981): 115–138.

7. Lawrence, M. J., R. H. Edmundson, and M. J. O'Connor. "The Accuracy of Combining Judgmental and Statistical Forecasts." *Management Science* 32 (December 1986): 1521–1532.

8. Mahmoud, E. "Accuracy in Forecasting: A Survey." *Journal of Forecasting* 3 (1984): 139–159.

9. Makridakis, S. G. "The Art and Science of Forecasting." *International Journal of Forecasting* 2 (1986): 5–39.

10. Makridakis, S. G., S. C. Wheelwright, and V. E. McGee. *Forecasting: Methods and Applications,* 2nd ed. New York: Wiley, 1983.

11. Mentzer, J., and J. Cox. "Familiarity, Application and Performance of Sales Forecasting Techniques." *Journal of Forecasting* 3 (1984): 27–36.

12. Microsoft Excel Users' Guide. Microsoft Corporation: 1993–1994.

13. Sager, I., and A. Cortese. "IBM: Why Good News Isn't Good Enough." *Business Week* (January 23, 1995): 72–73.

14. Schlender, B. R. "Its Failure to Deliver on Promised Software Hits Microsoft Hard." *Wall Street Journal* (March 8, 1989): A1, A6.
15. Wheelwright, S. C., and S. G. Makridakis. *Forecasting Methods for Management,* 4th ed. New York: Wiley, 1985.
16. Willis, R. E. *A Guide to Forecasting for Planners and Managers.* Englewood Cliffs, N.J.: Prentice-Hall, 1987.

CHAPTER 9

1. APICS. *Certification Study Guide: Capacity Management.* Washington, D.C.: American Production and Inventory Control Society, 1980.
2. Berry, W. L., T. G. Schmitt, and T. E. Vollman. "Capacity Planning Techniques for Manufacturing Control Systems: Information Requirements and Operational Features." *Journal of Operations Management* 3, No. 1 (November 1982): 13–25.
3. Fillley, R. D. "Putting the 'Fast' in Fast Foods: Burger King." *Industrial Engineering* (January 1983): 44–47.
4. Freidenfelds, J. *Capacity Expansion: Analysis of Simple Models with Applications.* New York: Elsevier North-Holland, 1981.
5. Gold, B. "Changing Perspectives on Size, Scale, and Returns: An Interpretive Survey." *Journal of Economic Literature* 19 (March 1981).
6. Harl, J. E. "Reducing Capacity Problems in Material Requirements Planning Systems." *Production and Inventory Management* (Third Quarter 1983): 52–60.
7. Karni, R. "Capacity Requirement Planning—A Systematization." *International Journal of Production Research* 20, No. 6 (1982): 715–739.
8. Leone, R. A., and J. R. Meyer. "Capacity Strategies for the 1980s." *Harvard Business Review* 58, No. 6 (November–December 1980): 133–140.
9. Lowe, P. H., and J. E. Eguren. "The Determination of Capacity Expansion Programmes with Economies of Scale." *International Journal of Production Research* 18, No. 3 (1980): 379–390.
10. Microsoft Excel Users' Guide. Microsoft Corporation: 1993–1994.
11. Port, O. "Huh? Chipmakers Copying Steelmakers?" *Business Week* (August 15, 1994): 97–98.
12. Tanzer, A. "The Right Kind of Problem." *Forbes* (March 20, 1989): 134, 138.
13. Templin, N. "GM Hopes to Awaken Profits by Operating Plants 24 Hours a Day." *Wall Street Journal* (October 6, 1993): A1, A12.
14. Shafer, S. M. *Operations Management Primer.* Burr Ridge, Ill.: Irwin, 1994.
15. Stevenson, W. J. *Production/Operations Management,* 4th ed. Homewood, Ill.: Irwin, 1993.
16. Tompkins, J. A., and J. A. White. *Facilities Planning.* New York: Wiley, 1984.
17. Vollmann, T. E., W. L. Berry, and D. C. Whybark. *Manufacturing Planning and Control Systems,* 2nd ed. Homewood, Ill.: Irwin, 1988.
18. Wemmerlov, U. Capacity Management Techniques. American Production and Inventory Control Society, 1984.
19. Whyte, W. *Human Relations in the Restaurant Business.* New York: McGraw-Hill, 1948.

SUPPLEMENT TO CHAPTER 9

1. Bazarra, M. S., and J. J. Jarvis. *Linear Programming and Network Flows,* 2nd ed. New York: Wiley, 1990.

2. Best, M. J., and K. Ritter. *Linear Programming: Action Set Analysis and Computer Programs.* Englewood Cliffs, N.J.: Prentice-Hall, 1985.

3. Calvert, J. E., et al. *Linear Programming.* New York: Harcourt Brace Jovanovich, 1989.

4. Friendly, J. "Shazam! A Shortcut for Computers." *New York Times* (November 11, 1979): E7.

5. Hayhurst, G. *Mathematical Programming Applications.* New York: Macmillan, 1987.

6. Hooker, J. N. "Karmarker's Linear Programming Algorithm." *Interfaces* 16, No. 4 (July–August 1986): 75–90, and 17, No. 1 (January–February 1987): 128.

7. Karmarker, N. "A New Polynomial-Time Algorithm for Linear Programming." *Combinatorica* 4, No. 4 (1984): 373–395.

8. Kolata, G. "A Fast Way to Solve Hard Problems." *Science* (September 21, 1984): 1379–1380.

9. Ignizio, J. P. *Linear Programming in Single and Multiple Objective Systems.* Englewood Cliffs, N.J.: Prentice-Hall, 1982.

10. Kolman, B., and R. E. Beck. *Elementary Linear Programming with Applications.* New York: Academic, 1980.

11. Lev, B., and H. J. Weiss. *Introduction to Mathematical Programming.* New York: Elsevier North-Holland, 1982.

12. Luenberger, D. G. *Linear and Nonlinear Programming,* 2nd ed. Reading, Mass.: Addison-Wesley, 1985.

13. Murty, K. *Linear Programming,* 2nd ed. New York: Wiley, 1983.

14. Schrage, L. *Linear, Integer, and Quadratic Programming with LINDO,* 3rd ed. Palo Alto, Calif.: Scientific, 1986.

15. "The Startling Discovery Bell Labs Kept in the Shadows." *Business Week* (September 21, 1987): 69, 72, 76.

16. Strayer, J. K. *Linear Programming and Its Applications.* New York: Springer-Verlag, 1989.

17. Turban, E., and J. R. Meredith. *Fundamentals of Management Science,* 5th ed. Homewood, Ill.: Irwin, 1991.

CHAPTER 10

1. Ballou, R. H. *Business Logistics Management: Planning and Control,* 2nd ed. Englewood Cliffs, N.J.: Prentice-Hall, 1985.

2. Fitzsimmons, J. A., and L. A. Allen, "A Warehouse Location Model Helps Texas Comptroller Select Out-of-State Audit Offices." *Interfaces* (October 1983): 40–46.

3. Francis, R. L., and J. A. White. *Facilities Layout and Location: An Analytical Approach.* Englewood Cliffs, N.J.: Prentice-Hall, 1987.

4. Geoffrion, A. M., and R. F. Powers. "Facility Location Analysis Is Just the Beginning." *Interfaces* 10, No. 2 (April 1980): 22–30.

5. Harding, C. F. "Your Business: Right Ingredients, Wrong Location." *INC.* (February 1980): 20–22.

6. Johnson, J. C., and D. F. Wood. *Contemporary Physical Distribution and Logistics,* 3rd ed. New York: Macmillan, 1986.

7. Kraus, R. L. "A Strategic Planning Approach to Facility Site Selection." *Dun's Review* (November 1980): 14–16.

8. Price, W. L., and M. Turcotte. "Locating a Blood Bank." *Interfaces* (September–October 1986): 17–26.
9. Schilling, D. A. "Dynamic Location Modeling for Public-Sector Facilities: A Multi-Criteria Approach." *Decision Sciences* 11, No. 4 (October 1980): 714–724.
10. Schmenner, R. W. "Look Beyond the Obvious in Plant Location." *Harvard Business Review* (January–February 1979): 126–132.
11. Schmenner, R. W. *Making Business Location Decisions.* Englewood Cliffs, N.J.: Prentice-Hall, 1982.
12. Shapiro, R. D., and J. L. Heskett. *Logistics Strategy: Cases and Concepts.* St. Paul, Minn.: West, 1985.
13. Sharman, G. "The Rediscovery of Logistics." *Harvard Business Review* (September–October 1984): 71–79.
14. Tetzeli, R. "Mapping for Dollars." *Fortune* (October 18, 1993): 91–96.
15. Treece, J. M. "Here Comes GM's Saturn." *Business Week* (April 9, 1990): 56–62, 102–110.
16. Tong, H. M., and C. K. Walter. "An Empirical Study of Plant Location Decisions of Foreign Manufacturing Investors in the United States." *Columbia Journal of World Business* (Spring 1980): 66–73.
17. Woodruff, D., and J. Templeman. "Why Mercedes Is Alabama Bound." *Business Week* (October 11, 1993): 138–139.

CHAPTER 11

1. Bedworth, D., and J. Bailey. *Integrated Production Control Systems,* 2nd ed. New York: Wiley, 1987.
2. Chung, C. H., and L. Krajewski. "Planning Horizons for Master Production Scheduling." *Journal of Operations Management* 4, No. 4 (August 1984): 389–405.
3. Connell, B. C., E. E. Adam, Jr., and A. N. Moore. "Aggregate Planning in a Health Care Foodservice System with Varying Technologies." *Journal of Operations Management* 5, No. 1 (1984): 41–55.
4. Fogarty, D. W., and T. R. Hoffman. *Production and Inventory Management.* Cincinnati, Ohio: South-Western, 1983.
5. Freeland, J., and R. Landel. *Aggregate Production Planning: Text and Cases.* Reston, Va.: Reston, 1984.
6. Gallagher, G. R. "How to Develop a Realistic Master Schedule." *Management Review* (April 1980): 19–25.
7. Greene, J. H., ed. *Production and Inventory Control Handbook,* 2nd ed. New York: McGraw-Hill, 1987.
8. Kilman, S. "Delays at Atlanta's Hartsfield Airport Should Lessen Under Revised Schedules." *Wall Street Journal* (September 14, 1984): 6.
9. Krajewski, L. J., and, L. P. Ritzman. "Shift Scheduling in Banking Operations: A Case Application." *Interfaces* (April 1980): 1–7.
10. Liberatore, M. J., and T. Miller, "A Hierarchical Production Planning System." *Interfaces* (July–August 1985): 1–11.
11. Mangiameli, P., and L. Krajewski. "The Effects of Workforce Strategies on Manufacturing Operations." *Journal of Operations Management* 3, No. 4 (August 1983): 183–196.
12. McLeavey, D. W., and S. L. Narasimhan. *Production Planning and Inventory Control.* Boston: Allyn and Bacon, 1985.

13. Meal, C. H. "Putting Production Decisions Where They Belong." *Harvard Business Review* (March–April 1984): 102–111.

14. Miller, J. G. "Fit Production Systems to the Task." *Harvard Business Review* (January–February 1981): 145–154.

15. Plossl, G. W. *Production and Inventory Control: Principles and Techniques,* 2nd ed. Englewood Cliffs, N.J.: Prentice-Hall, 1985.

16. Proud, J. F. "Controlling the Master Schedule." *Production and Inventory Management* 22, No. 2 (Second Quarter 1981), pp. 78–90.

17. Schramm, W. R., and Freund, L. E. "Application of Economic Control Charts by a Nursing Modeling Team." *Industrial Engineering* (April 1993): 27–31.

18. Schroeder, R. G., and P. Larson. "A Reformulation of the Aggregate Planning Problem." *Journal of Operations Management* 6, No. 3 (May 1986): 245–256.

19. Shafer, S. M. "A Spreadsheet Approach to Aggregate Scheduling." *Production and Inventory Management Journal* 32, No. 4 (Fourth Quarter 1991), 4–10.

20. Silver, E. A., and R. Peterson. *Decision Systems for Inventory Management and Production Planning,* 2nd ed. New York: Wiley, 1985.

21. Van Dierdonck, R., and J. G. Miller. "Designing Production Planning and Control Systems." *Journal of Operations Management* 1, No. 1 (August 1980): 37–46.

22. Vollmann, T. E., W. L. Berry, and D. C. Whybark. *Manufacturing Planning and Control Systems,* 2nd ed. Homewood, Ill.: Irwin, 1988.

23. Wall Street Journal. "American Airlines Fixer of Broken Schedules" (June 28, 1988): 4.

24. Walter, J. D., Jr. "The Business Economist at Work: Dow Corning Corporation." *Business Economics* (July 1986): 46–48.

25. Wight, O. W. *MRP II: Unlocking America's Productivity Potential.* Boston: CBI, 1984.

SUPPLEMENT TO CHAPTER 11

1. Bazarra, M. S., and J. J. Jarvis. *Linear Programming and Network Flows,* 2nd ed. New York: Wiley, 1990.

2. Best, M. J., and K. Ritter. *Linear Programming: Action Set Analysis and Computer Programs.* Englewood Cliffs, N.J.: Prentice-Hall, 1985.

3. Calvert, J. E., et al. *Linear Programming.* New York: Harcourt Brace Jovanovich, 1989.

4. Hayhurst, G. *Mathematical Programming Applications.* New York: Macmillan, 1987.

5. Ignizio, J. P. *Linear Programming in Single and Multiple Objective Systems.* Englewood Cliffs, N.J.: Prentice-Hall, 1982.

6. Kolman, B., and R. E. Beck. *Elementary Linear Programming with Applications.* New York: Academic, 1980.

7. Murty, K. *Linear Programming,* 2nd ed. New York: Wiley, 1983.

8. Schrage, L. *Linear, Integer, and Quadratic Programming with LINDO,* 3rd ed. Palo Alto, Calif.: Scientific, 1986.

9. Strayer, J. K. *Linear Programming and Its Applications.* New York: Springer-Verlag, 1989.

10. Taha, H. A. *Operations Research: An Introduction,* 4th ed. New York: Prentice-Hall, 1987.

11. Turban, E., and J. R. Meredith. *Fundamentals of Management Science,* 5th ed. Homewood, Ill.: Irwin, 1991.

CHAPTER 12

1. Adkins, A. C., Jr. "EOQ in the Real World." *Production and Inventory Management* 25, No. 4 (Fourth Quarter 1984): 50–54.
2. *APICS Dictionary,* 8th ed. Falls Church, Va.: American Production and Inventory Control Society, 1995.
3. Bird, L. "High-Tech Inventory System Coordinates Retailer's Clothes with Customers' Taste." *Wall Street Journal* (June 12, 1996): B1, B5.
4. Cantwell, J. "The How and Why of Cycle Counting: The ABC Method." *Production and Inventory Control* 26, No. 2 (Second Quarter 1985): 50–54.
5. Edwards, J. R., H. M. Wagner, and W. P. Wood. "Blue Bell Trims Its Inventory." *Interfaces* (January–February 1985): 34–52.
6. Finke, G. F. "Determining Target Inventories of Wood Chips Using Risk Analysis." *Interfaces* (September–October 1984): 53–58.
7. Flores, B. E., and D. C. Whybark. "Implementing Multiple Criteria ABC Analysis." *Journal of Operations Management* 7, No. 1–2 (October 1987): 79–85.
8. Flowers, A. D., and J. B. O'Neill II. "An Application of Classical Inventory Analysis to a Spare Parts Inventory." *Interfaces* (February 1978): 76–79.
9. Fogarty, D. W., and T. R. Hoffman. *Production and Inventory Management.* Cincinnati, Ohio: South-Western, 1983.
10. Gardner, E. S. "Inventory Theory and the Gods of Olympus." *Interfaces* 10, No. 4 (1980): 42–45.
11. Gardner, E. S. "A Top-Down Approach to Modelling U.S. Navy Inventories." *Interfaces* (July–August 1987): 1–7.
12. Greene, J. H., ed. *Production and Inventory Control Handbook,* 2nd ed. New York: McGraw-Hill, 1987.
13. Hall, R. W. *Zero Inventories.* Homewood, Ill.: Dow Jones–Irwin, 1983.
14. Janson, R. L. *Handbook of Inventory Management.* Englewood Cliffs, N.J.: Prentice-Hall, 1989.
15. Hogg, R. V., and A. T. Craig. *Introduction to Mathematical Statistics,* 4th ed. New York: Macmillan, 1978.
16. Kleuthgen, P. P., and J. C. McGee. "Development and Implementation of an Integrated Inventory Management Program at Pfizer Pharmaceuticals." *Interfaces* 15, No. 1 (January–February 1985): 69–87.
17. McLeavey, D. W., and S. L. Narasimhan. *Production Planning and Inventory Control.* Boston: Allyn and Bacon, 1985.
18. Nakane, J., and R. W. Hall. "Management Specs for Stockless Production." *Harvard Business Review* (May–June 1983): 84–91.
19. Nelson, N. S. "MRP and Inventory and Production Control in Process Industries." *Production and Inventory Control* 22, No. 4 (Fourth Quarter 1981): 15–22.
20. Plossl, G. W. *Production and Inventory Control: Principles and Techniques,* 2nd ed. Englewood Cliffs, N.J.: Prentice-Hall, 1985.
21. Reid, R. A. "The ABC Method in Hospital Inventory Management: A Practical Approach." *Production and Inventory Management Journal* (Fourth Quarter 1987): 67–70.

22. Reinfeld, N. V. *Handbook of Production and Inventory Control.* Englewood Cliffs, N.J.: Prentice-Hall, 1987.

23. Schonberger, R. J. "Selecting the Right Manufacturing Inventory System: Western and Japanese Approaches." *Production and Inventory Control* 24, No. 2 (Second Quarter 1983): 33–44.

24. Silver, E. A., and R. Peterson. *Decision Systems for Inventory Management and Production Planning,* 2nd ed. New York: Wiley, 1985.

25. Smith, S. B. *Computer Based Production and Inventory Control.* Englewood Cliffs, N.J.: Prentice-Hall, 1989.

26. Tersine, R. J. *Principles of Inventory and Materials Management,* 3rd ed. New York: North-Holland, 1987.

27. Verity, J. W. "Invoice? What's an Invoice?" *Business Week* (June 10, 1996): 110–112.

28. Stevenson, W. J. *Production/Operations Management,* 5th ed. Homewood, Ill.: Irwin, 1996.

SUPPLEMENT TO CHAPTER 12

1. Aburdene, M. F. *Computer Simulation of Dynamic Systems.* Dubuque, Iowa: Brown, 1988.

2. Banks, J., and J. S. Carson. *Discrete Event System Simulation.* Englewood Cliffs, N.J.: Prentice-Hall, 1984.

3. Bulgren, W. *Discrete System Simulation.* Englewood Cliffs, N.J.: Prentice-Hall, 1982.

4. Camm, J. D., and J. R. Evan. *Management Science: Modeling, Analysis, and Interpretation.* Cincinnati, Ohio: South-Western, 1996.

5. Graybeal, W., and U. W. Pooch. *Simulation: Principles and Methods.* Cambridge, Mass.: Winthrop, 1980.

6. Haider, S. W., and J. Banks. "Simulation Software Products for Analyzing Manufacturing Systems." *Industrial Engineering* 18, No. 7 (July 1986): 98–103.

7. Hoover, S. V., and R. F. Perry. *Simulation: A Problem Approach.* Reading, Mass.: Addison-Wesley, 1989.

8. Horn, R. E., and A. Clearas. *The Guide to Simulation and Games,* 4th ed. Beverly Hills, Calif.: Sage, 1980.

9. Law, A. M. "Computer Simulation of Manufacturing Systems: Part I." *Industrial Engineering* 18, No. 5 (May 1986): 46–63.

10. Law, A. M., and W. D. Kelton. *Simulation Modeling and Analysis.* New York: McGraw-Hill, 1982.

11. Neelamkavil, F. *Computer Simulation and Modeling.* New York: Wiley, 1987.

12. Payne, J. A. *An Introduction to Simulation.* New York: McGraw-Hill, 1982.

13. Pidd, M. *Computer Simulation in Management Science.* New York: Wiley, 1984.

14. Shafer, S. M., and J. R. Meredith, *Spreadsheet Templates and Applications in Operations Management.* New York: Wiley, 1987.

15. Solomon, S. L. *Simulation of Waiting Lines.* Englewood Cliffs, N.J.: Prentice-Hall, 1983.

16. Watson, H. J., and J. H. Blackstone, Jr. *Computer Simulation,* 2nd ed. New York: Wiley, 1989.

CHAPTER 13

1. Anderson, J. C., R. G. Schroeder, S. E. Tupy, and E. M. White. "Material Requirements Planning: The State of the Art." *Production and Inventory Management* 23, No. 4 (Fourth Quarter 1982): 51–67.

2. Bitran, G. R., D. M. Marini, H. Matsuo, and J. W. Noonan. "Multiplant MRP." *Journal of Operations Management* 5, No. 2 (February 1985): 183–204.

3. Blumberg, D. F. "Factors Affecting the Design of a Successful MRP System." *Production and Inventory Management* 21, No. 4 (Fourth Quarter 1980): 50–62.

4. Burlingame, J. W., and J. K. Weeks. "Behavioral Dimensions of MRP Change: Assessing Your Organization's Strengths and Weaknesses." *Production and Inventory Management* 22, No. 1 (First Quarter 1981): 81–95.

5. Bylinsky, G. "The Digital Factory." *Fortune* (November 14, 1994): 92–110.

6. Etienne, E. C. "MRP May Not Be Right for You: At Least Not Yet." *Production and Inventory Management* 24, No. 3 (Third Quarter 1983): 33–46.

7. Goddard, W. E. "Getting a Grip on Customer Service." *Modern Materials Handling* (September 1992): 41.

8. Gray, C. *The Right Choice: A Complete Guide to Evaluating, Selecting and Installing MRP II Software*. Essex Junction, Vt.: Wight, 1987.

9. Horovitz, B. "Why Corning Is Sticking with MRP." *Industry Week* (January 25, 1982): 44–48.

10. Jarkon, J. G., and R. Nanda. "Resource Requirements Planning Achieves Production Goals for Non-Profit Organization." *Industrial Engineering* (October 1985): 54–62.

11. Khumawala, B. M., C. Hixon, and J. S. Law. "MRP II in the Service Industries." *Production and Inventory Management* 27, No. 3 (Third Quarter 1986): 57–63.

12. Krupp, J. A. G. "Why MRP Systems Fail: Traps to Avoid." *Production and Inventory Management* 25, No. 3 (Third Quarter 1984): 49–53.

13. Lieber, R. B. "Here Comes SAP." *Fortune* (October 2, 1995): 122–124.

14. Martin, A. J. *Distribution Resource Planning*. Englewood Cliffs, N.J.: Prentice-Hall, 1983.

15. Melnyk, S. A., and R. F. Gonzalez. "MRP II: The Early Returns Are In." *Production and Inventory Management* 26, No. 1 (First Quarter 1985): 124–137.

16. Nelson, N. S. "MRP and Inventory and Production Control in Process Industries." *Production and Inventory Control* 22, No. 4 (Fourth Quarter 1981): 15–22.

17. Plossl, G. W. *Production and Inventory Control: Applications*. Atlanta, Ga.: George Plossl Educational Services, 1983.

18. Plossl, G. W. *Production and Inventory Control; Principles and Techniques,* 2nd ed. Englewood Cliffs, N.J.: Prentice-Hall, 1985.

19. Schroeder, R. G., J. C. Anderson, S. E. Tupy, and E. M. White. "A Study of MRP Benefits and Costs." *Journal of Operations Management* 2, No. 1 (October 1981): 1–9.

20. Smolik, D. P. *Material Requirements of Manufacturing*. New York: Van Nostrand Reinhold, 1983.

21. Steinberg, E. E., B. Khumawala, and R. Scamell. "Requirements Planning Systems in the Health Care Environment." *Journal of Operations Management* 2, No. 4 (August 1982): 251–259.

22. Steinberg, E. E., W. B. Lee, and B. Khumawala. "A Requirements Planning System for the Space Shuttle Operations Schedule." *Journal of Operations Management* 1, No. 2 (November 1980): 69–76.

23. Tersine, R. J. *Principles of Inventory and Materials Management,* 3rd ed. New York: North-Holland, 1987.

24. Thompson, K. "MRP II in the Repetitive Manufacturing Environment." *Production and Inventory Management* 24, No. 4 (Fourth Quarter 1983): 1–14.

25. Vollmann, T. E., W. L. Berry, and D. C. Whybark. *Manufacturing Planning and Control Systems,* 2nd ed. Homewood, Ill.: Irwin, 1988.

26. White, E. M., J. C. Anderson, R. G. Schroeder, and S. E. Tupy. "A Study of the MRP Implementation Process." *Journal of Operations Management* 2, No. 3 (May 1982): 145–153.

27. White, J. B., D. Clark, and S. Ascarelli. "This German Software Is Complex, Expensive, and Wildly Popular." *Wall Street Journal* (March 17, 1997): A1, A12.

28. Wight, O. W. *The Executive's Guide to Successful MRP II.* Williston, Vt.: Wight, 1982.

29. Wight, O. W. *MRP II: Unlocking America's Productivity Potential.* Boston: CBI, 1984.

CHAPTER 14

1. Aggarwal, S. C. "MRP, JIT, OPT, FMS?" *Harvard Business Review* (September–October 1985).

2. Ansari, A. "Survey Identifies Critical Factors in Successful Implementation of Just-in-Time Purchasing Techniques." *Industrial Engineering* 18, No. 10 (1986): 44–50.

3. Auguston, K. "How We Produce Printers on a JIT Basis." *Modern Materials Handling* (January 1995a): 47–49.

4. Auguston, K. "Feeding the JIT Pipeline from Across the Border." *Modern Materials Handling* (May 1995b): 34–38.

5. Barrett, J. "IEs at Calcomp Are Integrating JIT, TOC, and Employee Involvement for World Class Manufacturing." *Industrial Engineering* (September 1988): 26–32.

6. Boyer, M. "Harley's Chairman Hogs the Limelight." *Cincinnati Enquirer* (November 8, 1989).

7. Burnham, J. M. "Some Conclusions About JIT Manufacturing." *Production and Inventory Management* 28, No. 3 (1987): 7–11.

8. Burrows, P. "The Computer Is in the Mail (Really)." *Business Week* (January 23, 1995): 76–77.

9. Conway, J. A. "Harley Back in Gear." *Forbes* (April 20, 1987): 8.

10. Conant, R. G. "JIT in a Mail Order Operation Reduces Processing Time from Four Days to Four Hours." *Industrial Engineering* (September 1988): 34–37.

11. Crosby, L. B. "The Just-in-Time Manufacturing Process: Control of Quality and Quantity." *Production and Inventory Management* 25, No. 4 (1984): 21–33.

12. Esparrago, R. A., Jr. "Kanban." *Production and Inventory Management* 29, No. 1 (1988): 6–10.

13. Gould, L. "Staging Fills in Honda JIT Orders in 2 Hours." *Modern Materials Handling* (July 1994): 44–45.

14. Hannah, K. H. "Just-in-Time: Meeting the Competitive Challenge." *Production and Inventory Management* 28, No. 3 (1987): 1–3.

15. Hay, H. J. *The Just-in-Time Breakthrough: Implementing the New Manufacturing Basics*. New York: Wiley, 1989.
16. Hutchins, D. "Having a Hard Time with Just-in-Time." *Fortune* (June 9, 1986): 64–66.
17. Lubben, R. *Just-in-Time Manufacturing*. New York: McGraw-Hill, 1988.
18. Monden, Y. *Toyota Production System: Practical Approach to Production Management*. Atlanta, Ga.: Industrial Engineering and Management Press, 1983.
19. Nakane, J., and R. W. Hall. "Management Specs for Stockless Production." *Harvard Business Review* (May–June 1983): 84–91.
20. Plenert, G., and T. D. Best. "MRP, JIT, and OPT: What's Best?" *Production and Inventory Management* 27, No. 2 (1986): 22–29.
21. Schonberger, R. J. "Applications of Single-Card and Dual-Card Kanban." *Interfaces* 13, No. 4 (August 1983): 56–67.
22. Schonberger, R. J. "Some Observations on the Advantages and Implementation Issues of Just-in-Time Production Systems." *Journal of Operations Management* 2, No. 1 (November 1982): 1–12.
23. Schonberger, R. J. *World Class Manufacturing: The Lessons of Simplicity Applied*. New York: Free Press, 1986.
24. Seglund, R., and S. Ibarreche. "Just-in-Time: The Accounting Implications." *Management Accounting* (August 1984): 43–45.
25. Sepehri, M. "How Kanban System Is Used in an American Toyota Motor Facility." *Industrial Engineering* (February 1985): 50–56.
26. Sepehri, M. "Case in Point: Buick City Genuine JIT Delivery." *P&IM Review with APICs News* (March 1988): 34–36.
27. Suzaki, K. "Japanese Manufacturing Techniques: Their Importance to U.S. Manufacturers." *Journal of Business Strategy* 5, No. 3 (1985): 10–20.
28. Suzaki, K. *The New Manufacturing Challenge*. New York: Free Press, 1986.
29. Walleigh, R. C. "Getting Things Done: What's Your Excuse for Not Using JIT?" *Harvard Business Review* (March–April 1986): 39–54.
30. Waters, C. R. "Why Everybody's Talking About Just-in-Time." *INC.* (March 1984).
31. Weiss, A. "Simple Truths of Japanese Manufacturing." *Harvard Business Review* (July–August 1984): 119–125.

SUPPLEMENT TO CHAPTER 14

1. Ammer, D. S. *Materials Management and Purchasing*, 4th ed. Homewood, Ill.: Irwin, 1980.
2. Ansari, A., and B. Modarress. "The Potential Benefits of Just-in-Time Purchasing for U.S. Manufacturing." *Production and Inventory Management* 28, No. 2 (Second Quarter 1987): 30–35.
3. Batdorf, L., and J. A. Vora. "Use of Analytical Techniques in Purchasing." *Journal of Purchasing and Materials Management* (Spring 1983): 25–29.
4. Bowersox, D. J., D. J. Closs, and O. K. Helferich. *Logistical Management: A Systems Integration of Physical Distribution, Manufacturing Support, and Materials Procurement*, 3rd ed. New York: Macmillan, 1986.
5. Burt, D. *Proactive Purchasing*. Englewood Cliffs, N.J.: Prentice-Hall, 1984.
6. Cavinato, J. L. *Purchasing and Materials Management*. St. Paul, Minn.: West, 1984.
7. Colton, R. R., and W. F. Rohrs. *Industrial Purchasing and Effective Materials Management*. Reston, Va.: Reston, 1985.

8. Dobler, D. W., L. Lee, Jr., and D. N. Burt. *Purchasing and Materials Management: Text and Cases.* New York: McGraw-Hill, 1984.

9. Hahn, C. K., K. H. Kim, and J. S. Kim. "Costs of Competition: Implications for Purchasing Strategy." *Journal of Purchasing and Materials Management* (Fall 1986): 2–7.

10. Heinritz, S. F., P. V. Farrell, and C. L. Smith. *Purchasing: Principles and Applications,* 7th ed. Englewood Cliffs, N.J.: Prentice-Hall, 1986.

11. Leenders, M. R., H. E. Gearon, and W. B. England. *Purchasing and Materials Management,* 8th ed. Homewood, Ill.: Irwin, 1985.

12. Messner, W. A. *Profitable Purchasing Management.* New York: AMACOM, 1982.

13. Narasimhan, R. "An Analytical Approach to Supplier Selection." *Journal of Purchasing and Materials Management* (Winter 1983): 27–32.

14. Schonberger, R., and J. Gilbert. "Just-in-Time Purchasing: A Challenge for U.S. Industry." *California Management Review* 26, No. 1 (Fall 1983): 54–68.

15. Tully, S. "Purchasing's New Muscle." *Fortune* (February 20, 1995): 75–83.

CHAPTER 15

1. Alstrup, J., S.-E. Andersson, S. Boas, O. B. G. Madsen, and R. V. V. Vidal. "Booking Control Increases Profit at Scandinavian Airlines." *Interfaces* (July–August 1989): 10–19.

2. Bechtold, S. E. "Work-Force Scheduling for Arbitrary Cyclic Demands." *Journal of Operations Management* 1, No. 4 (May 1981): 205–214.

3. Bedworth, D., and J. Bailey. *Integrated Production Control Systems,* 2nd ed. New York: Wiley, 1987.

4. Blackstone, J. H., D. T. Phillips, and G. L. Hogg. "A State-of-the-Art Survey of Dispatching Rules for Manufacturing Job Shop Operations." *International Journal of Production Research* 20 (1982): 27–45.

5. Box, R. E., and D. G. Herbe, Jr. "A Scheduling Model for LTV Stell's Cleveland Works' Twin Strand Continuous Slab Caster." *Interfaces* (January–February 1988): 42–56.

6. Collier, D. A. *Service Management: Operating Decisions.* Englewood Cliffs, N.J.: Prentice-Hall, 1987.

7. Filley, R. D. "Cost Effective Patient Care: Harper-Grace Hospitals." *Industrial Engineering* (January 1983): 48–52.

8. Forger, G. "New Software Delivers Real-Time Shop Floor Control." *Modern Materials Handling* (May 1995): 44–45.

9. Goldratt, E. Y., and J. Cox. *The Goal.* New York: North River, 1984.

10. Green, G. I., and L. B. Appel. "An Empirical Analysis of Job Shop Dispatch Rule Selection." *Journal of Operations Management* 1, No. 4 (May 1981): 197–204.

11. Jacobs, F. R. "The OPT Scheduling System: A Review of a New Production Scheduling System." *Production and Inventory Management* 24, No. 3 (1983): 47–51.

12. Jacobs, F. R. "OPT Uncovered: Many Production Planning and Scheduling Concepts Can Be Applied With or Without the Software." *Industrial Engineering* (October 1984): 32–41.

13. Kanet, J. K., and J. C. Hayya. "Priority Dispatching with Operations Due Dates in a Job Shop." *Journal of Operations Management* 2, No. 3 (May 1982): 167–175.

14. Krajewski, L. J., L. P. Ritzman, and P. McKenzie. "Shift Scheduling in Banking Operations: A Case Application." *Interfaces* 10, No. 2 (April 1980): 1–8.

15. Mabert, V. A. "Static vs. Dynamic Priority Rules for Check Processing in Multiple Dispatch-Multiple Branch Banking." *Journal of Operations Management* 2, No. 1 (May 1982): 187–196.

16. Mabert, V. A., and M. J. Showalter. "Priority Rules for Check Processing in Multiple Branch Banking: An Experimental Analysis." *Journal of Operations Management* 1, No. 1 (August 1980): 15–22.

17. Mabert, V. A., and C. A. Watts. "A Simulation Analysis of Tour-Shift Construction Procedures." *Management Science* (May 1982): 520–532.

18. Mosier, C. T., D. A. Elvers, and D. Kelly. "Analysis of Group Technology Scheduling Heuristics." *International Journal of Production Research* 22, No. 5 (1984): 857–875.

19. Muhlemann, A. P., A. G. Lockett, and C. I. Farn. "Job Shop Scheduling Heuristics and Frequency of Scheduling." *International Journal of Production Research* 20, No. 2 (1982): 227–241.

20. Plenert, G., and T. D. Best. "MRP, JIT, and OPT: What's Best?" *Production and Inventory Management* 27, No. 2 (1986): 22–29.

21. Ragatz, G. L., and V. A. Mabert. "A Simulation Analysis of Due Date Assignment Rules." *Journal of Operations Management* 5, No. 1 (November 1984): 27–40.

22. Trail, D. T. "Package Products Capitalizes on Data." *APICS—The Performance Advantage* (August 1996): 38–41.

23. Vollmann, T. E. "OPT as an Enhancement to MRP II." *Production and Inventory Management* 27, No. 2 (1986): 38–47.

24. Vollmann, T. E., W. L. Berry, and D. C. Whybark. *Manufacturing Planning and Control Systems,* 2nd ed. Homewood, Ill.: Irwin, 1988.

25. Wymann, F. P. "Growing Strong by Scheduling Well." *APICS—The Performance Advantage* (August 1996): 44–47.

SUPPLEMENT TO CHAPTER 15

1. Boxoma, O. J., and R. Syski, eds. *Queuing Theory and Its Applications.* Amsterdam: North-Holland, 1988.

2. Bunday, B. D. *Basic Queuing Theory.* London: Edward Arnold, 1986.

3. Cooper, R. B. *Introduction to Queuing Theory,* 2nd ed. New York: Elsevier North-Holland, 1981.

4. Erikson, W. J., and O. P. Hall, Jr. *Computer Models for Management Science.* Reading, Mass.: Addison-Wesley, 1983.

5. Hillier, F. S., and O. S. Yu. *Queuing Tables and Graphs.* New York: Elsevier North-Holland, 1981.

6. Solomon, S. L. *Simulation of Waiting Line Systems.* Englewood Cliffs, N.J.: Prentice-Hall, 1983.

7. Turban, E., and J. R. Meredith. *Fundamentals of Management Science,* 5th ed. Homewood, Ill.: Irwin, 1991.

8. Walrand, J. *An Introduction to Queuing Networks.* Englewood Cliffs, N.J.: Prentice-Hall, 1988.

CHAPTER 16

1. Badiru, A. B. *Project Management in Manufacturing and High Technology Operations.* New York: Wiley, 1988.
2. Byers, L. "U.S. Pharmaceutical Industry: A Standard for Success." *Project Management Journal* (September 1989): 11–22.
3. Cleland, D. I., and W. R. King. *Project Management Handbook.* New York: Van Nostrand Reinhold, 1983.
4. Gabel, D. "Project Management Software." *PC Week* (September 10, 1985): 59–67.
5. Gido, J. *An Introduction to Project Planning,* 2nd ed. New York: Industrial, 1985.
6. Gilbreath, R. D. *Winning at Project Management.* New York: Wiley, 1986.
7. Gobeli, D. H., and E. W. Larson. "Relative Effectiveness of Different Project Structures." *Project Management Journal* 18, No. 2 (June 1987): 81–85.
8. Hughes, M. W. "Why Projects Fail: The Effects of Ignoring the Obvious." *Industrial Engineering* 18, No. 4 (April 1986): 14–18.
9. Kerzner, H. *Project Management: A Systems Approach to Planning, Scheduling, and Controlling.* New York: Van Nostrand Reinhold, 1984.
10. Kerzner, H. *Project Management for Executives.* New York: Van Nostrand Reinhold, 1984.
11. Kezbom, D. S., D. L. Schilling, and V. A. Edward. *Dynamic Project Management.* New York: Wiley, 1989.
12. Knutson, J. *How to Be a Successful Project Manager.* Saranac Lake, N.Y.: American Management Association, 1989.
13. Levine, H. A. *Project Management Using Microcomputers.* Berkeley, Calif.: Osborne McGraw-Hill, 1986.
14. Lock, D. *Project Management,* 4th ed. Brookfield, Vt.: Gower, 1987.
15. Martin, P. K. *Leading Project Management into the 21st Century.* Flemington, N.J.: Renaissance Education Services, 1996.
16. Meredith, J. R. "Installation of Flexible Manufacturing System Teaches Management Lessons in Integration, Labor, Costs, Benefits." *Industrial Engineering* (April 1988): 18–27.
17. Meredith, J. R. "Project Planning for Factory Automation." *Project Management Journal* (December 1986): 56–62.
18. Meredith, J. R., and S. J. Mantel, Jr. *Project Management: A Managerial Approach,* 2nd ed. New York: Wiley, 1989.
19. Murphy, P. L. "Pharmaceutical Project Management—Is It Different?" *Project Management Journal* (September 1989): 35–38.
20. Moder, J. J., C. R. Phillips, and E. W. Davis. *Project Management with CPM, PERT, and Precedence Diagramming,* 3rd ed. New York: Van Nostrand Reinhold, 1983.
21. O'Keeffe, S. W. T. "Chrysler and Artemis: Striking Back with the Viper." *Industrial Engineering* (December 1994): 15–17.
22. O'Neal, K. "Project Management Computer Buyer's Guide." *Industrial Engineering* 19, No. 1 (January 1987).
23. Pinto, J. K. "Strategy and Tactics in a Process Model of Project Implementation." *Interfaces* 17, No. 3 (May–June 1987): 34–46.
24. Posner, B. Z. "What It Takes to Be a Good Project Manager." *Project Management Journal* 18, No. 1 (March 1987): 51–54.

25. Sinclair, J. M. "Is the Matrix Really Necessary?" *Project Management Journal* 15, No. 1 (March 1984): 49–52.

26. Spirer, H. F., and A. G. Hulvey. "Project Management and Control Systems for Capital Projects," in *Proceedings of PMI, Internet 81*. Drexel Hill, Pa.: Project Management Institute, 1981.

27. Winslow, R. "Utility Cuts Red Tape, Builds Nuclear Plant Almost on Schedule." *Wall Street Journal* (February 22, 1984): 1, 22.

CHAPTER 17

1. Besterfield, D. H. *Quality Control,* 2nd ed. Englewood Cliffs, N.J.: Prentice-Hall, 1986.

2. Bowles, J. G. "The Quality Imperative: Adapting to Change at Whirlpool." *Fortune* (September 29, 1986): 61–96.

3. Dobbins, J. G., and W. J. Padgett. "SPC in Printed Circuit Board Assembly." *Quality Progress* (July 1993): 65–67.

4. Duncan, A. J. *Quality Control and Industrial Statistics,* 5th ed. Homewood, Ill.: Irwin, 1986.

5. Enrick, N. L. *Quality, Reliability, and Process Improvement,* 8th ed. New York: Industrial, 1985.

6. Evans, J. R., and W. M. Lindsay. *The Management and Control of Quality,* 3rd ed., St. Paul, Minn.: West, 1996.

7. Feigenbaum, A. V. *Total Quality Control: Engineering and Management,* 3rd ed. New York: McGraw-Hill, 1983.

8. Grant, E. L., and R. S. Levenworth. *Statistical Quality Control,* 6th ed. New York: McGraw-Hill, 1988.

9. Juran, J. M., F. M. Gryna, Jr., and R. S. Bingham, Jr., eds. *Quality Control Handbook,* 4th ed. New York: McGraw-Hill, 1988.

10. Maki, R. G., and M. R. Milota. "Statistical Quality Control Applied to Lumber Drying." *Quality Progress* (December 1993): 75–79.

11. McCabe, W. J. "Improving Quality and Cutting Costs in a Service Organization." *Quality Progress* (June 1985).

12. Messina, W. S. *Statistical Quality Control for Manufacturing Managers.* New York: Wiley, 1987.

13. Montgomery, D. S. *Introduction to Statistical Quality Control.* New York: Wiley, 1985.

14. Nadkarni, R. A. "A Not-So-Secret Recipe for Successful TQM." *Quality Progress* (November 1995): 91–96.

15. Richardson, T. L. *Total Quality Management.* Albany, N.Y.: Delmar, 1997.

16. Rosander, A. C. *Applications of Quality Control in the Service Industries.* New York: Marcel Dekker, 1985.

17. Schiller, Z. "Why Image Counts: A Tale of Two Industries: Appliance Repairmen Are Getting Lonelier." *Business Week* (June 8, 1987): 139–140.

18. Sinha, M. N., and W. O. Willborn. *The Management of Quality Assurance.* New York: Wiley, 1985.

19. Squires, F. H. "What Do Quality Control Charts Control?" *Quality* (November 1982): 63.

20. Sullivan, L. P. "The Seven Stages in Company-Wide Quality Control." *Quality Progress* (May 1986).

21. Vasilash, G. S. "Big Job. A Big Plant. An Enormous Challenge." *Production* (February 1991): 42–46.

SUPPLEMENT TO CHAPTER 17

1. Baker, J. T. "Automated Preventive Maintenance Program for Service Industries and Public Institutions." *Industrial Engineering* 12, No. 2 (February 1980): 18–21.
2. Chowdhury, A. R. "Reliability as It Relates to QA/QC." *Quality Progress* 18, No. 12 (December 1985): 27–30.
3. Cordero, S. T. *Maintenance Management.* Englewood Cliffs, N.J.: Fairmont, 1987.
4. Dhavale, D. G., and G. L. Otterson, Jr. "Maintenance by Priority." *Industrial Engineering* 12, No. 2 (February 1980): 24–27.
5. Enrick, N. L. *Quality, Reliability, and Process Improvement,* 8th ed. New York: Industrial, 1985.
6. Evans, J. R., and W. M. Lindsay. *The Management and Control of Quality.* St. Paul, Minn.: West, 1989.
7. Feigenbaum, A. V. *Total Quality Control: Engineering and Management,* 3rd ed. New York: McGraw-Hill, 1983.
8. Gitlow, H. S., and P. T. Hertz. "Product Defects and Productivity." *Harvard Business Review* (September–October 1983): 131–141.
9. Hansen, B. L., and P. M. Ghare. *Quality Control and Application.* Englewood Cliffs, N.J.: Prentice-Hall, 1987.
10. Henley, E. J., and H. Kavmamoto. *Reliability Engineering and Risk Assessment.* Englewood Cliffs, N.J.: Prentice-Hall, 1981.
11. Hora, M. E. "The Unglamorous Game of Managing Maintenance." *Business Horizons* 30, No. 3 (May–June 1987): 67–75.
12. Juran, J. M., and F. M. Gryna. *Quality Planning and Analysis,* 2nd ed. New York: McGraw-Hill, 1980.
13. Katzel, J. "Maintenance Management Software." *Plant Engineering* 41, No. 12 (June 18, 1987): 124–170.
14. Mann, L., Jr. *Maintenance Management,* rev. ed. Lexington, Mass.: Lexington, 1983.
15. Montgomery, D. C. *Introduction to Statistical Quality Control.* New York: Wiley, 1985.
16. Patton, J. D., Jr. *Preventive Maintenance.* Research Triangle Park, N.C.: Instrument Society of America, 1983.
17. Sinha, S. K., and B. K. Kale. *Life Testing and Reliability Estimation.* New York: Wiley, 1980.
18. Sinha, M. N., and W. O. Willborn. *The Management of Quality Assurance.* New York: Wiley, 1985.
19. Smith, D. J. *Reliability and Maintainability in Perspective,* 2nd ed. New York: Wiley, 1985.
20. Tombari, H. "Designing a Maintenance Management System." *Production and Inventory Management* 23, No. 4 (1982): 139–147.
21. Tomlinson, P. D. "Organizing for Productive Maintenance." *Production Engineering* 34, No. 10 (October 1987): 38–40.
22. Wireman, T. *Preventive Maintenance.* Englewood Cliffs, N.J.: Reston, 1984.

Photo and Illustration Credits

CHAPTER 1
Page 11: Courtesy CalComp, Inc. Page 16: Courtesy First National Bank of Chicago.

CHAPTER 2
Page 53: Courtesy Black & Decker.

CHAPTER 3
Page 93: Courtesy Motorola, Inc.

CHAPTER 4
Page 118: Fig. 4.1 Adapted from Hammer, M., Beyond Reengineering, Harper Business, 1996, p. 83.

CHAPTER 5
Page 171: Michael Rosenfeld/Tony Stone Images/ New York, Inc. Page 172: Courtesy Cincinnati Milacron. Page 173: John Madere/The Stock Market.

CHAPTER 6
Page 195: Alvis Upittis/The Image Bank. Page 197: Courtesy Corning, Inc. Pages 216-217: Courtesy Cincinnati Milacron.

CHAPTER 7
Page 226: Courtesy Federal Express Corporation. Page 230: Mark Joseph/Tony Stone Images/ New York, Inc. Page 231: Courtesy Northern Telecom, Inc. Page 233: Courtesy First National Bank of Chicago.

CHAPTER 9
Page 336: Courtesy Cathay Pacific.

CHAPTER 10
Page 376: Courtesy Saturn Corporation. Page 379: Courtesy Federal Express Corporation. Page 387: Courtesy Texas State Comptroller's Office.

CHAPTER 11
Page 457: Courtesy Dow Corning Corporation.

CHAPTER 12
Page 508: Courtesy Weyerhaeuser. Page 522: Courtesy Department of Defense.

CHAPTER 13
Page 552: Courtesy Recording for the Blind, New Jersey. Page 560: Courtesy Corning, Inc. Page 593: Courtesy NASA.

CHAPTER 14
Page 603: Courtesy General Motors Corporation. Page 614: Courtesy Toyota Motor Corporation. Page 621: Courtesy Harley-Davidson, Inc. Page 625: Courtesy Smart Practice.

CHAPTER 15
Page 671: Courtesy Harper Hospital.

CHAPTER 16
Page 695: Ted Horowitz/The Stock Market.

CHAPTER 17
Page 755: Courtesy Ben & Jerry's. Page 757: Courtesy Whirlpool Corporation. Page 760: Courtesy of International Business Machines Corporation.

Index